Infants and Children:
Prenatal Through Middle Childhood
FIFTH EDITION

Laura E. Berk

Illinois State University

PEARSON

Boston | New York | San Francisco
Mexico City | Montreal | Toronto | London | Madrid | Munich | Paris
Hong Kong | Singapore | Tokyo | Cape Town | Sydney

**To the staff of the Children's Discovery Museum, Normal, IL,
for an outstanding model of how a small community
can enhance children's development.**

Managing Editor: Jennifer Albanese
Development Editor: Susan Messer
Editorial Assistant: Leah Prebluda
Executive Marketing Manager: Pam Laskey
Manufacturing Manager: Megan Cochran
Composition Buyer: Linda Cox
Senior Production Editor: Elizabeth Gale Napolitano
Electronic Composition: Schneck-DePippo Graphics
Cover Design Director: Linda Knowles
Photo Researcher: Sarah Evertson/ImageQuest
Copyeditor: Connie Day
Proofreader: Bill Heckman

For related titles and support materials, visit our online catalog at *www.ablongman.com*

Portions of this book are also published under the title *Infants, Children, and Adolescents,* Fifth Edition, by Laura E. Berk, copyright © 2005, 2002, 1999, 1996, 1993 by Pearson Education, Inc.

Library of Congress Cataloging-in-Publication Data

Berk, Laura E.
    Infants and children / Laura E. Berk. — 5th ed.
      p. cm.
    Previous eds has subtitle: Prenatal through middle childhood.
    Includes bibliographic references and indexes.
    ISBN 0-205-42063-X (alk. paper)
    1. Child development.   I. Title.

    RJ131.B3863 2004
    305.231 — dc22   2004040065

Printed in the United States of America

10 9 8 7 6 5 4 3 2   VH   08 07 06 05 04

About the Author

Laura E. Berk is a distinguished professor of psychology at Illinois State University, where she teaches human development to both undergraduate and graduate students. She received her bachelor's degree in psychology from the University of California, Berkeley, and her master's and doctoral degrees in early childhood development and education from the University of Chicago. She has been a visiting scholar at Cornell University, UCLA, Stanford University, and the University of South Australia. Berk has published widely on the effects of school environments on children's development, the development of private speech, and most recently the role of make-believe play in the development of self-regulation. Her research has been funded by the U.S. Office of Education and the National Institute of Child Health and Human Development. It has appeared in many prominent journals, including *Child Development, Developmental Psychology, Merrill-Palmer Quarterly, Journal of Abnormal Child Psychology, Development and Psychopathology,* and *Early Childhood Research Quarterly.* Her empirical studies have attracted the attention of the general public, leading to contributions to *Psychology Today* and *Scientific American.* Berk has served as research editor for *Young Children* and consulting editor for *Early Childhood Research Quarterly.* She is author of the chapter on the extracurriculum for the *Handbook of Research on Curriculum* (American Educational Research Association), the chapter on development for *The Many Faces of*

Psychological Research in the Twenty-First Century (Society for the Teaching of Psychology), and the article on Vygotsky for the *Encyclopedia of Cognitive Science.* Her books include *Private Speech: From Social Interaction to Self-Regulation, Scaffolding Children's Learning: Vygotsky and Early Childhood Education,* and *Landscapes of Development: An Anthology of Readings.* In addition to *Infants, Children, and Adolescents,* she is author of the best-selling texts *Child Development* and *Development Through the Lifespan,* published by Allyn and Bacon. Her recently published book for parents and teachers is *Awakening Children's Minds: How Parents and Teachers Can Make a Difference.*

Brief Contents

List of Features

Contents

PART IV
Early Childhood: Two to Six Years

chapter 8 Physical Development in Early Childhood 286

chapter 9 Cognitive Development in Early Childhood 314

**chapter 13 Emotional
and Social Development in
Middle Childhood** **468**

$\mathcal{A}$ Personal Note to Students

$\mathcal{M}$y 33 years of teaching child development have brought me in contact with thousands of students like you—students with diverse college majors, future goals, interests, and needs. Some are affiliated with my own department, psychology, but many come from other child-related fields—education, sociology, anthropology, family studies, and biology, to name just a few. Each semester, my students' aspirations are as varied as their fields of study. Many look toward careers in applied work—teaching, caregiving, medicine, counseling, social work, school psychology, and program administration. Some plan to teach child development, and a few want to do research. Most hope someday to become parents, whereas others are already parents who come with a desire to better understand and rear their children. And almost all arrive with a deep curiosity about how they themselves developed from tiny infants into the complex human beings they are today.

My goal in preparing this fifth edition of *Infants, Children, and Adolescents* is to provide a textbook that meets the instructional goals of your course as well as your personal interests and needs. To achieve these objectives, I have grounded this book in a carefully selected body of classic and current theory and research brought to life with stories and vignettes about children and families, most of whom I have known personally. In addition, the text highlights the joint contributions of biology and environment to the developing child, explains how the research process helps solve real-world problems, illustrates commonalities and differences between ethnic groups and cultures, and pays special attention to policy issues that are crucial for safeguarding children's well-being in today's world. I have also provided a unique pedagogical program that will assist you in mastering information, integrating the various aspects of development, critically examining controversial issues, reflecting on your own childhood experiences, and applying what you have learned.

I hope that learning about child development will be as rewarding for you as I have found it over the years. I would like to know what you think about both the field of child development and this book. I welcome your comments; please feel free to send them to me at Department of Psychology, Box 4620, Illinois State University, Normal, IL 61790, or care of the publisher, who will forward them to me.

Laura E. Berk

Preface for Instructors

My decision to write *Infants, Children, and Adolescents* was inspired by a wealth of professional and personal experiences. First and foremost were the interests and concerns of hundreds of students of child development with whom I have worked in more than three decades of college teaching. I aimed for a text that is intellectually stimulating, that provides depth as well as breadth of coverage, that portrays the complexities of child development with clarity and excitement, and that is relevant and useful in building a bridge from theory and research to children's everyday lives. Instructor and student enthusiasm for the book not only has been among my greatest sources of pride and satisfaction, but also has inspired me to rethink and improve each edition.

The twelve years since *Infants, Children, and Adolescents* first appeared have been a period of unprecedented expansion and change in theory and research. This fifth edition represents these rapidly transforming aspects of the field, with a wealth of new content and teaching tools:

■ *Diverse pathways of change are highlighted.* Investigators have reached broad consensus that variations in biological makeup, everyday tasks, and the people who support children in mastery of those tasks lead to wide individual differences in children's paths of change and resulting competencies. This edition pays more attention to variability in development and to recent theories—including ecological, sociocultural, and dynamic systems—that attempt to explain it. Multicultural and cross-cultural findings, including international comparisons, are enhanced throughout the text and in revised and expanded Cultural Influences boxes.

■ *The complex, bidirectional relationship between biology and environment is given greater attention.* Accumulating evidence on development of the brain, motor skills, cognitive competencies, temperament, and developmental problems underscores the way biological factors emerge in, are modified by, and share power with experience. The interconnection between biology and environment is revisited throughout the text narrative and in Biology and Environment boxes with new and updated topics.

■ *Inclusion of interdisciplinary research is expanded.* The move toward viewing thoughts, feelings, and behavior as an integrated whole, affected by a wide array of influences in biology, social context, and culture, has motivated developmental researchers to strengthen their ties with other fields of psychology and with other disciplines. Topics and findings included in this edition increasingly reflect the contributions of educational psychology, social psychology, health psychology, clinical psychology, neuropsychology, biology, pediatrics, sociology, anthropology, social welfare, and other fields.

■ *The links between theory, research, and applications—a theme of this book since its inception—are strengthened.* As researchers intensify their efforts to generate findings that can be applied to real-life situations, I have placed even greater weight on social policy issues and sound theory- and research-based practices. Further applications are provided in the Applying What We Know tables, which give students concrete ways of building bridges between their learning and the real world.

■ *The educational context of development becomes a stronger focus.* The home, school, and community are featured as vital educational contexts in which the child develops. Research on effective teaching practices appears in many chapters and in new and revised Social Issues: Education boxes.

■ *The role of active student learning is made more explicit.* Ask Yourself questions at the end of each major section have been revised and expanded to promote four approaches to engaging actively with the subject matter: *Review, Apply, Connect,* and *Reflect.* This feature assists students in reflecting on what they have read from multiple vantage points.

Text Philosophy

The basic approach of this book has been shaped by my own professional and personal history as a teacher, researcher, and parent. It consists of seven philosophical ingredients that I regard as essential for students to emerge from a course with a thorough understanding of child development:

1. **An understanding of major theories and the strengths and shortcomings of each.** The first chapter begins by emphasizing that only knowledge of multiple theories can do justice to the richness of child development. As I take up each age period and domain of development, I present a variety of theoretical perspectives, indicate how each highlights previously overlooked facets of development, and discuss research that evaluates it. Consideration of contrasting theories also serves as the context for an evenhanded analysis of many controversial issues.

2. **An appreciation of research strategies for investigating child development.** To evaluate theories, students must have a firm grounding in research methods and designs. In addition to a special section in Chapter 1 covering research strategies, throughout the book numerous studies are discussed in sufficient detail for students to use what they have learned to critically assess the findings, conclusions, and implications of research.

3. **Knowledge of both the sequence of child development and the processes that underlie it.** Students are provided with a description of the organized sequence of development along with processes of change. An understanding of process—how complex interactions of biological and environmental events produce development—has been the focus of most recent research. Accordingly, the text reflects this emphasis. But new information about the timetable of change has also emerged. In many ways, children have proved to be far more competent than they were believed to be in the past. Current evidence on the sequence and timing of development, along with its implications for process, is presented throughout the book.

4. **An appreciation of the impact of context and culture on child development.** A wealth of research indicates that children live in rich physical and social contexts that affect all domains of development. In each chapter, the student travels to distant parts of the world as I review a growing body of cross-cultural evidence. The text narrative also discusses many findings on socioeconomically and ethnically diverse children within the United States and Canada, and children with varying abilities and disabilities. Besides highlighting the role of immediate settings, such as family, neighborhood, and school, I make a concerted effort to underscore the impact of larger social structures—societal values, laws, and government programs—on children's well-being.

5. **An understanding of the joint contributions of biology and environment to development.** The field recognizes more powerfully than ever before the interaction of hereditary/constitutional and environmental factors—that these contributions to development combine in complex ways and cannot be separated in a simple manner. Numer-

ous examples of how biological dispositions can be maintained as well as transformed by social contexts are presented throughout the book.

6. **A sense of the interdependency of all domains of development—physical, cognitive, emotional, and social.** Every chapter takes an integrated approach to understanding children. I show how physical, cognitive, emotional, and social development are interwoven. Within the text narrative and in a special series of Ask Yourself *Connect* questions at the end of major sections, students are referred to other sections of the book to deepen their grasp of relationships between various aspects of change.

7. **An appreciation of the interrelatedness of theory, research, and applications.** Throughout this book, I emphasize that theories of child development and the research stimulated by them provide the foundation for sound, effective practices with children. The links between theory, research, and applications are reinforced by an organizational format in which theory and research are presented first, followed by practical implications. In addition, a current focus in the field—harnessing child development knowledge to shape social policies that support children's needs—is reflected in every chapter. The text addresses the current condition of children in the United States, Canada, and around the world and shows how theory and research have sparked successful interventions.

Text Organization

I have chosen a chronological organization for this text. The chronological approach assists students in thoroughly understanding each age period. It also eases the task of integrating the various domains of development because each is discussed in close proximity. At the same time, a chronologically organized book requires that theories covering several age periods be presented piecemeal. This creates a challenge for students, who must link the various parts together. To assist with this task, I frequently remind students of important earlier achievements before discussing new developments, referring back to related sections with page references. Also, chapters devoted to the same topic (for example, Cognitive Development in Early Childhood, Cognitive Development in Middle Childhood) are similarly organized, making it easier for students to draw connections across age periods and construct an overall view of developmental change.

New Coverage in the Fifth Edition

In this edition, I continue to represent a rapidly transforming contemporary literature with theory and research from more than 1,500 new citations. Cutting-edge topics throughout the text underscore the book's major themes. Here is a sampling:

CHAPTER 1 ● Latest research that dispels misconceptions on how children were perceived in the Middle Ages ● New illustration of information-processing research—a study of children's problem solving ● New section on evolutionary developmental psychology ● Enhanced discussion of cohort effects, including a new Social Issues: Health box on the Great Depression and World War II ● Updated Biology and Environment box on resilience.

CHAPTER 2 ● Expanded coverage of gene–environment exchanges and reproductive technologies ● Revised and updated section on development of adopted children ● Expanded attention to the impact of poverty on development, including a new Social Issues: Health box on welfare reform, poverty, and child development ● Discussion of public policy and the overall well-being of North American children ● Enhanced discussion of environmental influences on gene expression.

CHAPTER 3 ● New Biology and Environment box on the teratogenic effects of Accutane ● Expanded treatment of prenatal AIDS exposure, with discussion of the rapid spread of AIDS among women in developing countries ● Updated consideration of the importance of prenatal health care.

CHAPTER 4 ● Enhanced section on infant crying, including cultural variations in infant soothing and new evidence on abnormal crying ● New research on methods of caring for preterm and low-birth-weight infants, including "kangaroo care" in the intensive care nursery ● New findings on infant pain perception ● Revised section on the transition to parenthood, including new evidence on the challenges of adapting to both a first and a second birth.

CHAPTER 5 ● Updated discussion of brain development, including a new Biology and Environment box on brain plasticity ● New evidence on infants' and toddlers' eating habits and early risk for obesity ● Updated findings on development of reaching and grasping ● New findings on the development of speech perception, including infants as statistical analyzers of speech patterns ● Expanded and updated consideration of early face perception.

CHAPTER 6 ● Inclusion of the core knowledge perspective on cognitive development ● New Biology and Environment box considering whether infants have built-in numerical knowledge ● Revised and updated Biology and Environment box on infantile amnesia ● Updated findings on quality of child care in the United States and Canada, with consequences for cognitive and social competence.

CHAPTER 7 ● New research on the stability of temperament, and discussion of different methods for measuring temperament ● Enhanced coverage of attachment, including new evidence on cultural variations and a new Cultural Influences box on the powerful role of paternal warmth in development.

CHAPTER 8 ● Expanded treatment of preschoolers' sleep habits and problems, with advice in a new Applying What We Know table ● International comparisons of rates of childhood injury mortality, with discussion of factors contributing to the relatively poor rankings of Canada and the United States ● Updated Cultural Influences box on child health care in the United States and other Western nations, with special attention to the large number of uninsured children in the United States ● New research on the development of drawing and printing, including the relationship between these skills.

CHAPTER 9 ● New Cultural Influences box on how children in village and tribal cultures learn by observing and participating in adult work ● Enhanced discussion of autobiographical memory, including the influence of the parent–child relationship on the richness of reminiscing ● Updated Biology and Environment box on "mindblindness" and autism, including explanations for autistic children's deficient theory of mind ● New developments in early childhood literacy and mathematical reasoning ● New findings on the impact of educational television during the preschool years on academic achievement ● Updated research on the diverse strategies preschoolers use to figure out word meanings.

CHAPTER 10 ● New evidence on emotional self-regulation and consequences for development ● Revised and updated section on parenting and children's peer relations, including direct and indirect influences ● New findings on development of aggression, including effects of media violence ● Updated discussion of gender typing, including a new Biology and Environment box describing a case study of a boy reared as a girl ● New evidence on the powerful role of sex segregation in children's peer relations ● Updated section on child maltreatment, including incidence in the United States and Canada and a new Social Issues: Health box on Healthy Start, Hawaii's home visiting program for preventing child maltreatment.

CHAPTER 11 ● Updated consideration of brain development in middle childhood ● New findings on the causes and consequences of obesity, including a new Social Issues: Health box on how Americans became the heaviest people in the world ● Updated evidence on consequences of participation in youth sports programs.

CHAPTER 12 ● Enhanced consideration of metacognition, including experiences that foster children's awareness of mental activities ● Updated description of Sternberg's triarchic theory of successful intelligence ● New Cultural Influences box on the Flynn effect—massive generational gains in IQ—and its implications for the IQ nature-nurture controversy ● New research on culture, communication styles, and children's mental test performance ● New evidence revealing that stereotype threat can impair children's test taking ● Updated section on bilingual development and education, including Canada's French immersion programs ● Revised and updated section on educational philosophies, including constructivist and social-constructivist classrooms and the community of learners approach.

CHAPTER 13 ● Expanded and updated treatment of emotional self-regulation, including school-age children's flexible use of problem-centered and emotion-centered coping ● New Cultural Influences box on children's understanding of God ● New research on the relationship of peer-acceptance categories to bullying ● New evidence on children's development in never-married single-parent families ● Updated attention to divorce, with special attention to long-term consequences ● Updated research on school-age children's fears, including cultural influences and the role of temperament ● Expanded consideration of resilience, including a new Applying What We Know table on fostering resilience in middle childhood.

Pedagogical Features

Maintaining a highly accessible writing style – one that is lucid and engaging without being simplistic – continues to be one of my major goals. I frequently converse with students, encouraging them to relate what they read to their own lives. In doing so, I hope to make the study of child development involving and pleasurable.

Stories and Vignettes About Children. To help students construct a clear image of development and to enliven the text narrative, each chronological age division is unified by case examples woven throughout that set of chapters. For example, within the infancy and toddlerhood section, we'll look in on three children, observe dramatic changes and striking individual differences, and address the impact of family background, child-rearing practices, and parents' and children's life experiences on development. Besides a set of main characters, many additional vignettes offer vivid examples of development among children and adolescents.

Chapter Introductions and End-of-Chapter Summaries. To provide a helpful preview of chapter content, I include an outline and overview in each chapter introduction. Comprehensive end-of-chapter summaries, organized according to the major divisions of each chapter and highlighting important terms, remind students of key points in the text discussion. Review questions are included in the summary to encourage active study.

Ask Yourself questions Active engagement with the subject matter is also supported by Ask Yourself questions at the end of each major section. Four types of questions prompt students to think about child development in diverse ways: *Review* questions help students recall and comprehend information they have just read. *Apply* questions encourage the application of knowledge to controversial issues and problems faced by children, parents, and professionals who work with them. *Connect* questions help students build an image of the whole child by integrating what they have learned across age periods and domains of development. *Reflect* questions make the study of child development personally meaningful by asking students to reflect on their own development. An icon (www) indicates that each question is answered on the text's Companion Website (*http://www.ablongman.com/berk*). Students may compare their reasoning to a model response.

Three types of thematic boxes accentuate the philosophical themes of this book:

● **Social Issues** boxes discuss the impact of social conditions on children and emphasize the need for sensitive social policies to ensure their well-being. They are divided into two types: (1) **Social Issues: Health** boxes address values and practices relevant to children's physical and mental health. Examples include Welfare Reform, Poverty, and Child Development; Healthy Start: Preventing Child Maltreatment Through Home Visitation; and Parents and Teenagers (Don't) Talk About Sex. (2) **Social Issues: Education** boxes focus on home, school, and community influences on children's learning—for example, School Readiness and Grade Retention; Children's Understanding of Health and Illness; and High-Stakes Testing.

● **Biology and Environment** boxes highlight the growing attention to the complex, bi-directional relationship between biology and environment. Examples include Brain Plasticity: Insights from Research on Brain-Damaged Children and Adults; Do Infants Have Built-In Numerical Knowledge; "Mindblindness" and Autism; and Bullies and Their Victims.

● **Cultural Influences** boxes have been expanded and updated to deepen attention to culture threaded throughout the text. They highlight both cross-cultural and multicultural variations in child development—for example, The Powerful Role of Paternal Warmth in Development; Children in Village and Tribal Cultures Observe and Participate in Adult Work; The Flynn Effect: Massive Generational Gains in IQ; and Children's Understanding of God.

Sample textbook pages displayed as examples of the thematic boxes described: "Social Issues: Health — Otitis Media and Development" (Chapter Eight); "Social Issues: Education — High-Stakes Testing" (Chapter Fifteen); "Biology and Environment — Do Infants Have Built-In Numerical Knowledge?"; and "Cultural Influences — The Powerful Role of Paternal Warmth in Development" (Chapter Seven).

Applying What We Know Tables. In this new feature, I summarize research-based applications on many issues, speaking directly to students as parents or future parents and to those pursuing different careers or areas of study, such as teaching, health care, counseling, or social work.

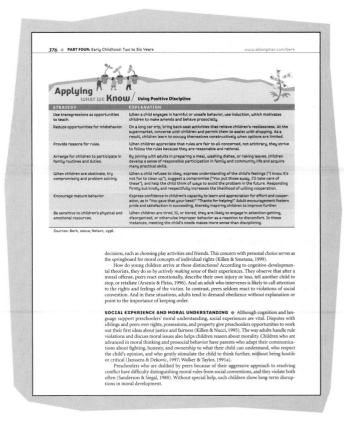

Milestones Tables. A Milestones table appears at the end of each age division of the text. These tables summarize major physical, cognitive, language, emotional, and social attainments, providing a convenient aid for reviewing the chronology of child development.

484 ● **PART FIVE:** Middle Childhood: Six to Eleven Years www.ablongman.com/berk

Moral Education

Debate over whether and how to teach morality in the public schools is vigorous. On one side are educators who call for *character education*—teaching students to follow a common set of moral virtues, such as honesty, kindness, fairness, and responsibility (De Roche & Williams, 1998). But critics claim that transmitting a ready-made morality, such as "Be honest and work hard," ignores school-age children's developing capacity to consider multiple variables in moral decision making (Nucci, 2001). As children get older, cognitive-developmental theorists point out, they benefit from increasing opportunities for *moral discussion*—evaluating beliefs and practices on moral grounds.

Darcia Narvaez and her colleagues (2001) recommend that moral education be broadened to promote four moral components, starting at a concrete level and moving toward more abstract understandings. Each component involves a different type of knowledge essential for moral functioning:

- *Interpreting the situation: moral sensitivity*—using cause–effect reasoning and perspective taking to predict how one's actions are likely to affect others, resulting in awareness that a situation involves a moral issue;

- *Reasoning about right and wrong: moral judgment*—evaluating possible courses of action to determine which one is fair and just;

- *Granting moral values a high priority: moral motivation*—elevating moral values above other personal values; and

- *Having the strength of one's convictions: moral character*—controlling impulses and steadfastly behaving in accord with moral values.

At present, moral education programs for children are narrowly focused. Character education emphasizes *moral character*, whereas the cognitive-developmental approach stresses *moral judgment* (Bebeau, Rest, & Narvaez, 1999). Narvaez's four-component model offers a comprehensive basis for moral education. Children in highly successful programs should gain in each aspect of morality.

Alexandria Necker of DeWitt, Iowa, read a story about foster children being given a trash bag in which to put their belongings while being moved from home to home. On her tenth birthday, she had guests bring gifts not for her, but for area foster children. She continues to gather and distribute such gifts. Alexandria exemplifies the diverse ingredients of moral maturity—high moral sensitivity, moral judgment, moral motivation, and moral character.

COURTESY ALEXANDRA NECKER

CHAPTER FIFTEEN: Cognitive Development in Adolescence ● **573**

FIGURE 15.8

Employment rates of young adults by educational attainment, United States and Canada. Young people who do not graduate from high school are much less likely to get jobs than those with high school diplomas. (From Human Resources Development Canada, 2000; U.S. Department of Education, 2002.)

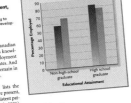

scores than high school graduates. As a result, American and Canadian high school dropouts lack skills valued by employers in today's knowledge-based economy. Consequently, as Figure 15.8 reveals, employment rates are much lower for dropouts than for high school graduates. And even when they are employed, dropouts are far more likely to remain in menial, low-paid jobs and to be out of work from time to time.

FACTORS RELATED TO DROPPING OUT ● Table 15.1 lists the diverse factors related to leaving school early. The more that are present, the greater the risk of dropping out. Many dropouts show a persistent pattern of disruptive behavior and poor achievement (Vitaro et al., 2001). But a considerable number are like Norman, who had few behavior problems but failed academically and quietly disengaged from school (Janosz et al., 2000; Newcomb et al., 2002). The pathway to dropping out starts early. Risk factors in first grade predict later dropout nearly as well as risk factors in secondary school (Alexander, Entwisle, & Kabbani, 2001).

Norman had a long history of marginal to failing school grades and low academic self-esteem. He gave up on tasks that presented even the least challenge and counted on luck—his

TABLE 15.1

Factors Related to Dropping Out of High School

STUDENT CHARACTERISTICS	FAMILY CHARACTERISTICS	SCHOOL CHARACTE...
Poor school attendance	Parents who do not support or emphasize achievement	Large, unstimulatin...
Inattentiveness in class	Parents who were high school dropouts	Lack of opportuni... personal relation... teachers
School discipline problems, especially aggressive behavior	Parents who are uninvolved in the adolescent's education	Curriculum irrel... student interest...
Inability to get along with teachers		
1 to 2 years behind in grade level	Parents who react with anger and punishment to the adolescent's low grades	School authori... that emphasize... and discourag... input
Low academic achievement		
A sharp drop in achievement after school transition	Single-parent household	Large stude...
Dislike of school	Low income	Frequent sc...
Enrollment in a general education or vocational track		
Low educational aspirations		
Low self-esteem, especially academic self-esteem		
Friendships with peers who have left school		
Low involvement in extracurricular activities		
Drug use		
Law breaking behavior		
Adolescent parenthood		

Sources: Kushman, Sieber, & Heariold-Kinney, 2000; Lee & Burkam, 2003.

CHAPTER THIRTEEN: Emotional and Social Development in Middle Childhood ● **511**

Some Common Problems of Development

Cite common fears and anxieties in middle childhood.

- School-age children's fears are directed toward new concerns, including physical harm, media events, academic failure, parents' health, the possibility of dying, and peer rejection. Children with inhibited temperaments are at high risk for developing **phobias**, or intense, unmanageable fears. School phobia—severe apprehension about attending school—is an example. Severe anxiety can also result from harsh living conditions, such as constant violence.

Discuss factors related to child sexual abuse, its consequences for children's

development, and its prevention and treatment.

- Child sexual abuse is generally committed by male family members, and more often against girls than against boys. Abusers have characteristics that predispose them toward sexual exploitation of children. Reported cases are linked to poverty and marital instability, but middle-SES children in stable homes are also victims. Children with inhibited temperaments are at high risk for developing **phobias**, or intense, unmanageable fears. School phobia—severe apprehension about attending school—is an example. Adjustment problems of abused children often are severe. Common reactions are depression, low self-esteem, mistrust of adults, anger and hostility, suicidal reactions, and inappropriate sexual behavior.

- Because sexual abuse is related to other serious family problems, long-term therapy with children and families is usually necessary. Educational pro-

grams that teach children to recognize inappropriate sexual advances and whom to turn to for help reduce the risk of sexual abuse.

Cite factors that foster resilience in middle childhood.

- Overall, a modest relationship exists between stressful life experiences and psychological disturbance in childhood. Personal characteristics of children, a warm family life that includes authoritative parenting, and social supports at school and in the community are related to resilience in the face of stress. Often just one or a few resources favoring resilience are necessary because each strengthens others.

Important Terms and Concepts

attribution retraining (p. 476)	joint custody (p. 498)	popular children (p. 487)
attributions (p. 474)	learned helplessness (p. 475)	popular-antisocial children (p. 487)
blended, or reconstituted, family (p. 499)	mastery-oriented attributions (p. 475)	popular-prosocial children (p. 487)
controversial children (p. 487)	neglected children (p. 487)	problem-centered coping (p. 479)
coregulation (p. 492)	peer acceptance (p. 487)	rejected children (p. 487)
distributive justice (p. 482)	peer group (p. 485)	rejected-aggressive children (p. 488)
divorce mediation (p. 497)	peer victimization (p. 489)	rejected-withdrawn children (p. 488)
emotion-centered coping (p. 479)	perspective taking (p. 480)	self-care children (p. 501)
industry versus inferiority (p. 470)	phobia (p. 502)	social comparisons (p. 471)
		sociometric techniques (p. 487)

FYI **For Further Information and Help**

Consult the Companion Website for *Infants, Children, and Adolescents*, Fifth Edition, (*www.ablongman.com/berk*), where you will find the following resources for this chapter:

- **Chapter Objectives**
- **Flashcards** for studying important terms and concepts
- **Annotated Weblinks** to guide you in further research
- **Ask Yourself questions**, which you can answer and then check against a sample response

- **Suggested Readings**
- **Practice Tests** with immediate scoring and feedback

Additional Tables, Illustrations, and Photographs. Tables are liberally included to help students grasp essential points in the text narrative and extend information on a topic. The many full-color figures and illustrations depict important theories, methods, and research findings. Photos have been carefully selected to portray the text discussion and to represent the diversity of children around the world.

In-Text Key Terms with Definitions, End-of-Chapter Term List, and End-of-Book Glossary. Mastery of terms that make up the central vocabulary of the field is promoted through highlighted key-term and concept definitions, which appear in the text narrative, an end-of-chapter term list, and an end-of-book glossary.

Acknowledgments

The dedicated contributions of a great many individuals helped make this book a reality and contributed to refinements and improvements in this fifth edition. An impressive cast of reviewers provided many helpful suggestions, constructive criticisms, and encouragement and enthusiasm for the organization and content of the text. I am grateful to each one of them.

Reviewers for the First Through Fourth Editions

Mark B. Alcorn, University of Northern Colorado
Armin W. Arndt, Eastern Washington University
Kathleen Bey, Palm Beach Community College
Donald Bowers, Community College of Philadelphia
Michele Y. Breault, Truman State University
Jerry Bruce, Sam Houston State College
Lanthan D. Camblin, University of Cincinnati
Joseph J. Campos, University of California, Berkeley
Linda A. Camras, DePaul University
Nancy Taylor Coghill, University of Southwest Louisiana
Diane Brothers Cook, Gainesville College
Jennifer Cook, Kent State University
Roswell Cox, Berea College
Zoe Ann Davidson, Alabama A & M University
Sheridan DeWolf, Grossmont College
Constance DiMaria-Kross, Union County College
Bronwyn Fees, Kansas State University
Kathleen Fite, Southwest Texas State University
Trisha Folds-Bennett, College of Charleston
Vivian Harper, San Joaquin Delta College
Janice Hartgrove-Freile, North Harris Community College
Vernon Haynes, Youngstown State University
Bert Hayslip, Jr., University of North Texas
Paula Hillmann, University of Wisconsin, Waukesha
Malia Huchendorf, Normandale Community College
Lisa Huffman, Ball State University
Clementine Hansley Hurt, Radford University
John S. Klein, Castleton State College
Claire Kopp, Claremont Graduate School
Eugene Krebs, California State University, Fresno
Carole Kremer, Hudson Valley Community College
Gary W. Ladd, University of Illinois, Urbana-Champaign
Linda Lavine, State University of New York at Cortland
Gail Lee, Jersey City State College
Judith R. Levine, State University of New York at Farmingdale
Frank Manis, University of Southern California
Mary Ann McLaughlin, Clarion University of Pennsylvania
Annie McManus, Parkland College
Cloe Merrill, Weber State University
Rich Metzger, University of Tennessee at Chattanooga
Karla Miley, Black Hawk College

Jennifer Trapp Myers, University of Michigan
Virginia Navarro, University of Missouri, St. Louis
Peter V. Oliver, University of Hartford
Virginia Parsons, Carroll College
Joe M. Price, San Diego State University
Mary Kay Reed, York College of Pennsylvania
Alan Russell, Flinders University
Tizrah Schutzengel, Bergen Community College
Johnna Shapiro, Illinois Wesleyan University
Gregory Smith, Dickinson College
Thomas Spencer, San Francisco State University
Carolyn Spies, Bloomfield College
Kathy Stansbury, University of New Mexico
Connie Steele, University of Tennessee, Knoxville
Janet Strayer, Simon Fraser University
Marcia Summers, Ball State University
Judith Ward, Central Connecticut State University
Shawn Ward, Le Moyne College
Alida Westman, Eastern Michigan University
Belinda Wholeben, Rockford College
Sue Williams, Southwest Texas State University
Deborah Winters, New Mexico State University
Connie K. Varnhagen, University of Alberta

Reviewers for the Fifth Edition

Lamia Barakat, Drexel University
Cecelia Benelli, Western Illinois University
Lynn Caruso, Seneca College
Ronald Craig, Edinboro University of Pennsylvania
Matthew DiCintio, Delaware County Community College
F. Richard Ferraro, University of North Dakota
Nancy Freeman, University of South Carolina
Eugene Geist, Ohio University
Kristine Hansen, University of Winnipeg
Algea Harrison, Oakland University
Sandra Hellyer, Butler University
Joan Herwig, Iowa State University
Christie Honeycutt, Stanly Community College
Joline Jones, Worcester State University
Kate Kenney, Howard Community College
Shirin Khosropour, Austin Community College
Deborah Laible, Southern Methodist University
Sara Lawrence, California State University, Northridge
David Lockwood, Humber College
Martin Marino, Atlantic Cape Community College
Behnaz Pakizegi, William Patterson University
Cathy Proctor-Castillo, Long Beach Community College
Christy Teranishi, Texas A&M International University
Alida Westman, Eastern Michigan University
Colin William, Columbus State Community College

Colleagues and students at Illinois State University aided my research and contributed significantly to the text's supplements. Richard Payne, Department of Politics and Government, is a kind and devoted friend with whom I have shared many profitable discussions about the writing process, the condition of children and families, and other topics that significantly influenced my perspective on child development and social policy. JoDe Paladino's outstanding, dedicated work in conducting literature searches and in revising the Study Guide has been invaluable. Sara Harris and Leslie Barnes Young joined me in preparing a thoroughly revised Instructor's Resource Manual, bringing to the task enthusiasm, imagination, depth of knowledge, and impressive writing skill. Sara extended her remarkable talents to MyDevelopmentLab, collaborating with me in the preparation of the first edition of this unique teaching tool for all three of my texts. Kristy Barnes and Tara Kindelberger spent countless hours gathering library materials.

The supplements package also benefited from the talents and diligence of two other individuals. Gabrielle Principe of Ursinus College and Naomi Tyler of Vanderbilt University authored a superb test bank with great concern for clarity and accuracy.

I have been fortunate to work with a highly capable editorial team at Allyn and Bacon. Tom Pauken laid the groundwork for this edition, arranging for manuscript reviews and advising on the book's features. Although he has moved on to a career in teaching, I value our continued friendship and his concern for children's welfare. Jennifer Albanese served as Managing Editor for the fifth edition, bringing skillful and caring attention to this multifaceted task. She inspired the new Applying What We Know tables, oversaw its numerous supplements, arranged for a video shoot that greatly expanded my ability to illustrate important developmental concepts and milestones, kept me abreast of the status of all aspects of the project, contributed uniquely to its photo illustrations, and much, much more. Jenn's understanding of and interest in children have added to my pleasure in working with her this year.

Susan Messer undertook the development activities for this book for the second time. It is difficult to find words that do justice to her contributions. Susan worked closely with me as I wrote each chapter, making sure that every thought and concept would be precisely expressed and well developed. Her keen writing and editing skills and prompt and patient responses to my concerns and queries have enhanced every aspect of this edition and made working with her an exceptional learning experience.

Liz Napolitano, Senior Production Editor, managed the complex production tasks that resulted in a beautiful fifth edition. I am grateful for her keen esthetic sense, attention to detail, flexibility, efficiency, and thoughtfulness, and I look forward to a continuing partnership with her in future editions. I thank Sarah Evertson for obtaining the exceptional photographs that so aptly illustrate the text narrative. Connie Day and Bill Heckman provided outstanding copyediting and proofreading.

I would like to express a heartfelt thank you to Pamela Laskey, Executive Marketing Manager, for her exceptional work in marketing my texts. Pam has made sure that accurate and clear information about my books and their ancillaries reached Allyn and Bacon's sales force and that the needs of prospective and current adopters were met. My special appreciation to Pam for her masterful efforts in helping me plan and deliver a lively and instructive presentation to the Allyn and Bacon sales force, replete with child demonstrations and an interview with an emerging adult.

A final word of gratitude goes to my family, whose love, patience, and understanding have enabled me to be wife, mother, teacher, researcher, and text author at the same time. My sons, David and Peter, grew up with my child development texts, passing from childhood to adolescence and then to emerging and young adulthood as successive editions were written. David has a special connection with the books' subject matter as an elementary school teacher, and Peter is now an attorney. Both continue to enhance my understanding through reflections on events and progress in their own lives. I thank them for helping me grasp the awe-inspiring continuities and discontinuities in development in a most profound and personally enriching way. My husband, Ken, willingly made room for yet another time-consuming endeavor in our life together and communicated his belief in its importance in a great many unspoken, caring ways.

Laura E. Berk

About the Chapter Opening Art

I would like to extend grateful acknowledgments to the International Museum of Children's Art, Oslo, Norway, for the exceptional cover image and chapter opening art, which depict the talents, concerns, and viewpoints of young artists from around the world. I was privileged to visit the museum several years ago and was greatly moved by the endless variety and imaginativeness of the works gracing its walls. They express family, school, and community themes; good times and personal triumphs; profound appreciation for beauty; and great depth of emotion. I am pleased to share this window into children's creativity, insightfulness, sensitivity, and compassion with readers.

Thanks, also, to Joel Bergner for permission to include his breathtaking mural in the opening of Chapter 17, Emerging Adulthood. Joel is recipient of the 2004 Public Community Mural Award, San Francisco, California.

Supplementary Materials

Instructor's Supplements

A variety of teaching tools are available to assist instructors in organizing lectures, planning demonstrations and examinations, and ensuring student comprehension:

Instructor's Resource Manual (IRM)

Prepared by Sara Harris and Laura E. Berk, Illinois State University, and Leslie Barnes Young, Francis Marion University, this thoroughly revised IRM contains additional material to enrich your class presentations. For each chapter, the IRM provides a Chapter-at-a-Glance grid, Brief Chapter Summary, Learning Objectives, detailed Lecture Outline, Lecture Enhancements, Learning Activities, Ask Yourself questions with answers, Suggested Student Readings, Transparencies listing, and Media Materials. The Media Materials include descriptions that connect the *Observation* and *Windows* videos to the chapter content, and a listing of other media materials relevant to the chapter.

Test Bank

Prepared by Gabrielle Principe, Ursinus College, and Naomi Tyler, Vanderbilt University, the test bank contains over 2,000 multiple-choice questions, each of which is cross-referenced to a Learning Objective, page-referenced to chapter content, and classified by type (factual, applied, or conceptual). Each chapter also includes a selection of essay questions and sample answers.

Computerized Test Bank

This computerized version of the Test Bank, in easy-to-use software, lets you prepare tests for printing as well as for network and online testing. It has full editing capability. Test items are also available in CourseCompass, Blackboard, and WebCT formats.

Transparencies

Updated for this edition, over 200 full-color new transparencies taken from the text and other sources are referenced in the IRM for the most appropriate use in your classroom presentations.

"Infants, Children, and Adolescents in Action" Observation Program

This revised and expanded real-life videotape is over two hours in length and contains hundreds of observation segments that illustrate the many theories, concepts, and milestones of child development. New additions include twin interactions and early language among toddlers, a discussion of adolescent dating with a high school couple, and interviews with emerging adults. An Observation Guide helps students use the video in conjunction with the textbook, deepening their understanding and applying what they have learned to everyday life. The videotape and Observation Guide are free to instructors who adopt the text and are available to students at a discount when packaged with the text.

"A Window on Infants, Children, and Adolescents" Running Observational Footage Video

This video complements the Observation Program described above, through two hours of unscripted footage on many aspects of child development. An accompanying Video Guide is also available.

Powerpoint™ CD-ROM

A PowerPoint™ CD-ROM contains outlines of key points and illustrations from each chapter, as well as an electronic version of the Instructor's Resource Manual, making it easy to customize content.

Allyn & Bacon Digital Media Archive for Berk

This collection of media products – including charts, graphs, tables, figures, audio, and video clips – assists you in meeting your classroom goals.

My Development Lab

This is an interactive and instructive multimedia resource that can be used as a supplement to a traditional lecture course or to completely administer an online course. Prepared in collaboration with Laura Berk, this product makes use of extensive video that illustrates developmental milestones and processes. Its power lies in its design as an all inclusive tool, combining an online version of the textbook, plus multimedia tutorials, simulations, and controlled assessments to completely engage students and reinforce learning. Visit *http://www.mydevelopmentlab.com* to tour the product, and discover where child development comes to life.

Student Supplements

Beyond the study aids found in the textbook, Allyn & Bacon offers a number of supplements for students:

Grade Aid Workbook with Practice Tests

Prepared by JoDe Paladino and Laura Berk of Illinois State University, this helpful guide offers Chapter Summaries, Learning Objectives, Study Questions organized according to major headings in the text, Suggested Student Readings, Crossword Puzzles for mastering important terms, and two multiple-choice Practice Tests per chapter.

Website

The Companion Website, *http://www.ablongman.com/berk* offers support for students through chapter-specific learning objectives, annotated web resources, flashcard vocabulary building, activities, practice tests, Ask Yourself questions that also appear in the text, along with model answers, and milestones tables. The site also features an *eThemes of the Times* section with full text articles from the *New York Times*.

Video Workshop for *Infants, Children, and Adolescents*

This complete teaching and learning system includes quality video footage on an easy-to-use CD-ROM plus a Student Learning Guide and an Instructor's Teaching Guide—both with text-specific Correlation Grids. Video Workshop is available FREE when packaged with the text. Contact your Allyn & Bacon sales representative for additional details and ordering information or visit *http://www.ablongman.com/ videoworkshop*.

ResearchNavigator™

Through three exclusive databases, this intuitive search interface allows students to efficiently make the most of their research time and provides extensive help in the research process. EBSCO's *ContentSelect* Academic Journal Database permits a discipline-specific search through professional and popular journals. Also featured are the *New York Times* Search-by-Subject Archive, and *Best of the Web* Link Library. (A required access code is contained in *ResearchNavigator* Guide). Visit *http://www.researchnavigator.com*.

ResearchNavigator Guide: Human Development, with Research Navigator Access Code

Designed to help students select and evaluate research from the Web, this booklet contains a practical discussion of search engines, detailed information on evaluating online sources, citation guidelines for web resources, additional web activities and links for human development, and an access code and guide to *ResearchNavigator* (available only when packaged with the text).

TutorCenter

(Access code required). The Tutor Center provides students free, one-on-one, interactive tutoring from qualified instructors on all material in the text. Tutors offer help with understanding major developmental principles and suggest effective study techniques. Tutoring assistance is available by phone, FAX, Internet, and e-mail during Tutor Center hours. For more details and ordering information, please contact your Allyn & Bacon publisher's representative or visit *http://www.aw.com/tutorcenter*.

Infants and Children

A village fair draws people of all ages out of their homes into the full richness of their physical and social worlds. Chapter 1 will introduce you to a multiplicity of ways of thinking about and studying children's development.

"Village Fair"
Saima Saima Shahid
13 years, Bangladesh

Reprinted with permission from the International Museum of Children's Art, Oslo, Norway.

History, Theory, and Research Strategies

Not long ago, I left my Midwestern home to live for a year near the small city in northern California where I spent my childhood. One morning, I visited the neighborhood where I grew up—a place I had not seen since I was 12 years old.

I stood at the entrance to my old schoolyard. Buildings and grounds that had looked large to me as a child now seemed strangely small. I peered through the window of my first-grade classroom. The desks were no longer arranged in rows but grouped in intimate clusters. Computers rested against the far wall, near where I once sat. I walked my old route home from school, the distance shrunken by my longer stride. I stopped in front of my best friend Kathryn's house, where we once drew sidewalk pictures, crossed the street to play kickball, and produced plays in the garage. In place of the small shop where I had purchased penny candy stood a child-care center, filled with the voices and vigorous activity of toddlers and preschoolers.

As I walked, I reflected on early experiences that contributed to who and what I am today—weekends helping my father in his downtown clothing shop, the year my mother studied to become a high school teacher, moments of companionship and rivalry with my sister and brother, Sunday outings to museums and the seashore, and visits to my grandmother's house, where I became someone extra special.

As I passed the homes of my childhood friends, I thought of what I knew about their present lives. Kathryn, star student and president of our sixth-grade class—today a successful corporate lawyer and mother of two. Shy, withdrawn Phil, cruelly teased because of his cleft lip—now owner of a thriving chain of hardware stores and member of the city council. Julio, immigrant from Mexico who joined our class in third grade—today director of an elementary school bilingual education program and single parent of an adopted Mexican boy. And finally, my next-door neighbor Rick, who picked fights at recess, struggled with reading, repeated fourth grade, dropped out of high school, and (so I heard) moved from one job to another over the following 10 years.

As you begin this course in child development, perhaps you, too, wonder about some of the same questions that crossed my mind during that nostalgic neighborhood walk:

- In what ways are children's home, school, and neighborhood experiences the same today as they were in generations past, and in what ways are they different?

- How is the infant and young child's perception of the world the same as the adult's, and how is it different?

- What determines the features that humans have in common and those that make each of us unique—physically, mentally, and behaviorally?

- How did Julio, transplanted to a foreign culture at 8 years of age, master its language and customs and succeed in its society, yet remain strongly identified with his ethnic community?

- Why do some of us, like Kathryn and Rick, retain the same styles of responding that characterized us as children, whereas others, like Phil, change in essential ways?

These are central questions addressed by **child development,** a field of study devoted to understanding constancy and change from conception through adolescence and emerging adulthood. Child development is part of a larger discipline known as *developmental psychology* or, in its interdisciplinary sense, *human development,* which includes all changes we experience throughout the lifespan. Great diversity characterizes the interests and concerns of the thousands of investigators who study child development. But all have a common goal: to describe and identify those factors that influence the consistencies and changes in young people during the first two and one-half decades of life.

The Field of Child Development

Look again at the questions just listed, and you will see that they are not just of scientific interest. Each has *applied,* or practical, importance as well. In fact, scientific curiosity is just one factor that led child development to become the exciting field of study it is today. Research about development has also been stimulated by social pressures to better the lives of children. For example, the beginning of public education in the early part of the twentieth century led to a demand for knowledge about what and how to teach children of different ages. Pediatricians' interest in improving children's health required an understanding of physical growth and nutrition. The social service profession's desire to treat children's anxieties and behavior problems required information about personality and social development. And parents have continually asked for advice about child-rearing practices and experiences that would promote the well-being of their child.

Our large storehouse of information about child development is *interdisciplinary.* It has grown through the combined efforts of people from many fields. Because of the need for solutions to everyday problems concerning children, researchers from psychology, sociology, anthropology, and biology joined forces with professionals from education, family studies, medicine, public health, and social service, to name just a few. The field of child development, as it exists today, is a monument to the contributions of these many disciplines. Its body of knowledge is not just scientifically important but also relevant and useful.

Periods of Development

How can we divide the flow of time we are about to consider into sensible, manageable parts? To solve this dilemma, researchers usually use the following age periods, according to which I have organized this book. Each brings with it new capacities and social expectations that serve as important transitions in major theories.

● *The prenatal period: from conception to birth.* This 9-month period is the most rapid phase of change, during which a one-celled organism is transformed into a human baby with remarkable capacities for adjusting to life in the surrounding world.

● *Infancy and toddlerhood: from birth to 2 years.* This period brings dramatic changes in the body and brain that support the emergence of a wide array of motor, perceptual, and intellectual capacities; the beginnings of language; and first intimate ties to others.

● *Early childhood: from 2 to 6 years.* During this period, the body becomes longer and leaner, motor skills are refined, and children become more self-controlled and self-sufficient. Make-believe play blossoms and supports every aspect of psychological development. Thought and language expand at an astounding pace, a sense of morality becomes evident, and children establish ties with peers.

● *Middle childhood: from 6 to 11 years.* These are the school years, a phase in which children learn about the wider world and master new responsibilities that increasingly resemble those they will perform as adults. Improved athletic abilities, participation in organized games with rules, more logical thought processes, mastery of basic literacy skills, and advances in understanding the self, morality, and friendship are hallmarks of this phase.

● *Adolescence: from 11 to 18 years.* This period initiates the transition to adulthood. Puberty leads to an adult-sized body and sexual maturity. Thought becomes abstract and idealistic, and schooling becomes increasingly directed at preparation for higher education and the world of work. Establishing autonomy from the family and beginning to define personal values and goals are major concerns.

● *Emerging adulthood: from 18 to 25 years.* For many contemporary youths, especially those in industrialized nations, the transition to adult roles has extended further, resulting in this new period. Young people pursue higher education, and their exploration of options in love, career, and personal values becomes more intense and serious prior to their making enduring commitments. Because emerging adulthood has surfaced only in the past few decades, researchers have just begun to study it.

Domains of Development

To make the vast, interdisciplinary study of human constancy and change more orderly and convenient, development is often divided into three broad domains: *physical, cognitive,* and *emotional and social.* Refer to Figure 1.1 on page 6 for a description and illustration of each. Within each period from infancy through adolescence, we will consider the three domains in the order just listed. Yet the domains are not really distinct. Instead, they combine in an integrated, holistic fashion to yield the living, growing child. Furthermore, each domain influences and is influenced by the others. For example, in Chapter 5 you will see that new motor capacities, such as reaching, sitting, crawling, and walking (physical), contribute greatly to infants' understanding of their surroundings (cognitive). When babies think and act more competently, adults begin to stimulate them more with games, language, and expressions of delight at their new achievements (emotional and social). These enriched experiences, in turn, promote all aspects of development.

Although each chapter focuses on a particular domain, you will encounter instances of the interwoven nature of all domains on nearly every page of this book. Also, look for the *Ask Yourself* feature at the end of major sections. Within it, I have included *Review* questions, which help

Child development is so dramatic that researchers divide it into age periods. These brothers and sisters illustrate, clockwise from bottom, toddlerhood, early childhood (age 4), middle childhood (age 6), and middle childhood (age 8).

Emotional and Social Development
Changes in emotional communication, self-understanding, knowledge about other people, interpersonal skills, friendships, intimate relationships, and moral reasoning and behavior

Physical Development
Changes in body size, proportions, appearance, functioning of body systems, perceptual and motor capacities, and physical health

Cognitive Development
Changes in intellectual abilities, including attention, memory, academic and everyday knowledge, problem solving, imagination, creativity, and language

© DENNIS MACDONALD/PHOTOEDIT

© JOSE LUIS PELAEZ, INC./CORBIS

© CHRIS BARTLETT/GETTY IMAGES/TAXI

FIGURE 1.1

Major domains of development.

The three domains are not really distinct. Rather, they overlap and interact.

you recall and think about information you have just read; *Apply* questions, which encourage you to apply your knowledge to controversial issues and problems faced by parents, teachers, and children; *Connect* questions, which help you form a coherent, unified picture of child development that integrates domains; and *Reflect* questions, which invite you to reflect on your own development and that of people you know well. The questions are designed to deepen your understanding and inspire new insights.

With this introduction in mind, let's turn to some basic issues that have captivated, puzzled, and sparked debate among child development theorists. Then our discussion will trace the emergence of the field and survey major theories. We will return to each contemporary theory in greater detail in later chapters.

Basic Issues

Research on child development is a relatively recent endeavor. It did not begin until the late nineteenth and early twentieth centuries. Nevertheless, ideas about how children grow and change have existed for centuries. As these speculations combined with research, they inspired the construction of *theories* of development. A **theory** is an orderly, integrated set of statements that describes, explains, and predicts behavior. For example, a good theory of infant–caregiver attachment would (1) *describe* the behaviors of babies around 6 to 8 months of age as they seek the affection and comfort of a familiar adult, (2) *explain* how and why infants develop this strong desire to bond with a caregiver, and (3) *predict* the consequences of this emotional bond for future relationships.

Theories are vital tools for two reasons. First, they provide organizing frameworks for our observations of children. In other words, they *guide and give meaning* to what we see. Second, theories that are verified by research often serve as a sound basis for practical action. Once a theory helps us *understand* development, we are in a much better position to *know what to do* to improve the welfare and treatment of children.

As we will see later, theories are influenced by the cultural values and belief systems of their times. But theories differ in one important way from mere opinion and belief: A theory's continued existence depends on *scientific verification*. This means that the theory must be tested with a fair set of research procedures agreed on by the scientific community, and its findings must endure, or be replicated, over time.

The field of child development contains many theories with very different ideas about what children are like and how they change. The study of child development provides no ultimate truth because investigators do not always agree on the meaning of what they see. In addition, children are complex beings; they change physically, cognitively, emotionally, and socially. As yet, no single theory has explained all these aspects. However, the existence of many theories helps advance knowledge because researchers are continually trying to support, contradict, and integrate these different points of view.

Although there are many theories, we can easily organize them, since nearly all take a stand on three basic issues: (1) Is the course of development continuous or discontinuous? (2) Does one course of development characterize all children, or are there many possible courses? (3) Are genetic or environmental factors more important in influencing development? Let's look closely at each of these issues.

Continuous or Discontinuous Development?

Recently, the mother of 20-month-old Angelo reported to me with amazement that her young son had pushed a toy car across the living room floor while making a motorlike sound, "Brmmmm, brmmmm," for the first time. When he hit a nearby wall with a bang, Angelo let go of the car, exclaimed, "C'ash," and laughed heartily.

"How come Angelo can pretend, but he couldn't a few months ago?" queried his mother. "And I wonder what 'Brmmmm, brmmmm' and 'Crash!' mean to Angelo? Is his understanding of motorlike sounds and collision similar to mine?"

Angelo's mother has raised a puzzling issue about development: How can we best describe the differences in capacities and behavior between small infants, young children, adolescents, and adults? As Figure 1.2 on page 8 illustrates, most major theories recognize two possibilities.

Theories are of practical importance; they help us improve the welfare and treatment of children. For example, theories have contributed to new approaches to education that emphasize exploration, discovery, and collaboration. As a result, children express greater enthusiasm for learning.

FIGURE 1.2

Is development continuous or discontinuous?

(a) Some theorists believe that development is a smooth, continuous process. Children gradually add more of the same types of skills. (b) Other theorists think that development takes place in discontinuous stages. Children change rapidly as they step up to a new level of development and then change very little for a while. With each step, the child interprets and responds to the world in a qualitatively different way.

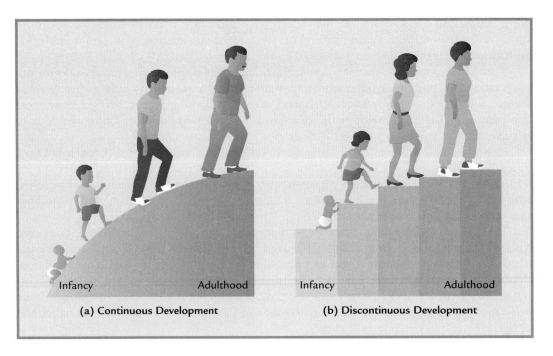

(a) **Continuous Development**   (b) **Discontinuous Development**

One view holds that infants and preschoolers respond to the world in much the same way as adults do. The difference between the immature and the mature being is simply one of *amount or complexity.* For example, little Angelo's thinking might be just as logical and well organized as our own. Perhaps (as his mother reports) he can sort objects into simple categories, recognize whether he has more of one kind than of another, and remember where he left his favorite toy at child care the week before. Angelo's only limitation may be that he cannot perform these skills with as much information and precision as we can. If this is so, then Angelo's development is **continuous**—a process of gradually augmenting the same types of skills that were there to begin with.

According to a second view, Angelo's thoughts, emotions, and behavior differ considerably from those of adults. If so, then development is **discontinuous**—a process in which new ways of understanding and responding to the world emerge at specific times. From this perspective, Angelo is not yet able to organize objects or remember and interpret experiences as we do. Instead, he will move through a series of developmental steps, each with unique features, until he reaches the highest level of functioning.

Theories that accept the discontinuous perspective regard development as taking place in **stages**—*qualitative changes* in thinking, feeling, and behaving that characterize specific periods of development. In stage theories, development is much like climbing a staircase, with each step corresponding to a more mature, reorganized way of functioning. The stage concept also assumes that children undergo periods of rapid transformation as they step up from one stage to the next, followed by plateaus during which they stand solidly within a stage. In other words, change is fairly sudden rather than gradual and ongoing.

Does development actually occur in a neat, orderly sequence of stages? For now, let's note that this is a very ambitious assumption that has faced significant challenges. We will review some influential stage theories later in this chapter.

●One Course of Development or Many?

Stage theorists assume that people everywhere follow the same sequence of development. For example, in the domain of cognition, a stage theorist might try to identify the common influences that lead children to represent their world through language and make-believe play in early childhood, to think more logically and systematically in middle childhood, and to reason abstractly in adolescence.

At the same time, the field of child development is becoming increasingly aware that children grow up in distinct **contexts, or unique combinations of personal and environmental circumstances that can result in different paths of change.** For example, a shy child who fears social encounters develops in very different contexts from those of a sociable agemate who readily seeks out other people (Rubin & Coplan, 1998). Children in non-Western village societies encounter experiences in their families and communities that differ sharply from those of children in large Western cities. These different circumstances foster different cognitive capacities, social skills, and feelings about the self and others (Shweder et al., 1998).

As you will see, contemporary theorists regard the contexts that mold development as many-layered and complex. On the personal side, these include heredity and biological makeup. On the environmental side, they include immediate settings, such as home, child-care center, school, and neighborhood, as well as circumstances more remote from children's everyday lives—community resources, societal values and priorities, and historical time period. Finally, a special interest in culture has made researchers more conscious than ever before of diversity in development.

Nature or Nurture as More Important?

In addition to describing the course of child development, each theory takes a stand on a major question about its underlying causes: Are genetic or environmental factors more important in influencing development? This is the age-old **nature–nurture controversy.** By *nature*, we mean inborn biological givens—the hereditary information we receive from our parents at the moment of conception. By *nurture*, we mean the complex forces of the physical and social world that influence our biological makeup and psychological experiences before and after birth.

Although all theories grant at least some role to both nature and nurture, they vary in emphasis. For example, consider the following questions: Is the older child's ability to think in more complex ways largely the result of an inborn timetable of growth? Or is it primarily influenced by stimulation from parents and teachers? Do children acquire language because they are genetically predisposed to do so or because parents intensively tutor them from an early age? And what accounts for the vast individual differences among children—in height, weight, physical coordination, intelligence, personality, and social skills? Is nature or nurture more responsible?

A theory's position on the roles of nature and nurture affects how it explains individual differences. Some theorists emphasize *stability*—that children who are high or low in a characteristic (such as verbal ability, anxiety, or sociability) will remain so at later ages. These theorists typically stress the importance of *heredity.* If they regard environment as important, they usually point to *early experiences* as establishing a lifelong pattern of behavior. Powerful negative events in the first few years, they argue, cannot be fully overcome by later, more positive ones (Bowlby, 1980; Sroufe, Egeland, & Kreutzer, 1990). Other theorists are more optimistic. They believe that *change* is possible and likely if new experiences support it (Chess & Thomas, 1984; Nelson, 2002; Werner & Smith, 2001).

Throughout this book, you will see that investigators disagree, often sharply, on the question of *stability or change.* The answers they provide are of great applied significance. If you believe that development is largely due to nature, then providing experiences aimed at promoting change would seem to be of little value. If, on the other hand, you are convinced of the supreme importance of early experience, then you would intervene as soon as possible, offering high-quality stimulation and support to ensure that children develop at their best. Finally, if you think that environment is profoundly influential throughout development, you would provide assistance any time children face difficulties, believing that, with the help of favorable life circumstances, they can recover from early negative events.

Biology and Environment

Resilient Children

John and his best friend Gary grew up in a run-down, crime-ridden inner-city neighborhood. By age 10, each had experienced years of family conflict followed by parental divorce. Reared for the rest of childhood and adolescence in mother-headed households, John and Gary rarely saw their fathers. Both achieved poorly, dropped out of high school, and were in and out of trouble with the police.

Then John and Gary's paths diverged. By age 30, John had fathered two children with women he never married, had spent time in prison, was unemployed, and drank alcohol heavily. In contrast, Gary had returned to finish high school, had studied auto mechanics at a community college, and became manager of a gas station and repair shop. Married with two children, he had saved his earnings and bought a home. He was happy, healthy, and well adapted to life.

A wealth of evidence shows that environmental risks—poverty, negative family interactions and parental divorce, job loss, mental illness, and drug abuse—predispose children to future problems (Masten & Coatsworth, 1998). Why did Gary "beat the odds" and come through unscathed?

New evidence on **resilience**—the ability to adapt effectively in the face of threats to development—is receiving increasing attention because investigators want to find ways to protect young people from the damaging effects of stressful life conditions (Masten, 2001). This interest has been inspired by several long-term studies on the relationship of life stressors in childhood to competence and adjustment in adolescence and adulthood (Garmezy, 1993; Rutter, 1987; Werner & Smith, 2001). In each study, some individuals were shielded from negative outcomes, whereas others had lasting problems. Four broad factors seemed to offer protection from the damaging effects of stressful life events.

Personal Characteristics

A child's biologically endowed characteristics can reduce exposure to risk or lead to experiences that compensate for early stressful events. High intelligence and socially valued talents (in music or athletics, for example) are protective factors. They increase the chances that a child will have rewarding experiences at school and in the community that offset the impact of a stressful home life. Temperament is particularly powerful. Children with easygoing, sociable dispositions have an optimistic outlook on life and a special capacity to adapt to change—qualities that elicit positive responses from others. In contrast, emotionally reactive and irritable children often tax the patience of people around them (Masten & Reed, 2002; Masten et al., 1999). For example, both John and Gary moved several times during their childhoods. Each time, John became anxious and angry. Gary looked forward to making new friends and exploring new parts of the neighborhood.

A Warm Parental Relationship

A close relationship with at least one parent who provides warmth, appropriately high expectations, monitoring of the child's activities, and an organized home environment fosters resilience. But note that this factor (as well as the next one) is not independent of children's personal characteristics. Children who are relaxed, socially responsive, and able to deal with change are easier to rear and more likely to enjoy positive relationships

A Balanced Point of View

So far, we have discussed the basic issues of child development in terms of extremes—solutions on one side or the other. As we trace the unfolding of the field in the rest of this chapter, you will see that the positions of many theories have softened. Contemporary ones, especially, recognize the merits of both sides. Some theorists believe that both continuous and discontinuous changes occur. And some acknowledge that development can have both universal features and features unique to the individual and his or her contexts. Furthermore, an increasing number of investigators regard heredity and environment as inseparably interwoven, each affecting the potential of the other to modify the child's traits and capacities (Gottlieb, 2002; Huttenlocher, 2002; Rutter, 2002). We will discuss these new ideas about nature and nurture in Chapter 2.

Finally, as you will see in later parts of this book, the relative impact of early and later experiences varies greatly from one domain of development to another and even—as the Biology and Environment box above indicates—across individuals! Because of the complex network of factors contributing to human change and the challenge of isolating the effects of each, many theoretical points of view have gathered research support. Although debate continues, this circumstance has also sparked more balanced visions of child development.

with parents and other people. At the same time, children can develop more attractive dispositions as a result of parental warmth and attention (Conger & Conger, 2002).

Social Support Outside the Immediate Family

The most consistent asset of resilient children is a strong bond to a competent,

This child's special relationship with her grandfather provides the social support she needs to cope with stress and solve problems constructively. A warm tie with a person outside the immediate family can promote resilience.

© ALAN HICKS/GETTY IMAGES/STONE

caring adult, who need not be a parent. A grandparent, aunt, uncle, or teacher who forms a special relationship with the child can promote resilience (Masten & Reed, 2002). Gary received support in adolescence from his grandfather, who listened to Gary's concerns and helped him solve problems constructively. In addition, Gary's grandfather had a stable marriage and work life and handled stressors skillfully. Consequently, he served as a model of effective coping.

Associations with rule-abiding peers who value school achievement are also linked to resilience. But children who have positive relationships with adults are far more likely to establish these supportive peer ties.

A Strong Community

Opportunities to participate in community life increase the chances that older children and adolescents will overcome adversity. Extracurricular activities at school, religious youth groups, scouting, and other organizations teach important social skills, such as cooperation, leadership, and contributing to others' welfare. As participants acquire these com-

petencies, they gain in self-reliance, self-esteem, and community commitment. As a college student, Gary volunteered for Habitat for Humanity, joining a team building affordable housing in low-income neighborhoods. Community involvement offered Gary additional opportunities to form meaningful relationships, which further strengthened his resilience (Seccombe, 2002).

Research on resilience highlights the complex connections between heredity and environment. Armed with positive characteristics, which stem from innate endowment, favorable rearing experiences, or both, children and adolescents take action to reduce stressful situations. Nevertheless, when many risks pile up, they are increasingly difficult to overcome (Quyen et al., 1998). Therefore, interventions must reduce risks and enhance relationships at home, in school, and in the community that protect children from the negative effects of risk. This means attending to both the person and the environment—strengthening children's capacities as well as reducing hazardous experiences.

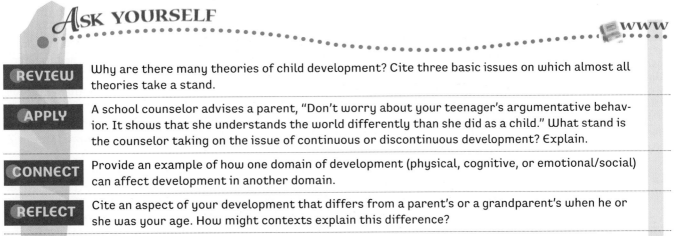

Ask YOURSELF   www

REVIEW Why are there many theories of child development? Cite three basic issues on which almost all theories take a stand.

APPLY A school counselor advises a parent, "Don't worry about your teenager's argumentative behavior. It shows that she understands the world differently than she did as a child." What stand is the counselor taking on the issue of continuous or discontinuous development? Explain.

CONNECT Provide an example of how one domain of development (physical, cognitive, or emotional/social) can affect development in another domain.

REFLECT Cite an aspect of your development that differs from a parent's or a grandparent's when he or she was your age. How might contexts explain this difference?

Historical Foundations

Contemporary theories of child development are the result of centuries of change in Western cultural values, philosophical thinking about children, and scientific progress. To understand the field as it exists today, we must return to its early beginnings—to influences that long preceded scientific child study. We will see that early ideas about children linger as important forces in current theory and research.

Medieval Times

Historical artifacts and writings show that childhood was regarded as a separate phase of life as early as medieval Europe—the sixth through the fifteenth centuries. Medieval painters often depicted children as childlike—dressed in loose, comfortable gowns while playing games and looking up to adults. Written texts contained terms that distinguished children under age 7 or 8 from other people and that recognized even young teenagers as not fully mature (Lett, 1997). Archeological digs have unearthed small bowls and eating utensils, toys, dolls, and other objects, which reveal that adults were sensitive to children's physical limitations and psychological needs.

By the fourteenth century, manuals offering advice on many aspects of child care, including health, feeding, clothing, games, and participation in family life, had become common (Alexandre-Bidon & Lett, 1997). In communities, laws recognized that children needed protection from people who might mistreat them. And courts exercised leniency with lawbreaking youths because of their tender years (Hanawalt, 1993).

In sum, in medieval times, if not before, clear awareness existed of children as vulnerable beings and of childhood as a distinct developmental period. Religious writings, however, contained contradictory beliefs about children's basic nature. Sometimes infants were portrayed as possessed by the devil and in need of purification through exorcism and baptism. At other times, they were characterized as innocent and close to angels (Hanawalt, 2003). Both ideas foreshadowed views of childhood in succeeding centuries.

THE ART ARCHIVE/BIBLIOTHÈQUE UNIVERSITAIRE DE MÉDECINE, MONTPELLIER/DAGLI ORTI

As far back as medieval times, adults regarded childhood as a distinct developmental period and were sensitive to children's needs. In this fourteenth-century image painted in a book of songs, children play a lively game of Blind Man's Bluff in a garden, dressed in loose, comfortable gowns.

The Reformation

In the sixteenth century, a revised image of childhood sprang from the Puritan belief in original sin. According to Puritan doctrine, children were born evil and stubborn and had to be civilized (Shahar, 1990). Harsh, restrictive child-rearing practices were recommended to tame the depraved child. Children were dressed in stiff, uncomfortable clothing that held them in adultlike postures, and disobedient pupils were routinely beaten by their schoolmasters. Although punitiveness was the prevailing child-rearing philosophy, love and affection for their children prevented most Puritan parents from exercising extremely repressive measures (Moran & Vinovskis, 1986).

As the Puritans emigrated from England to the United States, they brought the belief that child rearing was one of their most important obligations. Although they continued to regard the child's soul as tainted by original sin, they tried to promote reason in their sons and daughters so they could tell right from wrong (Clarke-Stewart, 1998). The Puritans were the first to devise special reading materials for children that instructed them in religious and moral ideals. As they trained their children in self-reliance and self-control, Puritan parents gradually adopted a moderate balance between discipline and indulgence, severity and permissiveness (Pollock, 1987).

Philosophies of the Enlightenment

The seventeenth-century Enlightenment brought new philosophies that emphasized ideals of human dignity and respect. Conceptions of childhood appeared that were more humane than those of centuries past.

JOHN LOCKE ● The writings of John Locke (1632–1704), a leading British philosopher, served as the forerunner of a twentieth-century perspective that we will discuss shortly: behaviorism. Locke viewed the child as a **tabula rasa.** Translated from Latin, this means "blank slate." According to this idea, children are, to begin with, nothing at all, and all kinds of experiences can shape their characters. Locke (1690/1892) described parents as rational tutors who can mold the child in any way they wish, through careful instruction, effective example, and rewards for good behavior. He was ahead of his time in recommending child-rearing practices that present-day research supports. For example, Locke suggested that parents reward children not with money or sweets but with praise and approval. He also opposed physical punishment: "The child repeatedly beaten in school cannot look upon books and teachers without experiencing fear and anger." Locke's philosophy led to a change from harshness toward children to kindness and compassion.

Look carefully at Locke's ideas, and you will see that he regarded development as *continuous;* adultlike behaviors are gradually built up through the warm, consistent teachings of parents. Furthermore, his view of the child as a tabula rasa means that he championed *nurture*—the power of the environment to shape the child. And his faith in nurture suggests the possibility of *many courses of development* and of *change at later ages* due to new experiences.

Finally, Locke's philosophy characterizes children as doing little to influence their own destiny, which is written on "blank slates" by others. This vision of a passive child has been discarded. All contemporary theories view children as active, purposeful beings who contribute substantially to their own development.

JEAN JACQUES ROUSSEAU ● In the eighteenth century, French philosopher Jean Jacques Rousseau (1712–1778) introduced a new view of childhood. Children, Rousseau claimed, are not blank slates to be filled by adult instruction. Instead, they are **noble savages,** naturally endowed with a sense of right and wrong and an innate plan for orderly, healthy growth. Unlike Locke, Rousseau thought that children's built-in moral sense and unique ways of thinking and feeling would only be harmed by adult training. His was a child-centered philosophy in which the adult should be receptive to the child's needs at each of four stages of development: infancy, childhood, late childhood, and adolescence.

Rousseau's philosophy includes two vitally important concepts that are found in contemporary theories. The first is the concept of *stage,* which we discussed earlier. The second is the concept of **maturation,** which refers to a genetically determined, naturally unfolding course of growth. Unlike Locke, Rousseau saw children as determining their own destinies. And he viewed development as a *discontinuous, stagewise* process that follows a *single, unified course* mapped out by *nature.*

Scientific Beginnings

The study of child development evolved quickly during the late nineteenth and early twentieth centuries. Early observations of children were soon followed by improved methods and theories. Each advance contributed to the firm foundation on which the field rests today.

DARWIN: FOREFATHER OF SCIENTIFIC CHILD STUDY ● A century after Rousseau, the British naturalist Charles Darwin (1809–1882) joined an expedition to distant parts of the world, where he observed infinite variation among plant and animal species. He also saw that within a species, no two individuals are exactly alike. From these observations, he constructed his famous theory of evolution.

The theory emphasized two related principles: *natural selection* and *survival of the fittest.* Darwin explained that certain species survived in particular parts of the world because they

Early theories of child development sparked a parenting advice literature, which today fills shelf after shelf in public libraries and bookstores. This woman prepares for parenthood by reading about what to expect in the first year of her baby's life.

have characteristics that fit with, or are adapted to, their surroundings. Other species die off because they are not as well suited to their environments. Individuals within a species who best meet the survival requirements of the environment live long enough to reproduce and pass their more favorable characteristics to future generations. Darwin's emphasis on the adaptive value of physical characteristics and behavior eventually found its way into important developmental theories.

During his explorations, Darwin discovered that the early prenatal growth of many species is strikingly similar. Other scientists concluded from Darwin's observation that the development of the human child followed the same general plan as the evolution of the human species. Although this belief eventually proved inaccurate, efforts to chart parallels between child growth and human evolution prompted researchers to make careful observations of all aspects of children's behavior. Out of these first attempts to document an idea about development, scientific child study was born.

THE NORMATIVE PERIOD ● G. Stanley Hall (1846–1924), one of the most influential American psychologists of the early twentieth century, is generally regarded as the founder of the child-study movement (Dixon & Lerner, 1999). Inspired by Darwin's work, Hall and his well-known student Arnold Gesell (1880–1961) devised theories based on evolutionary ideas. These early leaders regarded development as a genetically determined process that unfolds automatically, much like a flower (Gesell, 1933; Hall, 1904).

Hall and Gesell are remembered less for their one-sided theories than for their intensive efforts to describe all aspects of child development. They launched the **normative approach, in which measures of behavior are taken on large numbers of individuals, and age-related averages are computed to represent typical development.** Using this procedure, Hall constructed elaborate questionnaires asking children of different ages almost everything they could tell about themselves—interests, fears, imaginary playmates, dreams, friendships, everyday knowledge, and more (White, 1992). In the same fashion, Gesell collected detailed normative information on the motor achievements, social behaviors, and personality characteristics of infants and children.

Gesell was also among the first to make knowledge about child development meaningful to parents. If, as he believed, the timetable of development is the product of millions of years of evolution, then children are naturally knowledgeable about their needs. His child-rearing advice, in the tradition of Rousseau, recommended sensitivity to children's cues (Thelen & Adolph, 1992). Along with Benjamin Spock's *Baby and Child Care,* Gesell's books became a central part of a rapidly expanding popular literature for parents.

THE MENTAL TESTING MOVEMENT ● While Hall and Gesell were developing their theories and methods in the United States, French psychologist Alfred Binet (1857–1911) was also taking a normative approach to child development, but for a different reason. In the early 1900s, Binet and his colleague Theodore Simon were asked by Paris school officials to find a way to identify children with learning problems who needed to be placed in special classes. The first successful intelligence test, which they constructed for this purpose, grew out of practical educational concerns.

Binet's effort was unique in that he began with a well-developed theory. In contrast to earlier views, which reduced intelligence to simple elements of reaction time and sensitivity to physical stimuli, Binet captured the complexity of children's thinking. He defined intelligence as good judgment, planning, and critical reflection (Sternberg & Jarvin, 2003). Then he created age-graded test items that directly measured these abilities.

In 1916, at Stanford University, Binet's test was adapted for use with English-speaking children. Since then the English version has been known as the *Stanford-Binet Intelligence Scale.* Besides providing a score that could successfully predict school achievement, the Binet test sparked tremendous interest in individual differences in development. Comparisons of the scores of children who vary in gender, ethnicity, birth order, family background, and other characteristics became a major focus of research. Intelligence tests also rose quickly to the forefront of the controversy over nature versus nurture that has continued to this day.

ASK YOURSELF

www

REVIEW Suppose we could arrange a debate between John Locke and Jean Jacques Rousseau on the nature–nurture controversy. Summarize the argument that each historical figure is likely to present.

CONNECT What do the ideas of Rouseau, Darwin, and Hall have in common?

REFLECT Find out if your parents read Gesell, Spock, or other parenting advice books when you were growing up. What questions about child rearing most concerned them? Do you think today's parents have concerns that differ from those of your parents? Explain.

Mid-Twentieth-Century Theories

In the mid-twentieth century, the field of child development expanded. As child development attracted increasing interest, a variety of theories emerged, each of which continues to have followers today. In these theories, the European concern with the child's inner thoughts and feelings contrasts sharply with the North American academic focus on scientific precision and concrete, observable behavior.

The Psychoanalytic Perspective

By the 1930s and 1940s, parents increasingly sought help from professionals in dealing with children's emotional difficulties. The earlier normative movement had answered the question, What are children like? But now another question had to be addressed: How and why do children become the way they are? To treat psychological problems, psychiatrists and social workers turned to an emerging approach to personality development that emphasized the unique history of each child.

According to the **psychoanalytic perspective,** children move through a series of stages in which they confront conflicts between biological drives and social expectations. The way these conflicts are resolved determines the person's ability to learn, to get along with others, and to cope with anxiety. Although many individuals contributed to the psychoanalytic perspective, two have been especially influential: Sigmund Freud, founder of the psychoanalytic movement, and Erik Erikson.

FREUD'S THEORY ● Freud (1856–1939), a Viennese physician, saw patients in his practice with a variety of symptoms, such as hallucinations, fears, and paralyses, that appeared to have no physical basis. Seeking a cure for these troubled adults, Freud found that their symptoms could be relieved by having patients talk freely about painful events of their childhoods. Working with these remembrances, Freud examined the unconscious motivations of his patients and constructed his **psychosexual theory,** which emphasizes that how parents manage their child's sexual and aggressive drives in the first few years of life is crucial for healthy personality development.

Three Parts of the Personality. In Freud's theory, three parts of the personality—id, ego, and superego—become integrated during a sequence of five stages, summarized in Table 1.1 on page 16. The *id,* the largest portion of the mind, is the source of basic biological needs and desires. The *ego,* the conscious, rational part of personality, emerges in early infancy to redirect the id's impulses so that they are discharged in acceptable ways. For example, aided by the ego, the hungry baby of a few months of age stops crying when he sees his mother warm a bottle or unfasten her clothing for breastfeeding. And the more competent preschooler goes into the kitchen and gets a snack on her own.

TABLE 1.1

Freud's Psychosexual Stages

PSYCHOSEXUAL STAGE	APPROXIMATE AGE	DESCRIPTION
Oral	Birth–1 year	The new ego directs the baby's sucking activities toward breast or bottle. If oral needs are not met appropriately, the individual may develop such habits as thumb sucking, fingernail biting, and pencil chewing in childhood and overeating and smoking later in life.
Anal	1–3 years	Young toddlers and preschoolers enjoy holding and releasing urine and feces. Toilet training becomes a major issue between parent and child. If parents insist that children be trained before they are ready or make too few demands, conflicts about anal control may appear in the form of extreme orderliness and cleanliness or messiness and disorder.
Phallic	3–6 years	Id impulses transfer to the genitals, and the child finds pleasure in genital stimulation. Freud's Oedipus conflict for boys and Electra conflict for girls arise, and young children feel a sexual desire for the other-sex parent. To avoid punishment, they give up this desire and, instead, adopt the same-sex parent's characteristics and values. As a result, the superego is formed. The relations between id, ego, and superego established at this time determine the individual's basic personality.
Latency	6–11 years	Sexual instincts die down, and the superego develops further. The child acquires new social values from adults outside the family and from play with same-sex peers.
Genital	Adolescence	Puberty causes the sexual impulses of the phallic stage to reappear. If development has been successful during earlier stages, it leads to mature sexuality, marriage, and the birth and rearing of children.

In psychoanalytic theory, the ego redirects the id's impulses so the child's needs are satisfied in socially acceptable ways. Here a 3-year-old who wants to play with a puzzle refrains from grabbing and, instead, asks to help her classmate.

© LAURA DWIGHT

Between 3 and 6 years of age, the *superego*, or conscience, develops from interactions with parents, who insist that children conform to the values of society. Now the ego faces the increasingly complex task of reconciling the demands of the id, the external world, and conscience (Freud, 1923/1974). For example, when the ego is tempted to gratify an id impulse by hitting a playmate to get an attractive toy, the superego may warn that such behavior is wrong. The ego must decide which of the two forces (id or superego) will win this inner struggle, or it must work out a compromise, such as asking for a turn with the toy. According to Freud, the relations established between id, ego, and superego during the preschool years determine the individual's basic personality.

Psychosexual Development. Freud (1938/1973) believed that during childhood, sexual impulses shift their focus from the oral to the anal to the genital regions of the body. In each stage, parents walk a fine line between permitting too much or too little gratification of their child's basic needs. If parents strike an appropriate balance, then children grow into well-adjusted adults with the capacity for mature sexual behavior, investment in family life, and rearing of the next generation.

Freud's psychosexual theory highlighted the importance of family relationships and early experiences for children's development. But Freud's perspective was eventually criticized. First, the theory overemphasized the influence of sexual feelings in development. Second, because it was based on the problems of sexually repressed, well-to-do adults, it did not apply in cultures differing from nineteenth-century Victorian society. Finally, Freud had not studied children directly.

ERIKSON'S THEORY ● Several of Freud's followers took what was useful from his theory and improved on his vision. The most important of these neo-Freudians is Erik Erikson (1902–1994).

Although Erikson (1950) accepted Freud's psychosexual framework, he expanded the picture of development at each stage. In his **psychosocial theory,** Erikson emphasized that the ego does not just mediate between id impulses and superego demands. It is also a positive force in development. At each stage, it acquires attitudes and skills that make the individual an active,

TABLE 1.2

Erikson's Psychosocial Stages, with Corresponding Psychosexual Stages Indicated

PSYCHOSOCIAL STAGE	PERIOD OF DEVELOPMENT	DESCRIPTION
Basic trust versus mistrust (Oral)	Birth–1 year	From warm, responsive care, infants gain a sense of trust, or confidence, that the world is good. Mistrust occurs when infants have to wait too long for comfort and are handled harshly.
Autonomy versus shame and doubt (Anal)	1–3 years	Using new mental and motor skills, children want to choose and decide for themselves. Autonomy is fostered when parents permit reasonable free choice and do not force or shame the child.
Initiative versus guilt (Phallic)	3–6 years	Through make-believe play, children experiment with the kind of person they can become. Initiative—a sense of ambition and responsibility—develops when parents support their child's new sense of purpose. The danger is that parents will demand too much self-control, which leads to overcontrol, meaning too much guilt.
Industry versus inferiority (Latency)	6–11 years	At school, children develop the capacity to work and cooperate with others. Inferiority develops when negative experiences at home, at school, or with peers lead to feelings of incompetence.
Identity versus identity confusion (Genital)	Adolescence	The adolescent tries to answer the question, Who am I, and what is my place in society? Self-chosen values and goals lead to a lasting personal identity. The negative outcome is confusion about future adult roles.
Intimacy versus isolation	Emerging adulthood	As the quest for identity continues, young people also work on establishing intimate ties to others. Because of earlier disappointments, some individuals cannot form close relationships and remain isolated.
Generativity versus stagnation	Adulthood	Generativity means giving to the next generation through child rearing, caring for other people, or productive work. The person who fails in these ways feels an absence of meaningful accomplishment.
Integrity versus despair	Old age	In this final stage, individuals reflect on the kind of person they have been. Integrity results from feeling that life was worth living as it happened. Old people who are dissatisfied with their lives fear death.

Erik Erikson

contributing member of society. A basic psychological conflict, which is resolved along a continuum from positive to negative, determines whether healthy or maladaptive outcomes occur at each stage. As Table 1.2 shows, Erikson's first five stages parallel Freud's stages, but Erikson added three adult stages. He was one of the first to recognize the lifespan nature of development.

Finally, unlike Freud, Erikson pointed out that normal development must be understood in relation to each culture's life situation. For example, in the 1940s, he observed that Yurok Indians of the northwest coast of the United States deprived babies of breastfeeding for the first 10 days after birth and instead fed them a thin soup from a small shell. At age 6 months, infants were abruptly weaned—if necessary, by having the mother leave for a few days. These experiences, from our cultural vantage point, seem cruel. But Erikson explained that the Yurok lived in a world in which salmon fill the river just once a year, a circumstance that required the development of considerable self-restraint for survival. In this way, he showed that child rearing can be understood only by making reference to the competencies valued and needed by the child's society.

CONTRIBUTIONS AND LIMITATIONS OF PSYCHOANALYTIC THEORY ● A special strength of the psychoanalytic perspective is its emphasis on the individual's unique life history as worthy of study and understanding (Emde, 1992). Consistent with this view, psychoanalytic theorists accept the *clinical method,* which synthesizes information from a variety of sources into a detailed picture of the personality of a single child. (We will discuss the clinical method further at the end of this chapter.) Psychoanalytic theory has also inspired a wealth of research on many aspects of emotional and social development, including infant–caregiver attachment, aggression, sibling relationships, child-rearing practices, morality, gender roles, and adolescent identity.

Despite its extensive contributions, the psychoanalytic perspective is no longer in the mainstream of child development research (Cairns, 1998). Psychoanalytic theorists may have become isolated from the rest of the field because they were so strongly committed to the clinical approach that they failed to consider other methods. In addition, many psychoanalytic ideas, such as psychosexual stages and ego functioning, are so vague that they are difficult or impossible to test empirically (Thomas, 2000; Westen & Gabbard, 1999). Nevertheless, Erikson's broad outline of psychosocial change captures the essence of personality development during childhood and adolescence. Consequently, we will return to it in later chapters.

Behaviorism and Social Learning Theory

As the psychoanalytic perspective gained prominence, child study was also influenced by a very different perspective. According to behaviorism, directly observable events—stimuli and responses—are the appropriate focus of study. American behaviorism began with the work of psychologist John Watson (1878–1958) in the early twentieth century. Watson wanted to create an objective science of psychology and rejected the psychoanalytic concern with the unseen workings of the mind (Horowitz, 1992).

TRADITIONAL BEHAVIORISM ● Watson was inspired by Russian physiologist Ivan Pavlov's studies of animal learning. Pavlov knew that dogs release saliva as an innate reflex when they are given food. But he noticed that his dogs were salivating before they tasted any food—when they saw the trainer who usually fed them. The dogs, Pavlov reasoned, must have learned to associate a neutral stimulus (the trainer) with another stimulus (food) that produces a reflexive response (salivation). As a result of this association, the neutral stimulus by itself could bring about a response resembling the reflex. Eager to test this idea, Pavlov successfully taught dogs to salivate at the sound of a bell by pairing it with the presentation of food. He had discovered *classical conditioning.*

Watson wanted to find out if classical conditioning could be applied to children's behavior. In a historic experiment, he taught Albert, an 11-month-old infant, to fear a neutral stimulus— a soft white rat—by presenting it several times with a sharp, loud sound, which naturally scared the baby. Little Albert, who at first had reached out eagerly to touch the furry rat, soon cried and turned his head away when he caught sight of it (Watson & Raynor, 1920). In fact, Albert's fear was so intense that researchers eventually challenged the ethics of studies like this one. Consistent with Locke's tabula rasa, Watson concluded that environment is the supreme force in development. Adults can mold children's behavior, he thought, by carefully controlling stimulus–response associations. And development is a continuous process, consisting of a gradual increase with age in the number and strength of these associations.

Another form of behaviorism was B. F. Skinner's (1904–1990) *operant conditioning theory.* According to Skinner, the frequency of a behavior can be increased by following it with a wide variety of *reinforcers,* such as food, praise, a friendly smile, or a new toy. It can also be decreased through *punishment,* such as disapproval or withdrawal of privileges. As a result of Skinner's work, operant conditioning became a broadly applied learning principle. We will consider these conditioning techniques further when we explore the infant's learning capacities in Chapter 5.

SOCIAL LEARNING THEORY ● Psychologists quickly became interested in whether behaviorism might offer a more direct and effective explanation of the development of children's social behavior than the less precise concepts of psychoanalytic theory. This sparked the emergence of several approaches that built on the principles of conditioning, offering expanded views of how children and adults acquire new responses.

Several kinds of **social learning theory** emerged. The most influential, devised by Albert Bandura, emphasized *modeling,* otherwise known as *imitation* or *observational learning,* as a powerful source of development. Bandura (1977) recognized that children acquire many favorable and unfavorable responses by watching and listening to others around them. The baby who claps her hands after her mother does so, the child who angrily hits a playmate in the same way that he has been punished at home, and the teenager who wears the same clothes and hairstyle as her friends at school are all displaying observational learning.

Bandura's work continues to influence much research on children's social development. However, like the field of child development as a whole, today his theory stresses the importance of *cognition,* or thinking. Bandura has shown that children's ability to listen, remember, and abstract general rules from complex sets of observed behavior affects their imitation and learning. In fact, Bandura's (1992, 2001) most recent revision of his theory places such strong emphasis on how children think about themselves and other people that he calls it a *social-cognitive* rather than a social learning approach.

Social learning theory recognizes that children acquire many skills through modeling. By observing and imitating her mother's behavior, this Vietnamese preschooler is becoming a skilled user of chopsticks.

According to this view, children gradually become more selective in what they imitate. From watching others engage in self-praise and self-blame and through feedback about the worth of their own actions, children develop *personal standards* for behavior and a *sense of self-efficacy*—the belief that their own abilities and characteristics will help them succeed. These cognitions guide responses in particular situations (Bandura, 1999, 2001). For example, imagine a parent who often remarks, "I'm glad I kept working on that task, even though it was hard," who explains the value of persistence, and who encourages it by saying, "I know you can do a good job on that homework!" Soon the child starts to view herself as hardworking and high achieving and selects people with these characteristics as models. In this way, as children acquire attitudes, values, and convictions about themselves, they control their own learning and behavior.

CONTRIBUTIONS AND LIMITATIONS OF BEHAVIORISM AND SOCIAL LEARNING THEORY ● Behaviorism and social learning theory have had a major applied impact. **Behavior modification** consists of procedures that combine conditioning and modeling to eliminate undesirable behaviors and increase desirable responses. It has been used to relieve a wide range of serious developmental problems, such as persistent aggression, language delays, and extreme fears (Pierce & Epling, 1995; Wolpe & Plaud, 1997). But it is also effective in dealing with common, everyday difficulties, including poor time management; unwanted habits, such as nail biting and smoking; and anxiety over such recurrent events as test-taking, public speaking, and medical and dental treatments. In one study, preschoolers' anxious reactions during dental treatment were reduced by reinforcing them with small toys for answering questions about a story read to them while the dentist worked. Because the children could not listen to the story and kick and cry at the same time, their disruptive behaviors subsided (Stark et al., 1989).

Nevertheless, modeling and reinforcement do not provide a complete account of development. Many theorists believe that behaviorism and social learning theory offer too narrow a view of important environmental influences. These extend beyond immediate reinforcements and modeled behaviors to children's rich physical and social worlds. Finally, behaviorism and social learning theory have been criticized for underestimating children's contributions to their own development. However, in emphasizing cognition, Bandura is unique among theorists whose work grew out of the behaviorist tradition in granting children an active role in their own learning.

Piaget's Cognitive-Developmental Theory

If one individual has influenced the contemporary field of child development more than any other, it is Swiss cognitive theorist Jean Piaget (1896–1980). North American investigators had

In Piaget's sensori-motor stage, babies learn by acting on the world. As this 1-year-old bangs a mallet on a xylophone, he discovers that his movments have predictable effects on objects and that objects influence one another in regular ways.

In Piaget's preoperational stage, preschool children represent their earlier sensorimotor discoveries with symbols. Language and make-believe play develop rapidly. These 4-year-olds create an imaginative play scene with dress-up clothes and the assistance of a cooperative family pet.

been aware of Piaget's work since 1930. However, they did not grant it much attention until the 1960s, mainly because his ideas were very much at odds with behaviorism, which dominated psychology in the middle of the twentieth century (Zigler & Gilman, 1998). Piaget did not believe that children's learning depends on reinforcers, such as rewards from adults. According to his **cognitive-developmental theory,** children actively construct knowledge as they manipulate and explore their world.

PIAGET'S STAGES ● Piaget's view of development was greatly influenced by his early training in biology. Central to his theory is the biological concept of *adaptation* (Piaget, 1971). Just as structures of the body are adapted to fit with the environment, so structures of the mind develop to better fit with, or represent, the external world. In infancy and early childhood, Piaget claimed, children's understanding is different from adults'. For example, he believed that young babies do not realize that an object hidden from view—a favorite toy or even the mother—continues to exist. He also concluded that preschoolers' thinking is full of faulty logic. For example, children younger than age 7 commonly say that the amount of milk or lemonade changes when it is poured into a different-shaped container. According to Piaget, children eventually revise these incorrect ideas in their ongoing efforts to achieve an *equilibrium,* or balance, between internal structures and information they encounter in their everyday worlds.

In Piaget's theory, as the brain develops and children's experiences expand, they move through four broad stages, each characterized by qualitatively distinct ways of thinking. Table 1.3 provides a brief description of Piaget's stages. In the *sensorimotor stage,* cognitive development begins with the baby's use of the senses and movements to explore the world. These action patterns evolve into the symbolic but illogical thinking of the preschooler in the *pre-operational stage.* Then cognition is transformed into the more organized reasoning of the school-age child in the *concrete operational stage.* Finally, in the *formal operational stage,* thought becomes the complex, abstract reasoning system of the adolescent and adult.

PIAGET'S METHODS OF STUDY ● Piaget devised special methods for investigating how children think. In the early part of his career, he carefully observed his three infant children and also presented them with everyday problems, such as an attractive object that could be grasped,

TABLE 1.3

Piaget's Stages of Cognitive Development

STAGE	PERIOD OF DEVELOPMENT	DESCRIPTION
Sensorimotor	Birth–2 years	Infants "think" by acting on the world with their eyes, ears, hands, and mouth. As a result, they invent ways of solving sensorimotor problems, such as pulling a lever to hear the sound of a music box, finding hidden toys, and putting objects in and taking them out of containers.
Preoperational	2–7 years	Preschool children use symbols to represent their earlier sensorimotor discoveries. Development of language and make-believe play takes place. However, thinking lacks the logic of the two remaining stages.
Concrete operational	7–11 years	Children's reasoning becomes logical. School-age children understand that a certain amount of lemonade or play dough remains the same even after its appearance changes. They also organize objects into hierarchies of classes and subclasses. However, thinking falls short of adult intelligence. It is not yet abstract.
Formal operational	11 years and older	The capacity for abstraction permits adolescents to reason with symbols that do not refer to objects in the real world, as in advanced mathematics. They can also think of all possible outcomes in a scientific problem, not just the most obvious ones.

Jean Piaget

mouthed, kicked, or searched for. From their responses, Piaget derived his ideas about cognitive changes during the first 2 years. In studying childhood and adolescent thought, Piaget took advantage of children's ability to describe their thinking. He adapted the clinical method of psychoanalysis, conducting open-ended *clinical interviews* in which a child's initial response to a task served as the basis for the next question Piaget would ask. We will look more closely at this technique when we discuss research methods later in this chapter.

CONTRIBUTIONS AND LIMITATIONS OF PIAGET'S THEORY ● Piaget's cognitive-developmental perspective convinced the field that children are active learners whose minds

In Piaget's concrete operational stage, school-age children think in an organized, logical fashion about concrete objects. This 6-year-old girl and 7-year-old boy understand that the amount of milk remains the same after being poured into a differently shaped container, even though its appearance changes.

In Piaget's formal operational stage, adolescents can think logically and abstractly. These high school students, who have entered a science competition, must construct a lightweight model tower that can support up to 60 pounds. They solve the problem by thinking of all possible outcomes, not just the most obvious ones. Then they conduct systematic tests and observe their real-world consequences.

consist of rich structures of knowledge. Besides investigating children's understanding of the physical world, Piaget explored their reasoning about the social world. His stages have sparked a wealth of research on children's conceptions of themselves, other people, and human relationships. Practically speaking, Piaget's theory encouraged the development of educational philosophies and programs that emphasize children's discovery learning and direct contact with the environment.

Despite Piaget's overwhelming contributions, his theory has been challenged. Research indicates that Piaget underestimated the competencies of infants and preschoolers. When young children are given tasks scaled down in difficulty, their understanding appears closer to that of the older child and adult than Piaget assumed. This discovery has led many researchers to conclude that the maturity of children's thinking may depend on their familiarity with the task presented and the complexity of knowledge sampled. Furthermore, many studies show that children's performance on Piagetian problems can be improved with training—findings that call into question Piaget's assumption that discovery learning rather than adult teaching is the best way to foster development. Finally, critics point out that Piaget's stagewise account pays insufficient attention to social and cultural influences—and the resulting wide variation that exists in same-age children's thinking.

Today, the field of child development is divided over its loyalty to Piaget's ideas. Those who continue to find merit in Piaget's stages often accept a modified view—one in which changes in children's thinking are not sudden and abrupt but take place gradually (Case, 1998; Demetriou et al., 2002; Fischer & Bidell, 1998). Others have turned to an approach that emphasizes continuous gains in children's cognition: information processing. And still others have been drawn to theories that focus on the role of children's social and cultural contexts. We take up these approaches in the next section.

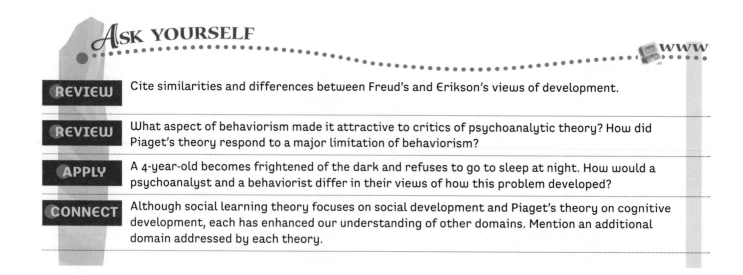

ASK YOURSELF

REVIEW Cite similarities and differences between Freud's and Erikson's views of development.

REVIEW What aspect of behaviorism made it attractive to critics of psychoanalytic theory? How did Piaget's theory respond to a major limitation of behaviorism?

APPLY A 4-year-old becomes frightened of the dark and refuses to go to sleep at night. How would a psychoanalyst and a behaviorist differ in their views of how this problem developed?

CONNECT Although social learning theory focuses on social development and Piaget's theory on cognitive development, each has enhanced our understanding of other domains. Mention an additional domain addressed by each theory.

Recent Theoretical Perspectives

New ways of understanding the child are constantly emerging—questioning, building on, and enhancing the discoveries of earlier theories. Today, a burst of fresh approaches and research emphases is broadening our understanding of children's development.

Information Processing

During the 1970s, researchers turned to the field of cognitive psychology for ways to understand the development of children's thinking. The design of digital computers that use mathematically specified steps to solve problems suggested to psychologists that the human mind might also be viewed as a symbol-manipulating system through which information flows—a perspective called **information processing** (Klahr & MacWhinney, 1998). From presentation to the senses at input to behavioral responses at output, information is actively coded, transformed, and organized.

Information-processing researchers often use flowcharts to map the precise steps individuals use to solve problems and complete tasks, much like the plans devised by programmers to get computers to perform a series of "mental operations." Let's look at an example to clarify the usefulness of this approach. In a study of problem solving, a researcher provided a pile of blocks varying in size, shape, and weight and asked school-age children to build a bridge across a "river" (painted on a floor mat) that was too wide for any single block to span (Thornton, 1999). Figure 1.3 shows one solution to the problem: Two planklike blocks span the water, each held in place by the counterweight of heavy blocks on the bridge's towers. Whereas older children easily built successful bridges, only one 5-year-old did. Careful tracking of her efforts revealed that she repeatedly tried unsuccessful strategies, such as pushing two planks together and pressing down on their ends to hold them in place. But eventually, her experimentation triggered the idea of using the blocks as counterweights. Her mistaken procedures helped her understand why the counterweight approach worked.

A variety of information-processing models exist. Some, like the one just considered, track children's mastery of one or a few tasks. Others describe the human cognitive system as a whole

FIGURE 1.3

Information-processing flowchart showing the steps that a 5-year-old used to solve a bridge-building problem.

Her task was to use blocks varying in size, shape, and weight, some of which were planklike, to construct a bridge across a "river" (painted on a floor mat) too wide for any single block to span. The child discovered how to counterweight and balance the bridge. The arrows reveal that even after building a successful counterweight, she returned to earlier, unsuccessful strategies, which seemed to help her understand why the counterweight approach worked. (Adapted from Thornton, 1999.)

(Atkinson & Shiffrin, 1968; Lockhart & Craik, 1990). These general models are used as guides for asking questions about broad age changes in children's thinking. For example, does a child's ability to search the environment for information needed to solve a problem become more organized and "planful" with age? What strategies do younger and older children use to remember new information, and how do those strategies affect children's recall?

The information-processing approach is also being used to clarify the processing of social information. For example, flowcharts exist that track the steps children use to solve social problems (such as how to enter an ongoing play group) and acquire gender-linked preferences and behaviors (Crick & Dodge, 1994; Ruble & Martin, 1998). Such efforts have practical uses. That is, if we can identify how social problem solving and gender stereotyping arise in childhood, then we can design interventions that promote more favorable social development.

Like Piaget's theory, the information-processing approach regards children as active, sense-making beings who modify their own thinking in response to environmental demands (Halford, 2002; Klahr & MacWhinney, 1998). But unlike Piaget's theory, there are no stages of development. Rather, the thought processes studied—perception, attention, memory, categorization of information, planning, problem solving, and comprehension of written and spoken prose—are assumed to be similar at all ages but present to a lesser or greater extent. Therefore, the view of development is one of continuous change.

A great strength of the information-processing approach is its commitment to careful, rigorous research methods. Because it has provided precise accounts of how children of different ages engage in many aspects of thinking, its findings have led to teaching interventions that help children approach tasks in more advanced ways (Geary, 1994; Siegler, 1998). But information processing has fallen short in some respects. Although good at analyzing thinking into its components, it has difficulty putting them back together into a comprehensive theory. In addition, aspects of children's cognition that are not linear and logical, such as imagination and creativity, are all but ignored by this approach (Lutz & Sternberg, 1999). Furthermore, much information-processing research has been conducted in laboratories rather than in real-life situations. Recently, investigators have addressed this concern by studying children's conversations, stories, memory for everyday events, and academic problem solving.

An advantage of having many theories is that they encourage one another to attend to previously neglected dimensions of children's lives. A unique feature of the final four perspectives we will discuss is the emphasis they place on *contexts* for development—the way children's genetic heritage combines with diverse environmental circumstances to affect pathways of change. The first of these views emphasizes that development of many capacities is influenced by our long evolutionary history.

Ethology and Evolutionary Developmental Psychology

Ethology is concerned with the adaptive, or survival, value of behavior and its evolutionary history (Dewsbury, 1992; Hinde, 1989). Its roots can be traced to the work of Darwin. Two European zoologists, Konrad Lorenz and Niko Tinbergen, laid its modern foundations. Watching diverse animal species in their natural habitats, Lorenz and Tinbergen observed behavior patterns that promote survival. The best known of these is *imprinting*, the early following behavior of certain baby birds that ensures that the young will stay close to the mother and be fed and protected from danger. Imprinting takes place during an early, restricted period of development. If the mother goose is not present during this time, but an object resembling her in important features is, young goslings may imprint on it instead (Lorenz, 1952).

Observations of imprinting led to a major concept in child development: the *critical period*. It refers to a limited time during which the child is biologically prepared to acquire certain adaptive behaviors but needs the support of an appropriately stimulating environment. Many researchers have conducted studies to find out whether complex cognitive and social behaviors must be learned during certain periods. For example, if children are deprived of adequate food or physical and social stimulation during the early years, will their intelligence be impaired? If language is not mastered during the preschool years, is the child's capacity to acquire it reduced?

Konrad Lorenz was one of the founders of ethology and a keen observer of animal behavior. He developed the concept of imprinting. Here, young geese who were separated from their mother and placed in the company of Lorenz during an early, critical period show that they have imprinted on him. They follow him about as he swims through the water, a response that promotes survival.

In later chapters, you will discover that the term *sensitive period* applies better to human development than the strict notion of a critical period (Bornstein, 1989). A **sensitive period** is a time that is optimal for certain capacities to emerge and in which the individual is especially responsive to environmental influences. However, its boundaries are less well defined than are those of a critical period. Development can occur later, but it is harder to induce.

Inspired by observations of imprinting, British psychoanalyst John Bowlby (1969) applied ethological theory to understanding the human infant–caregiver relationship. He argued that infant smiling, babbling, grasping, and crying are built-in social signals that encourage the caregiver to approach, care for, and interact with the baby. By keeping the parent near, these behaviors help ensure that the baby will be fed, protected from danger, and provided with the stimulation and affection necessary for healthy growth. The development of attachment in human infants is a lengthy process involving changes in psychological structures that lead the baby to form a deep affectionate tie with the caregiver (van den Boom, 2002). It is far more complex than imprinting in baby birds. In Chapter 7, we will consider how infant, caregiver, and family context contribute to attachment and will examine the impact of attachment on later development.

Observations by ethologists have shown that many aspects of children's social behavior, including emotional expressions, aggression, cooperation, and social play, resemble those of our primate relatives. Recently, researchers have extended this effort in a new area of research called **evolutionary developmental psychology.** It seeks to understand the adaptive value of species-wide cognitive, emotional, and social competencies as those competencies change with age. Evolutionary developmental psychologists ask such questions as, What role does the newborn's visual preference for facelike stimuli play in survival? Does it support older infants' capacity to distinguish familiar caregivers from unfamiliar people? Why do children play in gender-segregated groups? What do they learn from such play that might lead to adult gender-typed behaviors, such as male dominance and female investment in caregiving?

As these examples suggest, evolutionary psychologists are not just concerned with the genetic and biological basis of development. They are also interested in how individuals learn because learning lends flexibility and greater adaptiveness to behavior. And they recognize that today's lifestyles differ so radically from those of our evolutionary ancestors that certain evolved behaviors, such as life-threatening risk taking in adolescents and male-to-male violence, are no longer adaptive (Bjorklund & Pellegrini, 2000; Geary, 1999). By clarifying the origins and development of such behaviors, evolutionary developmental psychology may contribute to more effective interventions.

In sum, the interests of evolutionary psychologists are broad. They want to understand the entire *organism–environment system.* The next contextual perspective we will discuss, Vygotsky's sociocultural theory, serves as an excellent complement to the evolutionary viewpoint because it highlights the social and cultural aspects of children's experiences.

According to Lev Vygotsky, many cognitive processes and skills are socially transferred from more knowledgeable members of society to children. Vygotsky's sociocultural theory helps us understand the wide cultural variation in cognitive competencies. Vygotsky is pictured here with his daughter.

Vygotsky's Sociocultural Theory

The field of child development has recently seen a dramatic increase in studies addressing the cultural context of children's lives. Investigations that make comparisons across cultures, and between ethnic groups within cultures, provide insight into whether developmental pathways apply to all children or are limited to particular environmental conditions. As a result, cross-cultural and multicultural research helps us untangle genetic and environmental contributions to the timing, order of appearance, and diversity of children's behaviors (Greenfield, 1994).

In the past, cross-cultural studies focused on broad cultural differences in development—for example, whether children in one culture are more advanced in motor development or do better on intellectual tasks than children in another. However, this approach can lead us to conclude incorrectly that one culture is superior in enhancing development, whereas another is deficient. In addition, it does not help us understand the precise experiences that contribute to cultural differences in behavior.

Today, more research is examining the relationship of *culturally specific practices* to development. The contributions of Russian psychologist Lev Vygotsky (1896–1934) have played a major role in this trend. Vygotsky's (1934/1987) perspective is called **sociocultural theory.** It focuses on how *culture*—the values, beliefs, customs, and skills of a social group—is transmitted to the next generation. According to Vygotsky, *social interaction*—in particular, cooperative dialogues with more knowledgeable members of society—is necessary for children to acquire the ways of thinking and behaving that make up a community's culture (Rowe & Wertsch, 2002). Vygotsky believed that as adults and more-expert peers help children master culturally meaningful activities, the communication between them becomes part of children's thinking. As children internalize features of these dialogues, they can use the language within them to guide their own thought and behavior and to acquire new skills (Berk, 2001a). The young child instructing herself while working a puzzle or tying her shoes has begun to implement on her own the supportive functions of adult–child interaction. Consequently, the child can be heard producing comments similar to those an adult used to help her master important tasks.

Vygotsky's theory has been especially influential in the study of children's cognition. Vygotsky agreed with Piaget that children are active, constructive beings. But unlike Piaget, who emphasized children's independent efforts to make sense of their world, Vygotsky viewed cognitive development as a *socially mediated process*—as dependent on the assistance that adults and more-expert peers provide as children tackle new challenges.

In Vygotsky's theory, children undergo certain stagewise changes. For example, when they acquire language, their ability to participate in dialogues with others is greatly enhanced, and mastery of culturally valued competencies surges forward. When children enter school, they spend much time discussing language, literacy, and other academic concepts—experiences that encourage them to reflect on their own thinking (Kozulin, 2003). As a result, they gain dramatically in reasoning and problem solving.

At the same time, Vygotsky stressed that dialogues with experts lead to continuous changes that vary greatly from culture to culture. Consistent with this view, a major finding of cross-cultural research is that cultures select different tasks for children's learning (Rogoff & Chavajay, 1995). Social interaction surrounding those tasks leads to competencies essential for success in a particular culture. For example, in industrialized nations, teachers can be seen helping people learn to read, drive a car, or use a com-

This girl of Bali, Indonesia, is learning traditional dance steps through the guidance of an adult expert. According to Vygotsky's sociocultural theory, social interaction between children and more knowledgeable members of their culture leads to ways of thinking and behaving essential for success in that culture.

puter. Among the Zinacanteco Indians of southern Mexico, adult experts guide young girls as they master complicated weaving techniques (Childs & Greenfield, 1982). In Brazil and other developing nations, child candy sellers with little or no schooling develop sophisticated mathematical abilities as the result of buying candy from wholesalers, pricing it in collaboration with adults and experienced peers, and bargaining with customers on city streets (Saxe, 1988).

Vygotsky's theory, and the research stimulated by it, reveal that children in every culture develop unique strengths. At the same time, Vygotsky's emphasis on culture and social experience led him to neglect the biological side of development. Although he recognized the importance of heredity and brain growth, he said little about their role in cognitive change. Furthermore, Vygotsky's focus on social transmission of knowledge meant that he placed less emphasis than other theorists on children's capacity to shape their own development (Wertsch & Tulviste, 1992). Followers of Vygotsky stress that children actively participate in the conversations and social activities from which their development springs. From these joint experiences, they not only acquire culturally valued practices but also modify and transform those practices (Rogoff, 1998, 2003). Contemporary sociocultural theorists grant the individual and society balanced, mutually influential roles.

Ecological Systems Theory

Urie Bronfenbrenner, an American psychologist, is responsible for an approach to child development that has moved to the forefront of the field over the past two decades because it offers the most differentiated and thorough account of contextual influences on children's development. **Ecological systems theory** views the child as developing within a complex *system* of relationships affected by multiple levels of the surrounding environment. Since the child's biologically influenced dispositions join with environmental forces to mold development, Bronfenbrenner recently characterized his perspective as a *bioecological model* (Bronfenbrenner & Evans, 2000).

Bronfenbrenner envisions the environment as a series of nested structures that includes but extends beyond home, school, and neighborhood settings in which children spend their everyday lives (see Figure 1.4). Each layer of the environment is viewed as having a powerful impact on development.

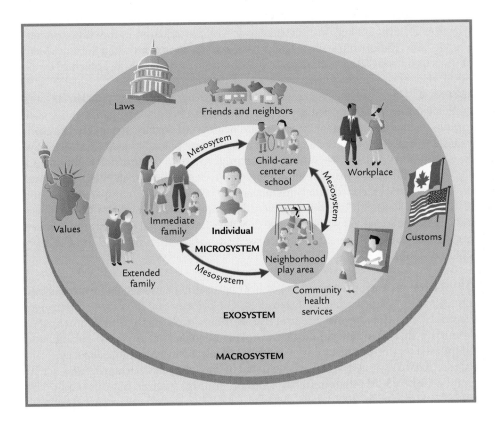

FIGURE 1.4

Structure of the environment in ecological systems theory.

The *microsystem* concerns relations between the child and the immediate environment; the *mesosystem,* connections among immediate settings; the *exosystem,* social settings that affect but do not contain the child; and the *macrosystem,* the values, laws, customs, and resources of the culture that affect activities and interactions at all inner layers. The *chronosystem* (not pictured) is not a specific context. Instead, it refers to the dynamic, ever-changing nature of the person's environment.

© ELLEN SENISI/THE IMAGE WORKS

In ecological systems theory, development occurs within a complex system of relationships affected by multiple levels of the environment. This father greets his daughter at the end of the school day. The girl's experiences at school (microsystem) and the father's experiences at work (exosystem) affect father–daughter interaction.

THE MICROSYSTEM ● The innermost level of the environment is the **microsystem,** which consists of activities and interaction patterns in the child's immediate surroundings. Bronfenbrenner emphasizes that to understand child development at this level, we must keep in mind that all relationships are *bidirectional.* That is, adults affect children's behavior, but children's biologically and socially influenced characteristics—their physical attributes, personalities, and capacities—also affect adults' behavior. For example, a friendly, attentive child is likely to evoke positive, patient reactions from parents, whereas a distractible child is more likely to receive restriction and punishment. When these reciprocal interactions occur often over time, they have an enduring impact on development (Bronfenbrenner, 1995; Collins et al., 2000).

At the same time, *third parties*—other individuals in the microsystem—affect the quality of any two-person relationship. If they are supportive, then interaction is enhanced. For example, when parents encourage one another in their child-rearing roles, each engages in more effective parenting (Cowan, Powell, & Cowan, 1998). In contrast, marital conflict is associated with inconsistent discipline and hostile reactions toward children. In response, children typically become hostile, and their adjustment suffers (Hetherington & Stanley-Hagen, 2002).

THE MESOSYSTEM ● The second level of Bronfenbrenner's model, the **mesosystem,** encompasses connections between microsystems, such as home, school, neighborhood, and child-care center. For example, a child's academic progress depends not just on activities that take place in classrooms. It is also promoted by parent involvement in school life and the extent to which academic learning is carried over into the home (Epstein & Sanders, 2002). Similarly, parent–child interaction at home is likely to affect caregiver–child interaction in the child-care setting, and vice versa. Each relationship is more likely to support development when there are links, in the form of visits and cooperative exchanges of information, between home and child care.

THE EXOSYSTEM ● The **exosystem** is made up of social settings that do not contain children but that affect their experiences in immediate settings. These can be formal organizations, such as parents' workplaces, their religious institutions, and health and welfare services in the community. For example, flexible work schedules, paid maternity and paternity leave, and sick leave for parents whose children are ill are ways that work settings can help parents rear children and, indirectly, enhance development. Exosystem supports also can be informal, such as parents' social networks—friends and extended-family members who provide advice, companionship, and even financial assistance. Research confirms the negative impact of a breakdown in exosystem activities. Families who are socially isolated because they have few personal or community-based ties or who are affected by unemployment show increased rates of conflict and child abuse (Emery & Laumann-Billings, 1998).

THE MACROSYSTEM ● The outermost level of Bronfenbrenner's model, the **macrosystem,** consists of cultural values, laws, customs, and resources. The priority that the macrosystem gives to children's needs affects the support they receive at inner levels of the environment. For example, in countries that mandate generous workplace benefits for employed parents and high-quality standards for child care, children are more likely to have favorable experiences in their immediate settings. As you will see in greater detail in later chapters, such programs are far less available in the United States than in Canada and other industrialized nations (Children's Defense Fund, 2003; Kamerman, 2000).

AN EVER-CHANGING SYSTEM ● According to Bronfenbrenner, the environment is not a static force that affects people in a uniform way. Instead, it is ever-changing. Important life events, such as the birth of a sibling, entering school, moving to a new neighborhood, or parents' divorce, modify existing relationships between children and their environments, producing new conditions that affect development. In addition, the timing of environmental change affects its impact. The arrival of a new sibling has very different consequences for a homebound toddler than for a school-age child with many relationships and activities beyond the family.

Bronfenbrenner refers to the temporal dimension of his model as the **chronosystem** (the prefix *chrono-* means "time"). Changes in life events can be imposed on the child, as in the examples just given. Alternatively, they can arise from within the child, since as children get older they select, modify, and create many of their own settings and experiences. How they do so depends on their physical, intellectual, and personality characteristics and their environmental opportunities. Therefore, in ecological systems theory, development is neither controlled by environmental circumstances nor driven by inner dispositions. Instead, children are products and producers of their environments, so both children and the environments form a network of interdependent effects. Notice how our discussion of resilient children on pages 10–11 illustrates this idea. You will see many more examples in this book.

New Directions: Development as a Dynamic System

Today, researchers recognize both consistency and variability in children's development and want to do a better job of explaining variation. Consequently, a new wave of theorists has adopted a **dynamic systems perspective.** According to this view, the child's mind, body, and physical and social worlds form an *integrated system* that guides mastery of new skills. The system is *dynamic,* or constantly in motion. A change in any part of it—from brain maturation to physical and social surroundings—disrupts the current organism–environment relationship. When this happens, the child actively reorganizes his or her behavior so the various components of the system work together again but in a more complex, effective way (Fischer & Bidell, 1998; Thelen & Smith, 1998; Wachs, 2000).

Researchers adopting a dynamic systems perspective try to find out just how children attain new levels of organization by studying their behavior while they are in transition (Thelen & Corbetta, 2002). For example, when presented with an attractive toy, how does a 3-month-old baby who engages in many, varied movements discover how to reach for it? On hearing a new word, how does a 2-year-old figure out the category of objects or events to which it refers?

Dynamic systems theorists acknowledge that a common human genetic heritage and basic regularities in children's physical and social worlds yield certain universal, broad outlines of development. But biological makeup, everyday tasks, and the people who support children in mastery of those tasks vary greatly, leading to wide individual differences in specific skills. Even when children master the same skills, such as walking, talking, or adding and subtracting, they often do so in unique ways. And because children build competencies by engaging in real activities in real contexts, different skills vary in maturity within the same child (Fischer & Bidell, 1998). From this perspective, development cannot be characterized as a single line of change. As Figure 1.5 on page 30 shows, it is more like a web of fibers branching out in many directions, each of which represents a different skill area that may undergo continuous and stagewise transformations.

The dynamic systems view has been inspired by other scientific disciplines, especially biology and physics. In addition, it draws on information-processing and contextual theories—evolutionary developmental psychology, sociocultural theory,

Although these children are about the same age, they vary widely in competencies. The dynamic systems perspective aims to explain this variation by examining how the child's mind, body, and physical and social worlds form an integrated system that guides mastery of new skills.

© MICHAEL NEWMAN/PHOTOEDIT

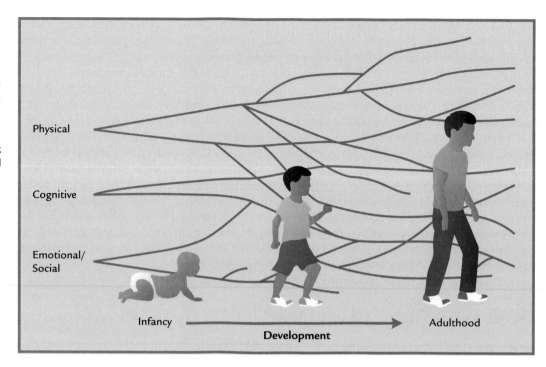

FIGURE 1.5

The dynamic systems view of development.
Rather than envisioning a single line of stagewise or continuous change (refer to Figure 1.2 on page 8), dynamic systems theorists conceive of development as a web of fibers branching out in many directions. Each strand in the web represents a skill within the major domains of development—physical, cognitive, and emotional/social. The differing directions of the strands signify possible variations in paths and outcomes as the child masters skills necessary to participate in diverse contexts. The interconnections of the strands within the vertical windows portray stagelike changes—periods of major transformation in which various skills work together as a functioning whole. As the web expands, skills become more numerous, complex, and effective. (Adapted from Fischer & Bidell, 1998.)

and ecological systems theory. At present, dynamic systems research is in its early stages. The perspective has largely been applied to children's motor and cognitive skills, but some investigators have drawn on it to explain emotional and social development as well (Fogel, 2000; Lewis, 2000). Consider the young teenager, whose body and reasoning powers are changing massively and who also confronts the challenges of secondary school. Researchers following parent–child interaction over time found that the transition to adolescence disrupted family communication. It became unstable and variable for several years—a mix of positive, neutral, and negative exchanges. Gradually, as parent and adolescent devised new, more mature ways of relating to one another, the system reorganized and stabilized. Once again, interaction became predictable and mostly positive (Granic et al., 2003).

As dynamic systems research illustrates, today investigators are tracking and analyzing development in all its complexity. In doing so, they hope to move closer to an all-encompassing approach to understanding change.

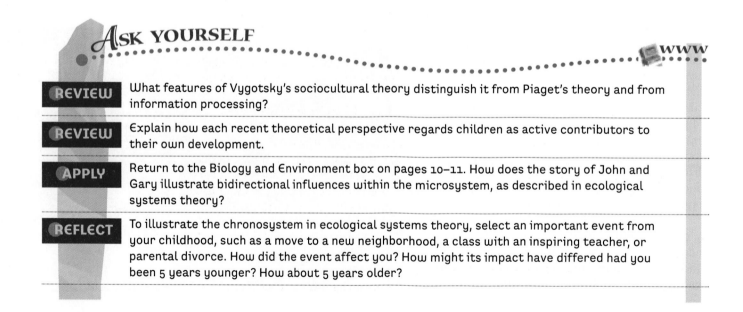

Ask YOURSELF

REVIEW What features of Vygotsky's sociocultural theory distinguish it from Piaget's theory and from information processing?

REVIEW Explain how each recent theoretical perspective regards children as active contributors to their own development.

APPLY Return to the Biology and Environment box on pages 10–11. How does the story of John and Gary illustrate bidirectional influences within the microsystem, as described in ecological systems theory?

REFLECT To illustrate the chronosystem in ecological systems theory, select an important event from your childhood, such as a move to a new neighborhood, a class with an inspiring teacher, or parental divorce. How did the event affect you? How might its impact have differed had you been 5 years younger? How about 5 years older?

Comparing Child Development Theories

In the preceding sections, we reviewed theoretical perspectives that are major forces in child development research. They differ from each other in many respects. First, they focus on different domains of development. Some, such as the psychoanalytic perspective and ethology, emphasize emotional and social development. Others, such as Piaget's cognitive-developmental theory, information processing, and Vygotsky's sociocultural theory, stress changes in thinking. The remaining approaches—behaviorism, social learning theory, evolutionary developmental psychology, ecological systems theory, and the dynamic systems perspective—discuss many aspects of children's functioning. Second, every theory contains a point of view about child development. As we conclude our review of theoretical perspectives, identify the stand that each theory takes on the controversial issues presented at the beginning of this chapter. Then check your analysis of theories against Table 1.4 on page 32.

Finally, we have seen that theories have strengths and limitations. This may remind you of an important point made earlier in this chapter—that no theory provides a complete account of development. Perhaps you found that you were attracted to some theories, but you had doubts about others. As you read more about child development in later chapters of this book, you may find it useful to keep a notebook in which you test your own theoretical likes and dislikes against the evidence. Don't be surprised if you revise your ideas many times, just as theorists have done throughout this century. By the end of the course, you will have built your own personal perspective on child development. Very likely, it will turn out to be an *eclectic position,* or blend of several theories, since every viewpoint we have considered has contributed to what we know about children.

Studying the Child

In every science, theories, like those we have just reviewed, guide the collection of information, its interpretation, and its application to real-life situations. In fact, research usually begins with a *hypothesis,* or prediction, drawn directly from a theory. But theories and hypotheses are only the beginning of the many activities that result in sound evidence on child development. Conducting research according to scientifically accepted procedures involves many steps and choices. Investigators must decide which participants, and how many, to include. Then they must figure out what the participants will be asked to do and when, where, and how many times each will have to be seen. Finally, they must examine and draw conclusions from their data.

In the following sections, we look at research strategies commonly used to study children. We begin with *methods of gathering information*—the specific activities of participants, such as taking tests, answering questionnaires, responding to interviews, or being observed. Then we turn to *research designs*—overall plans for research studies that permit the best possible test of the investigator's hypothesis. Finally, we discuss special ethical issues involved in doing research on children.

At this point, you may be wondering, Why learn about research strategies? Why not leave these matters to research specialists and concentrate on what is already known about the child and how this knowledge can be applied? There are two reasons. First, each of us must be a wise and critical consumer of knowledge. Knowing the strengths and limitations of various research strategies becomes important in separating dependable information from misleading results. Second, individuals who work directly with children may be in a unique position to build bridges between research and practice by conducting studies, either on their own or in partnership with experienced investigators. Currently, community agencies such as schools, mental health facilities, and parks and recreation programs are collaborating with researchers in designing, implementing, and evaluating interventions aimed at enhancing children's development (Lerner, Fisher, & Weinberg, 2000). To broaden these efforts, a basic understanding of the research process is essential.

TABLE 1.4

Stances of Major Theories on Basic Issues in Child Development

THEORY	CONTINUOUS OR DISCONTINUOUS DEVELOPMENT?	ONE COURSE OF DEVELOPMENT OR MANY?	NATURE OR NURTURE AS MORE IMPORTANT?
Psychoanalytic perspective	*Discontinuous:* Psychosexual and psychosocial development takes place in stages.	*One course:* Stages are assumed to be universal.	*Both nature and nurture:* Innate impulses are channeled and controlled through child-rearing experiences. *Early experiences* set the course of later development.
Behaviorism and social learning theory	*Continuous:* Development involves an increase in learned behaviors .	*Many possible courses:* Behaviors reinforced and modeled may vary from child to child.	*Emphasis on nurture:* Development results from conditioning and modeling. *Both early and later experiences* are important.
Piaget's cognitive-developmental theory	*Discontinuous:* Cognitive development takes place in stages.	*One course:* Stages are assumed to be universal.	*Both nature and nurture:* Development occurs as the brain matures and children exercise their innate drive to discover reality in a generally stimulating environment. *Both early and later experiences* are important.
Information processing	*Continuous:* Children gradually improve in perception, attention, memory, and problem-solving skills.	*One course:* Changes studied characterize most or all children.	*Both nature and nurture:* Children are active, sense-making beings who modify their thinking as the brain matures and they confront new environmental demands. *Both early and later experiences* are important.
Ethology and evolutionary developmental psychology	*Both continuous and discontinuous:* Children gradually develop a wider range of adaptive behaviors. Sensitive periods occur, in which qualitatively distinct capacities emerge fairly suddenly.	*One course:* Adaptive behaviors and sensitive periods apply to all members of a species.	*Both nature and nurture:* Evolution and heredity influence behavior, and learning lends greater flexibility and adaptiveness to it. In sensitive periods, *early experiences* set the course of later development.
Vygotsky's sociocultural theory	*Both continuous and discontinuous:* Language acquisition and schooling lead to stagewise changes. Dialogues with more expert members of society also lead to continuous changes that vary from culture to culture.	*Many possible courses:* Socially mediated changes in thought and behavior vary from culture to culture.	*Both nature and nurture:* Heredity, brain growth, and dialogues with more expert members of society jointly contribute to development. *Both early and later experiences* are important.
Ecological systems theory	*Not specified.*	*Many possible courses:* Children's characteristics join with environmental forces at multiple levels to mold development in unique ways.	*Both nature and nurture:* Children's characteristics and the reactions of others affect each other in a bidirectional fashion. Layers of the environment influence child-rearing experiences. *Both early and later experiences* are important.
Dynamic systems perspective	*Both continuous and discontinuous:* Change in the system is always ongoing. Stagelike transformations occur as children reorganize their behavior so components of the system work as a functioning whole.	*Many possible courses:* Biological makeup, everyday tasks, and social experiences vary, yielding wide individual differences in specific skills.	*Both nature and nurture:* The child's mind, body, and physical and social surroundings form an integrated system that guides mastery of new skills. *Both early and later experiences* are important.

Common Methods of Gathering Information

How does a researcher choose a basic approach to gathering information about children? Common methods include systematic observation, self-reports (such as questionnaires and interviews), psychophysiological measures, clinical or case studies of a single child, and ethnographies of the life circumstances of a specific group of children. As you read about these methods, you may find it helpful to refer to Table 1.5 on page 34, which summarizes the strengths and limitations of each.

SYSTEMATIC OBSERVATION ● Observations of the behavior of children, and of adults who are important in their lives, can be made in different ways. One approach is to go into the field, or natural environment, and observe the behavior of interest—a method called **naturalistic observation.**

A study of preschoolers' responses to their peers' distress provides a good example of this technique (Farver & Branstetter, 1994). Observing 3- and 4-year-olds in child-care centers, the researchers recorded each instance of a child crying and the reactions of nearby children—whether they ignored, watched curiously, commented on the child's unhappiness, scolded or teased, or shared, helped, or expressed sympathy. Caregiver behaviors, such as explaining why a child was crying, mediating conflict, or offering comfort, were noted to see if adult sensitivity was related to children's caring responses. A strong relationship emerged. The great strength of naturalistic observation is that investigators can see directly the everyday behaviors they hope to explain.

Naturalistic observation also has a major limitation: Not all individuals have the same opportunity to display a particular behavior in everyday life. In the study just mentioned, some children might have encountered crying classmates or witnessed caregiver sensitivity more often than others. For this reason, they might have displayed more compassion.

Researchers commonly deal with this difficulty by making **structured observations,** in which the investigator sets up a laboratory situation that evokes the behavior of interest so that every participant has an equal opportunity to display the response. In one study, children's comforting behavior was observed by playing a tape recording of a baby crying in the next room. Using an intercom, children could either talk to the baby or push a button so they did not have to listen (Eisenberg et al., 1993). Notice how structured observation permits more control over the research situation. But its great disadvantage is that people do not necessarily behave in the laboratory as they do in everyday life.

The procedures used to collect systematic observations vary, depending on the purpose of the research. Some investigators need to describe the entire behavior stream—everything said and done over a certain time period. In one of my own studies, I wanted to find out how sensitive, responsive, and verbally stimulating caregivers were with children in child-care centers

© 1999 LAURA DWIGHT

In naturalistic observation, the researcher goes into the field and records the behavior of interest. This investigator might be observing children's attention, language, emotional expressions, or conflicts. However, a limitation of this method is that some children may have more opportunities than others to display the behavior in everyday life.

TABLE 1.5

Strengths and Limitations of Common Information-Gathering Methods

METHOD	DESCRIPTION	STRENGTHS	LIMITATIONS
Systematic Observation			
Naturalistic observation	Observation of behavior in natural contexts	Reflects participants' everyday behaviors.	Cannot control conditions under which participants are observed.
Structured observation	Observation of behavior in a laboratory, where conditions are the same for all participants	Grants each participant an equal opportunity to display the behavior of interest.	May not yield observations typical of participants' behavior in everyday life.
Self-Reports			
Clinical interview	Self-report instruments in which each participant is asked the same questions in the same way	Comes as close as possible to the way participants think in everyday life; great breadth and depth of information can be obtained in a short time.	May not result in accurate reporting of information; flexible procedure makes comparing individuals' responses difficult.
Structured interview, questionnaires, and tests	Flexible interviewing procedure in which the investigator obtains a complete account of the participant's thoughts	Permits comparisons of participants' responses and efficient data collection and scoring.	Does not yield the same depth of information as a clinical interview; responses are still subject to inaccurate reporting.
Psychophysiological Methods	Methods that measure the relationship between physiological processes and behavior	Reveals which central nervous system structures contribute to development and individual differences in certain competencies. Helps identify the perceptions, thoughts, and emotions of infants and young children, who cannot report them clearly.	Cannot reveal with certainty how an individual processes stimuli. Many factors besides those of interest to the researcher can influence a physiological response.
Clinical Method (Case Study)	A full picture of a single individual's psychological functioning, obtained by combining interviews, observations, test scores, and sometimes psychophysiological assessments	Provides rich, descriptive insights into processes of development.	May be biased by researcher's theoretical preferences; findings cannot be applied to individuals other than the participant.
Ethnography	Participant observation of a culture or distinct social group; by making extensive field notes, the researcher tries to capture the culture's unique values and social processes	Provides a more complete and accurate description than can be derived from a single observational visit, interview, or questionnaire.	May be biased by researcher's values and theoretical preferences; findings cannot be applied to individuals and settings other than the ones studied.

(Berk, 1985). In this case, everything each caregiver said and did—even the amount of time spent away from children, taking coffee breaks and talking on the phone—was important. In other studies, only one or a few kinds of behavior are needed, and it is not necessary to preserve the entire behavior stream. In these instances, researchers record only certain events or mark off behaviors on checklists.

Systematic observation provides invaluable information on how children and adults behave, but it tells us little about the reasoning behind their responses. For this kind of information, researchers must turn to another type of method: self-reports.

SELF-REPORTS: INTERVIEWS AND QUESTIONNAIRES ● Self-reports are instruments that ask participants to provide information on their perceptions, thoughts, abilities, feelings, attitudes, beliefs, and past experiences. They range from relatively unstructured interviews to highly structured interviews, questionnaires, and tests.

In a **clinical interview, a flexible, conversational style is used to probe for the participant's point of view.** Consider the following example, in which Piaget questioned a 5-year-old child about his understanding of dreams:

Where does the dream come from?—I think you sleep so well that you dream.—*Does it come from us or from outside?*—From outside. —*When you are in bed and you dream, where is the dream?*—In my bed, under the blanket. I don't really know. If it was in my stomach, the bones would be in the way and I shouldn't see it.—*Is the dream there when you sleep?*—Yes, it is in the bed beside me. (Piaget, 1926/1930, pp. 97–98)

Using the clinical interview, this researcher asks a mother to describe her child's development. The method permits large amounts of information to be gathered in a fairly brief period. A major drawback of this method is that participants do not always report information accurately.

The clinical interview has two major strengths. First, it permits people to display their thoughts in terms that are as close as possible to the way they think in everyday life. Second, the clinical interview can provide a large amount of information in a fairly brief period. For example, in an hour-long session, we can obtain a wide range of child-rearing information from a parent—much more than we could capture by observing for the same amount of time.

A major limitation of the clinical interview has to do with the accuracy with which people report their thoughts, feelings, and experiences. Some participants, desiring to please the interviewer, may make up answers. When asked about past events, they may have trouble recalling exactly what happened. And because the clinical interview depends on verbal ability and expressiveness, it may underestimate the capacities of individuals who have difficulty putting their thoughts into words.

The clinical interview has also been criticized because of its flexibility. When questions are phrased differently for each participant, different responses may be due to the manner of interviewing rather than to real differences in the way people think about a topic. **Structured interviews, in which each participant is asked the same questions in the same way,** can eliminate this problem. In addition, these instruments are much more efficient. Answers are briefer, and researchers can obtain written responses from an entire class of children or group of parents at the same time. Also, when structured interviews use multiple-choice, yes/no, and true/false formats, as is done on many tests and questionnaires, a computer can tabulate the answers. However, these approaches do not yield the same depth of information as a clinical interview. And they can still be affected by inaccurate reporting.

PSYCHOPHYSIOLOGICAL METHODS ● Researchers' desire to uncover the biological bases of perceptual, cognitive, and emotional responses has led to **psychophysiological methods, which measure the relationship between physiological processes and behavior.** Investigators who rely on these methods want to find out which central nervous system structures contribute to development and individual differences. Psychophysiological methods also help identify the psychological experiences of infants and young children, who cannot report them clearly.

Involuntary activities of the autonomic nervous system—changes in heart rate, blood pressure, respiration, pupil dilation, and stress hormone levels—are highly sensitive to psychological state. For example, heart rate can be used to infer whether an infant is staring blankly at a stimulus (heart rate is stable), processing information (heart rate slows during concentration), or experiencing distress (heart rate rises). Heart rate variations are also linked to certain emotions, such as interest, anger, and sadness (Fox & Card, 1998). And as Chapter 7 will reveal, distinct patterns of autonomic activity are related to aspects of temperament, such as shyness and sociability (Kagan & Saudino, 2001).

AP/WIDE WORLD PHOTOS   © B. J. CASEY/UPMC

In functional magnetic resonance imaging (fMRI), the child looks up at a stimulus, and changes in blood flow within brain tissue are detected magnetically (a). The result is a computerized image of activated areas (b), permitting study of age-related changes in brain organization and the brain functioning of children with serious learning and emotional problems.

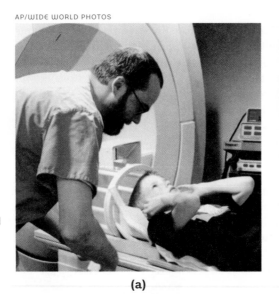

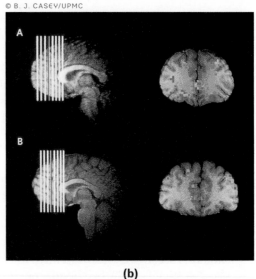

(a)   **(b)**

Autonomic indicators have been enriched by measures of brain functioning. In an *electroencephalogram (EEG)*, researchers tape electrodes to the scalp to record electrical activity of the brain. EEG brain waves are linked to different states of arousal, from deep sleep to alert wakefulness, permitting researchers to see how these states change with age. EEG patterns also vary with emotional states—whether children are happy or distressed (Jones et al., 1997). At times, investigators study *event-related potentials (ERPs)*, or EEG waves that accompany particular events. For example, different wave patterns appear when 3-month-olds from English-speaking homes hear passages in English, Italian, and Dutch, suggesting that infants can discriminate among the three languages and indicating the brain regions involved (Shafer, Shucard, & Jaeger, 1999).

Functional brain-imaging techniques, which yield three-dimensional pictures of brain activity, provide the most precise information on which brain regions are specialized for certain capacities. *Functional magnetic resonance imaging (fMRI)* is the best of these methods because it does not depend on X-ray photography, which requires injection of radioactive substances. Instead, when a child is shown a stimulus, changes in blood flow within the brain are detected magnetically, producing a computerized image of active areas. Currently, fMRI is being used to study age-related changes in brain organization and the brain functioning of children with learning and emotional problems (Pine, 2001; Rivkin, 2000).

Despite their virtues, psychophysiological methods have limitations. First, interpreting the results involves a high degree of inference. Even though a stimulus produces a consistent pattern of autonomic or brain activity, researchers cannot be sure that an infant or child has processed it in a certain way. Second, many factors can influence a physiological response. A researcher who takes a change in heart rate or brain activity as an indicator of information processing must make sure that the change was not due instead to hunger, boredom, fatigue, body movements, or a child's fearful reaction to the laboratory equipment.

THE CLINICAL, OR CASE STUDY, METHOD ● An outgrowth of psychoanalytic theory, the clinical, or case study, method brings together a wide range of information on one child, including interviews, observations, test scores, and sometimes psychophysiological measures. The aim is to obtain as complete a picture as possible of that child's psychological functioning and the experiences that led up to it.

The clinical method is well suited to studying the development of certain types of individuals who are few in number but vary widely in characteristics. For example, the method has been used to find out what contributes to the accomplishments of *prodigies*—extremely gifted children who attain adult competence in a field before age 10 (Gardner, 1998). Consider Adam, a boy who read, wrote, and composed musical pieces before he was out of diapers. By age 4, Adam was deeply involved in mastering human symbol systems—BASIC for the computer, French, German, Russian, Sanskrit, Greek, ancient hieroglyphs, music, and mathematics. Adam's parents provided a home rich in stimulation and reared him with affection, firmness, and humor. They searched for schools in which he could both develop his abilities and form rewarding social relationships. He graduated from college at age 18 and continued to pursue musical composition. Would Adam have realized his potential without the chance combination of his special gift and nurturing, committed parents? Probably not, researchers concluded (Goldsmith, 2000).

The clinical method yields richly detailed case narratives that offer valuable insights into the multiplicity of factors that affect development. Nevertheless, like all other methods, it has drawbacks. Information often is collected unsystematically and subjectively, permitting too much leeway for researchers' theoretical preferences to bias their interpretations. In addition, investigators cannot assume that their conclusions apply, or generalize, to anyone other than the child studied. Even when patterns emerge across several cases, it is wise to try to confirm them with other research strategies.

METHODS FOR STUDYING CULTURE ● A growing interest in the impact of culture has led researchers to adjust the methods just considered as well as to tap procedures specially devised for cross-cultural and multicultural research. Which approach investigators choose depends on their research goals (Triandis, 1995, 1998).

Sometimes researchers are interested in characteristics that are believed to be universal but that vary in degree from one culture to the next. These investigators might ask, Do parents make greater maturity demands of children in some cultures than in others? How strong are gender stereotypes in different nations? In each instance, several cultural groups will be compared, and all participants must be questioned or observed in the same way. Therefore, researchers draw on the self-report and observational procedures we have already considered, adapting them through translation so they can be understood in each cultural context. For example, to study cultural variation in parenting attitudes, the same questionnaire, asking for ratings on such items as "If my child gets into trouble, I expect him or her to handle the problem mostly by himself or herself," is given to all participants (Chen et al., 1998).

At other times, researchers want to uncover the *cultural meanings* of children's and adults' behaviors by becoming as familiar as possible with their way of life (Miller, Hengst, & Wang, 2003). To achieve this goal, researchers rely on a method borrowed from the field of anthropology—**ethnography.** Like the clinical method, ethnographic research is a descriptive, qualitative technique. But instead of aiming to understand a single individual, it is directed toward understanding a culture or a distinct social group through *participant observation.* Typically, the researcher spends months and sometimes years in the cultural community, participating in its daily life. Extensive field notes are gathered, consisting of a mix of observations, self-reports from members of the culture, and careful interpretations by the investigator (Shweder, 1996). Later, these notes are put together into a description of the community that tries to capture its unique values and social processes.

The ethnographic method assumes that by entering into close contact with a social group, researchers can understand the beliefs and behaviors of its members more accurately, in a way not possible with an observational visit, interview, or questionnaire. Some ethnographies take in many aspects of children's experience, as one researcher did in describing what it is like to grow up in a small American town. Others focus on one or a few settings, such as home, school, or neighborhood life (Peshkin, 1978, 1997; Valdés, 1998). And still others are limited to a particular practice, such as uncovering cultural and religious influences on children's make-believe play. For example, ethnographic findings reveal that East Indian Hindu parents encourage preschoolers to communicate with "invisible" characters. They regard the activity as linked to *karma* (the cycle of birth and death) and believe that the child may be remembering a past life. In contrast, Christian fundamentalist parents often discourage children from pretending to be unreal characters, believing that such play promotes dangerous spiritual ideas and deceitful behavior (Taylor & Carlson, 2000). Researchers may supplement traditional self-report and observational methods with ethnography if they suspect that unique meanings underlie cultural differences, as the Cultural Influences box on pages 38–39 reveals.

Ethnographers strive to minimize their influence on the culture they are studying by becoming part of it. Nevertheless, as with clinical research, investigators' cultural values and theoretical

Cultural Influences

Immigrant Youths: Amazing Adaptation

During the past quarter century, a rising tide of immigrants has come to North America, fleeing war and persecution in their homelands or otherwise seeking better life chances. Today, one-fifth of the U.S. youth population has foreign-born parents; nearly one-third of these youths are foreign born themselves. Similarly, immigrant youths are the fastest-growing segment of the Canadian population (Fuligni, 2001; Statistics Canada, 2000). They are ethnically diverse. In the United States, most come from Asia and Latin America; in Canada, from Asia, Africa, and the Middle East.

Academic Achievement and Adjustment

Although educators and laypeople often assume that the transition to a new country has a negative impact on psychological well-being, recent evidence reveals that children of immigrant parents from diverse countries adapt amazingly well. Students who are first-generation (foreign-born) or second-generation (American-born with immigrant parents) often achieve in school as well as or better than students of native-born parents. Their success is evident in many academic subjects, including English, even though they are likely to come from non-English-speaking homes (Fuligni, 1997; Rumbaut, 1997).

Findings on psychological adjustment resemble those on achievement. Compared with their agemates, adolescents from immigrant families are less likely to commit delinquent and violent acts, to use drugs and alcohol, and to have early sex. They are also in better health—less likely to be obese and to have missed school because of illness. And in terms of self-esteem, they feel as positively about themselves as do young people with native-born parents and report less emotional distress. These successes do not depend on having extensive time to adjust to a new way of life. The school performance and psychological well-being of recently arrived high school students is as high as—and sometimes higher than—that of students who come at younger ages (Fuligni, 1997, 1998b; Rumbaut, 1997).

The outcomes just described are strongest for Chinese, Japanese, Korean, and East Indian youths, less dramatic for other ethnicities (Fuligni, 1997; Kao & Tienda, 1995; Louie, 2001). Variations in parental education and income largely account for these differences. Still, even first- and second-generation youths from ethnic groups that face considerable economic hardship (such as Mexican and Vietnamese) are remarkably successful (Fuligni & Yoshikawa, 2003). Factors other than income are responsible.

Family and Community Influences

Ethnographies of immigrant populations reveal that uniformly, parents express the belief that education is the surest way to improve life chances. Consequently, they place a high value on their children's academic achievement (Goldenberg et al., 2001; Louie, 2001). Aware of the challenges their children face, immigrant parents underscore the importance of trying hard. They remind their children that educational opportunities were not available in their native countries and that as a result, they themselves are often limited to menial jobs.

Adolescents from immigrant families internalize their parents' valuing of education, endorsing it more strongly than agemates with native-born parents (Asakawa, 2001; Fuligni, 1997). Because minority ethnicities usually stress allegiance to family and community over individual goals, first- and second-generation young people spend much time with their fami-

commitments sometimes lead them to observe selectively or misinterpret what they see. Finally, the findings of ethnographic studies cannot be assumed to generalize beyond the people and settings in which the research was conducted.

Ask YOURSELF

REVIEW Why might a researcher choose structured observation over naturalistic observation? How about the reverse? What might lead the researcher to opt for clinical interviewing over systematic observation?

APPLY A researcher wants to study the thoughts and feelings of children who have experienced their parents' divorce. Which method is best suited for investigating this question? Why?

CONNECT What strengths and limitations do the clinical, or case study, method and ethnography have in common?

lies and feel a strong sense of obligation to their parents. They view school success as one of the most important ways they can repay their parents for the hardships they endured in coming to a new land (Fuligni et al., 1999; Fuligni, Yip, & Tseng, 2002). Both family relationships and school achievement protect these youths from risky behaviors, such as delinquency, early pregnancy, and drug use (refer to the Biology and Environment box on pages 10–11).

Immigrant parents typically develop close ties to an ethnic community, which exerts additional control through a high consensus on values and constant monitoring of young people's activities. Consider Versailles Village, a low-income Vietnamese neighborhood in New Orleans, where the overwhelming majority of high school students say that obedi-

ence to parents and working hard are very important. A local education association promotes achievement by offering after-school homework tutoring sessions and English- and Vietnamese-language classes. Almost 70 percent of Vietnamese adolescents enroll, and attendance is positively related to school performance. The comments of Vietnamese teenagers capture the power of these family and community forces:

Thuy Trang, age 14, middle-school Student of the Year: "When my par-

ents first immigrated from Vietnam, they spent every waking hour working hard to support a family. They have sacrificed for me, and I am willing to do anything for them."

Elizabeth, age 16, straight-A student, like her two older sisters: "My parents know pretty much all the kids in the neighborhood. . . . Everybody here knows everybody else. It's hard to get away with much." (Zhou & Bankston, 1998, pp. 93, 130)

This family recently immigrated to the United States from Ecuador. Ethnographic research shows that immigrant parents typically place a high value on academic achievement and emphasize family and community goals over individual goals. Their children, who feel a strong sense of obligation to meet their parents' expectations, achieve as well as or better than native-born agemates, and they are less likely to commit antisocial acts.

© MICHAEL NEWMAN/PHOTOEDIT

General Research Designs

In deciding on a research design, investigators choose a way of setting up a study that permits them to test their hypotheses with the greatest degree of certainty possible. Two main designs are used in all research on human behavior: correlational and experimental.

CORRELATIONAL DESIGN ● In a **correlational design,** researchers gather information on individuals, generally in natural life circumstances, and make no effort to alter their experiences. Then they look at relationships between participants' characteristics and their behavior or development. Suppose we want to answer such questions as, Do parents' styles of interacting with their children have any bearing on children's intelligence? Does attending a child-care center promote children's friendliness with peers? How do child abuse and neglect affect children's feelings about themselves and their relationships with peers? In these and many other instances, the conditions of interest are difficult or impossible to arrange and control and must be studied as they currently exist.

Correlational studies have one major limitation: We cannot infer cause and effect. For example, if we find that parental interaction is related to children's intelligence, we still do not know whether parents' behavior actually *causes* intellectual differences among children. In fact, the opposite is possible. The behaviors of highly intelligent children may be so attractive that they cause parents to interact more favorably. Or a third variable that we did not even consider, such as amount of noise and distraction in the home, may cause both parental interaction and children's intelligence to change.

In correlational studies, and in other types of research designs, investigators often examine relationships by using a **correlation coefficient**—a number that describes how two measures, or variables, are associated with one another. We will encounter the correlation coefficient in discussing research findings throughout this book. So let's look at what it is and how it is interpreted. A correlation coefficient can range in value from +1.00 to −1.00. The *magnitude,* or *size, of the number* shows the *strength of the relationship.* A zero correlation indicates no relationship, but the closer the value is to either +1.00 or −1.00, the stronger the relationship. For instance, a correlation of −.78 is high, −.52 is moderate, and −.18 is low. Note, however that correlations of +.52 and −.52 are equally strong. The *sign of the number* refers to the *direction of the relationship.* A positive sign (+) means that as one variable *increases,* the other also *increases.* A negative sign (−) indicates that as one variable *increases,* the other *decreases.*

Let's take some examples to illustrate how a correlation coefficient works. In one study, a researcher found a +.50 correlation between a measure of maternal language stimulation at 13 months and the size of children's vocabularies at 20 months (Tamis-LeMonda & Bornstein, 1994). This is a moderate correlation, which indicates that the more mothers spoke to their infants, the more advanced their children were in language development. In another study, a researcher reported that the extent to which mothers ignored their 10-month-olds' bids for attention was negatively correlated with children's willingness to comply with parental demands 1 year later—at −.46 for boys and −.36 for girls (Martin, 1981). These moderate correlations reveal that the more mothers ignored their babies, the less cooperative their children were.

Both investigations found a relationship between maternal behavior and children's early development. Although the researchers suspected that maternal behavior affected children's responses, in neither study could they be sure about cause and effect. However, finding a relationship in a correlational study suggests that tracking down its cause—with a more powerful experimental strategy, if possible—would be worthwhile.

EXPERIMENTAL DESIGN ● An **experimental design** permits inferences about cause and effect because researchers use an evenhanded procedure to assign people to two or more treatment conditions. In an experiment, the events and behaviors of interest are divided into two types: independent and dependent variables. The **independent variable** is the one the investigator expects to cause changes in another variable. The **dependent variable** is the one the investigator expects to be influenced by the independent variable. Cause-and-effect relationships can be detected because the researcher directly *controls* or *manipulates* changes in the independent variable by exposing participants to the treatment conditions. Then the researcher compares their performance on measures of the dependent variable.

In one *laboratory experiment,* researchers explored the impact of adults' angry interactions on children's adjustment (El-Sheikh, Cummings, & Reiter, 1996). They hypothesized that the way angry encounters end (independent variable) affects children's emotional reactions (dependent variable). Four- and 5-year-olds were brought one at a time to a laboratory, accompanied by their mothers. One group was exposed to an *unresolved-anger treatment,* in which two adult actors entered the room and argued but did not work out their disagreements. The other group witnessed a *resolved-anger treatment,* in which the adults ended their disputes by apologizing and compromising. As Figure 1.6 shows, when they witnessed a follow-up adult conflict, more children in the resolved-anger treatment showed a decline in distress, as measured by fewer anxious facial expressions, less freezing in place, and less seeking of closeness to their mothers. The experiment revealed that anger resolution can reduce the stressful impact of adult conflict on children.

In experimental studies, investigators must take special precautions to control for participants' characteristics that could reduce the accuracy of their findings. For example, in the study just described, if a greater number of children from homes high in parental conflict ended up in the unresolved-anger treatment, we could not tell whether the in-

FIGURE 1.6

Does the way adults end their angry encounters affect children's emotional reactions?

A laboratory experiment showed that children who previously witnessed adults resolving their disputes by apologizing and compromising are more likely to decline in distress when witnessing subsequent adult conflicts than are children who witnessed adults leaving their arguments unresolved. Notice in this graph that only 10 percent of children in the unresolved-anger treatment declined in distress (see bar on left), whereas 42 percent of children in the resolved-anger treatment did so (see bar on right). (Adapted from El-Sheikh, Cummings, & Reiter, 1996.)

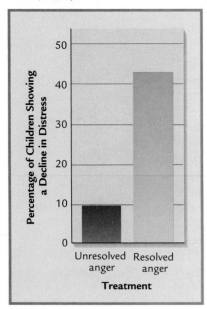

dependent variable or the children's backgrounds produced the results. To protect against this problem, researchers engage in **random assignment** of participants to treatment conditions. By using an unbiased procedure, such as drawing numbers out of a hat or flipping a coin, investigators increase the chances that participants' characteristics will be equally distributed across treatment groups.

Sometimes researchers combine random assignment with another technique called *matching*. In this procedure, participants are measured before the experiment on the factor in question—in our example, exposure to parental conflict. Then children from homes high and low in parental conflict are assigned in equal numbers to each treatment condition. In this way, the experimental groups are deliberately matched, or made equivalent, on characteristics that are likely to distort the results.

MODIFIED EXPERIMENTAL DESIGNS: FIELD AND NATURAL EXPERIMENTS ● Most experiments are conducted in laboratories, where researchers can achieve the maximum possible control over treatment conditions. But as we have already indicated, findings obtained in laboratories may not apply to everyday situations. In *field experiments,* investigators capitalize on rare opportunities to randomly assign people to treatment conditions in natural settings. In the laboratory experiment just described, we can conclude that the emotional climate established by adults affects children's behavior in the laboratory. But does it also do so in daily life?

Another study helps answer this question (Yarrow, Scott, & Waxler, 1973). This time, the research was carried out in a child-care center. A caregiver deliberately interacted differently with two groups of preschoolers. In one condition (the *nurturant treatment*), she modeled many instances of warmth and helpfulness. In the second condition (the *control*, since it involved no treatment), she behaved as usual, with no special emphasis on concern for others. Two weeks later, the researchers created several situations that called for helpfulness. For example, a visiting mother asked each child to watch her baby for a few moments, but the baby's toys had fallen out of the playpen. The investigators found that children exposed to the nurturant treatment were much more likely than those in the control condition to return toys to the baby.

Often researchers cannot randomly assign participants and manipulate conditions in the real world. However, sometimes they can compromise by conducting *natural experiments.* Treatments that already exist, such as different family environments, child-care centers, or schools, are compared. These studies differ from correlational research only in that groups of participants are carefully chosen to ensure that their characteristics are as much alike as possible. In this way, investigators rule out, as best they can, alternative explanations for their treatment effects. But despite these efforts, natural experiments are unable to achieve the precision and rigor of true experimental research.

To help you compare correlational and experimental designs, Table 1.6 on page 42 summarizes their strengths and limitations. It also includes an overview of designs for studying development, to which we now turn.

Designs for Studying Development

Scientists interested in child development require information about the way research participants change over time. To answer questions about development, they must extend correlational and experimental approaches to include measurements at different ages. Longitudinal and cross-sectional designs are special *developmental research strategies.* In each, age comparisons form the basis of the research plan.

THE LONGITUDINAL DESIGN ● In a **longitudinal design**, participants are studied repeatedly at different ages, and changes are noted as the participants mature. The time spanned may be relatively short (a few months to several years) or very long (a decade or even a lifetime). The longitudinal approach has two major strengths. First, because it tracks the performance of each person over time, researchers can identify common patterns of development as well as individual differences. Second, longitudinal studies permit investigators to examine relationships between early and later events and behaviors. Let's take an example to illustrate these ideas.

TABLE 1.6

Strengths and Limitations of Research Designs

DESIGN	DESCRIPTION	STRENGTHS	LIMITATIONS
General			
Correlational	The investigator obtains information on already existing groups, without altering participants' experiences.	Permits study of relationships between variables.	Does not permit inferences about cause-and-effect relationships.
Experimental	The investigator manipulates an independent variable and looks at its effect on a dependent variable; can be conducted in the laboratory or in the natural environment.	Permits inferences about cause-and-effect relationships.	When conducted in the laboratory, findings may not apply to the real world. When conducted in the field, control is usually weaker, and results may be due to variables other than the treatment.
Developmental			
Longitudinal	The investigator studies the same group of participants repeatedly at different ages.	Permits study of common patterns and individual differences in development and relationships between early and later events and behaviors.	Age-related changes may be distorted because of dropout and test-wiseness of participants, and cohort effects.
Cross-sectional	The investigator studies groups of participants differing in age at the same point in time.	More efficient than the longitudinal design.	Does not permit study of individual developmental trends. Age differences may be distorted because of cohort effects.
Longitudinal-sequential	The investigator selects two or more groups of participants born in different years and studies them repeatedly at different ages.	Permits both longitudinal and cross-sectional comparisons; reveals existence of cohort effects.	May have the same problems as longitudinal and cross-sectional strategies, but the design helps identify cohort effects.
Microgenetic	The investigator presents children with a novel task and follows their mastery over a series of closely spaced sessions.	Offers unique insights into the process of development.	Requires intensive study of participants' moment-by-moment behaviors; the time required for participants to change is difficult to anticipate; practice effects may distort developmental trends.

A group of researchers wondered whether children who display extreme personality styles—either angry and explosive or shy and withdrawn—retain the same dispositions when they become adults. In addition, they wanted to know what kinds of experiences promote stability or change in personality and what consequences explosiveness and shyness have for long-term adjustment. To answer these questions, the researchers delved into the archives of the Guidance Study, a well-known longitudinal investigation that was initiated in 1928 at the University of California, Berkeley, and continued over several decades (Caspi, Elder, & Bem, 1987, 1988).

Results revealed that the two personality styles were moderately stable. Between ages 8 and 30, a good number of individuals remained the same, whereas others changed substantially. When stability did occur, it appeared to be due to a "snowballing effect," in which children evoked responses from adults and peers that acted to maintain their dispositions. Explosive youngsters were likely to be treated with anger, whereas shy children were apt to be ignored. As a result, the two types of children came to view their social worlds differently. Explosive children regarded others as hostile; shy children regarded them as unfriendly (Caspi & Roberts, 2001). Together, these factors led explosive children to sustain or increase their unruliness and shy children to continue to withdraw.

Persistence of extreme personality styles affected many areas of adult adjustment. For men, the results of early explosiveness were most apparent in their work lives, in the form of conflicts with supervisors, frequent job changes, and unemployment. Since few women in this sample of an earlier generation worked after marriage, their family lives were most affected. Explosive girls grew up to be hotheaded wives and parents who were especially prone to divorce. Sex differences in the long-term consequences of shyness were even greater. Men who had been withdrawn in childhood were delayed in marrying, becoming fathers, and developing stable careers. However, because a withdrawn, unassertive style was socially acceptable for females, women who had shy personalities showed no special adjustment problems.

PROBLEMS IN CONDUCTING LONGITUDINAL RESEARCH ● Despite their strengths, longitudinal investigations pose a number of problems. For example, participants may move away or drop out of the research for other reasons. This often leads to *biased samples* that no longer represent the populations to whom researchers would like to generalize their findings. Also, from repeated study, people may become "test-wise." Their performance may improve as a result of *practice effects*—better test-taking skills and increased familiarity with the test—not because of factors commonly associated with development.

But the most widely discussed threat to the accuracy of longitudinal findings is cultural-historical change, or what are commonly called **cohort effects.** Longitudinal studies examine the development of *cohorts*—children born at the same time who are influenced by particular cultural and historical conditions. Results based on one cohort may not apply to children developing at other times. For example, unlike the findings on female shyness described in the previous section, which were gathered more than a half-century ago, today's shy young women tend to be poorly adjusted—a difference that may be due to changes in gender roles in Western societies. Shy adults, whether male or female, feel more depressed, have fewer social supports, and may do less well in educational and career attainment than their agemates (Caspi, 2000; Kerr, Lambert, & Bem, 1996). Similarly, a longitudinal study of social development would probably result in quite different findings if it were carried out in the first decade of the twenty-first century, around the time of World War II, or during the Great Depression of the 1930s (see the Social Issues: Health box on page 44). Cohort effects don't just operate broadly on an entire generation. They also occur when specific experiences influence some children but not others in the same generation—for example, those attending a small rather than a large secondary school or growing up in a certain region of the country.

THE CROSS-SECTIONAL DESIGN ● The length of time it takes for many behaviors to change, even in limited longitudinal studies, has led researchers to turn to a more convenient strategy for studying development. In the **cross-sectional design,** groups of people differing in age are studied at the same point in time.

An investigation in which students in grades 3, 6, 9, and 12 filled out a questionnaire asking about their sibling relationships provides a good illustration (Buhrmester & Furman, 1990). Findings revealed that sibling interaction was characterized by greater equality and less power assertion with age. Also, feelings of sibling companionship declined during adolescence. The researchers thought that several factors contributed to these age differences. As later-born children become more competent and independent, they no longer need, and are probably less willing to accept, direction from older siblings. In addition, as adolescents move from psychological dependence on the family to greater involvement with peers, they may have less time and emotional need to invest in siblings These intriguing ideas about the impact of development on sibling relationships, as you will see in Chapter 16, have been confirmed in subsequent research.

PROBLEMS IN CONDUCTING CROSS-SECTIONAL RESEARCH ● The cross-sectional design is an efficient strategy for describing age-related trends. Because participants are measured only once, researchers need not be concerned about such difficulties as participant

$\mathcal{S}$ocial Issues: Health

Impact of Historical Times on Development: The Great Depression and World War II

Cataclysmic events, such as economic disaster, war, and rapid social change, shake the foundations of life, inducing shared adaptations among people born at the same time (Rogler, 2002). Glen Elder (1999) capitalized on the hardships that families experienced during the Great Depression of the 1930s to study its influence on development. He delved into the vast archives of two major longitudinal studies: (1) the Oakland Growth Study, an investigation of individuals born in the early 1920s who were adolescents when the Depression took its toll; and (2) the Guidance Study, whose participants were born in the late 1920s and were young children when their families faced severe financial losses.

In both cohorts, relationships changed when economic deprivation struck. As unemployed fathers lost status, mothers took greater control over family affairs. This reversal of traditional gender roles often sparked conflict. Fathers sometimes became explosive and punitive toward their children. At other times, they withdrew into passivity and depression. Mothers often became frantic with worry over their family's well-being and sought work to make ends meet (Elder, Liker, & Cross, 1984).

Outcomes for Adolescents

Although unusual burdens were placed on them as family lives changed, the Oakland Growth Study cohort—especially the boys—weathered economic hardship quite well. As adolescents, they were too old to be wholly dependent on their highly stressed parents. Boys spent less time at home as they searched for part-time jobs, and many turned toward adults and peers outside

the family for emotional support. Girls took over responsibility for household chores and caring for younger siblings. Their greater involvement in family affairs exposed them to more parental conflict and unhappiness. Consequently, adolescent girls' adjustment in economically deprived homes was somewhat less favorable than that of adolescent boys (Elder, Van Nguyen, & Caspi, 1985).

These changes had major consequences for adolescents' future aspirations and adult lives. As girls focused on home and family, they were less likely to think about college and careers and more likely to marry early. Boys learned that economic resources could not be taken for granted, and they tended to make a very early commitment to an occupational choice. And the chance to become a parent was especially important to men whose lives had been disrupted by the Depression. Perhaps because they believed that a rewarding career could not be guaranteed, they viewed children as the most enduring benefit of their adult lives.

Outcomes for Children

Unlike the Oakland Growth Study cohort, the Guidance Study participants were within the years of intense family dependency when the Depression struck. For young boys (who, as you will see in later chapters, are especially prone to adjustment problems in the face of family

stress), the impact of economic strain was severe. They showed emotional difficulties and poor attitudes toward school and work that persisted through the teenage years (Elder & Caspi, 1988).

But as the Guidance Study sample became adolescents, another major historical event occurred: In 1941, the United States entered World War II. As a result, thousands of men left their communities for military bases, leading to dramatic life changes. Some combat veterans came away with symptoms of emotional trauma that persisted for decades. Yet for most young soldiers, war mobilization broadened their range of knowledge and experience. It also provided time out from civilian responsibilities, giving many soldiers a chance to consider where their lives were going. And the GI Bill of Rights enabled them to expand their education and acquire new skills after the war. By middle adulthood, the Guidance Study war veterans had reversed the early negative impact of the Great Depression. They were more successful educationally and occupationally than their counterparts who had not entered the service (Elder & Hareven, 1993).

Clearly, cultural-historical change does not have a uniform impact on development. Outcomes can vary considerably, depending on the pattern of historical events and the age at which people experience them.

Historical time period has profound implications for development. The Great Depression of the 1930s left this farm family without a steady income. Children were more negatively affected than adolescents, who were no longer entirely dependent on their highly stressed parents.

© CORBIS

dropout or practice effects. But evidence about change at the level at which it actually occurs—the individual—is not available (Kraemer et al., 2000). For example, in the cross-sectional study of sibling relationships just discussed, comparisons are limited to age-group averages. We cannot tell if important individual differences exist. Indeed, longitudinal findings reveal that adolescents vary considerably in the changing quality of their sibling relationships, many becoming more distant but some becoming increasingly supportive and intimate (Dunn, Slomkowski, & Beardsall, 1994).

Cross-sectional studies—especially those that cover a wide age span—have another problem. Like longitudinal research, they can be threatened by cohort effects. For example, comparisons of 5-year-old cohorts and 15-year-old cohorts—groups born and reared in different years—may not really represent age-related changes. Instead, they may reflect unique experiences associated with the different times in which the age groups were growing up.

IMPROVING DEVELOPMENTAL DESIGNS ● Researchers have devised ways of building on the strengths and minimizing the weaknesses of longitudinal and cross-sectional approaches. Several modified developmental designs have resulted.

Combining Longitudinal and Cross-sectional Designs. In the **longitudinal-sequential design,** researchers merge longitudinal and cross-sectional strategies by following a sequence of samples (two or more age groups) over time. For example, suppose we select three samples—sixth, seventh, and eighth graders—and track them for 2 years. That is, we observe each sample this year and next year, as follows: Sample 1 from grades 6 to 7, Sample 2 from grades 7 to 8, and Sample 3 from grades 8 to 9.

The design has three advantages: (1) We can find out whether cohort effects are operating by comparing children of the same age (or grade in school) who were born in different years. Using our example, we can compare children from different samples at grades 7 and 8. If they do not differ on the measure being studied, then we can rule out cohort effects. (2) We can make both longitudinal and cross-sectional comparisons. If outcomes are similar, then we can be especially confident about the accuracy of our findings. (3) The design is efficient. In our example, we can find out about change over a 4-year period by following each cohort for just 2 years.

A study of adolescents' gender-stereotyped beliefs included the longitudinal-sequential features just described (Alfieri, Ruble, & Higgins, 1996). The researchers focused on stereotype flexibility—young people's willingness to say that "masculine" traits (such as *strong*) and "feminine" traits (such as *gentle*) are appropriate for both males and females. As Figure 1.7 reveals, Samples

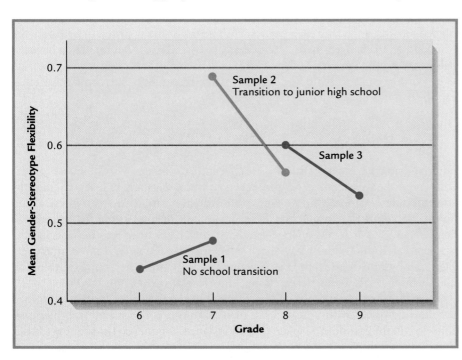

FIGURE 1.7

A longitudinal-sequential study of the development of gender-stereotyped beliefs during adolescence.

Three samples were followed longitudinally from one school year to the next. To test for cohort effects, the researchers compared Sample 1 with Sample 2 at grade 7 and Sample 2 with Sample 3 at grade 8. The scores of Samples 1 and 2 did not match! The reason, the investigators discovered from additional evidence, was that a cohort effect—transition to junior high school—prompts a temporary rise in gender-stereotype flexibility. Because the scores of Samples 2 and 3 were similar at grade 8, the researchers were confident that gender-stereotype flexibility declines sharply in the years following transition to junior high school. (Adapted from Alfieri, Ruble, & Higgins, 1996.)

In a block-gluing project, these 5-year-olds experiment with balance, observe the results with rapt attention, and—if the structure tumbles—take corrective steps. What strategies do they use, and how do they become proficient at the task? Because a microgenetic design permits researchers to follow children's mastery of a challenging task, it is uniquely suited to answering these questions.

2 and 3 showed a sharp longitudinal decline in stereotype flexibility and had similar scores when measured at grade 8. But Sample 1, on reaching seventh grade, scored much lower than seventh graders in Sample 2.

The reason, the researchers discovered, was that Sample 1 remained in the same school from sixth to seventh grade, whereas Samples 2 and 3 had transitioned from an elementary to a junior high school. Entry into junior high sparked a temporary rise in gender-stereotype flexibility, perhaps because of exposure to a wide range of older peers, some of whom challenged stereotypes. Over time, stereotype flexibility decreased in Samples 2 and 3. The researchers speculated that these young junior high students were responding to social pressures to conform to traditional gender roles—a topic we will take up in Chapter 16.

Notice how the developmental trend shown in Figure 1.7—high gender-stereotype flexibility at grade 7 that drops off steeply—characterizes only adolescents who moved to a self-contained junior high school. Researchers have become increasingly interested in identifying such cohort effects because they help explain diversity in development.

Examining Microcosms of Development. In all the examples of developmental research we have discussed, observations of children are fairly widely spaced. When we observe once a year or every few years, we can describe development, but we have little opportunity to capture the processes that produce it. The **microgenetic design,** an adaptation of the longitudinal approach, presents children with a novel task and follows their mastery over a series of closely spaced sessions. Within this "microcosm" of development, researchers observe how change occurs (Kuhn, 1995; Siegler & Crowley, 1991). The microgenetic design is especially useful for studying cognitive development. For example, researchers can examine the strategies children use to acquire new knowledge in reading, mathematics, and science (Siegler, 1996, 2002). As you will see in Chapter 5, the microgenetic design has also been used to trace infants' mastery of motor skills.

Nevertheless, microgenetic studies are difficult to carry out. Researchers must pore over hours of videotaped records, analyzing each participant's behavior many times. In addition, the time required for children to change is hard to anticipate. It depends on a careful match between the child's capabilities and the demands of the task. Finally, as in other longitudinal research, practice effects can distort microgenetic findings. But when researchers overcome these challenges, they reap the benefits of seeing development as it takes place.

Ethics in Research on Children

Research into human behavior creates ethical issues because, unfortunately, the quest for scientific knowledge can sometimes exploit people. When children take part in research, the ethical concerns are especially complex. Children are more vulnerable than adults to physical and psychological harm. In addition, immaturity makes it difficult or impossible for children to evaluate for themselves what participation in research will mean. For these reasons, special ethical guidelines for research on children have been developed by the federal government, by funding agencies, and by research-oriented associations such as the American Psychological Association (2002) and the Society for Research in Child Development (1993).

Table 1.7 presents a summary of children's basic research rights. Once you have examined them, read the following research situations, each of which poses a serious ethical dilemma. What precautions do you think should be taken in each instance? Is either so threatening to children's well-being that it should not be carried out?

TABLE 1.7

Children's Research Rights

RESEARCH RIGHT	DESCRIPTION
Protection from harm	Children have the right to be protected from physical or psychological harm in research. If in doubt about the harmful effects of research, investigators should seek the opinion of others. When harm seems possible, investigators should find other means for obtaining the desired information or abandon the research.
Informed consent	All research participants, including children, have the right to have explained to them, in language appropriate to their level of understanding, all aspects of the research that may affect their willingness to participate. When children are participants, informed consent of parents as well as others who act on the child's behalf (such as school officials) should be obtained, preferably in writing. Children, and the adults responsible for them, have the right to discontinue participation in the research at any time.
Privacy	Children have the right to concealment of their identity on all information collected in the course of research. They also have this right with respect to written reports and any informal discussions about the research.
Knowledge of results	Children have the right to be informed of the results of research in language that is appropriate to their level of understanding.
Beneficial treatments	If experimental treatments believed to be beneficial are under investigation, children in control groups have the right to alternative beneficial treatments if they are available.

Sources: American Psychological Association, 2002; Society for Research in Child Development, 1993.

- To study children's willingness to separate from their caregivers, an investigator decides to ask mothers of 1- and 2-year-olds to leave their child alone briefly in an unfamiliar play-room. The researcher knows that these circumstances will upset some children.

- In a study of moral development, a researcher wants to assess children's ability to resist temptation by videotaping their behavior without their knowledge. Seven-year-olds are promised an attractive prize for solving difficult puzzles. They are also told not to look at a classmate's correct solutions, which are deliberately placed at the back of the room. Telling children ahead of time that cheating is being studied or that their behavior is being monitored will defeat the purpose of the study.

Did you find it difficult to evaluate these examples? Virtually every organization that has devised ethical principles for research has concluded that conflicts arising in research situations cannot be resolved with simple right or wrong answers. The ultimate responsibility for the ethical integrity of research lies with the investigator. However, researchers are advised—and often required—to seek advice from others. Committees for this purpose exist in colleges, universities, and other institutions. These review boards balance the costs of the research to participants in terms of time, stress, and inconvenience against the study's value for advancing knowledge and improving conditions of life. If any risks to the safety and welfare of participants outweigh the worth of the research, then preference is always given to the interests of the participants.

The ethical principle of *informed consent* requires special interpretation when participants cannot fully appreciate the research goals and activities. Parental consent is meant to protect the safety of children whose ability to decide is not yet mature. Besides parental consent, researchers should obtain the agreement of other individuals who act on children's behalf, such as institutional officials when research is conducted in schools, child-care centers, or hospitals. This is especially important when research includes special groups of children, such as abused youngsters, whose parents may not always represent their best interests (Fisher, 1993; Thompson, 1990b).

For children 7 years and older, their own informed consent should be obtained in addition to parental consent. Around age 7, changes in children's thinking permit them to better understand basic scientific principles and the needs of others. Researchers should respect and enhance these capacities by providing school-age children with a full explanation of research activities in language they can understand (Fisher, 1993). Extra care must be taken when telling children that the information they provide will be kept confidential and that they can end their participation at any time. Children may not understand or believe these promises (Abramovitch et al., 1995; Bruzzese & Fisher, 2003). And in certain ethnic minority communities, where deference to authority, maintaining pleasant relationships, and meeting the needs of a guest (the researcher) are highly valued, children and parents may be particularly likely to consent when they would rather not do so (Fisher et al., 2002).

Finally, young children rely on a basic faith in adults to feel secure in unfamiliar situations. For this reason, some types of research may be particularly disturbing to them. All ethical guidelines advise that special precautions be taken in the use of deception and concealment, as occurs when researchers observe children from behind one-way mirrors, give them false feedback about their performance, or do not tell them the truth regarding what the research is about. When these procedures are used with adults, *debriefing,* in which the experimenter provides a full account and justification of the activities, occurs after the research session is over. Debriefing should also take place with children, but it rarely works as well. Despite explanations, children may leave the research situation with their belief in the honesty of adults undermined. Ethical standards permit deception in research with children if investigators satisfy institutional committees that such practices are necessary. Nevertheless, because deception may have serious emotional consequences for some youngsters, many child development specialists believe that researchers should come up with other research strategies when children are involved.

Ask YOURSELF
www

REVIEW Explain how cohort effects can distort the findings of both longitudinal and cross-sectional studies. How does the longitudinal-sequential design reveal cohort effects?

APPLY A researcher compares children who went to summer leadership camps with children who attended athletic camps. She finds that those who attended leadership camps are friendlier. Should the investigator tell parents that sending children to leadership camps will cause them to be more sociable? Why or why not?

CONNECT Henry, age 7, did not want to answer a researcher's questions about how he feels about his younger brother, who has physical disabilities. But he did not feel free to say "no" because his parents told him they had granted permission. What steps do you think the researcher should take to make sure Henry is granted his research rights?

REFLECT Suppose a researcher asks you to enroll your baby in a 10-year longitudinal study. What factors would lead you to agree and to stay involved? Do your answers shed light on why longitudinal studies often have biased samples? Explain.

Summary

The Field of Child Development

What is the field of child development, and what factors stimulated its expansion?

- **Child development** is an interdisciplinary field devoted to the study of constancy and change from conception through adolescence and emerging adulthood. It is part of a larger field known as developmental psychology, or human development, which includes the entire lifespan. Research on child development has been stimulated by both scientific curiosity and social pressures to better children's lives.

How can we divide child development into sensible, manageable periods and domains?

- Researchers generally use the following age periods, which serve as important transitions in major theories: (1) the prenatal period, (2) infancy and toddlerhood, (3) early childhood, (4) middle childhood, (5) adolescence, and (6) emerging adulthood.

- Development is often further divided into three domains: (1) physical development, (2) cognitive development, and (3) emotional and social development. These domains are not really distinct; they combine in an integrated, holistic fashion.

Basic Issues

Identify three basic issues on which theories of child development take a stand.

- Child development **theories** can be organized according to the stand they take on three controversial issues: (1) Is development a **continuous** process, or does it follow a series of **discontinuous stages**? (2) Does one general course of development characterize all children, or do many possible courses exist, depending on the **contexts** in which children grow up? (3) Is development primarily influenced by **nature** or **nurture**?

- More recent theories take a balanced stand on these issues. And contemporary researchers realize that answers

may vary across domains of development and even, as research on **resilience** illustrates, across individuals.

Historical Foundations

Describe major historical influences on modern theories of child development.

- Contemporary theories of child development have roots extending far into the past. As early as medieval times, childhood was regarded as a separate phase of life. In the sixteenth and seventeenth centuries, the Puritan conception of original sin led to a harsh philosophy of child rearing.

- The Enlightenment brought new ideas favoring more humane treatment of children. Locke's notion of the **tabula rasa** provided the basis for twentieth-century behaviorism, and Rousseau's idea of the **noble savage** foreshadowed the concepts of stage and **maturation.**

- Inspired by Darwin's theory of evolution, efforts to observe the child directly began in the late nineteenth and early twentieth centuries. Soon after, Hall and Gesell introduced the **normative approach,** which produced a large body of descriptive facts about children. Binet and Simon constructed the first successful intelligence test, which sparked interest in individual differences in development and led to a heated controversy over nature versus nurture.

Mid-Twentieth-Century Theories

What theories influenced child development research in the mid-twentieth century?

- In the 1930s and 1940s, psychiatrists and social workers turned to the **psychoanalytic perspective** for help in treating children's emotional problems. In Freud's **psychosexual theory,** children move through five stages, during which three portions of the personality—id, ego, and superego—become integrated. Erikson's **psychosocial theory** builds on Freud's theory by emphasizing the development of culturally relevant attitudes and skills and the lifespan nature of development.

- As the psychoanalytic perspective gained in prominence, **behaviorism** and **social learning theory** emerged, emphasizing principles of conditioning and modeling and practical procedures of **behavior modification** to eliminate undesirable behaviors and increase desirable responses.

- In contrast to behaviorism, Piaget's **cognitive-developmental theory** emphasizes that children actively construct knowledge as they manipulate and explore their world. According to Piaget, children move through four stages, beginning with the baby's sensorimotor action patterns and ending with the elaborate, abstract reasoning system of the adolescent. Piaget's work has stimulated a wealth of research on children's thinking and has encouraged educational programs that emphasize discovery learning.

Recent Theoretical Perspectives

Describe recent theoretical perspectives on child development.

- **Information processing** views the mind as a complex, symbol-manipulating system, much like a computer. This approach helps investigators achieve a detailed understanding of what children of different ages do when faced with tasks and problems.

- Four theories place special emphasis on contexts for development. **Ethology** stresses the evolutionary origins and adaptive value of behavior and inspired the **sensitive period** concept. In **evolutionary developmental psychology,** researchers have extended this emphasis, seeking to understand the adaptiveness of species-wide competencies as they change over time.

- Vygotsky's **sociocultural theory** has enhanced our understanding of cultural influences, especially in the area of cognitive development. Through cooperative dialogues with more mature members of society, children come to use language to guide their own thought and actions and to acquire culturally relevant knowledge and skills.

● In **ecological systems theory**, nested layers of the environment—**microsystem, mesosystem, exosystem,** and **macrosystem**—are seen as major influences on children's well-being. The **chronosystem** represents the dynamic, ever-changing nature of children and their experiences.

● Inspired by ideas in other sciences and recent perspectives in child development, a new wave of theorists has adopted a **dynamic systems perspective** to account for wide variation in development. According to this view, the mind, body, and physical and social worlds form an integrated system that guides mastery of new skills. A change in any part of the system prompts the child to reorganize her behavior so the various components work together again, but in a more complex, effective way.

Comparing Child Development Theories

Identify the stand taken by each major theory on the basic issues of child development.

● Theories that are major forces in child development research vary in their focus on different domains of development, in their view of development, and in their strengths and weaknesses. (For a full summary, see Table 1.5 on page 34.)

Studying the Child

Describe methods commonly used to gather information on children.

● **Naturalistic observations,** gathered in everyday environments, permit researchers to see directly the everyday behaviors they hope to explain. In contrast, **structured observations** take place in laboratories, where every participant has an equal opportunity to display the behaviors of interest.

● Self-report methods can be flexible and open-ended like the **clinical interview.** Alternatively, **structured interviews,** tests, and questionnaires, which permit efficient administration and scoring, can be given.

● **Psychophysiological methods** measure the relation between physiological processes and behavior. They help researchers uncover the biological bases of children's perceptual, cognitive, and emotional responses.

● Investigators use the **clinical,** or **case study, method** when they desire an in-depth understanding of a single child. It involves synthesizing a wide range of information, including interviews, observations, test scores, and sometimes psychophysiological measures.

● A growing interest in the impact of culture has prompted researchers to adapt observational and self-report methods to permit direct comparisons of cultures. To uncover the cultural meanings of children's and adults' behaviors, researchers rely on **ethnography.** It uses participant observation to capture the unique values and social processes of a culture or distinct social group.

Distinguish between correlational and experimental research designs, noting the strengths and limitations of each.

● The **correlational design** examines relationships between variables as they happen to occur, without altering participants' experiences. The **correlation coefficient** is often used to measure the association between variables. Correlational studies do not permit inferences about cause and effect. However, their use is justified when it is difficult or impossible to control the variables of interest.

● An **experimental design** permits inferences about cause and effect. Researchers manipulate an **independent variable** by exposing participants to two or more treatment conditions. Then they determine what effect this variable has on a **dependent variable. Random assignment** reduces the chances that characteristics of participants will affect the accuracy of experimental findings.

● To achieve high degrees of control, most experiments are conducted in laboratories, but their findings may not apply to everyday life. Field and natural experiments compare treatments in natural environments. These approaches, however, are less rigorous than laboratory experiments.

Describe designs for studying development, noting the strengths and limitations of each.

● The **longitudinal design** permits study of common patterns as well as individual differences in development and the relationship between early and later events and behaviors. Among problems researchers face in conducting longitudinal research are biased samples and practice effects. Another problem, **cohort effects,** makes it difficult to generalize findings to children developing at other times, who are affected by different cultural and historical conditions.

● The **cross-sectional design** offers an efficient approach to investigating development. However, it is limited to comparisons of age-group averages. Findings of cross-sectional research also can be distorted by cohort effects, especially when they cover a wide age span.

● Modified developmental designs overcome some limitations of longitudinal and cross-sectional research. By combining the two approaches in the **longitudinal-sequential design,** investigators can test for cohort effects. In the **microgenetic design,** researchers track change as it occurs for unique insights into the processes of development. However, the time required for children to change is hard to anticipate, and practice effects can bias findings.

What special ethical concerns arise in doing research on children?

● Because of their immaturity, children are especially vulnerable to harm and often cannot evaluate the risks and benefits of research. Ethical guidelines and special committees that weigh the risks and benefits of research help ensure that children's research rights are protected. Besides obtaining consent from parents and others who act on children's behalf, researchers should seek the informed consent of children 7 years and older. The use of deception in research with children is especially risky because it may undermine their basic faith in the trustworthiness of adults.

Important Terms and Concepts

behavior modification (p. 19)
behaviorism (p. 18)
child development (p. 4)
chronosystem (p. 29)
clinical interview (p. 35)
clinical, or case study, method (p. 36)
cognitive-developmental theory
　(p. 20)
cohort effects (p. 43)
contexts (p. 9)
continuous development (p. 8)
correlation coefficient (p. 40)
correlational design (p. 39)
cross-sectional design (p. 43)
dependent variable (p. 40)
discontinuous development (p. 8)
dynamic systems perspective (p. 29)

ecological systems theory (p. 27)
ethnography (p. 37)
ethology (p. 24)
evolutionary developmental
　psychology (p. 25)
exosystem (p. 28)
experimental design (p. 40)
independent variable (p. 40)
information processing (p. 23)
longitudinal design (p. 41)
longitudinal-sequential design (p. 45)
macrosystem (p. 28)
maturation (p. 13)
mesosystem (p. 28)
microgenetic design (p. 46)
microsystem (p. 28)
naturalistic observation (p. 33)

nature–nurture controversy (p. 9)
noble savage (p. 13)
normative approach (p. 14)
psychoanalytic perspective (p. 15)
psychophysiological methods (p. 35)
psychosexual theory (p. 15)
psychosocial theory (p. 16)
random assignment (p. 41)
resilience (p. 10)
sensitive period (p. 25)
social learning theory (p. 19)
sociocultural theory (p. 26)
stage (p. 8)
structured interview (p. 35)
structured observation (p. 33)
tabula rasa (p. 13)
theory (p. 6)

 **For Further Information and Help**

Consult the Companion Website for *Infants, Children, and Adolescents,* Fifth Edition, *(www.ablongman.com/berk),* where you will find the following resources for this chapter:

- **Chapter Objectives**
- **Flashcards** for studying important terms and concepts
- **Annotated Weblinks** to guide you in further research
- **Ask Yourself questions,** which you can answer and then check against a sample response

- **Suggested Readings**
- **Practice Tests** with immediate scoring and feedback

This portrayal of life in a complex urban environment captures a diversity of sensations and impressions related to history, commerce, transportation, resources, communication, and culture. Chapter 2 will introduce you to a similarly complex blend of genetic, family, school, neighborhood, and societal forces that influence child development.

"My City"
Priyanka Anandjiwala
13 years, India

Reprinted with permission from the International Museum of Children's Art, Oslo, Norway.

Biological and Environmental Foundations

"It's a girl," announces the doctor, who holds up the squalling little creature while her new parents gaze with amazement at their miraculous creation.

"A girl! We've named her Sarah!" exclaims the proud father to eager relatives waiting by the telephone for word about their new family member.

As we join these parents in thinking about how this wondrous being came into existence and imagining her future, we are struck by many questions. How could this well-formed baby, equipped with everything necessary for life outside the womb, have developed from the union of two tiny cells? What ensures that Sarah will, in due time, roll over, reach for objects, walk, talk, make friends, imagine, and create—just like every other normal child born before her? Why is she a girl and not a boy, dark-haired rather than blond, calm and cuddly instead of wiry and energetic? What difference will it make that Sarah is given a name and place in one family, community, nation, and culture rather than another?

To answer these questions, this chapter takes a close look at the foundations of development: heredity and environment. Because nature has prepared us for survival, all humans have features in common. Yet each human being is also unique. Take a moment to think about several children you know well. Now jot down the most obvious physical and behavioral similarities between them and their parents. Did you find that one child shows combined features of both parents, another resembles just one parent, whereas a third is not like either parent? These directly observable characteristics are called **phenotypes.** They depend in part on the individual's **genotype**—the complex blend of genetic information that determines our species and influences all our unique characteristics. Yet throughout life, phenotypes are also affected by the person's experiences.

We begin our discussion of development at the moment of conception, an event that establishes the hereditary makeup of the new individual. In the first section of this chapter, we review basic genetic principles that help explain similarities and differences between children in appearance and behavior. Next, we turn to aspects of the environment that play powerful roles in children's lives. As our discussion proceeds, you will quickly see that both nature and nurture affect all aspects of development. In fact, some findings and conclusions may surprise you. For example, many people believe that when children inherit unfavorable characteristics, not much can be done to help them. Others are convinced that the damage done to a child by a harmful environment can easily be corrected. We will see that neither of these assumptions is true. In the final section of this chapter, we take up the question of how nature and nurture *work together* to shape the course of development.

Genetic Foundations

Each of us is made up of trillions of units called *cells.* Inside every cell is a control center, or *nucleus,* that contains rodlike structures called **chromosomes, which store and transmit genetic information.** Human chromosomes come in 23 matching pairs (an exception is the XY pair in males, which we will discuss shortly). Each member of a pair corresponds to the other in size, shape, and genetic functions. One is inherited from the mother and one from the father (see Figure 2.1).

The Genetic Code

Chromosomes are made up of a chemical substance called **deoxyribonucleic acid, or DNA.** As Figure 2.2 shows, DNA is a long, double-stranded molecule that looks like a twisted ladder. Each rung of the ladder consists of a specific pair of chemical substances called *bases,* joined together between the two sides. Although the bases always pair up in the same way across the ladder rungs—A with T and C with G—they can occur in any order along its sides. It is this sequence of base pairs that provides genetic instructions. A **gene** is a segment of DNA along the length of the chromosome. Genes can be of different lengths—perhaps 100 to several thousand ladder rungs long. An estimated 25,000 to 30,000 genes lie along the human chromosomes (Pennisi, 2003).

We share some of our genetic makeup with even the simplest organisms, such as bacteria and molds, and most of it with other mammals, especially primates. Between 98 and 99 percent

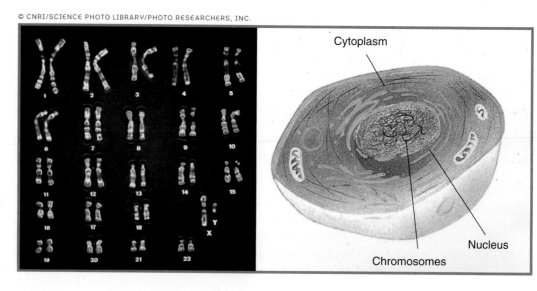

FIGURE 2.1

A karyotype, or photograph, of human chromosomes.

The 46 chromosomes shown on the left were isolated from a human cell, stained, greatly magnified, and arranged in pairs according to decreasing size of the upper "arm" of each chromosome. Note the twenty-third pair, XY. The cell donor is a male. In a female, the twenty-third pair would be XX.

Cytoplasm

Nucleus

Chromosomes

of chimpanzee and human DNA is identical. This means that only a small portion of our heredity is responsible for the traits that make us human, from our upright gait to our extraordinary language and cognitive capacities. And the genetic variation from one human to the next is even less! Individuals around the world are about 99.1 percent genetically identical (Gibbons, 1998). Only a tiny quantity of DNA contributes to human variation in traits and capacities.

A unique feature of DNA is that it can duplicate itself through a process called **mitosis.** This special ability permits a single cell, formed at conception, to develop into a complex human being composed of a great many cells. Refer again to Figure 2.2, and you will see that during mitosis, the chromosomes copy themselves. As a result, each new body cell contains the same number of chromosomes and the identical genetic information.

Genes accomplish their task by sending instructions for making a rich assortment of proteins to the *cytoplasm,* the area surrounding the cell nucleus. Proteins, which trigger chemical reactions throughout the body, are the biological foundation on which our characteristics are built. How do humans, with far fewer genes than scientists once thought (only twice as many as the worm or fly), manage to develop into such complex beings? The answer lies in the proteins our genes make, which break up and reassemble in staggering variety—about 10 to 20 million altogether. In simpler species, the number of proteins is far more limited. Furthermore, the communication system between the cell nucleus and cytoplasm, which fine-tunes gene activity, is more intricate in humans than in simpler organisms. Within the cell, a wide range of environmental factors modify gene expression (Davies, Howell, & Gardner, 2001). So even at this microscopic level, biological events are the result of *both* genetic and nongenetic forces.

The Sex Cells

New individuals are created when two special cells called **gametes,** or sex cells—the sperm and ovum—combine. A gamete contains only 23 chromosomes, half as many as a regular body cell. Gametes are formed through a cell division process called **meiosis,** which halves the number of chromosomes normally present in body cells, thereby ensuring that a constant quantity of genetic material is transmitted from one generation to the next. When sperm and ovum unite at conception the cell that results, called a **zygote,** will again have 46 chromosomes.

Meiosis takes place according to the steps shown in Figure 2.3 on page 56. First, chromosomes pair up, and each one copies itself. Then a special event occurs called **crossing over,** in which chromosomes next to each other break at one or more points along their length and exchange segments, so that genes from one are replaced by genes from another. This shuffling of genes in crossing over creates new hereditary combinations. Next, the chromosome pairs separate into different cells, but chance determines which member of each pair will gather with others and end up in the same gamete. Finally, each chromosome leaves its partner and becomes part of a gamete containing 23 chromosomes instead of the usual 46.

These events make the chances extremely low that nontwin offspring of the same two parents will be genetically the same—about 1 in 700 trillion (Gould & Keeton, 1996). Therefore, meiosis helps us understand why siblings differ, even though they have features in common because their genotypes come from the same pool of parental genes. The genetic variability produced by

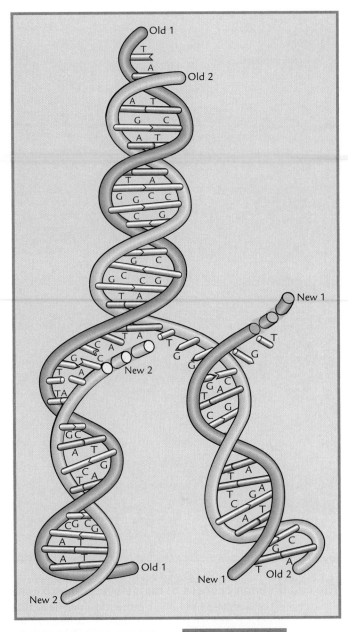

FIGURE 2.2

DNA's ladderlike structure.

This figure shows that the pairings of bases across the rungs of the ladder are very specific: adenine (A) always appears with thymine (T), and cytosine (C) always appears with guanine (G). Here, the DNA ladder duplicates by splitting down the middle of its ladder rungs. Each free base picks up a new complementary partner from the area surrounding the cell nucleus.

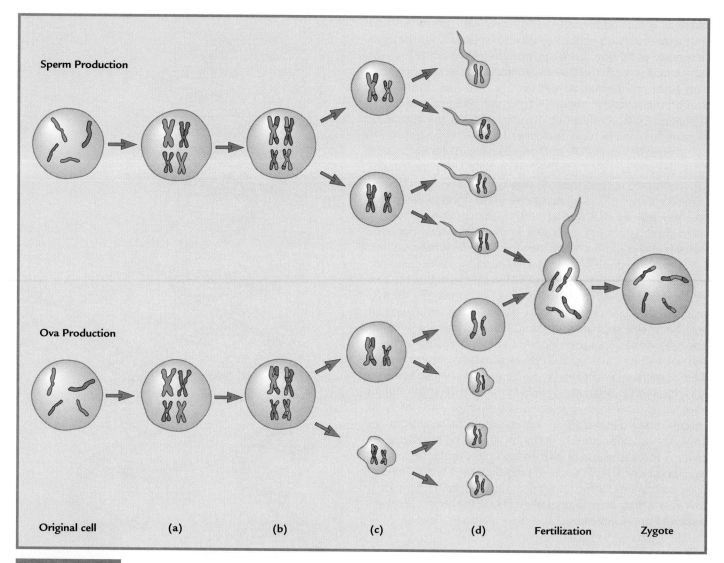

The cell division process of meiosis, leading to gamete formation.
Here, original cells are depicted with 2 rather than the full complement of 23 pairs. Meiosis creates gametes through the following steps: (a) Chromosomes each duplicate and pair with one another. (b) Crossing over takes place between the two innermost pair members. (c) The pairs of chromosomes separate to form two cells, each with 23 duplicated chromosomes, with chance determining which chromosomes from a pair end up in the same cell. (d) The duplicated chromosomes separate to form gametes, each with 23 single chromosomes. In the female, this second meiotic division occurs after conception, and the remaining genetic material degenerates. Consequently, four sperm and a single ovum are produced. After sperm and ovum unite at conception, the first cell of the new individual, called a zygote, has 46 chromosomes, or 23 pairs—the same number as in the original cells.

meiosis is important in an evolutionary sense. It increases the chances that at least some members of a species will be able to cope with ever-changing environments and survive.

In the male, four sperm are produced when meiosis is complete. Also, the cells from which sperm arise are produced continuously throughout life. For this reason, a healthy man can father a child at any age after sexual maturity. In the female, gamete production results in just one ovum; the remaining genetic material degenerates. In addition, the female is born with all her ova already present in her ovaries, and she can bear children for only three to four decades. Still, there are plenty of female sex cells. About 1 to 2 million are present at birth, 40,000 remain at adolescence, and approximately 350 to 450 will mature during a woman's childbearing years (Moore & Persaud, 2003).

Boy or Girl?

Return to Figure 2.1, and note that 22 of the 23 pairs of chromosomes are matching pairs, called **autosomes.** They are numbered by geneticists from longest (1) to shortest (22). The twenty-third pair consists of **sex chromosomes.** In females, this pair is called XX; in males, it is called XY. The X is a relatively long chromosome, whereas the Y is short and carries little genetic material. When gametes form in males, the X and Y chromosomes separate into different sperm cells. In females, all gametes carry an X chromosome. Therefore, the sex of the new organism is determined by whether an X-bearing or a Y-bearing sperm fertilizes the ovum. In fact, scientists have isolated three genes on the Y chromosome that are crucial for male sexual development—one that switches on the production of male hormones and two involved in the formation of male sex organs. But they also know that other genes, yet to be discovered, are involved in the development of sexual characteristics (Cotinot et al., 2002).

Multiple Births

Ruth and Peter, a couple I know well, tried for several years to have a child, without success. When Ruth reached age 33, her doctor prescribed a fertility drug, and twins—Jeannie and Jason—were born. Jeannie and Jason are **fraternal,** or **dizygotic, twins,** the most common type of multiple birth, resulting from the release and fertilization of two ova. Therefore, Jeannie and Jason are genetically no more alike than ordinary siblings. Older maternal age, fertility drugs, and in vitro fertilization (to be discussed shortly) are major causes of the dramatic rise in fraternal twinning and other multiple births in industrialized nations over the past several decades (Russell et al., 2003; SOGC, 2003). As Table 2.1 indicates, other genetic and environmental factors also increase the chances of bearing fraternal twins.

Twins can be created in another way. Sometimes a zygote that has started to duplicate separates into two clusters of cells that develop into two individuals. These are called **identical,** or **monozygotic, twins** because they have the same genetic makeup. The frequency of identical twins is unrelated to the factors listed in Table 2.1. It is the same around the world—about 3 of every 1,000 births (Tong, Caddy, & Short, 1997). Animal research has uncovered a variety of environmental influences that prompt this type of twinning, including temperature changes, variation in oxygen levels, and late fertilization of the ovum.

During their early years, children of single births often are healthier and develop more rapidly than twins (Mogford-Bevan, 1999). Jeannie and Jason were born early (as are most

TABLE 2.1

Maternal Factors Linked to Fraternal Twinning

FACTOR	DESCRIPTION
Ethnicity	Occurs in 4 per 1,000 births among Asians, 8 per 1,000 births among whites, 12 to 16 per 1,000 births among blacks[a]
Family history of twinning	Occurs more often among women whose mothers and sisters gave birth to fraternal twins
Age	Rises with maternal age, peaking between 35 and 39 years, and then rapidly falls
Nutrition	Occurs less often among women with poor diets; occurs more often among women who are tall and overweight or of normal weight as opposed to slight body build
Number of births	Is more likely with each additional birth
Fertility drugs and in vitro fertilization	Is more likely with fertility hormones and in vitro fertilization (see page 66), which also increase the chances of triplets to quintuplets

[a]Worldwide rates, not including multiple births resulting from use of fertility drugs.
Source: Bortolus et al., 1999; Mange & Mange, 1998.

© RACHEL EPSTEIN/PHOTOEDIT

These identical, or monozygotic, twins were created when a duplicating zygote separated into two clusters of cells, and two individuals with the same genetic makeup developed. Identical twins look alike, and as we will see later in this chapter, tend to resemble each other in a variety of psychological characteristics.

twins)—3 weeks before Ruth's due date. As you will see in Chapter 4, like other premature infants, they required special care after birth. When the twins came home from the hospital, Ruth and Peter had to divide time between them. Perhaps because neither baby got quite as much attention as the average single infant, Jeannie and Jason walked and talked several months later than other children their age, although both caught up in development by middle childhood (Lytton & Gallagher, 2002).

Patterns of Genetic Inheritance

Jeannie has her parents' dark, straight hair, whereas Jason is curly-haired and blond. Patterns of genetic inheritance—the way genes from each parent interact—explain these outcomes. Recall that except for the XY pair in males, all chromosomes come in corresponding pairs. Two forms of each gene occur at the same place on the autosomes, one inherited from the mother and one from the father. Each form of a gene is called an **allele.** If the alleles from both parents are alike, the child is **homozygous** and will display the inherited trait. If the alleles are different, the child is **heterozygous,** and relationships between alleles determine what trait will appear.

DOMINANT–RECESSIVE INHERITANCE ● In many heterozygous pairings, **dominant–recessive inheritance** occurs: Only one allele affects the child's characteristics. It is called *dominant;* the second allele, which has no effect, is called *recessive.* Hair color is an example. The allele for dark hair is dominant (we can represent it with a capital *D*), whereas the one for blond hair is recessive (symbolized by a lowercase *b*). A child who inherits a homozygous pair of dominant alleles *(DD)* and a child who inherits a heterozygous pair *(Db)* will be dark-haired, even though their genotypes differ. Blond hair (like Jason's) can result only from having two recessive alleles *(bb).* Still, heterozygous individuals with just one recessive allele *(Db)* can pass that trait to their children. Therefore, they are called **carriers** of the trait.

Some human characteristics that follow the rules of dominant–recessive inheritance are given in Table 2.2 on the following page and Table 2.3 on page 60. As you can see, many disabilities and diseases are the product of recessive alleles. One of the most frequently occurring recessive disorders is *phenylketonuria,* or *PKU.* It affects the way the body breaks down proteins contained in many foods. Infants born with two recessive alleles lack an enzyme that converts one of the basic amino acids that make up proteins (phenylalanine) into a byproduct essential for body functioning (tyrosine). Without this enzyme, phenylalanine quickly builds to toxic levels that damage the central nervous system. By 1 year, infants with PKU are permanently retarded.

Despite its potentially damaging effects, PKU provides an excellent illustration of the fact that inheriting unfavorable genes does not always lead to an untreatable condition. All U.S. states and Canadian provinces require that each newborn be given a blood test for PKU. If the disease is found, doctors place the baby on a diet low in phenylalanine. Children who receive this treatment nevertheless show mild deficits in certain cognitive skills, such as memory, planning, and problem solving, because even small amounts of phenylalanine interfere with brain functioning (Luciana, Sullivan, & Nelson, 2001; White et al., 2001). But as long as dietary treatment begins early and continues, children with PKU usually attain an average level of intelligence and have a normal lifespan.

In dominant–recessive inheritance, if we know the genetic makeup of the parents, we can predict the percentage of children in a family who are likely to display or be carriers of a trait. Figure 2.4 illustrates this for PKU. Notice that for a child to inherit the condition, each parent must carry a recessive allele *(p).* As the figure also shows, a single gene can affect more than one trait. Because of their inability to convert phenylalanine into tyrosine (which is responsible for pigmentation), children with PKU usually have light hair and blue eyes. Furthermore, children vary in the degree to which phenylalanine accumulates in their tissues and in the extent to which they respond to treatment. This is due to the action of **modifier genes,** which enhance or dilute the effects of other genes.

Only rarely are serious diseases due to dominant alleles. Think about why this is so. Children who inherited the dominant allele would always develop the disorder. They seldom live long enough to reproduce, and the harmful dominant allele is eliminated from the family's heredity in a single generation. Some dominant disorders, however, do persist. One of them is *Huntington disease,* a condition in which the central nervous system degenerates. Why has this disorder endured? Its symptoms usually do not appear until age 35 or later, after the person has passed the dominant gene to his or her children.

CODOMINANCE ● In some heterozygous circumstances, the dominant–recessive relationship does not hold completely. Instead, we see **codominance, a pattern of inheritance in which both alleles influence the person's characteristics.**

The *sickle cell trait,* a heterozygous condition present in many black Africans, provides an example. *Sickle cell anemia* (see Table 2.3) occurs in full form when a child inherits two recessive alleles. They cause the usually round red blood cells to become sickle (crescent moon) shaped, especially under low-oxygen conditions. The sickled cells clog the blood vessels and block the flow of blood, causing intense pain, swelling, and tissue damage. About 50 percent of affected people survive to age 40, only 1 percent to age 60 (Ashley-Koch, Yang, & Olney, 2000). Heterozygous individuals are protected from the disease under most circumstances. However, when they experience oxygen deprivation—for example, at high altitudes or after intense physical exercise—the single recessive allele asserts itself, and a temporary, mild form of the illness occurs.

The sickle cell allele is common among black Africans for a special reason. Those who carry it are more resistant to malaria than individuals with two alleles for normal red blood cells. In Africa, where malaria is common, these carriers have survived and reproduced more frequently than others, leading the gene to be maintained in the black population. In regions of the world where the risk of malaria is low, the frequency of the gene is declining—for example, only 8 percent of African Americans carry it, compared to 20 percent of black Africans (Fixler & Styles, 2002).

X-LINKED INHERITANCE ● Males and females have an equal chance of inheriting recessive disorders carried on the autosomes, such as PKU and sickle cell anemia. But when a harmful allele is carried on the X chromosome, **X-linked inheritance** applies. Males are more

TABLE 2.2

Examples of Dominant and Recessive Characteristics

DOMINANT	RECESSIVE
Dark hair	Blond hair
Normal hair	Pattern baldness
Curly hair	Straight hair
Nonred hair	Red hair
Facial dimples	No dimples
Normal hearing	Some forms of deafness
Normal vision	Nearsightedness
Farsightedness	Normal vision
Normal vision	Congenital eye cataracts
Normally pigmented skin	Albinism
Double-jointedness	Normal joints
Type A blood	Type O blood
Type B blood	Type O blood
Rh-positive blood	Rh-negative blood

Note: Many normal characteristics that were previously thought to be due to dominant–recessive inheritance, such as eye color, are now regarded as due to multiple genes. For the characteristics listed here, there still seems to be general agreement that the simple dominant–recessive relationship holds.
Source: McKusick, 1998.

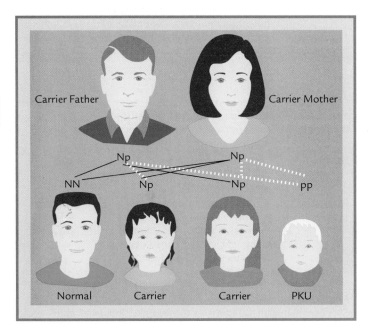

FIGURE 2.4

Dominant–recessive mode of inheritance, as illustrated by PKU.

When both parents are heterozygous carriers of the recessive gene (*p*), we can predict that 25 percent of their offspring are likely to be normal (*NN*), 50 percent are likely to be carriers (*Np*), and 25 percent are likely to inherit the disorder (*pp*). Notice that the PKU-affected child, in contrast to his siblings, has light hair. The recessive gene for PKU affects more than one trait. It also leads to fair coloring.

TABLE 2.3

Examples of Dominant and Recessive Diseases

DISEASE	DESCRIPTION	MODE OF INHERITANCE	INCIDENCE	TREATMENT
Autosomal Diseases				
Cooley's anemia	Pale appearance, retarded physical growth, and lethargic behavior begin in infancy.	Recessive	1 in 500 births to parents of Mediterranean descent	Frequent blood transfusion; death from complications usually occurs by adolescence.
Cystic fibrosis	Lungs, liver, and pancreas secrete large amounts of thick mucus, leading to breathing and digestive difficulties.	Recessive	1 in 2,000 to 2,500 Caucasian births; 1 in 16,000 births to North Americans of African descent	Bronchial drainage, prompt treatment of respiratory infection, dietary management. Advances in medical care allow survival with good life quality into adulthood.
Phenylketonuria (PKU)	Inability to metabolize the amino acid phenylalanine, contained in many proteins, causes severe central nervous system damage in the first year of life.	Recessive	1 in 8,000 births	Placing the child on a special diet results in average intelligence and normal lifespan. Subtle difficulties with planning and problem solving are often present.
Sickle cell anemia	Abnormal sickling of red blood cells causes oxygen deprivation, pain, swelling, and tissue damage. Anemia and susceptibility to infections, especially pneumonia, occur.	Recessive	1 in 500 births to North Americans of African descent	Blood transfusions, painkillers, prompt treatment of infection. No known cure; 50 percent die by age 20.
Tay-Sachs disease	Central nervous system degeneration, with onset at about 6 months, leads to poor muscle tone, blindness, deafness, and convulsions.	Recessive	1 in 3,600 births to Jews of European descent and to French Canadians	None. Death by 3 to 4 years of age.
Huntington disease	Central nervous system degeneration leads to muscular coordination difficulties, mental deterioration, and personality changes. Symptoms usually do not appear until age 35 or later.	Dominant	1 in 18,000 to 25,000 births	None. Death occurs 10 to 20 years after symptom onset.
Marfan syndrome	Tall, slender build; thin, elongated arms and legs. Heart defects and eye abnormalities, especially of the lens. Excessive lengthening of the body results in a variety of skeletal defects.	Dominant	1 in 20,000 births	Correction of heart and eye defects sometimes possible. Death from heart failure in young adulthood is common.
X-Linked Diseases				
Duchenne muscular dystrophy	Degenerative muscle disease. Abnormal gait, loss of ability to walk between 7 and 13 years of age.	Recessive	1 in 3,000 to 5,000 male births	None. Death from respiratory infection or weakening of the heart muscle usually occurs in adolescence.
Hemophilia	Blood fails to clot normally. Can lead to severe internal bleeding and tissue damage.	Recessive	1 in 4,000 to 7,000 male births	Blood transfusions. Safety precautions to prevent injury.
Diabetes insipidus	Insufficient production of the hormone vasopressin results in excessive thirst and urination. Dehydration can cause central nervous system damage.	Recessive	1 in 2,500 male births	Hormone replacement.

Note: For recessive disorders, carrier status can be detected in prospective parents through a blood test or genetic analyses. For all disorders listed, prenatal diagnosis is available (see page 65).

Sources: Behrman, Kliegman, & Arvin, 1996; Chodirker et al., 2001; Gott, 1998; Grody, 1999; Knoers et al., 1993; McKusick, 1998; Schulman & Black, 1997.

likely to be affected because their sex chromosomes do not match. In females, any recessive allele on one X chromosome has a good chance of being suppressed by a dominant allele on the other X. But the Y chromosome is only about one-third as long and therefore lacks many corresponding alleles to override those on the X. A well-known example is *hemophilia,* a disorder in which the blood fails to clot normally. Figure 2.5 shows its greater likelihood of inheritance by male children whose mothers carry the abnormal allele.

Besides X-linked disorders, many sex differences reveal the male to be at a disadvantage. Rates of miscarriage, infant and childhood deaths, birth defects, learning disabilities, behavior disorders, and mental retardation are greater for boys (Halpern, 1997). It is possible that these sex differences can be traced to the genetic code. The female, with two X chromosomes, benefits from a greater variety of genes. Nature, however, seems to have adjusted for the male's disadvantage. Worldwide, about 106 boys are born for every 100 girls, and judging from miscarriage and abortion statistics, a still greater number of boys appear to be conceived (Pyeritz, 1998).

Nevertheless, in recent decades the proportion of male births has declined in many industrialized countries, including the United States, Canada, and Europe (Grech, Vassallo-Agius, & Savona-Ventura, 2000). Some researchers blame increased occupational and community exposure to pesticides for a reduction in sperm counts overall, especially Y-bearing sperm.

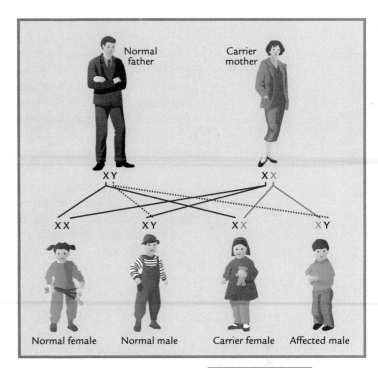

FIGURE 2.5

X-linked inheritance.
In the example shown here, the allele on the father's X chromosome is normal. The mother has one normal and one abnormal recessive allele on her X chromosomes. By looking at the possible combinations of the parents' alleles, we can predict that 50 percent of male children are likely to have the disorder and 50 percent of female children are likely to be carriers of it.

GENETIC IMPRINTING ● More than 1,000 human characteristics follow the rules of dominant–recessive and codominant inheritance (McKusick, 1998). In these cases, whichever parent contributes a gene to the new individual, the gene responds in the same way. Geneticists, however, have identified some exceptions. In **genetic imprinting,** alleles are *imprinted,* or chemically *marked,* in such a way that one pair member (either the mother's or the father's) is activated, regardless of its makeup. The imprint is often temporary: It may be erased in the next generation, and it may not occur in all individuals (Everman & Cassidy, 2000).

Imprinting helps us understand certain puzzling genetic patterns. For example, children are more likely to develop diabetes if their father, rather than their mother, suffers from it. And people with asthma or hay fever tend to have mothers, not fathers, with the illness. Scientists do not yet know what causes this parent-specific genetic transmission. At times, it reveals itself in heartbreaking ways. Imprinting is involved in several childhood cancers and in *Prader-Willi syndrome,* a disorder with symptoms of mental retardation and severe obesity (Hanel & Wevrick, 2001). It may also explain why Huntington disease, when inherited from the father, tends to emerge at an earlier age and to progress more rapidly (Navarrete, Martinez, & Salamanca, 1994).

Genetic imprinting can also operate on the sex chromosomes, as *fragile X syndrome* reveals. In this disorder, an abnormal repetition of a sequence of DNA bases occurs in a special spot on the X chromosome, damaging a particular gene. Fragile X syndrome is the most common inherited cause of mild to moderate mental retardation. It has also been linked to 2 to 3 percent of cases of autism, a serious emotional disorder of early childhood involving bizarre, self-stimulating behavior and delayed or absent language and communication. Research reveals that the defective gene at the fragile site is expressed only when it is passed from mother to child (Jinn & Warren, 2000).

MUTATION ● How are harmful genes created in the first place? The answer is **mutation, a sudden but permanent change in a segment of DNA.** A mutation may affect only one or two genes, or it may involve many genes, as in the chromosomal disorders we will discuss shortly. Some mutations occur spontaneously, simply by chance. Others are caused by hazardous environmental agents in our food supply or the air we breathe.

Although nonionizing forms of radiation—electromagnetic waves and microwaves—have no demonstrated impact on DNA, ionizing (high-energy) radiation is an established cause of mutation. Women who receive repeated doses before conception are more likely to miscarry or give birth to children with hereditary defects. Genetic abnormalities, such as physical malformations and childhood cancer, are also higher when fathers are exposed to radiation in their occupations (Brent, 1999). However, infrequent and mild exposure does not cause genetic damage. Instead, high doses over a long period impair DNA.

POLYGENIC INHERITANCE ● So far, we have discussed patterns of inheritance in which people either display a particular trait or do not. These cut-and-dried individual differences are much easier to trace to their genetic origins than are characteristics that vary continuously among people, such as height, weight, intelligence, and personality. These traits are due to **polygenic inheritance, in which many genes affect the characteristic in question.** Polygenic inheritance is complex, and much about it is still unknown. In the final section of this chapter, we discuss how researchers infer the influence of heredity on human attributes when they do not know the precise patterns of inheritance.

Chromosomal Abnormalities

Besides harmful recessive alleles, abnormalities of the chromosomes are a major cause of serious developmental problems. Most chromosomal defects result from mistakes during meiosis, when the ovum and sperm are formed. A chromosome pair does not separate properly, or part of a chromosome breaks off. Since these errors involve far more DNA than problems due to single genes, they usually produce many physical and mental symptoms.

DOWN SYNDROME ● The most common chromosomal disorder, occurring in 1 out of every 1,000 live births, is *Down syndrome.* In 95 percent of cases, it results from a failure of the twenty-first pair of chromosomes to separate during meiosis, so the new individual inherits three of these chromosomes rather than the normal two. For this reason, Down syndrome is sometimes called *trisomy 21.* In other, less frequent forms, an extra twenty-first chromosome is attached to part of another chromosome (called *translocation* pattern). Or an error occurs during the early stages of mitosis, causing some but not all body cells to have the defective chromosomal makeup (called *mosaic* pattern). Because less genetic material is involved in the mosaic type, symptoms of the disorder are usually less extreme (Hodapp, 1996).

The consequences of Down syndrome include mental retardation, speech problems, limited vocabulary, and slow motor development. Affected individuals also have distinct physical features—a short, stocky build, a flattened face, a protruding tongue, almond-shaped eyes, and an unusual crease running across the palm of the hand. In addition, infants with Down syndrome often are born with eye cataracts, hearing loss, and heart and intestinal defects. Because of medical advances, fewer individuals with Down syndrome die early than was the case in the past. Many survive into their fifties, and a few into their sixties to eighties (Roizen & Patterson, 2003). Although this lengthening of life expectancy is cause for celebration, many affected individuals who live past age 40 show symptoms of *Alzheimer's disease,* the most common form of dementia (Heinz & Blass, 2002). Genes on chromosome 21 are linked to this disorder.

Parents face extra challenges in caring for a baby with Down syndrome. Facial deformities often lead to breathing and feeding difficulties. Also, these infants smile less readily, show poorer eye-to-eye contact, and explore objects less persistently. But when parents encourage them to engage with their surroundings, Down syndrome children develop more favorably (Sigman, 1999). They also benefit from infant and preschool intervention programs, although emotional, social, and motor skills im-

The facial features of the 9-year-old boy on the left are typical of Down syndrome. Although his intellectual development is impaired, this child is doing well because he is growing up in a stimulating home where his special needs are met and he is loved and accepted. Here he collaborates with his normally developing 4-year-old brother in making won ton dumplings.

© 2000 LAURA DWIGHT

prove more than intellectual performance (Carr, 2002). Clearly, environmental factors affect how well children with Down syndrome fare.

As Table 2.4 shows, the risk of a Down syndrome baby rises dramatically with maternal age. Why is this so? Geneticists believe that the ova, present in the woman's body since her own prenatal period, weaken over time. As a result, chromosomes do not separate properly as they complete the process of meiosis. But in about 5 to 10 percent of cases, the extra genetic material originates with the father. The reasons for this mutation are unknown, as Down syndrome and other chromosomal abnormalities are not related to advanced paternal age (Muller et al., 2000; Savage et al., 1998).

ABNORMALITIES OF THE SEX CHROMOSOMES ● Disorders of the autosomes other than Down syndrome usually disrupt development so severely that miscarriage occurs. When such babies are born, they rarely survive beyond early childhood. In contrast, abnormalities of the sex chromosomes usually lead to fewer problems. In fact, sex chromosome disorders often are not recognized until adolescence when, in some deviations, puberty is delayed. The most common problems involve the presence of an extra chromosome (either X or Y) or the absence of one X in females.

A variety of myths exist about individuals with sex chromosome disorders. For example, as Table 2.5 reveals, males with *XYY syndrome* are not necessarily more aggressive and antisocial than XY males. And most children with sex chromosome disorders do not suffer from mental retardation. Instead, their intellectual problems are usually very specific. Verbal difficulties—for example, with reading and vocabulary—are common among girls with *triple X syndrome* and boys with *Klinefelter syndrome*, both of whom inherit an extra X chromosome. In contrast, girls with *Turner syndrome*, who are missing an X, have

TABLE 2.4

Risk of Giving Birth to a Down Syndrome Child by Maternal Age

MATERNAL AGE	RISK
20	1 in 1,900 births
25	1 in 1,200
30	1 in 900
33	1 in 600
36	1 in 280
39	1 in 130
42	1 in 65
45	1 in 30
48	1 in 15

Note: The risk of giving birth to a Down syndrome baby after age 35 has increased slightly over the past 20 years, due to improved medical interventions during pregnancy and consequent greater likelihood of a Down syndrome fetus surviving to be liveborn.

Source: Adapted from Halliday et al., 1995; Meyers et al., 1997.

TABLE 2.5

Sex Chromosomal Disorders

DISORDER	DESCRIPTION	INCIDENCE	TREATMENT
XYY syndrome	Extra Y chromosome. Above-average height, large teeth, and sometimes severe acne. Intelligence, male sexual development, and fertility are normal.	1 in 1,000 male births	No special treatment necessary.
Triple X syndrome (XXX)	Extra X chromosome. Tallness and impaired verbal intelligence. Female sexual development and fertility are normal.	1 in 500 to 1,250 female births	Special education to treat verbal ability problems.
Klinefelter syndrome (XXY)	Extra X chromosome. Tallness, body fat distribution resembling females, incomplete development of sex characteristics at puberty, sterility, and impaired verbal intelligence.	1 in 900 male births	Hormone therapy at puberty to stimulate development of sex characteristics; special education to treat verbal ability problems.
Turner syndrome (XO)	Missing X chromosome. Short stature, webbed neck, incomplete development of sex characteristics at puberty, sterility, and impaired spatial intelligence.	1 in 2,500 to 8,000 female births	Hormone therapy in childhood to stimulate physical growth and at puberty to promote development of sex characteristics; special education to treat spatial ability problems.

Sources: Money, 1993; Moore & Persaud, 1993; Netley, 1986; Pennington et al., 1982; Ratcliffe, Pan, & McKie, 1992; Rovet et al., 1996; Schiavi et al., 1984.

trouble with spatial relationships—for example, drawing pictures, telling right from left, following travel directions, and noticing changes in facial expressions (Collaer et al., 2002; Geschwind et al., 2000; Money, 1993). These findings tell us that adding to or subtracting from the usual number of X chromosomes results in particular intellectual deficits. At present, geneticists do not know why.

Ask YOURSELF

REVIEW   Explain the genetic origins of PKU and Down syndrome. Cite evidence indicating that both heredity and environment contribute to the development of children with these disorders.

REVIEW   Using your knowledge of X-linked inheritance, explain why males are more vulnerable to miscarriage, infant death, genetic disorders, and other problems.

APPLY   Gilbert's genetic makeup is homozygous for dark hair. Jan's is homozygous for blond hair. What color is Gilbert's hair? How about Jan's? What proportion of their children are likely to be dark-haired? Explain.

CONNECT   Referring to ecological systems theory (Chapter 1, pages 27–29), explain why parents of children with genetic disorders often experience increased stress. What factors, within and beyond the family, can help these parents support their children's development?

Reproductive Choices

Two years after they married, Ted and Marianne gave birth to their first child. Kendra appeared to be a healthy infant, but by 4 months her growth had slowed. Diagnosed as having Tay-Sachs disease (see Table 2.3), Kendra died at 2 years of age. Ted and Marianne were devastated by Kendra's death. Although they did not want to bear another infant who would endure such suffering, they badly wanted a child. They began to avoid family get-togethers, where little nieces and nephews were constant reminders of the void in their lives.

In the past, many couples with genetic disorders in their families chose not to have children rather than risk the birth of an abnormal baby. Today, genetic counseling and prenatal diagnosis help people make informed decisions about conceiving, carrying a pregnancy to term, or adopting a child.

Genetic Counseling

Genetic counseling is a communication process designed to help couples assess their chances of giving birth to a baby with a hereditary disorder and choose the best course of action in view of risks and family goals (Shiloh, 1996). Individuals likely to seek counseling are those who have had difficulties bearing children, such as repeated miscarriages, or who know that genetic problems exist in their families. In addition, women who delay childbearing past age 35 are candidates for genetic counseling. After this time, the overall rate of chromosomal abnormalities rises sharply, from 1 in every 190 to as many as 1 in every 10 pregnancies at age 48 (Meyers et al., 1997).

If a family history of mental retardation, physical defects, or inherited diseases exists, the genetic counselor interviews the couple and prepares a *pedigree,* a picture of the family tree in which affected relatives are identified. The pedigree is used to estimate the likelihood that parents will have an abnormal child, using the same genetic principles discussed earlier in this chapter. In the case of many disorders, blood tests or genetic analyses can reveal whether the parent is a carrier of the harmful gene. Carrier detection is possible for all the recessive diseases listed in Table 2.3, as well as others, and for fragile X syndrome.

When all the relevant information is in, the genetic counselor helps people consider appropriate options. These include "taking a chance" and conceiving, choosing from among a variety of reproductive technologies (see the Social Issues: Health box on pages 66–67), or adopting a child.

Prenatal Diagnosis and Fetal Medicine

If couples who might bear an abnormal child decide to conceive, several **prenatal diagnostic methods**—medical procedures that permit detection of developmental problems before birth—are available (see Table 2.6). Women of advanced maternal age are prime candidates for *amniocentesis* or *chorionic villus sampling* (see Figure 2.6 on page 68). Except for *ultrasound* and *maternal blood analysis,* prenatal diagnosis should not be used routinely, since other methods have some chance of injuring the developing organism.

Prenatal diagnosis has led to advances in fetal medicine. For example, by inserting a needle into the uterus, doctors can administer drugs to the fetus. Also, surgery has been performed to

---

TABLE 2.6
Prenatal Diagnostic Methods

METHOD	DESCRIPTION
Amniocentesis	The most widely used technique. A hollow needle is inserted through the abdominal wall to obtain a sample of fluid in the uterus. Cells are examined for genetic defects. Can be performed by the 14th week after conception; 1 to 2 more weeks are required for test results. Small risk of miscarriage.
Chorionic villus sampling	A procedure that can be used if results are desired or needed very early in pregnancy. A thin tube is inserted into the uterus through the vagina, or a hollow needle is inserted through the abdominal wall. A small plug of tissue is removed from the end of one or more chorionic villi, the hairlike projections on the membrane surrounding the developing organism. Cells are examined for genetic defects. Can be performed at 6 to 8 weeks after conception, and results are available within 24 hours. Entails a slightly greater risk of miscarriage than does amniocentesis. Also associated with a small risk of limb deformities, which increases the earlier the procedure is performed.
Fetoscopy	A small tube with a light source at one end is inserted into the uterus to inspect the fetus for defects of the limbs and face. Also allows a sample of fetal blood to be obtained, permitting diagnosis of such disorders as hemophilia and sickle cell anemia as well as neural defects (see below). Usually performed between 15 and 18 weeks after conception, but can be done as early as 5 weeks. Entails some risk of miscarriage.
Ultrasound	High-frequency sound waves are beamed at the uterus; their reflection is translated into a picture on a videoscreen that reveals the size, shape, and placement of the fetus. By itself, permits assessment of fetal age, detection of multiple pregnancies, and identification of gross physical defects. Also used to guide amniocentesis, chorionic villus sampling, and fetoscopy. When used five or more times, may increase the chances of low birth weight.
Maternal blood analysis	By the second month of pregnancy, some of the developing organism's cells enter the maternal bloodstream. An elevated level of alpha-fetoprotein may indicate kidney disease, abnormal closure of the esophagus, or neural tube defects, such as anencephaly (absence of most of the brain) and spina bifida (bulging of the spinal cord from the spinal column). Isolated cells can be examined for genetic defects, such as Down syndrome.
Preimplantation genetic diagnosis	After in vitro fertilization and duplication of the zygote into a cluster of about eight to ten cells, one or two cells are removed and examined for hereditary defects. Only if that sample is free of detectable genetic disorders is the fertilized ovum implanted in the woman's uterus.

Sources: Eiben et al., 1997; Lissens & Sermon, 1997; Moore & Persaud, 2003; Newnham et al., 1993; Quintero, Puder, & Cotton, 1993; Sutcliffe, 2002; Wapner, 1997; Willner, 1998.

Social Issues: Health

The Pros and Cons of Reproductive Technologies

Some couples decide not to risk pregnancy because of a history of genetic disease. Many others—in fact, one-sixth of all couples who try to conceive—discover that they are sterile. And some never-married adults and gay and lesbian partners want to bear children. Today, increasing numbers of individuals are turning to alternative methods of conception—technologies that, although they fulfill the wish of parenthood, have become the subject of heated debate.

Donor Insemination and In Vitro Fertilization

For several decades, *donor insemination*—injection of sperm from an anonymous man into a woman—has been used to overcome male reproductive difficulties. In recent years, it has also permitted women without a heterosexual partner to become pregnant. Donor insemination is 70 to 80 percent successful, resulting in 30,000 to 50,000 births in North America each year (Cooper & Glazer, 1999).

In vitro fertilization is another reproductive technology that has become increasingly common. Since the first "test tube" baby was born in England in 1978, 1 percent of all children in developed countries—about 39,000 babies in the United States and 3,500 in Canada—have been conceived through this technique annually (Sutcliffe, 2002). With in vitro fertilization, hormones are given to a woman, stimulating the ripening of several ova. These are removed surgically and placed in a dish of nutrients, to which sperm are added. Usually, in vitro fertilization is used to treat women whose fallopian tubes are permanently damaged. But a recently developed technique permits a single sperm to be injected directly into an ovum, thereby overcoming most male fertility problems as well. And a new "sex sorter" method helps ensure that couples who carry X-linked diseases (which usually affect males) have a daughter. Once an ovum is fertilized

and begins to duplicate into several cells, it is injected into the mother's uterus.

The overall success rate of in vitro fertilization is about 30 percent. However, success declines steadily with age, from 38 percent in women younger than age 35 to 6 percent in women age 43 and older (Wright et al., 2003). By mixing and matching gametes, pregnancies can be brought about when either or both partners have a reproductive problem. Fertilized ova and sperm can even be frozen and stored in embryo banks for use at some future time, thereby guaranteeing healthy zygotes should age or illness lead to fertility problems.

Children conceived through these methods may be genetically unrelated to one or both of their parents. In addition, most parents who have used in vitro fertilization do not tell their children about their origins, although health professionals now encourage them to do so. Does lack of genetic ties or secrecy surrounding these techniques interfere with parent–child relationships? Perhaps because of a strong desire for parenthood, caregiving is actually somewhat warmer for young children conceived through donor insemination or in vitro fertilization. And in vitro infants are as securely attached to their parents, and children and adolescents as well adjusted, as their counterparts who were naturally conceived (Golombok et al., 2002a, 2002b; Hahn, 2001).

Although donor insemination and in vitro fertilization have many benefits, serious questions have arisen about their use. Most U.S. states and Canadian provinces have few legal guidelines for these procedures. As a result, donors are not always screened for genetic or sexually transmitted diseases. In many countries, including Canada, Denmark, Great Britain, Norway, and the United States, donors remain anonymous, and doctors are not required to keep records of their characteristics. Canada, however, retains a file on donor identities, permitting contact only in cases of serious disease, where knowledge of the child's

genetic background might be helpful for medical reasons (Bioethics Consultative Committee, 2003). Another concern is that the in vitro "sex sorter" method will lead to parental sex selection, thereby eroding the moral value that boys and girls are equally precious.

Finally, more than 50 percent of in vitro procedures result in multiple births. Most are twins, but 9 percent are triplets and higher-order multiples. Consequently, among in vitro babies, the rate of low birth weight is 2.6 times higher than in the general population (Schieve et al., 2002). Risk of major birth defects also doubles, probably because of multiple factors, including drugs used to induce ripening of ova and maintain the pregnancy and delays in fertilizing ova outside the womb (Hansen et al., 2002). In sum, in vitro fertilization poses greater risks than natural conception to infant survival and healthy development.

Surrogate Motherhood

An even more controversial form of medically assisted conception is *surrogate motherhood*. Typically in this procedure, sperm from a man whose wife is infertile are used to inseminate a woman, called a surrogate, who is paid a fee for her childbearing services. In return, the surrogate agrees to turn the baby over to the man (who is the natural father). The child is then adopted by his wife.

Although most of these arrangements proceed smoothly, those that end up in court highlight serious risks for all concerned. In one case, both parties rejected the infant with severe disabilities that resulted from the pregnancy. In several others, the surrogate mother wanted to keep the baby or the couple changed their minds during the pregnancy. These children came into the world in the midst of conflict that threatened to last for years.

Because surrogacy usually involves the wealthy as contractors for infants and the less economically advantaged as surrogates, it may promote exploitation of financially needy women (Sureau,

1997). In addition, most surrogates already have children of their own, who may be deeply affected by the pregnancy. Knowledge that their mother would give away a baby for profit may cause these children to worry about the security of their own family circumstances.

New Reproductive Frontiers

Reproductive technologies are evolving faster than societies can weigh the ethics of these procedures. Doctors have used donor ova from younger women in combination with in vitro fertilization to help postmenopausal women become pregnant. Most recipients are in their forties, but a 62-year-old has given birth in Italy and a 63-year-old in the United States. Even though candidates for postmenopausal-assisted childbirth are selected on the basis of good health, serious questions arise about bringing children into the world whose parents may not live to see them reach adulthood. Based on U.S. life expectancy data, 1 in 3 mothers

and 1 in 2 fathers having a baby at age 55 will die before their child enters college (U.S. Census Bureau, 2003b).

Currently, experts are debating other reproductive options. In once instance, a woman with a busy stage career who could have conceived naturally chose to combine in vitro fertilization (using her own ova and her husband's sperm) and surrogate motherhood. This permitted the woman to continue her career while the surrogate carried her biological child (Wood, 2001). At donor banks, customers can select ova or sperm on the basis of physical characteristics and even IQ. Some worry that this practice is a dangerous step toward selective breeding through "designer babies"—controlling offspring characteristics by manipulating the genetic makeup of fertilized ova.

Finally, scientists have successfully cloned (made multiple copies of) fertilized ova in sheep, cattle, and monkeys, and they are working on effective ways to do so in humans. By providing extra

ova for injection, cloning might improve the success rate of in vitro fertilization. But it also raises the possibility of mass-producing genetically identical people. Therefore, it is widely condemned (Fasouliostis & Schenker, 2000).

Although new reproductive technologies permit many barren couples to rear healthy newborn babies, laws are needed to regulate such practices. In Australia, New Zealand, Sweden, and Switzerland, individuals conceived with donated gametes have a right to information about their genetic origins (Frith, 2001). Pressure from those working in the field of assisted reproduction may soon lead to a similar policy in the United States.

In the case of surrogate motherhood, the ethical problems are so complex that 18 U.S. states have sharply restricted the practice, and Australia, Canada, and many European nations have banned it, arguing that the status of a baby should not be a matter of commercial arrangement and that the body's reproductive system should not be rented or sold (Chen, 2003; McGee, 1997). Denmark, France, and Great Britain have prohibited in vitro fertilization for women past menopause (Bioethics Consultative Committee, 2003). At present, nothing is known about the psychological consequences of being a product of these procedures. Research on how such children grow up, including what they know and how they feel about their origins, is important for weighing the pros and cons of these techniques.

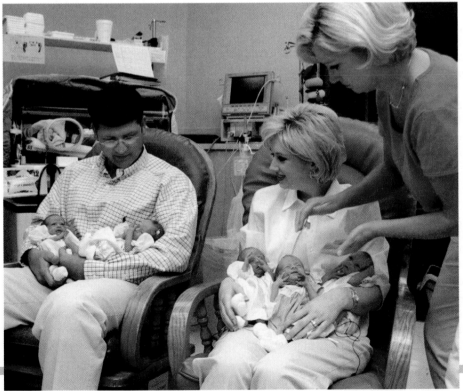

Although reproductive technologies permit many barren couples to have healthy newborns, they can pose grave ethical dilemmas. Fertility drugs and in vitro fertilization often lead to multiple fetuses. When three or more fill the uterus, pregnancy complications are often so severe that doctors recommend aborting one or more to save the others. These 3-week-old babies, being held by their parents in the intensive care nursery, are the only documented quintuplets to have all been born alive in Mississippi.

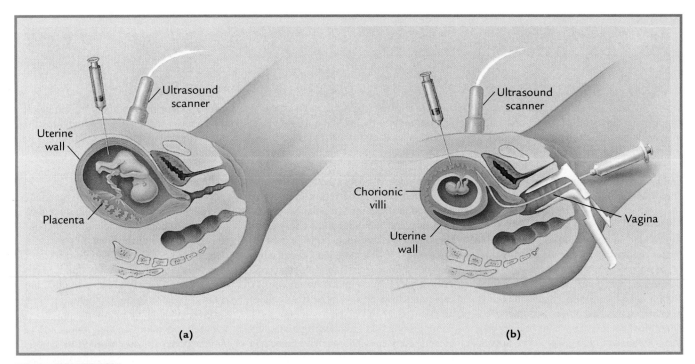

(a) (b)

FIGURE 2.6

Amniocentesis and chorionic villus sampling.
Today, hundreds of defects and diseases can be detected before birth using these two procedures. (a) In amniocentesis, a hollow needle is inserted through the abdominal wall into the uterus during the fourteenth week after conception, or later. Fluid is withdrawn and fetal cells are cultured, a process that takes about 3 weeks. (b) Chorionic villus sampling can be performed much earlier in pregnancy, at 6 to 8 weeks after conception, and results are available within 24 hours. Two approaches to obtaining a sample of chorionic villus are shown: inserting a thin tube through the vagina into the uterus, and inserting a needle through the abdominal wall. In both amniocentesis and chorionic villus sampling, an ultrasound scanner is used for guidance. (From K. L. Moore & T. V. N. Persaud, 2003, *Before We Are Born,* 6th ed., Philadelphia: Saunders, p. 87. Adapted by permission of the publisher and author.)

repair such problems as heart and lung malformations, urinary tract obstructions, neural defects, and tumors of the tailbone. Fetuses with hereditary immune deficiencies have even received bone marrow transplants that succeeded in creating a normally functioning immune system (Flake, 2003).

Nevertheless, these techniques frequently result in complications, the most common being premature labor and miscarriage (Flake et al., 2000). Yet parents may be willing to try almost any option, even one with only a slim chance of success. Currently, the medical profession is struggling with how to help parents make informed decisions about fetal surgery. One suggestion is that the advice of an independent counselor be provided—a doctor or nurse who understands the risks but is not involved in doing research on or performing the procedure.

Advances in *genetic engineering* also offer new hope for correcting hereditary defects. As part of the Human Genome Project—an ambitious, international research program aimed at deciphering the chemical makeup of human genetic material (genome)—researchers have mapped the sequence of all human DNA base pairs. Using this information, they are "annotating" the genome—identifying all its genes and their functions, including their protein products and what these products do. A major goal is to understand the estimated 4,000 human disorders, those due to single genes and those resulting from a complex interplay of multiple genes and environmental factors.

Already, thousands of genes have been identified, including those involved in hundreds of diseases, such as cystic fibrosis, Duchenne muscular dystrophy, Huntington disease, Marfan syndrome, sickle cell anemia, and many forms of cancer (NIH, 2003). As a result, new treatments are being explored, such as *gene therapy*—correcting genetic abnormalities by delivering DNA carrying a functional gene to the cells. In recent experiments, gene therapy relieved symptoms in hemophilia patients and in patients with severe immune system dysfunction (Cavazzano-Calvo et al., 2000; Kay et al., 2000). Another approach is *proteomics,* in which gene-specified proteins involved in disease are modified (Banks, 2003).

Genetic treatments seem some distance away for most single-gene defects, however, and far off for diseases involving multiple genes that combine in complex ways with each other and the environment (Collins & McKusick, 2001). For steps that prospective parents can take before conception to protect the health of their child, refer to Applying What We Know below.

The Alternative of Adoption

Adults who cannot bear children, who are likely to pass along a genetic disorder, or who are older and single but want a family are turning to adoption in increasing numbers. Adoption agencies usually try to find parents of the same ethnic and religious background as the child. Where possible, they also try to choose parents who are the age of most natural parents. Because the availability of healthy babies has declined (fewer young unwed mothers give up their babies than in the past), more people are adopting from other countries or taking children who are older or who have developmental problems.

Still, adopted children and adolescents—whether born in another country or in the country of their adoptive parents—have more learning and emotional difficulties than other children, a difference that increases with the child's age at time of adoption (Levy-Shiff, 2001; Miller et al., 2000). There are many possible reasons for adoptees' more problematic childhoods. The

The Human Genome Project is leading to new gene-based treatments for hereditary disorders such as Alzheimer's disease. When the daughter and granddaughter of this Alzheimer's victim reach late adulthood, they may be spared this devastating illness.

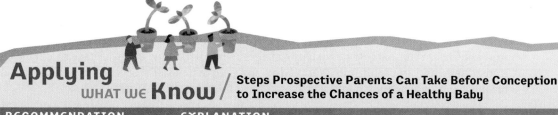

Applying WHAT WE Know / Steps Prospective Parents Can Take Before Conception to Increase the Chances of a Healthy Baby

RECOMMENDATION	EXPLANATION
Arrange for a physical exam.	A physical exam before conception permits detection of diseases and other medical problems that might reduce fertility, be difficult to treat after the onset of pregnancy, or affect the developing organism.
Consider your genetic makeup.	Find out if anyone in your family has had a child with a genetic disease or disability. If so, seek genetic counseling before conception.
Reduce or eliminate toxins under your control.	Since the developing organism is highly sensitive to damaging environmental agents during the early weeks of pregnancy (see Chapter 3), couples trying to conceive should avoid drugs, caffeine, alcohol, cigarette smoke, radiation, pollution, chemical substances in the home and workplace, and infectious diseases. Furthermore, stay away from ionizing radiation and some industrial chemicals, which are known to cause mutations.
Ensure proper nutrition.	A well-balanced diet helps ensure healthy prenatal growth. A doctor-recommended vitamin-mineral supplement, begun before conception, helps prevent many prenatal problems. It should include folic acid, which reduces the chances of neural tube defects, prematurity, and low birth weight (see Chapter 3, page 118).
Consult a physician after 12 months of unsuccessful efforts at conception.	Long periods of infertility may be due to undiagnosed spontaneous abortions, which can be caused by genetic defects in either partner. If a physical exam reveals a healthy reproductive system, seek genetic counseling.

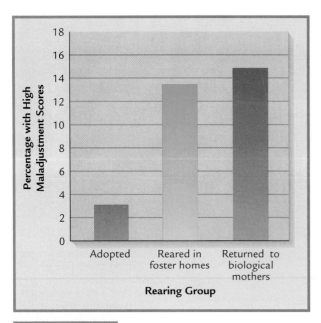

FIGURE 2.7

Relationship of type of rearing to maladjustment among a sample of Swedish adolescents who had been candidates for adoption at birth.

Compared with the other two groups, adopted young people were rated by teachers as having far fewer problems, including anxiety, withdrawal, aggression, inability to concentrate, peer difficulties, and poor school motivation. (Adapted from Bohman & Sigvardsson, 1990.)

biological mother may have been unable to care for the child because of problems believed to be partly genetic, such as alcoholism or severe depression. If so, she may have passed this tendency to her offspring. Or perhaps she experienced stress, poor diet, or inadequate medical care during pregnancy—factors that can affect the child (as you will see in Chapter 3). Furthermore, children adopted after infancy are more likely than their nonadopted peers to have a history of conflict-ridden family relationships, lack of parental affection, and neglect and abuse. Finally, adoptive parents and children, who are genetically unrelated, are less alike in intelligence and personality than biological relatives—differences that may threaten family harmony.

But despite these risks, most adopted children fare well, and those with problems usually make rapid progress (Johnson, 2002; Kim, 2002). In a Swedish study, researchers followed more than 600 infant adoption candidates into adolescence. Some were adopted shortly after birth; some were reared in foster homes; and some were reared by their biological mothers, who initially gave up their babies and then changed their minds and took them back. As Figure 2.7 shows, adoptees developed much more favorably than children growing up in foster families or returned to their birth mothers (Bohman & Sigvardsson, 1990). And in a study of internationally adopted children in the Netherlands, sensitive maternal care and secure attachment in infancy predicted cognitive and social competence at age 7 (Stams, Juffer, & van IJzendoorn, 2002). So even when children are not genetically related to their parents, an early warm, trusting parent–child relationship fosters development. Children with troubled family histories who are adopted at older ages also develop feelings of trust and affection for their adoptive parents as they come to feel loved and supported in their new families (Sherrill & Pinderhughes, 1999).

By adolescence, however, adoptees' lives often are complicated by unresolved curiosity about their roots. Some have difficulty accepting the possibility that they may never know their birth parents. Others worry about what they would do if their birth parents suddenly reappeared (Grotevant & Kohler, 1999). Nevertheless, the decision to search for birth parents is usually postponed until early adulthood, when marriage and childbirth may trigger it (Schaffer & Kral, 1988). Despite concerns about their origins, most adoptees appear well adjusted as adults. And as long as their parents took steps to help them learn about their heritage in childhood, transracially and transculturally adopted young people generally develop identities that are healthy blends of their birth and rearing backgrounds (Brooks & Barth, 1999).

As we conclude our discussion of reproductive choices, perhaps you are wondering how things turned out for Ted and Marianne. Through genetic counseling, Marianne discovered a history of Tay-Sachs disease on her mother's side of the family. Ted had a distant cousin who died of the disorder. The genetic counselor explained that the chances of giving birth to another affected baby were 1 in 4. Ted and Marianne took the risk. Their son Douglas is now 12 years old. Although Douglas is a carrier of the recessive allele, he is a normal, healthy boy. In a few years, Ted and Marianne will tell Douglas about his genetic history and explain the importance of genetic counseling and testing before he has children of his own.

This transracially adopted African-American baby plays with her Caucasian older sisters. Will she develop an identity that is a healthy blend of her birth and rearing backgrounds? The answer depends on the extent to which her adoptive parents expose her to her African-American heritage.

Aᴋ YOURSELF

www

REVIEW   Why is genetic counseling called a *communication process?* Who should seek it?

REVIEW   Describe the ethical pros and cons of fetal surgery, surrogate motherhood, and post-menopausal-assisted childbearing?

CONNECT   How does research on adoption reveal resilience? Which of the factors related to resilience (see Chapter 1, pages 10–11) is central in positive outcomes for adoptees?

REFLECT   Put yourself in the place of a woman who is a carrier of fragile X syndrome but who wants to have children. Would you become pregnant, adopt, use a surrogate mother, or give up your desire for parenthood? Explain. If you became pregnant, would you opt for prenatal diagnosis? Why or why not?

Environmental Contexts for Development

Just as complex as the genetic inheritance that sets the stage for development is the surrounding environment—a many-layered set of influences that combine to help or hinder physical and psychological well-being. Take a moment to reflect on your own childhood, and jot down a brief description of events and people you regard as having had a significant impact on your development. When I ask my students to do this, most items they list involve their families. This emphasis is not surprising, since the family is the first and longest-lasting context for development. But other settings turn out to be important as well. Friends, neighbors, school, workplace, community organizations, and church, synagogue, or mosque generally make the top ten.

Think back to Bronfenbrenner's ecological systems theory, discussed in Chapter 1. It emphasizes that environments extending beyond the *microsystem,* or the immediate settings just mentioned, powerfully affect development. Indeed, my students rarely mention one very important context. Its impact is so pervasive that we seldom stop to think about it in our daily lives. This is the *macrosystem,* or broad social climate of society—its values and programs that support and protect children's development. All families need help in rearing their children—through affordable housing and health care, safe neighborhoods, good schools, well-equipped recreational facilities, and high-quality child care and other services that permit parents to meet both work and family responsibilities. And some families, because of poverty or special tragedies, need considerably more help than others.

In the following sections, we take up these contexts for development. Because they affect every age and aspect of change, we will return to them in later chapters. For now, our discussion emphasizes that besides heredity, environments can enhance or create risks for development. And when a vulnerable child, with physical or psychological problems, is exposed to unfavorable environmental contexts, development is seriously threatened.

The Family

In power and breadth of influence, no context equals the family. The family introduces children to the physical world through the opportunities it provides for play and exploration of objects. It also creates bonds between people that are unique. Attachments to parents and siblings usually last

The family is a network of interdependent relationships; each person influences the behavior of others, in direct and indirect ways. The positive mealtime atmosphere in this Filipino-American family is the result of many forces, including parents who respond to children with warmth and patience, grandparents who support parents in their child-rearing roles, and children who have developed cooperative dispositions.

a lifetime and serve as models for relationships in the wider world of neighborhood, school, and community. Within the family, children learn the language, skills, and social and moral values of their culture. And at all ages, they turn to family members for information, assistance, and pleasurable interaction. Warm, gratifying family ties predict psychological health throughout development. In contrast, isolation or alienation from the family is often associated with developmental problems (Parke & Buriel, 1998).

Contemporary researchers view the family as a network of interdependent relationships (Bronfenbrenner & Morris, 1998; Lerner et al., 2002). Recall from ecological systems theory that *bidirectional influences* exist in which the behaviors of each family member affect those of others. Indeed, the very term *system* implies that the responses of all family members are related. These system influences operate both directly and indirectly.

DIRECT INFLUENCES ● Recently, as I passed through the checkout counter at the supermarket, I witnessed the following two episodes, in which parents and children directly affected each other.

- Four-year-old Danny stood next to tempting rows of candy as his mom lifted groceries from the cart onto the counter. "Pleeeeease, can I have it, Mom?" begged Danny, holding up a large package of bubble gum. "Do you have a dollar? Just one?"

  "No, not today," his mother answered. "Remember, we picked out your special cereal. That's what I need the dollar for." Danny's mother handed him the cereal while gently taking the bubble gum from his hand and returning it to the shelf. "Here, let's pay the man," she said, as she lifted Danny into the empty grocery cart where he could see the cash register.

- Three-year-old Meg sat in the cart while her mom transferred groceries to the counter. Meg turned around, grabbed a bunch of bananas, and started to pull them apart.

  "Stop it, Meg!" shouted her mom, who snatched the bananas from Meg's hand. Meg reached for a chocolate bar from a nearby shelf while her mother wrote the check. "Meg, how many times have I told you, DON'T TOUCH!" Loosening the candy from Meg's tight little grip, Meg's mother slapped her hand. Meg's face turned red with anger as she began to wail. "Keep this up, and you'll get it when we get home," threatened Meg's mom as they left the store.

These observations fit with a wealth of research on the family system. Many studies show that when parents' requests are accompanied by warmth and affection, children tend to cooperate. And when children willingly comply, their parents are likely to be warm and gentle in the future. In contrast, parents who discipline harshly and impatiently have children who refuse and rebel. And because children's misbehavior is stressful for parents, they may increase their use of punishment, leading to more unruliness by the child (Dodge, Pettit, & Bates, 1994; Stormshak et al., 2000). In each case, the behavior of one family member helps sustain a form of interaction in the other that either promotes or undermines children's well-being.

INDIRECT INFLUENCES ● The impact of family relationships on child development becomes even more complicated when we consider that interaction between any two members is affected by others present in the setting. Bronfenbrenner calls these indirect influences the effect of *third parties* (see Chapter 1, page 28).

Third parties can serve as supports for development. For example, when their marital relationship is warm and considerate, mothers and fathers tend to cooperate in child rearing, and they praise and stimulate children more and nag and scold them less. In contrast, when a marriage is tense and hostile, parents often interfere with one another's child-rearing efforts, are less responsive to children's needs, and criticize, express anger, and punish (Cox, Paley, & Harter, 2001; McHale et al., 2002). Similarly, children can affect their parents' relationship in powerful ways. For example, as you will see in Chapter 13, some children show lasting emotional problems when their parents divorce. But longitudinal research reveals that long before the marital breakup, some children of divorcing couples were impulsive and defiant. These behaviors may have contributed to, as well as been caused by, their parents' marital problems (Amato & Booth, 1996; Hetherington, 1999).

Yet even when marital conflict strains children's adjustment, other family members may help restore effective interaction. Grandparents are a case in point. They can promote children's development in many ways—both directly, by responding warmly to the child, and indirectly, by providing parents with child-rearing advice, models of child-rearing skill, and even financial assistance (Drew, Richard, & Smith, 1998). Of course, like any indirect influence, grandparents can sometimes be harmful. When quarrelsome relations exist between parents and grandparents, parent–child communication may suffer.

ADAPTING TO CHANGE ● Think back to the *chronosystem* in Bronfenbrenner's theory (see page 29). The interplay of forces within the family is dynamic and ever changing, as each member adapts to the development of other members. Indeed, no social unit other than the family is required to adjust to such vast changes in its members.

For example, as children acquire new skills, parents adjust the way they treat their more competent youngsters. When you next have a chance, notice the way that a parent relates to a tiny baby as opposed to a walking, talking toddler. During the first few months, much time is spent feeding, changing, bathing, and cuddling the infant. Within a year, things change dramatically. The 1-year-old points, shows, names objects, and makes his way through the household cupboards. In response, parents devote less time to physical care and more to talking, playing games, and disciplining. These new ways of interacting encourage the child's expanding motor, cognitive, and social skills.

Parents' development affects children as well. In Chapter 14, we will see that the rise in parent–child conflict that often occurs in early adolescence is not solely due to teenagers' striving for independence. Most parents of adolescents have reached middle age and are reconsidering their own commitments. They are conscious that their children will soon leave home and establish their own lives (Grotevant, 1998; Steinberg & Silk, 2002). Consequently, while the adolescent presses for greater autonomy, the parent presses for more togetherness. This imbalance promotes friction, which parent and teenager gradually resolve by accommodating to changes in one another.

Historical time period also contributes to a dynamic family system. In recent decades, a declining birth rate, a high divorce rate, expansion of women's roles, greater acceptance of homosexuality, and postponement of parenthood have led to a smaller family size and a greater number of single parents, remarried parents, gay and lesbian parents, employed mothers, and dual-earner families. Clearly, families in industrialized nations have become more diverse than ever before. In later chapters we will take up these family forms, emphasizing how each affects family relationships and, ultimately, children's development.

Nevertheless, some general patterns in family functioning do exist. In the United States, Canada, and other industrialized nations, one important source of these consistencies is socioeconomic status.

Socioeconomic Status and Family Functioning

People in industrialized nations are stratified on the basis of what they do at work and how much they earn for doing it—factors that determine their social position and economic well-being. Researchers assess a family's standing on this continuum through an index called **socioeconomic status (SES).** It combines three interrelated, but not completely overlapping, variables: (1) years of education and (2) the prestige of and skill required by one's job, both of which measure social status; and (3) income, which measures economic status. As SES rises and falls, parents and children face changing circumstances that profoundly affect family functioning.

SES is linked to timing of parenthood and to family size. People who work in skilled and semi-skilled manual occupations (for example, machinists, truck drivers, and custodians) tend to marry and have children earlier, as well as give birth to more children, than people in white-collar and professional occupations. The two groups also differ in child-rearing values and expectations. For example, when asked about personal qualities they desire for their children, lower-SES parents tend to emphasize external characteristics, such as obedience, politeness, neatness, and cleanliness. In contrast, higher-SES parents emphasize psychological traits, such as curiosity, happiness, self-direction, and cognitive and social maturity (Hoff, Laursen, & Tardiff, 2002; Tudge et al., 2000). In addition, fathers in higher-SES families tend to be more involved in child rearing and household responsibilities. Lower-SES fathers, partly because of their gender-stereotyped beliefs and partly because of economic necessity, focus more on their provider role (Rank, 2000).

These differences are reflected in family interaction. Parents higher in SES talk to and stimulate their infants and preschoolers more and grant them greater freedom to explore. When their children are older, higher-SES parents use more warmth, explanations, and verbal praise and set higher developmental goals for their children. Commands, such as "You do that because I told you to," as well as criticism and physical punishment occur more often in low-SES households (Bradley & Corwyn, 2003).

The life conditions of families help explain these findings. Lower-SES parents often feel a sense of powerlessness and lack of influence in their relationships beyond the home. For example, at work they must obey the rules of others in positions of power and authority. When they get home, their parent–child interaction seems to duplicate these experiences, with them in the authority roles. Higher levels of stress, along with a stronger belief in the value of physical punishment, contribute to low-SES parents' greater use of coercive discipline (Pinderhughes et al., 2000). Higher-SES parents, in contrast, have more control over their own lives. At work, they are used to making independent decisions and convincing others of their point of view. At home, they teach these skills to their children (Greenberger, O'Neil, & Nagel, 1994).

Education also contributes to SES differences in family interaction. Higher-SES parents' interest in verbal stimulation and nurturing inner traits is supported by years of schooling, during which they learned to think about abstract, subjective ideas (Uribe, LeVine, & LeVine, 1994). Furthermore, the greater economic security of higher-SES parents permits them to devote more time, energy, and material resources to nurturing their children's psychological characteristics.

As early as the second year of life, higher SES is associated with enhanced cognitive and language development and with reduced incidence of emotional and behavior problems. And throughout childhood and adolescence, higher-SES children do better in school (Bradley & Corwyn, 2003). As a result, they attain higher levels of education, which greatly enhances their opportunities for a prosperous adult life. Researchers believe that differences in family functioning have much to do with these outcomes.

The Impact of Poverty

When families slip into poverty, development is seriously threatened. Consider the case of Zinnia Mae, who grew up in Trackton, a close-knit black community located in a small southeastern American city (Heath, 1990). As unemployment struck Trackton and citizens moved away, 16-year-old Zinnia Mae caught a ride to Atlanta. Two years later, Zinnia Mae was the mother of a daughter and twin boys. She had moved into high-rise public housing.

Each of Zinnia Mae's days was much the same. She watched TV and talked with girlfriends on the phone. The children had only one set meal (breakfast) and otherwise ate whenever they were hungry or bored. Their play space was limited to the living room sofa and a mattress on the floor. Toys consisted of scraps of a blanket, spoons and food cartons, a small rubber ball, a few plastic cars, and a roller skate abandoned in the building. Zinnia Mae's most frequent words were, "I'm so tired." She worried about where to find a baby-sitter so she could go to the laundry or grocery, and what she would do if she located the twins' father, who had stopped sending money.

At the researcher's request, Zinnia Mae agreed to tape record her family interactions. Cut off from family and community ties and overwhelmed by financial strain and feelings of help-lessness, she found herself unable to join in activities with her children. In 500 hours of tape, she started a conversation with her children only 18 times.

Over the past 30 years, economic changes in the United States have caused the poverty rate to climb substantially; in recent years, it has dropped and then risen again. Today, nearly 12 per-cent of the population in the United States and Canada are affected. Those hit hardest are par-ents under age 25 with young children and elderly people who live alone. Poverty is also magnified among ethnic minorities and women. For example, 16 percent of American and Canadian children are poor, a rate that climbs to 32 percent for Native-American children, 34 percent for African-American and Hispanic children, and 60 percent for Canadian Aboriginal children. (Aboriginal peoples in Canada include First Nations, Inuit, and Métis.) For single mothers with preschool children, the poverty rate in both countries is nearly 50 percent (Canada Campaign 2000, 2003; U.S. Census Bureau, 2003b).

Joblessness, a high divorce rate, a high rate of adolescent parenthood, and (as we will see later) inadequate government programs to meet family needs are responsible for these dis-heartening statistics. The child poverty rate is higher than that of any other age group. And of all Western nations, the United States has the highest percentage of extremely poor children. More than 6 percent of American children live in deep poverty (well below the *poverty thresh-old*, the income level judged necessary for bare subsistence), compared with 2.5 percent in Canada. However, these circumstances are worrisome in both countries because the earlier poverty begins, the deeper it is, and the longer it lasts, the more devastating its effects. In many societies, children of poverty are more likely than other children to suffer from lifelong poor physical health, persistent deficits in cognitive development and academic achievement, high school dropout, mental illness, and antisocial behavior (Children's Defense Fund, 2003; Poulton et al., 2002; Seccombe, 2002).

The constant stresses that accompany poverty gradually weaken the family system. Poor families have many daily hassles—bills to pay, the car breaking down, loss of welfare and unem-ployment payments, something stolen from the house, to name just a few. When daily crises arise, parents become depressed, irritable, and distracted, hostile interactions in-crease, and children's development suffers (Evans, 2004). Negative out-comes are especially severe in families that must live in poor housing and dangerous neighborhoods—conditions that make everyday existence even more difficult, while reducing social supports that assist in coping with economic hardship (Leventhal & Brooks-Gunn, 2003).

Besides poverty, another problem—one uncommon 25 years ago—has reduced the life chances of many children. On any given night, ap-proximately 35,000 people in Canada and 350,000 people in the United States have no place to live (Pohl, 2001; Wright, 1999). Nearly 29 percent of the homeless in Canada and 40 percent in the United States are families with children. The rise in homelessness is due to a number of factors, the most important of which is a decline in the availability of government-supported low-cost housing and the release of large numbers of mentally ill people from hospitals, without an increase in community treatment programs aimed at helping them adjust to ordinary life and get better.

Homelessness in the United States has risen over the past two decades. Families like this one travel from place to place in search of employment and a safe and secure place to live. Because of constant stress and few social supports, homeless children are usu-ally behind in development, have frequent health prob-lems, and show poor psy-chological adjustment.

Most homeless families consist of women with children younger than age 5. Besides health problems (which affect most homeless people), homeless children suffer from developmental delays and serious emotional stress (Bratt, 2002). An estimated 25 to 30 percent of those who are old enough do not go to school. Those who do enroll achieve less well than other poverty-stricken children due to poor attendance and severe health and emotional difficulties (Vostanis, Grattan, & Cumella, 1997).

Beyond the Family: Neighborhoods and Schools

In ecological systems theory, the mesosystem and the exosystem underscore that ties between family and community are vital for children's well-being. From our discussion of poverty, perhaps you can see why. In poverty-stricken urban areas, community life usually is disrupted. Families move often, parks and playgrounds are in disarray, and community centers providing organized leisure activities do not exist. Family violence and child abuse and neglect are greatest in neighborhoods where residents are dissatisfied with their community, describing it as a socially isolated place to live. In contrast, when family ties to the community are strong—as indicated by regular church attendance, frequent contact with friends and relatives, and organized youth activities—family stress and youth adjustment problems are reduced (Garbarino & Kostelny, 1993; Magnuson & Duncan, 2002).

NEIGHBORHOODS ● Let's look closely at the functions of communities in the lives of children by beginning with the neighborhood. What were your childhood experiences like in the yards, streets, and parks surrounding your home? How did you spend your time, whom did you get to know, and how important were these moments to you?

Neighborhood resources are important influences on children's development and well-being. A young girl proudly carries the Canadian flag in the Chinese New Year parade in the Chinatown district of Vancouver, British Columbia. The event fosters self-confidence, cooperation, and identification with her community and culture.

© ANNIE GRIFFITHS BELT/CORBIS

The resources offered by neighborhoods play an important part in children's development. In several studies, low-SES families were randomly assigned vouchers to move out of public housing into neighborhoods varying widely in affluence. Compared with their peers who remained in poverty-stricken areas, children and youths who moved into low-poverty neighborhoods showed substantially better physical and mental health and school achievement (Goering, 2003; Rubinowitz & Rosenbaum, 2000).

Neighborhood resources have a greater impact on economically disadvantaged than on well-to-do young people. Affluent families are not as dependent on their immediate surroundings for social support, education, and leisure pursuits. They can afford to reach beyond the streets near their homes, transporting their children to lessons and entertainment and, if necessary, to better-quality schools in distant parts of the community (Elliott et al., 1996). In low-income neighborhoods, after-school programs that provide art, music, sports, scouting, and other special experiences are associated with improved school performance and psychological adjustment in middle childhood (Posner & Vandell, 1994; Vandell & Posner, 1999). Neighborhood organizations, such as religious youth groups and special interest clubs, contribute to favorable development in adolescence, including self-confidence, school achievement, and educational aspirations (Gonzales et al., 1996).

In areas riddled with unemployment, crime, and population turnover, social ties that link families to one another and to other institutions are weak or absent. Consequently, informal social controls—adults who keep an eye on children's play activities and who intervene when they see young people skipping school or behaving antisocially—disintegrate. Unstable, poverty-stricken neighborhoods also introduce stressors that undermine parental warmth, involvement, and supervision and increase parental harshness and inconsistency. And when a run-down, impoverished neighborhood combines with poor parenting, child behavior problems and youth antisocial activity are especially high (Brody et al., 2003; Kohen et al., 2002).

The Better Beginnings, Better Futures Project of Ontario, Canada, is a government-sponsored set of pilot programs aimed at preventing the dire consequences of neighborhood poverty. The most successful of these efforts used a local elementary school as its base, providing children with in-class and summer enrichment activities. In addition, workers visited each child's parents regularly, informed them about community resources, and encouraged their involvement in the child's school and neighborhood life (Peters, Petrunka, & Arnold, 2003). An evaluation after 4 years revealed wide-ranging benefits—gains in neighborhood satisfaction, family functioning, effective parenting, and children's reading skills and a reduction in emotional and behavior problems.

SCHOOLS ● Unlike the informal worlds of family and neighborhood, school is a formal institution designed to transmit knowledge and skills that children need to become productive members of their society. Children spend many long hours in school—6 hours a day, 5 days a week, 36 weeks a year—totaling, altogether, about 14,000 hours by high school graduation. In fact, today, many children younger than age 5 attend child-care centers or preschools that are "school-like," so the impact of schooling begins earlier and is more powerful than these figures suggest.

Schools are complex social systems that affect many aspects of development. Schools differ in their physical environments—student body size, number of children per class, and space available for work and play. They also vary in their educational philosophies—whether teachers regard children as passive learners to be molded by adult instruction; as active, curious beings who determine their own learning; or as collaborative partners assisted by adult experts, who guide their mastery of new skills. Finally, the social life of schools varies—for example, in the degree to which students cooperate or compete; in the extent to which students of different abilities, SES, and ethnic backgrounds learn together; and in whether classrooms, hallways, and play yards are safe, humane settings or are riddled with violence. We will discuss each of these aspects of schooling in later chapters.

Regular parent–school contact supports development at all ages. Students whose parents are involved in school activities and attend parent–teacher conferences show better academic achievement. Phone calls and visits to school are common among higher-SES parents, whose backgrounds and values are similar to those of teachers. In contrast, low-SES and ethnic minority parents often feel uncomfortable about coming to school (Epstein & Sanders, 2002). Contact between parents and teachers is also more frequent in small towns, where most citizens know each other and schools serve as centers of community life (Peshkin, 1994). Teachers and administrators must take extra steps with low-SES and ethnic minority families and in urban areas to build supportive family–school ties.

When these efforts lead to cultures of good parenting and teaching, they deliver an extra boost to children's well-being. For example, students attending schools with many highly involved parents achieve especially well (Darling & Steinberg, 1997). And when excellent education becomes a team effort of teachers, administrators, and community members, its effects on learning are stronger and reach many more students (Brown, 1997; Tharp, 1993).

Thomas J. Pappas School in Phoenix, Arizona, reaches out to the neediest children and families, providing vital supports for development. Although all its students are homeless, classrooms are exciting contexts for learning that stress effective communication, problem solving, responsibility, and cultural awareness. And parent–teacher contact occurs often. The school began in a homeless shelter, moved to a renovated car dealership, and now has its own building. Here students gather for an assembly.

The Cultural Context

Our discussion in Chapter 1 emphasized that child development can be fully understood only when viewed in its larger cultural context. In the following sections, we expand on this important theme by taking up the macrosystem's role in development. First, we discuss ways that cultural values and practices affect environmental contexts for development. Second, we consider how healthy development depends on laws and government programs that shield children from harm and foster their well-being.

CULTURAL VALUES AND PRACTICES ● Cultures shape family interaction, school experiences, and community settings beyond the home—in short, all aspects of daily life. Many of us remain blind to aspects of our own cultural heritage until we see them in relation to the practices of others.

Each semester, I ask my students to think about the question, Who should be responsible for rearing young children? Here are some typical answers: "If parents decide to have a baby, then they should be ready to care for it." "Most people want to rear their own children and are not happy about others intruding into family life." These statements reflect a widely held opinion in North America—that the care and rearing of young children, and paying for that care, are the duty of parents, and only parents. This view has a long history—one in which independence, self-reliance, and the privacy of family life emerged as central North American values (Halfon & McLearn, 2002; Rickel & Becker, 1997). It is one reason that the public has been slow to endorse publicly supported benefits for all families, such as high-quality child care. And it has also contributed to the large number of American and Canadian children who remain poor, despite the fact that their parents are gainfully employed (Pohl, 2002; Zigler & Hall, 2000).

Although many people value independence and privacy, not all share the same values. Some are part of subcultures—groups of people with beliefs and customs that differ from those of the larger culture. Many ethnic minority groups in the United States and Canada have cooperative family structures, which help protect their members from the harmful effects of poverty. As the Cultural Influences box on the following page indicates, the African-American tradition of extended-family households, in which parent and child live with one or more adult relatives, is a vital feature of black family life that has enabled its members to survive, despite a long history of prejudice and economic deprivation. Within the extended family, grandparents play meaningful roles in guiding younger generations; adults with employment, marital, or child-rearing difficulties receive assistance and emotional support; and caregiving is enhanced for children and the elderly. Active and involved extended families also characterize Asian-American, Native-American, Hispanic, and Canadian Aboriginal subcultures (Harrison et al., 1994).

Consider our discussion so far, and you will see that it reflects a broad dimension on which cultures and subcultures differ: the extent to which *collectivism versus individualism* is emphasized. In collectivist societies, people define themselves as part of a group and stress group over individual goals. In individualistic societies, people think of themselves as separate entities and are largely concerned with their own personal needs (Triandis, 1995). Although individualism tends to increase as cultures become more complex, cross-national differences remain. The United States is strongly individualistic, and Canada falls between the United States and most Western European countries. As we will see in the next section, collectivist versus individualistic values have a powerful impact on a nation's approach to protecting children's development.

PUBLIC POLICIES AND CHILD DEVELOPMENT ● When widespread social problems arise, such as poverty, homelessness, hunger, and disease, nations attempt to solve them by developing public policies—laws and government programs designed to improve current conditions. For example, when poverty increases and families become homeless, a country might decide to build more low-cost housing, raise the minimum wage, and increase welfare benefits. When reports indicate that many children are not achieving well in school, federal and state governments might grant more tax money to school districts and make sure that help reaches children who need it most.

Nevertheless, American and Canadian public policies safeguarding children and youths have lagged behind policies in other developed nations. As Table 2.7 on page 80 reveals, the United States does not rank well on any key measure of children's health and well-being. Canada fares somewhat better, devoting considerably more of its resources to education and health. For example, it grants all its citizens government-funded health care.

The problems of children and youths extend beyond the indicators in the table. For example, approximately 12 percent of American children—most of them living in poverty or near-poverty—have no health insurance, making children the largest segment of the U.S. uninsured population (Mills & Bhandari, 2003). Furthermore, the United States and Canada have been slow to move toward national standards and funding for child care. In both countries, much child care is substandard in quality (Goelman et al., 2000; NICHD Early Child Care Research

Cultural Influences

The African-American Extended Family

The African-American extended family can be traced to the African heritage of most black Americans. In many African societies, newly married couples do not start their own households. Instead, they live with a large extended family, which assists its members with all aspects of daily life. This tradition of maintaining a broad network of kinship ties traveled to the United States during the period of slavery. Since then, it has served as a protective shield against the destructive impact of poverty and racial prejudice on African-American family life. Today, more black than white adults have relatives other than their own children living in the same household. African-American parents also live closer to kin, often establish familylike relationships with friends and neighbors, see more relatives during the week, and perceive them as more important in their lives (Wilson et al., 1995).

By providing emotional support and sharing income and essential resources, the African-American extended family helps reduce the stress of poverty and single parenthood. In addition, extended-family members often help with child rearing. The presence of grandmothers in the households of many African-American teenagers and their infants protects babies from the negative influence of an overwhelmed and inexperienced mother. Furthermore, black adolescent mothers living in extended families are more likely to complete high school and get a job, and less likely to be on welfare, than mothers living on their own—factors that benefit children's well-being (Trent & Harlan, 1994).

For single mothers who were very young at the time of their child's birth, extended-family living continues to be associated with more positive mother–child interaction during the preschool years. Otherwise, establishing an independent household with the help of nearby relatives is related to improved child rearing. Perhaps this arrangement permits the more mature teenage mother who has developed effective parenting skills to implement them (Chase-Lansdale, Brooks-Gunn, & Zamsky, 1994). In families rearing adolescents, kinship support increases the likelihood of effective parenting, which is related to adolescents' self-reliance, emotional well-being, and reduced delinquency (Taylor & Roberts, 1995).

Finally, the extended family plays an important role in transmitting African-American culture. Compared with nuclear-family households (which include only parents and their children), extended-family arrangements place more emphasis on cooperation and on moral and religious values. And older black adults, such as grandparents and great-grandparents, regard educating children about their African heritage as especially important (Taylor, 2000). These influences strengthen family bonds, protect children's development, and increase the chances that the extended-family lifestyle will carry over to the next generation.

© LAWRENCE MIGDALE/GETTY IMAGES/STONE

Strong bonds with extended-family members protect the development of many African-American children growing up under conditions of poverty and single parenthood. This family gathers for Kwanzaa, a holiday celebrated between December 26 and January 1 by Africans and African descendants throughout the world. In Swahili, *matunda ya kwanzaa* means "first fruits." Kwanzaa rituals are derived from African harvest celebrations.

Network, 2000a). In families affected by divorce, weak enforcement of child support payments heightens poverty in mother-headed households. By the time they finish high school, many North American non-college-bound young people do not have the vocational preparation they need to contribute fully to society. And about 11 percent of U.S. and Canadian adolescents leave high school without a diploma (U.S. Department of Education, 2003a; Statistics Canada, 2002f). Those who do not finish their education are at risk for lifelong poverty.

Why have attempts to help children and youths in the United States and (to a lesser extent) Canada been difficult to realize? A complex set of political and economic forces is involved. Cultural values of self-reliance and privacy have made government hesitant to become involved in family

TABLE 2.7

How Do the United States and Canada Compare to Other Nations on Indicators of Children's Health and Well-Being?

INDICATOR	U.S. RANK[a]	CANADIAN RANK[a]	SOME COUNTRIES THE UNITED STATES AND CANADA TRAIL
Childhood poverty[b] (among 23 industrialized nations considered)	19th	19th	Australia, Czech Republic, Germany, Norway, Sweden, Spain
Infant deaths in the first year of life (worldwide)	24th	15th	Hong Kong, Ireland, Singapore, Spain
Teenage pregnancy rate (among 45 industrialized nations considered)	45th	25th	Albania, Australia, Czech Republic, Denmark, Poland, Netherlands
Expenditures on education as a percentage of gross domestic product (among 22 industrialized nations considered)	10th	6th	*For Canada:* Israel, Sweden *For the U.S.:* Australia, France, New Zealand, Sweden
Expenditures on health as a percentage of gross domestic product[c] (among 22 industrialized nations considered)	16th	4th	*For Canada:* Iceland, Switzerland, France *For the U.S.:* Austria, Australia, Hungary, New Zealand

[a]1 = highest, or best, rank

[b]The U.S. and Canadian childhood poverty rates of 17 percent greatly exceed those of any of these nations. For example, the rate is 12 percent in Australia, 6 percent in the Czech Republic, 4 percent in Norway, and 2.5 percent in Sweden.

[c]Gross domestic product is the value of all goods and services produced by a nation during a specified time period. It provides an overall measure of a nation's wealth.

Sources: Perie et al., 2000; Singh & Darroch, 2000; United Nations Children's Fund, 2000; United Nations Development Programme, 2002; U.S. Census Bureau, 2003a.

matters. In addition, less consensus exists among North Americans than among European citizens on issues of child and family policy. Furthermore, good social programs are expensive, and they must compete for a fair share of a country's economic resources. Children can easily remain un-recognized in this process because they cannot vote or speak out to protect their own interests, as adult citizens do (Zigler & Finn-Stevenson, 1999). Instead, they must rely on the goodwill of others to make them an important government priority.

Without vigilance from child advocates, policies directed at solving one social problem can work at cross-purposes with children's well-being, leaving them in dire straights or worsening their condition. Consider, for example, the U.S. welfare-to-work program. As the Social Issues: Health box on the following page makes clear, it can help or harm children, depending on whether it lifts a family out of poverty.

LOOKING TOWARD THE FUTURE ● Public policies aimed at fostering children's development can be justified on two grounds. The first is that children are the future—the parents, workers, and citizens of tomorrow. Investing in children yields valuable returns to a nation's quality of life. In contrast, failure to invest in children results in "economic inefficiency, loss of productivity, shortages in needed skills, high health care costs, growing prison costs, and a nation that will be less safe, less caring, and less free" (Hernandez, 1994, p. 20).

Second, child-oriented policies can be defended on humanitarian grounds—children's basic rights as human beings. In 1989, the United Nations General Assembly, with the assistance of experts from many child-related fields, drew up the *Convention on the Rights of the Child*, a legal agreement among nations that commits each cooperating country to work toward guaranteeing environments that foster children's development, protect them from harm, and enhance their community participation and self-determination. Examples of rights include the

Social Issues: Health

Welfare Reform, Poverty, and Child Development

In 1996, the United States instituted a welfare-to-work program that ended six decades of guaranteed government financial aid to needy families. In the new system, each state receives federal funds for time-limited welfare payments. After 24 months, recipients must go to work or face reduced or terminated benefits. Each family's lifetime welfare limit is 60 months. The states, however, can impose shorter time limits, and they can also restrict benefits. For example, they can prevent payments from increasing if recipients have more children, and they can deny teenage single mothers any benefits. The goal of these requirements is to encourage welfare families to become self-sufficient.

Until recently, most evaluations of welfare-to-work focused on the decline in the number of families on the welfare rolls. By these standards, welfare-to-work seemed to be a resounding success. But as researchers looked more closely, they found that in the years after welfare reform, some people made successful transitions to financial independence—typically, those who had more schooling and fewer mental health problems. Others, however, had difficulty meeting work requirements and fell deeper into poverty. Consequently, as welfare caseloads declined, the incomes of the poorest 20 percent of mother-headed families dropped sharply (Lindsay & Martin, 2003; Primus et al., 1999).

Designers of welfare-to-work assumed that it would have positive benefits for children. But moving off welfare without increasing family income poses serious risks to development. In one study, mothers who left welfare and also left poverty engaged in more positive parenting and had preschoolers who showed more favorable cognitive development, compared with working mothers whose incomes remained below the poverty threshold. Among these mothers, harsh, coercive parenting remained high (Smith et al., 2001).

Other research revealed that families who moved from welfare to a combination of welfare and work experienced a greater reduction in young children's behavior problems than families who moved to total reliance on work (Gennetian & Morris, 2003; Dunifon, Kalil, & Danziger, 2003). Why was the welfare–work combination so beneficial? Most welfare recipients must take unstable jobs with erratic work hours and minimal or no benefits. Working while retaining some welfare support probably gave mothers an added sense of economic stability. And it sustained government-provided health insurance (Medicaid), a major source of American parents' worry about leaving welfare (Kalil, Schweingruber, & Seefeldt, 2001). The resulting lessening of financial anxiety seemed to enhance children's adjustment.

In sum, U.S. welfare reform promotes children's development only under certain conditions—when it results in a more adequate standard of living. Punitive aspects of welfare-to-work that reduce or cut off benefits push families deeper into poverty, with destructive consequences for children's well-being. Mothers on welfare who have infants and preschoolers are least able to earn enough by working. Yet poverty is most harmful to development when it occurs early in life (see page 75).

Welfare policies in other Western nations do not just encourage parents to be better providers. They also protect children from the damaging effects of poverty. France, for example, guarantees most of its citizens a modest minimum income. Single parents receive an extra amount during their child's first 3 years—a benefit that acknowledges a special need for income support during this period. Government-funded, high-quality child care begins at age 3, enabling mothers to go to work knowing that their children are safe and secure (Duncan & Brooks-Gunn, 2000). Canada provides welfare payments that rise with family size and that are not time-limited. It also offers working parents more generous tax refunds than are available in the United States. Still, widespread poverty in both nations underscores the need for more effective poverty prevention policies—ones that help poor families rear children while they transition to financial independence.

---

highest attainable standard of health; an adequate standard of living; free and compulsory education; a happy, understanding, and loving family life; protection from all forms of abuse and neglect; and freedom of thought, conscience, and religion, subject to appropriate parental guidance and national law. A U.N. committee monitors participating nations' progress toward reaching the Convention's goals. Although the United States played a key role in drawing up the Convention, it is one of two countries in the world whose legislature has not yet ratified it. (The other nation is Somalia, which currently does not have a recognized national government.) American individualism has stood in the way. Opponents maintain that the Convention's provisions would shift the burden of child rearing from the family to the state (Woodhouse, 2001).

Despite the worrisome state of many children and families, progress is being made in improving their condition. Throughout this book, we will discuss many successful programs that could be expanded. Also, growing awareness of the gap between what we know and what we do to better children's lives has led experts in child development to join with concerned citizens as

The Children's Defense Fund is the most vigorous interest group working for the well-being of children in the United States. It released this poster expressing outrage that millions of American children, most living in poverty or near-poverty, have no health insurance, making children the largest segment of the U.S. uninsured population.

advocates for more effective policies. As a result, several influential interest groups devoted to the well-being of children have emerged.

In the United States, the most vigorous of these groups is the Children's Defense Fund. A private, nonprofit organization founded by Marion Wright Edelman in 1973, it engages in research, public education, legal action, drafting of legislation, congressional testimony, and community organizing. Each year, it publishes *The State of America's Children,* which provides a comprehensive analysis of the current conditions, including government-sponsored programs that serve children and families and proposals for improving those programs. To learn more about the Children's Defense Fund, visit its website at *www.cdc.com.*

In 1991, Canada initiated a public education movement, called *Campaign 2000,* to build nationwide awareness of the extent and consequences of child poverty and to lobby government representatives for improved policies benefiting children. Diverse organizations—including professional, religious, health, and labor groups at national, provincial, and community levels—have joined forces to work toward campaign goals: raising basic living standards so no child lives in poverty, ensuring each child affordable, appropriate housing, and strengthening child care and other community resources that assist families in rearing children. Consult *www.campaign2000.ca* to explore the work of Campaign 2000, including its annual *Report Card on Child Poverty in Canada.*

Besides depending on strong advocacy, public policies that enhance child development flow from policy-relevant research that documents needs and evaluates programs to spark improvements (refer again to the Social Issues: Health box on page 81 for an example). Today, more researchers are collaborating with community and government agencies to enhance the social relevance of their investigations. They are also doing a better job of disseminating their findings to the public, through television documentaries, newspaper stories, magazine articles, and direct reports to government officials (Denner et al., 1999). As a result, they are helping to create the sense of immediacy about the condition of children and families that is necessary to spur a society into action.

Campaign 2000 is Canada's public education movement aimed at building national awareness of the extent of child poverty and the need to improve policies benefiting children. This Campaign 2000 poster calls for strengthening a diverse array of community resources that assist families in rearing children.

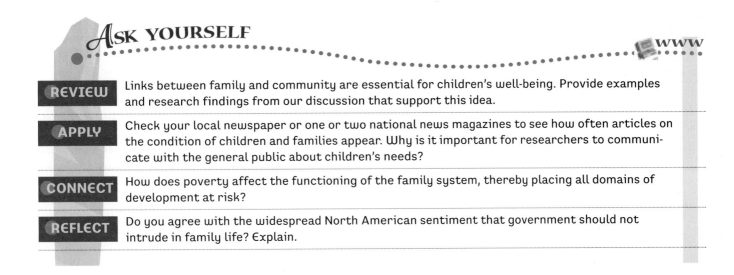

ASK YOURSELF

| REVIEW | Links between family and community are essential for children's well-being. Provide examples and research findings from our discussion that support this idea. |

| APPLY | Check your local newspaper or one or two national news magazines to see how often articles on the condition of children and families appear. Why is it important for researchers to communicate with the general public about children's needs? |

| CONNECT | How does poverty affect the functioning of the family system, thereby placing all domains of development at risk? |

| REFLECT | Do you agree with the widespread North American sentiment that government should not intrude in family life? Explain. |

Understanding the Relationship Between Heredity and Environment

Throughout this chapter, we have discussed a wide variety of hereditary and environmental influences, each of which has the power to alter the course of development. Yet children who are born into the same family (and who therefore share genes and environments) often are quite different in characteristics. We also know that some children are affected more than others by their homes, neighborhoods, and communities. Cases exist in which a child provided with many advantages does poorly, whereas another exposed to unfavorable rearing conditions does well. How do scientists explain the impact of heredity and environment when they seem to work in so many different ways?

Behavioral genetics is a field devoted to uncovering the contributions of nature and nurture to this diversity in human traits and abilities. All contemporary researchers agree that both heredity and environment influence every aspect of development. But for polygenic traits (those due to many genes) such as intelligence and personality, scientists are a long way from knowing precisely what hereditary influences are involved. They must study the impact of genes on these characteristics indirectly.

Some believe that it is useful and possible to answer the question of *how much* each factor contributes to differences among children. A growing consensus, however, regards that question as unanswerable. These investigators believe that heredity and environment are inseparable. The important question, they maintain, is how nature and nurture work together. Let's consider each position in turn.

The Question, "How Much?"

Two methods—heritability estimates and concordance rates—are used to infer the role of heredity in complex human characteristics. Let's look closely at the information these procedures yield, along with their limitations.

HERITABILITY ● **Heritability estimates** measure the extent to which individual differences in complex traits in a specific population are due to genetic factors. We will take a brief look at heritability findings on intelligence and personality here and will return to them in later chapters, when we consider these topics in greater detail. Heritability estimates are obtained from

kinship studies, which compare the characteristics of family members. The most common type of kinship study compares identical twins, who share all their genes, with fraternal twins, who share only some. If people who are genetically more alike are also more similar in intelligence and personality, then the researcher assumes that heredity plays an important role.

Kinship studies of intelligence provide some of the most controversial findings in the field of child development. Some experts claim a strong genetic influence, whereas others believe that heredity is barely involved. Currently, most kinship findings support a moderate role for heredity. When many twin studies are examined, correlations between the scores of identical twins are consistently higher than those of fraternal twins. In a summary of more than 13,000 twin pairs, the average correlation was .86 for identical twins and .55 for fraternal twins (Scarr, 1997).

Researchers use a complex statistical procedure to compare these correlations, arriving at a heritability estimate ranging from 0 to 1.00. The value for intelligence is about .50 for child and adolescent twin samples in Western industrialized nations. This suggests that differences in genetic makeup explain half the variation in intelligence (Plomin, 1994). Adopted children's intelligence is more strongly related to their biological parents' scores than to those of their adoptive parents, a finding that offers further support for the role of heredity (Scarr & Weinberg, 1983).

Heritability research also reveals that genetic factors are important in personality. For frequently studied traits, such as sociability, emotional expressiveness, and activity level, heritability estimates obtained on child, adolescent, and emerging adult twins are moderate, at .40 to .50 (Rothbart & Bates, 1998).

CONCORDANCE ● A second measure that has been used to infer the contribution of heredity to complex characteristics is the **concordance rate.** It refers to the percentage of instances in which both twins show a trait when it is present in one twin. Researchers typically use concordance to study the contribution of heredity to emotional and behavioral disorders, which can be judged as either present or absent.

A concordance rate ranges from 0 to 100 percent. A score of 0 indicates that if one twin has the trait, the other twin never has it. A score of 100 means that if one twin has the trait, the other one always has it. When a concordance rate is much higher for identical twins than for fraternal twins, heredity is believed to play a major role. As Figure 2.8 reveals, twin studies of schizophrenia (a disorder involving delusions and hallucinations, difficulty distinguishing fantasy from reality, and irrational and inappropriate behaviors) and severe depression show this pattern of findings. Look carefully at the figure, and you will see that the influence of heredity on antisocial behavior and criminality, although apparent, is less strong. In that case, the difference between concordance rates for identical and fraternal twins is smaller. Once again, adoption studies lend support to these results. Biological relatives of schizophrenic and depressed adoptees are more likely than adoptive relatives to share the same disorder (Plomin et al., 2000; Tienari et al., 2003).

Taken together, concordance and adoption research suggests that the tendency for schizophrenia, depression, and criminality to run in families is partly due to genetic factors. However, we also know that environment is involved because the concordance rate for identical twins would have to be 100 percent for heredity to be the only influence operating. Already we have seen that environmental stressors, such as poverty, family conflict, and a disorganized home and neighborhood life, often are associated with emotional and behavior problems. You will encounter many more examples of this relationship throughout this book.

LIMITATIONS OF HERITABILITY AND CONCORDANCE

● Serious questions have been raised about the accuracy of heritability estimates and concordance rates. First, each value refers only to the particular population studied and its unique

FIGURE 2.8

Concordance rates for schizophrenia, severe depression, and antisocial behavior and criminality.

We know that heredity plays some role in schizophrenia and is even more influential in severe depression because the concordance rate is much higher for identical than for fraternal twins. Heredity contributes less to antisocial behavior and criminality because the difference between identical and fraternal twins' concordance rates is smaller. (From Gottesman, 1991; McGuffin & Sargeant, 1991; Torrey et al., 1994.)

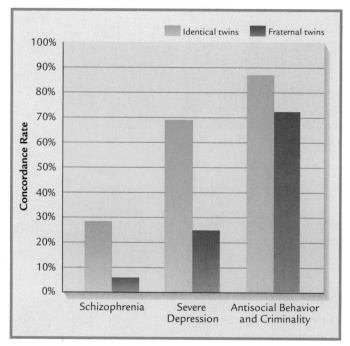

range of genetic and environmental influences. For example, imagine a country in which people's home, school, and community experiences are very similar. Under these conditions, individual differences in intelligence and personality would be largely genetic, and heritability estimates would be close to 1.00. Conversely, the more environments vary, the greater their opportunity to account for individual differences, and the lower heritability estimates are likely to be (Plomin, 1994).

Second, the accuracy of heritability estimates and concordance rates depends on the extent to which the twin pairs used reflect genetic and environmental variation in the population. Yet most twins studied are reared together under highly similar conditions. Even when separated twins are available, social service agencies often place them in advantaged homes that are alike in many ways (Rutter et al., 2001). Because the environments of most twin pairs are less diverse than those of the general population, heritability estimates are likely to exaggerate the role of heredity.

Heritability estimates are controversial measures because they can easily be misapplied. For example, high heritabilities have been used to suggest that ethnic differences in intelligence, such as the poorer performance of black children compared to white children, have a genetic basis (Jensen, 1969, 1985, 1998). Yet this line of reasoning is widely regarded as incorrect. Heritabilities computed on mostly white twin samples do not tell us what is responsible for test score differences between ethnic groups. We have already seen that large economic and cultural differences are involved. In Chapter 12, we will discuss research indicating that when black children are adopted into economically advantaged homes at an early age, their scores are well above average and substantially higher than those of children growing up in impoverished families.

Perhaps the most serious criticism of heritability estimates and concordance rates has to do with their limited usefulness. Although they are interesting statistics, they give us no precise information about how intelligence and personality develop or how children might respond to environments designed to help them develop as far as possible (Rutter, 2002; Wachs, 1999). Indeed, the heritability of intelligence is higher in advantaged homes and communities, which permit children to make the most of their genetic endowment. In disadvantaged environments, children are prevented from realizing their potential. Consequently, enhancing their experiences through interventions—such as parent education and high-quality preschool or child care—has a greater impact on development (Bronfenbrenner & Morris, 1998).

According to one group of experts, heritability estimates have too many problems to yield any firm conclusions about the relative strength of nature and nurture (Collins et al., 2000). Although these statistics confirm that heredity contributes to complex traits, they do not tell us how environment can modify genetic influences.

Identical twins Bob and Bob were separated by adoption shortly after birth and not reunited until adulthood. The two Bobs discovered they were alike in many ways. Both hold bachelor's degrees in engineering, are married to teachers named Brenda, wear glasses, have mustaches, smoke pipes, and are volunteer firemen. The study of identical twins reared apart reveals that heredity contributes to many psychological characteristics. Nevertheless, not all separated twins match up as well as this pair, and generalizing from twin evidence to the population is controversial.

The Question, "How?"

Today, most researchers view development as the result of a dynamic interplay between heredity and environment. How do nature and nurture work together? Several concepts shed light on this question.

REACTION RANGE ● The first of these ideas is **range of reaction,** or each person's unique, **genetically determined response to the environment** (Gottesman, 1963). Let's explore this idea in Figure 2.9 on page 86. Reaction range can apply to any characteristic; here it is illustrated for intelligence. Notice that when environments vary from extremely unstimulating to highly

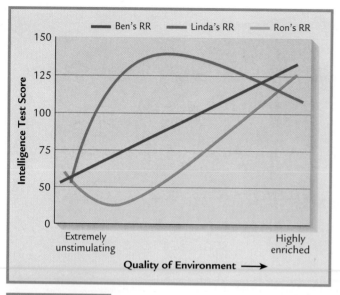

FIGURE 2.9

Intellectual ranges of reaction (RR) for three children in environments that vary from extremely unstimulating to highly enriched.

Each child, due to his or her genetic makeup, responds differently as quality of the environment changes. Ben's intelligence test score increases steadily, Linda's rises sharply and then falls off, and Ron's begins to increase only after the environment becomes modestly stimulating. (Adapted from Wahlsten, 1994.)

enriched, Ben's intelligence increases steadily, Linda's rises sharply and then falls off, and Ron's begins to increase only after the environment becomes modestly stimulating.

Reaction range highlights two important points. First, it shows that because each of us has a unique genetic makeup, we respond differently to the same environment. Note in Figure 2.9 how a poor environment results in similarly low scores for all three individuals. But Linda is by far the best-performing child when environments provide an intermediate level of stimulation. And when environments are highly enriched, Ben does best, followed by Ron, both of whom now outperform Linda. Second, sometimes different genetic–environmental combinations can make two people look the same! For example, if Linda is reared in a minimally stimulating environment, her score will be about 100—average for children in general. Ben and Ron can also obtain this score, but to do so they must grow up in a fairly enriched home. In sum, range of reaction reveals that unique blends of heredity and environment lead to both similarities and differences in behavior (Wahlsten, 1994).

CANALIZATION ● The concept of canalization provides another way of understanding how heredity and environment combine. **Canalization is the tendency of heredity to restrict the development of some characteristics to just one or a few outcomes.** A behavior that is strongly canalized follows a genetically set growth plan, and only strong environmental forces can change it (Waddington, 1957). For example, infant perceptual and motor development seems to be strongly canalized because all normal human babies eventually roll over, reach for objects, sit up, crawl, and walk. It takes extreme conditions to modify these behaviors or cause them not to appear. In contrast, intelligence and personality are less strongly canalized, since they vary much more with changes in the environment.

When we look at behaviors that are constrained by heredity, we can see that canalization is highly adaptive. Through it, nature ensures that children will develop certain species-typical behaviors under a wide range of rearing conditions, thereby promoting survival.

GENETIC–ENVIRONMENTAL CORRELATION ● Nature and nurture work together in still another way. Several investigators point out that a major problem in trying to separate heredity and environment is that they are often correlated (Plomin, 1994; Scarr & McCartney, 1983). According to the concept of genetic–environmental correlation, our genes influence the environments to which we are exposed. The way this happens changes with age.

Passive and Evocative Correlation. At younger ages, two types of genetic–environmental correlations are common. The first is called *passive* correlation because the child has no control over it. Early on, parents provide environments influenced by their own heredity. For example, parents who are good athletes emphasize outdoor activities and enroll their children in swimming and gymnastics. Besides getting exposed to an "athletic environment," the children may have inherited their parents' athletic ability. As a result, they are likely to become good athletes for both genetic and environmental reasons.

The second type of genetic–environmental correlation is *evocative.* Children evoke responses from others that are influenced by the child's heredity, and these responses strengthen the child's original style. For example, an active, friendly baby is likely to receive more social stimulation than a passive, quiet infant. And a cooperative, attentive child probably receives more patient and sensitive interactions from parents than an inattentive, distractible child. In support of this idea, the less genetically alike siblings are, the more their parents treat them differently, in both warmth and negativity. That is, parents' treatment of identical twins is highly similar, whereas their treatment of fraternal twins and nontwin biological siblings is only moderately so. And little resemblance exists in parents' warm and negative interactions with unrelated stepsiblings (see Figure 2.10)(Reiss, 2003).

Active Correlation. At older ages, *active* genetic–environmental correlation becomes common. As children extend their experiences beyond the immediate family and are given the freedom to make more choices, they actively seek environments that fit with their genetic tendencies. The well-coordinated, muscular child spends more time at after-school sports, the musically talented youngster joins the school orchestra and practices his violin, and the intellectually curious child is a familiar patron at her local library.

This tendency to actively choose environments that complement our heredity is called **niche-picking** (Scarr & McCartney, 1983). Infants and young children cannot do much niche-picking because adults select environments for them. In contrast, older children and adolescents are much more in charge of their environments. The niche-picking idea explains why pairs of identical twins reared apart during childhood and later reunited may find, to their great surprise, that they have similar hobbies, food preferences, and vocations—a trend that is especially evident when twins' environmental opportunities are similar (Bouchard et al., 1990; Plomin, 1994a). Niche-picking also helps us understand some curious longitudinal findings indicating that identical twins become somewhat more alike, and fraternal twins and adopted siblings less alike, in intelligence with age (Loehlin, Horn, & Willerman, 1997). The influence of heredity and environment is not constant but changes over time. With age, genetic factors may become more important in determining the environments we experience and choose for ourselves.

ENVIRONMENTAL INFLUENCES ON GENE EXPRESSION ● Notice how, in the concepts just considered, heredity is granted priority. In range of reaction, it *limits* responsiveness to varying environments. In canalization, it *restricts* the development of certain behaviors. Similarly, some theorists regard genetic–environmental correlation as entirely driven by genetics (Harris, 1998; Rowe, 1994). They believe that children's genetic makeup causes them to receive, evoke, or seek experiences that actualize their inborn tendencies. Others argue that heredity does not dictate children's experiences or development in a rigid way. For example, parents and other caring adults can *uncouple* unfavorable genetic–environmental correlations. They often provide children with positive experiences that modify the expression of heredity, yielding favorable outcomes (see the Biology and Environment box on page 88). Other research shows that parents' unequal treatment of siblings is not simply the result of children's heredity. It is partly due to aspects of family life. In large families, single-parent families, low-SES families, and families with unhappy marriages, siblings receive more differential treatment from parents (Jenkins, Rasbash, & O'Connor, 2003). When parents are under stress, perhaps they concentrate their limited energies on one child.

Accumulating evidence reveals that the relationship between heredity and environment is not a one-way street, from genes to environment to behavior. Instead, like other system influences considered in this and the previous chapter, it is *bidirectional:* Genes affect children's behavior and experiences, but their experiences and behavior also affect gene expression (Gottlieb, 2000).

This mother is an accomplished skier who exposes her children to skiing. In addition, the children may have inherited their mother's athletic talent. When heredity and environment are correlated, they jointly foster the same capacities, and the influence of one cannot be separated from the influence of the other.

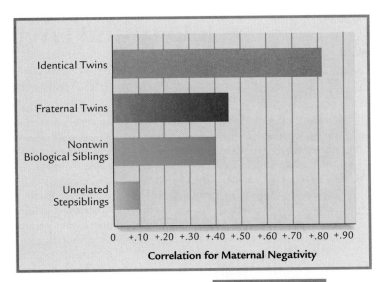

FIGURE 2.10

Similarity in mothers' interactions for pairs of siblings differing in genetic relatedness.

The correlations shown are for maternal negativity. The pattern illustrates *evocative genetic–environmental correlation.* Identical twins evoke highly similar maternal treatment because of their identical heredity. As genetic resemblance between siblings declines, the strength of the correlation drops. Mothers vary their interactions as they respond to each child's unique genetic makeup. (Adapted from Reiss, 2003.)

©MITCH WOJNAROWICZ/THE IMAGE WORKS

*B*iology and Environment

Uncoupling Genetic–Environmental Correlations for Mental Illness and Antisocial Behavior

Diagnosed with schizophrenia, Lars's and Sven's biological mothers had such difficulty functioning in everyday life that each gave up her infant son for adoption. Lars had the misfortune of being placed with adoptive parents who, like his biological mother, were mentally ill. His home life was chaotic, and his parents were punitive and neglectful. Sven's adoptive parents, in contrast, were psychologically healthy and reared him with love, patience, and consistency.

Lars was subject to a commonly observed genetic–environmental correlation: a predisposition for schizophrenia coupled with maladaptive parenting. Will he be more likely than Sven, whose adoption *uncoupled* this adverse genotype-environment link, to develop mental illness? In a large Finnish adoption study, nearly 200 adopted children of schizophrenic mothers were followed into adulthood (Tienari et al., 1994, 2003). Those (like Sven) who were reared by healthy adoptive parents showed little mental illness—no more than a control group with healthy biological and adoptive parents. In contrast, psychological impairments piled up in adoptees (like Lars) with disturbed biological *and* adoptive parents. These children were considerably more likely to develop mental illness than were controls whose biological parents were healthy but who were being reared by severely disturbed adoptive parents.

Similar findings emerged in several American and Swedish adoption studies addressing genetic and environmental contributions to antisocial behavior (Bohman, 1996; Yates, Cadoret, & Troughton, 1999). As Figure 2.11 shows, adopted infants whose biological mothers were imprisoned criminal offenders displayed a high rate of antisocial behavior in adolescence only when reared in unfavorable homes, as indicated by adoptive parents or siblings with severe adjustment problems. In families free of psychological disturbance, adoptees with a predisposition to criminality did not differ from adoptees without this genetic background.

In sum, the chances that genes for psychological disorder will be expressed are far greater when child rearing is maladaptive. Well-functioning families seem to promote healthy development in children, despite a genetic risk associated with mental illness or criminality in a biological parent.

FIGURE 2.11

Antisocial behavior of adoptees varying in genetic and home-environment risk for criminality.
Adolescent adoptees at genetic risk for criminality displayed a high rate of antisocial behavior only when reared in unfavorable homes. When reared in favorable homes, they did not differ from adoptees at no genetic risk. (Adapted from Cadoret, Cain, & Crowe, 1983.)

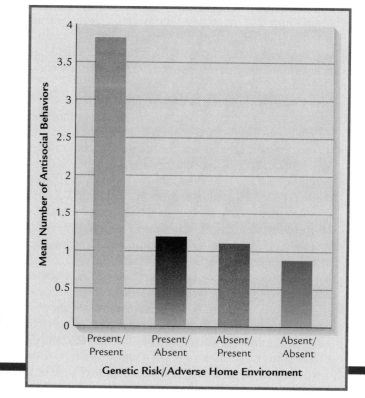

Stimulation—both *internal* to the child (activity within the cytoplasm of the cell, hormones released into the bloodstream) and *external* to the child (home, neighborhood, school, and, society)—triggers gene activity.

Researchers call this view of the relationship between heredity and environment the *epigenetic framework* (Gottlieb, 1998, 2000). It is depicted in Figure 2.12. **Epigenesis** means development resulting from ongoing, bidirectional exchanges between heredity and all levels of the environment. To illustrate, providing a baby with a healthy diet promotes brain growth, which translates into new connections between nerve cells, which transform gene expression. This

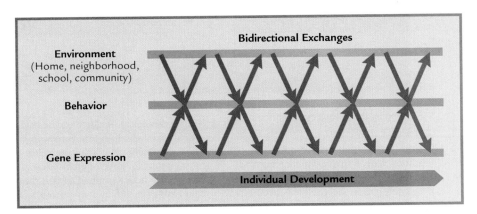

FIGURE 2.12

The epigenetic framework.
Development takes place through on-going, bidirectional exchanges between heredity and all levels of the environment. Genes affect behavior and experiences. Experiences and behavior also affect gene expression. (Adapted from Gottlieb, 2000.)

opens the door to new gene–environment exchanges—for example, advanced exploration of objects and interaction with caregivers, which further enhance brain growth and gene expression. These ongoing bidirectional influences foster cognitive and social development. In contrast, harmful environments can dampen gene expression, at times so profoundly that later experiences can do little to change characteristics (such as intelligence and personality) that were flexible to begin with.

A major reason that researchers are interested in the nature–nurture issue is that they want to improve environments so that children can develop as far as possible. The concept of epigenesis reminds us that development is best understood as a series of complex exchanges between nature and nurture. Although children cannot be changed in any way we might desire, environments can modify genetic influences. The success of any attempt to improve development depends on the characteristics we want to change, the genetic makeup of the child, and the type and timing of our intervention.

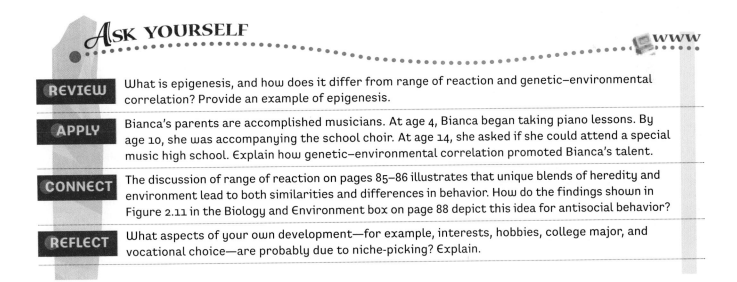

ASK YOURSELF

REVIEW What is epigenesis, and how does it differ from range of reaction and genetic–environmental correlation? Provide an example of epigenesis.

APPLY Bianca's parents are accomplished musicians. At age 4, Bianca began taking piano lessons. By age 10, she was accompanying the school choir. At age 14, she asked if she could attend a special music high school. Explain how genetic–environmental correlation promoted Bianca's talent.

CONNECT The discussion of range of reaction on pages 85–86 illustrates that unique blends of heredity and environment lead to both similarities and differences in behavior. How do the findings shown in Figure 2.11 in the Biology and Environment box on page 88 depict this idea for antisocial behavior?

REFLECT What aspects of your own development—for example, interests, hobbies, college major, and vocational choice—are probably due to niche-picking? Explain.

Summary

Genetic Foundations

What are genes, and how are they transmitted from one generation to the next?

- Each individual's **phenotype,** or directly observable characteristics, is a product of both **genotype** and environment. **Chromosomes,** rodlike structures within the cell nucleus, contain our hereditary endowment. Along their length are **genes,** segments of **DNA** that send instructions for making a rich assortment of proteins to the cytoplasm of the cell—a process that makes us distinctly human and influences our development and characteristics.

- **Gametes,** or sex cells, are produced through the process of cell division known as **meiosis. Crossing over** and independent assortment of chromosomes ensure that each gamete receives a unique set of genes from each parent. Once sperm and ovum unite, the resulting **zygote** starts to develop into a complex human being through cell duplication, or **mitosis.**

- If the fertilizing sperm carries an X chromosome, the child will be a girl; if it contains a Y chromosome, a boy will be born. **Fraternal,** or **dizygotic, twins** result when two ova are released from the mother's ovaries and each is fertilized. In contrast, **identical,** or **monozygotic, twins** develop when a zygote divides in two during the early stages of cell duplication.

Describe various patterns of genetic inheritance.

- **Dominant–recessive** and **codominant** relationships are patterns of inheritance that apply to traits controlled by single genes. In dominant–recessive inheritance, **heterozygous** individuals with one recessive **allele** are **carriers** of the recessive trait. **Modifier genes** enhance or dilute the effects of other genes.

- When recessive disorders are **X-linked** (carried on the X chromosome), males are more likely to be affected. **Genetic imprinting** is a pattern of inheritance in which one parent's allele is activated, regardless of its makeup.

- Unfavorable genes arise from **mutations,** which can occur spontaneously or be induced by hazardous environmental agents.

- Human traits that vary continuously among people, such as intelligence and personality, are **polygenic,** or influenced by many genes. Because the genetic principles involved are unknown, scientists must study the influence of heredity on these characteristics indirectly.

Describe major chromosomal abnormalities, and explain how they occur.

- Most chromosomal abnormalities are due to errors in meiosis. The most common chromosomal disorder is Down syndrome, which results in physical defects and mental retardation. Disorders of the **sex chromosomes**—XYY, triple X, Klinefelter, and Turner syndromes—are milder than defects of the **autosomes.**

Reproductive Choices

What procedures can assist prospective parents in having healthy children?

- **Genetic counseling** helps couples at risk for giving birth to children with genetic abnormalities consider appropriate reproductive options. **Prenatal diagnostic methods** make early detection of genetic problems possible. Although reproductive technologies, such as donor insemination, in vitro fertilization, surrogate motherhood, and postmenopausal-assisted childbirth, permit many individuals to become parents who otherwise would not, they raise serious legal and ethical concerns.

- Many parents who cannot conceive or who have a high likelihood of transmitting a genetic disorder decide to adopt. Adopted children have more learning and emotional problems than children in general. However, warm, sensitive parenting predicts favorable development, and in the long run, most adopted children fare quite well.

Environmental Contexts for Development

Describe family functioning from the perspective of ecological systems theory, along with aspects of the environ-

ment that support family well-being and children's development.

- Just as complex as heredity are the environments in which children grow up. The family is the child's first and foremost context for development. Ecological systems theory emphasizes that the behaviors of each family member affect those of others, both directly and indirectly. The family system is also dynamic, constantly adjusting to the development of its members and to societal change.

- Despite these variations, one source of consistency in family functioning is **socioeconomic status (SES).** Higher-SES families tend to be smaller, to place greater emphasis on nurturing psychological traits, and to promote warm, verbally stimulating interaction with children. Lower-SES parents often stress external characteristics and engage in harsh, restrictive child rearing. Effective parenting and all aspects of children's development are seriously undermined by poverty and homelessness.

- Children profit from supportive ties between the family and the surrounding environment. Neighborhoods that offer constructive leisure activities, high-quality schools that communicate often with parents, and other strong connections between family and community life foster development.

- The values and practices of cultures and **subcultures** affect all aspects of children's daily lives. **Extended-family households,** in which parent and child live with one or more adult relatives, are common among ethnic minorities. They protect children's development under conditions of high life stress.

- In the complex world in which we live, children's well-being depends on favorable **public policies.** Effective social programs are influenced by many factors, including cultural values that stress **collectivism** over **individualism,** a nation's economic resources, and organizations and individuals that work for an improved quality of life. American and (to a lesser extent) Canadian policies safeguarding children and youths have lagged behind policies in other developed nations.

Understanding the Relationship Between Heredity and Environment

Explain the various ways heredity and environment may combine to influence complex traits.

● **Behavioral genetics** is a field devoted to uncovering the contributions of nature and nurture to complex traits. Some researchers believe that it is useful and possible to determine "how much" each factor contributes to individual differences. These investigators compute **heritability estimates** and **concordance rates** from **kinship studies.** Although these measures show that genetic factors contribute to such traits as intelligence and personality, their accuracy and usefulness have been challenged.

● Most researchers view development as the result of a dynamic interplay between nature and nurture and ask "how" these forces work together. According to **range of reaction** and **canalization**, heredity influences children's responsiveness to varying environments. In **genetic–environmental correlation** and **niche-picking**, children's genes affect the environments to which they are exposed. **Epigenesis** reminds us that development is best understood as a series of complex exchanges between nature and nurture.

Important Terms and Concepts

allele (p. 58)
autosomes (p. 57)
behavioral genetics (p. 83)
canalization (p. 86)
carrier (p. 58)
chromosomes (p. 54)
codominance (p. 59)
collectivist societies (p. 78)
concordance rate (p. 84)
crossing over (p. 55)
deoxyribonucleic acid (DNA) (p. 54)
dominant–recessive inheritance
  (p. 58)
epigenesis (p. 88)
extended-family household (p. 78)

fraternal, or dizygotic, twins (p. 57)
gametes (p. 55)
gene (p. 54)
genetic counseling (p. 64)
genetic imprinting (p. 61)
genetic–environmental correlation
  (p. 86)
genotype (p. 53)
heritability estimate (p. 83)
heterozygous (p. 58)
homozygous (p. 58)
identical, or monozygotic, twins
  (p. 57)
individualistic societies (p. 78)
kinship studies (p. 84)

meiosis (p. 55)
mitosis (p. 55)
modifier genes (p. 58)
mutation (p. 61)
niche-picking (p. 87)
phenotype (p. 53)
polygenic inheritance (p. 62)
prenatal diagnostic methods (p. 65)
public policies (p. 78)
range of reaction (p. 85)
sex chromosomes (p. 57)
socioeconomic status (SES) (p. 74)
subculture (p. 78)
X-linked inheritance (p. 59)
zygote (p. 55)

 **FYI** **For Further Information and Help**

Consult the Companion Website for *Infants, Children, and Adolescents,* Fifth Edition, *(www.ablongman.com/berk),* where you will find the following resources for this chapter:

● **Chapter Objectives**
● **Flashcards** for studying important terms and concepts
● **Annotated Weblinks** to guide you in further research
● **Ask Yourself questions,** which you can answer and then
  check against a sample response

● **Suggested Readings**
● **Practice Tests** with immediate scoring and feedback

CHAPTER 3

"Pregnant Mummy"
Eliska Kocová
Age 5, Czech Republic

A young painter places the new being at the center, conveying an intuitive understanding of how it increasingly claims a central place in the parent's world. How is the one-celled organism gradually transformed into a baby with the capacity to participate in family life? What factors support or undermine this earliest period of development? Chapter 3 provides answers to these questions.

Prenatal Development

After months of wondering if the time in their lives was right, Yolanda and Jay decided to have a baby. I met them one fall in my child development class, when Yolanda was just 2 months pregnant. Both were full of questions: "How does the baby grow before birth? When is each organ formed? Has its heart begun to beat? Can it hear, feel, or sense our presence?"

Most of all, Yolanda and Jay wanted to do everything possible to make sure their baby would be born healthy. At first, they believed that the uterus completely shielded the developing organism from any dangers in the environment. All babies born with problems, they thought, had unfavorable genes. After browsing through several pregnancy books, Yolanda and Jay realized they were wrong. Yolanda started to wonder about her diet and whether she should keep up her daily aerobics routine. And she asked me whether an aspirin for a headache, a sleeping pill before bedtime, a glass of wine at dinner, or a few cups of coffee during study hours might be harmful.

In this chapter we answer Yolanda and Jay's questions, along with a great many more that scientists have asked about the events before birth. We begin our discussion during the time period before pregnancy with these puzzling questions: Why is it that generation after generation, most couples who fall in love and marry want to become parents? And how do they decide whether to have just one child or more than one?

Then we trace prenatal development—the 9-month period before birth. Our discussion pays special attention to environmental supports for healthy growth, as well as damaging influences that threaten the child's health and survival. Finally, we look at how couples prepare psychologically for the arrival of the baby and start to forge a new sense of self as mother or father.

Motivations For Parenthood

As part of her semester project for my class, Yolanda interviewed her grandmother, asking why she had wanted children and how she settled on a particular family size. Yolanda's grandmother, whose children were born in the 1950s, replied,

> We didn't think much about whether or not to have children in those days. We just had them—everybody did. It would have seemed odd not to! I was 22 years old when I had the first of my four children, and I had four because—well, I wouldn't have had just one because we all thought children needed brothers and sisters, and only children could end up spoiled and selfish. Life is more interesting with children, you know. And now that we're older, we've got family we can depend on and grandchildren to enjoy.

Why Have Children?

In some ways, the reasons for wanting children given by Yolanda's grandmother are like those of contemporary parents. In other ways, they are very different. In the past, the issue of whether to have children was, for many adults, "a biological given or unavoidable cultural demand" (Michaels, 1988, p. 23). Today, in Western industrialized nations, it is a matter of true individual choice. Effective birth control techniques enable adults to avoid having children in most instances. And changing cultural values allow people to remain childless with much less fear of social criticism and rejection than was the case a generation or two ago. In 1950, 78 percent of North American married couples were parents. Today, 70 percent bear children—a choice affected by a complex array of factors including financial circumstances, career goals, personal and religious values, and health conditions.

When North Americans are asked about their desire to have children, they mention a variety of advantages and disadvantages, which are listed in Table 3.1. Although some ethnic and regional differences exist, reasons for having children that are most important to all groups include the warm, affectionate relationship and the stimulation and fun that children provide. Also frequently mentioned are growth and learning experiences that children bring into the lives of adults, the desire to have someone carry on after one's own death, and feelings of accomplishment and creativity that come from helping children grow (Cowan & Cowan, 2000; Michaels, 1988).

Most young adults are also aware that having children means years of extra burdens and responsibilities. When asked about the disadvantages of parenthood, they mention "loss of freedom" most often, followed by "financial strain." Indeed, the cost of child rearing is a major factor in modern family planning. According to a conservative government estimate, today's new parents will spend about $275,000 to rear a child from birth through 4 years

An expectant mother joins her sister, mother, and grandmother to celebrate the impending arrival of her baby. All share the grandmother's joy as she senses the movements of her soon-to-be-born great-grandchild. Compared with a generation or two ago, adults today are far more likely to make careful, well-reasoned choices about whether, when, and how to have children.

STOCKBYTE

TABLE 3.1

Advantages and Disadvantages of Parenthood Mentioned by American Couples

ADVANTAGES	DISADVANTAGES
Giving and receiving warmth and affection	Loss of freedom, being tied down
Experiencing the stimulation and fun that children add to life	Financial strain
Being accepted as a responsible and mature member of the community	Family–work conflict—not enough time to meet both child-rearing and job responsibilities
Experiencing new growth and learning opportunities that add meaning to life	Interference with mother's employment opportunities and career progress
Having someone to provide care in old age	Worries over children's health, safety, and well-being
Gaining a sense of accomplishment and creativity from helping children grow	Risks of bringing up children in a world plagued by crime, war, and pollution
Learning to become less selfish and to sacrifice	Reduced time to spend with husband or wife
Having someone carry on after one's own death	Loss of privacy
Having offspring who help with parents' work or add their own income to the family's resources	Fear that children will turn out badly, through no fault of one's own

Source: Cowan & Cowan, 2000; O'Laughlin & Anderson, 2001.

of college (U.S. Department of Labor, 2003). Finally, many adults worry greatly about conflict between family and work—not having enough time to meet both child-rearing and job responsibilities (Hewlett, 2003).

Greater freedom to choose whether, when, and how to have children (see the discussion of reproductive choices in Chapter 2) makes modern family planning more challenging than it was in Yolanda's grandmother's day. As each partner expects to have equal say, childbearing often becomes a matter of delicate negotiation (Cowan & Cowan, 2000). Yet careful weighing of the pros and cons of having children means that many more couples are making informed and personally meaningful decisions—a trend that should increase the chances that they will have children when ready and will find parenting an enriching experience.

How Large A Family?

In contrast to her grandmother, Yolanda plans to have no more than two children. And she and Jay are talking about whether to limit their family to a single child. In 1960, the average number of children per North American couple was 3.1. Currently, it is 1.8 in the United States, 1.7 in Australia and Great Britain, 1.6 in Canada and Sweden, 1.4 in Japan, and 1.3 in Germany (U.S. Census Bureau, 2003b; United Nations, 2003). In addition to more effective birth control, a major reason for this decline is that many women are reaping the economic and personal rewards of a career. A family size of one or two children is more compatible with a woman's decision to divide her energies between family and work.

Children benefit from growing up in small families. Parents who have fewer children are more

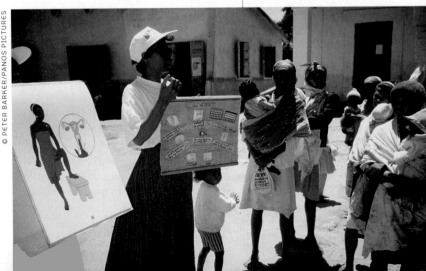

Health counselors explain birth control options to mothers in rural Madagascar. Family planning combined with education helps limit rising birthrates in developing countries. Smaller families mean an enhanced quality of life for both mothers and children.

© PETER BARKER/PANOS PICTURES

TABLE 3.2

Advantages and Disadvantages of a One-Child Family

ADVANTAGES		DISADVANTAGES	
Mentioned by Parents	*Mentioned by Children*	*Mentioned by Parents*	*Mentioned by Children*
Having time to pursue one's own interests and career	Having no sibling rivalry	Walking a "tightrope" between healthy attention and overindulgence	Not getting to experience the closeness of a sibling relationship
	Having more privacy		
Less financial pressure	Enjoying greater affluence	Having only one chance to "make good" as a parent	Feeling too much pressure from parents to succeed
Not having to worry about "playing favorites" among children	Having a closer parent–child relationship	Being left childless in case of the child's death	Having no one to help care for parents when they get old

Source: Hawke & Knox, 1978.

patient and less punitive. They also have more time to devote to each child's activities, schoolwork, and other special needs. Furthermore, in smaller families, siblings are more likely to be widely spaced (born more than 2 years apart), which adds to the attention and resources parents can invest in each child. Together, these findings may account for the fact that children who grow up in small families are healthier, have somewhat higher intelligence test scores, do better in school, and attain higher levels of education (Powell & Steelman, 1993).

However, recall from Chapter 1 that a correlation between family size and children's characteristics does not tell us for sure about causation. Large families are usually less well off economically. Factors associated with low income—crowded housing, inadequate nutrition, and poorly educated and stressed parents—seem to account for the negative relationship between family size and children's well-being. Parents with lower intelligence test scores (many of whom are poorly educated) tend to have larger families (Rodgers et al., 2000). And when children of bright, stimulating, economically advantaged parents grow up in large families, unfavorable outcomes are eliminated (Guo & VanWey, 1999). As the Social Issues: Education box on the following page indicates, education and family planning are closely linked. Both are vital for improving children's quality of life, especially in poverty-stricken regions of the world.

Is Yolanda's grandmother right: Are parents who have just one child likely to end up with a spoiled, selfish youngster? As we will see in Chapter 13, a great deal of research challenges this commonly held belief. Only children are just as well adjusted as are children with siblings. Still, the one-child family has both pros and cons, as does every family lifestyle. Table 3.2 summarizes results of a survey in which only children and their parents were asked what they liked and disliked about living in a single-child family. The list is a useful one for parents to consider when deciding how many children would best fit their life plans.

Is There a Best Time During Adulthood to Have a Child?

Yolanda's grandmother had her first child in her early twenties. Yolanda is pregnant for the first time at age 28. Many people believe that women giving birth in their twenties is ideal, not only because the risk of having a baby with a chromosomal disorder increases with age (see Chapter 2) but also because younger parents have more energy to keep up with active children.

However, as Figure 3.2 on page 98 reveals, first births to women in their thirties have increased greatly over the past two decades. Many people are delaying childbearing until their education is

Social Issues: Education

A Global Perspective on Family Planning

Approximately one-fifth of the world's population—one billion people—live in extreme poverty, the majority in slums and shantytowns of developing countries. If current trends in population growth continue, the number of poor will quadruple within the next 60 to 70 years (United Nations, 2003). Poverty and rapid population growth are intertwined: Poverty leads to high birthrates, and rising birthrates heighten poverty and deprivation. Why is this so?

First, in poor regions of the world where child death rates are high, parents have more children to compensate for the fact that some will certainly die. Second, lack of status, education, and opportunities for women, characteristic of most nonindustrialized societies, restrict life choices to early marriage and prolonged childbearing. Third, in regions with few basic services and labor-saving technologies, families often depend on children to help in the fields and at home. Fourth, poverty is associated with absence of family planning services, which causes birthrates to remain high even when people begin to realize the advantages of smaller families (Caldwell & Barket-e-Khuda, 2002). And finally, lack of hope in the future is a major obstacle to life planning in general and family planning in particular.

As a country's population grows, poverty worsens. The labor force expands more quickly than available work, and a new generation of unemployed or underemployed parents emerges. Basic resources, including food, water, land, and fuel, are in shorter supply, and health and educational services are increasingly strained. As a result, overcrowding in urban areas—along with malnutrition, disease, illiteracy, and hopelessness—spreads. A cycle forms through which poverty and high birthrates perpetuate one another.

Two interrelated strategies are especially effective for intervening in this cycle:

● Emphasizing education and literacy, particularly for girls. Years of schooling is a powerful predictor of small family size. Because women with more education have better life opportunities, they are more likely to marry at a later age and take advantage of family planning services. As a result, they have fewer, more widely spaced, and healthier children (Caldwell, 1999).

● Making family planning services available to all who want them, in ways that are compatible with each family's cultural and religious traditions and place of residence. Home visits by workers, including resupply of contraceptives, are essential for women living in rural areas located far from clinics. During the past 40 years, the percentage of married women in the developing world using birth control increased from 10 to 50 percent, contributing to an overall birthrate decline from 6 to 3 children per woman in developing countries (United Nations, 2003).

Still, the unmet need for family planning remains high. About 100 million women in developing countries want to limit family size or increase spacing between births (DaVanzo & Adamson, 2000). Yet those who have weak reading skills or are illiterate have difficulty understanding family planning information (Ashraf, 2002). Hence, they have many unintended pregnancies. As Figure 3.1 shows, the world's population continues to increase at an astounding pace because of high birthrates in poverty-stricken, developing countries. Population growth is especially great in sub-Saharan Africa. In Somalia, Uganda, and Niger, for example, the average woman will give birth to nearly 7 children in her lifetime.

Education combined with family planning leads to substantial declines in birthrates and to improvements in quality of life for both mothers and children. These benefits carry over to future generations.

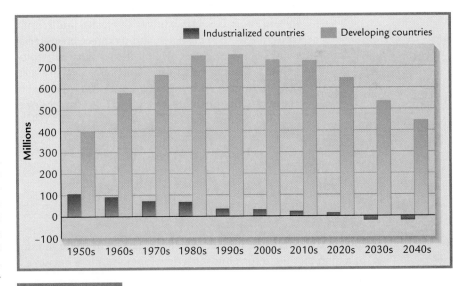

FIGURE 3.1

Population increases by decade in industrialized and developing countries, projected through the first half of the twenty-first century.

Although birthrates are declining, the downward trend is very recent for developing nations. The world's population is still growing, and nearly all of this growth is concentrated in developing countries. In the 2030s, the population in industrialized countries will start to decrease, whereas that of developing nations will continue to swell by more than 500 million. (United Nations, 2003.)

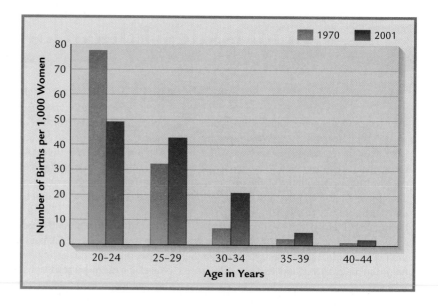

FIGURE 3.2

First births to American women of different ages in 1970 and 2001.

The birthrate decreased during this period for women 20 to 24 years of age, whereas it increased for women 25 years of age and older. For women in their thirties, the birthrate more than doubled. Similar trends have occurred in Canada and other industrialized nations. (Adapted from U. S. Department of Health and Human Services, 2003a.)

complete, their careers are well established, and they know they can support a child. Older parents may be somewhat less energetic than they were at earlier ages, but they are financially better off and emotionally more mature. For these reasons, they may be better able to invest in parenting.

Nevertheless, reproductive capacity does decline with age. Fertility problems among women increase from age 15 to 50, with a sharp rise in the mid-thirties. Bet8ween ages 25 and 34, nearly 14 percent of women are affected, a figure that climbs to 26 percent for 35- to 44-year-olds. Age also affects male reproductive capacity. Amount of semen and concentration of sperm in each ejaculation gradually decline after age 30. Consequently, compared to a 25-year-old man, a 45-year-old is twelve times more likely to take more than 2 years to achieve a conception (Hassan & Killick, 2003; U.S. Department of Health and Human Services, 2003d). Dual-career couples, in which the woman has a demanding career, are especially likely to delay parenthood (Barber, 2001). Many believe, incorrectly, that if they have difficulty conceiving, they can rely on reproductive technologies. But recall from Chapter 2 that the success of these procedures drops steadily with age. Although no one time during adulthood is best to begin parenthood, individuals who decide to put off childbirth until well into their thirties or early forties risk having fewer children than they desire or none at all.

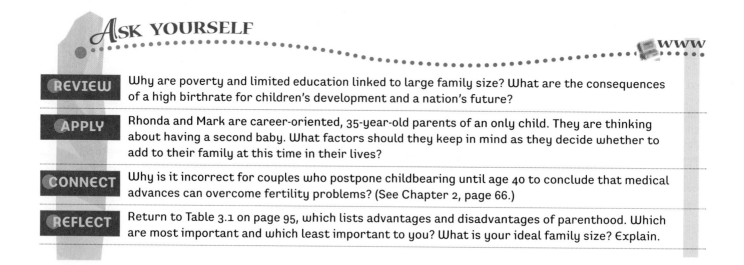

ASK YOURSELF

REVIEW   Why are poverty and limited education linked to large family size? What are the consequences of a high birthrate for children's development and a nation's future?

APPLY   Rhonda and Mark are career-oriented, 35-year-old parents of an only child. They are thinking about having a second baby. What factors should they keep in mind as they decide whether to add to their family at this time in their lives?

CONNECT   Why is it incorrect for couples who postpone childbearing until age 40 to conclude that medical advances can overcome fertility problems? (See Chapter 2, page 66.)

REFLECT   Return to Table 3.1 on page 95, which lists advantages and disadvantages of parenthood. Which are most important and which least important to you? What is your ideal family size? Explain.

Prenatal Development

The sperm and ovum that unite to form the new individual are uniquely suited for the task of reproduction. The ovum is a tiny sphere, measuring $1/175$ inch in diameter, that is barely visible to the naked eye as a dot the size of a period at the end of this sentence. But in its microscopic world, it is a giant—the largest cell in the human body. The ovum's size makes it a perfect target for the much smaller sperm, which measure only $1/500$ inch.

Conception

About once every 28 days, in the middle of a woman's menstrual cycle, an ovum bursts from one of her *ovaries*, two walnut-sized organs located deep inside her abdomen, and is drawn into one of two *fallopian tubes*—long, thin structures that lead to the hollow, soft-lined uterus (see Figure 3.3). While the ovum is traveling, the spot on the ovary from which it was released, now called the *corpus luteum*, begins to secrete hormones that prepare the lining of the uterus to receive a fertilized ovum. If pregnancy does not occur, the corpus luteum shrinks, and the lining of the uterus is discarded 2 weeks later with menstruation.

The male produces sperm in vast numbers—an average of 300 million a day—in the *testes*, two glands located in the *scrotum*, sacs that lie just behind the penis. In the final process of maturation, each sperm develops a tail that permits it to swim long distances, upstream in the female reproductive tract, through the *cervix* (opening of the

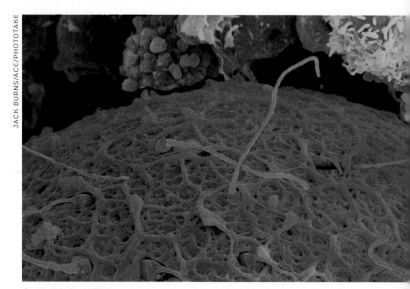

JACK BURNS/ACE/PHOTOTAKE

In this photo taken with the aid of a powerful microscope, sperm penetrate the surface of the enormous-looking ovum, the largest cell in the human body. When one sperm is successful at fertilizing the ovum, the resulting zygote will begin duplicating into the new organism.

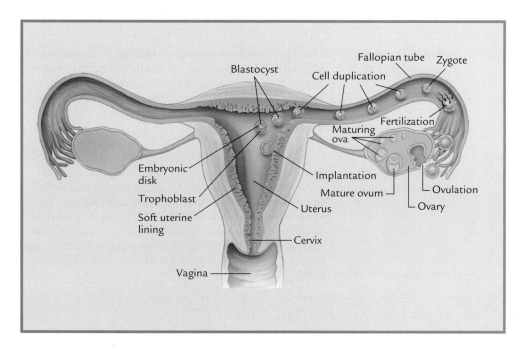

FIGURE 3.3

Female reproductive organs, showing fertilization, early cell duplication, and implantation.

As the zygote moves down the fallopian tube, it begins to duplicate, at first slowly and then more rapidly. By the fourth day, it forms a hollow, fluid-filled ball called a blastocyst. The inner cells, called the embryonic disk, will become the new organism. The outer cells, or trophoblast, will provide protective covering. At the end of the first week, the blastocyst begins to implant in the uterine lining. (Adapted from K. L. Moore and T. V. N. Persaud, 2003, *Before We Are Born*, 6th ed., Philadelphia: Saunders, p. 36. Reprinted by permission of the publisher and authors.)

uterus), and into the *fallopian tube,* where fertilization usually takes place. The journey is diffi-cult, and many sperm die. Only 300 to 500 reach the ovum, if one happens to be present. Sperm live for up to 6 days and can lie in wait for the ovum, which survives for only 1 day after being released into the fallopian tube. However, most conceptions result from intercourse during a 3-day period—on the day of or during the 2 days preceding ovulation (Wilcox, Weinberg, & Baird, 1995).

With conception, the story of prenatal development begins to unfold. The vast changes that take place during the 38 weeks of pregnancy are usually divided into three phases: (1) the pe-riod of the zygote, (2) the period of the embryo, and (3) the period of the fetus. As we look at what happens in each, you may find it useful to refer to Table 3.3, which summarizes major milestones of prenatal development.

TABLE 3.3

Major Milestones of Prenatal Development

TRIMESTER	PERIOD	WEEKS	LENGTH AND WEIGHT	MAJOR EVENTS
First	Zygote	1		The one-celled zygote multiplies and forms a blastocyst.
		2		The blastocyst burrows into the uterine lining. Structures that feed and protect the developing organism begin to form—amnion, chorion, yolk sac, placenta, and umbilical cord.
	Embryo	3–4	¼ inch (6 mm)	A primitive brain and spinal cord appear. Heart, muscles, ribs, backbone, and digestive tract begin to develop.
		5–8	1 inch (2.5 cm); ⅐ ounce (4 g)	Many external body structures (face, arms, legs, toes, fingers) and internal organs form. The sense of touch begins to develop, and the embryo can move.
	Fetus	9–12	3 inches (7.6 cm); less than 1 ounce (28 g)	Rapid increase in size begins. Nervous system, organs, and muscles become organized and connected, and new behavioral capacities (kicking, thumb sucking, mouth opening, and rehearsal of breathing) appear. External genitals are well formed, and the fetus's sex is evident.
Second		13–24	12 inches (30 cm); 1.8 pounds (820 g)	The fetus continues to enlarge rapidly. In the middle of this period, fetal movements can be felt by the mother. Vernix and lanugo keep the fetus's skin from chapping in the amniotic fluid. Most of the brain's neurons are present by 24 weeks. Eyes are sensitive to light, and the fetus reacts to sound.
Third		25–38	20 inches (50 cm); 7.5 pounds (3,400 g)	The fetus has a chance of survival if born during this time. Size increases. Lungs mature. Rapid brain devel-opment causes sensory and behavioral capacities to expand. In the middle of this period, a layer of fat is added under the skin. Antibodies are transmitted from mother to fetus to protect against disease. Most fetuses rotate into an upside-down position in preparation for birth.

Source: Moore & Persaud, 2003.

The Period of the Zygote

The period of the zygote lasts about 2 weeks, from fertilization until the tiny mass of cells drifts down and out of the fallopian tube and attaches itself to the wall of the uterus. The zygote's first cell duplication is long and drawn out; it is not complete until about 30 hours after conception. Gradually, new cells are added at a faster rate. By the fourth day, 60 to 70 cells exist that form a hollow, fluid-filled ball called a **blastocyst** (refer again to Figure 3.3). The cells on the inside of the blastocyst, called the **embryonic disk,** will become the new organism; the thin outer ring of cells, termed the **trophoblast,** will become the structures that provide protective covering and nourishment.

IMPLANTATION ● Between the seventh and ninth days, **implantation** occurs: The blastocyst burrows deep into the uterine lining. Surrounded by the woman's nourishing blood, it starts to grow in earnest. At first, the trophoblast (protective outer layer) multiplies fastest. It forms a membrane, called the **amnion,** that encloses the developing organism in **amniotic fluid,** which helps keep the temperature of the prenatal world constant and provides a cushion against any jolts caused by the woman's movement. A *yolk sac* emerges that produces blood cells until the developing liver, spleen, and bone marrow are mature enough to take over this function (Moore & Persaud, 2003).

© LENNART NILSSON, *A CHILD IS BORN*/BONNIERS

Period of the zygote: seventh to ninth day. The fertilized ovum duplicates at an increasingly rapid rate, forming a hollow ball of cells, or blastocyst, by the fourth day after fertilization. Here the blastocyst, magnified thousands of times, burrows into the uterine lining between the seventh and ninth day.

The events of these first 2 weeks are delicate and uncertain. As many as 30 percent of zygotes do not make it through this phase. In some, the sperm and ovum do not join properly. In others, for some unknown reason, cell duplication never begins. By preventing implantation in these cases, nature eliminates most prenatal abnormalities in the very earliest stages of development (Sadler, 2000).

THE PLACENTA AND UMBILICAL CORD ● By the end of the second week, cells of the trophoblast form another protective membrane—the **chorion,** which surrounds the amnion. From the chorion, tiny fingerlike *villi,* or blood vessels, begin to emerge.[1] As these villi burrow into the uterine wall, the placenta starts to develop. By bringing the mother's and the embryo's blood close together, the **placenta** permits food and oxygen to reach the developing organism and waste products to be carried away. A membrane forms that allows these substances to be exchanged but prevents the mother's and the embryo's blood from mixing directly (see Figure 3.4 on page 102).

The placenta is connected to the developing organism by the **umbilical cord.** In the period of the zygote, it first appears as a primitive body stalk, but during the course of pregnancy, it grows to a length of 1 to 3 feet. The umbilical cord contains one large vein that delivers blood loaded with nutrients and two arteries that remove waste products. The force of blood flowing through the cord keeps it firm, much like a garden hose, so it seldom tangles while the embryo, like a space-walking astronaut, floats freely in its fluid-filled chamber (Moore & Persaud, 2003).

By the end of the period of the zygote, the developing organism has found food and shelter. Already, it is a very complex being. These dramatic beginnings take place before most mothers know they are pregnant.

---

[1]Recall from Chapter 2 that *chorionic villus sampling* is the prenatal diagnostic method that can be performed earliest, by 6 to 8 weeks after conception. In this procedure, tissues from the ends of the villi are removed and examined for genetic abnormalities.

FIGURE 3.4

Cross section of the uterus, showing detail of the placenta.

The embryo's blood flows from the umbilical cord arteries into the chorionic villi and returns via the umbilical cord vein. The mother's blood circulates in spaces surrounding the chronic villi. A membrane between the two blood supplies permits food and oxygen to be delivered and waste products to be carried away. The two blood supplies do not mix directly. The umbilical arteries carry oxygen-poor blood (shown in blue) to the placenta, and the umbilical vein carries oxygen-rich blood (shown in red) to the fetus. (Adapted from K. l. Moore and T. V. N. Persaud, 2003, *Before We Are Born,* 6th ed., Philadelphia: Saunders, p. 95. Reprinted by permission of the publisher and author.)

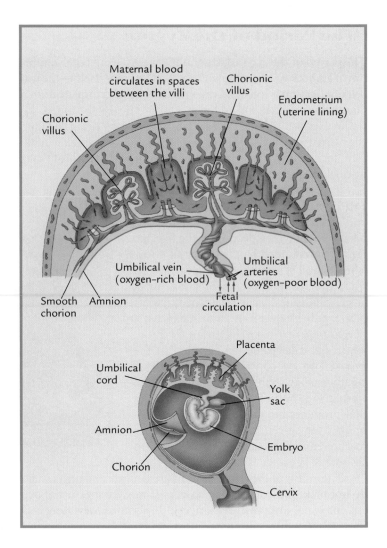

The Period of the Embryo

The period of the embryo lasts from implantation through the eighth week of pregnancy. During these brief 6 weeks, the most rapid prenatal changes take place, as the groundwork is laid for all body structures and internal organs. Because all parts of the body are forming, the embryo is especially vulnerable to interference with healthy development. But a short time span of embryonic growth helps limit opportunities for serious harm.

LAST HALF OF THE FIRST MONTH ● In the first week of this period, the embryonic disk forms three layers of cells: (1) the *ectoderm,* which will become the nervous system and skin; (2) the *mesoderm,* from which will develop the muscles, skeleton, circulatory system, and other internal organs; and (3) the *endoderm,* which will become the digestive system, lungs, urinary tract, and glands. These three layers give rise to all parts of the body.

At first, the nervous system develops fastest. The ectoderm folds over to form the **neural tube,** or spinal cord. At 3½ weeks, the top swells to form the brain. Production of *neurons* (nerve cells that store and transmit information) begins deep inside the neural tube. Once formed, neurons travel along tiny threads to their permanent locations, where they will form the major parts of the brain (Nelson & Bosquet, 2000).

While the nervous system is developing, the heart begins to pump blood, and muscles, backbone, ribs, and digestive tract start to appear. At the end of the first month, the curled embryo—only ¼ inch long—consists of millions of organized groups of cells.

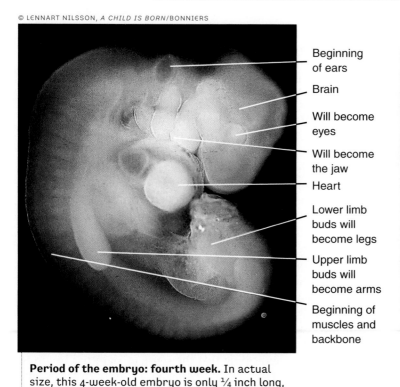

Beginning
of ears

Brain

Will become
eyes

Will become
the jaw

Heart

Lower limb
buds will
become legs

Upper limb
buds will
become arms

Beginning of
muscles and
backbone

Period of the embryo: fourth week. In actual
size, this 4-week-old embryo is only ¼ inch long,
but many body structures have begun to form.

Period of the embryo: seventh week. The embryo's
posture is more upright. Body structures—eyes, nose,
arms, legs, and internal organs—are more distinct. An
embryo of this age responds to touch. It also can move,
although at less than one inch long and an ounce in
weight, it is still too tiny to be felt by the mother.

THE SECOND MONTH ● In the second month, growth continues rapidly. The eyes, ears,
nose, jaw, and neck form. Tiny buds become arms, legs, fingers, and toes. Internal organs are
more distinct: the intestines grow, the heart develops separate chambers, and the liver and
spleen take over production of blood cells so that the yolk sac is no longer needed. Changing
body proportions cause the embryo's posture to become more upright. Now 1 inch long and 1/7
of an ounce in weight, the embryo can sense its world. It responds to touch, particularly in the
mouth area and on the soles of the feet. And it can move, although its tiny flutters are still too
light to be felt by the mother (Nilsson & Hamberger, 1990).

The Period of the Fetus

Lasting until the end of pregnancy, the period of the **fetus** is the "growth and finishing" phase.
During this longest prenatal period, the developing organism begins to increase rapidly in size.
The rate of body growth is extraordinary, especially from the ninth to the twentieth week
(Moore & Persaud, 2003).

THE THIRD MONTH ● In the third month, the organs, muscles, and nervous system start to
become organized and connected. The brain signals, and in response, the fetus kicks, bends its
arms, forms a fist, curls its toes, opens its mouth, and even sucks its thumb. The tiny lungs begin
to expand and contract in an early rehearsal of breathing movements (Joseph, 2000). By the
twelfth week, the external genitals are well formed, and the sex of the fetus is evident. Using ultrasound, Yolanda's doctor could see that she would have a boy (although Yolanda and Jay asked
not to be told the fetus's sex). Other finishing touches appear, such as fingernails, toenails, tooth
buds, and eyelids that open and close. The heartbeat is now stronger and can be heard through
a stethoscope.

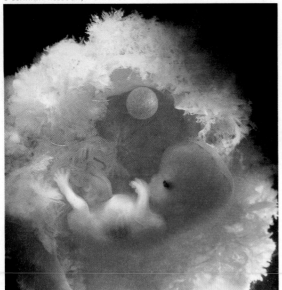

Period of the fetus: eleventh week. The organism increases rapidly in size, and body structures are completed. At 11 weeks, the brain and muscles are better connected. The fetus can kick, bend its arms, open and close its hands and mouth, and suck its thumb. Notice the yolk sac, which shrinks as pregnancy advances. The internal organs have taken over its function of producing blood cells.

Period of the fetus: twenty-second week. This fetus is almost a foot long and weighs slightly more than a pound. Its movements can be felt easily by the mother and other family members who place a hand on her abdomen. The fetus has reached the age of viability; if born, it has a slim chance of surviving.

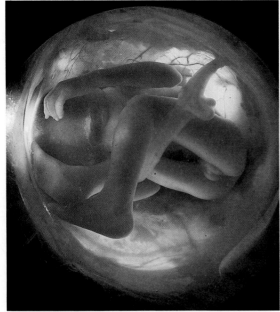

Prenatal development is sometimes divided into **trimesters,** or three equal time periods. At the end of the third month, the first trimester is complete. Two more must pass before the fetus is fully prepared to survive outside the womb.

THE SECOND TRIMESTER ● By the middle of the second trimester, between 17 and 20 weeks, the new being has grown large enough that the mother can feel its movements. A white, cheeselike substance called **vernix** covers the skin, protecting it from chapping during the long months spent in the amniotic fluid. White, downy hair called **lanugo** also appears, helping the vernix stick to the skin.

At the end of the second trimester, many organs are quite well developed. And most of the brain's neurons are in place; few will be produced after this time. However, *glial cells,* which support and feed the neurons, continue to increase at a rapid rate throughout pregnancy, as well as after birth.

Brain growth means new behavioral capacities. The 20-week-old fetus can be stimulated as well as irritated by sounds. And if a doctor has reason to look inside the uterus using fetoscopy (see Chapter 2, page 65), fetuses try to shield their eyes from the light with their hands, indicating that the sense of sight has begun to emerge (Nilsson & Hamberger, 1990). Still, a fetus born at this time cannot survive. Its lungs are immature, and the brain cannot yet control breathing movements or body temperature.

THE THIRD TRIMESTER ● During the final trimester, a fetus born early has a chance for survival. The point at which the baby can first survive, called the **age of viability,** occurs sometime between 22 and 26 weeks (Moore & Persaud, 2003). If born between the seventh and eighth month, however, the baby usually needs oxygen assistance to breathe. Although the respiratory center of the brain is now mature, tiny air sacs in the lungs are not yet ready to inflate and exchange carbon dioxide for oxygen.

The brain continues to make great strides during the last 3 months. The *cerebral cortex,* the seat of human intelligence, enlarges (see Figure 3.5). As neurological organization improves, the fetus spends more time awake. At 20 weeks, the fetal heart rate reveals no periods of alertness. But by 28 weeks, fetuses are awake about 11 percent of the time, a figure that rises to 16 percent just before birth (DiPietro et al., 1996).

By the end of pregnancy, the organism takes on the beginnings of a personality. Higher fetal activity in the last weeks of pregnancy predicts a more active infant in the first month of life—a relationship that, for boys, persists into early childhood. Furthermore, fetal activity is linked to infant temperament. In one study, more active fetuses during the third trimester became 1-year-olds who could better handle frustration and 2-year-olds who were less fearful, in that they more readily interacted with toys and an unfamiliar adult in a laboratory (Groome et al., 1999; Pietro et al., 2002). Perhaps fetal activity level is an indicator of healthy neurological development, which fosters adaptability in childhood. The relationships just described, however, are only modest. As we will see in Chapter 7, sensitive caregiving can modify the temperaments of children who have difficulty adapting to new experiences.

© LENNART NILSSON, *A CHILD IS BORN*/BONNIERS

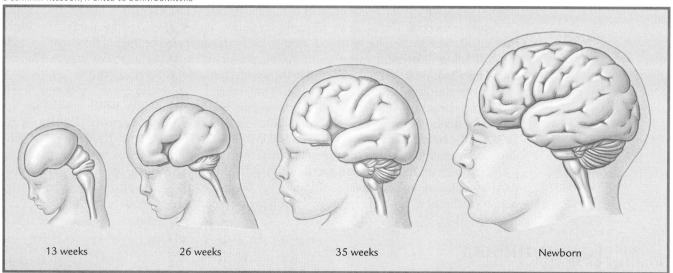

13 weeks   26 weeks   35 weeks   Newborn

FIGURE 3.5

Growth of the brain during the prenatal period, shown one-half actual size.

The cerebral cortex, the outer layer of gray matter, is responsible for higher brain functions, including sensation, voluntary movement, and thought. At 13 weeks, its surface is smooth. By 26 weeks (beginning of the third trimester), grooves and convolutions start to appear. These permit a dramatic increase in surface area without extensive increase in head size. As a result, maximum prenatal brain growth takes place, while still permitting the full-term baby's head to pass through the birth canal. As cortical folds become more apparent (35 weeks), fetal sensory and behavioral capacities expand. The fetus spends more time awake, responds to external stimulation, and moves more vigorously (although less often as it fills the uterus). It also learns to prefer familiar sounds, such as the tone and rhythm of the mother's voice. (Adapted from Moore, Persaud, & Shiota, 1994.)

    The third trimester also brings greater responsiveness to external stimulation. Around 24 weeks, fetuses can first feel pain, so after this time painkillers should be used in any surgical procedures (Royal College of Obstetricians and Gynecologists, 1997). When Yolanda turned on an electric mixer, the fetus reacted with a forceful startle. By 28 weeks, fetuses blink their eyes in reaction to nearby sounds (Kisilevsky & Low, 1998). Soon they distinguish the tone and rhythm of different voices. They show systematic heart rate changes to a male versus a female speaker, and to the mother versus a

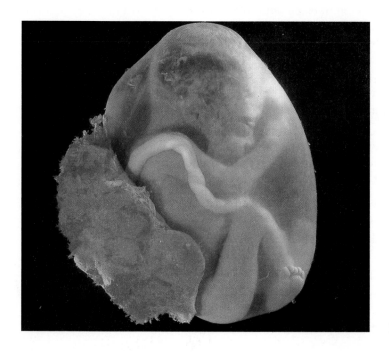

Period of the fetus: thirty-sixth week. This fetus fills the uterus. To support its need for nourishment, the umbilical cord and placenta have grown large. Notice the vernix (cheeselike substance) on the skin, which protects it from chapping. The fetus has accumulated a layer of fat to assist with temperature regulation after birth. In 2 more weeks, it would be full term.

stranger (Kisilevsky et al., 2003; Lecanuet et al., 1993). And in one clever study, mothers read aloud Dr. Seuss's lively book *The Cat in the Hat* each day during the last 6 weeks of pregnancy. After birth, their infants were given a chance to suck on nipples that turned on recordings of their mother reading this book or different rhyming stories. The infants sucked hardest to hear *The Cat in the Hat,* the sound they had come to know while still in the womb (DeCasper & Spence, 1986).

During the final 3 months, the fetus gains more than 5 pounds and grows 7 inches. As it fills the uterus, it gradually moves less often. In addition, brain development, which enables the organism to inhibit behavior, may also contribute to a decline in physical activity (DiPietro et al., 1996). In the eighth month, a layer of fat is added to assist with temperature regulation. The fetus also receives antibodies from the mother's blood to protect against illnesses, since the newborn's own immune system will not work well until several months after birth. In the last weeks, most fetuses assume an upside-down position, partly because of the shape of the uterus and partly because the head is heavier than the feet. Growth slows, and birth is about to take place.

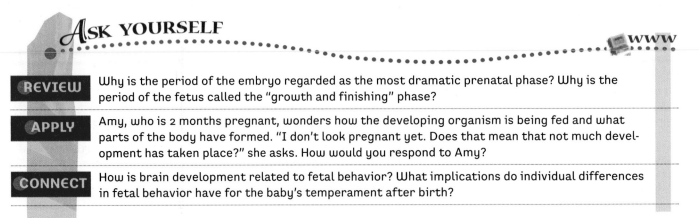

Ask YOURSELF www

REVIEW Why is the period of the embryo regarded as the most dramatic prenatal phase? Why is the period of the fetus called the "growth and finishing" phase?

APPLY Amy, who is 2 months pregnant, wonders how the developing organism is being fed and what parts of the body have formed. "I don't look pregnant yet. Does that mean that not much development has taken place?" she asks. How would you respond to Amy?

CONNECT How is brain development related to fetal behavior? What implications do individual differences in fetal behavior have for the baby's temperament after birth?

Prenatal Environmental Influences

Although the prenatal environment is far more constant than the world outside the womb, a great many factors can affect the embryo and fetus. Yolanda and Jay learned that they could do a great deal to create a safe environment for development before birth. Let's look at some factors that can influence the prenatal environment.

Teratogens

The term **teratogen** refers to any environmental agent that causes damage during the prenatal period. It comes from the Greek word *teras,* meaning "malformation" or "monstrosity." Scientists selected this label because they first learned about harmful prenatal influences from cases in which babies had been profoundly damaged. Yet the harm done by teratogens is not always simple and straightforward. It depends on the following factors:

- *Dose.* We will see as we discuss particular teratogens that larger doses over longer time periods usually have more negative effects.
- *Heredity.* The genetic makeup of the mother and the developing organism plays an important role. Some individuals are better able to withstand harmful environments.
- *Other negative influences.* The presence of several negative factors at once, such as poor nutrition, lack of medical care, and additional teratogens, can worsen the impact of a single harmful agent.
- *Age.* The effects of teratogens vary with the age of the organism at time of exposure.

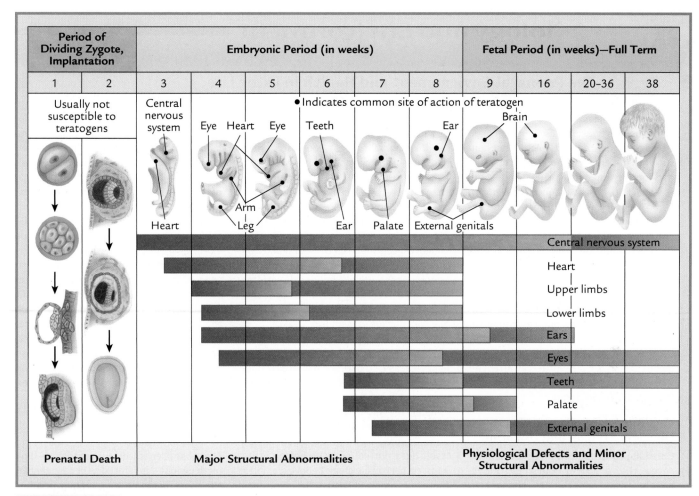

FIGURE 3.6

Sensitive periods in prenatal development.

Each organ or structure has a sensitive period, during which its development may be disturbed. Blue horizontal bars indicate highly sensitive periods. Green horizontal bars indicate periods that are somewhat less sensitive to teratogens, although damage can occur. (Adapted from K. L. Moore & T. V. N. Persaud, 2003, *Before We Are Born,* 6th ed., Philadelphia: Saunders, p. 130. Reprinted by permission of the publisher and authors.)

We can best understand this last idea if we think of the *sensitive period* concept introduced in Chapter 1. A sensitive period is a limited time span in which a part of the body or a behavior is biologically prepared to develop rapidly. During that time, it is especially sensitive to its surroundings. If the environment is harmful, then damage occurs, and recovery is difficult and sometimes impossible.

Figure 3.6 summarizes prenatal sensitive periods. Look carefully at it, and you will see that some parts of the body, such as the brain and eye, have long sensitive periods that extend throughout the prenatal phase. Other sensitive periods, such as those for the limbs and palate, are much shorter. Figure 3.6 also indicates that we can make some general statements about the timing of harmful influences. In the period of the zygote, before implantation, teratogens rarely have any impact. If they do, the tiny mass of cells is usually so completely damaged that it dies. The embryonic period is the time when serious defects are most likely to occur because the foundations for all body parts are being laid down. During the fetal period, teratogenic damage is usually minor. However, some organs, such as the brain, eye, and genitals, can still be strongly affected.

The effects of teratogens are not limited to immediate physical damage. Some health outcomes are subtle and delayed. As the Biology and Environment box on pages 108–109 illustrates,

Biology and Environment

The Prenatal Environment and Health in Later Life

When Michael entered the world 55 years ago, 6 weeks premature and weighing only 4 pounds, the doctor delivering him wasn't sure he would make it. Michael not only survived but enjoyed good health until his mid-forties, when, during a routine medical checkup, he was diagnosed with high blood pressure and adult-onset diabetes. Michael wasn't overweight, didn't smoke, and didn't eat high-fat foods—risk factors for these conditions. Nor did the illnesses run in his family. Could the roots of Michael's health problems date back to his prenatal development? Increasing evidence suggests that prenatal environmental factors—ones not toxic (like tobacco or alcohol) but rather fairly subtle, such as the flow of nutrients and hormones across the placenta—can affect an individual's health decades later (Wheeler, Barker, & O'Brien, 1999).

Low Birth Weight and Heart Disease, Stroke, and Diabetes

Carefully controlled animal experiments reveal that a poorly nourished, underweight fetus experiences changes in body structure and function that result in cardiovascular disease in adulthood (Franco et al., 2002). To explore this relationship in humans, researchers tapped public records, gathering information on the birth weights of 15,000 British men and women and the occurrence of disease in middle adulthood. Those weighing less than 5 pounds at birth had a 50 percent greater chance of dying of heart disease and stroke, after SES and a variety of other health risks were controlled. The connection between birth weight and cardiovascular disease was strongest for people whose weight-to-length ratio at birth was very low—a sign of prenatal growth stunting (Godfrey & Barker, 2000; Martyn, Barker, & Osmond, 1996).

In other large-scales studies, a consistent link between low birth weight and heart disease, stroke, and diabetes in middle adulthood has emerged—for both sexes and in several countries, including Finland, India, Jamaica, and the United States (Barker et al., 2002; Forsén et al., 2000; Godfrey & Barker, 2001). Smallness itself does not cause later health problems; rather, researchers believe, complex factors associated with it are involved.

Some speculate that a poorly nourished fetus diverts large amounts of blood to the brain, causing organs in the abdomen, such as the liver and kidneys (involved in controlling cholesterol and blood pressure), to be undersized (Barker, 2002). The result is heightened later risk for heart disease and stroke. In the case of diabetes, inadequate prenatal nutrition may permanently impair functioning of the pancreas, leading glucose intolerance to rise as the person ages (Rich-Edwards et al., 1999). Yet another hypothesis, supported by both animal and human research, is that the malfunctioning placentas of some expectant mothers permit high levels of stress hormones to reach the fetus. These hormones retard fetal growth, increase fetal blood pressure, and promote hyperglycemia (excess blood sugar), predisposing the developing person to later disease (Osmond & Barker, 2000).

High Birth Weight and Breast Cancer

The other prenatal growth extreme—high birth weight—is related to breast cancer, the most common malignancy in adult women (Andersson et al., 2001; Vatten et al., 2002). In one study, the mothers of 589

they may not show up for decades. Furthermore, psychological consequences may occur indirectly, as a result of physical damage. For example, a defect resulting from drugs the mother took during pregnancy can change the reactions of others to the child as well as the child's ability to move about the environment. Over time, parent–child interaction, peer relations, and opportunities to explore may suffer. These experiences, in turn, can have far-reaching consequences for cognitive, emotional, and social development.

Notice how an important idea about development discussed in earlier chapters is at work here—that of *bidirectional influences* between child and environment. Now let's take a look at what scientists have discovered about a variety of teratogens.

PRESCRIPTION AND NONPRESCRIPTION DRUGS ● In the early 1960s, the world learned a tragic lesson about drugs and prenatal development. At that time, a sedative called **thalidomide** was widely available in Canada, Europe, and South America. When taken by mothers 4 to 6 weeks after conception, thalidomide produced gross deformities of the embryo's developing arms and legs and, less frequently, damage to the ears, heart, kidneys, and genitals. About 7,000 infants worldwide were affected (Moore & Persaud, 2003). As children exposed to thalidomide grew older, many scored below average in intelligence. Perhaps the drug damaged the central nervous system directly. Or the child-rearing conditions of these severely deformed youngsters may have impaired their intellectual development.

nurses with invasive breast cancer and of 1,569 nurses who did not have breast cancer were asked to provide their daughters' birth weights, early life exposures (for example, smoking during pregnancy), and a family health history (such as relatives diagnosed with breast cancer). The nurses themselves provided information on their adult health. After other risk factors were controlled, high birth weight—especially more than 8.7 pounds—emerged as a clear predictor of breast cancer (see Figure 3.7) (Michels et al., 1996). Researchers think that the culprit is excessive maternal estrogen during pregnancy, which promotes large fetal size and alters beginning breast tissue so that it may respond to estrogen in adulthood by becoming malignant.

Prevention

The prenatal development–later-life illness relationships emerging in research do not mean that the illnesses are inevitable. Rather, prenatal environmental conditions *influence* adult health, and the steps we take to protect our health can prevent prenatal risks from becoming reality. Researchers advise individuals who were low-weight at birth to get regular medical checkups and to be attentive to diet, weight, fitness, and stress—controllable factors that contribute to heart disease and adult-onset diabetes. And high-birth-weight women should be conscientious about breast self-exams and mammograms, which permit breast cancer to be detected early and, in many instances, cured.

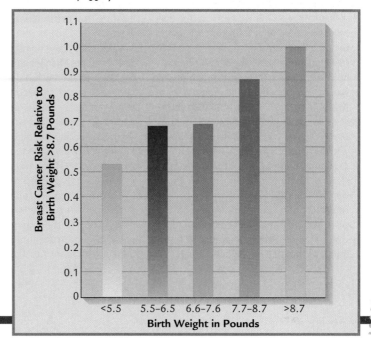

FIGURE 3.7

Relationship of birth weight to breast cancer risk in adulthood.

In a study of 589 nurses with invasive breast cancer and 1,569 nurses who did not have breast cancer, birth weight predicted breast cancer incidence after many other prenatal and postnatal health risks were controlled. The breast cancer risk was especially high for women whose birth weights were greater than 8.7 pounds. (Adapted from Michels et al., 1996.)

Currently, thalidomide is being prescribed to treat *erythema nodosum,* a rare but painful skin inflammation associated with flulike symptoms. It also may prove useful for a variety of other diseases. Consequently, some researchers worry about a resurgence of thalidomide-caused birth defects (Ances, 2002). Turn to the Social Issues: Health box on pages 110–111 to find out about another drug, prescribed to treat severe acne, that has sparked similar concerns.

Another medication, a synthetic hormone called *diethylstilbestrol (DES),* was widely prescribed between 1945 and 1970 to prevent miscarriages. As daughters of these mothers reached adolescence and young adulthood, they showed unusually high rates of cancer of the vagina, malformations of the uterus, and infertility. And their pregnancies more often resulted in prematurity, low birth weight, and miscarriage than those of non-DES-exposed women. Young men showed an increased risk of genital abnormalities and cancer of the testes (Hammes & Laitman, 2003; Palmer et al., 2001).

Any drug taken by the mother that has a molecule small enough to penetrate the placental barrier can enter the embryonic or fetal bloodstream. Despite the bitter lesson of thalidomide, many pregnant women take over-the-counter drugs without consulting their doctors. Aspirin is one of the most common. Several studies suggest that regular aspirin use is linked to low birth weight, infant death around the time of birth, poorer motor development, and lower intelligence test scores in early childhood, although other research fails to confirm these findings (Barr et al., 1990; Hauth et al., 1995; Streissguth et al., 1987). Coffee, tea, cola, and cocoa contain another

Social Issues: Health

Can a Thalidomide-Like Tragedy Occur Again? The Teratogenic Effects of Accutane

Twenty-five-year-old Corrine, several weeks pregnant, suffered from severe, disfiguring acne. After several milder medications failed to clear up the inflamed, hard bumps covering her face, Corrine's dermatologist prescribed the drug Accutane, also known by the generic name *isotretinoin*—a vitamin A derivative. Within days, Corinne's acne receded.

We depend on vitamin A for the health of our skin, hair, mucous membranes, and immune system. But in excess, vitamin A and its derivatives are toxic to the developing organism. Taken during the first trimester of pregnancy, Accutane causes extensive damage, including eye, ear, skull, brain, heart, central nervous system, and immune system abnormalities. Corrine's baby was born with multiple defects, including heart disease, facial deformities, and hydrocephalus (accumulation of excess fluid, which compresses and damages the brain). After extensive treatment, including heart surgery, he died at 9 weeks of age.

Accutane is the most widely used, potent teratogen since the thalidomide disaster of nearly a half-century ago (Accutane Action Group Forum, 2003). Since its release in the early 1980s, 12 million people in some 100 countries have been treated with it. Hundreds of thousands of American and Canadian women of childbearing age currently take Accutane, and the number of prescriptions is increasing. Despite its established teratogenic effects, about 2,000 reports of drug-exposed pregnancies have occurred in the United States alone. Miscarriage rates among affected women are high, and many others choose to end their pregnancies once they learn about possible prenatal damage. Although the number of babies born with Accutane-caused malformations is not known, at least 156 documented American cases exist (Hoffmann-La Roche, 2000).

Accutane's packaging warns users to avoid pregnancy and also states that the drug must not be used by women who are pregnant. Furthermore, early case reports of infants damaged by the drug caused the manufacturer to step up efforts to get doctors to inform patients about the importance of abstaining from intercourse or using two methods of birth control if taking Accutane. The drug company will even pay for birth control counseling and contraceptives. Why, then, do Accutane-exposed pregnancies continue to occur?

To find out, researchers interviewed women who became pregnant while taking Accutane. Findings revealed that most did not use two forms of contraception, and more than half reported at least one instance in which they used none at all! Either their doctors had failed to communicate the risks, or the patients had not been receptive to the warnings. Furthermore, only half the women had acne severe enough to warrant Accutane treatment (Honein, Paulozzi, & Erickson, 2001). Doctors were over-prescribing the drug, using it even to treat mild skin inflammations! Other evidence indicates that some women purchase the medication in foreign countries, use a "leftover" prescription, or "borrow" medication from a friend, without following manu-

---

frequently consumed drug, caffeine. Heavy caffeine intake (more than 3 cups of coffee per day) is associated with low birth weight, miscarriage, and newborn withdrawal symptoms, such as irritability and vomiting (Fernandes et al., 1998; Gilbert-Barness, 2000; Klebanoff et al., 2002).

Because children's lives are involved, we must take findings like these seriously. At the same time, we cannot be sure that these drugs actually cause the problems just mentioned. Imagine how difficult it is to study the effects of many substances on the unborn! Often mothers take more than one kind of drug. If the prenatal organism is injured, it is hard to tell which drug might be responsible or whether other factors correlated with drug taking are really at fault. Until we have more information, the safest course is the one Yolanda took: Cut down or avoid these drugs entirely.

ILLEGAL DRUGS ● The use of highly addictive mood-altering drugs, such as cocaine and heroin, has become more widespread, especially in poverty-stricken inner-city areas, where drugs provide a temporary escape from a daily life of hopelessness. The number of "cocaine babies" born in the United States has reached crisis levels in recent years, amounting to hundreds of thousands annually (Cornelius et al., 1999).

Babies born to users of cocaine, heroin, or methadone (a less addictive drug used to wean people away from heroin) are at risk for a wide variety of problems, including prematurity, low birth weight, physical defects, breathing difficulties, and death around the time of birth (Behnke et al., 2001; Walker, Rosenberg, & Balaban-Gil, 1999). In addition, these infants arrive drug addicted. They often are feverish and irritable at birth and have trouble sleeping, and their cries are abnormally shrill and piercing—a common symptom among stressed newborns (Friedman, 1996; Ostrea, facturer recommendations for monthly pregnancy testing and effective birth control (Robertson et al., 2002).

Unlike thalidomide, which was released before its catastrophic consequences were known, Accutane's teratogenic effects were established when the drug was first marketed. Yet barriers to preventing prenatal exposure persist. As many as 40 percent of pregnancies in

Canada and 50 percent in the United States are unintended (Childbirth by Choice, 1999; Henshaw, 1998). Because these women are not planning a pregnancy, they are less likely to avoid drug taking and less responsive to teratogen counseling. Furthermore, both doctors and patients are slow to comply with instruction aimed at preventing prenatal exposures (Atanackovic & Koren, 1999).

And some patients misunderstand warnings. For example, one study showed that users frequently misinterpret the teratogen symbol that appears on bottles of Accutane and thalidomide: They took it to mean that a woman could not get pregnant while taking the drug—a conclusion that increases the risk of pregnancy exposures (Honein et al., 2002).

Notice how a combination of factors—biological, psychological, and environmental—jointly contribute to Accutane prenatal risks. Consequently, multifaceted efforts are needed to prevent Accutane from spiraling into a thalidomide-like tragedy. These include:

● restricting teratogenic drugs to treatment of severe medical conditions, for which there are no alternatives;

● improved public and patient education about teratogenic effects and protective strategies; and

● interventions that promote widespread, effective contraceptive use and family planning.

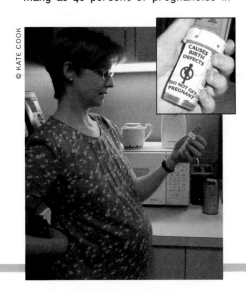

© KATE COOK

Accutane is the most widely used, potent teratogenic drug in the industrialized world. If a woman becomes pregnant and takes the drug during the first trimester, her baby is likely to suffer from multiple, severe physical defects. Accutane-exposed pregnancies continue to occur because doctors sometimes fail to communicate the risks and patients are not always receptive to warnings. And many women misinterpret the teratogen symbol that appears on Accutane bottles as indicating that a woman cannot get pregnant while using the drug!

Ostrea, & Simpson, 1997). When mothers with many problems of their own must take care of these babies, who are difficult to calm down, cuddle, and feed, behavior problems are likely to persist.

Throughout the first year, heroin- and methadone-exposed infants are less attentive to the environment, and their motor development is slow. After infancy, some children get better, whereas others remain jittery and inattentive. The kind of parenting these youngsters receive seems to explain why problems last for some but not for others (Cosden, Peerson, & Elliott, 1997).

Evidence on cocaine suggests that some prenatally exposed babies develop lasting difficulties. Cocaine constricts the blood vessels, causing oxygen delivered to the developing organism to fall for 15 minutes following a high dose. It also can alter the production and functioning of neurons and the chemical balance in the fetus's brain. These effects may contribute to an array of cocaine-associated physical defects, including eye, bone, genital, urinary tract, kidney, and heart deformities, brain hemorrhages and seizures, and severe growth retardation (Covington et al., 2002; Espy, Kaufmann, & Glisky, 1999; Mayes, 1999). Several studies report perceptual, motor, attention, memory, and language problems in infancy that persist into the preschool years (Lester et al., 2003; Richardson et al., 1996; Singer et al., 2002a, 2002b).

But other investigations reveal no major negative effects of prenatal cocaine exposure (Frank et al., 2001; Zuckerman, Frank, & Mayes, 2002). These contradictory findings indicate how difficult it is to isolate the precise damage caused by illegal drugs. Cocaine users vary greatly in the amount, potency, and purity of the cocaine they ingest. Also, they often take several drugs, display other high-risk behaviors, suffer from poverty and other stresses, and engage in insensitive caregiving (Lester, 2000). The joint impact of these factors worsens outcomes for children (Alessandri, Bendersky, &

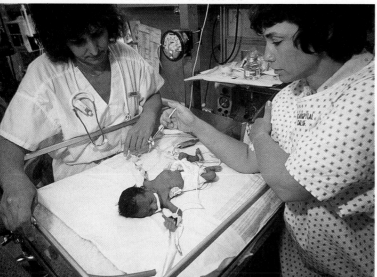

This baby, whose mother took crack during pregnancy, was born many weeks before his due date. He breathes with the aid of a respirator. His central nervous system may be damaged. Researchers are not yet sure if these outcomes are caused by crack or by the many other high-risk behaviors of drug users.

Lewis, 1998; Chasnoff et al., 1998). But researchers have yet to determine exactly what accounts for findings of cocaine-related damage in some studies but not in others.

Another illegal drug, marijuana, is used more widely than heroin and cocaine. Studies examining its relationship to low birth weight and prematurity reveal mixed findings (Fried, 1993). Several researchers have linked prenatal marijuana exposure to smaller head size (a measure of brain growth), disturbed sleep and attention and memory difficulties in childhood, and poorer problem-solving performance in adolescence (Dahl et al., 1995; Fried, Watkinson, & Gray, 1998; Fried, 2002a, 2002b). As with cocaine, however, lasting consequences are not well established. Overall, the effects of illegal drugs are far less consistent than the impact of two legal substances to which we now turn: tobacco and alcohol.

TOBACCO ● Although smoking has declined in Western nations, an estimated 12 percent of American women and 19 percent of Canadian women smoke during their pregnancies (Health Canada, 2001b; Ventura et al., 2003). The most well-known effect of smoking during pregnancy is low birth weight. But the likelihood of other serious consequences, such as miscarriage, prematurity, impaired heart rate and breathing during sleep, infant death, and cancer later in childhood, is also increased (Franco et al., 2000; Walker, Rosenberg, & Balaban-Gil, 1999). The more cigarettes a mother smokes, the greater the chances that her baby will be affected. If a pregnant woman decides to stop smoking at any time, even during the last trimester, she can help her baby. She immediately reduces the chances that the infant will be born underweight and suffer from future problems (Klesges et al., 2001).

Even when a baby of a smoking mother appears to be born in good physical condition, slight behavioral abnormalities may threaten the child's development. Newborns of smoking mothers are less attentive to sounds, display more muscle tension, are more excitable when touched and visually stimulated, and more often have colic (persistent crying)—findings that suggest subtle negative effects on brain development (Law et al., 2003; Sondergaard et al., 2002). Furthermore, an unresponsive, restless baby may not evoke the kind of interaction from adults that promotes healthy psychological development. Some studies report that prenatally exposed youngsters have shorter attention spans, poorer memories, lower mental test scores, and more behavior problems in childhood and adolescence, after many other factors have been controlled (Cornelius et al., 2001; Trasti et al., 1999; Wasserman et al., 2001). However, factors associated with smoking, such as lower maternal education and income, may contribute to these outcomes (Ernst, Moolchan, & Robinson, 2001).

Exactly how can smoking harm the fetus? Nicotine, the addictive substance in tobacco, constricts blood vessels, lessens blood flow to the uterus, and causes the placenta to grow abnormally. This reduces the transfer of nutrients, so the fetus gains weight poorly. Also, nicotine raises the concentration of carbon monoxide in the bloodstreams of both mother and fetus. Carbon monoxide displaces oxygen from red blood cells, damaging the central nervous system and slowing body growth in the fetuses of laboratory animals. Similar effects may occur in humans (Friedman, 1996).

From one-third to one-half of nonsmoking pregnant women are "passive smokers" because their husbands, relatives, and co-workers use cigarettes. Passive smoking is also related to low birth weight, infant death, and possible long-term impairments in attention and learning (Dejin-Karlsson et al., 1998; Makin, Fried, & Watkinson, 1991). Clearly, expectant mothers should avoid smoke-filled environments.

ALCOHOL ● In a moving story, Michael Dorris (1989), a Dartmouth University anthropology professor, described what it was like to raise his adopted son Adam, whose biological mother drank heavily throughout pregnancy and died of alcohol poisoning shortly after his birth. A

Sioux Indian, Adam was born with **fetal alcohol syndrome (FAS).** Mental retardation; impaired motor coordination, attention, memory, and language; and overactivity are typical of children with the disorder (Connor et al., 2001; Schonfeld et al., 2001). Distinct physical symptoms also accompany it, including slow physical growth and a particular pattern of facial abnormalities: widely spaced eyes, short eyelid openings, a small upturned nose, a thin upper lip, and a small head, indicating that the brain has not developed fully. Other defects—of the eyes, ears, nose, throat, heart, genitals, urinary tract, or immune system—may also be present.

In a related condition, known as **fetal alcohol effects (FAE),** individuals display only some of these abnormalities. Usually, their mothers drank alcohol in smaller quantities. The defects of FAE children vary with the timing and length of alcohol exposure during pregnancy (Goodlett & Johnson, 1999; Mattson et al., 1998).

Even when provided with enriched diets, FAS babies fail to catch up in physical size during infancy or childhood. Mental impairment is also permanent: In his teens and twenties, Adam had trouble concentrating and keeping a routine job. He also suffered from poor judgment. For example, he would buy something and not wait for change, or he would wander off in the middle of a task. The more alcohol consumed by a woman during pregnancy, the poorer the child's motor coordination, speed of information processing, reasoning, and intelligence and achievement test scores during the preschool and school years (Aronson, Hagberg, & Gillberg, 1997; Hunt et al., 1995; Jacobson et al., 1993). In adolescence, FAS is associated with poor school performance, trouble with the law, inappropriate sexual behavior, alcohol and drug abuse, and lasting mental health problems (Kelly, Day, & Streissguth, 2000). Adolescents with FAS who escape mental retardation still have serious cognitive impairments, including deficits in attention, memory, planning, and spatial abilities (Olson et al., 1998).

How does alcohol produce its devastating effects? First, it interferes with cell duplication and migration in the primitive neural tube. Psychophysiological measures, such as fMRI and EEGs, reveal structural damage and abnormalities in brain functioning, including electrical and chemical activity involved in transferring messages from one part of the brain to another (Bookstein et al., 2002; Goodlett & Horn, 2001). Second, the body uses large quantities of oxygen to metabolize alcohol. A pregnant woman's heavy drinking draws away oxygen that the developing organism needs for cell growth.

About 25 percent of American and Canadian mothers reported drinking at some time during their pregnancies. As with heroin and cocaine, alcohol abuse is higher in poverty-stricken women (Health Canada, 2003b; U.S. Department of Health and Human Services, 2003c). On the reservation where Adam was born, many children show symptoms of prenatal alcohol exposure. Unfortunately, when girls with FAS or FAE later become pregnant, the poor judgment caused by the syndrome often prevents them from understanding why they should avoid alcohol themselves. Thus, the tragic cycle is likely to be repeated in the next generation.

How much alcohol is safe during pregnancy? Even mild drinking, less than one drink per day, is associated with reduced head size and body growth among children followed into adolescence (Day et al., 2002). And as little as 2 ounces of alcohol a day, taken very early in pregnancy, is linked to FAS-like facial features (Astley et al., 1992). Recall that other factors—both genetic and environmental—can make some fetuses more vulnerable to teratogens. Therefore, no amount of alcohol is safe, and pregnant women should avoid it entirely.

RADIATION ● In Chapter 2, we saw that ionizing radiation can cause mutation, damaging DNA in ova and sperm. When mothers are exposed to radiation during pregnancy, additional harm can come to the embryo or fetus. Defects due to radiation were tragically apparent in the

(Top) The mother of these twin baby girls drank heavily during pregnancy. Their widely spaced eyes, thin upper lip, and short eyelid openings are typical of fetal alcohol syndrome (FAS). In addition, the twins are growing slowly. They are much shorter and lighter than the typical North American 1-year-old. (Bottom) The adolescent girl shown here also has symptoms of FAS. The brain damage alcohol caused before she was born is permanent, making learning in school and adapting to everyday challenges extremely difficult.

This child's mother was just a few weeks pregnant during the Chernobyl nuclear power plant disaster. Radiation exposure probably is responsible for his limb deformities. He also is at risk for low intelligence and language and emotional disorders.

© CHARLTON-BOURDILLON/GAMMA PRESSE

children born to pregnant Japanese women who survived the bombing of Hiroshima and Nagasaki during World War II. Similar abnormalities surfaced in the 9 months following the 1986 Chernobyl, Ukraine, nuclear power plant accident. After each disaster, the incidence of miscarriage and babies born with underdeveloped brains, physical deformities, and slow physical growth rose dramatically (Hoffmann, 2001; Schull & Otake, 1999).

Even when a radiation-exposed baby seems normal, problems may appear later. For example, even low-level radiation, as the result of industrial leakage or medical X-rays, can increase the risk of childhood cancer (Fattibene et al., 1999). In middle childhood, prenatally exposed Chernobyl children showed abnormal EEG brain-wave activity, lower intelligence test scores, and rates of language and emotional disorders two to three times greater than those of nonexposed Russian children. Furthermore, Chernobyl children's parents were highly anxious, due to forced evacuation from their homes and worries about living in irradiated areas. The more tension parents reported, the poorer their children's emotional functioning (Kolominsky, Igumnov, & Drozdovitch, 1999; Loganovskaja & Loganovsky, 1999). Stressful rearing conditions seemed to combine with the damaging effects of prenatal radiation to impair children's development.

ENVIRONMENTAL POLLUTION ● Yolanda and Jay like to refinish antique furniture in their garage, and Jay enjoys growing fruit trees in the backyard. When Yolanda became pregnant, they postponed work on several pieces of furniture, and Jay did not spray the fruit trees in the fall and spring of that year. Continuing to do so, they learned, might expose Yolanda and the embryo or fetus to chemical levels thousands of times greater than judged safe by the federal government. In industrialized nations, an astounding number of potentially dangerous chemicals are released into the environment. Over 100,000 are in common use in the United States, and many new pollutants are introduced each year.

Mercury is an established teratogen. In the 1950s, an industrial plant released waste containing high levels of mercury into a bay providing food and water for the town of Minimata, Japan. Many children born at the time displayed physical deformities, mental retardation, abnormal speech, difficulty in chewing and swallowing, and uncoordinated movements. Autopsies of those who died revealed widespread brain damage (Dietrich, 1999).

Another teratogen, *lead,* is present in paint flaking off the walls of old buildings and in certain materials used in industrial occupations. High levels of prenatal lead exposure are consistently related to prematurity, low birth weight, brain damage, and a wide variety of physical defects (Dye-White, 1986). Even low levels seem to be dangerous. Affected babies show slightly poorer mental and motor development (Dietrich, Berger, & Succop, 1993; Wasserman et al., 1994).

For many years, *polychlorinated biphenyls (PCBs)* were used to insulate electrical equipment, until research showed that, like mercury, they found their way into waterways and entered the food supply. In Taiwan, prenatal exposure to very high levels of PCBs in rice oil resulted in low birth weight, discolored skin, deformities of the gums and nails, brain-wave abnormalities, and delayed cognitive development (Chen & Hsu, 1994; Chen et al., 1994). Steady, low-level PCB exposure is also harmful. Compared with those who ate little or no fish, women who frequently ate PCB-contaminated fish had infants with lower birth weights, smaller heads, more intense physiological reactions to stress, and less interest in their surroundings (Jacobson et al., 1984; Stewart et al., 2000). Follow-ups later in the first year and in early childhood revealed persisting memory difficulties and lower intelligence test scores (Jacobson, 1998; Walkowiak et al., 2001).

INFECTIOUS DISEASE ● On her first prenatal visit, Yolanda's doctor asked if she and Jay had already had measles, mumps, and chicken pox, as well as other illnesses. In addition, Yolanda was checked for the presence of several infections, and for good reason. As you can see in Table 3.4 on page 116, certain diseases are major causes of miscarriage and birth defects.

Viruses. Five percent of women catch a virus of some sort while pregnant. Most of these illnesses, such as the common cold and various strains of the flu, have no impact on the embryo or fetus. However, a few can result in extensive damage.

The best known of these is rubella, otherwise known as 3-day or German measles. In the mid-1960s, a worldwide epidemic of rubella led to the birth of more than 20,000 North American babies with serious defects. Consistent with the sensitive-period concept, the greatest damage occurs when rubella strikes during the embryonic period. More than 50 percent of infants whose mothers become ill during that time show eye cataracts; deafness; heart, genital, urinary, and intestinal defects; and mental retardation (Eberhart-Phillips, Frederick, & Baron, 1993). Infection during the fetal period is less harmful, but low birth weight, hearing loss, and bone defects may still occur. And the brain abnormalities resulting from prenatal rubella increase the risk of severe mental illness, especially schizophrenia, in adulthood (Brown & Susser, 2002).

Since 1996, infants and young children have been routinely vaccinated against rubella, so prenatal cases today are far fewer than they were a generation ago. Still, 10 to 20 percent of women in North America and Western Europe lack the rubella antibody, so new disease outbreaks are possible (Health Canada, 2002f; Pebody et al., 2000).

The *human immunodeficiency virus (HIV),* which can lead to **acquired immune deficiency syndrome (AIDS),** a disease that destroys the immune system, has infected increasing numbers of women over the past decade. Currently, women account for 16 percent of AIDS victims in the United States and for 25 percent in Canada (Centers for Disease Control and Prevention, 2003; Health Canada, 2003c). Although the incidence of AIDS has declined in industrialized nations, the disease is rampant in developing countries, where 95 percent of new infections occur, more than half affecting women. In South Africa, for example, one-fourth of all pregnant women are HIV-positive (Kasmauski & Jaret, 2003). They pass the deadly virus to the developing organism 20 to 30 percent of the time.

AIDS progresses rapidly in infants. By 6 months, weight loss, diarrhea, and repeated respiratory illnesses are common. The virus also causes brain damage, as indicated by seizures, gradual loss in brain weight, and delayed mental and motor development. Most prenatal AIDS babies survive for only 5 to 8 months after the appearance of these symptoms (Parks, 1996). The antiviral drug zidovudine (ZDV) reduces prenatal AIDS transmission by as much as 95 percent, with no harmful consequences of drug treatment for children (Culnane et al., 1999). Although ZDV has led to a dramatic decline in prenatally acquired AIDS in industrialized nations, it is not widely available in impoverished regions of the world.

As Table 3.4 reveals, the developing organism is especially sensitive to the family of herpes viruses, for which no vaccine or treatment exists. Among these, *cytomegalovirus* (the most frequent prenatal infection, transmitted through respiratory or sexual contact) and *herpes simplex 2* (which is sexually transmitted) are especially dangerous. In both, the virus invades the mother's genital tract. Babies can be infected either during pregnancy or at birth.

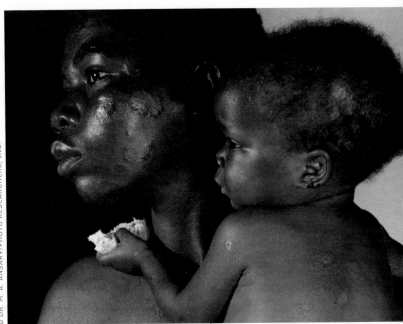

© DR. M. A. ANSARY/PHOTO RESEARCHERS, INC.

In Africa, lack of access to information on how to prevent AIDS and to antiviral drugs that reduce the chances of prenatal AIDS transmission has led to rampant spread of the disease and to many prenatally affected babies. This South African mother and infant have AIDS. Both have extensive ringworm skin rashes. Their weakened immune systems make normally harmless infections life threatening. Because AIDS progresses rapidly in infants, the baby may live only for a few more months.

TABLE 3.4

Effects of Some Infectious Diseases During Pregnancy

DISEASE	MISCARRIAGE	PHYSICAL MALFORMATIONS	MENTAL RETARDATION	LOW BIRTH WEIGHT AND PREMATURITY
Viral				
Acquired immune deficiency syndrome (AIDS)	o	?	+	?
Chicken pox	o	+	+	+
Cytomegalovirus	+	+	+	+
Herpes simplex 2 (genital herpes)	+	+	+	+
Mumps	+	?	o	o
Rubella (German measles)	+	+	+	+
Bacterial				
Syphilis	+	+	+	?
Tuberculosis	+	?	+	+
Parasitic				
Malaria	+	o	o	+
Toxoplasmosis	+	+	+	+

+ = established finding, o = no present evidence, ? = possible effect that is not clearly established.
Sources: Behrman, Kliegman, & Jenson, 2000; O'Rahilly & Müller, 2001; Parks, 1996; Jones, Lopez, & Wilson, 2003.

Bacterial and Parasitic Diseases. Table 3.4 also includes several bacterial and parasitic diseases. Among the most common is **toxoplasmosis,** an infection caused by a parasite found in many animals. Pregnant women may become infected from eating raw or undercooked meat or from contact with the feces of infected cats. About 40 percent of women who have the disease transmit it to the developing organism. If it strikes during the first trimester, it is likely to cause eye and brain damage. Infection during the second and third trimesters is linked to mild visual and cognitive impairments. And about 80 percent of affected newborns with no obvious signs of damage develop learning or visual disabilities in later life (Jones, Lopez, & Wilson, 2003). Expectant mothers can avoid toxoplasmosis by making sure that the meat they eat is well cooked, having pet cats checked for the disease, and turning over care of litter boxes to other family members.

●Other Maternal Factors

Besides avoiding teratogens, expectant parents can support the developing organism in other ways. Regular exercise, good nutrition, and emotional well-being of the mother are essential. Difficulties that may result from blood type differences between mother and fetus can be prevented. Finally, many expectant parents wonder how a mother's age affects the course of pregnancy. We examine each of these factors in the following sections.

EXERCISE ● Yolanda continued her half-hour of aerobics three times a week into the third trimester, although her doctor cautioned against bouncing, jolting, and jogging movements that might subject the fetus to too many shocks and startles. In healthy, physically fit women, regular moderate exercise, such as walking, swimming, biking, and aerobics, is related to increased birth weight (Hatch et al., 1993). However, very frequent, vigorous, extended exercise—working up a sweat for more than 30 minutes, four or five days a week, especially late in pregnancy—results in lower birth weight than in healthy controls (Clapp et al., 2002; Pivarnik, 1998). Hospital-sponsored childbirth education programs frequently offer exercise classes and suggest appropriate routines that help prepare for labor and delivery. Exercises that strengthen the back, abdominal, pelvic, and thigh muscles are emphasized, since the growing fetus places some strain on these parts of the body.

During the last trimester, when the abdomen grows very large, mothers have difficulty moving freely and often must cut back on exercise. In most cases, a mother who has remained fit during the earlier months experiences fewer physical discomforts, such as back pain, upward pressure on the chest, and difficulty breathing.

Pregnant women with health problems, such as circulatory difficulties or a history of miscarriages, should consult their doctors about fitness routines. For these mothers, exercise (especially the wrong kind) can endanger the pregnancy.

NUTRITION ● Children grow more rapidly during the prenatal period than at any other phase of development. During this time, they depend totally on the mother for nutrients to support their growth. A healthy diet, consisting of a gradual increase in calories—an extra 100 calories a day in the first trimester, 265 in the second, and 430 in the third—resulting in a weight gain of 25 to 30 pounds (10 to 13.5 kilograms), helps ensure the health of mother and baby (Reifsnider & Gill, 2000).

Consequences of Prenatal Malnutrition. During World War II, a severe famine occurred in the Netherlands, giving scientists a rare opportunity to study the impact of nutrition on prenatal development. Findings revealed that the sensitive-period concept operates with nutrition, just as it does with teratogens. Women affected by the famine during the first trimester were more likely to have miscarriages or give birth to babies with physical defects. When women were past the first trimester, fetuses usually survived, but many were born underweight and had small heads (Stein et al., 1975).

We now know that prenatal malnutrition can cause serious damage to the central nervous system. The poorer the mother's diet, the greater the loss in brain weight, especially if malnutrition occurred during the last trimester. During that time, the brain is increasing rapidly in size, and

This government-sponsored nutrition class in a village in India prevents prenatal malnutrition by promoting a proper diet for pregnant women. Mothers also learn how breast-feeding can protect their newborn baby's healthy growth (see Chapter 5, pages 178–179).

© RICHARD LORD/PHOTOEDIT

for it to reach its full potential, the mother must have a diet high in all the basic nutrients (Morgane et al., 1993). An inadequate diet during pregnancy can also distort the structure of other organs, including the liver, kidney, and pancreas, thereby increasing the risk of heart disease, stroke, and diabetes in adulthood (refer again to the Biology and Environment box on pages 108–109).

Because prenatal malnutrition suppresses development of the immune system, prenatally malnourished babies frequently catch respiratory illnesses (Chandra, 1991). In addition, they often are irritable and unresponsive to stimulation. Like drug-addicted newborns, they have a high-pitched cry that is particularly distressing to their caregivers. In poverty-stricken families, these effects quickly combine with a stressful home life. With age, low intelligence test scores and serious learning problems become more apparent (Pollitt, 1996).

Prevention and Treatment. Many studies show that providing pregnant women with adequate food has a substantial impact on the health of their newborn babies. Yet the growth demands of the prenatal period require more than just increasing the quantity of a typical diet. Optimizing maternal nutrition through vitamin–mineral enrichment as early as possible is also crucial.

For example, folic acid can prevent abnormalities of the neural tube, such as anencephaly and spina bifida (see Table 2.6 on page 65). In a study of nearly 2,000 women in seven countries who had previously given birth to a baby with a neural tube defect, half were randomly selected to receive a daily folic acid supplement around the time of conception, and half received a mixture of other vitamins or no supplement. The folic acid group showed 72 percent fewer neural tube defects (MCR Vitamin Study Research Group, 1991). In addition, adequate folate during the last 10 weeks of pregnancy cuts in half the risk of premature delivery and low birth weight (Scholl, Hediger, & Belsky, 1996). Because of these findings, U.S. and Canadian government guidelines recommend that all women of childbearing age consume at least 0.4 but not more than 1 milligram of folic acid per day (excessive intake can be harmful). Currently, bread, flour, rice, pasta, and other grain products are being fortified with folic acid.

Other vitamins and minerals also have established benefits. Enriching women's diets with calcium helps prevent maternal high blood pressure and premature births (Repke, 1992). Adequate magnesium and zinc reduce the risk of many prenatal and birth complications (Facchinetti et al., 1992; Jameson, 1993; Spätling & Spätling, 1988). Fortifying table salt with iodine virtually eradicates cretinism—a common cause of mental retardation and stunted growth in many parts of the world. And sufficient vitamin C and iron beginning early in pregnancy promote growth of the placenta and healthy birth weight (Mathews, Yudkin, & Neil, 1999). Nevertheless, a supplement program should complement, not replace, efforts to improve maternal diets during pregnancy. For women who do not get enough food or an adequate variety of foods, multivitamin tablets are a necessary, but not a sufficient, intervention.

When poor nutrition continues throughout pregnancy, infants often require more than dietary enrichment. Their tired, restless behavior leads mothers to be less sensitive and stimulating. In response, babies become even more passive and withdrawn. Successful interventions must break this cycle of apathetic mother–baby interaction. Some do so by teaching parents how to interact effectively with their infants, whereas others focus on stimulating infants to promote active engagement with their physical and social surroundings (Grantham-McGregor et al., 1994; Zeskind & Ramey, 1978, 1981).

Although prenatal malnutrition is highest in poverty-stricken regions of the world, it is not limited to developing countries. The U.S. Special Supplemental Food Program for Women, Infants, and Children provides food packages and nutrition education to low-income pregnant women, but funding is limited, and only 70 percent of those eligible are served (Children's Defense Fund, 2003). Besides food, the Canada Prenatal Nutrition Program provides counseling, social support, access to health care, and shelter to all pregnant women at risk for poor birth outcomes (Health Canada, 2002b).

EMOTIONAL STRESS ● When women experience severe emotional stress during pregnancy, their babies are at risk for a wide variety of difficulties. Intense prenatal anxiety is associated with a higher rate of miscarriage, prematurity, low birth weight, infant respiratory illness and digestive disturbances, and irritability during the first 3 years (Mulder et al., 2002; Wadhwa, Sandman, & Garite, 2001). It is also related to certain physical defects, such as cleft lip and palate, heart deformities, and pyloric stenosis (tightening of the infant's stomach outlet, which must be treated surgically) (Carmichael & Shaw, 2000).

How can maternal stress affect the developing organism? To understand this process, think back to how your body felt the last time you were under stress. When we experience fear and anxiety, stimulant hormones released into our bloodstream cause us to be "poised for action." Large amounts of blood are sent to parts of the body involved in the defensive response—the brain, the heart, and muscles in the arms, legs, and trunk. Blood flow to other organs, including the uterus, is reduced. As a result, the fetus is deprived of a full supply of oxygen and nutrients. Stress hormones also cross the placenta, leading the fetus's heart rate and activity to rise dramatically. In addition, stress weakens the immune system, making pregnant women more susceptible to infectious disease (Cohen & Williamson, 1991; Monk et al., 2000). Finally, women who experience long-term anxiety are more likely to smoke, drink, eat poorly, and engage in other behaviors that harm the embryo and fetus.

But stress-related prenatal complications are greatly reduced when mothers have husbands, other family members, and friends who offer support (McLean et al., 1993; Nuckolls, Cassel, & Kaplan, 1972). The link between social support and positive pregnancy outcomes is particularly strong for low-income women, who often lead highly stressful lives (Hoffman & Hatch, 1996). Enhancing supportive social networks for pregnant mothers can help prevent prenatal complications.

RH BLOOD INCOMPATIBILITY ● When the inherited blood types of mother and fetus differ, serious problems sometimes result. The most common cause of these difficulties is **Rh factor incompatibility.** When the mother is Rh-negative (lacks the protein) and the father is Rh-positive (has the protein), the baby may inherit the father's Rh-positive blood type. (Recall from Table 2.2 on page 59 that Rh-positive blood is dominant and Rh-negative blood is recessive, so the chances are good that a baby will be Rh-positive.) If even a little of a fetus's Rh-positive blood crosses the placenta into the Rh-negative mother's bloodstream, she begins to form antibodies to the foreign Rh protein. If these enter the fetus's system, they destroy red blood cells, reducing the oxygen supply to organs and tissues. Mental retardation, miscarriage, heart damage, and infant death can occur.

Since it takes time for the mother to produce Rh antibodies, first-born children are rarely affected. The danger increases with each additional pregnancy. Fortunately, the harmful effects of Rh incompatibility can be prevented in most cases. After the birth of each Rh-positive baby, Rh-negative mothers are routinely given a vaccine to prevent the buildup of antibodies. In emergency cases, blood transfusions can be performed immediately after delivery or, if necessary, even before birth.

MATERNAL AGE ● Recall that women who delay having children until their thirties or forties face increased risk of infertility, miscarriage, and babies born with chromosomal defects (see Chapter 2). Are other pregnancy problems more common for older mothers? For many years, scientists thought so. But healthy women in their late thirties and early forties have about the same rate of prenatal and birth problems as those in their twenties (Bianco et al., 1996; Cnattingius et al., 1992; Prysak, Lorenz, & Kisly, 1995). Women in their mid-forties do show higher rates of prenatal complications and medical interventions during birth. But their newborns are just as healthy as those of younger women (Dulitzki et al., 1998).

In the case of teenage mothers, does physical immaturity cause prenatal problems? Again, research shows that it does not. As we will see in Chapter 14, nature tries to ensure that once a girl can conceive, she is physically ready to carry and give birth to a baby. Infants of teenagers are born with a higher rate of problems for quite different reasons. Many pregnant adolescents do not have access to medical care or are afraid to seek it. In addition, most pregnant teenagers come from low-income backgrounds, where stress, poor nutrition, and health problems are common (Coley & Chase-Lansdale, 1998).

The Importance of Prenatal Health Care

Yolanda had her first prenatal appointment 3 weeks after missing her menstrual period. After that, she visited the doctor's office once a month until she was 7 months pregnant, then twice during the eighth month. As birth grew near, Yolanda's appointments increased to once a week. The doctor kept track of her general health, her weight gain, and the capacity of her uterus and cervix to support the fetus. The fetus's growth was also carefully monitored. During these visits, Yolanda asked questions, picked up literature in the waiting room, got to know the person who would deliver her baby, and planned the birth experience she and Jay desired.

Yolanda's pregnancy, like most others, was free of complications. But unexpected difficulties can arise, especially if mothers have health problems. For example, women with diabetes need careful monitoring. Extra sugar in the diabetic mother's bloodstream causes the fetus to grow larger than average, making pregnancy and birth problems more common. Another complication, **toxemia** (sometimes called *eclampsia*), in which blood pressure increases sharply and the face, hands, and feet swell in the second half of pregnancy, is experienced by 5 to 10 percent of pregnant women. If untreated, it can cause convulsions in the mother and fetal death. Usually, hospitalization, bed rest, and drugs can lower blood pressure to a safe level. If not, the baby must be delivered at once (Carlson, Eisenstat, & Ziporyn, 1996).

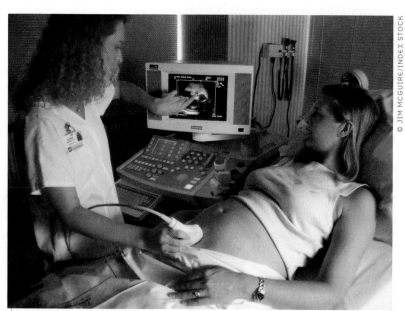

During a routine prenatal visit, this doctor uses ultrasound to show an expectant mother an image of her fetus and to evaluate its development. All pregnant women should receive early and regular prenatal care to protect their own health and the health of their babies.

Unfortunately, 17 percent of pregnant women in the United States wait until after the first trimester to seek prenatal care, and 4 percent receive none at all. As Figure 3.8 shows, inadequate care rises sharply for adolescent and low-income, ethnic minority mothers. Their infants are far more likely to be born underweight and to die before birth or during the first year of life than the babies of mothers who receive early medical attention (U.S. Department of Health and Human Services, 2003f). Why do these mothers delay going to the doctor? One reason is lack of health insurance. Although the very poorest mothers are eligible for government-sponsored health services, many low-income women do not qualify. As we will see when we take up birth complications in Chapter 4, in countries where affordable medical care is universally available, such

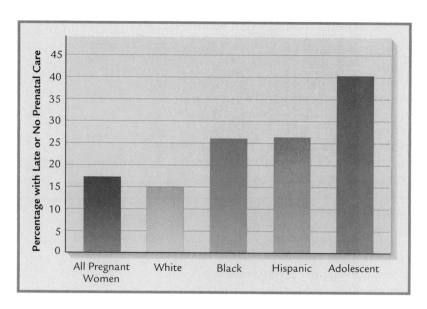

FIGURE 3.8

Expectant mothers in the United States with late (after the first trimester) or no prenatal care.

More than 25 percent of low-income, ethnic minority mothers, and more than 40 percent of adolescent mothers, receive inadequate prenatal care. Weak health insurance policies contribute to this dire situation. In nations where medical care is universally available, late-care pregnancies are rare. (From U.S. Department of Health and Human Services, 2003f.)

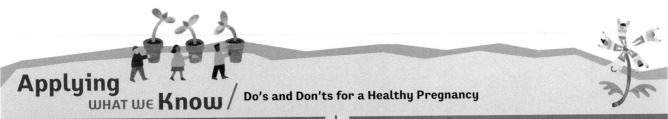

as Australia, Canada, Japan, and Western Europe, late-care pregnancies and maternal and infant health problems are greatly reduced.

Besides financial hardship, some mothers have other reasons for not seeking early prenatal care. When researchers asked women who first went to the doctor late in pregnancy why they waited so long, they mentioned a wide variety of obstacles. These included situational barriers, such as difficulty finding a doctor and getting an appointment and lack of transportation. The women also mentioned many personal barriers—psychological stress, the demands of taking care of young children, ambivalence about the pregnancy, family crises, and lack of belief in the benefits of prenatal care (Maloni et al., 1996; Rogers & Shiff, 1996). Many were also engaging in high-risk behaviors, such as smoking and drug abuse. These women were among those most in need of early prenatal visits!

Clearly, public education about the importance of early and sustained prenatal care for all pregnant women is badly needed. Refer to Applying What We Know below, which lists "do's and don'ts" for a healthy pregnancy, based on our discussion of the prenatal environment.

Applying WHAT WE Know / Do's and Don'ts for a Healthy Pregnancy

DO

Do make sure that you have been vaccinated against infectious diseases dangerous to the embryo and fetus, such as rubella, before you get pregnant. Most vaccinations are not safe during pregnancy.

Do see a doctor as soon as you suspect that you are pregnant—within a few weeks after a missed menstrual period.

Do continue to get regular medical checkups throughout pregnancy.

Do obtain literature from your doctor, local library, and bookstore about prenatal development and care. Ask questions about anything you do not understand.

Do eat a well-balanced diet and take vitamin–mineral supplements, as prescribed by your doctor, both prior to and during pregnancy. On average, a woman should increase her intake by 100 calories a day in the first trimester, 265 in the second, and 430 in the third. Gain 25 to 30 pounds gradually.

Do keep physically fit through mild exercise. If possible, join a special exercise class for expectant mothers.

Do avoid emotional stress. If you are a single parent, find a relative or friend on whom you can count for emotional support.

Do get plenty of rest. An overtired mother is at risk for pregnancy complications.

Do enroll in a prenatal and childbirth education class along with your partner. When parents know what to expect, the 9 months before birth can be one of the most joyful times of life.

DON'T

Don't take any drugs without consulting your doctor.

Don't smoke. If you have already smoked during part of your pregnancy, cut down or (better yet) quit. If other members of your family are smokers, ask them to quit or to smoke outside.

Don't drink alcohol from the time you decide to get pregnant. If you find it difficult to give up alcohol, ask for help from your doctor, local family service agency, or nearest chapter of Alcoholics Anonymous.

Don't engage in activities that might expose your embryo or fetus to environmental hazards, such as radiation or chemical pollutants. If you work in an occupation that involves these agents, ask for a safer assignment or a leave of absence.

Don't engage in activities that might expose your embryo or fetus to harmful infectious diseases, such as toxoplasmosis.

Don't choose pregnancy as a time to go on a diet.

Don't gain too much weight during pregnancy. A very large weight gain is associated with complications.

ASK YOURSELF

REVIEW | Why is it difficult to determine the effects of some environmental agents, such as drugs and pollution, on the embryo and fetus?

APPLY | Nora, pregnant for the first time, has heard about the teratogenic impact of alcohol and tobacco. Nevertheless, she believes that a few cigarettes and a glass of wine a day won't be harmful. Provide Nora with research-based reasons for not smoking or drinking.

CONNECT | List teratogens and other maternal factors that affect brain development during the prenatal period. Using Figure 3.6 on page 107, explain why the central nervous system is often affected when the prenatal environment is compromised.

REFLECT | A recent survey reported that only 7 percent of women of childbearing age are aware that taking a daily folic acid supplement around the time of conception reduces the incidence of neural tube defects (March of Dimes, 2002). Were you aware of this finding? If you could publicize five environmental influences in a campaign aimed at safeguarding prenatal development, which ones would you choose, and why?

Preparing For Parenthood

Although we have discussed a great many ways that development can be thrown off course during the prenatal period, over 90 percent of pregnancies in industrialized nations result in healthy newborn babies. For most expectant parents, the prenatal period is not a time of medical hazard. Instead, it is a period of major life change accompanied by excitement, anticipation, and looking inward. The 9 months before birth not only permit the fetus to grow but also give men and women time to develop a new sense of themselves as mothers and fathers.

This period of psychological preparation is vital. In one study, more than 100 first-time expectant married couples, varying widely in age and SES, were interviewed about their pregnancy experiences. Participants reported a wide range of reactions to learning they were expecting. Nearly two-thirds were positive, about one-third mixed or neutral, and a handful were negative (Feeney et al., 2001). An unplanned pregnancy was especially likely to spark negative or ambivalent feelings. But as the pregnancy moved along, these reactions subsided. By the third trimester, no participants felt negatively, and only about 10 percent remained mixed or neutral. Couples' increasingly upbeat attitudes reflected acceptance of parenthood—a coming to terms with this imminent, radical change in their lives.

How effectively individuals construct a parental identity during pregnancy has important consequences for the parent–child relationship. A great many factors contribute to the personal adjustments that take place.

Seeking Information

We know most about how mothers adapt to the psychological challenges of pregnancy, although some evidence suggests that fathers use many of the same techniques (Colman & Colman, 1991). One common strategy is to seek information, as Yolanda and Jay did when they read books on pregnancy and childbirth and enrolled in my class. In fact, expectant mothers regard books as an extremely valuable source of information, rating them as second in importance only to their doctors. And the more a pregnant woman seeks information—by reading, accessing relevant websites, asking friends, consulting her own mother, or attending a prenatal class—the more confident she tends to feel about her own ability to be a good mother (Cowan & Cowan, 2000; Deutsch et al., 1988).

The Baby Becomes a Reality

At the beginning of pregnancy, the baby seems far in the future. Except for a missed period and some morning sickness (nausea that most women experience during the first trimester), the woman's body has not changed much. But gradually, her abdomen enlarges, and the baby starts to become a reality. A major turning point occurs when expectant parents have concrete proof that a fetus is, indeed, developing inside the uterus. For Yolanda and Jay, this happened 13 weeks into the pregnancy, when their doctor showed them an ultrasound image. As Jay described the experience, "We saw it, these little hands and feet waving and kicking. It had the cord and everything. It's really a baby in there!" Sensing the fetus's movements for the first time can be just as thrilling. Of course, the mother feels these "kicks" first, but soon after, the father (and siblings) can participate by touching her abdomen.

Parents get to know the fetus as an individual through these signs of life. And both may form an emotional attachment to the new being, dream about the future parent–infant relationship, and discuss names. In a Swedish study, the stronger mothers' and fathers' attachment to their fetus, the more positively they related to each other and to their baby after birth, and the more upbeat the baby's mood at 8 months of age (White et al., 1999).

Models of Effective Parenthood

As pregnancy proceeds, expectant parents think about important models of parenthood in their own lives. When men and women have had good relationships with their own parents, they are more likely to develop positive images of themselves as parents during pregnancy (Deutsch et al., 1988). These images, in turn, predict favorable relationships with children during infancy and early childhood (Cowan et al., 1994; Fonagy, Steele, & Steele, 1991; Klitzing et al., 1999).

If their own parental relationships are mixed or negative, expectant mothers and fathers may have trouble building a healthy picture of themselves as parents. Some adults handle this problem by seeking other examples of effective parenthood. One expectant father named Roger shared these thoughts with his wife and several couples, who met regularly with a counselor to talk about their concerns during pregnancy:

> I rethink past experiences with my father and my family and am aware of how I was raised. I just think I don't want to do that again, I want to change that; I don't want to be like my father in that way. I wish there had been more connection and closeness and a lot more respect for who I was. For me, my father-in-law combines spontaneity, sincerity, and warmth. He is a mix of empathy and warmth plus stepping back and being objective that I want to be as a father. (Colman & Colman, 1991, p. 148)

Like Roger, many people come to terms with negative experiences in their own childhood, recognize that other options are available to them, and build healthier and happier relationships with their children (Cox et al., 1992). Roger achieved this understanding after he participated in a special intervention program for expectant mothers and fathers. Couples who take part in such programs feel better about themselves and their marital relationships, regard the demands of caring for the new baby as less stressful, and adapt more easily when family problems arise (Cowan & Cowan, 1997).

As this couple shares the thrill of sensing the fetus's movements, parenthood starts to become a reality. Mother and father get to know the fetus as an individual. They may become emotionally attached to the new being and dream about the future parent–infant relationship.

Practical Concerns

When women first learn they are pregnant, they often wonder how long they will be able to continue their usual activities. Culture has a major impact on answers to this question. In the United States, women in good health often work and travel until the very end of their pregnancies, without any apparent harm to the fetus. And as long as the pregnancy has gone well, health professionals advise that sexual intercourse can be continued until 2 to 4 weeks before the estimated birth date (ACOG, 2002; Sayle et al., 2001).

In contrast, when a Japanese woman learns she is pregnant, she changes her daily life considerably, out of a belief that this is necessary to protect the health of her baby. Nancy Engel, an American nurse, described her experience of becoming pregnant for the first time while living in Japan:

> When I announced my pregnancy it was assumed that I would quit my teaching position and drop out of language school. My teacher told me that language study was stressful, and the increased [hormone levels] it caused were harmful to the baby. Similarly, I was advised that the noise of train travel, typing, or using a sewing machine should be avoided. My colleagues at college . . . were particularly concerned when I revealed plans to go to Thailand on vacation during the fourth month. They told me that airplane travel would cause miscarriage, and they cited numerous examples. . . . My doctor assumed that I would not engage in sexual activity, to ensure a healthy newborn. (Engel, 1989, p. 83)

At the fifth month, a pregnant Japanese woman often participates in a traditional custom called *chakautai,* in which she or her doctor ties a ceremonial sash, which has been blessed at a Shinto shrine, around her abdomen. Then family members offer prayers for an easy delivery. As the eighth month approaches, the Japanese woman goes to her mother's home, where she rests until birth and recuperates for 6 to 8 weeks afterward (Ito & Sharts-Hopko, 2002).

Although Engel could not accept these practices for herself, she realized that they were based on cultural values that hold the maternal role in high esteem and place the infant's well-being first. For example, medical checkups and tests (such as ultrasound) are more frequent in Japan than in the United States. And prenatal care is more consistent: The same health professionals deliver all prenatal services, as well as attend the woman during birth (Ito & Sharts-Hopko, 2002). Not surprisingly, Japanese women giving birth in the United States have complaints. One commented, "In the United States, they always consider cost-effectiveness. . . . In Japan, they may perform redundant examinations to make doubly sure" (Ito & Sharts-Hopko, 2002, p. 672). Because of its high investment in mothers' and babies' well-being, Japan has one of the lowest rates of pregnancy and birth complications in the world.

After learning of her pregnancy, this Japanese woman probably changed her daily activities considerably, out of a cultural conviction that a slower-paced lifestyle will help protect the health of her baby. She benefits from cultural values that hold the maternal role in high esteem and from one of the best prenatal health care systems in the world. As she approaches the eighth month of pregnancy, she will go to her mother's home, where she will rest until birth and recuperate afterward.

© CAMELOT/PACIFIC PRESS SERVICE

The Parental Relationship

The most important preparation for parenthood takes place in the context of the parents' relationship. Expectant couples who are unhappy in their marriages continue to be dissatisfied after the baby is born (Cowan & Cowan, 2000). Deciding to have a baby in hopes of improving a troubled relationship is a serious mistake. Pregnancy adds to rather than subtracts from family conflict in a troubled marriage (Belsky & Kelly, 1994).

When a couple's relationship is faring well and both partners want and planned for the baby, the excitement of a first pregnancy may bring husband and wife closer (Feeney et al., 2001). At the same time, pregnancy does change a marriage. Expectant parents must adjust their established roles to make room for children. In addition, each partner is likely to develop new expectations of the other. Women look for greater demonstrations of affection, interest in the pregnancy, and help with household chores. They see these behaviors as important signs of continued acceptance of themselves, the pregnancy, and the baby to come. Similarly, men are particularly sensitive to expressions of warmth from their partner. These reassure them of a central place in the new mother's emotional life after the baby is born (Cowan & Cowan, 2000).

When a relationship rests on a solid foundation of love and respect, parents are well equipped for the challenges of pregnancy. They are also prepared to handle the much more demanding changes that will take place as soon as the baby is born.

ASK YOURSELF

APPLY Muriel, who is expecting her first child, recalls her own mother as cold and distant. Muriel is worried about whether she will be effective at caring for her new baby. What factors during pregnancy are related to maternal behavior?

REFLECT Find out how your mother and your grandmothers managed regular activities, such as work and travel, during pregnancy. How were their daily lives different from those of contemporary pregnant women?

Summary

Motivations For Parenthood

How has decision making about childbearing changed over the past half-century, and what are the consequences for child rearing and child development?

● Today, adults in Western industrialized nations have greater freedom to choose whether, when, and how to have children, and they are more likely to weigh the advantages and disadvantages of becoming parents. Parents are also having smaller families, a trend that grants children more parental attention and is linked to favorable health, intellectual, and educational outcomes.

● When couples limit their families to just one child, their children are just as well adjusted socially as children with siblings. Many adults delay childbearing until their education is complete, their careers are well established, and they are emotionally more mature. Consequently, they may be better able to invest in parenting.

Prenatal Development

List the three phases of prenatal development, and describe the major milestones of each.

● The first prenatal phase, the period of the zygote, lasts about 2 weeks, from fertilization until the **blastocyst** becomes deeply **implanted** in the uterine lining. During this time, structures that will support prenatal growth begin to form. The **embryonic disk** is surrounded by the **trophoblast,** which forms structures that protect and nourish the organism. The **amnion** fills with **amniotic fluid** to regulate temperature and cushion against the mother's movements. From the **chorion,** villi emerge that burrow into the uterine wall, and the **placenta** starts to develop. The developing organism is connected to the placenta by the **umbilical cord.**

- During the period of the **embryo,** which lasts from weeks 2 to 8, the foundations for all body structures are laid down. In the first week of this period, the **neural tube** forms, and the nervous system starts to develop. Other organs follow and grow rapidly. At the end of this phase, the embryo responds to touch and can move.

- The period of the **fetus,** lasting until the end of pregnancy, involves a dramatic increase in body size and completion of physical structures. By the middle of the second **trimester,** the mother can feel movement. The fetus becomes covered with **vernix,** which protects the skin from chapping. White, downy hair called **lanugo** helps the vernix stick to the skin. At the end of the second trimester, production of neurons in the brain is complete.

- The **age of viability** occurs at the beginning of the third trimester, sometime between 22 and 26 weeks. The brain continues to develop rapidly, and new sensory and behavioral capacities emerge. Gradually the lungs mature, the fetus fills the uterus, and birth is near.

Prenatal Environmental Influences

What are teratogens, and what factors influence their impact?

- **Teratogens** are environmental agents that cause damage during the prenatal period. Their effects conform to the sensitive period concept. The developing organism is especially vulnerable during the embryonic period, since all essential body structures emerge rapidly.

- The impact of teratogens varies with the amount and length of exposure, the genetic makeup of mother and fetus, the presence or absence of other harmful agents, and the age of the organism at time of exposure. The effects of teratogens are not limited to immediate physical damage. Some health outcomes appear later in development. Psychological consequences may occur indirectly, as a result of physical defects.

List agents known to be or suspected of being teratogens, and discuss evidence supporting their harmful impact.

- Drugs, cigarettes, alcohol, radiation, environmental pollution, and infectious diseases are teratogens that can endanger the developing organism. **Thalidomide,** a sedative widely available in the early 1960s, showed without a doubt that drugs could cross the placenta and cause serious damage. Babies whose mothers took heroin, methadone, or cocaine during pregnancy have withdrawal symptoms after birth and are irritable and inattentive. In some studies, cocaine is associated with physical defects and central nervous system damage, whereas in others, it has no major negative effects.

- Infants of parents who use tobacco are often born underweight and may have attention, learning, and behavior problems in early childhood. When mothers consume alcohol in large quantities, **fetal alcohol syndrome (FAS),** a disorder involving mental retardation, poor attention, overactivity, slow physical growth, and facial abnormalities, often results. Smaller amounts of alcohol may lead to some of these problems—a condition known as **fetal alcohol effects (FAE).**

- High levels of radiation, mercury, lead, and PCBs lead to physical malformations and severe brain damage. Low-level exposure has also been linked to diverse impairments. For radiation, these include language and emotional disorders. For PCB exposure, more intense physiological reactions to stress, reduced interest in the environment, and memory difficulties are involved.

- Among infectious diseases, **rubella** causes a wide variety of abnormalities, which vary with its time of occurrence during pregnancy. The human immunodeficiency virus (HIV), responsible for **acquired immune deficiency syndrome (AIDS),** can be transmitted prenatally and results in brain damage, delayed development, and early death. **Toxoplasmosis** in the first trimester may lead to eye and brain damage, and in the second and third trimesters to mild visual and cognitive impairments.

Describe the impact of other maternal factors on prenatal development.

- In healthy, physically fit women, regular moderate exercise contributes to an expectant woman's general health and readiness for childbirth and is related to increased birth weight. However, very vigorous exercise results in lower birth weight. When the mother's diet is inadequate, low birth weight and damage to the brain and other organs are major concerns.

- Severe emotional stress is linked to many pregnancy complications, although its impact can be reduced by providing the mother with emotional support. **Rh factor incompatibility**—an Rh-negative mother and Rh-positive fetus—can lead to oxygen deprivation, brain and heart damage, and infant death.

- Aside from the risk of chromosomal abnormalities in older women, maternal age is not a major cause of prenatal problems. Instead, poor health and environmental risks associated with poverty are the strongest predictors of pregnancy complications.

Why is early and regular health care vital during the prenatal period?

- Unexpected difficulties, such as **toxemia,** can arise, especially when pregnant women have health problems to begin with. Prenatal care is especially crucial for women unlikely to seek it—in particular, those who are young or poverty stricken.

Preparing for Parenthood

What factors contribute to preparation for parenthood during the prenatal period?

- Over the course of pregnancy, reactions to expectant parenthood become increasingly positive. Mothers and fathers prepare for their new role by seeking information from books and other sources. Ultrasound images, fetal movements, and the mother's enlarging abdomen make the baby a reality, and parents may form an emotional attachment to the new being. They also rely on effective models of parenthood to build images of themselves as mothers and fathers.

- The most important preparation for parenthood takes place in the context of the couple's relationship. During the 9 months preceding birth, parents adjust their roles and their expectations of each other as they prepare to welcome the baby into the family.

Important Terms and Concepts

acquired immune deficiency syndrome (AIDS) (p. 115)
age of viability (p. 104)
amnion (p. 101)
amniotic fluid (p. 101)
blastocyst (p. 101)
chorion (p. 101)
embryo (p. 102)
embryonic disk (p. 101)

fetal alcohol effects (FAE) (p. 113)
fetal alcohol syndrome (FAS) (p. 113)
fetus (p. 103)
implantation (p. 101)
lanugo (p. 104)
neural tube (p. 102)
placenta (p. 101)
Rh factor incompatibility (p. 119)
rubella (p. 115)

teratogen (p. 106)
thalidomide (p. 108)
toxemia (p. 120)
toxoplasmosis (p. 116)
trimesters (p. 104)
trophoblast (p. 101)
umbilical cord (p. 101)
vernix (p. 104)

FYI For Further Information and Help

Consult the Companion Website for *Infants, Children, and Adolescents,* Fifth Edition, *(www.ablongman.com/berk)*, where you will find the following resources for this chapter:

● **Chapter Objectives**
● **Flashcards** for studying important terms and concepts
● **Annotated Weblinks** to guide you in further research
● **Ask Yourself questions,** which you can answer and then check against a sample response

● **Suggested Readings**
● **Practice Tests** with immediate scoring and feedback

"Motherhood"

Nasr Abdulsemih Mahmud

12 years, Egypt

Held close and allowed to feel welcome and protected, the baby thrives and grows into a child whose world is filled with color and beauty. In Chapter 4, we explore the birth process, the marvelous competencies of the newborn, and the intense experience of the transition to parenthood.

Reprinted with permission from the International Museum of Children's Art, Oslo, Norway.

Birth and the Newborn Baby

Although Yolanda and Jay completed my course 3 months before their baby was born, they returned the following spring to share with my next class their reactions to birth and new parenthood. Two-week-old Joshua came along as well. Yolanda and Jay's story revealed that the birth of a baby is one of the most dramatic and emotional events in human experience. Jay was present throughout Yolanda's labor and delivery. Yolanda explained,

By morning, we knew I was in labor. It was Thursday, so we went in for my usual weekly appointment. The doctor said, yes, the baby was on the way, but it would be a while. He told us to go home and relax or take a leisurely walk and come to the hospital in 3 or 4 hours. We checked in at 3 in the afternoon; Joshua arrived at 2 o'clock the next morning. When, finally, I was ready to deliver, it went quickly; a half hour or so and some good hard pushes, and there he was! His body had stuff all over it, his face was red and puffy, and his head was misshapen, but I thought, "Our son! I can't believe he's really here."

Jay was also elated by Joshua's birth. "I wanted to support Yolanda and to experience as much as I could. It was awesome, indescribable," he said, holding little Joshua over his shoulder and patting and kissing him gently.

In this chapter we explore the experience of childbirth, from both the parents' and the baby's points of view. As recently as 40 years ago, the birth process was treated more like an illness than a natural part of life. Today, women in industrialized nations have many choices about where and how they give birth, and hospitals go to great lengths to make the arrival of a new baby a rewarding, family-centered event.

Joshua reaped the benefits of Yolanda and Jay's careful attention to his needs during pregnancy. He was strong, alert, and healthy at birth. Nevertheless, the birth process does not always go smoothly. We will pay special attention to the problems of infants who are born underweight or too early. Our discussion will also examine the pros and cons of medical interventions, such as pain-relieving drugs and surgical deliveries, designed to ease a difficult birth and protect the health of mother and baby.

Finally, Yolanda and Jay spoke candidly about how, since Joshua's arrival, life at home had changed. "It's exciting and wonderful," reflected Yolanda, "but the adjustments are enormous. I wasn't quite prepared for the intensity of Joshua's 24-hour-a-day demands." In the last part of this chapter, we take a close look at the remarkable ability of newborn babies to adapt to the external world and to communicate their needs. We also consider how parents adjust to the realities of everyday life with a new baby.

The Stages of Childbirth

It is not surprising that childbirth is often referred to as *labor*. It is the hardest physical work that a woman may ever do. As the Biology and Environment box on pages 132–133 explains, a complex series of hormonal changes initiates the process. Yolanda's whole system, which for 9 months supported and protected Joshua's growth, now turned toward a new goal: getting him safely out of the uterus.

The events that lead to childbirth begin slowly in the ninth month of pregnancy and gradually pick up speed. Several signs indicate that labor is near:

- Yolanda occasionally felt the upper part of her uterus contract. These contractions are often called *false labor* or *prelabor*, since they remain brief and unpredictable for several weeks.

- About 2 weeks before birth, an event called *lightening* occurred; Joshua's head dropped low into the uterus. Yolanda's cervix had begun to soften in preparation for delivery and no longer supported Joshua's weight so easily.

- A sure sign that labor is only hours or days away is the *bloody show.* As the cervix opens more, the plug of mucus that sealed it during pregnancy is released, producing a reddish discharge. Soon after, contractions of the uterus become more frequent, and mother and baby have entered the first of three stages of labor (see Figure 4.1).

Stage 1: Dilation and Effacement of the Cervix

Stage 1 is the longest, lasting an average of 12 to 14 hours with a first birth and 4 to 6 hours with later births. **Dilation and effacement of the cervix** take place—that is, uterine contractions gradually become more frequent and powerful, causing the cervix to open (dilate) and thin (efface), forming a clear channel from the uterus into the birth canal, or vagina. Uterine contractions that open the cervix are forceful and regular, starting out 10 to 20 minutes apart and lasting about 15 to 20 seconds. Gradually, they get closer together, occurring every 2 to 3 minutes. In addition, they become more powerful, continuing for as long as 60 seconds.

During this stage, Yolanda could do nothing to speed up the process. Jay held her hand, provided sips of juice and water, and helped her get comfortable. Throughout the first few hours, Yolanda walked, stood, or sat upright. As the contractions became more intense, she leaned against pillows or lay on her side.

The climax of Stage 1 is a brief period called **transition,** in which the frequency and strength of contractions are at their peak and the cervix opens completely. Although transition

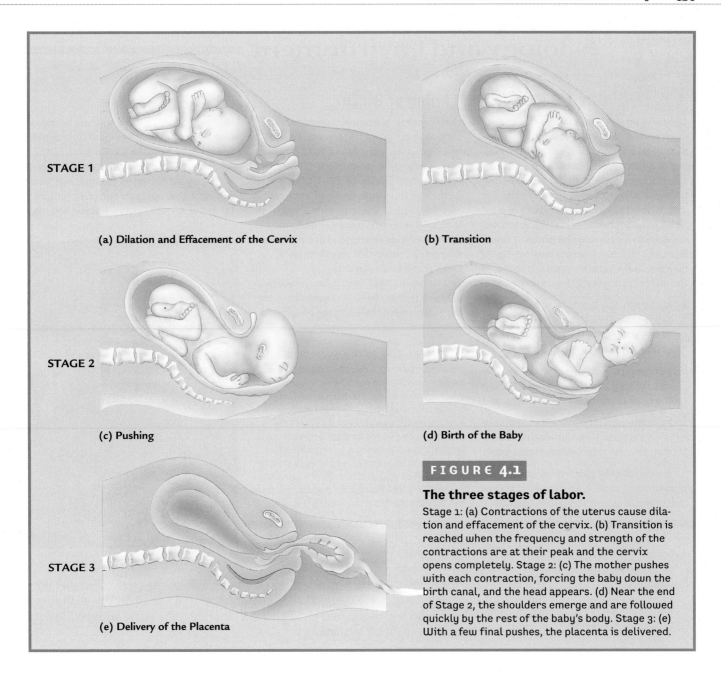

STAGE 1

(a) Dilation and Effacement of the Cervix

(b) Transition

STAGE 2

(c) Pushing

(d) Birth of the Baby

STAGE 3

(e) Delivery of the Placenta

FIGURE 4.1

The three stages of labor.

Stage 1: (a) Contractions of the uterus cause dilation and effacement of the cervix. (b) Transition is reached when the frequency and strength of the contractions are at their peak and the cervix opens completely. Stage 2: (c) The mother pushes with each contraction, forcing the baby down the birth canal, and the head appears. (d) Near the end of Stage 2, the shoulders emerge and are followed quickly by the rest of the baby's body. Stage 3: (e) With a few final pushes, the placenta is delivered.

is the most uncomfortable part of childbirth, it is especially important that the mother relax. If she tenses or bears down with her muscles before the cervix is completely dilated and effaced, she may bruise the cervix and slow the progress of labor.

Stage 2: Delivery of the Baby

In Stage 2, which lasts about 50 minutes for a first baby and 20 minutes in later births, the infant is born. Strong contractions of the uterus continue, but the mother also feels a natural urge to squeeze and push with her abdominal muscles. As she does so with each contraction, she forces the baby down and out.

Yolanda dozed lightly between contractions. As each new wave came, "I pushed with all my might," she said. When the doctor announced that the baby's head was *crowning*—the vaginal opening had stretched around the entire head—Yolanda felt renewed energy; she knew that soon the baby would arrive. Quickly, with several more pushes, Joshua's forehead, nose, and chin emerged, then his upper body and trunk. The doctor held him up, wet with amniotic fluid and

Biology and Environment

What Controls the Timing of Birth?

Only in the past decade has animal and human research begun to uncover the precise biological changes that control the timing of birth. Through most of pregnancy, the placenta secretes high levels of the hormone *progesterone,* which keeps the uterus relaxed and the cervix firm a nd inflexible, so it remains tightly closed and capable of supporting the growing fetus. But the placenta also secretes *estrogen,* which rises during pregnancy and counters the effects of progesterone in three ways:

● by producing a protein called *connexin,* which links uterine muscle cells to one another so they contract in a coordinated fashion;

● by making the uterine muscle sensitive to *oxytocin,* a hormone released from the brain that induces contractions; and

● by stimulating the placenta to release *prostaglandins,* hormones that soften the cervix so it will dilate during labor.

What switches on the production of estrogen and leads it to overwhelm progesterone? Researchers began to suspect that another placental hormone called *corticotropin-releasing hormone (CRH)* is involved when they found that mothers who experience premature labor have higher blood levels of CRH than other women in the same week of pregnancy (see Figure 4.2) (McLean et al., 1999). In fact, CRH levels measured as early as the 16th to 20th week are good predictors of whether a woman will give birth early, on time, or past her due date.

How does CRH work? When it reaches a high enough level, it leads the fetal adrenal glands (located on top of each kidney) to produce *cortisol,* a stress hormone that clears the infant's lungs of fluid so they are ready to breathe air. Cortisol further stimulates CRH production, which triggers estrogen secretion in the placenta, resulting in the rapid estrogen rise required for labor (Smith, 1999). Notice how the

AP/WIDE WORLD PHOTOS

These Muslim women of Indonesia pray in a mosque during the month of Ramadan, a time of daily fasting from dawn to sunset. Pregnant women may postpone the fast to a later time—an exception that recognizes food deprivation as a threat to the mother's and baby's health. Fast may precipitate early birth by causing the fetus to produce an excess of cortisol, a stress hormone. Cortisol initiates a rise in corticotropin-releasing hormone (CRH), which, in turn, triggers increased estrogen production, required for labor.

still attached to the umbilical cord. Air rushed into his lungs, and Joshua cried. When the umbilical cord stopped pulsing, it was clamped and cut. A nurse placed Joshua on Yolanda's chest, where she and Jay could see, touch, and gently talk to him. Then the nurse wrapped Joshua snugly, to help with temperature regulation.

Stage 3: Birth of the Placenta

Stage 3 brings labor to an end with a few final contractions and pushes. These cause the placenta to separate from the wall of the uterus and be delivered in about 5 to 10 minutes. Yolanda and Jay were surprised at the large size of the thick 1½-pound red-gray organ, which had taken care of Joshua's basic needs for the previous 9 months.

The Baby's Adaptation to Labor and Delivery

At first glance, labor and delivery seem like a dangerous ordeal for the baby. The strong contractions of Yolanda's uterus exposed Joshua's head to a great deal of pressure, and they squeezed the placenta and the umbilical cord repeatedly. Each time, Joshua's supply of oxygen was temporarily reduced.

Fortunately, healthy babies are well equipped to withstand these traumas. The force of the contractions causes the infant to produce high levels of stress hormones. Recall from Chapter 3 that during pregnancy, the effects of maternal stress can endanger the baby. In contrast, during childbirth, the infant's production of stress hormones is adaptive. It helps the baby with-

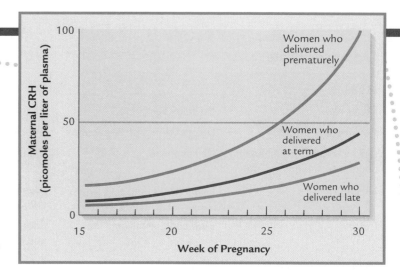

FIGURE 4.2

Release of CRH by the placenta in relation to timing of birth.

CRH levels in the blood of 500 women were measured repeatedly as their pregnancies progressed. As early as the 16th to 20th week after conception, CRH concentration predicted who would deliver prematurely, who would deliver on time, and who would deliver late. (From Smith, R., "The Timing of Birth," *Scientific American, 280*(3), 68–75. Copyright © 1999 by Scientific American, Inc. All rights reserved. Reprinted by permission.)

"CRH–cortisol circuit" helps ensure that labor will occur only when the fetus is ready to survive outside the womb.

What causes the placenta to make CRH, and what affects how much is produced? Researchers are still trying to answer to this question. The genetic makeup of CRH-producing cells may lead CRH to rise too early in some women, resulting in prematurity. Another potential influence is maternal nutrition. Food deprivation precipitates early birth in some mammals, and the same effect may occur in humans. In support of this possibility, an Israeli study reported that pregnant Jewish women observing the day-long fast of Yom Kippur showed a sharp rise in delivery rates during the last 6 hours of the fast and the day after. This increase was not observed in non-Jewish women living in the same region or in Jewish women observing the harvest holiday of Succoth, which is celebrated with a special meal (Wiser et al., 1997). Perhaps even brief periods of inadequate nutrition can activate the fetal stress system, which prompts excess production of CRH.

In sum, a complex hormonal system, initiated by CRH and involving both mother and fetus, controls the timing of birth. New knowledge about birth timing is leading to more effective prevention of prematurity—a major cause of infant death and disability. Already, studies show that chemically inhibiting CRH production delays birth in sheep (McLean & Smith, 2001). If tests of CRH inhibitors in nonhuman primates prove safe and effective, then trials in human mothers are not far off.

stand oxygen deprivation by sending a rich supply of blood to the brain and heart. In addition, it prepares the baby to breathe effectively by causing the lungs to absorb any remaining fluid and by expanding the bronchial tubes (passages leading to the lungs). Finally, stress hormones arouse the infant into alertness at birth. Joshua was born wide awake, ready to interact with the surrounding world (Lagercrantz & Slotkin, 1986).

The Newborn Baby's Appearance

Parents are often surprised at the odd-looking newborn, who is a far cry from the storybook image many had in their minds before birth. The average newborn is 20 inches long and weighs 7½ pounds; boys tend to be slightly longer and heavier than girls. Body proportions contribute to the baby's strange appearance. The head is very large in comparison to the trunk and legs, which are short and bowed. Proportionally, if your head were as large as that of a newborn infant, you would be balancing something about the size of a watermelon between your shoulders! As we will see in later chapters, the combination of a large head (with its well-developed brain) and a small body means that human infants learn quickly in the first few months of life. But unlike most mammals, they cannot get around on their own until much later.

Even though newborn babies may not match parents' idealized image, some features do make them attractive. Their round faces, chubby cheeks,

This newborn is held by his mother's birthing coach (on the left) and midwife (on the right) just after delivery. The umbilical cord has not yet been cut. The baby's head is molded from being squeezed through the birth canal for many hours. As the infant takes his first breaths, his body turns from blue to pink. He is wide awake and ready to get to know his new surroundings.

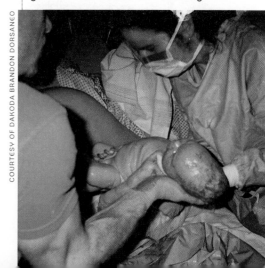

COURTESY OF DAKODA BRANDON DORSANEO

TABLE 4.1

The Apgar Scale

SIGN[a]	SCORE		
	0	1	2
Heart rate	No heartbeat	Under 100 beats per minute	100 to 140 beats per minute
Respiratory effort	No breathing for 60 seconds	Irregular, shallow breathing	Strong breathing and crying
Reflex irritability (sneezing, coughing, and grimacing)	No response	Weak reflexive response	Strong reflexive response
Muscle tone	Completely limp	Weak movements of arms and legs	Strong movements of arms and legs
Color	Blue body, arms, and legs	Body pink with blue arms and legs	Body, arms, and legs completely pink

[a]To remember these signs, you may find it helpful to use a technique in which the original labels are reordered and renamed as follows: color = **A**ppearance, heart rate = **P**ulse, reflex irritability = **G**rimace, muscle tone = **A**ctivity, and respiratory effort = **R**espiration. Together, the first letters of the new labels spell **Apgar.**

Source: Apgar, 1953.

large foreheads, and big eyes make adults feel like picking them up and cuddling them (Berman, 1980; Lorenz, 1943).

Assessing The Newborn's Physical Condition: The Apgar Scale

Infants who have difficulty making the transition to life outside the uterus must be given special help at once. To quickly assess the newborn's physical condition, doctors and nurses use the **Apgar Scale.** As Table 4.1 shows, a rating of 0, 1, or 2 on each of five characteristics is made at 1 and 5 minutes after birth. A combined Apgar score of 7 or better indicates that the infant is in good physical condition. If the score is between 4 and 6, the baby requires assistance in establishing breathing and other vital signs. If the score is 3 or below, the infant is in serious danger, and emergency medical attention is needed. Two Apgar ratings are given, since some babies have trouble adjusting at first but do quite well after a few minutes (Apgar, 1953).

Color is the least dependable of the Apgar ratings. Dark-skinned babies like Joshua cannot be judged easily for pinkness and blueness. However, all newborns can be rated for a rosy glow that results from the flow of oxygen through body tissues after breathing starts, since skin tone is usually lighter at birth than the baby's inherited pigmentation.

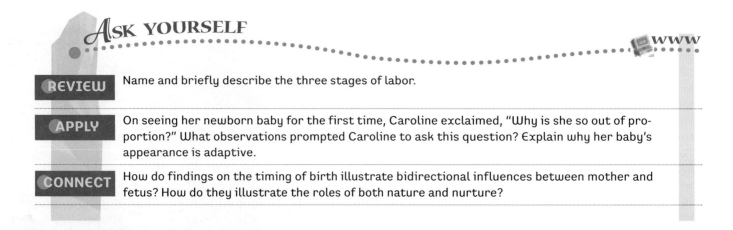

ASK YOURSELF

REVIEW Name and briefly describe the three stages of labor.

APPLY On seeing her newborn baby for the first time, Caroline exclaimed, "Why is she so out of proportion?" What observations prompted Caroline to ask this question? Explain why her baby's appearance is adaptive.

CONNECT How do findings on the timing of birth illustrate bidirectional influences between mother and fetus? How do they illustrate the roles of both nature and nurture?

Approaches to Childbirth

Childbirth practices, like other aspects of family life, are molded by the society of which mother and baby are a part. In many village and tribal cultures, expectant mothers are well acquainted with the childbirth process. For example, the Jarara of South America and the Pukapukans of the Pacific Islands treat birth as a vital part of daily life. The Jarara mother gives birth in full view of the entire community, including small children. The Pukapukan girl is so familiar with the events of labor and delivery that she can frequently be seen playing at it. Using a coconut to represent the baby, she stuffs it inside her dress, imitates the mother's pushing, and lets the nut fall at the proper moment. Although they may not be attended by medical personnel, most women in nonindustrialized cultures are assisted by someone during childbirth. Among the Mayans of the Yucatán, the mother leans against the body of a woman called the "head helper," who supports her weight and breathes with her during each contraction (Jordan, 1993; Mead & Newton, 1967).

In large Western nations, childbirth has changed dramatically over the centuries. Before the late 1800s, birth took place at home and was a family-centered event. The industrial revolution brought greater crowding to cities, along with new health problems. As a result, childbirth moved from home to hospital, where the health of mothers and babies could be protected. Once doctors assumed responsibility for childbirth, women's knowledge of it declined, and relatives and friends were no longer welcome to participate (Borst, 1995).

By the 1950s and 1960s, women started to question medical procedures that had become routine during labor and delivery. Many felt that frequent use of strong drugs and delivery instruments had robbed them of a precious experience and were often not necessary or safe for the baby. Gradually, a natural childbirth movement arose in Europe and spread to North America. Its purpose was to make hospital birth as comfortable and rewarding for mothers as possible. Today, most hospitals carry this theme further by offering birth centers that are family centered and homelike. *Freestanding birth centers* permit greater maternal control over labor and delivery, including freedom to eat and move during labor, choice of delivery positions, presence of family members and friends, and early contact between parents and baby. However, they offer less backup medical care than hospitals. And a small but growing number of North American women are rejecting institutional birth and choosing to have their babies at home.

Let's take a closer look at two childbirth approaches that have gained popularity in recent years: natural childbirth and home delivery.

Natural, or Prepared, Childbirth

Yolanda and Jay chose **natural, or prepared, childbirth**—a group of techniques aimed at reducing pain and medical intervention and making childbirth as rewarding an experience as possible. Although many natural childbirth programs exist, most draw on methods developed by Grantly Dick-Read (1959) in England and Fernand Lamaze (1958) in France. These physicians recognized that cultural attitudes had taught women to fear the birth experience. An anxious, frightened woman in labor tenses her muscles, turning the mild pain that sometimes accompanies strong contractions into a great deal of pain.

In a typical natural childbirth program, the expectant mother and a companion (a partner, a relative, or a friend) participate in three activities:

- *Classes.* Yolanda and Jay attended a series of classes in which they learned about the anatomy and physiology of labor and delivery. Knowledge about the birth process reduces a mother's fear.

- *Relaxation and breathing techniques.* During each class, Yolanda was taught relaxation and breathing exercises aimed at counteracting the pain of uterine contractions.

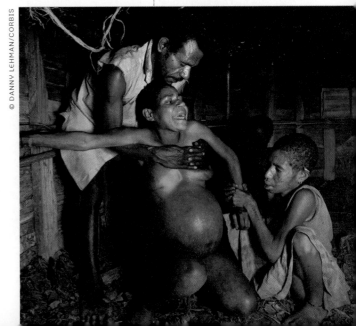

© DANNY LEHMAN/CORBIS

In this village society in Papua New Guinea, a woman gives birth in an upright squatting position. Her husband supports her body while an elderly woman helper soothes and encourages.

FIGURE 4.3

Sitting position often used for delivery in a birth center or at home.

It facilitates pushing during the second stage of labor; increases blood flow to the placenta, which grants the baby a richer supply of oxygen; and permits the mother to see the delivery, enabling her to track the effectiveness of each contraction.

As the midwife and grandmother look on, a mother and father greet their newborn baby and express ecstatic joy. The birth took place at home, where the mother used a birthing tub, which permitted her to relax in a soothing bath during labor and delivery. Mothers who choose home birth want to avoid unnecessary medical procedures and exercise greater control over the birth experience.

- *Labor coach.* Jay learned how to help Yolanda during childbirth by reminding her to relax and breathe, massaging her back, supporting her body, and offering encouragement and affection.

Studies comparing mothers who experience natural childbirth with those who do not reveal many benefits. Because mothers feel more in control of labor and delivery, their attitudes toward the childbirth experience are more positive. They also feel less pain. As a result, they require less pain-relieving medication—very little or none at all (Taylor, 2002; Waldenström, 1999).

SOCIAL SUPPORT AND NATURAL CHILDBIRTH ● Social support is important to the success of natural childbirth techniques. In Guatemalan and American hospitals that routinely isolated patients during childbirth, some mothers were randomly assigned a trained companion who stayed with them throughout labor and delivery, talking to them, holding their hands, and rubbing their backs to promote relaxation. These mothers had fewer birth complications, and their labors were several hours shorter than those of women who did not have supportive companionship. Guatemalan mothers who received support also interacted more positively with their babies after delivery, talking, smiling, and gently stroking (Kennell et al., 1991; Sosa et al., 1980). Other studies indicate that mothers who are supported during labor less often have cesarean (surgical) deliveries, and their babies' Apgar scores are higher (Sauls, 2002).

The continuous rather than intermittent support of a trained companion during labor and delivery strengthens these outcomes. It is particularly helpful during a first childbirth, when mothers are more anxious (DiMatteo & Kahn, 1997; Scott, Berkowitz, & Klaus, 1999). And this aspect of natural childbirth makes Western hospital birth customs more acceptable to women from parts of the world where assistance from family and community members is the norm (Granot et al., 1996).

POSITIONS FOR DELIVERY ● When natural childbirth is combined with delivery in a birth center or at home, mothers often give birth in the upright, sitting position shown in Figure 4.3 rather than lying flat on their backs with their feet in stirrups (which is the traditional hospital delivery room practice). In Europe, women often are encouraged to give birth on their sides because pressure of the baby's head against the mother's tissues is less intense. This reduces the need for an *episiotomy* (incision that increases the size of the vaginal opening) (Bobak, Jensen, & Zalar, 1989).

Research findings favor the sitting position. When mothers are upright, labor is shortened because pushing is easier and more effective. The baby benefits from a richer supply of oxygen because blood flow to the placenta is increased. Furthermore, since the mother can see the delivery, she can track the effectiveness of each contraction in pushing the baby out of the birth canal (Kelly, Terry, & Naglieri, 1999). This helps her work with the doctor or midwife to ensure that the baby's head and shoulders emerge slowly, to prevent tearing of the vaginal opening.

 ## Home Delivery

Home birth has always been popular in certain industrialized nations, such as England, the Netherlands, and Sweden. The number of North American women choosing to have their babies at home has increased in recent years, although it remains small, at about 1 percent (Curtin & Park, 1999). These mothers want birth to be an important part of family life. In addition, most want to avoid unnecessary medical procedures. And they want greater control over their own care and that of their babies than hospitals permit (Wickham, 1999). Although some home births are attended by doctors, many more are handled by *certified nurse–midwives* who have degrees in nursing and additional training in childbirth management.

The joys and perils of home delivery are well illustrated by the story that Don, who painted my house as I worked on this book, related to me. "Our first child was delivered in the hospital," he said. "Even though I was present, Kathy and I found the atmosphere to be rigid and insensitive. We wanted a warmer, more personal birth environment." With the coaching of a nurse–midwife, Don delivered their second child, Cindy, at their farmhouse, 3 miles out of town. Three years later, when Kathy went into labor with Marnie, their third child, a heavy snowstorm prevented the midwife from reaching the house on time. Don delivered the baby alone, but the birth was difficult. Marnie failed to breathe for several minutes; with great effort, Don managed to revive her. The frightening memory of Marnie's limp, blue body convinced Don and Kathy to return to the hospital to have their last child. By then, the hospital's birth practices had changed, and the event was a rewarding one for both parents.

Don and Kathy's experience raises the question of whether it is just as safe to give birth at home as in a hospital. For healthy women who are assisted by a well-trained doctor or midwife, it seems so, since complications rarely occur (Janssen et al., 2002). However, if attendants are not carefully trained and prepared to handle emergencies, the rate of infant death is high (Mehlmadrona & Madrona, 1997). When mothers are at risk for any kind of complication, the appropriate place for labor and delivery is the hospital, where life-saving treatment is available.

Medical Interventions

Medical interventions during childbirth occur in both industrialized and nonindustrialized cultures. For example, some preliterate tribal and village societies have discovered labor-inducing drugs and devised surgical techniques to deliver babies (Jordan, 1993). Yet, more so than elsewhere in the world, childbirth in North America is a medically monitored and controlled event. What medical techniques are doctors likely to use during labor and delivery? When are they justified, and what dangers do they pose to mothers and babies? These are questions we take up in the following sections.

Fetal Monitoring

Fetal monitors are electronic instruments that track the baby's heart rate during labor. An abnormal heartbeat pattern may indicate that the baby is in distress due to lack of oxygen and needs to be delivered immediately. Most American hospitals require continuous fetal monitoring; it is used in over 80 percent of American births. In Canada, continuous monitoring is usually reserved for babies at risk for birth complications (Banta & Thacker, 2001; Liston et al., 2002). The most popular type of monitor is strapped across the mother's abdomen throughout labor. A second, more accurate method involves threading a recording device through the cervix and placing it directly under the baby's scalp.

Fetal monitoring is a safe medical procedure that has saved the lives of many babies in high-risk situations. Nevertheless, the practice is controversial. In healthy pregnancies, it does not reduce the already low rates of infant brain damage and death. Furthermore, most infants have some heartbeat irregularities during labor, and critics worry that fetal monitors identify many babies as in danger who, in fact, are not. Monitoring is linked to an increase in the number of instrument and cesarean (surgical) deliveries, practices we will discuss shortly (Thacker & Stroup, 2003). In addition, some women complain that the devices are uncomfortable, prevent them from moving easily, and interfere with the normal course of labor.

Still, fetal monitors will probably continue to be used routinely in the United States, even though they are not necessary in most cases. Doctors fear being sued for malpractice if an infant dies or is born with problems and they cannot show that they did everything possible to protect the baby.

Although not at risk for birth complications, this mother wears a fetal monitor strapped across her abdomen throughout labor. The monitor uses ultrasound to record fetal heart rate. In high-risk situations, fetal monitoring saves many lives. But it also may lead to an increase in unnecessary instrument and cesarean (surgical) deliveries. In addition, some women complain that the monitors are uncomfortable and interfere with the normal course of labor.

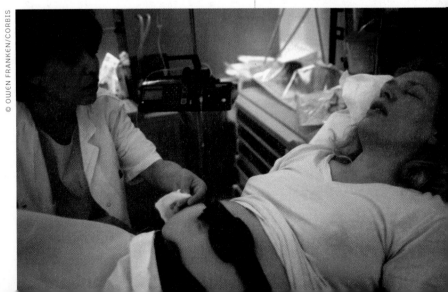

© OWEN FRANKEN/CORBIS

Labor and Delivery Medication

Some form of medication is used in 80 to 95 percent of North American births (Glosten, 1998). **Analgesics** are drugs used to relieve pain. When given during labor, the dose is usually mild and intended to help a mother relax. **Anesthetics** are a stronger type of painkiller that blocks sensation. Currently, the most common approach to controlling pain during labor is *epidural analgesia,* in which a regional pain-relieving drug is delivered continuously through a catheter into a small space in the lower spine. The amount can be adjusted over the course of labor, as needed. Rather than numbing the lower half of the body, as older spinal block procedures do, epidural analgesia limits pain reduction to the pelvic region. The mother retains the capacity to move her trunk and legs and to feel the pressure of the contractions. Consequently, she can push during the second stage of labor.

Although pain-relieving drugs assist women in coping with childbirth and enable doctors to perform essential life-saving medical interventions, they also cause problems. Epidural analgesia, for example, weakens uterine contractions. As a result, labor is prolonged. During the days after birth, mothers often suffer from headaches and fever. And because drugs rapidly cross the placenta, exposed newborns tend to have lower Apgar scores, to be sleepy and withdrawn, to suck poorly during feedings, and to be irritable when awake (Caton et al., 2002; Eltzschig, Lieberman, & Camann, 2003; Emory, Schlackman, & Fiano, 1996).

Do heavy doses of childbirth medication have a lasting impact on physical and mental development? Some researchers claim so (Brackbill, McManus, & Woodward, 1985), but their findings have been challenged (Golub, 1996). Use of medication may be related to other risk factors that could account for the long-term consequences in some studies, and more research is needed to sort out these effects. In the meantime, the negative impact of these drugs on the early infant–mother relationship supports the current trend to limit their use.

Instrument Delivery

Forceps, metal clamps placed around the baby's head to pull the infant from the birth canal, have been used since the sixteenth century to speed up delivery (see Figure 4.4). A more recent instrument, the **vacuum extractor,** consists of a plastic cup (placed on the baby's head) attached to a suction tube. Instrument delivery is appropriate if the mother's pushing during the second stage of labor does not move the baby through the birth canal in a reasonable period of time.

Instrument use has declined considerably over the past decade, partly because doctors more often deliver babies surgically when labor problems arise. Nevertheless, forceps and vacuum extractors continue to be used in about 7 percent of American and 17 percent of Canadian births, compared with less than 5 percent in Western Europe (Martin et al., 2002; Wen et al., 2001). These figures suggest that instruments are applied too freely in North American hospitals.

Using forceps to pull the baby through most or all of the birth canal greatly increases the risk of brain damage. As a result, forceps are seldom used this way today. Low-forceps delivery (carried out

FIGURE 4.4

Instrument delivery.
(a) The pressure that must be applied to pull the infant from the birth canal with *forceps* involves risk of injury to the baby's head. (b) An alternative method, the *vacuum extractor,* is less likely than forceps to injure the mother. However, it is just as risky for the infant; scalp injuries are common.

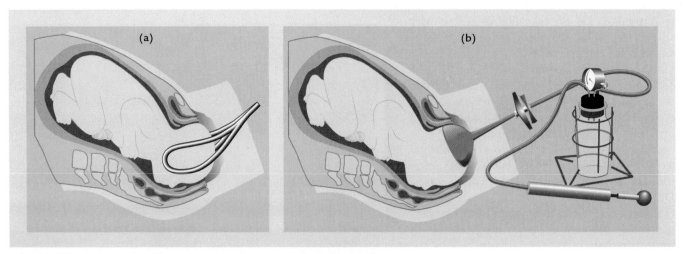

when the baby is most of the way through the vagina) is associated with some risk of injury to the baby's head and the mother's tissues. Although vacuum extractors are less likely to tear the mother's tissues, rates of infant injury are higher. In 5 percent of cases, bleeding within the head or eye results in serious complications (Davis, 2001; Putta & Spencer, 2000). Neither method should be used when mothers can be encouraged to deliver normally and there is no special reason to hurry the birth.

Induced Labor

An **induced labor** is one that is started artificially, usually by breaking the amnion, or bag of waters (an event that typically occurs naturally in the first stage of labor), and giving the mother synthetic oxytocin, a hormone that stimulates contractions. About 20 percent of North American labors are induced—a figure that has more than doubled over the past decade (Harris et al., 2001; Martin et al., 2002).

Induced labors are justified when continuing the pregnancy threatens the well-being of mother or baby. Often, though, they are performed for the doctor's or the patient's convenience—a major reason they have increased. An induced labor often proceeds differently from a naturally occurring one. Contractions are longer, harder, and closer together, increasing the possibility of inadequate oxygen supply to the baby. In addition, mothers often find it more difficult to stay in control of an induced labor, even when they have been coached in natural childbirth techniques. As a result, labor and delivery medication is likely to be used in larger amounts, and the chances of instrument delivery are slightly greater (Cammu et al., 2002).

Occasionally, induction is performed before the mother is physically ready to give birth, and the procedure fails. When this happens, a cesarean delivery is necessary. The rate of cesareans is nearly twice as great in induced labors as in spontaneous labors (Dublin et al., 2000). The placental hormone CRH (turn back to the Biology and Environment box on pages 132–133) helps predict the success of induction procedures. Mothers with high levels of CRH are more likely to respond well than are those whose CRH levels are low (Smith, 1999).

Cesarean Delivery

A **cesarean delivery** is a surgical birth; the doctor makes an incision in the mother's abdomen and lifts the baby out of the uterus. It received its name from the belief that Roman emperor Julius Caesar was born this way. Thirty years ago, the cesarean rate in most of the world's nations was 5 percent or less. Since then, the incidence of cesareans has climbed internationally, reaching 15 percent in Finland, 19 percent in Canada and New Zealand, 21 percent in Australia, and 24 percent in the United States (Canadian Institute for Health Information, 2003; Martin et al., 2002). Cesareans have skyrocketed in some Latin American countries. For example, they account for 27 percent of births in Brazil and for 40 percent in Chile (ICAN, 2003).

Cesareans have always been warranted by medical emergencies, such as Rh incompatibility, premature separation of the placenta from the uterus, and serious maternal illness or infection (for example, the herpes simplex 2 virus, which can infect the baby during a vaginal delivery). Furthermore, when babies are in **breech position,** or turned so that the buttocks or feet would be delivered first (about 1 in every 25 births), cesareans are usually justified. The breech position increases the possibility that the umbilical cord may be squeezed as the large head moves through the birth canal, depriving the infant of oxygen. Head injuries are also more likely (Golfier et al., 2001). But the infant's exact position (which can be felt by the doctor) makes a difference. Certain breech babies fare just as well with a normal delivery as they do with a cesarean (Giuliani et al., 2002). Sometimes, too, the doctor can gently turn the baby into a head-down position during the early part of labor.

During the past two decades, doctors have offered many women who have had a cesarean the option of a vaginal birth in subsequent pregnancies. Although once considered safe, recently this practice has been questioned. Studies indicate that compared with repeated cesareans, a natural labor after a cesarean is associated with slightly increased rates of rupture of the uterus and infant death. If labor is induced, these risks multiply (Lydon-Rochelle et al., 2001; Smith et al., 2002). As a result, the rule, "Once a cesarean, always a cesarean," is making a comeback.

However, repeated cesareans do not explain the dramatic, worldwide rise in cesarean deliveries. Instead, medical control over childbirth is largely responsible. In Latin America, the largest increases have occurred in countries with the strongest economies and the greatest numbers of doctors (Belizán et al., 1999). Because many needless cesareans are performed, pregnant women should ask questions about the procedure when choosing a doctor.

When a mother does have a cesarean, she and her baby need extra support. The operation itself is safe, but it requires more time for recovery. Since anesthetic may have crossed the placenta, cesarean newborns are more likely to be sleepy and unresponsive and to have breathing difficulties (Cox & Schwartz, 1990). These factors can negatively affect the early mother–infant relationship.

$\mathcal{A}$SK YOURSELF

www

REVIEW	Describe the features and benefits of natural childbirth. What aspect contributes greatly to favorable outcomes, and why?
APPLY	Sharon, a heavy smoker, has just arrived at the hospital in labor. Which one of the medical interventions discussed in the preceding sections is her doctor justified in using? (For help in answering this question, review the prenatal effects of tobacco in Chapter 3, page 112.)
CONNECT	Use of any one medical intervention during labor increases the chances that others will also be used. Provide as many examples as you can to illustrate this idea.
REFLECT	If you were an expectant parent, would you choose home birth? Why or why not?

$\mathcal{B}$irth Complications

We have seen that some babies—in particular, those whose mothers are in poor health, do not receive good medical care, or have a history of pregnancy problems—are especially likely to experience birth complications. Inadequate oxygen, a pregnancy that ends too early, and a baby who is born underweight are serious risks to development that we have touched on many times. A baby remaining in the uterus too long is yet another risk. Let's look at the impact of each complication on later development.

Oxygen Deprivation

Some years ago, I got to know 2-year-old Melinda and her mother, Judy, both of whom participated in a special program for infants with disabilities at our laboratory school. Melinda has **cerebral palsy,** a general term for a variety of problems that result from brain damage before, during, or just after birth. Difficulties in muscle coordination are always involved, such as a clumsy walk, uncontrolled movements, and unclear speech. The disorder can range from very mild tremors to severe crippling and mental retardation. One out of every 500 North American children has cerebral palsy. About 10 percent of these youngsters experienced **anoxia,** or inadequate oxygen supply, during labor and delivery (Anslow, 1998).

Melinda walks with a halting, lumbering gait and has difficulty keeping her balance. "Some mothers don't know how the palsy happened," confided Judy, "but I do. I got pregnant accidentally, and my boyfriend didn't want to have anything to do with it. I was frightened and alone most of the time. I arrived at the hospital at the last minute. Melinda was breech, and the cord was wrapped around her neck."

Squeezing of the umbilical cord, as in Melinda's case, is one cause of anoxia. Another cause is *placenta abruptio,* or premature separation of the placenta, a life-threatening event with a high rate of infant death (Matsuda, Maeda, & Kouno, 2003). Although the reasons for placenta abruptio are not well understood, teratogens that cause abnormal development of the placenta, such as cigarette smoking, are related to it (Handler et al., 1994). Just as serious is *placenta previa*, a condition caused by implantation of the blastocyst so low in the uterus that the placenta covers the cervical opening. As the cervix dilates and effaces in the third trimester, part of the placenta may detach (Sheiner et al., 2001). When hemorrhaging from placenta abruptio or placenta previa is severe, an emergency cesarean must be performed.

In still other instances, the birth seems to go along all right, but the baby fails to start breathing within a few minutes. Healthy newborns can survive periods of little or no oxygen longer than adults can; they reduce their metabolic rate, thereby conserving the limited oxygen available. Nevertheless, brain damage is likely if regular breathing is delayed more than 10 minutes (Parer, 1998). Can you think of other possible causes of oxygen deprivation that you learned about as you studied prenatal development and birth?

After initial brain injury from anoxia, another phase of cell death can occur several hours later. Currently, researchers are experimenting with ways to prevent this secondary damage. Placing a device around the head that cools the brain by several degrees and administering growth factors (substances naturally produced by the brain to promote recovery from injury) are effective in newborn rats, pigs, and sheep. The techniques show promise for human babies as well (Battin et al., 2001; Gunn, 2000).

How do children who experience anoxia during labor and delivery fare as they get older? Research suggests that the greater the oxygen deprivation, the poorer children's cognitive and language skills in early and middle childhood (Hopkins-Golightly, Raz, & Sander, 2003; Porter-Stevens, Raz, & Sander, 1999). Still, many children with mild to moderate anoxia improve over time (Raz, Shah, & Sander, 1996). In Melinda's case, her physical disability was permanent, but otherwise she fared well.

When development is severely impaired, the anoxia was probably extreme. Perhaps it was caused by prenatal insult to the baby's respiratory system, or it may have happened because the infant's lungs were not yet mature enough to breathe. For example, infants born more than 6 weeks early commonly have **respiratory distress syndrome** (otherwise known as *hyaline membrane disease*). Their tiny lungs are so poorly developed that the air sacs collapse, causing serious breathing difficulties. Today, mechanical respirators keep many such infants alive. In spite of these measures, some babies suffer permanent damage from lack of oxygen, and in other cases their delicate lungs are harmed by the treatment itself. Respiratory distress syndrome is only one of many risks for babies born too soon, as we will see in the following section.

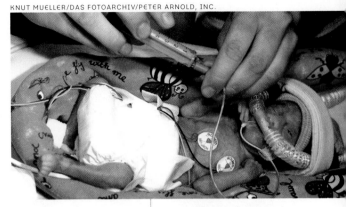

This baby was born 12 weeks before her due date and weighs little more than 2 pounds. Because her lungs are too immature to function independently, she breathes with the aid of a respirator. Her survival and development are seriously at risk.

Preterm and Low-Birth-Weight Infants

Janet, almost 6 months pregnant, and her husband, Rick, boarded a flight in Hartford, Connecticut, on their way to a vacation in Hawaii. During a stopover in San Francisco, Janet told Rick she was bleeding. Rushed to a hospital, she gave birth to Keith, who weighed less than 1½ pounds. Delivered 23 weeks after conception, he had barely reached the age of viability (see Chapter 3, page 104).

During Keith's first month, he experienced one crisis after another. Three days after birth, an ultrasound scan suggested that fragile blood vessels feeding Keith's brain had hemorrhaged, a complication that can cause brain damage. Within 3 weeks, Keith had surgery to close a heart valve that seals automatically in full-term babies. Keith's immature immune system made infections difficult to contain. Repeated illnesses and the drugs used to treat them caused permanent hearing loss. Keith also had respiratory distress syndrome and breathed with the help of a respirator. Soon there was evidence of lung damage. More than 3 months of hospitalization passed before Keith's rough course of complications and treatment eased.

Babies born 3 weeks or more before the end of a full 38-week pregnancy or who weigh less than 5½ pounds (2,500 grams) have for many years been referred to as "premature." A wealth of research indicates that premature babies are at risk for many problems. Birth weight is the

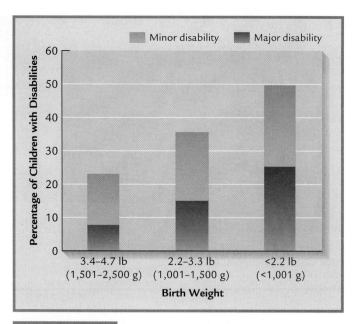

FIGURE 4.5

Incidence of major and minor disabilities by birth weight, obtained from studies of low-birth-weight children at school age.

Major disabilities include cerebral palsy, mental retardation, and vision and hearing impairments. *Minor disabilities* include slightly below-average intelligence, learning disabilities (usually in reading, spelling, and math), mild difficulties in motor control, and behavior problems (including poor attention and impulse control, aggressiveness, noncompliance, depression, passivity, anxiety, and difficulty separating from parents). (Adapted from D'Agostino & Clifford, 1998.)

best available predictor of infant survival and healthy development. Many newborns who weigh less than 3⅓ pounds (1,500 grams) experience difficulties that are not overcome, an effect that becomes stronger as birth weight decreases (Minde, 2000; Palta et al., 2000). Frequent illness, inattention, overactivity, sensory impairments, poor motor coordination, language delays, low intelligence test scores, deficits in school learning, and emotional and behavior problems are some of the difficulties that persist into childhood and adolescence (Bhutta et al., 2002; Hille et al., 2001; Walther, den Ouden, & Verloove-Vanhorick, 2000). In a study that followed very-low-birth-weight individuals to age 20, educational disadvantages were still evident in poorer academic achievement and lower high school graduation and college attendance rates compared with normal birth-weight controls (Hack et al., 2002).

About 1 in 13 American infants and 1 in 18 Canadian infants are born underweight. The problem can occur unexpectedly, as it did for Janet and Rick. But it is highest among poverty-stricken women (Martin et al., 2002; Statistics Canada, 2003a). These mothers, as indicated in Chapter 3, are more likely to be undernourished and exposed to other harmful environmental influences—factors strongly linked to low birth weight. In addition, they often do not receive the prenatal care necessary to protect their vulnerable babies.

Recall from Chapter 2 that prematurity is also common among twins. Twins usually are born about 3 weeks early. Because space inside the uterus is restricted, they gain less weight than singletons after the twentieth week of pregnancy.

PRETERM VERSUS SMALL-FOR-DATE INFANTS ● Although low-birth-weight infants face many obstacles to healthy development, individual differences exist in how well they do. Most go on to lead normal lives; half of those who weighed only a few pounds at birth have no disability (see Figure 4.5). To better understand why some babies do better than others, researchers divide them into two groups. **Preterm infants** are born several weeks or more before their due date. Although they are small, their weight may still be appropriate, based on time spent in the uterus. **Small-for-date infants** are below their expected weight when length of the pregnancy is taken into account. Some small-for-date infants are actually full term. Others are preterm babies who are especially underweight.

Of the two types of babies, small-for-date infants usually have more serious problems. During the first year, they are more likely to die, catch infections, and show evidence of brain damage. By middle childhood, they have lower intelligence test scores, are less attentive, achieve more poorly in school, and are socially immature (Hediger et al., 2002; Minde, 2000). Small-for-date infants probably experienced inadequate nutrition before birth. Perhaps their mothers did not eat properly, the placenta did not function normally, or the babies themselves had defects that prevented them from growing as they should.

CONSEQUENCES FOR CAREGIVING ● Imagine a scrawny, thin-skinned infant whose body is only a little larger than the size of your hand. You try to play with the baby by stroking and talking softly, but he is sleepy and unresponsive. When you feed him, he sucks poorly. He is usually irritable during the short, unpredictable periods in which he is awake.

The appearance and behavior of preterm babies can lead parents to be less sensitive and responsive in caring for them. Compared to full-term infants, preterm babies—especially those who are very ill at birth—are less often held close, touched, and talked to gently. At times, mothers of these infants resort to interfering pokes and verbal commands, in an effort to obtain a higher level of response from the baby (Barratt, Roach, & Leavitt, 1996). This may explain why preterm babies as a group are at risk for child abuse. When they are born to isolated, poverty-stricken mothers who cannot provide good nutrition, health care, and parenting, the likelihood of unfavorable outcomes increases (Bacharach & Baumeister, 1998). In contrast, parents with stable life circumstances and social supports usually can overcome the stresses of caring for a preterm infant. In these cases, even sick preterm babies have a good chance of catching up in development by middle childhood (Liaw & Brooks-Gunn, 1993).

These findings suggest that how well preterm babies develop has a great deal to do with the parent–child relationship. Consequently, interventions directed at supporting both sides of this tie are more likely to help these infants recover.

INTERVENTIONS FOR PRETERM INFANTS ● A preterm baby is cared for in a special Plexiglas-enclosed bed called an *isolette*. Temperature is carefully controlled because these infants cannot yet regulate their own body temperature effectively. To help protect the baby from infection, air is filtered before it enters the isolette. When a preterm infant is fed through a stomach tube, breathes with the aid of a respirator, and receives medication through an intravenous needle, the isolette can be very isolating indeed! Physical needs that otherwise would lead to close contact and other human stimulation are met mechanically.

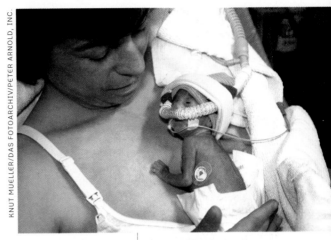

Special Infant Stimulation. At one time doctors believed that stimulating such fragile babies could be harmful. Now we know that in proper doses, certain kinds of stimulation can help preterm infants develop. In some intensive care nurseries, preterm babies can be seen rocking in suspended hammocks or lying on waterbeds designed to replace the gentle motion they would have experienced while still in the mother's uterus. Other forms of stimulation have also been used—for example, an attractive mobile or a tape recording of a heartbeat, soft music, or the mother's voice. These experiences promote faster weight gain, more predictable sleep patterns, and greater alertness (Marshall-Baker, Lickliter, & Cooper, 1998; Standley, 1998).

Touch is an especially important form of stimulation. In baby animals, touching the skin releases certain brain chemicals that support physical growth—effects believed to occur in humans as well. When preterm infants were gently massaged several times each day in the hospital, they gained weight faster and, at the end of the first year, were more advanced in mental and motor development than preterm babies not given this stimulation (Field, 2001; Field, Hernandez-Reif, & Freedman, 2004).

In developing countries where hospitalization is not always possible, skin-to-skin "kangaroo care," in which the preterm infant is tucked close to the chest and peers over the top of the caregiver's clothing, is encouraged. The technique is used in Western nations as a supplement to hospital intensive care. It fosters improved oxygenation of the baby's body, temperature regulation, breathing, feeding, alertness, and infant survival (Anderson, 1999; Feldman & Eidelman, 2003). In addition, mothers and fathers practicing kangaroo care feel more confident about meeting their infants' needs and interact more sensitively and affectionately with them. And as Figure 4.6 shows, their babies develop more favorably during the first year than preterm infants not receiving such care (Feldman et al., 2002, 2003). cause of its diverse benefits, more than 80 percent of North American nurses now offer kangaroo care to preterm newborns (Engler et al., 2002).

This mother practices "kangaroo care" with her preterm baby in the intensive care nursery. By holding the infant close to her chest, she promotes oxygenation of the baby's body, temperature regulation, feeding, alertness, and more favorable development. At the same time, she gains confidence in her ability to meet her fragile newborn's needs.

FIGURE 4.6

Six-month mental and motor development of preterm infants receiving kangaroo care versus controls.

In this study, nurses arranged for some mothers of preterm newborns to provide kangaroo care for an hour a day over a 2-week period in the intensive care nursery. Compared with a control group, the kangaroo care babies scored higher on both mental and motor development at age 6 months. Kangaroo care induced mothers to interact more sensitively and affectionately with their babies. The infants responded with increased alertness and social involvement, which sparked further improvement in maternal caregiving. These maternal and infant behaviors predicted more favorable development. (From Feldman et al., 2002.)

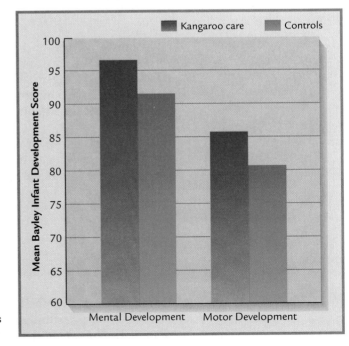

Social Issues: Health

A Cross-National Perspective on Health Care and Other Policies for Parents and Newborn Babies

Infant mortality is an index used around the world to assess the overall health of a nation's children. It refers to the number of deaths in the first year of life per 1,000 live births. The United States has the most up-to-date health care technology in the world, including a newborn intensive care capacity per number of births that far exceeds that of other industrialized nations (Thompson, Goodman, & Little, 2002). Nevertheless, it has made less progress in reducing infant deaths. Over the past three decades, it has slipped in the international rankings, from seventh in the 1950s to twenty-fourth in the year 2001. Members of America's poor ethnic minorities, African-American babies especially, are at greatest risk. Black infants are more than twice as likely as white infants to die in the first year of life (U.S. Census Bureau, 2003a). Canada, in contrast, has achieved one of the lowest infant mortality rates in the world. It ranks fifteenth and differs only slightly from top-ranked countries. Still, infant mortality rates among Canada's lowest-income groups are two to four times higher than the nation's as a whole (Health Canada, 2002e).

Neonatal mortality, the rate of death within the first month of life, accounts for 67 percent of the infant death rate in the United States and for 80 percent in Canada. Two factors are largely responsible for neonatal mortality. The first is serious physical defects, most of which cannot be prevented. The percentage of babies born with physical defects is about the same in all ethnic and income groups. The second leading cause of neonatal mortality is low birth weight, which is largely preventable. African-American and Canadian Aboriginal babies are more than twice as likely as white infants to be born early and underweight (Health Canada, 2000b; Martin et al., 2002).

Widespread poverty and, in the United States, weak health care programs for mothers and young children are largely responsible for these trends. Each country in Figure 4.7 that outranks the United States in infant survival provides all its citizens with government-sponsored health care benefits. And each takes extra steps to make sure that pregnant mothers and babies have access to good nutrition, high-quality medical care, and social and economic supports that promote effective parenting.

For example, all Western European nations guarantee women a certain number of prenatal visits at very low or no cost. After a baby is born, a health professional routinely visits the home to provide counseling about infant care and to arrange continuing medical services. Home assistance is especially extensive in the Netherlands. For a token fee, each mother is granted a specially trained maternity helper, who assists with infant care, shopping, housekeeping, meal preparation, and the care of other children during the days after delivery (Buekens et al., 1993; Kamerman, 1993).

Paid, job-protected employment leave is another vital societal intervention for new parents. Canadian mothers or fathers are eligible for up to 1 year of parental leave. Paid leave is widely available in other industrialized nations as well. Sweden has the most generous parental leave program in the world. Parents have the right to paid birth leave of 2 weeks for fathers plus 15 months of paid leave to share between them (Seward, Yeats, & Zottarelli, 2002). Even less-developed nations offer parental leave benefits. For example, in the People's Republic of China, a new mother is granted 3 months leave at regular pay. Furthermore, many countries supplement basic paid leave. In Germany, for example, after a fully paid 3-month leave, a parent may take 2 more years at a modest flat rate and a third year at no pay (Kamerman, 2000).

Yet in the United States, the federal government mandates *only 12 weeks of unpaid leave* for employees in companies with at least 50 workers. Most women,

Some very small or sick babies, however, are too weak for much stimulation. The noise, bright lights, and constant medical monitoring of the intensive care nursery are already overwhelming, triggering irritability and withdrawal. And like full-term infants, preterm infants differ in how they respond to sights, sounds, and touch (Korner, 1996). Doctors and nurses must carefully adjust the amount and kind of stimulation to fit the baby's individual needs.

Training Parents in Infant Caregiving Skills. Interventions that support parents of preterm infants generally teach them about the infant's characteristics and promote caregiving skills. For parents with the economic and personal resources to care for a preterm infant, just a few sessions of coaching in recognizing and responding to the baby's needs are linked to steady gains in mental test performance that, after several years, equal those of full-term children (Achenbach et al., 1990). Warm parenting that helps preterm infants sustain attention (for example, gently commenting on and showing the baby features of a toy) is especially helpful in promoting early cognitive and language development (Smith et al., 1996).

When preterm infants live in stressed, low-income households, long-term, intensive intervention is necessary. In the Infant Health and Development Project, preterm babies born into poverty received a comprehensive intervention that combined medical follow-up, weekly parent training sessions, and cognitively stimulating child care from 1 to 3 years of age. More than four times as many intervention children as no-intervention controls (39 versus 9 percent) were

144

however, work in smaller businesses (Hewlett, 2003). And even those who work in large-enough companies may be unable to afford to take unpaid leave. In 2002, California became the first state to guarantee a mother or father paid leave—up to 6 weeks at half salary, regardless of the size of the company. Nevertheless, research indicates that 6 weeks of childbirth leave is too short. When a family is stressed by a baby's arrival, leaves of 6 weeks or less are linked to maternal anxiety and depression and to negative interactions with the baby. Longer leaves of 12 weeks or more predict favorable maternal mental health and sensitive, responsive caregiving (Clark et al., 1997; Hyde et al., 1995). Single women and their babies are most hurt by the absence of a generous national paid leave policy. These mothers are usually the sole source of support for their families and can least afford to take time from their jobs.

In countries with low infant mortality rates, expectant mothers need not wonder how or where they will get health care and other resources to support their baby's development. The powerful impact of universal, high-quality health care and social services on maternal and infant well-being provides strong justification for implementing similar programs in the United States.

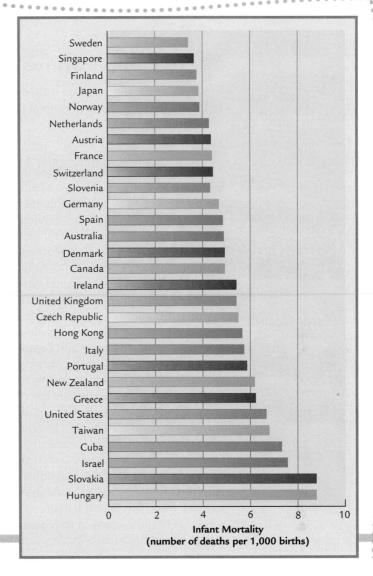

FIGURE 4.7

Infant mortality in 29 nations.

Despite its advanced health care technology, the United States ranks poorly. It is twenty-fourth in the world, with a death rate of 6.7 infants per 1,000 births. Canada grants all its citizens government-funded health care and ranks fifteenth. Its infant death rate is 4.9 per 1,000 births. (Adapted from U.S. Census Bureau, 2003a.)

within normal range at age 3 in intelligence, psychological adjustment, and physical growth (Bradley et al., 1994). In addition, mothers in the intervention group were more affectionate and more often encouraged play and cognitive mastery in their children—one reason their 3-year-olds may have been developing so favorably (McCarton, 1998).

Yet by age 5, the intervention children had lost ground. And by age 8, the intervention and control children no longer differed in development (Brooks-Gunn et al., 1994; McCarton et al., 1997). These very vulnerable children need high-quality intervention well beyond age 3—even into the school years. And special strategies, such as extra adult–child interaction, may be necessary to achieve lasting changes in children with the lowest birth weights (Berlin et al., 1998).

What happened to Keith, the very sick baby you met at the beginning of this section? Because of advanced medical technology and new ways of helping parents, many preterm infants survive and eventually catch up in development, but Keith was not one of the lucky ones. Even with the best care, all but a few babies born as early and with as low a birth weight as Keith either die or end up with serious disabilities (Doyle, 2001). Six months after he was born, Keith died without ever having left the hospital.

Keith's premature birth was unavoidable, but the high rate of underweight babies in the United States—one of the worst in the industrialized world—could be greatly reduced by improving the health and social conditions described in the Social Issues: Health box above. Fortunately, today we can save many preterm babies, but an even better course of action would be to prevent this serious threat to infant survival and development before it happens.

Birth Complications, Parenting, and Resilience

In the preceding sections, we considered a variety of birth complications. Now let's try to put the evidence together. Can any general principles help us understand how infants who survive a traumatic birth are likely to develop? A landmark study carried out in Hawaii provides answers to this question.

In 1955, Emmy Werner began to follow the development of nearly 700 infants on the island of Kauai who experienced either mild, moderate, or severe birth complications. Each was matched, on the basis of SES and ethnicity, with a healthy newborn (Werner & Smith, 1982). Findings revealed that the likelihood of long-term difficulties increased if birth trauma was severe. But among mildly to moderately stressed children, the best predictor of how well they did in later years was the quality of their home environments. Children growing up in stable families did almost as well on measures of intelligence and psychological adjustment as those with no birth problems. Those exposed to poverty, family disorganization, and mentally ill parents often developed serious learning difficulties, behavior problems, and emotional disturbance.

The Kauai study tells us that as long as birth injuries are not overwhelming, a supportive home environment can restore children's growth. But the most intriguing cases in this study were the handful of exceptions. A few children with fairly serious birth complications and troubled family environments grew into competent adults who fared as well as controls in career attainment and psychological adjustment. Werner found that these children relied on factors outside the family and within themselves to overcome stress. Some had especially attractive personalities that caused them to receive positive responses from relatives, neighbors, and peers. In other instances, a grandparent, aunt, uncle, or babysitter established a warm relationship with the child and provided the needed emotional support (Werner, 1989, 1993; Werner & Smith, 1992, 2001).

Do these outcomes remind you of the characteristics of resilient children, discussed in Chapter 1? The Kauai study—and other similar investigations—reveal that the impact of early biological risks often wanes as children's personal characteristics and social experiences contribute increasingly to their functioning (Laucht, Esser, & Schmidt, 1997; Resnick et al., 1999). In sum, when the overall balance of life events tips toward the favorable side, children with serious birth problems can develop successfully. And when negative factors outweigh positive ones, even a sturdy newborn can become a lifelong casualty.

ASK YOURSELF

REVIEW Sensitive care can help preterm infants recover, but unfortunately they are less likely than full-term newborns to receive such care. Explain why.

APPLY Cecilia and Adena each gave birth to a 3-pound baby 7 weeks preterm. Cecilia is single and on welfare. Adena and her husband are happily married and earn a good income. Plan an intervention appropriate for helping each baby develop.

CONNECT List factors discussed in this chapter and in Chapter 3 that increase the chances that an infant will be born underweight. How many of these factors could be prevented by better health care for mothers and babies?

REFLECT Many people object to the use of extraordinary medical measures to save extremely low-birth-weight babies (less than 1½ pounds, or 1,000 grams), since most who survive develop serious physical, cognitive, and emotional problems. Do you agree or disagree? Explain.

Precious Moments After Birth

Yolanda and Jay's account of Joshua's birth revealed that the time spent holding and touching him right after delivery was filled with intense emotion. A mother given her infant at this time will usually stroke the baby gently, look into the infant's eyes, and talk softly (Klaus & Kennell, 1982). Fathers respond similarly. Most are overjoyed at the birth of the baby; characterize the experience as "awesome," "indescribable," or "unforgettable"; and display intense interest in their newborn child (Bader, 1995; Rose, 2000). Regardless of SES or participation in childbirth classes, fathers touch, look at, talk to, and kiss their newborn infants just as much as mothers do. When they hold the baby, sometimes they exceed mothers in stimulation and affection (Parke & Tinsley, 1981).

Immediately after birth, many nonhuman animals engage in specific caregiving behaviors that are critical for survival of the young. For example, a mother cat licks her newborn kittens and then encircles them with her body (Schneirla, Rosenblatt, & Tobach, 1963). Rats, sheep, and goats engage in similar licking behaviors. But if the mother is separated from her young during the period following delivery, her responsiveness declines until finally she rejects the infant (Poindron & Le Neindre, 1980; Rosenblatt, 2002).

Do human parents also require close physical contact in the hours after birth for **bonding, or feelings of affection and concern for the infant,** to develop? Current evidence indicates that the human parent–infant relationship does not depend on a precise, early period of togetherness. Some parents report sudden, deep feelings of affection on first holding their babies. For others, these emotions emerge gradually (Lamb, 1994). In adoptive parents, a warm, affectionate relationship can develop even if the child enters the family months or years after birth (Hodges & Tizard, 1989). Human bonding is a complex process that depends on many factors, not just on what happens during a short sensitive period.

Still, contact with the baby after birth might be one of several factors that helps build a good parent–infant relationship. Research shows that mothers learn to discriminate their newborn baby from other infants on the basis of touch, smell, and sight (a photograph) after as little as 1 hour of contact (Kaitz et al., 1987, 1988, 1993a). Fathers, as well, can recognize their baby by touch and sign after brief exposure (Bader & Phillips, 2002; Kaitz, 1993b). This early recognition probably facilitates responsiveness to the infant. Also, mothers with close and continuous proximity to their newborns report thinking often about the baby's safety and well-being. These concerns intensify with brief separations (Feldman et al., 1999).

Clearly, early contact supports parents' feelings of caring and affection. Realizing this, today hospitals offer an arrangement called **rooming in, in which the infant stays in the mother's hospital room all or most of the time.** If parents do not choose this option or cannot do so for medical reasons, there is no evidence that their competence as caregivers will be compromised or that the baby will suffer emotionally.

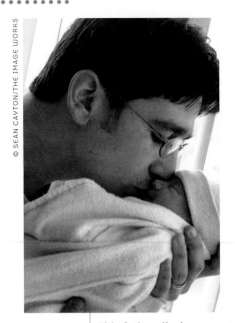

© SEAN CAYTON/THE IMAGE WORKS

This father displays great affection for and involvement with his newborn baby. Like mothers, fathers typically express their elation by touching, looking at, talking to, and kissing the infant.

The Newborn Baby's Capacities

As recently as the mid-twentieth century, scientists considered the newborn baby to be a passive, disorganized being who could see, hear, feel, and do very little. Today we know that this image is wrong. Newborn babies have a remarkable set of capacities that are crucial for survival and for evoking attention and care from parents. In relating to the physical and social world, babies are active from the very start.

TABLE 4.2

Some Newborn Reflexes

REFLEX	STIMULATION	RESPONSE	AGE OF DISAPPEARANCE	FUNCTION
Eye blink	Shine bright light at eyes or clap hand near head	Infant quickly closes eyelids	Permanent	Protects infant from strong stimulation
Rooting	Stroke cheek near corner of mouth	Head turns toward source of stimulation	3 weeks (becomes voluntary head turning at this time)	Helps infant find the nipple
Sucking	Place finger in infant's mouth	Infant sucks finger rhythmically	Replaced by voluntary sucking after 4 months	Permits feeding
Swimming	Place infant face down in pool of water	Baby paddles and kicks in swimming motion	4–6 months	Helps infant survive if dropped into water
Moro	Hold infant horizontally on back and let head drop slightly, or produce a sudden loud sound against surface supporting infant	Infant makes an "embracing" motion by arching back, extending legs, throwing arms outward, and then bringing arms in toward the body	6 months	In human evolutionary past, may have helped infant cling to mother
Palmar grasp	Place finger in infant's hand and press against palm	Spontaneous grasp of finger	3–4 months	Prepares infant for voluntary grasping
Tonic neck	Turn baby's head to one side while infant is lying awake on back	Infant lies in a "fencing position." One arm is extended in front of eyes on side to which head is turned, other arm is flexed	4 months	May prepare infant for voluntary reaching
Stepping	Hold infant under arms and permit bare feet to touch a flat surface	Infant lifts one foot after another in stepping response	2 months in infants who gain weight quickly; sustained in lighter infants	Prepares infant for voluntary walking
Babinski	Stroke sole of foot from toe toward heel	Toes fan out and curl as foot twists in	8–12 months	Unknown

Sources: Knobloch & Pasamanick, 1974; Prechtl & Beintema, 1965; Thelen, Fisher, & Ridley-Johnson, 1984.

●Reflexes

A **reflex** is an inborn, automatic response to a particular form of stimulation. Reflexes are the newborn baby's most obvious organized patterns of behavior. As Jay placed Joshua on a table in my classroom, we saw several. When Jay bumped the side of the table, Joshua reacted by flinging his arms wide and bringing them back toward his body. As Yolanda stroked Joshua's cheek, he turned his head in her direction. When she put her finger in Joshua's palm, he grabbed on tightly. Look at Table 4.2 and see if you can name the newborn reflexes that Joshua displayed. Then let's consider the meaning and purpose of these curious behaviors.

ADAPTIVE VALUE OF REFLEXES ● Some reflexes have survival value. The rooting reflex helps a breastfed baby find the mother's nipple. And if sucking were not automatic, our species would be unlikely to survive for a single generation! The swimming reflex helps a baby who is accidentally dropped into a body of water stay afloat, increasing the chances of retrieval by the caregiver.

Other reflexes probably helped babies survive during our evolutionary past. For example, the Moro, or "embracing," reflex is believed to have helped infants cling to their mothers when they were carried about all day. If the baby happened to lose support, the reflex caused the infant to embrace and, along with the palmar grasp reflex (so strong during the first week that it can support the baby's entire weight), regain its hold on the mother's body (Kessen, 1967; Prechtl, 1958).

Several reflexes help parents and infants establish gratifying interaction. A baby who searches for and successfully finds the nipple, sucks easily during feedings, and grasps when her hand is touched encourages parents to respond lovingly and feel competent as caregivers. Reflexes can also help parents comfort the baby because they permit infants to control distress and amount of stimulation. For example, on short trips with Joshua to the grocery store, Yolanda brought along a pacifier. If he became fussy, sucking helped quiet him until she could feed, change, or hold and rock him.

In the Moro reflex, loss of support or a sudden loud sound causes the baby to arch her back, extend her arms outward, and then bring them in toward her body.

REFLEXES AND THE DEVELOPMENT OF MOTOR SKILLS ● A few reflexes form the basis for complex motor skills that develop later. For example, the tonic neck reflex may prepare the baby for voluntary reaching. When infants lie on their backs in this "fencing position," they naturally gaze at the hand in front of their eyes. The reflex may encourage them to combine vision with arm movements and, eventually, reach for objects (Knobloch & Pasamanick, 1974).

Certain reflexes—such as the palmar grasp, swimming, and stepping—drop out early, but the motor functions involved seem to be renewed later. The stepping reflex, for example, looks like a primitive walking response. In infants who gain weight quickly in the weeks after birth, the stepping reflex drops out because thigh and calf muscles are not strong enough to lift the baby's increasingly chubby legs. However, if the lower part of the infant's body is dipped in water, the reflex reappears, since the buoyancy of the water lightens the load on the baby's muscles (Thelen, Fisher, & Ridley-Johnson, 1984). When the stepping reflex is exercised regularly, babies display more spontaneous stepping movements and gain muscle strength. Consequently, they tend to walk several weeks earlier than if stepping is not practiced (Zelazo et al., 1993). However, there is no special need for infants to practice the stepping reflex because all normal babies walk in due time.

When held upright under the arms, newborn babies show reflexive stepping movements.

In the case of the swimming reflex, trying to build on it is risky. Although young babies placed in a swimming pool will paddle and kick, they swallow large amounts of water. This lowers the concentration of salt in the baby's blood, which can cause brain swelling and seizures. Despite this remarkable reflex, swimming lessons are best postponed until at least 3 years of age.

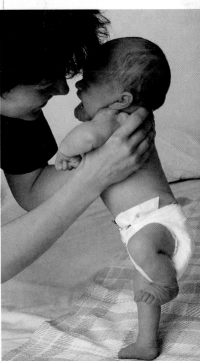

This baby shows the Babinski reflex. When an adult strokes the sole of the foot, the toes fan out. Then they curl as the foot twists in.

© INNERVISIONS

© LAURA DWIGHT

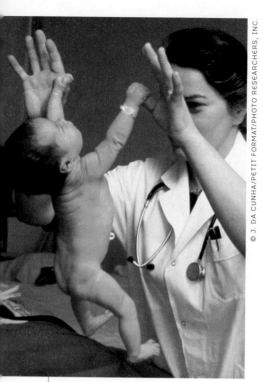

© J. DA CUNHA/PETIT FORMAT/PHOTO RESEARCHERS, INC.

The palmar grasp reflex is so strong during the first week after birth that many infants can use it to support their entire weight.

THE IMPORTANCE OF ASSESSING NEWBORN REFLEXES ● Look at Table 4.2 again, and you will see that most newborn reflexes disappear during the first 6 months. Researchers believe that this is due to a gradual increase in voluntary control over behavior as the cerebral cortex develops. Pediatricians test reflexes carefully, especially if a newborn has experienced birth trauma, because reflexes can reveal the health of the baby's nervous system. Weak or absent reflexes, overly rigid or exaggerated reflexes, and reflexes that persist beyond the point in development when they should normally disappear can signal brain damage (Zafeiriou, 2000). However, individual differences in reflexive responses exist that are not cause for concern. An observer must assess newborn reflexes along with other characteristics to accurately distinguish normal from abnormal central nervous system functioning (Touwen, 1984).

States

Throughout the day and night, newborn infants move in and out of the five **states of arousal, or degrees of sleep and wakefulness,** described in Table 4.3. During the first month, these states alternate frequently. Quiet alertness is the most fleeting. It usually moves quickly toward fussing and crying. Much to the relief of their fatigued parents, newborns spend the greatest amount of time asleep—about 16 to 18 hours a day. Although newborns sleep more at night than during the day, their sleep–wake cycles are affected more by fullness–hunger than by darkness–light (Goodlin-Jones, Burnham, & Anders, 2000).

However, striking individual differences in daily rhythms exist that affect parents' attitudes toward and interactions with the baby. A few newborns sleep for long periods, increasing the energy their well-rested parents have for sensitive, responsive care. Other babies cry a great deal, and their parents must exert great effort to soothe them. If these parents do not succeed, they may feel less competent and positive toward their infant. Babies who spend more time alert probably receive more social stimulation and opportunities to explore and, therefore, may be slightly advantaged in mental development (Gertner et al., 2002).

Of the states listed in Table 4.3, the two extremes of sleep and crying have been of greatest interest to researchers. Each tells us something about normal and abnormal early development.

SLEEP ● One day, Yolanda and Jay watched Joshua while he slept and wondered why his eyelids and body twitched and his rate of breathing varied. Sleep is made up of at least two states. Yolanda and Jay happened to observe irregular, or **rapid-eye-movement (REM), sleep,** in which electrical brain-wave activity, measured with an EEG, is remarkably similar to that of the waking state. The eyes dart beneath the lids; heart rate, blood pressure, and breathing are uneven; and slight body movements occur. The expression "sleeping like a baby" was probably not meant to describe this state! In contrast, during regular, or **non-rapid-eye-movement (NREM), sleep,** the body is almost motionless, and heart rate, breathing, and brain-wave activity are slow and even.

Like children and adults, newborns alternate between REM and NREM sleep. However, they spend far more time in the REM state than they ever will again. REM sleep accounts for 50 percent of the newborn baby's sleep time. By 3 to 5 years of age, it has declined to an adultlike level of 20 percent (Louis et al., 1997).

Why do young infants spend so much time in REM sleep? In older children and adults, the REM state is associated with dreaming. Babies probably do not dream, at least not in the same way we do. But sleep researchers believe that the stimulation of REM sleep is vital for growth of the central nervous system. Young infants seem to have a special need for this stimulation because they spend so little time in an alert state, when they can get input from the environment. In support of this idea, the percentage of REM sleep is especially great in the fetus and in preterm babies, who are even less able to take advantage of external stimulation than are full-term newborns (DiPietro et al., 1996; Sahni et al., 1995).

Whereas the brain-wave activity of REM sleep safeguards the central nervous system, the rapid eye movements protect the health of the eye. Eye movements cause the vitreous (gelatin-like substance within the eye) to circulate, thereby delivering oxygen to parts of the eye that do not

TABLE 4.3

Infant States of Arousal

STATE	DESCRIPTION	DAILY DURATION IN NEWBORN
Regular, or NREM, sleep	The infant is at full rest and shows little or no body activity. The eyelids are closed, no eye movements occur, the face is relaxed, and breathing is slow and regular.	8–9 hours
Irregular, or REM, sleep	Gentle limb movements, occasional stirring, and facial grimacing occur. Although the eyelids are closed, occasional rapid eye movements can be seen beneath them. Breathing is irregular.	8–9 hours
Drowsiness	The infant is either falling asleep or waking up. Body is less active than in irregular sleep but more active than in regular sleep. The eyes open and close; when open, they have a glazed look. Breathing is even but somewhat faster than in regular sleep.	Varies
Quiet alertness	The infant's body is relatively inactive, with eyes open and attentive. Breathing is even.	2–3 hours
Waking activity and crying	The infant shows frequent bursts of uncoordinated body activity. Breathing is very irregular. Face may be relaxed or tense and wrinkled. Crying may occur.	1–4 hours

Source: Wolff, 1966.

have their own blood supply. During sleep, when the eyes and the vitreous are still, visual structures are at risk for anoxia. As the brain cycles through periods of REM sleep, rapid eye movements stir up the vitreous, ensuring that the eye is fully oxygenated (Blumberg & Lucas, 1996).

Because the normal sleep behavior of the newborn baby is organized and patterned, observations of sleep states can help identify central nervous system abnormalities. In infants who are brain damaged or who have experienced serious birth trauma, disturbed REM–NREM sleep cycles often are present. Babies with poor sleep organization are likely to be behaviorally disorganized and, therefore, to have difficulty learning and eliciting caregiver interactions that enhance their development (Groome et al., 1997; Halpern, MacLean, & Baumeister, 1995). And the brain-functioning problems that underlie newborn sleep irregularities may culminate in sudden infant death syndrome, a major cause of infant mortality (see the Social Issues: Health box on page 152).

CRYING ● Crying is the first way that babies communicate, letting parents know that they need food, comfort, and stimulation. During the weeks after birth, all babies seem to have some fussy periods when they are difficult to console. But most of the time, the nature of the cry, combined with the experiences that led up to it, helps guide parents toward its cause. The baby's cry is actually a complex stimulus that varies in intensity, from a whimper to a message of all-out distress (Gustafson, Wood, & Green, 2000). As early as the first few weeks of life, infants can be identified by the unique vocal "signature" of their cry, which helps parents locate their baby from a distance (Gustafson, Green, & Cleland, 1994).

Young infants usually cry because of physical needs. Hunger is the most common cause, but babies may also cry in response to temperature change when undressed, a sudden noise, or a painful stimulus. Newborn crying can also be caused by the sound of another crying baby (Dondi, Simion, & Caltran, 1999). Some researchers believe that

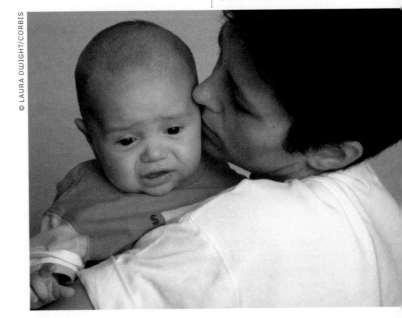

In responding to her crying baby's needs, this mother holds him upright against her gently moving body. Besides encouraging infants to stop crying, this technique causes them to become quietly alert and attentive to the environment.

© LAURA DWIGHT/CORBIS

Social Issues: Health

The Mysterious Tragedy of Sudden Infant Death Syndrome

Millie awoke with a start one morning and looked at the clock. It was 7:30, and Sasha had missed her night waking and early morning feeding. Wondering if she was all right, Millie and her husband Stuart tiptoed into the room. Sasha lay still, curled up under her blanket. She had died silently during her sleep.

Sasha was a victim of **sudden infant death syndrome (SIDS),** the unexpected death, usually during the night, of an infant younger than 1 year of age that remains unexplained after thorough investigation. In industrialized nations, SIDS is the leading cause of infant mortality between 1 week and 12 months of age. It accounts for one-third of these deaths in the United States and for one-fourth in Canada (Health Canada, 2002; MacDorman et al., 2002).

Although the precise cause of SIDS is not known, its victims usually show physical problems from the very beginning. Early medical records of SIDS babies reveal higher rates of prematurity and low birth weight, poor Apgar scores, and limp muscle tone. Abnormal heart rate and respiration and disturbances in sleep–wake activity are also involved (Leach et al., 1999; Malloy & Hoffman, 1995). At the time of death, many SIDS babies have a mild respiratory infection (Kohlendorfer, Kiechl, & Sperl, 1998). This seems to increase the chances of respiratory failure in an already vulnerable baby.

One hypothesis about the cause of SIDS is that problems in brain functioning prevent these infants from learning how to respond when their survival is threatened—for example, when respiration is suddenly interrupted. Between 2 and 4 months, when SIDS is most likely, reflexes decline and are replaced by voluntary, learned responses. Respiratory and muscular weaknesses may stop SIDS babies from acquiring behaviors that replace defensive reflexes (Lipsitt, 2003). As a result, when breathing difficulties occur during sleep, the infants do not wake up, shift their position, or cry out for help. Instead, they simply give in to oxygen deprivation and death. In support of this interpretation, autopsies reveal that SIDS babies, more often than other infants, show a chemical abnormality in brain centers that control breathing (Kinney, Filiano, & White, 2001).

In an effort to reduce the occurrence of SIDS, researchers are studying environmental factors related to it. Maternal cigarette smoking, both during and after pregnancy, as well as smoking by other caregivers, strongly predicts the disorder. Babies exposed to cigarette smoke have more respiratory infections and are two to three times more likely than are nonexposed infants to die of SIDS (Dwyer, Ponsonby, & Couper, 1999; Sundell, 2001). Prenatal abuse of drugs that depress central nervous system functioning (opiates and barbiturates) increases the risk of SIDS tenfold (Kandall et al., 1993). SIDS babies are also more likely to sleep on their stomachs than on their backs and are often wrapped very warmly in clothing and blankets (Galland, Taylor, & Bolton, 2002).

Some researchers suspect that nicotine, depressant drugs, excessive body warmth, and respiratory infection lead to physiological stress, which disrupts the normal sleep pattern. When sleep-deprived infants experience a sleep "rebound," they sleep more deeply, which results in loss of muscle tone in the airway passages. In at-risk babies, the airway may collapse, and the infant may fail to arouse sufficiently to reestablish breathing (Simpson, 2001). In other cases, healthy babies sleeping face down in soft bedding may die from continually breathing their own exhaled breath.

Quitting smoking, changing an infant's sleeping position, and removing a few bedclothes can reduce the incidence

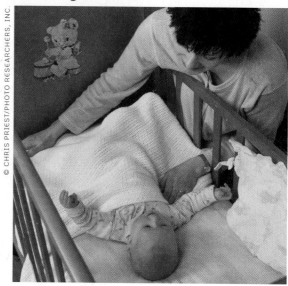

Having babies sleep on their backs with only a light covering has dramatically reduced the incidence of sudden infant death syndrome (SIDS). Taking these precautions reduces the chances that an infant's face will become trapped in blankets and that excessive body warmth will lead to physiological stress followed by deeper sleep. Under these conditions, at-risk babies may fail to arouse and reestablish respiration.

of SIDS. For example, if women refrained from smoking while pregnant, an estimated 30 percent of SIDS would be prevented. Public education campaigns that discourage parents from putting babies down on their stomachs have led to dramatic reductions in SIDS in many countries (American Academy of Pediatrics, 2000; Schlaud et al., 1999).

When SIDS does occur, surviving family members require a great deal of help to overcome a sudden and unexpected death. As Millie commented 6 months after Sasha's death, "It's the worst crisis we've ever been through. What's helped us most are the comforting words of others who've experienced the same tragedy."

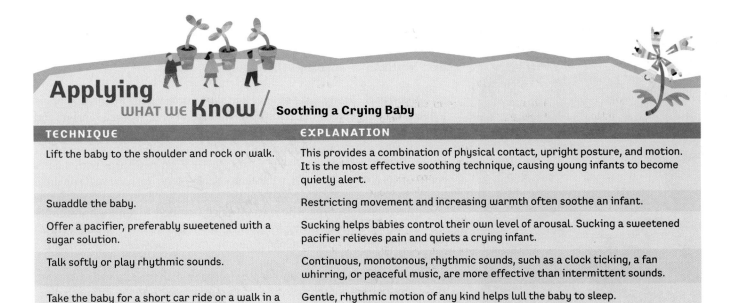

Applying WHAT WE Know / Soothing a Crying Baby

TECHNIQUE	EXPLANATION
Lift the baby to the shoulder and rock or walk.	This provides a combination of physical contact, upright posture, and motion. It is the most effective soothing technique, causing young infants to become quietly alert.
Swaddle the baby.	Restricting movement and increasing warmth often soothe an infant.
Offer a pacifier, preferably sweetened with a sugar solution.	Sucking helps babies control their own level of arousal. Sucking a sweetened pacifier relieves pain and quiets a crying infant.
Talk softly or play rhythmic sounds.	Continuous, monotonous, rhythmic sounds, such as a clock ticking, a fan whirring, or peaceful music, are more effective than intermittent sounds.
Take the baby for a short car ride or a walk in a baby carriage; swing the baby in a cradle.	Gentle, rhythmic motion of any kind helps lull the baby to sleep.
Massage the baby's body.	Stroke the baby's torso and limbs with continuous, gentle motions. This technique is used in some non-Western cultures to relax the baby's muscles.
Combine several methods just listed.	Stimulating several of the baby's senses at once is often more effective than stimulating only one.
If these methods do not work, let the baby cry for a short period.	Occasionally, a baby responds well to just being put down and will, after a few minutes, fall asleep.

Sources: Blass, 1999; Campos, 1989; Lester, 1985; Reisman, 1987.

this response reflects an inborn capacity to react to the suffering of others. Furthermore, crying typically increases during the early weeks, peaks at about 6 weeks, and then declines. Because this trend appears in many cultures with vastly different infant care practices, researchers believe that normal readjustments of the central nervous system underlie it (Barr, 2001).

The next time you hear an infant cry, notice your own mental and physical reaction. The sound stimulates strong feelings of arousal and discomfort in just about anyone—men and women, parents and nonparents (Boukydis & Burgess, 1982; Murray, 1985). This powerful response is probably innately programmed in all human beings to help ensure that babies receive the care and protection they need to survive.

Soothing Crying Infants. Although parents do not always interpret their baby's cry correctly, experience quickly improves their accuracy. Fortunately, there are many ways to soothe a crying baby when feeding and diaper changing do not work (see Applying What We Know above). The technique that Western parents usually try first, lifting the baby to the shoulder and rocking or walking, is most effective.

Another common soothing method is swaddling—wrapping the baby snugly in a blanket. The Quechua, who live in the cold, high-altitude desert regions of Peru, dress young babies in several layers of clothing and blankets that cover the head and body. The result—a warm pouch placed on the mother's back that moves rhythmically as she walks—reduces crying and promotes sleep. It also allows the baby to conserve energy for early growth in the harsh Peruvian highlands (Tronick, Thomas, & Daltabuit, 1994).

In many tribal and village societies and non-Western developed nations, infants spend most of the day and night in close physical contact with their caregivers. Among the !Kung of the desert regions of Botswana, Africa, mothers carry their young babies in grass-lined, animal-skin slings

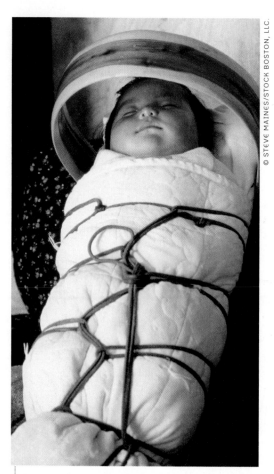

© STEVE MAINES/STOCK BOSTON, LLC.

Some cultures routinely swaddle young infants, restricting movement and increasing warmth by wrapping blankets tightly around the body. This Navajo baby rests on a traditional cradle board that can be strapped to the mother's back. Swaddling reduces crying and promotes sleep.

hung on their hips, so the infants can see their surroundings and can nurse at will. Japanese mothers also spend much time in close body contact with their babies (Small, 1998). Infants in these cultures show shorter bouts of crying than North American babies (Barr, 2001).

Abnormal Crying. Like reflexes and sleep patterns, the infant's cry offers a clue to central nervous system distress. The cries of brain-damaged babies and those who have experienced prenatal and birth complications are often shrill, piercing, and shorter in duration than the cries of healthy infants (Boukydis & Lester, 1998; Green, Irwin, & Gustafson, 2000). Even newborns with a fairly common problem—*colic,* or persistent crying—tend to have high-pitched, harsh-sounding cries (Zeskind & Barr, 1997). Although the cause of colic is unknown, certain newborns, who react especially strongly to unpleasant stimuli, are susceptible. Because their crying is intense, they have more difficulty calming down than other babies. Colic generally subsides between 3 and 6 months of age (Barr & Gunnar, 2000; St James-Roberts et al., 2003).

Most parents try to respond to a crying baby's call for help with extra care and attention, but sometimes the cry is so unpleasant and the infant so difficult to soothe that parents become frustrated, resentful, and angry. Preterm and ill babies are more likely to be abused by highly stressed parents, who sometimes mention a high-pitched, grating cry as one factor that caused them to lose control and harm the baby (Zeskind & Lester, 2001). We will discuss a host of additional influences on child abuse in Chapter 10.

Sensory Capacities

On his visit to my class, Joshua looked wide-eyed at my bright pink blouse and turned to the sound of his mother's voice. During feedings, he lets Yolanda know by the way he sucks that he prefers the taste of breast milk to a bottle of plain water. Clearly, Joshua has some well-developed sensory capacities. In the following sections, we explore the newborn baby's responsiveness to touch, taste, smell, sound, and visual stimulation.

TOUCH ● In our discussion of preterm infants, we saw that touch helps stimulate early physical growth. And as we will see in Chapter 7, it is vital for emotional development as well. Therefore, it is not surprising that sensitivity to touch is well developed at birth. The reflexes listed in Table 4.2 reveal that the newborn baby responds to touch, especially around the mouth, on the palms, and on the soles of the feet. During the prenatal period, these areas, along with the genitals, are the first to become sensitive to touch (Humphrey, 1978).

At birth, infants are quite sensitive to pain. If male newborns are circumcised, anesthetic is sometimes not used because of the risk of giving drugs to a very young infant. Babies often respond with a high-pitched, stressful cry and a dramatic rise in heart rate, blood pressure, palm sweating, pupil dilation, and muscle tension (Jorgensen, 1999). Recent research establishing the safety of certain local anesthetics for newborns promises to ease the stress of these procedures. Offering a nipple that delivers a sugar solution is also helpful; it quickly reduces crying and discomfort in young babies, preterm and full term alike. And combining the sweet liquid with gentle holding by the parent lessens pain even more (Gormally et al., 2001). Allowing infants to endure severe or repeated pain overwhelms the nervous system with stress hormones, which can disrupt the child's developing capacity to handle common, everyday stressors. The result is heightened pain sensitivity, sleep disturbances, feeding problems, and difficulty calming down when upset (Mitchell & Boss, 2002).

TASTE AND SMELL ● All babies come into the world with the ability to communicate their taste preferences to caregivers. Facial expressions reveal that newborns can distinguish several basic tastes. Like adults, they relax their facial muscles in response to sweetness, purse their lips when the taste is sour, and show a distinct archlike mouth opening when it is bitter (Rosenstein & Oster, 1990; Steiner, 1979). These reactions are important for survival, since (as we will see in Chapter 5) the food that best supports the infant's early growth is the sweet-tasting milk of the mother's breast. Not until 4 months of age will babies prefer the salty taste to plain water, a change that may prepare them to accept solid foods (Mennella & Beauchamp, 1998).

Nevertheless, newborns can readily learn to like a taste that at first evoked either a neutral or a negative response. For example, babies allergic to cow's milk formula who are given a soy or other vegetable-based substitute (typically very strong and bitter-tasting) soon prefer it to regular formula. A taste previously disliked can come to be preferred when it is paired with relief of hunger (Harris, 1997).

Like taste, certain odor preferences are innate. For example, the smell of bananas or chocolate causes a relaxed, pleasant facial expression, whereas the odor of rotten eggs makes the infant frown (Steiner, 1979). Newborns can also identify the location of an odor and, if it is unpleasant, defend themselves by turning their heads in the other direction (Reiser, Yonas, & Wikner, 1976).

In many mammals, the sense of smell plays an important role in eating and in protecting the young from predators by helping mothers and babies identify each other. Although smell is less well developed in humans, traces of its survival value remain. Newborns given a choice between the smell of their own mother's amniotic fluid and that of another mother spend more time oriented toward the familiar fluid (Marlier, Schaal, & Soussignan, 1998). The smell of the mother's amniotic fluid is comforting; babies exposed to it cry less than babies who are not (Varendi et al., 1998).

Immediately after birth, infants placed face down between their mother's breasts latch on to a nipple and begin sucking within an hour. If one breast is washed to remove its natural scent, most newborns move toward the unwashed breast, indicating that they are guided by smell (Varendi & Porter, 2001). At 4 days of age, breastfed babies prefer the smell of their own mother's breast to that of an unfamiliar lactating woman (Cernoch & Porter, 1985). Bottle-fed babies orient to the smell of any lactating woman over the smell of formula or of a nonlactating woman (Marlier & Schaal, 1997; Porter et al., 1992). Newborn infants' dual attraction to the odors of their mother and of the lactating breast helps them locate an appropriate food source and, in the process, distinguish their caregiver from other people.

HEARING ● Newborn infants' can hear a wide variety of sounds, although their sensitivity improves greatly over the first few months (Tharpe & Ashmead, 2001). At birth, infants prefer complex sounds, such as noises and voices, to pure tones. And babies only a few days old can tell the difference between a few sound patterns—a series of tones arranged in ascending versus descending order; utterances with two versus three syllables; the stress patterns of words, such as *ma*-ma versus ma-*ma*; and happy-sounding speech as opposed to speech with negative or neutral emotional qualities (Mastropieri & Turkewitz, 1999; Sansavini, Bertoncini, & Giovanelli, 1997; Trehub, 2001).

Tiny infants are especially sensitive to the sounds of human speech, and they are biologically prepared to detect the sounds of any human language. Young infants can make fine-grained distinctions among many speech sounds—"ba" and "ga," "ma" and "na," and the short vowel sounds "a" and "i," to name just a few. For example, when given a nipple that turns on the "ba" sound, babies suck vigorously for a period of time, and then sucking slows down as the novelty wears off. When the sound switches to "ga," sucking picks up, indicating that infants detect this subtle difference. Using this method, researchers have found only a few speech sounds that newborns cannot discriminate. Their ability to perceive sounds not found in their own language is more precise than an adult's (Jusczyk, 1995; Aldridge, Stillman, & Bower, 2001). These capacities reveal that the baby is marvelously prepared for the awesome task of acquiring language.

Responsiveness to sound also supports the newborn baby's exploration of the environment. Infants as young as 3 days turn their eyes and head in the general direction of a sound. The ability to identify the precise location of a sound improves greatly over the first 6 months and shows further gains into the second year (Litovsky & Ashmead, 1997).

(a) Newborn View

(b) Adult View

FIGURE 4.8

View of the human face by the newborn and the adult.

The newborn baby's limited focusing ability and poor visual acuity lead the mother's face, even when viewed from close up, to look much like the fuzzy image in (a) than the clear image in (b). Also, newborn infants have some color vision, although they have difficulty discriminating colors. Researchers speculate that colors probably appear similar, but less intense, to newborns than to older infants and adults. (From Hainline, 1998; Slater, 2001.)

Listen carefully to yourself the next time you talk to a young baby. You will probably speak in a high-pitched, expressive voice and use a rising tone at the ends of phrases and sentences. Adults probably communicate this way with infants because they notice that babies are more attentive when they do so. Indeed, newborns prefer speech with these characteristics (Aslin, Jusczyk, & Pisoni, 1998). In addition, newborn babies will suck more on a nipple to hear a recording of their own mother's voice than that of an unfamiliar woman, and to hear their native language as opposed to a foreign language (Moon, Cooper, & Fifer, 1993; Spence & DeCasper, 1987). These preferences might have developed from hearing the muffled sounds of the mother's voice before birth.

VISION ● Vision is the least developed of the senses at birth. Visual structures in both the eye and the brain are not yet fully formed. For example, cells in the *retina,* the membrane lining the inside of the eye that captures light and transforms it into messages that are sent to the brain, are not as mature or densely packed as they will be in several months. And the optic nerve that relays these messages, and visual centers in the brain that receive them, will not be adultlike for several years. Furthermore, the muscles of the lens, which permit us to adjust our visual focus to varying distances, are weak (Atkinson, 2000).

Because of these factors, newborn babies cannot focus their eyes well, and their **visual acuity, or fineness of discrimination,** is limited. At birth, infants perceive objects at a distance of 20 feet about as clearly as adults do at 600 feet (Slater, 2001). In addition, unlike adults (who see nearby objects most clearly), newborn babies see unclearly across a wide range of distances (Banks, 1980; Hainline, 1998). As a result, images such as the parent's face, even from close up, look like the blurry image in Figure 4.8. Nevertheless, as we will see in Chapter 5, newborns can detect human faces. And like their preference for their mother's smell and voice, they quickly learn to prefer her face to that of an unfamiliar woman, although they are sensitive to its broad outlines rather than its fine-grained features (Bartrip, Morton, & de Schonen, 2001; Walton, Armstrong, & Bower, 1998).

Although newborn infants cannot see well, they actively explore their environment by scanning it for interesting sights and tracking moving objects. However, their eye movements are slow and inaccurate (von Hofsten & Rosander, 1998). Joshua's captivation with my pink blouse reveals that he is attracted to bright objects. Nevertheless, once newborns focus on an object, they tend to look only at a single feature—for example, the corner of a triangle instead of the entire shape. And although newborn babies prefer to look at colored rather than gray stimuli, they are not yet good at discriminating colors. It will take a month or two for color vision to improve (Adams & Courage, 1998; Teller, 1998).

●Neonatal Behavioral Assessment

A variety of instruments permit doctors, nurses, and researchers to assess the behavior of newborn babies. The most widely used of these tests, T. Berry Brazelton's **Neonatal Behavioral Assessment Scale (NBAS),** evaluates the baby's reflexes, state changes, responsiveness to physical and social stimuli, and other reactions (Brazelton & Nugent, 1995).

The NBAS has been given to many infants around the world. As a result, researchers have learned about individual and cultural differences in newborn behavior and how child-rearing practices can maintain or change a baby's reactions. For example, NBAS scores of Asian and Native-American babies reveal that they are less irritable than Caucasian infants. Mothers in these cultures often encourage their babies' calm dispositions through swaddling, close physical contact, and nursing at the first signs of discomfort (Chisholm, 1989; Muret-Wagstaff & Moore, 1989). In contrast, maternal care quickly changes the poor NBAS scores of undernourished infants in Zambia, Africa. The Zambian mother carries her baby about on her hip all day, providing a rich variety of sensory stimulation. As a result, a once unresponsive newborn becomes an alert, contented 1-week-old (Brazelton, Koslowski, & Tronick, 1976).

Can you tell from these examples why a single NBAS score is not a good predictor of later development? Because newborn behavior and parenting styles combine to shape development, *changes in NBAS scores* over the first week or two of life (rather than a single score) provide the best estimate of the baby's ability to recover from the stress of birth. NBAS "recovery curves" predict intelligence with moderate success well into the preschool years (Brazelton, Nugent, & Lester, 1987).

The NBAS also has been used to help parents get to know their infants. In some hospitals, health professionals discuss with or demonstrate to parents the newborn capacities assessed by the NBAS. Parents of both preterm and full-term newborns who participate in these programs interact more effectively with their babies (Eiden & Reifman, 1996). In one study, Brazilian mothers who experienced a 50-minute NBAS-based discussion a few days after delivery were more likely than controls who received only health care information to establish eye contact, smile, vocalize, and soothe in response to infant signals a month later (Wendland-Carro, Piccinini, & Millar, 1999). Although lasting effects on development have not been demonstrated, NBAS interventions are useful in helping the parent–infant relationship get off to a good start.

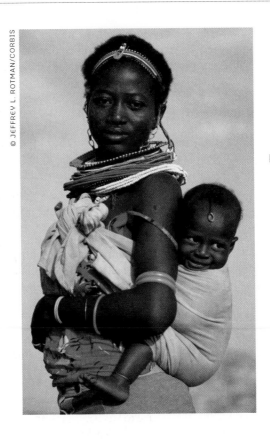

Similar to women in the Zambian culture, this mother of the El Molo people of northern Kenya carries her baby about all day, providing close physical contact, a rich variety of stimulation, and ready feeding.

Ask YOURSELF

www

REVIEW What functions does REM sleep serve in young infants? Can sleep tell us anything about the health of the newborn's central nervous system? Explain.

APPLY Jackie, who had a difficult birth, observes her 2-day-old daughter, Kelly, being given the NBAS. Kelly scores poorly on many items. Jackie wonders if this means that Kelly will not develop normally. How would you respond to Jackie's concern?

CONNECT How do the diverse capacities of newborn babies contribute to their first social relationships? Provide as many examples as you can.

REFLECT Are young infants more competent than you thought they were before you read this chapter? Describe aspects of their wide range of capacities that most surprised you.

The Transition to Parenthood

The early weeks after a new baby enters the family are full of profound changes. The mother needs to recover from childbirth and adjust to massive hormone shifts in her body. If she is breastfeeding, energies must be devoted to working out this intimate relationship. The father needs to become a part of this new threesome while supporting the mother in her recovery. At times, he may feel ambivalent about the baby, who constantly demands and gets the mother's attention.

While all this is going on, the tiny infant is assertive about his urgent physical needs, demanding to be fed, changed, and comforted at odd times of the day and night. The family schedule becomes irregular and uncertain. Yolanda spoke candidly about the changes she and Jay experienced:

> When we brought Joshua home, we had to deal with the realities of new parenthood. Joshua seemed so small and helpless, and we worried about whether we would be able to take proper care of him. It took us 20 minutes to change the first diaper. I rarely feel rested because I'm up two to four times every night, and I spend a good part of my waking hours trying to anticipate Joshua's rhythms and needs. If Jay weren't so willing to help by holding and walking Joshua, I think I'd find it much harder.

Changes in the Family System

The demands of new parenthood—constant caregiving, added financial responsibilities, and less time for couples to devote to one another—usually cause the gender roles of husband and wife to become more traditional (Cowan & Cowan, 2000; Salmela-Aro et al., 2000). This is true even for couples like Yolanda and Jay, who are strongly committed to gender equality and are used to sharing household tasks. Yolanda took a leave of absence from work, whereas Jay's career continued as it had before. As a result, Yolanda spent more time at home with the baby, while Jay focused more on his provider role.

For most new parents, however, the arrival of a baby does not cause significant marital strain. Marriages that are gratifying and supportive tend to remain so and resemble childless marriages in overall happiness (Feeney et al., 2001; Miller, 2000). In contrast, troubled marriages usually become more distressed after a baby is born. In a study of newlyweds who were interviewed annually for 6 years, the husband's affection, expression of "we-ness" (values and goals similar to his wife's), and awareness of his wife's daily life predicted mothers' stable or increasing marital satisfaction after childbirth. In contrast, the husband's negativity and the couple's out-of-control conflict predicted a drop in mothers' satisfaction (Shapiro, Gottman, & Carrere, 2000). For some, adjustment problems are severe (see the Biology and Environment box on the following page).

Also, the larger the difference between men's and women's caregiving responsibilities, the greater the decline in marital satisfaction after childbirth, especially for women—with negative consequences for parent–infant interaction. In contrast, sharing caregiving predicts greater parental happiness and sensitivity to the baby (Feldman, 2002). Postponing parenthood to the late twenties or thirties eases the transition to parenthood. Waiting permits couples to pursue occupational goals, gain life experience, and plan to become parents when they feel psychologically ready. Under these circumstances, men are more enthusiastic about becoming fathers and therefore more willing to participate. And women whose careers are well under way are more likely to encourage their husbands to share housework and child care (Coltrane, 1990).

A second birth typically requires that fathers take an even more active role in parenting—by caring for the first-born while the mother is recuperating and by sharing in the high demands of tending to both a baby and a young child. Consequently, well-functioning families with a newborn second child typically show a pulling back from the traditional division of responsibilities that occurred after the first birth (Kreppner, Paulsen, & Schuetz, 1982). In a study that tracked parents from the end of pregnancy through the first year after their second child's birth, fathers became increasingly aware of their vital role in fostering favorable day-to-day family functioning. As one father commented, "It took only one child to make my wife a mother, but two to make me a father" (Stewart, 1990, p. 142).

Fathers' willingness to place greater emphasis on the parenting role is strongly linked

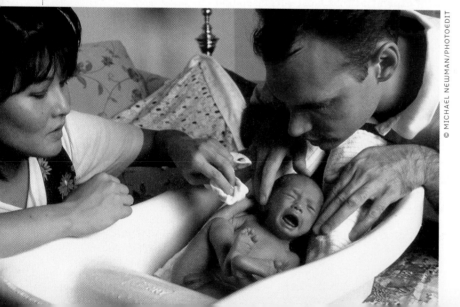

After arriving home from the hospital, these first-time parents comfort their baby during a bath. The transition to parenthood can enrich a warm, gratifying marriage or worsen a tense, unhappy marriage. Sharing caregiving tasks enhances marital satisfaction and is related to parents' sensitivity toward their baby.

© MICHAEL NEWMAN/PHOTOEDIT

*B*iology and Environment

Postpartum Depression and the Parent–Child Relationship

For 50 to 80 percent of first-time mothers, the excitement of the baby's arrival gives way to an emotional letdown during the first week after delivery known as the *postpartum* (or after-birth) *blues.* The blues are temporary. They die down as mothers adjust to hormonal changes following childbirth, gain confidence in caring for the baby, and are reassured by their husbands, family members, and friends. However, about 10 percent of women do not bounce back so easily. They experience **postpartum depression,** mild to severe feelings of sadness and withdrawal that continue for weeks or months.

During Stella's pregnancy, her husband Kyle's lack of interest in the baby caused her to worry that having a child might be a mistake. Shortly after Lucy was born, Stella's mood plunged. She was anxious and weepy, overwhelmed by Lucy's needs, and angry that she no longer had control over her own schedule. When Stella approached Kyle about her own fatigue and his unwillingness to help with the baby, he snapped that she overreacted to every move he made. Stella's friends, who did not have children, stopped by once to see Lucy and did not call again. Although genetic makeup increases the risk of depressive illness, Stella's case shows that social and cultural factors are also involved (Swendsen & Mazure, 2000).

Stella's depressed mood quickly affected her baby. In the weeks after birth, infants of depressed mothers sleep poorly, are less attentive and responsive to their surroundings, and have elevated levels of stress hormones. The more extreme the depression and the greater the number of stressors in a mother's life (such as marital discord, little or no social support, ambivalence about parenthood, and poverty), the more the parent–child relationship suffers (Goodman et al., 1993; Simpson et al., 2003). Stella, for example, rarely smiled and talked to Lucy, who responded to her mother's sad, vacant gaze by turning away, crying, and often looking sad or angry herself

(Murray & Cooper, 1997). Each time this happened, Stella felt guilty and inadequate, and her depression deepened. By 6 months of age, Lucy displayed emotional symptoms common in babies of depressed mothers—a negative, irritable mood and attachment difficulties (Martins & Gaffan, 2000).

When maternal depression persists, the parent–child relationship worsens. Depressed parents view their infants more negatively than do independent observers (Hart, Field, & Roitfarb, 1999). And they use inconsistent discipline—sometimes lax, at other times too forceful. As we will see in later chapters, children who experience these maladaptive parenting practices often have serious adjustment problems. To avoid their parent's insensitivity, they sometimes withdraw into a depressive mood themselves. Or they may mimic their parent's anger and become impulsive and antisocial (Conger, Patterson, & Ge, 1995; Murray et al., 1999).

Over time, the parenting behaviors just described lead children to develop a negative world view—one in which they lack confidence in themselves and perceive their parents and other people as threatening. Children who constantly feel in danger are likely to become overly aroused in stressful situations, easily losing control in the face of cognitive and social challenges (Cummings & Davies, 1994). Although children of depressed parents may inherit a tendency to develop emotional and behavior problems, quality of parenting is a major factor in their adjustment.

Early treatment of maternal depression is vital to prevent the disorder from interfering with the parent–child relationship and harming children. Often family members must assist the mother in seeking help, as she may not have the emotional energy to do so. In Stella's case, her doctor referred her to a program for depressed mothers and their babies. A counselor worked with the family for several months, helping Stella and Kyle with their marital problems and encouraging them to be more sensitive and

patient with Lucy. At times, antidepressant medication is prescribed. In most cases of postpartum depression, short-term treatment is successful (Steinberg & Bellavance, 1999). When depressed mothers do not respond easily to treatment, their children's development can be safeguarded by a warm relationship with the father or another caregiver.

© LAURA DWIGHT/PHOTOEDIT

Depression disrupts parents' capacity to engage with children. This infant tries hard to get his despondent mother to react. If her unresponsiveness continues, the baby is likely to turn away, cry, and become negative and irritable. Over time, this disruption in the parent–child relationship leads to serious emotional and behavior problems.

Applying
WHAT WE **Know** / **How Couples Can Ease the Transition to Parenthood**

STRATEGY	DESCRIPTION
Devise a plan for sharing household tasks.	As soon as possible, discuss division of household responsibilities. Decide who does a particular chore based on who has the needed skill and time, not gender. Schedule regular times to reevaluate your plan to fit changing family circumstances.
Begin sharing child care right after the baby's arrival.	For fathers, strive to spend equal time with the baby early. For mothers, refrain from imposing your standards on your partner. Instead, share the role of "child-rearing expert" by discussing parenting values and concerns often. Attend a new-parenthood course together.
Talk over conflicts about decision making and responsibilities.	Face conflict through communication. Clarify your feelings and needs, and express them to your partner. Listen and try to understand your partner's point of view. Then be willing to negotiate and compromise.
Establish a balance between work and parenting.	Critically evaluate the time you devote to work in view of new parenthood. If it is too much, try to cut back.
Press for workplace and public policies that assist parents in rearing children.	Difficulties faced by new parents may be partly due to lack of workplace and societal supports. Encourage your employer to provide benefits that help combine work and family roles, such as paid employment leave; flexible work hours; and on-site high-quality, affordable child care. Communicate with lawmakers and other citizens about improving policies for children and families, including paid, job-protected leave to support the transition to parenthood.

to mothers' adjustment after the arrival of a second baby. And the support and encouragement of family, friends, and spouse are crucial for reducing fathers' stress (Stewart, 1990). Finally, both parents must help their first-born child adjust. Preschool-age siblings understandably may feel displaced and react with jealousy and anger—a topic we will take up in Chapter 7.

Parent Interventions

For strategies that couples can use to ease the transition to parenthood, refer to Applying What We Know above. In addition, special interventions are available to help parents adjust. For those who are not at high risk for problems, couples' groups led by counselors are highly effective (Cowan & Cowan, 1995). In one program, first-time expectant couples gathered once a week for 6 months to discuss their dreams for the family and the changes in relationships sparked by the baby's arrival. Eighteen months after the program ended, participating fathers described themselves as more involved with their child than did fathers in a no-intervention condition. Perhaps because of fathers' caregiving assistance, participating mothers maintained their prebirth satisfaction with family and work roles. Three years after the birth, the marriages of all participating couples were still intact and just as happy as they had been before parenthood. In contrast, 15 percent of couples receiving no intervention had divorced (Cowan & Cowan, 1997, 2000).

For high-risk parents struggling with poverty or the birth of a child with disabilities, interventions must be more intensive. Programs in which a trained intervener visits the home and focuses on enhancing social support and the parent–child relationship have resulted in improved parent–infant interaction and benefits for children's cognitive and social development up to 5 years after the intervention (Meisels, Dichtelmiller, & Liaw, 1993).

When couples support each other's needs, the stress caused by the birth of a baby remains manageable. Nevertheless, as one pair of counselors who have worked with many new parents point out, "As long as children are dependent on their parents, those parents find themselves preoccupied with thoughts of their children. This does not keep them from enjoying other aspects of their lives, but it does mean that they never return to being quite the same people they were before they became parents" (Colman & Colman, 1991, p. 198).

Ask YOURSELF

REVIEW Explain how persisting postpartum depression seriously impairs children's development.

APPLY Derek, father of a 3-year-old and a newborn, reported greater difficulty adjusting to the birth of his second child than to that of his first child. Explain why.

CONNECT Louise has just given birth to her first child. Because her husband works long hours and is seldom available to help, she feels overwhelmed by the pressures of caring for a new baby. Why does Louise's 4-week maternity leave pose a risk to her mental health? (*Hint:* Consult the Social Issues: Health box on pages 144–145.)

REFLECT If you are a parent, what was the transition to parenthood like for you? What factors eased the stress of this major life change? What factors made it more difficult? If you are not a parent, pose these questions to someone you know who recently became a parent.

Summary

The Stages of Childbirth

Describe the three stages of childbirth, the baby's adaptation to labor and delivery, and the newborn baby's appearance.

● In the first stage of childbirth, **dilation and effacement of the cervix** occur as uterine contractions increase in strength and frequency. This stage culminates in **transition,** a brief period in which contractions are strongest and closest together and the cervix opens completely. In the second stage, the mother feels an urge to bear down with her abdominal muscles, and the baby is born. In the final stage, the placenta is delivered.

● During labor, infants produce high levels of stress hormones, which help them withstand oxygen deprivation, clear the lungs for breathing, and arouse them into alertness at birth. Newborn infants have large heads, small bodies, and facial features that make adults feel like picking them up and cuddling them. The **Apgar Scale** is used to assess the newborn baby's physical condition at birth.

Approaches to Childbirth

Describe natural childbirth and home delivery, noting benefits and concerns associated with each.

● **Natural, or prepared, childbirth** involves classes in which the expectant mother and a companion learn about labor and delivery, relaxation and breathing techniques to counteract pain, and coaching during childbirth. The method reduces stress, pain, and use of medication and fosters more positive maternal attitudes toward the birth experience.

● Social support, a vital part of natural childbirth, reduces the length of labor and the incidence of birth complications. When mothers give birth in a sitting position, labor is also shortened.

● Home birth reduces unnecessary medical procedures and permits mothers to exercise greater control over their own care and that of their babies. As long as mothers are healthy and assisted by a well-trained doctor or midwife, giving birth at home is just as safe to as giving birth in a hospital.

Medical Interventions

List common medical interventions during childbirth, circumstances that justify their use, and any dangers associated with each.

● Medical interventions during childbirth are more common in North America than anywhere else in the world. When women have a history of pregnancy and birth complications, **fetal monitors** help save the lives of many babies. However, when used routinely, they may identify infants as in danger who, in fact, are not. Fetal monitoring is linked to an increase in cesarean deliveries.

● When **analgesics** and **anesthetics** are used to control pain during childbirth, they can prolong labor and cause newborns to be withdrawn and irritable. **Forceps** or **vacuum extractors** are appropriate if the mother's pushing does not move the infant through the birth canal in a reasonable period of time, but they can injure the baby's head and the mother's tissues.

● Because **induced labors** are more difficult than naturally occurring ones, they increase the use of labor and delivery medication and instrument deliveries. Consequently, inductions should be scheduled only when continuing the pregnancy threatens the well-being of mother or baby. **Cesarean deliveries** are justified in cases of medical emergency, serious maternal illness, and babies in **breech position**. A dramatic, worldwide rise in cesareans has occurred, many of which are unnecessary.

Birth Complications

What are the risks of oxygen deprivation, preterm birth, and low birth weight, and what factors can help infants who survive a traumatic birth?

● Although most births proceed normally, serious complications can occur.

A major cause of **cerebral palsy** is lack of oxygen during labor and delivery. As long as **anoxia** is not extreme, most affected children improve in development over time. **Respiratory distress syndrome** is common in infants born more than 6 weeks early. It can cause permanent damage due to immaturity of the lungs and resulting oxygen deprivation.

● The incidence of premature births is high among poverty-stricken women and mothers of twins. Compared with **preterm** babies, whose weight is appropriate for time spent in the uterus, **small-for-date** infants have more serious problems. The fragile appearance and unresponsive, irritable behavior of preterm infants can lead parents to be less sensitive and responsive in caring for them.

● Some interventions provide special infant stimulation through gentle motion, attractive mobiles, soothing sounds, massage, and skin-to-skin contact with the caregiver in the intensive care nursery. Others teach parents how to care for and interact with their babies.

● Parents with stable life circumstances and social supports need only a few sessions of coaching in caring for a preterm baby to help their child develop favorably. When preterm infants live in stressed, low-income households, long-term, intensive intervention is required. A major cause of **neonatal** and **infant mortality** is low birth weight.

● When babies experience birth trauma, a supportive family environment or relationships with other caring adults can help restore their growth. Even infants with fairly serious birth complications can recover with the help of positive life events.

Precious Moments After Birth

Is close parent–infant contact shortly after birth necessary for bonding?

● Human parents do not require close physical contact with the baby immediately after birth for **bonding** and effective parenting to occur. Nevertheless, early contact supports parents' feelings of caring and affection. Hospital practices that promote parent–infant closeness, such as **rooming in,** may help parents build a good relationship with their newborn.

The Newborn Baby's Capacities

Describe the newborn baby's reflexes and states of arousal, including sleep characteristics and ways to soothe a crying baby.

● **Reflexes** are the newborn baby's most obvious organized patterns of behavior. Some have survival value, others help parents and infants establish gratifying interaction, and still others provide the foundation for voluntary motor skills.

● Although newborns move in and out of five **states of arousal,** they spend most of their time asleep. Sleep consists of at least two states: **rapid-eye-movement (REM) sleep** and **non-rapid-eye-movement (NREM) sleep.** REM sleep is greater during the newborn period than at any later age. It provides young infants with the stimulation essential for central nervous system development. Rapid eye movements ensure that structures of the eye remain oxygenated during sleep. Disturbed REM–NREM cycles are a sign of central nervous system abnormalities, which may contribute to **sudden infant death syndrome (SIDS).**

● A crying baby stimulates strong feelings of discomfort in nearby adults. The intensity of the cry and the experiences that led up to it help parents identify what is wrong. Once feeding and diaper changing have been tried, lifting the baby to the shoulder and rocking or walking is the most effective soothing technique. Many other soothing methods, including swaddling, offering a pacifier, and talking softly, are helpful.

Describe the newborn baby's sensory capacities.

● The senses of touch, taste, smell, and sound are well developed at birth. Newborns are sensitive to pain, prefer sweet tastes and smells, and orient toward the odor of their own mother's amniotic fluid and the lactating breast. Already they can distinguish a few sound patterns, as well as nearly all speech sounds. They are especially responsive to high-pitched expressive voices, their own mother's voice, and speech in their native language.

● Vision is the least developed of the newborn's senses. At birth, focusing ability and **visual acuity** are limited. Nevertheless, newborns can detect human faces and prefer their mother's familiar face to the face of a stranger. In exploring the visual field, newborn babies are attracted to bright objects, but they limit their looking to single features. Newborn babies have difficulty discriminating colors.

Why is neonatal behavioral assessment useful?

● The most widely used instrument for assessing the behavior of the newborn infant is Brazelton's **Neonatal Behavioral Assessment Scale (NBAS).** The NBAS has helped researchers understand individual and cultural differences in newborn behavior. Sometimes it is used to teach parents about their baby's capacities.

The Transition to Parenthood

Describe typical changes in the family after the birth of a new baby, along with interventions that foster the transition to parenthood

● The new baby's arrival is exciting but stressful. The demands of new parenthood usually cause the gender roles of husband and wife to become more traditional. Parents in gratifying marriages who continue to support each others' needs generally adapt well. A large difference in a husband's and wife's caregiving responsibilities, however, can strain the marriage and negatively affect parent–child interaction. Favorable adjustment to a second birth typically requires that fathers take an even more active role in parenting.

● About 10 percent of women experience **postpartum depression.** If not treated early, it can have serious, lasting consequences for children's development.

● When parents are at low risk for problems, couples' groups involving discussion of changing family relationships can ease the transition to parenthood. High-risk parents struggling with poverty or the birth of a baby with disabilities benefit from intensive home interventions focusing on enhancing social support and parent–infant interaction.

Important Terms and Concepts

analgesic (p. 138)
anesthetic (p. 138)
anoxia (p. 140)
Apgar Scale (p. 134)
bonding (p. 147)
breech position (p. 139)
cerebral palsy (p. 140)
cesarean delivery (p. 139)
dilation and effacement of the cervix
 (p. 130)
fetal monitors (p. 137)
forceps (p. 138)

induced labor (p. 139)
infant mortality (p. 144)
natural, or prepared, childbirth
 (p. 135)
Neonatal Behavioral Assessment
 Scale (NBAS) (p. 156)
neonatal mortality (p. 144)
non-rapid-eye-movement (NREM)
 sleep (p. 150)
postpartum depression (p. 159)
preterm infant (p. 142)

rapid-eye-movement (REM) sleep
 (p. 150)
reflex (p. 148)
respiratory distress syndrome (p. 141)
rooming in (p. 147)
small-for-date infant (p. 142)
states of arousal (p. 150)
sudden infant death syndrome (SIDS)
 (p. 152)
transition (p. 130)
vacuum extractor (p. 138)
visual acuity (p. 156)

 ## For Further Information and Help

Consult the Companion Website for *Infants, Children, and Adolescents*, Fifth Edition, *(www.ablongman.com/berk)*, where you will find the following resources for this chapter:

● **Chapter Objectives**
● **Flashcards** for studying important terms and concepts
● **Annotated Weblinks** to guide you in further research
● **Ask Yourself questions,** which you can answer and then check against a sample response

● **Suggested Readings**
● **Practice Tests** with immediate scoring and feedback

Lifted by his mother into a world of wonder, the baby responds with joy as he senses the physical potential of his growing body. During the first year, infants grow quickly, move on their own, increasingly investigate their surroundings, and make sense of complicated sights and sounds.

"Mother with Child"
Ma Hninn Moe Htwe
12 years, Myanmar

Reprinted with permission from the International Museum of Children's Art, Oslo, Norway.

Physical Development in Infancy and Toddlerhood

- **BODY GROWTH**
  Changes in Body Size and Muscle–Fat Makeup • Changes in Body Proportions • Skeletal Growth

- **BRAIN DEVELOPMENT**
  Development of Neurons • Development of the Cerebral Cortex • Sensitive Periods in Brain Development • Changing States of Arousal

  BIOLOGY AND ENVIRONMENT *Brain Plasticity: Insights from Research on Brain-Damaged Children and Adults*

  CULTURAL INFLUENCES *Cultural Variation in Infant Sleeping Arrangements*

- **INFLUENCES ON EARLY PHYSICAL GROWTH**
  Heredity • Nutrition • Malnutrition • Emotional Well-Being

- **LEARNING CAPACITIES**
  Classical Conditioning • Operant Conditioning • Habituation • Imitation

- **MOTOR DEVELOPMENT**
  The Sequence of Motor Development • Motor Skills as Dynamic Systems • Dynamic Motor Systems in Action • Cultural Variations in Motor Development • Fine Motor Development: Reaching and Grasping • Bowel and Bladder Control

- **PERCEPTUAL DEVELOPMENT**
  Hearing • Vision • Object Perception • Intermodal Perception • Understanding Perceptual Development

  BIOLOGY AND ENVIRONMENT *Development of Infants with Severe Visual Impairments*

On a brilliant June morning, 16-month- old Caitlin emerged from her front door, ready for the short drive to the child-care home where she spent her weekdays while her mother, Carolyn, and her father, David, worked. Clutching a teddy bear in one hand and her mother's arm with the other, Caitlin descended the steps. "One! Two! Threeeee!" Carolyn counted as she helped Caitlin down, mother and daughter laughing after each giant step. "How much she's changed!" Carolyn thought to herself, looking at the child who, not long ago, had been a newborn cradled in her arms. With her first steps, Caitlin had passed from *infancy* to *toddlerhood*—a period spanning the second year of life. At first, Caitlin did, indeed, "toddle" with an awkward gait, rocking from side to side and tipping over frequently. But her face reflected the thrill of being upright and conquering a new skill.

As they walked toward the car, Carolyn and Caitlin caught sight of 3-year-old Eli and his father, Kevin, in the neighboring yard. Eli dashed toward them, waving a bright yellow envelope. Carolyn bent down to open the envelope and took out a card. It read, "Announcing the arrival of Grace Ann. Born: Cambodia. Age: 16 months." Carolyn turned toward Kevin and Eli. "That's wonderful news! When can we see her?"

"Let's wait a few days," Kevin suggested. "Monica's taken Grace to the doctor this morning. She's underweight and malnourished." Kevin described Monica's first night with Grace in a hotel room in Phnom Penh before they flew to the United States. Grace lay on the bed, withdrawn and fearful. Eventually she fell asleep, clutching crackers in both hands.

Carolyn felt a tug at her sleeve. Caitlin was impatient. Off they drove to child care, where Vanessa had just dropped off her 18-month-old son, Timmy. Within moments, Caitlin and Timmy were in the sandbox, shoveling sand into plastic cups and buckets with the help of their caregiver, Ginette. A few weeks later, Grace joined Caitlin and Timmy at Ginette's child-care home. Although still tiny and unable to crawl or walk, she had grown taller and heavier, and her sad, vacant gaze had given way to an alert expression, a ready smile, and an enthusiastic desire to imitate and explore. When Caitlin headed for the sandbox, Grace stretched out her arms, asking Ginette to carry her there, too. Soon Grace was pulling herself up at every opportunity. Finally, at age 18 months, she walked!

This chapter traces physical growth during the first 2 years—one of the most remarkable and busiest times of development. We will see how rapid changes in the infant's body and brain support learning, motor skills, and perceptual capacities. Caitlin, Grace, and Timmy will join us along the way to illustrate individual differences and environmental influences on physical development.

Body Growth

The next time you happen to be walking in your neighborhood or at a shopping center, briefly observe the contrast between infants and toddlers. You will see that their capabilities differ vastly. One reason for the change in what children can do over the first 2 years is that their bodies change enormously—faster than at any other time after birth.

Changes in Body Size and Muscle–Fat Makeup

As Figure 5.1 illustrates, by the end of the first year a typical infant's height is 50 percent greater than it was at birth, and by 2 years of age it is 75 percent greater. Weight shows similar dramatic gains. By 5 months of age, birth weight has doubled, at 1 year it has tripled, and at 2 years it has quadrupled.

Rather than making steady gains, infants and toddlers grow in little spurts. In one study, children who were followed over the first 21 months of life went for periods of 7 to 63 days with no growth and then added as much as half an inch in a 24-hour period! Almost always, parents described their babies as irritable and very hungry on the day before the spurt (Lampl, 1993; Lampl, Veldhuis, & Johnson, 1992).

One of the most obvious changes in infants' appearance is their transformation into round, plump babies by the middle of the first year. Body fat begins to increase in the last few weeks of prenatal life and continues to do so after birth, reaching a peak at about 9 months. This early rise in "baby fat" helps the infant maintain a constant body temperature. During the second year, most toddlers slim down, a trend that continues into middle childhood (Fomon & Nelson, 2002). In contrast, muscle tissue increases very slowly during infancy and will not reach a peak until adolescence. Babies are not very muscular creatures, and their strength and physical coordination are limited.

As in all aspects of development, differences among children in body size and muscle–fat makeup exist. In infancy, girls are slightly shorter and lighter than boys and have a higher ratio of fat to muscle. These small sex differences remain throughout early and middle childhood and will be greatly magnified at adolescence. Ethnic differences in body size are apparent as well. Grace was below the growth norms (height and weight averages for children her age). Although early malnutrition contributed to Grace's small size, even after substantial catch-up she remained below North American norms, a

This comparison between a 4-month-old and a 2-year-old shows that body growth is dramatic during infancy and toddlerhood—faster than at any other time after birth. Height increases by 75 percent, and weight quadruples.

© BARBARA PEACOCK/CORBIS

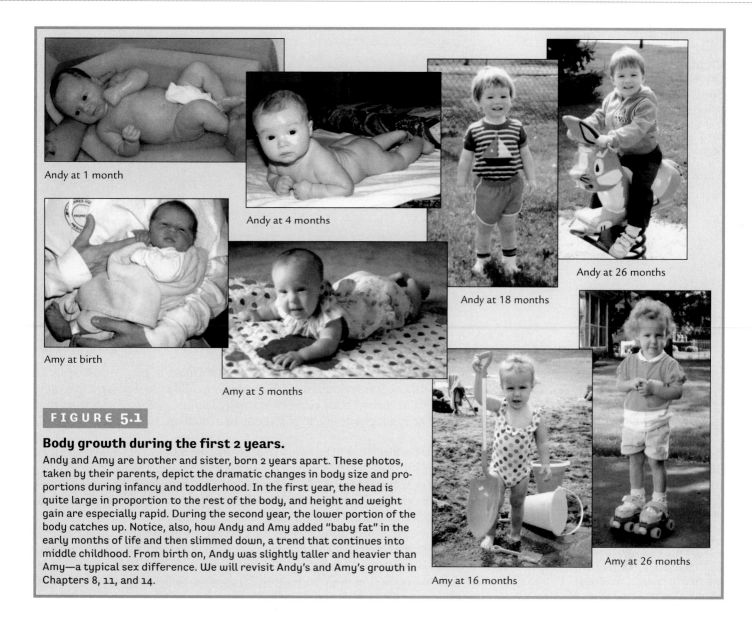

FIGURE 5.1

Body growth during the first 2 years.
Andy and Amy are brother and sister, born 2 years apart. These photos, taken by their parents, depict the dramatic changes in body size and proportions during infancy and toddlerhood. In the first year, the head is quite large in proportion to the rest of the body, and height and weight gain are especially rapid. During the second year, the lower portion of the body catches up. Notice, also, how Andy and Amy added "baby fat" in the early months of life and then slimmed down, a trend that continues into middle childhood. From birth on, Andy was slightly taller and heavier than Amy—a typical sex difference. We will revisit Andy's and Amy's growth in Chapters 8, 11, and 14.

Andy at 1 month
Andy at 4 months
Andy at 18 months
Andy at 26 months
Amy at birth
Amy at 5 months
Amy at 16 months
Amy at 26 months

trend typical for Asian children. In contrast, Timmy is slightly above average, as African-American children tend to be (Tanner, 1990).

Changes in Body Proportions

As the child's overall size increases, parts of the body grow at different rates. Two growth patterns describe these changes in body proportions. The first, depicted in Figure 5.2 on page 168, is called the **cephalocaudal trend.** Translated from Latin, it means "head to tail." As you can see, during the prenatal period, the head develops more rapidly than the lower part of the body. At birth, the head takes up one-fourth of total body length, the legs only one-third. Note, however, how the lower portion of the body catches up. By age 2, the head accounts for only one-fifth and the legs for nearly one-half of total body length.

The second pattern is the **proximodistal trend,** in which growth proceeds, literally, from "near to far," or from the center of the body outward. In the prenatal period, the head, chest, and trunk grow first, followed by the arms and legs, and finally by the hands and feet. During infancy and childhood, the arms and legs continue to grow somewhat ahead of the hands and feet. As we will see later, motor development follows these same trends.

Changes in body proportions from the early prenatal period to adulthood.

This figure illustrates the cephalocaudal trend of physical growth. The head gradually becomes smaller, and the legs longer, in proportion to the rest of the body.

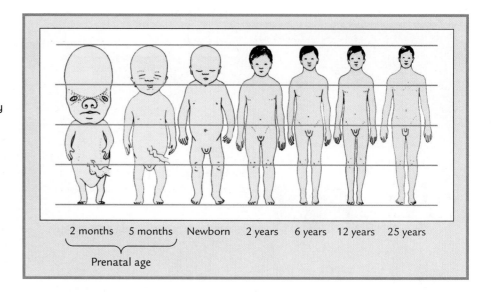

2 months   5 months   Newborn   2 years   6 years   12 years   25 years

Prenatal age

Diagram of a long bone showing upper and lower epiphyses.

Cartilage cells are produced at the growth plates of the epiphyses and gradually harden into bone. (From J. M. Tanner, *Foetus into Man* [2nd ed.], Cambridge, MA: Harvard University Press, p. 32. Copyright © 1990 by J. M. Tanner. All rights reserved. Reprinted by permission of the publisher and author.)

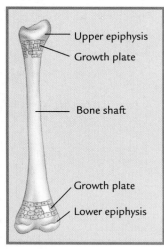

Upper epiphysis

Growth plate

Bone shaft

Growth plate

Lower epiphysis

Skeletal Growth

Children of the same age differ in *rate* of physical growth; some make faster progress toward a mature body size than others. Still, we cannot tell how quickly a child's physical growth is moving along just by looking at current body size. For example, Timmy is larger and heavier than Caitlin and Grace, but he is not physically more mature. In a moment, you will see why.

GENERAL SKELETAL GROWTH ● The best way of estimating a child's physical maturity is to use **skeletal age,** a measure of development of the bones of the body. The embryonic skeleton is first formed out of soft, pliable tissue called *cartilage.* Then, beginning in the sixth week of pregnancy, cartilage cells harden into bone, a gradual process that continues throughout childhood and adolescence (Moore & Persaud, 2003).

Just before birth, special growth centers in the bones called **epiphyses** appear, where cartilage cells continue to be produced (see Figure 5.3). In the long bones of the body, the epiphyses emerge at the two extreme ends of each bone. As growth continues, the epiphyses get thinner and disappear. When this occurs, no more bone growth is possible. Skeletal age can be estimated by X-raying the bones and seeing how many epiphyses there are and the extent to which their growth plates are fused (Malina & Bouchard, 1991).

When the skeletal ages of infants and children are examined, African-American children tend to be slightly ahead of Caucasian-American children at all ages. And girls are considerably ahead of boys—the reason Timmy's skeletal age lags behind that of Caitlin and Grace. At birth, the sexes differ by about 4 to 6 weeks, a gap that widens over infancy and childhood and is responsible for the fact that girls reach their full body size several years before boys (Tanner, Healy, & Cameron, 2001). Girls are advanced in development of other organs as well. Their greater physical maturity may contribute to their resistance to harmful environmental influences. As noted in Chapter 2, girls experience fewer developmental problems than boys, and infant and childhood mortality for girls is also lower.

GROWTH OF THE SKULL ● Pediatricians routinely measure children's head size between birth and 2 years of age. Skull growth is especially rapid during the first 2 years because of large increases in brain size. At birth, the bones of the skull are separated by six gaps, or "soft spots," called **fontanels** (see Figure 5.4). The gaps permit the bones to overlap as the large head of the baby passes through the mother's narrow birth canal. You can easily feel the largest gap, the anterior fontanel, which measures slightly more than an inch across at the top of a baby's skull. It gradually shrinks and is filled in during the second year. The other fontanels are smaller and close more quickly. As the skull bones come in contact with one another, they form *sutures,* or seams. These permit the skull to expand easily as the brain grows. The sutures disappear completely in adolescence, when skull growth is complete.

APPEARANCE OF TEETH ● On average, an African-American baby's first tooth appears at about 4 months, and a Caucasian baby's around 6 months, although wide individual differences exist. Timmy's first tooth erupted when he was 2 months old; a few infants do not get their first tooth until 1 year of age. After the first tooth erupts, new ones appear every month or two. By age 2, the average child has 20 teeth (Ranly, 1998). Dental development provides a rough clue to overall rate of skeletal development. A child who gets teeth early is likely to be advanced in physical maturity.

*B*rain Development

At birth, the brain is nearer than any other physical structure to its adult size, and it continues to develop at an astounding pace throughout infancy and toddlerhood. To best understand brain growth, we need to look at it from two vantage points: (1) the microscopic level of individual brain cells, and (2) the larger level of the cerebral cortex, the most complex brain structure and the one responsible for the highly developed intelligence of our species.

● Development of Neurons

The human brain has 100 to 200 billion **neurons, or nerve cells, that store and transmit information,** many of which have thousands of direct connections with other neurons. Neurons differ from other body cells in that they are not tightly packed together. They have tiny gaps, or **synapses,** between them where fibers from different neurons come close together but do not touch (see Figure 5.5). Neurons send messages to one another by releasing chemicals called *neurotransmitters,* which cross the synapse.

The basic story of brain growth concerns how neurons develop and form this elaborate communication system. Major milestones of brain development are summarized in Figure 5.6 on page 170. During the prenatal period, neurons are produced in the primitive neural tube of the embryo. From there, they migrate to form the major parts of the brain, traveling along threads produced by a network of guiding cells. By the end of the second trimester of pregnancy, production and migration of neurons is largely complete (see Chapter 3, page 104).

Once neurons are in place, they differentiate, establishing their unique functions by extending their fibers to form synaptic connections with neighboring cells. During infancy and toddlerhood, growth of neural fibers increases at an astounding pace (Huttenlocher, 1994; Moore & Persaud, 2003). Because neurons require space for these connective structures, a surprising aspect of brain growth is that when synapses are formed, many surrounding neurons die—20 to 80 percent, depending on the brain region (Diamond & Hopson, 1999; Stiles, 2001a). Fortunately, during the prenatal period, the neural tube produces far more neurons than the brain will ever need.

As neurons form connections, *stimulation* becomes vital to their survival. Neurons that are stimulated by input from the surrounding environment continue to establish new synapses, forming increasingly

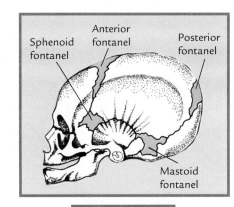

FIGURE 5.4

The skull at birth, showing the fontanels and sutures.

The fontanels gradually close during the first 2 years, forming sutures that permit the skull to expand easily as the brain grows.

FIGURE 5.5

Neurons and their connective fibers.

This photograph of several neurons, taken with the aid of a powerful microscope, shows the elaborate synaptic connections that form with neighboring cells.

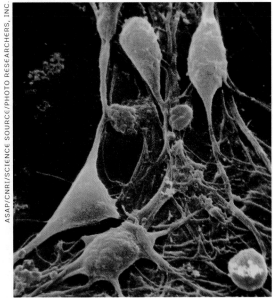

ASAP/CNRI/SCIENCE SOURCE/PHOTO RESEARCHERS, INC.

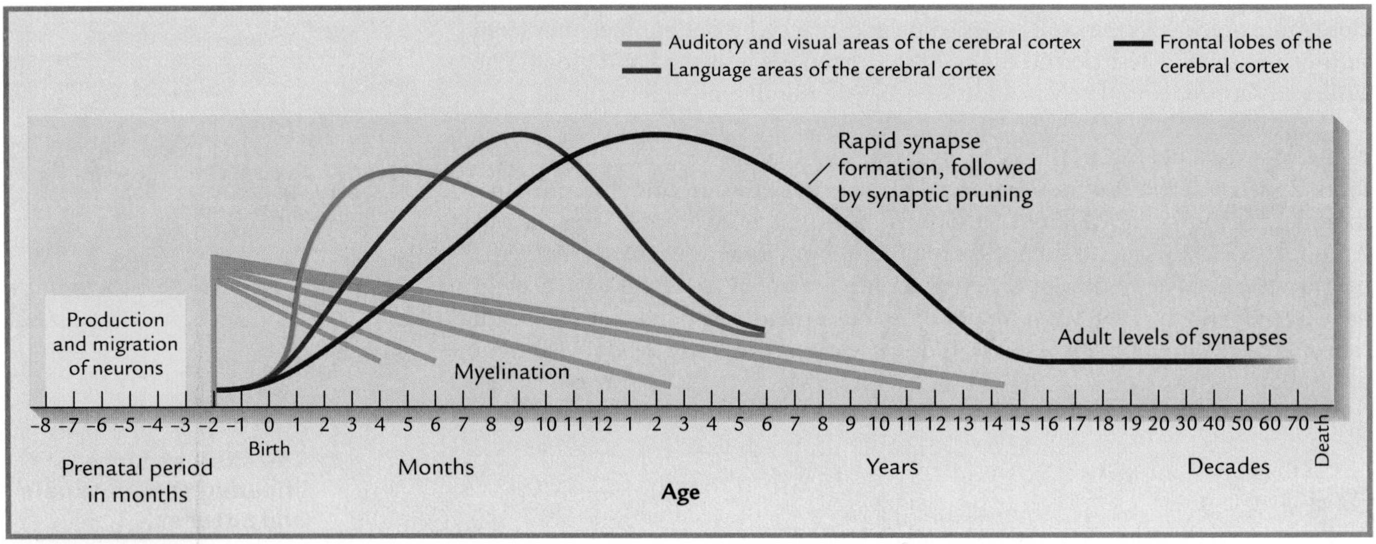

FIGURE 5.6

Major milestones of brain development.
Formation of synapses is rapid during the first 2 years of life, especially in the auditory, visual, and language areas of the cerebral cortex. The frontal lobes, responsible for thought, undergo more extended synaptic growth. In each area, overproduction of synapses is followed by synaptic pruning as stimulation strengthens needed connections and returns neurons not needed at the moment to an uncommitted state so that they can support future skills. The frontal lobes are among the last regions to attain adult levels of synaptic connections—in mid- to late adolescence. Myelination occurs at a dramatic pace during the first 2 years and then at a slower pace through middle childhood. It will increment again during adolescence. The multiple yellow lines indicate that the timing of myelination varies among different brain areas. For example, neural fibers continue to myelinate over a longer period in the language areas and, especially, in the frontal lobes than in the visual and auditory areas. (Adapted from Thompson & Nelson, 2001).

elaborate systems of communication that lead to more complex abilities. At first, stimulation results in a massive overabundance of synapses, many of which serve identical functions, thereby ensuring that the child will acquire the motor, cognitive, and social skills that our species needs to survive. Neurons that are seldom stimulated soon lose their synapses, a process called **synaptic pruning.** Pruning returns neurons not needed at the moment to an uncommitted state so they can support future development. In all, about 40 percent of synapses are pruned during childhood and adolescence to reach the adult level (refer again to Figure 5.6) (Webb, Monk, & Nelson, 2001). Notice how, for this process to go forward, appropriate stimulation of the child's brain is vital during periods in which the formation of synapses is at its peak (Greenough et al., 1993; Huttenlocher, 2002).

Perhaps you are wondering, if few neurons are produced after the prenatal period, what causes the dramatic increase in brain size during the first 2 years? About half the brain's volume is made up of **glial cells,** which do not carry messages. Instead, they are responsible for **myelination,** the coating of neural fibers with an insulating fatty sheath (called *myelin*) that improves the efficiency of message transfer. Glial cells multiply dramatically from the fourth month of pregnancy through the second year of life, a process that continues at a slower pace through middle childhood. Dramatic increases in neural fibers and myelination are responsible for the rapid gain in overall size of the brain. At birth, the brain is nearly 30 percent of its adult weight; by the time toddlerhood is complete, it reaches 70 percent (Thatcher et al., 1996).

In sum, brain development can be compared to molding a "living sculpture." After neurons and synapses are overproduced, programmed cell death and synaptic pruning sculpt away excess building material to form the mature brain—a process jointly influenced by genetically programmed events and the child's experiences. The resulting sculpture is a set of interconnected regions, each with specific functions—much like countries on a globe that communicate with one another (Johnston et al., 2001). This "geography" of the brain permits researchers to study its organization with brain-imaging techniques, such as *functional magnetic resonance imaging (fMRI)*. Recall from Chapter 1 that by detecting blood-flow changes as a child processes a stimulus, fMRI generates a computerized image of active areas (see page 36). Let's turn now to the developing organization of the cerebral cortex.

Development of the Cerebral Cortex

The **cerebral cortex** surrounds the rest of the brain, looking much like a half-shelled walnut. It is the largest, most complex brain structure—accounting for 85 percent of the brain's weight, containing the greatest number of neurons and synapses, and making possible uniquely human mental capacities. The cerebral cortex is the last part of the brain to stop growing. For this reason, it is sensitive to environmental influences for a much longer period than any other part of the brain.

REGIONS OF THE CORTEX ● Figure 5.7 shows specific functions of regions of the cerebral cortex, such as receiving information from the senses, instructing the body to move, and thinking. The order in which cortical regions develop corresponds to the order in which various capacities emerge in the infant and growing child. A burst of synaptic growth in the auditory and visual cortexes occurs from 3 to 4 months until the end of the first year—a period of dramatic gains in auditory and visual perception. Among the areas responsible for body movement, neurons that control the head, arms, and chest form connections before those that control the trunk and legs. (Can you name this growth trend?) And areas that support language show dramatic synaptic growth during late infancy and toddlerhood, when language development begins to flourish.

Among the last regions of the cortex to develop are the *frontal lobes,* which are responsible for thought—in particular, for consciousness, inhibition of impulses, and regulation of behavior through planning. From age 2 months on, this area functions more effectively. Formation and pruning of synapses in the frontal lobes continue for many years, yielding an adult level of synaptic connections around mid- to late adolescence (Nelson, 2002; Thompson et al., 2000).

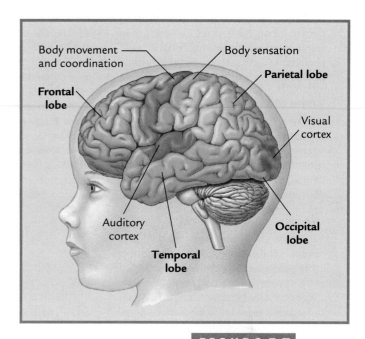

FIGURE 5.7

The left side of the human brain, showing the cerebral cortex.
The cortex is divided into different lobes, each of which contains a variety of regions with specific functions. Some major regions are labeled here.

LATERALIZATION AND PLASTICITY OF THE CEREBRAL CORTEX ● The cortex has two *hemispheres,* or sides—left and right—that differ in their functions. Some tasks are done mostly by one hemisphere and some by the other. For example, each hemisphere receives sensory information from and controls only one side of the body—the one opposite to it.[1] For most of us, the left hemisphere is largely responsible for verbal abilities (such as spoken and written language) and positive emotion (for example, joy). The right hemisphere handles spatial abilities (judging distances, reading maps, and recognizing geometric shapes) and negative emotion (such as distress) (Banish & Heller, 1998; Nelson & Bosquet, 2000). This pattern may be reversed in a small number of left-handed people, but more often, the cortex of left-handers is less clearly specialized than that of right-handers.

Specialization of the two hemispheres is called **lateralization.** Why are behaviors and abilities lateralized? According to one view, the left hemisphere is better at processing information in a sequential, analytic (piece-by-piece) way, which is a good approach for dealing with communicative information—both verbal (language) and emotional (a joyful smile). In contrast, the right hemisphere is specialized for processing information in a holistic, integrative manner, ideal for making sense of spatial information and regulating negative emotion (Banish, 1998).

---

[1] The eyes are an exception. Messages from the right half of each retina go to the right hemisphere; messages from the left half of each retina go to the left hemisphere. Thus, visual information from *both* eyes is received by *both* hemispheres.

Biology and Environment

Brain Plasticity: Insights from Research on Brain-Damaged Children and Adults

In the first few years of life, the brain is highly plastic. It can reorganize areas committed to specific functions in a way that the mature brain cannot. Consistently, adults who suffered brain injuries in infancy and early childhood show fewer cognitive impairments than adults with later-occurring injuries (Huttenlocher, 2002). Nevertheless, the young brain is not totally plastic. When it is injured, its functioning is compromised. The extent of plasticity depends on several factors, including age at time of injury, site of damage, and skill area.

Brain Plasticity in Infancy and Early Childhood

In a large study of children with injuries to the cerebral cortex that occurred before birth or in the first 6 months of life, language and spatial skills were assessed repeatedly into the school years (Stiles, 2001a; Stiles et al., 1998). All the children had experienced early brain seizures or hemorrhages. Brain-imaging techniques revealed the precise site of damage.

Regardless of whether injury occurred in the left or right cerebral hemisphere, the children showed delays in language development that persisted until about 3½ years of age. That damage to either hemisphere affected early language competence indicates that at first, language functioning is broadly distributed in the brain. But by age 5, the children caught up in vocabulary and grammatical skills. Undamaged areas—in either the left or the right hemisphere—had taken over these language functions.

Compared with language, spatial skills were more impaired after early brain injury. When 5- and 6-year-olds were asked to copy designs, children with early right-hemispheric damage had trouble with holistic processing—accurately representing the overall shape. In contrast, children with left-hemispheric damage captured the basic shape but omitted fine-grained details (see Figure 5.8) (Akshoomoff & Stiles, 1995). Nevertheless, the children showed some improvement in their drawings over the school years—gains that do not occur in brain-injured adults (Akshoomoff et al., 2001).

Clearly, recovery after early brain injury is greater for language than for spatial skills. Why is this so? Researchers speculate that spatial processing is the older of the two capacities in our evolutionary history and, therefore, more lateralized at birth (Stiles, 2001b). But early brain injury has far less impact than later injury on *both* language and spatial skills. In sum, the young brain is remarkably plastic.

The Price of High Plasticity in the Young Brain

Despite impressive recovery of language and (to a lesser extent) spatial skills, children with early brain injuries show deficits in a wide variety of complex mental abilities during the school years. For example, their reading and math progress is slow. And when asked to tell stories, they produce simpler narratives than their agemates without early brain injuries (Reilly, Bates, & Marchman, 1998). Furthermore, the more brain tissue destroyed in infancy or early childhood, the poorer children score on intelligence tests (Levine et al., 1987).

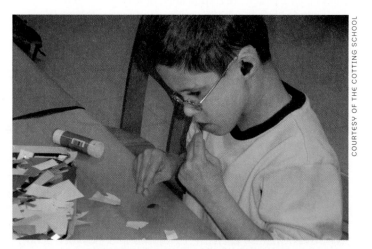

This 8-year-old, who experienced brain damage in infancy, has well-developed language skills but has difficulty with spatial tasks. Still, he has been spared massive impairments in either area because of early, high brain plasticity. The boy's teachers are strengthening his spatial skills by providing him with many activities involving copying and creating designs.

COURTESY OF THE COTTING SCHOOL

A lateralized brain is certainly adaptive. It permits a wider array of functions to be carried out effectively than if both sides processed information exactly the same way.

Researchers are interested in determining when brain lateralization occurs because they want to know more about **brain plasticity.** In a highly *plastic* cerebral cortex, many areas are not yet committed to specific functions. Consequently, the cortex has a high capacity for learning. In addition, if a part of the cortex is damaged, other parts can take over the tasks it would have handled. But once the hemispheres lateralize, damage to a specific region means that the abilities it controls cannot be recovered to the same extent or with the same ease that they could earlier.

High brain plasticity, researchers explain, comes at a price. When healthy brain regions take over the functions of damaged areas, a "crowding effect" occurs: Multiple tasks must be done by a smaller than usual volume of brain tissue. Consequently, the brain processes information less quickly and accurately than it would if it were fully intact. Complex mental abilities of all kinds suffer because they require considerable space in the cerebral cortex to be performed well (Huttenlocher, 2002).

Later Plasticity

Plasticity is not restricted to early childhood. Although far more limited, reorganization in the brain can occur later, even in adulthood. For example, adult stroke victims often display some recovery, especially in response to stimulation of language and motor skills. Brain-imaging techniques reveal that structures adjacent to the permanently damaged area or in the opposite cerebral hemisphere reorganize to support the impaired ability (Bach-y-Rita, 2001; Hallett, 2000).

In infancy and childhood, the goal of brain growth is to form neural connections that ensure mastery of essential skills. Animal research reveals that plasticity is greatest while the brain is forming many new synapses; it declines during synaptic pruning (Kolb & Gibb, 2001). At older ages, specialized brain structures are in place, but after injury they can still reorganize to some degree. Recent research reveals that the adult brain can produce a small number of new neurons (Gould et al., 1999). And when an individual practices relevant tasks, the brain strengthens existing synapses and generates new ones. Plasticity seems to be a basic property of the nervous system. Researchers hope to discover how experience and brain plasticity work together throughout life, helping people of all ages—with and without brain injuries—develop at their best.

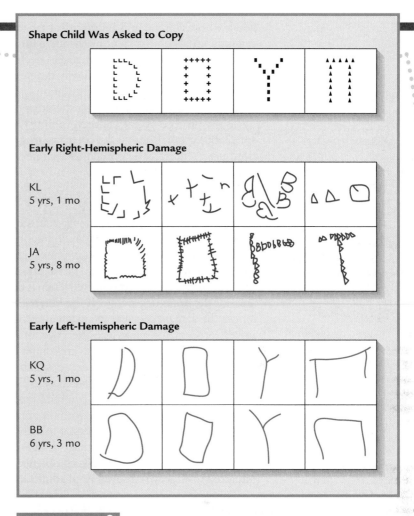

FIGURE 5.8

Impairments in spatial skills in 5- and 6-year-olds who had experienced brain injury before birth or in the first 6 months of life.

Compared with language skills, spatial skills are more impaired after early brain injury. When researchers had children copy designs, those with right-hemispheric damage had difficulty representing the overall shape. Those with left-hemispheric damage captured the basic shape but omitted fine-grained details. Although drawings improved over the school years, difficulties with spatial processing remained. (Adapted from J. Stiles, 2001, "Neural Plasticity and Cognitive Development," *Developmental Neuropsychology, 18,* p. 261. Reprinted by permission.)

At birth, the hemispheres have already begun to specialize. For example, most newborns favor the right side of the body in their head position and reflexive reactions (Grattan et al., 1992; Rönnqvist & Hopkins, 1998). Most also show greater EEG brain-wave activity in the left hemisphere while listening to speech sounds and displaying positive emotions. In contrast, the right hemisphere reacts more strongly to nonspeech sounds as well as to stimuli (such as a sour-tasting fluid) that evoke negative emotion (Davidson, 1994; Fox & Davidson, 1986).

Nevertheless, dramatic evidence for substantial plasticity in the young brain comes from research on brain-damaged children, summarized in the Biology and Environment box above. Furthermore, a growing body of research reveals that early experience greatly influences the organization of the cerebral cortex. For example, EEG brain-wave recordings reveal that deaf adults who, as infants and children, learned sign language (a spatial skill) depend more than hearing individuals on the right hemisphere for language processing (Neville & Bruer, 2001). Also, toddlers who are advanced in language development show greater left-hemispheric specialization for language than their more slowly developing agemates. Apparently, the very process of acquiring language promotes lateralization (Bates, 1999; Mills, Coffey-Corina, & Neville, 1997).

In sum, the brain is more plastic during the first few years than at any later time of life. Its flexibility protects young children's ability to learn, which is fundamental to their survival (Nelson, 2000). And although the cortex is programmed from the start for hemispheric specialization, experience greatly influences the rate and success of this genetic program.

Sensitive Periods in Brain Development

Recall that stimulation of the brain is vital during periods in which it is growing most rapidly. The existence of sensitive periods in development of the cerebral cortex has been amply demonstrated in studies of animals exposed to extreme forms of sensory deprivation. For example, there seems to be a time when rich and varied visual experiences must occur for the visual centers of the brain to develop normally. If a month-old kitten is deprived of light for as brief a time as 3 or 4 days, these areas of the brain degenerate. If the kitten is kept in the dark during the fourth week of life and longer, the damage is severe and permanent (Crair, Gillespie, & Stryker, 1998). Enriched versus deprived early environments also affect overall brain growth. When animals reared in physically and socially stimulating surroundings are compared with animals reared in isolation, the brains of the stimulated animals show much denser synaptic connections (Greenough & Black, 1992).

Because we cannot ethically expose children to such experiments, researchers interested in identifying sensitive periods for human brain development must rely on less direct evidence. They have found some parallels with the animal evidence just described. For example, as long as surgery takes place within the first 4 months, babies born with cataracts in both eyes (clouded lenses, preventing clear visual images) show rapid improvement in vision. The longer surgery is postponed after this time, the less complete the recovery. And vision is severely and permanently impaired if surgery is delayed until adulthood (Maurer & Lewis, 1993; Maurer et al., 1999).

BRAIN GROWTH SPURTS ● Focusing on the cerebral cortex as a whole, investigators have identified intermittent brain growth spurts, based on gains in brain weight and skull size as well as changes in neural activity, as measured by the EEG and fMRI. For example, several surges in frontal-lobe activity, which gradually spread to other cortical regions, occur during the first 2 years of life: at 3 to 4 months, when infants typically reach for objects; around 8 months, when they begin to crawl and search for hidden objects; around 12 months, when they walk and display more advanced object-search behaviors; and between 1½ and 2 years, when language flourishes (Bell & Fox, 1994, 1996; Fischer & Bidell, 1998). Between ages 3 and 6, frontal-lobe areas devoted to planning and organizing actions show a dramatic increase in activity—a period when children become better at using language to guide their behavior (Thompson & Nelson, 2001). Later frontal-lobe activity spurts, at ages 9, 12, 15, and 18 to 20, may reflect the emergence and refinement of abstract thought (Fischer & Rose, 1995).

Massive production of synapses may underlie brain growth spurts in the first 2

This boy has spent his first 2 years in a Romanian orphanage, with little adult contact and stimulation. The longer he remains in a barren environment, the more he will withdraw and wither and display permanent impairments in all domains of development.

© DAVID & PETER TURNLEY/CORBIS

years. Development of more complex and efficient neural networks, due to synaptic pruning, myelination, and longer-distance connections between the frontal lobes and other cortical regions, may account for the later ones. Researchers are convinced that what "wires" a child's brain during each of these periods is experience. But they still have many questions to answer about just how brain and behavioral development might best be supported during each growth spurt.

APPROPRIATE STIMULATION ● The evidence we do have confirms that the brain is particularly spongelike during the first few years of life; children learn new skills rapidly. As we will see later in this chapter and in chapters to come, understimulating infants and young children by depriving them of the rich and varied experiences available in caring family environments impairs their development. Studies of infants from Eastern European orphanages show that the earlier they are removed from these barren settings and placed in loving families, the greater their catch-up in development. When children spend their first 2 years or more in deprived institutional care with little social contact and sensory stimulation, all domains of development usually are delayed (Ames, 1997; Johnson, 2000). Deficits in concentration and control of anger and other impulses are especially severe (Gunnar, 2001).

Unlike the orphanage children just described, Grace, whom Monica and Kevin had adopted in Cambodia at 16 months of age, showed favorable progress. Two years earlier, they had adopted Grace's older brother, Eli. When Eli was 2 years old, Monica and Kevin sent a letter and a photo of Eli to his biological mother, describing a bright, happy child. The next day, the Cambodian mother tearfully asked an adoption agency to send her baby daughter to join Eli and his American family. Although Grace's early environment was very deprived, her biological mother's loving care—gentle holding, soft speaking, and breastfeeding—may have prevented irreversible damage to her brain.

Besides impoverished environments, ones that overwhelm children with expectations beyond their current capacities interfere with the brain's potential. In recent years, expensive early learning centers have sprung up, in which infants are trained with letter and number flash cards and slightly older toddlers are given a full curriculum of reading, math, science, art, gym, and more. There is no evidence that these programs yield smarter, better "superbabies." To the contrary, trying to prime infants with stimulation for which they are not ready can cause them to withdraw, thereby threatening their interest in learning and creating conditions much like stimulus deprivation!

How, then, can we characterize appropriate and inappropriate stimulation during the early years? To answer this question, researchers distinguish between two types of brain development. The first, **experience-expectant brain growth,** refers to the young brain's rapidly developing organization, which depends on ordinary experiences—opportunities to see and touch objects, to hear language and other sounds, and to move about and explore the environment. As a result of millions of years of evolution, the brains of all infants, toddlers, and young children *expect* to encounter these experiences and, if they do, grow normally. The second type of brain development—**experience-dependent brain growth**—occurs throughout our lives. It consists of new growth and the refinement of established brain structures as a result of specific learning experiences that vary widely across individuals and cultures (Greenough & Black, 1992). Reading, playing computer games, weaving an intricate rug, composing poetry, and practicing the violin are examples. The brain of a violinist differs in certain ways from the brain of a poet because each has exercised different brain regions for an extensive time (Thompson, 2001).

Experience-expectant brain development takes place early and naturally, as caregivers offer babies and preschoolers age-appropriate play materials and stimulating, enjoyable daily routines—a shared meal, a game of peek-a-boo, a bath before bed, a picture book to talk about, a song to sing, or an outing to the grocery store. The resulting growth provides the foundation for later-occurring, experience-dependent development (Huttenlocher, 2002; Shonkoff & Phillips, 2001). No

Relaxed participation with adults that ensures opportunities to see and touch objects, to hear language and other sounds, and to explore the environment are best for promoting brain growth during the early years of life. The brains of all infants, toddlers, and young children expect these ordinary experiences. In contrast, overstimulating babies with academic training and other lessons can impede brain development and the child's desire to learn.

© JOSE LUIS PELAEZ, INC./CORBIS

evidence exists for a sensitive period in the first 5 or 6 years of life for mastering skills that depend on extensive training, such as reading, musical performance, or gymnastics (Bruer, 1999).

As we saw in earlier chapters, the young, rapidly growing brain is vulnerable in many ways—to hazardous drug exposure, environmental toxins, poor diet, and chronic stress. Researchers speculate that rushing early learning also harms the brain by overwhelming its neural circuits, thereby reducing the brain's sensitivity to the everyday experiences it needs for a healthy start in life. In addition, when "mind-building" lessons do not produce young geniuses, they can lead to disappointed parents who view their children as failures at a tender age.

Changing States of Arousal

Rapid brain growth means that the organization of sleep and wakefulness changes substantially between birth and 2 years, and fussiness and crying also decline. The newborn baby takes round-the-clock naps that total about 16 hours. The decline in total sleep time during the first 2 years is not great; the average 2-year-old still needs 12 to 13 hours. The greatest changes are that periods of sleep and wakefulness become fewer but longer, and the sleep–wake pattern increasingly conforms to a night–day schedule. Most 6- to 9-month-olds take two naps. By the middle of the second year, children generally need only one nap. Around age 4 to 5, napping subsides (Iglowstein et al., 2003).

Although these changing arousal patterns are due to brain development, they are affected by the social environment. In most Western nations, parents usually succeed in getting their babies to sleep through the night around 4 months of age by offering an evening feeding before putting them down in a separate, quiet room. In this way, they push young infants to the limits of their neurological capacities. Not until the middle of the first year is the secretion of *melatonin,* a hormone within the brain that promotes drowsiness, much greater at night than during the day (Sadeh, 1997).

As the Cultural Influences box on the following page reveals, the practice of isolating infants to promote sleep is rare elsewhere in the world. When babies sleep with their parents, their average sleep period remains constant at 3 hours from 1 to 8 months of age. Only at the end of the first year, as REM sleep (the state that usually prompts waking) declines, do infants move in the direction of an adultlike sleep–wake schedule (Ficca et al., 1999).

Even after infants sleep through the night, they continue to wake occasionally. In surveys carried out in Great Britain, Israel, and the United States, parent reports indicated that night wakings peaked between 1½ and 2 years and then declined (Johnson, 1991; Scher et al., 1995). As Chapter 7 will reveal, the challenges of this period—ability to range farther from the familiar caregiver and awareness of the self as separate from others—often prompt anxiety in toddlers, evident in disturbed sleep and clinginess. When parents offer comfort, these behaviors subside.

Ask YOURSELF   www

REVIEW How does stimulation affect early brain development? Cite evidence at the level of neurons and at the level of the cerebral cortex.

REVIEW Explain why overproduction of synapses and synaptic pruning are adaptive processes that foster brain development.

APPLY Which infant enrichment program would you choose: one that emphasizes gentle talking and touching, exposure to sights and sounds, and simple social games, or one that includes word and number drills and classical music lessons? Explain.

REFLECT What is your attitude toward parent–infant cosleeping? Is it influenced by your cultural background? Explain.

Cultural Influences

Cultural Variation in Infant Sleeping Arrangements

While awaiting the birth of a new baby, North American parents typically furnish a room as the infant's sleeping quarters. For decades, child-rearing advice from experts strongly encouraged the nighttime separation of baby from parent. For example, the most recent edition of Benjamin Spock's *Baby and Child Care* recommends that babies be moved out of their parents' room early in the first year, explaining, "Otherwise, there is a chance that they may become dependent on this arrangement" (Spock & Parker, 1998, p. 102).

Yet parent–infant "cosleeping" is common around the globe. Japanese and Korean children usually lie next to their mothers throughout infancy and early childhood, and many continue to sleep with a parent or other family member until adolescence (Takahashi, 1990; Yang & Hahn, 2002). Among the Maya of rural Guatemala, mother–infant cosleeping is interrupted only by the birth of a new baby, at which time the older child is moved beside the father or to another bed in the same room (Morelli et al., 1992). Cosleeping is also frequent in some North American groups. African-American children frequently fall asleep with their parents and remain with them for part or all of the night (Brenner et al., 2003). Appalachian children of eastern Kentucky typically sleep with their parents for the first 2 years of life (Abbott, 1992).

Cultural values—specifically, collectivism versus individualism (see Chapter 2, page 78)—strongly influence infant sleeping arrangements. In one study, researchers interviewed American middle-SES mothers and Guatemalan Mayan mothers about their sleeping practices. American mothers conveyed an individualistic perspective,

mentioning the importance of instilling early independence, preventing bad habits, and protecting their own privacy. In contrast, Mayan mothers stressed a collectivist perspective, explaining that cosleeping builds a close parent–child bond, which is necessary for children to learn the ways of people around them (Morelli et al., 1992).

Perhaps because more mothers are breastfeeding, cosleeping among American mothers and their infants increased from 6 to 13 percent during the past decade (McKenna, 2002; Willinger et al., 2003). Research suggests that bedsharing evolved to protect infants' survival and health. Cosleeping babies breastfeed three times longer at night than infants who sleep alone. Because infants arouse to nurse more often when sleeping next to their mothers, some researchers believe that cosleeping may help safeguard babies at risk for sudden infant death syndrome (see page 152) (Moskow, Richard, & McKenna, 1997a). And contrary to popular belief, mothers' total sleep time is not decreased by cosleeping, although they experience a greater number of brief awakenings, which permits them to check on their baby (Mosko, Richard, & McKenna, 1997b).

Infant sleeping practices affect other aspects of family life. For example, sleep problems are not an issue for Mayan parents. Babies doze off in the midst of on-

going family activities and are carried to bed by their mothers. In contrast, in the United States, getting young children ready for bed often requires an elaborate ritual that takes a good part of the evening. Perhaps bedtime struggles, so common in American homes but rare elsewhere in the world, are related to the stress young children feel when they are required to fall asleep without assistance (Latz, Wolf, & Lozoff, 1999).

Critics worry that cosleeping children will develop emotional problems—especially, excessive dependency. Yet a longitudinal study following children from the end of pregnancy through age 18 showed that young people who had bed-shared in the early years were no different from others in any aspect of adjustment (Okami, Weisner, & Olmstead, 2002). Another concern is that infants might become trapped under the parent's body or in soft covers and suffocate. Parents who are obese or who smoke while bedsharing do pose a serious risk to their babies. Also, use of quilts and comforters is hazardous (Fleming et al., 1996; Willinger et al., 2003). But with appropriate precautions, parents and infants can cosleep safely (McKenna, 2001). In cultures where cosleeping is widespread, parents and infants usually sleep with light covering on hard surfaces, such as firm mattresses, floor mats, and wooden planks (Nelson, Schiefenhoevel, & Haimerl, 2000).

© STEPHEN L. RAYMER/NATIONAL GEOGRAPHIC IMAGE COLLECTION

This Cambodian father and child sleep together— a practice common in their culture and around the globe. When children fall asleep with their parents, sleep problems are rare during the early years. And many parents who practice cosleeping believe that it helps build a close parent–child bond.

Influences on Early Physical Growth

Physical growth, like other aspects of development, results from the continuous and complex interplay between genetic and environmental factors. Heredity, nutrition, relative freedom from disease, and emotional well-being all affect early physical growth.

Heredity

Since identical twins are much more alike in body size than are fraternal twins, we know that heredity is important in physical growth. When diet and health are adequate, height and rate of physical growth (as measured by skeletal age) are largely determined by heredity. In fact, as long as negative environmental influences such as poor nutrition or illness are not severe, children and adolescents typically show *catch-up growth*—a return to a genetically determined growth path. After her adoption, Grace grew rapidly; by age 2, she was nearly average in size by Cambodian standards. Physical growth is a strongly canalized process (see Chapter 2, page 86).

Genetic makeup also affects body weight, since the weights of adopted children correlate more strongly with those of their biological than adoptive parents (Stunkard et al., 1986). However, as far as weight is concerned, environment—in particular, nutrition—plays an especially important role.

Nutrition

Nutrition is important at any time of development, but it is especially crucial during the first 2 years because the baby's brain and body are growing so rapidly. Pound for pound, an infant's energy needs are twice those of an adult. Twenty-five percent of the infant's total caloric intake is devoted to growth, and extra calories are needed to keep rapidly developing organs functioning properly (Pipes, 1996).

BREAST- VERSUS BOTTLE-FEEDING ● Babies need not only enough food but also the right kind of food. In early infancy, breast milk is especially suited to their needs, and bottled formulas try to imitate it. Refer to Applying What We Know on the following page, which summarizes the major nutritional and health advantages of breastfeeding.

Because of these benefits, breastfed babies in poverty-stricken regions of the world are much less likely to be malnourished and 6 to 14 times more likely to survive the first year of life. The World Health Organization recommends breastfeeding until age 2 years, with solid foods added at 6 months—practices that, if widely followed, would save the lives of more than a million infants annually. Even breastfeeding for just a few weeks offers some protection against respiratory and intestinal infections, which are devastating to young children in developing countries. Furthermore, because a mother is less likely to get pregnant while she is nursing, breastfeeding helps increase the spacing among siblings, a major factor in reducing infant and childhood deaths in nations with widespread poverty (Darnton-Hill & Coyne, 1998). (Note, however, that breastfeeding is not a reliable method of birth control.)

Yet many mothers in the developing world do not know about the benefits of breastfeeding. In Africa, the Middle East, and Latin America, fewer than 40 percent of mothers breastfeed (Save the Children, 2001). Instead, they give their babies commercial formula or low-grade nutrients, such as rice water or highly diluted cow or goat milk. These foods often lead to illness because they are contaminated due to poor sanitation. The United Nations has encouraged all hospitals and maternity units in developing countries to promote breastfeeding as

Breastfeeding is especially important in developing countries, where infants are at risk for malnutrition, infectious disease, and early death due to widespread poverty. This baby of Rajasthan, India, is likely to grow normally during the first year because his mother decided to breastfeed.

© JANE SCHREIBMAN/PHOTO RESEARCHERS, INC.

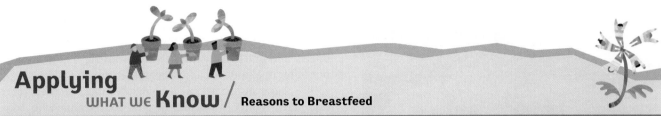

Applying
WHAT WE **Know** / **Reasons to Breastfeed**

NUTRITIONAL AND HEALTH ADVANTAGES	EXPLANATION
Provides the correct balance of fat and protein.	Compared with the milk of other mammals, human milk is higher in fat and lower in protein. This balance, as well as the unique proteins and fats contained in human milk, is ideal for a rapidly myelinating nervous system.
Assures nutritional completeness.	A mother who breastfeeds need not add other foods to her infant's diet until the baby is 6 months old. The milks of all mammals are low in iron, but the iron contained in breast milk is much more easily absorbed by the baby's system. Consequently, bottle-fed infants need iron-fortified formula.
Helps ensure healthy physical growth.	In the first few months, breastfed infants add weight and length slightly faster than bottle-fed infants, who catch up by the end of the first year. One-year-old breastfed babies are leaner (have a higher percentage of muscle to fat), a growth pattern that may help prevent later overweight and obesity.
Protects against many diseases.	Breastfeeding transfers antibodies and other infection-fighting agents from mother to child and enhances functioning of the immune system. As a result, compared with bottle-fed infants, breastfed babies have far fewer allergic reactions and respiratory and intestinal illnesses, including colds, flu, diarrhea, middle ear infection, meningitis, and infections of the urinary tract and colon. Components of human milk that protect against disease can be added to formula, but breastfeeding provides superior immunity.
Protects against faulty jaw development and tooth decay.	Sucking the mother's nipple instead of an artificial nipple helps avoid malocclusion, a condition in which the upper and lower jaws do not meet properly. It also protects against tooth decay due to sweet liquid remaining in the mouths of infants who fall asleep while sucking on a bottle.
Assures digestibility.	The composition of breast milk makes it more digestible than cow's milk. Because breastfed babies have a different kind of bacteria growing in their intestines than do bottle-fed infants, they rarely suffer from constipation or other gastrointestinal problems.
Smoothes the transition to solid foods.	Breastfed infants accept new solid foods more easily than do bottle-fed infants, perhaps because of their greater experience with a variety of flavors, which pass from the maternal diet into the mother's milk.

Sources: Dewey, 2001; Kramer et al., 2002, 2003; Kramer & Kakuma, 2002; U.S. Department of Health and Human Services, 2000.

long as mothers do not have viral or bacterial infections (such as HIV or tuberculosis) that can be transmitted to the baby. Today, most developing countries have banned the practice of giving free or subsidized formula to new mothers.

Partly as a result of the natural childbirth movement, breastfeeding has become more common in industrialized nations, especially among well-educated women. Today, 68 percent of American and 73 percent of Canadian mothers breastfeed. However, about two-thirds of breastfeeding American mothers and nearly half of Canadian mothers stop after a few months (Ahluwalia et al., 2003; Health Canada, 2002). Breast milk is so easily digestible that a breastfed infant becomes hungry quite often—every 1½ to 2 hours, compared to every 3 or 4 hours for a bottle-fed baby. This makes breastfeeding inconvenient for many employed women. Not surprisingly, mothers who return to work sooner wean their babies from the breast earlier (Arora et al., 2002).

However, mothers who cannot be with their babies all the time can combine breast- and bottle-feeding. Still, the American Academy of Pediatrics (1997) and the Canadian Pediatric Society (2003) advise exclusive breastfeeding for the first 6 months. In the United States, recommendations also suggest that breast milk be included in the baby's diet until at least 1 year; in Canada, until 2 years and beyond.

This father serves his 22-month-old toddler a breakfast of fruit, grains, and milk, responds sensitively to her desire to feed herself, and avoids foods loaded with sugar, salt, and saturated fats. In these ways, he supports his daughter's healthy physical growth, teaches her to prefer nutritious foods, and protects her from excessive early weight gain, which is linked to later obesity.

Women who cannot or do not want to breastfeed sometimes worry that they are depriving their baby of an experience essential for healthy psychological development. Yet breast- and bottle-fed youngsters in industrialized nations do not differ in emotional adjustment (Fergusson & Woodward, 1999). Some studies report a small advantage in intelligence test performance for children and adolescents who were breastfed, after many factors are controlled. Others, however, find no cognitive benefits (Jain, Concat, & Leventhal, 2002; Mortensen et al., 2002). Notice in the Applying What We Know table on page 179 that breast milk provides nutrients ideally suited for early brain development.

ARE CHUBBY BABIES AT RISK FOR LATER OVER-WEIGHT AND OBESITY? ●

Timmy was an enthusiastic eater from early infancy. He nursed vigorously and gained weight quickly. By 5 months, he began reaching for food on his mother's plate. Vanessa wondered: Was she overfeeding Timmy and increasing his chances of being permanently overweight?

Most chubby infants thin out during toddlerhood and the preschool years, as weight gain slows and they become more active. Infants and toddlers can eat nutritious foods freely, without risk of becoming overweight. Recent evidence does indicate, however, a strengthening relationship between rapid weight gain in infancy and obesity at older ages (Stettler et al., 2003; Yanovski, 2003). The trend might be due to the growing number of overweight and obese adults, who promote unhealthful eating habits in their young children. Interviews with more than 3,000 American parents of 4- to 24-month-olds revealed that many served them French fries, pizza, candy, sugary fruit drinks, and soda on a daily basis. For example, 60 percent of 12-month-olds ate candy at least once per day! On average, infants consumed 20 percent and toddlers 30 percent more calories than they needed. At the same time, one-third ate no fruits or vegetables (Briefel et al., 2004).

How can concerned parents prevent infants from becoming overweight children and adults? One way is to avoid giving them foods loaded with sugar, salt, and saturated fats. When young children eat such foods regularly, they start to prefer them (Birch & Fisher, 1995). Physical exercise is another safeguard against excessive weight gain. Once toddlers learn to walk, climb, and run, parents should provide opportunities for energetic play.

Malnutrition

Osita is an Ethiopian 2-year-old whose mother has never had to worry about his gaining too much weight. When she weaned him at 1 year, he had little to eat besides starchy rice flour cakes. Soon his belly enlarged, his feet swelled, his hair fell out, and a rash appeared on his skin. His bright-eyed curiosity vanished, and he became irritable and listless.

In developing countries and war-torn areas, where food resources are limited, malnutrition is widespread. Recent evidence indicates that about one-third of the world's children suffer from malnutrition before age 5 (Bellamy, 1998). Among the 4 to 7 percent who are severely affected, undernourishment leads to two dietary diseases: marasmus and kwashiorkor.

Marasmus is a wasted condition of the body caused by a diet low in all essential nutrients. It usually appears in the first year of life when a baby's mother is too malnourished to produce enough breast milk and bottle-feeding is also inadequate. Her starving baby becomes painfully thin and is in danger of dying.

Osita has **kwashiorkor,** caused by an unbalanced diet very low in protein. Kwashiorkor usually strikes after weaning, between 1 and 3 years of age. It is common in areas of the world where children get just enough calories from starchy foods, but protein resources are scarce. The child's body responds by breaking down its own protein reserves, leading to the swelling and other symptoms that Osita experienced.

Children who survive these extreme forms of malnutrition grow to be smaller in all body dimensions (Galler, Ramsey, & Solimano, 1985a). And when their diets improve, they are at risk for excessive weight gain. Nationwide surveys in Russia, China, and South Africa reveal that growth-stunted children are far more likely to be overweight than their nonstunted agemates (Popkin, Richards, & Montiero, 1996). To protect itself, a malnourished body establishes a low basal metabolism rate, which may endure after nutrition improves. Also, malnutrition may disrupt appetite control centers in the brain, causing the child to overeat when food becomes plentiful.

Learning and behavior are also seriously affected. One long-term study of marasmic children revealed that an improved diet led to some catch-up growth in height, but the children failed to catch up in head size (Stoch et al., 1982). The malnutrition probably interfered with growth of neural fibers and myelination, causing a permanent loss in brain weight. These children score low on intelligence tests, show poor fine motor coordination, and have difficulty paying attention (Galler et al., 1990; Galler, Ramsey, & Solimano, 1985b). They also display a more intense stress response to fear-arousing situations, perhaps caused by the constant, gnawing pain of hunger (Fernald & Grantham-McGregor, 1998).

Recall from our discussion of prenatal malnutrition in Chapter 3 that the passivity and irritability of malnourished children worsen the impact of poor diet. These behaviors may appear even when protein-calorie deprivation is only mild to moderate. They also accompany *iron-deficiency anemia,* a condition common among poverty-stricken infants and children that interferes with many central nervous system processes. Withdrawal and listlessness reduce the nutritionally deprived child's ability to pay attention, explore, and evoke sensitive caregiving from parents, whose lives are already disrupted by poverty and stressful living conditions (Grantham-McGregor & Ani, 2001; Lozoff et al., 1998). For this reason, interventions for malnourished children must improve the family situation as well as the child's nutrition. Even better are efforts at prevention—providing food and medical care before the dire effects of early malnutrition run their course.

Inadequate nutrition is not confined to developing countries. Because American and Canadian supplementary food programs do not reach all families in need, an estimated 16 percent of North American children suffer from *food insecurity*—uncertain access to enough food for a healthy, active life (McIntyre, Connor, & Warren, 1998; U.S. Department of Agriculture, 2003). Although few have marasmus or kwashiorkor, their physical growth and ability to learn in school are still affected (Wachs, 1995). Malnutrition is clearly an international crisis—one of the most serious problems confronting the human species today.

The swollen abdomen and listless behavior of this Honduran child are classic symptoms of kwashiorkor, a nutritional illness that results from a diet very low in protein.

Emotional Well-Being

We are not used to thinking of affection and stimulation as necessary for healthy physical growth, but they are just as vital to infants as food. **Nonorganic failure to thrive** is a growth disorder that results from lack of parental love and that is usually present by 18 months of age. Infants who have it show all the signs of marasmus—their bodies look wasted, and they are withdrawn and apathetic. But no organic (or biological) cause for the baby's failure to grow can be found. The baby is offered enough food and does not have a serious illness.

Lana, an observant nurse at a public health clinic, became concerned about 8-month-old Melanie, who was 3 pounds lighter than she had been at her last checkup. Her mother claimed to feed her often and could not understand why she did not grow. Lana noted Melanie's behavior. She showed little interest in toys but, instead, kept her eyes on nearby adults, anxiously watching their every move. She rarely smiled when her mother came near and rarely cuddled when picked up (Steward, 2001).

Family circumstances surrounding failure to thrive help explain these typical reactions. During feeding, diaper changing, and play, Melanie's mother sometimes acted cold and distant, at other times impatient and hostile (Hagekull, Bohlin, & Rydell, 1997). Melanie tried to protect herself by tracking her mother's whereabouts and, when she approached, avoiding her gaze.

Often an unhappy marriage and parental psychological disturbance contribute to these serious caregiving problems (Drotar, Pallotta, & Eckerle, 1994; Duniz et al., 1996). Sometimes the baby is irritable and displays abnormal feeding behaviors, such as poor sucking or vomiting, that stress the parent–child relationship further (Wooster, 1999).

In Melanie's case, her alcoholic father was out of work, and her parents argued constantly. Melanie's mother had little energy to meet Melanie's psychological needs. When treated early, by helping parents or placing the baby in a caring foster home, failure-to-thrive infants show quick catch-up growth. But if the disorder is not corrected in infancy, most children remain small and show lasting cognitive and emotional difficulties (Dykman et al., 2001).

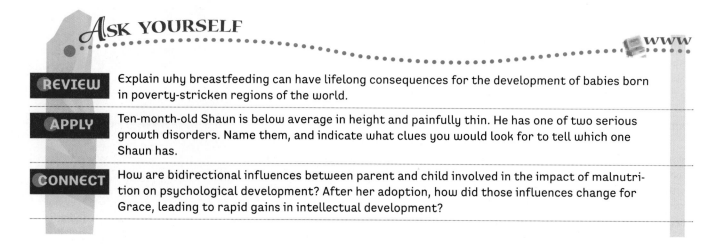

𝒜SK YOURSELF

REVIEW	Explain why breastfeeding can have lifelong consequences for the development of babies born in poverty-stricken regions of the world.
APPLY	Ten-month-old Shaun is below average in height and painfully thin. He has one of two serious growth disorders. Name them, and indicate what clues you would look for to tell which one Shaun has.
CONNECT	How are bidirectional influences between parent and child involved in the impact of malnutrition on psychological development? After her adoption, how did those influences change for Grace, leading to rapid gains in intellectual development?

ℒearning Capacities

Learning refers to changes in behavior as the result of experience. Babies come into the world with built-in learning capacities that permit them to profit from experience immediately. Infants are capable of two basic forms of learning, which were introduced in Chapter 1: classical and operant conditioning. They also learn through their natural preference for novel stimulation. Finally, shortly after birth, babies learn by observing others; they can soon imitate the facial expressions and gestures of adults.

Classical Conditioning

Newborn reflexes, discussed in Chapter 4, make **classical conditioning** possible in the young infant. In this form of learning, a neutral stimulus is paired with a stimulus that leads to a reflexive response. Once the baby's nervous system makes the connection between the two stimuli, the new stimulus produces the behavior by itself.

Classical conditioning is of great value to infants because it helps them recognize which events usually occur together in the everyday world. As a result, they can anticipate what is about to happen next, and the environment becomes more orderly and predictable. Let's take a closer look at the steps of classical conditioning.

As Carolyn settled down in the rocking chair to nurse Caitlin, she often stroked Caitlin's forehead. Soon Carolyn noticed that each time Caitlin's forehead was stroked, she made active sucking movements. Caitlin had been classically conditioned. Here is how it happened (see Figure 5.9):

● Before learning takes place, an **unconditioned stimulus (UCS)** must consistently produce a reflexive, or **unconditioned, response (UCR)**. In Caitlin's case, sweet breast milk (UCS) resulted in sucking (UCR).

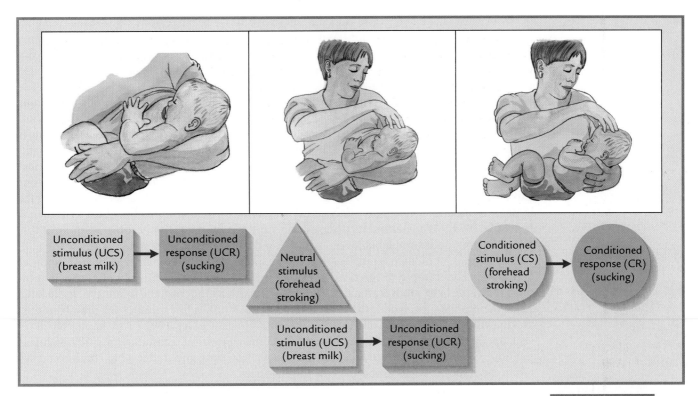

FIGURE 5.9

The steps of classical conditioning.

This example shows how Caitlin's mother classically conditioned her to make sucking movements by stroking her forehead at the beginning of feedings.

- To produce learning, a *neutral stimulus* that does not lead to the reflex is presented just before, or at about the same time as, the UCS. Carolyn stroked Caitlin's forehead as each nursing period began. The stroking (neutral stimulus) was paired with the taste of milk (UCS).

- If learning has occurred, the neutral stimulus by itself produces a response similar to the reflexive response. The neutral stimulus is then called a **conditioned stimulus (CS)**, and the response it elicits is called a **conditioned response (CR)**. We know that Caitlin has been classically conditioned because stroking her forehead outside the feeding situation (CS) results in sucking (CR).

If the CS is presented alone enough times, without being paired with the UCS, the CR will no longer occur. In other words, if Carolyn strokes Caitlin's forehead again and again without feeding her, Caitlin will gradually stop sucking in response to stroking. This is referred to as *extinction.*

Young infants can be classically conditioned most easily when the association between two stimuli has survival value. Caitlin learned quickly in the feeding situation, since learning which stimuli regularly accompany feeding improves the infant's ability to get food and survive (Blass, Ganchrow, & Steiner, 1984). In contrast, some responses are very difficult to classically condition in young babies. Fear is one of them. Until infants have the motor skills to escape unpleasant events, they do not have a biological need to form these associations. But after 6 months of age, fear is easy to condition, as seen in the famous example of little Albert, conditioned by John Watson to withdraw and cry at the sight of a furry white rat. Return to Chapter 1, page 18, to review this well-known experiment. Then test your knowledge of classical conditioning by identifying the UCS, UCR, CS, and CR in Watson's study. In Chapter 7, we will discuss the development of fear, as well as other emotional reactions.

Operant Conditioning

In classical conditioning, babies build expectations about stimulus events in the environment, but they do not influence the stimuli that occur. In **operant conditioning**, infants act (or operate) on the environment, and stimuli that follow their behavior change the probability that the behavior will occur again. A stimulus that increases the occurrence of a response is called a **reinforcer.** For example, sweet liquid *reinforces* the sucking response in newborn babies. Removing a desirable stimulus or presenting an unpleasant one to decrease the occurrence of a response is called **punishment.** A sour-tasting fluid *punishes* newborn babies' sucking response. It causes them to purse their lips and stop sucking entirely.

Because the young infant can control only a few behaviors, successful operant conditioning in the early weeks of life is limited to sucking and head-turning responses. However, many stimuli besides food can serve as reinforcers. For example, researchers have created special laboratory conditions in which the baby's rate of sucking on a nipple produces a variety of interesting sights and sounds. Newborns will suck faster to see visual designs or hear music and human voices (Floccia, Christophe, & Bertoncini, 1997). Even preterm babies will seek reinforcing stimulation. In one study, they increased their contact with a soft teddy bear that "breathed" at a rate reflecting the infant's respiration, whereas they decreased their contact with a nonbreathing bear (Thoman & Ingersoll, 1993). As these findings suggest, operant conditioning has become a powerful tool for finding out what stimuli babies can perceive and which ones they prefer.

As infants get older, operant conditioning expands to include a wider range of responses and stimuli. For example, researchers have hung special mobiles over the cribs of 2- to 6-month-olds. When the baby's foot is attached to the mobile with a long cord, the infant can, by kicking, make the mobile turn. Under these conditions, it takes only a few minutes for infants to start kicking vigorously (Rovee-Collier, 1999; Shields & Rovee-Collier, 1992). As Chapter 6 will reveal, operant conditioning with mobiles has become a powerful technique for studying infant memory. Once babies learn to kick, researchers see how long and under what conditions they retain the response when exposed to the mobile again.

Operant conditioning soon modifies parents' and babies' reactions to each other. As the infant gazes into the adult's eyes, the adult looks and smiles back, and then the infant looks and smiles again. The behavior of each partner reinforces the other, and as a result, both continue their pleasurable interaction. In Chapter 7, we will see that this contingent responsiveness contributes to the development of infant–caregiver attachment.

Look carefully at the findings just described, and you will see that young babies are active learners; they use any means they can to explore and control their surroundings in an effort to meet their needs for nutrition, stimulation, and social contact (Rovee-Collier, 1996). In fact, when infants' environments are so disorganized that their behavior does not lead to predictable outcomes, serious difficulties ranging from intellectual delays to apathy and depression can result (Cicchetti & Aber, 1986; Seligman, 1975).

Habituation

At birth, the human brain is set up to be attracted to novelty. Infants tend to respond more strongly to a new element that has entered their environment. **Habituation** refers to a gradual reduction in the strength of a response due to repetitive stimulation. Looking, heart rate, and respiration may all decline, indicating a loss of interest. Once this has occurred, a new stimulus—some kind of change in the environment—causes responsiveness to return to a high level, an increase called **recovery.** For example, when you walk through a familiar space, you notice things that are new and different, such as a recently purchased picture on the wall or a piece of furniture that has been moved. Habituation and recovery enable us to focus our attention on those aspects of the environment we know least about. As a result, learning is more efficient.

By studying infants' habituation and recovery, researchers can explore their understanding of the world. For example, a baby who first *habituates* to a visual pattern (a photo of a baby) and then *recovers* to a new one (a photo of a bald man) appears to remember the first stimulus and to perceive the second one as new and different from it. This method of studying infant perception and cognition, illustrated in Figure 5.10, can be used with newborn babies, even those who are preterm. It has even been used to study the fetus's sensitivity to external stimuli—for example, by measuring changes in fetal heart rate when various repeated sounds are presented (Sandman et al., 1997).

The capacity to habituate is evident in the third trimester of pregnancy. As fetuses and babies get older, they habituate to stimuli more quickly, indicating that they process information more efficiently. Yet a fascinating exception to this trend exists. Two-month-olds actually take longer than newborns to habituate to novel visual forms (Slater et al., 1996). Later, we will see that 2 months is also a time of dramatic gains in visual perception. Perhaps when young babies are first able to perceive certain information, they require more time to take it in (Johnson, 1996). We will return to habituation and recovery when we discuss perception later in this chapter and when we consider attention, memory, and other aspects of infant cognition in Chapter 6.

Imitation

Newborn babies come into the world with a primitive ability to learn through **imitation**—by copying the behavior of another person. For example, Figure 5.11 shows infants from 2 days to several weeks old imitating several adult facial expressions (Field et al., 1982; Meltzoff & Moore, 1977). The newborn's capacity to imitate extends to certain gestures, such as head movements, and has been demonstrated in many ethnic groups and cultures (Meltzoff & Kuhl, 1994).

But a few studies have failed to reproduce these findings (see, for example, Anisfeld et al., 2001). And imitation is more difficult to induce in babies 2 to 3 months old than just after birth. Therefore, some researchers regard the capacity as little more than an automatic response that declines with age, much like a reflex. Others claim that newborns imitate a variety of facial expressions with effort and determination, even after short delays—when the adult is no longer

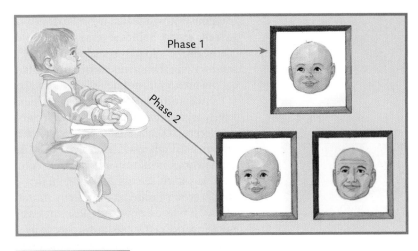

FIGURE 5.10

Example of how the habituation/recovery sequence can be used to study infant perception and cognition.

In Phase 1, infants are shown (habituated to) a photo of a baby. In Phase 2, infants are again shown the baby photo, but this time it appears alongside a photo of a bald-headed man. Infants recovered to (spent more time looking at) the photo of the man, indicating that they remembered the baby and perceived the man's face as different from it. (Adapted from Fagan & Singer, 1979.)

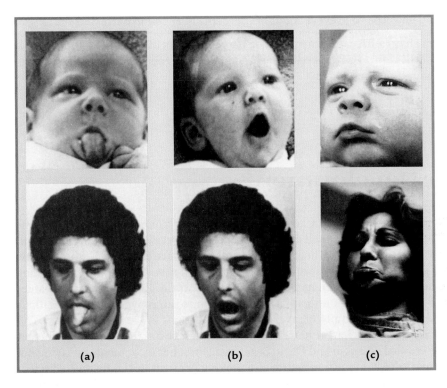

(a)   (b)   (c)

FIGURE 5.11

Photographs from two of the first studies of newborn imitation.

Those on the left show 2- to 3-week-old infants imitating tongue protrusion (a), and mouth opening (b). The one on the right shows a 2-day-old infant imitating a sad (c) adult facial expression. (From A. N. Meltzoff & M. K. Moore, 1977, "Imitation of Facial and Manual Gestures by Human Neonates," *Science, 198,* p. 75; and T. M. Field et al., 1992, "Discrimination and Imitation of Facial Expressions by Neonates," *Science, 218,* p. 180. Copyright 1977 and 1982, respectively, by the AAAS. Reprinted by permission.)

demonstrating the behavior. Furthermore, these investigators argue, imitation does not decline, as reflexes do. Babies several months old often do not imitate an adult's behavior right away because they try to play social games they are used to in face-to-face interaction—smiling, cooing, and waving their arms. When an adult models a gesture repeatedly, older babies soon get down to business and imitate (Meltzoff & Moore, 1994).

According to Andrew Meltzoff, newborns imitate in much the same way adults do—by actively trying to match body movements they *see* with ones they *feel* themselves make (Meltzoff & Decety, 2003; Meltzoff & Moore, 1999). Later we will encounter evidence that young babies are surprisingly good at coordinating information across sensory systems. Still, Meltzoff's view of newborn imitation as a flexible, voluntary capacity is controversial.

As we will see in Chapter 6, infants' capacity to imitate improves greatly over the first 2 years. But however limited it is at birth, imitation may reflect the baby's deep-seated need to communicate. It is also a powerful means of learning. Using imitation, young infants begin to explore their social world, getting to know people by matching behavioral states with them. In the process, babies notice similarities between their own actions and those of others and start to find out about themselves. Furthermore, by tapping into infants' ability to imitate, adults can get infants to exhibit desirable behaviors, and once they do, adults can encourage these further. Finally, caregivers take great pleasure in a baby who imitates their facial gestures and actions. Newborn imitation seems to be one of those capacities that helps get the infant's relationship with parents off to a good start.

Ask YOURSELF

www

REVIEW Provide an example of classical conditioning, operant conditioning, and habituation/recovery in young infants. Why is each type of learning useful?

APPLY Infants with nonorganic failure to thrive rarely smile at friendly adults. Also, they anxiously keep track of nearby adults. Explain these reactions using the learning capacities discussed in the previous sections.

APPLY Nine-month-old Byron has a toy with large, colored push buttons on it. Each time he pushes a button, he hears a nursery tune. Which capacity is the manufacturer of this toy taking advantage of? What can Bryon's play with the toy reveal about his perception of sound patterns?

CONNECT Return to the section on intervening with preterm infants on pages 143–145 of Chapter 4. Why might a preterm baby seek contact with a soft, "breathing" teddy bear, as reported in our discussion of operant conditioning on pages 183–184?

Motor Development

Carolyn, Monica, and Vanessa each kept baby books, filling them with proud notations about when their children held up their heads, reached for objects, sat by themselves, and walked alone. Parents' enthusiasm for these achievements makes perfect sense. With each new motor skill, babies master their bodies and the environment in a new way. For example, sitting upright gives infants an entirely different perspective on the world. Reaching permits babies to find out about objects by acting on them. And when infants can move on their own, their opportunities for exploration multiply.

Babies' motor achievements have a powerful effect on their social relationships. When at 7½ months Caitlin crawled, Carolyn and David began to restrict her movements by saying no, expressing mild impatience, and picking her up and moving her—strategies that were unnecessary before. When Caitlin started walking three days after her first birthday, first "testing of wills" occurred (Biringen et al., 1995). Despite her mother's warnings, she sometimes pulled items from shelves that were "off limits." "Oh, Caitlin, I said not to do that!" Carolyn would remark as she redirected Caitlin's activities.

At the same time, expressions of affection and playful activities expanded as Caitlin sought her parents out for greetings, hugs, and a gleeful game of hide-and-seek (Campos, Kermoian, & Zumbahlen, 1992). Soon after, Caitlin turned the pages of a book and pointed as she and her parents named each picture. Caitlin's expressions of delight as she worked on new motor competencies triggered pleasurable reactions in others, which encouraged her efforts further (Mayes & Zigler, 1992). Motor skills, social competencies, cognition, and language developed together and supported one another.

The Sequence of Motor Development

Gross motor development refers to control over actions that help infants get around in the environment, such as crawling, standing, and walking. In contrast, *fine motor development* has to do with smaller movements, such as reaching and grasping. Table 5.1 shows the average age at which infants and toddlers achieve a variety of gross and fine motor skills. Most (but not all) children follow this sequence.

Notice that the table also presents the age ranges during which the majority of babies accomplish each skill. These indicate that although the *sequence* of motor development is fairly uniform across children, large individual differences exist in *rate* of motor progress. Also, a baby who is a late reacher is not necessarily going to be a late crawler or walker. We would be concerned about a child's development only if many motor skills were seriously delayed.

TABLE 5.1

Gross and Fine Motor Development in the First Two Years

MOTOR SKILL	AVERAGE AGE ACHIEVED	AGE RANGE IN WHICH 90 PERCENT OF INFANTS ACHIEVE THE SKILL
When held upright, holds head erect and steady	6 weeks	3 weeks–4 months
When prone, lifts self by arms	2 months	3 weeks–4 months
Rolls from side to back	2 months	3 weeks–5 months
Grasps cube	3 months, 3 weeks	2–7 months
Rolls from back to side	4½ months	2–7 months
Sits alone	7 months	5–9 months
Crawls	7 months	5–11 months
Pulls to stand	8 months	5–12 months
Plays pat-a-cake	9 months, 3 weeks	7–15 months
Stands alone	11 months	9–16 months
Walks alone	11 months, 3 weeks	9–17 months
Builds tower of two cubes	11 months, 3 weeks	10–19 months
Scribbles vigorously	14 months	10–21 months
Walks up stairs with help	16 months	12–23 months
Jumps in place	23 months, 2 weeks	17–30 months
Walks on tiptoe	25 months	16–30 months

Sources: Bayley, 1969, 1993.

Photos: (top) © Laura Dwight; (lower left) © Barbara Peacock/Getty Images/Taxi; (lower right) © Elizabeth Crews/The Image Works.

Look at Table 5.1 once more, and you will see both organization and direction to infants' motor achievements. The *cephalocaudal trend* is evident. Motor control of the head comes before control of the arms and trunk, which comes before control of the legs. You can also see the *proximodistal trend*: Head, trunk, and arm control is advanced over coordination of the hands and fingers. These similarities between physical and motor development suggest a genetic contribution to motor progress. But, as we will see, deviations from these trends exist.

We must be careful not to think of motor skills as unrelated accomplishments that follow a fixed maturational timetable. Instead, each skill is a product of earlier motor attainments and a contributor to new ones. Furthermore, children acquire motor skills in highly individual ways. For example, Grace, who spent most of her days lying in a hammock until her adoption, did not try to crawl because she rarely spent time on her tummy or on firm surfaces that enabled her to move on her own. As a result, she pulled to a stand and walked before she crawled!

Many influences—both internal and external to the child—join together to support the vast transformations in motor competencies of the first 2 years. The *dynamic systems perspective,* a relatively recent theoretical approach introduced in Chapter 1 (see pages 29–30), helps us understand how motor development takes place.

Motor Skills as Dynamic Systems

According to **dynamic systems theory of motor development,** mastery of motor skills involves acquiring increasingly complex *systems of action.* When motor skills work as a *system,* separate abilities blend together, each cooperating with others to produce more effective ways of exploring and controlling the environment. For example, control of the head and upper chest combine into sitting with support. Kicking, rocking on all fours, and reaching combine to become crawling. Then crawling, standing, and stepping unite into walking (Thelen, 1989).

Each new skill is a joint product of the following factors: (1) central nervous system development, (2) movement capacities of the body, (3) the goal the child has in mind, and (4) environmental supports for the skill. Change in any element makes the system less stable, and the child starts to explore and select new, more effective motor patterns.

The factors that induce change vary with age. In the early weeks of life, brain and body growth are especially important as infants achieve control over the head, shoulders, and upper torso. Later, the baby's goals (getting a toy or crossing the room) and environmental supports (parental encouragement, objects in the infants' everyday setting) play a greater role. Characteristics of the broader physical world also profoundly influence motor skills. For example, had Caitlin, Grace, and Timmy been reared in the moon's reduced gravity, they would have preferred jumping to walking or running!

When a skill is first acquired, infants must refine it. For example, in trying to crawl, Caitlin often collapsed on her tummy and moved backward. Soon she figured out how to propel herself forward by alternately pulling with her arms and pushing with her feet. As she experimented, she perfected the crawling motion (Adolph, Vereijkin, & Denny, 1998). In mastering walking, toddlers practice six or more hours a day, traveling the length of twenty-nine football fields! Gradually their small, unsteady steps change to a longer stride, their feet move closer together, their toes point to the front, and their legs become symmetrically coordinated (Adolph, Vereijken, & Shrout, 2003). As movements are repeated thousands of times, they promote new synaptic connections in the brain that govern motor patterns.

Look carefully at dynamic systems theory, and you will see why motor development cannot be genetically determined. Because exploration and the desire to master new tasks motivate it, heredity can map it out only at a general level. Instead of behaviors being *hardwired* into the nervous system, they are *softly assembled,* and different paths to the same motor skill exist (Hopkins & Butterworth, 1997; Thelen & Smith, 1998).

Dynamic Motor Systems in Action

To study infants' motor mastery, researchers have conducted *microgenetic studies* (see Chapter 1, page 46), following babies from their first attempts at a skill until it becomes smooth and effortless. Using this strategy, James Galloway and Esther Thelen (2004) held sounding toys alternately in front of infants' hands and feet, from the time they first showed interest until they engaged in well-coordinated reaching and grasping. In a violation of the cephalocaudal trend, infants first contacted the toys with their feet—as early as 8 weeks of age! These were not accidental contacts. The babies explored deliberately, spending longer times with their feet in contact with the toys than they spent moving their feet in the area where the toys had been offered (see Figure 5.12).

Infants' foot reaching preceded their hand reaching by at least a month. Why did they reach "feet first?" Because the hip joint constrains the legs to move less freely than the shoulder joint constrains the arms, infants could more easily control their leg movements. When they first tried reaching with their hands, their arms actually moved away from the object! Consequently, hand reaching required far more practice than foot reaching. As these findings confirm, rather than following a strict, predetermined cephalocaudal pattern, the order of motor skills depends on the anatomy of body part being used, the surrounding environment, and the baby's efforts.

Cultural Variations in Motor Development

Cross-cultural research further illustrates how early movement opportunities and a stimulating environment contribute to motor development. Several decades ago, Wayne Dennis (1960) observed infants in Iranian orphanages who were deprived of the tantalizing surroundings that induce infants to acquire motor skills. The Iranian babies spent almost all their time lying on their backs in cribs, without toys to play with—conditions far worse than Grace experienced lying in a hammock in her Cambodian home. As a result, most did not move on their own until after 2 years of age. When they finally did move, the constant experience of lying on their backs led them to scoot in a sitting position rather than crawl on their hands and knees. Because babies who scoot come up against objects such as furniture with their feet, not their hands, they are far less likely to pull themselves to a standing position in preparation for walking. Indeed, only 15 percent of the Iranian orphans walked alone by 3 to 4 years of age.

Cultural variations in infant-rearing practices also affect motor development. Take a quick survey of several parents you know, asking this question: Should sitting, crawling, and walking be deliberately encouraged? Answers vary widely from culture to culture. Japanese mothers, for example, believe such efforts are unnecessary. Among the Zinacanteco Indians of southern Mexico, rapid motor progress is actively discouraged. Babies who walk before they know enough to keep away from cooking fires and weaving looms are viewed as dangerous to themselves and disruptive to others (Greenfield, 1992).

In contrast, among the Kipsigis of Kenya and the West Indians of Jamaica, babies hold their heads up, sit alone, and walk considerably earlier than North American infants. Kipsigi parents deliberately teach these motor skills. In the first few months, babies are seated in holes dug in the ground, and rolled blankets are used to keep them upright. Walking is promoted by frequently bouncing babies on their feet (Super, 1981). As Figure 5.13 on page 190 shows, West Indian mothers use a highly stimulating, formal handling routine, explaining that exercise helps infants grow strong, healthy, and physically attractive (Hopkins & Westra, 1988).

Fine Motor Development: Reaching and Grasping

Of all motor skills, reaching may play the greatest role in infant cognitive development because it opens up a whole new way of exploring the environment. By grasping things, turning them, and releasing them, infants learn a great deal about the sights, sounds, and feel of objects.

The development of reaching and grasping, illustrated in Figure 5.14 on page 190, provides an excellent example of how motor skills start out as gross, diffuse activity and move toward mastery of fine movements. Newborns make poorly coordinated swipes or swings, called **prereaching,** toward an object dangled in front of them. Because they cannot control their arms and hands, they rarely contact the object. Like the reflexes discussed in Chapter 4, prereaching drops out—around 7 weeks of age. Yet these early behaviors suggest that babies are biologically prepared to coordinate hand with eye in the act of reaching (Thelen, 2001).

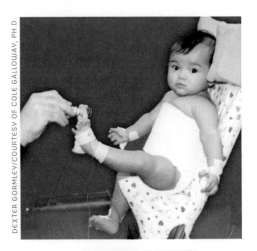

DEXTER GORMLEY/COURTESY OF COLE GALLOWAY, PH.D.

FIGURE 5.12

Reaching "feet first."
When sounding toys were held in front of babies' hands and feet, they reached with their feet as early as 8 weeks of age, a month or more before they reached with their hands—a clear violation of the cephalocaudal pattern. Reduced freedom of movement in the hip joint makes leg movements easier to control than arm movements. This 2½-month-old skillfully explores an object with her foot.

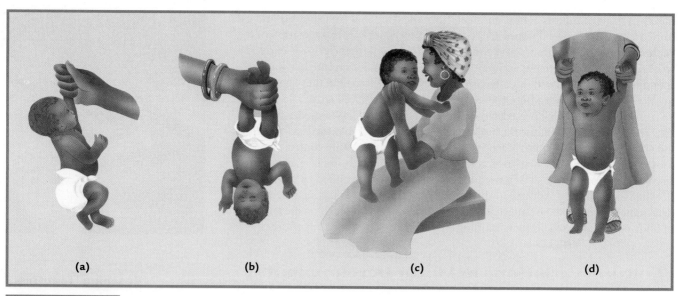

West Indians of Jamaica use a formal handling routine with their babies.

Exercises practiced in the first few months include (a) stretching each arm while suspending the baby and (b) holding the infant upside-down by the ankles. Later in the first year, the baby is (c) "walked" up the mother's body and (d) encouraged to take steps on the floor while supported. (Adapted from B. Hopkins & T. Westra, 1988, "Maternal Handling and Motor Development: An Intra-cultural Study," *Genetic, Social and General Psychology Monographs, 14,* pp. 385, 388, 389. Reprinted by permission of the Helen Dwight Reid Educational Foundation. Published by Heldref Publications, 1319 Eighteenth St., N.W., Washington, DC 20036-1802.)

FIGURE 5.14

Some milestones of voluntary reaching.

The average age at which each skill is attained is given. (Ages from Bayley, 1969; Rochat, 1989.)

DEVELOPMENT OF REACHING AND GRASPING • At about 3 months, as infants develop the necessary eye-gaze and head and shoulder control, voluntary reaching appears and gradu-ally improves in accuracy (Bertenthal & von Hofsten, 1998; Spencer et al., 2000). By 5 to 6 months, infants can reach for and grasp an object in a room that has been darkened during the reach by switching off the lights—a skill that improves over the next few months (Clifton et al., 1994; McCarty & Ashmead, 1999). This indicates that reaching does not require that the baby use vision to guide the arms and hands. Instead, reaching is largely controlled by *proprioception,* our sense of movement and location in space, arising from stimuli within the body. Early on, vi-sion is freed from the basic act of reaching so it can focus on more complex adjustments, such as fine-tuning actions to fit the distance and shape of objects.

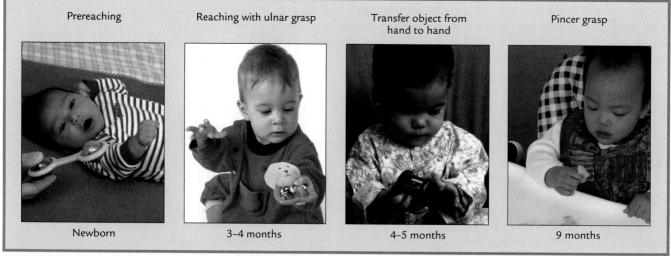

Prereaching	Reaching with ulnar grasp	Transfer object from hand to hand	Pincer grasp
Newborn	3–4 months	4–5 months	9 months

Reaching improves as depth perception advances and as infants gain greater control of body posture and arm and hand movements. Around 5 months, babies reduce their efforts when an object is moved beyond their reach (Robin, Berthier, & Clifton, 1996). By 7 months, their arms become more independent: They reach for an object by extending one arm rather than both (Fagard & Pezé, 1997). During the next few months, infants become better at reaching for moving objects—ones that spin, change direction, or move closer or farther away (Wentworth, Benson, & Haith, 2000).

Individual differences in movement styles also affect how reaching is perfected (Thelen, Corbetta, & Spencer, 1996). For example, 4-month-old Timmy's arm motions were large and forceful; he had to make them less vigorous to reach for a toy accurately. In contrast, Caitlin's gentle actions became more energetic as she moved toward smoothly executed reaching (Thelen et al., 1993). Each infant builds the act of reaching uniquely by exploring the match between current movements and those demanded by the task.

Improved control of body posture and arm and hand movements enable this 7-month-old to reach more effectively. She leans toward an attractive toy and reaches with one arm.

Once infants can reach, they modify their grasp. The newborn's grasp reflex is replaced by the **ulnar grasp,** a clumsy motion in which the young infant's fingers close against the palm. Still, even 3-month-olds readily adjust their grasp to the size and shape of an object—a capacity that improves over the first year (Newman, Atkinson, & Braddick, 2001). Around 4 to 5 months, when infants begin to sit up, both hands become coordinated in exploring objects. Babies of this age can hold an object in one hand while the other scans it with the tips of the fingers, and they frequently transfer objects from hand to hand (Rochat & Goubet, 1995). By the end of the first year, infants use the thumb and index finger in a well-coordinated **pincer grasp.** Then the ability to manipulate objects greatly expands. The 1-year-old can pick up raisins and blades of grass, turn knobs, and open and close small boxes.

Between 8 and 11 months, reaching and grasping are well practiced. As a result, attention is released from the motor skill to events that occur before and after obtaining the object. For example, 10-month-olds easily adjust their reach to anticipate their next action. They reach for a ball faster when they intend to throw it than when they intend to drop it carefully through a narrow tube (Claxton, Keen, & McCarty, 2003). Around this time, too, infants begin to solve simple problems that involve reaching, such as searching for and finding a hidden toy.

EARLY EXPERIENCE AND VOLUNTARY REACHING ● Like other motor milestones, early experience affects voluntary reaching. In a well-known study, institutionalized infants given a moderate amount of visual stimulation—at first, simple designs and, later, a mobile hung over their crib—reached for objects 6 weeks earlier than infants given nothing to look at. A third group given massive stimulation—patterned crib bumpers and mobiles at an early age—also reached sooner than unstimulated babies. But this heavy enrichment took its toll. These infants looked away and cried a great deal, and they were not as advanced in reaching as the moderately stimulated group (White & Held, 1966). Recall from our discussion of brain development that more stimulation is not necessarily better. Trying to push infants beyond their readiness to handle stimulation can undermine the development of important motor skills.

Finally, as motor skills permit infants and toddlers to move about and manipulate objects, caregivers must devote more energy to protecting them from harm. See Applying What We Know on page 192 for a variety of suggestions for keeping infants and toddlers safe. In Chapter 8, we will consider the topic of unintentional injuries in greater detail.

● Bowel and Bladder Control

More than any other aspect of early muscular development, parents wonder about bowel and bladder control. Two or three generations ago, many mothers tried to toilet train infants. However, they only caught the baby's reflexive release of urine or a bowel movement at a convenient moment.

Applying
WHAT WE Know / Keeping Infants and Toddlers Safe

STRATEGY	DESCRIPTION
Provide safe toys.	Match all toys to the child's age and abilities (see Applying What We Know, Chapter 6, page 219). Inspect all toys for small parts that can be swallowed, sharp edges that can cut, and materials that can shatter.
	Avoid cord-activated toys and toys intended to be attached to a crib or playpen; the infant's neck can become entangled in the cord or clothing can catch on a part of the toy, resulting in strangulation.
	Remove crib mobiles and crib gyms when the baby begins to push up on hands and knees; although researchers often use such toys to investigate infant capacities, the risk of becoming entangled is high.
	Do not let young children play with balloons, which can be inhaled if the child tries to blow them up.
Child-proof all rooms.	Keep toilet lids closed and buckets of water used for cleaning away from infants and toddlers; a curious toddler who tries to play in the water can fall in and drown.
	Keep all medicines, cosmetics, cleaners, paints, glues, and other toxic substances out of reach, preferably in locked cabinets; make sure that medicine bottles have child-resistant safety caps.
	Put safety plugs in all unused electrical outlets.
	Unplug all appliances or remove dials when not in use so the child cannot turn them on. Keep cords for window blinds and curtains out of reach.
	Remove unstable furniture, such as tall floor lamps and freestanding bookshelves.
	When the infant starts to crawl, install safety gates at top and bottom of stairs.
Continuously monitor the infant or toddler in situations that pose any risk of injury.	Never leave a young child alone in the bath or on a changing table, even for a moment. At mealtimes, strap the infant or toddler into a high chair, and do not leave the child unattended.
Use a car seat, following government regulations.	When driving, always strap the infant and young child into a car seat that meets government safety standards. Always have children under age 13 ride in the back seat, and never hold an infant in your arms or permit a child to ride on your lap; in an accident, your body could crush the child as you are thrown forward.
Report any unsafe toys and equipment.	Check with the U.S. Consumer Product Safety Commission, (800) 638-2772, www.cpsc.gov, or the Canadian Consumer Product Safety Programme, (613) 957-4467, www.hc-sc.gc.ca/hecs-sesc/cps, to stay informed about unsafe toys and equipment. If you discover any products that seem unsafe, report them to these agencies. Each keeps a record of complaints and initiates recalls of dangerous products.

© ELIZABETH CREWS

Toilet training is best delayed until the end of the second or the beginning of the third year. Not until then can toddlers consistently identify the signals from a full bladder or rectum and wait until they get to the right place to permit these muscles to open—physiological developments essential for the child to cooperate with training. A toddler who stays dry for several hours at a time, stops playing during urination or a bowel movement, and is bothered by a wet or full diaper shows signs of readiness. Parents who postpone training until age 2 have infants who are fully trained within 4 months. Starting earlier does not produce a more reliably trained preschooler; the process just takes longer (Brazelton, 1997).

Effective training techniques include establishing regular toileting routines (for example, after getting up, after a snack or meal, before going to bed), using gentle

Toddlers are not ready for toilet training until around age 2, when they can control bladder and rectal muscles consistently. The parents of this 2-year-old girl bought a small toilet on which she can sit comfortably, and they make toileting a pleasant experience. She is likely to be fully trained within a few months.

encouragement, and praising children for their efforts (Christophersen & Mortweet, 2003; Stephens, 1999). As we will see in Chapter 7, pressuring too much in this area, as well as in others, can negatively affect the toddler's emotional well-being.

ASK YOURSELF

www

REVIEW Cite evidence that motor development is not genetically determined but rather is a joint product of biological, psychological, and social factors.

APPLY Rosanne hung mobiles and pictures above her newborn baby's crib, hoping that this would stimulate her infant's motor development. Is Rosanne doing the right thing? Why or why not?

CONNECT Provide several examples of how motor development influences infants' and toddlers' social experiences. How do social experiences, in turn, influence motor development?

REFLECT Do you favor early training of infants in motor skills, such as crawling, walking, running, hopping, and stair climbing? Why or why not?

Perceptual Development

In Chapter 4, you learned that the senses of touch, taste, smell, and hearing—but not vision—are remarkably well developed at birth. Now let's turn to a related question: How does perception change over the first year of life?

Our discussion will focus on hearing and vision because almost all research addresses these two aspects of perceptual development. Unfortunately, little research exists on how touch, taste, and smell develop after birth. Also, in Chapter 4 we used the word *sensation* to talk about these capacities. Now we use the word *perception.* The reason is that *sensation* suggests a fairly passive process—what the baby's receptors detect when they are exposed to stimulation. In contrast, *perception* is much more active. When we perceive, we organize and interpret what we see.

As we review the perceptual achievements of infancy, you will probably find it hard to tell where perception leaves off and thinking begins. For this reason, the research we are about to discuss provides an excellent bridge to the topic of Chapter 6—cognitive development during the first 2 years.

Hearing

On Timmy's first birthday, Vanessa bought several tapes of nursery songs, and she turned one on each afternoon at naptime. Soon Timmy let her know his favorite tune. If she put on "Twinkle, Twinkle," he stood up in his crib and whimpered until she replaced it with "Jack and Jill." Timmy's behavior illustrates the greatest change in hearing over the first year of life: Babies start to organize sounds into complex patterns. Between 4 and 7 months, they have a sense of musical phrasing. They prefer Mozart minuets with pauses between phrases to those with awkward breaks (Krumhansl & Jusczyk, 1990). At the end of the first year, infants recognize the same melody when it is played in different keys. And when the tone sequence is changed only slightly, they can tell that the melody is no longer the same (Trehub, 2001).

Over the first year, infants learn much about the organization of sounds in their native language. Recall from Chapter 4 that newborns can distinguish nearly all sounds in human languages, and they prefer listening to their native tongue. As they listen to the talk of people around them, they learn to focus on meaningful sound variations. By 6 months, they start to "screen out" sounds not used in their own language (Polka & Werker, 1994).

Soon infants focus on larger speech units that are critical to figuring out meaning. They recognize familiar words in spoken passages and can detect clauses and phrases in sentences (Jusczyk & Hohne, 1997; Soderstrom et al., 2003). In one study, researchers recorded two versions of a mother telling a story. In the first, she spoke naturally, with pauses occurring between clauses: "Cinderella lived in a great big house [pause], but it was sort of dark [pause] because she had this mean stepmother." In the second version, the mother inserted pauses in unnatural places—in the middle of clauses: "Cinderella lived in a great big house, but it was [pause] sort of dark because she had [pause] this mean stepmother." Like adults, 7-month-olds clearly preferred speech with natural breaks (Hirsh-Pasek et al., 1987).

Around 7 to 9 months, infants extend this rhythmic sensitivity to individual words. They listen much longer to speech with stress patterns common in their own language (Mattys & Jusczyk, 2001). And they divide the speech stream into wordlike segments. Seven-month-olds can distinguish sound patterns that typically begin words from those that do not. For example, English learners often rely on the onset of a strong syllable to indicate a new word, as in "<u>an</u>imal" and "<u>pud</u>ding." By 10 months, infants can detect words that start with weak syllables, such as "sur<u>prise</u>," by listening for sound regularities before and after the words (Jusczyk, 2002; Jusczyk, Houston, & Newsome, 1999).

How do infants make such rapid progress in perceiving the structure of sentences and words—information vital for linking speech units with their meanings? Research reveals that they are remarkable *statistical analyzers* of sound patterns. In detecting words, for example, they distinguish syllables that frequently occur together (indicating that they belong to the same word) from those that seldom occur together (indicating a word boundary) (Saffran, Aslin, & Newport, 1996; Saffran & Thiessen, 2003). Also, they notice patterns in word sequences. In a study using nonsense words, 7-month-olds discriminated the ABA structure of "ga ti ga" and "li na li" from the ABB structure of "wo fe fe" and "ta la la" (Marcus et al., 1999). The infants seemed to detect a simple word-order pattern—a capacity that may help them figure out the basic grammar of their language.

Clearly, babies have a powerful ability to extract regularities from a continuous, complex speech stream. Some researchers believe that they are innately equipped with a general learning mechanism for detecting structure in the environment, which they also apply to visual information (Kirkham, Slemmer, & Johnson, 2002).

Vision

If you had to choose between hearing and vision, which would you select? Most people pick vision, for good reason. More than any other sense, humans depend on vision for active exploration of the environment. Although at first the baby's visual world is fragmented, it undergoes extraordinary changes during the first 7 to 8 months of life.

Visual development is supported by rapid maturation of the eye and visual centers in the cerebral cortex. Recall from Chapter 4 that the newborn baby focuses and perceives color poorly. Around 2 months, infants can focus on objects and discriminate colors about as well as adults can (Teller, 1998). Visual acuity (fineness of discrimination) increases steadily throughout the first year, reaching a near-adult level of about 20/20 by 6 months (Slater, 2001). Also, babies' ability to scan and track moving objects improves over the first half-year as eye movements come under voluntary control (von Hofsten & Rosander, 1998; Johnson, 1995).

As infants see more clearly and explore their visual field more adeptly, they figure out the characteristics of objects and how they are arranged in space. We can best understand how they do so by examining the development of three aspects of vision: depth, pattern, and object perception.

DEPTH PERCEPTION ● *Depth perception* is the ability to judge the distance of objects from one another and from ourselves. It is important for understanding the layout of the environment and for guiding motor activity. To reach for objects, babies must have some sense of depth. Later, when infants crawl, depth perception helps prevent them from bumping into furniture and falling down stairs.

Figure 5.15 shows the well-known *visual cliff*, designed by Eleanor Gibson and Richard Walk (1960) and used in the earliest studies of depth perception. It consists of a Plexiglas-covered table with a platform at the center, a "shallow" side with a checkerboard pattern just under the glass, and a "deep" side with a checkerboard several feet below the glass. The researchers found that crawling babies readily crossed the shallow side, but most reacted with fear to the deep side. They concluded that around the time that infants crawl, most distinguish deep from shallow surfaces and avoid drop-offs.

Gibson and Walk's research shows that crawling and avoidance of drop-offs are linked, but it does not tell us how they are related or when depth perception first appears. To better understand the development of depth perception, recent research has looked at babies' ability to detect specific depth cues, using methods that do not require that they crawl.

Emergence of Depth Perception. How do we know when an object is near rather than far away? Try these exercises to find out. Pick up a small object (such as your cup) and move it toward and away from your face. Did its image grow larger as it approached and smaller as it receded? When you next take a bike or car ride, notice that nearby objects move past your field of vision more quickly than those far away.

Motion provides a great deal of information about depth, and it is the first depth cue to which infants are sensitive. Babies 3 to 4 weeks of age blink their eyes defensively when an object moves toward their face as though it is going to hit (Nánez & Yonas, 1994). As they are carried about and people and things turn and move before their eyes, infants learn more about depth. For example, by the time they are 3 months old, motion has helped them figure out that objects are not flat but three-dimensional (Arterberry, Craton, & Yonas, 1993).

Binocular depth cues arise because our two eyes have slightly different views of the visual field. The brain blends these two images but also registers the difference between them. Research in which infants wear special goggles, like those for 3-D movies, reveals that sensitivity to binocular cues emerges between 2 and 3 months and improves rapidly over the first half-year (Birch, 1993). Infants soon make use of binocular cues in their reaching, adjusting arm and hand movements to match the distance of objects from the eyes.

Finally, around 6 to 7 months, infants develop sensitivity to *pictorial depth cues*—the same ones artists use to make a painting look three-dimensional. Examples are lines that create the illusion of perspective, changes in texture (nearby textures are more detailed than faraway ones), and overlapping objects (an object partially hidden by another object is perceived to be more distant) (Sen, Yonas, & Knill, 2001; Yonas, Elieff, & Arterberry, 2002).

Why does perception of depth cues emerge in the order just described? Researchers speculate that motor development is involved. For example, control of the head during the early weeks of life may help babies notice motion and binocular cues. And around 5 to 6 months, the ability to turn, poke, and feel the surface of objects may promote perception of pictorial cues (Bushnell & Boudreau, 1993). Indeed, as we will see next, one aspect of motor progress—independent movement—plays a vital role in the refinement of depth perception.

Crawling and Depth Perception. Just before he reached the 6-month mark, Timmy started crawling. "He's like a fearless daredevil," exclaimed Vanessa. "If I put him down in the middle of the bed, he crawls right over the edge. Several times I stopped him just before he went overboard. And the same thing has happened by the stairs." Will Timmy become more wary of the side of the bed and the staircase as he becomes a more experienced crawler? Research suggests that he will. Infants with more crawling experience (regardless of when they started to crawl) were far more likely to refuse to cross the deep side of the visual cliff (Bertenthal, Campos, & Barrett, 1984).

© MARK RICHARDS/PHOTOEDIT

FIGURE 5.15

The visual cliff.

Plexiglas covers the deep and shallow sides. By refusing to cross the deep side and showing a preference for the shallow side, this infant demonstrates the ability to perceive depth.

Biology and Environment

Development of Infants with Severe Visual Impairments

Research on infants who can see little or nothing at all dramatically illustrates the interdependence of vision, motor exploration, social interaction, and understanding of the world. In a longitudinal study, infants with a visual acuity of 20/800 or worse (they had only dim light perception or were blind) were followed through the preschool years. Compared to agemates with less severe visual impairments, they showed serious delays in all aspects of development. Motor and cognitive functioning suffered the most; with age, performance in both domains became increasingly distant from that of other children (Hatton et al., 1997).

What explains these profound developmental delays? Minimal or absent vision can alter the child's experiences in at least two crucial, interrelated ways.

Impact on Motor Exploration and Spatial Understanding

Infants with severe visual impairments attain gross and fine motor milestones many months later than their sighted counterparts (Levtzion-Korach et al., 2000). For ex-

ample, on average, blind infants do not reach for and manipulate objects until 12 months, crawl until 13 months, or walk until 19 months (compare these averages to the norms given in Table 5.1 on page 187). Why is this so?

Infants with severe visual impairments must rely on sound to identify the whereabouts of objects. But sound does not function as a precise clue to object location until much later than vision—around the middle of the first year (Litovsky & Ashmead, 1997). And because infants who cannot see have difficulty engaging their caregivers, adults may not provide them with rich, early exposure to sounding objects. As a result, the baby comes to understand relatively late that there is a world of tantalizing objects to explore.

Until "reaching on sound" is achieved, infants with severe visual impairments are not motivated to move independently. Because of their own uncertainty and their parents' protection and restraint to prevent injury, blind infants are typically tentative in their movements. These factors delay motor development further.

Motor and cognitive development are closely linked, especially for infants with little or no vision. These babies build an understanding of the location and arrangement of objects in space only after reaching and crawling (Bigelow, 1992). Inability to imitate the motor actions of others presents additional challenges as these children get older, contributing to declines in motor and cognitive progress relative to peers with better vision (Hatton et al., 1997).

Impact on the Caregiver–Infant Relationship

Infants who see poorly have great difficulty evoking stimulating caregiver interaction. They cannot make eye contact, imitate, or pick up nonverbal social cues. Their emotional expressions are muted; for example, their smile is fleeting and unpredictable. Consequently, these infants may receive little adult attention, play, and other stimulation vital for all aspects of development (Tröster & Brambring, 1992).

When a visually impaired child does not learn how to participate in social

What do infants learn from crawling that promotes this sensitivity to depth information? Research suggests that from extensive everyday experience, babies gradually figure out how to use depth cues to detect the danger of falling. But because the loss of body control that leads to falling differs greatly for each body position, babies must undergo this learning separately for each posture. In one study, 9-month-olds, who were experienced sitters but novice crawlers, were placed on the edge of a shallow drop-off that could be widened (Adolph, 2000). While in the familiar sitting position, infants avoided leaning out for an attractive toy at distances likely to result in falling. But in the unfamiliar crawling position, they headed over the edge, even when the distance was extremely wide! As infants discover how to avoid falling in different postures and situations, their understanding of depth expands.

Crawling experience promotes other aspects of three-dimensional understanding. For example, seasoned crawlers are better than their inexperienced agemates at remembering

© BOB DAEMMRICH/STOCK BOSTON, LLC.

Crawling promotes three-dimensional understanding, such as wariness of drop-offs and memory for object locations. As this baby moves about, he takes note of how to get from place to place, where objects are in relation to himself and to other objects, and what they look like from different points of view.

interaction during infancy, communication is compromised in early childhood. In an observational study of blind children enrolled in preschools with sighted agemates, the blind children seldom initiated contact with peers and teachers. When they did interact, they had trouble interpreting the meaning of others' reactions and responding appropriately (Preisler, 1991, 1993).

Interventions

Parents, teachers, and caregivers can help infants with minimal vision overcome early developmental delays through stimulating, responsive interaction. Until a close emotional bond with an adult is forged, babies with visual impairments cannot establish vital links with their environments.

Techniques that help infants become aware of their physical and social surroundings include heightened sensory input through combining sound and touch (holding, touching, or bringing the baby's hands to the adult's face while talking or singing), engaging in many repetitions,

As a result of complications from prematurity, this 2-year-old experienced nearly complete detachment of her retinas and has only minimal light perception. By guiding the child's exploration of a harpsichord through touch and sound, a caregiver helps prevent the developmental delays often associated with severely impaired vision.

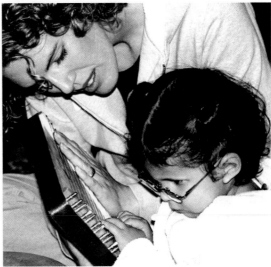
COURTESY OF RICH KENNEY, FOUNDATION FOR BLIND CHILDREN

and consistently reinforcing the infant's efforts to make contact. Manipulative play with objects that make sounds is also vital. Finally, rich language stimulation can compensate for visual loss (Conti-Ramsden & Pérez-Pereira, 1999). It grants young children a ready means of finding out about objects, events, and behaviors they cannot see. Once language emerges, many children with limited or no vision show impressive rebounds. Some acquire a unique capacity for abstract thinking, and most master social and practical skills that enable them to lead productive, independent lives (Warren, 1994).

object locations and finding hidden objects (Bai & Bertenthal, 1992; Campos et al., 2000). Why does crawling make such a difference? Compare your own experience of the environment when you are driven from one place to another with what you experience when you walk or drive yourself. When you move on your own, you are much more aware of landmarks and routes of travel, and you take more careful note of what things look like from different points of view. The same is true for infants. In fact, crawling promotes a new level of brain organization, as indicated by more organized EEG brain-wave activity in the cerebral cortex. Perhaps crawling strengthens certain neural connections, especially those involved in vision and understanding of space (Bell & Fox, 1996). As the Biology and Environment box above reveals, the link between independent movement and spatial knowledge is also evident in a population with very different perceptual experience: infants with severe visual impairments.

PATTERN PERCEPTION ● Even newborns prefer to look at patterned as opposed to plain stimuli—for example, a drawing of the human face or one with scrambled facial features rather than a black-and-white oval (Fantz, 1961). As infants get older, they prefer more complex patterns. For example, 3-week-olds look longest at black-and-white checkerboards with a few large squares, whereas 8- and 14-week-olds prefer those with many squares (Brennan, Ames, & Moore, 1966).

A general principle, called **contrast sensitivity,** explains early pattern preferences (Banks & Ginsburg, 1985). *Contrast* refers to the difference in the amount of light between adjacent regions in a pattern. If babies are *sensitive to* (can detect) the contrast in two or more patterns, they prefer the one with more contrast. To understand this idea, look at the checkerboards in the top

Two checkerboards differing in complexity

Appearance of checkerboards to very young infants

FIGURE 5.16

The way two checkerboards differing in complexity look to infants in the first few weeks of life.
Because of their poor vision, very young infants cannot resolve the fine detail in the complex checkerboard. It appears blurred, like a gray field. The large, bold checkerboard appears to have more contrast, so babies prefer to look at it. (Adapted from M. S. Banks & P. Salapatek, 1983, "Infant Visual Perception," in M. M. Haith & J. J. Campos [Eds.], *Handbook of Child Psychology: Vol. 2. Infancy and Developmental Psychobiology* [4th ed.], New York: Wiley, p. 504. Copyright © 1983 by John Wiley & Sons. Reprinted by permission.)

row of Figure 5.16. To us, the one with many small squares has more contrasting elements. Now look at the bottom row, which shows how these checkerboards appear to infants in the first few weeks of life. Because of their poor vision, very young babies cannot resolve the small features in more complex patterns, so they prefer to look at the large, bold checkerboard. Around 2 months of age, when detection of fine-grained detail has improved considerably, infants become sensitive to the greater contrast in complex patterns and spend more time looking at them (Gwiazda & Birch, 2001; Teller, 1997).

Combining Pattern Elements. In the early weeks of life, infants respond to the separate parts of a pattern. For example, when shown drawings of human faces, 1-month-olds limit their visual exploration to the border of the stimulus and stare at single high-contrast features, such as the hairline or chin. At about 2 months, when scanning ability and contrast sensitivity have improved, infants thoroughly explore a pattern's internal features, pausing briefly to look at each salient part (Bronson, 1991).

Once babies can detect all parts of a pattern, they integrate them into a unified whole. By 4 months, babies are so good at detecting pattern organization that they even perceive subjective boundaries that are not really present. For example, they perceive a square in the center of Figure 5.17a, just as you do (Ghim, 1990). Older infants carry this responsiveness to subjective form even further. For example, 9-month-olds show a special preference for an organized series of moving lights that resembles a human being walking, in that they look much longer at this display than at upside-down or scrambled versions (Bertenthal, 1993). By 12 months, infants detect objects represented by incomplete drawings, even when as much as two-thirds of the drawing is missing (see Figure 5.17b) (Rose, Jankowski, & Senior, 1997). By the end of the first year, a suggestive image is all that babies need to recognize a familiar form. As these finding reveal, infants' increasing knowledge of objects and actions supports pattern perception.

Perception of the Human Face. Infants' tendency to search for structure in a patterned stimulus applies to face perception. Newborns prefer to look at simple, facelike stimuli with features arranged naturally (upright) rather than unnaturally (upside down or sideways) (see Figure 5.18a) (Mondloch et al., 1999). They also track a facelike pattern moving across their visual field farther than they track other stimuli (Johnson, 1999). And although their ability to distinguish real faces on the basis of inner features is limited, shortly after birth babies prefer photos of faces with eyes open and a direct gaze. Yet another amazing capacity is their tendency to look longer at faces judged by adults as attractive, compared with less attractive ones—a preference that may be the origin of the widespread social bias favoring physically attractive people (Slater et al., 2000).

Some researchers believe that these behaviors reflect a built-in capacity to orient toward members of one's own species, just as many newborn animals do (Johnson, 2001a; Slater & Quinn, 2001). Others refute the claim that newborns have a special sensitivity to the facial pattern. Instead, they assert, newborns prefer any stimulus in which the most salient elements are arranged

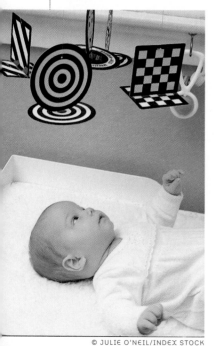

This 3-month-old looks at stimuli that match his level of visual development. His visual acuity has improved greatly since birth, so he can detect the contrast in complex patterns and spends more time looking at them.

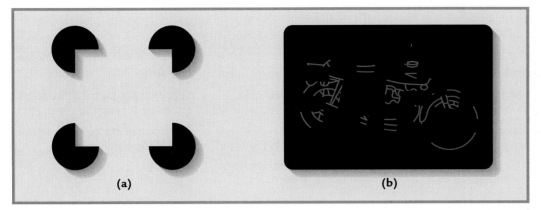

(a)   (b)

FIGURE 5.17

Subjective boundaries in visual patterns.

(a) Do you perceive a square in the middle of the figure on the left? By 4 months of age, infants do, too. (b) What does the image on the right, missing two-thirds of its outline, look like to you? By 12 months, infants detect the image of a motorcycle. After habituating to the incomplete motorcycle image, they were shown an intact motorcycle figure paired with a novel form. Twelve-month-olds recovered to (looked longer at) the novel figure, indicating that they recognized the motorcycle pattern on the basis of very little visual information. (Adapted from Ghim, 1990; Rose, Jankowski, & Senior, 1997.)

horizontally in the upper part of a pattern—like the "eyes" in Figure 5.18a. Indeed, newborns do prefer nonfacial patterns with these characteristics over other nonfacial arrangements (Simion et al., 2001). But possibly, a bias favoring the facial pattern promotes such preferences. Still other researchers argue that newborns are exposed to faces more often than to other stimuli—early experiences that could quickly "wire" the brain to detect faces and prefer attractive ones (Nelson, 2001).

Although newborns respond to a simple facelike structure, they cannot discriminate a complex facial pattern from other, equally complex configurations (see Figure 5.18b). At 2 to 3 months, when infants explore an entire stimulus and can combine its elements into an organized whole, they do prefer a drawing of the human face to other stimulus arrangements (Dannemiller & Stephens, 1988). The baby quickly applies this tendency to search for pattern to face perception. By 2 months, infants recognize and prefer their mother's facial features to those of an unfamiliar woman (Bartrip, Morton, & deSchonen, 2001).

Around 3 months of age, infants make fine distinctions among the features of different faces. For example, they can tell the difference between the photos of two strangers, even when the faces are moderately similar. And between 7 and 10 months, infants start to perceive emotional expressions as meaningful wholes. They treat positive faces (happy and surprised) as different from negative ones (sad and fearful), even when these expressions are demonstrated in slightly varying ways by different people (Ludemann, 1991). As infants recognize and respond to the expressive behavior of others, face perception supports their earliest social relationships.

The development of depth and pattern perception is summarized in Table 5.2 on page 200. Note that several important changes take place around 2 months of age. Recall that 2 months also is a time when the frontal lobes of the cerebral cortex function more effectively. Brain development fosters babies' improved visual capacities, and babies' visual processing, in turn, promotes brain development.

FIGURE 5.18

Early face perception.

(a) Newborns prefer to look at the simple pattern resembling a face on the left over the upside-down version on the right. This preference for a facelike stimulus disappears by age 6 weeks. Some researchers believe it is innate, orients newborns toward people, and is replaced by more complex perceptual learning as the cerebral cortex develops and visual capacities improve. (b) When the complex drawing of a face on the left and the equally complex, scrambled version on the right are moved across newborns' visual field, they follow the face longer—another finding that suggests a built-in capacity to orient toward people. But if the two stimuli are presented side by side, infants show no preference for the face until 2 to 3 months of age. (From Johnson, 1999; Mondloch et al., 1999.)

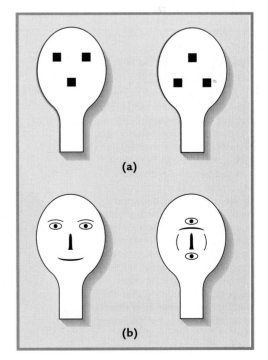

(a)

(b)

TABLE 5.2

Development of Visual Perception

	BIRTH–1 MONTH	2–4 MONTHS	5–12 MONTHS
Depth perception	Sensitivity to motion cues	Sensitivity to binocular cues	Sensitivity to pictorial cues; wariness of heights
Pattern perception	Preference for patterns with large elements Visual exploration limited to border of a stimulus and single features	Visual exploration of entire stimulus, including internal features Pattern elements combined into an organized whole	Detection of increasingly complex, meaningful patterns
Face perception	Preference for a simple, facelike pattern	Preference for a complex facial pattern over other, equally complex patterns and for mother's facial features over those of an unfamiliar woman	More fine-grained discrimination of faces, including ability to perceive emotional expressions as organized wholes

Object Perception

Research on pattern perception involves only two-dimensional stimuli, but our environment is made up of stable, three-dimensional objects. Do young infants perceive a world of independently existing objects—knowledge essential for distinguishing among the self, other people, and things?

SIZE AND SHAPE CONSTANCY • As we move around the environment, the images that objects cast on our retina constantly change in size and shape. To perceive objects as stable and unchanging, we must translate these varying retinal images into a single representation.

Size constancy—perception of an object's size as the same, despite changes in the size of its retinal image—is evident in the first week of life. To test for it, researchers capitalized on the habituation response, using the procedure described and illustrated in Figure 5.19. Perception of an object's shape as stable, despite changes in the shape projected on the retina, is called shape constancy. Habituation research reveals that it, too, is present within the first week of life, long

FIGURE 5.19

Testing newborns for size constancy.

(a) First, infants were habituated to a small black-and-white cube at varying distances from the eye. In this way, researchers hoped to desensitize them to changes in the cube's retinal image size and direct their attention to its actual size.
(b) Next, the small cube and a new, large cube were presented together, but at different distances so they cast retinal images of the same size. All babies recovered responsiveness to (looked longer at) the novel large cube, indicating that they distinguish objects on the basis of actual size, not retinal image size. (Adapted from Slater, 2001.)

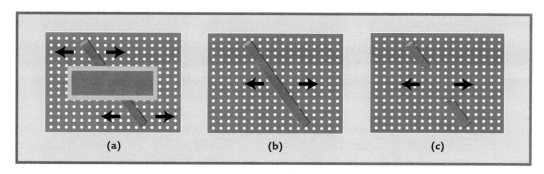

FIGURE 5.20

Display used to test infants' ability to perceive object unity.
(a) Infants are habituated to a rod moving back and forth be-hind a box against a textured background. Next, they are shown (b) a complete rod or (c) a broken rod with a gap corresponding to the location of the box. Each of these stimuli is moved back and forth against the textured background, in the same way as the habituation stimulus. Infants 2 months of age and older typically recover responsiveness to (look longer at) the broken rod than the complete rod. This suggests that they perceive the rod behind the box in the first display as a single unit. (Adapted from Johnson, 1997.)

before babies can actively rotate objects with their hands and view them from different angles (Slater & Johnson, 1999).

In sum, both size and shape constancy seem to be innate capacities that assist babies in detecting a coherent world of objects. Yet they provide only a partial picture of young infants' object perception.

PERCEPTION OF OBJECT UNITY ● When Vanessa dangled a colorful rattle in front of 4-month-old Timmy, he grabbed it. But when she placed the rattle on a book, Timmy no longer reached for it. Instead, he reached for the larger, supporting object. Timmy's behavior suggests that he did not perceive the boundary between two objects. Rather, he treated objects close together as a single unit.

Research reveals that at first, babies rely heavily on motion and spatial arrangement to identify objects (Jusczyk et al., 1999; Spelke & Hermer, 1996). When two objects are touching and either move in unison or stand still, babies younger than 4 months of age cannot distinguish between them. Infants, of course, are fascinated by moving objects; they almost always prefer a moving stimulus to an identical stationary one. As they track a moving object, they pick up additional information about its boundaries, such as shape, color, texture. For example, as Figure 5.20 reveals, after 2 months of age, babies realize that a moving rod whose center is hidden behind a box is a complete rod rather than two rod pieces. Motion, a textured background, alignment of the top and bottom of the rod, and a small box (so most of the rod is visible) are necessary for 2- to 4-month-olds to infer object unity. They cannot do so without all these cues to heighten the distinction between the objects in the display (Johnson & Aslin, 1996; Johnson et al., 2002).

As infants become familiar with many types of objects, they rely more on shape, color, and texture and less on motion (Cohen & Cashon, 2001). Babies as young as 4½ months can distinguish between two touching objects on the basis of their features in very simple, easy-to-process situations (Needham, 2001). In the second half of the first year, this capacity extends to more complex displays of objects.

Intermodal Perception

When we take in information from the environment, we often use **intermodal perception.** That is, we combine stimulation from more than one *modality,* or sensory system. For example, we know that the shape of an object is the same whether we see it or touch it, that lip movements are closely coordinated with the sound of a voice, and that dropping a rigid object on a hard surface will cause a sharp, banging sound.

From the start, babies perceive the world in an intermodal fashion (Meltzoff, 1990). Recall that newborns turn in the general direction of a sound, and they reach for objects in a primitive way. These behaviors suggest that infants expect sight, sound, and touch to go together. Experiencing the integration of sensory modalities in these ways prepares young babies for detecting the wealth of intermodal associations that pervade their everyday worlds (Slater, 2001).

Within a few months, infants make impressive intermodal matches. Three- and 4-month-olds can relate a child's or an adult's moving lips to the corresponding sounds in speech. And

7-month-olds can link a happy or angry voice with the appropriate face of a speaking person (Bahrick, Netto, & Hernandez-Reif, 1998; Soken & Pick, 1992). Of course, many intermodal associations, such as the way a train sounds or a teddy bear feels, must be based on direct exposure. Yet even newborns acquire these relationships remarkably quickly, often after just one contact with a new situation (Morrongiello, Fenwick, & Chance, 1998). In addition, when researchers try to teach intermodal matches by pairing sights and sounds that do not naturally go together, babies will not learn them (Bahrick, 1992).

How does intermodal perception begin so early and develop so quickly? Young infants seem biologically primed to focus on intermodal information. They better detect changes in stimulation that occur simultaneously in two modalities (sight and sound) than those that occur in only one (Lewkowicz, 1996). Furthermore, detection of *amodal relations*—for example, the common tempo and rhythm in the sight and sound of clapping hands—develops first and may provide a basis for detecting other intermodal matches (Bahrick, 2001). Finally, early parent–infant interaction presents the baby with a rich context—consisting of many concurrent sights, sounds, touches, and smells—for expanding intermodal knowledge (Lickliter & Bahrich, 2000). Intermodal perception is yet another capacity that illustrates infants' active efforts to build an orderly, predictable world.

Understanding Perceptual Development

Now that we have reviewed the development of infant perceptual capacities, how can we put together this diverse array of amazing achievements? Eleanor and James Gibson provide widely accepted answers. According to the Gibsons' **differentiation theory,** infants actively search for **invariant features** of the environment—those that remain stable—in a constantly changing perceptual world. For example, in pattern perception, at first babies are confronted with a confusing mass of stimulation. But very quickly, they search for features that stand out along the border of a stimulus and orient toward images that crudely represent a face. Soon they explore internal features, noticing *stable relationship*s between those features. As a result, they detect patterns, such as squares and complex faces. The development of intermodal perception also reflects this principle. Babies seem to seek out invariant relationships—at first a common tempo and rhythm in concurrent sights and sounds, later more detailed associations—that unite information across modalities.

The Gibsons use the word *differentiation* (which means analyze or break down) to describe their theory, because over time, the baby detects finer and finer invariant features among stimuli. In addition to pattern perception, differentiation applies to depth perception: Recall how sensitivity to motion and binocular cues precedes detection of fine-grained pictorial features. So one way of understanding perceptual development is to think of it as a built-in tendency to search for order and consistency, a capacity that becomes more fine-tuned with age (Gibson, 1970; Gibson, 1979).

Acting on the environment plays a major role in perceptual differentiation. According to the Gibsons, perception is guided by the discovery of **affordances**—the action possibilities that a situation offers an organism with certain motor capabilities (Gibson, 2000). By moving about and exploring the environment, babies figure out which objects can be grasped, squeezed, bounced, or stroked and whether a surface is safe to cross or presents the possibility of falling. Sensitivity to these affordances makes our actions future oriented and largely successful rather than reactive and blundering. Consequently, we spend far less time correcting ineffective actions than we otherwise would.

To illustrate, let's consider how infants' changing capabilities for independent movement affect their perception. When babies crawl, and again when they walk, they gradually realize that a steeply sloping surface *affords the possibility* of falling (see Figure 5.21). With added weeks of practicing each skill, they hesitate to crawl or walk down a risky incline. Experience in trying to keep their balance on various surfaces seems to make crawlers and walkers more aware of the consequences of their movements. Crawlers come to detect when surface slant places so much body weight on their arms that they will fall forward, and walkers come to sense when an incline shifts body weight so their legs and feet can no longer hold them upright (Adolph & Eppler, 1998, 1999). Each skill leads infants to perceive surfaces in new ways that guide their movements. As a result, they act more competently.

As we conclude this chapter, it is only fair to note that some researchers believe that babies do more than make sense of experience by searching for invariant features and discovering affordances. They also *impose meaning* on what they perceive, constructing categories of objects and events in the surrounding environment. We have seen the glimmerings of this cognitive

COURTESY OF KAREN ADOLPH, EMORY UNIVERSITY

FIGURE 5.21

Acting on the environment plays a major role in perceptual differentiation.

Crawling and walking change the way babies perceive a steeply sloping surface. The newly crawling infant on the left plunges headlong down a steeply sloping surface. He has not yet learned that it affords the possibility of falling. The toddler on the right, who has been walking for more than a month, approaches the slope cautiously. Experience in trying to remain upright but frequently tumbling over has made him more aware of the consequences of his movements. He perceives the incline differently than he did at a younger age.

point of view in this chapter. For example, older babies *interpret* a familiar face as a source of pleasure and affection and a pattern of blinking lights as a moving human being. This cognitive perspective also offers insight into the achievements of infancy. In fact, many researchers combine these two positions, regarding infant development as proceeding from a perceptual to a cognitive emphasis over the first year of life.

Ask YOURSELF

www

REVIEW Using research on crawling, show how motor and perceptual development support one another.

REVIEW How does face perception change over the first year, and what gains in pattern perception support it?

APPLY After several weeks of crawling, Benjie learned to avoid going headfirst down a steep incline. Now he has started to walk. Can his mother trust him not to try walking down a steep surface? Explain, using the concept of affordances.

CONNECT According to differentiation theory, perceptual development reflects infants' active search for invariant features. Provide examples from research on hearing, pattern perception, and intermodal perception.

Summary

Body Growth

Describe major changes in body size, proportions, muscle–fat makeup, and skeletal growth over the first 2 years.

● Height and weight gains are greater during the first 2 years than at any other time after birth. Body fat is laid down quickly during the first 9 months, whereas muscle development is slow and gradual. Growth of parts of the body follows **cephalocaudal** and **proximodistal trends,** resulting in changing body proportions.

● **Skeletal age,** a measure based on the number of **epiphyses** and the extent to which they are fused, is the best way to estimate the child's overall physical maturity. At birth, infants have six **fontanels,** which permit the skull bones to expand as the brain grows. The first tooth emerges around 6 months of age. By age 2, the average child has 20 teeth.

Brain Development

Describe brain development during infancy and toddlerhood, along with

appropriate stimulation to support the brain's potential.

● Early in development the brain grows faster than any other organ of the body. Once **neurons** are in place, they form **synapses,** or connections, at a rapid rate. During the peak period of synaptic growth in any brain area, many surrounding neurons die to make room for synaptic connections. Stimulation determines which neurons will survive and establish new synapses and which will lose their connective fibers through synaptic pruning. **Glial cells,** which are responsible for **myelination,** multiply dramatically through the second year and contribute to large gains in brain weight.

● Regions of the **cerebral cortex** develop in the same order in which various capacities emerge in the infant and child, with the frontal lobes among the last to develop. **Lateralization** refers to specialization of the hemispheres of the cerebral cortex. During the first few years, **brain plasticity** is high. However, some lateralization exists at birth. Both heredity and early experience contribute to brain organization.

● Gains in brain weight and skull size, along with changes in neural activity, indicate that brain growth spurts occur intermittently from infancy through adolescence. These coincide with major cognitive changes and may be sensitive periods in which appropriate stimulation is necessary for full development.

● Both impoverished environments and environments that overwhelm young children with expectations beyond their current capacities can interfere with the brain's potential. **Experience-expectant brain growth** characterizes the early years. It takes place naturally as caregivers offer babies and preschoolers age-appropriate play materials and stimulating, enjoyable daily routines. **Experience-dependent brain growth**—new growth and refinement of established brain structures as a result of specific learning—builds on this foundation and takes place later, continuing throughout our lives.

How does the organization of sleep and wakefulness change over the first 2 years?

● Infants' changing arousal patterns are primarily affected by brain growth, but the social environment also plays a role. Short periods of sleep and wakefulness are put together and better coincide with a night–day schedule. Infants in Western nations sleep through the night much earlier than babies throughout most of the world, who sleep with their parents.

Influences on Early Physical Growth

Cite evidence indicating that heredity, nutrition, and parental affection and stimulation contribute to early physical growth.

● Twin and adoption studies reveal that heredity contributes to body size and rate of physical growth.

● Breast milk is ideally suited to infants' growth needs and offers protection against disease. Breastfeeding prevents malnutrition and infant death in poverty-stricken areas of the world. Although breastfed and bottle-fed babies do not differ in emotional adjustment, some studies report a slight advantage in intelligence test performance for children and adolescents who were breastfed.

● Most infants and toddlers can eat nutritious foods freely, without risk of becoming overweight. However, the relationship between rapid weight gain in infancy and obesity at older ages is strengthening, perhaps because of a rise in unhealthful early feeding practices, in which babies are given high-fat foods and sugary drinks.

● **Marasmus** and **kwashiorkor** are dietary diseases caused by malnutrition that affect many children in developing countries. If these conditions continue, body growth and brain development can be permanently stunted. **Nonorganic failure to thrive** illustrates the importance of parental affection and stimulation for normal physical growth.

Learning Capacities

Describe infant learning capacities, the conditions under which they occur, and the unique value of each.

● **Classical conditioning** permits infants to recognize which events usually occur together in the everyday world. In this form of learning, a neutral stimulus is paired with an **unconditioned stimulus (UCS)** that produces a reflexive, **unconditioned response (UCR).** Once learning has occurred, the neutral stimulus, now called the **conditioned stimulus (CS),** by itself elicits a similar response, called the **conditioned response (CR).** Young infants can be classically conditioned when the pairing of a UCS with a CS has survival value, as in the feeding situation. However, classical conditioning of fear is difficult before 6 months of age.

● **Operant conditioning** helps infants explore and control their surroundings. In addition to food, interesting sights and sounds serve as effective **reinforcers,** increasing the occurrence of a preceding behavior. **Punishment** involves removing a desirable stimulus or presenting an unpleasant one to decrease the occurrence of a response.

● **Habituation** and **recovery** reveal that at birth, babies are attracted to novelty.

Newborn infants also have a primitive ability to imitate the facial expressions and gestures of adults. **Imitation** is a powerful means of learning and contributes to the parent–infant bond.

Motor Development

Describe the general course of motor development during the first 2 years, along with factors that influence it.

● Like physical development, motor development follows the cephalocaudal and proximodistal trends. According to **dynamic systems theory of motor development,** new motor skills develop as existing skills combine into increasingly complex systems of action. Each new skill is a joint product of central nervous system development, movement possibilities of the body, the goal the child has in mind, and environmental supports for the skill.

● Movement opportunities and a stimulating environment profoundly affect motor development, as shown by research on infants raised in institutions where they were deprived of stimulation. Cultural values and child-rearing customs contribute to the emergence and refinement of early motor skills.

● During the first year, infants perfect their reaching and grasping. The poorly coordinated **prereaching** of the newborn period eventually drops out. As control of body posture and of arm and hand movements improves, voluntary reaching becomes more flexible and accurate, and the clumsy **ulnar grasp** is transformed into a refined **pincer grasp.**

● Young children are not physically and psychologically ready for toilet training until the end of the second year or the beginning of the third. Effective training techniques include regular toileting routines and gentle encouragement and praise.

Perceptual Development

What changes in perception of speech sounds, depth, patterns, objects, and intermodal systems take place during infancy?

● Over the first year, infants organize sounds into complex patterns. They also become more sensitive to the sounds of their own language and use their remarkable ability to analyze sound patterns to detect meaningful speech units.

● Rapid development of the eye and visual centers in the brain supports the development of focusing, color discrimination, and visual acuity during the first few months. The ability to scan the environment and track moving objects also improves.

- Research on depth perception reveals that responsiveness to motion develops first, followed by sensitivity to binocular and then to pictorial cues. Experience in crawling enhances depth perception and other aspects of three-dimensional understanding. However, babies must learn to avoid drop-offs for each body position.

- **Contrast sensitivity** accounts for infants' early pattern preferences. At first, babies look at the border of a stimulus and at single features. Around 2 months, they explore internal features of a pattern and start to detect pattern organization.

Over time, they discriminate increasingly complex and meaningful patterns.

- Newborns prefer to look at and track simple, facelike stimuli, which suggests a built-in tendency to orient toward human faces. At 2 to 3 months, with the capacity to combine pattern elements into organized wholes, they can discriminate a complex facial pattern and make fine distinctions between the features of different faces. In the second half-year, they perceive emotional expressions as meaningful wholes.

- At birth, **size** and **shape constancy** assist babies in building a coherent world of objects. At first, infants depend on motion and spatial arrangement to identify objects. After 4 months of age, they rely increasingly on other features, such as distinct shape, color, and texture.

- Infants have a remarkable, built-in capacity to engage in **intermodal perception.** They quickly combine information across sensory modalities, often after just one exposure to a new situation. Detection of amodal relations (such as common tempo and rhythm in sights and sounds) precedes, and may provide a basis for detecting, other intermodal matches.

Explain the Gibsons' differentiation theory of perceptual development.

- According to **differentiation theory,** perceptual development is a matter of detecting **invariant features** in a constantly changing perceptual world. Perceptual differentiation is guided by discovery of **affordances**—the action possibilities a situation offers the individual.

Important Terms and Concepts

affordances (p. 202)
brain plasticity (p. 172)
cephalocaudal trend (p. 167)
cerebral cortex (p. 171)
classical conditioning (p. 182)
conditioned response (CR) (p. 183)
conditioned stimulus (CS) (p. 183)
contrast sensitivity (p. 197)
differentiation theory (p. 202)
dynamic systems theory of motor development (p. 188)
epiphyses (p. 168)
experience-dependent brain growth (p. 175)
experience-expectant brain growth (p. 175)

fontanels (p. 168)
glial cells (p. 170)
habituation (p. 184)
imitation (p. 185)
intermodal perception (p. 201)
invariant features (p. 202)
kwashiorkor (p. 180)
lateralization (p. 171)
marasmus (p. 180)
myelination (p. 170)
neurons (p. 169)
nonorganic failure to thrive (p. 181)
operant conditioning (p. 183)
pincer grasp (p. 191)
prereaching (p. 189)

proximodistal trend (p. 167)
punishment (p. 184)
recovery (p. 184)
reinforcer (p. 184)
shape constancy (p. 200)
size constancy (p. 200)
skeletal age (p. 168)
synapses (p. 169)
synaptic pruning (p. 170)
ulnar grasp (p. 191)
unconditioned response (UCR) (p. 182)
unconditioned stimulus (UCS) (p. 182)

 **For Further Information and Help**

Consult the Companion Website for *Infants, Children, and Adolescents,* Fifth Edition, *(www.ablongman.com/berk),* where you will find the following resources for this chapter:

- **Chapter Objectives**
- **Flashcards** for studying important terms and concepts
- **Annotated Weblinks** to guide you in further research
- **Ask Yourself questions,** which you can answer and then check against a sample response

- **Suggested Readings**
- **Practice Tests** with immediate scoring and feedback

With a glorious wash of earth and sky as a backdrop, a family accompanies a toddler on an expedition of discovery. In Chapter 6, you will see that a stimulating environment combined with the guidance of more mature members of their culture ensures that young children's cognition will develop at its best.

"My Family"
Aldo Pablo Fernandez
5 years, Mexico

Reprinted with permission from the International Museum of Children's Art, Oslo, Norway.

Cognitive Development in Infancy and Toddlerhood

When Caitlin, Grace, and Timmy gathered at Ginette's child-care home, the playroom was alive with activity. The three spirited explorers, each nearly 18 months old, were bent on discovery. Grace dropped shapes through holes in a plastic box that Ginette held and adjusted so the harder ones would fall smoothly into place. Once a few shapes were inside, Grace grabbed and shook the box, squealing with delight as the lid fell open and the shapes scattered around her. The clatter attracted Timmy, who picked up a shape, carried it to the railing at the top of the basement steps, and dropped it overboard, then followed with a teddy bear, a ball, his shoe, and a spoon. In the meantime, Caitlin opened a drawer, unloaded a set of wooden bowls, stacked them in a pile, knocked it over, then banged two bowls together like cymbals. With each action, the children seemed to be asking, "How do things work? What makes interesting events happen? Which ones can I control?"

As the toddlers experimented, I could see the beginnings of language—a whole new way of influencing the world. Caitlin was the most vocal. "All gone baw!" she exclaimed as Timmy tossed the bright red ball down the basement steps. "Bye-bye," Grace chimed in, waving as the ball disappeared from sight. Later in the day, Grace revealed that she could use words and gestures to pretend. "Night-night," she said as she put her head down and closed her eyes, ever so pleased that in make-believe, she could decide for herself when and where to go to bed.

Over the first 2 years, the small, reflexive newborn baby becomes a self-assertive, purposeful being who solves simple problems and starts to master the most amazing human ability: language. Parents often wonder, "How does all this happen so quickly?" This question has also captivated researchers, yielding a wealth of findings along with vigorous debate over how to explain the astonishing pace of infant and toddler cognition.

In this chapter we take up three perspectives on early cognitive development: Piaget's *cognitive-developmental theory, information processing,* and Vygotsky's *sociocultural theory.* We will also consider the usefulness of tests that measure infants' and toddlers' intellectual progress. Our discussion concludes with the beginnings of language. We will see how toddlers' first words build on early cognitive achievements and how, very soon, new words and expressions increase the speed and flexibility of their thinking. Throughout development, cognition and language mutually support one another.

Piaget's Cognitive-Developmental Theory

Swiss theorist Jean Piaget inspired a vision of children as busy, motivated explorers whose thinking develops as they act directly on the environment. Influenced by his background in biology, Piaget believed that the child's mind forms and modifies psychological structures to achieve a better fit with external reality. Recall from Chapter 1 that in Piaget's theory, children move through four stages between infancy and adolescence. During those stages, all aspects of cognition develop in an integrated fashion, changing in a similar way at about the same time. The first stage is the **sensorimotor stage,** which spans the first 2 years of life.

As the name of this stage implies, Piaget believed that infants and toddlers "think" with their eyes, ears, hands, and other sensorimotor equipment. They cannot yet carry out many activities inside their heads. But by the end of toddlerhood, children can solve practical, everyday problems and represent their experiences in speech, gesture, and play. To appreciate Piaget's view of how these vast changes take place, let's consider some important concepts.

Piaget's Ideas About Cognitive Change

According to Piaget, specific psychological structures—organized ways of making sense of experience called **schemes**—change with age. At first, schemes are motor action patterns. For example, at 6 months, Timmy dropped objects in a fairly rigid way, simply by letting go of a rattle or teething ring and watching with interest. At age 18 months, his "dropping scheme" became much more deliberate and creative. He tossed all sorts of objects down the basement stairs, throwing some up in the air, bouncing others off walls, releasing some gently and others forcefully. Soon his schemes will move from an *action-based level* to a *mental level*. Instead of just acting on objects, he will show evidence of thinking before he acts. This change, as we will see later, marks the transition from sensorimotor to preoperational thought.

In Piaget's theory, two processes account for changes in schemes: *adaptation* and *organization*.

ADAPTATION ● The next time you have a chance, notice how infants and toddlers tirelessly repeat actions that lead to interesting effects. **Adaptation** involves building schemes through direct interaction with the environment. It consists of two complementary activities: *assimilation* and *accommodation*. During **assimilation,** we use our current schemes to interpret the external world. For example, when Timmy dropped objects, he was assimilating them all into his sensorimotor dropping scheme. In **accommodation,** we create new schemes or adjust old ones after noticing that our current ways of thinking do not fit the environment completely. When Timmy dropped objects in different ways, he modified his dropping scheme to take account of the varied properties of objects.

According to Piaget, the balance between assimilation and accommodation varies over time. When children are not changing very much, they assimilate more than they accommodate. Piaget called this a state of cognitive *equilibrium,* implying a steady, comfortable condition. During times of rapid cognitive change, however, children are in a state of *disequilibrium,* or cognitive discomfort. They realize that new information does not match their current schemes, so they shift away from assimilation toward accommodation. Once they have modified their schemes, they move back toward assimilation, exercising their newly changed structures until they are ready to be modified again.

Each time this back-and-forth movement between equilibrium and disequilibrium occurs, more effective schemes are produced. Because the times of greatest accommodation are the earliest ones, the sensorimotor stage is Piaget's most complex period of development.

ORGANIZATION ● Schemes change through a second process called **organization,** a process that takes place internally, apart from direct contact with the environment. Once children form new schemes, they rearrange them, linking them with other schemes to create a strongly interconnected cognitive system. For example, eventually Timmy will relate "dropping" to "throwing" and to his developing understanding of "nearness" and "farness." According to Piaget, schemes reach a true state of equilibrium when they become part of a broad network of structures that can be jointly applied to the surrounding world (Piaget, 1936/1952).

In the following sections, we will first describe infant development as Piaget saw it, noting research that supports his observations. Then we will consider evidence demonstrating that in some ways, the cognitive competence of babies is more advanced than Piaget believed it to be.

According to Piaget's theory, at first schemes are motor action patterns. As this 8-month-old takes apart, turns, and bangs these pots and pans, he discovers that his movements have predictable effects on objects and that objects influence one another in predictable ways.

The Sensorimotor Stage

The difference between the newborn baby and the 2-year-old child is so vast that the sensorimotor stage is divided into six substages (see Table 6.1 for a summary). Piaget's observations of his own three children served as the basis for this sequence of development. Although this is a very small sample, Piaget watched carefully and also presented his son and two daughters with everyday problems (such as hidden objects) that helped reveal their understanding of the world.

TABLE 6.1

Summary of Piaget's Sensorimotor Stage

SENSORIMOTOR SUBSTAGE	TYPICAL ADAPTIVE BEHAVIORS
1. Reflexive schemes (birth–1 month)	Newborn reflexes (see Chapter 4, page 148)
2. Primary circular reactions (1–4 months)	Simple motor habits centered around the infant's own body; limited anticipation of events
3. Secondary circular reactions (4–8 months)	Actions aimed at repeating interesting effects in the surrounding world; imitation of familiar behaviors
4. Coordination of secondary circular reactions (8–12 months)	Intentional, or goal-directed, behavior; ability to find a hidden object in the first location in which it is hidden (object permanence); improved anticipation of events; imitation of behaviors slightly different from those the infant usually performs
5. Tertiary circular reactions (12–18 months)	Exploration of the properties of objects by acting on them in novel ways; imitation of unfamiliar behaviors; ability to search in several locations for a hidden object (accurate A–B search)
6. Mental representation (18 months–2 years)	Internal depictions of objects and events, as indicated by sudden solutions to problems; ability to find an object that has been moved while out of sight (invisible displacement); deferred imitation; and make-believe play

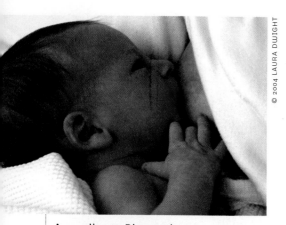

According to Piaget, the newborn baby's schemes consist of reflexes, which will gradually modify as they are applied to the surrounding environment.

According to Piaget, at birth infants know so little about their world that they cannot purposefully explore it. The **circular reaction** provides a special means of adapting their first schemes. It involves stumbling onto a new experience caused by the baby's own motor activity. The reaction is "circular" because the infant tries to repeat the event again and again. As a result, a sensorimotor response that first occurred by chance becomes strengthened into a new scheme. Consider Caitlin, who at age 2 months accidentally made a smacking sound after a feeding. The sound was new and intriguing, so Caitlin tried to repeat it until, after a few days, she became quite expert at smacking her lips.

During the first 2 years, the circular reaction changes in several ways. At first, it centers around the infant's own body. Later it turns outward, toward manipulation of objects. Finally it becomes experimental and creative, aimed at producing novel effects in the environment. Young children's difficulty inhibiting new and interesting behaviors may underlie the circular reaction. But this immaturity in inhibition seems to be adaptive. It helps ensure that new skills will not be interrupted before they strengthen (Carey & Markman, 1999). Piaget considered revisions in the circular reaction so important that he named the sensorimotor substages after them (refer again to Table 6.1).

REPEATING CHANCE BEHAVIORS ● For Piaget, newborn reflexes are the building blocks of sensorimotor intelligence. At first, in Substage 1, babies suck, grasp, and look in much the same way, no matter what experiences they encounter. Carolyn reported an amusing example of Caitlin's indiscriminate sucking at 2 weeks of age. She lay on the bed next to her father while he took a nap. Suddenly, he awoke with a start. Caitlin had latched on and begun to suck on his back!

Around 1 month, as babies enter Substage 2, they start to gain voluntary control over their actions through the primary circular reaction, by repeating chance behaviors largely motivated by basic needs. This leads to some simple motor habits, such as sucking their fists or thumbs. Babies of this substage also begin to vary their behavior in response to environmental demands. For example, they open their mouths differently for a nipple than for a spoon. Young infants also start to anticipate events. At age 3 months, when Timmy awoke from his nap, he cried out with hunger. But as soon as Vanessa entered the room, his crying stopped. He knew that feeding time was near.

During Substage 3, which lasts from 4 to 8 months, infants sit up and become skilled at reaching for and manipulating objects. These motor achievements play a major role in turning their attention outward toward the environment. Using the *secondary* circular reaction, they try to repeat interesting events caused by their own actions. For example, 4-month-old Caitlin accidentally knocked a toy hung in front of her, producing a swinging motion. Over the next 3 days, Caitlin tried to repeat this effect, at first by grasping and then by waving her arms. Finally, she succeeded in hitting the toy and gleefully repeated the motion. She had built the sensorimotor scheme of "hitting." Improved control over their own behavior permits infants to imitate the behavior of others more effectively. However, 4- to 8-month-olds cannot adapt flexibly and quickly enough to imitate novel be-

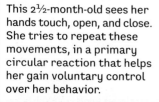

This 2½-month-old sees her hands touch, open, and close. She tries to repeat these movements, in a primary circular reaction that helps her gain voluntary control over her behavior.

At 4 months, this baby accidentally hits a toy hung in front of him. He tries to recapture the interesting effect of the swinging toy. In doing so, he builds a new "hitting scheme" through the secondary circular reaction.

haviors (Kaye & Marcus, 1981). Therefore, although they enjoy watching an adult demonstrate a game of pat-a-cake, they are not yet able to participate.

INTENTIONAL BEHAVIOR ● In Substage 4, 8- to 12-month-olds combine schemes into new, more complex action sequences. As a result, actions that lead to new schemes no longer have a random, hit-or-miss quality—*accidentally* bringing the thumb to the mouth or *happening* to hit the toy. Instead, 8- to 12-month-olds can engage in **intentional, or goal-directed, behavior,** coordinating schemes deliberately to solve simple problems. The clearest example is provided by Piaget's famous object-hiding task, in which he shows the baby an attractive toy and then hides it behind his hand or under a cover. Infants of this substage can find the object. In doing so, they coordinate two schemes—"pushing" aside the obstacle and "grasping" the toy. Piaget regarded these *means–end action sequences* as the foundation for all problem solving.

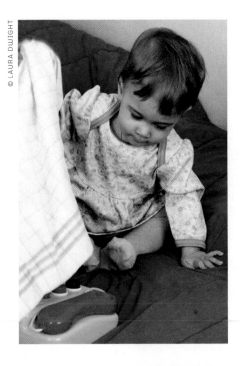

The capacity to find hidden objects between 8 and 12 months marks a major advance in cognitive development. In coordinating schemes to uncover and obtain the toy, this infant displays intentional, or goal-directed, behavior— the foundation for all problem solving.

Retrieving hidden objects reveals that infants have begun to master **object permanence,** the understanding that objects continue to exist when they are out of sight. But awareness of object permanence is not yet complete because babies make the **A-not-B search error.** If they reach several times for an object at a first hiding place (A) and see it moved to a second (B), they still search for it in the first hiding place (A). Consequently, Piaget concluded that they do not have a clear image of the object as persisting when hidden from view.

Substage 4 brings additional advances. First, infants can better anticipate events, so they sometimes use their capacity for intentional behavior to try to change those events. At 10 months, Timmy crawled after Vanessa when she put on her coat, whimpering to keep her from leaving. Second, babies can imitate behaviors slightly different from those they usually perform. After watching someone else, they try to stir with a spoon, push a toy car, or drop raisins in a cup. Once again, they draw on intentional behavior, purposefully modifying schemes to fit an observed action (Piaget, 1945/1951).

In Substage 5, which lasts from 12 to 18 months, the *tertiary circular reaction* emerges. Toddlers repeat behaviors *with variation,* provoking new effects. Recall how Timmy dropped objects over the basement steps, trying this, then that, and then another action. Because they approach the world in this deliberately exploratory way, 12- to 18-month-olds are far better sensorimotor problem solvers than they were before. For example, Grace figured out how to fit a shape through a hole in a container by turning and twisting it until it fell through, and she discovered how to use a stick to get toys that were out of reach. According to Piaget, this capacity to experiment leads to a more advanced understanding of object permanence. Toddlers look in several locations to find a hidden toy, displaying an accurate A–B search. Their more flexible action patterns also permit them to imitate many more behaviors, such as stacking blocks, scribbling on paper, and making funny faces.

At 14 months, this toddler drops a variety of objects over the edge of a living room table, pushing some gently and others forcefully, in a deliberately experimental approach. She displays a tertiary circular reaction.

MENTAL REPRESENTATION ● Substage 6 culminates with the ability to create **mental representations**—internal depictions of information that the mind can manipulate. Our most powerful mental representations are of two kinds: (1) *images,* or mental pictures of objects, people, and spaces, and (2) *concepts,* or categories in which similar objects or events are grouped together. Using a mental image, we can retrace our steps when we've misplaced something. Or we can imitate another's behavior long after we've

© SPENCER GRANT/PHOTOEDIT

At age 23 months, this child engages in make-believe play. At first, pretending involves simple schemes that the child has experienced often in everyday life.

observed it. And by thinking in concepts and labeling them (for example, *ball* for all rounded, movable objects used in play), we become more efficient thinkers, organizing our diverse experiences into meaningful, manageable, and memorable units.

Piaget noted that 18- to 24-month-olds arrive at solutions suddenly rather than through trial-and-error behavior. In doing so, they seem to experiment with actions inside their heads—evidence that they can mentally represent experiences. For example, at 19 months Grace received a new push toy. As she played with it for the first time, she rolled it over the carpet and ran into the sofa. She paused for a moment, as if to "think," and then immediately turned the toy in a new direction. Had she been in Substage 5, she would have pushed, pulled, and bumped the toy in a random fashion until it was free to move again.

Representation results in several other capacities. First, it enables older toddlers to solve advanced object permanence problems involving *invisible displacement*—finding a toy moved while out of sight, such as into a small box while under a cover. Second, it permits **deferred imitation**—the ability to remember and copy the behavior of models who are not present. An amusing example comes from Jacqueline, Piaget's daughter:

Jacqueline had a visit from a little boy . . . who, in the course of the afternoon, got into a terrible temper. He screamed as he tried to get out of a playpen and pushed it backwards, stamping his feet. Jacqueline stood watching him in amazement. . . . The next day, she herself screamed in her playpen and tried to move it, stamping her foot lightly. (Piaget, 1936/1952, p. 63)

Finally, representation leads to a major change in play. Throughout the first year and a half, infants and toddlers engage in **functional play**—pleasurable motor activity with or without objects through which they practice sensorimotor schemes. Around 18 months, they start to engage in **make-believe play**, in which they act out everyday and imaginary activities. Remember Grace's pretending to go to sleep at the beginning of this chapter? This is typical of the very simple make-believe of toddlers. Make-believe expands greatly in early childhood, and it is so important for psychological development that we will return to it again. In sum, as the sensorimotor stage draws to a close, mental symbols have become major instruments of thinking.

Follow-Up Research on Infant Cognitive Development

Many studies suggest that infants display a wide array of understandings earlier than Piaget believed. For example, recall the operant conditioning research reviewed in Chapter 5, in which newborns sucked vigorously on a nipple to gain access to interesting sights and sounds. This behavior, which closely resembles Piaget's secondary circular reaction, shows that babies try to explore and control the external world long before age 4 to 8 months. In fact, they do so as soon as they are born.

A major method used to find out what infants know about hidden objects and other aspects of physical reality capitalizes on habituation/recovery, which we discussed in Chapter 5. In the **violation-of-expectation method,** researchers habituate babies to a physical event. Then they determine whether infants recover responsiveness to (look longer at) a *possible event* (a variation of the first event that follows physical laws) or an *impossible event* (a variation that violates physical laws). Recovery to the impossible event suggests that the infant is surprised at a deviation from physical reality and, therefore, is aware of that aspect of the physical world.

But as we will see, the violation-of-expectation method is controversial. Some critics believe that it indicates limited awareness of physical events, not the full-blown understandings that Piaget detected when he observed infants acting on their surroundings, such as searching for hidden objects (Bremner, 1998). Other critics are convinced that the method is flawed—that it

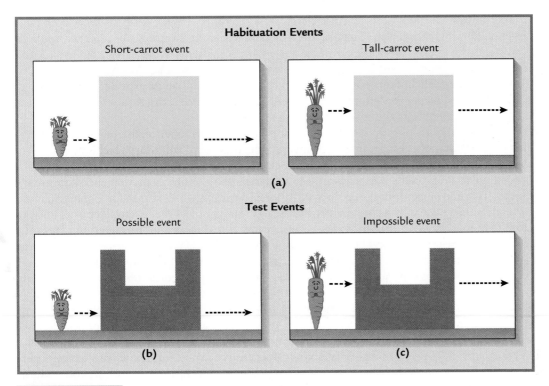

FIGURE 6.1

Testing infants for understanding of object permanence using the violation-of-expectation method.

(a) First, infants were habituated to two events: a short carrot and a tall carrot moving behind a yellow screen, on alternative trials. Next the researchers presented two test events. The color of the screen was changed to help infants notice its window. (b) In the *possible event,* the carrot shorter than the window's lower edge moved behind the blue screen and reappeared on the other side. (c) In the *impossible event,* the carrot taller than the window's lower edge moved behind the screen, did not appear in the window, but then emerged intact on the other side. Infants as young as 2½ to 3½ months recovered to (looked longer at) the impossible event, suggesting that they had some understanding of object permanence. (Adapted from R. Baillargeon & J. DeVos, 1991, "Object Permanence in Young Infants: Further Evidence," *Child Development, 62,* p. 1230. © The Society for Research in Child Development. Reprinted with permission of the Society for Research in Child Development.)

reveals only babies' perceptual preference for novelty, not their understanding of experience (Haith, 1999). Let's examine this debate in light of recent evidence.

OBJECT PERMANENCE ● In a series of studies using the violation-of-expectation method, Renée Baillargeon and her collaborators claimed to have found evidence for object permanence in the first few months of life. One of Baillargeon's studies is illustrated in Figure 6.1 (Aguiar & Baillargeon, 1999, 2002; Baillargeon & DeVos, 1991). After habituating to a short and a tall carrot moving behind a screen, infants were given two test events: (1) a *possible event,* in which the short carrot moved behind a screen, could not be seen in its window, and reappeared on the other side, and (2) an *impossible event,* in which the tall carrot moved behind a screen, could not be seen in its window (although it was taller than the window's lower edge), and reappeared. Three-month-olds looked longer at the *impossible event,* suggesting that they expected an object moved behind a screen to continue to exist. Infants as young as 2½ to 3½ months looked longer at the impossible event, suggesting that they expected an object moved behind a screen to continue to exist.

But studies using procedures similar to Baillargeon's failed to confirm some of her findings (Bogartz, Shinskey, & Shilling, 2000; Cashon & Cohen, 2000; Rivera, Wakeley, & Langer, 1999). Baillargeon and others answer that these opposing investigations did not include crucial controls. And they emphasize that infants look longer at a wide variety of impossible events that make it appear as though an object covered by a screen no longer exists (Aslin, 2000; Baillargeon, 2000). Furthermore, using a different task, researchers once again reported findings consistent with young babies' grasp of object permanence. After viewing a ball moving back and forth on a computer screen, 4-month-olds saw the ball disappear behind a barrier in the middle of the screen. The infants continued to searched for the ball on its expected path of movement (Johnson, Amso, & Slemmer 2003). In response, however, critics question what babies' looking behavior tells us about what they actually know.

If 2- to 3-month-olds do have some notion of object permanence, then what explains Piaget's finding that much older infants (who are quite capable of voluntary reaching) do not try to search for hidden objects? Consistent with Piaget's theory, research suggests that searching for hidden objects represents a true advance in understanding of object permanence because infants solve some object-hiding tasks before others. Ten-month-olds search for an object placed on a table and covered by a cloth before they search for an object that a hand deposits under a cloth (Moore & Meltzoff, 1999). In the second, more difficult task, infants seem to expect the object to reappear in the hand because that is where the object initially disappeared. When the hand emerges without the object, they conclude that there is no other place the object could be. Not until 14 months can most infants infer that the hand deposited the object under the cloth.

SEARCHING FOR OBJECTS HIDDEN IN MORE THAN ONE LOCATION ● For some years, researchers thought that 8- to 12-month-olds made the A-not-B search error because they had trouble remembering an object's new location after it was hidden in more than one place. But recent findings reveal that poor memory cannot fully account for infants' unsuccessful performance. For example, between 6 and 12 months, infants increasingly *look* at the correct location while *reaching* incorrectly (Ahmed & Ruffman, 1998; Hofstadter & Reznick, 1996).

Perhaps babies search at A (where they found the object on previous reaches) instead of at B (its most recent location) because they have trouble inhibiting a previously rewarded motor response (Diamond, Cruttenden, & Neiderman, 1994). In support of this view, the more prior reaches to A, the greater the likelihood that the infant will reach again toward A when the object is hidden at B (Smith et al., 1999). Another possibility is that after finding the object several times at A, babies do not attend closely when it is hidden at B (Ruffman & Langman, 2002). A more comprehensive explanation is that a complex, dynamic system of factors—having built a habit of reaching toward A, continuing to look at A, having the hiding place at B look similar to the one at A, and maintaining a constant body posture—increase the chances that the baby will make the A-not-B search error. Research shows that disrupting any one of these factors increased 10-month-olds' accurate searching at B (Smith et al., 1999).

In sum, before 12 months, infants have trouble translating what they know about object location into a successful search strategy. The ability to integrate knowledge with action coincides with rapid development of the frontal lobes of the cerebral cortex at the end of the first year (Bell, 1998; Diamond, 1991). Also crucial are a wide variety of experiences perceiving, acting on, and remembering objects.

MENTAL REPRESENTATION ● In Piaget's theory, infants lead purely sensorimotor lives. They cannot represent experience until about 18 months of age. Yet 8-month-olds' ability to recall the location of hidden objects, even after delays of more than a minute, indicates that they mentally represent objects (McDonough, 1999). And new studies of deferred imitation and problem solving reveal that representational thought is evident even earlier.

Deferred Imitation. Piaget studied imitation by noting when his three children demonstrated it in their everyday behavior. Under these conditions, a great deal must be known about the infant's daily life to be sure that deferred imitation—which requires infants to represent another's past behavior—has occurred.

Laboratory research reveals that deferred imitation is present at 6 weeks of age! Infants who watched an unfamiliar adult's facial expression imitated it when exposed to the same adult the next day (Meltzoff & Moore, 1994). Perhaps young babies use this imitation to identify and communicate with people they have seen before. As motor capacities improve, infants start to copy actions with objects. In one study, 6- and 9-month-olds were shown an "activity" board

Deferred imitation greatly enriches young children's adaptations to their surrounding world. This toddler probably watched an adult watering flowers. Later, he imitates the behavior, having learned through observation what the sprinkling can is for.

© ESBIN/ANDERSON/THE IMAGE WORKS

with twelve novel objects fastened to it—for example, a frog whose legs jump when a cord is pulled. An adult modeled the actions of six objects. When tested a day later, babies of both ages were far more likely to produce the actions they had seen than actions associated with objects that had not been demonstrated (Collie & Hayne, 1999). The babies retained and enacted not just one but, on average, three modeled behaviors.

Between 12 and 18 months, toddlers use deferred imitation skillfully to enrich their range of schemes. They retain modeled behaviors for at least several months, copy the actions of peers as well as adults, and imitate across a change in context—for example, enact in the home a behavior learned at child care or on TV (Barr & Hayne, 1999; Hayne, Boniface, & Barr, 2000; Klein & Meltzoff, 1999). Toddlers even imitate rationally! If they see an adult perform an unusual action for fun (turn on a light with her head, even though her hands are free), they copy the behavior after a week's delay. But if the adult seems to engage in the odd behavior because she must (her hands are otherwise occupied), 14-month-olds modify their imitative response to a more efficient action (use their hand to turn on the light) (Gergely, Bekkering, & Király, 2002).

Around 18 months, toddlers imitate actions an adult tries to produce, even if these are not fully realized (Meltzoff, 1995). On one occasion, Ginette attempted to pour some raisins into a small bag but missed, spilling them onto the counter. A moment later, Grace climbed on a stool and began dropping the raisins into the bag, indicating that she had inferred Ginette's intention. By age 2, children mimic entire social roles—such as mommy, daddy, or baby—during make-believe play.

Problem Solving. As Piaget indicated, infants develop intentional means–end action sequences around 7 to 8 months, using them to solve simple problems, such as pulling on a cloth to obtain a toy resting on its far end (Willatts, 1999). Soon after, infants' representational skills permit more effective problem solving than Piaget's theory suggests.

By 10 to 12 months, infants can *solve problems by analogy*—take a strategy from one problem and apply it to other relevant problems. In one study, babies were given three similar problems, each requiring them to overcome a barrier, grasp a string, and pull it to get an attractive toy. The problems differed in all aspects of their specific features (see Figure 6.2). On the first problem, the parent demonstrated the solution and encouraged the infant to imitate. Babies obtained the toy more readily on each additional problem, suggesting that they had formed a flexible mental representation of actions that access an out-of-reach object (Chen, Sanchez, & Campbell, 1997).

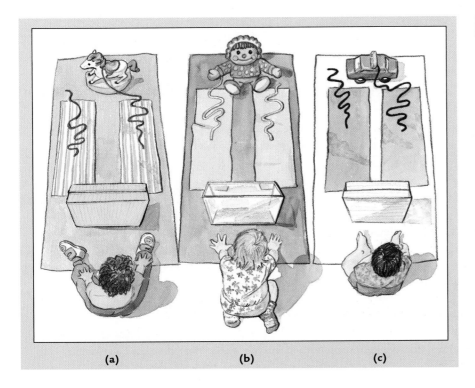

(a) (b) (c)

FIGURE 6.2

Analogical problem solving by 10- to 12-month-olds.

After the parent demonstrated the solution to problem (a), infants solved problems (b) and (c) with increasing efficiency, even though those problems differed in all aspects of their superficial features. (From Z. Chen, R. P. Sanchez, & T. Campbell, 1997, "From Beyond to Within Their Grasp: The Rudiments of Analogical Problem Solving in 10- to 13-Month-Olds," *Developmental Psychology, 33,* p. 792. Copyright © 1997 by the American Psychological Association. Reprinted by permission of the publisher and author.)

With age, children can better reason by analogy, applying relevant strategies across increasingly dissimilar situations (Goswami, 1996). But even in the first year, infants have some ability to move beyond trial-and-error experimentation, represent a solution mentally, and use it in new contexts.

Evaluation of the Sensorimotor Stage

Table 6.2 summarizes the remarkable cognitive attainments considered in this and the previous section. Compare this table with the description of Piaget's sensorimotor substages in Table 6.1 on page 209. You will see that infants anticipate events, actively search for hidden objects, master the A–B object search, flexibly vary their sensorimotor schemes, and engage in make-believe play within Piaget's time frame. Yet other capacities—including secondary circular reactions, first signs of object permanence, deferred imitation, and problem solving by analogy—emerge earlier than Piaget expected.

Notice, also, that the cognitive attainments of infancy and toddlerhood do not develop in the neat, stepwise fashion Piaget predicted. For example, deferred imitation is present long before toddlers can solve Piaget's most advanced object-hiding task. To obtain an object that has been moved while out of sight, infants must go beyond recall of a past event to a more complex form of representation: They must *imagine an event they have not seen* (Rast & Meltzoff, 1995). Yet Piaget assumed that all representational capacities develop at the same time, at the end of the sensorimotor stage. These findings, and others like them, are among an accumulating body of evidence that raises doubts about the accuracy of Piaget's stages.

Disagreements between Piaget's observations and those of recent researchers raise controversial questions about how infant development takes place. Consistent with Piaget's ideas, sensorimotor action helps infants construct some forms of knowledge. For example, in Chapter 5 we saw that crawling experience enhances depth perception and ability to find hidden objects. Yet we have also seen evidence that infants comprehend a great deal before they are capable of the motor behaviors that Piaget assumed led to those understandings. How can we account for babies' amazing cognitive accomplishments?

ALTERNATIVE EXPLANATIONS ● Most researchers believe that young babies have more built-in cognitive equipment for making sense of experience than granted by Piaget, who thought that they constructed all mental representations out of sensorimotor activity. But intense

TABLE 6.2

Some Cognitive Attainments of Infancy and Toddlerhood

AGE	COGNITIVE ATTAINMENTS
Birth–1 month	Secondary circular reactions using limited motor skills, such as sucking a nipple to gain access to interesting sights and sounds
1–4 months	Violation-of-expectation findings suggest awareness of many object properties, including object permanence, object solidity, and gravity; deferred imitation of an adult's facial expression after a short delay (1 day)
4–8 months	Violation-of-expectation findings suggest basic numerical knowledge and improved physical knowledge; deferred imitation of an adult's novel actions on objects over a short delay (1 day)
8–12 months	Ability to search for a hidden object after it is covered by a cloth; ability to solve simple problems by analogy to a previous similar problem
12–18 months	Ability to search for a hidden object in diverse situations—after a hand deposits it under a cloth and after it is moved from one location to another (accurate A–B search); deferred imitation of an adult's novel actions on objects after a long delay (at least several months) and across a change in context
18 months–2 years	Deferred imitation of actions an adult tries to produce, even if these are not fully realized, indicating a capacity to infer others' intentions

Note: Which capacities listed in this table indicate that mental representation emerges earlier than predicted by Piaget's sensorimotor substages?

disagreement exists over how much initial understanding infants have. As we have seen, much evidence on young infants' cognition rests on the violation-of-expectation method. Researchers who lack confidence in this method argue that babies' cognitive starting point is limited. For example, some believe that newborns begin life with a set of general-purpose learning procedures—such as powerful techniques for analyzing complex perceptual information of all kinds—that serves as a means for constructing schemes (Haith & Benson, 1998; Huttenlocher, 2002; Karmiloff-Smith, 1992).

Others, convinced by violation-of-expectation findings, believe that infants start out with impressive understandings. According to this **core knowledge perspective,** babies are born with a set of innate knowledge systems, or *core domains of thought.* Each of these "prewired" understandings permits a ready grasp of new, related information and therefore supports early, rapid, development (Carey & Markman, 1999; Spelke & Newport, 1998). Core knowledge theorists argue that infants could not make sense of the varied stimulation around them without having been "set up" in the course of evolution to comprehend its crucial aspects.

Researchers have conducted many studies of infants' *physical knowledge,* including object permanence, object solidity (that one object cannot move through another object), and gravity (that an object will fall without support). Violation-of-expectation findings suggest that in the first few months, infants have some awareness of these basic object properties and quickly build on this knowledge (Baillargeon, 1994; Hespos & Baillargeon, 2001; Spelke et al., 1992). Researchers have also investigated infants' *numerical knowledge,* or ability to distinguish small quantities (see the Biology and Environment box on page 218). Furthermore, core knowledge theorists assume that *linguistic knowledge* is etched into the structure of the human brain—a possibility we will consider when we take up language development. And infants' early orientation toward people, these theorists point out, initiates swift development of *psychological knowledge*—in particular, understanding of mental states, such as intentions, emotions, desires, and beliefs, which we will begin to address in Chapter 7.

But as the Biology and Environment box reveals, studies of young infants' knowledge yield mixed results. And even when violation-of-expectation findings are consistent, critics take issue with the assumption that infants are endowed with *knowledge.* They argue that young infants' looking behaviors may indicate only a perceptual preference, not the existence of concepts and reasoning (Haith, 1999, Meltzoff & Moore, 1998). Similarly, investigators of brain development add that little evidence exists for prewiring of complex cognitive functions in the brain. Instead, they say, the cerebral cortex is initially highly plastic and gradually specializes, largely as the result of children's experiences (see Chapter 5, pages 172–174) (Johnson, 2001b).

Finally, although the core knowledge perspective emphasizes native endowment, it acknowledges that experience is essential for children to extend this initial knowledge. But so far, it has not offered greater clarity than Piaget's theory on how biology and environment jointly produce cognitive change. For example, it says little about which experiences are most important in each domain of thought and how those experiences advance children's thinking. Despite these limitations, the ingenious studies and provocative findings of core knowledge researchers have sharpened the field's focus on clarifying the starting point for human cognition and on carefully tracking the changes that build on it.

PIAGET'S LEGACY ● Follow-up research on Piaget's sensorimotor stage yields broad agreement on two issues. First, many cognitive changes of infancy are gradual and continuous rather than abrupt and stagelike, as Piaget thought (Courage & Howe, 2002; Flavell, Miller, & Miller, 2002). Second, rather than developing together, various aspects of infant cognition change unevenly because of the challenges posed by different types of tasks and infants' varying experiences with them. These ideas serve as the basis for another major approach to cognitive development—*information processing*—which we take up next.

© REFLECTIONS PHOTOLIBRARY/CORBIS

Did these toddlers acquire the necessary physical knowledge to build a block tower through many opportunities to act on objects, as Piaget assumed? Or did the toddlers begin life with considerable innate knowledge, which enabled them to understand objects and their relationships quickly, with little hands-on exploration?

Biology and Environment

Do Infants Have Built-In Numerical Knowledge?

How does cognition develop so rapidly during the early years of life? According to the *core knowledge perspective,* infants have an inherited foundation of knowledge, which quickly becomes more elaborate as they explore, play, and interact with others (Geary & Bjorklund, 2000). Do infants display numerical understandings so early that some knowledge must be innate? The violation-of-expectation method has been used to answer this question.

In the best known of these investigations, 5-month-olds saw a screen raised to hide a single toy animal (see Figure 6.3). Then they watched a hand place a second toy behind the screen. Finally the screen was removed to reveal either one toy or two toys. If infants kept track of the two objects, then they should look longer at the one-toy display (*impossible outcome*)—which is what they did. In additional experiments, 5-month-olds given this task looked longer at three objects than at two. These results, and those of other similar studies, suggest that in the first half-year, babies can discriminate quantities of single items up to three and use that knowledge to perform simple arithmetic—not just addition, but also subtraction, in which two objects are covered by a screen and one is removed (Wynn, 1992; Wynn, Bloom, & Chiang, 2002).

Other research shows that 6-month-olds can distinguish among large sets of items, as long as the difference between those sets is very great. For example, they can tell the difference between 8 versus 16 dots, but not between 6 versus 12 (Xu & Spelke, 2000). As a result, some researchers believe that infants can represent approximate large-number values, in addition to the small-number discriminations evident in Figure 6.3.

But findings on infants' numerical knowledge, like other violation-of-expectation results, are controversial. Critics question what looking preferences tell us about infants' numerical knowledge. And some researchers report that 5-month-olds cannot add and subtract small quantities. In experiments similar to those just described, looking preferences were inconsistent (Feigenson, Carey, & Spelke, 2002; Wakeley, Rivera, & Langer, 2000). Furthermore, infants' knowledge of number is surprising, given that toddlers usu- ally do not show these understandings. Before 14 to 16 months, toddlers have difficulty with less-than and greater-than relationships between small sets. And not until the preschool years do children add and subtract small sets correctly.

Overall, in some studies infants display amazing knowledge, but in others they do not. And if such knowledge is innate, older children should reason in the same way as infants, yet they do not always do so. Core knowledge theorists respond that infant looking behaviors may be more reliable indicators of understanding than older children's verbal and motor behaviors, which may not tap their true competencies (Wynn, 2002). At present, just what babies start out with—innate understandings or general learning strategies that permit them to discover knowledge quickly—continues to be hotly debated.

FIGURE 6.3

Testing infants for basic number concepts.

(a) First, infants saw a screen raised in front of a toy animal. Then an identical toy was added behind the screen. Next, the researchers presented two outcomes. (b) In the *possible outcome,* the screen dropped to reveal two toy animals. (c) In the *impossible outcome,* the screen dropped to reveal one toy animal. Five-month-olds shown the impossible outcome looked longer than did 5-month-olds shown the possible outcome. The researchers concluded that infants can discriminate the quantities "one" and "two" and use that knowledge to perform simple addition: 1 + 1 = 2. A variation of this procedure suggested that 5-month-olds could also do simple subtraction: 2 − 1 = 1. (From K. Wynn, 1992, "Addition and Subtraction by Human Infants," *Nature, 358,* p. 749. Reprinted by permission.)

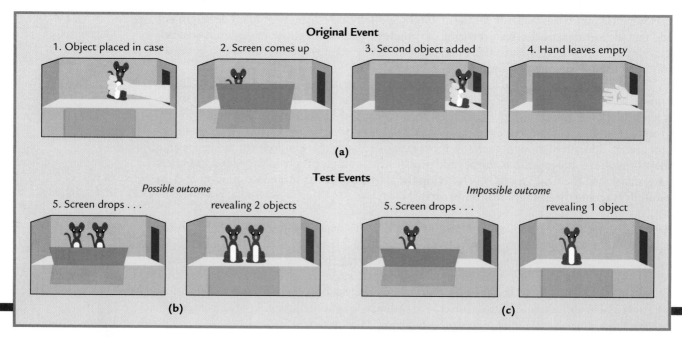

Original Event

1. Object placed in case   2. Screen comes up   3. Second object added   4. Hand leaves empty

(a)

Test Events

Possible outcome

5. Screen drops . . .   revealing 2 objects

Impossible outcome

5. Screen drops . . .   revealing 1 object

(b)   (c)

Applying WHAT WE Know / Play Materials That Support Infant and Toddler Cognitive Development

FROM 2 MONTHS	FROM 6 MONTHS	FROM 1 YEAR
Crib mobile	Squeeze toys	Large dolls
Rattles and other handheld sound-making toys, such as a bell on a handle	Nesting cups	Toy dishes
	Clutch and texture balls	Toy telephone
Adult-operated music boxes, records, tapes, and CDs with gentle, regular rhythms, songs, and lullabies	Stuffed animals and soft-bodied dolls	Hammer-and-peg toy
	Filling and emptying toys	Pull and push toys
	Large and small blocks	Cars and trucks
	Pots, pans, and spoons from the kitchen	Rhythm instruments for shaking and banging, such as bells, cymbals, and drums
	Simple, floating objects for the bath	Simple puzzles
	Picture books	Sandbox, shovel, and pail
		Shallow wading pool and water toys

Note: Return to Applying What We Know in Chapter 5, page 192, to review safety concerns related to toys for infants and toddlers.
Source: Bronson, 1995.

Before we turn to this alternative point of view, let's take a moment to recognize Piaget's enormous contributions. Although his account of development is no longer fully accepted, contemporary theorists are a long way from consensus on how to modify or replace it. And they continue to draw inspiration from Piaget's lifelong quest to understand how children acquire new cognitive capacities. Piaget's work inspired a wealth of research on infant cognition, including the studies that challenged his theory. His observations also have been of great practical value. Teachers and caregivers continue to look to the sensorimotor stage for guidelines on how to create developmentally appropriate environments for infants and toddlers. Now that you are familiar with some milestones of the first 2 years, what play materials do you think would support the development of sensorimotor and early representational schemes? Prepare a list, justifying it by referring to the cognitive attainments described in the previous sections. Then compare your suggestions to the ones given above in Applying What We Know.

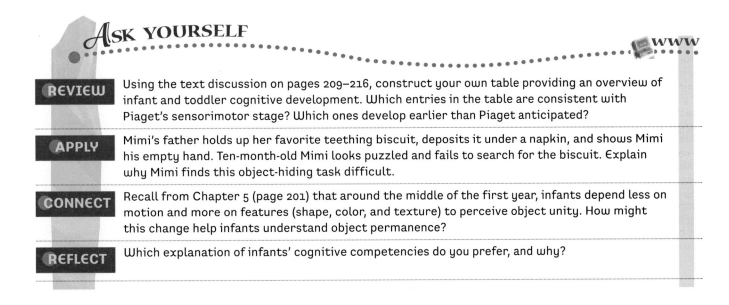

Ask YOURSELF

www

REVIEW   Using the text discussion on pages 209–216, construct your own table providing an overview of infant and toddler cognitive development. Which entries in the table are consistent with Piaget's sensorimotor stage? Which ones develop earlier than Piaget anticipated?

APPLY   Mimi's father holds up her favorite teething biscuit, deposits it under a napkin, and shows Mimi his empty hand. Ten-month-old Mimi looks puzzled and fails to search for the biscuit. Explain why Mimi finds this object-hiding task difficult.

CONNECT   Recall from Chapter 5 (page 201) that around the middle of the first year, infants depend less on motion and more on features (shape, color, and texture) to perceive object unity. How might this change help infants understand object permanence?

REFLECT   Which explanation of infants' cognitive competencies do you prefer, and why?

Information Processing

Information-processing researchers agree with Piaget that children are active, inquiring beings, but they do not provide a single, unified theory of cognitive development. Instead, they focus on many aspects of thinking, from attention, memory, and categorization skills to complex problem solving.

Recall from Chapter 1 that the information-processing approach frequently relies on computerlike flowcharts to describe the human cognitive system. The computer model of human thinking is attractive because it is explicit and precise. Information-processing researchers are not satisfied with general concepts, such as assimilation and accommodation, to describe how children think. Instead, they want to know exactly what individuals of different ages do when faced with a task or problem (Klahr & MacWhinney, 1998; Siegler, 1998).

Structure of the Information-Processing System

Most information-processing researchers assume that we hold information in three parts of the mental system for processing: the *sensory register; working,* or *short-term, memory;* and *long-term memory* (see Figure 6.4). As information flows through each, we can operate on and transform it using **mental strategies,** increasing the chances that we will retain information and use it efficiently. To understand this more clearly, let's take a look at each aspect of the mental system.

First, information enters the **sensory register.** Here, sights and sounds are represented directly and stored briefly. Look around you, and then close your eyes. An image of what you saw persists for a few seconds, but then it decays or disappears, unless you use mental strategies to preserve it. For example, you can *attend to* some information more carefully than to other information, increasing the chances that it will transfer to the next step of the information-processing system.

The second part of the mind is **working,** or **short-term, memory,** where we actively "work" on a limited amount of information, applying mental strategies. For example, if you are study-

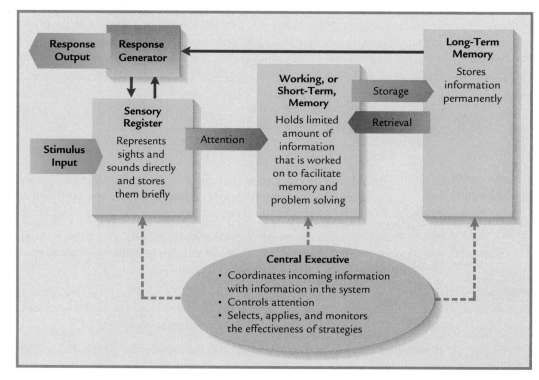

FIGURE 6.4

Store model of the human information-processing system.

Information flows through three parts of the mental system: the *sensory register; working,* or *short-term, memory;* and *long-term memory.* In each, mental strategies can be used to manipulate information, increasing the efficiency of thinking and the chances that information will be retained. Strategies also permit us to think flexibly, adapting information to changing circumstances. The *central executive* is the conscious, reflective part of working memory. It coordinates incoming information already in the system, decides what to attend to, and oversees the use of strategies.

ing this book effectively, you are taking notes, repeating information to yourself, or grouping pieces of information together. Think, for a moment, about why you apply these strategies. The sensory register, although limited, can take in a wide panorama of information. The capacity of working memory is more restricted. By using strategies, we increase the chances that we will retain certain information. And by meaningfully connecting pieces of information into a single representation, we reduce the number of separate pieces we must attend to, thereby making room in working memory for more. Also, the more thoroughly we learn information, the more *automatically* we use it. Automatic cognitive processing expands working memory by permitting us to focus on other information simultaneously.

To manage its complex activities, a special part of working memory called the **central executive** directs the flow of information. It decides what to attend to, coordinates incoming information with information already in the system, and selects, applies, and monitors strategies (Baddeley, 1993, 2000). The central executive is the conscious, reflective part of our mental system.

The longer we hold information in working memory, the greater the likelihood that it will transfer to the third and largest storage area—**long-term memory,** our permanent knowledge base, which is limitless. In fact, we store so much in long-term memory that we sometimes have problems with *retrieval,* or getting information back from the system. To aid retrieval, we apply strategies, just as we do in working memory. Information in long-term memory is *categorized* according to a master plan based on contents, much like a library shelving system. As a result, you can retrieve it quite easily by following the same network of associations used to store it in the first place.

Information-processing researchers believe that the basic structure of the human mental system is similar throughout life. However, the *capacity* of the system—the amount of information that can be processed at once and the speed with which it can be processed—increases, making possible more complex forms of thinking with age (Case, 1998; Miller & Vernon, 1997). Gains in information-processing capacity are due partly to brain development and partly to improvements in strategies, such as attending to information and categorizing it effectively. The development of these strategies is already under way in the first 2 years of life.

Attention

How does attention develop in early infancy? Recall from our discussion of perceptual development in Chapter 5 that between 1 and 2 months of age, infants shift from attending to a single high-contrast feature of their visual world to exploring objects and patterns more thoroughly. Besides attending to more aspects of the environment, infants gradually become more efficient at managing their attention, taking in information more quickly with age. Habituation research reveals that preterm and newborn babies require about 3 or 4 minutes to habituate and recover to novel visual stimuli. But by 5 months, infants require just a few seconds to take in a complex visual stimulus and recognize that it differs from a previous one (Rose, Feldman, & Janowski, 2001).

One reason that very young babies' habituation times are so much longer is that they have difficulty disengaging their attention from interesting stimuli (Frick, Colombo, & Saxon, 1999). Once, Carolyn held a doll dressed in red-and-white checked overalls in front of 2-month-old Caitlin, who stared intently until, unable to break her gaze, she burst into tears. Just as important as attending to a stimulus is the ability to shift attention from one stimulus to another. By 4 to 6 months, infants' attention becomes more flexible—a change believed to be due to development of structures in the cerebral cortex controlling eye movements (Hood, Atkinson, & Braddick, 1998).

During the first year, infants attend to novel and eye-catching events, orienting to them more quickly and tracking their movements more effectively (Richards & Holley, 1999). With the transition to toddlerhood, children become increasingly capable of intentional behavior (refer back to page 211). Consequently, attraction to novelty declines (but does not disappear) and *sustained attention* improves, especially when children play with toys. When a toddler engages in goal-directed behavior even in a limited way, such as stacking blocks or putting them in a container, attention must be maintained to reach the goal. As plans and activities gradually become more complex, so does the duration of attention (Ruff & Lawson, 1990).

Adults can foster infants' and toddlers' sustained attention by taking note of the child's current interest, encouraging it ("Oh, you like that bell!"), and prompting the child to stay focused ("See, it makes a noise!"). Consistently helping infants focus attention at 10 months predicts higher mental test scores at 18 months (Bono & Stifter, 2003). Also, infants and toddlers gradually become more interested in what others are attending to. Later we will see that this joint attention between caregiver and child is important for language development. By 18 months, toddlers are skilled at dividing their attention between adult partners and toys in play (Ruff & Rothbart, 1996).

Memory

Habituation provides a window into infant memory. Studies show that infants gradually make finer distinctions among visual stimuli and remember them longer—at 3 months, for about 24 hours; by the end of the first year, for several days; and in the case of some stimuli (such as a photo of the human face), even for weeks (Fagan, 1973; Pascalis, de Haan, & Nelson, 1998). Yet recall that what babies know about the stimuli to which they habituate and recover is not always clear. Some researchers argue that infants' understanding is best revealed through their active efforts to master their environment. Consistent with this view, habituation greatly underestimates infants' memory when compared with methods that rely on their active exploration of objects (Wilk, Klein, & Rovee-Collier, 2001).

Recall the operant conditioning research discussed in Chapter 5, in which babies learned to make a mobile move by kicking. In a series of studies, Carolyn Rovee-Collier found that 3-month-olds remembered how to activate the mobile 1 week after training. By 6 months of age, retention increases to 2 weeks (Rovee-Collier, 1999; Rovee-Collier & Bhatt, 1993). Around the middle of the first year, tasks in which babies control stimulation by manipulating buttons or switches work well for studying memory. When infants and toddlers pressed a lever to make a toy train move around a track, duration of memory continued to increase with age; 13 weeks after training, 18-month-olds still remembered how to press the lever (Hartshorn et al., 1998b). Figure 6.5 shows this dramatic rise in retention of operant responses over the first year and a half.

Even after 3- to 6-month-olds forget an operant response, they need only a brief prompt—an adult who shakes the mobile—to reinstate the memory (Hildreth & Rovee-Collier, 2002). And when 6-month-olds are given a chance to reactivate the response themselves for just a couple of minutes—jiggling the mobile by kicking or moving the train by lever-pressing—their memory not only returns but also extends further, to about 17 weeks (Hildreth, Sweeney, & Rovee-Collier, 2003). Perhaps retention is fostered in the second case (permitting the baby to produce the previously learned behavior) because it re-exposes the child to more aspects of the original learning situation.

At first, infant memory is highly *context dependent.* If 2- to 6-month-olds are not tested in the same situation in which they were trained—with the same mobile and crib bumper and in the same room—they remember poorly (Boller, Grabelle, & Rovee-Collier, 1995; Hayne & Rovee-Collier, 1995). After 9 months, the importance of context declines. Older infants and toddlers remember how to make the toy train move even when its features are altered and testing takes place in a different room (Hartshorne et al., 1998a;

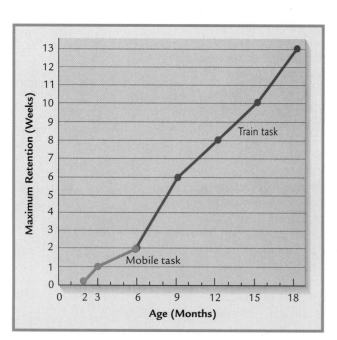

FIGURE 6.5

Maximum duration of retention in two operant conditioning tasks from 2 to 18 months of age.
During the first year and a half, memory improves dramatically. Six-month-olds were trained and tested in both the mobile task and the train task and retained the two responses for an identical length of time. (From C. Rovee-Collier & R. Barr, 2001, "Infant Learning and Memory," in G. Bremner & A. Fogel, eds., *Blackwell Handbook of Infant Development,* Oxford, U.K.: Blackwell, p. 150. Reprinted by permission.)

Hayne, Boniface, & Barr, 2000). As babies move on their own and experience frequent changes in context, their memory becomes increasingly *context free*. They can apply learned responses more flexibly, generalizing them to relevant new situations.

So far, we have discussed only **recognition,** the simplest form of memory because all that babies have to do is indicate (by looking, kicking, or pressing a lever) whether a new experience is identical or similar to a previous one. **Recall** is more challenging, since it involves remembering something in the absence of perceptual support. To recall, you must generate a mental image of the past experience. Can infants engage in recall? By the end of the first year, they can, as indicated by their ability to find hidden objects and imitate the actions of others hours or days after they have observed the behavior.

Between 1 and 2 years of age, children's recall of people, places, objects, and actions is excellent. In several studies, 1-year-olds who briefly observed an adult's actions on a novel toy imitated those behaviors 1 month later. Among 2-year-olds, retention persisted for at least 3 months (Herbert & Hayne, 2000; Klein & Meltzoff, 1999). Other evidence suggests that toddlers' recall endures even longer—3 months for short sequences of adult-modeled actions at 1 year and up to 12 months for sequences observed at 1½ years (Bauer, 2002).

Long-term recall depends on connections among multiple regions of the cerebral cortex. During the second year, these neural circuits develop rapidly (Nelson, 1997). Yet a puzzling finding is that older children and adults no longer recall their earliest experiences! See the Biology and Environment box on pages 224–225 for a discussion of *infantile amnesia*.

Categorization

As infants remember more information, they store it in a remarkably orderly fashion. Some creative variations of the operant conditioning research described earlier have been used to find out about infant categorization. One such study is described and illustrated in Figure 6.6. In fact, young babies categorize stimuli on the basis of shape, size, and other physical properties at such an early age that categorization is among the strongest evidence that infants structure their experience in adultlike ways (Mandler, 1998).

Habituation/recovery has also been used to study infant categorization. Researchers show babies a series of stimuli belonging to one category and then see whether they recover to (look longer at) a picture that is not a member of the category. Findings reveal that 7- to 12-month-olds structure objects into an impressive array of meaningful categories—food items, furniture, birds, animals, plants, vehicles, kitchen utensils, spatial location ("above" and "below"), and more (Mandler & McDonough, 1996, 1998; Oakes, Coppage, & Dingel, 1997). Besides organizing the physical world, infants of this age categorize their emotional and social worlds. They sort people and their voices by gender and age (Bahrick,

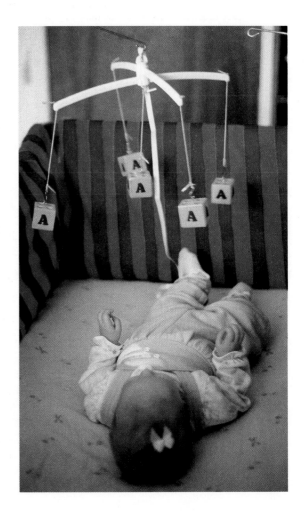

Investigating infant categorization using operant conditioning.

Three-month-olds were taught to kick to move a mobile that was made of small blocks, all with the letter A on them. After a delay, kicking returned to a high level only if the babies were shown a mobile whose elements were labeled with the same form (the letter A). If the form was changed (from As to 2s), infants no longer kicked vigorously. While making the mobile move, the babies had grouped together its features. They associated the kicking response with the category A and, at later testing, distinguished it from the category 2 (Bhatt, Rovee-Collier, & Weiner, 1994; Hayne, Rovee-Collier, & Perris, 1987).

ℬiology and Environment

Infantile Amnesia

If toddlers remember many aspects of their everyday lives, then what explains infantile amnesia—the fact that few of us can retrieve events that happened to us before age 3? This forgetting cannot be due merely to the passage of time because we can recall many events that happened long ago (Eacott, 1999). At present, several complementary explanations of infantile amnesia exist.

One theory credits brain development. Vital changes in the frontal lobes of the cerebral cortex may pave the way for an *explicit* memory system—one in which children remember deliberately rather than *implicitly,* without conscious awareness (Boyer & Diamond, 1992; Rovee-Collier & Barr, 2001). In support of this idea, 9- and 10-year-olds shown pictures of their preschool classmates react physiologically in ways consistent with remembering, even when they do not consciously recall the child (Newcombe & Fox, 1994).

A related conjecture is that older children and adults often use verbal means for storing information, whereas infants' and toddlers' memory processing is largely nonverbal—an incompatibility that may prevent long-term retention of their experiences. To test this idea, researchers sent two adults to the homes of 2- to 4-year-olds with a highly unusual toy that the children were likely to remember: The Magic Shrinking Machine, depicted in Figure 6.7. One of the adults showed the child how, after inserting an object in an opening on top of the machine and turning a crank that activated flash-

ing lights and musical sounds, the child could retrieve a smaller, identical object from behind a door on the front of the machine. (The second adult discretely dropped the smaller object down a chute leading to the door.) The child was encouraged to participate as the machine "shrunk" additional objects.

A day later, the researchers tested the children to see how well they recalled the event. Results revealed that their nonverbal memory—based on acting out the "shrinking" event and recognizing the "shrunken" objects in photos—was excellent. But even when they had the vocabulary, children younger than age 3 had trouble describing features of the "shrinking" experience. Verbal recall increased sharply between ages 3 and 4—the period during which children "scramble over the amnesia barrier" (Simcock & Hayne, 2003, p. 813). A second study showed that preschoolers could not translate their nonverbal memory for the game into language after 6 months to 1 year had elapsed and their language had improved dramatically. Their verbal reports were "frozen in time," reflecting their limited language skill at the time they played the game (Simcock & Hayne, 2002).

These findings help us reconcile infants' and toddlers' remarkable memory skills with infantile amnesia. During the first few years, children rely heavily on nonverbal techniques—such as visual images and motor actions—to remember. As language develops, children first use words to talk about the here and now.

Only after age 3 do they often represent their past experiences verbally—a mode of storage that increases the accessibility of these memories at later ages.

Additional evidence indicates that the decline of infantile amnesia requires a special form of verbal recall: **autobiographical memory**—narrative accounts of significant, one-time events that are long-lasting because they are imbued with personal meaning. For example, perhaps you recall the day a sibling was born, a move to a new house, a serious illness, or the first time you took an airplane. For memories to become autobiographical, at least two developments are necessary. First, the child must have a well-developed image of the self. Yet in the first few years, the sense of self is not yet mature enough to serve as an anchor for one-time events (Howe, 2003). Second, autobiographical memory requires that children integrate personal experiences into a meaningful, time-organized life story. Preschoolers learn to structure memories in narrative form by talking about them with adults, who expand on their recollections by explaining what happened when, where, and with whom (Nelson, 1993).

During the preschool years, children's capacity to participate in memory-related conversations increases greatly—a change that may support the rise in autobiographical memories. Interestingly, parents talk about the past in more detail with preschool daughters than with preschool sons (Bruce, Dolan, & Phillips-Grant, 2000; Reese, Haden, & Fivush,

---

Netto, & Hernandez-Reif, 1998; Poulin-DuBois et al., 1994), have begun to distinguish emotional expressions, and can separate the natural movements of people from other motions (see Chapter 5, pages 198–199).

The earliest categories are *perceptual*—based on similar overall appearance or prominent object parts, such as legs for animals and wheels for vehicles. By the end of the first year, categories are becoming *conceptual*—based on common function and behavior (Cohen, 2003). Older infants can even make categorical distinctions when the perceptual contrast between two categories—animals and vehicles—is minimal (for an illustration, see Figure 6.8 on page 226).

In the second year, children become active categorizers. Around 12 months, toddlers touch objects that go together, without grouping them. Sixteen-month-olds can group objects into a single

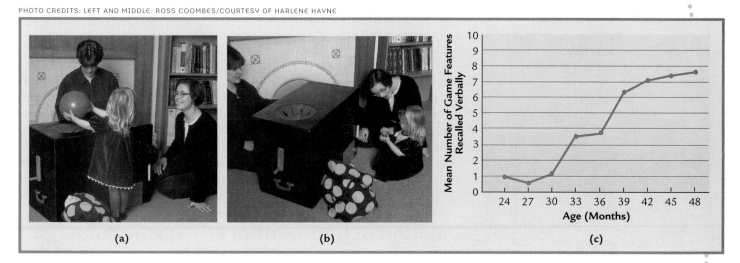

(a)   (b)   (c)

FIGURE 6.7

The Magic Shrinking Machine, used to test young children's verbal and nonverbal memory of an unusual event.

After being shown how the machine worked, the child participated in selecting objects from a polka-dot bag, dropping them into the top of the machine (a), and turning a crank, which produced a "shrunken" object (b). When tested the next day, 2- and 4-year-olds' nonverbal memory for the event was excellent. But below age 3, verbal recall was poor, based on the number of features recalled about the game during an open-ended interview (c). Recall improved between ages 3 and 4, the period during which infantile amnesia subsides. (From G. Simcock & H. Hayne, 2003, "Age-Related Changes in Verbal and Nonverbal Memory During Early Childhood," *Developmental Psychology, 39,* pp. 806, 808. Copyright © by the American Psychological Association. Reprinted by permission.)

1996). And collectivist cultural values lead Asian parents to discourage their children from talking about themselves (Han, Leichtman, & Wang, 1998). Perhaps because women's early experiences were integrated into more coherent narratives, they report an earlier age of first memory and more vivid early memories than men. Similarly, first memories of North American adults are, on average, 6 months earlier than those of Asians (Wang, 2003).

In sum, the decline of infantile amnesia seems to represent a change to which both biology and social experience contribute. Brain development and adult–child interaction jointly foster language and self-awareness, which permit children to converse with adults about important personal experiences. As a result, preschoolers begin to form an autobiography of their lives. In Chapters 8 and 12, we will see that deliberate, verbal recall improves greatly during childhood. It undoubtedly supports the success of conversations about the past in structuring children's autobiographical memories.

category. For example, when given four balls and four boxes, they put all the balls together but not the boxes. Around 18 months, toddlers can sort objects into two classes (Gopnik & Meltzoff, 1987). Compared with habituation/recovery, touching, sorting, and other play behaviors better reveal the meanings that toddlers attach to categories because they are applying those meanings in their everyday activities. For example, after having watched an experimenter give a toy dog a drink from a cup, 14-month-olds shown a rabbit and a motorcycle usually offer the drink only to the rabbit (Mandler & McDonough, 1998). Their behavior reveals a clear understanding that certain actions are appropriate for some categories of items (animals) and not for others (vehicles).

How does perceptual-to-conceptual change take place? Most researchers acknowledge that exploration of objects and expanding knowledge of the world contribute to older infants' capacity

FIGURE 6.8

Categorical distinction made by 9- to 11-month-olds.
After infants were given an opportunity to examine (by looking or touching) the objects in one category, they were shown a new object from each of the categories. They recovered to (spent more time looking at or touching) the object from the contrasting category, indicating that they distinguished the birds from the airplanes, despite their perceptual similarity. (Adapted from Mandler & McDonough, 1993.)

to move beyond physical features and group objects by their functions and behaviors (Madole & Oakes, 1999; Mandler, 1999). In addition, language both builds on and facilitates categorization. Adult labeling calls infants' attention to commonalities among objects and also promotes vocabulary growth. Toddlers' advancing vocabulary, in turn, is associated with advanced object-sorting behavior (Gopnik & Meltzoff, 1992; Waxman, 2003). Korean children, who learn a language in which object names are often omitted from sentences, develop object-grouping skills later than their English-speaking counterparts (Gopnik & Choi, 1990).

● Evaluation of Information-Processing Findings

The information-processing perspective underscores the continuity of human thinking from infancy into adult life. In attending to the environment, remembering everyday events, and categorizing objects, Caitlin, Grace, and Timmy think in ways that are remarkably similar to our own, even though they are far from being the proficient mental processors we are. Findings on infant memory and categorization join with other research in challenging Piaget's view of early cognitive development. If 2- to 3-month-olds can hold events in memory for as long as 1 week and categorize stimuli, then they clearly have some ability to mentally represent their experiences.

Information-processing research has contributed greatly to our view of infants and toddlers as sophisticated cognitive beings. Still, its greatest drawback stems from its central strength: By analyzing cognition into its components (such as perception, attention, memory, and categorization), information processing has had difficulty putting them back together into a broad, comprehensive theory. One approach to overcoming this weakness has been to combine Piaget's theory with the information-processing approach, an effort we will take up in Chapter 12. A more recent trend has been the application of a *dynamic systems view* to early cognition (see Chapter 1, page 29). In this approach, researchers analyze each cognitive attainment to see how it results from a complex system of prior accomplishments and the child's current goals (Courage & Howe, 2002; Thelen & Smith, 1998). These ideas have yet to be fully tested, but they may move the field closer to a more powerful view of how the mind of the infant and child develops.

The Social Context of Early Cognitive Development

Take a moment to review the short episode at the beginning of this chapter, in which Grace dropped shapes into a container. Notice that Grace learns about the toy with Ginette's help. With adult support, Grace will gradually become better at matching shapes to openings and dropping them into the container. Then she will be able to perform the activity (and others like it) on her own.

Vygotsky's sociocultural theory emphasizes that children live in rich social and cultural contexts that affect the way their cognitive world is structured (Rogoff, 1998; Wertsch & Tulviste, 1992). Vygotsky believed that complex mental activities, such as voluntary attention, deliberate memory, categorization, and problem solving, have their origins in social interaction. Through joint activities with more mature members of their society, children master activities and think in ways that have meaning in their culture.

A special Vygotskian concept explains how this happens. The **zone of proximal (or potential) development** refers to a range of tasks that the child cannot yet handle alone but can do with the help of more skilled partners. To understand this idea, think of a sensitive adult (such as Ginette) who introduces a child to a new activity. The adult picks a task that the child can master but that is challenging enough that the child cannot do it by herself. Or the adult capitalizes on an activity that the child has chosen. Then, as the adult guides and supports, the child joins in the interaction and picks up mental strategies, and her competence increases. When this happens, the adult steps back, permitting the child to take more responsibility for the task.

As we will see in Chapters 9 and 12, Vygotsky's ideas have been applied mostly at older ages, when children are more skilled in language and social communication. But recently, Vygotsky's theory has been extended to infancy and toddlerhood. Recall that babies are equipped with capabilities that ensure that caregivers will interact with them. Then adults adjust the environment and their communication in ways that promote learning adapted to their cultural circumstances.

This father assists his young son in putting together a puzzle through gentle physical support and simple words. By bringing the task within the child's zone of proximal development and adjusting his communication to suit the child's needs, the father transfers mental strategies to the child and promotes his cognitive development.

A study by Barbara Rogoff and her collaborators (1984) illustrates this process. The researchers watched how several adults played with Rogoff's son and daughter over the first 2 years while a jack-in-the-box toy was nearby. In the early months, adults tried to focus the baby's attention by working the toy and, as the bunny popped out, saying something like "My, what happened?" By the end of the first year (when the baby's cognitive and motor skills had improved), interaction centered on how to use the jack-in-the-box. When the infant reached for the toy, adults guided the baby's hand in turning the crank and putting the bunny back in the box. During the second year, adults helped from a distance. They used gestures and verbal prompts, such as rotating a hand in a turning motion near the crank. Research indicates that this fine-tuned support is related to advances in play, language, and problem solving during the second year (Bornstein et al., 1992b; Tamis-LeMonda & Bornstein, 1989).

As early as the first year, cultural variations in social experiences affect mental strategies. Note how, in the example just described, adults and children focused their attention on a single activity. This strategy, common in Western middle-SES homes, is well suited to lessons in which children learn skills apart from the everyday situations in which those skills will later be used. In contrast, Guatemalan Mayan adults and toddlers often attend to several events at once. For example, one 12-month-old skillfully put objects in a jar while watching a passing truck and blowing into a toy whistle his mother had slipped in his mouth (Chavajay & Rogoff, 1999). Processing several competing events simultaneously may be vital in cultures where children largely learn not through lessons but through keen observation of others at home, at work, and in public life.

Earlier we saw how infants and toddlers create new schemes by acting on the physical world (Piaget) and how certain skills become better developed as children represent their experiences more efficiently and meaningfully (information processing). Vygotsky adds a third dimension to our understanding by emphasizing that many aspects of cognitive development are socially mediated. The Cultural Influences box on page 228 presents additional evidence for this idea. And we see even more evidence in the next section, as we look at individual differences in mental development during the first 2 years.

Cultural Influences

Social Origins of Make-Believe Play

One of my husband Ken's activities with our two sons when they were young was to bake pineapple upside-down cake, a favorite treat. One Sunday afternoon when a cake was in the making, 21-month-old Peter stood on a chair at the kitchen sink, busily pouring water from one cup to another.

"He's in the way, Dad!" complained 4-year-old David, trying to pull Peter away from the sink.

"Maybe if we let him help, he'll give us some room," Ken suggested. As David stirred the batter, Ken poured some into a small bowl for Peter, moved his chair to the side of the sink, and handed him a spoon.

"Here's how you do it, Petey," instructed David, with an air of superiority. Peter watched as David stirred, then tried to copy his motion. When it was time to pour the batter, Ken helped Peter hold and tip the small bowl.

"Time to bake it," said Ken.

"Bake it, bake it," repeated Peter, as he watched Ken slip the pan into the oven.

Several hours later, we observed one of Peter's earliest instances of make-believe play. He got his pail from the sandbox and, after filling it with a handful of sand, carried it into the kitchen and put it down on the floor in front of the oven. "Bake it, bake it," Peter called to Ken. Together, father and son placed the pretend cake inside the oven.

Until recently, most researchers studied make-believe play apart from the social environment in which it occurs, while children played alone. Probably for this reason, Piaget and his followers concluded that toddlers discover make-believe independently, once they are capable of representational schemes. Vygotsky's theory has challenged this view. He believed that society provides children with opportunities to represent culturally meaningful activities in play. Make-believe, like other complex mental activities, is first learned under the guidance of experts (Berk, 2001a). In the example just described, Peter's capacity to represent daily events was extended when Ken drew him into the baking task and helped him act it out in play.

Current evidence supports the idea that early make-believe is the combined result of children's readiness to engage in it and social experiences that promote it. In one observational study of middle-SES toddlers, 75 to 80 percent of make-believe involved mother–child interaction (Haight & Miller, 1993). At 12 months, make-believe was fairly one-sided; almost all play episodes were initiated by mothers. By the end of the second year, mothers and children displayed mutual interest in getting make-believe started; half of pretend episodes were initiated by each.

When adults participate, toddlers' make-believe is more elaborate (O'Reilly & Bornstein, 1993). For example, play themes are more varied. And toddlers are more likely to combine schemes into complex sequences, as Peter did when he put the sand in the bucket ("making the batter"), carried it into the kitchen, and (with Ken's help) put it in the oven ("baking the cake"). The more parents pretend with their toddlers, the more time their children devote to make-believe. And in certain collectivist societies, such as Argentina and Japan, mother–toddler other-directed pretending, as in feeding or putting a doll to sleep, is particularly rich in maternal expressions of affection and praise (Bornstein et al., 1999a).

In some cultures, older siblings are toddlers' first play partners. For example, in Indonesia and Mexico, where extended-family households and sibling caregiving are common, make-believe is more frequent and complex with older siblings than with mothers. As early as 3 to 4 years of age, children provide rich, challenging stimulation to their younger brothers and sisters. The fantasy play of these toddlers is just as well developed as that of their middle-SES North American counterparts (Farver, 1993; Farver & Wimbarti, 1995).

In Western middle-SES families, as well, toddlers find older siblings' activities fascinating. In a study of New Zealand families of Western European descent, when both a parent and an older sibling were available, toddlers more often imitated the actions of the sibling. And the toddlers were especially interested in imitating when siblings engaged in make-believe or in routines (such as answering the phone or raking leaves) that could inspire pretending. Furthermore, toddlers' imitations included many actions with cultural significance that could be integrated into make-believe (Barr & Hayne, 2003). For example, some enacted behaviors unique to the New Zealand Maori culture, such as swinging a *poi* (an object used in a ceremonial dance). And imitating Western customs, such as shaking hands and clinking two classes together in a "cheers" gesture, was also common.

As we will see in Chapter 9, make-believe is a major means through which children extend their cognitive skills and learn about important activities in their culture. Vygotsky's theory, and the findings that support it, tell us that providing a stimulating environment is not enough to promote early cognitive development. In addition, toddlers must be invited and encouraged by more skilled members of their culture to participate in the social world around them. Parents and teachers can enhance early make-believe by playing often with toddlers and guiding and elaborating on their make-believe themes.

© KAREN HALVERSON/OMNI-PHOTO COMMUNICATIONS

In Mexico, where sibling caregiving is common, make-believe play is more frequent as well as complex with older siblings than with mothers. This 5-year-old provides rich, challenging stimulation to her toddler sister within a pretend-play scene.

Ask YOURSELF

www

REVIEW Cite evidence that categorization becomes less perceptual and more conceptual with age. What factors support this shift? How can adults facilitate the development of categorization?

APPLY Caitlin played with toys in a more intentional, goal-directed way as a toddler than as an infant. What impact is Caitlin's more advanced toy play likely to have on her development of attention? How is her cultural background likely to affect her attention?

CONNECT Review the research on page 215, indicating that by age 10 to 12 months, infants can solve problems by analogy. How might that capacity be related to a context-free memory, which develops about the same time?

REFLECT Describe your earliest autobiographical memory. How old were you when the event occurred? Do your responses fit with research on infantile amnesia?

Individual Differences in Early Mental Development

Recall from Chapter 5 that because of Grace's deprived early environment, Kevin and Monica had a child psychologist give her one of many tests available for assessing mental development in infants and toddlers. Worried about Timmy's progress, Vanessa also arranged for him to be tested. At age 22 months, he had only a handful of words in his vocabulary, played in a less mature way than Caitlin and Grace, and seemed restless and overactive.

The testing approach differs from the cognitive theories we have just discussed, which try to explain the *process* of development—how children's thinking changes over time. In contrast, designers of mental tests focus on cognitive *products.* They seek to measure behaviors that reflect mental development and to arrive at scores that *predict* future performance, such as later intelligence, school achievement, and adult vocational success. This concern with prediction arose nearly a century ago, when French psychologist Alfred Binet designed the first successful intelligence test, which predicted school achievement (see Chapter 1). It inspired the design of many new tests, including some that measure intelligence at very early ages.

Infant Intelligence Tests

Accurately measuring the intelligence of infants is challenging because they cannot answer questions or follow directions. All we can do is present them with stimuli, coax them to respond, and observe their behavior. As a result, most infant tests consist of perceptual and motor responses, along with a few tasks that tap early language and cognition. For example, the *Bayley Scales of Infant Development,* a commonly used test for children between 1 month and 3½ years, consists of two parts: (1) the Mental Scale, which includes such items as turning to a sound, looking for a fallen object, building a tower of cubes, and naming pictures; and (2) the Motor Scale, which assesses gross and fine motor skills, such as grasping, sitting, drinking from a cup, and jumping (Bayley, 1993).

A trained examiner tests this baby with the Bayley Scales of Infant Development while his father holds him and looks on. The perceptual and motor items on most infant tests are different from the tasks given to older children, which emphasize verbal, conceptual, and problem-solving skills. Among normally developing children, infant tests predict later intelligence poorly.

© LAURA DWIGHT/PHOTOEDIT

TABLE 6.3

Meaning of Different IQ Scores

SCORE	PERCENTILE RANK (CHILD DOES BETTER THAN ... PERCENT OF SAME-AGE CHILDREN)	
70	2	
85	16	
100 (average IQ)	50	
115	84	
130	98	

COMPUTING INTELLIGENCE TEST SCORES ● Intelligence tests for infants, children, and adults are scored in much the same way. When a test is constructed, it is given to a large, representative sample of individuals. Performances of people at each age level form a *normal,* or *bell-shaped, curve* in which most scores fall near the center (the mean or average) and progressively fewer fall toward the extremes. On the basis of this distribution, the test designer computes *norms,* or standards against which future test takers can be compared. For example, if Timmy does better than 50 percent of his agemates, his score will be 100, an average test score. If he exceeds most children his age, his score will be much higher. If he does better than only a small percentage of 2-year-olds, his score will be much lower.

A score computed in this way, permitting an individual's test performance to be compared with those of other same-age individuals, is called an **intelligence quotient,** or **IQ**—a term you have undoubtedly heard before. Table 6.3 describes the meaning of a range of IQ scores. Notice that the IQ offers a way of finding out whether a child is ahead, behind, or on time (average) in mental development in relation to other children of the same age. The great majority of individuals (96 percent) have IQs that fall between 70 and 130. Only a very few achieve higher or lower scores.

PREDICTING LATER PERFORMANCE FROM INFANT TESTS ● Many people assume, incorrectly, that IQ is a measure of inborn ability that does not change with age. Despite careful construction, most infant tests predict later intelligence poorly. Longitudinal research reveals that the majority of children show substantial fluctuations in IQ between toddlerhood and adolescence—10 to 20 points in most cases and sometimes much more (McCall, 1993).

Because infants and toddlers are especially likely to become distracted, fatigued, or bored during testing, their scores often do not reflect their true abilities. In addition, the perceptual and motor items on infant tests differ from the test questions given to older children, which emphasize verbal, conceptual, and problem-solving skills. Because of concerns that infant test scores do not tap the same dimensions of intelligence measured at older ages, they are conservatively labeled **developmental quotients,** or **DQs,** rather than IQs. Not until age 6 do IQ scores become stable, serving as reasonably good predictors of later performance (Hayslip, 1994).

Infant tests are somewhat better at making long-term predictions for extremely low-scoring babies. Today, they are used largely for *screening*—helping to identify for further observation and intervention babies whose very low scores mean that they are likely to have developmental problems in the future (Kopp, 1994).

Because infant tests do not predict later mental test scores for most children, researchers have turned to the information-processing approach to assess early mental progress. Their findings show that speed of habituation and recovery to visual stimuli are among the best available infant predictors of IQ from early childhood into adolescence, with correlations ranging from the .30s to the .60s (McCall & Carriger, 1993; Sigman, Cohen, & Beckwith, 1997). Habituation and recovery seem to be an especially effective early index of intelligence because they assess quickness of thinking, a characteristic of bright individuals. They also tap basic cognitive processes—attention, memory, and response to novelty—that underlie intelligent behavior at all ages (Colombo, 1995; Rose & Feldman, 1997).

Piagetian object permanence tasks also predict later IQ better than traditional infant tests, perhaps because they, too, reflect a basic intellectual process—problem solving (Rose, Feldman, & Wallace, 1992). The consistency of these findings prompted designers of the most recent edition of the Bayley test to include several items that tap cognitive skills, such as habituation/recovery, object permanence, and categorization.

Early Environment and Mental Development

In Chapter 2, we indicated that intelligence is a complex blend of hereditary and environmental influences. Many studies have examined the relationship of environmental factors to infant and toddler mental test scores. As we consider this evidence, you will encounter findings that highlight the role of heredity as well.

HOME ENVIRONMENT ● The Home Observation for Measurement of the Environment (HOME) is a checklist for gathering information about the quality of children's home lives through observation and parental interview (Caldwell & Bradley, 1994). Refer to Applying What We Know below for factors measured by HOME during the first 3 years. Each is positively related to toddlers' mental test performance. In addition, high HOME scores are associated with IQ gains between 1 and 3 years of age, whereas low HOME scores predict declines as large as 15 to 20 points (Bradley et al., 1989). Regardless of SES and ethnicity, an organized, stimulating physical setting and parental encouragement, involvement, and affection repeatedly predict IQ during the early years (Espy, Molfese, & DeLalla, 2001; Klebanov et al., 1998; Roberts, Burchinal, & Durham, 1999). The extent to which parents talk to infants and toddlers is particularly important. As the final section of this chapter will reveal, it contributes strongly to early language progress. Language progress, in turn, predicts intelligence and academic achievement in elementary school (Hart & Risley, 1995).

Yet we must interpret these correlational findings with caution. In all the studies, children were reared by their biological parents, with whom they share not just a common environment but also a common heredity. Parents who are genetically more intelligent might provide better experiences as well as give birth to genetically brighter children, who also evoke more stimulation from their parents. Note that this hypothesis refers to *genetic–environmental correlation* (see Chapter 2, pages 86–87), and research supports it. The HOME–mental development relationship is not as strong for adopted children as for biological children (Cherny, 1994). But heredity does not account for all of the correlation between home environment and mental tests scores. Family living conditions continue to predict children's IQ beyond the contribution of parental IQ and education (Chase-Lansdale et al., 1997; Klebanov et al., 1998). In one study, infants and children growing up in less crowded homes had parents who were far more verbally responsive to them—a major contributor to language, intellectual, and academic progress (Evans, Maxwell, & Hart, 1999).

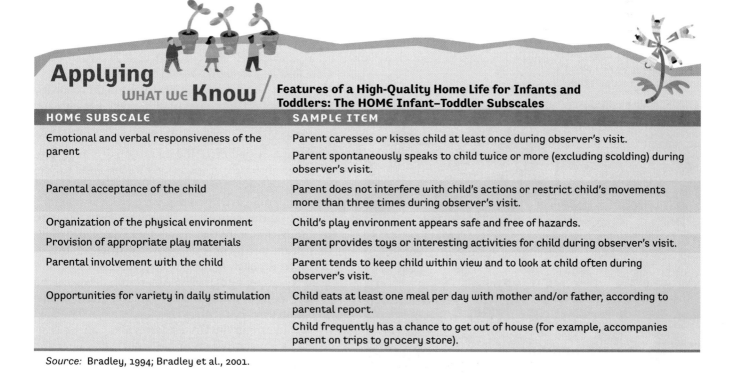

Applying
WHAT WE Know

Features of a High-Quality Home Life for Infants and Toddlers: The HOME Infant–Toddler Subscales

HOME SUBSCALE	SAMPLE ITEM
Emotional and verbal responsiveness of the parent	Parent caresses or kisses child at least once during observer's visit.
	Parent spontaneously speaks to child twice or more (excluding scolding) during observer's visit.
Parental acceptance of the child	Parent does not interfere with child's actions or restrict child's movements more than three times during observer's visit.
Organization of the physical environment	Child's play environment appears safe and free of hazards.
Provision of appropriate play materials	Parent provides toys or interesting activities for child during observer's visit.
Parental involvement with the child	Parent tends to keep child within view and to look at child often during observer's visit.
Opportunities for variety in daily stimulation	Child eats at least one meal per day with mother and/or father, according to parental report.
	Child frequently has a chance to get out of house (for example, accompanies parent on trips to grocery store).

Source: Bradley, 1994; Bradley et al., 2001.

Can the research summarized so far help us understand Vanessa's concern about Timmy's development? Indeed, it can. Ben, the psychologist who tested Timmy, found that he scored only slightly below average. Ben also talked with Vanessa about her child-rearing practices and watched her play with Timmy. A single parent, Vanessa worked long hours and had little energy for Timmy at the end of the day. Ben noticed that Vanessa, anxious about how well Timmy was doing, tended to pressure him. She constantly tried to dampen his active behavior and bombarded him with directions, such as "That's enough ball play. Stack these blocks." Ben explained that when parents are intrusive in these ways, infants and toddlers are likely to be distractible, to play immaturely, and to do poorly on mental tests (Fiese, 1990; Bono & Stifter, 2003). He coached Vanessa in how to interact sensitively with Timmy. At the same time, he assured her that Timmy's current performance need not forecast his future development. Warm, responsive parenting that builds on toddlers' current capacities is a much better indicator of how they will do later than is an early mental test score.

INFANT AND TODDLER CHILD CARE ● Home environments are not the only influential settings in which young children spend their days. Today, more than 60 percent of North American mothers with a child under age 2 are employed (Statistics Canada, 2002d; U.S. Census Bureau, 2003b). Child care for infants and toddlers has become common, and its quality has a major impact on mental development. American and Canadian research consistently shows that infants and young children exposed to poor-quality child care, regardless of whether they come from middle- or low-SES homes, score lower on measures of cognitive and social skills (Hausfather et al., 1997; Kohen et al., 2000; NICHD Early Child Care Research Network, 2000b, 2003b).

In contrast, good child care can reduce the negative impact of a stressed, poverty-stricken home life, and it sustains the benefits of growing up in an economically advantaged family (NICHD Early Child Care Research Network, 2003b; Lamb, 1998). In Swedish longitudinal research, entering high-quality child care in infancy and toddlerhood was associated with cognitive, emotional, and social competence in middle childhood and adolescence (Andersson, 1989, 1992; Broberg et al., 1997).

Visit some child-care settings, and take notes on what you see. In contrast to most European countries and to Australia and New Zealand, where child care is nationally regulated and funded to ensure its quality, reports on American and Canadian child care are cause for concern. Standards are set by the states and provinces and vary greatly across each nation. In some places, caregivers need no special training in child development, and one adult is permitted to care for 6 to 12 babies at once (Children's Defense Fund, 2003). In nationwide studies of child-care quality in the United States and Canada, only 20 to 25 percent of child-care centers and family child-care settings (in which a caregiver cares for children in her home) provided infants and toddlers with sufficiently positive, stimulating experiences to promote healthy psychological development; most settings offered substandard care (Doherty et al., 2000; Goelman et al., 2000; NICHD Early Child Care Research Network, 2000a).

Refer to Applying What We Know on the following page for signs of high-quality child care for infants and toddlers, based on standards for **developmentally appropriate practice.** These standards, devised by the U.S. National Association for the Education of Young Children, specify program characteristics that meet the developmental and individual needs of young children, based on both current research and consensus among experts. Caitlin, Grace, and Timmy are fortunate to be in family child care that meets these standards. Children from low-income and poverty-stricken families are especially likely to have inadequate child care (Pungello & Kurtz-Costes, 1999). As a result, they receive a double dose of vulnerability—at home and in the child-care environment.

Child care in the United States and Canada is affected by a macrosystem of individualistic values and weak government regulation and funding. Further-

This child-care center meets rigorous, professionally established standards of quality. A generous caregiver–child ratio, a limited number of children in each room, an environment with appropriate equipment and toys, and training in child development enable caregivers to respond to infants' and toddlers' needs to be held, comforted, and stimulated.

© B. MAHONEY/THE IMAGE WORKS

Applying
WHAT WE **Know** / **Signs of Developmentally Appropriate Infant and Toddler Child Care**

PROGRAM CHARACTERISTIC	SIGNS OF QUALITY
Physical setting	Indoor environment is clean, in good repair, well lighted, and well ventilated. Fenced outdoor play space is available. Setting does not appear overcrowded when children are present.
Toys and equipment	Play materials are appropriate for infants and toddlers and are stored on low shelves within easy reach. Cribs, high chairs, infant seats, and child-sized tables and chairs are available. Outdoor equipment includes small riding toys, swings, slide, and sandbox.
Caregiver–child ratio	In child-care centers, caregiver–child ratio is no greater than 1 to 3 for infants and 1 to 6 for toddlers. Group size (number of children in one room) is no greater than 6 infants with 2 caregivers and 12 toddlers with 2 caregivers. In family child care, caregiver is responsible for no more than 6 children; within this group, no more than 2 are infants and toddlers. Staffing is consistent, so infants and toddlers can form relationships with particular caregivers.
Daily activities	Daily schedule includes times for active play, quiet play, naps, snacks, and meals. It is flexible rather than rigid, to meet the needs of individual children. Atmosphere is warm and supportive, and children are never left unsupervised.
Interactions among adults and children	Caregivers respond promptly to infants' and toddlers' distress; hold, talk to, sing, and read to them; and interact with them in a manner that respects the individual child's interests and tolerance for stimulation.
Caregiver qualifications	Caregiver has some training in child development, first aid, and safety.
Relationships with parents	Parents are welcome anytime. Caregivers talk frequently with parents about children's behavior and development.
Licensing and accreditation	Child-care setting, whether a center or a home, is licensed by the state or province. In the United States, voluntary accreditation by the National Academy of Early Childhood Programs, *www.naeyc.org/accreditation*, or the National Association for Family Child Care, *www.nafcc.org*, is evidence of an especially high-quality program. Canada is working on a voluntary accreditation system, under the leadership of the Canadian Child Care Federation, *www.cccf-fcsge.ca*. The province of Alberta has already begun to test an accreditation model.

Sources: Bredekamp & Copple, 1997; National Association for the Education of Young Children, 1998.

more, many parents think their children's child-care experiences are better than they actually are (Helburn, 1995). Inability to identify good care means that many parents do not demand it. Yet nations that invest in child care have selected a highly cost-effective means of protecting children's well-being. Much like the programs we are about to consider, excellent child care can serve as effective early intervention for children whose development is at risk.

Early Intervention for At-Risk Infants and Toddlers

Many studies indicate that children living in poverty are likely to show gradual declines in intelligence test scores and to achieve poorly when they reach school age. These problems are largely due to disorganized, stressful home environments that undermine children's ability to learn and increase the chances that they will remain poor throughout their lives (Bradley et al., 2001; Brody, 1997). A variety of intervention programs have been developed to break this tragic cycle of poverty. Although most begin during the preschool years (we will discuss those in Chapter 9), a few start during infancy and continue through early childhood.

Some interventions are center based; children attend an organized child-care or preschool program where they receive educational, nutritional, and health services, and child-rearing and other social service supports are provided to parents as well. Other interventions are home based. A skilled adult visits the home and works with parents, teaching them how to stimulate a very young child's development. In most programs, participating children score higher on mental tests by age 2 than do untreated controls. These gains persist as long as the program lasts and occasionally longer. The more intense the intervention (for example, full-day, year-round, high-quality child care plus support services for parents), the better children's cognitive and academic performance during the school years (Ramey, Campbell, & Ramey, 1999).

The Carolina Abecedarian Project illustrates these positive outcomes. In the 1970s, more than one hundred 3-week- to 3-month-old infants from poverty-stricken families were randomly assigned to either a treatment group or a control group. Treatment infants were enrolled in full-time, year-round child care through the preschool years. There they received stimulation aimed at promoting motor, cognitive, language, and social skills and, after age 3, literacy and math concepts. At all ages, special emphasis was placed on rich, responsive adult–child verbal communication. All children received nutrition and health services; the primary difference between treatment and controls was the child-care experience.

As Figure 6.9 shows, by 12 months of age, the IQs of the two groups diverged. Treatment children maintained their advantage when last tested—at 21 years of age. In addition, throughout their years of schooling, treatment youths achieved considerably better in reading and math. These gains translated into more years of schooling completed and higher rates of college enrollment and employment in skilled jobs for the treatment group than for the control group (Campbell et al., 2001, 2002; Ramey & Ramey, 1999). While the children were in elementary school, the researchers conducted a second experiment to compare the impact of early and later intervention. From kindergarten through second grade, half the treatment group and half the control group were provided a resource teacher, who introduced into the home educational activities addressing the child's specific learning needs. School-age intervention had no impact on IQ. And although it enhanced children's academic achievement, the effects were weaker than the impact of very early intervention (Campbell & Ramey, 1995).

Without some form of early intervention, many children born into economically disadvantaged families will not reach their potential. Recognition of this reality led the U.S. Congress to provide limited funding for intervention services directed at infants and toddlers who already have serious developmental problems or who are at risk for problems because of poverty. At present, available programs are not nearly enough to meet the need (Children's Defense Fund, 2003). Nevertheless, those that exist are a promising beginning.

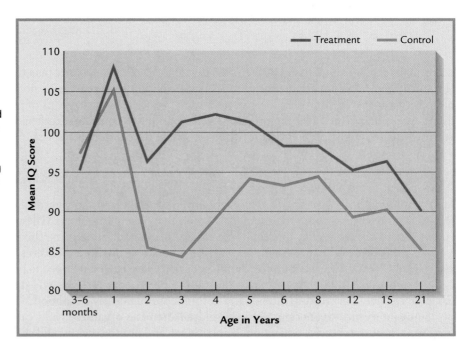

FIGURE 6.9

IQ scores of treatment and control children from infancy to 21 years in the Carolina Abecedarian Project.

At 1 year, treatment children outperformed controls, an advantage consistently maintained through 21 years of age. The IQ scores of both groups declined gradually during the school years—a trend probably due to the damaging impact of poverty on mental development. (Adapted from Campbell et al., 2001.)

www

ASK YOURSELF

REVIEW What probably accounts for the finding that speed of habituation and recovery to visual stimuli predicts later IQ better than an infant mental test score?

APPLY Fifteen-month-old Joey's developmental quotient (DQ) is 115. His mother wants to know exactly what this means and what she should do at home to support his mental development. How would you respond to her questions?

CONNECT Using what you learned about brain development in Chapter 5, explain why intensive intervention for poverty-stricken children beginning in the first 2 years has a greater impact on IQ than intervention at a later age.

REFLECT Suppose you were seeking a child-care setting for your baby. What would you want it to be like, and why?

Language Development

As perception and cognition improve during infancy, they pave the way for an extraordinary human achievement—language. On the average, children say their first word at 12 months of age, with a range of about 8 to 18 months. Once words appear, language develops rapidly. Sometime between 1½ and 2 years, toddlers combine two words (Bloom, 1998). By age 6, children have a vocabulary of about 10,000 words, speak in elaborate sentences, and are skilled conversationalists.

To appreciate what an awesome task this is, think about the many abilities involved in your own flexible use of language. When you speak, you must select words that match the underlying concepts you want to convey. Then you must combine them into phrases and sentences using a complex set of grammatical rules. Next, you must pronounce these utterances correctly, or you will not be understood. Finally, you must follow the rules of everyday conversation. For example, if you do not take turns, make comments that are relevant to what your partner just said, and use an appropriate tone of voice, then no matter how clear and correct your language, others may refuse to listen to you.

Infants and toddlers make remarkable progress in getting these skills under way. How do they do so? Let's begin to address this question by examining several prominent theories, based on what we know about the beginnings of language in the first 2 years.

Infants are communicative beings from the start, as this interaction between a 6-month-old and his grandfather indicates. How will he accomplish the awesome task of becoming a speaker of his native language? Theorists disagree sharply on answers to this question.

© LAURA DWIGHT/OMNI-PHOTO COMMUNICATIONS

Three Theories of Language Development

In the 1950s, researchers did not take seriously the idea that very young children might be able to figure out important properties of the language they hear. As a result, the first two theories of how children acquire language were extreme views. One, *behaviorism,* regards language development as entirely due to environmental influences. The second, *nativism,* assumes that children are "prewired" to master the intricate rules of their language.

THE BEHAVIORIST PERSPECTIVE ● Behaviorist B. F. Skinner (1957) proposed that language, like any other behavior, is acquired through *operant conditioning.* As the baby makes sounds, parents reinforce those that are most like words with smiles, hugs, and speech in return. For example, at 12 months, my older son, David, often babbled something like this: "book-a-book-a-dook-a-dook-a-book-a-nook-a-book-aaa." One day while he babbled away, I held up his picture book and said, "Book!" Very soon David was saying "book-aaa" in the presence of books.

Some behaviorists say children rely on *imitation* to rapidly acquire complex utterances, such as whole phrases and sentences (Moerk, 1992). And imitation can combine with reinforcement to promote language, as when the parent coaxes, "Say 'I want a cookie,'" and delivers praise and a treat after the toddler responds, "Wanna cookie!"

Although reinforcement and imitation contribute to early language development, they are best viewed as supporting rather than fully explaining it. As Carolyn remarked one day, "It's amazing how creative Caitlin is with language. She combines words in ways she's never heard before, such as 'needle it' when she wants me to sew up her teddy bear and 'allgone outside' when she has to come in." Carolyn's observations are accurate: Young children create many novel utterances that are not reinforced by or copied from others.

THE NATIVIST PERSPECTIVE ● Linguist Noam Chomsky (1957) proposed a nativist theory that regards the young child's amazing language skill as etched into the structure of the human brain. Focusing on grammar, Chomsky reasoned that the rules of sentence organization are much too complex to be directly taught to or independently discovered by a young child. Instead, he argued, all children are born with a **language acquisition device (LAD)**, an innate system that contains a set of rules common to all languages. It permits children, no matter which language they hear, to speak in a rule-oriented fashion as soon as they pick up enough words.

Are children biologically primed to acquire language? Recall from Chapter 4 that newborn babies are remarkably sensitive to speech sounds and prefer to listen to the human voice. In addition, children the world over reach major language milestones in a similar sequence—evidence that fits with a biologically based language program (Gleitman & Newport, 1996). Furthermore, efforts to teach language to nonhuman primates—using either specially devised artificial symbol systems or American Sign Language, a gestural language used by the deaf—have met with limited success (Miles, 1999). After extensive training, apes master only a basic vocabulary, and they do not acquire complex grammatical forms—findings consistent with Chomsky's view that humans are uniquely prepared for language.

Evidence for specialized language areas in the brain and a sensitive period for language development have also been interpreted as supporting Chomsky's theory. Let's take a closer look at these findings.

Language Areas in the Brain. Humans have evolved specialized regions in the brain that support language skills. Recall from Chapter 5 that for most people, language is housed in the left hemisphere of the cerebral cortex. Within it are two language-specific structures (see Figure 6.10). **Broca's area,** located in the left frontal lobe, controls language production. **Wernicke's area,** located in the left temporal lobe, is responsible for interpreting language.

Although Broca's and Wernicke's areas have been taken as support for an LAD, we must be cautious about this conclusion. In Chapter 5 we noted that at birth, the brain is not fully lateralized; instead, it is highly plastic. As children acquire language, the brain becomes more specialized. Furthermore, if the left hemisphere is injured in the early years, other regions take over its language functions (see page 172). So rather than the brain being innately programmed for language, language-learning experience leads certain brain areas to become dedicated to language (Bates, 1999). Other research indicates that many parts of the brain participate in language activities to differing degrees, depending on the particular language skill and the individual's mastery of that skill (Huttenlocher, 2002; Neville & Bavelier, 1998).

A Sensitive Period for Language Development. Must language be acquired early in life, during an age span in which the brain is particularly responsive to language stimulation? Evi-

FIGURE 6.10

Language-specific structures in the left hemisphere of the cerebral cortex.

Broca's area controls language production by creating a detailed program for speaking, which it sends to the face area of the cortical region that controls body movement and coordination. *Wernicke's area* interprets language by receiving impulses from the primary auditory area, where sensations from the ears are sent. To produce a verbal response, Wernicke's area communicates with Broca's area through a bundle of nerve fibers, represented by dotted lines in the figure.

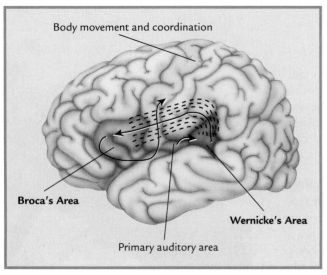

Body movement and coordination

Broca's Area

Wernicke's Area

Primary auditory area

dence for a sensitive period that coincides with brain lateralization would support the view that babies have a biological readiness to acquire language.

To test this idea, researchers tracked the recovery of severely abused children who experienced little human contact in childhood. The most thoroughly studied is Genie, a normally developing child who said her first words just before she was isolated in the back room of her parents' house at 1½ years of age. Until she was found at 13½, no one talked to her, and she was beaten when she made any noise. With several years of training by dedicated teachers, Genie's language developed to some extent. She acquired a large vocabulary and good comprehension of conversation, but her grammar and communication skills were limited (Curtiss, 1977, 1989). Genie's case and others like it fit with the notion of a sensitive period, although a precise age cutoff for a decline in language competence has not been established.

What about acquiring a second language? Is this task harder after a sensitive period has passed? In one study, researchers examined U.S. census data, selecting immigrants from non-English-speaking countries who had resided in the United States for at least 10 years. The census form had asked the immigrants to rate how competently they spoke English, from "not at all" to "very well"—self-reports that correlate strongly with objective language measures. As age of immigration increased from infancy and early childhood into adulthood, English proficiency declined (Hakuta, Bialystok, & Wiley, 2003). Similar trends exist for adults who became deaf at varying ages and learned American Sign Language as their second language (Mayberry, 1994; Newport, 1991). Furthermore, brain-wave (EEG) and brain-imaging (fMRI) measures of neural activity indicate that second-language processing is less lateralized in older than in younger learners (Neville & Bruer, 2001). However, the capacity to acquire a second language does not drop sharply at a certain age. Instead, a gradual, age-related decrease occurs.

In sum, research on both first- and second-language learning reveals a biologically based time frame for optimum language development. However, the boundaries of this sensitive period remain unclear.

LIMITATIONS OF THE NATIVIST PERSPECTIVE ● Chomsky's theory has had a major impact on current views of language development. It is now widely accepted that humans have a unique, biological predisposition to acquire language. Yet as we have seen, the biological basis of Chomsky's LAD is far from clear. And his account of development has been challenged on other grounds.

First, researchers have had great difficulty identifying the single system of grammar that Chomsky believes underlies all languages. Even seemingly simple grammatical distinctions, such as the use of *the* versus *a* in English, are made in quite different ways around the world. For example, several African languages rely on tone patterns to express these articles. In Japanese and Chinese, they are inferred entirely from sentence context. Critics of Chomsky's theory doubt the existence of an LAD that can account for such varied approaches to conveying the same meaning (Maratsos, 1998; Tomasello, 1995).

Second, Chomsky's assumption that grammatical knowledge is innately determined does not fit with certain observations of language development. Although children make extraordinary strides during the early years, they acquire many sentence constructions gradually. As we will see in Chapter 12, complete mastery of some grammatical forms is not achieved until well into middle childhood (Tager-Flusberg, 2001). This suggests that more learning and discovery are involved than Chomsky assumed.

THE INTERACTIONIST PERSPECTIVE ● Recent ideas about language development emphasize *interactions* between inner capacities and environmental influences. Although several interactionist theories exist, all stress the social context of language learning. An active child, well endowed for acquiring language, observes and participates in social exchanges. From these experiences, children gradually discover the functions and regularities of language. According to the interactionist position, native capacity, a strong desire to interact with others, and a rich language and social environment combine to help children build a communicative system. And because genetic and environmental contributions vary across children, the interactionist perspective predicts individual differences in language learning (Bohannon & Bonvillian, 2001; Chapman, 2000).

TABLE **6.4**

Milestones of Language Development During the First Two Years

APPROXIMATE AGE	MILESTONE
2 months	Infants coo, making pleasant vowel sounds.
4 months on	Infants babble, adding consonants to their cooing sounds and repeating syllables. By 7 months, babbling starts to include many sounds of spoken languages.
	Infants observe with interest as the caregiver plays turn-taking games, such as pat-a-cake and peekaboo.
8–12 months	Infants comprehend some words.
	Infants become more accurate at establishing joint attention with the caregiver, who often verbally labels what the baby is looking at.
	Infants actively participate in turn-taking games, trading roles with the caregiver.
	Infants use preverbal gestures, such as showing and pointing, to influence the behavior of others.
12 months	Babbling includes sound and intonation patterns of the child's language community.
	Toddlers say their first recognizable word.
18–24 months	Vocabulary expands from about 50 to 200 spoken words.
	Toddlers combine two words.

Even among interactionists, debate continues over the precise nature of innate language abilities. Some theorists accept a modified view of Chomsky's position. They believe that children are primed to acquire language but form and refine hypotheses about its structure on the basis of experiences (Slobin, 1997). Others believe that children make sense of their complex language environments by applying powerful, general cognitive strategies—such as searching for patterns in the buzz of talk around them—rather than strategies specifically tuned to language (Bates, 1999; Tomasello, 2003).

As we chart the course of early language development, we will see a great deal of evidence that supports interactionists' ideas. But none of these theories has yet been fully tested. In reality, biology, cognition, and social experience may operate in different balances with respect to various aspects of language: pronunciation, vocabulary, grammar, and communication skills. Table 6.4 provides an overview of early language milestones that we will take up in the next few sections.

● Getting Ready to Talk

Before babies say their first word, they make impressive progress toward understanding and speaking their native tongue. They listen attentively to human speech, and they make speech-like sounds. As adults, we can hardly help but respond.

COOING AND BABBLING ● Around 2 months, babies begin to make vowel-like noises, which are called **cooing** because of their pleasant "oo" quality. Gradually, consonants are added, and around 4 months **babbling** appears, in which infants repeat consonant–vowel combinations in long strings, such as "babababa" or "nanananana."

The timing of early babbling seems to be due to brain maturation because babies everywhere (even those who are deaf) start babbling at about the same age and produce a similar range of early sounds. But for babbling to develop further, infants must be able to hear human speech. If a baby's hearing is impaired, these speechlike sounds are greatly delayed or, in the case of deaf infants, are totally absent (Eilers & Oller, 1994; Oller, 2000).

When a baby coos or babbles and gazes at you, what are you likely to do? One day, as I stood in line at the post office behind a mother and her 7-month-old daughter, the baby babbled, and three adults—myself and two people standing beside me—started to talk to the infant. We cooed and babbled ourselves, imitating the baby, and also said such things as "My, you're a big girl, aren't you? Out to help Mommy mail letters today?" The baby smiled and babbled all the more. As infants listen to spoken language, babbling increases. Around 7 months, it starts to include many sounds of spoken languages. And by 1 year, it contains the consonant–vowel and intonation patterns of the child's language community (Levitt & Utmann, 1992).

Deaf infants exposed to sign language from birth babble with their hands in much the same way hearing infants do through speech (Petitto & Marentette, 1991). Furthermore, hearing babies who have deaf, signing parents produce babblelike hand motions with the rhythmic patterns of natural language (Petitto et al., 2001). Infants' sensitivity to language rhythm, evident in both spoken and signed babbling, may help them discover and produce meaningful language units. And through babbling, babies seem to experiment with a great many sounds that they can blend into their first words.

BECOMING A COMMUNICATOR ● Besides responding to cooing and babbling, adults interact with infants in many other situations. By age 4 months, infants start to gaze in the same direction as adults are looking, a skill that becomes more accurate between 9 and 15 months (Tomasello, 1999b). Adults also follow the baby's line of vision and comment on what the infant sees. In this way, they label the baby's environment. This **joint attention, in which the child attends to the same object or event as the caregiver, who offers verbal information,** contributes greatly to early language development. Infants and toddlers who often experience it sustain attention longer, talk earlier, and show faster vocabulary development (Carpenter, Nagel, & Tomasello, 1998; Flom & Pick, 2003; Silvén, 2001). Gains in joint attention at the end of the first year suggest that infants are beginning to appreciate that other people have intentions, or goals, just as they themselves do. This permits the child to establish a "common ground" with the adult, through which the child can figure out the meaning of the adult's verbal labels (Tomasello, 2003).

Interactions between caregivers and babies also include give-and-take, as in turn-taking games such as pat-a-cake and peekaboo. At first, the parent starts the game and the baby is an amused observer. Nevertheless, 4-month-olds are sensitive to the structure and timing of these interactions, smiling more to an organized than to a disorganized peekaboo exchange (Rochat, Querido, & Striano, 1999). By 12 months, babies participate actively, trading roles with the caregiver. As they do so, they practice the turn-taking pattern of human conversation, a vital context for acquiring language and communication skills. Infants' play maturity and vocalizations during games predict advanced language progress between 1 and 2 years of age (Rome-Flanders & Cronk, 1995).

As 8- to 12-month-olds become capable of intentional behavior, they use preverbal gestures to influence the behavior of others (Carpenter, Nagel, & Tomasello, 1998). For example, Caitlin held up a toy to show it and pointed to the cupboard when she wanted a cookie. Carolyn responded to her gestures and also labeled them ("That's your bear!"; "Oh, you want a cookie!"). In this way, toddlers learn that using language leads to desired results. Soon they utter words with their reaching and pointing gestures, the gestures recede, and spoken language is under way (Namy & Waxman, 1998).

This 15-month-old delights in playing peekaboo with her mother. As she participates, she practices the turn-taking pattern of human conversation.

© TONY FREEMAN/PHOTOEDIT

First Words

In the middle of the first year, infants begin to understand word meanings. When 6-month-olds listened to the words "mommy" and "daddy" while looking at side-by-side videos of their parents, they looked longer at the video of the named parent (Tincoff & Jusczyk, 1999). First spoken words, around 1 year, build on the sensorimotor foundations Piaget described and on categories children form during infancy and toddlerhood. Earliest words usually refer to important people ("Mama," "Dada"), objects that move ("ball," "car," "cat," "shoe"), familiar actions ("bye-bye," "up," "more"), or outcomes of familiar actions ("dirty," "hot," "wet"). In their first 50 words, toddlers rarely name things that just *sit there,* like "table" or "vase" (Nelson, 1973).

Some early words are linked to specific cognitive achievements. For example, about the time toddlers master advanced object permanence problems, they use disappearance words, such as "all gone." And success and failure expressions, such as "There!" and "Uh-oh!", appear when toddlers can solve problems suddenly rather than through trial and error. According to one pair of researchers, "Children seem to be motivated to acquire words that are relevant to the particular cognitive problems they are working on at the moment" (Gopnik & Meltzoff, 1986, p. 1057).

Besides cognition, emotion influences early word learning. At first, when acquiring a new word for an object, person, or event, 1½-year-olds say it neutrally; they need to listen carefully to learn, and strong emotion diverts their attention. As words become better learned, toddlers integrate talking and expressing feelings (Bloom, 1998). "Shoe!" 22-month-old Grace said enthusiastically, as Monica tied her shoelaces before an outing. At the end of the second year, toddlers label their emotions with words like "happy," "mad," and "sad"—a development we will consider further in Chapter 7.

When young children first learn words, they sometimes apply them too narrowly, an error called **underextension.** For example, at 16 months, Caitlin used "bear" only to refer to the worn and tattered teddy bear she carried around much of the day. A more common error is **overextension**—applying a word to a wider collection of objects and events than is appropriate. For example, Grace used the word "car" for buses, trains, trucks, and fire engines. Toddlers' overextensions reflect their sensitivity to categories. They apply a new word to a group of similar experiences, such as "dog" to refer to furry, four-legged animals and "open" to mean opening a door, peeling fruit, and untying shoelaces. This suggests that children sometimes overextend deliberately because they have difficulty recalling or have not acquired a suitable word. In addition, when a word is hard to pronounce, toddlers are likely to substitute a related one they can say (Bloom, 2000; Elsen, 1994). As vocabulary and pronunciation improve, overextensions disappear.

The Two-Word Utterance Phase

At first, toddlers add to their vocabularies slowly, at a rate of 1 to 3 words a month. Between 18 and 24 months, a spurt in vocabulary often takes place. The speed of identifying words in spoken sentences picks up, and memory, categorization, and ability to detect a speaking partner's intentions also improve. As a result, many children add 10 to 20 new words a week (Dapretto & Bjork, 2000; Fenson et al., 1994; Fernald, Swingley, & Pinto, 2001). When vocabulary approaches 200 words, toddlers start to combine two words, such as "Mommy shoe," "go car," and "my truck." These two-word utterances are called **telegraphic speech** because, like a telegram, they focus on high-content words and leave out smaller and less important ones, such as "can," "the," and "to."

Children the world over use two-word utterances to express an impressive variety of meanings. But they do not yet apply a consistent grammar. Two-word speech is largely made up of simple formulas, such as "want + X" and "more + X," with many different words inserted in the X position. Although toddlers rarely make gross grammatical errors, such as saying "chair my" instead of "my chair," they can be heard violating the rules. For example, at 20 months, Caitlin said "more hot" and "more read," expressions not acceptable in English grammar. The word-order regularities in toddlers' two-word utterances are usually copies of adult word pairings, as when Carolyn remarked to Caitlin, "That's *my book*" or "How about *more sandwich*?" (Tomasello & Brooks, 1999). When 18- to 23-month-olds were taught noun and verb nonsense words (for example, "meek" for a doll and "gop" for a snapping action), they easily combined the new nouns with words they knew well, as in "more meek." But they seldom formed word combinations with the new verbs (Tomasello et al., 1997). This suggests that they did not yet grasp subject–verb and verb–object relations, which are the foundation of grammar.

In sum, toddlers are absorbed in figuring out word meanings and using their limited vocabularies in whatever way possible to get their thoughts across (Maratsos, 1998). But it does not take long for children to figure out grammatical rules. As we will see in Chapter 9, the beginnings of grammar are in place by age 2½.

Comprehension versus Production

So far, we have focused on language **production**—the words and word combinations children use. What about **comprehension**—the language they understand? At all ages, comprehension develops ahead of production. For example, toddlers follow many simple directions, such as "Bring me your book" or "Don't touch the lamp," even though they cannot yet express all these words in their own speech. A 5-month lag exists between the time children comprehend 50 words (around 13 months) and the time they produce that many (around 18 months) (Menyuk, Liebergott, & Schultz, 1995).

Why is comprehension ahead of production? Think back to the distinction made earlier in this chapter between two types of memory—recognition and recall. Comprehension requires only that children recognize the meaning of a word. Production is more difficult because children must recall, or actively retrieve from their memories, the word as well as the concept for which it stands. Failure to say a word does not mean that toddlers do not understand it. If we rely only on what children say, we will underestimate their language progress.

Individual and Cultural Differences

Each child's progress in acquiring language results from a complex blend of biological and environmental influences. For example, earlier we saw that Timmy's spoken language was delayed, in part because of Vanessa's tense, directive communication with him. But Timmy is also a boy, and many studies show that girls are slightly ahead of boys in early vocabulary growth (Fenson et al., 1994). The most common biological explanation is girls' faster rate of physical maturation, which is believed to promote earlier development of the left cerebral hemisphere, where language is housed. But perhaps because of girls' slight language advantage, mothers also talk more to toddler-age girls than boys (Leaper, Anderson, & Sanders, 1998). So girls add vocabulary more quickly for both genetic and environmental reasons.

Besides the child's sex, temperament and life circumstances make a difference. Reserved, cautious toddlers often wait until they understand a great deal before trying to speak. When they finally do speak, their vocabularies grow rapidly (Nelson, 1973). In the week after her adoption, 16-month-old Grace spoke only a single Cambodian word, saying it when by herself. For the next 2 months, Grace listened to English conversation without speaking—a "silent period" typical of children beginning to acquire a second language (Saville-Troike, 1988). Around 18 months, words came quickly—first "Eli," then "doggie," "kitty," "Mama," "Dada," "book," "ball," "car," "cup," "clock," and "chicken," all within one week.

Young children have unique styles of early language learning. Caitlin and Grace, like most

This Korean toddler, adopted during the second year of life, said little for several months as she listened to new language sounds and tried to make sense of them. But now, at age 2, she speaks enthusiastically while playing with her father.

toddlers, used a **referential style;** their vocabularies consisted mainly of words that referred to objects. A smaller number of toddlers use an **expressive style;** compared to referential children, they produce many more social formulas and pronouns, such as "stop it," "thank you," and "I want it," uttered as compressed phrases, much like single words (as in "Iwannit"). These styles reflect early ideas about the functions of language. Grace, for example, thought words were for naming things. In contrast, expressive-style children believe words are for talking about people's feelings and needs. The vocabularies of referential-style children grow faster because all languages contain many more object labels than social phrases (Bates et al., 1994).

What accounts for a toddler's choice of a particular language style? Once again, both biological and environmental factors are involved. Rapidly developing referential-style children often have an especially active interest in exploring objects. They also eagerly imitate their parents' frequent naming of objects, and their parents imitate back—a strategy that supports swift vocabulary growth by helping children remember new labels (Masur & Rodemaker, 1999). Expressive-style children tend to be highly sociable, and their parents more often use verbal routines ("How are you?" "It's no trouble") that support social relationships (Goldfield, 1987). The two language styles are also linked to culture. Whereas object words (nouns) are particularly common in the vocabularies of English-speaking toddlers, action words (verbs) and social routines are more numerous among Japanese, Korean, and Chinese toddlers. When mothers' speech is examined in each culture, it reflects this difference (Choi & Gopnik, 1995; Fernald & Morikawa, 1993; Tardif, Gelman, & Xu, 1999).

At what point should parents be concerned if their child does not talk or says very little? If a toddler's development is greatly delayed when compared with the norms in Table 6.4, then parents should consult the child's doctor or a speech and language therapist. Late babbling may be a sign of slow language development that can be prevented with early intervention (Oller et al., 1999). Some toddlers who do not follow simple directions or who, after age 2, have difficulty putting their thoughts into words may suffer from a hearing impairment or a language disorder that requires immediate treatment (Ratner, 2001).

Supporting Early Language Development

There is little doubt that children are specially prepared for acquiring language, since no other species can develop as flexible and creative a capacity for communication as we can. Yet consistent with the interactionist view, a rich social environment builds on young children's natural readiness to speak their native tongue. For a summary of how caregivers can consciously support early language learning, see Applying What We Know on the following page. Caregivers also do so unconsciously—through a special style of speech.

Adults in many countries speak to young children in **child-directed speech (CDS),** a form of language made up of short sentences with high-pitched, exaggerated expression, clear pronunciation, distinct pauses between speech segments, and repetition of new words in a variety of contexts ("See the ball." "The ball bounced!") (Fernald et al., 1989; Kuhl, 2000). Deaf parents use a similar style of communication when signing to their babies (Masataka, 1996). CDS builds on several communicative strategies we have already considered: joint attention, turn-taking, and caregivers' sensitivity to toddlers' preverbal gestures. Here is an example of Carolyn using CDS with 18-month-old Caitlin as she picked her up from child care:

Caitlin: "Go car."

Carolyn: "Yes, time to go in the car. Where's your jacket?"

Caitlin: [looks around, walks to the closet] "Dacket!" [pointing to her jacket]

Carolyn: "There's that jacket! [She helps Caitlin into the jacket.] On it goes! Let's zip up. [Zips up the jacket.] Now, say bye-bye to Grace and Timmy."

Caitlin: "Bye-bye, G-ace."

Carolyn: "What about Timmy? Bye to Timmy?"

Caitlin: "Bye-bye, Te-te."

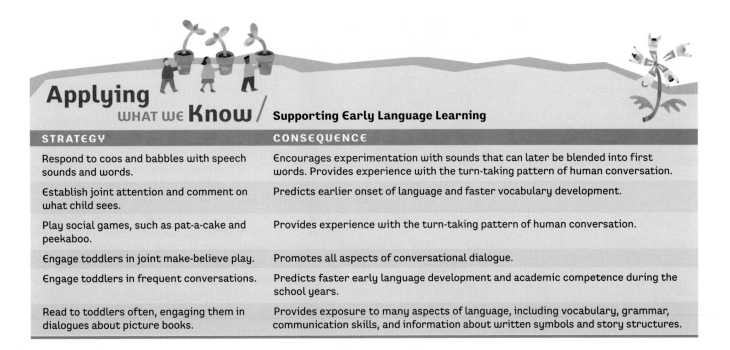

Applying WHAT WE Know / Supporting Early Language Learning

STRATEGY	CONSEQUENCE
Respond to coos and babbles with speech sounds and words.	Encourages experimentation with sounds that can later be blended into first words. Provides experience with the turn-taking pattern of human conversation.
Establish joint attention and comment on what child sees.	Predicts earlier onset of language and faster vocabulary development.
Play social games, such as pat-a-cake and peekaboo.	Provides experience with the turn-taking pattern of human conversation.
Engage toddlers in joint make-believe play.	Promotes all aspects of conversational dialogue.
Engage toddlers in frequent conversations.	Predicts faster early language development and academic competence during the school years.
Read to toddlers often, engaging them in dialogues about picture books.	Provides exposure to many aspects of language, including vocabulary, grammar, communication skills, and information about written symbols and story structures.

Carolyn: "Where's your bear?"

Caitlin: [looks around]

Carolyn: [pointing] "See? Go get the bear. By the sofa." [Caitlin gets the bear.]

Parents do not seem to be deliberately trying to teach children to talk when they use CDS, since many of the same speech qualities appear when adults communicate with foreigners. CDS probably arises from adults' desire to keep young children's attention and ease their task of understanding, and it works effectively in these ways. From birth on, children prefer to listen to CDS over other kinds of adult talk (Aslin, Jusczyk, & Pisoni, 1998). By 5 months, they are more emotionally responsive to it and can discriminate the tone quality of CDS with different meanings—for example, approving versus soothing utterances (Moore, Spence, & Katz, 1997; Werker, Pegg, & McLeod, 1994).

Parents constantly fine-tune CDS to fit with children's needs. Notice how Carolyn kept her utterance length just ahead of Caitlin's, creating a sensitive match between language stimulation and Caitlin's current capacities. In a study carried out in four cultures, American, Argentinean, French, and Japanese mothers tended to speak to 5-month-olds in emotion-laden ways, emphasizing greetings, repeated sounds, and affectionate names. At 13 months, when toddlers could understand as well as respond, maternal speech became more information-laden—concerned with giving directions, asking questions, and describing what was happening at the moment (Bornstein et al., 1992a).

Many features of CDS support early language development. For example, toddlers whose parents frequently offer verbal prompts and imitate and expand on their utterances during play make faster language progress during

© MYRLEEN FERGUSON CATE/PHOTOEDIT

This Chinese mother speaks to her baby daughter in short, clearly pronounced sentences with high-pitched, exaggerated intonation. Adults in many countries use this form of language, called child-directed speech, with infants and toddlers. It eases the task of early language learning.

Dialogues about picture books are an especially effective way to stimulate young children's language development. As this father talks about the pictures with his 2-year-old daughter, he exposes her to great breadth of language and literacy knowledge.

the second year (Tamis-LeMonda, Bornstein, & Baumwell, 2001). This does not mean that we should deliberately load our speech to toddlers with repetitions, questions, and other characteristics of CDS! These qualities occur naturally as adults draw young children into dialogues, accepting their attempts to talk as meaningful and worthwhile.

Conversational give-and-take between parent and toddler is one of the best predictors of early language development and academic competence during the school years (Hart & Risley, 1995). It provides many examples of speech just ahead of the child's current level and a sympathetic environment in which children can try out new skills (Huttenlocher et al., 1991; Walker et al., 1994). Dialogues about picture books are particularly effective. They expose children to great breadth of language and literacy knowledge, from vocabulary, grammar, and communication skills to information about written symbols and story structures. Two- and 3-year-olds who experience daily reading at home or child care are greatly advanced in language skills, compared with those who do not (Whitehurst & Lonigan, 1998; Whitehurst et al., 1994).

Do social experiences that promote language development remind you of those that strengthen cognitive development in general? Notice how CDS and parent–child conversation create a *zone of proximal development* in which children's language expands. In contrast, impatience with and rejection of children's efforts to talk lead them to stop trying and result in immature language skills (Baumwell, Tamis-LeMonda, & Bornstein, 1997). In the next chapter we will see that sensitivity to children's needs and capacities supports their emotional and social development as well.

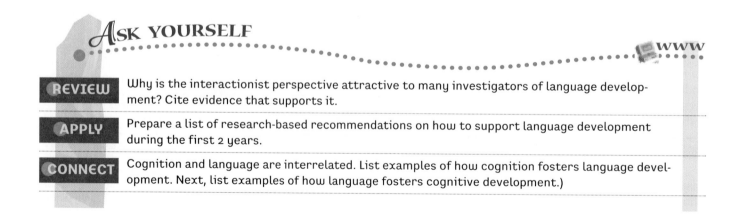

ASK YOURSELF

REVIEW Why is the interactionist perspective attractive to many investigators of language development? Cite evidence that supports it.

APPLY Prepare a list of research-based recommendations on how to support language development during the first 2 years.

CONNECT Cognition and language are interrelated. List examples of how cognition fosters language development. Next, list examples of how language fosters cognitive development.)

Summary

Piaget's Cognitive-Developmental Theory

According to Piaget, how do schemes change over the course of development?

- In Piaget's theory, by acting directly on the environment, children move through four stages in which psychological structures, or **schemes,** achieve a better fit with external reality.

- Schemes change in two ways. The first is through **adaptation,** which is made up of two complementary activities—**assimilation** and **accommodation.** The second is through **organization,** the internal rearrangement of schemes into a strongly interconnected cognitive system.

Describe the major cognitive achievements of the sensorimotor stage.

- Piaget's **sensorimotor stage** is divided into six substages. Through the **circular reaction,** the newborn baby's reflexes gradually transform into the more flexible action patterns of the older infant. During Substage 4, infants develop **intentional,** or **goal-directed, behavior** and begin to understand **object permanence.** Substage 5 brings a more exploratory approach to **functional play,** and infants no longer make the **A-not-B search error.** By Substage 6, toddlers become capable of **mental representation,** as shown by mastery of object permanence problems involving invisible displacement, **deferred imitation** and **make-believe play.**

What does follow-up research say about the accuracy of Piaget's sensorimotor stage?

- Many studies suggest that infants display certain understandings earlier than Piaget believed. Some awareness of object permanence, as revealed by the **violation-of-expectation method,** may be evident in the first few months. In addition, young infants display deferred imitation and analogical problem solving, which suggests that they are capable of mental representation in the first year.

- Today, researchers believe that newborns have more built-in equipment for making sense of their world than Piaget assumed, although they disagree on how much initial understanding infants have. According to the **core knowledge perspective,** infants begin life with core domains of thought that support early, rapid cognitive development. Overall, however, findings on the existence of "prewired," ready-made knowledge are mixed.

- Nevertheless, broad agreement exists on two issues. First, many cognitive changes of infancy are continuous rather than stagelike. Second, various aspects of cognition develop unevenly rather than in an integrated fashion.

Information Processing

Describe the information-processing view of cognitive development and the general structure of the information-processing system.

- Rather than providing a single, unified theory, information-processing researchers study many aspects of thinking. They want to know exactly what individuals of different ages do when faced with a task or problem.

- Most information-processing researchers assume that we hold information in three parts of the mental system, where **mental strategies** operate on it so that it can be retained and used efficiently. Information enters the **sensory register,** is actively processed in **working,** or **short-term, memory,** and is permanently stored in **long-term memory.** The **central executive,** a special part of working memory, manages its complex activities.

What changes in attention, memory, and categorization take place over the first 2 years?

- With age, infants attend to more aspects of the environment, take information in more quickly, and flexibly shift their attention from one stimulus to another. In the second year, attention to novelty declines and sustained attention improves, especially during play with toys.

- As infants get older, they remember experiences longer. After 9 months, memory persists despite changes in context. Young infants are capable of **recognition** memory; by the end of the first year, they can engage in **recall.** Between 1 and 2 years, recall for people, places, and objects is excellent. Both biology and social experience probably contribute to the decline of infantile amnesia and the emergence of **autobiographical memory.**

- During the first year, infants group stimuli into increasingly complex categories, and categorization shifts from a perceptual to a conceptual basis. In the second year, toddlers become active categorizers, spontaneously sorting objects during their play.

Describe the contributions and limitations of the information-processing approach to our understanding of early cognitive development.

- Information-processing findings challenge Piaget's view of infants as sensorimotor beings who cannot mentally represent experiences. However, information processing has not yet provided a broad, comprehensive theory of children's thinking.

The Social Context of Early Cognitive Development

How does Vygotsky's concept of the zone of proximal development expand our understanding of early cognitive development?

- According to Vygotsky's sociocultural theory, complex mental activities originate in social interaction. Through the support and guidance of more skilled partners, infants master tasks within the **zone of proximal development**—that is, tasks just ahead of their current capacities. As early as the first year, cultural variations in social experiences affect mental strategies.

Individual Differences in Early Mental Development

Describe the mental testing approach, the meaning of intelligence test scores, and the extent to which infant tests predict later performance.

- The mental testing approach measures intellectual development in an effort to predict future performance. **Intelligence quotients, or IQs,** are scores on mental tests that compare a child's performance to that of a large, representative sample of same-age children.

- Infant tests consist largely of perceptual and motor responses; they predict later intelligence poorly. As a result, scores on infant tests are called **developmental quotients, or DQs,** rather than IQs. Speed of habituation and recovery to visual stimuli and object permanence, which tap basic cognitive processes, are better predictors of future performance.

Discuss environmental influences on early mental development, including home, child care, and early intervention for at-risk infants and toddlers.

- Research with the **Home Observation for Measurement of the Environment (HOME)** shows that an organized, stimulating home environment and parental encouragement, involvement, and affection repeatedly predict higher mental test scores. Although the HOME–IQ relationship is partly due to heredity, family living conditions do affect mental development.

- The quality of infant and toddler child care has a major impact on cognitive and social skills. Standards for **developmentally appropriate practice** specify program characteristics that meet the developmental needs of young children.

- Intensive early intervention can prevent the gradual declines in intelligence and the poor academic performance of poverty-stricken children. Findings of the Carolina Abecedarian Project reveal long-lasting gains in IQ and achievement.

Language Development

Describe three theories of language development, and indicate the emphasis each places on innate abilities and environmental influences.

- According to the behaviorist perspective, parents train children in language skills through operant conditioning and imitation. Behaviorism has difficulty accounting for children's novel, rule-based utterances.

- Chomsky's nativist theory regards children as endowed with a **language acquisition device (LAD).** Consistent with this perspective, a complex language system is unique to humans, and language-specific structures—**Broca's** and **Wernicke's areas**—exist in the left hemisphere of the cerebral cortex. Research supports the existence of an early, sensitive period for language development. However, the role of language learning in brain lateralization, vast diversity among the world's languages, and children's gradual mastery of many constructions have raised questions about Chomsky's theory.

- Interactionist theories offer a compromise between these extreme views, stressing that innate abilities and a rich social environment combine to promote language development.

Describe major milestones of language development in the first 2 years, individual differences, and ways adults can support infants' and toddlers' emerging capacities.

- Infants begin **cooing** at 2 months and **babbling** around 4 months. After 9 months, their skill at establishing **joint attention** becomes more accurate, and by 12 months they actively engage in turn-taking games and use preverbal gestures. Adults can encourage language progress by responding to infants' coos and babbles, playing turn-taking games, establishing joint attention and labeling what babies see, and responding verbally to their preverbal gestures.

- In the middle of the first year, infants begin to understand word meanings. Around 12 months, toddlers say their first word. Young children often make errors of **underextension** and **overextension.** Between 18 and 24 months, a spurt in vocabulary growth often occurs, and two-word utterances called **telegraphic speech** appear. At all ages, language **comprehension** develops ahead of **production.**

- Individual differences in early language development exist. Girls show faster progress than boys, and reserved, cautious toddlers may wait before trying to speak. Most toddlers use a **referential style** of language learning, in which early words consist largely of names for objects. A few use an **expressive style,** in which social formulas and pronouns are common and vocabulary grows more slowly.

- Adults in many cultures speak to young children in **child-directed speech (CDS),** a simplified form of language that is well suited to their learning needs. Conversational give-and-take between parent and toddler is one of the best predictors of early language development and academic competence during the school years.

Important Terms and Concepts

A-not-B search error (p. 211)
accommodation (p. 208)
adaptation (p. 208)
assimilation (p. 208)
autobiographical memory (p. 224)
babbling (p. 238)
Broca's area (p. 236)
central executive (p. 221)
child-directed speech (CDS) (p. 242)
circular reaction (p. 210)
comprehension (p. 241)
cooing (p. 238)
core knowledge perspective (p. 217)
deferred imitation (p. 212)
developmental quotient, or DQ (p. 230)
developmentally appropriate
    practice (p. 232)

expressive style (p. 242)
functional play (p. 212)
Home Observation for Measurement of
    the Environment (HOME) (p. 231)
intelligence quotient, or IQ (p. 230)
intentional, or goal-directed,
    behavior (p. 211)
joint attention (p. 239)
language acquisition device (LAD)
    (p. 236)
long-term memory (p. 221)
make-believe play (p. 212)
mental representation (p. 211)
mental strategies (p. 220)
object permanence (p. 211)
organization (p. 209)

overextension (p. 240)
production (p. 241)
recall (p. 223)
recognition (p. 223)
referential style (p. 242)
scheme (p. 208)
sensorimotor stage (p. 208)
sensory register (p. 220)
telegraphic speech (p. 240)
underextension (p. 240)
violation-of-expectation method
    (p. 212)
Wernicke's area (p. 236)
working, or short-term, memory
    (p. 220)
zone of proximal development (p. 227)

FYI   For Further Information and Help

Consult the Companion Website for *Infants, Children, and Adolescents,* Fifth Edition, *(www.ablongman.com/berk),* where you will find
the following resources for this chapter:

- **Chapter Objectives**
- **Flashcards** for studying important terms and concepts
- **Annotated Weblinks** to guide you in further research
- **Ask Yourself questions,** which you can answer and then
  check against a sample response

- **Suggested Readings**
- **Practice Tests** with immediate scoring and feedback

CHAPTER 7

"Tenderness"
Veronica Beatriz Rebella
14 years, Uruguay

In the calm harmony of this image, the mother and her clothing become a soft, safe nest of emotional closeness for the baby. The importance of early family relationships as a secure base for emotional and social development is a major theme of Chapter 7.

Reprinted with permission from the International Museum of Children's Art, Oslo, Norway.

Emotional and Social Development in Infancy and Toddlerhood

ERIKSON'S THEORY OF INFANT AND TODDLER PERSONALITY
Basic Trust versus Mistrust • Autonomy versus Shame and Doubt

EMOTIONAL DEVELOPMENT
Development of Basic Emotions • Understanding and Responding to the Emotions of Others • Emergence of Self-Conscious Emotions • Beginnings of Emotional Self-Regulation

DEVELOPMENT OF TEMPERAMENT
The Structure of Temperament • Measuring Temperament • Stability of Temperament • Genetic Influences • Environmental Influences • Temperament and Child Rearing: The Goodness-of-Fit Model

BIOLOGY AND ENVIRONMENT *Biological Basis of Shyness and Sociability*

DEVELOPMENT OF ATTACHMENT
Bowlby's Ethological Theory • Measuring the Security of Attachment • Stability of Attachment • Cultural Variations • Factors That Affect Attachment Security • Multiple Attachments • From Attachment to Peer Sociability • Attachment and Later Development

SOCIAL ISSUES: HEALTH *Does Child Care in Infancy Threaten Attachment Security and Later Adjustment?*

CULTURAL INFLUENCES *The Powerful Role of Paternal Warmth in Development*

SELF-UNDERSTANDING
Self-Awareness • Categorizing the Self • Emergence of Self-Control

As Caitlin reached 8 months of age, her parents noticed that she had become more fearful. One evening, when Carolyn and David left her with a babysitter, she wailed when they headed for the door—an experience she had accepted easily a few weeks earlier. Caitlin and Timmy's caregiver Ginette also observed an increasing wariness of strangers. When she turned to go to another room, both babies dropped their play to crawl after her. And a knock at the door from the mail carrier prompted them to cling to Ginette's legs and reach out to be picked up.

At the same time, each baby seemed more willful. An object removed from the hand at 5 months produced little response, but at 8 months Timmy resisted when his mother Vanessa took away a table knife he had managed to reach. He burst into angry screams and could not be consoled by the toys she offered in its place.

Monica and Kevin knew little about Grace's development during her first year, except that she had been deeply loved by her destitute, homeless mother. Separating from her, followed by a long journey to an unfamiliar home, left Grace in shock. At first, she was extremely sad, turning away when Monica or Kevin picked her up. She did not smile for over a week.

But as Grace's new parents held her close, spoke gently, and satisfied her craving for food, Grace returned their affection. Two weeks after her arrival, her despondency gave way to a sunny, easygoing disposition. She burst into a wide grin, reached out at the sight of Monica and Kevin, and laughed at her brother Eli's funny faces. Among her first words were the names of family members—"Eli," "Mama," and "Dada." As her second birthday approached, she pointed to photos of herself, exclaiming "Gwace!", and laid claim to treasured possessions. "Gwace's chicken!" she would announce at mealtimes, chewing the meat from the drumstick and then sucking out the marrow, a practice she brought with her from Cambodia.

Taken together, Caitlin's, Timmy's, and Grace's reactions reflect two related aspects of personality that develop during the first 2 years: close ties to others and a sense of self. Our discussion begins with Erikson's psychosocial theory, which provides an overview of personality development during infancy and toddlerhood. Then we chart the course of emotional development. As we do so, we will discover why fear and anger became more apparent in Caitlin's and Timmy's range of emotions by the end of the first year. Our attention then turns to individual differences in temperament. We will examine biological and environmental contributions to these differences and their consequences for future development.

Next, we take up attachment to the caregiver, the child's first affectionate tie. We will see how the feelings of security that grow out of this important bond support the child's exploration, sense of independence, and expanding social relationships.

Finally, we focus on early self-development. By the end of toddlerhood, Grace recognized herself in mirrors and photographs, labeled herself as a girl, and showed the beginnings of self-control. "Don't touch!" she instructed herself one day as she resisted the desire to pull a lamp cord out of its socket. Cognitive advances combine with social experiences to produce these changes during the second year.

Erikson's Theory of Infant and Toddler Personality

Our discussion of major theories in Chapter 1 revealed that psychoanalytic theory is no longer in the mainstream of child development research. But one of its lasting contributions is its ability to capture the essence of personality development during each phase of life. Recall that Sigmund Freud, founder of the psychoanalytic movement, believed that psychological health and maladjustment could be traced to the early years—in particular, to the quality of the child's relationships with parents. Although Freud's preoccupation with the channeling of biological drives and his neglect of important experiences beyond infancy and early childhood came to be heavily criticized, the basic outlines of his theory were accepted and elaborated in several subsequent theories of personality development. The leader of these neo-Freudian perspectives is Erik Erikson's *psychosocial theory,* also introduced in Chapter 1.

Basic Trust versus Mistrust

Freud called the first year the *oral stage* and regarded gratification of the infant's need for food and oral stimulation as vital. Erikson accepted Freud's emphasis on the importance of feeding, but he expanded and enriched Freud's view. A healthy outcome during infancy, Erikson believed, does not depend on the *amount* of food or oral stimulation offered but rather on the *quality* of the caregiver's behavior. A mother who supports her baby's development relieves discomfort promptly and sensitively. For example, she holds the infant gently during feedings, patiently waits until the baby has had enough milk, and weans when the infant shows less interest in the breast or bottle.

Erikson recognized that no parent can be perfectly in tune with the baby's needs. Many factors affect parental responsiveness—feel-

According to Erikson, basic trust grows out of the early caregiving relationship. A parent who relieves the baby's discomfort promptly and holds the baby tenderly promotes basic trust—the feeling that the world is good and gratifying. This mother and infant share the joy of tender closeness.

©VCL/SPENCER ROWELL/GETTY IMAGES/TAXI

ings of personal happiness, momentary life conditions (for example, additional young children in the family), and culturally valued child-rearing practices. But when the *balance of care* is sympathetic and loving, then the psychological conflict of the first year—**basic trust versus mistrust**— is resolved on the positive side. The trusting infant expects the world to be good and gratifying, so he feels confident about venturing out and exploring it. The mistrustful baby cannot count on the kindness and compassion of others, so she protects herself by withdrawing from people and things around her.

Autonomy versus Shame and Doubt

In the second year, during Freud's *anal stage,* instinctual energies shift to the anal region of the body. Freud viewed toilet training, in which children must bring their impulses in line with social requirements, as crucial for personality development. (Return to Chapter 5, pages 192–193, to review how adults can best support toddlers' attainment of bladder and bowel control.)

Erikson agreed that the parent's manner of toilet training is essential for psychological health. But he regarded it as only one of many important experiences for newly walking, talking toddlers. Their familiar refrains—"No!" and "Do it myself!"—reveal that they have entered a period of budding selfhood. Toddlers want to decide for themselves—not just in toileting but in other situations as well. The great conflict of toddlerhood, **autonomy versus shame and doubt,** is resolved favorably when parents provide young children with suitable guidance and reasonable choices. A self-confident, secure 2-year-old has been encouraged not just to use the toilet but also to eat with a spoon and to help pick up his toys. His parents do not criticize or attack him when he fails at these new skills. And they meet his assertions of independence with tolerance and understanding. For example, they grant him an extra 5 minutes to finish his play before leaving for the grocery store and wait patiently while he tries to zip his jacket.

This 2-year-old is intent on using a spoon to feed herself. Toddlers who are allowed to decide and do things for themselves in appropriate situations develop a sense of autonomy— the feeling that they can control their bodies and act competently on their own.

According to Erikson, the parent who is over- or undercontrolling in toileting is likely to be so in other aspects of the toddler's life. The outcome is a child who feels forced and shamed and who doubts his ability to control his impulses and act competently on his own.

In sum, basic trust and autonomy grow out of warm, sensitive parenting and reasonable expectations for impulse control starting in the second year. If children emerge from the first few years without sufficient trust in caregivers and without a healthy sense of individuality, the seeds are sown for adjustment problems. Adults who have difficulty establishing intimate ties, who are overly dependent on a loved one, or who continually doubt their own ability to meet new challenges may not have fully mastered the tasks of trust and autonomy during infancy and toddlerhood.

Ask YOURSELF · · · · · · www

APPLY Derek's mother fed him in a warm and loving manner during the first year. But when he became a toddler, she kept him in a playpen for many hours because he got into too much mischief while exploring freely. Use Erikson's theory to evaluate Derek's early experiences.

CONNECT Do Erikson's recommendations for fostering autonomy in toddlerhood fit with Vygotsky's concept of the zone of proximal development, described on page 227 of Chapter 6? Explain.

Emotional Development

In the previous chapter, we considered babies' increasingly effective schemes for controlling the environment and ways that adults support cognitive and language development. Now let's focus on another aspect of infant and caregiver behavior: the exchange of emotions. Observe several infants and toddlers, noting the emotions each displays, the cues you rely on to interpret the baby's emotional state, and the way caregivers respond. Researchers have conducted many such observations to find out how effectively infants and toddlers communicate their emotions and interpret those of others. They have discovered that emotions play powerful roles in organizing the attainments that Erikson regarded as so important: social relationships, exploration of the environment, and discovery of the self (Frijda, 2000; Izard, 1991; Saarni, Mumme, & Campos, 1998).

Think back to the *dynamic systems perspective* introduced in Chapters 1 and 5. As you read about early emotional development in the sections that follow, notice how emotions are an integral part of young children's dynamic systems of action. Emotions energize development. At the same time, they are an aspect of the system that develops, becoming more varied and complex as children reorganize their behavior to attain new goals (Witherington, Campos, & Hertenstein, 2001).

Because infants cannot describe their feelings, determining exactly which emotions they are experiencing is a challenge. Although vocalizations and body movements provide some information, facial expressions offer the most reliable cues. Cross-cultural evidence reveals that people around the world associate photographs of different facial expressions with emotions in the same way (Ekman & Friesen, 1972). These findings, which suggest that emotional expressions are built-in social signals, inspired researchers to analyze infants' facial patterns carefully to determine the range of emotions they display at different ages. A commonly used method for doing so, the MAX System, is illustrated in Figure 7.1.

Development of Basic Emotions

Basic emotions are universal in humans and other primates, have a long evolutionary history of promoting survival, and can be directly inferred from facial expressions. They include happiness, interest, surprise, fear, anger, sadness, and disgust. Do infants come into the world with the ability to express basic emotions? Although signs of some emotions are present, babies' earliest emotional life consists of little more than two global arousal states: attraction to pleasant stimulation and withdrawal from unpleasant stimulation (Fox, 1991; Sroufe, 1979). Over time, emotions become clear, well-organized signals.

FIGURE 7.1

Which emotions are these babies displaying?

The MAX (Maximally Discriminative Facial Movement) System is a widely used method for classifying infants' emotional expressions. Facial muscle movements are carefully rated to determine their correspondence with basic feeling states, since people around the world associate different facial gestures with emotions in the same way. For example, cheeks raised and corners of the mouth pulled back and up signal happiness (a). Eyebrows raised, eyes widened, and mouth opened with corners pulled straight back denote fear (b). (From Izard, 1979.)

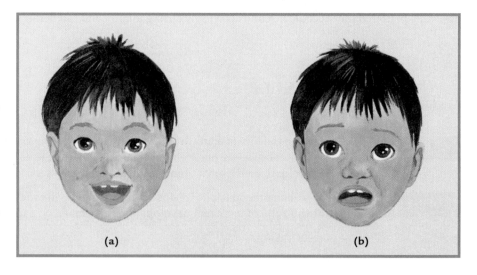

(a)   (b)

TABLE 7.1

Milestones of Emotional Development During the First Two Years

APPROXIMATE AGE	MILESTONE
Birth	Infants' emotions consist of two global arousal states: attraction to pleasant stimulation and withdrawal from unpleasant stimulation.
2–3 months	Infants engage in social smiling and respond in kind to adults' facial expressions.
3–4 months	Infants begin to laugh at very active stimuli. Expressions of sadness appear when parent–infant interaction is seriously disrupted.
6–8 months	Expressions of basic emotions are well organized and vary meaningfully with environmental events. Infants start to become angry more often and in a wider range of situations. Fear, especially stranger anxiety, begins to rise. Attachment to the familiar caregiver is clearly evident, and separation anxiety appears. Infants use caregivers as a secure base for exploration.
8–12 months	Infants perceive facial expressions as organized patterns, and meaningful understanding of them improves. Social referencing appears. Infants laugh at subtle elements of surprise.
18–24 months	Self-conscious emotions of shame, embarrassment, guilt, and pride appear. A vocabulary for talking about feelings develops rapidly, and emotional self-regulation improves. Toddlers begin to appreciate that others' emotional reactions may differ from their own. First signs of empathy appear.

The dynamic systems perspective helps us understand how this happens. According to this view, children coordinate separate skills into more effective systems as the central nervous system develops and the child's goals and experiences change. Videotaping the facial expressions of her daughter from 6 to 14 weeks, Linda Camras (1992) found that in the early weeks, the baby displayed a fleeting angry face as she was about to cry and a sad face as her crying waned. These expressions first appeared on the way to or away from full-blown distress and were not clearly linked to the baby's experiences and desires. With age, she was better able to sustain an angry signal when she encountered a blocked goal and a sad signal when she could not overcome an obstacle.

Around 6 months, face, gaze, voice, and posture form organized patterns that vary meaningfully with environmental events. For example, Caitlin typically responded to her parents' playful interaction with a joyful face, pleasant babbling, and a relaxed posture, as if to say, "This is fun!" In contrast, an unresponsive parent often evokes a sad face, fussy sounds, and a drooping body (sending the message, "I'm despondent") or an angry face, crying, and "pick-me-up" gestures (as if to say, "Change this unpleasant event!"). In sum, by the middle of the first year, emotional expressions are well organized and specific—and therefore able to tell us a great deal about the infant's internal state (Weinberg & Tronick, 1994; Yale et al., 1999).

Four basic emotions—happiness, anger, sadness, and fear—have received the most research attention. Refer to Table 7.1 for an overview of changes during the first 2 years in these emotions as well as others we will take up in this chapter.

HAPPINESS ● Happiness—first in terms of blissful smiles and later through exuberant laughter—contributes to many aspects of development. Infants smile and laugh when they conquer new skills, expressing their delight in motor and cognitive mastery. The smile also encourages caregivers to be affectionate and stimulating, so the baby smiles even more. Happiness binds parent and baby into a warm, supportive relationship that fosters the infant's developing competence.

During the early weeks, newborn babies smile when full, during sleep, and in response to gentle touches and sounds, such as stroking of the skin, rocking, and the mother's soft, high-pitched voice. By the end of the first month, infants

This 6-month-old breaks into a broad grin after seeing the surprising results of pressing his feet against the paper. Infants express great delight in motor and cognitive mastery, and their happiness encourages caregivers to be all the more affectionate and stimulating.

PHOTO COUTESY OF SARAH HYMAN AND ELIZABETH NAPOLITANO

start to smile at interesting sights, but these must be dynamic and eye-catching, such as a bright object jumping suddenly across the baby's field of vision. Between 6 and 10 weeks, the human face evokes a broad grin called the **social smile** (Sroufe & Waters, 1976). By 3 months, infants smile most often when interacting with people (Ellsworth, Muir, & Hains, 1993). These changes parallel the development of infant perceptual capacities—in particular, babies' sensitivity to visual patterns, including the human face (see Chapter 5).

Laughter, which first occurs around 3 to 4 months, reflects faster processing of information than does smiling. But like smiling, the first laughs occur in response to very active stimuli, such as the parent saying playfully, "I'm gonna get you!" and kissing the baby's tummy. As infants understand more about their world, they laugh at events with subtler elements of surprise. At 10 months, Timmy chuckled as Vanessa played a silent game of peekaboo. At 1 year, he laughed heartily as she crawled on all fours and then walked like a penguin (Sroufe & Wunsch, 1972).

Around the middle of the first year, infants smile and laugh more often when interacting with familiar people, a preference that strengthens the parent–child bond. Like adults, 10- to 12-month-olds have several smiles, which vary with context. They show a broad, "cheek-raised" smile in response to a parent's greeting; a reserved, muted smile in response to a friendly stranger; and a "mouth-open" smile during stimulating play (Dickson, Fogel, & Messinger, 1998). During the second year, the smile becomes a deliberate social signal. Toddlers break their play with an interesting toy to communicate their delight to an attentive adult (Jones & Raag, 1989).

ANGER AND SADNESS ● Newborn babies respond with generalized distress to a variety of unpleasant experiences, including hunger, painful medical procedures, changes in body temperature, and too much or too little stimulation (see Chapter 4). From 4 to 6 months into the second year, angry expressions increase in frequency and intensity. Older infants react with anger in a wider range of situations—for example, when an interesting object is removed, an expected pleasant event does not occur, their arms are restrained, the caregiver leaves for a brief time, or they are put down for a nap (Camras et al., 1992; Stenberg & Campos, 1990).

Why do angry reactions increase with age? Cognitive and motor development are involved. As infants become capable of intentional behavior (see Chapter 6), they want to control their own actions and the effects they produce. Loss of *contingent control*—for example, when pulling on a string at first produces pleasant pictures and music but later is unrelated to these rewarding outcomes—evokes especially strong angry responses (Sullivan & Lewis, 2003). Older infants are also better at identifying the person who blocked their goal or caused them pain—realizations that trigger anger. Finally, the rise in anger is adaptive. New motor capacities permit babies to use the energy mobilized by anger to overcome obstacles or defend themselves (Izard & Ackerman, 2000). At the same time, anger is a powerful social signal that motivates caregivers to ease a baby's distress.

Expressions of sadness also occur in response to pain, removal of an object, and brief separations, but anger is the more common response to these experiences. In contrast, sadness occurs often when infants are deprived of a familiar, loving caregiver, as Grace's despondency in the weeks after her adoption illustrates. Sadness also occurs when parent–infant interaction is seriously disrupted. In several studies, researchers had parents assume either a still-faced, unreactive pose or a depressed emotional state. Their 2- to 7-month-olds tried facial expressions, vocalizations, and body movements to get their mother or father to respond again. When these efforts failed, they turned away, frowned, and cried (Hernandez & Carter, 1996; Moore, Cohn, & Campbell, 2001). The still-face reaction is identical among American, Canadian, and Chinese babies, suggesting that it is a built-in withdrawal response to caregivers' lack of communication (Kisilevsky et al., 1998). Return to Chapter 4, page 159, and note that infants of depressed parents respond this way. When allowed to persist, a sad, vacant outlook disrupts all aspects of early development.

FEAR ● Like anger, fear rises during the second half of the first year. Older infants hesitate before playing with a new toy, and newly crawling infants soon show fear of heights (see Chapter 5). But the most frequent expression of fear is to unfamiliar adults, a response called **stranger anxiety.** Many infants and toddlers are quite wary of strangers, although the reaction does not always occur. It depends on several factors: temperament (some babies are generally more fearful), past experiences with strangers, and the current situation (Thompson & Limber, 1991). When an unfamiliar adult picks up the infant in a new situation, stranger anxiety is likely. But if the adult sits still while the baby moves around and a parent is nearby, infants often show positive and curious behavior (Horner, 1980). The stranger's style of interaction—expressing warmth, holding out an attractive toy, playing a familiar game, and approaching slowly rather than abruptly—reduces the baby's fear.

Culture can modify stranger anxiety through infant-rearing practices. Maternal deaths are high among the Efe hunters and gatherers of Zaire, Africa. To ensure infant survival, a collective caregiving system exists in which, beginning at birth, Efe babies are passed from one adult to another. Consequently, Efe infants show little stranger anxiety (Tronick, Morelli, & Ivey, 1992). In contrast, in Israeli kibbutzim (cooperative agricultural settlements), living in an isolated community subject to terrorist attacks has led to widespread wariness of strangers. By the end of the first year, when infants look to others for cues about how to respond emotionally, kibbutz babies display far greater stranger anxiety than their city-reared counterparts (Saarni, Mumme, & Campos, 1998).

The rise in fear after 6 months of age keeps newly crawling and walking babies' enthusiasm for exploration in check, motivating them to remain close to the caregiver and to be careful about approaching unfamiliar people and objects. Eventually, stranger anxiety and other fears decline as cognitive development permits toddlers to discriminate more effectively between threatening and nonthreatening people and situations. This change is also adaptive, since adults other than caregivers will be soon be important in children's development. Fear also wanes as children acquire a wider array of strategies for coping with it, as you will see shortly when we discuss emotional self-regulation.

Understanding and Responding to the Emotions of Others

Infants' emotional expressions are closely tied to their ability to interpret the emotional cues of others. Already we have seen that in the first few months, babies match the feeling tone of the caregiver in face-to-face communication. Early on, babies respond to others' emotions through a fairly automatic process of *emotional contagion,* just as we tend to smile, laugh, or feel sad when we sense these emotions in others. Around 4 months, infants become sensitive to the structure and timing of face-to-face interactions (see Chapter 6, page 239). As a result, when they gaze, smile, or vocalize, they expect their social partner to respond in kind (Rochat, Striano, & Blatt, 2002). Within these exchanges, babies become increasingly aware of the range of emotional expressions (Montague & Walker-Andrews, 2001).

Between 7 and 10 months, infants perceive facial expressions as organized patterns, and they can match the emotion in a voice with the appropriate face of a speaking person (see Chapter 5). Responding to emotional expressions as organized wholes indicates that these signals have become meaningful to babies. As skill at establishing joint attention improves (see Chapter 6), infants realize that an emotional expression not only has meaning but is also a meaningful reaction to a specific object or event (Moses et al., 2001; Tomasello, 1999a).

Once these understandings are in place, infants engage in **social referencing,** in which they actively seek emotional information from a trusted person in an uncertain situation. Beginning at 8 to 10 months, when infants start to evaluate objects and events in terms of their safety and security, social referencing occurs often. Many studies show that a caregiver's emotional expression (happy, angry, or fearful) influences whether a 1-year-old will be wary of strangers, play with an unfamiliar toy, or cross the deep side of the visual cliff (Repacholi, 1998; Sorce et al., 1985; Striano & Rochat, 2000).

Parents can capitalize on social referencing to teach their baby how to react to a great many everyday events. Social referencing also permits toddlers to compare their own assessments of events with those of others. By the middle of the second year, they begin to appreciate that others' emotional reactions may differ from their own. Consider a study in which an adult showed 14- and 18-month-olds broccoli and crackers. In one condition, she acted delighted with the taste of broccoli but disgusted with the taste of crackers. In the other condition, she showed the reverse preference. When asked to share the food, 14-month-olds offered only the type of food they themselves preferred—usually crackers. In contrast, 18-month-olds gave the adult whichever food they saw she liked, regardless of their own preferences (Repacholi & Gopnik, 1997).

On an outing, this 1-year-old shows stranger anxiety, which increases during the second half of the first year. As infants move on their own, this rise in fear has adaptive value, increasing the chances that they will remain close to the parent and be protected from danger.

In sum, social referencing helps toddlers move beyond simply reacting to others' emotional messages. They use those signals to guide their own actions and to find out about others' intentions and preferences.

Emergence of Self-Conscious Emotions

Besides basic emotions, humans are capable of a second, higher-order set of feelings, including shame, embarrassment, guilt, envy, and pride. These are called **self-conscious emotions** because each involves injury to or enhancement of our sense of self. For example, when we are ashamed or embarrassed, we feel negatively about our behavior, and we want to retreat so that others will no longer notice our failings. Guilt occurs when we know that we have harmed someone, and we want to correct the wrongdoing and repair the relationship. In contrast, pride reflects delight in the self's achievements, and we are inclined to tell others what we have accomplished and to take on further challenges (Saarni, Mumme, & Campos, 1998).

Self-conscious emotions appear in the middle of the second year, as the sense of self emerges. Shame and embarrassment can be seen as 18- to 24-month-olds lower their eyes, hang their heads, and hide their faces with their hands. Guiltlike reactions are also evident. After noticing Grace's unhappiness, 22-month-old Caitlin returned a toy she had grabbed and patted her upset playmate. Pride, as well, emerges around this time, and envy is present by age 3 (Barrett, 1998; Lewis et al., 1989). Besides self-awareness, self-conscious emotions require an additional ingredient: adult instruction in when to feel proud, ashamed, or guilty. Parents begin this tutoring early when they say, "My, look how far you can throw that ball!" or "You should feel ashamed for grabbing that toy!"

As these comments indicate, self-conscious emotions play important roles in children's achievement-related and moral behaviors. The situations in which adults encourage these feelings vary from culture to culture. In Western individualistic nations, most children are taught to feel proud of personal achievement—throwing a ball the farthest, winning a game, and (later on) getting good grades. In collectivist cultures such as China and Japan, calling attention to purely personal success evokes embarrassment and self-effacement. And violating cultural standards by failing to show concern for others—a parent, a teacher, or an employer—sparks intense shame (Akimoto & Sanbinmatsu, 1999; Lewis, 1992).

Self-conscious emotions appear at the end of the first year. This Guatemalan 2-year-old undoubtedly feels a sense of pride as she helps care for her elderly grandmother—an activity highly valued in her culture.

Beginnings of Emotional Self-Regulation

Besides expressing a wider range of emotions, infants and toddlers begin to manage their emotional experiences. **Emotional self-regulation** refers to the strategies we use to adjust our emotional state to a comfortable level of intensity so we can accomplish our goals (Thompson, 1994). If you reminded yourself that an anxiety-provoking event would be over soon or decided not to see a scary horror film, you were engaging in emotional self-regulation. A good start in regulating emotion during the first 2 years contributes greatly to autonomy and mastery of cognitive and social skills, whereas early difficulties in regulation predict later adjustment problems (Crockenberg & Leerkes, 2000).

In the early months, infants have only a limited capacity to regulate their emotional states. Although they can turn away from unpleasant stimulation and can mouth and suck when their feelings get too intense, they are easily overwhelmed. They depend on the soothing interventions of caregivers—being lifted to the shoulder, rocked, gently stroked, and talked to softly.

Rapid development of the cerebral cortex increases the baby's tolerance for stimulation. Between 2 and 4 months, caregivers build on this capacity by initiating face-to-face play and attention to objects. In these interactions, parents arouse pleasure in the baby while adjusting the pace of their own behavior so the infant does not become overwhelmed and distressed. As a result, the baby's tolerance for stimulation increases further (Field, 1994). By 4 months, the ability to shift their attention helps infants control emotion. Babies who more readily turn away from unpleasant events are less prone to distress (Axia, Bonichini, & Benini, 1999). At the end of the first year, crawling and walking enable infants to regulate emotion more effectively by approaching or retreating from various situations. And further gains in attention permit toddlers to sustain interest in their surroundings and in play activities for a longer time (Rothbart & Bates, 1998).

As caregivers help infants regulate their emotional states, they contribute to the child's style of emotional self-regulation. Parents who read and respond contingently and sympathetically to the baby's emotional cues have infants who express more pleasurable emotion and are more attentive, more interested in exploration, and more easily soothed (Eisenberg, Cumberland, & Spinrad, 1998; Volling et al., 2002). In contrast, parents who wait to intervene until the infant has become extremely agitated reinforce the baby's rapid rise to intense distress. This makes it harder for parents to soothe the baby in the future—and for the baby to learn to calm herself. When caregivers fail to regulate stressful experiences for infants who cannot yet regulate them for themselves, brain structures that buffer stress may fail to develop properly, resulting in an anxious, reactive temperament (Nelson & Bosquet, 2000).

Caregivers also provide lessons in socially approved ways of expressing feelings. Beginning in the first few months, parents encourage infants to suppress negative emotion by often imitating their expressions of interest, happiness, and surprise and rarely imitating their expressions of anger and sadness. Infant boys get more of this training than infant girls, in part because boys have a harder time regulating negative emotion. As a result, the well-known sex difference—females as emotionally expressive and males as emotionally controlled—is promoted at a tender age (Malatesta et al., 1986; Weinberg et al., 1999). Furthermore, collectivist cultures usually emphasize socially appropriate emotional behavior. Compared with North Americans, Chinese and Japanese adults more often discourage the expression of strong emotion in babies (Fogel, 1993). By the end of the first year, Chinese and Japanese infants smile and cry less than American babies (Camras et al., 1998).

In the second year, growth in representation and language leads to new ways of regulating emotions. A vocabulary for talking about feelings, such as "happy," "love," "surprised," "scary," "yucky," and "mad," develops rapidly after 18 months (Dunn, Bretherton, & Munn, 1987). Toddlers are not yet good at using language to comfort themselves (Grolnick, Bridges, & Connell, 1996). But once they can describe their internal states, they can guide caregivers in helping them. For example, while listening to a story about monsters, Grace whimpered, "Mommy, scary." Monica put the book down and gave Grace a comforting hug.

Toddlers' use of words to label feelings shows that they already have a remarkable understanding of themselves and others as emotional beings. As we will see in later chapters, with the ability to think about feelings, emotional self-regulation improves greatly during early and middle childhood.

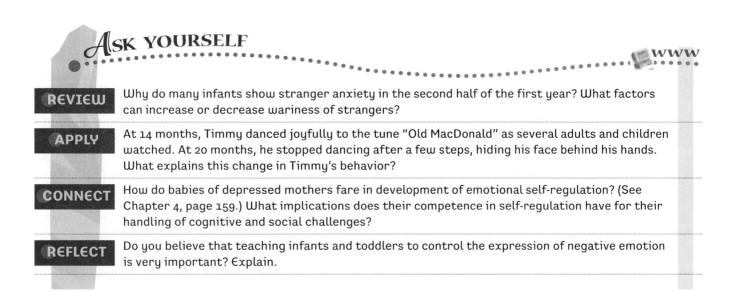

*A*SK YOURSELF

www

REVIEW Why do many infants show stranger anxiety in the second half of the first year? What factors can increase or decrease wariness of strangers?

APPLY At 14 months, Timmy danced joyfully to the tune "Old MacDonald" as several adults and children watched. At 20 months, he stopped dancing after a few steps, hiding his face behind his hands. What explains this change in Timmy's behavior?

CONNECT How do babies of depressed mothers fare in development of emotional self-regulation? (See Chapter 4, page 159.) What implications does their competence in self-regulation have for their handling of cognitive and social challenges?

REFLECT Do you believe that teaching infants and toddlers to control the expression of negative emotion is very important? Explain.

Development of Temperament

Beginning in early infancy, Caitlin, Grace, and Timmy showed unique patterns of emotional responding. Caitlin's sociability was unmistakable to everyone who met her. She smiled and laughed while interacting with adults and readily approached other children during the second year. Meanwhile, Monica marveled at Grace's calm, relaxed disposition. At 19 months, she sat through a 2-hour family celebration at a restaurant, content in her high chair. In contrast, Timmy was active and distractible. Vanessa found herself chasing him as he dropped one toy, moved on to the next, and climbed on chairs and tables.

When we describe one person as cheerful and "upbeat," another as active and energetic, and still others as calm, cautious, or prone to angry outbursts, we are referring to **temperament—stable individual differences in quality and intensity of emotional reaction, activity level, attention, and emotional self-regulation** (Rothbart & Bates, 1998). Researchers have become increasingly interested in temperamental differences among children because the psychological traits that make up temperament are believed to form the cornerstone of the adult personality.

The New York Longitudinal Study, initiated in 1956 by Alexander Thomas and Stella Chess, is the longest and most comprehensive study of temperament to date. A total of 141 children were followed from early infancy well into adulthood. Results showed that temperament increases the chances that a child will experience psychological problems or, alternatively, be protected from the effects of a stressful home life. However, Thomas and Chess (1977) also found that parenting practices can modify children's emotional styles considerably.

These findings inspired a growing body of research on temperament, including its stability, biological roots, and interaction with child-rearing experiences. Let's begin to explore these issues by looking at the structure, or makeup, of temperament and how it is measured.

The Structure of Temperament

Thomas and Chess's nine dimensions, listed in Table 7.2, served as the first influential model of temperament, inspiring all others that followed. When detailed descriptions of infants' and children's behavior obtained from parental interviews were rated on these dimensions, certain characteristics clustered together, yielding three types of children:

- The **easy child** (40 percent of the sample) quickly establishes regular routines in infancy, is generally cheerful, and adapts easily to new experiences.

- The **difficult child** (10 percent of the sample) is irregular in daily routines, is slow to accept new experiences, and tends to react negatively and intensely.

- The **slow-to-warm-up child** (15 percent of the sample) is inactive, shows mild, low-key reactions to environmental stimuli, is negative in mood, and adjusts slowly to new experiences.

Note that 35 percent of the children did not fit any of these categories. Instead, they showed unique blends of temperamental characteristics.

Of the three types, the difficult pattern has sparked the most interest, since it places children at high risk for adjustment problems—both anxious withdrawal and aggressive behavior in early and middle childhood (Bates, Wachs, & Emde, 1994; Thomas, Chess, & Birch, 1968). Compared with difficult children, slow-to-warm-up children do not present many problems in the early years. However, they tend to show excessive fearfulness and slow, constricted behavior in the late preschool and school years, when they are expected to respond actively and quickly in classrooms and peer groups (Chess & Thomas, 1984; Schmitz et al., 1999).

A second model of temperament, developed by Mary Rothbart (1981), is also shown in Table 7.2. It combines overlapping dimensions of Thomas and Chess and other researchers. For example, "distractibility" and "attention span and persistence" are considered opposite ends of the same dimension and are simply called "attention span/persistence." It also includes a

TABLE 7.2

Two Models of Temperament

THOMAS AND CHESS		ROTHBART	
DIMENSION	**DESCRIPTION**	**DIMENSION**	**DESCRIPTION**
Activity level	Ratio of active periods to inactive ones	Activity level	Level of gross motor activity
Rhythmicity	Regularity of body functions, such as sleep, wakefulness, hunger, and excretion	Soothability	Reduction of fussing, crying, and distress in response to caregiver's soothing
Distractibility	Degree to which stimulation from the environment alters behavior—for example, whether crying stops when a toy is offered	Attention span/persistence	Duration of orienting or interest
Approach/withdrawal	Response to a new object, food, or person	Fearful distress	Wariness and distress in response to intense or novel stimuli, including time to adjust to new situations
Adaptability	Ease with which child adapts to changes in the environment, such as sleeping or eating in a new place	Irritable distress	Extent of fussing, crying, and distress when desires are frustrated
Attention span and persistence	Amount of time devoted to an activity, such as watching a mobile or playing with a toy	Positive affect	Frequency of expression of happiness and pleasure
Intensity of reaction	Energy level of response, such as laughing, crying, talking, or gross motor activity		
Threshold of responsiveness	Intensity of stimulation required to evoke a response		
Quality of mood	Amount of friendly, joyful behavior as opposed to unpleasant, unfriendly behavior		

Sources: Left: Thomas & Chess, 1977. Right: Rothbart, 1981; Rothbart, Ahadi, & Evans, 2000.

dimension not identified by Thomas and Chess—"irritable distress"—that taps emotional self-regulation. And it omits overly broad dimensions, such as "rhythmicity," "intensity of reaction," "threshold of responsiveness" (Rothbart, Ahadi, & Evans, 2000). A child who is rhythmic in sleeping is not necessarily rhythmic in eating or bowel habits. And a child who smiles and laughs quickly and intensely is not necessarily quick and intense in fear or irritability.

Notice how Rothbart's six dimensions represent three underlying components of temperament: (1) emotion ("fearful distress," "irritable distress," "positive affect," and "soothability"), (2) attention ("attention span/persistence"), and (3) action ("activity level"). According to Rothbart, these components form an integrated system of capacities and limitations. Overall, the characteristics shown in Table 7.2 provide a fairly complete picture of the temperamental traits most often studied.

Measuring Temperament

Temperament is often assessed through interviews or questionnaires given to parents. Behavior ratings by pediatricians, teachers, and others familiar with the child and direct observations by researchers have also been used. Parental reports are convenient and take advantage of parents' depth of knowledge of the child across many situations (Gartstein & Rothbart, 2003). At the same time, information from parents has been criticized as biased and subjective. For example, mothers who are anxious and depressed tend to view their babies as more difficult (Mebert, 1991). Nevertheless, parent ratings are moderately related to researchers' observations of children's

*B*iology and Environment

Biological Basis of Shyness and Sociability

At age 4 months, Larry and Mitch visited the laboratory of Jerome Kagan, who observed their reactions to a variety of unfamiliar experiences. When exposed to new sights and sounds, such as a moving mobile decorated with colorful toys, Larry tensed his muscles, moved his arms and legs with agitation, and began to cry. Mitch's body remained relaxed and quiet, and he smiled and cooed pleasurably at the excitement around him.

Larry and Mitch returned to the laboratory as toddlers. This time, each experienced a variety of procedures designed to induce uncertainty. For example, electrodes were placed on their bodies and blood pressure cuffs on their arms to measure heart rate; toy robots, animals, and puppets moved before their eyes; and unfamiliar people entered and behaved in atypical ways or wore novel costumes. Larry whimpered and quickly withdrew. Mitch watched with interest, laughed at the strange sights, and approached the toys and strangers.

On a third visit, at age 4½ years, Larry barely talked or smiled during an interview with an unfamiliar adult. In contrast, Mitch asked questions and communicated his pleasure at each intriguing activity. In a playroom with two unfamiliar

peers, Larry pulled back. Mitch made friends quickly.

In longitudinal research on several hundred Caucasian children, Kagan (1998) found that about 20 percent of 4-month-old babies were easily upset by novelty (like Larry), whereas 40 percent were comfortable, even delighted, with new experiences (like Mitch). About 20 to 30 percent of these extreme groups retained their temperamental styles as they grew older (Kagan, 2003; Kagan & Saudino, 2001). Those resembling Larry tended to become fearful, inhibited toddlers and preschoolers; those resembling Mitch developed into outgoing, uninhibited youngsters.

Physiological Correlates of Shyness and Sociability

Kagan believes that individual differences in arousal of the *amygdala,* an inner brain structure that controls avoidance reactions, contribute to these contrasting temperaments. In shy, inhibited children, novel stimuli easily excite the amygdala and its connections to the cerebral cortex and sympathetic nervous system, which prepares the body to act in the face of threat. The same level of stimulation evokes minimal neural excitation in highly sociable, uninhibited children. In support

of this theory, while viewing photos of unfamiliar faces, adults who had been classified as inhibited in the second year of life showed greater fMRI activity in the amygdala than adults who had been uninhibited as toddlers (Schwartz et al., 2003). And additional physiological responses, known to be mediated by the amygdala, distinguish the two emotional styles:

- *Heart rate.* As early as the first few weeks of life, the heart rates of shy children are consistently higher than those of sociable children, and they speed up further in response to unfamiliar events (Snidman et al., 1995).

- *Cortisol.* Saliva concentration of cortisol, a hormone that regulates blood pressure and is involved in resistance to stress, tends to be higher in shy than in sociable children (Gunnar & Nelson, 1994; Kagan & Snidman, 1991).

- *Pupil dilation, blood pressure, and skin surface temperature.* Compared with sociable children, shy children show greater pupil dilation, rise in blood pressure, and cooling of the fingertips when faced with novelty (Kagan et al., 1999).

Yet another physiological correlate of approach–withdrawal to people and ob-

behavior (Mangelsdorf, Schoppe, & Buur, 2000). And parent perceptions are vital for understanding the way parents view and respond to their child. For example, parents' early judgments of their babies as emotionally positive, irritable, or fearful predict the development of temperament over the first year (Pauli-Pott et al., 2003). This suggests that at least to some extent, parents shape their infant's emotional style to fit with their beliefs.

Although observations by researchers in the home or laboratory avoid the subjectivity of parent reports, they can lead to other inaccuracies. In homes, observers find it hard to capture all relevant information, especially rare but important events, such as infants' response to frustration. And in the unfamiliar lab setting, distress-prone children may become too upset to complete the session (Wachs & Bates, 2001). Still, researchers can better control the study of temperament in the lab. And they can conveniently combine observations of behavior with psychophysiological measures to gain insight into the biological basis of temperament.

Most psychophysiological assessments have focused on **inhibited, or shy, children,** who react negatively to and withdraw from novel stimuli (much like Thomas and Chess's slow-to-warm-up children), and on **uninhibited, or sociable, children,** who react positively to and approach novel stimuli. As the Biology and Environment box above reveals, heart rate, hormone levels, and EEG brain waves in the frontal region of the cerebral cortex differentiate children with inhibited and uninhibited temperaments.

A strong physiological response to uncertain situations prompts this 2-year-old's withdrawal when a friend of her parents bends down to chat with her. Her mother's patient but insistent encouragement can modify her physiological reactivity and help her overcome her urge to retreat from unfamiliar events.

© ROBERT BRENNER/PHOTOEDIT

jects is the pattern of EEG brain waves in the frontal region of the cerebral cortex. Recall from Chapter 5 that the left hemisphere is specialized to respond with positive emotion, the right hemisphere with negative emotion. Shy infants and preschoolers show greater right than left frontal brain-wave activity; their sociable counterparts show the opposite pattern (Calkins, Fox, & Marshall, 1996). Neural activity in the amygdala is transmitted to the frontal lobe and probably influences these patterns.

Long-Term Consequences

According to Kagan (1998), extremely shy or sociable children inherit a physiology that biases them toward a particular temperamental style. When early inhibition persists, it can lead to adjustment difficulties, such as excessive cautiousness, social withdrawal, low self-esteem, and loneliness (Fordham & Stevenson-Hinde,

1999; Rubin, Stewart, & Coplan, 1995). Yet heritability research indicates that genes contribute only modestly to shyness and sociability. And many inhibited infants and young children cope with novelty more effectively as they get older.

Child-rearing practices affect the chances that an emotionally reactive baby will become a fearful child. Warm, supportive parenting reduces the physiological reactivity of shy infants and preschoolers, whereas cold, intrusive parenting heightens anxiety and social re-

serve (Rubin, Burgess, & Hastings, 2002). In addition, when parents protect infants who dislike novelty from minor stresses, they make it harder for the child to overcome an urge to retreat from unfamiliar events. In contrast, parents who make appropriate demands for their baby to approach new experiences help the child overcome fear (Rubin et al., 1997). In sum, for children to develop at their best, parenting must be tailored to their temperaments—a theme we will encounter again in this and later chapters.

Stability of Temperament

It would be difficult to claim that something like temperament really exists if children's emotional styles were not stable over time. Indeed, many studies support the long-term stability of temperament. Infants and young children who score low or high on attention span, irritability, sociability, or shyness are likely to respond similarly when assessed again a few years later and, occasionally, even into the adult years (Caspi et al., 2003; Kochanska & Radke-Yarrow, 1992; Pedlow et al., 1993; Rothbart, Ahadi, & Evans, 2000; Ruff & Rothbart, 1996).

When the evidence as a whole is examined carefully, however, temperamental stability is generally low to moderate (Putnam, Samson, & Rothbart, 2000). Although quite a few children remain the same, a good number have changed when assessed again. In fact, some characteristics, such as shyness and sociability, are stable over the long term only in children at the extremes—those who are very inhibited or very outgoing to begin with (Kerr et al., 1994; Sanson et al., 1996).

Why is temperament not more stable? A major reason is that temperament itself develops with age. To illustrate, let's look at irritability and activity level. Recall from Chapter 4 that the early months are a period of fussing and crying for most babies. As infants better regulate their attention and emotions, many who initially seemed irritable become calm and content. In the case of activity level, the meaning of the behavior changes. At first, an active, wriggling infant tends to be highly aroused and uncomfortable, whereas an inactive baby is often alert and attentive. As infants move on their own, the reverse is so! An active crawler is usually alert and interested in exploration, whereas a very inactive baby might be fearful and withdrawn.

These inconsistencies help us understand why long-term prediction from early temperament is best achieved in the second year of life and after, when the child's system of emotion, attention, and action is better established (Caspi, 1998; Lemery et al., 1999). At the same time, the changes shown by many children suggest that experience can modify biologically based temperamental traits, although children rarely change from one extreme to another—that is, a shy toddler practically never becomes highly sociable. With these ideas in mind, let's turn to genetic and environmental contributions to temperament and personality.

Genetic Influences

The word *temperament* implies a genetic foundation for individual differences in personality. Research indicates that identical twins are more similar than fraternal twins across a wide range of temperamental traits (activity level, shyness/sociability, irritability, attention span, and persistence) and personality measures (introversion/extroversion, anxiety, agreeableness, and impulsivity) (Caspi, 1998; DiLalla, Kagan, & Reznick, 1994; Goldsmith et al., 1999; Saudino & Cherny, 2001). In Chapter 2, we noted that heritability estimates derived from twin studies suggest a moderate role for genetic factors in temperament and personality: About half of individual differences have been attributed to differences in genetic makeup.

Consistent ethnic and sex differences in early temperament exist, again implying a role for heredity. Compared with Caucasian infants, Asian babies tend to be less active, irritable, and vocal, more easily soothed when upset, and better at quieting themselves (Kagan et al., 1994; Lewis, Ramsay, & Kawakami, 1993). Grace's capacity to remain contentedly seated in her high chair through a long family dinner certainly fits with this evidence. And some Asian infants are more emotionally restrained. Furthermore, Timmy's high rate of activity is consistent with sex differences in emotional styles (Gartstein & Rothbart, 2003). Beginning in infancy, boys tend to be more active and daring, and girls more anxious and timid—a difference reflected in boys' higher injury rates throughout childhood and adolescence.

Still, genetic influences vary with the temperamental trait and the age of the individual being studied. For example, heritability estimates are much higher for expressions of negative emotion than for positive emotion. And the role of hereditary is considerably less in infancy than in childhood and later years, when temperament becomes more stable (Wachs & Bates, 2001).

Environmental Influences

Although genetic influences on temperament are clear, environment is powerful as well. For example, persistent nutritional and emotional deprivation profoundly alters temperament, resulting in maladaptive emotional styles (Wachs & Bates, 2001). Recall from Chapter 5 that even after dietary improvement, children exposed to severe malnutrition in infancy remain more distractible and fearful than their agemates. And infants reared in deprived orphanages are easily overwhelmed by stressful experiences. Their poor regulation of emotion results in inattention and weak impulse control, including frequent expressions of anger (see pages 175 and 181).

Other research shows that child rearing has much to do with whether or not infants and young children maintain their temperamental traits. In fact, heredity and environment often jointly contribute to temperament, since a child's approach to the world affects the experiences to which she is exposed. To see how this works, let's take a closer look at the evidence on ethnic and sex differences in temperament, which shows that parenting practices are involved.

When asked about their approach to child rearing, Japanese mothers say that babies come into the world as independent beings who must learn to rely on their parents through close physical contact. North American mothers are likely to believe just the opposite—that they must wean the baby away from dependence into autonomy (Kojima, 1986). Consistent with these beliefs, Asian mothers interact gently, soothingly, and gesturally with their babies, whereas Caucasian mothers use a more active, stimulating, verbal approach (Rothbaum et al., 2000a). Also, recall from

© GEORGE F. MOBLEY/NATIONAL GEOGRAPHIC IMAGE COLLECTION

At birth, Chinese infants are calmer, more easily soothed when upset, and better at quieting themselves than are Caucasian infants. Although these differences may have biological roots, cultural variations in child rearing support them.

our discussion of emotional self-regulation that Chinese and Japanese adults discourage babies from expressing strong emotion, an effort that contributes further to their infants' tranquility.

A similar process seems to contribute to sex differences in temperament. Within the first 24 hours after birth (before they have had much experience with the baby), parents already perceive male and female newborns differently. Sons are rated as larger, better coordinated, more alert, and stronger. Daughters are viewed as softer, more awkward, weaker, and more delicate (Stern & Karraker, 1989; Vogel et al., 1991). These gender-stereotyped beliefs influence parents' treatment of infants and toddlers. Parents more often encourage their young sons to be physically active and their daughters to seek help and physical closeness (Ruble & Martin, 1998). These practices promote temperamental differences between boys and girls.

In families with several children, an additional influence on temperament is at work. Parents often look for and emphasize personality differences in their children. This is reflected in the comparisons parents make: "She's a lot more active," or "He's more sociable." In a study of identical-twin toddlers, mothers treated each twin differently, and this differential treatment predicted twin differences in emotional style. The twin who received more warmth and less harshness was more positive in mood and social behavior (Deater-Deckard et al., 2001). Each child, in turn, evokes responses from caregivers that are consistent with parental beliefs and the child's actual temperamental style.

Besides different experiences within the family, as siblings get older, they have unique experiences with peers, teachers, and others in their community that profoundly affect development (Caspi, 1998). And in middle childhood and adolescence, siblings often seek ways to differ from one another. For these reasons, both identical and fraternal twins tend to become more distinct in personality with age (McCartney, Harris, & Bernieri, 1990). In sum, temperament and personality can be understood only in terms of complex interdependencies between genetic and environmental factors.

Temperament and Child Rearing: The Goodness-of-Fit Model

We have already indicated that the temperaments of many children change with age. This suggests that environments do not always promote a child's current emotional style. If a child's disposition interferes with learning or getting along with others, adults can gently but consistently counteract the child's maladaptive behavior.

Thomas and Chess (1977) proposed a **goodness-of-fit model** to explain how temperament and environment can together produce favorable outcomes. Goodness of fit involves creating child-rearing environments that recognize each child's temperament while encouraging more adaptive functioning.

Goodness of fit helps explain why difficult children (who withdraw from new experiences and react negatively and intensely) are at high risk for later adjustment problems. These children, at least in many Western middle-SES families, frequently experience parenting that fits poorly with their dispositions. As infants, they are less likely to receive sensitive caregiving (van den Boom & Hoeksma, 1994). By the second year, parents of difficult children tend to resort to angry, punitive discipline, and the child reacts with defiance and disobedience. Consequently, parents continue their coercive tactics as well as behave inconsistently, at times rewarding the child's noncompliance by giving in to it (Calkins, 2002; Lee & Bates, 1985). These practices maintain and even increase the child's irritable, conflict-ridden style. In contrast, when parents are positive and involved and engage in the sensitive, face-to-face play that helps infants regulate emotion, difficultness declines by age 2 (Feldman, Greenbaum, & Yirmiya, 1999).

Effective caregiving, however, depends on life conditions. In a comparison of the temperaments of Russian and American babies, Russian infants were more emotionally negative, fearful, and upset when frustrated (Gartstein, Slobodskaya, & Kinsht, 2003). Faced with a depressed national economy, which resulted in longer work hours and increased stress, Russian parents may have lacked time and energy to engage in sensitive, coordinated interaction with their babies, which protects against difficultness.

This mother is perplexed because her 1-year-old is not responding to her efforts to help him calm down. Difficult children react negatively and intensely. When parents are patient and make firm but reasonable demands for mastering new experiences, difficultness often subsides.

© NUBAR ALEXANIAN/STOCK BOSTON, LLC.

Cultural values also affect the fit between parenting and child temperament. In Western nations, shy, withdrawn children are viewed as socially incompetent. Yet Chinese adults evaluate such children positively—as advanced in social maturity. In line with this view, in a study comparing Canadian and Chinese children, the Chinese children scored much higher in inhibition. Furthermore, Canadian mothers of shy children reported more protection and punishment and less acceptance and encouragement of achievement. Chinese mothers of shy children indicated just the opposite—less punishment and more acceptance and encouragement (Chen et al., 1998).

In cultures where particular temperamental styles are linked to adjustment problems, a good match between rearing conditions and child temperament is best accomplished early, before unfavorable temperament–environment relationships produce maladjustment that is hard to undo. Both difficult and shy children benefit from warm, accepting parenting that makes firm but reasonable demands for mastering new experiences. In the case of reserved, inactive toddlers, highly stimulating maternal behavior—frequent questioning and pointing out objects—fosters exploration of the environment. Yet these same parental behaviors have a negative impact on active toddlers, inhibiting their exploration (Miceli et al., 1998). Recall from Chapter 6 that Vanessa often behaved in a harsh, directive way with Timmy. A "poor fit" between her parenting and Timmy's active temperament may have contributed to his tendency to move from one activity to the next with little true engagement.

The goodness-of-fit model reminds us that babies come into the world with unique dispositions that adults have to accept. Parents can neither take full credit for their children's virtues nor be blamed for all their faults. But parents can turn an environment that exaggerates a child's problems into one that builds on the youngster's strengths. In the following sections, we will see that goodness of fit is also at the heart of infant–caregiver attachment. This first intimate relationship grows out of interaction between parent and baby, to which the emotional styles of both partners contribute.

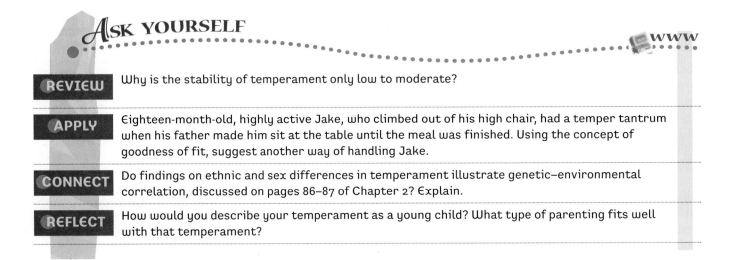

Ask YOURSELF

www

REVIEW Why is the stability of temperament only low to moderate?

APPLY Eighteen-month-old, highly active Jake, who climbed out of his high chair, had a temper tantrum when his father made him sit at the table until the meal was finished. Using the concept of goodness of fit, suggest another way of handling Jake.

CONNECT Do findings on ethnic and sex differences in temperament illustrate genetic–environmental correlation, discussed on pages 86–87 of Chapter 2? Explain.

REFLECT How would you describe your temperament as a young child? What type of parenting fits well with that temperament?

Development of Attachment

Attachment is the strong, affectionate tie we feel for special people in our lives that leads us to experience pleasure and joy when we interact with them and to be comforted by their nearness during times of stress. By the second half of the first year, infants have become attached to familiar people who have responded to their needs. Watch babies of this age, and notice how they single out their parents for special attention. For example, when the mother enters the room, the baby breaks into a broad, friendly smile. When she picks him up, he pats her face, explores her hair, and snuggles against her. When he feels anxious or afraid, he crawls into her lap and clings closely.

Freud first suggested that the infant's emotional tie to the mother is the foundation for all later relationships. We will see shortly that research on the consequences of attachment is consistent with Freud's idea. But attachment has also been the subject of intense theoretical debate. Turn back to the description of Erikson's theory at the beginning of this chapter, and notice how the *psychoanalytic perspective* regards feeding as the central context in which caregivers and babies build this close emotional bond. *Behaviorism,* too, emphasizes the importance of feeding, but for different reasons. According to a well-known behaviorist account, as the mother satisfies the baby's hunger (primary drive), infants learn to prefer her soft caresses, warm smiles, and tender words of comfort (secondary drive) because these events have been paired with tension relief.

Although feeding is an important context for building a close relationship, attachment does not depend on hunger satisfaction. In the 1950s, a famous experiment showed that rhesus monkeys reared with terry-cloth and wire-mesh "surrogate mothers" clung to the soft terry-cloth substitute, even though the wire-mesh "mother" held the bottle and infants had to climb on it to be fed (Harlow & Zimmerman, 1959). Similarly, human infants become attached to family members who seldom feed them, including fathers, siblings, and grandparents. And perhaps you have noticed that toddlers in Western cultures who sleep alone and experience frequent daytime separations from their parents sometimes develop strong emotional ties to cuddly objects, such as blankets or teddy bears. Yet such objects have never played a role in infant feeding!

Another problem with drive reduction and psychoanalytic accounts of attachment is that much is said about the caregiver's contribution to the attachment relationship, but little attention is given to the role of the infant's characteristics.

Bowlby's Ethological Theory

Today, **ethological theory of attachment,** which recognizes the infant's emotional tie to the caregiver as an evolved response that promotes survival, is the most widely accepted view. John Bowlby (1969), who first applied this idea to the infant–caregiver bond, was originally a psychoanalyst. In his theory, he retained the psychoanalytic idea that quality of attachment to the caregiver has profound implications for the child's feelings of security and capacity to form trusting relationships.

At the same time, Bowlby was inspired by Konrad Lorenz's studies of imprinting in baby geese (see Chapter 1). He believed that the human infant, like the young of other animal species, is endowed with a set of built-in behaviors that keep the parent nearby to protect the infant from danger and to provide support for exploring and mastering the environment (Waters & Cummings, 2000). Contact with the parent also ensures that the baby will be fed, but Bowlby was careful to point out that feeding is not the basis for attachment. Instead, the attachment bond has strong biological roots. It can best be understood in an evolutionary context in which survival of the species—through ensuring both safety and competence—is of utmost importance.

According to Bowlby, the infant's relationship with the parent begins as a set of innate signals that call the adult to the baby's side. Over time, a true affectionate bond forms, which is supported by new cognitive and emotional capacities as well as by a history of warm, sensitive care. Attachment develops in four phases:

1. *The preattachment phase* (birth to 6 weeks). Built-in signals—grasping, smiling, crying, and gazing into the adult's eyes—help bring newborn babies into close contact with other humans. Once an adult responds, infants encourage her to remain nearby because closeness comforts them. Babies of this age recognize their own mother's smell and voice (see Chapter 4). But they are not yet attached to her, since they do not mind being left with an unfamiliar adult.

2. *The "attachment in the making" phase* (6 weeks to 6–8 months). During this phase, infants respond differently to a familiar caregiver than to a stranger. For example, at 4 months, Timmy smiled, laughed, and babbled more freely when interacting with his mother and quieted more quickly when she picked him up. As infants interact with the parent and experience relief from distress, they learn that their own actions affect the behavior of those around them. They begin to develop a *sense of trust*—the expectation that the caregiver will respond when signaled. But even though they recognize the parent, babies still do not protest when separated from her.

3. *The phase of "clear-cut" attachment* (6–8 months to 18 months–2 years). Now, attachment to the familiar caregiver is evident. Babies display **separation anxiety,** becoming upset when the

Baby monkeys reared with "surrogate mothers" preferred to cling to a soft terry-cloth "mother" instead of a wire-mesh "mother" that held a bottle. These findings contradict the drive reduction explanation of attachment, which assumes that the parent–infant relationship is based on feeding.

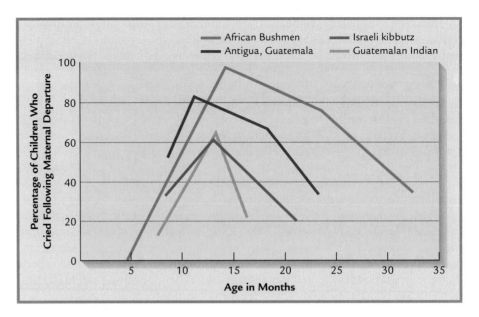

FIGURE 7.2

Development of separation anxiety.

In cultures around the world, separation anxiety emerges in the second half of the first year, increases until about 15 months, and then declines. (From J. Kagan, R. B. Kearsley, & P. R. Zelazo, 1978, *Infancy: Its Place in Human Development,* Cambridge, MA: Harvard University Press, p. 107. Copyright 1978 by the President and Fellows of Harvard College. All rights reserved. Reprinted by permission.)

adult they have come to rely on leaves. Separation anxiety does not always occur; like stranger anxiety (see page 254), it depends on infant temperament and the current situation. But in many cultures, it increases between 6 and 15 months (see Figure 7.2). Its appearance suggests that infants have a clear understanding that the caregiver continues to exist when not in view. Consistent with this idea, babies who have not yet mastered Piagetian object permanence usually do not become anxious when separated from their mothers (Lester et al., 1974).

Besides protesting the parent's departure, older infants and toddlers try hard to maintain her presence. They approach, follow, and climb on her in preference to others. And they use the familiar caregiver as a **secure base,** or point from which to explore, venturing into the environment and then returning for emotional support.

4. *Formation of a reciprocal relationship* (18 months–2 years and on). By the end of the second year, rapid growth in representation and language enables toddlers to understand the parent's coming and going and to predict her return. As a result, separation protest declines. Now children negotiate with the caregiver, using requests and persuasion to alter her goals. For example, at age 2, Caitlin asked Carolyn and David to read her a story before leaving her with a babysitter. The extra time with her parents, along with a better understanding of where they were going ("to have dinner with Uncle Sean") and when they would be back ("right after you go to sleep"), helped Caitlin withstand her parents' absence.

According to Bowlby (1980), out of their experiences during these four phases, children construct an enduring affectionate tie to the caregiver that they can use as a secure base in the parent's absence. This inner representation becomes a vital part of personality. It serves as an **internal working model,** or set of expectations about the availability of attachment figures, their likelihood of providing support during times of stress, and the self's interaction with those figures. This image becomes the model, or guide, for all future close relationships—through childhood and adolescence and into adult life (Bretherton, 1992).

Measuring the Security of Attachment

Although all family-reared babies become attached to a familiar caregiver by the second year, the quality of this relationship differs from child to child. Some infants appear relaxed and secure in the presence of the caregiver; they know they can count on her for protection and support. Others seem anxious and uncertain.

A widely used technique for assessing the quality of attachment between 1 and 2 years of age is the **Strange Situation.** In designing it, Mary Ainsworth and her colleagues reasoned that securely attached infants and toddlers should use the parent as a secure base from which to explore in an unfamiliar playroom. In addition, when the parent leaves, an unfamiliar adult should be less comforting than the parent. Consequently, the Strange Situation takes the baby through eight short episodes, in which brief separations from and reunions with the caregiver occur (see Table 7.3).

Observing infants' responses to these episodes, researchers identified a secure attachment pattern and three patterns of insecurity; a few babies cannot be classified (Ainsworth et al., 1978; Main & Solomon, 1990; Barnett & Vondra, 1999). Which pattern do you think Grace displayed after adjusting to her adoptive family? (See the description at the beginning of this chapter.)

- **Secure attachment.** These infants use the parent as a secure base. When separated, they may or may not cry, but if they do, it is because the parent is absent and they prefer her to the stranger. When the parent returns, they actively seek contact, and their crying is reduced immediately. About 65 percent of North American infants show this pattern.

- **Avoidant attachment.** These infants seem unresponsive to the parent when she is present. When she leaves, they usually are not distressed, and they react to the stranger in much the same way as to the parent. During reunion, they avoid or are slow to greet the parent, and when picked up, they often fail to cling. About 20 percent of North American infants show this pattern.

- **Resistant attachment.** Before separation, these infants seek closeness to the parent and often fail to explore. When she leaves, they are usually distressed, and on her return, they mix clinginess with angry, resistive behavior, struggling when held and sometimes hitting and pushing. In addition, many continue to cry after being picked up and cannot be comforted easily. About 10 to 15 percent of North American infants show this pattern.

- **Disorganized/disoriented attachment.** This pattern reflects the greatest insecurity. At reunion, these infants show a variety of confused, contradictory behaviors. They might look away while being held by the parent or approach her with flat, depressed emotion. Most communicate their disorientation with a dazed facial expression. A few cry out unexpectedly after having calmed down or display odd, frozen postures. About 5 percent of North American infants show this pattern.

Infants' reactions in the Strange Situation closely resemble their use of the parent as a secure base and their response to separation at home (Pederson & Moran, 1996; Pederson et al., 1998). For this reason, the procedure is a powerful tool for assessing attachment security.

The **Attachment Q-Sort** is a more efficient method that is suitable for children between 1 and 5 years of age. An observer—the parent or an expert informant—sorts a set of 90 descriptors of attachment-related behaviors (such as "Child greets mother with a big smile when she

---

TABLE 7.3

Episodes in the Strange Situation

EPISODE	EVENTS	ATTACHMENT BEHAVIOR OBSERVED
1	Experimenter introduces parent and baby to playroom and then leaves.	
2	Parent is seated while baby plays with toys.	Parent as a secure base
3	Stranger enters, is seated, and talks to parent.	Reaction to unfamiliar adult
4	Parent leaves room. Stranger responds to baby and offers comfort if upset.	Separation anxiety
5	Parent returns, greets baby, and offers comfort if necessary. Stranger leaves room.	Reaction to reunion
6	Parent leaves room.	Separation anxiety
7	Stranger enters room and offers comfort.	Ability to be soothed by stranger
8	Parent returns, greets baby, offers comfort if necessary, and tries to reinterest baby in toys.	Reaction to reunion

Note: Episode 1 lasts about 30 seconds; each of the remaining episodes lasts about 3 minutes. Separation episodes are cut short if the baby becomes very upset. Reunion episodes are extended if the baby needs more time to calm down and return to play.

Source: Ainsworth et al., 1978.

enters the room" and "If mother moves very far, child follows along") into nine categories, ranging from highly descriptive to not at all descriptive of the child. Then a score is computed that assigns children to securely or insecurely attached groups. Q-Sort responses of expert observers correspond well with Strange Situation attachment classifications (Pederson et al., 1998; Waters et al., 1995). And when mothers are carefully trained and supervised, their responses are reasonably consistent with those of expert observers (Seifer et al., 1996).

Stability of Attachment

Research on the stability of attachment patterns between 1 and 2 years of age yields a wide range of findings. In some studies, as many as 70 to 90 percent of children remain the same in their reactions to parents; in others, only 30 to 40 percent do (Thompson, 1998). A close look at which babies stay the same and which ones change yields a more consistent picture. Quality of attachment is usually secure and stable for middle-SES babies experiencing favorable life conditions. And infants who move from insecurity to security typically have well-adjusted mothers with positive family and friendship ties. Perhaps many became parents before they were psychologically ready but, with social support, grew into the role. In contrast, in low-SES families with many daily stresses, little social support, and parental psychological problems, attachment status generally moves away from security or changes from one insecure pattern to another (Belsky et al., 1996; Vondra, Hommerding, & Shaw, 1999; Vondra et al., 2001).

These findings indicate that securely attached babies more often maintain their attachment status than do insecure babies, whose relationship with the caregiver is, by definition, fragile and uncertain. The exception to this trend is disorganized/disoriented attachment—an insecure pattern that is highly stable over the second year (Barnett, Ganiban, & Cicchetti, 1999; Hesse & Main, 2000). As you will see, many disorganized/disoriented infants experience extremely negative caregiving, which may disrupt emotional self-regulation so severely that the baby's confused behavior persists.

Overall, many children show short-term instability in attachment quality. A few studies reveal high long-term stability from infancy to middle childhood and (on the basis of interviews about relationships with parents) into adolescence and emerging adulthood (Hamilton, 2000; Howes, Hamilton, & Phillipsen, 1998; Waters et al., 2000). But once again, participants came from middle-SES homes, and most probably had stable family lives. In one investigation of poverty-stricken children, many moved from secure attachment in infancy to insecure attachment in emerging adulthood. Child maltreatment, maternal depression, and poor family functioning in early adolescence distinguished these young people from the few who stayed securely attached (Weinfield, Sroufe, & Egeland, 2000).

Cultural Variations

Cross-cultural evidence indicates that attachment patterns may have to be interpreted differently in certain cultures. For example, as Figure 7.3 reveals, German infants show considerably more avoidant attachment than American babies do. But German parents encourage their infants to be nonclingy and independent, so the baby's behavior may be an intended outcome of cultural beliefs and practices (Grossmann et al., 1985). In contrast, a study of infants of the Dogon people of Mali, Africa, revealed that none showed avoidant attachment to their mothers (True, Pisani, & Oumar, 2001). Even when grandmothers are primary caregivers (as is the case with first-born sons), Dogan mothers remain available to their babies, holding them close and nursing them promptly in response to hunger and distress.

Japanese infants, as well, rarely show avoidant attachment (refer again to Figure 7.3). Instead, an unusually high number are resistantly attached, but the reaction may not represent true insecurity. Japanese mothers rarely leave their babies in others' care, so the Strange Situation probably creates far greater stress for them than for infants who frequently experience maternal sepa-

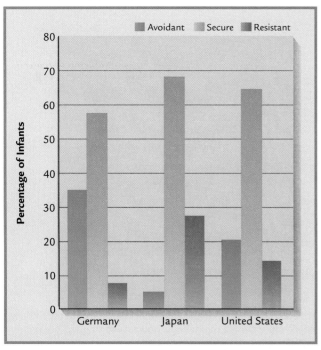

FIGURE 7.3

A cross-cultural comparison of infants' reactions in the Strange Situation.

A high percentage of German babies seem avoidantly attached, whereas a substantial number of Japanese infants appear resistantly attached. Note that these responses may not reflect true insecurity. Instead, they are probably due to cultural differences in child-rearing practices. (Adapted from van IJzendoorn & Kroonenberg, 1988.)

rations (Takahashi, 1990). Also, Japanese parents value the infant clinginess and attention seeking that are part of resistant attachment, considering them to be normal indicators of infant closeness and dependence (Rothbaum et al., 2000b). Despite these cultural variations and others, the secure pattern is still the most common attachment classification in all societies studied to date (van IJzendoorn & Sagi, 1999).

Factors That Affect Attachment Security

What factors might influence attachment security? Researchers have looked closely at four important influences: (1) opportunity to establish a close relationship, (2) quality of caregiving, (3) the baby's characteristics, and (4) family context, including parents' internal working models.

OPPORTUNITY FOR ATTACHMENT ● What happens when a baby does not have the opportunity to establish a close tie to a caregiver? In a series of studies, René Spitz (1945, 1946) observed institutionalized infants who had been given up by their mothers between 3 and 12 months of age. The babies were placed on a large ward where they shared a nurse with at least seven other babies. In contrast to the happy, outgoing behavior they had shown before separation, they wept and withdrew from their surroundings, lost weight, and had difficulty sleeping. If a consistent caregiver did not replace the mother, the depression deepened rapidly.

These institutionalized babies had emotional difficulties because they were prevented from forming a bond with one or a few adults (Rutter, 1996). Another study supports this conclusion. Researchers followed the development of infants in an institution with a good caregiver–child ratio and a rich selection of books and toys. However, staff turnover was so rapid that the average child had 50 different caregivers by age 4½! Many of these children became "late adoptees" who were placed in homes after age 4. Most developed deep ties with their adoptive parents, indicating that a first attachment bond can develop as late as 4 to 6 years of age (Tizard & Rees, 1975).

But these children were more likely to display emotional and social problems, including an excessive desire for adult attention, "overfriendliness" to unfamiliar adults and peers, and few friendships. Adopted children who spent their first 8 months or more in deprived Romanian orphanages often display these same difficulties (Hodges & Tizard, 1989; Zeanah, 2000). Although follow-ups into adulthood are necessary before we can be sure, these findings suggest that fully normal development depends on establishing close bonds with caregivers during the first few years of life.

QUALITY OF CAREGIVING ● Dozens of studies report that sensitive caregiving—responding promptly, consistently, and appropriately to infants and holding them tenderly and carefully—is moderately related to attachment security, in both biological and adoptive mother–infant pairs and in diverse cultures (De Wolff & van IJzendoorn, 1997; Posada et al., 2002; Stams, Juffer, & van IJzendoorn, 2002). In contrast, insecurely attached infants tend to have mothers who engage in less physical contact, handle them awkwardly, behave in a "routine" manner, and are sometimes negative, resentful, and rejecting (Ainsworth et al., 1978; Isabella, 1993; Pederson & Moran, 1996).

Also, in several studies, a special form of communication called interactional synchrony separated the experiences of secure from insecure babies. It is best described as a sensitively tuned "emotional dance," in which the caregiver responds to infant signals in a well-timed, rhythmic, appropriate fashion. In addition, both partners match emotional states, especially the positive ones (Isabella & Belsky, 1991; Kochanska, 1998). In one instance, Carolyn responded to Caitlin's excited shaking of a rattle with an enthusiastic "That-a-girl!" When Caitlin babbled and looked at her mother, Carolyn smiled and spoke expressively in return. When she fussed and cried, Carolyn soothed with gentle touches and soft words.

Earlier we saw that sensitive face-to-face play, in which interactional synchrony occurs, helps infants regulate emotion. But moderate adult–infant coordination is a better predictor of attachment security than "tight" coordination, in which the adult responds to most infant cues (Jaffe et al., 2001). Perhaps warm, sensitive caregivers use a relaxed, flexible style of communication in which they comfortably accept and repair emotional mismatches, returning to a synchronous state. Furthermore, finely tuned, coordinated interaction does not characterize parent–infant interaction everywhere. Among the Gusii people of Kenya, mothers rarely cuddle, hug, and interact playfully with their babies, although they are very responsive to their babies'

Research on infants of the Dogon people, who live in small farming villages in Mali, Africa, revealed that none were avoidantly attached to their mothers. Dogon maternal care consists of constant nearness to babies and prompt, gentle responsiveness to infant distress. Dogon mothers are almost never overstimulating and intrusive—practices linked to avoidant attachment.

This mother and baby engage in a sensitively tuned form of communication called interactional synchrony, in which they match emotional states, especially the positive ones. Interactional synchrony may support the development of secure attachment, but it does not characterize parent–infant interaction in all cultures.

needs. Most Gusii infants appear securely attached, using the mother as a secure base (LeVine et al., 1994). This suggests that secure attachment depends on attentive caregiving but that its association with moment-by-moment contingent interaction is probably limited to certain cultures.

Compared with securely attached infants, avoidant babies tend to receive overstimulating and intrusive care. Their mothers might, for example, talk energetically to them while they are looking away or falling asleep. By avoiding the mother, these infants appear to be escaping from overwhelming interaction. Resistant infants often experience inconsistent care. Their mothers are unresponsive to infant signals. Yet when the baby begins to explore, these mothers interfere, shifting the infant's attention back to themselves. As a result, the baby is overly dependent as well as angry at the mother's lack of involvement (Cassidy & Berlin, 1994; Isabella & Belsky, 1991).

When caregiving is highly inadequate, it is a powerful predictor of disruptions in attachment. Child abuse and neglect (topics we will consider in Chapter 10) are associated with all three forms of attachment insecurity. Among maltreated infants, disorganized/disoriented attachment is especially high (Barnett, Ganiban, & Cicchetti, 1999). Depressed mothers and parents suffering from a traumatic event, such as loss of a loved one, also tend to promote the uncertain behaviors of this pattern (Teti et al., 1995; van IJzendoorn, 1995). Observations reveal that these mothers display frightening, contradictory, and other unpleasant behaviors, such as looking scared, mocking or teasing the baby, holding the baby stiffly at a distance, roughly pulling the baby by the arm, or seeking reassurance from the upset child (Lyons-Ruth, Bronfman, & Parsons, 1999; Schuengel et al., 1999). The baby's disorganized behavior seems to reflect her conflicting reaction to the parent, who sometimes comforts but at other times arouses fear.

INFANT CHARACTERISTICS ● Since attachment is the result of a *relationship* that builds between two partners, infant characteristics should affect how easily it is established. In Chapters 3 and 4 we saw that prematurity, birth complications, and newborn illness make caregiving more taxing. In stressed, poverty-stricken families, these difficulties are linked to attachment insecurity (Wille, 1991). But when parents have the time and patience to care for a baby with special needs and view their infants positively, at-risk newborns fare quite well in attachment security (Cox, Hopkins, & Hans, 2000; Pederson & Moran, 1995).

Infants also vary in temperament, but its role in attachment security has been intensely debated. Some researchers believe that infants who are irritable and fearful may simply react to brief separations with intense anxiety, regardless of the parent's sensitivity to the baby (Kagan, 1998). Consistent with this view, emotionally reactive, difficult babies are more likely to develop later insecure attachments (Seifer et al., 1996; Vaughn & Bost, 1999).

But other evidence suggests that caregiving may be involved in the relationship between infant difficultness and attachment insecurity. In one study, the emotional quality of the mother–infant relationship was a better predictor of attachment quality than infants' temperamental traits, assessed in situations other than mother–infant interaction (Kochanska & Coy, 2002) And in a study focusing on disorganized/disoriented babies, emotional reactivity increased sharply over the second year (see Figure 7.4). Attachment disorganization was not caused by difficult temperament but rather seemed to promote it (Barnett, Ganiban, & Cicchetti, 1999).

Furthermore, caregiving can override the impact of infant characteristics on attachment security. When researchers combined data from 34 studies including more than 1,600 mother–infant pairs, they found that maternal problems—such as mental illness, teenage parenthood, and child abuse—were associated with increased attachment insecurity (see Figure 7.5). In contrast, infant problems—ranging from prematurity and developmental delays to serious physical and mental disabilities—had little impact on attachment quality (van IJzendoorn et al., 1992). Finally, interventions that teach parents to interact sensitively with difficult-to-care-for infants are highly successful in enhancing both quality of caregiving and attachment security (Bakermans-Kranenburg et al., 2003).

FIGURE 7.4

Mean vocal distress (ranging from brief frustration sounds to continuous crying and screaming) in the Strange Situation by disorganized/disoriented babies and babies with other attachment patterns.

Babies were rated at two ages: 12 months and 18 months. At 12 months, the disorganized/disoriented infants appeared to suppress their distress, perhaps out of fear of their mother's response; they scored lower than infants with other attachment patterns. By 18 months, the distress of disorganized/disoriented toddlers had risen sharply, whereas the distress of other toddlers had declined. A disorganized/disoriented attachment pattern appeared to promote an emotionally reactive temperament. (Adapted from Barnett, Ganiban, & Cicchetti, 1999.)

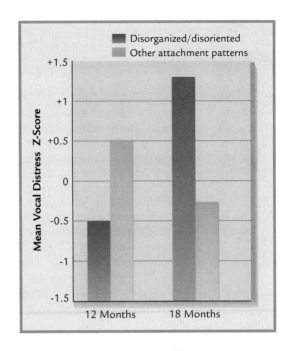

A major reason that temperament and other infant characteristics do not show strong relationships with attachment security may be that their influence depends on goodness of fit. From this perspective, *many* child attributes can lead to secure attachment as long as caregivers sensitively adjust their behavior to fit the baby's needs (Seifer & Schiller, 1995). But when a parent's capacity to do so is strained—for example, by stressful life conditions or her own personality—then infants with illnesses, disabilities, and difficult temperaments are at risk for attachment problems.

FAMILY CIRCUMSTANCES ● Timmy's parents divorced shortly after he was born, and his father moved to a distant city. Although Vanessa tried not to let his departure affect her caregiving, she became anxious and distracted. To make ends meet, she placed 1-month-old Timmy in Ginette's child-care home and began working 50- to 60-hour weeks. When Vanessa stayed late at the office, a babysitter picked Timmy up, gave him dinner, and put him to bed. Once or twice a week, Vanessa went to get Timmy. As he neared his first birthday, she noticed that the other children reached out, crawled, or ran to their mothers and fathers to be picked up and hugged. Timmy, in contrast, ignored Vanessa. When she said, "It's time to go," he passively allowed himself to be taken.

Timmy's behavior reflects a repeated finding: Job loss, a failing marriage, financial difficulties, and other stressors can undermine attachment by interfering with the sensitivity of parental care. Or they can affect babies' sense of security directly, by exposing them to angry adult interactions or unfavorable child-care arrangements (Thompson, 1998). At the same time, when parents manage to sustain a favorable relationship with their baby despite environmental stressors, they protect the child's development and foster resilience (Belsky & Fearon, 2002b). The availability of social supports, especially assistance with caregiving, reduces parental stress and fosters attachment security. Ginette's sensitivity and the parenting advice that Ben, a psychologist, offered Vanessa were helpful. As Timmy turned 2, his relationship with his mother seemed warmer.

PARENTS' INTERNAL WORKING MODELS ● Parents bring to the family context a long history of attachment experiences, out of which they construct internal working models that they apply to

FIGURE 7.5

Comparison of the effects of maternal problems and child problems on the attachment bond.

Maternal problems were associated with increased attachment insecurity. In contrast, child problems had little impact on the rate of attachment security and insecurity, which resembled that of normal samples. (Adapted from van IJzendoorn et al., 1992.)

Social Issues: Health

Does Child Care in Infancy Threaten Attachment Security and Later Adjustment?

Research suggests that infants placed in full-time child care before 12 months of age are more likely than home-reared babies to display insecure attachment—especially avoidance—in the Strange Situation (Belsky, 1992, 2001). Does this mean that infants who experience daily separations from their employed parents and early placement in child care are at risk for developmental problems? A close look at the evidence reveals that we should be cautious about coming to this conclusion.

Attachment Quality

In studies reporting a child care–attachment association, the rate of insecurity among child-care infants is somewhat higher than among non-child-care infants (36 versus 29 percent), but it nevertheless resembles the overall rate of insecurity reported for children in industrialized countries (Lamb, Sternberg, & Prodromidis, 1992). In fact, most infants of employed mothers are securely attached! Furthermore, not all investigations report a difference in attachment quality between child-care and non-child-care infants (NICHD Early Child Care Research Network, 1997; Roggman et al., 1994).

Family Circumstances

We have seen that family conditions affect attachment security. Many employed women find the pressures of handling two full-time jobs (work and motherhood) stressful. Some respond less sensitively to their babies because they receive little caregiving assistance from the child's father and are fatigued and harried, thereby risking the infant's security (Stifter, Coulehan, & Fish, 1993). Other employed mothers probably value and encourage their infant's independence. Or their babies are unfazed by brief separations in the Strange Situation because they are used to separating from their parents. In these cases, avoidance in the Strange Situation may represent healthy autonomy rather than insecurity (Clark-Stewart, Allhusen, & Goosens, 2001).

Quality and Extent of Child Care

Poor-quality child care and many hours in child care may contribute to a higher rate of insecure attachment among infants of employed mothers. In the U.S. National Institute of Child Health and Development (NICHD) Study of Early Child Care—the largest longitudinal study to date, including more than 1,300 infants and their families residing in ten American communities—child care alone did not con-

tribute to attachment insecurity. But when babies were exposed to combined home and child-care risk factors—insensitive caregiving at home with insensitive caregiving in child care, long hours in child care, or more than one child-care arrangement—the rate of insecurity increased. Overall, mother–child interaction was more favorable when children attended higher-quality child care and were in child care for fewer hours (NICHD Early Child Care Research Network, 1997, 1999).

Furthermore, when the NICHD sample reached 3 years of age, a history of higher-quality child care predicted better social skills as rated by caregivers (NICHD Early Child Care Research Network, 2002b). At the same time, regardless of child-care quality, at age 4½ to 5, children averaging more than 30 child-care hours per week were rated by their mothers, caregivers, and kindergarten teachers as having more behavior problems, especially defiance, disobedience, and aggression (NICHD Early Child Care Research Network, 2003a). This does not necessarily mean that child care causes behavior problems. Children prone to be aggressive may have parents who leave them in child care for longer hours.

Overall, findings of the NICHD study indicate that parenting has a far stronger

the bonds they establish with their babies. Carolyn remembered her mother as deeply affectionate and caring and viewed her as a positive influence in her own parenting. Monica recalled her mother as tense and preoccupied and expressed regret that they had not had a closer relationship. Do these images of parenthood affect the quality of Caitlin's and Grace's attachments to their mothers?

To answer this question, researchers have assessed adults' internal working models by having them evaluate childhood memories of attachment experiences. Parents who show objectivity and balance in discussing their childhoods, whether they were positive or negative, tended to have securely attached infants and behaved sensitively toward them. In contrast, parents who dismiss the importance of early relationships or describe them in angry, confused ways usually have insecurely attached babies and engage in less sensitive caregiving (van IJzendoorn, 1995; Pederson et al., 1998; Slade et al., 1999).

But we must be careful not to assume any direct transfer of parents' childhood experiences to their inner representations and quality of attachment to their own children. Internal working models are *reconstructed memories* affected by many factors besides early attachment experiences, including other close relationships, personality, and current life satisfaction. Research reveals that negative life events can weaken the link between an individual's own attachment security in infancy

© ELIZABETH CREWS

At the end of her day in child care, a toddler eagerly greets her mother. High-quality child care and fewer hours in child care are associated with favorable mother–child interaction, which contributes to attachment security.

impact on preschoolers' problem behavior than early, extensive child care (NICHD Early Child Care Research Network, 2002c). Indeed, having the opportunity to form a warm bond with a stable professional caregiver can be helpful to infants whose relationship with one or both parents is insecure. When followed into the preschool and early school years, such children show higher self-esteem and socially skilled behavior than their insecurely attached agemates who did not attend child care (Egeland & Hiester, 1995).

Conclusions

Taken together, research suggests that some infants may be at risk for attachment insecurity due to inadequate child care, long hours in child care, and the joint pressures their mothers experience from full-time employment and parenthood. However, using this as evidence to justify a reduction in infant child-care services is inappropriate. When family incomes are limited or mothers who want to work are forced to stay at home, children's emotional security is not promoted. In an Australian study, first-time mothers with high career commitment and high levels of social support tended to return to work early in their baby's first year. Compared with other babies, infants of these career-committed mothers were more likely to be securely attached at 12 months of age (Harrison & Ungerer, 2002). They also benefited from Australia's government-subsidized high-quality child care, which is available to all families.

Consequently, it makes sense to increase the availability of high-quality child care, to provide paid employment leave so parents can limit the hours their children spend in child care (see pages 144–145), and to educate parents about the vital role of sensitive caregiving in early emotional development. Return to Chapter 6, page 233, to review signs of developmentally appropriate child care for infants and toddlers. For child care to foster attachment security, the professional caregiver's relationship with the baby is vital. When caregiver–child ratios are generous, group sizes are small, and caregivers are educated about child development and child rearing, caregivers' interactions are more positive and children develop more favorably (NICHD Early Child Care Research Network, 2000b, 2002a). Child care with these characteristics can become part of an ecological system that relieves rather than intensifies parental and child stress, thereby promoting healthy attachment and development.

and a secure internal working model in adulthood. And insecurely attached babies who become adults with insecure internal working models often have lives that, based on adulthood self-reports, are filled with family crises (Waters et al., 2000; Weinfield, Sroufe, & Egeland, 2000).

In sum, our early rearing experiences do not destine us to become sensitive or insensitive parents. Rather, the way we *view* our childhoods—our ability to come to terms with negative events, to integrate new information into our working models, and to look back on our own parents in an understanding, forgiving way—appears to be much more influential in how we rear our children than the actual history of care we received (Main, 2000).

ATTACHMENT IN CONTEXT ● Carolyn and Vanessa returned to work when their babies were 2 to 3 months old. Monica did the same a few weeks after Grace's adoption. When mothers divide their time between work and parenting and place their infants and toddlers in child care, is the quality of attachment affected? Turn to the Social Issues: Health box above for research that addresses this issue.

After reading the box on child care and attachment, take a moment to consider each factor that influences the development of attachment. These include infant and parent characteristics, the parents' relationship with each other, outside-the-family stressors, the availability of social supports, parents' views of their attachment history, and child-care arrangements. Although attachment builds within the warmth and intimacy of caregiver–infant interaction, it can be fully understood only from an ecological systems perspective (Bornstein, 2002). Return to Chapter 1, pages 27–29, to review Bronfenbrenner's ecological systems theory. Notice how research confirms the importance of each level of the environment for attachment security.

Multiple Attachments

We have already indicated that babies develop attachments to a variety of familiar people—not just mothers, but fathers, siblings, grandparents, and professional caregivers. Although Bowlby (1969) made room for multiple attachments in his theory, he believed that infants are predisposed to direct their attachment behaviors to a single special person, especially when they are distressed. For example, when an anxious, unhappy 1-year-old is permitted to choose between the mother and the father as a source of comfort and security, the infant usually chooses the mother (Lamb, 1997). This preference typically declines over the second year of life. An expanding world of attachments enriches the emotional and social lives of many babies.

FATHERS ● Like mothers' sensitive caregiving, fathers' sensitive caregiving predicts secure attachment—an effect that becomes stronger the more time they spend with their babies (van IJzendoorn & De Wolff, 1997). And fathers of 1- to 5-year-olds enrolled in full-time child care report feeling just as much anxiety as mothers about separating from their child and just as much concern about the impact of these daily separations on the child's well-being (Deater-Deckard et al., 1994).

But as infancy progresses, mothers and fathers in many cultures—Australia, India, Israel, Italy, Japan, and the United States—relate to babies in different ways. Mothers devote more time to physical care and expressing affection. Fathers spend more time in playful interaction—a vital context in which they build secure attachments with their babies (Lamb, 1997; Roopnarine et al., 1990). Mothers and fathers also play differently. Mothers more often provide toys, talk to infants, and engage in conventional games like pat-a-cake and peekaboo. In contrast, fathers tend to engage in more exciting, highly physical bouncing and lifting games that provide bursts of stimulation, especially with their infant sons (Yogman, 1981).

However, this picture of "mother as caregiver" and "father as playmate" has changed in some families due to the revised work status of women. Employed mothers tend to engage in more playful stimulation of their babies than unemployed mothers, and their husbands are somewhat more involved in caregiving (Cox et al., 1992). When fathers are the primary caregivers, they retain their arousing play style (Lamb & Oppenheim, 1989). Such highly involved fathers are less gender-stereotyped in their beliefs; have sympathetic, friendly personalities; often had fathers who were more involved in raising them; and regard parenthood as an especially enriching experience (Cabrera et al., 2000; Levy-Shiff & Israelashvili, 1988).

Fathers' involvement with babies takes place within a complex system of family attitudes and relationships. When pregnancies were intended rather than accidental and when both parents believe that men can nurture infants, fathers devote more time to caregiving (Beitel & Parke, 1998; Brown & Eisenberg, 1995). A warm, gratifying marital bond supports both parents' sensitivity and involvement, but it is particularly important for fathers (Frosch, Mangelsdorf, & McHale, 2000; Grych & Clark, 1999). See the Cultural Influences box on the following page for cross-cultural evidence that documents this conclusion—and also shows the powerful role of paternal warmth in children's development.

SIBLINGS ● Despite a declining family size, 80 percent of North American children still grow up with at least one sibling. The arrival of a baby brother or sister is a difficult experience for most preschoolers, who quickly realize that now they must share their parents' attention and affec-

Although the arrival of a baby brother or sister is a difficult experience for most preschoolers, a rich emotional relationship quickly builds between siblings. This toddler is already actively involved in play with her 4-year-old-brother, and both derive great pleasure from the interaction.

© ERIKA STONE/PHOTO RESEARCHERS, INC.

Cultural Influences

The Powerful Role of Paternal Warmth in Development

Research in many societies demonstrates that fathers' warmth contributes greatly to children's long-term favorable development. In studies of many societies and ethnic groups, representing Western and non-Western diversity around the world, researchers coded paternal expressions of love and nurturance—evident in such behaviors as cuddling, hugging, comforting, playing, verbally expressing love, and praising the child's behavior. Fathers' sustained affectionate involvement predicted later cognitive, emotional, and social competence as strongly, and occasionally more strongly, than did mothers' warmth (Veneziano, 2003; Rohner & Veneziano, 2001). And in Western cultures, fathers' warmth protected children against a wide range of difficulties, including childhood emotional and behavior problems and adolescent substance abuse and delinquency (Grant et al., 2000; Rohner & Brothers, 1999; Tacon & Caldera, 2001).

In families where fathers devote little time to physical caregiving, they express warmth through play. In a German longitudinal study, fathers' play sensitivity—accepting toddlers' play initiatives, adapting play behaviors to fit toddlers' capacities, and responding appropriately to toddlers' expressions of emotion—predicted children's secure internal working models of attachment during middle childhood and adolescence (Grossmann et al., 2002). Through

stimulating play, fathers seemed to transfer to young children a sense of confidence in exploration and in the parental relationship, which may strengthen their capacity to master many later challenges.

What factors promote paternal warmth? Cross-cultural research reveals a consistent relationship between the amount of time fathers spend near infants and toddlers and their expressions of caring and affection (Rohner & Veneziano, 2001). Consider the Aka hunters and gatherers of Central Africa, where fathers spend more time in physical proximity to their babies than in any other known society. Observations reveal that Aka fathers are within arm's reach of infants more than half the day. They pick up, cuddle, and play with their babies at least five times more often than fathers in other hunting-and-gathering societies. Why are Aka fathers so involved? The bond between Aka husband and wife is unusually cooperative and intimate. Throughout

the day, couples share hunting, food preparation, and social and leisure activities. The more Aka parents are together, the greater the father's loving interaction with his baby (Hewlett, 1992).

In Western cultures as well, mothers' and fathers' warm interactions with babies are closely linked (Rohner & Veneziano, 2001). At the same time, paternal warmth promotes long-term favorable development, beyond the influence of maternal warmth. Greater recognition of the power of fathers' affection in virtually every culture and ethnic group studied may help motivate more men to engage in nurturing care of young children.

© RONNIE KAUFMAN/CORBIS

In both Western and non-Western nations, fathers' warmth predicts long-term, favorable development. And in Western societies, it protects against a wide range of adjustment problems in childhood and adolescence. In families where fathers devote little time to caregiving, they express warmth through play. This Japanese father engages in the exciting, active play style that tends to characterize fathers in many cultures.

tion. They often become demanding and clingy for a time and engage in deliberate naughtiness. And their security of attachment typically declines, more so if they are over age 2 (old enough to feel threatened and displaced) and the mother is under stress due to marital or psychological problems (Teti et al., 1996).

Yet resentment is only one feature of a rich emotional relationship that starts to form between siblings after a baby's birth. An older child can also be seen kissing, patting, and calling out "Mom, he needs you" when the baby cries—signs of growing affection. By the end of the baby's first year, siblings typically spend much time together, with the preschooler helping, sharing toys, imitating, and expressing friendliness in addition to anger and ambivalence (Dunn & Kendrick, 1982). Infants of this age are comforted by the presence of their preschool-age brother or sister during the mother's short absences (Stewart, 1983). And during the second year, toddlers often imitate and join in play with the older child (Dunn, 1989).

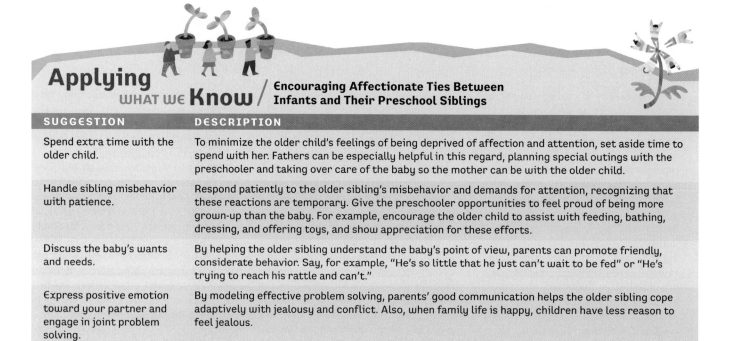

Applying WHAT WE Know / Encouraging Affectionate Ties Between Infants and Their Preschool Siblings

SUGGESTION	DESCRIPTION
Spend extra time with the older child.	To minimize the older child's feelings of being deprived of affection and attention, set aside time to spend with her. Fathers can be especially helpful in this regard, planning special outings with the preschooler and taking over care of the baby so the mother can be with the older child.
Handle sibling misbehavior with patience.	Respond patiently to the older sibling's misbehavior and demands for attention, recognizing that these reactions are temporary. Give the preschooler opportunities to feel proud of being more grown-up than the baby. For example, encourage the older child to assist with feeding, bathing, dressing, and offering toys, and show appreciation for these efforts.
Discuss the baby's wants and needs.	By helping the older sibling understand the baby's point of view, parents can promote friendly, considerate behavior. Say, for example, "He's so little that he just can't wait to be fed" or "He's trying to reach his rattle and can't."
Express positive emotion toward your partner and engage in joint problem solving.	By modeling effective problem solving, parents' good communication helps the older sibling cope adaptively with jealousy and conflict. Also, when family life is happy, children have less reason to feel jealous.

Nevertheless, individual differences in the quality of sibling relationships appear shortly after the younger siblings' arrival. Temperament plays an important role. For example, conflict increases when one sibling is emotionally intense or highly active (Brody, Stoneman, & McCoy, 1994; Dunn, 1994). Parenting also makes a difference. Secure infant–mother attachment and warmth toward both children are related to positive sibling interaction and to preschoolers' support of a distressed younger sibling (Volling, 2001; Volling & Belsky, 1992). Also, mothers who frequently play with their children and explain the toddler's wants and needs to the preschool sibling foster cooperative sibling ties. In contrast, maternal harshness and lack of involvement are linked to antagonistic sibling relationships (Howe, Aquan-Assee, & Bukowski, 2001). Finally, a good marriage is linked to older preschool siblings' capacity to cope adaptively with jealousy and conflict (Volling, McElwain, & Miller, 2002). Perhaps good communication between parents serves as a model of effective problem solving. It may also foster a generally happy family environment, which results in less reason for children to feel jealous.

Refer to Applying What We Know above for ways to promote positive relationships between babies and their preschool siblings. Research on brothers and sisters as attachment figures reminds us of the complex, multidimensional nature of the infant's social world. Siblings offer a rich social context in which children learn and practice a wide range of skills, including affectionate caring, conflict resolution, and control of hostile and envious feelings.

From Attachment to Peer Sociability

In cultures where agemates have regular contact during the first year of life, peer sociability begins early. By age 6 months, Caitlin and Timmy occasionally looked, reached, smiled, and babbled when they saw one another. These isolated social acts increased until, by the end of the first year, an occasional reciprocal exchange occurred in which the children grinned, gestured, or otherwise imitated a playmate's behavior (Vandell & Mueller, 1995).

Between 1 and 2 years, coordinated interaction occurs more often, largely in the form of mutual imitation involving jumping, chasing, or banging a toy. These imitative, turn-taking games create joint understandings that aid verbal communication. Around age 2, toddlers use words to talk about and influence a peer's behavior, as when Caitlin said to Grace, "Let's play chase," and after the game got going, "Hey, good running!" (Eckerman & Peterman, 2001; Eckerman & Whitehead, 1999). Reciprocal play and positive emotion are especially frequent in toddlers' interactions with familiar agemates, suggesting that they are building true peer relationships (Ross et al., 1992).

As we will see when we take up self-development, toddlers' budding social understanding sometimes leads to clever efforts to annoy others. And struggles with peers, often over objects, occur as well. But peer sociability is present in the first 2 years, and it is fostered by the early caregiver–child bond. From interacting with sensitive adults, babies learn how to send and interpret emotional signals in their first peer associations. Consistent with this idea, infants with a warm parental relationship engage in more extended peer exchanges. These children, in turn, display more socially competent behavior as preschoolers (Howes, 1988; Howes & Matheson, 1992). And for toddlers in child care, a secure attachment to a stable professional caregiver predicts advanced peer and play behavior (Howes & Hamilton, 1993).

Attachment and Later Development

According to psychoanalytic and ethological theories, the inner feelings of affection and security that result from a healthy attachment relationship support all aspects of psychological development. Consistent with this view, in an extensive longitudinal study, Alan Sroufe and his colleagues found that preschool teachers viewed children who were securely attached as babies as high in self-esteem, socially competent, cooperative, and popular. In contrast, they viewed avoidantly attached agemates as isolated and disconnected and resistantly attached agemates as disruptive and difficult. Studied again at age 11 in summer camp, children who had been secure infants had more favorable relationships with peers, closer friendships, and better social skills, as judged by camp counselors (Elicker, Englund, & Sroufe, 1992; Sroufe, 2002).

These findings have been taken by some researchers to mean that secure attachment in infancy causes improved cognitive, emotional, and social competence in later years. Yet more evidence is needed before we can be certain of this conclusion. In other longitudinal studies, secure infants sometimes developed more favorably than insecure infants and sometimes did not (Lewis, 1997; Schneider, Atkinson, & Tardif, 2001; Stams, Juffer, & van IJzendoorn, 2002). Disorganized/disoriented attachment, however, is an exception. It is consistently related to high hostility and aggression during the preschool and school years (Lyons-Ruth, 1996; Lyons-Ruth, Easterbrooks, & Cibelli, 1997).

Why, overall, is research on the consequences of attachment quality unclear? Perhaps *continuity of caregiving* determines whether attachment security is linked to later development (Lamb et al., 1985; Thompson, 2000). When parents respond sensitively not just in infancy but also during later years, children are likely to develop favorably. In contrast, parents who react insensitively for a long time have children who establish lasting patterns of avoidant, resistant, or disorganized behavior and are at greater risk for developmental difficulties.

Several findings support this interpretation. Recall that many mothers of disorganized/disoriented infants have serious psychological problems and engage in highly maladaptive caregiving—conditions that usually persist and are strongly linked to children's poor adjustment (Lyons-Ruth, Bronfman, & Parsons, 1999). Furthermore, when more than 1,000 children were tracked from 1 to 3 years of age, those with histories of secure attachment followed by sensitive mothering scored highest in cognitive, emotional, and social outcomes. Those with histories of insecure attachment followed by insensitive mothering scored lowest. And those with mixed histories of attachment and maternal sensitivity scored in between (Belsky & Fearon, 2002a). Specifically, insecurely attached infants whose mothers became more positive and supportive in early childhood showed signs of developmental recovery.

Does this trend remind you of our discussion of *resiliency* in Chapter 1? A child whose parental caregiving improves or who has compensating affectionate ties outside the immediate family can bounce back from adversity. In sum, efforts to create warm, responsive environments are not just important in infancy and toddlerhood; they are vital at later ages, as we will see in subsequent chapters.

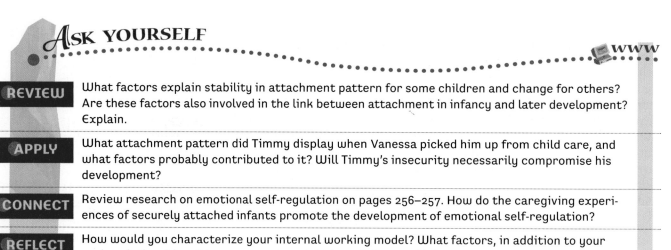

REVIEW What factors explain stability in attachment pattern for some children and change for others? Are these factors also involved in the link between attachment in infancy and later development? Explain.

APPLY What attachment pattern did Timmy display when Vanessa picked him up from child care, and what factors probably contributed to it? Will Timmy's insecurity necessarily compromise his development?

CONNECT Review research on emotional self-regulation on pages 256–257. How do the caregiving experiences of securely attached infants promote the development of emotional self-regulation?

REFLECT How would you characterize your internal working model? What factors, in addition to your early relationship with your parents, might have influenced it?

Self-Understanding

Infancy is a rich, formative period for the development of physical and social understanding. In Chapter 6 you learned that infants develop an appreciation of the permanence of objects. And in this chapter, we have seen that over the first year, infants recognize and respond appropriately to others' emotions and distinguish familiar from unfamiliar people. That both objects and people achieve an independent, stable existence for the infant implies that knowledge of the self as a separate, permanent entity emerges around this time.

Self-Awareness

After Caitlin's bath, Carolyn often held her in front of the bathroom mirror. As early as the first few months, Caitlin smiled and returned friendly behaviors to her image. At what age did she realize that the charming baby gazing and grinning back was really herself?

EMERGENCE OF THE I-SELF AND THE ME-SELF ● To answer this question, researchers have exposed infants and toddlers to images of themselves in mirrors, on videotapes, and in photos. When shown two side-by-side video images of their kicking legs, one from their own perspective (camera behind the baby) and one from an observer's perspective (camera in front of the baby), 3-month-olds looked longer at the observer's view (see Figure 7.6a). In another video-image comparison, they looked longer at a reversal of their leg positions than at a normal view (see Figure 7.6b) (Rochat, 1998). This suggests that young babies have a sense of their own body as a distinct entity, since they have habituated to it, as indicated by their interest in novel views of the body. By 4 months, infants look and smile more at video images of others than video images of themselves, indicating that they distinguish between the two and treat another person (as opposed to the self) as a potential social partner (Rochat & Striano, 2002).

Researchers agree that the earliest aspect of the self to emerge is the **I-self,** or *sense of self as agent,* involving awareness that the self is separate from the surrounding world and can control its own thoughts and actions. According to many theorists, the beginnings of the I-self lie in infants' recognition that their own actions cause objects and people to react in predictable ways (Harter, 1998). In support of this idea, when parents encourage exploration and respond sensitively to infant signals, their children tend to be advanced in constructing a sense of self as agent. For example, between 1 and 2 years of age, babies with such parents display more complex self-related actions during play, such as making a doll labeled as the self take a drink or kiss a teddy bear (Pipp, Easterbrooks, & Harmon, 1992).

FIGURE 7.6

Three-month-olds' emerging self-awareness, as indicated by reactions to video images.
(a) When shown two side-by-side views of their kicking legs, babies looked longer at the novel, observer's view than at their own view. (b) When shown a normal view of their leg positions alongside a reversed view, infants looked longer at the novel, reversed view. (Adapted from Rochat, 1998.)

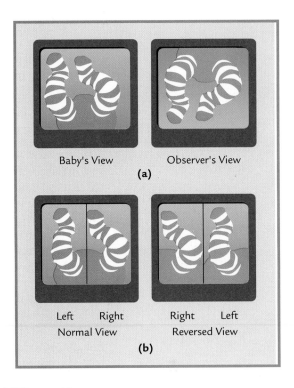

Baby's View   Observer's View

(a)

Left   Right   Right   Left
Normal View   Reversed View

(b)

Then, as infants act on the environment, they notice effects that help them sort out self from other people and objects (Rochat, 2001). For example, batting a mobile and seeing it swing informs the baby about the relation between self and physical world. Smiling and vocalizing at a caregiver who smiles and vocalizes back helps specify the relation between self and social world. And watching the movements of one's own hands and feet provides still another kind of feedback—one under much more direct control than other people or objects.

A second aspect of the self is the **me-self**, *a sense of self as an object of knowledge and evaluation.* It consists of all qualities that make the self unique, including physical characteristics, possessions, and (as the child gets older) attitudes, beliefs, and personality traits. During the second year, toddlers begin to construct a me-self; they become aware of the self's physical features. In one study, 9- to 24-month-olds were placed in front of a mirror. Then, under the pretext of wiping the baby's face, each mother was asked to rub red dye on her child's nose. Younger babies touched the mirror as if the red mark had nothing to do with any aspect of themselves. But by 15 months, toddlers rubbed their own strange-looking red noses. They were keenly aware of their unique appearance (Lewis & Brooks-Gunn, 1979). By age 2, almost all children use their name or a personal pronoun ("I" or "me") to refer to themselves.

Like the I-self, the me-self seems to be fostered by sensitive caregiving. Securely attached toddlers display more complex knowledge of their own and their parents' features (for example, by labeling body parts) than do their insecurely attached agemates (Pipp, Easterbrooks, & Brown, 1993).

SELF-AWARENESS AND EARLY EMOTIONAL AND SOCIAL DEVELOPMENT ● Self-awareness quickly becomes a central part of children's emotional and social lives. Recall that self-conscious emotions depend on an emerging sense of self. As the self strengthens in the second year, toddlers show the beginnings of self-conscious behavior: bashfulness and embarrassment. Self-awareness also leads to the child's first efforts to appreciate another's perspective. It is accompanied by early signs of **empathy**—the ability to understand another's emotional state and *feel with* that person, or respond emotionally in a similar way. For example, toddlers start to give to others what they themselves find comforting—a hug, a reassuring comment, or a favorite doll or blanket (Bischof-Köhler, 1991; Zahn-Waxler et al., 1992). At the same time, they demonstrate clear awareness of how to upset others. One 18-month-old heard her mother comment to another adult, "Anny (sibling) is really frightened of spiders. In fact, there's a particular toy spider that we've got that she just hates" (Dunn, 1989, p. 107). The innocent-looking toddler ran to get the spider from the toy box, returned, and pushed it in front of Anny's face!

Categorizing the Self

Once children have a me-self, they use their representational and language capacities to create a mental image of themselves. One of the first signs of this change is that toddlers compare themselves to other people. Between 18 and 30 months, children categorize themselves and others on the basis of age ("baby," "boy," or "man"), gender ("boy" versus "girl"), physical characteristics ("big," "strong"), and even goodness and badness ("I good girl." "Tommy mean!"). They also start to refer to the self's competencies ("Did it!" "I can't") (Stipek, Gralinski, & Kopp, 1990).

Toddlers' understanding of these social categories is limited, but they use this knowledge to organize their own behavior. For example, children's ability to label their own gender is associated

This 1-year-old notices the correspondence between her own movements and the movements of the image in the mirror, a cue that helps her figure out that the grinning baby is really herself.

© LAURA DWIGHT

with a sharp rise in gender-stereotyped responses (Fagot & Leinbach, 1989). As early as 18 months, children select and play in a more involved way with toys that are stereotyped for their own gender—dolls and tea sets for girls, trucks and cars for boys. Then parents encourage these preferences by responding more positively when toddlers display them (Fagot, Leinbach, & O'Boyle, 1992). As we will see in Chapter 10, gender-typed behavior increases dramatically during early childhood.

Emergence of Self-Control

Self-awareness also provides the foundation for **self-control,** the capacity to resist an impulse to engage in socially disapproved behavior. Self-control is essential for morality, another dimension of the self that will flourish during childhood and adolescence. To behave in a self-controlled fashion, children must think of themselves as separate, autonomous beings who can direct their own actions. And they must have the representational and memory capacities to recall a caregiver's directive (such as "Caitlin, don't touch that light socket!") and apply it to their own behavior. The ability to shift attention from a captivating stimulus and focus on a less attractive alternative, supported by development of the frontal lobes of the cerebral cortex, is also essential (Putnam, Spritz, & Stifter, 2002).

As these capacities improve, the first glimmerings of self-control appear between 12 and 18 months as **compliance.** Toddlers show clear awareness of caregivers' wishes and expectations and can obey simple requests and commands. And, as every parent knows, they can also decide to do just the opposite! One way toddlers assert their autonomy is by resisting adult directives. But among toddlers who experience parental warmth and gentle encouragement, opposition is far less common than compliance with an eager, willing spirit, which suggests that the child is beginning to adopt the adult's directive as his own (Kochanska, Tjebkes, & Forman, 1998; Lehman et al., 2002). Compliance quickly leads to toddlers' first consciencelike verbalizations, as when Caitlin said, "No, can't" as she reached out for a light socket.

Around 18 months, self-control appears, and it improves steadily into early childhood. In one study, toddlers were given three tasks that required them to resist temptation. In the first, they were asked not to touch an interesting toy telephone that was within arm's reach. In the second, raisins were hidden under cups, and they were instructed to wait until the experimenter said it was all right to pick up a cup and eat a raisin. In the third, they were told not to open a gift until the adult had finished her work. On all three problems, the ability to wait increased between 18 and 30 months (Vaughn, Kopp, & Krakow, 1984).

Early, large individual differences in self-control remain modestly stable into middle childhood and adolescence (Shoda, Mischel, & Peake, 1990). Children who are advanced in sustained attention and language development are more self-controlled, so girls usually are ahead of boys (Cournoyer, Solomon, & Trudel, 1998; Rothbart, 1989). Already, some toddlers use verbal techniques, such as singing and talking to themselves, to keep from engaging in a prohibited act. In addition, mothers who are sensitive and supportive have toddlers who show greater gains in self-control (Kochanska, Murray, & Harlan, 2000). Such parenting seems to encourage as well as model patient, nonimpulsive behavior.

Encouraging this toddler to help wipe up spilled milk fosters compliance and the beginnings of self-control. He joins in the clean-up task with an eager, willing spirit, which suggests he is beginning to adopt the adult's directive as his own.

© 2000 LAURA DWIGHT

As self-control improves, mothers increase the rules they require toddlers to follow, from safety and respect for property and people to family routines, manners, and simple chores (Gralinski & Kopp, 1993). Still, toddlers' control over their own actions depends on constant parental oversight and reminders. To get Caitlin to stop playing so that she and her parents could go on an errand, several prompts ("Remember, we're going to go in just a minute") and gentle insistence were usually necessary. A summary of ways to help toddlers develop compliance and self-control can be found in Applying What We Know on the following page.

As the second year of life drew to a close, Carolyn, Monica, and Vanessa were delighted with their children's readiness to learn the rules of social life. As we will see in Chapter 10, advances in cognition and language, along with parental warmth and reasonable demands for maturity, lead children to make tremendous strides in this area during early childhood.

Applying WHAT WE Know / Helping Toddlers Develop Compliance and Self-Control

SUGGESTION	RATIONALE
Respond to the toddler with sensitivity and encouragement.	Toddlers whose parents are sensitive and supportive are more compliant and self-controlled.
Provide advance notice when the toddler must stop an enjoyable activity.	Toddlers find it more difficult to stop a pleasant activity that is already under way than to wait before engaging in a desired action.
Offer many prompts and reminders.	Toddlers' ability to remember and comply with rules is limited; they need continuous adult oversight.
Respond to self-controlled behavior with verbal and physical approval.	Praise and hugs reinforce appropriate behavior, increasing its likelihood of occurring again.
Encourage sustained attention (see Chapter 6, pages 221–222).	Early sustained attention is related to self-control. Children who can shift attention from a captivating stimulus and focus on a less attractive alternative are better at controlling their impulses.
Support language development (see Chapter 6, pages 242–244).	Early language development is related to self-control. During the second year, children begin to use language to remind themselves about adult expectations.
Gradually increase rules in a manner consistent with the toddler's developing capacities.	As cognition and language improve, toddlers can follow more rules related to safety, respect for people and property, family routines, manners, and simple chores.

*A*sk YOURSELF

www

REVIEW Why is insisting that infants comply with parental directives inappropriate? What competencies are necessary for the emergence of compliance and self-control?

CONNECT What type of early parenting fosters the development of emotional self-regulation, attachment, and self-control? Why, in each instance, is it effective?

*S*ummary

Erikson's Theory of Infant and Toddler Personality

What personality changes take place during Erikson's stages of basic trust versus mistrust and autonomy versus shame and doubt?

● According to Erikson, warm, responsive caregiving leads infants to resolve the psychological conflict of **basic trust versus mistrust** on the positive side. The trusting infant expects the world to

be good and gratifying, so he feels confident about exploring it.

● During toddlerhood, the conflict of **autonomy versus shame and doubt** is resolved favorably when parents provide appropriate guidance and reasonable choices. The outcome is a child who feels self-confident, secure, and able to control her impulses and act competently on her own. If children emerge from the first few years without suffi-

cient trust and autonomy, the seeds are sown for adjustment problems.

Emotional Development

Describe changes in happiness, anger, sadness, and fear over the first year, noting the adaptive function of each.

● During the first half-year, **basic emotions** become clear, well-organized signals. The **social smile** appears between 6 and 10 weeks, laughter around 3 to 4 months.

Happiness strengthens the parent–child bond and reflects as well as supports physical and cognitive mastery.

● Anger and fear, especially in the form of **stranger anxiety,** increase in the second half of the first year as infants better evaluate objects and events. Anger motivates babies to defend themselves and overcome obstacles, and fear keeps in check their enthusiasm for exploration—reactions that are adaptive as infants' motor capacities improve. Expressions of sadness appear in response to pain, removal of an object, brief separations, and disruptions of caregiver–infant interaction, but they are less frequent than anger.

Summarize changes that occur during the first 2 years in understanding others' emotions, expression of self-conscious emotions, and emotional self-regulation.

● The ability to understand the feelings of others expands over the first year. Between 7 and 10 months, babies perceive facial expressions as organized patterns. Soon after, **social referencing** appears; infants actively seek emotional information from caregivers in uncertain situations. By the middle of the second year, infants begin to appreciate that others' emotional reactions may differ from their own.

● During toddlerhood, self-awareness and adult instruction provide the foundation for **self-conscious emotions,** such as shame, embarrassment, guilt, envy, and pride. Caregivers help infants with **emotional self-regulation** by relieving distress, engaging in stimulating play, and discouraging negative emotion. During the second year, growth in representation and language leads to more effective ways of regulating emotion.

Development of Temperament

What is temperament, and how is it measured?

● Infants differ greatly in **temperament,** or quality and intensity of emotional reaction, activity level, attention, and emotional self-regulation. On the basis of parental descriptions of children's behavior, three patterns of temperament—the **easy child,** the **difficult child,** and the **slow-to-warm-up child**—were identified in the New York Longitudinal Study. Difficult children, especially, are likely to display adjust-

ment problems. Rothbart's dimensions of temperament represent three underlying components—emotion, attention, and action—that form an integrated system of capacities and limitations.

● In addition to parental reports, researchers assess temperament through behavior ratings by other people familiar with the child, through direct observation, and through physiological measures. Physiological assessments have been used most often to distinguish **inhibited,** or **shy, children** from **uninhibited,** or **sociable, children,** who inherit a physiology that biases them toward a particular temperamental style.

Discuss the role of heredity and environment in the stability of temperament, including the goodness-of-fit model.

● Because temperament develops with age and can be modified by experience, stability is generally low to moderate. Long-term prediction from early temperament is best achieved in the second year of life and after.

● Temperament has a genetic foundation, but child rearing and cultural beliefs and practices have much to do with maintaining or changing it.

● The **goodness-of-fit model** describes how temperament and environment work together to affect later development. Parenting practices that create a good fit with the child's temperament help difficult, shy, and highly active children achieve more adaptive functioning.

Development of Attachment

What are the unique features of ethological theory of attachment?

● The development of **attachment,** the strong affectionate tie we feel for special people in our lives, has been the subject of intense theoretical debate. Although psychoanalytic and behaviorist explanations exist, the most widely accepted perspective is **ethological theory of attachment.** It views babies as biologically prepared to establish emotional bonds with familiar caregivers, which promote survival by ensuring both safety and competence.

● In early infancy, a set of built-in behaviors encourages the parent to remain close to the baby. Around 6 to 8 months, **separation anxiety** and use of the parent as a **secure base** indicate that

a true attachment bond has formed. As representation and language develop, toddlers better understand the parent's coming and going, and separation anxiety declines. Out of early caregiving experiences, children construct an **internal working model** that serves as a guide for all future close relationships.

Cite the four attachment patterns assessed by the Strange Situation and the Attachment Q-Sort, and discuss factors that affect attachment security.

● The **Strange Situation** is a widely used technique for measuring the quality of attachment between 1 and 2 years of age. A more efficient method is the **Attachment Q-Sort,** which is suitable for children between 1 and 5 years of age. Four attachment patterns have been identified: **secure attachment, avoidant attachment, resistant attachment,** and **disorganized/disoriented attachment.**

● Securely attached babies who experience favorable life conditions more often maintain their attachment pattern than insecure babies. An exception is the disorganized/disoriented pattern, which is highly stable. Cultural conditions must be considered in interpreting reactions to the Strange Situation.

● A variety of factors affect attachment security. Infants deprived of a close bond with one or a few adults show lasting emotional and social problems. **Sensitive caregiving** is moderately related to secure attachment. In some (but not all) cultures, **interactional synchrony** also characterizes the experiences of securely attached babies. Overstimulating, intrusive care is linked to avoidant attachment, inconsistent care to resistant attachment. Many disorganized/disoriented babies experience extremely negative caregiving.

● Even ill and temperamentally irritable infants are likely to become securely attached if parents adapt their caregiving to suit the baby's needs. Family conditions, including stress and instability, influence caregiving behavior and attachment security. Parents' internal working models also predict the quality of infants' attachment bonds. However, these reconstructed memories are influenced by many factors besides parents' childhood experiences. The development of attachment clearly takes place within a complex ecological system.

Discuss infants' attachments to fathers and siblings, and indicate how attachment paves the way for early peer sociability.

● Infants develop strong affectionate ties to fathers, whose sensitive caregiving predicts secure attachment. Fathers devote more time than mothers to stimulating, playful interaction, a vital context in which they build secure attachments with their babies. Early in the first year, infants start to form rich emotional relationships with siblings that mix rivalry and resentment with affection and sympathetic concern. Individual differences in the quality of sibling relationships are influenced by temperament, parenting practices, and marital quality.

● Peer sociability begins in infancy with isolated social acts that are gradually replaced by reciprocal exchanges, largely in the form of mutual imitation, in the second year of life. Sensitive interaction between caregiver and child fosters the development of peer sociability.

Describe and interpret the relationship between secure attachment in infancy and cognitive, emotional, and social competence in childhood.

● Evidence is mixed regarding the impact of early attachment pattern on cognitive, emotional, and social competence in later years. Continuity of parental care seems to be the crucial factor that determines whether attachment security is linked to later development.

Self-Understanding

Describe the development of self-awareness in infancy and toddlerhood, along with the emotional and social capacities it supports.

● The earliest aspect of the self to emerge is the **I-self,** a sense of self as agent. Its beginnings lie in infants' recognition that their own actions cause objects and people to react in predictable ways. During the second year, toddlers start to construct the **me-self,** a sense of self as an object of knowledge and evaluation. They become keenly aware of the self's physical features and, by age 2, use their name or a personal pronoun to refer to themselves.

● Self-awareness leads to toddlers' first efforts to appreciate another's perspective and to compare themselves to others. Social categories based on age, gender, physical characteristics, and goodness and badness are evident in toddlers' language. Self-awareness also provides the foundation for self-conscious emotions, leading to **empathy, compliance,** and **self-control.** Development of attention and language, along with sensitive, supportive parenting, promotes gains in self-control from toddlerhood into early childhood.

Important Terms and Concepts

attachment (p. 264)
Attachment Q-Sort (p. 267)
autonomy versus shame and doubt (p. 251)
avoidant attachment (p. 267)
basic emotions (p. 252)
basic trust versus mistrust (p. 251)
compliance (p. 280)
difficult child (p. 258)
disorganized/disoriented attachment (p. 267)
easy child (p. 258)

emotional self-regulation (p. 256)
empathy (p. 279)
ethological theory of attachment (p. 265)
goodness-of-fit model (p. 263)
inhibited, or shy, child (p. 260)
interactional synchrony (p. 269)
internal working model (p. 266)
I-self (p. 278)
me-self (p. 279)
resistant attachment (p. 267)
secure attachment (p. 267)

secure base (p. 266)
self-conscious emotions (p. 256)
self-control (p. 280)
sensitive caregiving (p. 269)
separation anxiety (p. 265)
slow-to-warm-up child (p. 258)
social referencing (p. 255)
social smile (p. 254)
Strange Situation (p. 266)
stranger anxiety (p. 254)
temperament (p. 258)
uninhibited, or sociable, child (p. 260)

 # For Further Information and Help

Consult the Companion Website for *Infants, Children, and Adolescents,* Fifth Edition, *(www.ablongman.com/berk),* where you will find the following resources for this chapter:

● **Chapter Objectives**
● **Flashcards** for studying important terms and concepts
● **Annotated Weblinks** to guide you in further research
● **Ask Yourself questions,** which you can answer and then check against a sample response

● **Suggested Readings**
● **Practice Tests** with immediate scoring and feedback

Milestones Development in Infancy and Toddlerhood

AGE	PHYSICAL	COGNITIVE	LANGUAGE	EMOTIONAL/SOCIAL
Birth–6 months	• Rapid height and weight gain. (166) • Reflexes decline. (150) • Sleep organized into a day–night schedule. (176) • Holds head up, rolls over, and reaches for objects. (187) • Responses can be classically and operantly conditioned. (182–184) • Habituates to unchanging stimuli; recovers to novel stimuli. (184–185) • Hearing well developed; by the end of this period, displays greater sensitivity to speech sounds of own language. (193–194) • Sensitive to motion and binocular depth cues. (195) • Perceives stimuli as organized patterns; recognizes and prefers pattern of human face; recognizes features of mother's face. (197–199)	• Engages in immediate imitation and deferred imitation of adults' facial expressions. (214–215) • Repeats chance behaviors leading to pleasurable and interesting results. (210) • Violation-of-expectation tasks suggest some awareness of object permanence and other object properties. (217) • Attention becomes more efficient and flexible. (221) • Recognition memory for people, places, and objects improves. (223) • Forms perceptual categories based on objects' similar appearance. (223–224)	• Engages in cooing and, by the end of this period, babbling. (238) • Starts to gaze in same direction as caregiver. (239) 	• Social smile and laughter emerge. (254) • Matches adults' emotional expressions during face-to-face interaction. (255) • Emotional expressions become better organized and meaningfully tied to environmental events. (255) • I-self emerges. (278)
7–12 months	• Sits alone, crawls, walks. (187) • Shows refined pincer grasp. (191)  • Perceives larger speech units crucial to understanding meaning. (194) • Sensitive to pictorial depth cues. (195) • Organizes many auditory and visual stimuli into meaningful patterns. (201–202) • Relies on shape, color, and texture to distinguish objects from their surroundings. (201)	• Combines sensorimotor schemes. (211) • Engages in intentional, or goal-directed, behavior. (211) • Finds objects hidden in one location. (211) • Understanding of object properties expands. (214) • Engages in deferred imitation of adults' actions with objects. (215) • Recall memory for people, places, and objects improves. (223) • Solves simple problems by analogy. (215) • Groups stimuli into a wide range of meaningful categories, based on common function and behavior. (223–224)	• Babbling expands to include sounds of spoken languages and the child's language community. (239) • Begins to comprehend word meanings. (240) • Uses preverbal gestures (showing, pointing) to communicate. (239) 	• Anger and fear increase in frequency and intensity. (254) • Stranger anxiety and separation anxiety appear. (254–255, 265–266) • Uses caregiver as a secure base for exploration. (266) • Engages in social referencing. (255) • Shows "clear-cut" attachment to familiar caregivers. (265–266)

AGE	PHYSICAL	COGNITIVE	LANGUAGE	EMOTIONAL/SOCIAL
13–18 months	• Height and weight gain rapid but not as great as in first year. (166–167) • Walking better coordinated. (187, 188)  • Manipulates small objects with improved coordination. (191, 210)	• Experiments with objects in a trial-and-error fashion. (208, 210) • Finds object hidden in more than one location. (211) • Sorts objects into categories. (223–224) • Imitates actions across a change in context—for example, from child care to home. (215) • Sustained attention improves. (221) • Memory becomes less dependent on context. (222)	• Joint attention with caregiver becomes more accurate. (239) • Takes turns in games, such as pat-a-cake and peekaboo. (239) • Uses preverbal gestures to influence others' behavior. (239) • Says first word. (240) 	• Joins in play with familiar adults, siblings, and peers. (275–277) • Me-self emerges; recognizes image of self in mirror. (279) • Begins to realize others' emotional reactions may differ from one's own. (255) • Shows signs of empathy. (279) • Complies with simple directives. (280)
19–24 months	 • Jumps, runs, and climbs. (187–188) • Manipulates small objects with good coordination. (191, 210)	• Solves simple problems through representation. (212) • Finds object that has been moved while out of sight. (212) • Engages in deferred imitation of actions an adult tries to produce, even if not fully realized. (215–216) • Engages in make-believe play. (212) • Sorts objects into categories more effectively. (224–225) • Recall memory for people, places, and objects improves further. (223)	• Vocabulary increases to 200 words. (240) • Combines two words. (240) 	• Self-conscious emotions (shame, embarrassment, guilt, and pride) emerge. (256) • Acquires a vocabulary of emotional terms. (257) • Begins using language to assist with emotional self-regulation. (257) • Begins to tolerate caregiver's absences more easily. (266) • Starts to use words to influence a playmate's behavior. (276) • Uses own name or personal pronoun to label image of self. (279) • Categorizes the self and others on the basis of age, gender, physical characteristics, goodness and badness, and competencies. (279) • Shows gender-stereotyped toy choices. (279–280) • Self-control appears. (280)

Note: Numbers in parentheses indicate the page(s) on which each milestone is discussed.

This painting deftly captures young children's access to exotic new experiences as their bodies and motor skills develop. Chapter 8 highlights the close link between early childhood physical growth and other aspects of development.

"Under the Sea"
Her Shuang
7 years, Singapore

Reprinted with permission from The International Museum of Children's Art, Oslo, Norway.

Physical Development in Early Childhood

For more than a decade, my fourth- floor office window overlooked the preschool and kindergarten play yard of our university laboratory school. On mild fall and spring mornings, the doors of classrooms swung open, and sand table, woodworking bench, easels, and large blocks spilled out into a small, fenced courtyard. Around the side of the building was a grassy area with jungle gyms, swings, a playhouse, and a flower garden planted by the children. Beyond it, I could see a circular path lined with tricycles and wagons. Each day, the setting was alive with activity.

Even from my distant vantage point, the physical changes of early childhood were evident. Children's bodies were longer and leaner than they had been a year or two earlier. The awkward gait of toddlerhood had disappeared in favor of more refined movements that included running, climbing, jumping, galloping, and skipping. Children scaled the jungle gym, raced across the lawn, turned summersaults, and vigorously pedaled tricycles. Just as impressive as these gross motor achievements were gains in fine motor skills. At the sand table, children built hills, valleys, caves, and roads and prepared trays of pretend cookies and cupcakes. And as they grew older, their paintings at the outdoor easels took on greater structure and detail as family members, houses, trees, birds, sky, monsters, and letterlike forms appeared in the colorful creations.

The years from 2 to 6 are often called "the play years," and aptly so, since play blossoms during this time and supports every aspect of development. Our discussion of early childhood opens with the physical achievements of this period—growth in body size, improvements in motor coordination, and refinements in perception. We pay special attention to biological and environmental factors that support these changes, as well as to their intimate connection with other domains of development. The children I came to know well, first by watching from my office window and later by observing at close range in their classrooms, will provide many examples of developmental trends and individual differences.

*B*ody Growth

The rapid increase in body size of the first two years tapers off into a slower growth pattern during early childhood. On average, children add 2 to 3 inches in height and about 5 pounds in weight each year. Boys continue to be slightly larger than girls. At the same time, the "baby fat" that began to decline in toddlerhood drops off further. The child gradually becomes thinner, although girls retain somewhat more body fat, and boys are slightly more muscular. As the torso lengthens and widens, internal organs tuck neatly inside, and the spine straightens. As Figure 8.1 shows, by age 5 the top-heavy, bowlegged, potbellied toddler has become a more streamlined, flat-tummied, longer-legged child with body proportions similar to those of adults. Consequently, posture and balance improve—changes that support the gains in motor coordination that we will take up later.

Individual differences in body size are even more apparent during early childhood than in infancy and toddlerhood. Looking down at the play yard one day, I watched 5-year-old Darryl speed around the bike path. At 48 inches tall and 55 pounds, he towered over his kindergarten classmates and was, as his mother put it, "off the growth charts" at the doctor's office. (The average North American 5-year-old boy is 43 inches tall and weighs 42 pounds). Priti, an Asian-Indian child, was unusually small because of genetic factors linked to her cultural ancestry. Lynette and Hallie, two Caucasian children with impoverished home lives, were well below average for reasons we will discuss shortly.

The existence of cultural variations in body size reminds us that growth norms for one population are not good standards for children elsewhere in the world. Consider the Efe of the Republic of Congo, inhabitants of the Central African tropical rain forests, who normally grow to an adult height of less than 5 feet. Between 1 and 6 years, Efe children's growth tapers off to a greater extent than that of most other preschoolers. By age 5, the average Efe child is shorter than more than 97 percent of North American 5-year-olds. For genetic reasons, the impact of hormones controlling body size is reduced in Efe children (Bailey, 1991). The Efe's small size probably evolved to reduce their caloric requirements in the face of food scarcity in the hot, humid rain forests, and to permit them to move easily through the dense forest underbrush (Shea & Bailey, 1996). So we would be mistaken to take Efe children's short stature as a sign of problems with growth or health. However, these concerns are warranted for other extremely slow-growing children, such as Lynette and Hallie.

Skeletal Growth

The skeletal changes that are under way in infancy continue throughout early childhood. Between ages 2 and 6, approximately 45 new *epiphyses,* or growth centers in which cartilage hardens into bone, emerge in various parts of the skeleton. Other epiphyses will appear in middle childhood. X-rays of these growth centers enable doctors to estimate children's *skeletal age,* or progress toward physical maturity (see Chapter 5, page 168). During early and middle childhood, information about skeletal age is helpful in diagnosing growth disorders.

Parents and children are especially aware of another aspect of skeletal growth: By the end of the preschool years, children start to lose their primary, or "baby," teeth. The age at which they do so varies considerably and is strongly influenced by genetic factors. For example, girls, who are ahead of boys in physical development, lose their primary teeth sooner. Cultural ancestry also makes a difference. North American children typically get their first secondary (permanent) tooth at 6½ years, children in Ghana at just over 5 years, and

Toddlers and 5-year-olds have very different body shapes. During early childhood, body fat declines, the torso enlarges to better accommodate the internal organs, and the spine straightens. Compared to her younger brother, this girl looks more streamlined. Her body proportions resemble those of an adult.

These Efe mothers, who live in the African tropical rain forests of the Republic of Congo, take time to braid one another's hair while their young children relax nearby. The average Efe 5-year-old is shorter than more than 97 percent of North American agemates, and Efe adults are under 5 feet tall. Their short stature probably evolved to reduce their caloric needs in a habitat of frequent food scarcity. The Efe illustrate the wide variation in normal physical growth.

Andy at 3 years

Andy at 4 years

Andy at 5 years

Andy at 5¾ years

Amy at 3 years

Amy at 3½ years

Amy at 4½ years

Amy at 5½ years

FIGURE 8.1

Body growth during early childhood.

Andy and Amy grew more slowly during the preschool years than they did in infancy and toddlerhood (see Chapter 5, page 167). By age 5, their bodies became more streamlined, flat-tummied, and longer-legged. Boys continue to be slightly taller and heavier and more muscular than girls. But generally, the two sexes are similar in body proportions and physical capacities.

children in Hong Kong around the 6th birthday (Burns, 2000). Environmental influences, especially prolonged malnutrition, can delay the age at which children cut their permanent teeth.

Even though primary teeth are temporary, dental care is important. Diseased baby teeth can affect the health of permanent teeth, since decay in baby teeth is a strong predictor of decay in permanent teeth. Brushing consistently, avoiding sugary foods, drinking fluoridated water, and getting topical fluoride treatments and sealants (plastic coatings that protect tooth surfaces) prevent cavities. Protecting children from exposure to tobacco smoke is also helpful. Inhaling the smoke suppresses children's immune system, reducing their ability to fight infectious agents, including bacteria responsible for tooth decay. The risk associated with this suppression is greatest in infancy and early childhood, when the immune system is not yet fully mature (Aligne et al., 2003).

Growth of three different organ systems and tissues contrasted with the body's general growth.
Growth is plotted in terms of percentage of change from birth to 20 years. Note that the growth of lymph tissue rises to nearly twice its adult level by the end of childhood. Then it declines. (Reprinted by permission of the publisher from J. M. Tanner, 1990, *Foetus into Man,* 2nd ed., Cambridge, MA: Harvard University Press, p. 16. Copyright © 1990 by J. M. Tanner. All rights reserved.)

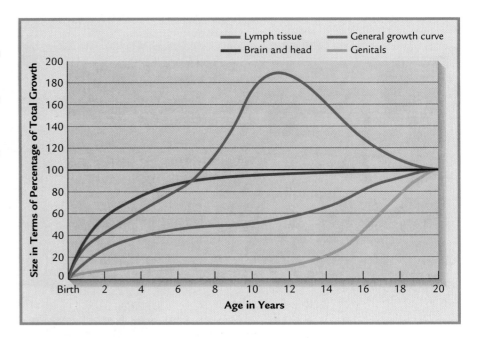

Unfortunately, childhood tooth decay remains high, especially among low-SES children. An estimated 40 percent of North American 5-year-olds have at least some tooth decay. Among poverty-stricken preschoolers, cavities advance at an especially rapid pace, affecting an average of 2.5 teeth per year. By the time American and Canadian young people graduate from high school, about 80 percent have decayed or filled teeth (World Health Organization, 2003a). Poor diet and health practices, lack of fluoridation in some communities, and inadequate dental care are responsible.

Asynchronies in Physical Growth

Body systems differ in their unique, carefully timed patterns of maturation. As Figure 8.2 shows, physical growth is *asynchronous.* Body size (as measured by height and weight) and a variety of internal organs follow the **general growth curve, which involves rapid growth during infancy, slower gains in early and middle childhood, and rapid growth again during adolescence.** Yet there are exceptions to this trend. The genitals develop slowly from birth to age 4, change little throughout middle childhood, and then grow rapidly during adolescence. In contrast, the lymph glands grow at an astounding pace in infancy and childhood, and then their rate of growth declines in adolescence. The lymph system helps fight infection and assists with absorption of nutrients, thereby supporting children's health and survival (Malina & Bouchard, 1991).

Figure 8.2 illustrates another growth trend with which you are already familiar: During the first few years, the brain grows more rapidly than any other part of the body. Let's look at some highlights of brain development during early childhood.

Brain Development

Between ages 2 and 6, the brain increases from 70 to 90 percent of its adult weight. At the same time, preschoolers improve in a wide variety of skills—physical coordination, perception, attention, memory, language, logical thinking, and imagination.

In addition to increasing in weight, the brain undergoes much reshaping and refining. For example, by age 4, many parts of the cortex have overproduced synapses. In some regions, such as the frontal lobes, the number of synapses is nearly double the adult value. Together, synaptic growth and myelination of neural fibers result in a high energy need. In fact, brain-imaging studies reveal that energy metabolism in the cerebral cortex reaches a peak around this age (Huttenlocher, 2002; Johnson, 1998).

Recall from Chapter 5 that overabundance of synaptic connections supports *plasticity* of the young brain, helping to ensure that the child will acquire certain abilities even if some areas are damaged. *Synaptic pruning* follows: Neurons that are seldom stimulated lose their connective fibers, and the number of synapses is reduced (see page 169). As the structures of stimulated neurons become more elaborate and require more space, surrounding neurons die, and brain plasticity declines. By age 8 to 10, energy consumption of most cortical regions declines to near-adult levels (Chugani, 1994).

In Chapter 5 we saw that the cerebral cortex is made up of two *hemispheres.* EEG and fMRI measures of neural activity in various cortical regions reveal especially rapid growth from 3 to 6 years in frontal-lobe areas devoted to attention and to planning and organizing behavior. Furthermore, for most children, the left hemisphere is especially active between 3 and 6 years and then levels off. In contrast, activity in the right hemisphere increases steadily throughout early and middle childhood, with a slight spurt between ages 8 and 10 (Thatcher, Walker, & Giudice, 1987; Thompson et al., 2000). Studies of the brains of children who have died confirm these trends. For example, Figure 8.3 shows age-related changes in density of synapses in three cortical areas important for language processing: the primary auditory area, Broca's area (concerned with producing language), and Wernicke's area (concerned with interpreting language). (To review the location of these structures, refer to page 236.) Notice how synaptic density rises during the first 3 years and then, as a result of pruning, falls to an adult level around age 10.

The growth trends just described fit with what we know about cognitive development. Language skills (typically housed in the left hemisphere) increase at an astonishing pace in early childhood, and they support children's increasing control over behavior, mediated by the frontal lobes. In contrast, spatial skills (typically housed in the right hemisphere), such as finding one's way from place to place, drawing pictures, and recognizing geometric shapes, develop gradually over childhood and adolescence.

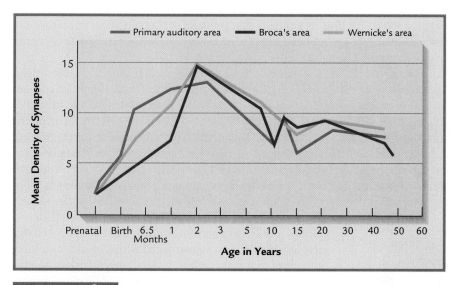

FIGURE 8.3

Age-related changes in synaptic density of three areas of the cerebral cortex involved in language processing.

Density of synapses in all three areas rises sharply during the first 3 years—the same period in which children rapidly develop language skills. Notice that the increase in synaptic density occurs first in the primary auditory area, which mediates hearing, next in Wernicke's area, which is concerned with interpreting language, and finally in Broca's area, which controls language production. Consistent with these trends, language comprehension develops ahead of language production (see Chapter 6, page 241). As a result of pruning, density of synapses falls during the late preschool and school years. During this time, plasticity of the cerebral cortex is reduced. (Adapted from P. R. Huttenlocher, 2000, "Synaptogenesis in Human Cerebral Cortex and the Concept of Critical Periods," in N. A. Fox, L. A. Leavitt, & J. G. Warhol, eds., *The Role of Early Experience in Development,* p. 21. St. Louis, MO: Johnson & Johnson Pediatric Institute. Reprinted by permission.)

Differences in rate of development between the two hemispheres reveal that they are continuing to *lateralize* (specialize in functions). Let's take a closer look at brain lateralization during early childhood by focusing on handedness.

● Handedness

One morning on a visit to the preschool, I watched 3-year-old Moira as she drew pictures, worked puzzles, joined in snack time, and played outside. Unlike most of her classmates, Moira does most things—drawing, eating, and zipping her jacket—with her left hand. But she also uses her right hand for a few activities, such as throwing a ball. Hand preference is evident in 10 percent of 1-year-olds and strengthens during early childhood. Ninety percent of 5-year-olds prefer one hand over the other (Öztürk et al., 1999).

A strong hand preference reflects the greater capacity of one side of the brain—the individual's **dominant cerebral hemisphere**—to carry out skilled motor action. Other important abilities may be located on the dominant side as well. In support of this idea, for right-handed people, who make up 90 percent of the population in Western nations, language is housed with hand control in the left hemisphere. For the remaining left-handed 10 percent, language is often shared between the hemispheres (Knecht et al., 2000). This indicates that the brains of left-handers tend to be less strongly lateralized than those of right-handers. Consistent with this idea, many left-handed individuals (like Moira) are also *ambidextrous.* Although they prefer their left hand, they sometimes use their right hand skillfully as well (McManus et al., 1988).

Is handedness hereditary? Researchers disagree on this issue. Left-handed parents show only a weak tendency to have left-handed children. One genetic theory proposes that most children inherit a gene that *biases* them for right-handedness and a left-dominant cerebral hemisphere. However, that bias is not strong enough to overcome experiences that might sway children toward a left-hand preference (Annett, 2002).

Research confirms that experience can profoundly affect handedness. Both identical and fraternal twins are more likely than ordinary siblings to differ in handedness. The hand preference of each twin is related to body position in the uterus; twins usually lie in opposite orientations (Derom et al., 1996). This finding suggests that prenatal events can affect lateralization. According to one theory, the way most fetuses lie—facing toward the left—may promote greater control over movement on the right side of the body (Previc, 1991).

Another possibility is that practice heavily affects hand preference. Handedness is strongest for complex skills requiring extensive training, such as eating with utensils, writing, and engaging in athletic activities. Also, wide cultural differences exist in rates of left-handedness. For example, in Tanzania, Africa, children are physically restrained and punished for favoring the left hand. Not surprisingly, less than 1 percent of Tanzanians are left-handed (Provins, 1997).

Perhaps you have heard that left-handedness is more frequent among severely retarded and mentally ill people than in the general population. Although this is true, recall that when two variables are correlated, one does not necessarily cause the other. Atypical brain lateralization is probably not responsible for the problems of these individuals. Instead, they may have suffered early damage to the left hemisphere, which both caused their disabilities and led to a shift in handedness. In support of this idea, left-handedness is associated with prenatal and birth difficulties that can result in brain damage, including prolonged labor, prematurity, Rh incompatibility, and breech delivery (O'Callaghan et al., 1993; Powls et al., 1996).

Keep in mind, however, that only a small number of left-handers show developmental problems. In fact, unusual lateralization may have certain advantages. Left- and mixed-handed young people are more likely than their right-handed agemates to develop outstanding verbal and mathematical talents (Flannery & Liederman, 1995). More even distribution of cognitive functions across both hemispheres may be responsible.

Twins typically lie in the uterus in opposite orientations during the prenatal period, which may explain why they are more often opposite-handed than are ordinary siblings. Although left-handedness is associated with developmental problems, the large majority of left-handed children are completely normal.

© LAURA DWIGHT

Other Advances in Brain Development

Besides the cerebral cortex, several other areas of the brain make strides during early childhood (see Figure 8.4). As we look at these changes, you will see that they all involve establishing links between parts of the brain, increasing the coordinated functioning of the central nervous system.

At the rear and base of the brain is the **cerebellum,** a structure that aids in balance and control of body movement. Fibers linking the cerebellum to the cerebral cortex grow and myelinate after birth, but they do not complete this process until about age 4 (Tanner, 1990). This change undoubtedly contributes to dramatic gains in motor control, so that by the end of the preschool years, children can play hopscotch, pump a playground swing, and throw a ball with a well-organized set of movements.

The **reticular formation,** a structure in the brain stem that maintains alertness and consciousness, generates synapses and myelinates throughout early childhood and into adolescence. Neurons in the reticular formation send out fibers to other areas of the brain. Many go to the frontal lobes of the cerebral cortex, contributing to improvements in sustained, controlled attention.

The **corpus callosum** is a large bundle of fibers that connects the two cortical hemispheres. Production of synapses and myelination of the corpus callosum increase at age 1, peak between 3 and 6 years, and continue at a slower pace through middle childhood and adolescence (Thompson et al., 2000). The corpus callosum supports smooth coordination of limb movements on both sides of the body and integration of many aspects of thinking, including perception, attention, memory, language, and problem solving. The more complex the task, the more critical is communication between the hemispheres.

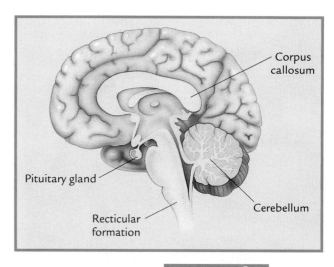

FIGURE 8.4

Cross section of the human brain, showing the location of the cerebellum, the reticular formation, and the corpus callosum.

These structures undergo considerable development during early childhood. Also shown is the pituitary gland, which secretes hormones that control body growth (see page 294).

*A*sk YOURSELF

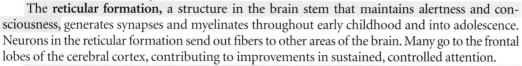

www

REVIEW	What aspects of brain development support the tremendous gains in language, thinking, and motor control of early childhood?
APPLY	Both Crystal and Shana are shorter and lighter than 97 percent of North American 4-year-old girls. What are the possible causes of their very short stature?
CONNECT	What stance on the nature–nurture issue does evidence on development of handedness support? Document your answer with research findings.

*F*actors Affecting Physical Growth and Health

In earlier chapters we considered a wide variety of influences on physical growth during the prenatal period and infancy. As we discuss growth and health during early childhood, you will encounter some familiar themes. Although heredity remains important, environmental factors continue to play crucial roles. Emotional well-being, restful sleep, good nutrition, relative freedom from disease, and physical safety are essential.

© ED BOCK/CORBIS

The boy second from left is the shortest child in his kindergarten class but is growing normally and is well accepted by his classmates. Thousands of parents seek hormone treatment for their short children, fearing that they will be stigmatized because of their shortness. But short, normal-GH children typically are well adjusted.

Heredity and Hormones

The impact of heredity on physical growth is evident throughout childhood. Children's physical size and rate of growth are related to those of their parents. Genes influence growth by controlling the body's production of hormones. The **pituitary gland,** located at the base of the brain (refer to Figure 8.4), plays a critical role by releasing two hormones that induce growth.

The first is **growth hormone (GH),** which from birth on is necessary for development of all body tissues except the central nervous system and the genitals. Children who lack GH reach an average mature height of only 4 feet, 4 inches, although they are normal and healthy in other respects. When treated with injections of GH starting at an early age, these GH-deficient children show catch-up growth and then grow at a normal rate, reaching a height much greater than they would have without treatment (Pasquino et al., 2001).

The availability of synthetic GH has also made it possible to treat short, normal-GH children with hormone injections, in hopes of increasing their final height. Consequently, thousands of parents, concerned that their children will suffer social stigma because of their shortness, have sought this GH therapy. But most normal-GH children given GH treatment grow only slightly taller than their previously predicted mature height (Guyda, 1999; Vance & Mauras, 1999). And contrary to popular belief, normal-GH short children are not deficient in self-esteem or other aspects of psychological adjustment (Sandberg & Voss, 2002). So despite the existence of "heightism" in Western cultures, little justification exists for medically intervening in short stature that is merely the result of biologically normal human diversity.

The second pituitary hormone affecting children's growth is **thyroid-stimulating hormone (TSH).** It stimulates the thyroid gland (located in the neck) to release *thyroxine,* which is necessary for normal development of the nerve cells of the brain and for GH to have its full impact on body size. Infants born with a deficiency of thyroxine must receive it at once or they will be mentally retarded. At later ages, children with too little thyroxine grow at a below-average rate. However, the central nervous system is no longer affected, since the most rapid period of brain development is complete. With prompt treatment, such children catch up in body growth and eventually reach normal size (Tanner, 1990).

Emotional Well-Being

In childhood as in infancy, emotional well-being can have a profound effect on growth and health. Preschoolers with very stressful home lives (due to divorce, financial difficulties, or a change in their parents' employment status) suffer more respiratory and intestinal illnesses and more unintentional injuries than others (Cohen & Herbert, 1996).

Extreme emotional deprivation can interfere with the production of GH and lead to **psychosocial dwarfism,** a growth disorder that appears between 2 and 15 years of age. Typical characteristics include very short stature, decreased GH secretion, immature skeletal age, and serious adjustment problems, which help distinguish psychosocial dwarfism from normal shortness (Doeker et al., 1999; Voss, Mulligan, & Betts, 1998). Lynette, the very small 4-year-old mentioned earlier in this chapter, was diagnosed with this condition. She had been placed in foster care after child welfare authorities discovered that she spent most of the day at home alone, unsupervised. She may also have been physically abused. When such children are removed from their emotionally inadequate environments, their GH levels quickly return to normal, and they grow rapidly. But if treatment is delayed, the dwarfism can be permanent.

Sleep Habits and Problems

Sleep contributes to body growth, since GH is released during the child's sleeping hours. A well-rested child is better able to play, learn, and contribute positively to family functioning. Also, by disrupting parents' sleep, children who sleep poorly can cause significant family stress—a major reason that sleep difficulties are among the most common concerns parents raise with their preschooler's doctor (Mindell, Owens, & Carskadon, 1999).

On average, total sleep declines in early childhood; 2- and 3-year-olds sleep 12 to 13 hours, 4- to 6-year-olds 10 to 11 hours. Younger preschoolers typically take a 1- to 2-hour nap in the early afternoon, although their daytime sleep needs vary widely. Some continue to take two naps, as they did in toddlerhood; others give up napping entirely. Most children stop napping between ages 3 and 4, although a quiet play period or rest after lunch helps them rejuvenate for the rest of the day (Howard & Wong, 2001). In some cultures, daytime naps persist through adulthood.

Western preschoolers often become rigid about bedtime rituals, such as using the toilet, listening to a story, getting a drink of water, taking a security object to bed, and hugging and kissing before turning off the light. These practices, which take as long as 30 minutes, help young children adjust to feelings of uneasiness at being left by themselves in a darkened room. Difficulty falling asleep—calling to the parent or asking for another drink of water—is common in early childhood. When it occurs repeatedly, it is usually due to typical fears of the preschool years or to parental problems in setting bedtime limits. The difficulty usually subsides when parents follow the recommendations given in Applying What We Know below. Intense bedtime struggles sometimes result from family turmoil, as children worry about how their parents may get along when they are asleep and not available to distract them. In these cases, addressing family stress and conflict is the key to improving children's sleep.

Parents of preschoolers often report that their children have sleep difficulties. Bedtime rituals, such as a story and a hug and kiss before turning out the light, help young children adjust to falling asleep in a room by themselves.

Applying WHAT WE Know / Helping Young Children Get a Good Night's Sleep

STRATEGY	EXPLANATION
Establish a regular bedtime, early enough to ensure, on average, 10 to 11 hours of nightly sleep.	Children who go to sleep too late in the evening—after 9:30 or 10 P.M.—get less sleep than those who go to sleep earlier and are sleepier and more irritable during the day.
Provide special bedtime attire.	Changing into bedtime attire, such as pajamas or a nightshirt, provides the child with clear psychological separation between daytime and bedtime.
Avoid watching television or playing computer games before bedtime.	Preschoolers' difficulty distinguishing fantasy from reality can lead to disturbing thoughts and emotions that interfere with sleep.
If the child resists going to bed, respond with kind but firm insistence.	Discuss the next day's activities with the child, emphasizing that tomorrow will be a good day. Initiate the bedtime ritual without introducing other enjoyable activities and, if necessary, stay with the child until he or she falls asleep.
If the child awakens repeatedly during the night, establish a routine to follow.	Respond to an upset child. Letting preschoolers cry themselves to sleep undermines trust in the parent and, instead of enhancing self-control, increases clingy and demanding behavior during the day. Use a predictable, but boring, routine that ends with the last two or three steps of the child's bedtime ritual—rubbing the child's back, hugging and kissing the child, and sitting quietly with the child until he or she returns to sleep.
Do not give a child who resists sleep over-the-counter sleeping medication of any kind.	These brain-altering chemicals can affect children differently than adults. They also cause "rebound" insomnia—sleeplessness after medication is discontinued. And they prevent children from developing their own effective strategies for falling asleep. Children with sleep disorders may require prescription medication, which must be carefully supervised by the child's doctor.

Sources: Fleiss, 1999; Owens, Rosen, & Mindell, 2003.

In early childhood, parent–child cosleeping remains the usual practice in non-Western cultures and many ethnic minority groups. North American Caucasian parents also cosleep with their preschoolers, although how many do so is uncertain. They tend to be reluctant to tell others about the practice, out of fear of disapproval. Cosleeping is not associated with any problems during the preschool years, other than more frequent night wakings by parents due to children's movements during sleep (Thiedke, 2001). Western cosleeping children generally ask to sleep in their own bed by age 6 or 7.

Finally, most children waken during the night from time to time, and those who cannot return to sleep on their own may suffer from a sleep disorder. Because of young children's vivid imaginations and difficulty separating fantasy from reality, *nightmares* are common; half of 3- to 6-year-olds experience them from time to time. And about 4 percent of children are frequent *sleepwalkers,* who are unaware of their wanderings during the night. Gently awakening and returning the child to bed helps avoid self-injury. *Sleep terrors,* which affect 3 percent of young children, are perhaps the most upsetting sleep problem to parents. In these panic-stricken arousals from deep sleep, the child may scream, thrash, speak incoherently, show a sharp rise in heart rate and breathing, and initially be unresponsive to parents' attempts to comfort. Sleep walking and sleep terrors tend to run in families, suggesting a genetic influence (Guilleminault et al., 2003; Thorpy & Yager, 2001). But they can also be triggered by stress or extreme fatigue.

Fortunately, sleep disorders of early childhood usually subside without treatment. In the few cases that persist, children require a medical and psychological evaluation. Their disturbed sleep may be a sign of neurological or emotional difficulties (Gregory & O'Connor, 2002). And the resulting daytime sleepiness often contributes to attention, learning, and behavior problems.

Nutrition

With the transition to early childhood, appetite tends to become unpredictable. Preschoolers eat well at one meal and barely touch their food at the next. And many become picky eaters. One father I know wistfully recalled his son's eager sampling of the cuisine at a Chinese restaurant during toddlerhood. "He ate rice, chicken chow mein, egg rolls, and more. Now, at age 3, the only thing he'll try is the ice cream!"

This decline in the appetite is normal. It occurs because growth has slowed. Furthermore, preschoolers' wariness of new foods is adaptive. By sticking to familiar foods, they are less likely to swallow dangerous substances when adults are not around to protect them (Birch & Fisher, 1995). Parents need not worry about variations in amount eaten from meal to meal. Over the course of a day, preschoolers compensate for a meal in which they ate little with a later one in which they eat more (Hursti, 1999).

Even though they eat less, preschoolers need a high-quality diet. They require the same foods that make up a healthy adult diet—only smaller amounts. Milk and milk products, meat or meat alternatives (such as eggs, dried peas or beans, and peanut butter), vegetables and fruits, and breads and cereals should be included. Fats and salt should be kept to a minimum because of their link to high blood pressure and heart disease in adulthood (Winkleby et al., 1999). Foods high in sugar should also be avoided. In addition to causing tooth decay, they lessen young children's appetite for healthy foods and increase their risk of overweight and obesity—a topic we will take up in Chapter 11.

The social environment powerfully influences young children's food preferences. Children tend to imitate the food choices and eating practices of people they admire—adults as well as peers. For example, mothers who drink milk or soft drinks tend to have 5-year-old daughters with a similar beverage preference (Fisher et al., 2001). In Mexico, children see family members delighting in the taste of peppery foods. As a result, Mexican preschoolers enthusiastically eat chili peppers, whereas most North American children reject them (Birch, Zimmerman, & Hind, 1980).

Children's food tastes are trained by foods served often in their culture. Many Western children would refuse the spicy noodle dish these Japanese preschoolers are eating with enthusiasm.

© TOM MCCARTHY/PHOTOEDIT

Applying WHAT WE Know / Encouraging Good Nutrition in Early Childhood

SUGGESTION	DESCRIPTION
Offer a varied, healthful diet.	Provide a well-balanced variety of nutritious foods that are colorful and attractively served. Avoid serving sweets and "junk" foods as a regular part of meals and snacks.
Offer predictable meals as well as several snacks each day.	Preschoolers' stomachs are small, and they may not be able to eat enough in three meals to satisfy their energy requirements. They benefit from extra opportunities to eat.
Offer small portions, and permit the child to serve him- or herself and to ask for seconds.	When too much food is put on the plate, preschoolers often overeat, increasing the risk of obesity. On average, preschoolers consume 25 percent less at a meal when permitted to serve themselves.
Offer new foods early in a meal and over several meals, and respond with patience if the child rejects the food.	Introduce new foods before the child's appetite is satisfied. Let children see you eat and enjoy the new food. If the child rejects it, accept the refusal and serve it again at another meal. As foods become more familiar, they are more readily accepted.
Keep mealtimes pleasant, and include the child in mealtime conversations.	A pleasant, relaxed eating environment helps children develop positive attitudes about food. Refrain from constantly offering food and prompting eating because these practices foster excessively fast eating and overeating. Avoid confrontations over disliked foods and table manners, which may lead to refusal to eat.
Avoid using food as a reward and forbidding access to certain foods.	Saying "No dessert until you clean your plate" tells children that they must eat regardless of whether they are hungry and that dessert is the best part of the meal. Restricting access to a food increases children's valuing of that food and their efforts to obtain it.

Sources: Birch, 1999; Fisher, Rolls, & Birch, 2003; Spruijt-Metz et al., 2002.

Repeated exposure to a new food (without any direct pressure to eat it) also increases children's acceptance. In one study, preschoolers were given one of three versions of a food they had never eaten before (sweet, salty, or plain tofu). After 8 to 15 exposures, they readily ate the food. But they preferred the version they had already tasted. For example, children in the "sweet" condition liked sweet tofu best, and those in the "plain" condition liked plain tofu best (Sullivan & Birch, 1990). These findings reveal that adding sugar or salt in hopes of increasing a young child's willingness to eat healthy foods simply strengthens the child's desire for a sugary or salty taste. Similarly, offering children sweet fruit or soft drinks promotes "milk avoidance." Compared to their milk-drinking agemates, milk-avoiders are shorter in stature and have a lower bone density—a condition that leads to a lifelong reduction in strength and to increased risk of bone fractures (Black et al., 2002).

The emotional climate at mealtimes has a powerful impact on children's eating habits. Many parents worry about how well their preschoolers eat, so meals become unpleasant and stressful. Sometimes parents bribe their children, saying, "Finish your vegetables, and you can have an extra cookie." This practice causes children to like the healthy food less and the treat more (Birch, 1998). Although children's healthy eating depends on a healthy food environment, too much parental control over children's eating limits their opportunities to develop self-control, thereby promoting overeating (Birch, Fisher, & Davison, 2003). For ways to encourage healthy, varied eating in young children, refer to Applying What We Know above.

Finally, as indicated in earlier chapters, many children in North America and in developing countries lack access to sufficient high-quality food to support healthy growth. Five-year-old Hallie was bused to our laboratory preschool from a poor neighborhood. His mother's income barely covered her rent, let alone food. Hallie's diet was deficient in protein as well as essential vitamins and minerals—iron (to prevent anemia), calcium (to support development of bones and teeth), vitamin A (to help maintain eyes, skin, and a variety of internal organs), and vitamin C (to facilitate iron absorption and wound healing). These are the most common dietary deficiencies of the preschool years (Kennedy, 1998). Not surprisingly, Hallie was thin, pale, and tired. By age 7, North American low-SES children are, on average, about 1 inch shorter than their economically advantaged counterparts (Yip, Scanlon, & Trowbridge, 1993).

Infectious Disease

Two weeks into the school year, I looked outside my window and noticed that Hallie was absent from the play yard. Several weeks passed, and I still did not see him. When I asked Leslie, his preschool teacher, what had happened, she explained, "Hallie's been hospitalized with the measles. He's had a difficult time recovering—lost weight when there wasn't much to lose in the first place." In well-nourished children, ordinary childhood illnesses have no effect on physical growth. But when children are undernourished, disease interacts with malnutrition in a vicious spiral, and the consequences for physical growth can be severe.

INFECTIOUS DISEASE AND MALNUTRITION ● Hallie's reaction to the measles is commonplace among children in developing nations, where a large proportion of the population lives in poverty. In these countries, many children do not receive a program of immunizations. Illnesses such as measles and chicken pox, which typically do not appear until after age 3 in industrialized nations, occur much earlier. This is because poor diet depresses the body's immune system, making children far more susceptible to disease. Worldwide, of the 10.5 million annual deaths of children under age 5, 98 percent are in developing countries and 70 percent are due to infectious diseases (World Health Organization, 2003b).

Disease, in turn, is a major contributor to malnutrition, thereby hindering physical growth and cognitive development. Illness reduces appetite, and it limits the body's ability to absorb foods. These outcomes are especially severe among children with intestinal infections. In developing countries, diarrhea is widespread, and it increases in early childhood due to unsafe water and contaminated foods, leading to several million childhood deaths each year (Shann & Steinhoff, 1999). Studies carried out in the slums and shantytowns of Brazil and Peru reveal that the more persistent diarrhea is in early childhood, the shorter children are in height and the lower they score on mental tests during the school years (Checkley et al., 2003; Niehaus et al., 2002).

Most developmental impairments and deaths due to diarrhea can be prevented with nearly cost-free *oral rehydration therapy (ORT),* in which sick children are given a glucose, salt, and water solution that quickly replaces fluids the body loses. Since 1990, public health workers have taught nearly half of families in the developing world how to administer ORT. Also, supplements of zinc, a mineral essential for immune system functioning that costs only 30 cents for a month's supply, substantially reduce the incidence of severe and prolonged diarrhea (Bhandari et al., 2002). As a result of these interventions, the lives of more than 1 million children are being saved each year (Victora et al., 2000).

IMMUNIZATION ● In industrialized nations, childhood diseases have declined dramatically during the past half-century, largely due to widespread immunization of infants and young children. Hallie got the measles because, unlike his classmates from more advantaged homes, he did not receive a full program of immunizations.

About 20 percent of American infants and toddlers are not fully immunized. Of the 80 percent who receive a complete schedule of vaccinations in the first 2 years, some do not receive the immunizations they need later, in early childhood. Overall, 24 percent of American preschoolers lack essential immunizations, a rate that rises to 38 percent for poverty-stricken children (U.S. Department of Health and Human Services, 2003e). In contrast, fewer than 10 percent of preschoolers in Denmark and Norway lack immunizations, and fewer than 7 percent in Great Britain, Canada, the Netherlands, and Sweden (Bellamy, 2000; Health Canada, 2000c).

How have these countries managed to achieve higher rates of immunization than the United States? In earlier chapters we noted that many children in the United States do not have access to the health care they need. The Cultural Influences box on the following page compares child health care in the United States with that in other Western nations.

In 1994, all medically uninsured American children were guaranteed free immunizations, a program that has led to steady improvement in early childhood immunization rates. Inability to pay for vaccines, however, is only one cause of inadequate immunization. Parents with stressful daily

Cultural Influences

Child Health Care in the United States and Other Western Nations

Historically, Americans have placed strong emphasis on parental responsibility for the care and rearing of children. This belief, in addition to powerful economic interests in the medical community, has prevented government-sponsored health services from being offered to all children.

American health insurance is an optional, employment-related fringe benefit. Many businesses that rely on low-wage and part-time help do not insure their employees. If they do, they often do not cover other family members, including children. Public health programs are available in the United States. The largest is Medicaid, which pays for medical services for very-low-income and poverty-stricken people. However, Medicaid does not reach all families in need. This leaves about 9 million children (12 percent of the child population)—many of whom have working parents—uninsured and, therefore, without affordable health care (Children's Defense Fund, 2003).

Because of the high cost of health care in the United States, uninsured, low-SES children are three times as likely to go without needed doctor visits as insured, higher-SES children with similar illnesses (Newachek et al., 2002). Consequently, an estimated 37 percent of children younger than age 5 who come from economically disadvantaged families are in less than very good health. Partly because of weak health care services, 13 percent of children living in poverty have activity limitations due to chronic illnesses—a rate nearly twice as high as the national average (U.S. Department of Health and Human Services, 2002a).

The inadequacies of American child health care stand in sharp contrast to services provided in other industrialized nations, where health insurance is government sponsored and available to all citizens, regardless of income. Let's look at two examples.

In the Netherlands, every child receives free medical examinations from birth through adolescence. During the early years, health care also includes parental counseling in nutrition, disease prevention, and child development (de Winter, Balledux, & de Mare, 1997). The Netherlands achieves its extraordinarily high childhood immunization rate by giving parents of every newborn baby a written schedule that shows exactly when and where the child should be immunized. If the child is not brought in at the specified time, a public health nurse calls the family. In cases of repeated missed appointments, the nurse goes to the home to ensure that the child receives the recommended immunizations (Bradley & Bray, 1996).

In Norway, federal law requires that well baby and child clinics be established in all communities and that examinations by doctors take place three times during the first year and at ages 2 and 4. Specialized nurses see children on additional occasions, monitoring their growth and development, providing immunizations, and counseling parents on physical and mental health. Although citizens pay a small fee for routine medical visits, hospital services are free of charge (Scarr et al., 1993).

In Australia, Canada, Western Europe, New Zealand, and other industrialized nations, child health care is regarded as a fundamental human right, no different from the right to education. Currently, many organizations, government officials, and concerned citizens committed to improving child health are working to guarantee every American child necessary health care. In 1997, a new health initiative—

the State Children's Health Insurance Program (SCHIP) was launched. Under SCHIP, the states receive $4 billion a year in federal matching funds for upgrading children's health insurance. State control over program implementation enables each state to adapt insurance coverage to meet its unique needs. But it also means that advocates for children's health must exert pressure for family-friendly policies.

A state can, for example, require that families share in the cost of participation. But for low-income parents trying to stretch their limited budgets, even a small premium or copayment generally makes SCHIP unaffordable. In addition, many insured children do not see a doctor regularly. When parents do not have health benefits of their own, they are less inclined to make appointments for their children (American Academy of Pediatrics, 2001). Furthermore, because of low insurance-reimbursement rates, many American doctors refuse to take public-aid patients. As a result, compared to children with private health insurance, children with public insurance receive a lower quality of care. They frequently do not have a primary care physician. Instead, they endure long waits in crowded public health clinics, and their parents frequently say they cannot access needed services (Hughes & Ng, 2003; Thompson et al., 2003).

Finally, millions of eligible children are not enrolled in these insurance programs because their parents either do not understand the eligibility requirements or find the application processes too complex and confusing. Clearly, the United States has a long way to go to ensure that all its children receive excellent health care.

AP/WIDE WORLD PHOTOS

Poverty-stricken, publicly insured American children and their parents often endure long waits in crowded public clinics to receive health care services. Because many American doctors refuse to take public aid patients, such children frequently do not have a primary care physician, and they receive lower-quality care than their more economically advantaged, privately insured agemates.

Widespread, government-sponsored immunization of infants and young children is a cost-effective means of supporting healthy growth by dramatically reducing the incidence of childhood diseases. Although this boy finds a routine inoculation painful, it will offer him lifelong protection.

lives often fail to schedule vaccination appointments. Misconceptions also contribute—for example, the notion that vaccines do not work or that they weaken the immune system (Gellin, Maibach, & Marcuse, 2000). Furthermore, some parents have been influenced by media reports suggesting that the measles–mumps–rubella vaccine has contributed to a rise in the number of children diagnosed with autism. Yet large-scale studies show no association between immunization and autism (Dales, Hammer, & Smith, 2001; Stehr-Green et al., 2003). Public education programs directed at increasing parental knowledge about the importance and safety of timely immunizations are badly needed.

A final point regarding communicable disease in early childhood deserves mention. Childhood illness rises with child-care attendance. On average, a child-care infant becomes sick 9 to 10 times a year, a child-care preschool child 6 to 7 times. The diseases that spread most rapidly are diarrhea and respiratory infections—the illnesses most frequently suffered by young children. The risk that a respiratory infection will result in *otitis media*, or middle ear infection, is almost double that for children remaining at home (Uhari, Mäntysaari, & Niemelä, 1996). To learn about the consequences of otitis media and how to prevent it, consult the Social Issues: Health box on the following page.

Childhood Injuries

Three-year-old Tory caught my eye as I visited the preschool classroom one day. More than any other child, he had trouble sitting still and paying attention at story time. Outside, he darted from one place to another, spending little time at a single activity. On a field trip to our campus museum, Tory ignored Leslie's directions and ran across the street without holding his partner's hand. Later in the year, I read in our local newspaper that Tory had narrowly escaped serious injury when he put his mother's car in gear while she was outside scraping its windows. The vehicle rolled through a guardrail and over the side of a 10-foot concrete underpass. There it hung until rescue workers arrived. Tory's mother was charged with failing to use a restraint seat for children under age 8.

Unintentional injuries—auto collisions, pedestrian accidents, drownings, poisonings, firearm wounds, burns, falls, and swallowing of foreign objects—are the leading causes of childhood mortality in industrialized nations (Agran et al., 2001). Figure 8.5 on page 302 reveals that compared with other developed countries, Canada and the United States rank poorly in these largely preventable events. Nearly 40 percent of North American childhood deaths and 70 percent of adolescent deaths are due to injury (Children's Defense Fund, 2003; Health Canada, 2002c). And among injured children and youths who survive, thousands suffer pain, brain damage, and permanent physical disabilities.

Auto and traffic accidents, drownings, burns, falls, and poisonings are the most common injuries during early childhood. Motor vehicle collisions are by far the most frequent source of injury at all ages, ranking as the leading cause of death among children more than 1 year old.

FACTORS RELATED TO CHILDHOOD INJURIES ● We are used to thinking of childhood injuries as "accidental," a word that encourages us to believe that they are due to chance and cannot be prevented (Sleet & Mercy, 2003). But a close look reveals that they occur within a complex *ecological system.* Individual, family, community, and societal factors underlie them, and we can, indeed, do something about them.

As Tory's case suggests, individual differences exist in the safety of children's behaviors. Because of their higher activity level and greater willingness to take risks during play, boys are more likely to be injured than girls (Laing & Logan, 1999). Temperamental characteristics—irritability, inattentiveness, and negative mood—are also related to childhood injuries. As we saw in Chapter 7, children

Social Issues: Health

Otitis Media and Development

During his first year in child care, 2-year-old Alex caught five colds, had the flu on two occasions, and experienced repeated otitis media (middle ear infection). Alex is not unusual. By age 6, nearly 70 percent of North American children have had respiratory illnesses that resulted in at least one bout of otitis media; 38 percent have had three or more bouts (Auinger et al., 2003). Although antibiotics eliminate the bacteria responsible for otitis media, they do not reduce fluid buildup in the middle ear, which causes mild to moderate hearing loss that can last for weeks or months.

The incidence of otitis media is greatest between 6 months and 3 years, when children are first acquiring language. Frequent infections predict delayed language progress and social isolation in early childhood (Casby, 2001; Miccio et al., 2002; Roberts et al., 2000). These outcomes can translate into poorer academic performance after school entry that, in one study, was still evident in adolescence (Bennett et al., 2001).

How might otitis media disrupt language and academic progress? Difficulties in hearing speech sounds, particularly in noisy settings, may be responsible. Children with many bouts are less attentive to the speech of others and less persistent at tasks (Petinou et al., 2001; Roberts, Burchinal, & Campbell, 1994). Their distractibility may be due to instances in which they could not make out what people around them were saying. When children have trouble paying attention, they may reduce the quality of others' interactions with them. In one study, mothers of preschoolers with frequent illnesses were less effective in teaching their child a task (Chase et al., 1995).

Current evidence argues strongly in favor of early prevention of otitis media, especially since the illness is so widespread. Crowded living conditions and exposure to cigarette smoke and other pollutants are linked to the disease—factors that probably account

for its high incidence among low-SES children. In addition, child care creates opportunities for close contact, greatly increasing otitis media episodes.

Early otitis media can be prevented in the following ways:

- *Preventive doses of xylitol, a sweetener derived from birch bark.* Research in Finland revealed that children given a daily dose of xylitol, in gum or syrup form, showed a 30 to 40 percent drop in otitis media compared with controls given gum or syrup without the sweetener. Xylitol appears to have natural, bacteria-fighting ingredients (Uhari, Tapiainen, & Kontiokari, 2000). However, dosage must be carefully monitored because too much xylitol can cause abdominal pain and diarrhea.

- *Frequent screening for the disease, followed by prompt medical intervention.* Plastic tubes that drain the inner ear often are used to treat chronic otitis media, although their effectiveness has been disputed.

- *Child-care settings that control infection.* Because infants and young children often put toys in their mouths, these objects should be rinsed frequently with a disinfectant. Spacious, well-ventilated rooms and small group sizes also limit spread of the disease.

- *Verbally stimulating adult–child interaction.* Developmental problems associated with otitis media are reduced or eliminated in high-quality child-care centers. When caregivers are verbally stimulating and keep noise to a minimum, children have more opportunities to hear, and benefit from, spoken language (Roberts et al., 1998; Vernon-Feagans, Hurley, & Yont, 2002).

High-quality child care reduces or eliminates language delays, social isolation, and later academic difficulties associated with frequent bouts of otitis media. These children profit from a verbally stimulating caregiver and a small group size, which ensures a relatively quiet environment where spoken language can be heard easily.

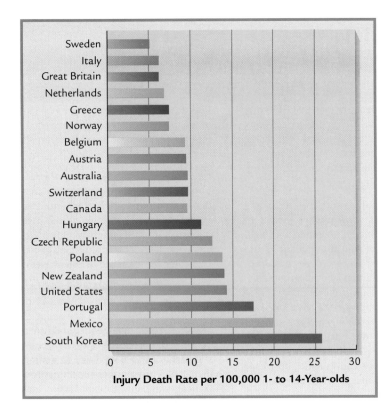

FIGURE 8.5

Death rates due to unintentional injuries among 1- to 14-year-olds in 19 nations.
Compared with other industrialized nations, Canada ranks 18th, with 9.7 deaths per 100,000, and the United States ranks 23rd, with 14.1 deaths per 100,000. Canada's rate of injury mortality is nearly twice as high, and the United States' is nearly three times as high, as that of Sweden, the best-ranked nation. Poverty, shortages of high-quality child care, and teenage parenthood are among the factors responsible for these disappointing statistics. (Adapted from Innocenti Research Center, 2001.)

with these traits present child-rearing challenges. They are likely to protest when placed in auto seat restraints, to refuse to take a companion's hand when crossing the street, and to disobey after repeated instruction and discipline (Matheny, 1991).

Poverty, low parental education, and more children in the home are also strongly associated with injury (Ramsey et al., 2003). Parents who must cope with many daily stresses often have little time and energy to monitor the safety of their youngsters. And the homes and neighborhoods of such families pose further risks. Noise, crowding, and confusion characterize these run-down, inner-city neighborhoods with few safe places to play (Kronenfeld & Glik, 1995).

Broad societal conditions also affect childhood injury. In developing countries, the rate of death from injury before age 15 is five times higher than in developed nations and soon may exceed disease as the leading cause of childhood mortality. Widespread poverty, rapid population growth, overcrowding in cities, and heavy road traffic combined with weak safety measures are major causes. Safety devices, such as car safety seats and bicycle helmets, are neither readily available nor affordable. To purchase a child safety seat requires more than 100 hours of wages in Vietnam and 53 hours in China, but only 2.5 hours in the United States (Safe Kids Worldwide, 2002).

Among developed nations, why are injury rates so high in Canada and the United States? Major contributing factors are poverty, shortages of high-quality child care (to supervise children in their parents' absence), and—especially in the United States—a high rate of births to teenagers (who are neither psychologically nor financially ready to raise a child). But North American children from advantaged families are also at somewhat greater risk for injury than children in Western Europe (Safe Kids Worldwide, 2002). This indicates that besides reducing poverty and teenage pregnancy and upgrading the status of child care, additional steps must be taken to ensure children's safety.

PREVENTING CHILDHOOD INJURIES ● Childhood injuries have many causes, so a variety of approaches are needed to control them. Laws prevent many injuries by requiring car safety seats, child-resistant caps on medicine bottles, flameproof clothing, and the fencing in of backyard swimming pools (the site of 50 percent of early childhood drownings) (Brenner et al., 2003).

Communities can help by modifying their physical environments. Inexpensive and widely available public transportation can reduce the amount of time that children spend in cars. Playgrounds, a common site of injury, can be covered with protective surfaces, such as rubber matting, sand, and wood chips (Dowd, 1999). Free, easily installed window guards can be given to families in high-rise apartment buildings to prevent falls. And widespread media and information campaigns can inform parents and children about safety issues.

Nevertheless, even though they know better, many parents and children behave in ways that compromise safety. For example, about 10 percent of Canadian parents and 40 percent of American parents (like Tory's mother) fail to place their preschoolers in car safety seats (Howard,

2002). Americans, especially, seem willing to ignore familiar safety practices, perhaps because of the high value they place on individual rights and personal freedom (Damashek & Peterson, 2002). Yet without consistent parental commitment to safety, young children are seriously at risk. Preschoolers spontaneously recall only about half the safety rules their parents teach them. They need prompting to remember the other rules and supervision to ensure that they comply with even well-learned rules (Morrongiello, Midgett, & Shields, 2001).

A variety of programs based on *behavior modification* (modeling and reinforcement) have improved child safety. In one, counselors helped parents identify dangers in the home—fire hazards, objects that young children might swallow, poisonous substances, firearms, and others. Then they demonstrated specific ways to eliminate the dangers (Tertinger, Greene, & Lutzker, 1984). Some interventions reward parents and children with prizes if the children arrive at child care or school restrained in car safety seats (Roberts, Alexander, & Knapp, 1990).

Efforts like these have been remarkably successful, yet their focus is fairly narrow—on decreasing specific environmental risks and risky behaviors (Peterson & Brown, 1994). Attention must also be paid to family conditions that can prevent childhood injury: relieving crowding in the home, providing social supports to ease parental stress, and teaching parents to use effective discipline—a topic we will take up in Chapter 10. Refer to Applying What We Know below for ways to reduce unintentional injuries in early childhood.

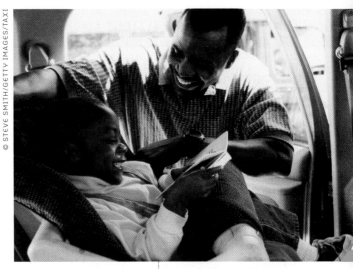

This child's parents insist that he always ride properly restrained in an age-appropriate safety seat, installed in the back seat of the car. In doing so, they greatly reduce his chances of injury and teach good safety practices.

Applying
WHAT WE **Know** / Reducing Unintentional Injuries in Early Childhood

SUGGESTION	DESCRIPTION
Provide age-appropriate supervision and safety instruction.	Despite increasing self-control, preschoolers need nearly constant supervision. Establish and enforce safety rules, explain the reasons behind them, and praise children for following them, thereby encouraging the child to remember, understand, and obey.
Know the child's temperament.	Children who are unusually active, distractible, negative, or curious have more than their share of injuries and need extra monitoring.
Eliminate the most serious dangers from the home.	Examine all spaces for safety. For example, in the kitchen, store dangerous products in high cabinets out of sight, and keep sharp implements in a latched drawer. Remove guns; if that is impossible, store them unloaded in a locked cabinet. Always accompany young preschoolers to the bathroom, and keep all medicines in containers with safety caps.
During automobile travel, always restrain the child properly in the back seat of the car.	Use an age-appropriate, properly installed car safety seat or booster seat up to age 8 or until the child is 4 feet 9 inches tall, and strap the child in correctly every time. Children should always ride in the back seat; passenger-side air bags in the front seat deploy so forcefully that they can cause injury or death to a child.
Select safe playground equipment and sites.	Make sure sand, wood chips, or rubberized matting has been placed under swings, seesaws, and jungle gyms. Check yards for dangerous plants. Always supervise outdoor play.
Be extra cautious around water.	Constantly observe children during water play; even shallow, inflatable pools are frequent sites of drownings. While they are swimming, young children's heads should not be immersed in water; they may swallow so much that they develop water intoxication, which can lead to convulsions and death.
Practice safety around animals.	Wait to get a pet until the child is mature enough to handle and care for it—usually around age 5 or 6. Never leave a young child alone with an animal; bites often occur during playful roughhousing. Model and teach humane pet treatment.

Source: Damashek & Peterson, 2002; Tremblay & Peterson, 1999.

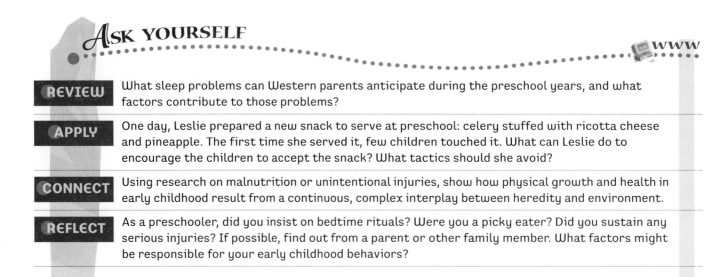

ASK YOURSELF

REVIEW What sleep problems can Western parents anticipate during the preschool years, and what factors contribute to those problems?

APPLY One day, Leslie prepared a new snack to serve at preschool: celery stuffed with ricotta cheese and pineapple. The first time she served it, few children touched it. What can Leslie do to encourage the children to accept the snack? What tactics should she avoid?

CONNECT Using research on malnutrition or unintentional injuries, show how physical growth and health in early childhood result from a continuous, complex interplay between heredity and environment.

REFLECT As a preschooler, did you insist on bedtime rituals? Were you a picky eater? Did you sustain any serious injuries? If possible, find out from a parent or other family member. What factors might be responsible for your early childhood behaviors?

www

Motor Development

Visit a playground at a neighborhood park, preschool, or child-care center, and observe several 2- to 6-year-olds. You will see that an explosion of new motor skills occurs in early childhood, each of which builds on the simpler movement patterns of toddlerhood.

The same principle that governs motor development during the first 2 years of life continues to operate during the preschool years. Children integrate previously acquired skills into more complex, *dynamic systems of action.* Then they revise each new skill as their bodies grow larger and stronger, their central nervous systems develop, their environments present new challenges, and they try to achieve new goals, aided by gains in perceptual and cognitive capacities.

Gross Motor Development

As children's bodies become more streamlined and less top-heavy, their center of gravity shifts downward, toward the trunk. As a result, balance improves greatly, paving the way for new motor skills involving large muscles of the body (Ulrich & Ulrich, 1985). By age 2, preschoolers' gaits become smooth and rhythmic—secure enough that soon they leave the ground, at first by running and later by jumping, hopping, galloping, and skipping.

As children become steadier on their feet, their arms and torsos are freed to experiment with new skills—throwing and catching balls, steering tricycles, and swinging on horizontal bars and rings. Then upper- and lower-body skills combine into more refined actions. Five- and 6-year-olds simultaneously steer and pedal a tricycle and flexibly move their whole body when jumping. By the end of the preschool years, all skills are performed with greater speed and endurance. Table 8.1 provides an overview of gross motor development in early childhood.

Changes in ball skills provide an excellent illustration of preschoolers' gross motor progress. Play a game of catch with a 2- or 3-year-old, and watch the child's body. Young preschoolers stand still facing the target, throwing with their arm thrust forward. Catching is equally awkward. Two-year-olds extend their arms and hands rigidly, using them as a single unit to trap the ball. By age 3, children flex their elbows enough to trap the ball against the chest. But if the ball arrives too quickly, they cannot adapt, and it may bounce off the body (Roberton, 1984).

Gradually, children call on the shoulders, torso, trunk, and legs to support throwing and catching. By age 4, the body rotates as the child throws, and at 5 years, preschoolers shift their weight forward, stepping as they release the ball. As a result, the ball travels faster and farther.

TABLE 8.1

Changes in Gross and Fine Motor Skills During Early Childhood

AGE	GROSS MOTOR SKILLS	FINE MOTOR SKILLS
2–3 years	Walks more rhythmically; hurried walk changes to run. Jumps, hops, throws, and catches with rigid upper body. Pushes riding toy with feet; little steering.	Puts on and removes simple items of clothing. Zips and unzips large zippers. Uses spoon effectively.
3–4 years	Walks up stairs, alternating feet, and downstairs, leading with one foot. Jumps and hops, flexing upper body. Throws and catches with slight involvement of upper body; still catches by trapping ball against chest. Pedals and steers tricycle.	Fastens and unfastens large buttons. Serves self food without assistance. Uses scissors. Copies vertical line and circle. Draws first picture of person, using tadpole image.
4–5 years	Walks downstairs, alternating feet. Runs more smoothly. Gallops and skips with one foot. Throws ball with increased body rotation and transfer of weight on feet; catches ball with hands. Rides tricycle rapidly, steers smoothly.	Uses fork effectively. Cuts with scissors following line. Copies triangle, cross, and some letters.
5–6 years	Increases running speed. Gallops more smoothly; engages in true skipping. Displays mature throwing and catching pattern. Rides bicycle with training wheels.	Uses knife to cut soft food. Ties shoes. Draws person with six parts. Copies some numbers and simple words.

Sources: Cratty, 1986; Getchell & Roberton, 1989; Newborg, Stock, & Wnek, 1984; Roberton, 1984.

When the ball is returned, older preschoolers predict its place of landing by moving forward, backward, or sideways (see Figure 8.6). Soon, they will catch it with their hands and fingers, "giving" with arms and body to absorb the force of the ball.

2 years

3 years

5–6 years

FIGURE 8.6

Changes in catching during early childhood.
At age 2, children extend their arms rigidly, and the ball tends to bounce off the body. At age 3, they flex their elbows in preparation for catching, trapping the ball against the chest. By ages 5 and 6, children involve the entire body. Soon, instead of pressing the ball against the chest, they will catch it with only the hands and fingers.

LEFT: © AMY ETRA/PHOTOEDIT;
CENTER: © ELIZABETH CREWS;
RIGHT: © MICHAEL NEWMAN/PHOTOEDIT

Fine Motor Development

Like gross motor development, fine motor skills take a giant leap forward during the preschool years. Because control of the hands and fingers improves, young children put puzzles together, build with small blocks, cut and paste, and string beads. To parents, fine motor progress is most apparent in two areas: (1) children's care of their own bodies, and (2) the drawings and paintings that fill the walls at home, child care, and preschool.

© ELIZABETH ZUCKERMAN/PHOTOEDIT

Putting on and fastening clothing is challenging but rewarding to preschoolers. Young children enjoy a new sense of independence when they can dress themselves.

SELF-HELP SKILLS ● As Table 8.1 shows, young children gradually become self-sufficient at dressing and feeding. Two-year-olds put on and take off simple items of clothing. By age 3, children can do so well enough to take care of toileting needs by themselves. Between ages 4 and 5, children can dress and undress without supervision. At mealtimes, young preschoolers use a spoon well, and they can serve themselves. By age 4 they are adept with a fork, and around 5 to 6 years they can use a knife to cut soft foods. Roomy clothing with large buttons and zippers and child-sized eating utensils help children master these skills.

Preschoolers get great satisfaction from managing their own bodies. They are proud of their independence, and their new skills also make life easier for adults. But parents need to be patient about these abilities. When tired and in a hurry, young children often revert to eating with their fingers. And the 3-year-old who dresses himself in the morning sometimes ends up with his shirt on inside out, his pants on backward, and his left snow boot on his right foot! Perhaps the most complex self-help skill of early childhood is shoe tying, mastered around age 6. Success requires a longer attention span, memory for an intricate series of hand movements, and the dexterity to perform them. Shoe tying illustrates the close connection between cognitive and motor development. Drawing and writing offer additional examples.

DRAWING AND WRITING ● When given crayon and paper, even young toddlers scribble in imitation of others. As the young child's ability to mentally represent the world expands, marks on the page take on definite meaning. A variety of factors combine with fine motor control in the development of children's artful representations. These include cognitive advances— the realization that pictures can serve as symbols and improved planning and spatial understanding, which allow the child to take a broader visual perspective rather than focusing on separate objects (Golomb, 2004). The emphasis that the child's culture places on artistic expression also affects progress in drawing.

From Scribbles to Pictures. Typically, drawing progresses through the following sequence:

1. *Scribbles.* Western children begin to draw during the second year. At first, gestures rather than the resulting scribble contain the intended representation. For example, one 18-month-old took her crayon and hopped it around the page, explaining as she made a series of dots, "Rabbit goes hop-hop" (Winner, 1986).

2. *First representational forms.* Around age 3, children's scribbles start to become pictures. Often this happens after they make a gesture with the crayon, notice that they have drawn a recognizable shape, and then decide to label it. In one case, a 2-year-old made some random marks on a page and then, realizing the resemblance between his scribbles and noodles, named the creation "chicken pie and noodles" (Winner, 1986).

   Few 3-year-olds spontaneously draw so others can tell what their picture represents. However, after an adult showed the child how pictures can be used to stand for objects in a game, more 3-year-olds drew recognizable forms (Callaghan, 1999; Callaghan & Rankin, 2002). Western parents and teachers spend much time promoting 2- and 3-year-olds' language and make-believe play, but relatively little time showing them how drawings can represent objects. When adults draw with children and point out the resemblances between drawings and objects, preschoolers create representational pictures at a somewhat earlier age, as their fine motor capacities permit.

   A major milestone in drawing occurs when children begin to use lines to represent the boundaries of objects. This enables 3- and 4-year-olds to draw their first picture of a person. Look at the tadpole image—a circular shape with lines attached—on the left in Figure 8.7. It is a universal one in which fine motor and cognitive limitations lead the preschooler

FIGURE 8.7

Examples of young children's drawings.

The universal tadpolelike shape that children use to draw their first picture of a person is shown on the left. The tadpole soon becomes an anchor for greater detail as arms, fingers, toes, and facial features sprout from the basic shape. By the end of the preschool years, children produce more complex, differentiated pictures like the one on the right, drawn by a 6-year-old child. (Tadpole drawings from H. Gardner, 1980, *Artful Scribbles: The Significance of Children's Drawings,* New York: Basic Books, p. 64. Reprinted by permission of Basic Books, a division of HarperCollins Publishers, Inc. Six-year-old's picture from E. Winner, August 1986, "Where Pelicans Kiss Seals," *Psychology Today, 20*[8], p. 35. Reprinted with permission from *Psychology Today* magazine. Copyright © 1986 Sussex Publishers, Inc.)

to reduce the figure to the simplest form that still looks human. Four-year-olds add features, such as eyes, nose, mouth, hair, fingers, and feet, as the tadpole drawings illustrate.

3. *More realistic drawings.* Young children do not demand that a drawing be realistic. But as cognitive and fine motor skills improve, they learn to desire greater realism. As a result, they create more complex drawings, like the one on the right in Figure 8.7, by a 6-year-old child. These drawings contain more conventional figures, in which the head and body are differentiated and arms and legs appear. (Note the human and animal figures in the 6-year-old's drawing.) Still, older preschoolers' drawings contain perceptual distortions because these children have just begun to represent depth (Braine et al., 1993).

   Greater realism in drawing occurs gradually, as perception, language (ability to describe visual details), memory, and fine motor capacities improve (Toomela, 2002). For geometric objects, drawing progress follows the steps illustrated in Figure 8.8. (1) Three- to 7-year olds draw a single unit to stand for an object. To represent a cube, they draw a square; to represent

Drawing Category and Approximate Age Range		
Single Units (3 to 7 years)		
Object Parts (4 to 13 years)		
Integrated Whole (8 years and older)		

FIGURE 8.8

Development of children's drawings of geometric objects—a cube and a cylinder.

As these examples show, drawings change from single units to representation of object parts. Then the parts are integrated into a realistic whole. (Adapted from Toomela, 1999.)

When young children experiment with crayons and paint, they not only develop fine motor skills but acquire the artistic traditions of their culture. This Australian Aboriginal 4-year-old creates a dot painting. To Westerners, it looks abstract. To the child, it expresses a "dreamtime" story about the life and land of his ancestors. If asked about the painting, he might respond, "Here are the boulders on the creek line, the hills with kangaroos and emus, and the campsites."

a cylinder, they draw a circle, an oval, or a rectangle. (2) During the late preschool and school years, children represent salient object parts. They draw several squares to stand for a cube's sides and draw two circles and some lines to represent a cylinder. However, the parts are not joined properly. (3) Older school-age children and adolescents integrate object parts into a realistic whole (Toomela, 1999).

Preschoolers' free depiction of reality makes their artwork look fanciful and inventive. Accomplished artists, who also try to represent people and objects freely, often must work hard to do deliberately what they did without effort as 5- and 6-year-olds.

Cultural Variations in Development of Drawing. In cultures with rich artistic traditions, children's drawings reflect the conventions of their culture and are more elaborate. For example, the women of Walbiri, an Aboriginal group in Australia, draw symbols in sand to illustrate stories for preschoolers. Walbiri children often mix these symbols with more realistic images (Wales, 1990).

In cultures with little interest in art, even older children and adolescents produce simple forms. The Jimi Valley is a remote region of Papua New Guinea with no indigenous pictorial art. Many Jimi children do not go to school and therefore have little opportunity to develop drawing skills. When a Western researcher asked nonschooled Jimi 10- to 15-year-olds to draw a human figure for the first time, most produced nonrepresentational scribbles and shapes or simple "stick" or "contour" images (see Figure 8.9) (Martlew & Connolly, 1996). These forms resemble those of preschoolers and seem to be a universal beginning in drawing. Once children realize that lines must evoke human features, they find solutions to figure drawing that vary somewhat from culture to culture but, overall, follow the sequence described earlier.

Early Printing. As preschoolers experiment with lines and shapes, notice print in storybooks, and observe people writing, they try to print letters and, later, words. Up to age 3, however, they scribble when they try to write, just as they do when they try to draw. Initially, they do not distinguish writing from drawing. Around age 4, children's writing shows some distinctive features of print, such as separate forms arranged in a line on the page. But they often mix picturelike devices into their writing—for example, writing *sun* by using a yellow marker or a circular shape (Levin & Bus, 2003). Using their understanding of the symbolic function of drawings, 4-year-olds who are asked to write typically make a "drawing of print." Only gradually—between ages 4 and 6—do children realize that writing stands for language.

Preschoolers' first attempts to print often involve their name, generally using a single letter. "How do you make a *D*?" my older son David asked at age 3½. When I printed a large uppercase *D*, he tried to copy. "*D* for David," he said as he wrote, quite satisfied with his backward, imperfect creation. A year later, David added several letters, and around age 5, he wrote his name clearly enough that others could read it.

Between ages 3 and 5, children acquire skill in gripping a pencil. As Figure 8.10 shows, 3-year-olds display diverse grip patterns and pencil angles against the surface. Depending on the direction and location of the marks they want to make, they vary their grip. During this phase, they seem to be experimenting. As they try out different forms of pencil-holding, they discover the pencil grip and angle that maximizes stability and writing efficiency. By age 5, most children use an adult grip pat-

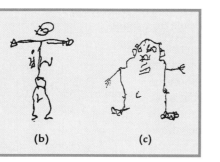

(a)   (b)   (c)

FIGURE 8.9

Drawings produced by nonschooled 10- to 15-year-old children of the Jimi Valley of Papua New Guinea when they were asked to draw a human figure for the first time.

Many produced nonrepresentational scribbles and shapes (a), "stick" figures (b), or "contour" figures (c). Compared with the Western tadpole form, the Jimi "stick" and "contour" figures emphasize the hands and feet. Otherwise, the drawings of these older children resemble those of young preschoolers. (From M. Martlew & K. J. Connolly, 1996, "Human Figure Drawings by Schooled and Unschooled Children in Papua New Guinea," *Child Development, 67,* pp. 2750–2751. © The Society for Research in Child Development, Inc. Adapted by permission.)

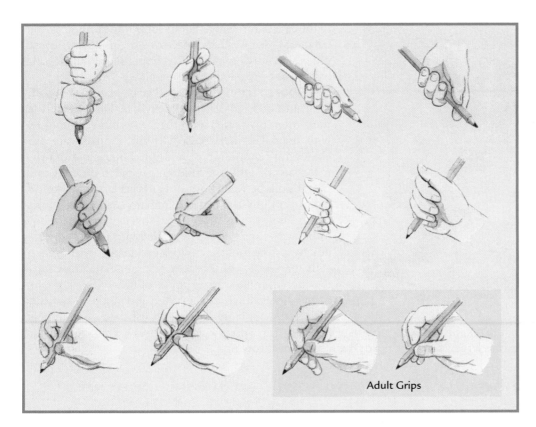

FIGURE 8.10

Variations in 3-year-olds' pencil grip.

Through experimenting with different grips, preschoolers gradually discover an adult grip with one or two fingers on top of the pencil, which maximizes writing stability and efficiency. (Adapted from Greer & Lockman, 1998.)

Adult Grips

tern and a fairly constant pencil angle across a range of drawing and writing conditions (Greer & Lockman, 1998).

In addition to gains in fine motor control, advances in perception contribute to the ability to print. Like many children, David continued to reverse letters until well into second grade. Once preschoolers distinguish writing from nonwriting around age 4, they make progress in identifying individual letters. Those alike in shape are difficult to tell apart. For example, because the distinctive features of *C* and *G*, *E* and *F*, and *M* and *W* are subtle, many preschoolers confuse these letter pairs (Bornstein & Arteberry, 1999; Gibson, 1970). Letters that are mirror images of one another, such as *b* and *d* and *p* and *q*, are especially hard to discriminate. One reason is that until children start to read, they do not find it especially useful to notice the difference between mirror-image forms.

The ability to tune in to mirror images, as well as to scan a printed line from left to right, improves as children gain experience with written materials (Casey, 1986). The more that parents and teachers assist preschoolers in their efforts to print, the more advanced children are in writing and in other aspects of literacy development (Aram & Levin, 2001, 2002). We will consider early childhood literacy in greater detail in Chapter 9.

Individual Differences in Motor Skills

We have discussed motor milestones in terms of the average age at which children reach them in Western nations, but, of course, wide individual differences occur. A child with a tall, muscular body tends to move more quickly and to acquire certain skills earlier than a short, stocky youngster. Researchers believe that body build contributes to the superior performance of African-American over Caucasian-American children in running and jumping. African-American youngsters tend to have longer limbs, so they have better leverage (Lee, 1980; Wakat, 1978).

Sex differences in motor skills are evident in early childhood. Boys are ahead of girls in skills that emphasize force and power. By age 5, they can jump slightly farther, run slightly faster, and throw a ball much farther (about 5 feet farther). Girls have an edge in fine motor skills and in certain gross motor skills that require a combination of good balance and foot movement, such as hopping and skipping (Fischman, Moore, & Steele, 1992; Thomas & French, 1985). Boys' greater muscle mass and,

This 4-year-old girl, who gets plenty of modeling and practice at batting, throwing, and catching, is likely to outperform most of her age-mates in those skills. Typically, girls receive far less encouragement than boys to engage in physical activities identified as "masculine." As a result, small sex differences in motor skills in early childhood become large differences during the school years.

in the case of throwing, slightly longer forearms, may contribute to their skill advantages. And girls' greater overall physical maturity may be partly responsible for their better balance and precision of movement.

From an early age, boys and girls are usually encouraged into different physical activities. For example, fathers often play catch with their sons but seldom do so with their daughters. Baseballs and footballs are purchased for boys, jump ropes, hula hoops, and drawing materials for girls. As children get older, differences in motor skills between boys and girls get larger, yet sex differences in physical capacity remain small until adolescence. These trends suggest that social pressures for boys to be active and physically skilled and for girls to play quietly at fine motor activities exaggerate small, genetically based sex differences (Greendorfer, Lewko, & Rosengren, 1996). In support of this view, boys can throw a ball much farther than girls only when using their dominant hand. When they use their nondominant hand, the sex difference is minimal (Williams, Haywood, & Painter, 1996). This suggests that practice is largely responsible for boys' superior throwing.

Enhancing Early Childhood Motor Development

Many Western parents provide preschoolers with early training in gymnastics, tumbling, and other lessons. These experiences offer excellent opportunities for physical exercise and social interaction. But aside from throwing (where direct instruction is helpful), formal lessons during the preschool years have little impact on motor development. Instead, children master the motor skills of early childhood naturally, as part of their everyday play.

Nevertheless, the physical environment in which informal play takes place can affect mastery of complex motor skills. When children have play spaces and equipment appropriate for running, climbing, jumping, and throwing and are encouraged to use them, they respond eagerly to these challenges. But if balls are too large and heavy to be properly grasped and thrown, or jungle gyms, ladders, and horizontal bars are suitable for only the largest and strongest children, then preschoolers cannot easily acquire new motor skills. Consequently, playgrounds must offer a range of equipment to meet the diverse needs of individual children.

When play spaces are properly designed and equipped for preschoolers, young children respond eagerly to motor challenges and develop new skills through informal play. This imaginative playground provides a rich variety of equipment suited to children of varying sizes and a surface that protects them from injury.

Similarly, fine motor development can be supported through daily routines, such as pouring juice and dressing, and play that involves puzzles, construction sets, drawing, painting, sculpting, cutting, and pasting. Exposure to artwork of their own culture and of other cultures enhances children's awareness of the creative possibilities of artistic media. And opportunities to represent their own ideas and feelings, rather than to color in predrawn forms, foster artistic development.

Finally, the social climate created by adults can enhance or dampen preschoolers' motor development. When parents and teachers criticize a child's performance, push specific motor skills, or promote a competitive attitude, they risk undermining children's self-confidence and, in turn, their motor progress (Kutner, 1993). Adult involvement in young children's motor activities should focus on "fun" rather than on winning or perfecting the "correct" technique.

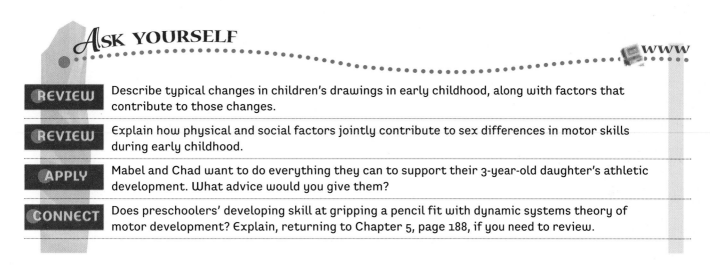

*A*sk YOURSELF

REVIEW Describe typical changes in children's drawings in early childhood, along with factors that contribute to those changes.

REVIEW Explain how physical and social factors jointly contribute to sex differences in motor skills during early childhood.

APPLY Mabel and Chad want to do everything they can to support their 3-year-old daughter's athletic development. What advice would you give them?

CONNECT Does preschoolers' developing skill at gripping a pencil fit with dynamic systems theory of motor development? Explain, returning to Chapter 5, page 188, if you need to review.

*S*ummary

Body Growth

Describe changes in body size, proportions, and skeletal maturity during early childhood.

● Gains in body size taper off in early childhood. Body fat also declines, and children become longer and leaner. In various parts of the skeleton, new epiphyses appear, where cartilage gradually hardens into bone. Compared with infancy and early childhood, individual differences in body size and rate of physical growth are more apparent in early childhood.

● By the end of early childhood, children start to lose their primary teeth. Care of primary teeth is important because diseased baby teeth can affect the health of permanent teeth. Childhood tooth decay remains high, especially among low-SES children.

What makes physical growth an asynchronous process?

● Different parts of the body grow at different rates. The **general growth curve** describes change in body size—rapid during infancy, slower during early and middle childhood, rapid again during adolescence. Exceptions to this trend include the genitals, the lymph tissue, and the brain.

Brain Development

Describe brain development in early childhood.

● During the preschool years, neural fibers in the brain continue to form synapses and myelinate. By this time, many cortical regions have overproduced synapses, and synaptic pruning occurs. To make room for the connective structures of active neurons, many

surrounding neurons die, and plasticity of the brain is reduced.

● The left hemisphere of the cerebral cortex develops ahead of the right hemisphere, supporting young children's rapidly expanding language skills.

● Hand preference strengthens during early childhood, indicating that lateralization increases during this time. Handedness indicates an individual's **dominant cerebral hemisphere**. According to one theory, most children inherit a gene that biases them for right-handedness, but experience can sway children toward a left-hand preference. Body position during the prenatal period and practice can affect handedness.

● Although left-handedness is associated with developmental problems, the great majority of left-handed children are normal. Left- and mixed-handed youngsters are more likely to display outstanding verbal and mathematical talents.

● During early childhood, connections are established between brain structures. Fibers linking the **cerebellum** to the cerebral cortex grow and myelinate, enhancing balance and motor control. The **reticular formation,** responsible for alertness and consciousness, and the **corpus callosum,** which connects the two cerebral hemispheres, also form synapses and myelinate.

Factors Affecting Physical Growth and Health

Explain how heredity influences physical growth.

● Heredity influences physical growth by controlling the release of hormones from the **pituitary gland.** The most important pituitary hormones for childhood growth are **growth hormone (GH),** which affects the development of almost all body tissues, and **thyroid-stimulating hormone (TSH),** which influences brain growth and body size.

Describe the effects of emotional well-being, restful sleep, nutrition, and infectious disease on physical growth and health in early childhood.

● Emotional well-being continues to influence body growth in early childhood. Extreme emotional deprivation can lead to **psychosocial dwarfism.**

● Restful sleep in early childhood contributes to body growth and positive family functioning. Bedtime routines help Western children, who generally sleep alone, fall asleep. About half of preschoolers awaken occasionally because of nightmares. Disorders of sleep walking and sleep terrors run in families, suggesting a genetic influence, but they can also be triggered by stress or extreme fatigue.

● Preschoolers' slower growth rate causes appetite to decline, and they often become picky eaters. Young children's social environments have a powerful impact on food preferences. Modeling by others, repeated exposure to new foods, and a positive emotional climate at mealtimes can promote healthy, varied eating in young children.

● Malnutrition can combine with infectious disease to undermine healthy growth. In developing countries, diarrhea is widespread and claims millions of young lives. Teaching families how to administer oral rehydration therapy (ORT) and providing zinc supplements can prevent most of these deaths.

● Immunization rates are lower in the United States than in other industrialized nations because many economically disadvantaged children do not have access to the health care they need. In addition, parental misconceptions about safe immunization practices are not always corrected through public education.

● Childhood illness rises with child-care attendance. Otitis media, or middle ear infection, is especially common. Frequent bouts predict delayed language progress, social isolation, and poorer academic performance after school entry. High-quality child care and screening for otitis media can prevent these negative outcomes.

What factors increase the risk of unintentional injuries, and how can childhood injuries be prevented?

● Unintentional injuries are the leading cause of childhood mortality. Injury victims are more likely to be boys; to be temperamentally irritable, inattentive, and negative; and to be growing up in stressed, poverty-stricken, crowded family environments. Among developed nations, injury deaths are high in the United States and Canada. And in developing countries, they are even higher and may soon overtake disease as the leading cause of childhood deaths.

● A variety of approaches are needed to prevent childhood injuries, including reducing poverty and other sources of family stress; passing laws that promote child safety; creating safer home, travel, and play environments; improving public education; and changing parent and child behaviors.

Motor Development

Cite major milestones of gross and fine motor development in early childhood.

● During early childhood, children continue to integrate previously acquired

motor skills into more complex dynamic systems of action. The child's center of gravity shifts toward the trunk, and balance improves, paving the way for many gross motor achievements. Preschoolers' gaits become smooth and rhythmic, and they run, jump, hop, gallop, eventually skip, throw, and catch, and generally become better coordinated.

● Increasing control of the hands and fingers leads to dramatic improvements in fine motor skills. Preschoolers gradually dress themselves and use a fork and knife.

● By age 3, children's scribbles become pictures. With age, their drawings increase in complexity and realism, as perception, language, memory, and fine motor capacities improve. Children's drawings are also influenced by their culture's artistic traditions.

● Around age 4, children's writing shows some distinctive features of print, but only gradually do childre realize that writing stands for language. Between 3 and 5 years, children experiment with pencil grip and discover the adultlike grip that maximizes stability and writing efficiency. Advances in perception and exposure to written materials contribute to progress in discriminating individual letters. When parents and teachers support children's efforts to print, preschoolers make greater strides in writing and other aspects of literacy development.

Describe individual differences in preschoolers' motor skills and ways to enhance motor development in early childhood.

● Body build and opportunity for physical play affect early childhood motor development. Sex differences that favor boys in skills requiring force and power and girls in skills requiring good balance and fine movements are partly genetic, but social pressures exaggerate them.

● Children master the motor skills of early childhood through informal play experiences. Richly equipped play environments that accommodate a wide range of physical abilities are important. Emphasizing pleasure in motor activities is the best way to foster motor development during the preschool years.

Important Terms and Concepts

cerebellum (p. 293)

corpus callosum (p. 293)

dominant cerebral hemisphere (p. 292)

general growth curve (p. 290)

growth hormone (GH) (p. 294)

pituitary gland (p. 294)

psychosocial dwarfism (p. 294)

reticular formation (p. 293)

thyroid-stimulating hormone (TSH) (p. 294)

For Further Information and Help

Consult the Companion Website for *Infants, Children, and Adolescents,* Fifth Edition, *(www.ablongman.com/berk),* where you will find the following resources for this chapter:

- **Chapter Objectives**
- **Flashcards** for studying important terms and concepts
- **Annotated Weblinks** to guide you in further research
- **Ask Yourself questions,** which you can answer and then check against a sample response

- **Suggested Readings**
- **Practice Tests** with immediate scoring and feedback

In the colorful context of this painting, children participate in activities that make up their culture's way of life. Chapter 9 explores the many ways that children think and master essential skills for becoming competent, contributing members of their community and culture.

"Fisherman"
Marisa Herryanto
6 years, Indonesia

Cognitive Development in Early Childhood

One rainy morning, as I observed in our laboratory preschool, Leslie, the children's teacher, joined me at the back of the room to watch for a moment herself. "Preschoolers' minds are such a curious blend of logic, fantasy, and faulty reasoning," Leslie reflected. "Every day, I'm startled by the maturity and originality of what they say and do. Yet at other times, their thinking seems limited and inflexible."

Leslie's comments sum up the puzzling contradictions of early childhood cognition. That day, for example, I found 3-year-old Sammy at the puzzle table, moments after a loud crash of thunder outside. Sammy looked up, startled, then said to Leslie, "The man turned on the thunder!" Leslie patiently explained that people can't turn thunder on or off. But Sammy persisted. "Then a lady did it," he stated with certainty.

In other respects, Sammy's cognitive skills seemed surprisingly advanced. At snack time, he accurately counted, "One, two, three, four!" and then got four cartons of milk, giving one to each child at his table. Sammy's keen memory and ability to categorize were also evident. As he sat in the reading corner, he recited by heart *The Very Hungry Caterpillar,* a story he had heard many times. Sammy's favorite picture books were about animals, and he could name and classify dozens of them.

Still, Sammy's cognitive skills seemed fragile. When more than four children joined his snack group, Sammy's counting broke down. And some of his notions about quantity seemed as fantastic as his understanding of thunder. Across the snack table, Priti dumped out her raisins, and they scattered in front of her. "How come you got lots, and I only got this little bit?" asked Sammy, failing to realize that he had just as many; they were simply all bunched up in a tiny red box. While Priti washed her hands after snack, Sammy put her remaining raisins in her cubby. When Priti returned and looked for her raisins, Sammy pronounced, "You know where

315

they are!" He failed to grasp that Priti, who hadn't seen him move the raisins, believed they would be where she had left them.

In this chapter, we explore the many facets of early childhood cognition, drawing from three theories with which you are already familiar. We begin with Piaget's preoperational stage, which, for the most part, emphasizes preschool children's deficits rather than their strengths. Recent research, along with two additional perspectives—Vygotsky's sociocultural theory and information processing—extends our understanding of preschoolers' cognitive competencies. Then we turn to a variety of factors that contribute to individual differences in mental development—the home environment, the quality of preschool and child care, and the many hours young children spend watching television. Our chapter concludes with language development, the most awesome achievement of early childhood.

Piaget's Theory: The Preoperational Stage

As children move from the sensorimotor to the **preoperational stage,** which spans the years 2 to 7, the most obvious change is an extraordinary increase in mental representation. Recall that infants and toddlers have some ability to mentally represent the world. During early childhood, this capacity blossoms.

Advances in Mental Representation

As I looked around the preschool classroom, signs of developing representation were everywhere—in the children's drawings and paintings, in the elaborate castles and fortresses they built out of blocks, in their re-creations of family life in the housekeeping area, and in their delight at story time. Especially impressive were strides in language skill. During free play, a hum of chattering voices rose from the classroom.

Piaget acknowledged that language is our most flexible means of mental representation. By detaching thought from action, it permits far more efficient thinking than was possible earlier. When we think in words, we overcome the limits of our momentary experiences. We can deal with the past, present, and future at once and combine concepts in unique ways, as when we think about a hungry caterpillar eating bananas or monsters flying through the forest at night.

Despite the power of language, Piaget did not believe that it plays a major role in cognitive development. Instead, he claimed that sensorimotor activity leads to internal images of experience, which children then label with words (Piaget, 1936/1952). In support of Piaget's view, recall from Chapter 6 that the first words toddlers use have a strong sensorimotor basis. In addition, toddlers acquire an impressive range of cognitive categories long before they use words to label them (see pages 223–226).

Still, other theorists regard Piaget's account of the link between language and thought as incomplete, as we will see later in this chapter.

Make-Believe Play

Make-believe play is another excellent example of the development of representation during early childhood. Piaget believed that through pretending, young children practice and strengthen newly acquired representational schemes. Drawing on Piaget's ideas, several investigators have traced changes in make-believe play during the preschool years.

DEVELOPMENT OF MAKE-BELIEVE PLAY ● One day, Sammy's 18-month-old brother, Dwayne, visited the classroom. Dwayne wandered around, picked up the receiver of a toy telephone, said, "Hi, Mommy," and then dropped it. In the housekeeping area, he found a cup, pretended to drink, and toddled off again. In the meantime, Sammy joined a group of children in the block area for a space shuttle launch.

"That can be our control tower," he suggested to Vance and Lynette, pointing to a corner by a bookshelf. "Countdown!" Sammy announced, speaking into a small wooden block, his pretend walkie-talkie. "Five, six, two, four, one, blastoff!" Lynette made a doll push a pretend button, and the rocket was off!

A comparison of Dwayne's pretend with that of Sammy and his classmates illustrates three important advances in make-believe. Each reflects the preschool child's growing symbolic mastery:

● *Over time, play increasingly detaches from the real-life conditions associated with it.* In early pretending, toddlers use only realistic objects—a toy telephone to talk into or a cup to drink from. Most of these earliest pretend acts imitate adults' actions and are not yet flexible. Children younger than age 2, for example, will pretend to drink from a cup but refuse to pretend a cup is a hat (Tomasello, Striano, & Rochat, 1999). They have trouble using an object (cup) as a symbol for another object (hat) when the object (cup) already has an obvious use.

After age 2, children pretend with less realistic toys, such as a block for a telephone receiver. And gradually they flexibly imagine objects and events without support from the real world, as Sammy's imaginary control tower illustrates (O'Reilly, 1995; Striano, Tomasello, & Rochat, 2001).

● *Play becomes less self-centered.* At first, make-believe is directed toward the self—for example, Dwayne pretends to feed only himself. A short time later, children direct pretend actions toward objects, as when the child feeds a doll. And early in the third year, they become detached participants who make a doll feed itself or (in Lynette's case) push a button to launch a rocket. Make-believe becomes less self-centered as children realize that agents and recipients of pretend actions can be independent of themselves (McCune, 1993).

● *Play gradually includes more complex combinations of schemes.* For example, Dwayne can pretend to drink from a cup, but he does not yet combine drinking with pouring. Later, children combine schemes with those of peers in **sociodramatic play, the make-believe with others that is under way by age 2½ and increases rapidly during the next few years** (Haight & Miller, 1993). Already, Sammy and his classmates can coordinate several roles in an elaborate plot. By the end of early childhood, children have a sophisticated understanding of role relationships and story lines (Göncü, 1993).

The appearance of complex sociodramatic play signals a major change in representation. Children do not just represent their world; they display *awareness* that make-believe is a representational activity, an understanding that increases steadily from 4 to 8 years of age (Lillard, 1998, 2001). Listen closely to preschoolers as they jointly create an imaginary scene. You will hear them assign roles and negotiate make-believe plans: "*You pretend to be* the astronaut, *I'll act like* I'm operating the control tower!" "Wait, *I gotta set up* the spaceship." In communicating about pretend, children think about their own and others' fanciful representations. This indicates that they have begun to reason about people's mental activities, a topic we will return to later in this chapter.

BENEFITS OF MAKE-BELIEVE PLAY ● Today, Piaget's view of make-believe as mere practice of representational schemes is regarded as too limited. Play not only reflects but contributes to children's cognitive and social skills. Sociodramatic play has been studied most thoroughly. In comparison to social nonpretend activities (such as drawing or putting puzzles together), during social pretend preschoolers' interactions last longer, show more involvement, draw larger numbers of children into the activity, and are more cooperative (Creasey, Jarvis, & Berk, 1998).

When we consider these findings, it is not surprising that preschoolers who spend more time at sociodramatic play are seen as more socially competent by their teachers (Connolly & Doyle, 1984). And many studies reveal that make-believe

These 3- and 4-year-olds coordinate several make-believe roles as they jointly care for a sick baby. Sociodramatic play contributes to cognitive, emotional, and social development.

© LAURA DWIGHT

Applying
WHAT WE **Know** / Enhancing Make-Believe Play in Early Childhood

STRATEGY	DESCRIPTION
Provide sufficient space and play materials.	A generous amount of space and materials allows for many play options and reduces conflict.
Supervise and encourage children's play without controlling it.	Respond to, guide, and elaborate on preschoolers' play themes when they indicate a need for assistance. Provide open-ended suggestions (for example, "Would the animals like a train ride?"), and talk with the child about the thoughts, motivations, and emotions of play characters. Refrain from directing the child's play; excessive adult control destroys the creativity and joy of make-believe.
Offer a wide variety of both realistic materials and materials without clear functions.	Children use realistic materials, such as trucks, dolls, tea sets, dress-up clothes, and toy scenes (house, farm, garage, airport) to act out everyday roles in their culture. Materials without clear functions (such as blocks, cardboard cylinders, paper bags, and sand) inspire fantastic role play, such as "pirate" and "creature from outer space."
Ensure that children have many rich, real-world experiences to inspire positive fantasy play.	Opportunities to participate in real-world activities with adults and to observe adult roles in the community provide children with rich social knowledge to integrate into make-believe. Restricting television viewing, especially programs with violent content, limits the degree to which violent themes and aggressive behavior become part of children's play. (See Chapter 10, pages 378–380.)
Help children solve social conflicts constructively.	Cooperation is essential for sociodramatic play. Guide children toward positive relationships with agemates by helping them resolve disagreements constructively. For example, ask, "What could you do if you want a turn?" If the child cannot think of possibilities, suggest some options and assist the child in implementing them.

Sources: Berk, 2001; Frost, Shin, & Jacobs, 1998; Vandenberg, 1998.

strengthens a wide variety of mental abilities, including sustained attention, memory, logical reasoning, language and literacy, imagination, creativity, and the ability to reflect on one's own thinking and take another's perspective (Bergen & Mauer, 2000; Berk, 2001; Kavanaugh & Engel, 1998; Newman, 1990; Ruff & Capozzoli, 2003).

Between 25 and 45 percent of preschoolers spend much time in solitary make-believe, creating *imaginary companions*—special fantasized friends endowed with humanlike qualities. For example, one preschooler created Nutsy and Nutsy, a pair of boisterous birds living outside her bedroom window who often went along on family outings. Another child conjured up Maybe, a human of changing gender who could be summoned by shouting out the front door of the family house (Gleason, Sebanc, & Hartup, 2000; Taylor, 1999). In the past, imaginary companions were viewed as a sign of maladjustment, but recent research challenges this assumption. Children with these invisible playmates typically treat their companion with care and affection. And they display more complex pretend play, are advanced in understanding others' viewpoints, and are more sociable with peers (Gleason, 2002; Taylor & Carlson, 1997).

Refer to Applying What We Know above for ways to enhance preschoolers' make-believe. Later we will return to the origins and consequences of make-believe from an alternative perspective—Vygotsky's.

Symbol–Real World Relations

Leslie set up a dollhouse, replete with tiny furnishings, in a corner of the classroom. Sammy often arranged the furniture to match his real-world living room, kitchen, and bedroom. Representations of reality, like Sammy's, are powerful cognitive tools. When we understand that a photograph, model, or map corresponds to circumstances in everyday life, we can use it to acquire information about objects and places we have not experienced.

When do children realize that a symbol stands for a specific state of affairs in the real world? In one study, 2½- and 3-year-olds watched as an adult hid a small toy (Little Snoopy) in a scale

© PAUL GISH

model of a room; then children were asked to retrieve it. Next, they had to find a larger toy (Big Snoopy) hidden in the room that the model represented. Not until age 3 could most children use the model as a guide to finding Big Snoopy in the real room (DeLoache, 1987). The younger children had trouble with **dual representation**—viewing a symbolic object as both an object in its own right and a symbol. In the study just described, 2½-year-olds did not realize that the model could be both *a toy room and a symbol of another room.* In support of this interpretation, when researchers decreased the prominence of the model room as an object, by placing it behind a window and preventing children from touching it, more 2½-year-olds succeeded at the search task (DeLoache, 2000a, 2002b).

Recall a similar limitation in early pretending—that 1½- to 2-year-olds cannot use an object with an obvious use (cup) to stand for another object (hat). Likewise, 2-year-olds do not yet grasp that a drawing—an object in its own right—represents real-world objects. When an adult held up a drawing indicating which of two objects preschoolers should drop down a chute, 3-year-olds used the drawing as a symbol to guide their behavior, but 2-year-olds did not (Callaghan, 1999).

How do children grasp the dual representation of models, drawings, and other symbols? Adult teaching is helpful. When adults point out similarities between models and real-world spaces, 2½-year-olds perform better on the find-Snoopy task (Peralta de Mendoza & Salsa, 2003). Furthermore, understanding one type of symbol helps preschoolers understand others. For example, children understand photos as symbols very early, around age 2, since a photo's primary purpose is to stand for something; it is not an interesting object in its own right (DeLoache, 1991). And 3-year-olds who can use a model of a room to locate Big Snoopy readily transfer their understanding to a simple map (Marzolf & DeLoache, 1994).

In sum, giving young children many opportunities to learn the functions of diverse symbols—picture books, photographs, drawings, make-believe, and maps—enhances their understanding that one object or event can stand for another (DeLoache, 2002a). With age, children come to understand a wide range of symbols that do not bear a strong physical similarity to what they represent (Liben, 1999). As a result, doors open to vast realms of knowledge.

Is this preschooler aware that the doll house is not just an interesting object in its own right, but can stand for a real house—that is, serve as a symbol of the real world? Not until age 3 do most young children grasp the dual representation of models.

Limitations of Preoperational Thought

Aside from gains in representation, Piaget described preschool children in terms of what they cannot, rather than can, understand (Beilin, 1992). He compared them to older, more competent children in the concrete operational stage, as the term *pre*operational suggests. According to Piaget, young children are not capable of **operations**—mental representations of actions that obey logical rules. Instead, their thinking is rigid, limited to one aspect of a situation at a time, and strongly influenced by the way things appear at the moment.

EGOCENTRIC AND ANIMISTIC THINKING ● For Piaget, the most serious deficiency of preoperational thinking, the one that underlies all others, is **egocentrism**—failure to distinguish the symbolic viewpoints of others from one's own. He believed that when children first mentally represent the world, they tend to focus on their own viewpoint. Hence, they often assume that others perceive, think, and feel the same way they do.

Piaget's most convincing demonstration of egocentrism involves his *three-mountains problem,* described in Figure 9.1. He also

FIGURE 9.1

Piaget's three-mountains problem.

Each mountain is distinguished by its color and by its summit. One has a red cross, another a small house, and the third a snow-capped peak. Children at the preoperational stage respond egocentrically. They cannot select a picture that shows the mountains from the doll's perspective. Instead, they simply choose the photo that reflects their own vantage point.

regarded egocentrism as responsible for preoperational children's **animistic thinking**—the belief that inanimate objects have lifelike qualities, such as thoughts, wishes, feelings, and intentions. Recall Sammy's firm insistence that someone must have turned on the thunder. Similarly, the 3-year-old who explains that the sun is angry at the clouds and has chased them away is demonstrating this kind of reasoning. According to Piaget, because young children egocentrically assign human purposes to physical events, magical thinking is especially common during the preschool years.

Piaget argued that young children's egocentric bias prevents them from accommodating, or reflecting on and revising their faulty reasoning in response to their physical and social worlds. But to appreciate this shortcoming fully, let's consider some additional tasks that Piaget gave children.

INABILITY TO CONSERVE ● Piaget's famous conservation tasks reveal a variety of deficiencies of preoperational thinking. **Conservation** refers to the idea that certain physical characteristics of objects remain the same, even when their outward appearance changes. At snack time, Sammy and Priti each had identical boxes of raisins, but after Priti spread hers out on the table, Sammy was convinced that she had more.

Another conservation task involves liquid. The child is shown two identical tall glasses of water and asked if they contain equal amounts. Once the child agrees, the water in one glass is poured into a short, wide container, changing the appearance of the water but not its amount. Then the child is asked whether the amount of water is the same or has changed. Preoperational children think the quantity has changed. They explain, "There is less now because the water is way down here" (that is, its level is so low) or "There is more because the water is all spread out." In Figure 9.2, you will find other conservation tasks that you can try with children.

FIGURE 9.2

Some Piagetian conservation tasks.
Children at the preoperational stage cannot yet conserve.

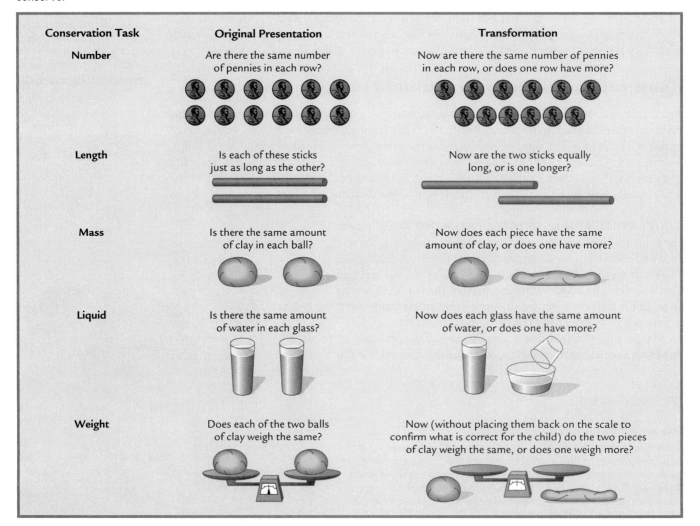

Conservation Task	Original Presentation	Transformation
Number	Are there the same number of pennies in each row?	Now are there the same number of pennies in each row, or does one row have more?
Length	Is each of these sticks just as long as the other?	Now are the two sticks equally long, or is one longer?
Mass	Is there the same amount of clay in each ball?	Now does each piece have the same amount of clay, or does one have more?
Liquid	Is there the same amount of water in each glass?	Now does each glass have the same amount of water, or does one have more?
Weight	Does each of the two balls of clay weigh the same?	Now (without placing them back on the scale to confirm what is correct for the child) do the two pieces of clay weigh the same, or does one weigh more?

Preoperational children's inability to conserve highlights several related aspects of their thinking. First, their understanding is *centered*, or characterized by **centration.** They focus on one aspect of a situation, neglecting other important features. In conservation of liquid, the child *centers* on the height of the water, failing to realize that all changes in height are compensated for by changes in width. Second, children are easily distracted by the *perceptual appearance* of objects. Third, children treat the initial and final *states* of the water as unrelated events, ignoring the *dynamic transformation* (pouring of water) between them.

The most important illogical feature of preoperational thought is its **irreversibility,** an inability to mentally go through a series of steps in a problem and then reverse direction, returning to the starting point. *Reversibility* is part of every logical operation. After Priti spills her raisins, Sammy cannot reverse by thinking, "I know Priti doesn't have more raisins than I do. If we put them back in that little box, her raisins and mine would look just the same."

LACK OF HIERARCHICAL CLASSIFICATION ● Lack of logical operations leads preschoolers to have difficulty with **hierarchical classification—the organization of objects into classes and subclasses on the basis of similarities and differences.** Piaget's famous *class inclusion problem*, illustrated in Figure 9.3, demonstrates this limitation. Preoperational children center on the overriding feature of yellow and do not think reversibly by moving from the whole class (flowers) to the parts (yellow and blue) and back again.

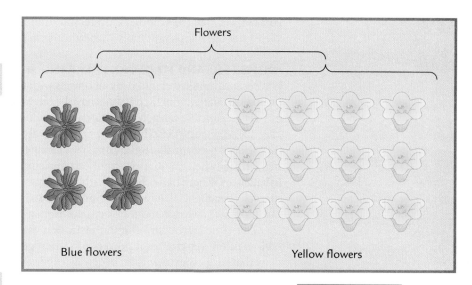

FIGURE 9.3

A Piagetian class inclusion problem.

Children are shown 16 flowers, 4 of which are blue and 12 of which are yellow. Asked, "Are there more yellow flowers or flowers?" the preoperational child responds, "More yellow flowers," failing to realize that both yellow and blue flowers are included in the category "flowers."

Follow-Up Research on Preoperational Thought

Over the past two decades, researchers have challenged Piaget's account of a cognitively deficient preschooler. Many Piagetian problems contain unfamiliar elements or too many pieces of information for young children to handle at once. As a result, preschoolers' responses often do not reflect their true abilities. Piaget also missed many naturally occurring instances of preschoolers' effective reasoning. Let's look at some examples.

EGOCENTRISM ● Do young children really believe that a person standing elsewhere in a room sees the same thing they see? When researchers change the nature of Piaget's three-mountains problem to include familiar objects and use methods other than picture selection (which is difficult even for 10-year-olds), 4-year-olds show clear awareness of others' vantage points (Borke, 1975; Newcombe & Huttenlocher, 1992).

Nonegocentric responses also appear in young children's conversations. For example, preschoolers adapt their speech to fit the needs of their listeners. Sammy uses shorter, simpler expressions when talking to his little brother Dwayne than when talking to agemates or adults (Gelman & Shatz, 1978). Also, in describing objects, children do not use such words as "big" and "little" in a rigid, egocentric fashion. Instead, they *adjust* their descriptions, taking context into account. By age 3, children judge a 2-inch shoe as small when seen by itself (because it is much smaller than most shoes) but as big for a tiny, 5-inch doll (Ebeling & Gelman, 1994).

In previous chapters, we showed that even toddlers have some appreciation of others' perspectives. By 18 months, they have begun to infer others' intentions (see page 215) and realize that others' emotional reactions may differ from their own (see page 255). In fairness, however, Piaget (1945/1951) in his later writings referred to young children's egocentrism as a tendency rather than an inability. As we revisit the topic of perspective taking in this and later chapters, you will see that preschoolers' understanding is far from complete. Understanding of others' viewpoints develops gradually throughout childhood and adolescence.

ANIMISTIC AND MAGICAL THINKING ● Piaget overestimated preschoolers' animistic beliefs because he asked children about objects with which they have little direct experience, such as the clouds, sun, and moon. Even infants have begun to distinguish animate from inanimate, as indicated by their remarkable categorical distinctions among living and nonliving things (see Chapter 6, pages 223–226). By age 2½, children give psychological explanations—"he likes to" or "she wants to"—for people and, occasionally, for animals but rarely for objects (Hickling & Wellman, 2001). They do make errors when questioned about certain vehicles, such as trains and airplanes. But these appear to be self-moving, a basic characteristic of animate beings. And they have some lifelike features—for example, headlights that look like eyes (Gelman & Opfer, 2002). Preschoolers' responses result from incomplete knowledge about objects, not from a belief that inanimate objects are alive.

The same is true for other fantastic beliefs of the preschool years. Most 3- and 4-year-olds believe in the supernatural powers of fairies, goblins, and other enchanted creatures. But they deny that magic can alter their everyday experiences—for example, turn a picture into a real object (Subbotsky, 1994). Instead, they think magic accounts for events they cannot explain, as in 3-year-old Sammy's magical account of what causes thunder in the opening to this chapter (Rosengren & Hickling, 2000).

Between 4 and 8 years, as familiarity with physical events and principles increases, magical beliefs decline. Children figure out who is really behind the activities of Santa Claus and the Tooth Fairy! They also realize that the antics of magicians are due to trickery, not special powers (Phelps & Woolley, 1994; Woolley et al., 1999). But despite their impressive understandings, children entertain the possibility that something they imagine might materialize. As a result, they may react with anxiety to scary stories, TV shows, and nightmares. In one study, researchers had 4- to 6-year-olds imagine that a monster was inside one empty box and a puppy was inside another. Although almost all the children approached the "puppy" box, many avoided putting their finger in the "monster" box, even though they knew that imagination cannot create reality (Harris et al., 1991).

How quickly children give up certain fantastic ideas varies with religion and culture. For example, Jewish children express greater disbelief in Santa Claus and the Tooth Fairy than their Christian agemates. Having been taught at home about the unreality of Santa, they seem to generalize this attitude to other magical figures (Woolley, 1997). And cultural myths about wishing—for example, the custom of making a wish before blowing out birthday candles—probably underlie the conviction of most 3- to 6-year-olds that just by wishing, you can sometimes make your desires come true (Woolley, 2000).

The importance of knowledge, experience, and culture can be seen in preschoolers' grasp of other natural concepts. Refer to the Social Issues: Education box on pages 324–325 to find out about young children's developing understanding of death.

ILLOGICAL THOUGHT ● Many studies have reexamined the illogical characteristics that Piaget saw in the preoperational stage. Results show that when preschoolers are given tasks that are simplified and made relevant to their everyday lives, they do better than Piaget might have expected.

For example, when a conservation-of-number task is scaled down to include only three items instead of six or seven, 3-year-olds perform well (Gelman, 1972). And when preschoolers are asked carefully worded questions about what happens to substances (such as sugar) after they are dissolved in water, they give accurate explanations. Most 3- to 5-year-olds know that the substance is conserved—that it continues to exist, can be tasted, and makes the liquid heavier, even though it is invisible in the water (Au, Sidle, & Rollins, 1993; Rosen & Rozin, 1993).

Which of the children in this audience realize that a magician's powers depend on trickery? The younger children look surprised and bewildered. The older children think the magician's antics are funny. Between 4 and 8 years, as familiarity with physical events and principles increases, children's magical beliefs decline.

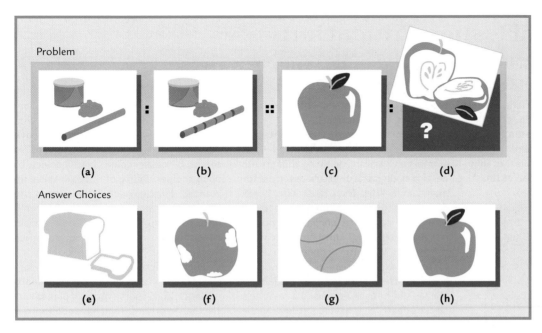

Problem

(a)   (b)   (c)   (d)

Answer Choices

(e)   (f)   (g)   (h)

FIGURE 9.4

Analogical problem about physical transformations.

Preschoolers were told they would be playing a picture-matching game. Then the researchers showed each child the first three pictures of a four-picture sequence—in this example, playdough, cut up playdough, and apple—and asked the child to complete the sequence by choosing from five alternatives. Several wrong answers shared features with the right choice—for example, correct physical change but wrong object (e), correct object but wrong physical change (f). Children as young as 3 years of age could combine the correct physical change with the correct object and solve the problem. (Adapted from Goswami & Brown, 1989.)

Preschoolers' ability to reason about transformations is evident on other problems. They can engage in impressive *reasoning by analogy* about physical changes. As Figure 9.4 shows, when they are presented with the problem *"playdough is to cut-up playdough as apple is to ?"* even 3-year-olds choose the correct answer from a set of alternatives, several of which share physical features with the right choice (Goswami, 1996). These findings indicate that preschoolers can overcome appearances and think logically about cause and effect in familiar contexts.

Furthermore, preschoolers have a remarkable understanding of diverse cause-and-effect relationships. For example, they know that the insides of animals differ from the insides of machines. Even though they have little detailed biological or mechanical knowledge, they realize that animal insides are responsible for different cause–effect sequences (such as willing oneself to move) than are possible for nonliving things (Keil & Lockhart, 1999).

Finally, 3- and 4-year-olds use causal expressions, such as *if–then* and *because,* with the same degree of accuracy as adults do (McCabe & Peterson, 1988). Illogical reasoning seems to occur only when they grapple with unfamiliar topics, too much information, or contradictory facts, which they have trouble reconciling (Ruffman, 1999).

CATEGORIZATION ● Although preschoolers have difficulty with Piagetian class inclusion tasks, they organize their everyday knowledge into nested categories at an early age. By the second half of the first year, children have formed a variety of global categories, such as furniture, animals, vehicles, plants, and kitchen utensils. Notice that each of these categories includes objects that differ widely in perceptual features. The objects go together because of their common natural kind (animate versus inanimate), function, and behavior, challenging Piaget's assumption that young children's thinking is governed by the way things appear. Indeed, 2- to 5-year-olds readily draw inferences about nonobservable characteristics that category members share (Gopnik & Nazzi, 2003). For example, after being told that a bird has warm blood and a stegosaurus (dinosaur) has cold blood, preschoolers infer that a pterodactyl (labeled a dinosaur) has cold blood, even though it closely resembles a bird.

Over the early preschool years, children's global categories differentiate. They form many *basic-level categories*—ones at an intermediate level of generality, such as "chairs," "tables," "dressers," and "beds." Performance on object-sorting tasks indicates that by the third or fourth year, children easily move back and forth between basic-level categories and *general categories,* such as "furniture" (Blewitt, 1994). They also break down the basic-level categories into *subcategories,* such as "rocking chairs" and "desk chairs." In fact, a case study of a highly verbal toddler

The capacity to categorize expands greatly in early childhood. Children form many categories based on underlying characteristics rather than perceptual features. Guided by knowledge that "dinosaurs have cold blood," this 4-year-old categorizes the pterodactyl (in the foreground) as a dinosaur rather than a bird, even though pterodactyls have wings and can fly.

© TONY FREEMAN/PHOTOEDIT

Social Issues: Education

Young Children's Understanding of Death

Five-year-old Miriam arrived at preschool the day after her dog Pepper died. Instead of running to play with the other children, she stayed close to Leslie, who noticed Miriam's discomfort. "What's wrong?" Leslie asked.

"Daddy said Pepper had a sick tummy. He fell asleep and died." For a moment, Miriam looked hopeful, "When I get home, Pepper might be up."

Leslie answered directly, "No, Pepper won't get up again. He's not asleep. He's dead, and that means he can't sleep, eat, run, or play anymore."

Miriam wandered off. Later, she returned to Leslie and confessed, "I chased Pepper too hard." Tears streamed from her eyes.

Leslie put her arm around Miriam. "Pepper didn't die because you chased him. He was very old and very sick," she explained.

Over the next few days, Miriam asked many more questions: "When I go to sleep, will I die?" "Can a tummy ache make you die?" "Does Pepper feel better now?" "Will Mommy and Daddy die?"

Development of the Death Concept

A realistic understanding of death is based on three ideas: (1) *Permanence:* Once a living thing dies, it cannot be brought back to life. (2) *Universality:* All living things eventually die. (3) *Nonfunctionality:* All living functions, including thought, feeling, movement, and body processes, cease at death.

To understand death, children must acquire some basic notions of biology—that animals and plants are living things with certain body parts that are essential for maintaining life. They must also break down their global category of *not alive* into *dead, inanimate, unreal,* and *nonexistent* (Carey, 1999). Until children grasp these ideas, they interpret death in terms of familiar experiences—as a change in behavior. Consequently, they may believe, as Miriam did, that they caused a relative's or pet's death, that having a stomachache can cause someone to die, and that death is like sleep. When researchers asked 4- to 6-year-olds whether dead people need food, air, and water; whether they go to the bathroom; whether they sleep and dream; and whether a cut on their body would heal, more than half of those who had not yet started to acquire biological understandings answered yes (Slaughter, Jaakkola, & Carey, 1999).

Most children master the three components of the death concept by age 7. *Permanence* is the first and most easily understood idea. When Leslie explained that Pepper would not get up again, Miriam accepted this fact quickly, perhaps because she had seen it in other, less emotionally charged situations, such as the dead butterflies and beetles she picked up and inspected while playing outside (Furman, 1990). Appreciation of *universality* comes slightly later. At first, children think that certain people do not die, especially themselves, people like themselves (other children), and people with whom they have close emotional ties. Anxiety about loss seems to cause young preschoolers to deny the possibility of death in these instances. Finally, *nonfunctionality* is the most difficult component of death for children to grasp. Many preschoolers view dead things as retaining living capacities (Kenyon, 2001; Speece & Brent, 1996).

Furthermore, young children understand death in animals better than death in plants, and in some types of plants better than in others. They have seen wilted plants revive after watering. And plants vary greatly in the physical evidence they offer about death (Nguyen & Gelman, 2002). Whereas most flowers are fragile, weeds often grow back after attempts to destroy them.

Cultural Influences

Although a mature appreciation of death is usually reached by middle childhood, ethnic variations suggest that religious teachings affect children's understanding. A comparison of four ethnic groups in Israel revealed that Druze and Moslem children's death concepts differed from those of Christian and Jewish children (Florian & Kravetz, 1985). The Druze emphasis on reincarnation and the greater religiosity of the Druze and Moslem groups may have led more of their children to deny permanence and nonfunctionality. Similarly, children of Southern Baptist families, who believe in

with a strong interest in birds revealed that by age 2, he had constructed a hierarchical understanding of the bird domain that included such basic-level categories and subcategories as "waterbirds" ("ducks" and "swans"), "landbirds" ("roosters" and "turkeys"), and "other birds" ("bluebirds," "cardinals," and "seagulls") (Mervis, Pani, & Pani, 2003). The boy's category structure was not quite the same as that of many adults, but it was, indeed, hierarchical.

Preschoolers' rapidly expanding vocabularies and general knowledge support their impressive skill at categorizing. As they learn more about their world, they devise theories about underlying characteristics that category members share, which help them identify new instances (Gelman & Koenig, 2003). For example, they realize that animals have an inborn potential for certain physical features and behaviors that determine their identity. And they derive much information from adult explanations. In one study, researchers made up two categories of animals: One had horns, armor, and a spiky tail; the other had wings, large ears, long toes, and a monkey-like tail (see Fig-

an afterlife, are less likely to endorse permanence than are children from Unitarian families, who focus on the here and now—peace and justice in today's world (Candy-Gibbs, Sharp, & Petrun, 1985).

Experiences with death also influence understanding. Children growing up on Israeli kibbutzim (agricultural settlements) who have experienced terrorist attacks, family members' departure on army tours to high-tension areas, and parental anxiety about safety express a full grasp of the death concept by age 5 (Mahon, Goldberg, & Washington, 1999). And actually experiencing the death of a close relative or friend greatly accelerates appreciation of permanence and universality, even among children as young as age 3 (Reilly et al., 1983).

Enhancing Children's Understanding

Parents often worry that discussing death candidly with children fuels their fears, but this is not so. Instead, children with a good grasp of the facts of death have an easier time accepting it (Essa & Murray, 1994). Direct explanations, like Leslie's, that match the child's capacity to understand, work best. When adults use clichés or make misleading statements, children may take these literally and react with confusion. For example, after a parent said to her 5-year-old daughter, "Grandpa went on a long trip," the child wondered, "Why didn't he take me?" In another instance, a father whose wife had died of cancer said to his 9-year-old son that his mother "was

sick," explaining nothing else. Later, the father was surprised when the boy caught the flu and became terribly afraid of dying (Wolfelt, 1997). Sometimes children ask very difficult questions, such as "Will I die? Will you die?" Parents can be truthful as well as comforting by taking advantage of children's sense of time. They can say something like "Not for many, many years. First I'm going to enjoy you as a grown-up and be a grandparent."

Yet another way to foster an accurate appreciation of death is to teach preschoolers about the biology of the human body. Three- to 5-year-olds given lessons in the role of the heart, kidneys, lungs, brain, digestion, bones, and muscles in sustaining life have more advanced death concepts than children not given such lessons (Slaughter & Lyons, 2003).

Adult–child discussions should also be culturally sensitive. Rather than presenting scientific evidence as counteracting religious beliefs, parents and teachers can assist children in blending the two

As long as parents provide candid, age-appropriate explanations, experiencing the death of a pet can contribute to children's accurate appreciation of what happens when living things die. These parents comfort their children after the death of the family's dog by talking and reading about the experience.

sources of knowledge. As children get older, they often combine their appreciation of the death concept with religious and philosophical views, which offer solace during times of bereavement. Indeed, mystical explanations, such as being called by God and existing in a nonmaterial state, increase during adolescence as young people think more deeply about the nature of existence and grapple with religious and spiritual ideas (Cuddy-Casey & Orvaschel, 1997). Open, honest, and respectful communication about death contributes to cognitive development as well as to emotional well-being.

ure 9.5 on page 326). Four-year-olds who were given a theory that identified an inner cause for the coexistence of the animals' features—animals in the first category "like to fight," and those in the second category "like to hide in trees"—easily classified new examples of animals. Four-year-olds for whom animal features were merely pointed out or who were given a separate function for each feature could not remember the categories (Krascum & Andrews, 1998).

In sum, preschoolers' category systems are not as complex as those of older children and adults. But the capacity to classify on the basis of nonobvious properties and in a hierarchical fashion is present in early childhood.

APPEARANCE VERSUS REALITY ● So far, we have seen that preschoolers show some remarkably advanced reasoning when presented with familiar situations and simplified problems. What happens when they encounter objects that have two identities: a real and an apparent one?

Categories of Animals   **New Instances**

"Likes to fight"

"Likes to hide in trees"

FIGURE 9.5

Categories of imaginary animals shown to preschoolers.
When an adult provided a theory about the coexistence of animals' features—"likes to fight" and "likes to hide in trees"—4-year-olds easily classified new examples of animals with only one or two features. Without the theory, preschoolers could not remember the categories. Theories about underlying characteristics support the formation of many categories in early childhood. (From R. M. Krascum & S. Andrews, 1998, "The Effects of Theories on Children's Acquisition of Family-Resemblance Categories," *Child Development, 69,* p. 336. © The Society for Research in Child Development, Inc. Reprinted by permission.)

Can they distinguish appearance from reality? In a series of studies, John Flavell and his colleagues presented children with objects that were disguised in various ways and questioned them about what each "looks like" and what each "is really and truly." Preschoolers had difficulty. For example, when asked whether a candle that looks like a crayon "is really and truly" a crayon or whether a stone painted to look like an egg "is really and truly" an egg, they often responded "Yes!" Not until age 6 or 7 did children do well on these tasks (Flavell, Green, & Flavell, 1987).

Younger children's poor performance, however, is not due to a difficulty in distinguishing appearance from reality, as Piaget suggested. Instead, they have trouble with the language of these tasks (Deák, Ray, & Brenneman, 2003). When permitted to solve appearance–reality problems nonverbally, by selecting from an array of objects the one that "really" has a particular identity, most 3-year-olds perform well (Sapp, Lee, & Muir, 2000).

These findings suggest that preschoolers grasp the appearance–reality distinction sometime during the third year. Note how it involves a capacity we discussed earlier: *dual representation,* the realization that an object can be one thing (a candle) while symbolizing another (a crayon). At first, however, children's understanding is fragile. After putting on a Halloween mask, young preschoolers are often wary, and sometimes frightened, when they see themselves in a mirror. And only over time do children learn about the range of situations in which appearance and reality differ. For example, not until the school years do they fully appreciate the unreality of much that they see on TV.

Finally, research on preschoolers' appreciation of appearance versus reality reminds us of another important point: Adults' questioning styles can easily underestimate children's understanding.

Evaluation of the Preoperational Stage

Table 9.1 provides an overview of the cognitive attainments of early childhood just considered. Compare them with Piaget's description of the preoperational child on pages 316–321. How can we make sense of the contradictions between Piaget's conclusions and the findings of recent research? The evidence as a whole indicates that Piaget was partly wrong and partly right about young children's cognitive capacities. When given simplified tasks based on familiar experiences, preschoolers show the beginnings of logical operations.

That preschoolers have some logical understanding suggests that they attain logical operations gradually. Over time, children rely on increasingly effective mental (as opposed to perceptual) approaches to solving problems. For example, children who cannot use counting to compare two sets of items do not conserve number (Sophian, 1995). Once preschoolers can count, they apply this skill to conservation-of-number tasks with only a few items. As counting improves, they extend the strategy to problems with more items. By age 6, they understand that number remains the same after a transformation as long as nothing is added or taken away. Consequently, they no longer need to count to verify their answer (Klahr & MacWhinney, 1998). This sequence indicates that children pass through several phases of understanding, although (as Piaget indicated) they do not fully grasp conservation until the early school years.

Evidence that preschool children can be trained to perform well on Piagetian problems also supports the idea that operational thought is not absent at one point in time and present at another (Roazzi & Bryant, 1997; Siegler, 1995). It makes sense that children who possess some understanding benefit from training, unlike those with no understanding at all. That logical operations develop gradually poses a serious challenge to Piaget's stage concept, which assumes abrupt change toward logical reasoning around age 6 or 7. Does a preoperational stage really exist? Some no longer think so. Recall from Chapter 6 that according to the information-processing perspective, children work out their understanding of each type of task separately. Their thought processes are regarded as basically the same at all ages—just present to a greater or lesser extent.

TABLE 9.1

Some Cognitive Attainments of the Preschool Years

APPROXIMATE AGE	COGNITIVE ATTAINMENTS
2–4 years	Shows a dramatic increase in representational activity, as reflected in the development of language, make-believe play, understanding of symbol–real world relations (such as photos, drawings, and maps), and categorization
	Takes the perspective of others in simplified, familiar situations and in everyday, face-to-face communication
	Distinguishes animate beings from inanimate objects; denies that magic can alter everyday experiences
	Notices transformations, reverses thinking, and understands many cause-and-effect relationships in familiar contexts
	Categorizes objects on the basis of common natural kind, function, and behavior (not just perceptual features) and devises ideas about underlying characteristics that category members share
	Sorts familiar objects into hierarchically organized categories
	Distinguishes appearance from reality
4–7 years	Becomes increasingly aware that make-believe (and other thought processes) are representational activities
	Replaces magical beliefs about fairies, goblins, and events that violate expectations with plausible explanations

Other experts think that the stage concept is still valid but must be modified. For example, some *neo-Piagetian theorists* combine Piaget's stage approach with the information-processing emphasis on task-specific change (Case, 1998; Halford, 1993). They believe that Piaget's strict stage definition must be transformed into a less tightly knit concept, one in which a related set of competencies develops over an extended period, depending on brain development and specific experiences. These investigators point to findings indicating that as long as the complexity of tasks and children's exposure to them are carefully controlled, children approach those tasks in similar, stage-consistent ways (Case & Okamoto, 1996). For example, in drawing pictures, preschoolers depict objects separately, ignoring their spatial arrangement (return to the drawing on page 307 of Chapter 8 for an example). In understanding stories, they grasp a single story line but have trouble with a main plot plus one or more subplots.

This flexible stage notion recognizes the unique qualities of early childhood thinking. At the same time, it provides a better account of why, to use Leslie's words, "preschoolers' minds are such a blend of logic, fantasy, and faulty reasoning."

Piaget and Early Childhood Education

Piaget's theory has had a major impact on education, especially during early childhood. Three educational principles derived from his theory continue to have a widespread influence on teacher training and classroom practices:

1. *Discovery learning.* In a Piagetian classroom, children are encouraged to discover for themselves through spontaneous interaction with the environment. Instead of presenting ready-made knowledge verbally, teachers provide a rich variety of activities designed to promote exploration and discovery—art, puzzles, table games, dress-up clothing, building blocks, books, measuring tools, musical instruments, and more.

2. *Sensitivity to children's readiness to learn.* A Piagetian classroom does not try to speed up development. Piaget believed that appropriate learning experiences build on children's current thinking. Teachers watch and listen to their students, introducing experiences that permit them to practice newly discovered schemes and that are likely to challenge their incorrect

ways of viewing the world. But teachers do not impose new skills before children indicate they are interested and ready because doing so leads to superficial acceptance of adult formulas rather than true understanding.

3. *Acceptance of individual differences.* Piaget's theory assumes that all children go through the same sequence of development, but at different rates. Therefore, teachers must plan activities for individual children and small groups rather than just for the whole class. In addition, teachers evaluate educational progress by comparing each child to his or her own previous development. They are less interested in how children measure up to normative standards—that is, to the average performance of same-age peers.

Like his stages, educational applications of Piaget's theory have met with criticism. Perhaps the greatest challenge has to do with his insistence that young children learn mainly through acting on the environment. In the next section we will see that they also use language-based routes to knowledge. Nevertheless, Piaget's influence on education has been powerful (Vergnaud, 1996). He gave teachers new ways to observe, understand, and enhance young children's development and offered strong theoretical justification for child-oriented approaches to classroom teaching and learning.

Ask YOURSELF
www

REVIEW Select two of the following features of Piaget's preoperational stage: egocentrism, a focus on perceptual appearances, difficulty reasoning about transformations, and lack of hierarchical classification. Cite findings that led Piaget to conclude that preschoolers are deficient in those ways. Then present evidence indicating that preschoolers are more capable thinkers than Piaget assumed.

APPLY At home, 4-year-old Will understands that his tricycle isn't alive and can't move by itself. Yet when Will went fishing with his family and his father asked, "Why do you think the river is flowing along?" Will responded, "Because it's alive and wants to." What explains this contradiction in Will's reasoning?

CONNECT When do children realize that a scale model of a room represents a real room? When do they distinguish the real and apparent identities of disguised objects (such as a stone painted to look like an egg)? What cognitive capacity underlies both attainments?

REFLECT Did you have an imaginary companion as a young child? If so, what was your companion like, and why did you create it? Were your parents aware of your companion? What was their attitude toward it?

Vygotsky's Sociocultural Theory

Piaget's de-emphasis on language as an important source of cognitive development brought on yet another challenge, this time from Vygotsky's sociocultural theory, which stresses the social context of cognitive development. In his theory, the child and the social environment collaborate to mold cognition in culturally adaptive ways. During early childhood, rapid growth in language broadens preschoolers' ability to participate in social dialogues with more knowledgeable individuals, who encourage them to master culturally important tasks. Soon children start to communicate with themselves in much the same way they converse with others. This greatly enhances the complexity of their thinking and their ability to control their own behavior. Let's see how it happens.

Children's Private Speech

Watch preschoolers as they go about their daily activities, and you will see that they frequently talk out loud to themselves. For example, as Sammy worked a puzzle one day, he said, "Where's the red piece? I need the red one. Now, a blue one. No, it doesn't fit. Try it here."

Piaget (1923/1926) called these utterances *egocentric speech,* reflecting his belief that young children have difficulty taking the perspectives of others. For this reason, he said, their talk is often "talk for self," in which they run off thoughts in whatever form they happen to occur, regardless of whether a listener can understand. Piaget believed that cognitive development and certain social experiences—namely, disagreements with peers—eventually bring an end to egocentric speech. Through arguments with agemates, children repeatedly see that others hold viewpoints different from their own. As a result, egocentric speech declines and is replaced by social speech, in which children adapt what they say to their listeners.

Vygotsky (1934/1987) voiced a powerful objection to Piaget's conclusions. He reasoned that children speak to themselves for self-guidance. Because language helps children think about mental activities and behavior and select courses of action, Vygotsky viewed it as the foundation for all higher cognitive processes, including controlled attention, deliberate memorization and recall, categorization, planning, problem solving, and self-reflection. As children get older and find tasks easier, their self-directed speech is internalized as silent, inner speech—the verbal dialogues we carry on with ourselves while thinking and acting in everyday situations.

Over the past three decades, almost all studies have supported Vygotsky's perspective (Berk, 2003). As a result, children's self-directed speech is now called **private speech** instead of egocentric speech. Research shows that children use more of it when tasks are difficult, after they make errors, or when they are confused about how to proceed. For example, Figure 9.6 shows how 4- and 5-year-olds' private speech increased as researchers made a color-sequencing task more difficult. Also, just as Vygotsky predicted, private speech goes underground with age, changing into whispers and silent lip movements (Winsler & Naglieri, 2003; Patrick & Abravanel, 2000). Furthermore, children who use private speech during a challenging activity are more attentive and involved and show better task performance than their less talkative agemates (Berk & Spuhl, 1995; Winsler, Diaz, & Montero, 1997).

Finally, compared with their agemates, children with learning and behavior problems engage in private speech over a longer period of development (Berk, 2001b; Winsler et al., 1999). They seem to call on private speech to help compensate for impairments in attention and cognitive processing that make many tasks more difficult for them.

Social Origins of Early Childhood Cognition

Where does private speech come from? Recall from Chapter 6 that Vygotsky believed children's learning takes place within the *zone of proximal development*—a range of tasks too difficult for the child to do alone but possible with the help of others. Consider the joint activity of Sammy and his mother, who assists him in putting together a difficult puzzle:

Sammy: "I can't get this one in." [Tries to insert a piece in the wrong place]

Mother: "Which piece might go down here?" [Points to the bottom of the puzzle]

Sammy: "His shoes." [Looks for a piece resembling the clown's shoes but tries the wrong one]

This 3-year-old makes a sculpture from playdough and plastic sticks with the aid of private speech. During the preschool years, children frequently talk to themselves as they play and tackle other challenging tasks. Research supports Vygotsky's theory that children use private speech to guide their own thinking and behavior.

FIGURE 9.6

Relationship of private speech to task difficulty among 4- and 5-year-olds.
Researchers increased the difficulty of a color-sequencing task, in which children listened to a list of colors and then placed colored stickers on a page to match the list. The longer the color list, the more private speech children used. (From E. Patrick and E. Abravanel, 2000, "The Self-Regulatory Nature of Preschool Children's Private Speech in a Naturalistic Setting," *Applied Psycholinguistics, 21,* p. 55. Reprinted by permission.)

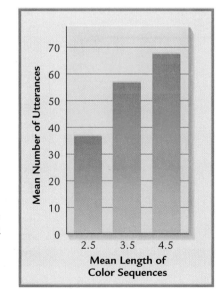

> *Mother:* "Well, what piece looks like this shape?" [Pointing again to the bottom of the puzzle]
>
> *Sammy:* "The brown one." [Tries it, and it fits; then attempts another piece and looks at his mother]
>
> *Mother:* "Try turning it just a little." [Gestures to show him]
>
> *Sammy:* "There!" [Puts in several more pieces. His mother watches.]

Sammy's mother keeps the puzzle within his zone of proximal development, at a manageable level of difficulty, by questioning, prompting, and suggesting strategies.

EFFECTIVE SOCIAL INTERACTION ● To promote cognitive development, social interaction must have two vital features. The first is **intersubjectivity,** the process whereby two participants who begin a task with different understandings arrive at a shared understanding (Newson & Newson, 1975). Intersubjectivity creates a common ground for communication, as each partner adjusts to the perspective of the other. Adults try to promote it when they translate their own insights in ways that are within the child's grasp. As the child stretches to understand the adult, she is drawn into a more mature approach to the situation (Rogoff, 1998).

The capacity for intersubjectivity is present early, in parent–infant mutual gaze, exchange of emotional signals, and imitation. Later, language facilitates it. As conversational skills improve, preschoolers increasingly seek others' help and direct that assistance to ensure that it is beneficial (Whitington & Ward, 1999). Between ages 3 and 5, children strive for intersubjectivity in dialogues with peers, as when they affirm a playmate's message, add new ideas, and make contributions to ongoing play to sustain it. They can also be heard saying, "I think [this way]. What do you think?"—evidence of a willingness to share viewpoints (Berk, 2001b). In these ways, children create zones of proximal development for one another.

A second important feature of social experience is **scaffolding**—adjusting the support offered during a teaching session to fit the child's current level of performance. When the child has little notion of how to proceed, the adult uses direct instruction, breaking down the task into manageable units, suggesting strategies, and offering rationales for using them. As the child's competence increases, effective scaffolders—such as Sammy's mother—gradually and sensitively withdraw support, turning over responsibility to the child. Then children take the language of these dialogues, make it part of their private speech, and use this speech to organize their independent efforts.

Scaffolding captures the form of teaching interaction that occurs as children work on school or school-like tasks, such as puzzles, model building, picture matching, and (later) academic assignments. It may not apply to other contexts that are just as vital for cognitive development—for example, play or everyday activities, during which adults usually support children's efforts without deliberately teaching. To account for children's diverse opportunities to learn through involvement with others, Barbara Rogoff (1998, 2003) suggests the term **guided participation,** a broader concept than scaffolding that refers to shared endeavors between more expert and less expert participants, without specifying the precise features of communication. Consequently, it allows for variations across situations and cultures.

RESEARCH ON SOCIAL INTERACTION AND COGNITIVE DEVELOPMENT ● What evidence supports Vygotsky's ideas on the social origins of cognitive development? In previous chapters, we reviewed a wealth of evidence indicating that when adults establish intersubjectivity by being stimulating, responsive, and supportive, they foster many competencies—attention, language, complex play, and understanding of others' perspectives. Furthermore, children of effective scaffolders use more private speech and are more successful when attempting difficult tasks on their own (Berk & Spuhl, 1995; Landry et al., 2002). Adult cognitive support—teaching in small steps and offering strategies—predicts children's mature thinking. And adult emotional support—offering encouragement and transferring responsibility to the child—predicts children's effort (Neitzel & Stright, 2003). The result is a winning combination for school success.

Other research shows that although young children benefit from working on tasks with same-age peers, their planning and problem solving improve more when their partner is either an "expert" peer (especially capable at the task) or an adult (Radziszewska & Rogoff, 1988). And peer disagreement (emphasized by Piaget) does not seem to be as important for cognitive development as the extent to which children achieve intersubjectivity—resolve differences of opinion and cooperate (Kobayashi, 1994; Tudge, 1992).

Vygotsky and Early Childhood Education

Piagetian and Vygotskian classrooms clearly have features in common, such as opportunities for active participation and acceptance of individual differences. Yet a Vygotskian classroom goes beyond independent discovery. It promotes *assisted discovery.* Teachers guide children's learning with explanations, demonstrations, and verbal prompts, carefully tailoring their efforts to each child's zone of proximal development. Assisted discovery is helped along by *peer collaboration.* Children with varying abilities work in groups, teaching and helping one another.

A Vygotskian classroom promotes assisted discovery. Teachers guide children's learning, tailoring their efforts to each child's zone of proximal development. They also promote peer collaboration, grouping together classmates of differing abilities and encouraging them to teach and help one another.

Vygotsky (1935/1978) saw make-believe play as the ideal social context for fostering cognitive development in early childhood. As children create imaginary situations, they learn to follow internal ideas and social rules rather than their immediate impulses. For example, a child pretending to go to sleep follows the rules of bedtime behavior. Another child imagining himself to be a father and a doll to be a child conforms to the rules of parental behavior. According to Vygotsky, make-believe play is a unique, broadly influential zone of proximal development in which children try out a wide variety of challenging activities and acquire many competencies.

Turn back to pages 317–318 to review findings that make-believe enhances a diverse array of cognitive and social skills. Pretending is also rich in private speech (Krafft & Berk, 1998). And preschoolers who spend more time engaged in sociodramatic play are more likely to take personal responsibility for following classroom rules (Elias & Berk, 2002). These findings support the role of make-believe in helping children gain control over their thought and behavior.

Evaluation of Vygotsky's Theory

In granting social experience a fundamental role in cognitive development, Vygotsky's theory helps us understand cultural variation in cognitive skills. It recognizes that children develop unique forms of thinking from engaging in activities that make up their culture's way of life. In addition, Vygotsky's ideas underscore the vital role of teaching in children's progress. Parents' and teachers' engagement with children results in profound advances in the complexity of children's thinking.

Nevertheless, Vygotsky's theory has not gone unchallenged. Verbal interaction may not be the only means, or even the most important means, through which children's thinking develops in some cultures. When Western parents help children with challenging tasks, they assume much responsibility for children's motivation by frequently instructing and conversing with the child. Their communication resembles the teaching that takes place in school, where their children will spend years preparing for adult life. But in cultures that place less emphasis on schooling and literacy, parents often expect children to acquire new skills through keen observation and participation in community activities (Rogoff, 2003). Turn to the Cultural Influences box on page 332 for research that illustrates this difference.

Vygotsky's theory has also been criticized for saying little about how basic skills, discussed in Chapters 5 and 6, contribute to socially transmitted higher cognitive processes. For example, his theory does not address how elementary motor, perceptual, attention, memory, and problem-solving capacities spark changes in children's social experiences, from which more advanced cognition springs (Moll, 1994). Piaget paid far more attention than Vygotsky to the development of basic cognitive processes. It is intriguing to speculate about the broader theory that might exist today had Piaget and Vygotsky—the two twentieth-century giants of cognitive development—had a chance to meet and weave together their extraordinary accomplishments.

Cultural Influences

Children in Village and Tribal Cultures Observe and Participate in Adult Work

In Western societies, children are largely excluded from participating in adult work, which generally takes place in settings beyond the home. Equipping children with the skills they need to become competent workers is assigned to school. In early childhood, middle-SES parents' interactions with children dwell on preparing children to succeed in school through child-focused activities—especially adult–child conversations and play that enhance language, literacy, and other school-related knowledge. In village and tribal cultures, children receive little or no schooling, spend their days in contact with or participating in adult work, and start to assume mature responsibilities in early childhood (Rogoff et al., 2003). Consequently, parents have little need to rely on conversation and play to teach children.

A study comparing 2- and 3-year-olds' daily lives in four cultures—two American middle-SES suburbs, the Efe hunters and gatherers of the Republic of Congo, and a Mayan agricultural town in Guatemala—documented these differences (Morelli, Rogoff, & Angelillo, 2003). In the American communities, young children had little access to adult work and spent much time involved in adult–child conversations and play that catered to children's interests and provided scholastic lessons. In contrast, the Efe and Mayan children rarely engaged in these child-focused activities. Instead, they spent their day in close proximity to adult work, which often took place in or near the Efe campsite or the Mayan family home. When Efe parents ventured outside their camp to gather food or collect fire-

wood, children often accompanied them. Compared to their American counterparts, Mayan and Efe children spent far more time observing adult work.

An ethnography of a remote Mayan village in Yucatan, Mexico, shows that when young children are legitimate onlookers and participants in a daily life structured around adult work, their competencies differ sharply from those of Western preschoolers (Gaskins, 1999). Yucatec Mayan adults are subsistence farmers. Men tend cornfields, aided by sons age 8 and older. Women oversee the household and yard, engaging in meal preparation, clothes washing, and care of livestock and garden, assisted by daughters as well as sons not yet old enough to work in the fields. To the extent that they can, children join in these activities from the second year on. When not participating with adults, they are expected to be independent. Even young children make many nonwork decisions for themselves—how much to sleep and eat, what to wear, when to bathe (as long as they do so every afternoon), and even when to start school. As a result, Yucatec Mayan preschoolers are highly competent at

self-care. In contrast, their make-believe play is limited; when it occurs, it involves brief imitations of adult work. Otherwise, they watch others—for hours each day.

Yucatec Mayan parents rarely converse or play with preschoolers or scaffold their learning. Rather, when children imitate adult tasks, parents conclude that they are ready for more responsibility. Then they assign chores, selecting tasks the child can do with little help so that adult work is not disturbed. If a child cannot do a task, the adult takes over and the child observers, reengaging when able to contribute.

Expected to be independent and helpful, Yucatec Mayan children seldom display attention-getting behaviors or ask others for something interesting to do. From an early age, they can sit quietly for long periods with little fussing—through a lengthy religious service or dance and even a 3-hour truck ride. And when an adult interrupts their activity and directs them to do a chore, they respond eagerly to a command that Western children frequently avoid or resent. By age 5, Yucatec Mayan children spontaneously take responsibility for tasks beyond those assigned.

In Yucatec Mayan culture, adults rarely converse with children or scaffold their learning. And rather than engaging in make-believe, children join in the work of their community from an early age, spending many hours observing adults. This Mayan preschooler watches intently as her grandmother washes dishes. When the child begins to imitate adult tasks, she will be given additional responsibilities.

© BERYL GOLDBERG

ASK YOURSELF

www

REVIEW Describe features of social interaction that support children's cognitive development. How does such interaction create a zone of proximal development?

REVIEW Why, according to Vygotsky, is make-believe play the ideal social context for cognitive development in early childhood?

APPLY Tanisha sees her 5-year-old son Toby talking out loud to himself while he plays. She wonders whether she should discourage this behavior. Use Vygotsky's theory to explain why Toby talks to himself. How would you advise Tanisha?

CONNECT How are intersubjectivity and scaffolding involved in child-directed speech, which is discussed on pages 242–243 of Chapter 6?

Information Processing

Return for a moment to the model of information processing discussed on pages 220–221 of Chapter 6. Recall that information processing focuses on *mental strategies* that children use to operate on stimuli flowing into their mental systems. During early childhood, advances in representation and in children's ability to guide their own behavior lead to more efficient and flexible ways of attending, manipulating information, and solving problems. Preschoolers also become more aware of their own mental life and begin to acquire academically relevant knowledge important for school success.

Attention

Parents and teachers quickly notice that compared with school-age children, preschoolers spend relatively short times involved in tasks and are easily distracted. But recall from Chapter 5 that sustained attention improves in toddlerhood, a trend that continues during early childhood. In a study of toddlers and young preschoolers engaged in play with toys, sustained attention increased sharply between 2 and 3½ years of age (Ruff & Capozzoli, 2003). Rapid growth of the frontal lobes of the cerebral cortex, the capacity to generate increasingly complex play goals (children must concentrate to attain those goals), and adult scaffolding of attention are jointly responsible. Parents who help their 2- and 3-year-olds maintain a focus of attention—by offering suggestions, questions, and comments about the child's current interest—have preschoolers who are more mature, cognitively and socially, at age 4 (Landry et al., 2000). Many skills, including language, exploration, problem solving, social interaction, and cooperation, benefit from an improved ability to concentrate.

During early childhood, children also become better at **planning**—thinking out a sequence of acts ahead of time and allocating attention accordingly to reach a goal. As long as tasks are familiar and not too complex, preschoolers sometimes generate and follow a plan. For example, by age 4, they search for a lost object in a play yard systematically and exhaustively, looking only in locations between where they last saw the object and where they discovered it missing (Wellman, Somerville, & Haake, 1979). Still, planning has a long way to go. When asked to compare detailed pictures, preschoolers fail to search thoroughly. On complex tasks, they rarely decide what to do first and what to do next in an orderly fashion. And even when young children do plan, they often fail to implement important steps (Friedman & Scholnick, 1997; Ruff & Rothbart, 1996).

Memory

Unlike infants and toddlers, preschoolers have the language skills to describe what they remember, and they can follow directions on simple memory tasks. As a result, memory development becomes easier to study in early childhood.

RECOGNITION AND RECALL ● Try showing a young child a set of 10 pictures or toys. Then mix them up with some unfamiliar items and ask the child to point to the ones in the original set. You will find that preschoolers' *recognition* memory—ability to tell whether a stimulus is the same as or similar to one they have seen before—is remarkably good. It becomes even more accurate by the end of early childhood. In fact, 4- and 5-year-olds perform nearly perfectly.

Now give the child a more demanding task. While keeping the items out of view, ask the child to name the ones she saw. This requires *recall*—remembering in the absence of perceptual support. One of the most obvious features of young children's memories is that their recall in such tasks, which require retention of pieces of information, is much poorer than their recognition. At age 2, they can recall no more than one or two items, at age 4 only about three or four (Perlmutter, 1984).

Of course, recognition is much easier than recall for adults as well, but in comparison to adults, children's recall is quite deficient. Better recall in early childhood is strongly associated with language development, which greatly enhances long-lasting representations of past experiences (Simcock & Hayne, 2003). But even preschoolers with good language skills recall poorly because they are less effective than older individuals at using **memory strategies,** deliberate mental activities that improve our chances of remembering. For example, when you want to retain information, you might *rehearse,* or repeat the items over and over. Or you might *organize* it, intentionally grouping items that are alike so that you can easily retrieve them by thinking of their similar characteristics.

Preschoolers do show the beginnings of memory strategies. When circumstances permit, they arrange items in space to aid their memories. In one study, an adult placed either an M&M or a wooden peg in each of 12 identical containers and handed them one by one to preschoolers, asking them to remember where the candy was hidden. By age 4, children put the candy containers in one place and the peg containers in another, a strategy that almost always led to perfect recall (DeLoache & Todd, 1988). But preschoolers do not yet rehearse or organize items into *categories* (for example, all the vehicles together, all the animals together) when asked to remember. Even when they are trained to do so, their memory performance rarely improves, and they do not apply these strategies in new situations (Gathercole, Adams, & Hitch, 1994).

Why do young children use memory strategies so rarely? One reason is that strategies tax their limited working memories. *Digit span* tasks, in which children try to repeat an adult-provided string of numbers, assess the size of working memory, which improves slowly, from an average of 2 digits at age 2½ to 5 digits at age 7 (Kail, 2003). With such limits, preschoolers have difficulty holding on to discrete pieces of information and applying a strategy at the same time.

MEMORY FOR EVERYDAY EXPERIENCES ● Think about the difference in your recall of listlike information and your memory for everyday experiences, or what researchers call **episodic memory.** In remembering lists, you recall isolated bits, reproducing them exactly as you originally learned them. In remembering everyday experiences, you recall complex, meaningful events.

Memory for Familiar Events. Like adults, preschoolers remember familiar, repeated events—what you do when you go to child care or get ready for bed—in terms of **scripts,** general descriptions of what occurs and when it occurs in a particular situation. Young children's scripts begin as a structure of main acts. For example, when asked to tell what happens when you go to a restaurant, a 3-year-old might say, "You go in, get the food, eat, and then pay." Although children's first scripts contain only a few acts, as long as events in a situation take place in logical order, they are almost always recalled in correct sequence. Still, adults must work hard to obtain preschoolers' scripted reports, asking questions and prompting (Bauer, 1997, 2002). With age, scripts become more spontaneous and elaborate, as in the following restaurant account given by a 5-year-old child: "You go in. You can sit at a booth or a table. Then you tell the waitress what you want. You eat. If you want dessert, you can have some. Then you pay and go home" (Hudson, Fivush, & Kuebli, 1992).

Once formed, scripts help children organize, interpret, and predict repeated events. When listening to and telling stories, children use scripts to assist recall. They also act out scripts in make-believe play as they pretend to put the baby to bed, go on a trip, or play school. And scripts support children's earliest efforts at planning as they represent sequences of actions that lead to desired goals (Hudson, Sosa, & Shapiro, 1997).

Memory for One-Time Events. In Chapter 6 we considered a second type of episodic memory—*autobiographical memory,* or representations of personally meaningful, one-time events. As 3- to 6-year-olds' cognitive and conversational skills improve, their descriptions of special events become better organized, detailed, and related to the larger context of their lives (Haden, Haine, & Fivush, 1997).

Adults use two styles for prompting children's autobiographical narratives. In the *elaborative style,* they ask varied questions, add information to children's statements, and volunteer their own recollections and evaluations of events. For example, after a field trip to the zoo, Leslie asked, "What was the first thing we did? Why weren't the parrots in their cages? I thought the roaring lion was scary. What did you think?" In this way, she helped the children reestablish and reorganize their memory of the field trip. In contrast, adults who use the *repetitive style* provide little information and ask the same questions over and over, as in "Do you remember the zoo? What did we do at the zoo?" Preschoolers who experience the elaborative style produce more organized and detailed personal stories when followed up 1 to 2 years later (Farrant & Reese, 2000; Reese, Haden, & Fivush, 1993).

As children converse with adults about the past, they do more than improve their episodic memory. They create a shared history that strengthens close relationships. Consistent with this idea, securely attached parents and preschoolers engage in more elaborate reminiscing, whereas parents who have insecure bonds with their preschoolers generally limit themselves to the repetitive style (Fivush & Reese, 2002). In sum, the emotional quality of the parent–child relationship affects the richness of children's autobiographical memories and, in turn, the extent to which children enter into the history of their family and community. As we conclude our consideration of early childhood memory, notice how adult support contributes to each aspect of preschoolers' memory development, in line with Vygotsky's ideas.

Problem Solving

How do preschoolers use their cognitive competencies to discover new problem-solving strategies? To find out, let's look in on 5-year-old Darryl as he added the marbles tucked into pairs of small bags that Leslie set out on a table.

As Darryl dealt with adding each pair, his strategies varied. Sometimes he guessed, without applying any strategy. At other times, he counted from 1 on his fingers. For example, for bags containing 2 + 4 marbles, his fingers popped up one by one as he exclaimed, "1, 2, 3, 4, 5, 6!" On still other occasions, he started with the lower digit, 2, and "counted on" (2, 3, 4, 5, 6). Or he began with the higher digit, 4, and "counted on" (4, 5, 6)—a strategy called *min* because it minimizes the work. Sometimes, he retrieved the answer from memory.

To study children's problem solving, Robert Siegler (1996) used the microgenetic research design (see Chapter 1, page 46), presenting children with many problems over an extended time. He found that strategy use on diverse types of tasks—including basic math facts, conservation, memory for lists of items, reading first words, spelling, and even playing tic-tac-toe—follows the overlapping-waves pattern shown in Figure 9.7 on page 336. According to **overlapping-waves theory,** when given challenging problems, children try out a variety of strategies, observe which work best, which work less well, and which are ineffective. Gradually, they select strategies that result in rapid, accurate solutions—in the case of basic addition, the *min* strategy, and later still, the most efficient strategy—automatic retrieval of the answer.

How do children move from less to more efficient strategies? Often they discover a faster procedure by using a more time-consuming technique. For example, by repeatedly counting on fingers, Darryl began to recognize the number of fingers he held up (Siegler & Jenkins, 1989). Also, certain problems dramatize the need for a better strategy. When Darryl opened a pair of bags with 10 marbles in one and 2 in the other, he realized that *min* would be best. Reasoning

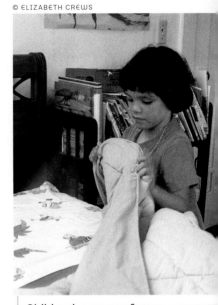

Children's memory for familiar experiences improves greatly during early childhood. This girl cannot remember the details of what she did on a particular day when she made her bed before going to preschool. Instead, she recalls the event in script form—in terms of what typically occurs after you get up in the morning. Her account will become more elaborate with age. Scripts help us predict what will happen on similar occasions in the future.

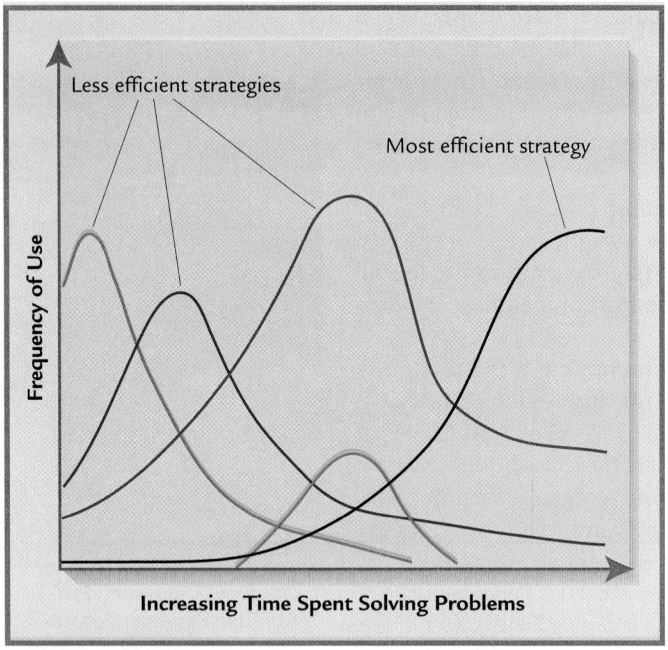

FIGURE 9.7

Overlapping-waves pattern of strategy use in problem solving.
When given challenging problems, a child generates a variety of strategies, each represented by a wave. The waves overlap because the child tries several different strategies at the same time. Use of each strategy, depicted by the height of the wave, is constantly changing. As the child observes which strategies work best, which work less well, and which are ineffective, the one that results in the most rapid, accurate solutions wins out. (Adapted from R. S. Siegler, *Emerging Minds: The Process of Change in Children's Thinking*, copyright © 1996 by Oxford University Press, Inc. Used by permission of Oxford University Press, Inc.)

about concepts relevant to the problems at hand is helpful (Canobi, Reeve, & Pattison, 1998). After Darrell understood that regardless of the order in which he combined 2 and 4, they yield the same result, he more often used *min.* Finally, when children are taught an effective strategy, they usually adopt it and abandon less successful techniques (Alibali, 1999).

Many factors, including practice, reasoning, tasks with new challenges, and adult assistance, contribute to improved problem solving. Children also profit from experimenting with less mature strategies because they see the limitations of those techniques. In sum, overlapping-waves theory emphasizes that trying out many strategies is vital for developing new, more effective solution techniques. Even 2-year-olds solve problems, such as how to use a tool to obtain an out-of-reach toy, with an overlapping-waves pattern (Chen & Siegler, 2000). It characterizes problem solving across a wide range of ages.

The Young Child's Theory of Mind

As memory, problem solving, and representation of the world improve, children start to reflect on their own thought processes. They begin to construct a *theory of mind,* or coherent set of ideas about mental activities. This understanding is also called **metacognition.** The prefix *meta-,* meaning "beyond or higher," is included in the term *metacognition,* which means "thinking about thought" (Flavell, 2000). As adults, we have a complex appreciation of our inner mental worlds. For example, we can differentiate among believing, knowing, remembering, guessing, forgetting, and imagining, and we are aware of a great many factors that influence these cognitive activities. We rely on these understandings to interpret our own and others' behavior and to improve our performance on various tasks. How early are children aware of their mental lives, and how complete and accurate is their knowledge?

AWARENESS OF MENTAL LIFE ● Infants' and toddlers' capacity for imitation, joint attention, preverbal gestures, and social referencing suggests a budding realization that people can share and influence each other's mental states. Furthermore, such words as "want" and "like" are among the first verbs in toddlers' vocabularies. And as early age 2, children use these terms to refer to internal states, often contrasting their own and another person's preferences, as in "I don't *like* carrots; Daddy *like* carrots" (Bartsch & Wellman, 1995). By age 3, children realize that thinking takes place inside their heads and that a person can think about something without seeing it, talking about it, or touching it (Flavell, Green, & Flavell, 1995). However, 2- to 3-year-olds have only a beginning grasp of the distinction between mental life and behavior. They think that people always behave in ways consistent with their *desires* and do not understand that less obvious mental states, such as *beliefs,* affect their actions (Gopnik & Wellman, 1994).

Between ages 3 and 4, children use such words as "think" and "know" to refer to their own and others' thoughts and beliefs (Wellman, 2002). And from age 4 on, they realize that both *beliefs* and *desires* determine behavior. In one instance, Sammy put a blanket over his head and, pretending to be a ghost, pushed Dwayne, who fell and began to cry. "I couldn't see him! The blanket was over my face," Sammy pleaded, trying to alter his mother's *belief* about his motive and, thereby, ward off any *desire* on her part to punish him. From early to middle childhood, efforts to alter others' beliefs increase, suggesting that children more firmly realize the power of belief to influence action.

Dramatic evidence for preschoolers' developing theory of mind comes from games that test whether they realize that *false beliefs*—ones that do not represent reality accurately—can guide people's behavior. For example: Show a child two small closed boxes, one a familiar Band-Aid box and the other a plain, unmarked box (see Figure 9.8). Then say, "Pick the box you think has the Band-Aids in it." Almost always, children pick the marked container. Next, open the boxes and show the child that, contrary to her own belief, the marked one is empty and the unmarked

FIGURE 9.8

Example of a false-belief task.
(a) An adult shows a child the contents of a Band-Aid box and an unmarked box. The Band-Aids are in the unmarked container. (b) The adult introduces the child to a hand puppet named Pam and asks the child to predict where Pam would look for the Band-Aids and to explain Pam's behavior. The task reveals whether children understand that without having seen that the Band-Aids are in the unmarked container, Pam will hold a false belief.

(a)   (b)

one contains the Band-Aids. Finally, introduce the child to a hand puppet and explain, "Here's Pam. She has a cut, see? Where do you think she'll look for Band-Aids? Why would she look in there? Before you looked inside, did you think that the plain box contained the Band-Aids? Why?" (Bartsch & Wellman, 1995; Gopnik & Wellman, 1994). Only a handful of 3-year-olds, but many 4-year-olds, can explain Pam's and their own false beliefs.

Children's understanding of false belief strengthens over the preschool years, becoming more secure by age 6 (Wellman, Cross, & Watson, 2001). During that time, it becomes a powerful tool for understanding oneself and others and a good predictor of social skills (Jenkins & Astington, 2000; Watson et al., 1999).

FACTORS CONTRIBUTING TO PRESCHOOLERS' THEORY OF MIND ● How do children manage to develop a theory of mind at such a young age? Research indicates that language and cognitive skills, make-believe play, and social experiences contribute.

Language and Cognitive Skills. Understanding the mind requires the ability to reflect on thoughts, which is made possible by language. A grasp of false belief requires language ability equivalent to that of an average 4-year-old or higher (Jenkins & Astington, 1996). And children who spontaneously use, or are trained to use, complex sentences with mental-state words are more likely to pass false-belief tasks (de Villiers & de Villiers, 2000; Hale & Tager-Flusberg, 2003). The Quechua village people of the Peruvian highlands refer to mental states, such as "think" and "believe," indirectly because their language lacks mental-state terms. Quechua children have difficulty with false-belief tasks for years after children in industrialized nations have mastered them (Vinden, 1996).

Like language, certain cognitive skills help children reflect on their experiences and mental states. For example, the ability to inhibit inappropriate responses, think flexibly, and plan fosters mastery of false belief (Carlson & Moses, 2001; Hughes, 1998).

Make-Believe Play. Make-believe offers a rich context for thinking about the mind. As children act out roles, they often create situations they know to be untrue in the real world and then reason about their implications (Harris & Leevers, 2000). These experiences may increase children's awareness that belief influences behavior. In support of this idea, preschoolers who engage in extensive fantasy play are advanced in understanding false belief and other aspects of the mind (Astington & Jenkins, 1995). And the better 3- and 4-year-olds can reason about situations that contradict a real-world state of affairs, the more likely they are to pass false-belief tasks (Riggs & Peterson, 2000).

Social Interaction. Many social experiences promote understanding of the mind. Preschoolers with siblings tend to be more aware of false belief, and those with older siblings especially so (Peterson, 2001; Ruffman et al., 1998). Having older siblings is associated with exposure to more family talk about thoughts, beliefs, and emotions. As younger siblings hear

Having older siblings fosters an understanding of false belief, probably because sibling interactions often highlight the influence of beliefs on behavior—through teasing, trickery, make-believe play, and discussing feelings.

and use these terms often, they better appreciate the role of mental states in behavior (Jenkins et al., 2003). Similarly, preschool friends who often engage in mental-state talk are ahead in their understanding of false belief (Hughes & Dunn, 1998). Interacting with more mature members of society also contributes. In a study of Greek preschoolers, daily contact with many adults and older children predicted mastery of false belief (Lewis et al., 1996). These encounters offer extra opportunities to observe different viewpoints and talk about inner states.

Core knowledge theorists (see Chapter 6, page 217) believe that to profit from the social experiences just described, children must be biologically prepared to develop a theory of mind. They claim that children with *autism*, for whom mastery of false belief is either greatly delayed or absent, are deficient in the brain mechanism that enables humans to detect mental states. See the Biology and Environment box on the following page to find out more about the biological basis of reasoning about the mind.

LIMITATIONS OF THE YOUNG CHILD'S THEORY OF MIND ● Although surprisingly advanced, preschoolers' awareness of mental activities is far from complete. For example, 3- and 4-year-olds are unaware that people continue to think while they wait, look at pictures, listen to stories, or read books. They conclude that mental activity stops when there are no obvious cues to indicate a person is thinking. They do not realize that people constantly talk to themselves and engage in thought (Flavell, Green, & Flavell, 1993, 1995; Flavell et al., 1997).

Furthermore, children younger than age 6 pay little attention to the *process* of thinking but, instead, focus on outcomes of thought. When questioned about subtle distinctions between mental states, such as "know" and "forget," they express confusion (Lyon & Flavell, 1994). And they often say they have always known information they just learned (Taylor, Esbenson, & Bennett, 1994). Finally, preschoolers believe that all events must be directly observed to be known. They do not understand that *mental inferences* can be a source of knowledge (Carpendale & Chandler, 1996).

These findings suggest that preschoolers view the mind as a passive container of information. Consequently, they greatly underestimate the amount of mental activity that goes on in people and are poor at inferring what people know or are thinking about. In contrast, older children view the mind as an active, constructive agent that selects and interprets information (Flavell, 1999; Wellman, 2002). We will consider this change further in Chapter 12 when we take up metacognition in middle childhood.

Early Literacy and Mathematical Development

Researchers have begun to study how children's information-processing capacities affect the development of basic reading, writing, and mathematical skills that prepare them for school. The study of how preschoolers start to master these complex activities provides us with additional information on their cognitive strengths and limitations. In addition, we can use this knowledge to foster early literacy and mathematical development.

EARLY CHILDHOOD LITERACY ● One week, Leslie's students brought empty food boxes to place on shelves in the classroom. Soon a make-believe grocery store opened. Children labeled items with prices, made shopping lists, and wrote checks at the cash register. A sign at the entrance announced the daily specials: "APLS BNS 5¢" ("apples bananas 5¢").

As their grocery store play reveals, preschoolers understand a great deal about written language long before they learn to read or write in conventional ways. This is not surprising when we consider that children in industrialized nations live in a world filled with written symbols. Each day, they observe and participate in activities involving storybooks, calendars, and lists. As part of these experiences, they try to figure out how written symbols convey meaning. Children's active efforts to construct literacy knowledge through informal experiences are called **emergent literacy**.

Biology and Environment

"Mindblindness" and Autism

Sidney stood at the water table in Leslie's classroom, repeatedly filling a plastic cup and dumping out its contents. Dip-splash, dip-splash, dip-splash he went, until Leslie came over and redirected his actions. Without looking at Leslie's face, Sidney moved to a new repetitive pursuit: pouring water from one cup into another and back again. As other children entered the play space and conversed, Sidney hardly noticed. He rarely spoke, and when he did, he usually used words to get things he wanted, not to exchange ideas.

Sidney has *autism,* the most severe behavior disorder of childhood. The term *autism* means "absorbed in the self," an apt description of Sidney. Like other children with the disorder, by age 3 he displayed deficits in three core areas of functioning. First, he had only limited ability to engage in nonverbal behaviors required for successful social interaction, such as eye gaze, facial expressions, gestures, and give-and-take. Most of the time, he seemed aloof and uninterested in other people. Second, his language was delayed and stereotyped. He used words to echo what others said and to get things he wanted, not to exchange ideas. Third, he engaged in much less make-believe play than children who were developing normally or who had other developmental problems (Frith, 2003). And Sidney showed another typical feature of autism: His interests, which focused on the physical world, were narrow and overly intense. For example, one day he sat for more than an hour spinning a toy ferris wheel.

Researchers agree that autism stems from abnormal brain functioning usually due to genetic or prenatal environmental causes. From the first year on, children with the disorder have larger than average brains, perhaps because of massive overgrowth of synapses and lack of the synaptic pruning that accompanies normal development of cognitive, language, and communication skills (refer to Chapter 8, page 291) (Courchesne, Carper, & Akshoomoff, 2003). Furthermore, fMRI studies reveal that autism is associated with reduced activity in brain regions known to mediate emotional and social responsiveness and thinking about mental

activities (Castelli et al., 2002; Mundy, 2003). But other brain structures may also be involved.

Growing evidence reveals that children with autism have a deficient theory of mind. Long after they reach the intellectual level of an average 4-year-old, they have great difficulty with false-belief tasks. Most find it hard to attribute mental states to others or to themselves (Steele, Joseph, & Tager-Flusberg, 2003). And such words as "believe," "think," "know," "feel," and "pretend" are rarely part of their vocabularies (Yirmiya, Solomonica-Levi, & Shulman, 1996).

As early as the second year, autistic children show deficits in social capacities that may contribute to awareness of others' mental states. For example, they less often establish joint attention, engage in social referencing, or imitate an adult's novel behaviors than do other children (Mundy & Stella, 2000). Furthermore, they are relatively insensitive to a speaker's gaze as a cue to what he or she is talking about. Instead, children with autism often assume that another person's language refers to what they themselves are looking at—a possible reason that they use many nonsensical expressions (Baron-Cohen, Baldwin, & Crowson, 1997).

Do these findings indicate that autism is due to a specific cognitive deficit that leaves the child "mindblind" and therefore unable to engage in human sociability? Some researchers think so (Baron-Cohen, 2001; Scholl & Leslie, 2000). But others point out that individuals with autism are not alone in poor performance on tasks assessing mental understanding; nonautistic, mentally retarded individuals also do poorly (Yirmiya et al., 1998). This suggests that some kind of general intellectual impairment may be involved.

One conjecture is that children with autism are impaired in *executive processing* (refer to the *central executive* in the information-processing model on page 221 of Chapter 6). This leaves them deficient in skills involved in flexible, goal-oriented thinking, such as shifting attention to address relevant aspects of a situation, inhibiting irrelevant responses,

This autistic girl does not take note of a speaker's gaze to determine what that person is talking about. For this reason, the girl's teacher takes extra steps to capture her attention in a science lesson. Researchers disagree on whether autistic children's "mindblindness" is due to a specific social-cognitive deficit that leaves the child mindblind, to general intellectual impairment, or to a memory deficit.

and generating plans. Perhaps these cognitive weaknesses explain autistic children's preoccupation with simple repetitive acts (Griffith et al., 1999; Pennington & Ozonoff, 1996). They may also account for autistic children's difficulty with problems, such as conservation, that require them to integrate several contexts at once (before, during, and after the transformation of a substance) (Yirmiya & Shulman, 1996). An inability to think flexibly would also interfere with understanding the social world, since social interaction requires quick integration of information from various sources and evaluation of alternative possibilities.

At present, it is not clear which of these hypotheses is correct. In fact, recent research suggests that impairments in social awareness, integrative thinking, and verbal ability contribute independently to autism (Morgan, Maybery, & Durkin, 2003). Perhaps several biologically based deficits underlie the tragic social isolation of children like Sidney.

© 2004 LAURA DWIGHT

Preschoolers acquire a great deal of literacy knowledge informally as they participate in everyday activities involving written symbols. This 4-year-old tries to write his name while a classmate helps by holding up his name card so he can easily see the letters. Although his ideas about the meaning of letters are probably different from adults', he will revise them as he encounters many instances of written language and as adults provide encouragement and assistance.

Young preschoolers search for units of written language as they "read" memorized versions of stories and recognize familiar signs, such as "ON" and "OFF" on light switches and "PIZZA" at their favorite fast-food counter. But their early ideas about written language differ from ours. For example, many preschoolers think that a single letter stands for a whole word or that each letter in a person's signature represents a separate name. And in Chapter 8, we noted that initially, preschoolers do not distinguish between drawing and writing. Often they believe that letters (just like pictures) look like the meanings they represent. One child explained that the word *deer* begins with the letter O because that letter is shaped like a deer; then he demonstrated by drawing an O and adding antlers to it (Sulzby & Teale, 1991).

Children gradually revise these ideas as their perceptual and cognitive capacities improve, as they encounter writing in many contexts, and as adults help them with written communication. Soon preschoolers become aware of general characteristics of written language and create their own printlike symbols, as in the "story" and "grocery list" written by a 4-year-old in Figure 9.9. Eventually children figure out that letters are parts of words and are linked to sounds in systematic ways, as you can see in the invented spellings that are typical between ages 5 and 7. At first, children rely on sounds in the names of letters: "ADE LAFWTS KRMD NTU A LAVATR" ("eighty elephants crammed into a[n] elevator"). Over time, they grasp sound–letter correspondences. They also learn that some letters have more than one common sound and that context affects their use ("a" is pronounced differently in "cat" than in "table") (McGee & Richgels, 2004).

Literacy development builds on a broad foundation of spoken language and knowledge about the world. Over time, children's language and literacy progress facilitate one another. **Phonological awareness**—the ability to reflect on and manipulate the sound structure of spoken language, as indicated by sensitivity to changes in sounds within words, to rhyming, and to incorrect pronunciation—is a strong predictor of emergent literacy and later reading and spelling achievement (Foy & Mann, 2003). Vocabulary and grammatical knowledge are also influential. And adult–child narrative conversations enhance diverse language skills essential for literacy progress.

The greater the number of informal literacy experiences preschoolers have, the better their language and emergent literacy development (Dickinson & McCabe, 2001). Pointing out letter–sound correspondences and playing language-sound games foster phonological awareness (Foy & Mann, 2003). *Interactive* storybook reading, in which adults discuss story content with preschoolers, promotes many aspects of language and literacy development. And adult-supported writing activities that focus on narrative, such as preparing a letter or a story, also have wide-ranging benefits (Purcell-Gates, 1996; Wasik & Bond, 2001). In longitudinal research, each of these literacy experiences is linked to improved reading achievement in middle childhood (Senechal & LeFevre, 2002; Storch & Whitehurst, 2001).

Compared with their higher-SES agemates, low-SES children have fewer home and preschool language and literacy learning opportunities—a major reason that they are behind in reading achievement throughout the school years (Serpell et al., 2002). In

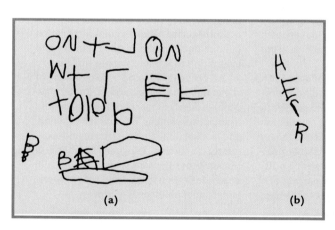

(a)   (b)

FIGURE 9.9

A story (a) and a grocery list (b) written by a 4-year-old child.

This child's writing has many features of real print. It also reveals an awareness of different kinds of written expression. (From L. M. McGee & D. J. Richgels, 2004, *Literacy's Beginnings* (4th ed.), Boston: Allyn and Bacon, p. 69. Reprinted by permission.)

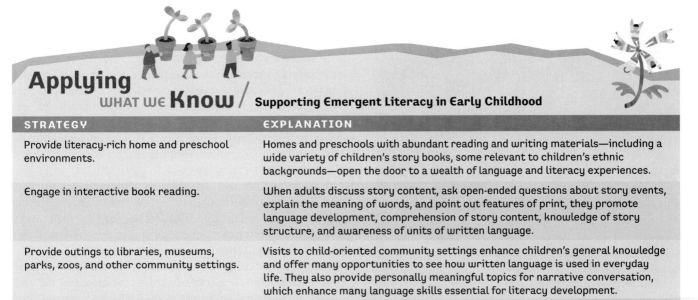

Applying
WHAT WE **Know** / Supporting Emergent Literacy in Early Childhood

STRATEGY	EXPLANATION
Provide literacy-rich home and preschool environments.	Homes and preschools with abundant reading and writing materials—including a wide variety of children's story books, some relevant to children's ethnic backgrounds—open the door to a wealth of language and literacy experiences.
Engage in interactive book reading.	When adults discuss story content, ask open-ended questions about story events, explain the meaning of words, and point out features of print, they promote language development, comprehension of story content, knowledge of story structure, and awareness of units of written language.
Provide outings to libraries, museums, parks, zoos, and other community settings.	Visits to child-oriented community settings enhance children's general knowledge and offer many opportunities to see how written language is used in everyday life. They also provide personally meaningful topics for narrative conversation, which enhance many language skills essential for literacy development.
Point out letter–sound correspondences, play rhyming and other language-sound games, and read rhyming poems and stories.	Experiences that help children isolate the sounds in words foster *phonological awareness*—a powerful predictor of early childhood literacy knowledge and later reading and spelling achievement.
Support children's efforts at writing, especially narrative products.	Assisting children in their efforts to write—especially letters, stories, and other narratives—fosters many language and literacy skills.
Model literacy activities.	When children see adults engaged in reading and writing activities, they better understand the diverse, everyday functions of literacy skills and the knowledge and pleasure that literacy brings. As a result, children's motivation to become literate is strengthened.

Sources: Dickinson & McCabe, 2001; McGee & Richgels, 2004.

one study, researchers compared literacy experiences in publicly funded preschools for poverty-stricken children with those in private preschools serving higher-SES groups. The publicly funded programs were deficient in many respects—in access to a rich array of books, in teacher talk about stories, in modeling the everyday uses of literacy, in classroom display of print information (such as the alphabet), in adult assistance with letter identification and writing, and in exposure to culturally relevant literacy materials. Children of poverty, the researchers concluded, "come away with little idea of what it means to be a literate person or what kind of power or responsibility literacy might confer" (McGill-Franzen, Lanford, & Adams, 2002, p. 460).

Providing low-SES parents with children's books, along with guidance in how to stimulate emergent literacy, greatly enhances literacy activities in the home (High et al., 2000). When children have few book-reading experiences in their families, preschools can help them catch up in literacy skills. In a program that "flooded" child-care centers with children's books and provided caregivers with training on how to get 3- and 4-year-olds to spend time with books, low-SES children showed much greater gains in emergent reading and writing knowledge than a control group (Neuman, 1999). And teachers who were given a tuition-free college course on effective early childhood literacy instruction readily applied what they learned, offering many more literacy activities in their classrooms (Dickinson & Sprague, 2001). For ways to support early childhood literacy development, refer to Applying What We Know above.

EARLY CHILDHOOD MATHEMATICAL REASONING ● Mathematical reasoning, like literacy, builds on informal knowledge. Between 14 and 16 months, toddlers display a beginning grasp of **ordinality,** or order relationships between quantities, such as three is more than two, and two is more than one. Soon they attach verbal labels (such as "lots," "little," "big," and "small") to amounts and sizes. And between ages 2 and 3, they begin to count. At first, counting is a memorized routine,

© BOB DAEMMRICH/THE IMAGE WORKS

It's time for this shopper to count and pay for her items at this preschool play grocery store. When early childhood programs provide rich, informal mathematical activities, children acquire a solid foundation of math concepts and skills, including counting, an understanding of cardinality, and basic addition and subtraction strategies. They also learn that math is interesting, enjoyable, and useful.

as in "Onetwothreefourfivesix!" Or children repeat a few number words while vaguely pointing toward objects (Fuson, 1992).

Soon, however, counting becomes more precise. Most 3- to 4-year-olds have established an accurate one-to-one correspondence between a short sequence of number words and the items they represent (Geary, 1995). Three-year-olds may not yet have memorized the correct number labels. For example, one child counted three items by saying, "1, 6, 10." But her pointing gestures show a one-to-one correspondence, which indicates that she is about to master correct counting (Graham, 1999).

Sometime between ages 4 and 5, children grasp the vital principle of **cardinality**—that the last number in a counting sequence indicates the quantity of items in the set (Bermejo, 1996). In the preschool scene described in the opening of this chapter, Sammy showed an appreciation of cardinality when he counted four children at his snack table and then retrieved four milk cartons. Mastery of cardinality increases the efficiency of children's counting. By age 4, children use counting to solve simple arithmetic problems. At first, their strategies are tied to the order of numbers presented; when given 2 + 4, they "count on" from 2 (Bryant & Nunes, 2002). Soon they begin to experiment with various other strategies. As a result, the *min* strategy, a more efficient approach, appears (see page 335). Around this time, children realize that subtraction cancels out addition. Knowing, for example, that 4 + 3 = 7, they infer without counting that 7 – 3 = 4 (Rasmussen, Ho, & Bisanz, 2003). Grasping this principle, along with other basic rules of addition and subtraction, greatly facilitates rapid computation.

The arithmetic knowledge just described emerges universally around the world. But in homes and preschools where adults provide many occasions for counting and comparing quantities, children construct these understandings sooner. In a math intervention program for low-SES 4-year-olds, teachers included math activities in almost all classroom routines. For example, children counted the number of steps needed to get from various locations in the classroom to the play yard and identified a partner who held a card with a certain number of dots on it. Compared with children in other classrooms, intervention children scored higher in math concepts and enjoyed math activities more (Arnold et al., 2002). Solid, secure early childhood math knowledge is essential for the wide variety of mathematical skills children will be taught once they enter school.

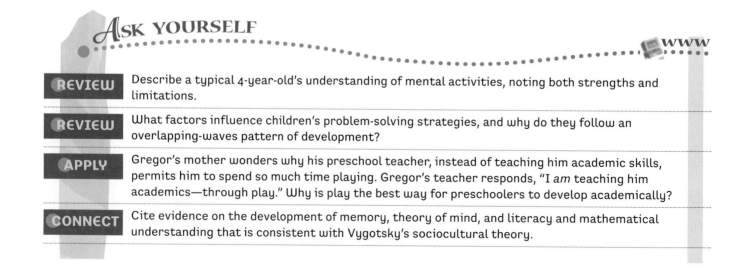

ASK YOURSELF

REVIEW Describe a typical 4-year-old's understanding of mental activities, noting both strengths and limitations.

REVIEW What factors influence children's problem-solving strategies, and why do they follow an overlapping-waves pattern of development?

APPLY Gregor's mother wonders why his preschool teacher, instead of teaching him academic skills, permits him to spend so much time playing. Gregor's teacher responds, "I *am* teaching him academics—through play." Why is play the best way for preschoolers to develop academically?

CONNECT Cite evidence on the development of memory, theory of mind, and literacy and mathematical understanding that is consistent with Vygotsky's sociocultural theory.

Individual Differences in Mental Development

Psychologists and educators typically measure how well preschoolers are developing mentally by giving them intelligence tests. Scores are computed in the same way as they are for infants and toddlers (return to Chapter 6, page 230, to review). But instead of emphasizing perceptual and motor responses, tests for preschoolers sample a wide range of mental abilities. Understanding the link between early childhood experiences and mental test performance highlights ways to intervene in support of children's cognitive development.

Early Childhood Intelligence Tests

Five-year-old Hallie sat in a small, strange testing room while Sarah gave him an intelligence test. Some of the questions Sarah asked were *verbal.* For example, she held out a picture of a shovel and said, "Tell me what this shows?"—an item measuring vocabulary. Then she tested his memory by asking him to repeat sentences and lists of numbers back to her. She probed Hallie's quantitative knowledge and problem solving by seeing if he could count and solve simple addition and subtraction problems. Other tasks were *nonverbal* and largely assessed spatial reasoning. Hallie copied designs with special blocks, figured out the pattern in a series of shapes, and indicated what a piece of paper folded and cut would look like when unfolded (Thorndike, Hagen, & Sattler, 1986).

Sarah was aware that Hallie came from an economically disadvantaged family. When low-SES and ethnic minority preschoolers are faced with an unfamiliar adult who bombards them with questions, they sometimes become anxious. Also, such children may not define the testing situation in achievement terms. Often they look for attention and approval from the examiner rather than focusing on the test questions. As a result, they may settle for lower levels of performance than their abilities allow. Sarah spent time playing with Hallie before she began testing, and she praised and encouraged him while the test was in progress. When these testing conditions are used, low-SES preschoolers improve in performance (Bracken, 2000).

Note that the questions Sarah asked Hallie tap knowledge and skills that not all children have had an equal opportunity to learn. The issue of *cultural bias* in mental testing is a hotly debated topic that we will take up in Chapter 12. For now, keep in mind that intelligence tests do not sample all human abilities and that performance is affected by cultural and situational factors (Sternberg, 2002a). Nevertheless, test scores remain important because by age 6 to 7, they are good predictors of later IQ and academic achievement, which are related to vocational success in industrialized societies. Let's see how the environments in which children spend their days—home, preschool, and child care—affect mental test performance.

Home Environment and Mental Development

A special version of the *Home Observation for Measurement of the Environment (HOME),* covered in Chapter 6, assesses aspects of 3- to 6-year-olds' home lives that foster intellectual growth (see Applying What We Know on page 344). Preschoolers who develop well intellectually have homes rich in educational toys and books. Their parents are warm and affectionate, stimulate language and academic knowledge, and arrange outings to places with interesting things to see and do. They also make reasonable demands for socially mature behavior—for example, that the child perform simple chores and behave courteously toward others. And these parents resolve conflicts with reason instead of physical force and punishment (Bradley & Caldwell, 1982; Espy, Molfese, & DiLalla, 2001; Roberts, Burchinal, & Durham, 1999).

As we saw in Chapter 2, these characteristics are less likely to be found in poverty-stricken families (Garrett, Ng'andu, & Ferron, 1994). When low-SES parents manage, despite daily stresses, to obtain high HOME scores, their preschoolers do substantially better on intelligence

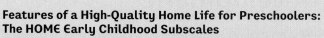

Applying WHAT WE Know / Features of a High-Quality Home Life for Preschoolers: The HOME Early Childhood Subscales

HOME SUBSCALE	SAMPLE ITEMS
Stimulation through toys, games, and reading material	Home includes toys to learn colors, sizes, and shapes.
Language stimulation	Parent teaches child about animals through books, games, and puzzles.
	Parent converses with child at least twice during observer's visit.
Organization of the physical environment	All visible rooms are reasonably clean and minimally cluttered.
Pride, affection, and warmth	Parent spontaneously praises child's qualities or behavior twice during observer's visit.
	Parent caresses, kisses, or hugs child at least once during observer's visit.
Stimulation of academic behavior	Child is encouraged to learn colors.
Modeling and encouragement of social maturity	Parent introduces interviewer to child.
Opportunities for variety in daily stimulation	Family member takes child on one outing at least every other week (picnic, shopping).
Avoidance of physical punishment	Parent neither slaps nor spanks child during observer's visit.

Source: Bradley, 1994; Bradley et al., 2001

tests (Klebanov et al., 1998; Linver, Brooks-Gunn, & Kohen, 2002). These findings (as well as others we will discuss in Chapter 12) indicate that the home plays a major role in the generally poorer intellectual performance of low-SES children, compared to their higher-SES peers.

Preschool, Kindergarten, and Child Care

Children between ages 2 and 6 spend even more time away from their homes and parents than infants and toddlers do. Over the past 30 years, the number of young children enrolled in preschool or child care has steadily increased. This trend is largely due to the dramatic rise in women's participation in the paid labor force. Currently, 64 percent of American and 68 percent of Canadian preschool children have mothers who are employed (Statistics Canada, 2002d; U.S. Census Bureau, 2003b). Figure 9.10 shows where preschoolers spend their days while their parents are at work.

A *preschool* is a program with planned educational experiences aimed at enhancing the development of 2- to 5-year-olds. In contrast, *child care* includes a variety of arrangements for supervising children of employed parents, ranging from care in someone else's or the child's own home to some type of center-based program. The line between preschool and child care is fuzzy. As Figure 9.10 indicates, parents often select a preschool as a child-care option. Many preschools—and public school kindergartens as well—have increased their hours to full days in response to the needs of employed parents (U.S. Department of Education, 2003a). At the same time, good child care is not

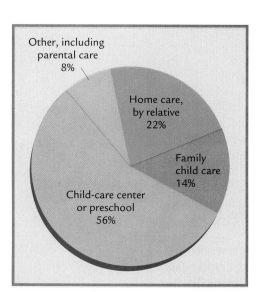

FIGURE 9.10

Who's minding America's preschoolers?

The percentages refer to settings in which 3- to 5-year-olds spend most time while their parents are at work. Over one-fourth of 3- to 5-year-olds experience more than one type of child care, a fact not reflected in the chart. In addition, some parents cannot find child care that is affordable or satisfactory in quality, so they care for their children while working. (Adapted from *Federal Interagency Forum on Child and Family Statistics,* 2003.)

simply a matter of keeping children safe and adequately fed. It should provide the same high-quality educational experiences that an effective preschool does, the only difference being that children attend for an extended day.

TYPES OF PRESCHOOL AND KINDERGARTEN ● Preschool and kindergarten programs range along a continuum from child-centered to teacher-directed. In **child-centered programs,** teachers provide activities from which children select, and most of the day is devoted to play. In contrast, in **academic programs,** teachers structure children's learning, teaching letters, numbers, colors, shapes, and other academic skills through formal lessons, often using repetition and drill.

Despite grave concern about the appropriateness of the approach, preschool and kindergarten teachers have felt increased pressure to stress formal academic training. Yet doing so in early childhood undermines motivation and emotional well-being. When preschoolers and kindergartners spend much time passively sitting and doing worksheets, as opposed to being actively engaged in learning centers, they display more stress behaviors (such as wiggling and rocking), have less confidence in their abilities, prefer less challenging tasks, and are less advanced in motor, academic, language, and social skills at the end of the school year (Marcon, 1999a; Stipek et al., 1995). Follow-ups reveal lasting effects into elementary school in terms of poorer study habits and lower achievement test scores (Burts et al., 1992; Hart et al., 1998). These outcomes are strongest for low-SES children. Yet teachers tend to prefer an academic approach for economically disadvantaged children—a disturbing trend in view of its negative impact on motivation and learning (Stipek & Byler, 1997).

EARLY INTERVENTION FOR AT-RISK PRESCHOOLERS ● In the 1960s, when the United States launched a "War on Poverty," a wide variety of intervention programs for economically disadvantaged preschoolers were initiated. Their underlying assumption was that learning problems are best treated early, before formal schooling begins. **Project Head Start,** begun by the U.S. federal government in 1965, is the most extensive of these programs. A typical Head Start center provides children with a year or two of preschool, along with nutritional and health services. Parent involvement is central to the Head Start philosophy. Parents serve on policy councils and contribute to program planning. They also work directly with children in classrooms, attend special programs on parenting and child development, and receive services directed at their own emotional, social, and vocational needs. Currently, more than 1,500 Head Start centers serve about 900,000 children (Head Start Bureau, 2003).

In 1995, Canada initiated **Aboriginal Head Start** for First Nations, Inuit, and Métis children younger than age 6, 60 percent of whom live in poverty. Like Project Head Start, the program provides children with preschool education and nutritional and health services and encourages parent involvement. Currently, Aboriginal Head Start has about 100 sites and serves more than 3,300 children (Health Canada, 2000a).

Benefits of Preschool Intervention. Over two decades of research have established the long-term benefits of preschool intervention. The most important of these studies combined data from seven university-based interventions. Results showed that poverty-stricken children who attended programs scored higher in IQ and academic achievement than controls during the first 2 to 3 years of elementary school. After that time, differences in test scores declined. Nevertheless, children who received intervention remained ahead on real-life measures of school adjustment. They were less likely to be placed in special education or retained in grade, and a greater number graduated from high school (Lazar & Darlington, 1982). A separate report on one program—the High/Scope Perry Preschool Project—revealed benefits lasting into young adulthood. It was associated with a reduction in delinquency and teenage pregnancy, a greater likelihood of employment, and greater educational attainment, earnings, and marital stability at age 27 (Weikart, 1998).

Does the impact of outstanding university-based programs on school adjustment generalize to Head Start and other community-based preschool intervention programs? Outcomes are similar, although not as strong. Head Start preschoolers are more economically disadvantaged than children in university-based programs and hence have more severe learning and behavior problems. And quality of services is more variable across community programs (NICHD Early Child Care Research Network, 2001; Ramey, 1999). But when interventions are of documented high quality, favorable

This Inuit 4-year-old attends an Aboriginal Head Start program in Nunavut, Canada. Like American Head Start children, she receives preschool education and nutritional and health services, and her parents participate. In the classroom, she has many opportunities to engage in culturally meaningful activities. Here she plays with a model igloo.

outcomes are diverse and long-lasting and include higher rates of high school graduation and college enrollment and a reduction in adolescent drug use and delinquency (Reynolds et al., 2001).

Nevertheless, a consistent finding is that gains in IQ and achievement test scores from attending Head Start and other interventions quickly dissolve. These children typically enter inferior public schools in poverty-stricken neighborhoods, which undermine the benefits of preschool education (Schnur & Belander, 2000). In a program that began at age 4 and continued through third grade, children's achievement gains were still evident in junior high school (Reynolds & Temple, 1998). And recall from Chapter 6 that when intensive intervention persists from infancy through early childhood and children enter good-quality schools, IQ gains endure into emerging adulthood (see page 234).

Still, Head Start children's better school adjustment is impressive. It may be partly due to program effects on parents. The more parents are involved in Head Start, the better their child-rearing practices and the more stimulating their home learning environments. These factors are positively related to preschoolers' independence and task persistence in the classroom and to their year-end academic, language, and social skills (Marcon, 1999b; Parker et al., 1999).

The Future of Preschool Intervention. A typical component of early intervention focuses on teaching parenting skills and encouraging parents to act as supplementary intervenors for their children. By emphasizing developmental goals for *both* parents and children, program benefits might be extended (Zigler & Styfco, 2001). A parent who is helped to move out of poverty with education, vocational training, and other social services is likely to gain in psychological well-being, planning for the future, and beliefs and behaviors that foster children's motivation in school. When combined with child-centered intervention, these gains should translate into exceptionally strong benefits for children.

At present, this *two-generation approach* is too new to have yielded much research. But one pioneering program, New Chance, is cause for optimism. In it, teenage mothers received services for themselves and their babies, including education, employment, family planning, life management, parent training, and child health care. A follow-up when children were 5 years old revealed that parent participants were more likely to have earned a high school diploma, were less likely to be on welfare, and had higher family earnings than controls who received less intensive intervention. In addition, program children experienced warmer and more stimulating home environments, were more likely to have attended Head Start, and had higher verbal IQs (Granger & Cytron, 1999; Quint, Bos, & Polit, 1997).

Head Start and other interventions like it are highly cost-effective. Program expenses are far less than the funds required to provide special education, treat delinquency, and support unemployed adults. Yet because of funding shortages, most poverty-stricken preschoolers in the United States and Canada do not receive services.

CHILD CARE ● We have seen that high-quality early intervention can enhance the development of economically disadvantaged children. However, as noted in Chapter 6, much North American child care lacks quality. Regardless of SES, preschoolers exposed to poor-quality child care score lower on measures of cognitive and social skills (Lamb, 1998; NICHD Early Child Care Research Network, 2002b).

What are the ingredients of high-quality child care during the preschool years? Large-scale studies of center and family child care reveal that the following factors are important: group size (number of children in a single space), caregiver–child ratio, caregivers' educational preparation, and caregivers' personal commitment to learning about and caring for children. When these characteristics are favorable, adults are more verbally stimulating and sensitive to children's needs. Children, especially those from low-SES families, gain in cognitive, language, and social skills—effects that persist into the early school years (Burchinal et al., 2000; Helburn, 1995; Peisner-Feinberg et al., 2001).

This room has all the elements of a high-quality child-care program, including richly equipped activity areas, small group size, and children working individually or in small groups and granted many opportunities to select their own activities.

© ELLEN B. SENISI/THE IMAGE WORKS

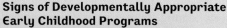

Applying WHAT WE Know / Signs of Developmentally Appropriate Early Childhood Programs

PROGRAM CHARACTERISTIC	SIGNS OF QUALITY
Physical setting	Indoor environment is clean, in good repair, and well ventilated. Classroom space is divided into richly equipped activity areas, including make-believe play, blocks, science, math, games and puzzles, books, art, and music. Fenced outdoor play space is equipped with swings, climbing equipment, tricycles, and sandbox.
Group size	In preschools and child-care centers, group size is no greater than 18 to 20 children with 2 teachers.
Caregiver–child ratio	In child-care centers, teacher is responsible for no more than 8 to 10 children. In child-care homes, caregiver is responsible for no more than 6 children.
Daily activities	Most of the time, children work individually or in small groups. Children select many of their own activities and learn through experiences relevant to their own lives. Teachers facilitate children's involvement, accept individual differences, and adjust expectations to children's developing capacities.
Interactions between adults and children	Teachers move among groups and individuals, asking questions, offering suggestions, and adding more complex ideas. Teachers use positive guidance techniques, such as modeling and encouraging expected behavior and redirecting children to more acceptable activities.
Teacher qualifications	Teachers have college-level specialized preparation in early childhood development, early childhood education, or a related field.
Relationships with parents	Parents are encouraged to observe and participate. Teachers talk frequently with parents about children's behavior and development.
Licensing and accreditation	Child-care setting, whether a center or a home, is licensed by the state or province. In the United States, voluntary accreditation by the National Academy of Early Childhood Programs, *www.naeyc.org/accreditation*, or the National Association for Family Child Care, *www.nafcc.org,* is evidence of an especially high-quality program. Canada is working on a voluntary accreditation system, under the leadership of the Canadian Child Care Federation, *www.cccf-fcsge.ca.*

Sources: Bredekamp & Copple, 1997; National Association for the Education of Young Children, 1998.

Consult Applying What We Know above, which summarizes the characteristics of high-quality early childhood programs, based on standards for developmentally appropriate practice devised by the U.S. National Association for the Education of Young Children. These standards offer a set of worthy goals as the United States and Canada strive to upgrade child-care and educational services for young children.

Educational Media

Besides home and preschool, young children spend much time in another learning environment: television. The average 2- to 6-year-old watches TV from 1½ to 2 hours a day—a long time in a young child's life. During middle childhood, TV viewing increases to an average of 3½ hours a day for American children and 2½ hours a day for Canadian children (Comstock & Scharrer, 2001; Statistics Canada, 2003d). Preschool and school-age boys watch slightly more than girls. Low-SES children also are more frequent viewers, perhaps because their parents are less able to pay for out-of-home entertainment or their neighborhoods provide few alternative activities (Bickham et al., 2003). And if parents watch a lot of TV, their children usually do, too.

Each afternoon, Sammy looked forward to his favorite TV program, *Sesame Street.* It uses lively visual and sound effects to stress basic literacy and number concepts and presents engaging puppet and human characters to teach general knowledge, emotional and social understanding, and social skills. Today, more than two-thirds of North American preschoolers watch *Sesame Street,* and it is broadcast in over 60 countries (Raugust, 1999).

The more children watch *Sesame Street,* the higher they score on tests that measure the program's academic goals (Fisch, Truglio, & Cole, 1999). One study reported a link between preschool viewing of *Sesame Street* and other similar educational programs and getting higher grades, reading more books, and placing more value on achievement in high school (Anderson et al., 2001). In recent years, *Sesame Street* has reduced its rapid-paced format in favor of leisurely episodes with a clear story line (Truglio, 2000). Children's shows with slow-paced action and easy-to-follow narratives, such as *Mr. Rogers' Neighborhood* and *Barney and Friends,* foster young children's comprehension of program content.

From early to middle childhood, computer use rises, averaging 30 minutes per day for youths over age 8 (Roberts et al., 1999). With adult assistance, even 3-year-olds quickly become adept at using computers, and they benefit cognitively from high-quality, educational software. For example, computer storybooks and other literacy programs encourage diverse language and emergent literacy skills (Huntinger et al., 1998). And when kindergartners use computers to draw or write, they produce more elaborate pictures and text, make fewer writing errors, and edit their work much like older children do. Similarly, computers permit preschoolers to extend their mastery of math. Indeed, combining everyday and computer experiences with math manipulatives is especially effective in promoting math concepts and skills (Clements & Sarama, 2003).

Does heavy TV viewing and computer use take children away from other activities that are vital for cognitive development? Research suggests that it does. The more time preschool and school-age children spend watching commercial entertainment TV and cartoons and playing inappropriate video and computer games, the less time they spend reading and interacting with others, and the weaker their academic skills after they start school (Huston et al., 1999; Wright et al., 2001). Clearly, children's time in front of the screen should be supervised and limited. We will look at the impact of television and computer games on emotional and social development in Chapter 10, and at the use of computers in classrooms in Chapter 12.

Ask YOURSELF

WWW

REVIEW	Describe differences between child-centered and academic preschools. What findings indicate that parents who want to foster their preschooler's academic development should choose a child-centered preschool?
APPLY	Senator Smith heard that IQ and achievement gains resulting from Head Start do not last, so he plans to vote against funding for the program. Write a letter to Senator Smith explaining why he should support Head Start.
REFLECT	What TV programs did you watch as a child? How do you think they affected your play and learning?

Language Development

Language is intimately related to virtually all the cognitive changes discussed in this chapter. Between ages 2 and 6, children make awesome and momentous advances in language. Preschoolers' remarkable achievements, as well as their mistakes along the way, indicate that they master their native tongue in an active, rule-oriented fashion.

Vocabulary

At age 2, Sammy had a vocabulary of 200 words. By age 6, he will have acquired around 10,000 words. To accomplish this extraordinary feat, Sammy will learn an average of 5 new words each day (Anglin, 1993).

RAPID GAINS IN VOCABULARY ● How do children build their vocabularies so quickly? Researchers have discovered that they can connect a new word with an underlying concept after only a brief encounter, a process called **fast mapping.** Even toddlers comprehend new labels remarkably quickly, but they need more repetitions of the word's use across several situations than preschoolers, who better remember and categorize speech-based information (Akhtar & Montague, 1999; Woodward, Markman, & Fitzsimmons, 1994).

Once children fast-map a word, they often have to refine their first guess about its meaning. One day, Sammy heard Leslie announce to the children that they would soon take a field trip. He excitedly told his mother, "We're going on a field trip!" When she asked where the class would go, Sammy responded matter-of-factly, "To a field, of course."

Sammy's error suggests that young children fast-map some words more easily than others. Western children learn labels for objects especially rapidly because these refer to concrete items they already know much about, and caregivers' speech often emphasizes names for things (Bloom, 1998). Soon action words ("go," "run," "broke") are added. However, Chinese-, Japanese-, and Korean-speaking children acquire verbs especially quickly. In these languages, nouns are often omitted from adult sentences, and verbs are stressed (Kim, McGregor, & Thompson, 2000; Tardif, Gelman, & Xu, 1999). Gradually, preschoolers add more modifiers ("red," "round," "sad"). If modifiers are related to one another in meaning, they take longer to learn. For example, 2-year-olds grasp the general distinction between "big" and "small," but not until age 3 to 5 are more refined differences, such as "tall–short," "high–low," and "long–short," understood. Similarly, children acquire "now–then" before "yesterday–today–tomorrow" (Stevenson & Pollitt, 1987).

STRATEGIES FOR WORD LEARNING ● Preschoolers figure out the meanings of words by contrasting them with words they already know and assigning the new label to a gap in their vocabulary (Clark, 1990). But exactly how they discover which concept each word picks out is not yet fully understood. One speculation is that early in vocabulary growth, children adopt a **mutual exclusivity bias,** in that they assume that words refer to entirely separate (nonoverlapping) categories (Markman, 1992). Two-year-olds seem to rely on mutual exclusivity when the objects named are perceptually distinct. For example, after hearing the labels for two very different novel objects ("clip" and "horn"), they assign each word correctly, to the whole object and not to a part of it (Waxman & Senghas, 1992).

But mutual exclusivity cannot account for what young children do when objects have more than one name. By age 3, preschoolers' memory, categorization, and language skills have expanded, and they readily assign multiple labels to many objects (Déak, Yen, & Pettit, 2001). For example, they refer to a sticker of a gray goose as "sticker," "goose," and "gray." Children draw on other aspects of language for help in these instances. According to one proposal, preschoolers discover many word meanings by observing how words are used in *syntax,* or the structure of sentences—a hypothesis called **syntactic bootstrapping** (Gleitman, 1990; Hoff & Naigles, 2002). Consider an adult who says, "This is a *citron* one," while showing the child a yellow car. Two- and 3-year-olds conclude that a new word used as an adjective refers to a property of the object (Hall & Graham, 1999). As preschoolers hear the word in various sentence structures ("That lemon is bright *citron*"), they use syntactic information to refine the word's meaning.

Furthermore, drawing on their ability to infer others' intentions and perspectives, preschoolers often call on social cues, such as gestures, to expand their vocabularies (Akhtar & Tomasello, 2000). In one study, an adult performed an action on an object and then used a new label while looking back and forth between the child and the object, as if to invite the child to play. Two-year-olds capitalized on this social information to conclude that the label referred to the action, not the object (Tomasello & Akhtar, 1995). And when adults first designate the whole

In a short few years, these 5-year-olds mastered thousands of words and many complex grammatical structures. They also learned to use language successfully in everyday life by taking turns, maintaining a topic of conversation, and conforming to cultural rules, such as speaking politely to their teacher. How children accomplish these amazing language feats is among the most puzzling questions about development.

object ("See the bird") and then point to a part of it ("That's a beak"), 3-year-olds realize that "beak" is a certain part, not the whole bird (Saylor, Sabbagh, & Baldwin, 2002).

Adults also inform children directly about word meanings. Consider an adult who says, "That soap is *made of lye.*" Relying on the phrase *made of,* preschoolers interpret lye to refer to the soap's material qualities rather than the dish on which the soap rests (Deák, 2000). When no social cues or direct information are available, children as young as 2 demonstrate remarkable flexibility in their word-learning strategies. They treat a new word applied to an already-labeled object as a second name for the object (Deák & Maratsos, 1998).

Furthermore, to fill in for words they have not yet learned, children as young as age 2 coin new words based on ones they already know. For example, Sammy said "plant-man" for gardener and "crayoner" for a child using crayons, adding the ending "–er" (Clark, 1995). Preschoolers also extend language meanings through metaphor. For example, one 3-year-old used the expression "fire engine in my tummy" to describe a stomachache (Winner, 1988). The metaphors young preschoolers use and understand involve concrete, sensory comparisons, such as "clouds are pillows" and "leaves are dancers." Once their vocabulary and general knowledge expand, they make nonsensory comparisons, such as "Friends are like magnets" (Karadsheh, 1991). Metaphors permit young children to communicate in especially vivid and memorable ways.

As these findings illustrate, children's cognitive capacities join with diverse patterns of information in the environment to guide word learning. And their word-learning strategies change as information processing, communication skills, vocabulary size, and knowledge of categories improve (Bloom, 2000; Hollich, Hirsh-Pasek, & Golinkoff, 2000). All along, children are strongly motivated to acquire a conventional vocabulary (Clark, 1995). To participate fully in their language community, they must abandon incorrect and invented words in favor of those used by others.

Grammar

Grammar refers to the way we combine words into meaningful phrases and sentences. Between ages 2 and 3, English-speaking children use simple sentences that follow a subject–verb–object word order. Children learning other languages adopt the word orders of the adult speech to which they are exposed (Maratsos, 1998). This shows that they have a beginning grasp of the grammar of their language.

FROM SIMPLE SENTENCES TO COMPLEX GRAMMAR ● As young children conform to word-order rules, they make the small additions and changes in words that enable speakers to express meanings flexibly and efficiently. For example, they add "-s" for plural ("cats"), use prepositions ("in" and "on"), and form various tenses of the verb *to be* ("is," "are," "were," "has been," "will"). All English-speaking children master these grammatical markers in a regular sequence, starting with the ones that involve the simplest meanings and structures (Brown, 1973; de Villiers & de Villiers, 1973). For example, children master the plural form "-s" before they learn tenses of the verb "to be."

By age 3½, children have acquired a great many grammatical rules, and they apply them so consistently that once in a while they overextend the rules to words that are exceptions, a type of error called **overregularization.** "My toy car *breaked,*" "I *runned* faster than you," and "We each got two *feets*" are expressions that appear between 2 and 3 years of age and persist into middle childhood (Marcus, 1995; Marcus et al., 1992). Overregularization shows that children apply grammatical rules creatively because they do not hear mature speakers use these forms.

Between 3 and 6 years, children master even more complex grammatical structures, although they make predictable errors along the way. In asking questions, at first preschoolers are reluctant to let go of the subject–verb–object sequence so basic to English. At first, they form questions by failing to invert the subject and verb, as in "What you doing?" and, slightly later, after acquiring forms of the verb *to be,* "Where Daddy is going?" (Stromswold, 1995). Because they cling to a consistent word order, they also have trouble with some passive sentences. When told, "The car was pushed by the truck," preschoolers often make a toy car push a truck. By age 5, they understand expressions like these. Nevertheless, 3- to 6-year-olds almost always use abbreviated passives ("It got broken") rather than full passives ("The glass was broken by Mary"). Full mastery of the passive form does not occur until the end of middle childhood (Horgan, 1978).

Nevertheless, preschoolers' grasp of grammar is remarkable. By age 4 to 5, they form embedded sentences ("I think *he will come*"), add tag questions ("Dad's going to be home soon, *isn't he?*"), and use indirect objects ("He showed *his friend* the present"). As the preschool years draw to a close, children use most of the grammatical constructions of their language competently (Tager-Flusberg, 2001).

STRATEGIES FOR ACQUIRING GRAMMAR ● Evidence that grammatical development proceeds gradually has raised questions about Chomsky's *language acquisition device (LAD)*, which assumes that children have innate knowledge of grammatical rules (see Chapter 6, page 236). Some experts believe that grammar is largely a product of general cognitive development—children's tendency to search the environment for consistencies and patterns of all sorts (Maratsos, 1998). Yet among these theorists, there is intense debate about just how children master grammar.

According to one view, young children rely on *semantics*, or word meanings, to figure out grammatical rules—an approach called **semantic bootstrapping.** For example, children might begin by grouping together words with "agent qualities" (things that cause actions) as *subjects* and words with "action qualities" as *verbs*. Then they merge these categories with observations of how words are used in sentences (Bates & MacWhinney, 1987). Others take the view that children master grammar through direct observation of the structure of language. That is, they notice which words appear in the same positions in sentences and are combined in the same way with other words. Over time, they group them into the same grammatical category (Braine, 1994; Tomasello, 2000).

Still other theorists agree with the essence of Chomsky's theory. One idea accepts semantic bootstrapping but proposes that the grammatical categories into which children group word meanings are innately given—present at the outset (Bloom, 1999; Pinker, 1989). Critics, however, point out that toddlers' two-word utterances do not show a grasp of grammar (return to Chapter 6, page 240, to review). According to another theory, although children do not start with innate knowledge, they have a *special language-making capacity*—a set of procedures for analyzing the language they hear, which supports the discovery of grammatical regularities. Research on children learning more than 40 different languages reveals common patterns, consistent with a basic set of strategies (Slobin, 1985, 1997). Yet controversy persists over whether a universal, built-in language-processing device exists or whether children who hear different languages develop unique strategies (de Villiers & de Villiers, 1999).

Conversation

Besides acquiring vocabulary and grammar, children must learn to engage in effective and appropriate conversation with others—by taking turns, staying on the same topic, stating their messages clearly, and conforming to cultural rules for social interaction. This practical side of language is called **pragmatics,** and preschoolers make considerable headway in mastering it.

At the beginning of early childhood, children are already skilled conversationalists. In face-to-face interaction, they initiate verbal exchanges, respond appropriately to their partner's remarks, and take turns (Bloom et al., 1996; Pan & Snow, 1999). The number of turns over which children can sustain interaction and their ability to maintain a topic over time increase with age, but even 2-year-olds are capable of effective conversation (Snow et al., 1996). These surprisingly advanced abilities probably grow out of early interactive experiences (see Chapter 7).

Indeed, the presence of a sibling seems to be especially conducive to acquiring the pragmatics of language. Preschoolers closely monitor conversations between their twin or older siblings and parents, and they often try to join in. When they do, these verbal exchanges last longer, with each participant taking more turns (Barton & Strosberg, 1997; Barton & Tomasello, 1991). And as they listen to conversations, young

These preschoolers are skilled conversationalists. Nevertheless, conversational give-and-take with adults remains vital for language progress in early childhood. And younger children learn a great deal about the everyday use of language from observing and interacting with older siblings.

In highly demanding situations, such as conversing on the phone, preschoolers often do not communicate clearly. They lack the supports available in face-to-face interaction, such as visual access to a partner's reaction and to objects that are topics of conversation.

language learners are exposed to important skills, such as use of personal pronouns ("I" versus "you"), which are more common in the early vocabularies of later-born than of first-born siblings (Pine, 1995).

By age 4, children already adjust their speech to fit the age, sex, and social status of their listeners. For example, in acting out roles with hand puppets, they use more commands when playing socially dominant and male roles, such as teacher, doctor, and father. In contrast, they speak more politely and used more indirect requests when playing less dominant and female roles, such as student, patient, and mother (Anderson, 1992).

Preschoolers' conversational skills occasionally do break down. For example, have you tried talking on the telephone with a preschooler? Here is an excerpt of one 4-year-old's telephone conversation with his grandfather:

Grandfather: "How old will you be?"

John: "Dis many." [Holding up four fingers]

Grandfather: "Huh?"

John: "Dis many." [Again holding up four fingers] (Warren & Tate, 1992, pp. 259–260)

Young children's conversations appear less mature in highly demanding situations in which they cannot see their listeners' reactions or rely on typical conversational aids, such as gestures and objects to talk about. However, when asked to tell a listener how to solve a simple puzzle, 3- to 6-year-olds' directions are more specific over the phone than in person, indicating that they realize that more verbal description is necessary in the phone context (Cameron & Lee, 1997). Between ages 4 and 8, both conversing and giving directions over the phone improve greatly. Telephone talk provides yet another example of how preschoolers' competencies depend on the demands of the situation.

Supporting Language Learning in Early Childhood

How can adults foster preschoolers' language acquisition? Interaction with more skilled speakers, which is so important during toddlerhood, remains vital during early childhood. Conversational give-and-take with adults, either at home or in preschool, is consistently related to language progress (Hart & Risley, 1995; Helburn, 1995). Furthermore, recall that language learning and literacy development are closely linked. Return to Applying What We Know on page 341, and notice how each strategy for supporting emergent literacy also fosters language progress.

Sensitive, caring adults use additional techniques that promote preschoolers' language skills. When children use words incorrectly or communicate unclearly, such adults give helpful, explicit feedback, such as "I can't tell which ball you want. Do you mean a large or small one or a red or green one?" At the same time, they do not overcorrect, especially when children make grammatical mistakes. Criticism discourages children from actively experimenting with language rules in ways that lead to new skills.

Instead, adults provide subtle, indirect feedback about grammar by using two strategies, often in combination: **expansions**—elaborating on children's speech, increasing its complexity; and **recasts**—restructuring inaccurate speech into correct form (Bohannon & Stanowicz, 1988). For example, if a child says, "I gotted new red shoes," the parent might respond, "Yes, you got a pair of new red shoes." However, some researchers question whether expansions and recasts are as important in children's mastery of grammar as mere exposure to a rich language environment. Western adults do not use these techniques often, and in some cultures adults never use them. Furthermore, whereas some studies report that parents' reformulations have a corrective effect, others show no impact on children's grammar (Strapp & Federico, 2000; Valian, 1999). Rather than eliminating errors, perhaps expansions and recasts model grammatical alternatives and encourage children to experiment with them.

Do the findings just described remind you once again of Vygotsky's theory? In language, as in other aspects of intellectual growth, parents and teachers gently prompt young children to take the next developmental step forward. Children strive to master language because they want to attain social connectedness to other people. Adults, in turn, respond to children's natural desire to become competent speakers by listening attentively, elaborating on what children say, modeling correct usage, and stimulating children to talk further. In the next chapter, we will see that this special combination of warmth and encouragement of mature behavior is at the heart of early childhood emotional and social development as well.

Ask YOURSELF

REVIEW Provide a list of recommendations for supporting language development in early childhood, noting research that supports each.

APPLY One day, Sammy's mother explained to him that the family would take a vacation in Miami. The next morning, Sammy emerged from his room with belongings spilling out of a suitcase and remarked, "I gotted my bag packed. When are we going to Your-ami?" What do Sammy's errors reveal about his approach to mastering language?

CONNECT Explain how children's strategies for word learning support the interactionist perspective on language development, described on pages 237–238 of Chapter 6.

Summary

Piaget's Theory: The Preoperational Stage

Describe advances in mental representation, and limitations of thinking, during the preoperational stage.

- Rapid advances in mental representation, notably language and make-believe play, mark the beginning of Piaget's **preoperational stage.** With age, make-believe becomes increasingly complex, evolving into **sociodramatic play.** Preschoolers' make-believe supports many aspects of cognitive and social development.

- **Dual representation** improves rapidly over the third year of life. Children realize that photographs, drawings, models, and simple maps correspond to circumstances in the real world. Adult teaching and experience with diverse symbols help preschoolers master many symbol–real world relations.

- Aside from representation, Piaget described preschoolers in terms of deficits rather than strengths. He viewed them as not yet capable of **operations.** Preoperational children are **egocentric;** they often fail to imagine the perspectives of others. Because egocentrism prevents children from reflecting on their own thinking and accommodating, it

contributes to **animistic thinking, centration,** a focus on perceptual appearances, and **irreversibility.** These difficulties cause preschoolers to fail **conservation** and **hierarchical classification** tasks.

What does follow-up research imply about the accuracy of the preoperational stage?

- When young children are given simplified problems relevant to their everyday lives, their performance appears more mature than Piaget assumed. Preschoolers recognize differing perspectives, distinguish animate and inanimate objects, and notice and reason about transformations. Furthermore, their language reflects accurate causal reasoning and hierarchical classification. And they form many categories based on nonobservable characteristics and notice distinctions between appearance and reality—capacities that reveal that their thinking is not dominated by perceptual appearances.

- These findings challenge Piaget's concept of stage. Rather than being absent, operational thinking develops gradually over the preschool years.

What educational principles can be derived from Piaget's theory?

- A Piagetian classroom promotes discovery learning, sensitivity to children's readiness to learn, and acceptance of individual differences.

Vygotsky's Sociocultural Theory

Describe Vygotsky's perspective on the social origins and significance of children's private speech.

- In contrast to Piaget, Vygotsky regarded language as the foundation for all higher cognitive processes. According to Vygotsky, **private speech,** or language used for self-guidance, emerges out of social communication as adults and more skilled peers help children master challenging tasks within the zone of proximal development. Eventually private speech is internalized as inner, verbal thought.

- **Intersubjectivity,** which creates a common ground for communication, and **scaffolding,** involving adult assistance that adjusts to the child's current level, are features of social interaction that promote transfer of cognitive processes to children. The term **guided participation** recognizes situational and cultural variations in adult support of children's efforts.

Describe applications of Vygotsky's theory to education, and evaluate his major ideas.

● A Vygotskian classroom emphasizes assisted discovery. Verbal guidance from teachers and peer collaboration are vitally important. Make-believe play is a unique, broadly influential zone of proximal development in early childhood.

● In granting social experience a central role in cognitive development, Vygotsky's theory helps us understand the wide cultural variation in cognitive skills. However, verbal communication may not be the only means, or even the most important means, through which children learn in some cultures. Vygotsky said little about how elementary cognitive capacities, which develop in infancy, contribute to socially transmitted, higher cognitive processes.

Information Processing

How do attention, memory, and problem solving change during early childhood?

● Sustained attention increases sharply between ages 2½ and 3, due to growth of the frontal lobes of the cerebral cortex, the capacity to generate complex play goals, and adult assistance. **Planning** also improves. Nevertheless, compared with older children, preschoolers spend relatively short periods involved in tasks and are less systematic in planning.

● Young children's recognition memory is very accurate. But their recall of listlike information is much poorer than that of older children and adults, largely because they use **memory strategies** less effectively.

● **Episodic memory,** or memory for everyday experiences, is well developed in early childhood. Like adults, preschoolers remember recurring everyday experiences in terms of **scripts,** which become more elaborate with age. As children's cognitive and conversational skills improve and as adults use an elaborative style to talk about the past, children's autobiographical memories become better organized, detailed, and related to the larger context of their lives.

● According to **overlapping-waves theory,** when solving problems, children generate a variety of strategies. As they try out those strategies, they gradually select ones that result in rapid, accurate solutions. Practice with strategies, reasoning, tasks with new challenges, and adult assistance contribute to improved problem solving.

Describe the young child's theory of mind.

● Preschoolers begin to construct a theory of mind, indicating that they are capable of **metacognition,** or thinking about thought. Around age 4, they realize that both beliefs and desires can influence behavior and that people can hold false beliefs.

● Many factors seem to contribute to young children's understanding of mental life, including language and cognitive skills, make-believe play and reasoning about imaginary situations, and social interaction with older siblings, friends, and adults.

● Preschoolers' understanding of the mind is far from complete. They regard the mind as a passive container of information rather than as an active, constructive agent.

Summarize children's literacy and mathematical knowledge during early childhood.

● Young children's **emergent literacy** reveals that they understand a great deal about written language before they read and write in conventional ways. Preschoolers gradually revise incorrect ideas about the meaning of written symbols as their perceptual and cognitive capacities improve, as they encounter writing in many contexts, and as adults help them make sense of written information.

● Children's language and literacy progress facilitate one another. **Phonological awareness** is a strong predictor of emergent literacy and of later reading and spelling achievement. Adult–child narrative conversations and a wealth of informal literacy experiences, such as interactive storybook reading, also contribute greatly to literacy development.

● Mathematical reasoning also builds on a foundation of informal knowledge. Toddlers display a beginning grasp of **ordinality,** which serves as the basis for more complex understandings. As children experiment with counting, they discover additional mathematical principles, including **cardinality.** Gradually, counting becomes more flexible and efficient, and children use it to solve simple arithmetic problems. When adults provide many occasions for counting and comparing quantities, children construct basic numerical concepts sooner.

Individual Differences in Mental Development

Describe the content of early childhood intelligence tests and the impact of home, preschool and kindergarten programs, child care, and educational television on mental development.

● Intelligence tests in early childhood sample a wide variety of verbal and nonverbal skills, including vocabulary, memory, quantitative knowledge, problem solving, and spatial reasoning. By age 6 to 7, scores are good predictors of later IQ and academic achievement.

● Children growing up in warm, stimulating homes with parents who make reasonable demands for mature behavior score higher on mental tests. Home environment plays a major role in the poorer intellectual performance of low-SES children in comparison to their higher-SES peers.

● Preschool and kindergarten programs range along a continuum. In **child-centered programs,** much learning takes place through play. In **academic programs,** teachers train academic skills through formal lessons, often emphasizing repetition and drill. Formal academic instruction, however, undermines young children's motivation and negatively influences later school achievement.

● **Project Head Start** is the most extensive federally funded preschool program for low-income children in the United States. In Canada, **Aboriginal Head Start** serves First Nations, Inuit, and Métis preschoolers living in poverty. High-quality preschool intervention results in immediate IQ and achievement gains and long-term improvements in school adjustment, educational attainment, and life success in adulthood. The more parents are involved in Head Start, the higher their children's year-end academic, language, and social skills. To strengthen the impact of intervention, two-generation models emphasizing developmental goals for both parents and children are being tried.

- Regardless of SES, poor-quality child care undermines preschoolers' cognitive and social development. When group size, caregiver–child ratio, caregivers' educational preparation, and caregivers' commitment to the child-care field are favorable, children—especially those from low-SES families—gain in cognitive, language, and social skills.

- Children pick up academic knowledge from educational television and computer software. TV shows with slow-paced action and easy-to-follow story lines help preschoolers comprehend program content. Heavy exposure to commercial entertainment TV, cartoons, and inappropriate computer games reduces time spent reading and interacting with others and is associated with poorer academic achievement after starting school.

Language Development

Trace the development of vocabulary, grammar, and conversational skills in early childhood.

- Supported by **fast mapping**, children's vocabularies increase dramatically during early childhood. Early in vocabulary growth, children seem to adopt a **mutual exclusivity bias,** assuming that each new word refers to an entirely separate category. In addition, preschoolers engage in **syntactic bootstrapping**, discerning a new word's meaning by observing how it is used in the structure of sentences. They also make use of adults' social cues and directly provided information. Once preschoolers have a sufficient vocabulary, they extend language meanings, coining new words and creating metaphors.

- Between ages 2 and 3, children adopt the word order of their language. As they master additional grammatical constructions, they occasionally **overregularize,** or apply the rules to words that are exceptions. By the end of the preschool years, children have acquired a wide variety of complex grammatical forms.

- Some experts believe that grammar is a product of general cognitive development. According to one view, children engage in **semantic bootstrapping**, relying on word meanings to figure out grammatical rules. Others agree with the essence of Chomsky's theory that children's brains are specially tuned for acquiring grammar.

- **Pragmatics** refers to the practical, social side of language. In face-to-face interaction with peers, young preschoolers are already skilled conversationalists. By age 4, they adapt their speech to their listeners in culturally accepted ways. Preschoolers' communicative skills appear less mature in highly demanding contexts, such as the telephone.

Cite factors that support language learning in early childhood.

- Conversational give-and-take with more skilled speakers fosters preschoolers' language skills. Adults often provide explicit feedback on the clarity of children's utterances. They give indirect feedback about grammar through **expansions** and **recasts.** However, some researchers question the impact of these strategies on grammatical development. For this aspect of language, exposure to a rich language environment may be sufficient.

Important Terms and Concepts

Aboriginal Head Start (p. 345)
academic programs (p. 345)
animistic thinking (p. 320)
cardinality (p. 342)
centration (p. 321)
child-centered programs (p. 345)
conservation (p. 320)
dual representation (p. 319)
egocentrism (p. 319)
emergent literacy (p. 338)
episodic memory (p. 334)
expansions (p. 352)

fast mapping (p. 349)
guided participation (p. 330)
hierarchical classification (p. 321)
intersubjectivity (p. 330)
irreversibility (p. 321)
memory strategies (p. 334)
metacognition (p. 336)
mutual exclusivity bias (p. 349)
operations (p. 319)
ordinality (p. 341)
overlapping-waves theory (p. 335)
overregularization (p. 350)

phonological awareness (p. 340)
planning (p. 333)
pragmatics (p. 351)
preoperational stage (p. 316)
private speech (p. 329)
Project Head Start (p. 345)
recasts (p. 352)
scaffolding (p. 330)
scripts (p. 334)
semantic bootstrapping (p. 351)
sociodramatic play (p. 317)
syntactic bootstrapping (p. 349)

 **FYI** **For Further Information and Help**

Consult the Companion Website for *Infants, Children, and Adolescents,* Fifth Edition, *(www.ablongman.com/berk),* where you will find the following resources for this chapter:

- **Chapter Objectives**
- **Flashcards** for studying important terms and concepts
- **Annotated Weblinks** to guide you in further research
- **Ask Yourself questions,** which you can answer and then check against a sample response

- **Suggested Readings**
- **Practice Tests** with immediate scoring and feedback

This painting, in which every detail of air and sky is distinct and alive, features the centrality of the family in young children's lives. In Chapter 10, the parent–child relationship remains a major theme in emotional and social development.

"I, My Mother, and Sister Went for a Walk"
Marija Zukovskaja
7 years, Lithuania

Reprinted with permission from the International Museum of Children's Art, Oslo, Norway.

Emotional and Social Development in Early Childhood

- **ERIKSON'S THEORY: INITIATIVE VERSUS GUILT**

- **SELF-UNDERSTANDING**
  Foundations of Self-Concept • Emergence of Self-Esteem

  CULTURAL INFLUENCES *Cultural Variations in Personal Storytelling: Implications for Early Self-Concept*

- **EMOTIONAL DEVELOPMENT**
  Understanding Emotion • Emotional Self-Regulation • Self-Conscious Emotions • Empathy and Sympathy

- **PEER RELATIONS**
  Advances in Peer Sociability • First Friendships • Social Problem Solving • Parental Influences on Early Peer Relations

- **FOUNDATIONS OF MORALITY**
  The Psychoanalytic Perspective • Social Learning Theory • The Cognitive-Developmental Perspective

- The Other Side of Morality: Development of Aggression

- **GENDER TYPING**
  Gender-Stereotyped Beliefs and Behaviors • Biological Influences on Gender Typing • Environmental Influences on Gender Typing • Gender Identity • Reducing Gender Stereotyping in Young Children

  BIOLOGY AND ENVIRONMENT *David: A Boy Who Was Reared as a Girl*

- **CHILD REARING AND EMOTIONAL AND SOCIAL DEVELOPMENT**
  Styles of Child Rearing • What Makes Authoritative Child Rearing Effective? • Cultural Variations • Child Maltreatment

  SOCIAL ISSUES: HEALTH *Healthy Start: Preventing Child Maltreatment Through Home Visitation*

As the children in Leslie's classroom moved through the preschool years, their personalities took on clearer definition. By age 3, they voiced firm likes and dislikes as well as new ideas about themselves. "Stop bothering me," Sammy said to Mark, who tried to reach for Sammy's beanbag as Sammy aimed it toward the mouth of a large clown face. "See, I'm great at this game," Sammy announced with confidence, an attitude that kept him trying, even though he missed most of the throws.

The children's conversations also revealed their first notions about morality. Often they combined statements about right and wrong they had heard from adults with forceful attempts to defend their own desires. "You're 'posed to share," declared Mark, while grabbing Sammy's beanbag.

"I was here first! Gimme it back," demanded Sammy, who pushed Mark. The two boys struggled for the beanbag until Leslie intervened, provided an extra set of beanbags, and showed them how they could both play.

As Sammy and Mark's interaction reveals, preschoolers quickly become complex social beings. Although all young children argue, grab, and push, cooperative exchanges are far more frequent. Between ages 2 and 6, first friendships form, in which children converse, act out complementary roles, and learn that their own desires for companionship and toys are best met when they consider the needs and interests of others.

The children's play highlighted their developing understanding of their social world. This was especially apparent in their attention to the dividing line between male and female. While Lynette and Karen cared for a sick baby doll in the housekeeping area, Sammy, Vance, and Mark transformed the block corner into a busy intersection. "Green light, go!" shouted police officer Sammy as Vance and Mark pushed large wooden cars and trucks across the floor. Already, the children preferred same-sex peers, and their play themes mirrored the gender stereotypes of their cultural community.

This chapter is devoted to the many facets of emotional and social development in early childhood. The theory of Erik Erikson provides an overview of personality change during the preschool years. Then we consider children's concepts of themselves, their insights into their social and moral worlds, their gender typing, and their increasing ability to manage their emotional and social behaviors. In the final sections of this chapter, we answer the question, What is effective child rearing? We also consider the complex conditions that support good parenting or lead it to break down, including the serious and widespread problems of child abuse and neglect.

Erikson's Theory: Initiative versus Guilt

Erikson (1950) described early childhood as a period of "vigorous unfolding." Once children have a sense of autonomy and feel secure about separating from parents, they become more relaxed and less contrary than they were as toddlers. Their energies are freed for tackling the psychological conflict of the preschool years: **initiative versus guilt.** As the word *initiative* suggests, young children have a new sense of purposefulness. They are eager to tackle new tasks, join in activities with peers, and discover what they can do with the help of adults. And they also make strides in conscience development.

Erikson regarded play as a means through which young children find out about themselves and their social world. Play permits preschoolers to try new skills with little risk of criticism and failure. It also creates a small social organization of children who must cooperate to achieve common goals. Around the world, children act out family scenes and highly visible occupations—police officer, doctor, and nurse in Western societies, rabbit hunter and potter among the Hopi Indians, and hut builder and spear maker among the Baka of West Africa (Roopnarine et al., 1998).

Recall that Erikson's theory builds on Freud's psychosexual stages (see Chapter 1, pages 16–17, to review). In Freud's well-known Oedipus and Electra conflicts, to avoid punishment and maintain the affection of parents, children form a *superego,* or conscience, by *identifying* with the same-sex parent. As a result, they adopt the moral and gender-role standards of their society. For Erikson, the negative outcome of early childhood is an overly strict superego, one that causes children to feel too much guilt because they have been threatened, criticized, and punished excessively by adults. When this happens, preschoolers' exuberant play and bold efforts to master new tasks break down.

Although Freud's Oedipus and Electra conflicts are no longer accepted as satisfactory explanations of conscience development, Erikson's image of initiative captures diverse changes in young children's emotional and social lives. The preschool years are, indeed, a time when children develop a confident self-image, more effective control over emotions, new social skills, the foundations of morality, and a clear sense of themselves as boy or girl. Now let's take a close look at each of these aspects of development.

These children of East India carry play *bhujariyas*—ceremonial wheat shoots that adults display in large processions during the Festival of Sawan, which celebrates the arrival of the monsoon rains that prepare the environment for planting and growth. By acting out adult roles in their play, children acquire insight into their futures and develop a sense of initiative.

© DORANNE JACOBSON

Self-Understanding

During early childhood, new powers of representation permit children to reflect on themselves. Language enables them to talk about the *I-self*—their own subjective experience of being. In Chapter 9, we noted that preschoolers acquire a vocabulary for talking about their inner mental lives and refine their understanding of mental states. As the I-self becomes more firmly established, children focus more intently on the *me-self*—knowledge and evaluation of the self's characteristics (Harter, 2003). They develop a **self-concept,** the set of attributes, abilities, attitudes, and values that an individual believes defines who he or she is.

Foundations of Self-Concept

Ask a 3- to 5-year-old to tell you about him- or herself, and you are likely to hear something like this: "I'm Tommy. See, I got this new red T-shirt. I'm 4 years old. I can brush my teeth, and I can wash my hair all by myself. I have a new Tinkertoy set, and I made this big, big tower." As these statements indicate, preschoolers' self-concepts are very concrete. Usually they mention observable characteristics, such as their name, physical appearance, possessions, and everyday behaviors (Harter, 1998; Watson, 1990).

By age 3½, children also describe themselves in terms of typical emotions and attitudes, as in "I'm happy when I play with my friends" or "I don't like being with grown-ups." This suggests a beginning understanding of their unique psychological characteristics (Eder & Mangelsdorf, 1997). As further support for this budding grasp of personality, when given a trait label, such as "shy" or "mean," 4-year-olds infer appropriate motives and feelings. For example, they know that a shy person doesn't like to be with unfamiliar people (Heyman & Gelman, 1999). But preschoolers do not refer directly to traits, by making such statements as "I'm helpful" or "I'm shy." This capacity must wait for greater cognitive maturity.

In fact, very young preschoolers' concepts of themselves are so bound up with specific possessions and actions that they spend much time asserting their rights to objects, as Sammy did in the beanbag incident at the beginning of this chapter. The stronger children's self-definition, the more possessive they tend to be, claiming objects as "Mine!" (Fasig, 2000; Levine, 1983). Rather than a sign of selfishness, early struggles over objects seem to be a sign of developing selfhood, an effort to clarify boundaries between self and others.

A firmer sense of self also permits children to cooperate in resolving disputes over objects, playing games, and solving simple problems (Brownell & Carriger, 1990; Caplan et al., 1991). Accordingly, when trying to promote friendly peer interaction, parents and teachers can accept the young child's possessiveness as a sign of self-assertion ("Yes, that's your toy") and then encourage compromise ("but in a little while, would you give someone else a turn?"), rather than insisting on sharing.

Recall from Chapter 9 that adult–child conversations about the past contribute to the development of an autobiographical memory. Parents often use these discussions to impart evaluative information about the child, as when they say, "You were a big boy when you did that!" Consequently, these narratives serve as a rich source of early self-knowledge and, as the Cultural Influences box on page 360 reveals, as a major means to imbue the self-concept with cultural values. Furthermore, as children construct a life story, the self-concept becomes increasingly coherent. Gradually children come to view the self as a unique person embedded in a world of others and as existing continuously in time (Nelson, 2001).

© LAURA DWIGHT

A firmer sense of self permits young children to cooperate in solving simple problems. These 3-year-olds work together to sweep up spilled sand in their preschool classroom.

Cultural Influences

Cultural Variations in Personal Storytelling: Implications for Early Self-Concept

Preschoolers of many cultural backgrounds participate in personal storytelling with their parents. Striking cultural differences exist in parents' selection and interpretation of events in these early narratives, affecting the way children come to view themselves.

In one study, researchers spent hundreds of hours over a 2-year period studying the storytelling practices of six middle-SES Irish-American families in Chicago and six middle-SES Chinese families in Taiwan. From extensive videotapes of adults' conversations with 2½-year-olds, the investigators identified personal stories and coded them for content, quality of their endings, and evaluation of the child (Miller, Fung, & Mintz, 1996; Miller et al., 1997).

Parents in both cultures discussed pleasurable holidays and family excursions about as often and in similar ways. Chinese parents, however, more often told lengthy stories about the child's misdeeds, such as using impolite language, writing on the wall, or playing in an overly rowdy way. These narratives were conveyed with warmth and caring, stressed the impact of misbehavior on others ("You made Mama lose face"), and often ended with direct teaching of proper behavior ("Saying dirty words is not good"). In the few instances in

which Irish-American stories referred to transgressions, parents downplayed their seriousness, attributing them to the child's spunk and assertiveness.

Early narratives about the child seem to launch preschoolers' self-concepts on culturally distinct paths. Influenced by Confucian traditions of strict discipline and social obligations, Chinese parents integrated these values into their personal stories, affirming the importance of not disgracing the family and explicitly conveying expectations in the story's conclusion. Although Irish-American parents disciplined their children, they rarely dwelt on misdeeds in storytelling. Rather, they cast the child's shortcomings in a positive light, perhaps to promote self-esteem.

Whereas most North Americans believe that favorable self-esteem is crucial for healthy development, Chinese adults generally regard it as unimportant or negative—as impeding the child's willingness to listen and to be corrected (Miller et al., 2002). Consistent with this view, the Chinese parents did little to cultivate their child's individuality. Instead, they used storytelling to guide the child toward socially responsible behavior. Hence, the Chinese child's self-image emphasizes obligations to others, whereas the North American child's is more autonomous.

This Chinese child on an outing with his mother listens as she speaks gently to him about proper behavior. Chinese parents often tell preschoolers stories about the child's misdeeds, stressing their negative impact on others. The Chinese child's self-concept, in turn, emphasizes social obligations.

Emergence of Self-Esteem

Another aspect of self-concept emerges in early childhood: **self-esteem, the judgments we make about our own worth and the feelings associated with those judgments.** Self-esteem ranks among the most important aspects of self-development, since evaluations of our own competencies affect our emotional experiences, future behavior, and long-term psychological adjustment. Take a moment to think about your own self-esteem. Besides a global appraisal of your worth as a person, you have a variety of separate self-judgments concerning different activities.

By age 4, preschoolers have several self-esteems—for example, about learning things in school, making friends, getting along with parents, and feeling physically attractive (Marsh, Ellis, & Craven, 2002). However, because they have difficulty distinguishing between their desired and their actual competence, when asked how well they can do something, preschoolers usually rate their own ability as extremely high and often underestimate the difficulty of tasks (Harter, 2003). Sammy's announcement that he was great at beanbag throwing despite his many misses is a typical self-evaluation during early childhood.

High self-esteem contributes greatly to preschoolers' initiative during a period in which they must master many new skills. Nevertheless, by age 4, some children give up easily or are discouraged after failure, and they conclude that they cannot manage challenging tasks, such as working a hard puzzle or building a tall block tower (Cain & Dweck, 1995; Smiley & Dweck, 1994). When these young nonpersisters are asked to act out with dolls an adult's reaction to failure, their responses sound something like this: "He's punished because he can't do the puzzle" or "Daddy's mad and is going to spank her" (Burhans & Dweck, 1995). They are also likely to report that their parents berate them for making small mistakes (Heyman, Dweck, & Cain, 1992). Adults can avoid these self-defeating reactions by adjusting their expectations to children's capacities, scaffolding children's attempts at difficult tasks (see Chapter 9, page 330), and accentuating the positive in children's work or behavior, pointing out effort and increasing skill.

This boy's belief in his ability to wash the family car, supported by his father's encouragement, fosters an enthusiastic sense of initiative.

ASK YOURSELF

REVIEW Why is self-esteem typically extremely high in early childhood?

APPLY Reread the description of Sammy and Mark's argument at the beginning of this chapter. On the basis of what you know about self-development, why was it a good idea for Leslie to resolve the dispute by providing an extra set of beanbags?

Emotional Development

Gains in representation, language, and self-concept support emotional development in early childhood. Between the ages of 2 and 6, children better understand their own and others' feelings, and they can better regulate the expression of emotion. Self-development also contributes to a rise in *self-conscious emotions,* such as shame, embarrassment, guilt, envy, and pride.

Understanding Emotion

Preschoolers' vocabulary for talking about emotion expands rapidly, and they use it skillfully to reflect on their own and others' behavior. Here are some excerpts from conversations in which 2-year-olds and 6-year-olds commented on emotionally charged experiences:

Two-year-old: [After father shouted at child, she became angry, shouting back] "I'm mad at you, Daddy. I'm going away. Good-bye."

Two-year-old: [Commenting on another child who refused to nap and cried] "Mom, Annie cry. Annie sad."

Six-year-old: [In response to mother's comment, "It's hard to hear the baby crying"] "Well, it's not as hard for me as it is for you." [When mother asked why] "Well, you like Johnny better than I do! I like him a little, and you like him a lot, so I think it's harder for you to hear him cry."

Six-year-old: [Trying to comfort a small boy in church whose mother had gone up to communion] "Aw, that's all right. She'll be right back. Don't be afraid. I'm here." (Bretherton et al., 1986, pp. 536, 540, 541)

COGNITIVE DEVELOPMENT AND EMOTIONAL UNDERSTANDING ● As the examples just given show, early in the preschool years, children refer to causes, consequences, and behavioral signs of emotion, and over time their understanding becomes more accurate and complex (Stein & Levine, 1999). By age 4 to 5, they correctly judge the causes of many basic emotions, as in "He's happy because he's swinging very high" or "He's sad because he misses his mother." However, preschoolers' explanations tend to emphasize external factors over internal states—a balance that changes with age (Levine, 1995). In Chapter 9, we saw that after age 4, children appreciate that both desires and beliefs motivate behavior. Once these understandings are secure, children's grasp of how internal factors can trigger emotion expands.

Preschoolers can also predict what a playmate expressing a certain emotion might do next. Four-year-olds know that an angry child might hit someone and that a happy child is more likely to share (Russell, 1990). And they realize that thinking and feeling are interconnected—that a person reminded of a previous sad experience is likely to feel sad (Lagattuta, Wellman, & Flavell, 1997). Furthermore, they can come up with effective ways to relieve others' negative feelings, such as hugging to reduce sadness (Fabes et al., 1988). Overall, preschoolers have an impressive ability to interpret, predict, and change others' feelings.

At the same time, in situations with conflicting cues about how a person is feeling, preschoolers have difficulty making sense of what is going on. For example, when asked what might be happening in a picture showing a happy-faced child with a broken bicycle, 4- and 5-year-olds tended to rely only on the emotional expression: "He's happy because he likes to ride his bike." Older children more often reconciled the two cues: "He's happy because his father promised to help fix his broken bike" (Gnepp, 1983; Hoffner & Badzinski, 1989). As in their approach to Piagetian tasks, young children focus on the most obvious aspect of a complex emotional situation, to the neglect of other relevant information.

SOCIAL EXPERIENCE AND EMOTIONAL UNDERSTANDING ● Although cognitive development leads to gains in emotional understanding, social experience also contributes. The more mothers label emotions and explain them in conversing with preschoolers, the more "emotion words" children use in these discussions. Maternal prompting of emotional thoughts, as in "What makes him afraid?" is a good predictor of 2-year-olds' emotion language. Explanations—"He's sad because his dog ran away"—are more important for older preschoolers (Cervantes & Callanan, 1998). Does this remind you of the concept of *scaffolding*—that to be effective, adult teaching must adjust to children's increasing competence?

Parents who frequently acknowledge their children's emotional reactions and explicitly teach them about diverse emotions have preschoolers who can better judge the emotions of others when tested at later ages (Denham & Kochanoff, 2002). Discussions in which family members disagree are particularly helpful. In one study, mothers who explained feelings and negotiated and compromised during conflicts with their 2½-year-olds had children who, at age 3, were advanced in emotion understanding and used similar strategies to resolve disagreements (Laible & Thompson, 2002). Such dialogues seem to help children reflect on the causes and consequences of emotion while modeling mature communication skills. Furthermore, 3- to 5-year-olds who are

During the preschool years children's grasp of the causes, consequences, and behavioral signs of emotion expands rapidly. This 4-year-old tries to figure out why his baby brother is crying. Perhaps the menu is not quite right.

© ELIZABETH CREWS

securely attached to their mothers better understand emotion, perhaps because secure attachment is related to richer mother–child conversations about feelings (Laible & Thompson, 1998, 2000).

As preschoolers learn more about emotion from conversing with adults, they transfer this knowledge to other contexts, engaging in more emotion talk with siblings and friends, especially during sociodramatic play (Brown, Donelan-McCall, & Dunn, 1996; Hughes & Dunn, 1998). Make-believe, in turn, contributes to emotional understanding, especially when children play with siblings (Youngblade & Dunn, 1995). The intense nature of the sibling relationship, combined with frequent acting out of feelings, makes pretending an excellent context for early learning about emotions. And when parents intervene in sibling disputes by reasoning and negotiating, preschoolers gain in sensitivity to their siblings' feelings (Perlman & Ross, 1997). They more often refer to their sibling's emotional perspective ("You get mad when I don't share") and engage in less fighting.

As these findings suggest, emotional knowledge helps children greatly in their efforts to get along with others. As early as 3 to 5 years of age, it is related to friendly, considerate behavior and willingness to make amends after harming another (Brown & Dunn, 1996; Dunn, Brown, & Maguire, 1995). Also, the more preschoolers refer to feelings when interacting with playmates, the better liked they are by their peers (Fabes et al., 2001). Children seem to recognize that acknowledging others' emotions and explaining their own enhance the quality of relationships.

Emotional Self-Regulation

Language also contributes to preschoolers' improved *emotional self-regulation,* or ability to control the expression of emotion. By age 3 to 4, children verbalize a variety of strategies for adjusting their emotional arousal to a more comfortable level. For example, they know they can blunt emotions by restricting sensory input (covering their eyes or ears to block out a scary sight or sound), talking to yourself ("Mommy said she'll be back soon"), or changing their goals (deciding that you don't want to play anyway after being excluded from a game) (Thompson, 1990a).

Children's use of these strategies means fewer emotional outbursts over the preschool years. In fact, by age 3, children can even pose an emotion they do not feel and have begun to realize when others might be hiding their true feelings (Denham, 1998). These emotional "masks" are largely limited to the positive feelings of happiness and surprise. Children of all ages (and adults as well) find it more difficult to act sad, angry, or disgusted than pleased (Lewis, Sullivan, & Vasen, 1987). To promote good social relations, most cultures teach children to communicate positive feelings and inhibit unpleasant ones.

Temperament affects the development of emotional self-regulation. Children who experience negative emotion intensely have greater difficulty inhibiting their feelings and shifting their focus of attention away from disturbing events. Beginning in early childhood, these children are more likely to respond with irritation to others' distress, to get along poorly with teachers and peers, and to have difficulty adjusting to classroom routines (Denham et al., 2002; Shields et al., 2001; Walden, Lemerise, & Smith, 1999).

If emotionally reactive children are to avoid social difficulties, they must develop effective emotion-regulation strategies (Eisenberg, 1998). By watching parents manage their feelings, children pick up strategies for regulating their own. When parents rarely express positive emotion and have difficulty controlling anger and hostility, especially during interactions with their preschooler, children have continuing problems in regulating emotion that seriously interfere with psychological adjustment (Eisenberg et al., 1999, 2001).

Adults' conversations with children also foster emotional self-regulation. Parents who prepare children for difficult experiences by describing what to expect and ways to handle anxiety offer coping strategies that children can apply. Preschoolers' vivid imaginations and incomplete grasp of the distinction between appearance and reality make fears common in early childhood. Consult Applying What We Know on page 364 for ways adults can help young children manage fears.

Self-Conscious Emotions

One morning in Leslie's classroom, a group of children crowded around for a bread-baking activity. Leslie asked them to wait patiently while she got a baking pan. In the meantime, Sammy

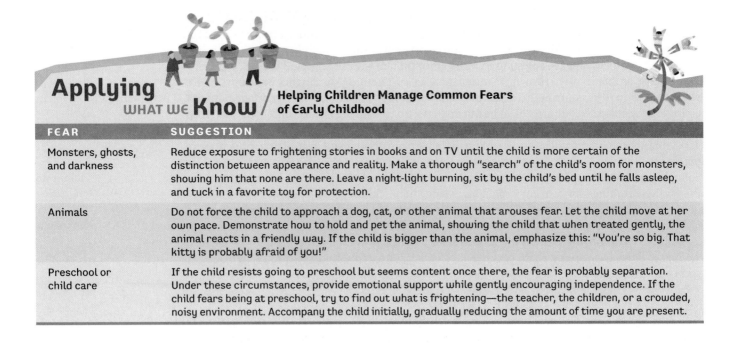

Applying WHAT WE **Know** / Helping Children Manage Common Fears of Early Childhood

FEAR	SUGGESTION
Monsters, ghosts, and darkness	Reduce exposure to frightening stories in books and on TV until the child is more certain of the distinction between appearance and reality. Make a thorough "search" of the child's room for monsters, showing him that none are there. Leave a night-light burning, sit by the child's bed until he falls asleep, and tuck in a favorite toy for protection.
Animals	Do not force the child to approach a dog, cat, or other animal that arouses fear. Let the child move at her own pace. Demonstrate how to hold and pet the animal, showing the child that when treated gently, the animal reacts in a friendly way. If the child is bigger than the animal, emphasize this: "You're so big. That kitty is probably afraid of you!"
Preschool or child care	If the child resists going to preschool but seems content once there, the fear is probably separation. Under these circumstances, provide emotional support while gently encouraging independence. If the child fears being at preschool, try to find out what is frightening—the teacher, the children, or a crowded, noisy environment. Accompany the child initially, gradually reducing the amount of time you are present.

reached to feel the dough, but the bowl tumbled over the side of the table. When Leslie returned, Sammy looked at her for a moment, covered his eyes with his hands, and said, "I did something bad." He felt ashamed and guilty.

As children's self-concepts become better developed, they become increasingly sensitive to praise and blame or (as in Sammy's case) to the possibility of such feedback. As a result, they more often experience *self-conscious emotions*—feelings that involve injury to or enhancement of their sense of self (see Chapter 7). By age 3, self-conscious emotions are clearly linked to self-evaluation (Lewis, 1995). Nevertheless, because preschoolers are still developing standards of excellence and conduct, they depend on adults' messages to know when to feel self-conscious emotions (Stipek, 1995). Parents who repeatedly give feedback about the worth of the child and her performance ("That's a bad job! I thought you were a good girl") have children who experience self-conscious emotions intensely—more shame after failure and more pride after success. In contrast, parents who focus on how to improve performance ("You did it this way; you should have done it that way") induce moderate, more adaptive levels of shame and pride (Lewis, 1998).

Beginning in early childhood, intense shame is associated with feelings of personal inadequacy ("I'm stupid," "I'm a terrible person") and with maladjustment—withdrawal and depression as well as aggression. In contrast, guilt—as long as it occurs in appropriate circumstances and shame does not accompany it—is related to good adjustment, perhaps because guilt helps children resist harmful impulses. And when children do transgress, guilt motivates them to repair the damage and behave more considerately (Ferguson et al., 1999; Tangney, 2001).

Empathy and Sympathy

Another emotional capacity—*empathy*—becomes more common in early childhood. It serves as an important motivator of **prosocial, or altruistic, behavior**—actions that benefit another person without any expected reward for the self (Eisenberg & Fabes, 1998). Compared with toddlers, preschoolers rely more on words to communicate their empathic feelings, a change that indicates a more reflective level of empathy. When a 6-year-old noticed that his mother was distressed at not being able to find a motel after a long day's travel, he said, "You're pretty upset, aren't you, Mom? You're pretty sad. Well, I think, it's going to be all right. I think we'll find a nice place and it'll be all right" (Bretherton et al., 1986, p. 540). As the ability to take the perspective of others improves, empathic responding increases.

Yet empathy, or *feeling with* another person and responding emotionally in a similar way, does not always yield acts of kindness and helpfulness. In some children, empathizing with an upset adult or peer escalates into *personal distress.* In trying to reduce these feelings, the child focuses on his own anxiety rather than on the person in need. As a result, empathy does not give way to **sympathy**—feelings of concern or sorrow for another's plight.

Whether empathy prompts a personally distressed, self-focused response or sympathetic, prosocial behavior is related to temperament. Children who are sociable, assertive, and good at regulating emotion are more likely to help, share, and comfort others in distress. In contrast, poor emotion regulators less often display sympathetic concern and prosocial behavior (Eisenberg et al., 1996, 1998). When faced with someone in need, these children react with facial and physiological distress—frowning, lip biting, a rise in heart rate, and a sharp increase in EEG brain-wave activity in the right cerebral hemisphere, which houses negative emotion, indicating that they are overwhelmed by their feelings (Miller et al., 1996; Pickens, Field, & Nawrocki, 2001).

During a field trip to the seashore with her preschool classmates, this Australian 3-year-old bursts into tears, and her friend offers comfort. As young children's language skills expand and their ability to take the perspective of others improves, empathy increases and becomes an important motivator of prosocial, or altruistic, behavior.

As with other aspects of emotional development, parenting affects empathy and sympathy. Parents who are warm and encouraging and show a sensitive, sympathetic concern for their preschoolers have children who are likely to react in a concerned way to the distress of others—relationships that persist into adolescence and young adulthood (Eisenberg & McNally, 1993; Koestner, Franz, & Weinberger, 1990). Besides modeling sympathy, parents can teach children the importance of kindness and can intervene when they display inappropriate emotion—strategies that predict high levels of sympathetic responding (Eisenberg et al., 1991; Zahn-Waxler & Radke-Yarrow, 1990).

In contrast, angry, punitive parenting disrupts the development of empathy at an early age. In one study, researchers observed physically abused preschoolers at a child-care center. Compared with nonabused agemates, they rarely expressed concern at a peer's unhappiness. Instead, they responded with fear, anger, and physical attacks (Klimes-Dougan & Kistner, 1990). The children's reactions resembled the behavior of their parents, who also responded insensitively to the suffering of others.

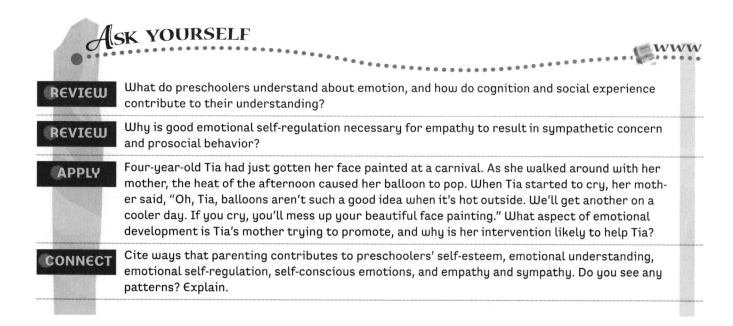

Ask YOURSELF

REVIEW What do preschoolers understand about emotion, and how do cognition and social experience contribute to their understanding?

REVIEW Why is good emotional self-regulation necessary for empathy to result in sympathetic concern and prosocial behavior?

APPLY Four-year-old Tia had just gotten her face painted at a carnival. As she walked around with her mother, the heat of the afternoon caused her balloon to pop. When Tia started to cry, her mother said, "Oh, Tia, balloons aren't such a good idea when it's hot outside. We'll get another on a cooler day. If you cry, you'll mess up your beautiful face painting." What aspect of emotional development is Tia's mother trying to promote, and why is her intervention likely to help Tia?

CONNECT Cite ways that parenting contributes to preschoolers' self-esteem, emotional understanding, emotional self-regulation, self-conscious emotions, and empathy and sympathy. Do you see any patterns? Explain.

℘eer Relations

As children become increasingly self-aware, more effective at communicating, and better at understanding the thoughts and feelings of others, their skill at interacting with peers improves rapidly. Peers provide young children with learning experiences they can get in no other way. Because peers interact on an equal footing, they must keep a conversation going, cooperate, and set goals in play. With peers, children form friendships—special relationships marked by attachment and common interests. Let's look at how peer interaction changes over the preschool years.

These children are engaged in parallel play. Although they sit side by side and use similar materials, they do not try to influence one another's behavior. Parallel play remains frequent and stable over the preschool years, accounting for as much of children's play as highly social, cooperative interaction.

Advances in Peer Sociability

Mildred Parten (1932), one of the first to study peer sociability among 2- to 5-year-olds, noticed a dramatic rise with age in the ability to engage in joint, interactive play. She concluded that social development proceeds in a three-step sequence. It begins with **nonsocial activity**—unoccupied, onlooker behavior and solitary play. Then it shifts to a limited form of social participation called **parallel play**, in which a child plays near other children with similar materials but does not try to influence their behavior. At the highest level are two forms of true social interaction. One is **associative play**, in which children engage in separate activities, but they exchange toys and comment on one another's behavior. The other is **cooperative play**, a more advanced type of interaction in which children orient toward a common goal, such as acting out a make-believe theme or building a sand castle.

FOLLOW-UP RESEARCH ON PEER SOCIABILITY ● Longitudinal evidence indicates that these play forms emerge in the order suggested by Parten, but they do not form a developmental sequence in which later-appearing ones replace earlier ones (Howes & Matheson, 1992). Instead, all types coexist during the preschool years. Watch children move from one play type to another in preschool, and you will see that they often transition from onlooker to parallel to cooperative play and back again (Robinson et al., 2003). Preschoolers seem to use parallel play as a way station—a respite from the high demands of complex social interaction and a crossroad to new activities. Furthermore, although nonsocial activity declines with age, it is still the most frequent form of behavior among 3- to 4-year-olds. Even among kindergartners it continues to take up about one-third of children's free-play time. And both solitary and parallel play remain fairly stable from 3 to 6 years, accounting for as much of the young child's play as highly social, cooperative interaction (Rubin, Fein, & Vandenberg, 1983).

We now understand that it is the *type,* rather than the amount, of solitary and parallel play that changes during early childhood. In studies of preschoolers' play in Taiwan and the United States, researchers rated the *cognitive maturity* of nonsocial, parallel, and cooperative play by applying the categories shown in Table 10.1. Within each of Parten's play types, older children displayed more cognitively mature behavior than younger children (Pan, 1994; Rubin, Watson, & Jambor, 1978).

As these children collaborate in operating a balance scale, they engage in an advanced form of interaction called cooperative play. With age, preschoolers more often cooperate to achieve a common goal.

Often parents wonder whether a preschooler who spends large amounts of time playing alone is developing normally. Only *certain types* of nonsocial activity—aimless wandering, hovering near peers, and functional play involving immature, repetitive motor action—are cause for concern. Children who behave in these ways are usually temperamentally inhibited preschoolers who have not learned to regulate their high social

TABLE 10.1

Developmental Sequence of Cognitive Play Categories

PLAY CATEGORY	DESCRIPTION	EXAMPLES
Functional play	Simple, repetitive motor movements with or without objects. Especially common during the first 2 years of life.	Running around a room, rolling a car back and forth, kneading clay with no intent to make something
Constructive play	Creating or constructing something. Especially common between 3 and 6 years.	Making a house out of toy blocks, drawing a picture, putting together a puzzle
Make-believe play	Acting out everyday and imaginary roles. Especially common between 2 and 6 years.	Playing house, school, or police officer; acting out storybook or television characters

Source: Rubin, Fein, & Vandenberg, 1983.

fearfulness. Often their parents overprotect them, criticize their social awkwardness, and unnecessarily control their play activities instead of patiently encouraging them to approach other children (Burgess et al., 2001; Rubin, Burgess, & Hastings, 2002).

But not all preschoolers with low rates of peer interaction are socially anxious. To the contrary, most like to play by themselves, and their solitary activities are positive and constructive. Teachers encourage such play when they set out art materials, books, puzzles, and building toys. Children who spend much time at these activities are not maladjusted (Rubin & Coplan, 1998). Instead, they are bright children who, when they do play with peers, show socially skilled behavior.

As noted in Chapter 9, *sociodramatic play* becomes especially common during the preschool years. This advanced form of cooperative play supports both cognitive and social development. In joint make-believe, preschoolers act out and respond to one another's pretend feelings. They also explore and gain control of fear-arousing experiences when they play doctor or pretend to search for monsters in a magical forest. As a result, they can better understand others' feelings and regulate their own (Smith, 2003). Finally, to create and manage complex plots, preschoolers must resolve their disputes through negotiation and compromise.

CULTURAL VARIATIONS ● Peer sociability in collectivist societies, which stress group harmony, takes different forms than in individualistic cultures. For example, children in India generally play in large groups that require high levels of cooperation. Much of their behavior is imitative, occurs in unison, and involves close physical contact. In a game called Bhatto Bhatto, they act out a script about a trip to the market, touching each others' elbows and hands as they pretend to cut and share a tasty vegetable (Roopnarine et al., 1994).

Cultural beliefs about the importance of play also affect early peer associations. Caregivers who view play as mere entertainment are less likely to provide props and encourage pretend than those who value its cognitive and social benefits (Farver & Wimbarti, 1995). Korean-American parents, who emphasize task persistence as vital for learning, have preschoolers who spend less time than their Caucasian-American counterparts at joint make-believe and more time unoccupied and in parallel play (Farver, Kim, & Lee, 1995).

Return to the description of Yucatec Mayan preschoolers' pretending on page 332 of Chapter 9. Mayan parents do not promote children's play, and when it interferes with important cultural activities, they discourage it. Yet even though they spend little time pretending, Mayan children are socially competent (Gaskins, 2000). Perhaps Western-style sociodramatic play, with its elaborate materials and wide-ranging themes, is particularly important for social development in societies where child and adult worlds are distinct. It may be less crucial when children participate in adult activities from an early age.

These cousins at a family birthday party in a village in central India play an intricate hand-clapping game, called "Chapte." The girls clap in unison to a jingle with eleven verses, which take them through their lifespan and conclude with their turning into ghosts. The girls end the game by mimicking a scary ghost's antics. Their play reflects the value their culture places on group harmony.

© DORANNE JACOBSON

First Friendships

As preschoolers interact, first friendships form that serve as important contexts for emotional and social development. Take a moment to consider what *friendship* means to you. You probably thought of a mutual relationship involving companionship, sharing, understanding of thoughts and feelings, and caring for and comforting one another in times of need. In addition, mature friendships endure over time and survive occasional conflicts.

Preschoolers understand something about the uniqueness of friendship. They know that a friend is someone "who likes you" and with whom you spend a lot of time playing (Youniss, 1980). Yet their ideas about friendship are far from mature. We have already seen that young children typically describe themselves in concrete, activity-based terms. Their notion of friendship is much the same, defined by pleasurable play and sharing of toys. As yet, friendship does not have a long-term, enduring quality based on mutual trust (Selman, 1980). Indeed, Sammy declared, "Mark's my best friend" on days when the boys got along well. But he would state just the opposite—"Mark, you're not my friend!"—when a dispute was not quickly settled.

Nevertheless, interactions between young friends are unique. Preschoolers give twice as much reinforcement, in the form of greetings, praise, and compliance, to children they identify as friends, and they also receive more from them. Friends are also more emotionally expressive—talking, laughing, and looking at each other more often—than nonfriends (Hartup & Stevens, 1999; Vaughn et al., 2001). Furthermore, early childhood friendships offer social support. When children begin kindergarten with friends in their class, they adjust to school more favorably (Ladd & Price, 1987). Perhaps the company of friends serves as a secure base from which to develop new relationships, enhancing children's feelings of comfort in the new classroom.

The ease with which kindergartners make new friends and are accepted by their classmates predicts cooperative participation in classroom activities and self-directed completion of learning tasks. These behaviors, in turn, are related to gains in achievement over the kindergarten year (Ladd, Birch, & Buhs, 1999; Ladd, Buhs, & Seid, 2000). Of course, kindergartners with friendly, prosocial behavioral styles are better at making new friends, whereas those with weak emotional self-regulation skills and argumentative, aggressive, or peer-avoidant styles establish poor-quality relationships and make few friends. These social outcomes impair children's liking for school, classroom participation, and academic learning (Birch & Ladd, 1998). Clearly, the capacity to forge friendships enables kindergartners to integrate themselves into classroom environments in ways that foster both academic and social competence.

Social Problem Solving

Children, even when they are best friends, sometimes come into conflict. Yet even preschoolers seem to handle most quarrels constructively, and only rarely do their disagreements result in hostile encounters. Although friends argue more than other peers do, they are more likely to work out their differences (Hartup, 1999).

Nevertheless, peer conflicts are important. Watch children engage in disputes over play objects ("That's mine!" "I had it first!"), entry into and control over play activities ("I'm on your team, Jerry." "No, you're not!"), and disagreements over facts, ideas, and beliefs ("I'm taller than he is." "No, you aren't!"). You will see that they take these matters quite seriously. Over time, preschoolers' conflicts shift from material concerns to mental and social issues (Chen et al., 2001). In Chapter 9 we noted that resolution of conflict, rather than conflict per se, promotes development. Social conflicts offer children invaluable learning opportunities for **social problem solving**—the generation and application of strategies that prevent or resolve disagreements, resulting in outcomes that are both acceptable to others and beneficial to the self. To engage in social problem solving, children must bring together diverse social understandings.

THE SOCIAL PROBLEM-SOLVING PROCESS ● Nicki Crick and Kenneth Dodge (1994) organize the steps of social problem solving into the circular model shown in Figure 10.1. Notice how this flowchart takes an *information-processing approach,* clarifying exactly what a child must

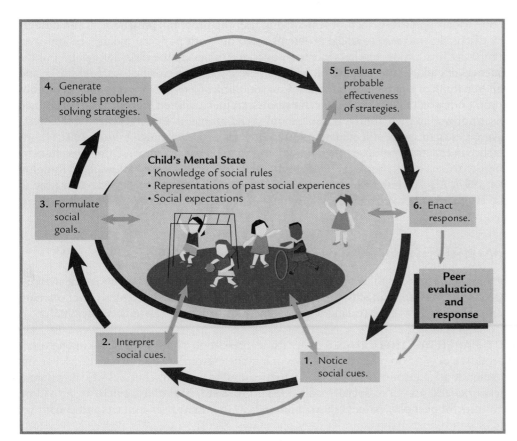

FIGURE 10.1

An information-processing model of social problem solving.

The model is circular because children often engage in several information-processing activities at once—for example, interpreting information as they notice it and continuing to consider the meaning of another's behavior while they generate and evaluate problem-solving strategies. The model also takes into account the impact of mental state on social information processing—in particular, children's knowledge of social rules, their representations of past social experiences, and their expectations for future experiences. Peer evaluations and responses to enacted strategies are also important factors in social problem solving. (Adapted from N. R. Crick & K. A. Dodge, 1994, "A Review and Reformulation of Social Information-Processing Mechanisms in Children's Social Adjustment," *Psychological Bulletin, 115,* 74–101, Figure 2 (adapted), p. 76. Copyright © 1994 by the American Psychological Association. Adapted by permission.)

do to grapple with and solve a social problem. Once this is known, processing deficits can be identified, and intervention can be tailored to meet children's individual needs.

Social problem solving profoundly affects peer relations. Children who get along well with agemates interpret social cues accurately, formulate goals that enhance relationships (being helpful to peers), and have a repertoire of effective problem-solving strategies. For example, they make polite requests to play and ask for an explanation when they do not understand another child's behavior. In contrast, children with peer difficulties often hold biased social expectations. Consequently, they attend selectively to social cues (such as hostile acts) and misinterpret others' behavior (an unintentional jostle as hostile). Their social goals (satisfying an impulse, getting even with or avoiding a peer) often lead to strategies that damage relationships (Rose & Asher, 1999; Youngstrom et al., 2000). They might barge into a play group without asking, use threats and physical force, or fearfully hover around peers' activities.

Children improve greatly in social problem solving over the preschool and early school years. Whereas younger children often grab, hit, or insist that another child obey, 5- to 7-year-olds tend to rely on friendly persuasion and compromise, to think of alternative strategies when an initial one does not work, and to resolve disagreements without adult intervention (Chen et al., 2001; Mayeux & Cillessen, 2003). And sometimes they suggest creating new, mutual goals. In doing so, they recognize that solutions to current problems have an important bearing on the future of the relationship (Yeates, Schultz, & Selman, 1991). By kindergarten to second grade, the accuracy and effectiveness of each component of social problem solving is related to socially competent behavior (Dodge et al., 1986).

TRAINING SOCIAL PROBLEM SOLVING ● Intervening with children who have weak social problem-solving skills can enhance development in several ways. Besides improving peer relations, effective social problem solving provides children with a sense of mastery in the face of stressful life events. It reduces the risk of adjustment difficulties in children from low-SES and troubled families (Goodman, Gravitt, & Kaslow, 1995).

In one widely applied social problem-solving training program, preschoolers and kinder-gartners discuss how to resolve social problems acted out with puppets in daily sessions over several months. In addition, teachers intervene as conflicts arise in the classroom, point out the consequences of children's behavior ("How do you think Johnny feels when you hit him?"), and help children think of alternative strategies ("Can you think of a different way to solve this problem so you both won't be mad?"). In several studies, trained children, in contrast to untrained controls, improved in their ability to think about social problems and in teacher-rated adjustment. And these gains were still evident months after the program ended (Shure, 2001).

Practice in enacting responses may strengthen these positive outcomes. Often preschoolers know how to solve a social problem effectively, but they do not apply their knowledge (Rudolph & Heller, 1997). Also, children who have enacted maladaptive responses repeatedly may need to rehearse alternatives to overcome their habitual behaviors and to spark more adaptive social information processing.

Parental Influences on Early Peer Relations

Children first acquire skills for interacting with peers within the family. Parents influence children's peer sociability both directly, through attempts to influence children's peer relations, and indirectly, through their child-rearing practices and play behaviors (Ladd & Pettit, 2002).

DIRECT PARENTAL INFLUENCES ● Outside preschool, child care, and kindergarten, young children depend on parents to help them establish rewarding peer associations. Parents who frequently arrange informal peer play activities tend to have preschoolers who have larger peer networks and are more socially skilled (Ladd, LeSieur, & Profilet, 1993). In providing opportunities for peer play, parents show children how to initiate peer contacts and encourage them to be good "hosts" who consider their playmates' needs.

Parents also influence their children's peer interaction skills by offering guidance on how to act toward others. Their skillful suggestions for managing conflict, discouraging teasing, and entering a play group are associated with preschoolers' social competence and peer acceptance (Laird et al., 1994; Mize & Pettit, 1997).

Parents influence children's peer interaction skills by arranging informal play activities and providing guidance on how to behave. This father teaches his 3-year-old son how to offer a present as a guest at a birthday party.

© CREWS/THE IMAGE WORKS

INDIRECT PARENTAL INFLUENCES ● Many aspects of parenting promote peer sociability, even when that is not parents' primary aim. For example, secure attachments to parents are linked to more responsive, harmonious peer interactions (Bost et al., 1998; Schneider, Atkinson, & Tardif, 2001). The emotionally expressive and supportive communication that contributes to attachment security may be responsible. In one study, researchers observed mother–child conversations for exchange of positive emotion and maternal sensitivity to the child's statements and feelings. Kindergartners who were more emotionally "connected" to their mothers displayed more empathy and prosocial behavior toward their classmates. This empathic orientation, in turn, was linked to more positive peer ties (Clark & Ladd, 2000).

Parent–child play seems particularly effective for promoting peer interaction skills. During play, parents interact with their child on a "level playing field," in much the same way peers do (Russell, Pettit, & Mize, 1998). Highly involved, emotionally positive, and cooperative play between parents and preschoolers is associated with more positive peer relations. And perhaps because parents play more with children of their own sex, mothers' play is more strongly linked to daughters' competence, and fathers play to sons' competence (Lindsey & Mize, 2000; Pettit et al., 1998).

As early as the preschool years, some children have great difficulty with peer relations. In Leslie's classroom, Robbie was one of them. Wherever he happened to be, such comments as "Robbie ruined our block tower," and "Robbie hit me for no reason" could be heard. You will learn more about how parenting contributed to Robbie's peer problems as we take up moral development in the next section.

Ask Yourself

REVIEW Among children who spend much time playing alone, what factors distinguish those who are likely to have adjustment difficulties from those who are well adjusted and socially skilled?

APPLY Three-year-old Bart lives in the country, with no other preschoolers nearby. His parents wonder whether it is worth driving Bart into town once a week to play with his 3-year-old cousin. What advice would you give Bart's parents, and why?

CONNECT Illustrate the influence of temperament on social problem solving by explaining how an impulsive child and a shy, inhibited child might respond at each social problem-solving step in Figure 10.1 on page 369.

REFLECT Think back to your first friendship. How old were you? Describe the quality of your relationship. What did your parents do, directly and indirectly, that might have influenced your earliest peer associations?

Foundations of Morality

If you watch young children's behavior and listen in on their conversations, you will discover their developing moral sense. By age 2, they react with distress to aggressive or potentially harmful behaviors. Soon they use words to evaluate their own and others' actions: "I naughty. I wrote on the wall" or (after having been hit by another child) "Connie not nice" (Kochanska, Casey, & Fukumoto, 1995). And we have seen that children of this age share toys, help others, and cooperate in games—early indicators of a considerate, responsible attitude.

Throughout the world, adults take note of this budding capacity to distinguish right from wrong and to accommodate the needs of others. Some cultures have special terms for it. The Utku Indians of Hudson Bay say the child develops *ihuma* (reason). The Fijians believe that *vakayalo* (sense) appears. In response, parents hold children more responsible for their behavior (Kagan, 1998). By the end of early childhood, children can state many moral rules, such as "You're not supposed to take things without asking" or "Tell the truth!" In addition, they argue over matters of justice, as when they say, "You sat there last time, so it's my turn" or "It's not fair. He got more!"

All theories of moral development recognize that conscience begins to take shape in early childhood. And most agree that at first, the child's morality is *externally controlled* by adults. Gradually, it becomes regulated by *inner standards*. That is, truly moral individuals do not do the right thing just to conform to others' expectations. Instead, they have developed compassionate concerns and principles of good conduct, which they follow in many situations.

Although points of agreement exist among major theories, each emphasizes a different aspect of morality. Psychoanalytic theory stresses the *emotional side* of conscience development—in particular, identification and guilt as motivators of good conduct. Social learning theory focuses on *moral behavior* and how it is learned through reinforcement and modeling. And the cognitive-developmental perspective emphasizes *thinking*—children's ability to reason about justice and fairness.

The Psychoanalytic Perspective

To briefly review Freud's psychoanalytic theory, moral development begins with the Oedipus and Electra conflicts, in which children desire to possess the parent of the other sex but give up this wish because they fear punishment and loss of parental love. Instead, they form a *superego*, or conscience, by *identifying* with the same-sex parent, whose moral standards they adopt. Children obey the superego to avoid *guilt,* a painful emotion that arises each time they are tempted to misbehave. According to Freud, moral development is largely complete by 5 to 6 years of age.

Today, most researchers disagree with this Freudian account. Notice how fear of punishment and loss of parental love are assumed to motivate conscience formation and moral behavior. Yet children whose parents frequently use threats, commands, or physical force tend to violate standards often and feel little guilt (Kochanska et al., 2002). And if a parent withdraws love—for example, refuses to speak to or states a dislike for the child—children often respond with high levels of self-blame after misbehaving. They might think, "I'm no good," or "Nobody loves me." Eventually, these children may protect themselves from overwhelming feelings of guilt by denying the emotion. So they, too, develop a weak conscience (Kochanska, 1991; Zahn-Waxler et al., 1990).

THE POWER OF INDUCTIVE DISCIPLINE ● In contrast, a special type of discipline supports conscience development. In **induction,** an adult helps the child notice feelings by pointing out the effects of the child's misbehavior on others, noting especially their distress and making clear that the child caused it. For example, the parent might say, "If you keep pushing him, he'll fall down and cry" or "She feels so sad because you won't give back her doll" (Hoffman, 2000). As long as the explanation matches the child's capacity to understand, induction works with children as early as 2 years of age. Preschoolers exposed to it are more likely to make up for their misdeeds and display prosocial behavior (Zahn-Waxler, Radke-Yarrow, & King, 1979).

The success of induction may lie in its power to cultivate children's active commitment to moral standards (Turiel, 1998). How does it do so? First, induction tells children how to behave so they can call on this information in future situations. Second, by pointing out the impact of the child's actions on others, parents encourage empathy and sympathetic concern, which motivate prosocial behavior (Krevans & Gibbs, 1996). Third, providing children with reasons for changing their behavior invites them to judge the appropriateness of parental expectations, which fosters adoption of standards because they make sense.

When children experience induction consistently, they may form a *script* for the negative emotional consequences of harming others: child harms, inductive message points out harm, child feels empathy for victim, child makes amends (Hoffman, 2000). The script deters future transgressions. In contrast, discipline that relies too heavily on threats of punishment or love withdrawal produces such intense fear and anxiety that children cannot think clearly to figure out what they should do. As a result, these practices do not get children to internalize moral rules.

THE CHILD'S CONTRIBUTION ● Notice how Freud's theory places a heavy burden on parents, who must ensure through their disciplinary practices that children develop an internalized conscience. Although good discipline is crucial, children's characteristics affect the success of parenting techniques. For example, twin studies suggest a modest genetic contribution to empathy (Zahn-Waxler et al., 2001). A more empathic child requires less power assertion and is more responsive to induction.

Temperament also is influential. Mild, patient tactics—requests, suggestions, and explanations—are sufficient to prompt guilt reactions and conscience development in anxious, fearful preschoolers (Kochanska et al., 2002). In contrast, gentle discipline has little impact on fearless, impulsive children. And power assertion works poorly as well! Instead, parents of these youngsters can foster conscience development by firmly correcting misbehavior and ensuring a secure attachment relationship (Fowles & Kochanska, 2000; Kochanska, 1997). Why is this so? When children are so low in anxiety that they do not respond to parental interventions with enough discomfort to promote a strong conscience, a close bond with the parent provides an alternative foundation for morality. It motivates children to listen to parents' inductions and follow their rules as a means of preserving an affectionate, cooperative relationship.

This teacher uses inductive discipline to explain to a child the impact of her transgression on others. Induction supports conscience development by clarifying how the child should behave, encouraging empathy and sympathetic concern, and permitting the child to grasp the reasons behind parental expectations.

© NANCY SHEEHAN

In sum, to foster early moral development, parents must tailor their disciplinary strategies to their child's personality. Does this remind you of *goodness of fit,* discussed in Chapter 7? Return to page 263 to review this idea.

THE ROLE OF GUILT ● Although little support exists for Freudian ideas about conscience development, Freud was correct that guilt is an important motivator of moral action. Early in the preschool years, guilt reactions are evident, and internalization of the parent's moral voice has begun, as this typical preschooler's statement reveals: "Didn't you hear my mommy? We'd better not play with these toys" (Emde & Buchsbaum, 1990).

Inducing guilt in children by explaining that their behavior is causing pain or distress is a means of influencing them without using coercion. Guilt reactions are associated with stopping harmful actions, repairing damage caused by misdeeds, and engaging in future prosocial behavior (Baumeister, 1998). At the same time, parents must help children deal with guilt feelings constructively—by guiding them to make up for immoral behavior rather than minimizing or excusing it (Bybee, Merisca, & Velasco, 1998).

Finally, contrary to what Freud believed, guilt is not the only force that compels us to act morally. And moral development is not an abrupt event that is virtually complete by the end of early childhood. Instead, it is gradual process, beginning in the preschool years and extending into adulthood.

When children are low in anxiety, a secure attachment relationship motivates conscience development. This boy wants to follow parental rules to preserve an affectionate, cooperative relationship with his father.

Social Learning Theory

According to the traditional behaviorist view, children pick up new responses through *operant conditioning.* That is, children behave in accord with adult moral standards because parents and teachers *reinforce* "good behavior" with approval, affection, and other rewards.

THE IMPORTANCE OF MODELING ● Despite its role in children's acquisition of moral responses, operant conditioning by itself is not sufficient. For a behavior to be reinforced, it must first occur spontaneously. Yet many prosocial behaviors, such as sharing, helping, and comforting an unhappy playmate, do not occur often enough at first for reinforcement to explain their rapid development. Instead, social learning theorists believe that children largely learn to act morally through *modeling*—by observing and imitating people who demonstrate appropriate behavior (Bandura, 1977; Grusec, 1988). Once children acquire a moral response, such as sharing or telling the truth, reinforcement in the form of praising the act ("That was a very nice thing to do") and the child's character ("You're a very kind and considerate boy") increases its frequency (Mills & Grusec, 1989).

Many studies show that having helpful or generous models increases young children's prosocial responses. And certain characteristics of the model affect children's willingness to imitate:

● *Warmth and responsiveness.* Preschoolers are more likely to copy the prosocial actions of an adult who is warm and responsive than those of one who is cold and distant (Yarrow, Scott, & Waxler, 1973). Warmth seems to make children more attentive and receptive to the model, and is itself an example of a prosocial response.

● *Competence and power.* Children admire and therefore tend to select competent, powerful models to imitate—the reason they are especially willing to copy the behavior of older peers and adults (Bandura, 1977).

● *Consistency between assertions and behavior.* When models say one thing and do another—for example, announce that "it's important to help others" but rarely engage in helpful acts—children generally choose the most lenient standard of behavior that adults demonstrate (Mischel & Liebert, 1966).

Models are most influential during the preschool years. At the end of early childhood, children with a history of consistent exposure to caring adults tend to behave prosocially whether or not a model is present. By that time, they have internalized prosocial rules from repeated observations and encouragement by others (Mussen & Eisenberg-Berg, 1977).

EFFECTS OF PUNISHMENT ● Many parents are aware that yelling at, slapping, and spanking children are ineffective disciplinary tactics. A sharp reprimand or physical force to restrain or move a child is justified when immediate obedience is necessary—for example, when a 3-year-old is about to run into the street. In fact, parents are most likely to use forceful methods under these conditions. When they wish to foster long-term goals, such as acting kindly toward others, they tend to rely on warmth and reasoning (Kuczynski, 1984). And parents often combine power assertion with reasoning in response to serious transgressions, such as lying or stealing (Grusec & Goodnow, 1994).

When used frequently, however, punishment promotes only immediate compliance, not lasting changes in behavior. For example, Robbie's parents often punished by hitting, shouting, and criticizing. Robbie usually engaged in the unacceptable behavior again as soon as his parents were out of sight. Many studies confirm that the more physical punishment children experience, the more likely they are to develop serious, lasting mental health problems. These include weak internalization of moral rules, depression, aggression, antisocial behavior, and poor academic performance during childhood and adolescence, and criminality, depressive and alcoholic symptoms, and partner and child abuse in adulthood (Brezina, 1999; Gershoff, 2002a).

Harsh punishment has undesirable side effects. First, when parents spank, they often do so in response to children's aggression (Holden, Coleman, & Schmidt, 1995). Yet the punishment itself models aggression! Second, children who are frequently punished soon learn to avoid the punishing adult. When Robbie's parents entered the room, Robbie braced himself for something unpleasant and kept his distance. Consequently, they had little opportunity to teach him desirable behaviors. Finally, because punishment "works" temporarily, it offers immediate relief to adults, and they are reinforced for using coercive discipline. For this reason, a punitive adult is likely to punish with greater frequency over time, a course of action that can spiral into serious abuse. Indeed, *corporal punishment*—the use of physical force to inflict pain but not injury—and physical abuse of children are closely linked (Gershoff, 2002a).

The negative outcomes just described occur in children of diverse temperaments (O'Connor et al., 1998). In view of these findings, the widespread use of corporal punishment by North American parents is cause for concern. A survey of a nationally representative sample of American households revealed that although corporal punishment increases from infancy to age 5 and then declines, it is high at all ages (see Figure 10.2). Similarly, more than 70 percent of Canadian parents admit to having hit or spanked their children (Durrant, Broberg, & Rose-Krasnor, 2000; Straus & Stewart, 1999). And many do not limit themselves to a slap or a spank. More than one-fourth of physically punishing parents report having used a hard object to hit their children (Gershoff, 2002b; Straus & Stewart, 1999).

FIGURE 10.2

Prevalence of corporal punishment by child's age. Estimates are based on the percentage of American parents in a nationally representative sample of nearly 1,000 reporting one or more instances of spanking, slapping, pinching, shaking, or hitting with a hard object in the past year. Physical punishment increases sharply during early childhood and then declines, but it is high at all ages. (From M. A. Straus & J. H. Stewart, 1999, "Corporal Punishment by American Parents: National Data on Prevalence, Chronicity, Severity, and Duration in Relation to Child and Family Characteristics," *Clinical Child and Family Psychology Review, 2*, p. 59. Adapted by permission of Kluwer Academic/Plenum Publishers and the author.)

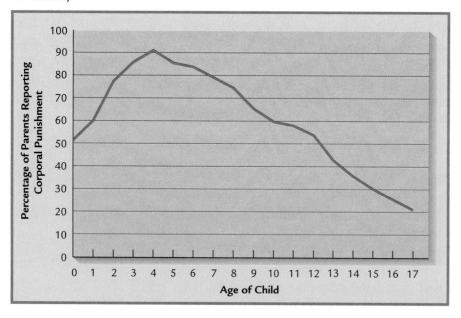

ALTERNATIVES TO HARSH PUNISHMENT ● Alternatives to criticism, slaps, and spankings can reduce the side effects of punishment. A technique called **time out** involves removing children from the immediate setting—for example, by sending them to their rooms—until they are ready to act appropriately. Time out is useful when a child is out of control (Betz, 1994). It usually requires only a few minutes to change behavior, and it also offers a "cooling off" period for angry parents. Another approach is *withdrawal of privileges,* such as playing outside or watching a favorite TV program. Removing privileges may generate some resentment in children, but it allows parents to avoid harsh techniques that could easily intensify into violence.

When parents do decide to use punishment, they can increase its effectiveness in three ways. The first is *consistency*. Permitting children to act inappropriately on some occasions but scolding them on others confuses children, and the unacceptable act persists (Acker & O'Leary, 1996). Second, a *warm parent–child relationship* is vital. Children of involved, caring parents find punishment especially unpleasant and want to regain parental warmth and approval as quickly as possible. Finally, *explanations* help children recall the misdeed and relate it to expectations for future behavior. Pairing reasons with mild punishment (such as time out) leads to a far greater reduction in misbehavior than using punishment alone (Larzelere et al., 1996).

POSITIVE DISCIPLINE ● The most effective forms of discipline encourage good conduct—by building a mutually respectful bond with the child, letting her know ahead of time how to act, and praising mature behavior (Zahn-Waxler & Robinson, 1995). When preschoolers have cooperative relationships with parents, they show firmer conscience development—behaving responsibly, playing fairly in games, and considering others' welfare (Kochanska & Murray, 2000). Parent–child closeness leads children to want to meet parental demands out of a sense of commitment to the relationship.

Consult Applying What We Know on page 376 for ways to discipline positively. Notice that parents who use these strategies focus on long-term social and life skills—cooperation, problem solving, and consideration for others. As a result, they greatly reduce the need for punishment.

Parents who engage in positive discipline encourage good conduct by building a cooperative relationship with their children and letting them know ahead of time how to act. They also reduce opportunities for misbehavior. These parents brought along plenty of activities to keep their children occupied during a long plane trip.

The Cognitive-Developmental Perspective

The psychoanalytic and behaviorist approaches to morality focus on how children acquire ready-made standards of good conduct from adults. In contrast, the cognitive-developmental perspective regards children as *active thinkers* about social rules. As early as the preschool years, children make moral judgments, deciding what is right or wrong on the basis of concepts they construct about justice and fairness (Gibbs, 2003).

Piaget's (1932/1965) work served as the inspiration for the cognitive-developmental approach to morality. Today, we know that Piaget underestimated young children's moral understanding, just as he did their ability to think about their physical world (see Chapter 9). We will consider his theory of moral development in Chapter 16, when we focus on major changes in moral reasoning from childhood to adolescence.

PRESCHOOLERS' MORAL UNDERSTANDING ● Young children have some well-developed ideas about morality. Three-year-olds know that a child who intentionally knocks a playmate off a swing is worse than one who does so accidentally (Yuill & Perner, 1988). Around age 4, children can tell the difference between truthfulness and lying (Bussey, 1992). And by the end of early childhood, children consider a person's intentions in evaluating lying. Influenced by collectivist values of social harmony and humility, Chinese children are more likely than Canadian children to judge lying favorably when an intention involves modesty—for example, when a child who generously picks up garbage in the school yard says, "I didn't do it." In contrast, both Chinese and Canadian children rate lying about antisocial acts as "very naughty" (Lee et al., 1997, 2001).

Furthermore, preschoolers in diverse cultures distinguish *moral imperatives,* which protect people's rights and welfare, from two other types of action: *social conventions,* or customs such as table manners and dress styles; and *matters of personal choice,* which do not violate rights and are up to the individual (Ardila-Rey & Killen, 2001; Nucci, 1996; Yan & Smetana, 2003). Three- and 4-year-olds judge moral violations (stealing an apple) as more wrong than social-conventional violations (eating ice cream with fingers). They also say that moral violations would still be wrong if an adult did not see them and no rules existed to prohibit them, because they harm others. And between ages 3 and 7, children increasingly judge that they should make certain personal

Applying
WHAT WE Know / Using Positive Discipline

STRATEGY	EXPLANATION
Use transgressions as opportunities to teach.	When a child engages in harmful or unsafe behavior, use induction, which motivates children to make amends and behave prosocially.
Reduce opportunities for misbehavior.	On a long car trip, bring back-seat activities that relieve children's restlessness. At the supermarket, converse with children and permit them to assist with shopping. As a result, children learn to occupy themselves constructively when options are limited.
Provide reasons for rules.	When children appreciate that rules are fair to all concerned, not arbitrary, they strive to follow the rules because they are reasonable and rational.
Arrange for children to participate in family routines and duties.	By joining with adults in preparing a meal, washing dishes, or raking leaves, children develop a sense of responsible participation in family and community life and acquire many practical skills.
When children are obstinate, try compromising and problem solving.	When a child refuses to obey, express understanding of the child's feelings ("I know it's not fun to clean up"), suggest a compromise ("You put those away, I'll take care of these"), and help the child think of ways to avoid the problem in the future. Responding firmly but kindly and respectfully increases the likelihood of willing cooperation.
Encourage mature behavior.	Express confidence in children's capacity to learn and appreciation for effort and cooperation, as in "You gave that your best!" "Thanks for helping!" Adult encouragement fosters pride and satisfaction in succeeding, thereby inspiring children to improve further.
Be sensitive to children's physical and emotional resources.	When children are tired, ill, or bored, they are likely to engage in attention-getting, disorganized, or otherwise improper behavior as a reaction to discomfort. In these instances, meeting the child's needs makes more sense than disciplining.

Sources: Berk, 2001a; Nelson, 1996.

decisions, such as choosing play activities and friends. This concern with personal choice serves as the springboard for moral concepts of individual rights (Killen & Smetana, 1999).

How do young children arrive at these distinctions? According to cognitive-developmental theorists, they do so by *actively making sense* of their experiences. They observe that after a moral offense, peers react emotionally, describe their own injury or loss, tell another child to stop, or retaliate (Arsenio & Fleiss, 1996). And an adult who intervenes is likely to call attention to the rights and feelings of the victim. In contrast, peers seldom react to violations of social convention. And in these situations, adults tend to demand obedience without explanation or point to the importance of keeping order.

SOCIAL EXPERIENCE AND MORAL UNDERSTANDING ● Although cognition and language support preschoolers' moral understanding, social experiences are vital. Disputes with siblings and peers over rights, possessions, and property give preschoolers opportunities to work out their first ideas about justice and fairness (Killen & Nucci, 1995). The way adults handle rule violations and discuss moral issues also helps children reason about morality. Children who are advanced in moral thinking and prosocial behavior have parents who adapt their communications about fighting, honesty, and ownership to what their child can understand, who respect the child's opinion, and who gently stimulate the child to think further, without being hostile or critical (Janssens & Deković, 1997; Walker & Taylor, 1991a).

Preschoolers who are disliked by peers because of their aggressive approach to resolving conflict have difficulty distinguishing moral rules from social conventions, and they violate both often (Sanderson & Siegal, 1988). Without special help, such children show long-term disruptions in moral development.

The Other Side of Morality: Development of Aggression

Beginning in late infancy, all children display aggression from time to time, and as opportunities to interact with siblings and peers increase, aggressive outbursts occur more often (Tremblay, 2002). During the early preschool years, two general types of aggression emerge. The most common is **instrumental aggression,** in which children want an object, privilege, or space, and in trying to get it, they push, shout at, or otherwise attack a person who is in the way. The other type, **hostile aggression,** is meant to hurt another person.

Hostile aggression comes in at least two varieties. The first is **overt aggression,** which harms others through physical injury or the threat of such injury. The second is **relational aggression,** which damages another's peer relationships, as in social exclusion and rumor spreading. "Go away, I'm not your friend!" and "Don't play with Margie; she's a nerd" are examples.

Both the form of aggression and the way it is expressed change with age. Between 2 and 6 years, physical aggression gradually is replaced by verbal aggression (Tremblay et al., 1999). And instrumental aggression declines as preschoolers learn to compromise over possessions. In contrast, hostile outbursts rise over early and middle childhood (Tremblay, 2000). Older preschoolers are better able to recognize malicious intentions, and as a result, they more often retaliate in hostile ways.

On average, boys are more overtly aggressive than girls, a trend that appears in many cultures (Whiting & Edwards, 1988b). The sex difference is due in part to biology—in particular, to male sex hormones, or androgens. Androgens contribute to boys' greater physical activity, which may increase their opportunities for physically aggressive encounters. (Collaer & Hines, 1995). At the same time, gender typing (a topic we will take up shortly) is important. As soon as 2-year-olds become dimly aware of gender stereotypes—that males and females are expected to behave differently—overt aggression drops off more sharply for girls than for boys (Fagot & Leinbach, 1989).

But preschool and school-age girls are not less aggressive than boys! Instead, they express their hostility differently—through relational aggression (Crick, Casas, & Mosher, 1997; Crick, Casas, & Ku, 1999). When trying to harm a peer, children do so in ways especially likely to thwart that child's social goals. Boys more often attack physically to block the dominance goals typical of boys. Girls resort to relational aggression because it interferes with the close, intimate bonds especially important to girls.

An occasional aggressive exchange between preschoolers is normal. As we saw earlier, they sometimes assert their sense of self through these encounters, which become important learning experiences as adults intervene and teach social problem solving (Vaughn et al., 2003). But some young children—especially those who are impulsive and disobedient—are at risk for lasting difficulties. In longitudinal research conducted in Canada, New Zealand, and the United States, boys who were highly aggressive in kindergarten were far more likely to engage in violent delinquency as adolescents (Brame, Nagin, & Tremblay, 2001; Nagin & Tremblay, 1999). And a study of Canadian girls revealed a similar link between disruptive, disobedient behavior in childhood and adolescent conduct problems (Coté et al., 2001). These negative outcomes, however, depend on child-rearing conditions.

THE FAMILY AS TRAINING GROUND FOR AGGRESSIVE BEHAVIOR ● "I can't control him; he's impossible," complained Nadine, Robbie's mother, to Leslie one day. When Leslie asked if Robbie might be troubled by something going on at home, she discovered that his parents fought constantly. Their conflict led to high levels of family stress and a "spillover" of hostility into child rearing. The same parenting practices that undermine moral internalization and self-control predict aggression. Love withdrawal, power assertion, negative comments and emotions, physical punishment, and inconsistent discipline are linked to antisocial behavior from early childhood through adolescence, in children of both sexes (Rubin et al., 2003; Stormshak et al., 2000).

Observations in families like Robbie's reveal that anger and punitiveness quickly create a conflict-ridden family atmosphere and an "out of control" child. The pattern begins with forceful discipline, which

An occasional expression of aggression is normal in early childhood. This preschooler displays instrumental aggression as she grabs an attractive toy from a classmate. Instrumental aggression declines with age as children learn how to compromise and share.

© LAURA DWIGHT

occurs more often with stressful life experiences (such as economic hardship or an unhappy marriage), a parent's unstable personality, or a temperamentally difficult child (Coie & Dodge, 1998). Once the parent threatens, criticizes, and punishes, the child whines, yells, and refuses until the parent "gives in." At the end of each exchange, both parent and child get relief from stopping the unpleasant behavior of the other, so the behaviors repeat and escalate.

Soon these cycles generate anxiety and irritability in other family members, who join in the hostile interactions. Compared with siblings in typical families, preschool siblings who have critical, punitive parents are more verbally and physically aggressive toward one another. Destructive sibling conflict, in turn, contributes to a rise in poor impulse control and antisocial behavior by the early school years (Dunn & Munn, 1986; Garcia et al., 2000).

Because they are more active, impulsive, and thus harder to control, boys are more likely than girls to be targets of harsh, physical discipline and parental inconsistency. Children who are products of these family processes soon view the world from a violent perspective. Because they expect others to react with anger and physical force, they see hostile intent where it does not exist and make many unprovoked attacks (Weiss et al., 1992). Soon they conclude that aggression "works" to produce rewards—getting others to comply and relieving teasing, taunting, and other unpleasant behaviors. And they come to value this control over others (Egan, Monson, & Perry, 1998).

Because of their hostility and poor self-control, highly aggressive children tend to be rejected by peers, to fail in school, and to form relationships with deviant peers. Together, these factors contribute to the long-term stability of aggression, evident in violence and other conduct problems (see Chapter 16).

VIOLENT MEDIA AND AGGRESSION ● According to a large-scale survey, 57 percent of American TV programs between 6 A.M. and 11 P.M. contain violent scenes. In fact, most TV violence does not show victims experiencing any serious harm, and few programs condemn violence or depict other ways of solving problems. Violent content is 9 percent above average in children's programming, and cartoons are the most violent (Center for Communication and Social Policy, 1998). Although Canadian broadcasters follow a code that sharply restricts televised violence, Canadians devote two-thirds of their viewing time to American channels (Statistics Canada, 2003d).

Children are especially likely to be influenced by television. One reason is that before age 8, they fail to understand a great deal of what they see on TV. Two- and 3-year-olds do not discriminate televised images from real objects; they say that a bowl of popcorn on television would spill if the TV were turned upside down (Flavell et al., 1990). And because preschoolers have difficulty connecting separate scenes into a meaningful story line, they do not relate the actions of a TV character to motives or consequences (Collins, 1983). A villain who gets what he wants by punching, shooting, and killing may not be a "bad guy" to a preschooler, who does not realize that the character was brought to justice in the end. Young children also find it hard to separate true-to-life from fantasized television content. Not until age 7 do they fully grasp the unreality of TV fiction—that characters do not retain their roles in real life and that their behavior is scripted (Wright et al., 1994). These misunderstandings increase children's willingness to uncritically accept and imitate what they see on TV.

Reviewers of thousands of studies have concluded that television provides children with "an extensive how-to course in aggression" (Comstock & Scharrer, 1999; Slaby et al., 1995, p. 163). And a growing number of investigations indicate that playing violent video and computer games has similar effects—heightening hostile thoughts and behavior and reducing prosocial acts (Anderson & Bushman, 2001). The case is strengthened by the fact that research using a wide variety of research designs, methods, and participants yields similar findings.

Violent programming not only creates short-term difficulties in parent and peer relations but also has lasting, negative consequences. In three longitudinal studies, time spent watching TV in childhood and adolescence predicted aggressive behavior in early adulthood, after other factors linked to TV viewing (such as child and parent prior aggression, IQ, parent education, family income, and neighborhood crime) were controlled (see Figure 10.3) (Huesmann, 1986; Huesmann et al., 2003; Johnson et al., 2002). Highly aggressive youngsters have

Using television to promote children's prosocial behavior and active engagement with their surroundings is a great challenge for American parents, given the antisocial content of many programs. Here a trip to a petting zoo brings to life an educational TV program on wildlife.

© LAWRENCE MIGDALE/PIX

a greater appetite for violent TV and computer games. As they view more, they become especially likely to resort to hostile ways of solving problems. But violent TV sparks hostile thoughts and behavior even in nonaggressive children; its impact is simply less intense (Bushman & Huesmann, 2001).

Furthermore, media violence "hardens" children to aggression, making them more willing to tolerate it in others. Heavy TV viewers believe that there is much more violence and danger in society, an effect that is especially strong for children who perceive televised aggression as relevant to their own lives (Donnerstein, Slaby, & Eron, 1994). As these responses indicate, violent media images modify children's attitudes toward social reality so they increasingly match what children see on TV.

The ease with which television and computer games can manipulate the beliefs and behavior of children has resulted in strong public pressures to improve its content. In the United States, the First Amendment right to free speech has hampered these efforts. Instead, broadcasters must rate television programs, and manufacturers must build the V-Chip (also called the Violence Chip) into new TV sets so parents can block undesired violent and sexual material. Canada also mandates the V-Chip, along with a program rating system. In addition, Canada's broadcasting code bans from children's shows realistic scenes of violence that minimize consequences and cartoons in which violence is the central theme. Further, violent programming intended for adults cannot be shown on Canadian channels before 9 P.M. (Canadian Broadcast Standards Council, 2003). Still, Canadian children can access violent TV fare on American channels.

At present, it is largely up to parents to regulate their children's exposure to media violence and other inappropriate content. The V-Chip is an incomplete solution, partly because ratings that indicate violent, sexual, and offensive-language material make certain TV shows more appealing to some youngsters (Cantor & Harrison, 1997). And as they get older, children may go to other homes to watch programs and play games forbidden by their own parents. Applying What We Know on page 380 lists strategies parents can use to protect children from unfavorable TV and computer fare.

HELPING CHILDREN AND PARENTS CONTROL AGGRESSION ● Treatment for aggressive children must begin early, before their antisocial behavior becomes so well practiced that it is difficult to change. Breaking the cycle of hostilities between family members and replacing it with effective interaction styles is crucial. The coercive cycles of punitive parents and aggressive children are so persistent that these children often get punished when they do behave appropriately (Strassberg, 1995).

Leslie suggested that Robbie's parents see a family therapist, who observed their inept practices and coached them in alternatives. They learned not to give in to Robbie, to pair commands with reasons, and to replace verbal insults and spankings with more effective punishments, such as time out and withdrawal of privileges (Patterson, 1982). The therapist also encouraged Robbie's parents to be warmer and to give him attention and approval for prosocial acts. And she helped them with their marital problems. This, in addition to their improved ability to manage Robbie's behavior, greatly reduced tension and conflict in the household.

At the same time, Leslie began teaching Robbie more successful ways of relating to peers, had him practice these skills, and praised him whenever she noticed him using them. And as opportunities arose, she encouraged Robbie to talk about a playmate's feelings and to express his own. This helped Robbie take the perspective of others, empathize, and feel sympathetic concern (Denham, 1998). Robbie also participated in social problem-solving training (return to pages 369–370 to review). These interventions reduce conduct problems in preschool and school-age children and help them develop more rewarding relationships with teachers and peers. But they work far more effectively when parents replace harsh, critical tactics with positive, consistent discipline (Webster-Stratton, Reid, & Hammond, 2001).

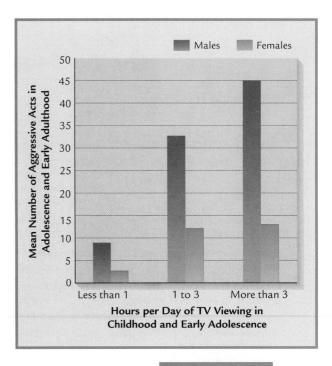

FIGURE 10.3

Relationship of television viewing in childhood and early adolescence to aggressive acts in adolescence and early adulthood.

Interviews with more than 700 parents and youths revealed that the more TV watched in childhood and early adolescence, the greater the annual number of aggressive acts committed by the young person, as reported in follow-up interviews at ages 16 and 22. (Adapted from Johnson et al., 2002.)

Applying
WHAT WE Know / Regulating Children's TV Viewing and Computer Use

STRATEGY	EXPLANATION
Limit TV viewing and computer use.	Provide clear rules that limit what children can view—for example, an hour a day and only certain programs—and stick to the rules. Avoid using the TV or the computer as a baby-sitter. Do not place a TV or computer in the child's bedroom; doing so increases use by as much as 40 minutes per day among school-age children
Refrain from using TV or computer time to reward or punish children.	When TV or computer access is used to reward or punish children, they become increasingly attracted to it.
Encourage child-appropriate TV and computer experiences.	Children who engage in TV and computer activities that are educational, prosocial, and age-appropriate gain in cognitive and social skills.
View TV with children, helping them understand what they see.	When adults express disapproval of on-screen behavior, raise questions about its realism, and encourage children to discuss it, they teach children to evaluate TV content rather than accepting it uncritically.
Link televised content to everyday learning experiences.	Building on TV programs in constructive ways enhances learning by encouraging children into active engagement with their surroundings. For example, a program on animals might spark a trip to the zoo, a visit to the library for books about animals, or new ways of observing and caring for the family pet.
Model good TV and computer practices.	Avoid excess television viewing, and exposure to violent media content, yourself. Parental viewing patterns influence children's viewing patterns.
Use a warm, rational approach to child rearing.	Children of warm parents who make reasonable demands for mature behavior prefer TV and computer experiences with educational and prosocial content and are less attracted to violent media fare.

Source: Wiecha et al., 2001; Winn, 2002.

Finally, relieving stressors that stem from poverty and neighborhood disorganization and providing families with social supports help prevent childhood aggression (Boyle & Lipman, 2002). These efforts improve parents' capacity to discipline effectively, and they are linked to a dramatic reduction in children's behavior problems.

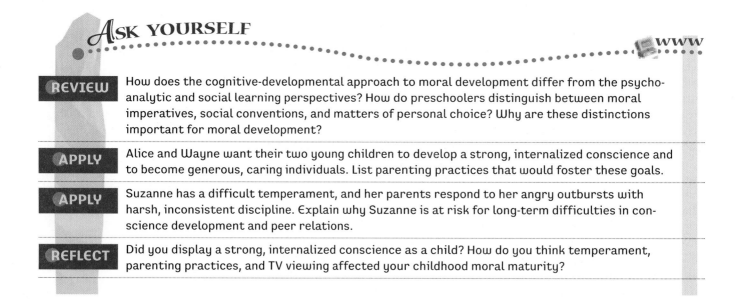

Ask YOURSELF

www

REVIEW How does the cognitive-developmental approach to moral development differ from the psycho-analytic and social learning perspectives? How do preschoolers distinguish between moral imperatives, social conventions, and matters of personal choice? Why are these distinctions important for moral development?

APPLY Alice and Wayne want their two young children to develop a strong, internalized conscience and to become generous, caring individuals. List parenting practices that would foster these goals.

APPLY Suzanne has a difficult temperament, and her parents respond to her angry outbursts with harsh, inconsistent discipline. Explain why Suzanne is at risk for long-term difficulties in conscience development and peer relations.

REFLECT Did you display a strong, internalized conscience as a child? How do you think temperament, parenting practices, and TV viewing affected your childhood moral maturity?

Gender Typing

The process of developing *gender roles,* or gender-linked preferences and behaviors valued by the larger society, is called **gender typing.** Early in the preschool years, gender typing is well under way. In Leslie's classroom, children tended to play and form friendships with peers of their own sex. Girls spent more time in the housekeeping, art, and reading corners, whereas boys gathered more often in spaces devoted to blocks, woodworking, and active play.

The same theories that provide accounts of morality have been used to explain gender-role development. According to *psychoanalytic theory,* gender-stereotyped beliefs and behaviors develop through identification with the same-sex parent. But as in the area of morality, Freud's ideas have difficulty. Research shows that the same-sex parent is only one of many influences on gender typing. The other-sex parent, peers, siblings, teachers, and the broader social environment are important as well.

Social learning theory, with its emphasis on modeling and reinforcement, and *cognitive-developmental theory,* with its focus on children as active thinkers about their social world, are major current approaches. We will see that neither is adequate by itself. Consequently, a third perspective that combines elements of both, called *gender schema theory,* has gained favor. In the following sections, we consider the early development of gender typing.

Gender-Stereotyped Beliefs and Behaviors

Before children can label their own sex consistently, they "tune in" to gender differences and stereotypes. To find out how early children form gender stereotypes, researchers showed toddlers pairs of gender-stereotyped toys (vehicles and dolls). Twelve-month-old boys and girls differed very little in their visual preference. But by 18 months, boys looked much longer than girls at vehicles, whereas girls looked much longer than boys at dolls (Serbin et al., 2001). Even more remarkable, children of this age have begun to acquire the subtle associations with gender that most of us hold—men as rough and sharp and women as soft and round. In a recent study, 18-month-olds linked such items as fir trees, bears, and hammers with males, although they had not yet learned similar feminine associations (Eichstedt et al., 2002).

Recall from Chapter 7 that between 18 and 30 months, children begin to label their own and others' sex, using such words as "boy" and "girl" and "lady" and "man." Once these categories are in place, children rapidly sort out what they mean in terms of activities and behaviors. Preschoolers associate toys, articles of clothing, tools, household items and activities, games, occupations, and colors (pink and blue) with one sex or the other (Poulin-Dubois et al., 2002; Ruble & Martin, 1998). And their actions tend to fall in line with their beliefs—not only in play preferences but also in personality traits. We have already seen that boys tend to be more active, impulsive, assertive, and overtly aggressive, whereas girls tend to be more fearful, dependent, compliant, considerate, emotionally sensitive, and relationally aggressive (Eisenberg & Fabes, 1998; Feingold, 1994; Geary, 1998; Saarni, 1993).

Over the preschool years, children's gender-stereotyped beliefs become stronger—so much so that they operate as blanket rules rather than flexible guidelines (Biernat, 1991; Martin, 1989). Once, when Leslie showed the children a picture of a Scottish bagpiper wearing a kilt, they insisted, "Men don't wear skirts!" During free play, they often exclaimed that girls can't be police officers and boys don't take care of babies. These one-sided ideas are a joint product of gender stereotyping in the environment and preschoolers' cognitive limitations—in particular, their difficulty coordinating conflicting sources of information. Most preschoolers do not yet realize that characteristics *associated with* one's sex—activities, toys,

© E. ZUCKERMAN/PHOTOEDIT

Gender-stereotyped game and toy choices are present before age 2 and strengthen over the preschool years. Already, these 3-year-olds play in highly gender-stereotyped ways.

occupations, hairstyle, and clothing—do not *determine* whether a person is male or female. They have trouble understanding that males and females can be different in terms of their bodies but similar in many other ways.

Biological Influences on Gender Typing

The sex differences just described appear in many cultures around the world (Whiting & Edwards, 1988a). Certain of them—the preference for same-sex playmates as well as male activity level and overt aggression—are also widespread among mammalian species (Beatty, 1992; de Waal, 1993). According to an evolutionary perspective, the adult life of our male ancestors was oriented toward competing for mates, that of our female ancestors toward rearing children. Therefore, males became genetically primed for dominance and females for intimacy and responsiveness. Evolutionary theorists claim that family and cultural forces can affect the intensity of biologically based sex differences, leading some individuals to be more gender typed than others. But experience cannot eradicate those aspects of gender typing that served adaptive functions in human history (Geary, 1999; Maccoby, 2002).

Experiments with animals reveal that prenatally administered androgens (male sex hormones) increase active play and suppress maternal caregiving in many mammals. Eleanor Maccoby (1998) argues that hormones also affect human play styles, leading to rough, noisy movements among boys and calm, gentle actions among girls. Then, as children interact with peers, they choose partners whose interests and behaviors are compatible with their own. Consistent with this view, over the preschool years, girls increasingly seek out other girls and like to play in pairs because of a common preference for quieter activities involving cooperative roles. And boys come to prefer larger-group play with other boys, who share a desire to run, climb, play-fight, compete, and build up and knock down (Fabes, Martin, & Hanish, 2003). At age 4, children spend 3 to 6 times as much time with same-sex as with other-sex playmates. By age 6, this ratio has climbed to 11 to 1 (Maccoby & Jacklin, 1987; Martin & Fabes, 2001).

Even stronger support for the role of biology in human gender typing comes from research on girls exposed to high levels of androgens prenatally, due either to normal variation in hormone levels or to a genetic defect. In both instances, these girls showed more "masculine" behavior—a preference for trucks and blocks over dolls, for active over quiet play, and for boys as playmates (Berenbaum, Duck, & Bryk, 2000; Hines et al., 2002). And additional evidence comes from a case study of a boy who experienced serious sexual-identity and adjustment problems because his biological makeup and sex of rearing were at odds. Refer to the Biology and Environment box on the following page to find out about David's development. Note, also, that David's reflections on his upbringing caution us against minimizing the role of experience in gender typing. As we will see next, environmental forces build on genetic influences to promote children's awareness of and conformity to gender roles.

Environmental Influences on Gender Typing

A wealth of evidence reveals that family influences, encouragement by teachers and peers, and examples in the broader social environment combine to promote the vigorous gender typing of early childhood.

THE FAMILY ● Beginning at birth, parents hold different perceptions and expectations of their sons and daughters (see Chapter 7). Many parents state that they want their children to play with "gender-appropriate" toys, and when asked about their child-rearing values, parents describe achievement, competition, and control of emotion as important for sons and cite warmth, "ladylike" behavior, and closely supervised activities as important for daughters (Brody, 1999; Turner & Gervai, 1995).

These beliefs carry over into parenting practices. Parents give toys that stress action and competition (such as guns, cars, tools, and footballs) to boys. They give toys that emphasize nurturance, cooperation, and physical attractiveness (dolls, tea sets, jewelry, and jump ropes) to girls (Leaper, 1994). Parents also actively reinforce independence in boys and dependency in girls. For

Biology and Environment

David: A Boy Who Was Reared as a Girl

A married man and a father in his mid-thirties, David Reimer talked freely about his interest in auto mechanics, his problems at work, and the challenges of child rearing. But when asked about his first 15 years of life, he distanced himself, speaking as though the child of his early life were another person. In essence, she was.

David—named Bruce at birth—underwent the first infant sex reassignment ever reported on a genetically and hormonally normal child. To find out about David's development, researchers intensively interviewed him and studied his medical and psychotherapy records (Diamond & Sigmundson, 1999; Colapinto, 2001).

At age 8 months, Bruce's penis was accidentally severed during circumcision. His desperate parents soon heard about psychologist John Money's success in assigning a sex to children born with ambiguous genitals. They traveled from their home in Canada to Johns Hopkins University in Baltimore, where under Money's oversight, 22-month-old Bruce had surgery to remove his testicles and sculpt his genitals to look like those of a girl. The operation complete, Bruce's parents named their daughter Brenda.

Research on infants with ambiguous genitals indicates that a parent-chosen sex assignment usually works out (Zucker, 2001). But because of an imbalance in prenatal sex hormones, the organization of those children's central nervous systems might also be ambiguous, permitting development as either a male or a female. Brenda's upbringing, in contrast, was tragic. From the outset, she resisted her parents' efforts to steer her in a "feminine" direction.

Brian (Brenda's identical twin brother) recalled that Brenda looked like a delicate, pretty girl—until she moved or spoke. "She walked like a guy. Sat with her legs apart. She talked about guy things. . . . She played with my toys: Tinkertoys, dump trucks" (Colapinto, 2001, p. 57). Brian was quiet and gentle in personality. Brenda, in contrast, was a dom-inant, rough-and-tumble child who picked fights with other children and usually won. Former teachers and classmates agreed that Brenda was the more traditionally masculine of the two children.

At school, Brenda's boyish behavior led classmates to taunt and tease her. When she played with girls, she tried organizing large-group, active games, but they weren't interested. Uncomfortable as a girl and without friends, Brenda displayed increasing behavior problems. During periodic medical follow-ups, she drew pictures of herself as a boy and refused additional surgery to create a vagina. Reflecting on Brenda's elementary school years, David explained that she realized she was not a girl and never would be.

As adolescence approached, Brenda's parents moved her from school to school and therapist to therapist, in an effort to help her fit in socially and accept a female identity. Brenda reacted with anxiety and insecurity, and conflict with her parents increased. At puberty, Brenda's shoulders broadened and her body added muscle, so her parents insisted that she begin estrogen therapy to feminize her appearance. Soon she grew breasts and added fat around her waist and hips. Repelled by her own feminizing shape, Brenda began overeating to hide it. Her classmates reacted to her confused appearance with stepped-up brutality.

At last, Brenda was transferred to a therapist who recognized her despair and encouraged her parents to tell her about her infancy. When Brenda was 14, her father explained the circumcision accident. David recalled reacting with relief. Deciding to return to his biological sex immediately, he chose for himself the name David, after the biblical lad who slew a giant and overcame adversity. David soon started injections of the androgen hormone testosterone to masculinize his body, and he underwent surgery to remove his breasts and to construct a penis. Although his adolescence continued to be troubled, in his twenties he fell in

Because of a tragic medical accident when he was a baby, David Reimer underwent the first sex reassignment on a genetically and hormonally normal baby: He was reared as a girl. His case shows the overwhelming impact of biology on gender identity. David is pictured here at age 36, a married man and a father.

love with Jane, a single mother of three children, and married her.

David's case confirms the impact of genetic sex and prenatal hormones on a person's sense of self as male or female. At the same time, his childhood highlights the importance of experience. David expressed outrage at adult encouragement of dependency in girls, having experienced it firsthand. In adulthood, David worked in a slaughterhouse with all male employees, who were extreme in their gender stereotyping. At one point he wondered—if he had had a typical childhood, would he have become like them? We can never know the answer to that question, but his case does clarify one issue: His gender reassignment failed because his male biology overwhelmingly demanded a consistent sexual identity.

Although David tried to surmount his tragic childhood, the troubled life that sprang from it persisted. During his final two years, his brother committed suicide. And after David lost his job and then his life savings in a shady investment deal, his wife separated from him, taking the children. Grief stricken, David sank into a deep depression. On May 4, 2004, at age 38, he shot himself.

example, they react more positively when a son plays with cars and trucks, demands attention, or tries to take toys from others. In contrast, they more often direct play activities, provide help, encourage participation in household tasks, and refer to emotions when interacting with daughters (Fagot & Hagan, 1991; Kuebli, Butler, & Fivush, 1995; Leaper, 2000). Furthermore, mothers more often *label emotions* when talking to girls, thereby teaching them to "tune in" to others' feelings. In contrast, they more often *explain emotions,* noting causes and consequences, to boys—an approach that emphasizes why it is important to control the expression of emotion (Cervantes & Callanan, 1998).

In most aspects of differential treatment of boys and girls, fathers discriminate more than mothers do. In Chapter 7 we saw that fathers tend to engage in more physically stimulating play with their infant sons than with their infant daughters, whereas mothers usually play in a quieter way with infants of both sexes. In childhood, fathers more than mothers encourage "gender-appropriate" behavior, and they place more pressure to achieve on sons than on daughters (Gervai, Turner, & Hinde, 1995; Lytton & Romney, 1991).

These factors influence gender-role learning, since parents who hold nonstereotyped values and apply them in their daily lives have less gender-typed children (Turner & Gervai, 1995; Tenenbaum & Leaper, 2002; Weisner & Wilson-Mitchell, 1990). Other family members also contribute to gender typing. For example, children with older, other-sex siblings have many more opportunities to imitate and participate in "cross-gender" activities and, as a result, are less gender typed in play preferences, attitudes, and personality traits (McHale et al., 2001; Rust et al., 2000).

In any case, of the two sexes, boys are clearly the more gender typed. One reason is that parents—particularly fathers—more strongly encourage "gender-appropriate" behavior in sons than in daughters (Wood, Desmarais, & Gugula, 2002). They are more concerned if a boy acts like a "sissy" than if a girl acts like a "tomboy."

TEACHERS ● Teachers also encourage children's gender typing. Several times, Leslie caught herself responding in ways that furthered sex segregation and stereotyping in her classroom (Thorne, 1993). One day she called out, "Will the girls line up on one side and the boys on the other?" Then, as the class became noisy, she pleaded, "Boys, I wish you'd quiet down like the girls!"

As at home, girls get more encouragement to participate in adult-structured activities at preschool. They can frequently be seen clustered around the teacher, following directions in an activity. In contrast, boys more often choose areas of the classroom where teachers are minimally involved (Carpenter, 1983; Powlishta, Serbin, & Moller, 1993). As a result, boys and girls engage in very different social behaviors. Compliance and bids for help occur more often in adult-structured contexts, whereas assertiveness, leadership, and creative use of materials appear more often in unstructured pursuits.

PEERS ● The extent to which children associate almost exclusively with peers of their own sex makes the peer context an especially potent source of gender-role learning. The more preschoolers play with same-sex partners, the more their behavior becomes gender typed—in toy choices, activity level, aggression, and involvement of adults (Martin & Fabes, 2001). By age 3, same-sex peers positively reinforce one another for gender-typed play by praising, imitating, or joining in. Similarly, when preschoolers engage in "cross-gender" activities—for example, when boys play with dolls, or girls with trucks—peers criticize them. Boys are especially intolerant of "cross-gender" play in their male companions (Fagot, 1984). A boy who frequently crosses gender lines is likely to be ignored by other boys even when he does engage in "masculine" activities!

Children also develop different styles of social influence in sex-segregated peer groups. To get their way in large-group play, boys often rely on commands, threats, and physical force. Girls' preference for playing in pairs leads to greater concern with a partner's needs, evident in girls' use of polite requests, persuasion, and acceptance. Girls soon find that these gentle tactics succeed with other girls but not with boys, who ignore their courteous overtures (Leaper, 1994; Leaper, Tenenbaum, & Shaffer, 1999). Consequently, an additional reason why girls may stop interacting with boys is that they do not find it very rewarding to communicate with an unresponsive social partner.

Over time, children form beliefs about peers' play preferences, which contribute further to sex segregation. In one study, 3- to 6-year-olds believed that peers would be more likely to approve of their behavior when they played with same-sex agemates—a conviction that predicted children's association with same-sex peers (Martin et al., 1999). As preschool-age boys and girls separate, they view their own group more positively and the other group more negatively — a bias that also characterizes adults (Nesdale & Flesser, 2001). This *own-sex favoritism* further sustains boys' and girls' separate social worlds, which—in the words of one expert—result in "two distinct subcultures" of shared knowledge, beliefs, interests, and behaviors (Maccoby, 2002, p. 57).

THE BROADER SOCIAL ENVIRONMENT ● Finally, although children's everyday environments have changed to some degree, they continue to present many examples of gender typing—in occupations, leisure activities, competencies, and achievements of men and women (Ruble & Martin, 1998). For example, TV viewing is linked to children's endorsement of many gender stereotypes. Although today's programs include more career-oriented women than in the past, female characters continue to be young, attractive, caring, emotional, victimized, and in romantic and family contexts. In contrast, male characters are usually dominant and powerful (Signorielli, 2001). Gender stereotypes are especially prevalent in cartoons, music television (MTV), and other entertainment programs for children and youths. And in video and computer games, gender stereotyping is rampant (Dietz, 1998).

As we will see in the next section, children do more than imitate the many gender-linked responses they observe. They also start to view themselves and their environment in gender-biased ways, a perspective that can seriously restrict their interests, experiences, and skills.

Gender Identity

As adults, each of us has a **gender identity**—an image of oneself as relatively masculine or feminine in characteristics. By middle childhood, researchers can measure gender identity by asking children to rate themselves on personality traits. A child or adult with a "masculine" identity scores high on traditionally masculine items (such as ambitious, competitive, and self-sufficient) and low on traditionally feminine items (such as affectionate, cheerful, and soft-spoken). Someone with a "feminine" identity does just the reverse. Although most people view themselves in gender-typed terms, a substantial minority (especially females) have a gender identity called **androgyny,** scoring high on *both* masculine and feminine personality characteristics.

Gender identity is a good predictor of psychological adjustment. Masculine and androgynous children and adults have higher self-esteem, whereas feminine individuals often think poorly of themselves, perhaps because many feminine traits are not highly valued by society (Alpert-Gillis & Connell, 1989; Boldizar, 1991). Also, androgynous individuals are more adaptable—for example, able to show masculine independence or feminine sensitivity, depending on the situation (Taylor & Hall, 1982). Research on androgyny shows that children can acquire a mixture of positive qualities traditionally associated with each gender—an orientation that may best help them realize their potential.

EMERGENCE OF GENDER IDENTITY ● How do children develop a gender identity? Both social learning and cognitive-developmental answers exist. According to *social learning theory,* behavior comes before self-perceptions. Preschoolers first acquire gender-typed responses through modeling and reinforcement. Only later do they organize these behaviors into gender-linked ideas about themselves. In contrast, *cognitive-developmental theory* maintains that self-perceptions come before behavior. That is, children first acquire a cognitive appreciation of the permanence of their sex, or **gender constancy**—the understanding that sex is biologically based and remains the same even if clothing, hairstyle, and play activities change. Then children use this idea to guide their behavior (Kohlberg, 1966).

Research indicates that gender constancy is not fully developed until the end of the preschool years, when children pass Piagetian conservation tasks (De Lisi & Gallagher, 1991). Shown a doll whose hairstyle and clothing are transformed before their eyes, children younger than age 6 typically indicate that the doll's sex has changed as well (McConaghy, 1979). And when asked such questions as "When you (a girl) grow up, could you ever be a daddy?" or "Could you be a boy if you wanted to?" young children freely answer yes (Slaby & Frey, 1975).

As children in their preschool gathered on the rug for storytime, these boys chose to sit by peers of their own sex. Sex segregation makes the peer context a powerful source of gender typing.

Because many young children in Western cultures do not see members of the other sex naked, they distinguish males and females using the only information they have—hairstyle, clothing, and behavior. But providing children with information about genital differences does not result in a full understanding of gender constancy. Preschoolers who have such knowledge still do not refer to sex as an innate, unchanging quality of people (Szkrybalo & Ruble, 1999). This suggests that cognitive immaturity, not social experience, is responsible for preschoolers' difficulty grasping the permanence of sex.

Is cognitive-developmental theory correct that gender constancy is responsible for children's gender-typed behavior? Perhaps you have already concluded that evidence for this assumption is weak. "Gender-appropriate" behavior appears so early in the preschool years that modeling and reinforcement must contribute to its initial appearance, as social learning theory suggests. At present, researchers disagree on just how gender constancy influences gender-role development. But they do know that once children integrate the knowledge they acquire from others into gender categories and can identify their own sex, their gender-typed self-images and behavior strengthen. Yet another theory shows how this happens.

GENDER SCHEMA THEORY ● Gender schema theory is an information-processing approach to gender typing that combines social learning and cognitive-developmental features. It emphasizes that environmental pressures and children's cognitions together shape gender-role development (Martin, Ruble, & Szkrybalo, 2002; Martin & Halverson, 1987). At an early age, children pick up gender-stereotyped preferences and behaviors from others. At the same time, they organize experiences into *gender schemas,* or masculine and feminine categories, that they use to interpret their world. A young child who says, "Only boys can be doctors" or "Cooking is a girl's job" already has some well-formed gender schemas. As soon as preschoolers can label their own gender, they select gender schemas consistent with it, applying those categories to themselves. Then their self-perceptions become gender typed and serve as additional schemas that they use to process information and guide their own behavior.

Let's look at the example in Figure 10.4 to see exactly how this network of gender schemas strengthens gender-typed preferences and behavior. Mandy has been taught that "dolls are for girls" and "trucks are for boys." She also knows that she is a girl. Mandy uses this information to make decisions about how to behave. Because her schemas lead her to conclude that "dolls are for me," when she is given a doll she approaches it, explores it, and learns more about it. In contrast, on seeing a truck, she uses her gender schemas to conclude that "trucks are not for me" and responds by avoiding the "gender-inappropriate" toy.

In research examining this pattern of reasoning, 4- and 5-year-olds were shown gender-neutral toys varying in attractiveness. An experimenter labeled some as boys' toys and others as

FIGURE 10.4

Impact of gender schemas on gender-typed preferences and behaviors.

Mandy's network of gender schemas leads her to approach and explore "feminine" toys, such as dolls, and to avoid "masculine" toys, such as trucks. (From C. L. Martin & C. F. Halverson, Jr., 1981, "A Schematic Processing Model of Sex Typing and Stereotyping in Children," *Child Development, 52,* p. 1121. © The Society for Research in Child Development, Inc. Adapted by permission.)

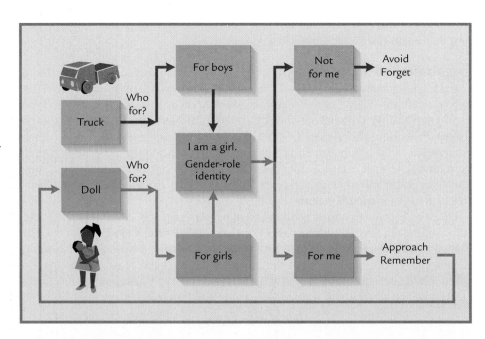

girls' toys and left a third group unlabeled. The children engaged in gender-based reasoning, preferring toys labeled for their gender. Highly attractive toys, especially, lost their appeal when they were labeled as for the other gender (Martin, Eisenbud, & Rose, 1995).

Gender schemas are so powerful that when children see others behaving in "gender-inconsistent" ways, they often cannot remember the behavior or they distort their memory to make it "gender-consistent" (Liben & Signorella, 1993). As a result, they increase their knowledge of "things for me" that fit with their gender schemas, but they learn much less about "cross-gender" activities and behaviors. Of course, gender schematic thinking could not operate so forcefully to restrict children's knowledge and learning opportunities if society did not teach a wide variety of gender-linked associations.

Reducing Gender Stereotyping in Young Children

How can we help young children avoid rigid gender schemas that restrict their behavior and learning opportunities? No easy recipe exists for this difficult task. Even children who grow up in homes and schools that minimize stereotyping eventually encounter it in the media and in what men and women typically do in their communities. Consequently, children need early experiences that counteract their readiness to absorb the extensive network of gender-linked associations that surrounds them.

Adults can begin by eliminating gender stereotyping from their own behavior and from the alternatives they provide for children. For example, mothers and fathers can take turns making dinner, bathing children, and driving the family car. They can provide sons and daughters with both trucks and dolls and with pink and blue clothing. Teachers can make sure that all children spend some time each day in mixed-gender play activities and in both adult-structured and unstructured pursuits. Also, efforts can be made to shield children from television and other media presentations that portray rigid gender differences.

Once children notice the vast array of gender stereotypes in their society, parents and teachers can point out exceptions. For example, they can arrange for children to see men and women pursuing nontraditional careers. And they can reason with children, explaining that interests and skills, not sex, should determine a person's occupation and activities. Research shows that such reasoning is very effective in reducing children's tendency to view the world in a gender-biased fashion (Bigler & Liben, 1992). And, as we will see in the next section, a rational approach to child rearing promotes healthy, adaptable functioning in many other areas as well.

Parents and teachers can reduce preschoolers' gender stereotyping by modeling nonstereotyped behaviors and pointing out exceptions to stereotypes in their neighborhood and community. Perhaps because this boy has observed family members engaged in nonstereotyped activities, he enacts similar roles in his preschool classroom.

© 2002 LAURA DWIGHT

Ask YOURSELF

www

REVIEW Explain how gender stereotyping in the environment and young children's cognitive limitations contribute to rigid gender stereotyping in early childhood.

REVIEW Cite research indicating that both biology and social experience influence gender-role adoption.

APPLY When 4-year-old Roger was in the hospital, he was cared for by a male nurse named Jared. After Roger recovered, he told his friends about Dr. Jared. Using gender schema theory, explain why Roger remembered Jared as a doctor, not a nurse.

REFLECT Think back to your peer associations in early and middle childhood. Did you play primarily with peers of your own sex? What gender-role attitudes and behaviors were emphasized in your peer associations? How did you view members of the other sex?

Child Rearing and Emotional and Social Development

In this and previous chapters, we have seen how parents can foster children's competence—by building a parent–child relationship based on affection and cooperation, by serving as models and reinforcers of mature behavior, by using reasoning and inductive discipline, and by guiding and encouraging mastery of new skills. Now let's put these elements together into an overall view of effective parenting.

Styles of Child Rearing

Child-rearing styles are combinations of parenting behaviors that occur over a wide range of situations, creating an enduring child-rearing climate. In a landmark series of studies, Diana Baumrind gathered information on child rearing by watching parents interact with their preschoolers. Her findings, and those of others who have extended her work, reveal three features that consistently differentiate an effective style from less effective ones: (1) acceptance and involvement, (2) control, and (3) autonomy granting (Gray & Steinberg, 1999; Hart, Newell, & Olsen, 2002). Table 10.2 shows how child-rearing styles differ in these features. Let's discuss each style in turn.

AUTHORITATIVE CHILD REARING ● The **authoritative child-rearing style**—the most successful approach to child rearing—involves high acceptance and involvement, adaptive control techniques, and appropriate autonomy granting. Authoritative parents are warm, attentive, and sensitive to their child's needs. They establish an enjoyable, emotionally fulfilling parent–child relationship that draws the child into close connection. At the same time, authoritative parents exercise firm, reasonable control; they insist on mature behavior and give reasons for their expectations. Finally, authoritative parents engage in gradual, appropriate autonomy granting, allowing the child to make decisions in areas where he is ready to make choices (Kuczynski & Lollis, 2002; Russell, Mize, & Bissaker, 2002).

Throughout childhood and adolescence, authoritative parenting is linked to many aspects of competence. These include an upbeat mood, self-control, task persistence, and cooperativeness during the preschool years, and, at older ages, high self-esteem, social and moral maturity, and favorable school performance (Baumrind & Black, 1967; Herman et al., 1997; Luster & McAdoo, 1996; Mackey, Arnold, & Pratt, 2001; Steinberg, Darling, & Fletcher, 1995).

TABLE 10.2

Features of Child-Rearing Styles

CHILD-REARING STYLE	ACCEPTANCE AND INVOLVEMENT	CONTROL	AUTONOMY GRANTING
Authoritative	Is warm, attentive, and sensitive to the child's needs	Makes reasonable demands for maturity, and consistently enforces and explains them	Permits the child to make decisions in accord with readiness
Authoritarian	Is cold and rejecting and frequently degrades the child	Makes many demands coercively by yelling, commanding, and criticizing	Makes decisions for the child. Rarely listens to the child's point of view
Permissive	Is warm but overindulgent or inattentive	Makes few or no demands	Permits the child to make many decisions before the child is ready
Uninvolved	Is emotionally detached and withdrawn	Makes few or no demands	Is indifferent to the child's decision making and point of view

AUTHORITARIAN CHILD REARING ● Parents who use an **authoritarian child-rearing style** are low in acceptance and involvement, high in coercive control, and low in autonomy granting. Authoritarian parents appear cold and rejecting; they frequently degrade their child by putting her down. To exert control, they yell, command, and criticize. "Do it because I said so!" is the attitude of these parents. If the child disobeys, authoritarian parents resort to force and punishment. In addition, they make decisions for their child and expect the child to accept their word in an unquestioning manner. If the child does not, authoritarian parents resort to force and punishment.

Children of authoritarian parents are anxious and unhappy, and they tend to react with hostility when frustrated. Boys, especially, show high rates of anger and defiance. Girls are dependent, lacking in exploration, and overwhelmed by challenging tasks (Hart et al., 2002; Nix et al., 1999; Thompson, Hollis, & Richards, 2003). Nevertheless, because of authoritarian parents' concern with control, children and adolescents experiencing this style do better in school and are less likely to engage in antisocial acts than those with undemanding parents—that is, parents who use the two styles we are about to consider.

PERMISSIVE CHILD REARING ● The **permissive child-rearing style** is warm and accepting. But rather than being involved, such parents are overindulging or inattentive. Permissive parents engage in little control of their child's behavior. And instead of gradually granting autonomy, they allow children to make many of their own decisions at an age when they are not yet capable of doing so. Their children eat meals and go to bed when they feel like it and watch as much television as they want. They do not have to learn good manners or do household chores. Although some permissive parents truly believe that this approach is best, many others simply lack confidence in their ability to influence their child's behavior.

Children of permissive parents are impulsive and disobedient. They are also overly demanding and dependent on adults, and they show less persistence on tasks, poorer school achievement, and more antisocial behavior than children whose parents convey clear expectations. The link between permissive parenting and dependent, nonachieving, rebellious behavior is especially strong for boys (Barber & Olsen, 1997; Baumrind, 1971).

UNINVOLVED CHILD REARING ● The **uninvolved child-rearing style** combines low acceptance and involvement with little control and general indifference to autonomy granting. Often these parents are emotionally detached and depressed and are so overwhelmed by life stress that they have little time and energy for children (Maccoby & Martin, 1983). At its extreme, uninvolved parenting is a form of child maltreatment called *neglect*. Especially when it begins early, it disrupts virtually all aspects of development (see Chapter 4, page 159). Even when parental disengagement is less extreme, children display many problems—poor emotional self-regulation, school achievement difficulties, and frequent antisocial acts in adolescence (Aunola, Stattin, & Nurmi, 2000; Kurdek & Fine, 1994).

What Makes Authoritative Child Rearing Effective?

Like other correlational findings, the relationship between parenting and children's competence is open to interpretation. Perhaps parents of well-adjusted children are authoritative because their youngsters have especially cooperative dispositions. Children's characteristics do contribute to the ease with which parents can apply the authoritative style. An impulsive, noncompliant child makes it hard for parents to be warm, firm, and rational. But longitudinal research reveals that authoritative child rearing reduces difficult children's intense, negative behavior, whereas parental coercion intensifies it (Stice & Barrera, 1995; Woodward, Taylor, & Dowdney, 1998).

Authoritative child rearing seems to create an emotional context for positive parental influence in the following ways:

- Warm, involved parents who are secure in the standards they hold for their children provide models of caring concern as well as of confident, self-controlled behavior.

- Authoritative parents exert control in ways that appear fair and reasonable to the child, generating far more compliance and internalization.

- Authoritative parents make demands that fit children's ability to take responsibility for their own behavior, thereby fostering high self-esteem and cognitive and social maturity.

African-American mothers often use strict, no-nonsense discipline combined with warmth and reasoning—an approach well suited to promoting self-reliance, self-control, and a watchful attitude in dangerous neighborhoods.

FIGURE 10.5

Daily time spent by Chinese-American and Caucasian-American preschoolers and kindergartners in focused practice on a task (usually math, music, or drawing), as reported by parents.

Chinese-American young children exceeded their Caucasian-American agemates in focused practice by nearly tenfold. In addition, Chinese-American parents indicated that they were more likely to set aside daily periods for such practice and taught their children in more formal ways. (Adapted from Huntsinger, Jose, & Larson, 1998.)

● Supportive aspects of the authoritative style are a powerful source of *resilience,* protecting children from the negative impact of family stress and poverty (Pettit, Bates, & Dodge, 1997).

Cultural Variations

Despite broad agreement on the advantages of authoritative child rearing, ethnic groups often have distinct child-rearing beliefs and practices. For example, compared with North Americans, Chinese adults describe their parenting as more controlling (Chao, 1994; Wu et al., 2002). As Figure 10.5 shows, this emphasis on control also characterizes Chinese immigrant parents, who are more directive in teaching their children (Huntsinger, Jose, & Larson, 1998). High control reflects the Confucian belief in strict discipline, respect for elders, and socially desirable behavior, taught by deeply involved parents. Compared with Western parents, Chinese parents appear less warm because they think frequent praise causes children to feel self-satisfied and interferes with motivation to achieve (Chen, 2001). But when control becomes coercive, it is harmful in Chinese as well as Western cultures. In studies of Chinese children, authoritative parenting predicted cognitive and social competence, whereas authoritarian parenting predicted poorer academic achievement, increased aggression, and peer difficulties (Chen, Dong, & Zhou, 1997; Chen, Liu, & Li, 2000).

In Hispanic and Asian Pacific Island families, firm insistence on respect for parental authority, particularly that of the father, is paired with high parental involvement. Although at one time viewed as coercive, contemporary Hispanic fathers typically spend much time with their children and are warm and sensitive (García Coll & Pachter, 2002; Jambunathan, Burts, & Pierce, 2000).

African-American mothers often expect immediate obedience, regarding strictness as important for promoting self-control and a watchful attitude in risky surroundings. Consistent with these beliefs, low-SES African-American parents who use more controlling strategies tend to have more cognitively and socially competent children (Brody & Flor, 1998; Brody, Stoneman, & Flor, 1996). And in several studies, physical discipline predicted aggression and other conduct problems only for Caucasian-American children, not for African-American children (Deater-Deckard & Dodge, 1997; Deater-Deckard et al., 1996). This does not mean that slaps and spankings are effective strategies. But it does suggest that ethnic differences in how children view parental behavior may modify its consequences. Most African-American parents who use "no-nonsense" discipline refrain from physical punishment and combine strictness with warmth and reasoning (Bluestone & Tamis-LeMonda, 1999; Pettit, Bates, & Dodge, 1998).

These cultural variations remind us that child-rearing styles must be viewed in their larger context. As we have seen, many factors contribute to good parenting: personal characteristics of the child and parent, SES, access to extended family and community supports, cultural values and practices, and public policies.

As we turn to the topic of child maltreatment, our discussion will underscore, once again, that effective child rearing is sustained not just by the desire of mothers and fathers to be good parents. Almost all want to be. Unfortunately, when vital supports for good parenting break down, children—as well as parents—can suffer terribly.

Child Maltreatment

Child maltreatment is as old as human history, but only recently has the problem been widely acknowledged and research aimed at understanding it. Perhaps public concern has increased because child maltreatment is especially common in large, industrialized nations. In the most recently reported year, 903,000 American children (12 out of every 1,000) and 136,000 Canadian children (10 out of every 1,000) were identified as victims (Trocomé & Wolfe, 2002; U.S.

Department of Health and Human Services, 2003b). Because most cases go unreported, the true figures are much higher.

Child maltreatment takes the following forms:

- *Physical abuse*: assaults, such as shaking, kicking, biting, punching, or stabbing, that inflict physical injury;

- *Sexual abuse*: fondling, intercourse, exhibitionism, commercial exploitation through prostitution or production of pornography, and other forms of sexual exploitation;

- *Neglect*: failure to provide for a child's basic needs, in terms of food, clothing, medical attention, education, or supervision; and

- *Emotional abuse*: acts that could cause serious mental or behavioral disorders, including social isolation, repeated unreasonable demands, ridicule, humiliation, intimidation, or terrorizing.

Neglect accounts for 40 to 50 percent of reported cases, physical abuse for 30 percent, emotional abuse for 10 to 20 percent, and sexual abuse for 10 percent. But these figures are only approximate, as many children experience more than one form. Parents commit the vast majority of child abuse and neglect incidents—more than 90 percent. Mothers engage in neglect more often than fathers, whereas fathers engage in sexual abuse more often than mothers. Maternal and paternal rates of physical and emotional abuse are fairly similar. And in an especially heartrending 18 percent of cases, parents jointly commit the abusive acts. Infants and young preschoolers are at greatest risk for neglect; preschool and school-age children are at greatest risk for physical, emotional, and sexual abuse. But each type occurs at every age (Trocomé & Wolfe, 2002; U.S. Department of Health and Human Services, 2003b). Because most sexual abuse victims are identified in middle childhood, we will pay special attention to this form of maltreatment in Chapter 13.

ORIGINS OF CHILD MALTREATMENT ● Early findings suggested that child maltreatment was rooted in adult psychological disturbance (Kempe et al., 1962). But although child abuse is more common among disturbed parents, it soon became clear that a single "abusive personality type" does not exist. Sometimes even "normal" parents harm their children! Also, parents who were abused as children do not necessarily become abusers (Buchanan, 1996; Simons et al., 1991).

For help in understanding child maltreatment, researchers turned to *ecological systems theory* (see Chapters 1 and 2). They discovered that many interacting variables—at the family, community, and cultural levels—promote child abuse and neglect. Table 10.3 summarizes factors

TABLE 10.3

Factors Related to Child Maltreatment

FACTOR	DESCRIPTION
Parent characteristics	Psychological disturbance; alcohol and drug abuse; history of abuse as a child; belief in harsh, physical discipline; desire to satisfy unmet emotional needs through the child; unreasonable expectations for child behavior; young age (most under 30); low educational level
Child characteristics	Premature or very sick baby; difficult temperament; inattentiveness and overactivity; other developmental problems
Family characteristics	Low income; poverty; homelessness; marital instability; social isolation; physical abuse of mother by husband or boyfriend; frequent moves; large families with closely spaced children; overcrowded living conditions; disorganized household; lack of steady employment; other signs of high life stress
Community	Characterized by social isolation; few parks, child-care centers, preschool programs, recreation centers, or churches to serve as family supports
Culture	Approval of physical force and violence as ways to solve problems

Sources: Cicchetti & Toth, 2000; Wekerle & Wolfe, 2003.

associated with child maltreatment. The more of these risks that are present, the greater the likelihood that abuse will occur. Let's examine each set of influences in turn.

The Family. Within the family, certain children—those whose characteristics make them more of a challenge to rear—are more likely to become targets of abuse. These include premature or very sick babies and children who are temperamentally difficult, are inattentive and overactive, or have other developmental problems. Child factors, however, only slightly increase the risk of abuse (Sidebotham et al., 2003). Whether such children are maltreated largely depends on parents' characteristics.

Maltreating parents are less skillful than other parents in handling discipline confrontations and getting children to cooperate in working toward common goals. They also suffer from biased thinking about their child (Rogosch et al., 1995). For example, they often evaluate transgressions as worse than they are, attribute their child's misdeeds to a stubborn or bad disposition, and feel powerless in parenting—perspectives that lead them to move quickly toward physical force.

Once abuse gets started, it quickly becomes part of a self-sustaining relationship. The small irritations to which abusive parents react—a fussy baby, a preschooler who knocks over her milk, or a child who will not mind immediately—soon become bigger ones. Then the harshness increases. By the preschool years, abusive and neglectful parents seldom interact with their children. When they do, they rarely express pleasure and affection; the communication is almost always negative (Wolfe, 1999).

Most parents, however, have enough self-control not to respond to their children's misbehavior with abuse. Other factors combine with these conditions to prompt an extreme response. Unmanageable parental stress is strongly associated with all forms of maltreatment. Abusive parents respond to stressful situations with high emotional arousal. And such stressors as low income and education (less than a high-school diploma), unemployment, young maternal age, alcohol and drug use, marital conflict, overcrowded living conditions, frequent moves, and extreme household disorganization are common in abusive homes (Wekerle & Wolfe, 2003). These personal and situational conditions increase the chances that parents will be too overwhelmed to meet basic child-rearing responsibilities or will vent their frustrations by lashing out at their children.

The Community. The majority of abusive parents are isolated from both formal and informal social supports. This social isolation has at least two causes. First, because of their own life histories, many of these parents have learned to mistrust and avoid others. They do not have the skills necessary for establishing and maintaining positive relationships (Polansky et al., 1985). Second, maltreating parents are more likely to live in unstable, run-down neighborhoods that provide few links between family and community, such as parks, child-care centers, preschool programs, recreation centers, and churches (Coulton, Korbin, & Su, 1999). For these reasons, they lack "lifelines" to others and have no one to turn to for help during stressful times.

The Larger Culture. Cultural values, laws, and customs profoundly affect the chances that child maltreatment will occur when parents feel overburdened. Societies that view violence as an appropriate way to solve problems set the stage for child abuse. Although the United States and Canada have laws to protect children from maltreatment, our earlier consideration of physical punishment revealed widespread use of physical force with children. In the United States, the Supreme Court has twice upheld the right of school officials to use corporal punishment. In Canada, the federal criminal code states that parents', teachers', and caregivers' use of physical force to discipline is justified, as long as such force is "reasonable under the circumstances." But because this definition is vague, many experts believe that it encourages adults to assault children and provides a ready defense for those who do so (Justice for Children and Youth, 2003). Indeed, Canadian courts have deemed hard spankings, slaps to the head and face, and hitting of the buttocks and legs with belts and sticks to be consistent with the criminal code. As in the United States, efforts by Canadian child advocates to challenge the legality of corporal punishment have been unsuccessful.

CONSEQUENCES OF CHILD MALTREATMENT ● The family circumstances of maltreated children impair the development of emotional self-regulation, empathy and sympathy, self-concept, social skills, and academic motivation. Over time, these youngsters show serious learning and adjustment problems, including academic failure, severe depression, aggressive behavior, peer difficulties, substance abuse, and delinquency (Bolger & Patterson, 2001; Shonk & Cicchetti, 2001).

How do these damaging consequences occur? Think back to our earlier discussion of hostile cycles of parent–child interaction, which are especially severe for abused children. Indeed, a family characteristic strongly associated with child abuse is spouse abuse (Cox, Kotch, & Everson, 2003). Clearly, the home lives of abused children abound with opportunities to learn to use aggression as a way of solving problems.

Furthermore, demeaning parental messages, in which children are ridiculed, humiliated, rejected, or terrorized, result in low self-esteem, high anxiety, self-blame, depression, and efforts to escape from extreme psychological pain—at times severe enough to lead to attempted suicide in adolescence (Wolfe, 1999). At school, maltreated children are serious discipline problems. Their noncompliance, poor motivation, and cognitive immaturity interfere with academic achievement—an outcome that further undermines their chances for life success (Wekerle & Wolfe, 2003).

Finally, the trauma of repeated abuse is associated with central nervous system damage, including abnormal EEG brain-wave activity, fMRI-detected reduced size and impaired functioning of the cerebral cortex and corpus callosum, and heightened production of stress hormones (Cicchetti, 2003; Kaufman & Charney, 2001). These effects increase the chances that cognitive and emotional problems will endure.

PREVENTING CHILD MALTREATMENT ● Because child maltreatment is embedded in families, communities, and society as a whole, efforts to prevent it must be directed at each of these levels. Many approaches have been suggested, including teaching high-risk parents effective child-rearing strategies, providing direct experience with children in high school child development, and broad social programs aimed at bettering economic conditions for low-SES families.

We have seen that providing social supports to families is very effective in easing parental stress. This approach sharply reduces child maltreatment as well (Azar & Wolfe, 1998). Research indicates that a trusting relationship with another person is the most important factor in preventing mothers with childhood histories of abuse from repeating the cycle with their own youngsters (Egeland, Jacobvitz, & Sroufe, 1988). Parents Anonymous, a national organization that has as its main goal helping child-abusing parents learn constructive parenting practices, does so largely through social supports. Its local chapters offer self-help group meetings, daily phone calls, and regular home visits to relieve social isolation and teach responsible child-rearing skills. And two-generation approaches to early intervention, aimed at strengthening both child and parent competencies (see Chapter 9, page 346), can reduce child maltreatment rates substantially (Reynolds & Robertson, 2003). Turn to the Social Issues: Health box on page 394 to find out about one such prevention effort: Healthy Start.

Still, many experts believe that child maltreatment cannot be eliminated as long as violence is widespread and corporal punishment is regarded as acceptable. In addition, combating poverty and its diverse correlates—family stress and disorganization, inadequate food and medical care, teenage parenthood, low-birth-weight babies, and parental hopelessness—would protect many children.

Although more cases reach the courts than in decades past, child maltreatment remains a crime that is difficult to prove. Most of the time, the only witnesses are the child victims or other loyal family members. Even in court cases in which the evidence is strong, judges hesitate to impose the ultimate safeguard against further harm: permanently removing the child from the family. There are several reasons for this reluctant attitude. First, in the United States and Canada, government intervention into family life is viewed as a last resort. Second, despite destructive family relationships, maltreated children and their parents usually are attached to one another. Most of the time, neither desires separation. Finally, American and Canadian legal systems tend to regard children as parental property rather than as human beings in their own right, and this also has stood in the way of court-ordered protection.

COURTESY SAN FRANCISCO CHILD ABUSE COUNCIL

you idiot!
you idiot!
you idiot!
you idiot!
you idiot!
you idiot!
you idiot!

Children learn by repetition.

You don't have to hit to hurt.

San Francisco
Child Abuse Council
(415) 668-0494

Public service announcements help prevent child abuse by educating people about the problem and informing them of where to seek help. This poster reminds adults that degrading remarks can hit as hard as a fist.

$\int$ocial Issues: Health

Healthy Start: Preventing Child Maltreatment Through Home Visitation

In 1985, the Hawaii legislature funded a pilot program called Healthy Start, aimed at improving parenting and reducing child abuse and neglect. The intervention had two unique features. First, families at risk for child maltreatment were identified as early as possible—during pregnancy or at birth—by screening mothers' medical records for risk factors (refer to Table 10.3) and interviewing mothers to confirm risk status. Second, each at-risk family was offered home-visiting services for 3 years, designed to help family members cope with the challenges of child rearing.

Home visitors were paraprofessionals (specially trained workers) recruited from the local community who had qualities essential for working with vulnerable families: warmth, self-confidence, cultural sensitivity, and good parenting skills. They established trusting relationships with parents, helped them manage crises, modeled and encouraged effective child rearing, and put families in touch with community services. Initially, home visits were frequent—once every 2 or 3 weeks. They declined as families increased in effective functioning. A professional in the field of early childhood education, social work, or nursing supervised each home visitor, meeting often with her to review each family's progress.

Of several hundred families invited to participate, over 90 percent enrolled in the pilot, and at the end of 3 years,

results were highly encouraging: Most families showed substantial decreases in risk factors, and only a handful had been reported for maltreatment—far fewer than in evaluations of other home-visiting interventions (Duggan et al., 1999). As a result, Healthy Start spread. Today, programs exist throughout Hawaii, supported by a mix of state, federal, and private funds. And these inspired a nationwide effort, Healthy Families America, with more than 270 sites around the United States.

Recently, researchers conducted a more rigorous evaluation of Healthy Start: a field experiment, in which several hundred at-risk families were randomly assigned to either a treatment or a control group and followed for 3 years. By the second year, program benefits were clear: Healthy Start mothers less often used violent disciplinary tactics and reported more confidence and less stress in parenting (Duggan et al., 1999). Additional benefits have been documented in research on Healthy Families America, including improved parenting skills and a reduction in a wide variety of family problems associated with poverty (Daro & Harding, 1999).

Furthermore, adding a *cognitive component* to home visitation dramatically increases its impact. Recall that maltreating parents tend to view their child negatively and feel powerless to change the child's irritating behaviors. In an

enhanced condition, home visitors helped parents change these appraisals—by teaching them to read their child's cues, countering inaccurate interpretations (for example, that the baby was behaving with malicious intent), and working on solutions to caregiving problems. Compared with home-visitation-only and no-intervention conditions, physical punishment (slaps and spankings) and physical abuse dropped sharply (see Figure 10.6) (Bugental et al., 2002). These outcomes were greatest for parents of difficult-to-care-for infants, who had experienced birth complications.

In sum, sustained home visitation with at-risk new parents carries high potential for preventing child maltreatment (Daro & Donnelly, 2002). This is especially so when it combines social support, parent education, and strategies for changing parents' biased thinking about their children.

FIGURE 10.6

Influence of home visitation with a cognitive component on physical abuse.

In an enhanced home-visitation condition, home visitors not only provided social support and encouraged effective child rearing but also helped at-risk parents change negative appraisals of their babies and come up with solutions to caregiving problems. This cognitive component led to a dramatic reduction in physical abuse of infants (hitting, shaking, beating, kicking, biting) compared with unenhanced home-visitation and no-intervention control conditions. (Adapted from Bugental et al., 2002.)

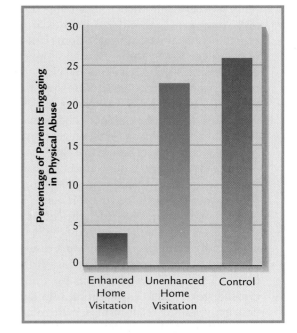

Even with intensive treatment, some adults persist in their abusive acts. An estimated 1,300 American children and 100 Canadian children die from maltreatment each year, most of them infants and preschoolers. About two-thirds suffered from beatings, drownings, suffocation, or *shaken baby syndrome,* in which shaking an infant or young child inflicts brain and neck injuries. And about one-third were severely neglected (Trocomé & Wolfe, 2002; U.S. Department of Health and Human Services, 2003b). When parents are unlikely to change their behavior, the drastic step of separating parent from child and legally terminating parental rights is the only justifiable course of action.

Child maltreatment is a distressing and horrifying topic—a sad note on which to end our discussion of a period of childhood that is so full of excitement, awakening, and discovery. But there is reason to be optimistic. Great strides have been made over the past several decades in understanding and preventing child maltreatment.

Ask YOURSELF

REVIEW Summarize findings on ethnic variations in child-rearing styles. Is the concept of authoritative parenting useful for understanding effective parenting across cultures? Explain.

APPLY Chandra heard a news report that 10 severely neglected children, living in squalor in an inner-city tenement, were discovered by Chicago police. Chandra thought to herself, "What could possibly lead parents to mistreat their children so badly?" How would you answer Chandra's question?

CONNECT Which child-rearing style is most likely to be associated with use of inductive discipline, and why?

REFLECT How would you classify your parents' child-rearing styles? What factors might have influenced their approach to child rearing?

Summary

Erikson's Theory: Initiative versus Guilt

What personality changes take place during Erikson's stage of initiative versus guilt?

● Preschoolers develop a new sense of purposefulness as they grapple with the psychological conflict of **initiative versus guilt.** A healthy sense of initiative depends on exploring the social world through play, forming a secure conscience, and experiencing supportive child rearing. Erikson's image of initiative captures the diverse emotional and social changes of early childhood.

Self-Understanding

Describe preschoolers' self-concepts, understanding of intentions, and self-esteem.

● Preschoolers' **self-concepts** largely consist of observable characteristics and typical emotions and attitudes. Their increasing self-awareness underlies struggles with other children over objects as well as first efforts to cooperate.

● During early childhood, **self-esteem** has already begun to differentiate into several self-judgments. Preschoolers' high self-esteem contributes to their mas-

tery-oriented approach to the environment. However, adult criticism of young children's efforts can undermine their self-esteem and enthusiasm for learning.

Emotional Development

Cite changes in understanding and expressing emotion during early childhood, along with factors that influence those changes.

● Cognitive development and opportunities to discuss emotion jointly contribute to young children's impressive grasp of the causes, consequences, and behavioral signs of emotion. Preschoolers are also aware of a variety of strategies that assist with emotional self-regulation. Temperament, adult modeling, and conversations about feelings influence their capacity to handle negative emotion.

● As their self-concepts become better developed, preschoolers experience self-conscious emotions more often, but they depend on parental messages to know when to feel pride, shame, or guilt. Parental messages affect both the situations in which self-conscious emotions occur and their intensity. Empathy also becomes more common. Temperament and parenting affect the extent to which empathy prompts **sympathy** and results in **prosocial,** or **altruistic, behavior.**

Peer Relations

Describe peer sociability, friendship, and social problem solving in early childhood, along with cultural and parental influences on early peer relations.

● During early childhood, peer interaction increases. According to Parten, it moves from **nonsocial activity** to **parallel play** and then to **associative** and **cooperative play.** However, these play forms do not unfold in a straightforward developmental sequence. Despite increases in associative and cooperative play, solitary play and parallel play remain common. Gains in sociodramatic play affect many aspects of emotional and social development. In collectivist societies, play occurs in large groups and is highly cooperative. Sociodramatic play seems especially important in societies where child and adult worlds are distinct.

● Preschoolers view friendship in concrete, activity-based terms. Their interactions with friends are especially positive and cooperative and serve as effective sources of social support as they enter kindergarten.

● Conflicts with peers offer children invaluable learning opportunities for **social problem solving.** Social problem solving improves from the preschool to the early school years. By kindergarten to second grade, each of its information-processing components is related to socially competent behavior. Training in social problem solving improves peer relations and psychological adjustment.

● Parents influence early peer relations both directly, through attempts to influence their child's peer relations, and indirectly, through their child-rearing practices. Secure attachment, emotionally positive parent–child conversations, and highly involved, cooperative parent–child play are linked to favorable peer interaction.

Foundations of Morality

What are the central features of psychoanalytic, social learning, and cognitive-developmental approaches to moral development?

● Psychoanalytic and behaviorist approaches to morality focus on how children acquire ready-made standards held by adults. In contrast to Freud's psychoanalytic theory, discipline promoting fear of punishment and loss of parental love does not foster conscience development. Instead, **induction** is far more effective in encouraging self-control and prosocial behavior. Freud was correct that guilt is an important motivator of moral action.

● Social learning theory regards reinforcement and modeling as the basis for moral action. Effective adult models of morality are warm and powerful, and they practice what they preach. Frequent, harsh punishment does not promote moral internalization and socially desirable behavior. Alternatives, such as **time out** and withdrawal of privileges, can help parents avoid the undesirable side effects of punishment. When parents use punishment, they can increase its effectiveness by being consistent, maintaining a warm relationship with the child, and offering explanations. The most effective discipline encourages good conduct by building a positive, cooperative relationship with the child.

● The cognitive-developmental perspective views children as active thinkers about social rules. By age 4, children consider intentions in making moral judgments and distinguish truthfulness from lying. Preschoolers also distinguish moral imperatives from social conventions and matters of personal choice. Through sibling and peer interaction, children work out their first ideas about justice and fairness. Parents who discuss moral issues with their children help them reason about morality.

Describe the development of aggression in early childhood, including family and media as influences.

● All children display aggression from time to time. During early childhood, **instrumental aggression** declines while **hostile aggression** increases. Two types of hostile aggression appear: **overt aggression,** more common in boys, and **relational aggression,** more common in girls.

● Ineffective discipline and a conflict-ridden family atmosphere promote and sustain aggression in children. Violent television programs and video and computer games also trigger childhood aggression. Young children's limited understanding of TV content increases their willingness to uncritically accept and imitate what they see.

● Teaching parents effective child-rearing practices, providing children with social problem-solving training, intervening in marital problems, and shielding children from violent TV reduce aggressive behavior.

Gender Typing

Discuss genetic and environmental influences on preschoolers' gender-stereotyped beliefs and behavior.

● Gender typing is well under way in early childhood. Preschoolers acquire a wide range of gender stereotypes and behaviors. Their gender-stereotyped beliefs operate like blanket rules rather than flexible guidelines.

● Prenatal hormones contribute to boys' higher activity level and overt aggression and to children's preference for same-sex playmates. At the same time, parents, same-sex older siblings, teachers, peers, and the broader social environment encourage many gender-typed responses.

Describe and evaluate major theories that explain the emergence of gender identity.

● Although most people have traditional **gender identities,** some are **androgynous,** combing both masculine and feminine characteristics. Masculine and androgynous identities are linked to better psychological adjustment.

● According to social learning theory, preschoolers first acquire gender-typed responses through modeling and reinforcement and then organize them into gender-linked ideas about themselves. Cognitive-developmental theory suggests that **gender constancy** must be mastered before children develop gender-typed behavior. However, gender-role behavior is acquired long before gender constancy.

● **Gender schema theory** is an information-processing approach to gender typing that combines social learning and cognitive-developmental features. As children acquire gender-stereotyped preferences and behaviors, they form masculine and feminine categories, or gender schemas, that they apply to themselves and their world.

Child Rearing and Emotional and Social Development

Describe the impact of child-rearing styles on children's development, and explain why authoritative parenting is effective.

● Three features distinguish major **child-rearing styles:** (1) acceptance and involvement, (2) control, and (3) autonomy granting. Compared with the **authoritarian, permissive,** and **uninvolved styles,** the **authoritative style** promotes cognitive, emotional, and social competence. Warmth, explanations, and reasonable demands for mature behavior account for its effectiveness.

● Certain ethnic groups, including Chinese, Hispanic, Asian Pacific Island, and African-American, rely on high levels of parental control. Research on Chinese children reveals that when such control is coercive, it impairs academic and social competence.

Discuss the multiple origins of child maltreatment, its consequences for development, and prevention strategies.

● Child maltreatment is related to factors within the family, community, and larger culture. Maltreating parents use ineffective discipline and hold a negatively biased view of their child. Unmanageable parental stress and social isolation greatly increase the chances that abuse and neglect will occur. When a society approves of force and violence as a means for solving problems, child abuse is promoted.

● Maltreated children are impaired in emotional self-regulation, empathy and sympathy, self-concept, social skills, and academic motivation. Over time they show serious adjustment problems. Successful prevention of child maltreatment requires efforts at the family, community, and societal levels.

Important Terms and Concepts

androgyny (p. 385)
associative play (p. 366)
authoritarian child-rearing style (p. 389)
authoritative child-rearing style (p. 388)
child-rearing styles (p. 388)
cooperative play (p. 366)
gender constancy (p. 385)
gender identity (p. 385)

gender schema theory (p. 386)
gender typing (p. 381)
hostile aggression (p. 377)
induction (p. 372)
initiative versus guilt (p. 358)
instrumental aggression (p. 377)
nonsocial activity (p. 366)
overt aggression (p. 377)
parallel play (p. 366)
permissive child-rearing style (p. 389)

prosocial, or altruistic, behavior (p. 364)
relational aggression (p. 377)
self-concept (p. 359)
self-esteem (p. 360)
social problem solving (p. 368)
sympathy (p. 365)
time out (p. 374)
uninvolved child-rearing style (p. 389)

 ## For Further Information and Help

Consult the Companion Website for *Infants, Children, and Adolescents,* Fifth Edition, *(www.ablongman.com/berk),* where you will find the following resources for this chapter:

● **Chapter Objectives**
● **Flashcards** for studying important terms and concepts
● **Annotated Weblinks** to guide you in further research
● **Ask Yourself questions,** which you can answer and then check against a sample response

● **Suggested Readings**
● **Practice Tests** with immediate scoring and feedback

Milestones Development in Early Childhood

AGE	PHYSICAL	COGNITIVE	LANGUAGE	EMOTIONAL/SOCIAL
2 years	• Slower gains in height and weight than in toddlerhood. (288) • Balance improves; walking becomes better coordinated. (304) • Running, jumping, hopping, throwing, and catching develop. (304)  • Puts on and removes some items of clothing. (306) • Uses spoon effectively. (306)	• Make-believe becomes less dependent on realistic toys, less self-centered, and more complex. (317) • Can take the perspective of others in simplified situations. (321–322) • Recognition memory is well developed. (334) • Aware of the difference between inner mental and outer physical events. (336–337)	• Vocabulary increases rapidly. (348–349) • Sentences follow word order of native language; adds grammatical markers. (350) • Displays effective conversational skills. (351) 	• Begins to develop self-concept and self-esteem. (359, 360) • Cooperation and instrumental aggression appear. (359, 377) • Understands causes, consequences, and behavioral signs of basic emotions. (362) • Empathy increases. (364–365) • Gender-stereotyped beliefs and behavior increase. (381)
3–4 years	• May no longer need a daytime nap. (295) • Running, jumping, hopping, throwing, and catching become better coordinated. (304–305)  • Galloping and one-foot skipping appear. (305) • Rides tricycle. (304) • Uses scissors. (305) • Draws first picture of a person. (306) • Can distinguish writing from nonwriting. (309)	• Masters dual representation. (319) • Notices and reasons about transformations, reverses thinking, and understands many cause-and-effect relationships. (323) • Classifies familiar objects hierarchically. (325) • Can distinguish appearance from reality. (326) • Uses private speech to guide behavior during challenging tasks. (329) • Attention becomes more sustained and planful. (333) • Uses scripts to recall familiar experiences. (334) • Understands that both beliefs and desires determine behavior. (336) • Aware of some meaningful features of written language. (338, 340) • Counts small numbers of objects and grasps cardinality. (341–342)	• Masters increasingly complex grammatical structures. (350) • Occasionally overextends grammatical rules to exceptions. (350) • Adjusts speech to fit the age, sex, and social status of speakers and listeners. (351) 	 • Has several self-esteems, such as learning things in school, making friends, and getting along with parents. (360) • Emotional self-regulation improves. (363) • Experiences self-conscious emotions more often. (364–365) • Nonsocial activity declines and interactive play increases. (366) • Instrumental aggression declines, and hostile aggression increases. (377) • Forms first friendships. (368) • Distinguishes moral from social-conventional and personal matters. (375–376) • Preference for same-sex playmates strengthens. (382)

AGE	PHYSICAL	COGNITIVE	LANGUAGE	EMOTIONAL/SOCIAL
5–6 years	• Body is streamlined and longer-legged with proportions similar to adults'. (288) • First permanent tooth erupts. (288) • Gross motor skills increase in speed and endurance. (304) • Skipping appears. (305)	• Attention continues to improve. (333) • Recognition, recall, scripted memory, and autobiographical memory improve. (334–335) • Understanding of false belief improves. (336–337) • Understands that letters and sounds are linked in systematic ways. (340)	• Vocabulary reaches about 10,000 words. (348) • Uses many complex grammatical structures. (350)	• Ability to interpret, predict, and influence others' emotional reactions improves. (362) • Relies more on language to express empathy. (364) • Becomes better at social problem solving. (369–370) • Has acquired many morally relevant rules and behaviors. (371) • Gender-stereotyped beliefs and behavior continue to increase. (381–382) • Understands gender constancy. (385)

• Shows mature throwing and catching patterns. (304–305)

• Ties shoes, draws more complex pictures, uses an adultlike pencil grip, and writes name. (306–309)

• Can discriminate letters of the alphabet. (309)

• Counts on and counts down, engaging in simple addition and subtraction. (342)

Note: Numbers in parentheses indicate the page(s) on which each milestone is discussed.

Inhabiting a street that seems to have emerged from a storybook—ageless and old but lovingly cared for—children engage in universal activities of moving, playing, throwing, and catching. Chapter 11 takes up the diverse physical attainments of the school years.

"Children of a Village"
Maryam Sefait
14 years, Iran

Reprinted with permission from the International Museum of Children's Art, Oslo, Norway.

Physical Development in Middle Childhood

- **BODY GROWTH**
  Worldwide Variations in Body Size • Secular Trends in Physical Growth • Skeletal Growth • Brain Development

- **COMMON HEALTH PROBLEMS**
  Vision and Hearing • Malnutrition • Obesity • Bedwetting • Illnesses • Unintentional Injuries
  SOCIAL ISSUES: HEALTH *The Obesity Epidemic: How Americans Became the Heaviest People in the World*

- **HEALTH EDUCATION**
  SOCIAL ISSUES: EDUCATION *Children's Understanding of Health and Illness*

- **MOTOR DEVELOPMENT AND PLAY**
  Gross Motor Development • Fine Motor Development • Individual Differences in Motor Skills • Child-Organized Games • Adult-Organized Youth Sports • Shadows of Our Evolutionary Past • Physical Education

"I'm on my way, Mom!" hollered 10-year-old Joey as he stuffed the last bite of toast into his mouth, slung his book bag over his shoulder, dashed out the door, jumped on his bike, and headed down the street for school. Joey's 8-year-old sister Lizzie followed, kissing her mother goodbye and pedaling furiously until she caught up with Joey. Rena, the children's mother and one of my colleagues at the university, watched from the front porch as her son and daughter disappeared in the distance.

"They're branching out," Rena remarked to me over lunch that day, as she described the children's expanding activities and relationships. Homework, household chores, soccer teams, music lessons, scouting, friends at school and in the neighborhood, and Joey's new paper route were all part of the children's routine. "It seems as if the basics are all there; I don't have to monitor Joey and Lizzie so constantly anymore. Although being a parent is still very challenging, it's more a matter of refinements—helping them become independent, competent, and productive individuals."

Joey and Lizzie have entered middle childhood, which spans the years from 6 to 11. Around the world, children of this age are assigned new responsibilities. Joey and Lizzie, like other children in industrialized nations, spend long hours in school. Indeed, middle childhood is often called the "school years" because its onset is marked by the start of formal schooling. In village and tribal cultures, the school may be a field or a jungle. But universally, mature members of society guide children of this age period toward tasks that increasingly resemble those they will perform as adults (Rogoff, 1996).

This chapter focuses on physical growth in middle childhood—changes less spectacular than those seen in earlier years. By age 6, the brain has reached 95 percent of its adult size, and the body continues to grow slowly. In this way, nature grants school-age children the mental powers to master challenging tasks, as well as added time to learn before reaching physical maturity.

We begin by reviewing typical growth trends and special health concerns of middle childhood. Then we turn to rapid gains in motor abilities, which support practical everyday activities, athletic skills, and participation in organized games. We will see that each of these achievements is affected by and contributes to cognitive, emotional, and social development. Our discussion will echo a familiar theme—that all domains are interrelated.

Body Growth

The rate of physical growth during the school years extends the slow, regular pattern that characterized early childhood. At age 6, the average North American child weighs about 45 pounds and is 3½ feet tall. During the next few years, children continue to add about 2 to 3 inches in height and 5 pounds in weight each year (see Figure 11.1). Between ages 6 and 8, girls are slightly shorter and lighter than boys. By age 9, this trend reverses. Already, Rena noticed, Lizzie was starting to catch up with Joey in physical size as she approached the dramatic adolescent growth spurt, which takes place 2 years earlier in girls than in boys.

Because the lower portion of the body is growing fastest, Joey and Lizzie appeared longer-legged than they had in early childhood. They grew out of their jeans more quickly than their jackets and frequently needed larger shoes. As in early childhood, girls have slightly more body fat and boys more muscle. After age 8, girls begin accumulating fat at a faster rate, and they will add even more during adolescence (Tanner, 1990).

Worldwide Variations in Body Size

A glance into any elementary school classroom reveals continuing, wide individual differences in body growth. Diversity in physical size is especially apparent when we travel to different nations, where a 9-inch gap exists between the smallest and the largest 8-year-olds. The shortest children tend to be found in South America, Asia, the Pacific Islands, and parts of Africa and include such ethnic groups as Colombian, Burmese, Thai, Vietnamese, Ethiopian, and Bantu. The tallest

FIGURE 11.1

Body growth during middle childhood.

Andy and Amy continued the slow, regular pattern of growth that they showed in early childhood (see Chapter 8, page 289). But around age 9, Amy began to grow at a faster rate than Andy. At age 10½, she was taller, heavier, and more mature looking.

Andy at 8 years

Andy at 6 years

Andy at 9 years

Andy at 10½ years

Amy at 6 years

Amy at 8 years

Amy at 9 years

Amy at 10½ years

children reside in Australia, northern and central Europe, Canada, and the United States and are from Czech, Dutch, Latvian, Norwegian, Swiss, and African-American populations (Meredith, 1978). These findings remind us that growth norms must be applied with caution, especially in countries with high immigration rates and many ethnic minorities.

What accounts for these vast differences in physical size? Both heredity and environment are involved. Body size sometimes results from evolutionary adaptations to a particular climate. For example, long, lean physiques are typical in hot, tropical regions and short, stocky ones in cold, Arctic areas. At the same time, children who grow tallest usually reside in developed countries, where food is plentiful and infectious diseases are largely controlled. In contrast, small children tend to live in less developed regions, where poverty, hunger, and disease are common (Bogin, 2001). And when families move from poor to wealthy nations, their children not only grow taller but also change to a longer-legged body shape. (Recall that during childhood, the legs are growing fastest). For example, American-born school-age children of immigrant Guatemalan Mayan parents are, on average, 4½ inches taller and nearly 3 inches longer-legged than their agemates in Guatemalan Mayan villages (Bogin et al., 2002).

These 9-year-olds, who are taking a temperature reading for a science project, illustrate faster growth of the lower portion of the body in middle childhood. They appear longer-legged than they did as preschoolers, quickly growing out of their jeans and frequently needing larger shoes. As at earlier ages, they vary greatly in body size.

Secular Trends in Physical Growth

Over the past 150 years, **secular trends in physical growth**—changes in body size from one generation to the next—have taken place in industrialized nations. Joey and Lizzie are taller and heavier than their parents and grandparents were as children. These trends have been found in Australia, Canada, Japan, New Zealand, the United States, and nearly all European nations. For example, measurements of more than 24,000 Bogalusa, Louisiana, schoolchildren between 1973 and 1992 revealed an average height gain of nearly ⅓ inch per decade (Freedman et al., 2000). The secular gain appears early in life and becomes greater over childhood and early adolescence. Then, as mature body size is reached, it declines. This pattern suggests that the larger size of today's children is mostly due to a faster rate of physical development.

Once again, improved health and nutrition are largely responsible for these growth gains. Secular trends are not as large for low-income children, who have poorer diets and are more likely to suffer from growth-stunting illnesses. And in regions of the world with widespread poverty, famine, and disease, either no secular change or a secular decrease in body size has occurred (Barnes-Josiah & Augustin, 1995; Cole, 2000).

Although the secular gain in height has slowed in recent decades, weight gain is continuing at a high rate. As we will see later, overweight and obesity have reached epic proportions.

Body size is sometimes the result of evolutionary adaptations to a particular climate. These boys of the Sudan, who live on the hot African plains, have long, lean physiques, which permit the body to cool easily.

Skeletal Growth

During middle childhood, the bones of the body lengthen and broaden. However, ligaments are not yet firmly attached to bones. This, combined with increasing muscle strength, grants children unusual flexibility of movement. School-age youngsters often seem like "physical contortionists," turning cartwheels and doing splits and handstands. As their bodies become stronger, many children experience a greater desire for physical exercise. Nighttime "growing pains"—stiffness and aches in the legs—are common as muscles adapt to an enlarging skeleton (Wall, 2000).

Between ages 6 and 12, all 20 primary teeth are replaced by permanent ones, with girls losing their teeth slightly earlier than boys. The first teeth to go are the lower and then upper front teeth, giving many first and second graders a "toothless" smile. For a while, permanent teeth seem much too large. Growth of the facial bones, especially those of the jaw and chin, gradually causes the child's face to lengthen and mouth to widen, accommodating the newly erupting teeth.

Care of the teeth is essential during the school years because dental health affects the child's appearance, speech, and ability to chew properly. Children often neglect to brush thoroughly, and they usually cannot floss by themselves until about 9 years of age. Parents need to remind them and help them with these tasks. More than 50 percent of North American school-age children have at least some tooth decay (World Health Organization, 2003a). As in the preschool years, low-SES children have especially high levels (see Chapter 8). Children without health insurance are three times more likely to have unmet dental needs. As decay progresses, they experience pain, embarrassment at damaged teeth, distraction from play and learning, and school absences due to dental-related illnesses.

One-third of school-age children suffer from **malocclusion,** a condition in which the upper and lower teeth do not meet properly. In about 14 percent of cases, serious difficulties in biting and chewing result. Malocclusion can be caused by thumb and finger sucking after permanent teeth erupt (Vogel, 1998). Children who were eager thumb suckers during infancy and early childhood may require gentle but persistent encouragement to give up the habit by school entry. A second cause of malocclusion is crowding of permanent teeth. In some children, this problem clears up as the jaw grows. Others need braces, a common sight by the end of elementary school.

Brain Development

The weight of the brain increases by only 10 percent during middle childhood and adolescence. Nevertheless, considerable growth occurs in certain brain structures. Using fMRI, researchers can detect the volume of two general types of brain tissue: *white matter,* consisting largely of myelinated nerve fibers, and *gray matter,* consisting mostly of neurons and supportive material. White matter increases steadily throughout childhood and adolescence, especially in the frontal lobes of the cerebral cortex (responsible for consciousness, impulse control, and planning), in the parietal lobes (supporting spatial abilities), and in the corpus callosum (leading to improved communication between the two cortical hemispheres) (Durston et al., 2001). As children acquire more complex abilities, stimulated neurons increase in synaptic connections, and their neural fibers become more elaborate and myelinated. At the same time, gray matter declines due to synaptic pruning (reduction of unused synapses) and death of surrounding neurons (Sowell et al., 2002). As a result, lateralization of the cerebral hemispheres increases.

Little information is available on how the brain changes in other ways. One idea is that much development takes place at the level of *neurotransmitters,* chemicals that permit neurons to communicate across synapses (see Chapter 5, page 169). And over time, neurons become increasingly selective, responding only to certain chemical messages. This change may contribute to the more efficient and flexible thinking and behavior of school-age children. Secretions of particular neurotransmitters are related to cognitive performance, social and emotional adjustment, and ability to withstand stress. Children may suffer serious developmental problems, such as inattention and overactivity, emotional disturbance, and epilepsy (an illness involving brain seizures and loss of motor control) when neurotransmitters are not present in appropriate balances (Barr et al., 2000; Dammerman & Kriegstein, 2000).

Researchers also believe that brain functioning may change in middle childhood because of the influence of hormones. Around age 7 to 8, an increase in *androgens* (male sex hormones), secreted by the adrenal glands (located on top of the kidneys), occurs in children of both sexes. Androgens will rise further among boys at puberty, when the testes release them in large amounts. Androgens affect brain organization and behavior in many animal species, and they do so in humans as well (Hines & Green, 1991). Recall from Chapter 10 that androgens contribute to boys' higher activity level. They may also promote social dominance and play-fighting, topics we will take up at the end of this chapter (Maccoby, 1998).

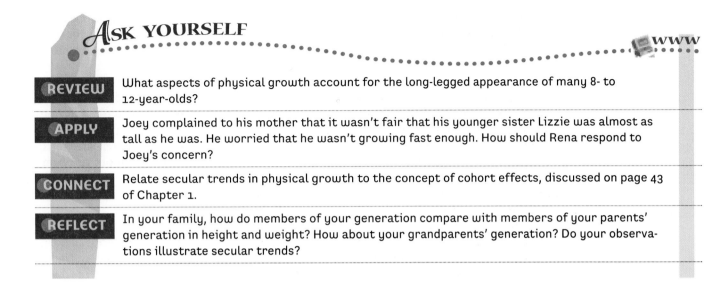

REVIEW
What aspects of physical growth account for the long-legged appearance of many 8- to 12-year-olds?

APPLY
Joey complained to his mother that it wasn't fair that his younger sister Lizzie was almost as tall as he was. He worried that he wasn't growing fast enough. How should Rena respond to Joey's concern?

CONNECT
Relate secular trends in physical growth to the concept of cohort effects, discussed on page 43 of Chapter 1.

REFLECT
In your family, how do members of your generation compare with members of your parents' generation in height and weight? How about your grandparents' generation? Do your observations illustrate secular trends?

Common Health Problems

Children like Joey and Lizzie, who come from economically advantaged homes, appear to be at their healthiest during middle childhood, full of energy and play. The cumulative effects of good nutrition, combined with rapid development of the body's immune system, offer greater protection against disease. At the same time, growth in lung size permits more air to be exchanged with each breath, so children are better able to exercise vigorously without tiring.

Nevertheless, a variety of health problems do occur. We will see that many of them are more common among low-SES children. Recall that in the United States, economically disadvantaged children often lack health insurance and, if they are publicly insured, generally receive a lower standard of care (see Chapter 8, page 299). And a substantial number also lack such basic necessities as a comfortable home and regular meals. Not surprisingly, poverty continues to be a powerful predictor of poor health during middle childhood.

Vision and Hearing

The most common vision problem in middle childhood is **myopia, or nearsightedness.** By the end of the school years, nearly 25 percent of children are affected, a rate that rises to 60 percent by early adulthood (Sperduto et al., 1996).

Kinship studies reveal that heredity contributes to myopia. Identical twins are more likely than fraternal twins to have the condition to a similar degree. And compared to children with no myopic parents, those with one myopic parent have twice the risk, and those with two myopic parents two to five times the risk, of becoming myopic themselves. Furthermore, around the world, myopia is far more frequent in Asian than in Caucasian populations (Feldkámper & Schaeffel, 2003). Early biological trauma can also induce myopia. School-age children with low birth weights show an especially high rate, believed to result from immaturity of visual structures, slower eye growth, and a greater incidence of eye disease (O'Connor et al., 2002).

But myopia is also related to experience and has increased in recent generations. Parents often warn their youngsters not to read in dim light or sit too close to the TV or computer screen, exclaiming, "You'll ruin your eyes!" Their concern is well founded. Myopia progresses much more rapidly during the school year, when children spend more time reading and doing other close work, than during the summer months (Goss & Rainey, 1998). And in diverse cultures, the more time children spend reading, writing, and using the computer, the more likely they are to be myopic (Mutti et al., 2002; Saw et al., 2002). Consequently, myopia is one of the few health conditions that increase with family income and education. Fortunately, for those children who develop nearsightedness because they love reading, sewing, drawing, or model building, the condition can be corrected easily with glasses.

During middle childhood, the Eustachian tube (the canal that runs from the inner ear to the throat) becomes longer, narrower, and more slanted, preventing fluid and bacteria from traveling so easily from the mouth to the ear. As a result, *otitis media* (middle ear infection) becomes less frequent (see Chapter 8). Still, about 3 to 4 percent of the school-age population, and as many as 20 percent of low-SES children, develop some hearing loss from repeated infections (Daly, Hunter, & Giebink, 1999; Ryding et al., 2002). Regular screening for both vision and hearing permits defects to be corrected before they lead to serious learning difficulties.

Malnutrition

School-age children need a well-balanced, plentiful diet to provide energy for successful learning in school and increased physical activity. Many youngsters are so focused on play, friendships, and new activities that they spend little time at the table. Joey's hurried breakfast, described at the beginning of this chapter, is a common event in middle childhood. Also, the percentage of children who eat dinner with their families drops sharply between 9 and 14 years, and family dinnertimes have waned in general over the past decade. Yet eating an evening meal with parents leads to a diet higher in fruits and vegetables and lower in fried foods and soft drinks (Gillman et al., 2000). It also results in the children's gaining useful nutrition information that parents provide during mealtime conversations (Gallup Organization, 1995).

School-age children report that they "feel better" and "focus better" after eating healthy foods and that they feel sluggish, "like a blob," after eating junk foods. But they also say that a major barrier to eating healthfully is the ready availability of unhealthy options, especially in their homes. As one sixth grader commented, "When I get home from school, I think, 'I should eat some fruits,' but then I see the chips" (O'Dea, 2003, p. 498). Readily available, healthy between-meal snacks—cheese, fruit, raw vegetables, and peanut butter—can help meet school-age children' nutritional needs. As long as parents promote healthy eating, the mild nutritional deficits that result from the child's busy daily schedule have no impact on development.

As we have seen in earlier chapters, many poverty-stricken children in developing countries and in North America suffer from serious and prolonged malnutrition. By middle childhood, the effects are apparent in retarded physical growth, low intelligence test scores, poor motor coordination, and inattention. The negative impact of malnutrition on learning and behavior may intensify during the school years. First, compared with their adequately nourished age-mates, growth-stunted school-age children respond with greater fear to stressful situations, as indicated by a sharper rise in heart rate and in saliva levels of the stress hormone cortisol (Fernald & Grantham-McGregor, 1998). Perhaps the repeated pain of hunger permanently altered their stress response. Second, animal evidence reveals that a deficient diet alters the production of neurotransmitters in the brain—an effect that can disrupt all aspects of psychological functioning (Levitsky & Strupp, 1995).

Unfortunately, when malnutrition persists from infancy or early childhood into the school years, permanent physical and mental damage usually results (Grantham-McGregor, Walker, & Chang, 2000). Prevention through government-sponsored food programs beginning in the early years and continuing throughout childhood and adolescence is necessary. In studies carried out in Egypt, Kenya, and Mexico, quality of food (protein, vitamin, and mineral content) was more important than quantity of food in predicting favorable cognitive development (Sigman, 1995; Wachs et al., 1995; Watkins & Pollitt, 1998).

Obesity

Mona, a very heavy child in Lizzie's class, often stood on the sidelines and watched during recess. When she did join the children's games, she was slow and clumsy. On a daily basis, Mona was the target of unkind comments: "Move it, Tubs!" "No fatsoes allowed!" Although Mona was a good student, the other children continued to reject her inside the classroom. When they chose partners for special activities, Mona was among the last to be selected. On most afternoons, she walked home from school by herself while the other children gathered in groups, talking, laughing, and chasing. Once at home, Mona sought comfort in high-calorie snacks, which promoted further weight gain.

Mona suffers from **obesity, a greater-than-20-percent increase over average body weight, based on an individual's age, sex, and physical build.** During the past several decades, a rise in overweight and obesity has occurred in many Western nations, with dramatic increases in Canada, Denmark, Finland, Great Britain, New Zealand, and especially the United States. Today, 15 percent of Canadian and 25 percent of American children are obese (Spurgeon, 2002; U.S. Department of Health and Human Services, 2002d). Smaller increases have occurred in other industrialized nations, including Australia, Germany, Israel, the Netherlands, and Sweden (Flegal, 1999). Obesity is also becoming common in developing countries as urbanization shifts the population toward sedentary lifestyles and diets high in meats and refined foods (Popkin, 2001).

Over 80 percent of affected children become overweight adults (Oken & Lightdale, 2000). Besides serious emotional and social difficulties, obese children are at risk for lifelong health problems. High blood pressure, high cholesterol levels, and respiratory abnormalities begin to appear in the early school years—symptoms that are powerful predictors of heart disease, other circulatory difficulties, adult-onset diabetes, liver and gallbladder disease, sleep and digestive disorders, most forms of cancer, and early death (Calle et al., 2003; Krebs & Jacobson, 2003). Indeed, "adult-onset" diabetes, which until recently was rare in childhood, is rising rapidly among overweight children, making the early appearance of other health problems, such as heart disease, more likely as well (American Academy of Pediatrics, 2004). As you can see from Table 11.1, childhood obesity is a complex physical disorder with multiple causes.

CAUSES OF OBESITY ● Not all children are equally at risk for excessive weight gain. Overweight children tend to have overweight parents, and concordance for obesity is greater in identical than in fraternal twins. (Return to Chapter 2, page 84, to review the concept of concordance.) But heredity accounts for only a tendency to gain weight (Salbe et al., 2002). One indication that environment is powerfully important is the consistent relation between low SES and overweight and obesity in industrialized nations, with especially high rates occurring

TABLE 11.1

Factors Associated with Childhood Obesity

FACTOR	DESCRIPTION
Heredity	Obese children are likely to have at least one obese parent, and concordance for obesity is greater in identical than in fraternal twins.
Socioeconomic status	Obesity is more common in low-SES families.
Early growth pattern	Infants who gain weight rapidly are at greater risk for obesity, probably because their parents promote unhealthy eating habits (see Chapter 5).
Family eating habits	When parents purchase high-calorie treats and junk food, use them to reward their children, anxiously overfeed, or control their children's intake, their youngsters are more likely to be obese.
Responsiveness to food cues	Obese children often decide when to eat on the basis of external cues, such as taste, smell, sight, time of day, and food-related words, rather than hunger.
Physical activity	Obese children are less physically active than their normal-weight peers.
Television viewing	Children who spend many hours watching television are more likely to become obese.
Early malnutrition	Early, severe malnutrition that results in growth stunting increases the risk of later obesity.

among low-SES ethnic minorities, including African-American, Hispanic, Native-American, and Canadian Aboriginal children and adults (Anand et al., 2001; Kim et al., 2002). Among the factors responsible are lack of knowledge about a healthy diet; a tendency to buy high-fat, low-cost foods; and family stress, which prompts overeating in some individuals.

Furthermore, children who were undernourished in their early years are at risk for later excessive weight gain. Surveys of nationally representative samples in Russia, China, and South Africa show that growth-stunted children are more likely to be overweight than their non-stunted agemates (Popkin, Richards, & Montiero, 1996). To protect itself, a malnourished body establishes a low basal metabolism rate, which may endure after nutrition improves. Also, malnutrition may disrupt the functioning of appetite control centers in the brain, causing the child to overeat when food becomes plentiful.

Parental feeding practices also contribute to childhood obesity. Overweight children are more likely to prefer and eat larger quantities of high-fat foods, perhaps because these foods are prominent in the diets offered by their parents, who also tend to be overweight (Fisher & Birch, 1995). Some parents anxiously overfeed their infants and young children, interpreting almost all their discomforts as a desire for food. Others pressure their children to eat—for example, by insisting that they finish everything on their plate. Still others are overly controlling, restricting when, what, and how much their child eats and worrying that the child will gain too much weight (Birch, Fisher, & Davison, 2003; Spruijt-Metz et al., 2002). In each case, parents fail to help children learn to regulate their own food intake. Also, parents of obese children often use high-fat, sugary foods to reinforce other behaviors—a practice that leads children to attach great value to the treat (Birch & Fisher, 1995).

Because of these experiences, obese children soon develop maladaptive eating habits. They are more responsive to external stimuli associated with food—taste, sight, smell, time of day, and food-related words—and less responsive to internal hunger cues than are normal-weight individuals (Braet & Crombez, 2003; Johnson & Birch, 1994). They also eat faster and chew their food less thoroughly, a behavior pattern that appears as early as 18 months of age (Drabman et al., 1979).

Overweight children are less physically active than their normal-weight peers, and their parents are similarly inactive (Davison & Birch, 2002). This inactivity is both cause and consequence of excessive weight gain. Recent evidence reveals that the rise in childhood obesity is due in part to the many hours North American children spend watching television. In a study that tracked children's TV viewing over a 4-year period, children who watched more than 5 hours per day were more than eight times likelier to become obese than children who watched 2 hours or less per day (see Figure 11.2) (Gortmaker et al., 1996). Television greatly reduces time devoted to physical exercise, and TV ads encourage children to eat fattening, unhealthy snacks. The more children watch, the more they believe that sugary cereals and fast foods are nutritious (Signorielli & Lears, 1992). As children get heavier, they increasingly replace active play with sedentary pursuits, including eating, and they gain more weight (Salby et al., 2002).

Finally, the broader food environment affects the incidence of obesity. The Pima Indians of Arizona, who recently changed from a traditional diet of plant foods to an American high-fat diet and sedentary lifestyle, have one of the highest rates of obesity in the world. Compared with descendants of their ancestors living in the remote Sierra Madre region of Mexico, the Arizona Pima have body weights 50 percent higher. Half the population

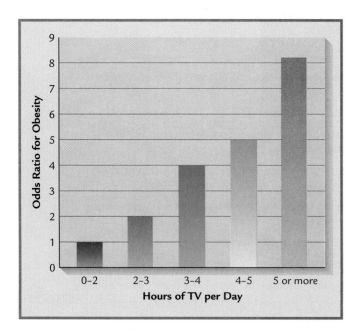

FIGURE 11.2

Relationship between television viewing and 5-development of childhood obesity.

Researchers tracked 10- to 15-year-olds' television viewing over a 4-year period. The more hours young people spent in front of the TV, the greater the likelihood that they became obese by the end of the study. (Adapted from Gortmaker et al., 1996.)

has diabetes (eight times the national average), and many are disabled by the disease in their twenties and thirties—blind, in wheelchairs, and on kidney dialysis (Gladwell, 1998). Although the Pima have a genetic susceptibility to overweight, it emerges only under Western conditions. Refer to the Social Issues: Health box on pages 410–411 for societal changes that have led Americans to become the heaviest people in the world.

CONSEQUENCES OF OBESITY ● Unfortunately, physical attractiveness is a powerful predictor of social acceptance in Western societies. Both children and adults rate obese youngsters as unlikable, stereotyping them as lazy, sloppy, dirty, ugly, stupid, and deceitful (Kilpatrick & Sanders, 1978; Tiggemann & Anesbury, 2000). By middle childhood, obese children report feeling more depressed and display more behavior problems than their peers. Unhappiness and overeating contribute to one another, and the child remains overweight (Mustillo et al., 2003). In addition, as we will see in Chapter 14, overweight girls are more likely to reach puberty early, which magnifies their risk for early sexual activity and other adjustment problems.

The psychological consequences of obesity combine with continuing discrimination to result in reduced life chances. Overweight young adults have completed fewer years of schooling, have lower incomes, and are less likely to be offered jobs and find mates (Allison & Pi-Sunyer, 1994).

This Pima Indian medicine man of Arizona is very obese. By the time his children reach adolescence, they are likely to follow in his footsteps. Because of a high-fat diet, the Pima residing in the Southwestern United States have one of the highest rates of obesity in the world. In contrast, the Pima living in the remote Sierra Madre region of Mexico are average weight.

TREATING OBESITY ● Childhood obesity is difficult to treat because it is a family disorder. In Mona's case, the school nurse suggested that Mona and her obese mother enter a weight-loss program together. But Mona's mother, unhappily married for many years, had her own reasons for continuing to overeat. She rejected this idea, claiming that Mona would eventually decide to lose weight on her own. Although many obese youngsters try to slim down in adolescence, they often go on crash diets that make matters worse. Temporary starvation leads to physical stress, discomfort, and fatigue. Soon the child returns to old eating patterns, and weight rebounds to a higher level. Then, to protect itself, the body burns calories more slowly and becomes more resistant to future weight loss.

When parents decide to seek treatment for an obese child, long-term changes in body weight do occur. The most effective interventions are family based and focus on changing behaviors. In one program, both parent and child revised eating patterns, exercised daily, and reinforced each other with praise and points for progress, which they exchanged for special activities and times together. Follow-ups after 5 and 10 years showed that children maintained their weight loss more effectively than adults—a finding that underscores the importance of intervening at an early age (Epstein, Roemmich, & Raynor, 2001). Furthermore, weight loss was greater when treatments focused on both dietary and lifestyle changes, including regular, vigorous exercise.

Getting obese children to exercise, however, is challenging because they find being sedentary pleasurable. A successful technique is to reinforce them for spending less time inactive. Giving obese children rewards (such as tickets to the zoo or a baseball game) for reducing sedentary time led to greater liking for physical activity and more weight loss than reinforcing them directly for exercising or punishing them (by loss of privileges) for remaining inactive (Epstein, Saelens, & O'Brien, 1995; Epstein et al., 1997). Rewarding children for giving up inactivity seems to increase their sense of personal control over exercising—a factor linked to sustained physical activity.

Schools can help reduce obesity by ensuring regular physical education and serving healthier meals. The makeup of school lunches and snacks can greatly affect body weight because children consume one-third of their daily energy intake at school. In Singapore, school interventions consisting of nutrition education, low-fat food choices, and daily physical activity led child and adolescent obesity to decline from 14 to 11 percent (Schmitz & Jeffery, 2000).

Social Issues: Health

The Obesity Epidemic: How Americans Became the Heaviest People in the World

In the late 1980s, obesity in the United States stared to soar. The maps in Figure 11.3 show how quickly it engulfed the nation. Today the majority of Americas—50 percent of school-age children and adolescents and 61 percent of adults—are either overweight or obese (U.S. Department of Health and Human Services, 2002d). The epidemic has spread to other Western nations, such as Canada, where the respective figures are 40 and 44 percent (Tremblay, Katzmarzyk, & Willms, 2002). But no country matches the United States in prevalence of this life-threatening condition.

A Changing Food Environment and Lifestyle

Several societal factors have encouraged this widespread, rapid weight gain.

- *Availability of cheap commercial fat and sugar.* In the 1970s, two massive changes in the U.S. food economy occurred: (1) the discovery and mass production of high-fructose corn syrup, a sweetener six times as sweet as, and therefore far less expensive than, ordinary sugar, and (2) the importing from Malaysia of large quantities of palm oil, which is lower in cost, higher in saturated fat, and therefore tastier than other vegetable oils. As food manufacturers relied on corn syrup and palm oil to make soft drinks and calorie-dense convenience foods, the pro-

duction cost of these items dropped and their variety expanded. A new era of "cheap, abundant, and tasty calories had arrived" (Critser, 2003).

- *Portion supersizing.* Fast-food chains discovered a highly successful strategy for attracting customers: increasing portion sizes substantially and prices just a little for foods that had become inexpensive to produce. Families thronged to buy "value meals," jumbo burgers and burritos, pizza "by the foot," and 20-ounce Cokes (Critser, 2003). And research revealed that when presented with larger portions, individuals 2 years and older increased their intake, on average, by 25 to 30 percent (Fisher, Rolls, & Birch, 2003; Rolls, Morris, & Roe, 2002).

- *Increasingly busy lives.* Between the 1970s and the 1990s, women entered the labor force in record numbers, and the average number of hours Americans worked increased by 350 per year (Schor, 2002). As time became scarce, eating out increased. In addition, American adults and children became frequent snackers, tempted by an ever-in-

creasing diversity of high-calorie snack foods. During this period, average number of calories consumed increased by 10 percent, and dietary fat rose from 19 to 38 percent (Nielsen & Popkin, 2003). As Americans spent more time working in sedentary jobs, they—and their children—exercised less. At home, TV became their major leisure pursuit.

- *Misguided information about healthy weight, exercise, and diet.* As Americans got heavier, national health experts hesitated to inform them of their dire condition. In 1990, the federal government relaxed its recommendations on ideal weight. And recently, it advised that moderate activity is key to health, despite clear evidence that intense exercise is more protective (Yu et al., 2003). Finally, an expanding health-advice industry dispensed a wealth of inconsistent messages, including the recommendation that Americans stop worrying about food intake and focus on fitness instead (Molnar & Babbitt, 2000). Yet the overwhelming majority of overweight children and adults do what they can

© DONNA DAY/GETTY IMAGES/STONE

A harmful food environment of cheap, calorie-dense convenience foods and supersize portions and an increasingly sedentary lifestyle have contributed to the obesity epidemic. Without intervention, this boy is at risk for many obesity-related illnesses. Already, he may have high blood pressure and high cholesterol, which are powerful predictors of heart disease, diabetes, various cancers, and other illnesses.

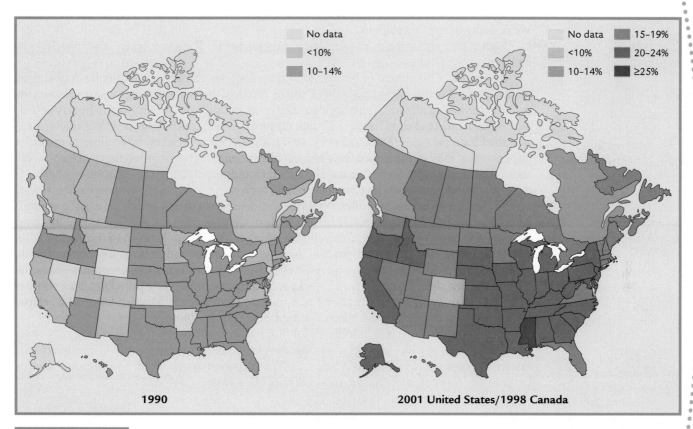

FIGURE 11.3

Obesity trends among Americans and Canadians, 1990 and 1998–2001.

The darkening maps show that obesity has increased in both nations. But the rise during the past decade is especially extreme in the United States. (From A. Katzmarzyk, "The Canadian Obesity Epidemic," *Canadian Medical Association Journal, 166,* pp. 1039–1040; Mokdad et al., 2001, "The Continuing Epidemics of Obesity and Diabetes in the United States," *Journal of the American Medical Association, 286,* p. 1198. Adapted by permission.)

to avoid physical activity—and especially, intense activity.

This conflicting information confused the public. In one national survey of parents of 2- to 11-year-olds, nearly one-third of mothers of overweight children judged their child as "about the right weight" (Maynard et al., 2003). And in one survey of low-SES African Americans, who are especially prone to obesity, 37 percent agreed with the statement, "I don't know if exercise is good or bad for me" (Airhihenbuwa et al., 1995).

Combating the Obesity Epidemic

In addition to individual treatment, broad societal measures are needed to combat obesity (Nestle & Jacobson, 2000). Suggestions include the following:

● Government funding to support massive public education about healthy eating and physical activity;

● Placing a high priority on building parks and recreation centers in low-income neighborhoods, where overweight and obesity are highest;

● Laws that mandate prominent posting of the calorie, sugar, and fat content of foods sold in restaurants, movie theaters, and convenience stores;

● A special tax on foods high in calories, sugar, or fat; and

● Incentives to schools and workplaces for promoting healthy eating and daily exercise.

Bedwetting

One Friday afternoon, Terry called Joey to see if he could sleep over, but Joey refused. "I can't," said Joey anxiously, without giving an explanation.

"Why not? We can take our sleeping bags out in the backyard. Come on, it'll be super!"

"My mom won't let me," Joey responded, unconvincingly. "I mean, well, I think we're busy. We're doing something tonight."

"Gosh, Joey, this is the third time you've said no. See if I'll ask you again!" snapped Terry as he hung up the phone.

Joey is one of 10 percent of North American school-age children who suffer from **nocturnal enuresis, or bedwetting during the night** (Thiedke, 2003). In the overwhelming majority of cases, the problem has biological roots. Heredity is a major contributing factor. Parents with a history of bedwetting are far more likely to have a child with the problem, and concordance is greater among identical than fraternal twins (Norgaard et al., 1997). Most often, it is caused by a failure of muscular responses that inhibit urination or by a hormonal imbalance that permits too much urine to accumulate during the night. Some children also have difficulty awakening to the sensation of a full bladder (Hjälmäs, 1998). Punishing a school-age child for wetting is only likely to make matters worse.

To treat enuresis, doctors often prescribe antidepressant drugs, which reduce the amount of urine produced. Although medication is a short-term solution for children attending camp or visiting a friend's house, once children stop taking it, they typically begin wetting again. Also, a small number show side effects, such as anxiety, loss of sleep, and personality changes (Goin, 1998; Harari & Moulden, 2000). The most effective treatment is a urine alarm that wakes the child at the first sign of dampness and works according to conditioning principles. Success rates of about 60 to 70 percent occur after 4 to 6 months of treatment. Most children who relapse achieve dryness after trying the alarm a second time (Houts, 2003).

Treatment of enuresis in middle childhood has immediate positive psychological consequences. It leads to gains in parents' evaluation of their child's behavior and in children's self-esteem (Longstaffe, Moffatt, & Whalen, 2000). Although many children outgrow enuresis without any form of intervention, this generally takes years.

Illnesses

Children experience a somewhat higher rate of illness during the first 2 years of elementary school than they will later, due to exposure to sick children and to the fact that the immune system is still developing. On average, illness causes children to miss about 11 days of school per year, but most absences can be traced to a few students with chronic health problems (Madan-Swain, Fredrick, & Wallander, 1999).

About 15 to 20 percent of North American children living at home have chronic diseases and conditions (including physical disabilities). By far the most common—accounting for about one-third of childhood chronic illness and the most frequent cause of school absence and childhood hospitalization—is **asthma, in which the bronchial tubes (passages that connect the throat and lungs) are highly sensitive. In response to a variety of stimuli, such as cold weather, infection, exercise, allergies, and emotional stress, they fill with mucus and contract, leading to coughing, wheezing, and serious breathing difficulties** (Akinbami & Schoendorf, 2002).

The number of children with asthma has more than doubled in the past 30 years, and asthma-related deaths have also risen. Although heredity contributes to asthma, researchers believe that environmental factors are necessary to spark the illness. Boys, African-American children, and children who were born underweight, whose parents smoke, and who live in poverty are at greatest risk (Federico & Liu, 2003). Perhaps African-American and poverty-stricken youngsters experience a higher rate of asthma and more severe asthma attacks because of pollution in inner-city areas (which triggers allergic reactions), stressful home lives, and lack of access to good health care. In addition, childhood obesity is related to asthma onset in middle childhood (Gilliland et al., 2003). Researchers speculate that high levels of blood-circulating inflammatory substances, associated with body fat, are responsible.

About 2 percent of North American children have chronic illnesses that are more severe than asthma, such as sickle cell anemia, cystic fibrosis, diabetes, arthritis, cancer, and acquired immune deficiency syndrome (AIDS). Painful medical treatments, physical discomfort, and changes in appearance often disrupt the sick child's daily life, making it difficult to concentrate in school and causing withdrawal from peers. As the illness worsens, family stress increases (LeBlanc, Goldsmith, & Patel, 2003). For these reasons, chronically ill children are at risk for academic, emotional, and social problems.

A strong link between parent psychological adjustment, good family functioning, and child well-being exists for chronically ill children, just as it does for physically healthy children (Barakat & Kazak, 1999). Interventions that foster positive family interactions and help parent and child cope with the disease improve children's adjustment. These include the following:

● Health education, in which parents and children learn about the illness and get training in how to manage it;

● Home visits by health professionals, who offer counseling and social support to enhance parents' and children's strategies for handling the stress of chronic illness;

● Schools that accommodate children's special health and education needs;

● Disease-specific summer camps, which teach children self-help skills and give parents time off from the demands of caring for an ill youngster;

● Parent and peer support groups; and

● Individual and family therapy.

Unintentional Injuries

As we conclude our discussion of threats to children's health during the school years, let's return for a moment to the topic of unintentional injuries (discussed in detail in Chapter 8). As Figure 11.4 shows, the frequency of injury fatalities increases from middle childhood into adolescence, and the rate for boys rises considerably above that for girls. In addition, poverty and rural or inner-city residence—factors associated with dangerous environments and reduced parental monitoring of children—are linked to high injury rates (Rivara & Aitken, 1998).

Motor vehicle accidents, involving children as passengers or pedestrians, continue to be the leading cause of injury, with bicycle accidents next in line (U.S. Department of Health and Human Services, 2002a). Pedestrian injuries most often result from midblock dart-outs; bicycle accidents generally result from disobeying traffic signals and rules. Young school-age children are not yet good at thinking before they act, especially when many stimuli impinge on them at once (Tuchfarber, Zins, & Jason, 1997). Whether on foot or bicycle, they need frequent reminders, supervision, and prohibitions against venturing into busy traffic on their own.

As children range farther from home, safety education becomes especially important. School-based programs with lasting effects use extensive modeling and rehearsal of safety practices; give children feedback about their performance, along with praise and tangible rewards for acquiring safety skills; and provide occasional booster sessions (Zins et al., 1994). An important part of injury prevention is educating parents about children's age-related safety capacities, since parents often overestimate their child's safety knowledge and physical abilities (Rivara, 1995; Schwebel & Bounds, 2003).

Insisting that children wear protective helmets while bicycling, roller blading, skateboarding, or using scooters is a vital safety measure. This simple precaution leads to an 85 percent reduction in risk of head injury—a leading cause of permanent physical disability and death during the school years (Schieber & Sacks, 2001). Combining helmet use with other prevention strategies is especially effective. In the Harlem Hospital Injury Prevention Program, inner-city children received safety education in classrooms and in a simulated traffic environment.

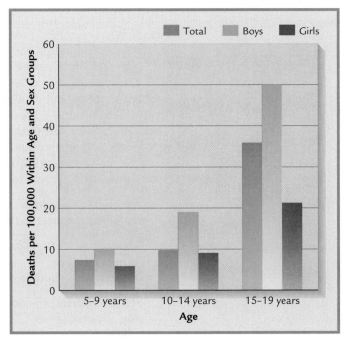

FIGURE 11.4

Rate of injury mortality in North America from middle childhood to adolescence.
Injury fatalities increase with age, and the gap between boys and girls expands. Motor vehicle (passenger and pedestrian) accidents are the leading cause, with bicycle injuries next in line. American and Canadian injury rates are nearly identical. (From U.S. Department of Health and Human Services, 2002a.)

© ARIEL SKELLEY/CORBIS

These boys play a fast-paced, pickup game of roller hockey. Unfortunately, their parents failed to insist that they wear helmets as well as arm and knee protection. A rough fall could result in a serious, life-threatening injury.

They also attended bicycle safety clinics, during which helmets were distributed. In addition, existing playgrounds were improved and new ones constructed to provide expanded off-street play areas. And more community-sponsored, supervised recreational activities were offered. As a result, motor vehicle and bicycle injuries declined by 36 percent among school-age children (Durkin et al., 1999).

Not all children respond to efforts to increase their safety. By middle childhood, the greatest risk takers tend to be those whose parents do not act as safety-conscious models, rarely supervise their children's activities, and try to enforce rules by using punitive or inconsistent discipline (Tuchfarber, Zins, & Jason, 1997). These child-rearing tactics, as we saw in Chapter 10, spark defiance in children, reduce their willingness to comply, and may actually promote high-risk behavior.

Highly active, impulsive children, many of whom are boys, remain particularly susceptible to injury in middle childhood. Although they have just as much safety knowledge as their peers, they are far less likely to implement it (Brehaut et al., 2003; Mori & Peterson, 1995). Compared with girls, boys judge risky play activities as less likely to result in injury, and they pay less attention to injury risk cues, such as a peer who looks hesitant or fearful (Morrongiello & Rennie, 1998). The greatest challenge for injury control programs is reaching these "more difficult to reach" youngsters, altering high-risk factors in their families, and reducing the dangers to which they are exposed.

ℋealth Education

Psychologists, educators, and pediatricians are intensely interested in finding ways to help school-age children understand their bodies, acquire mature conceptions of health and illness, and develop behaviors that foster good health throughout life. Successful health intervention requires information on children's current health-related knowledge. What can they understand? What reasoning processes do they use? What factors influence what they know? The Social Issues: Education box on the following page summarizes findings on children's concepts of health and illness during middle childhood.

The school-age period may be especially important for fostering healthy lifestyles because of the child's growing independence, increasing cognitive capacities, and rapidly developing self-concept, which includes a sense of physical well-being (Harter, 2003). During middle childhood, children can acquire a wide range of health information—about the structure and functioning of their bodies, about good nutrition, and about the causes and consequences of physical injuries and diseases. Yet most efforts to impart health concepts to school-age children have little impact on behavior (Tinsley, 2003). Several related reasons underlie this gap between knowledge and practice:

● Health is usually not an important goal for children, who feel good most of the time. They are far more concerned about schoolwork, friends, and play.

● Children do not yet have an adultlike time perspective, which relates past, present, and future. Engaging in preventive behaviors is difficult when so much time intervenes between what children do now and later health consequences.

● Much health information that children get is contradicted by other sources, such as television advertising (see Chapter 10) and the examples of adults and peers.

Social Issues: Education

Children's Understanding of Health and Illness

© SPENCER GRANT/INDEX STOCK

Lizzie lay on the living room sofa with a stuffy nose and sore throat, disappointed that she was missing her soccer team's final game and pizza party. "How'd I get this dumb cold anyhow?" she wondered aloud to Joey. "I probably got it by playing outside when it was freezing cold."

"No, no," Joey contradicted. "Viruses get into your blood and attack, just like an army."

"Gross. I didn't eat any viruses," responded Lizzie.

"You don't eat them, silly, you breathe them in. Somebody probably sneezed them all over you at school. That's how you got sick!"

Lizzie and Joey are at different developmental levels in their understanding of health and illness—due to cognitive development and exposure to biological knowledge. Researchers have asked preschool through high school students questions about the causes of health and of certain illnesses, such as colds, AIDS, and cancer.

During the preschool and early school years, children do not have much biological knowledge to bring to bear on their understanding of health and illness. For example, 3- to 8-year-olds know little about their internal organs and how they work. As a result, they fall back on their rich knowledge of people's behavior to account for health and illness (Carey, 1995, 1999; Simons & Keil, 1995). Children of this age regard health as a matter of engaging in specific practices (eating the right foods, getting enough sleep and exercise, and wearing warm clothing on cold days), and they regard illness as a matter of failing to follow these rules or coming too close to a sick person.

By age 9 or 10, children can name many internal organs and view them as interconnected, working as a system. Around this time, they almost always explain health and illness biologically (Carey, 1999). Joey understands that illness can be caused by contagion—breathing in a harmful substance (a virus), which affects the operation of the body. He also realizes

that we eat not just because food tastes good or to stay alive (younger children's explanations) but to build flesh, blood, muscle, and bone (Inagaki & Hatano, 1993; Toyamo, 2000).

In early adolescence, explanations become more elaborate and precise. Eleven- to 14-year-olds recognize health as a long-term condition that depends on the interaction of body, mind, and environment (Hergenrather & Rabinowitz, 1991). And their notions of illness involve clearly stated ideas about interference in normal biological processes: "You get a cold when your sinuses fill with mucus. Sometimes your lungs do, too, and you get a cough. Colds come from viruses. They get into the bloodstream and make your platelet count go down" (Bibace & Walsh, 1980).

Young school-age children can grasp basic biological ideas that are important for understanding disease. But whether or not they do so depends on the information in their environments. When supplied with relevant facts and biological concepts, such as "gene," "germ," and "virus," even 5- and 6-year-olds use the concepts to organize the facts, and their understanding advances (Solomon & Johnson, 2000).

Without such knowledge, children readily generalize what they know about familiar diseases to less familiar ones. As a result, they often conclude that risk factors for colds (sharing a Coke or sneezing on someone) can cause AIDS. And lacking much understanding of cancer, they assume that it (like colds) is communicable through casual contact. These incorrect ideas can lead to unnecessary anxiety about getting a serious disease. In surveys of school-age children, about half incorrectly believed that everyone is at risk for AIDS. And more than half said they worry about getting AIDS or cancer (Chin et al., 1998; Holcomb, 1990).

Although misconceptions decline with age, culturally transmitted attitudes can lead to gaps between knowledge and behavior. When certain diseases take on powerful symbolic meanings—for example, cancer as a malignant, destructive evil and AIDS as a sign of moral decay—even

This child comforts her grandmother, who is dying of cancer. Helping school-age children understand that cancer is not communicable can prevent them from developing negative attitudes toward its victims.

adults with accurate biological knowledge expect bad things to happen from associating with affected people (Pryor & Reeder, 1993). Children quickly pick up these attitudes, which help explain the severe social rejection experienced by some youngsters with chronic diseases.

Education about the causes of various illnesses leads to an increasingly accurate appreciation of disease transmission and prevention during middle childhood and adolescence. To combat irrational fears and prejudices and foster compassion, teachers can give AIDS, cancer, and other debilitating and deadly illnesses "a human face" by bringing chronically ill people into the classroom or talking about the experiences of people who died of an illness.

Applying
WHAT WE Know / Strategies for Fostering Healthy Lifestyles in School-Age Children

STRATEGY	DESCRIPTION
Increase health-related knowledge and encourage healthy behaviors.	Provide health education through developmentally appropriate, enjoyable activities that include modeling, role playing, rehearsal, and reinforcement of good health practices.
Involve parents in supporting health education.	Communicate with parents about health education goals in school, encouraging them to extend these efforts at home. Teach parents about unhealthy feeding practices, and encourage them to create healthy food environments at home. Promote proper parental supervision by providing information on children's age-related safety capacities.
Provide healthy environments in schools.	Ask school administrators to ensure that school breakfasts and lunches follow widely accepted dietary guidelines. Also work for daily, mandatory physical education from kindergarten through high school.
Make voluntary screening for risk factors available as part of health education.	Offer periodic measures of height, weight, body mass, blood pressure, and adequacy of diet. Educate children about the meaning of each index, and encourage improvement.
Promote pleasurable physical activity.	Provide opportunities for regular, vigorous physical exercise through activities that de-emphasize competition and stress skill-building and personal and social enjoyment.
Teach children to be critical of media advertising.	Besides teaching children to be skeptical of TV ads for unhealthy foods, reduce advertising for such foods in schools.
Work for safer, healthier community environments for children.	Form community action groups to improve child safety, school nutrition, and play environments, and initiate community programs that foster healthy physical activity.

This does not mean that teaching school-age children health-related facts is unimportant. But information must be supplemented by other efforts. As we have seen in this and earlier chapters, a powerful means of fostering children's health is to reduce hazards, such as pollution, inadequate medical and dental care, and unhealthy foods (Rivara & Aitken, 1998). At the same time, because environments will never be totally free of health risks, parents and teachers must coach children in good health practices and must model and reinforce these behaviors. Refer to Applying What We Know above for ways to foster healthy lifestyles in school-age children.

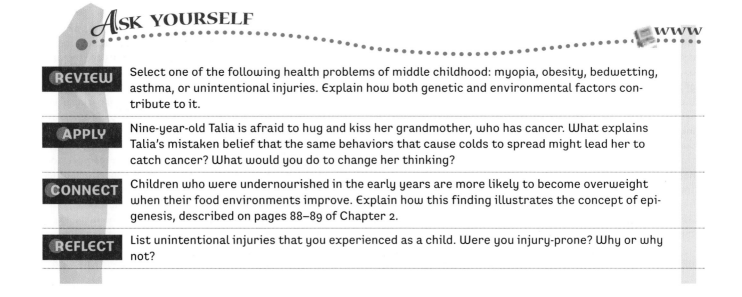

ASK YOURSELF   www

REVIEW Select one of the following health problems of middle childhood: myopia, obesity, bedwetting, asthma, or unintentional injuries. Explain how both genetic and environmental factors contribute to it.

APPLY Nine-year-old Talia is afraid to hug and kiss her grandmother, who has cancer. What explains Talia's mistaken belief that the same behaviors that cause colds to spread might lead her to catch cancer? What would you do to change her thinking?

CONNECT Children who were undernourished in the early years are more likely to become overweight when their food environments improve. Explain how this finding illustrates the concept of epigenesis, described on pages 88–89 of Chapter 2.

REFLECT List unintentional injuries that you experienced as a child. Were you injury-prone? Why or why not?

Motor Development and Play

Visit a park on a pleasant weekend afternoon, and watch several preschool and school-age children at play. You will see that gains in body size and muscle strength support improved motor coordination during middle childhood. In addition, greater cognitive and social maturity enables older children to use their new motor skills in more complex ways. A major change in children's play takes place at this time.

Gross Motor Development

During middle childhood, running, jumping, hopping, and ball skills become more refined. At Joey and Lizzie's school one day, I watched during the third to sixth graders' recess. Children burst into sprints as they raced across the playground, jumped quickly over rotating ropes, engaged in intricate patterns of hopscotch, kicked and dribbled soccer balls, batted at balls pitched by their classmates, and balanced adeptly as they walked toe-to-toe across narrow ledges. Table 11.2 summarizes gross motor achievements between 6 and 12 years of age. These diverse skills reflect gains in four basic motor capacities:

● *Flexibility.* Compared with preschoolers, school-age children are physically more pliable and elastic, a difference that can be seen as they swing bats, kick balls, jump over hurdles, and execute tumbling routines.

TABLE 11.2

Changes in Gross Motor Skills During Middle Childhood

SKILL	DEVELOPMENTAL CHANGE
Running	Running speed increases from 12 feet per second at age 6 to over 18 feet per second at age 12.
Other gait variations	Skipping improves. Sideways stepping appears around age 6 and becomes more continuous and fluid with age.
Vertical jump	Height jumped increases from 4 inches at age 6 to 12 inches at age 12.
Standing broad jump	Distance jumped increases from 3 feet at age 6 to over 5 feet at age 12.
Precision jumping and hopping (on a mat divided into squares)	By age 7 children can accurately jump and hop from square to square, a performance that improves until age 9 and then levels off.
Throwing	Throwing speed, distance, and accuracy increase for both sexes, but much more for boys than for girls. At age 6, a ball thrown by a boy travels 39 feet per second, one by a girl 29 feet per second. At age 12, a ball thrown by a boy travels 78 feet per second, one by a girl 56 feet per second.
Catching	Ability to catch small balls thrown over greater distances improves with age.
Kicking	Kicking speed and accuracy improve, with boys considerably ahead of girls. At age 6, a ball kicked by a boy travels 21 feet per second, one by a girl 13 feet per second. At age 12, a ball kicked by a boy travels 34 feet per second, one by a girl 26 feet per second.
Batting	Batting motions become more effective with age, increasing in speed and accuracy and involving the entire body.
Dribbling	Style of hand dribbling gradually changes, from awkward slapping of the ball to continuous, relaxed, even stroking.

© BOB DAEMMRICH/THE IMAGE WORKS

© DAVID YOUNG-WOLFF/PHOTOEDIT

Sources: Cratty, 1986; Malina & Bouchard, 1991; Roberton, 1984.

- *Balance.* Improved balance supports many athletic skills, including running, hopping, skipping, throwing, kicking, and the rapid changes of direction required in many team sports.

- *Agility.* Quicker and more accurate movements are evident in the fancy footwork of jump rope and hopscotch, as well as in the forward, backward, and sideways motions older children use as they dodge opponents in tag and soccer.

- *Force.* Older children can throw and kick a ball harder and propel themselves farther off the ground when running and jumping than they could at earlier ages (Cratty, 1986).

Although body growth contributes greatly to improved motor performance, more efficient information processing also plays an important role. Younger children often have difficulty with skills that require immediate responding, such as dribbling and batting. During middle childhood, the capacity to react only to relevant information increases. And steady improvements in reaction time occur, with 11-year-olds responding twice as quickly as 5-year-olds (Band et al., 2000; Largo et al., 2001). These differences in speed of reaction have practical implications for physical education (Seefeldt, 1996). Because 6- and 7-year-olds are seldom successful at batting a thrown ball, T-ball is more appropriate than baseball. And handball, four-square, and kickball should precede instruction in tennis, basketball, and football.

Fine Motor Development

Fine motor development also improves over the school years. On rainy afternoons, Joey and Lizzie experimented with yo-yos, built model airplanes, and wove pot holders on small looms. Like many children, they took up musical instruments, which demand considerable fine motor control.

Gains in fine motor skill are especially evident in children's writing and drawing. By age 6, most children can print the alphabet, their first and last names, and the numbers from 1 to 10 with reasonable clarity. However, their writing is large because they use the entire arm to make strokes rather than just the wrist and fingers. Children usually master uppercase letters first because horizontal and vertical motions are easier to control than the small curves of the lowercase alphabet. Legibility of writing gradually increases as children produce more accurate letters with uniform height and spacing. These improvements prepare children for mastering cursive writing by third grade.

Children's drawings show dramatic gains in organization, detail, and representation of depth during middle childhood. By the end of the preschool years, children can accurately copy many two-dimensional shapes, and they integrate these into their drawings. Some depth cues have also begun to appear, such as making distant objects smaller than near ones (Braine et al., 1993). Yet recall from Chapter 8 that before age 8, children have trouble accurately copying a three-dimensional form, such as a cube or cylinder (see page 307). Around 9 to 10 years, the third dimension is clearly evident in children's drawings through overlapping objects, diagonal placement, and converging lines. Furthermore, as Figure 11.5 shows, school-age children not only depict objects in considerable detail but also relate them to one another as part of an organized whole (Case, 1998; Case & Okamoto, 1996).

Individual Differences in Motor Skills

As at younger ages, school-age children show marked individual differences in motor capacities that are influenced by both heredity and environment. Body build continues to affect gross motor performance, with taller, more muscular children excelling at many tasks. At the same time, parents who encourage physical exercise tend to have children who enjoy it more and who are also more skilled.

Family income affects children's access to ballet, tennis, gymnastics, music lessons, and, therefore, their opportunities to develop a variety of physical abilities. School and community provisions for nurturing athletics through lessons, equipment, and regular practice are crucial for low-SES children. When these experiences combine with parental encouragement, many low-SES children become highly skilled.

FIGURE 11.5

Increase in organization, detail, and depth cues in school-age children's drawings.

Compare both drawings to the one by a 6-year-old on page 307. In the drawing on the left, an 8-year-old depicts her family—father, mother, and three children. Notice how all parts are depicted in relation to one another, and the human figures are given much more detail. (The artist is your author, as a third grader. In the drawing, Laura can be found between her older sister and younger brother.) Integration of depth cues increases dramatically over the school years, as shown in the drawing on the right, by a 10-year-old artist from Singapore. Here, depth is indicated by overlapping objects, diagonal placement, and converging lines, as well as by making distant objects smaller than near ones.

Sex differences in motor skills that appeared during the preschool years extend into middle childhood and, in some instances, become more pronounced. Girls remain ahead in the fine motor area, including handwriting and drawing. They also continue to have an edge in skipping, jumping, and hopping, which depend on balance and agility. But boys outperform girls on all other skills listed in Table 11.2, and the difference is large in throwing and kicking (Cratty, 1986).

School-age boys' genetic advantage in muscle mass is not great enough to account for their gross motor superiority. Instead, environment plays a larger role. Parents hold higher expectations for boys' athletic performance, and children absorb these messages at an early age. From first through twelfth grades, girls are less positive than boys about the value of sports and their own sports ability—differences explained in part by parental beliefs (Fredricks & Eccles, 2002). In one study, boys more often stated that it was vital to their parents that they participate in athletics. These attitudes affected children's self-confidence and behavior. Girls saw themselves as having less talent at sports, and by sixth grade they devoted less time to athletics than their male classmates (Eccles & Harold, 1991). At the same time, children regard boys' advantage in sports as unjust. They indicate, for example, that coaches should spend equal time with children of each sex and that female sports should command just as much media attention as male sports (Solomon & Bredemeier, 1999).

These findings indicate that extra measures must be taken to increase girls' participation, self-confidence, and sense of fair treatment in athletics. Educating parents about the minimal differences between school-age boys' and girls' physical capacities and sensitizing them to biases against girls' athletic ability may prove helpful. In addition, greater emphasis on skill training for girls, along with increased attention to their athletic achievements, is likely to increase involvement. Middle childhood is a crucial time to take these steps because during the school years children start to discover what they are good at and make some definite skill commitments.

Korean girls attending a cultural celebration in traditional dress organize a game of "neolttwigi," which involves throwing and catching a ball while balancing on a seesaw. Informal, child-organized games come in enormous variety. Through them, children try out different styles of cooperating, competing, winning, and losing, and discover why rules are necessary and which ones work well.

© CRAIG BROWN

Child-Organized Games

The physical activities of school-age children reflect an important advance in the quality of their play: Games with rules become common. In cultures around the world, children engage in an enormous variety of informally organized games. Some are variants on popular sports, such as soccer, baseball, basketball, and football. Others are well-known childhood games, such as tag, jacks, and hopscotch. And children have invented hundreds of less well-known games, including Red Rover, Statues, Leap Frog, Kick the Can, and Prisoner's Base, and have passed them from one generation to the next (Kirchner, 2000).

Gains in perspective taking—in particular, children's ability to understand the roles of several players in a game—permit this transition to rule-oriented games. These play experiences contribute greatly to emotional and social development. Child-invented games usually rely on simple physical skills and a sizable element of luck. As a result, they rarely become contests of individual ability. Instead, they permit children to try out different styles of cooperating, competing, winning, and losing with little personal risk. Also, in their efforts to organize a game, children discover why rules are necessary and which ones work well. In fact, they often spend as much time working out the details of how a game should proceed as they do playing the game! As we will see in Chapter 13, these experiences help children form more mature concepts of fairness and justice.

Adult-Organized Youth Sports

Today, school-age children spend less time gathering on sidewalks and playgrounds than in generations past. Parental concern about neighborhood safety and children's attraction to TV and video games account for some of this change. But adult-organized sports, such as Little League baseball and soccer and hockey leagues, also fill many hours that children used to devote to spontaneous play. The past several decades have witnessed a tremendous expansion of youth sports programs, with most North American youngsters participating at some time during childhood and adolescence (Statistics Canada, 2000a; U.S. Department of Health and Human Services, 2000b).

Some researchers worry that adult-structured athletics are endangering children's development by overemphasizing competition and substituting adult control for children's experimentation with rules and strategies. But so far, research indicates that for most children, participating in community athletic teams is associated with greater social competence (Fletcher, Nickerson, & Wright, 2003). Nevertheless, the arguments of critics are valid in some cases. Children who join teams so early that the skills demanded are beyond their capabilities soon lose interest. And coaches who criticize rather than encourage and who react angrily to defeat can prompt intense anxiety in some children. They also serve as poor models of good sportsmanship, self-control, and compassion. Furthermore, competence at sports is linked to peer admiration, especially among boys. When coaches create a climate in which winning is paramount, weaker performers generally experience social ostracism (Stryer, Tofler, & Lapchick, 1998).

Earlier we saw that parents influence children's athletic attitudes and abilities—an effect that is stronger than that of coaches. Occasionally, parents value sports so highly that they denounce and punish their child for making mistakes, insist that the child keep playing after injury, hold the child back in school to ensure a physical advantage, and request medical interventions to improve the child's performance. High parental pressure sets the stage for emotional difficulties and early athletic dropout, not elite performance (Marsh & Daigneault, 1999; Tofler, Knapp, & Drell, 1998). Children of such parents may find athletics so stressful and damaging to their self-worth that eventually they avoid sports entirely.

Is this Little League coach careful to encourage rather than criticize? To what extent does he emphasize teamwork, fair play, courtesy, and skill development over winning? These factors determine whether or not adult-organized sports are pleasurable, constructive experiences for children.

Finally, sports-related injuries are an issue to consider. Perhaps because organized sports specify health and safety rules, injuries tend to be infrequent and mild, except for football, which has a high rate of serious injury (Radelet et al., 2002). Nevertheless, in any sport, frequent, intense practice can lead to painful "overuse" injuries. In extreme cases, the physical stress fractures the soft cartilage in the epiphyses of the long bones, leading to premature closure and arrested growth (Lord & Kozar, 1996).

See Applying What We Know on page 422 for ways to ensure that athletic leagues provide children with positive learning experiences. When parents and coaches emphasize effort, improvement, participation, and teamwork, young athletes enjoy sports more and gain in self-esteem (Smith & Smoll, 1997). These effects are particularly strong for children whose self-confidence is low to begin with—and who are most in need of a rewarding sports experience.

Shadows of Our Evolutionary Past

Besides a new level of structure and organization, some additional qualities of physical play become common in middle childhood. While watching children at your city park, notice how they occasionally wrestle, roll, hit, and run after one another, alternating roles while smiling and laughing. This friendly chasing and play-fighting is called **rough-and-tumble play.** Research indicates that it is a good-natured, sociable activity that is distinct from aggressive fighting. School-age children in many cultures engage in it with peers whom they like especially well, and they continue interacting after a rough-and-tumble episode rather than separating, as they do at the end of an aggressive encounter (Pellegrini, 2002).

Children's rough-and-tumble play is similar to the social behavior of young mammals of many species. It seems to originate in parents' physical play with babies, especially fathers' play with sons (see Chapter 7). And childhood rough-and-tumble is more common among boys, probably because prenatal exposure to androgens (male sex hormones) predisposes boys toward active play (see Chapter 10, page 382). Boys' rough-and-tumble largely consists of playful wrestling, restraining, and hitting, whereas girls tend to engage in running, chasing, and only brief physical contact (Boulton, 1996).

Rough-and-tumble peaks during middle childhood, when it accounts for as much as 10 percent of free-play behavior, and then declines in adolescence. In our evolutionary past, it may have been important for the development of fighting skill (Boulton & Smith, 1992). Another possibility is that rough-and-tumble assists children in establishing a

Rough-and-tumble play can be distinguished from aggression by its good-natured quality. In our evolutionary past, it may have been important for the development of fighting skill.

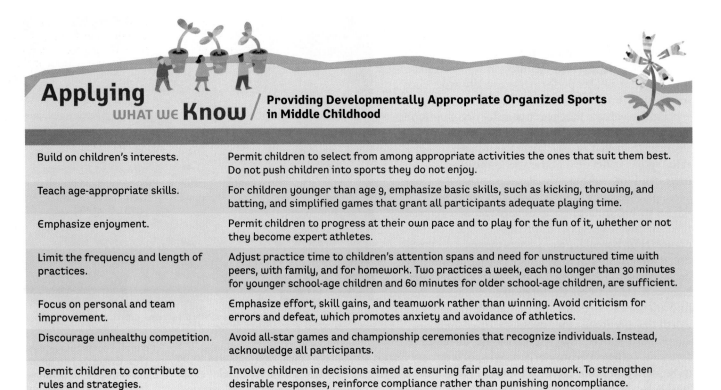

Applying WHAT WE Know / Providing Developmentally Appropriate Organized Sports in Middle Childhood

Build on children's interests.	Permit children to select from among appropriate activities the ones that suit them best. Do not push children into sports they do not enjoy.
Teach age-appropriate skills.	For children younger than age 9, emphasize basic skills, such as kicking, throwing, and batting, and simplified games that grant all participants adequate playing time.
Emphasize enjoyment.	Permit children to progress at their own pace and to play for the fun of it, whether or not they become expert athletes.
Limit the frequency and length of practices.	Adjust practice time to children's attention spans and need for unstructured time with peers, with family, and for homework. Two practices a week, each no longer than 30 minutes for younger school-age children and 60 minutes for older school-age children, are sufficient.
Focus on personal and team improvement.	Emphasize effort, skill gains, and teamwork rather than winning. Avoid criticism for errors and defeat, which promotes anxiety and avoidance of athletics.
Discourage unhealthy competition.	Avoid all-star games and championship ceremonies that recognize individuals. Instead, acknowledge all participants.
Permit children to contribute to rules and strategies.	Involve children in decisions aimed at ensuring fair play and teamwork. To strengthen desirable responses, reinforce compliance rather than punishing noncompliance.

dominance hierarchy—a stable ordering of group members that predicts who will win when conflict arises. Observations of arguments, threats, and physical attacks between children reveal a consistent lineup of winners and losers that becomes increasingly stable during middle childhood and adolescence, especially among boys. Many children say they can tell their own as well as their peers' strength through rough-and-tumble. They seem to use these encounters to make this judgment in a safe venue before challenging a peer's dominance. Over time, children increasingly choose rough-and-tumble partners who resemble themselves in dominance status (Pellegrini & Smith, 1998).

Like dominance relations among nonhuman animals, those among children serve the adaptive function of limiting aggression among group members. Once a dominance hierarchy is established, hostility is rare. As children move closer to physical maturity, individual differences in strength become clearer, and rough-and-tumble play declines. When it occurs, its meaning changes: It becomes a disguise for physical attacks. Adolescent boys' rough-and-tumble is linked to aggression (Pellegrini, 2003). After becoming embroiled in a bout, players "cheat" and hurt their opponent. When asked to explain the episode, boys often respond that they are retaliating, apparently to reestablish dominance among their peers.

Physical Education

Physical activity supports many aspects of children's development—the health of their bodies, their sense of self-worth as physically active and capable beings, and the cognitive and social skills necessary for getting along with others. Yet only 50 percent of American elementary schools require physical education, a figure that drops to 25 percent during junior high and to less than 10 percent during high school. The average American school-age child gets only 20 minutes of physical education a week. Although Canadian children fare better, averaging 2 hours per week, many Canadian schools have reduced their physical education programs to devote more time to academic instruction (Canadian Fitness and Lifestyle Research Institute, 2002, 2003; U.S. Department of Health and Human Services, 2000b, 2001a). In both nations, physical inactivity is pervasive. Among North American 5- to 17-year-olds, only about 40 percent of girls and 50 percent of boys are active enough for good health—that is, engage in at least 30 minutes of vigorous aerobic activity and 1 hour of walking per day.

Fourth graders in a Toronto, Canada, gym class pay close attention as their teacher models movements of the ancient martial art of kung fu and explains how it serves as a nonviolent aid to physical conditioning and mental discipline. Instead of training in competitive sports, these children learn skills that all members of their class can perform well—ones likely to persist in later years.

Besides requiring daily physical education classes, many experts believe that schools should change the content of physical education programs. Training in competitive sports is often a high priority, but it is unlikely to reach the least physically fit youngsters, who draw back when an activity demands a high level of skill (Portman, 1995). Instead, programs should emphasize informal games that most children can perform well and individual exercise—walking, running, jumping, tumbling, and climbing. These pursuits are the ones most likely to persist in later years. Furthermore, children of varying skill levels tend to sustain physical activity when teachers focus on each child's personal progress and contribution to team accomplishment (Connor, 2003). Then physical education fosters a healthy sense of self while satisfying school-age children's need to participate with others.

Physical fitness builds on itself. Children in good physical condition take great pleasure in their rapidly developing motor skills. As a result, they seek out these activities, developing rewarding interests in physical exercise and becoming active adults who reap many benefits (Dennison et al., 1998). These include greater physical strength, resistance to many illnesses (from colds and flu to cancer, diabetes, and heart disease), enhanced psychological well-being, and a longer life.

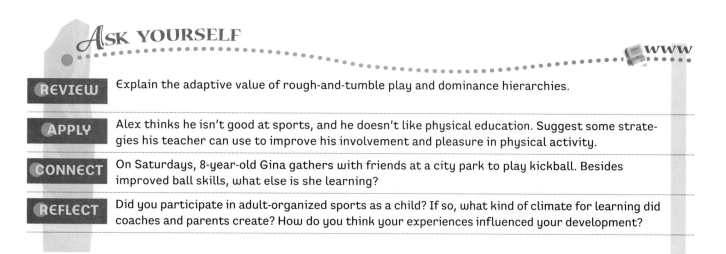

ASK YOURSELF

www

REVIEW Explain the adaptive value of rough-and-tumble play and dominance hierarchies.

APPLY Alex thinks he isn't good at sports, and he doesn't like physical education. Suggest some strategies his teacher can use to improve his involvement and pleasure in physical activity.

CONNECT On Saturdays, 8-year-old Gina gathers with friends at a city park to play kickball. Besides improved ball skills, what else is she learning?

REFLECT Did you participate in adult-organized sports as a child? If so, what kind of climate for learning did coaches and parents create? How do you think your experiences influenced your development?

Summary

Body Growth

Describe changes in body size, proportions, and skeletal maturity during middle childhood.

● School-age children's growth is slow and regular. On the average, they add about 2 to 3 inches in height and 5 pounds in weight each year. By age 9, girls overtake boys in physical size.

● Evolutionary adaptations to a particular climate, food resources, and infectious disease result in large individual and ethnic variations in physical growth. **Secular trends in physical growth** have occurred in industrialized nations. Because of improved health and nutrition, many children are growing larger and reaching physical maturity earlier than their ancestors.

● During middle childhood, bones continue to lengthen and broaden, and all 20 primary teeth are replaced by permanent ones. Tooth decay affects over half of North American school-age children and is especially high among low-SES children. One-third of school-age children suffer from **malocclusion,** making braces common by the end of elementary school.

Describe brain development in middle childhood.

● Only a small increase in brain size occurs during middle childhood. White matter (myelinated nerve fibers) increases steadily, especially in the frontal lobes of the cerebral cortex and in the corpus callosum. In contrast, gray matter (neurons and supportive material) declines due to synaptic pruning, and lateralization of the cerebral hemispheres increases. Brain development during the school years is believed to involve neurotransmitter and hormonal influences.

Common Health Problems

Describe the overall status of children's health during middle childhood.

● School-age children from economically advantaged homes are at their healthiest, due to the cumulative effects of good nutrition combined with rapid development of the body's immune system. At the same time, a variety of health problems do occur, many of which are more common among low-SES children.

● The most common vision problem is **myopia,** or nearsightedness. It is influenced by heredity, early biological trauma, and time spent reading and doing other close work. Myopia is one of the few health conditions that increase with family education and income. Although ear infections decline during the school years, many low-SES children experience some hearing loss because of chronic, untreated otitis media.

Describe the causes and consequences of serious nutritional problems in middle childhood, giving special attention to obesity.

● Poverty-stricken children in developing countries and in North America continue to suffer from malnutrition. When malnutrition is allowed to persist for many years, permanent physical and mental damage usually results. Severely malnourished, growth-stunted children display a heightened stress response, altered production of neurotransmitters in the brain, and greater vulnerability to obesity after their diets improve.

● Overweight and **obesity** have increased dramatically in both industrialized and developing nations, and especially in the United States. Heredity accounts for only a tendency to gain weight. More powerful influences are parental feeding practices, maladaptive eating habits, lack of exercise, and Western high-fat diets. Obese children are often socially rejected, report feeling more depressed, and display more behavior problems than their normal-weight peers.

● Family-based interventions in which parents and children revise eating patterns, engage in regular daily exercise, and reinforce one another's progress are the most effective approaches to treating childhood obesity. Rewarding obese children for reducing sedentary time is an effective approach to getting them to like and engage in more physical activity. Schools can help by ensuring regular physical activity and serving healthier meals.

What factors contribute to nocturnal enuresis and asthma, and how can these health problems be reduced?

● In the majority of cases, heredity is responsible for **nocturnal enuresis,** through a failure of muscular responses that inhibit urination or a hormonal imbalance that permits too much urine to accumulate. The most effective treatment is a urine alarm that works according to conditioning principles.

● The most frequent cause of school absence and childhood hospitalization is **asthma.** It occurs more often among African-American and poverty-stricken children, perhaps because of inner-city pollution, stressful home lives, and lack of access to good health care. Children with severe chronic illnesses are at risk for academic, emotional, and social difficulties. Interventions that foster positive family interactions and help parent and child cope with the disease improve adjustment.

Describe changes in unintentional injuries during middle childhood, and cite effective interventions.

● The rate of unintentional injury increases from middle childhood into adolescence. Motor vehicle accidents (with children as passengers or pedestrians) and bicycle accidents are the leading causes. Highly active, impulsive children, most of whom are boys, often do not implement their safety knowledge and are particularly susceptible to injury.

● Effective school-based safety education programs make use of modeling, role playing, and rehearsal of safety practices; reward children for good performance; and provide occasional booster sessions. In addition, parents must be educated about children's age-related safety capacities. Insisting that children wear protective bicycle helmets prevents many serious head injuries.

Health Education

What can parents and teachers do to encourage good health practices in school-age children?

● Besides providing health-related information, adults must reduce health hazards in children's environments, coach children in good health practices, and model and reinforce these behaviors.

Motor Development and Play

Cite major changes in gross and fine motor development during middle childhood.

● Gradual increases in body size and muscle strength support refinements in many gross motor skills. Gains in flexibility, balance, agility, and force occur. In addition, improvements in responding only to relevant information and in reaction time contribute to athletic performance.

● Fine motor development also improves. Children's writing becomes more legible, and their drawings show dramatic increases in organization, detail, and representation of depth.

Describe individual and group differences in motor performance during middle childhood.

● Children show wide individual differences in motor capacities that are influenced by both heredity and environment. Body build, parental encouragement, and opportunities to take lessons support a variety of physical abilities. Gender stereotypes, which affect parental expectations for children's athletic performance, largely account for school-age boys' superiority on a wide range of gross motor skills.

What qualities of children's play are evident in middle childhood?

● Organized games with rules become common during the school years. Children's informally organized games support many aspects of emotional and social development. Expansion of youth sports programs has led to concerns about adult-organized athletics. Although players typically show greater social competence, coaches and parents who emphasize competition and winning promote undue anxiety and avoidance of sports in some children. Promoting effort, improvement, participation, and teamwork makes organized sports enjoyable and beneficial for self-esteem.

● Some features of children's physical activity reflect our evolutionary past. **Rough-and-tumble play** may at one time have been important for the development of fighting skill and may assist children in establishing a **dominance hierarchy.** Dominance hierarchies become increasingly stable in middle childhood, especially among boys, and serve the adaptive function of limiting aggression among group members.

Why is high-quality physical education important during the school years?

● Physical education classes help ensure that all children have access to the physical, cognitive, and social benefits of regular exercise and play. Yet physical education does not take place often enough in American and Canadian schools. Daily classes that emphasize informal games that most children can perform well translate into lifelong psychological and physical health benefits.

Important Terms and Concepts

asthma (p. 412)
dominance hierarchy (p. 422)
malocclusion (p. 404)

myopia (p. 405)
nocturnal enuresis (p. 412)
obesity (p. 407)

rough-and-tumble play (p. 421)
secular trends in physical growth (p. 403)

 # For Further Information and Help

Consult the Companion Website for *Infants, Children, and Adolescents,* Fifth Edition, *(www.ablongman.com/berk),* where you will find the following resources for this chapter:

● **Chapter Objectives**
● **Flashcards** for studying important terms and concepts
● **Annotated Weblinks** to guide you in further research
● **Ask Yourself questions,** which you can answer and then check against a sample response

● **Suggested Readings**
● **Practice Tests** with immediate scoring and feedback

Untitled

Mahdi Saheb Mohammad

8 years, Kuwait

The school-age child's expanding ability to represent people, objects, and cultural practices is evident in this depiction of a busy fish market. Improved memory, categorization, reasoning, problem solving, and creativity make middle childhood a period of rapidly developing cognition—the topic of Chapter 12.

Cognitive Development in Middle Childhood

- **PIAGET'S THEORY: THE CONCRETE OPERATIONAL STAGE**
  Acheivements of the Concrete Operational Stage • Limitations of Concrete Operational Thought • Follow-Up Research on Concrete Operational Thought • Evaluation of the Concrete Operational Stage

- **INFORMATION PROCESSING**
  Attention • Memory Strategies • The Knowledge Base and Memory Performance • Culture, Schooling, and Memory Strategies • The School-Age Child's Theory of Mind • Cognitive Self-Regulation • Applications of Information Processing to Academic Learning

  BIOLOGY AND ENVIRONMENT *Children with Attention-Deficit Hyperactivity Disorder*

- **INDIVIDUAL DIFFERENCES IN MENTAL DEVELOPMENT**

Defining and Measuring Intelligence • Recent Efforts to Define Intelligence • Explaining Individual and Group Differences in IQ • Reducing Cultural Bias in Intelligence Testing

CULTURAL INFLUENCES *The Flynn Effect: Massive Generational Gains in IQ*

- **LANGUAGE DEVELOPMENT**
  Vocabulary • Grammar • Pragmatics • Learning Two Languages at a Time

- **CHILDREN'S LEARNING IN SCHOOL**
  Class Size • Educational Philosophies • Teacher–Student Interaction • Grouping Practices • Computers and Academic Learning • Teaching Children with Special Needs • How Well Educated Are North American Children?

  SOCIAL ISSUES: EDUCATION *School Readiness and Grade Retention*

"Finally!" 6-year-old Lizzie exclaimed

the day she entered first grade. "Now I get to go to real school just like Joey!" Lizzie walked confidently into her classroom, pencils, crayons, and writing pad in hand, ready for a more disciplined approach to learning than she had experienced in early childhood. As a preschooler, Lizzie had loved playing school, giving assignments as the "teacher" and pretending to read and write as the "student." Now she was eager to master the tasks that had sparked her imagination as a 4- and 5-year-old.

Lizzie entered a whole new world of challenging mental activities. In a single morning, she and her classmates wrote in journals, met in reading groups, worked on addition and subtraction, and sorted leaves gathered for a science project. As Lizzie and Joey moved through the elementary school grades, they tackled increasingly complex tasks and gradually became more accomplished at reading, writing, math skills, and general knowledge of the world.

We begin our discussion by returning to Piaget's theory and the information-processing approach, which, together, provide an overview of cognitive change during the school years. Then we take an in-depth look at individual differences in mental development. We examine the genetic and environmental roots of IQ scores, which often influence important educational decisions. Our discussion continues with language, which blossoms further during middle childhood. Finally, we consider the importance of schools in children's learning and development.

Piaget's Theory: The Concrete Operational Stage

When Lizzie visited my child development class as a 4-year-old, Piaget's conservation problems consistently confused her (see Chapter 9, page 320). For example, she insisted that the amount of water had changed after it had been poured from a tall, narrow container into a short, wide one. At age 8, when Lizzie returned, these tasks were easy. "Of course it's the same," she exclaimed. "The water's shorter but it's also wider. Pour it back," she instructed the college student who was interviewing her. "You'll see, it's the same amount!"

Achievements of the Concrete Operational Stage

Lizzie has entered Piaget's **concrete operational stage,** which extends from approximately 7 to 11 years. Thought is now more logical, flexible, and organized than it was during early childhood.

CONSERVATION ● The ability to pass *conservation tasks* provides clear evidence of *operations*—mental representations of actions that obey logical rules. Notice how Lizzie is capable of **decentration,** focusing on several aspects of a problem and relating them, rather than centering on just one. Lizzie also demonstrates **reversibility,** the capacity to think through a series of steps and then mentally reverse direction, returning to the starting point. Recall from Chapter 9 (page 321) that reversibility is part of every logical operation. It is solidly achieved in middle childhood.

CLASSIFICATION ● Between ages 7 and 10, children pass Piaget's *class inclusion problem* (see page 321). This indicates that they are more aware of classification hierarchies and can focus on relations between a general category and two specific categories at the same time—that is, on three relations at once (Ni, 1998; Hodges & French, 1988). You can see this in children's play activities. Collections—stamps, coins, baseball cards, rocks, bottle caps, and more—become common in middle childhood. At age 10, Joey spent hours sorting and resorting his large box of baseball cards. At times he grouped them by league and team, at other times by playing position and batting average. He could separate the players into a variety of classes and subclasses and flexibly move back and forth between them.

An improved ability to categorize underlies children's interest in collecting objects during middle childhood. These older school-age children sort baseball cards into an elaborate structure of classes and subclasses.

© BOB DAEMMRICH/THE IMAGE WORKS

SERIATION ● The ability to order items along a quantitative dimension, such as length or weight, is called **seriation.** To test for it, Piaget asked children to arrange sticks of different lengths from shortest to longest. Older preschoolers can create the series, but they do so haphazardly. They put the sticks in a row but make many errors and take a long time to correct them. In contrast, 6- to 7-year-olds are guided by an orderly plan. They create the series efficiently by beginning with the smallest stick, then moving to the next largest, and so on, until the ordering is complete.

The concrete operational child can also seriate mentally, an ability called **transitive inference.** In a well-known transitive inference problem, Piaget showed children pairings of differently colored sticks. From observing that stick A is longer than stick B and that stick B is longer than stick C, children must infer that A is longer than C. Notice how this task, like Piaget's class inclusion task, requires children to integrate three relations at once—in this instance, A–B, B–C, and A–C. When researchers take steps to ensure that children remember the premises (A–B and B–C), children grasp transitive inference around age 7 to 8 (Andrews & Halford, 1998; Wright & Dowker, 2002).

SPATIAL REASONING ● Piaget found that children improve greatly in spatial reasoning over the school years. Let's take two related examples: understanding of directions and maps.

Directions. When asked to name an object to the left or right of another person, 5- and 6-year-olds answer incorrectly; they apply their own frame of reference. Between 7 and 8 years, children start to perform *mental rotations,* in which they align the self's frame to match that of a person in a different orientation. As a result, they can identify left and right for positions they do not occupy (Roberts & Aman, 1993). Around 8 to 10 years, children can give clear, well-organized directions for how to get from one place to another by using a "mental walk" strategy in which they imagine another person's movements along a route (Gauvain & Rogoff, 1989b). Six-year-olds give more organized directions after they walk the route themselves or are specially prompted. Otherwise, they focus on the end point without describing exactly how to get there (Plumert et al., 1994).

Maps. Children's mental representations of familiar, large-scale spaces, such as their school or neighborhood, are called **cognitive maps.** Drawing a map of a large-scale space requires considerable perspective-taking skill because the entire space cannot be seen at once. Instead, children must infer its overall layout by relating its separate parts.

Preschoolers and young school-age children include landmarks on the maps they draw, but their arrangement is not always accurate. When asked to place stickers showing the location of desks and people on a map of their classroom, they perform better. But if the map is rotated to a position other than the orientation of the classroom, they have difficulty placing the stickers (Liben & Downs, 1993). During the early school years, children's maps become more coherent. They draw landmarks along an *organized route of travel*—an attainment that resembles their improved direction giving. By the end of middle childhood, children combine landmarks and routes into an *overall view of a large-scale space.* And they readily draw and read maps, even when the map's orientation and the space it represents do not match (Liben, 1999).

Limitations of Concrete Operational Thought

As suggested by the name of this stage, concrete operational thinking suffers from one important limitation. Children think in an organized, logical fashion only when dealing with concrete information they can perceive directly. Their mental operations work poorly with abstract ideas—ones not physically apparent in the real world. Children's solutions to transitive inference problems provide a good illustration. When shown pairs of sticks of unequal length, Lizzie easily engaged in transitive inference. But she had great difficulty with a hypothetical version of this task, such as "Susan is taller than Sally and Sally is taller than Mary. Who is the tallest?" Not until age 11 or 12 can children solve this problem.

That logical thought is at first tied to immediate situations helps account for a special feature of concrete operational reasoning. Perhaps you have already noticed that school-age children master Piaget's concrete operational tasks step by step, not all at once. For example, they usually grasp conservation number, followed by length, liquid, and mass, followed by weight. Piaget used the term **horizontal décalage** (meaning development within a stage) to describe this gradual mastery of logical concepts. The horizontal décalage also illustrates the concrete operational child's difficulty with abstractions. School-age children do not come up with general logical principles and then apply them to all relevant situations. Rather, they seem to work out the logic of each problem separately.

Follow-Up Research on Concrete Operational Thought

According to Piaget, brain development combined with experience in a rich and varied external world should lead children everywhere to reach the concrete operational stage. Yet recent evidence indicates that specific cultural and school practices have much to do with mastery of Piagetian tasks (Rogoff & Chavajay, 1995). The information-processing approach helps explain the gradual mastery of logical concepts in middle childhood.

© NOBORU KOMINE/PHOTO RESEARCHERS, INC.

In tribal and village societies, conservation is often delayed. These Vietnamese sisters gather firewood for their family. Although they have many opportunities to handle quantities, compared with their agemates in Western nations they may seldom see two identical quantities arranged in different ways.

IMPACT OF CULTURE AND SCHOOLING ● In tribal and village societies, conservation is often delayed. For example, among the Hausa of Nigeria, who live in small agricultural settlements and rarely send their children to school, even the most basic conservation tasks—number, length, and liquid—are not understood until age 11 or later (Fahrmeier, 1978). This suggests that taking part in relevant everyday activities helps children master conservation and other Piagetian problems (Light & Perret-Clermont, 1989). Joey and Lizzie, for example, think of fairness in terms of equal distribution—a value emphasized in their culture. They frequently divide materials, such as Halloween treats and lemonade, equally among their friends. Because they often see the same quantity arranged in different ways, they grasp conservation early.

The very experience of going to school seems to promote mastery of Piagetian tasks. When children of the same age are tested, those who have been in school longer do better on transitive inference problems (Artman & Cahan, 1993). Opportunities to seriate objects, to learn about order relations, and to remember the parts of a complex problem are probably responsible. Yet certain nonschool, informal experiences can also foster operational thought. Brazilian 6- to 9-year-old street vendors, who seldom attend school, do poorly on Piagetian class inclusion tasks. But they perform much better than economically advantaged schoolchildren on versions relevant to street vending—for example, "If you have 4 units of mint chewing gum and 2 units of grape chewing gum, is it better to sell me the mint gum or [all] the gum?" (Ceci & Roazzi, 1994).

On the basis of findings like these, some investigators have concluded that the forms of logic required by Piagetian tasks do not emerge spontaneously in children but are heavily influenced by training, context, and cultural conditions. Does this view remind you of Vygotsky's sociocultural theory, which we discussed in earlier chapters?

AN INFORMATION-PROCESSING VIEW OF CONRETE OPERATIONAL THOUGHT ● In Chapter 9 we showed that the beginnings of logical thinking are evident during the preschool years on simplified and familiar tasks. The horizontal décalage suggests that logical understanding continues to improve gradually over the school years.

Some *neo-Piagetian theorists* argue that the development of operational thinking can best be understood in terms of gains in information-processing capacity rather than a sudden shift to a new stage (Halford, 2002). For example, Robbie Case (1996, 1998) proposes that with practice, cognitive schemes demand less attention and become more automatic. This frees up space in *working memory* (see Chapter 6, page 220) so children can focus on combining old schemes and generating new ones. For instance, the child confronted with water poured from one container to another recognizes that the height of the liquid changes. As this understanding becomes routine, the child notices that the width of the water changes as well. Soon children coordinate these observations, and they grasp conservation of liquid. Then, as this logical idea becomes well practiced, the child transfers it to more demanding situations, such as weight.

Once the schemes of a Piagetian stage are sufficiently automatic, enough working memory is available for the child to integrate them into an improved representation. As a result, children acquire *central conceptual structures,* networks of concepts and relations that permit them to think more effectively about a wide range of situations. The central conceptual structures that emerge from integrating concrete operational schemes are highly efficient, abstract principles, which we will discuss in the context of formal operational thought in Chapter 15.

Case has applied his information-processing view to a wide variety of tasks, including solving arithmetic word problems, understanding stories, drawing pictures, sight-reading music, handling money, and interpreting social situations (Case, 1998; Case & Okamoto, 1996). In each task, preschoolers' schemes focus on only one dimension. In understanding stories, for example, they grasp only a single story line. In drawing pictures, they depict objects separately, ignoring their spatial arrangement. By the early school years, central conceptual structures coordinate two dimensions. Children combine two story lines into a single plot, and they create drawings that show both the features of objects and relationships among objects. Around 9 to 11 years, central conceptual structures integrate multiple dimensions. Children tell coherent stories with a main plot and several subplots. And their drawings follow a set of rules for representing perspective and, therefore, include several points of reference, such as near, midway, and far.

According to Case, children show a horizontal décalage for two reasons. First, different forms of the same logical insight, such as their various conservation tasks, vary in their processing demands. Those acquired later require more working-memory resources. Second, children's experiences vary widely. A child who often tells stories but rarely draws pictures displays more advanced central conceptual structures in storytelling. When tasks make similar processing demands, such as Piaget's class inclusion and transitive inference problems (each of which requires children to consider three relations simultaneously), children with relevant experiences master those tasks at the same time (Halford, Wilson, & Phillips, 1998).

Children who do not show central conceptual structures expected for their age can usually be trained to attain them. And their improved understanding readily transfers to academic tasks (Case, Griffin, & Kelly, 2001). Consequently, the application of Case's neo-Piagetian theory to teaching is helping children who are behind in academic performance learn more effectively.

Evaluation of the Concrete Operational Stage

Piaget was correct that school-age children approach a great many problems in systematic and rational ways not possible during early childhood. But controversy exists over whether development results from *continuous* improvement in logical skills or from *discontinuous* restructuring of children's thinking (as Piaget's stage idea assumes). Many researchers think that both types of change are involved (Carey, 1999; Case, 1996, 1998). From early to middle childhood, children apply logical schemes to a much wider range of tasks. Yet in the process, their thought seems to change qualitatively—toward a more comprehensive grasp of the underlying principles of logical thought.

Piaget himself seems to have recognized this possibility in the very concept of the horizontal décalage. So perhaps some blend of Piagetian and information-processing ideas holds the greatest promise for understanding cognitive development in middle childhood.

Some neo-Piagetian theorists explain the development of operational thinking in information-processing terms. As these children pour water from one container to another, they coordinate their observations of changes in the liquid's height and width, and conservation of liquid is achieved. Once this logical idea becomes automatic, enough space is available in working memory to form a more general representation of conservation that can be applied to a wider range of situations.

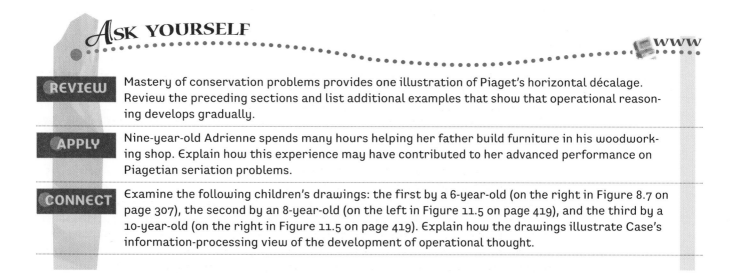

*A*SK YOURSELF
www

REVIEW Mastery of conservation problems provides one illustration of Piaget's horizontal décalage. Review the preceding sections and list additional examples that show that operational reasoning develops gradually.

APPLY Nine-year-old Adrienne spends many hours helping her father build furniture in his woodworking shop. Explain how this experience may have contributed to her advanced performance on Piagetian seriation problems.

CONNECT Examine the following children's drawings: the first by a 6-year-old (on the right in Figure 8.7 on page 307), the second by an 8-year-old (on the left in Figure 11.5 on page 419), and the third by a 10-year-old (on the right in Figure 11.5 on page 419). Explain how the drawings illustrate Case's information-processing view of the development of operational thought.

Information Processing

In contrast to Piaget's focus on cognitive change, the information-processing perspective examines separate aspects of thinking. Attention and memory, which underlie every act of cognition, are central concerns in middle childhood, just as they were during infancy and the preschool years. Researchers are also interested in how children's growing knowledge of the world and awareness of their own mental activities affect these basic components of thinking. Finally, increased understanding of how children process information is being applied to their academic learning—in particular, to reading and mathematics.

Researchers believe that brain development contributes to two basic changes in information processing that facilitate the diverse aspects of thinking we are about to consider:

● *Gains in information-processing capacity.* Time needed to process information on a wide variety of cognitive tasks declines rapidly between ages 6 and 12 in children from several cultures (Kail & Park, 1992, 1994). This suggests a biologically based, age-related gain in speed of thinking, possibly due to myelination and synaptic pruning in the brain (Kail, 2000). More efficient thinking increases working-memory capacity, since a faster thinker can hold onto and operate on more information at once. As processing speed improves sharply during the school years, digit span (see Chapter 9, page 334) increases from about 5 to 7 digits (Kail, 2003).

● *Gains in cognitive inhibition.* The ability to resist interference from internal and external distracting stimuli, or **cognitive inhibition,** improves from infancy on. But considerable progress occurs during middle childhood, due to further development of the cerebral cortex. EEG brain-wave and fMRI measures reveal a steady, age-related increase in activation of diverse cortical regions, especially the frontal lobes, in children and adolescents working on tasks that require suppression of inappropriate responses (Bartgis, Lilly, & Thomas, 2003; Luna et al., 2001). Individuals skilled at cognitive inhibition can prevent their minds from straying to irrelevant thoughts—a capacity that supports many information-processing skills (Dempster & Corkill, 1999; Klenberg, Korkman, & Lahti-Nuuttila, 2001).

Besides brain development, strategy use contributes to more effective information processing. As we will see, school-age children think far more strategically than preschoolers. At the same time, neurological change supports gains in strategy use.

Attention

During middle childhood, attention changes in three ways. It becomes more selective, adaptable, and planful.

SELECTIVITY AND ADAPTABILITY ● As Joey and Lizzie moved through the elementary school years, they became better at deliberately attending to just those aspects of a situation that were relevant to their task goals. Researchers study this increasing selectivity of attention by introducing irrelevant stimuli into a task and seeing how well children respond to its central elements. For example, they might present a stream of numbers on a computer screen and ask children to press a button whenever a particular sequence of two digits (such as "1" then "9") appears. Findings with this task, and others, show that selective attention improves sharply between ages 6 and 10, with gains continuing into adulthood (Goldberg, Maurer, & Lewis, 2001; Lin, Hsiao, & Chen, 1999; Smith et al., 1998).

Older children also flexibly adapt their attention to the momentary requirements of situations. For example, in judging whether pairs of stimuli are the same or different, sixth graders (but not second graders) quickly shift their basis of judgment (from size to shape to color) when asked to do so (Pick & Frankel, 1974). Furthermore, when studying for a spelling test, 10-year-old Joey devoted most attention to the words he knew least well. Lizzie was much less likely do so (Masur, McIntyre, & Flavell, 1973).

How do children acquire selective, adaptable attentional strategies? Children's performance on many tasks reveals a predictable, four-step sequence:

1. **Production deficiency.** Preschoolers rarely engage in attentional strategies. In other words, they fail to *produce* strategies when they could be helpful.

2. **Control deficiency.** Young elementary school children sometimes produce strategies, but not consistently. They fail to *control*, or execute, strategies effectively.

3. **Utilization deficiency.** Slightly later, children execute strategies consistently, but their performance does not improve.

4. **Effective strategy use.** By the mid-elementary school years, children use strategies consistently, and performance improves (Miller, 2000).

As we will see shortly, these phases also characterize the development of memory strategies. Why, when children first use a strategy, does it not work well? A likely reason is that applying a new strategy takes so much effort and attention that little remains to perform other parts of the task well (Miller, Woody-Ramsey, & Aloise, 1991).

PLANNING ● School-age children's attentional strategies also become increasingly planful. Compared with preschoolers, they more thoroughly scan detailed pictures and written materials for similarities and differences (Vurpillot, 1968). And on complex tasks, school-age children decide what to do first and what to do next in an orderly fashion. In one study, 5- to 9-year-olds were given lists of items to obtain from a play grocery store. Older children more often took time to scan the store before shopping. They also paused more often to look for each item before moving to get it. Consequently, they followed shorter routes through the aisles (Gauvain & Rogoff, 1989a; Szepkouski, Gauvain, & Carberry, 1994).

The development of planning illustrates how attention becomes coordinated with other cognitive processes. To solve problems involving multiple steps, children must postpone action in favor of weighing alternatives, organizing task materials (such as items on a grocery list), and remembering the steps of their plan so they can attend to each one in sequence. Along the way, they must monitor how well the plan works and revise it if necessary. Clearly, planning places heavy demands on working-memory capacity. Not surprisingly, even when younger children plan, they often forget important steps.

Children learn much about planning by collaborating on tasks with more expert planners. With age, children take on more responsibility in these joint endeavors, such as organizing task materials and suggesting planning strategies. The demands of school tasks—and teachers' explanations for how to plan—also contribute to gains in planning. And parents can foster planning by encouraging it in everyday activities and routines, from completing homework assignments to loading dishes into the dishwasher. In a longitudinal study involving observations of parent–child interaction at ages 4, 9, and 15, parent–child discussions involving planning predicted adolescents' initiations of planning interactions with other family members (Gauvain, 1999). Many opportunities to practice planning help children understand its components and use them.

The attentional strategies we have considered are crucial for success in school. Unfortunately, some school-age children have great difficulty paying attention. See the Biology and Environment box on pages 434–435 for a discussion of the serious learning and behavior problems of children with attention-deficit hyperactivity disorder.

Fifth graders jointly list materials they must gather for a class assignment. As a result of previous adult guidance and encouragement to plan, these children assume much responsibility for carrying out an activity in a deliberate, orderly fashion.

 Memory Strategies

As attention improves, so do *memory strategies,* the deliberate mental activities we use to store and retain information. During the school years, these techniques for holding information in working memory and transferring it to our long-term knowledge base take a giant leap forward (Schneider, 2002).

iology and Environment

Children with Attention-Deficit Hyperactivity Disorder

While the other fifth graders worked quietly at their desks, Calvin squirmed, dropped his pencil, looked out the window, fiddled with his shoelaces, and talked out. "Hey Joey," he yelled over the top of several desks, "wanna play ball after school?" Joey and the other children weren't eager to play with Calvin. Out on the playground, Calvin was a poor listener and failed to follow the rules of the game. He had trouble taking turns at bat. In the outfield, he tossed his mitt up in the air and looked elsewhere when the ball came his way. Calvin's desk was a chaotic mess. He often lost pencils, books, and other materials necessary for completing assignments. And he had difficulty remembering assignments and when they were due.

Symptoms of ADHD

Calvin is one of 3 to 5 percent of school-age children with **attention-deficit hyperactivity disorder (ADHD),** a disorder involving inattention, impulsivity, and excessive motor activity that results in academic and social problems (American Psychiatric Association, 1994). Boys are diagnosed three to nine times more often than girls. However, many girls with ADHD may be overlooked because their symptoms usually are not as flagrant (Abikoff et al., 2002).

Children with ADHD cannot stay focused on a task that requires mental effort for more than a few minutes. In addition, they often act impulsively, ignoring social rules and lashing out with hostility when frustrated. Many (but not all) are *hyperactive.* They charge through their days with excessive motor activity, exhausting parents and teachers and irritating other children so much that they are quickly rejected. For a child to be diagnosed with ADHD, these symptoms must have appeared before age 7 as a persistent problem.

Because of their difficulty concentrating, ADHD children score 7 to 15 points lower than other children on intelligence tests (Barkley, 2002b). According to one view that has amassed substantial research support, a common theme unifies ADHD symptoms: an impairment in inhibition, which makes it hard to delay action in favor of thought (Barkley, 1999, 2003). Consequently, such children do poorly on tasks requiring sustained attention, find it hard to ignore irrelevant information, and have difficulty with memory, planning, reasoning, and problem solving in academic and social situations (Denckla, 1996).

Origins of ADHD

Heredity plays a major role in ADHD. The disorder runs in families, and identical twins share it more often than fraternal twins (Sherman, Iacono, & McGue, 1997). Children with ADHD also show abnormal brain functioning, including reduced electrical and blood-flow activity in the frontal lobes of the cerebral cortex and in other areas responsible for attention and inhibition of behavior (Giedd et al., 2001; Rapport & Chung, 2000). And their brains grow more slowly and are smaller in overall volume than those of those unaffected agemates (Castellanos et al., 2002). Several genes that affect neurotransmitter and hormone levels have been implicated in the disorder (Biederman & Spencer, 2000; Quist & Kennedy, 2001).

At the same time, ADHD is associated with environmental factors. These children are more likely to come from homes in which marriages are unhappy and family stress is high (Bernier & Siegel, 1994). But a stressful home life rarely causes ADHD. Instead, the behaviors of these

---

REHEARSAL AND ORGANIZATION ● When Lizzie had a list of things to learn, such as a phone number, the capitals of the United States, or the names of geometric shapes, she immediately used **rehearsal,** repeating the information to herself. This memory strategy first appears in the early grade school years. Soon after, a second strategy becomes common: **organization—grouping related items** (for example, all state capitals in the same part of the country), an approach that improves recall dramatically.

Memory strategies require time and effort to perfect. For example, at age 6, Lizzie rehearsed in a piecemeal fashion. After being given the word "cat" in a list of items, she said, "Cat, cat, cat." Two years later, at age 8, she combined previous words with each new item, saying, "Desk, man, yard, cat, cat" (Kunzinger, 1985). Not surprisingly, she retained much more information. And in longitudinal research, at younger ages children organized inconsistently (a *control deficiency*) and, when they did organize, showed little or no memory benefits (a *utilization deficiency*). In contrast, between ages 8 and 10, after realizing how effective organization is, many children suddenly began using it consistently, and their recall improved immediately (Schlagmüller & Schneider, 2002; Weinert & Schneider, 1999). With experience, children organize more skillfully, grouping items into fewer categories. And they apply the strategy to a wider range of memory tasks, including ones with less clearly related materials (Bjorklund et al., 1994).

children can contribute to family problems, which intensify the child's preexisting difficulties. Furthermore, prenatal teratogens—particularly those involving long-term exposure, such as illegal drugs, alcohol, and cigarettes—are linked to inattention and hyperactivity (Milberger et al., 1997).

Treating ADHD

Calvin's doctor eventually prescribed stimulant medication, the most common treatment for ADHD. As long as dosage is carefully regulated, these drugs reduce activity level and improve attention, academic performance, and peer relations for about 70 percent of children who take them (Greenhill, Halperin, & Abikoff, 1999). Stimulant medication seems to increase activity in the frontal lobes, thereby improving the child's capacity to sustain attention and to inhibit off-task and self-stimulating behavior.

Although stimulant medication is relatively safe, its impact is short-term. Drugs cannot teach children to compensate for inattention and impulsivity. Combining medication with interventions that model and reinforce appropriate academic and social behavior seems

© MICHAEL NEWMAN/PHOTOEDIT

This boy frequently disturbs his classmates while they try to work. Children with ADHD have great difficulty staying on task and often act impulsively.

to be the most effective treatment approach (Arnold et al., 2003). Family intervention is also important. Inattentive, overactive children strain the patience of parents, who are likely to react punitively and inconsistently—a child-rearing style that strengthens inappropriate behavior. Breaking this cycle through training parents in effective child-rearing skills is as important for ADHD children as it is for the defiant, aggressive youngsters discussed in Chapter 10. In fact, in 45 to 65 percent of cases, these two sets of be-

havior problems occur together (Barkley, 2002a).

Most of the time, ADHD is a lifelong disorder, with affected individuals at risk for persistent antisocial behavior, depression, and other problems (Barkley et al., 2002; Fisher et al., 2002). In adulthood, people with ADHD continue to need help structuring their environments, regulating negative emotion, selecting appropriate careers, and understanding their condition as a biological deficit rather than a character flaw.

Furthermore, older children more often use several memory strategies at once—rehearsing, organizing, and stating category names (Coyle & Bjorklund, 1997). Although younger children's use of multiple strategies has little impact on performance (a *utilization deficiency*), their tendency to experiment is adaptive. By generating a variety of strategies, they discover which ones work best and how to combine them effectively. For example, second to fourth graders know that organizing the items first, rehearsing category names second, and then rehearsing individual items is a good way to study lists (Hock, Park, & Bjorklund, 1998). Recall from *overlapping-waves theory*, discussed in Chapter 9, that children experiment with strategies when faced with many cognitive challenges.

ELABORATION ● By the end of middle childhood, children start to use **elaboration**. It involves creating a relationship, or shared meaning, between two or more pieces of information that are not members of the same category. For example, suppose the words *fish* and *pipe* are among those you must learn. You might generate a mental image of a fish smoking a pipe. Once children discover this memory technique, they find it so effective that it tends to replace other strategies. Elaboration develops late because it requires considerable effort and working-memory capacity (Schneider & Pressley, 1997). It becomes increasingly common during adolescence and adulthood.

Because organization and elaboration combine items into *meaningful chunks,* they permit children to hold on to much more information. As a result, the strategies further expand working-memory. In addition, when children link a new item to information they already know, they can *retrieve* it easily by thinking of other items associated with it. As we will see next, this also contributes to improved memory during the school years.

The Knowledge Base and Memory Performance

During middle childhood, the long-term knowledge base grows larger and becomes organized into increasingly elaborate, hierarchically structured networks. This rapid growth of knowledge helps children use strategies and remember (Schneider, 2002). In other words, knowing more about a topic makes new information more meaningful and familiar so it is easier to store and retrieve.

To test this idea, researchers classified fourth graders as experts or novices in soccer knowledge. Then they gave both groups lists of new soccer and nonsoccer items to learn. Experts remembered far more items on the soccer list (but not on the nonsoccer list) than nonexperts. And during recall, the experts' listing of items was better organized, as indicated by clustering of items into categories (Schneider & Bjorklund, 1992). These findings suggest that highly knowledgeable children apply an organizational strategy to information in their area of expertise with little or no effort—by rapidly associating new items with the large number they already know. Consequently, experts not only learn more but can devote more working-memory resources to using what they learn to reason and solve problems (Bjorklund & Douglas, 1997).

Although powerfully influential, knowledge is not the only important factor in children's strategic memory processing. Children who are expert in an area are usually highly motivated. As a result, they not only acquire knowledge more quickly but also *actively use what they know* to add more. In contrast, academically unsuccessful children often fail to ask how previously stored information can clarify new material. This, in turn, interferes with the development of a broad knowledge base (Schneider & Bjorklund, 1998). By the end of the school years, then, extensive knowledge and use of memory strategies support one another.

Culture, Schooling, and Memory Strategies

Think about the situations in which the strategies of rehearsal, organization, and elaboration are useful. People usually employ these techniques when they need to remember information for its own sake. On many other occasions, they participate in daily activities and remember as a natural byproduct of the activity. For example, Joey can spout off a wealth of facts about baseball teams and players—information he picked up from watching the game, discussing it, and trading baseball cards with his friends. And without prior rehearsal, he can recount the story line of an exciting movie or novel—narrative material that is already meaningfully organized.

A repeated finding is that people in non-Western cultures who have no formal schooling do not use or benefit from instruction in memory strategies (Rogoff & Chavajay, 1995). Tasks that require children to recall isolated bits of information are common in classrooms, and they provide children with a great deal of motivation to use memory strategies. In fact, Western children get so much practice with this type of learning that they do not refine techniques that rely on spatial location and arrangement of objects— cues that are readily available in everyday life. Australian Aboriginal and Guatemalan Mayan children are considerably better at these memory skills (Kearins, 1981; Rogoff, 1986). Looked at in this way, the development of memory strategies is not just a matter of a more competent information-processing system. It is also a product of task demands and cultural circumstances.

Among the Inupiaq people of northwestern Alaska, who still practice subsistence hunting and fishing, elders teach community responsibility and respect for the environment to children. As this Inupiaq girl assists her grandmother in the intricate art of weaving a fishing net, she demonstrates keen memory for information embedded in meaningful contexts. Yet on a list memory task of the kind often given in school, her performance may appear less sharp.

© LAWRENCE MIGDALE/STOCK BOSTON, LLC

The School-Age Child's Theory of Mind

During middle childhood, children's *theory of mind,* or set of beliefs about mental activities, becomes much more elaborate and refined. Recall from Chapter 9 that this awareness of thought is often called *metacognition.* School-age children's improved ability to reflect on their own mental life is another reason why their thinking and problem solving advance.

KNOWLEDGE OF COGNITIVE CAPACITIES ● Unlike preschoolers, who view the mind as a passive container of information, older children regard it as an active, constructive agent, capable of selecting and transforming information (Kuhn, 2000a). Consequently, they better understand the process of thinking and the impact of psychological factors on performance.

Six- and 7-year-olds, for example, realize that doing well on a task depends on focusing attention—concentrating on it, wanting to do it, and not being distracted by anything else (Miller & Bigi, 1979). And by age 10, children realize that if you "remember," "know," or "understand," you are more certain of your knowledge than if you "guessed," "estimated," or "compared." They also grasp the interrelatedness of memory and understanding—that remembering is crucial for understanding and that understanding strengthens memory (Schwanenflugel, Fabricius, & Noyes, 1996; Schwanenflugel, Henderson, & Fabricius, 1998).

Furthermore, during the early school years, children's understanding of sources of knowledge expands. They realize that people can extend their knowledge not just by directly observing events and talking to others but also by making *mental inferences* (Carpendale & Chandler, 1996; Miller, Hardin, & Montgomery, 2003). This grasp of inference permits knowledge of *false belief* to expand. In several studies, researchers told children complex stories involving one character's belief about a second character's belief. Then the children answered questions about what the first character thought the second character would do (see Figure 12.1). By age 7, children were aware that people form beliefs about other people's beliefs and that these *second-order beliefs* can be wrong! Once children appreciate *second-order false belief,* they can better pinpoint the reasons that another person arrived at a certain belief (Astington, Pelletier, & Homer, 2002). This assists them greatly in understanding others' perspectives.

School-age children's capacity for more complex thinking contributes greatly to their more reflective, process-oriented view of the mind. But experiences that foster awareness of mental activities are also involved. In a study of rural children of Cameroon, Africa, those who attended school performed much better on theory-of-mind tasks (Vinden, 2002). In school, teachers often call attention to the workings of the mind when they remind children to pay attention, remember mental steps, and evaluate their reasoning. And as children engage in reading, writing, and math, they often use *private speech,* at first speaking aloud and later silently to themselves. As they "hear themselves think," they probably detect many aspects of mental life (Flavell, Green, & Flavell, 1995).

KNOWLEDGE OF STRATEGIES ● Consistent with their more active view of the mind, school-age children are far more conscious of mental strategies than are preschoolers. For example, when shown video clips of two children using different recall strategies and asked which one is likely to produce better memory, kindergarten and young elementary school children knew

FIGURE 12.1

Children's understanding of second-order false belief.

To study the understanding of second-order false belief (that people's beliefs about other people's beliefs can be wrong), researchers tell children complex stories. In this example, (a) Jason has a letter from a friend. Lisa wants to read the letter, but Jason doesn't want her to. Jason puts the letter under his pillow and (b) leaves the room to help his mother. (c) While Jason is gone, Lisa takes the letter and reads it. Jason returns and watches Lisa, but Lisa doesn't see Jason. Then Lisa puts the letter in Jason's desk. At the end of the story, the researcher asks the child a second-order false belief question: "Where does Lisa think Jason will look for the letter? Why?" Around age 7, children answer correctly: that Lisa thinks Jason will look under his pillow, because Lisa doesn't know that Jason saw her put the letter in the desk. (Adapted from Astington, Pelletier, & Homer, 2002.)

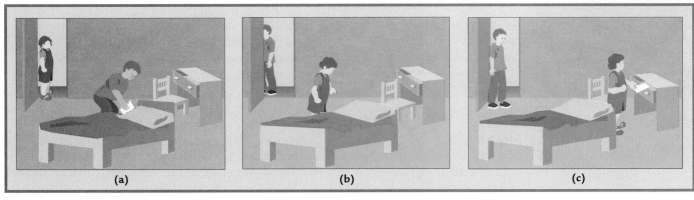

| (a) | (b) | (c) |

that rehearsing or organizing is better than looking or naming. Older children were aware of more subtle differences—that organizing is better than rehearsing (Justice, 1986; Schneider, 1986) And between third and fifth grade, children develop a much better appreciation of how and why strategies work (Alexander et al., 2003).

Once children become conscious of the many factors that influence mental activity, they combine them into an integrated understanding. By the end of middle childhood, children take account of *interactions* among variables—how age and motivation of the learner, effective use of strategies, and nature and difficulty of the task together affect cognitive performance (Wellman, 1990). In this way, metacognition truly becomes a comprehensive theory.

Cognitive Self-Regulation

Although metacognition expands, school-age children often have difficulty putting what they know about thinking into action. They are not yet good at **cognitive self-regulation,** the process of continuously monitoring progress toward a learning goal, checking outcomes, and redirecting unsuccessful efforts. For example, Lizzie is aware that she should attend closely to her teacher's directions, group items when memorizing, reread a complicated paragraph to make sure she understands it, and relate new information to what she already knows. But she does not always engage in these activities.

To study cognitive self-regulation, researchers sometimes look at the impact of children's awareness of memory strategies on how well they remember. By second grade, the more children know about memory strategies, the more they recall—a relationship that strengthens over middle childhood (Pierce & Lange, 2000). Furthermore, children who can explain why a memory strategy works use it more effectively, which results in better memory performance (Justice et al., 1997). And when children apply a useful strategy consistently, their knowledge of strategies strengthens, resulting in a bidirectional relationship between metacognition and strategic processing that enhances self-regulation (Schlagmüller & Schneider, 2002).

What explains the gradual development of self-regulation? Monitoring learning outcomes is cognitively demanding, requiring constant evaluation of effort and progress. By adolescence, self-regulation is a strong predictor of academic success (Joyner & Kurtz-Costes, 1997). Students who do well in school know when their learning is going well and when it is not. If they run up against obstacles, such as poor study conditions, a confusing text passage, or an unclear class presentation, they take steps to organize the learning environment, review the material, or seek other sources of support. This active, purposeful approach contrasts sharply with the passive orientation of students who achieve poorly (Zimmerman & Risemberg, 1997).

Parents and teachers can foster self-regulation by pointing out the special demands of tasks, encouraging the use of strategies, and emphasizing the value of self-correction. In one study, researchers observed parents instructing their children on a problem-solving task during the summer before third grade. Parents who patiently pointed out important features of the task and suggested strategies had children who, in the classroom, more often discussed ways to approach problems and monitored their own performance (Stright et al., 2002). Explaining the effectiveness of strategies is particularly helpful (Pressley, 1995). When adults tell children not just what to do but why to do it, they provide a rationale for future action.

Children who acquire effective self-regulatory skills succeed at challenging tasks. As a result, they develop confidence in their own ability—a belief that supports the use of self-regulation in the future (Schunk & Zimmerman, 2003). Unfortunately, some children receive messages from parents and teachers that seriously undermine their academic self-esteem and self-regulatory skills. We will consider these *learned helpless* youngsters, along with ways to help them, in Chapter 13.

Applications of Information Processing to Academic Learning

Joey entered first grade able to recognize only a handful of written words. By fifth grade, he was a proficient reader. Similarly, at age 6, Joey had an informally acquired knowledge of number concepts. By age 10, he could add, subtract, multiply, and divide with ease, and he had begun to master fractions and percentages. Fundamental discoveries about the development of information processing have

This girl's capacity for cognitive self-regulation is evident as she practices the violin. When she makes a mistake, does she continue, or does she isolate the passage for further practice? Her parents and music teacher can foster her self-regulatory skills by pointing out the special demands of the piece she is learning, suggesting strategies, and explaining why they are effective.

been applied to children's learning of reading and mathematics. Researchers are identifying the cognitive ingredients of skilled performance, tracing their development, and distinguishing good from poor learners by pinpointing differences in cognitive skills. They hope, as a result, to design teaching methods that will help all children master these essential skills.

READING ● While reading, we use many skills at once, taxing all aspects of our information-processing systems. We must perceive single letters and letter combinations, translate them into speech sounds, hold chunks of text in working memory while interpreting their meaning, and combine the meanings of various parts of a text passage into an understandable whole. In fact, reading is so demanding that most or all of these skills must be done automatically (Perfetti, 1988). If one or more are poorly developed, they will compete for resources in our limited working memories, and reading performance will decline.

Effective reading instruction involves a complex mix of elements—among them, balancing basic-skills and whole-language teaching. This first-grade teacher works with a small group on identifying, pronouncing, and writing words that begin with "fr." Teaching of phonics is embedded in exposure to interesting stories and challenging writing tasks.

Researchers are just beginning to understand how children acquire and combine these varied skills into fluent reading. Until recently, they were embroiled in an intense debate over how to teach children to read. On one side were those who took a **whole-language approach.** They argued that reading should be taught in a way that parallels natural language learning. From the very beginning, children should be exposed to text in its complete form—stories, poems, letters, posters, and lists—so that they can appreciate the communicative function of written language. According to these experts, as long as reading is kept meaningful, children will be motivated to discover the specific skills they need (Goodman, 1986; Watson, 1989). On the other side were those who advocated a **basic-skills approach.** According to this view, children should be given simplified reading materials. At first, they should be coached on *phonics*—the basic rules for translating written symbols into sounds. Only later, after they have mastered these skills, should they get complex material (Rayner & Pollatsek, 1989; Samuels, 1985).

Many studies have resolved this debate by showing that children learn best with a mixture of both approaches. Kindergarten children benefit from an emphasis on whole language, with gradual introduction of phonics (Jeynes & Littell, 2000). In first and second grade, teaching that includes phonics boosts reading achievement scores, especially for children who are behind in reading progress (Berninger et al., 2003; Ehri et al., 2001). And when teachers combine real reading and writing with teaching of basic skills and engage in other excellent teaching practices—encouraging children to tackle reading challenges and integrating reading into all school subjects—first graders show far greater literacy progress (Pressley et al., 2001).

Why might combining phonics with whole language work best? Learning the basics—relations between letters and sounds—enables children to *decode,* or decipher, words they have never seen before. As this process becomes more automatic, it releases working memory for higher-level comprehension activities. In Chapter 9, we saw that *phonological awareness*—the ability to reflect on and manipulate the sound structure of spoken language—predicts early reading success. Children who enter school low in phonological awareness make far better reading progress when given training in phonics. Soon they detect new letter–sound relations while reading on their own (Goswami, 2000). Compared with whole language, phonics instruction also results in more accurate spelling by third grade (Bruck et al., 1998). In view of these findings, it is not surprising that training in basic skills promotes *reading self-efficacy*—children's belief that they can succeed at challenging reading tasks (Tunmer & Chapman, 2002).

Yet if basic skills are overemphasized, children may lose sight of the goal of reading—understanding. Many teachers report cases of students who read aloud fluently but register little or no meaning. Such children have little knowledge of effective reading strategies—for example, that they must read more carefully if they will be tested on a passage. And they do not monitor their reading comprehension. Providing instruction aimed at increasing knowledge and use of reading strategies readily enhances reading performance of children from third grade on (Cross & Paris, 1988; Dickson et al., 1998).

TABLE 12.1

Sequence of Reading Development

GRADE/AGE	DEVELOPMENT	METHOD OF LEARNING
Preschool and Kindergarten 2–6 years	"Pretends" to read; recognizes some familiar signs ("ON," "OFF," "PIZZA"); "pretends" to write; prints own name and other words	Informal literacy experiences through literacy-rich physical environments, literacy-related play, and storybook reading (see Chapter 9, page 340)
Grades 1 and 2 6–7 years	Masters letter–sound correspondences; sounds out one-syllable words; reads simple stories; reads about 600 words	Direct teaching, through exposure to many types of texts and the basic rules of decoding written symbols into sounds
Grades 2 and 3 7–8 years	Reads simple stories more fluently; masters basic decoding rules; reads about 3,000 words	Same as above
Grades 4 to 9 9–14 years	Reads to learn new knowledge, usually without questioning the reading material	Reading and studying; participating in classroom discussion; completing written assignments
Grades 10 to 12 5–17 years	Reads more widely, tapping materials with diverse viewpoints	Reading more widely; writing papers
College 18 years and older	Reads with a self-defined purpose; decoding and comprehension skills reach a high level of efficiency	Reading even more widely; writing more sophisticated papers

Source: Chall, 1983.

Table 12.1 charts the general sequence of reading development. Notice how a major shift occurs around age 7 to 8, from "learning to read" to "reading to learn" (Ely, 2001). As decoding and comprehension skills reach a high level of efficiency, older readers become actively engaged with the text. They adjust the way they read to fit their current purpose—at times seeking new facts and ideas, at other times questioning, agreeing with, or disagreeing with the writer's viewpoint.

MATHEMATICS ● Mathematics teaching in elementary school builds on and greatly enriches children's informal knowledge of number concepts and counting. Written notation systems and formal computational techniques enhance children's ability to represent numbers and compute. Over the early elementary school years, children acquire basic math facts through a combination of frequent practice, reasoning about number concepts, and teaching that conveys effective strategies. (Return to Chapter 9, pages 335–336, for research supporting the importance of both extended practice and a grasp of concepts.) Eventually children retrieve answers automatically and apply this basic knowledge to more complex problems.

Arguments about how to teach math resemble those in reading. Drill in computational skills is pitted against "number sense," or understanding. Yet once again, a blend of these two approaches is most beneficial. In learning basic math, poorly performing students try to retrieve answers from memory too soon. Their responses are often wrong because they have not sufficiently experimented with strategies to test which ones result in rapid, accurate solutions. By trying out strategies, good students grapple with underlying concepts and develop effective solution techniques (Siegler, 1996). This suggests that encouraging students to apply strategies and making sure they understand why certain ones work well are vital for solid mastery of basic math.

A similar picture emerges for more complex skills, such as carrying in addition, borrowing in subtraction, and operating with decimals and fractions. When taught by rote, children cannot apply the procedure to new problems. Instead, they persistently make mistakes, using a "math rule" that they recall incorrectly because they do not understand it (Carpenter et al., 1999). Look at the following subtraction errors:

$$\begin{array}{r} 427 \\ -138 \\ \hline 311 \end{array} \qquad \begin{array}{r} 7002 \\ -5445 \\ \hline 1447 \end{array}$$

In the first problem, the child consistently subtracts a smaller from a larger digit, regardless of which is on top. In the second, columns with zeros are skipped in a borrowing operation, and whenever there is a zero on top, the bottom digit is written as the answer.

In contrast, when provided with rich opportunities to experiment with problem solving, to grasp the reasons behind strategies, and to evaluate solution techniques, children seldom make these errors. In one study, second graders who were taught in these ways not only mastered correct procedures but even invented their own successful strategies, some of which were superior to standard, school-taught methods! Consider this solution:

$$\begin{array}{r} 3 \quad 15\ 14\ 12 \\ \cancel{4}\ \cancel{6}\ \cancel{5}\ \cancel{2} \\ -\ 1\ 9\ 6\ 8 \\ \hline 2\ 6\ 8\ 4 \end{array}$$

In subtracting, the child performed all trades first, flexibly moving either from right to left or from left to right, and then subtracted all four columns—a highly efficient, accurate approach (Fuson & Burghard, 2003). In a German study, the more teachers emphasized conceptual knowledge, by having children actively construct meanings in word problems before practicing computation and memorizing math facts, the more children gained in math achievement from second to third grade (Staub & Stern, 2002).

In Asian countries, students receive a variety of supports for acquiring mathematical knowledge, and they excel at math reasoning and computation. For example, use of the metric system, which presents ones, tens, hundreds, and thousands values in all areas of measurement, helps Asian children grasp place value. The consistent structure of number words in Asian languages ("ten two" for 12, "ten three" for 13) also makes this idea clear (Ho & Fuson, 1998). Furthermore, Asian number words are shorter and more quickly pronounced. Therefore, more digits can be held in working memory at once, increasing the speed of thinking (Geary et al., 1996). Finally, as we will see later in this chapter, in Asian classrooms, much more time is spent exploring math concepts and much less on drill and repetition.

Culture and language-based factors contribute to Asian children's skill at mathematics. The abacus supports these Japanese pupils' understanding of place value. Ones, tens, hundreds, and thousands are each represented by a different column of beads, and calculations are performed by moving the beads to different positions. As children become skilled at using the abacus, they learn to think in ways that facilitate solving complex arithmetic problems.

Ask YOURSELF · ▯ www

REVIEW Cite evidence indicating that school-age children view the mind as an active, constructive agent.

APPLY One day, the children in Lizzie and Joey's school saw a slide show about endangered species. They were told to remember as many animal names as they could. Fourth and fifth graders recalled considerably more than first and second graders. What factors might account for this difference?

APPLY Lizzie knows that if you have difficulty learning part of a task, you should devote most of your attention to that aspect. But she plays each of her piano pieces from beginning to end instead of picking out the hard parts for extra practice. What explains Lizzie's failure to engage in cognitive self-regulation?

REFLECT Describe the relative emphasis on drill in computational skills and understanding of concepts in your elementary school math education. How do you think that balance affected your interest and performance in math?

Individual Differences in Mental Development

During middle childhood, educators rely heavily on intelligence tests for assessing individual differences in mental development. Around age 6, IQ becomes more stable than it was at earlier ages, and it correlates well with academic achievement, from .40 to .70. And children with higher IQs are more likely when they grow up to attain higher levels of education and enter more prestigious occupations (Brody, 1992).

Because IQ predicts school performance, it often plays a major role in educational decisions. Do intelligence tests accurately assess ability to profit from academic instruction? Let's look closely at this controversial issue.

Defining and Measuring Intelligence

Virtually all intelligence tests provide an overall score (the IQ), which represents *general intelligence* or reasoning ability, along with an array of separate scores measuring specific mental abilities. Intelligence is a collection of many capacities, not all of which are included on currently available tests. Test designers use a complicated statistical technique called *factor analysis* to identify the various abilities that intelligence tests measure. This procedure determines which sets of items on the test correlate strongly with one another. Those that do are assumed to measure a similar ability and, therefore, are designated as a separate factor. See Figure 12.2 for items typically included in intelligence tests for children.

The intelligence tests given every so often in classrooms are *group-administered tests.* They permit large numbers of students to be tested at once and require very little training of teachers who give them. Group tests are useful for instructional planning and for identifying children who require more extensive evaluation with *individually administered tests.* Unlike group tests, individually administered tests demand that the examiner have considerable training and experience. The examiner not only considers the child's answers but also observes the child's behavior, noting such things as attentiveness and wariness of the adult. These observations provide insight into whether the test score is accurate or underestimates the child's abilities. Two individual tests—the Stanford-Binet and the Wechsler—are often used to identify highly intelligent children and to diagnose those with learning problems.

The *Stanford-Binet Intelligence Scale,* the modern descendent of Alfred Binet's first successful intelligence test, is designed for individuals between 2 years of age and adulthood. Its latest version measures both general intelligence and four intellectual factors: verbal reasoning, quantitative reasoning, abstract/visual (spatial) reasoning, and short-term (working) memory (Thorndike, Hagen, & Sattler, 1986). Within these factors are 15 subtests that permit a detailed analysis of each child's mental abilities. The verbal and quantitative factors emphasize culturally loaded, fact-oriented information, such as vocabulary and sentence comprehension. The abstract/visual reasoning factor is believed to be less culturally biased because it demands little in the way of specific information. Instead, it tests children's ability to see complex relationships, as illustrated by the spatial visualization item in Figure 12.2.

The recently published *Wechsler Intelligence Scale for Children–IV (WISC–IV)* is the fourth edition of a widely used test for 6- through 16-year-olds. A downward extension of it, the *Wechsler Preschool and Primary Scale of Intelligence–Revised (WPPSI–III),* is appropriate for children 2 years 6 months through 7 years 3 months (Wechsler, 2002, 2003). The Wechsler tests offered both a measure of general intelligence and a variety of factor scores long before the Stanford-Binet. As a result, many psychologists and educators came to prefer them. The WISC–IV has four broad intellectual factors: verbal reasoning, perceptual reasoning, working memory, and processing speed. Each factor is made up of two or three subtests, yielding ten separate scores in all. The WISC-IV was designed to de-emphasize culture-dependent information, which is stressed on only one of its four factors (verbal reasoning). The remaining three factors emphasize information processing. According to the test designers, the result is the most theoretically current and "culture-fair" intelligence test available (Williams, Weis, & Rolfhus, 2003).

The Wechsler tests were the first to be standardized on samples representing the total population of the United States, including ethnic minorities. Previous editions of the WISC have been adapted for and standardized in Canada, where both English and French versions are available (Sarrazin, 1999; Wechsler, 1996).

Recent Efforts to Define Intelligence

As we have seen, mental tests now tap important aspects of information processing. In line with this trend, researchers are combining the factor-analytic approach to defining intelligence with the information-processing approach. They believe that factors on intelligence tests have limited usefulness unless we can identify the cognitive processes responsible for those factors. Once we understand the underlying basis for IQ, we will know much more about why a particular child does well or poorly. These researchers conduct *componential analyses* of children's test scores. This means that they look for relationships between aspects (or components) of information processing and children's IQs.

Many studies reveal that speed of processing, measured in terms of reaction time on diverse cognitive tasks, is modestly related to IQ (Deary, 2001; Vernon et al., 2001). These findings suggest that individuals whose nervous systems function more efficiently, permitting them to take in and manipulate information quickly, have an edge in intellectual skills. In support of this interpretation, fast, strong EEG brain waves in response to stimulation also predict speedy processing and high mental test scores (Rijsdijk & Boomsma, 1997; Schmid, Tirsch, & Scherb, 2002). But strategy use also predicts IQ, and it explains some of the association between response speed and test scores (Miller & Vernon, 1992). Children who apply strategies effectively acquire more knowledge and can retrieve that knowledge rapidly—advantages that carry over to performance on intelligence tests.

The componential approach has one major shortcoming: It regards intelligence as entirely due to causes within the child. Yet throughout this book, we have seen how cultural and situational factors affect children's cognitive skills. Robert Sternberg has expanded the componential approach into a comprehensive theory that regards intelligence as a product of inner and outer forces.

STERNBERG'S TRIARCHIC THEORY ● As Figure 12.3 on page 444 shows, Sternberg's (1997, 2001, 2002b) **triarchic theory of successful intelligence** is made up of three broad, interacting intelligences: (1) *analytical intelligence,* or information-processing skills; (2) *creative intelligence,* the capacity to solve novel problems; and (3) *practical intelligence,* application of intellectual skills in everyday situations. Intelligent behavior involves balancing all three intelligences to achieve success in life, according to one's personal goals and the requirements of one's cultural community.

TYPICAL VERBAL ITEMS

Vocabulary	Tell me what *carpet* means.
General Information	What day of the week comes right after Thursday?
Verbal Comprehension	Why are police officers needed?
Similarities	How are a ship and a train alike?
Arithmetic	If a $60 jacket is 25% off, how much does it cost?

TYPICAL PERCEPTUAL- AND SPATIAL-REASONING ITEMS

Block Design	Make these blocks look just like the picture.
Picture Concepts	Choose one object from each row to make a group of objects that goes together.
Spatial Visualization	Which of the boxes on the right can be made from the pattern on the left?

TYPICAL WORKING-MEMORY ITEMS

Digit Span	Repeat these digits in the same order. Now repeat these digits (a similar series) backward. **2, 6, 4, 7, 1, 8**
Letter–Number Sequencing	Repeat these numbers and letters, first giving the numbers, then the letters, each in correct sequence. **8 G 4 B 5 N 2**

TYPICAL PROCESSING-SPEED ITEM

Symbol Search	If the shape on the left is the same as any of those on the right, mark YES. If the shape is not the same, mark NO. Work as quickly as you can without making mistakes.

FIGURE 12.2

Test items like those on commonly used intelligence tests for children. The verbal items emphasize culturally loaded, fact-oriented information. The perceptual- and spatial-reasoning, working-memory, and processing-speed items emphasize aspects of information processing and are assumed to assess more biologically based skills.

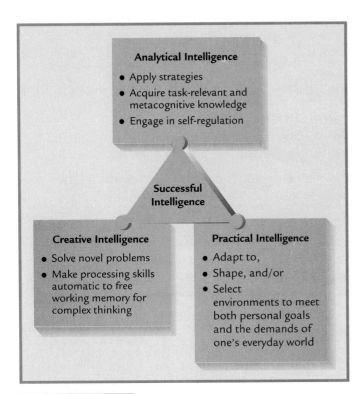

FIGURE 12.3

Sternberg's triarchic theory of successful intelligence.

People who behave intelligently balance three interrelated intelligences—analytical, creative, and practical—to achieve success in life, as defined by their personal goals and the requirements of their cultural communities.

The first intelligence, *analytical,* consists of the information-processing components that underlie all intelligent acts: applying strategies, acquiring task-relevant and metacognitive knowledge, and engaging in self-regulation. But in schoolwork and on mental tests, processing skills are used in only a few of their potential ways, resulting in a far too narrow view of intelligent behavior. We have already seen many examples of how children in tribal and village societies do not invest in or perform well on measures of school-type knowledge. At the same time, these children thrive when processing information in out-of-school situations that middle-SES Westerners would find highly challenging.

Second, in any context, success depends not only on processing familiar information but also on generating useful solutions to new problems. People who are *creative* think more skillfully than others when faced with novelty. And when given a new task, these individuals learn rapidly. They apply their information-processing skills in exceptionally effective ways, making them automatic so that working memory is freed for more complex aspects of the situation. Consequently, they quickly move to high-level performance. Although all of us are capable of creativity to some degree, only a few individuals excel at generating novel solutions. We will address the ingredients of creativity in greater detail at the end of this chapter.

Finally, intelligence is a *practical,* goal-oriented activity aimed at one or more of the following purposes: *adapting to an environment, shaping an environment,* and *selecting an environment.* Intelligent people skillfully *adapt* their thinking to fit with both their desires and the demands of their everyday worlds. When they cannot adapt to a situation, they try to *shape,* or change, it to meet their needs. And if they cannot shape it, they *select* new contexts that better match their skills, values, or goals. Practical intelligence reminds us that intelligent behavior is never culture-free. Because of their backgrounds, some children do well at the behaviors required for success on intelligence tests, and they easily adapt to the tasks and testing conditions. Others with different life histories misinterpret the testing context or reject it because it does not suit their needs. Yet such children often display sophisticated abilities in daily life—for example, telling stories, engaging in complex artistic activities, or interacting skillfully with other people.

Sternberg's triarchic theory emphasizes the complexity of intelligent behavior and the limitations of current tests in assessing that complexity. For example, out-of-school, practical forms of intelligence are vital for life success, and they help explain why cultures vary widely in the behaviors they regard as intelligent (Sternberg et al., 2000). When researchers asked ethnically diverse parents for their idea of an intelligent first grader, Caucasian Americans mentioned cognitive traits. In contrast, ethnic minorities (Cambodian, Filipino, Vietnamese, and Mexican immigrants) saw noncognitive capacities—motivation, self-management, and social skills—as particularly important (Okagaki & Sternberg, 1993). Clearly, Sternberg's ideas are relevant to the controversy surrounding cultural bias in intelligence testing, which we will address shortly.

GARDNER'S THEORY OF MULTIPLE INTELLIGENCES ● In yet another view of how information-processing skills underlie intelligence behavior, Howard Gardner's (1983, 1993, 2000) **theory of multiple intelligences** defines intelligence in terms of distinct sets of processing operations that permit individuals to engage in a wide range of culturally valued activities. Dismissing the idea of general intelligence, Gardner proposes at least eight independent intelligences (see Table 12.2).

Gardner believes that each intelligence has a unique biological basis, a distinct course of development, and different expert, or "end-state," performances. At the same time, he emphasizes that a lengthy process of education is required to transform any raw potential into a mature social role (Torff & Gardner, 1999). This means that cultural values and learning opportunities affect the extent to which a child's intellectual strengths are realized and the way they are expressed.

Gardner's theory has yet to be firmly grounded in research. Neurological evidence for the independence of his abilities is weak. Furthermore, some exceptionally gifted individuals have

TABLE 12.2

Gardner's Multiple Intelligences

INTELLIGENCE	PROCESSING OPERATIONS	END-STATE PERFORMANCE POSSIBILITIES
Linguistic	Sensitivity to the sounds, rhythms, and meaning of words and the functions of language	Poet, journalist
Logico-mathematical	Sensitivity to, and capacity to detect, logical or numerical patterns; ability to handle long chains of logical reasoning	Mathematician
Musical	Ability to produce and appreciate pitch, rhythm (or melody), and aesthetic quality of the forms of musical expressiveness	Instrumentalist, composer
Spatial	Ability to perceive the visual-spatial world accurately, to perform transformations on those perceptions, and to re-create aspects of visual experience in the absence of relevant stimuli	Sculptor, navigator
Bodily-kinesthetic	Ability to use the body skillfully for expressive as well as goal-directed purposes; ability to handle objects skillfully	Dancer, athlete
Naturalist	Ability to recognize and classify all varieties of animals, minerals, and plants	Biologist
Interpersonal	Ability to detect and respond appropriately to the moods, temperaments, motivations, and intentions of others	Therapist, salesperson
Intrapersonal	Ability to discriminate complex inner feelings and to use them to guide one's own behavior; knowledge of one's own strengths, weaknesses, desires, and intelligences	Person with detailed, accurate self-knowledge

Sources: Gardner, 1993, 1998, 2000.

abilities that are broad rather than limited to a particular domain (Goldsmith, 2000). And research with mental tests suggests that several of Gardner's intelligences (linguistic, logico-mathematical, and spatial) have at least some features in common.

Nevertheless, Gardner's theory highlights several intelligences not tapped by IQ scores. For example, his interpersonal and intrapersonal intelligences include a set of capacities for dealing with people and understanding oneself that has become known as *emotional intelligence.* Emotional intelligence involves recognizing and regulating one's own emotions, detecting others' emotions, feeling empathy and sympathy, and cooperating with others (Goleman, 1998). Recall from earlier chapters that these skills enhance both cognitive and social competence. And they are positively associated with self-esteem and life satisfaction (Mayer, Salovey, & Caruso, 2000).

Finally, Gardner's multiple intelligences have been helpful in efforts to understand and nurture children's special talents. We will take up this topic at the end of this chapter.

Explaining Individual and Group Differences in IQ

When we compare individuals in terms of academic achievement, years of education, and the status of their occupations, it quickly becomes clear that certain sectors of the population are advantaged over others. In trying to explain these differences, researchers have compared the IQ scores of ethnic and SES groups. American black children score, on average, 15 IQ points below American white children, although the difference has been shrinking (Hedges & Nowell, 1998; Loehlin, 2000). Hispanic children fall midway between black and white children (Ceci, Rosenblum, & Kumpf, 1998).

The gap between middle-SES and low-SES children is about 9 points (Jensen & Figueroa, 1975). SES accounts for some, but not

According to Gardner, children are capable of at least eight distinct intelligences. As this girl paints a birdhouse she built with her father's assistance, she enriches her spatial intelligence.

© ARIEL SKELLEY/CORBIS

all, of ethnic IQ differences. For example, when black children and white children are matched on family income, the black–white gap is reduced by a third to a half (Jensen & Reynolds, 1982; Smith, Duncan, & Lee, 2003). Of course, considerable variation exists *within* each ethnic and SES group. Still, these group differences in IQ are large enough and of serious enough consequence that they cannot be ignored.

In the 1970s, the IQ nature–nurture controversy escalated after psychologist Arthur Jensen (1969) published a controversial article entitled, "How Much Can We Boost IQ and Scholastic Achievement?" Jensen's answer to this question was "not much." He argued that heredity is largely responsible for individual, ethnic, and SES variations in intelligence, a position he still maintains (Jensen, 1998, 2001). Jensen's work was followed by an outpouring of responses and research studies. The controversy was rekindled in Richard Herrnstein's and Charles Murray's (1994) *The Bell Curve.* Like Jensen, these authors argued that the contribution of heredity to individual and SES differences in IQ is substantial. And although they did not arrive at a firm conclusion, they implied that heredity plays a sizable role in the black–white IQ gap. Let's evaluate these claims by looking at some important evidence.

NATURE VERSUS NURTURE ● In Chapter 2 we introduced the *heritability estimate.* Recall that heritabilities are obtained from *kinship studies,* which compare family members. The most powerful evidence on the role of heredity in IQ involves twin comparisons. The IQ scores of identical twins (who share all their genes) are more similar than those of fraternal twins (who are genetically no more alike than ordinary siblings). On the basis of this and other kinship evidence, researchers estimate that about half the differences in IQ among children can be traced to their genetic makeup.

However, recall that heritabilities risk overestimating genetic influences and underestimating environmental influences. Although these measures offer convincing evidence that genes contribute to IQ, disagreement persists over how large the role of heredity really is (Grigorenko, 2000). And heritability estimates do not reveal the complex processes through which genes and experiences influence intelligence as children develop.

Compared with heritabilities, adoption studies offer a wider range of information. In one investigation, children of two extreme groups of biological mothers—those with IQs below 95 and those with IQs above 120—were adopted at birth by parents who were well above average in income and education. During the school years, children of the low-IQ biological mothers scored above average in IQ, indicating that test performance can be greatly improved by an advantaged home life! At the same time, they did not do as well as children of high-IQ biological mothers placed in similar adoptive families (Horn, 1983; Loehlin, Horn, & Willerman, 1997). Adoption research confirms that heredity and environment contribute jointly to IQ.

Some intriguing adoption research also sheds light on the black–white IQ difference. African-American children placed in economically well-off white homes during the first year of life score high on intelligence tests. In two such studies, adopted black children attained mean IQs of 110 and 117 by middle childhood, well above average and 20 to 30 points higher than the typical scores of children growing up in low-income black communities (Moore, 1986; Scarr & Weinberg, 1983). However, a follow-up revealed that adoptees' IQs declined in adolescence, although they remained above the IQ average for low-SES African Americans. Perhaps the drop in test scores resulted from use of different tests at the two ages and from the emotional challenges of constructing an ethnic identity that blends birth and rearing backgrounds (DeBerry, Scarr, & Weinberg, 1996; Waldman, Weinberg, & Scarr, 1994).

Adoption findings do not completely resolve questions about ethnic differences in IQ. Nevertheless, the IQ gains of black children "reared in the culture of the tests and schools" are consistent with a wealth of evidence indicating that poverty severely depresses the intelligence of ethnic minority children (Nisbett, 1998). Furthermore, dramatic generational gains in mental test performance support the notion that, with new experiences and opportunities, oppressed groups can substantially raise their average IQs. See the Cultural Influences box on the following page to find out about the *Flynn effect.*

CULTURAL INFLUENCES ● Jermaine, an African-American child in Lizzie's third-grade class, participated actively in class discussion and wrote complex, imaginative stories. But two

(Cultural Influences

The Flynn Effect: Massive Generational Gains in IQ

After gathering IQ scores from 20 industrialized nations that had either military mental testing or frequent testing of other large, representative samples, James Flynn (1994, 1999) reported a finding so consistent and intriguing that it became known as the **Flynn effect: IQs have increased steadily from one generation to the next.** And the largest increases have occurred on tests of spatial reasoning—tasks often assumed to be "culture-fair" and, therefore, largely genetically based. Figure 12.4 shows these gains for one such test, administered to military samples consisting of almost all young men in Belgium, Israel, the Netherlands, and Norway. IQ rose, on average, 18 points per generation (30 years).

Consistent with this *secular trend,* when intelligence tests are revised, the representative sample on which the new version is standardized almost always performs better than the previous one. After locating every study in which the same individuals had taken two or more versions of Stanford-Binet

FIGURE 12.4

Generational gains in performance on a test of spatial reasoning in four nations.

Findings are based on military testing that includes nearly all young adults in each country. (From J. R. Flynn, 1999, "Searching for Justice: The Discovery of IQ Gains over Time," *American Psychologist, 54,* p. 7. Copyright © by the American Psychological Association. Adapted by permission.)

or Wechsler tests (a total of 73 samples, with more than 7,500 participants), Flynn used the data to estimate the rate of IQ change between 1932 and 1978 in the United States. On average, IQ increased about ⅓ point per year, steadily over time and similarly for all ages, for a total of 14 points over the 46-year period. And when subtest scores were examined, once again gains were largest for spatial tasks.

The Flynn effect is environmental; improved nutrition and education, technological innovations (including TV and computers), a more stimulating world, and greater test-taking motivation may contribute to the better reasoning ability of each successive generation (Williams, 1998). And the Flynn effect is spreading to the developing world. The IQs of rural

schoolchildren in Kenya underwent a large increase from 1984 to 1998. During this time, children's diets improved, TV sets appeared in some households, parental education and literacy increased, and family size declined, permitting parents to devote more time and resources to each child (Daley et al., 2003).

Notice that the generational gain in intelligence (18 points) is larger than the black–white IQ gap (about 15 points). Therefore, environmental explanations for ethnic differences in IQ are highly plausible. Flynn argues that large, environmentally induced IQ gains between generations present a major challenge to the assumption that black–white and other ethnic variations in IQ are largely genetic (Dickens & Flynn, 2001).

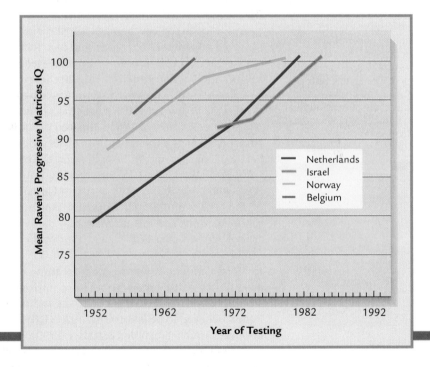

years earlier, as a first grader, Jermaine responded, "I don't know," to the simplest of questions, including "What's your name?" Fortunately, Jermaine's teacher understood his uneasiness. She helped him build a bridge between the learning style fostered by his cultural background and the style necessary for academic success. A growing body of evidence reveals that IQ scores are affected by specific learning experiences, including exposure to certain communication styles and knowledge. In addition, broadly held stereotypes about the test-taker's ethnic group can dramatically influence performance.

This mother of the Yakut people of Siberia, Russia, uses a collaborative style of communication with her daughter. They work together on the same aspect of a food preparation task, smoothly coordinating their actions until the dish is complete. Ethnic minority parents with little education often communicate this way. Because their children are not accustomed to the hierarchical style of communication typical of classrooms, they may do poorly on tests and assignments.

Communication Styles. Ethnic minority subcultures often foster unique language skills that do not match the expectations of most classrooms and testing situations. Shirley Brice Heath (1982, 1989), an anthropologist who has spent many hours observing in low-SES black homes in a southeastern American city, found that black adults asked their children questions unlike those of white middle-SES families. From an early age, white parents ask knowledge-training questions, such as "What color is it?" and "What's this story about?" that resemble the questioning style of tests and classrooms. In contrast, the black parents asked only "real" questions—ones they themselves could not answer. Often these were analogy questions ("What's that like?") or story-starter questions ("Didja hear Miss Sally this morning?") that called for elaborate responses about personal experiences and no "right answer."

These experiences lead low-SES black children to develop complex verbal skills, such as storytelling and exchanging quick-witted remarks. But their language emphasizes emotional and social concerns rather than facts about the world. Not surprisingly, black children may be confused by the "objective" questions they encounter on tests and in classrooms. Also, African-American children often take a unique approach to storytelling. Rather than using the *topic-focused style* of most school-age children, who describe a critical event, they use a *topic-associating style* in which they blend several similar experiences. One African-American 9-year-old, for example, related having a tooth pulled, then described seeing her sister's tooth being pulled, next told how she removed one of her baby teeth, and concluded "I'm a pullin' teeth expert . . . call me, and I'll be over'" (McCabe, 1997, p. 164). Yet many teachers criticize this approach as "disorganized," and it is not included in verbal intelligence test items.

Furthermore, many ethnic minority parents without extensive schooling prefer a *collaborative style of communication* when completing tasks with children. They work together in a coordinated, fluid way, each focused on the same aspect of the problem. This pattern of adult–child engagement has been observed in Native American, Canadian Inuit, Hispanic, and Guatemalan Mayan cultures (Chavajay & Rogoff, 2002; Crago, Annahatak, & Ningiuruvik, 1993; Delgado-Gaitan, 1994). With increasing education, parents establish a *hierarchical style of communication,* like that of classrooms and tests. The parent directs each child to carry out an aspect of the task, and children work independently. This sharp discontinuity between home and school communication practices may contribute to low-SES minority children's lower IQ and school performance (Greenfield, Quiroz, & Raeff, 2000).

Test Content. Many researchers argue that IQ scores are affected by specific information acquired as part of majority-culture upbringing. Unfortunately, attempts to change tests by eliminating fact-oriented verbal tasks and relying only on spatial reasoning and performance items (believed to be less culturally loaded) have not raised the scores of ethnic minority children very much (Reynolds & Kaiser, 1990).

Yet even these nonverbal test items depend on learning opportunities. In one study, children's performance on Block Design (see the sample items in Figure 12.2 on page 443) was related to how often they had played a popular but expensive game that (like the test) required them to arrange blocks to duplicate a design as quickly as possible (Dirks, 1982). Playing video games that require fast responding and mental rotation of visual images also fosters success on spatial tests (Subrahmanyam & Greenfield, 1996). Low-income minority children, who often grow up in more "people-oriented" than "object-oriented" homes, may lack opportunities to use games and objects that promote certain intellectual skills.

Furthermore, the sheer amount of time a child spends in school is a strong predictor of IQ. When children of the same age who are in different grades are compared, those who have been

FIGURE 12.5

Effect of stereotype threat on performance.

Some children were told that verbal tasks were "a test of how good children are at school problems." Others were told that the tasks were "not a test." Among children who were aware of ethnic stereotypes, African-American and Hispanic children scored much worse than Caucasian children in the "test" condition. The "not a test" condition yielded no group difference in performance. Being told that tasks were a test of school competence seemed to trigger a fear of being judged stereotypically among minority children, which undermined their performance. (Adapted from C. McKown & R. S. Weinstein, 2003, "The Development and Consequences of Stereotype Consciousness in Middle Childhood," *Child Development, 74,* p. 509. Copyright © by the Society for Research in Child Development, Inc. Reprinted by permission.)

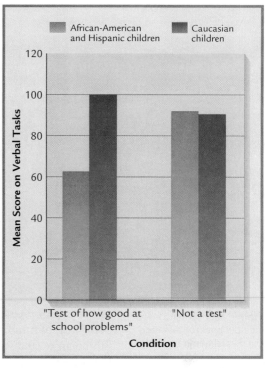

in school longer score higher on intelligence tests. Similarly, dropping out of school causes IQ to decline. The earlier young people leave school, the greater their loss of IQ points (Ceci 1991, 1999). Taken together, these findings indicate that children's exposure to the factual knowledge and ways of thinking valued in classrooms has a sizable impact on their intelligence test performance.

Stereotypes. Imagine trying to succeed at an activity when the prevailing attitude is that members of your group are incompetent. The fear of being judged on the basis of a negative stereotype is called **stereotype threat,** and it can trigger anxiety that interferes with performance (Steele, 1997; Steele & Aronson, 1995). Stereotype threat undermines the test taking of college students, and recent evidence shows that it does the same to elementary school children. In one study, researchers gave African-American, Hispanic, and Caucasian 6- to 10-year-olds verbal tasks. Some children were told that the tasks "were not a test," whereas others were informed that they were "a test of how good children are at school problems"—a statement designed to induce stereotype threat in the ethnic minority children. Among children who were aware of ethnic stereotypes (such as "black people aren't smart"), African Americans and Hispanics performed far worse than Caucasians in the "test" condition. In contrast, the "not a test" condition yielded no ethnic differences in scores (see Figure 12.5) (McKown & Weinstein, 2003).

Over middle childhood, children become increasingly conscious of ethnic stereotypes, and those from stigmatized groups are especially mindful of them. By junior high school, many low-SES, minority students start to devalue doing well in school, saying it is not important to them (Major et al., 1998; Osborne, 1994). Self-protective disengagement, sparked by stereotype threat, may be responsible. Notice how stereotype threat and disengagement create a vicious cycle. As stereotyped group members underperform and opt out of academic activities, their behavior provides the dominant group with further justification for the negative stereotype.

As minority children become increasingly aware of stereotypes during middle childhood, a teacher's remark, such as "This is a test," or "This will tell me how good you are at schoolwork," is enough to induce stereotype threat, which undermines academic performance in African-American and Hispanic children.

Reducing Cultural Bias in Intelligence Testing

Although not all experts agree, many acknowledge that IQ scores can underestimate the intelligence of culturally different children. A special concern exists about incorrectly labeling minority children as slow learners and assigning them to remedial classes, which are far less stimulating than regular school experiences. Because of this danger, test scores need to be combined with assessments of adaptive behavior—children's ability to cope with the demands of their everyday environments. The child who does poorly on an IQ test yet plays a complex game on the playground, figures out how to rewire a broken TV, or cares for younger

© WILL HART/PHOTOEDIT

Dynamic assessment introduces purposeful teaching into the situation to find out what the child can attain with social support. This teacher assists a second grader in writing the alphabet. Many ethnic minority children perform more competently after adult assistance. And the approach helps identify the teaching style to which the child is most responsive.

siblings responsibly is unlikely to be mentally deficient.

In addition, culturally relevant testing procedures enhance minority children's performance. In one approach called **dynamic assessment**, an innovation consistent with Vygotsky's zone of proximal development, the adult introduces purposeful teaching into the testing situation to find out what the child can attain with social support (Lidz, 2001). Dynamic assessment often follows a pretest–intervene–retest procedure. While intervening, the adult seeks the teaching style best suited to the child and communicates strategies that she can apply in new situations.

Research consistently shows that "static" assessments, such as IQ scores, frequently underestimate how well children do on test items after adult assistance. Children's receptivity to teaching and their capacity to transfer what they have learned to novel problems add considerably to the prediction of future performance (Sternberg & Grigorenko, 2002; Tzuriel, 2001). In one study, Ethiopian 6- and 7-year-olds who had recently immigrated to Israel scored well below their Israeli-born agemates on spatial reasoning tasks. The Ethiopian children had little experience with this type of thinking. After several dynamic assessment sessions in which the adult suggested effective strategies, the Ethiopian children's scores rose sharply, nearly equaling those of Israeli-born children (see Figure 12.6). They also transferred their learning to new test items (Tzuriel & Kaufman, 1999).

Dynamic assessment is time-consuming and requires extensive knowledge of minority children's cultural values and practices. Until we have the resources to implement these procedures broadly, should we suspend the use of intelligence testing? Most experts reject this solution because important educational decisions would be based only on subjective impressions—a policy that could increase the discriminatory placement of minority children. Intelligence tests are useful as long as examiners are sensitive to cultural influences on test performance. And despite their limitations, IQ scores continue to be valid measures of school learning potential for the majority of Western children.

FIGURE 12.6

Influence of dynamic assessment on mental test scores of Ethiopian-immigrant and Israeli-born 6- and 7-year-olds.

Each child completed test items in a preteaching phase, a postteaching phase, and a transfer phase, in which they had to generalize their learning to new problems. After dynamic assessment, Ethiopian and Israeli children's scores were nearly equal. Ethiopian children also transferred their learning to new test items, performing much better in the transfer phase than in the preteaching phase. (Adapted from Tzuriel & Kaufman, 1999.)

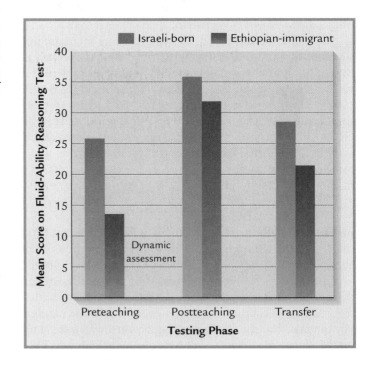

ASK YOURSELF

www

REVIEW Using Sternberg's triarchic theory and Gardner's theory of multiple intelligences, explain the limitations of current mental tests in assessing the complexity of human intelligence.

APPLY Desiree, an African-American child, was quiet and withdrawn while taking an intelligence test. Later she remarked to her mother, "I can't understand why that lady asked me all those questions. She's a grownup. She *must know* what a ball and stove are for!" Explain Desiree's reaction. Why is Desiree's score likely to underestimate her intelligence?

CONNECT Explain how dynamic assessment is consistent with Vygotsky's zone of proximal development and with scaffolding (see Chapter 9, pages 329–330).

REFLECT Do you think that intelligence tests are culturally biased? What evidence and observations influenced your conclusion?

Language Development

Vocabulary, grammar, and pragmatics continue to develop in middle childhood, although less obviously than at earlier ages. In addition, children's attitude toward language undergoes a fundamental shift. They develop **metalinguistic awareness, the ability to think about language as a system.**

Schooling contributes greatly to metalinguistic awareness and other language competencies. Talking about language is extremely common during literacy instruction but rare in other contexts. And fluent reading is a major new source of language learning (Gombert, 1992; Ravid & Tolchinsky, 2002). In the following sections, we will see how an improved capacity to reflect on language grows out of literacy and supports many complex language skills.

Vocabulary

Between the start of elementary school and its completion, vocabulary increases fourfold, eventually reaching about 40,000 words. On average, children learn about 20 new words each day—a rate of growth exceeding that of early childhood. In addition to the word-learning strategies discussed in Chapter 9, school-age children enlarge their vocabularies through analyzing the structure of complex words. From "happy" and "decide," they quickly derive the meanings of "happiness," and "decision" (Anglin, 1993). They also figure out many more word meanings from context (Nagy & Scott, 2000).

As at earlier ages, children benefit from engaging in conversation, especially when their adult partners use complex words and explain them (Weizman & Snow, 2001). But because written language contains a far more diverse and complex vocabulary than spoken language, reading contributes enormously to vocabulary growth. Children who engage in as little as 21 minutes of independent reading per day are exposed to nearly 2 million words per year (Cunningham & Stanovich, 1998).

As their knowledge expands and becomes better organized, school-age children think about and use words more precisely. Word definitions offer examples of this change. Five- and 6-year-olds give concrete descriptions that refer to functions or appearance—for example, *knife:* "when you're cutting carrots"; *bicycle:* "it's got wheels, a chain, and handlebars." By the end of elementary school, synonyms and explanations of categorical relationships appear—for example, *knife:* "something you could cut with. A saw is like a knife. It could also be a weapon" (Wehren, DeLisi, & Arnold,

1981). This advance reflects older children's ability to deal with word meanings on an entirely verbal plane. They can add new words to their vocabulary simply by being given a definition.

School-age children's more reflective and analytical approach to language permits them to appreciate the multiple meanings of words. For example, they realize that many words, such as "cool" and "neat," have psychological as well as physical meanings: "What a cool shirt!" or "That movie was really neat!" This grasp of double meanings permits 8- to 10-year-olds to comprehend subtle, mental metaphors, such as "sharp as a tack" and "spilling the beans" (Nippold, Taylor, & Baker, 1996; Wellman & Hickling, 1994). It also leads to a change in children's humor. By the mid-elementary school years, riddles and puns that go back and forth between different meanings of a key word are common, as in: "Hey, did you take a bath?" "No! Why, is one missing?"

Grammar

During the school years, mastery of complex grammatical constructions improves. For example, English-speaking children use the passive voice more frequently, and it expands from an abbreviated structure ("It got broken") into full statements ("The glass was broken by Mary") (Horgan, 1978). Older children also apply their grasp of the passive voice to a wider range of nouns and verbs. Preschoolers comprehend the passive best when the subject of the sentence is an animate being and the verb is an action word, as in "The boy is *kissed* by the girl." School-age children extend the passive to inanimate subjects, such as "drum" or "hat," and experiential verbs, such as "like" or "know" are included in passive constructions (Lempert, 1989; Pinker, Lebeaux, & Frost, 1987). Although the passive form is challenging, language input makes a difference. When adults speak a language that emphasizes full passives, such as Inukitut (spoken by the Inuit people of Arctic Canada), children produce them sooner (Allen & Crago, 1996).

Another grammatical achievement of middle childhood is advanced understanding of infinitive phrases, such as the difference between "John is eager to please" and "John is easy to please" (Chomsky, 1969). Like gains in vocabulary, appreciation of these subtle grammatical distinctions is supported by improved metalinguistic awareness, acquired during literacy activities.

Pragmatics

Improvements in *pragmatics,* the communicative side of language, also take place. Children adapt to the needs of listeners in challenging communicative situations, such as describing one object among a group of very similar objects. Whereas preschoolers tend to give ambiguous descriptions, such as "the red one," school-age children are much more precise. They might say, "the round red one with stripes on it" (Deutsch & Pechmann, 1982).

Gains in the ability to evaluate the clarity of others' messages occur as well, and children become better at resolving inconsistencies in messages. Consider the instruction, "Put the frog on the book in the box." Preschoolers cannot resolve the ambiguity, even though they use similar embedded phrases in their own speech. They respond by attending only to the first prepositional phrase ("on the book") and place a toy frog on a book. School-age children, in contrast, can attend to and integrate two competing representations ("on the book" and "in the box"). Hence, they quickly figure out the speaker's meaning and pick up a toy frog resting on a book and place it in a box (Hurewitz et al., 2000).

Children also refine their conversational strategies. For example, older children skillfully phrase things to get their way. When an adult refuses to hand over a desired object, 9-year-olds, but not 5-year-olds, state their second requests more politely (Axia & Baroni, 1985). School-age children are also more sensitive than preschoolers to distinctions between what people say and what they mean (Lee, Torrance, & Olson, 2001). Lizzie, for example, knew that when her mother said, "The garbage is beginning to smell," she really meant, "Take that garbage out!"

Opportunities to communicate in many situations with a variety of people help children refine their pragmatic skills (Ely, 2001). And because peers challenge unclear messages that adults accept, peer interaction probably contributes greatly to school-age children's conversational competence.

Learning Two Languages at a Time

Joey and Lizzie speak only their native tongue, English. Yet throughout the world, many children grow up *bilingual,* learning two languages, and sometimes more than two. Recall from Chapter 1 that both the United States and Canada have large immigrant populations. An estimated 15 percent of American children—6 million in all—speak a language other than English at home (U.S. Census Bureau, 2003b). Similarly, the native languages of 12 percent of Canadian children—nearly 700,000—are neither English nor French, the country's two official languages (Statistics Canada, 2002e).

BILINGUAL DEVELOPMENT ● Children can become bilingual in two ways: (1) by acquiring both languages at the same time in early childhood, or (2) by learning a second language after mastering the first. Children of bilingual parents who teach them both languages in infancy and early childhood show no special problems with language development. From the start, they separate the language systems, distinguishing their sounds, mastering equivalent words in each, and attaining early language milestones according to a typical timetable (Bosch & Sebastian-Galles, 2001; Holowka, Brosseau-Lapré, & Petitto, 2002). Preschoolers acquire normal native ability in the language of their surrounding community and good-to-native ability in the second language, depending on their exposure to it (Genessee, 2001). When school-age children acquire a second language after they already speak a first, it generally takes them 3 to 5 years to become as competent in the second language as native-speaking agemates (Hakuta, 1999).

Recall from Chapter 6 that, just as with first-language development, a sensitive period for second-language development exists. Mastery must begin sometime in childhood for full development to occur. Children who become fluent in two languages are advanced in cognitive development. They do better than others on tests of selective attention, analytical reasoning, concept formation, and cognitive flexibility (Bialystok, 1999, 2001). Also, their metalinguistic skills are particularly well developed. They are more aware that words are arbitrary symbols, more conscious of language structure and sounds, and better at noticing errors of grammar and meaning—capacities that enhance reading achievement (Bialystok & Herman, 1999; Campbell & Sais, 1995).

BILINGUAL EDUCATION ● The advantages of bilingualism provide strong justification for bilingual education programs in schools. In Canada, about 7 percent of elementary school students are enrolled in *language immersion programs,* in which English-speaking children are taught entirely in French for several years. The Canadian language immersion strategy succeeds in developing children who are proficient in both languages (Harley & Jean, 1999; Holobow, Genessee, & Lambert, 1991). At the same time, Canada recognizes immersion as only one form of bilingual education. It provides immigrant children with approaches aimed at fostering their native tongue while they acquire an official language. But these programs are in short supply, and many immigrant children miss out (Kalinowski, 2002).

In the United States, the question of how ethnic minority children with limited English proficiency should be educated is hotly debated. On one side are those who believe that time spent communicating in the child's native tongue detracts from English language achievement, which is crucial for success in the worlds of school and work. On the other side are educators committed to developing minority children's native language while fostering mastery of English. Providing instruction in the native tongue lets minority children know that their heritage is respected. In addition, it prevents *semilingualism,* or inadequate proficiency in both languages. When minority children gradually lose the first language as a result of being taught the second, they end up limited in both languages for a time, a circumstance that leads to serious academic difficulties (Ovando & Collier, 1998). Semilingualism

These Hispanic first graders attend a bilingual education program in which they receive instruction in both their native language and English. When ethnic minority children's first and second languages are integrated into the curriculum, they are more involved in learning, participate more actively in class discussions, and acquire the second language more easily.

is believed to contribute to the high rates of school failure and dropout among low-SES Hispanic youngsters, who make up nearly 50 percent of the American language-minority population.

At present, public opinion favors the first of these two viewpoints. Many U.S. states have passed laws declaring English to be their official language, creating conditions in which schools have no obligation to teach minority students in languages other than English. Yet in classrooms where both languages are integrated into the curriculum, minority children are more involved in learning, participate more actively in class discussions, and acquire the second language more easily. In contrast, when teachers speak only in a language that children can barely understand, minority children display frustration, boredom, and withdrawal (Crawford, 1995, 1997).

American supporters of English-only education often point to the success of Canadian language immersion programs, in which classroom lessons are conducted in the second language. Yet Canadian parents enroll their children in immersion classrooms voluntarily, and their children's first and second languages are both majority languages, judged equally important by their nation. Furthermore, teaching in the child's native language is merely delayed, not ruled out. For American non-English-speaking minority children, whose native languages are not valued by the larger society, a different strategy seems necessary: one that promotes children's native-language skills while they learn English (Cloud, Genesee & Hamayan, 2000).

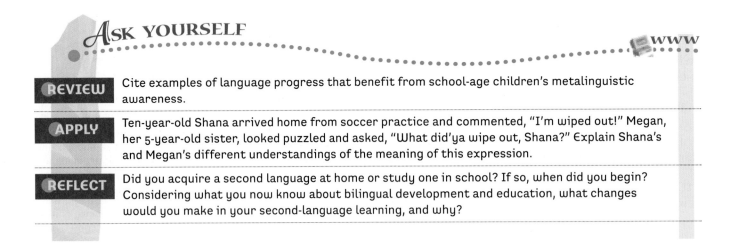

ASK YOURSELF   www

REVIEW   Cite examples of language progress that benefit from school-age children's metalinguistic awareness.

APPLY   Ten-year-old Shana arrived home from soccer practice and commented, "I'm wiped out!" Megan, her 5-year-old sister, looked puzzled and asked, "What did'ya wipe out, Shana?" Explain Shana's and Megan's different understandings of the meaning of this expression.

REFLECT   Did you acquire a second language at home or study one in school? If so, when did you begin? Considering what you now know about bilingual development and education, what changes would you make in your second-language learning, and why?

Children's Learning in School

Throughout this chapter, we have touched on evidence indicating that schools are vital forces in children's cognitive development. How do schools exert such a powerful influence? Research looking at schools as complex social systems—at their class size, educational philosophies, teacher–student interaction patterns, and larger cultural context—provides important insights into this question. As you read about these topics, refer to Applying What We Know on the following page, which summarizes characteristics of high-quality education in elementary school.

Class Size

As each school year began, Rena telephoned the principal's office and asked, "How large will Joey's and Lizzie's classes be?" Her concern is well founded. Class size influences children's learning. In a large field experiment, more than 6,000 Tennessee kindergartners were randomly assigned to three class types: small (13 to 17 students), regular (22 to 25 students), and regular with teacher plus a full-time teacher's aide. These arrangements continued into third grade.

Applying
WHAT WE **Know** / Signs of High-Quality Education in Elementary School

CLASSROOM CHARACTERISTICS	SIGNS OF QUALITY
Class Size	Optimum class size is no larger than 18 children.
Physical Setting	Space is divided into richly equipped activity centers—for reading, writing, playing math or language games, exploring science, working on construction projects, using computers, and engaging in other academic pursuits. Spaces are used flexibly for individual and small-group activities and whole-class gatherings.
Curriculum	The curriculum helps children both achieve academic standards and make sense of their learning in all subjects, including literacy, mathematics, social studies, art, music, health, and physical education. Subjects are integrated so that children apply knowledge in one area to others. The curriculum is implemented through activities responsive to children's interests, ideas, and everyday lives, including their cultural backgrounds.
Daily Activities	Teachers provide challenging activities that include opportunities for small-group and independent work. Groupings vary in size and makeup of children, depending on the activity and on children's learning needs. Teachers encourage cooperative learning and guide children in attaining it.
Interactions Between Teachers and Children	Teachers foster each child's progress, including children with academic difficulties and children capable of advanced performance. Teachers use intellectually engaging strategies, including posing problems, asking thought-provoking questions, discussing ideas, and adding complexity to tasks. They also demonstrate, explain, coach, and assist in other ways, depending on each child's learning needs.
Evaluations of Progress	Teachers regularly evaluate children's progress through written observations and work samples, which they use to enhance and individualize teaching. They help children reflect on their work and decide how to improve it. They also seek information and perspectives from parents on how well children are learning and include parents' views in evaluations.
Relationship with Parents	Teachers forge partnerships with parents. They hold periodic conferences and encourage parents to visit the classroom anytime, to observe and volunteer.

Source: Bredekamp & Copple, 1997.

Small-class students—especially minority children—scored higher in reading and math achievement and continued to do so after they returned to regular-size classes (Mosteller, 1995). Placing teacher's aides in regular-size classes had no impact. Instead, consistently being in small classes from kindergarten through third grade predicted substantially higher achievement from fourth through ninth grades (Nye, Hedges, & Konstantopoulos, 2001).

Why is small class size beneficial? With fewer children, teachers spend less time disciplining and more time getting to know students and giving individual attention, and children interact in more positive and cooperative ways. Also, children who learn in smaller groups show better concentration, higher-quality class participation, and more favorable attitudes toward school (Blatchford et al., 2001, 2002; Finn, Panozzo, & Achilles, 2003).

Educational Philosophies

Each teacher brings to the classroom an educational philosophy that plays a major role in children's learning. Two philosophical approaches have received the most research attention. They differ in what children are taught, in the way they are believed to learn, and in how their progress is evaluated.

TRADITIONAL VERSUS CONSTRUCTIVIST CLASSROOMS ● In a **traditional classroom,** the teacher is the sole authority for knowledge, rules, and decision making and does most of the talking. Students are relatively passive, listening, responding when called on, and completing teacher-assigned tasks. Their progress is evaluated by how well they keep pace with a uniform set of standards for their grade.

A **constructivist classroom,** in contrast, encourages students to *construct* their own knowledge. Although constructivist approaches vary, many are grounded in Piaget's theory, which views children as active agents who reflect on and coordinate their own thoughts, rather than absorbing those of others. A glance inside a constructivist classroom reveals richly equipped learning centers, small groups and individuals solving problems they choose themselves, and a teacher who guides and supports in response to children's needs. Students are evaluated by considering their progress in relation to their own prior development. How well they compare to other same-age students is of lesser importance.

During the past few decades, the pendulum has swung back and forth between these two views. In the 1960s and early 1970s, constructivist classrooms gained in popularity. Then, as concern over the academic progress of American children and youths became widespread, a "back to basics" movement arose. Classrooms returned to traditional instruction, a style still prevalent today.

The combined results of many studies reveal that older school-age children in traditional classrooms have a slight edge in academic achievement. But constructivist settings are associated with other benefits—gains in critical thinking, greater valuing of individual differences in classmates, and more positive attitudes toward school (Walberg, 1986). And as noted in Chapter 9, when teacher-directed instruction is emphasized in preschool and kindergarten, it undermines academic motivation and achievement, especially among low-SES children. The heavy emphasis on knowledge absorption in many kindergarten and primary classrooms has contributed to a growing trend among parents to delay their child's school entry. Traditional teaching practices may also increase the incidence of grade retention. See the Social Issues: Education box on the following page for research on these practices.

NEW PHILOSOPHICAL DIRECTIONS ● New approaches to education, grounded in Vygotsky's sociocultural theory, capitalize on the rich social context of the classroom to spur children's learning. In these **social-constructivist classrooms,** children participate in a wide range of challenging activities with teachers and peers, with whom they jointly construct understandings. As children *appropriate* (take for themselves) the knowledge and strategies generated from working together, they advance in cognitive and social development and become competent, contributing members of their cultural community (Palincsar, 1998). Vygotsky's emphasis on the social origins of complex mental activities has inspired the following educational themes:

● *Teachers and children as partners in learning.* A classroom rich in both teacher–child and child–child collaboration transfers culturally valued ways of thinking to children.

● *Experience with many types of symbolic communication in meaningful activities.* As children master reading, writing, and mathematics, they become aware of their culture's communication systems, reflect on their own thinking, and bring it under voluntary control. (Can you identify research presented earlier in this chapter that supports this theme?)

● *Teaching adapted to each child's zone of proximal development.* Assistance that both responds to current understandings and encourages children to take the next step forward helps ensure that each child makes the best progress possible.

Let's look at two examples of a growing number of programs that have translated these ideas into action.

Reciprocal Teaching. Originally designed to improve reading comprehension in students achieving poorly, this Vygotsky-inspired teaching method has been extended to other subjects and all schoolchildren (Palincsar & Herrenkohl, 1999). In **reciprocal teaching,** a teacher and two to four students form a cooperative group and take turns lead-

Reciprocal teaching is a Vygotsky-inspired educational innovation in which a teacher and two to four pupils form a cooperative learning group and engage in dialogue about a text passage. Elementary and junior high school pupils who participate in reciprocal teaching show impressive gains in reading comprehension.

MARK POKEMPNER/IMPACT VISUALS

Social Issues: Education

School Readiness and Grade Retention

While waiting to pick up their sons from preschool, Susan and Vicky struck up a conversation about kindergarten enrollment. "Freddy will be 5 in August," Susan announced. "He's a month older than the cutoff date."

"But he'll be one of the youngest in the class," Vicky countered. "Better check into what kids have to do in kindergarten these days. Have you asked his teacher what she thinks?"

"Well," Vicky admitted. "She did say Freddy was a bit young."

Since the 1980s, more parents have been delaying their children's kindergarten entry. Aware that boys lag behind girls in development, parents most often hold out sons whose birth dates are close to the cutoff for enrolling in kindergarten. Is delaying kindergarten entry beneficial? Although some teachers and principals recommend it, research has not revealed any advantages. Younger children make just as much academic progress as older children in the same grade (Cameron & Wilson, 1990; Graue & DiPerna, 2000). And younger first graders reap academic gains from on-time enrollment; they outperform same-age children a year behind them in school (Stipek & Byler, 2001). Furthermore, delaying kindergarten entry does not seem to prevent or solve emotional and social difficulties. To the contrary, students who are older than the typical age for their grade show high rates of behavior problems—considerably higher than students who are young for their grade (Stipek, 2002).

A related dilemma concerns whether to retain a student for a second year in kindergarten or in one of the primary grades. A wealth of research reveals no learning benefits and suggests negative consequences for motivation, self-esteem, peer relations, and school attitudes (Carlton & Winsler, 1999). In a Canadian study, students retained between kindergarten and second grade—regardless of the academic and social characteristics they brought to the situation—showed worsening academic performance, anxiety, and (among boys) disruptiveness throughout elementary school. These unfavorable trends did not characterize nonretained students (Pagani et al., 2001).

As an alternative to kindergarten retention, some school districts place poorly performing kindergarten children in a "transition" class—a waystation between kindergarten and first grade. Transition classes, however, are a form of homogeneous grouping. As with other "low groups," teachers may have reduced expectations and may teach transition children in a less stimulating fashion than other children (Dornbusch, Glasgow, & Lin, 1996).

Each of the options just considered is based on the view that readiness for school results largely from biological maturation. An alternative perspective, based on Vygotsky's sociocultural theory, is that children acquire the knowledge, skills, and attitudes for school success through assistance from parents and teachers. The U.S. National Association for the Education of Young Children recommends that all children of legal age start kindergarten and be granted classroom experiences that foster their individual progress. Research shows that school readiness is not something to wait for; it can be cultivated.

© ARIEL SKELLEY/CORBIS

Saying good-bye on the first day of school, this father may wonder how ready his son is for classroom learning. Yet delaying kindergarten entry for a year has no demonstrated benefits for academic or social development. Children of legal age for starting school can best acquire the knowledge, skills, and attitudes for school success through on-time enrollment and assistance from parents and teachers.

---

ing dialogues on the content of a text passage. Within the dialogues, group members apply four cognitive strategies: questioning, summarizing, clarifying, and predicting.

The dialogue leader (at first a teacher, later a student) begins by *asking questions* about the content of the text passage. Students offer answers, raise additional questions, and in case of disagreement, reread the original text. Next, the leader *summarizes* the passage, and children discuss the summary and *clarify* unfamiliar ideas. Finally, the leader encourages students to *predict* upcoming content based on clues in the passage.

Elementary and junior high school students exposed to reciprocal teaching show impressive gains in reading comprehension compared to controls taught in other ways (Lederer, 2000;

Rosenshine & Meister, 1994). Notice how reciprocal teaching creates a zone of proximal development in which children gradually assume more responsibility for comprehending text passages. Also, by collaborating with others, children forge group expectations for high-level thinking and acquire skills vital for learning and success in everyday life.

Communities of Learners. Recognizing that collaboration requires a supportive context, another Vygotsky-based innovation makes it a school-wide value. Classrooms are transformed into **communities of learners** where teachers guide the overall process of learning, but otherwise, no distinction is made between adult and child contributors: all participate in joint endeavors and have the authority to define and resolve problems. This approach is based on the assumption that different people have different expertises that can benefit the community and that students may become experts to whom others may turn (Engle & Conant, 2002). Classroom activities often consist of long-term projects that address complex, real-world problems. In working toward project goals, children and teachers draw on one another's expertises and those of others within and outside the school (Strauss, 1998).

In one classroom, students studied animal–habitat relationships so they could design an animal of the future, suited to environmental changes. The class formed small research groups, each of which selected a subtopic—for example, defense against predators, protection from the elements, reproduction, or food getting. Each group member assumed responsibility for part of the subtopic, consulting diverse experts and preparing teaching materials. Then group members taught one another, assembled their contributions, and brought them to the community as a whole so the knowledge gathered could be used to solve the problem (Brown, 1997). The result was a multifaceted understanding of the topic that would have been too difficult and time-consuming for any learner to accomplish alone.

In communities of learners, collaboration is created from within by teachers and children and supported from without by the culture of the school (Rogoff, Turkanis, & Bartlett, 2001). As a result, the approach broadens Vygotsky's concept of the zone of proximal development, from a child in collaboration with a more expert partner (adult or peer) to multiple, interrelated zones.

Teacher–Student Interaction

Elementary and secondary school students describe good teachers as warm, helpful, and stimulating—characteristics positively associated with learning (Daniels, Kalkman, & McCombs, 2001; Sanders & Jordan, 2000). Yet with respect to stimulation, a disappointing finding is that too many North American teachers emphasize repetitive drill over higher-level thinking, such as grappling with ideas and applying knowledge to new situations (Campbell, Hombo, & Mazzeo, 2000). In a study of fifth-grade social studies and math lessons, students were far more attentive when teachers encouraged high-level thinking (Stodolsky, 1988). And in a longitudinal investigation of more than 5,000 seventh graders, those in more stimulating, academically demanding classrooms showed better attendance and larger gains in math achievement over the following 2 years (Phillips, 1997).

Yet teachers do not interact in the same way with all children. Well-behaved, high-achieving students typically get more support and praise, whereas unruly students who achieve poorly are often criticized and rarely called on to contribute to class discussion (Good & Brophy, 1996). Unfortunately, once teachers' attitudes toward students are established, they can become more extreme than is warranted by children's behavior. Of special concern are **educational self-fulfilling prophecies:** Children may adopt teachers' positive or negative views and start to live up to them. As early as first grade, teachers' beliefs in children's ability to learn predict their students' year-end achievement progress. This effect is particularly strong when teachers emphasize competition and publicly compare children, regularly favoring the best students (Kuklinski & Weinstein, 2001; Weinstein, 2002).

Teacher expectations have a greater impact on low achievers than high achievers (Madom, Jussim, & Eccles, 1997). High-achieving students have less room to improve when teachers think well of them, and they can fall back on their long history of success when a teacher is critical. Low-achieving students' sensitivity to self-fulfilling prophecies can be beneficial when teachers believe in them, but unfortunately, biased teacher judgments are usually slanted in a negative direction. In one study, African-American children were especially responsive to negative teacher expectations in reading, and girls were especially responsive to negative teacher expectations in math (McKown & Weinstein, 2002). Recall our earlier discussion of *stereotype threat*. A child in the position of confirming a negative stereotype may respond with intense anxiety and reduced motivation, increasing the likelihood of a negative self-fulfilling prophecy.

Grouping Practices

In many schools, students are assigned to *homogeneous groups,* or classes in which children of similar ability levels are taught together. Homogeneous grouping can be a potent source of self-fulfilling prophecies (Smith et al., 1998). Low-group students get more drill on basic facts and skills, engage in less discussion, and progress at a slower learning pace. Gradually, they show a drop in self-esteem and come to be viewed by themselves and others as "not smart." Not surprisingly, homogeneous grouping widens the gap between high and low achievers (Dornbusch, Glasgow, & Lin, 1996).

Partly because of this finding, some schools have increased the *heterogeneity* of student groups by combining two or three adjacent grades. In *multigrade classrooms,* academic achievement, self-esteem, and attitudes toward school are usually more favorable than in the single-grade arrangement, perhaps because multigrade classrooms often decrease competition and increase harmony (Lloyd, 1999; Ong, Allison, & Haladyna, 2000). The opportunity that mixed-age grouping affords for peer tutoring may also contribute to its favorable outcomes. When older or more expert students teach younger or less expert students, both tutors and tutees benefit in achievement and self-esteem (Renninger, 1998).

However, small, heterogeneous groups of students working together often engage in poorer-quality interaction (less accurate explanations and answers) than homogeneous groups of above-average students (Webb, Nemer, & Chizhik, 1998). For collaboration between heterogeneous peers to succeed, children need extensive training and guidance in **cooperative learning**—resolving differences of opinion, sharing responsibility, considering one another's ideas, and working toward common goals. When teachers explain, model, and have children role-play how to work together effectively, cooperative learning among heterogeneous peers results in greater enjoyment of learning and achievement gains across a wide range of school subjects (Gillies, 2003; Gillies & Ashman, 1996). And children readily cooperate in future group activities, building on others' ideas and offering assistance (Gillies, 2002).

Computers and Academic Learning

In Joey and Lizzie's classrooms, several computers sat on desks in quiet corners. Virtually all American and Canadian public schools have integrated computers into their instructional programs and can access the Internet—trends also apparent in other industrialized nations (Statistics Canada, 2002a; U.S. Census Bureau, 2003b). In classrooms, small groups often gather around computers, and children more often collaborate in computer activities than in other pursuits (Svensson, 2000).

Computers can have rich educational benefits. Educational software permits children to practice basic skills and, in some instances, solve problems and acquire new knowledge. When children in the early grades use basic-skills programs for several months, they gain in reading and math achievement—benefits that are greatest for students with learning difficulties (Fletcher-Flinn & Gravatt, 1995; Hughes & Filbert, 2000).

As soon as children begin to read and write, they can use the computer for word processing. It permits them to write freely and experiment with letters and words without having to struggle with handwriting. In addition, they can revise the text's meaning and style as well as check their spelling. As a result, they worry less about making mistakes, and their written products tend to be longer and of higher quality (Clements, 1995). Often children jointly plan, compose, and revise text, learning from one another (Clements & Sarama, 2003).

These fifth graders download video from a camera to a computer as part of a class project. Schools must take special steps to ensure that all children develop diverse computer skills. When teachers encourage girls to write computer programs, analyze data, and use spreadsheets and graphics programs, they become competent, enthusiastic users.

© DAVID YOUNG-WOLFF/PHOTOEDIT

Specially designed computer languages introduce children to programming skills. As long as adults support children's efforts, computer programming leads to improvements in concept formation, problem solving, and creativity (Clements, 1995; Clements & Nastasi, 1992). And because children must detect errors in their programs to get them to work, programming helps them reflect on their thought processes, leading to gains in metacognition and self-regulation (Clements, 1990). Furthermore, while programming, children are especially likely to collaborate, to persist in the face of challenge, and to display positive attitudes toward school (Nastasi & Clements, 1994).

As children get older, they often use the computer for schoolwork, largely through word processing and searching the Web to find information. But despite their many learning advantages, computers also raise concerns about a "digital divide" between gender and SES groups. By the end of elementary school, boys spend more time with computers than girls, both in and out of school. In a Canadian survey of a nationally representative sample of 15- and 16-year-olds, boys more often engaged in computer activities—not just playing computer games, but writing programs, analyzing data, and using spreadsheets and graphics programs. And many more boys than girls expressed interest in computers and rated their computer skills as "excellent" (Looker & Thiessen, 2003). Similarly, time spent with computers and confidence in using them rise with SES (Subrahmanyam et al., 2001).

These findings indicate that schools must ensure that girls and low-SES students have many opportunities to benefit from the cognitively enriching aspects of computer technology. But attaining this goal is not just a matter of equipping classrooms with more technology. Intensive teacher guidance and encouragement are necessary to educate equitably and effectively with computers (Attewell, 2001).

Teaching Children with Special Needs

We have seen that effective teachers flexibly adjust their teaching strategies to accommodate students with a wide range of abilities and characteristics. But such adjustments are increasingly difficult at the very low and high ends of the ability distribution. How do schools serve children with special learning needs?

CHILDREN WITH LEARNING DIFFICULTIES ● American and Canadian legislation mandates that schools place children who require special supports for learning in the "least restrictive" (or closest to normal as possible) environments that meet their educational needs. In **mainstreaming,** students with learning difficulties are placed in regular classrooms for part of the school day, a practice designed to prepare them better for participation in society. Largely due to parental pressures, mainstreaming has been extended to **full inclusion**—placement in regular classrooms full-time.

Some mainstreamed pupils are *mildly mentally retarded*—children whose IQs fall between 55 and 70 and who also show problems in adaptive behavior, or skills of everyday living (American Psychiatric Association, 1994). But the largest number—5 to 10 percent of school-age children—have **learning disabilities,** great difficulty with one or more aspects of learning, usually reading. As a result, their achievement is considerably behind what would be expected on the basis of their IQ. The problems of these students cannot be traced to any obvious physical or emotional difficulty or to environmental disadvantage. Instead, subtle deficits in brain functioning are involved. Some disorders run in families, suggesting a genetic influence (Miller, Sanchez, & Hynd, 2003; Lyon, Fletcher, & Barnes, 2002). In many instances, the cause is unknown.

Does placement of these children in regular classes provide appropriate academic experiences as well as integrated participation in classroom life? At present, the evidence is not positive on either point. Although some mainstreamed and fully included students benefit academically, many do not. Achievement gains depend on both the severity of the disability and the support services available (Klingner et al., 1998). Furthermore, children with disabilities often are rejected by regular-classroom peers. Students with mental retardation are overwhelmed by the social skills of their classmates; they cannot interact adeptly in a conversation or game. And the processing deficits of some learning-disabled students lead to problems in social awareness and responsiveness (Gresham & MacMillan, 1997; Sridhar & Vaughn, 2001).

Does this mean that students with special needs cannot be served in regular classrooms? Not necessarily. Often these children do best when they receive instruction in a resource room for part of the day and in the regular classroom for the remainder—an arrange-ment that the majority of school-age children with learning disabilities say they prefer (Vaughn & Klingner, 1998). In the resource room, a spe-cial education teacher works with students on an individual and small-group basis. Then, depending on their progress, children join regular classmates for different subjects and amounts of time.

Once children enter the regular classroom, special steps must be taken to promote peer acceptance. Cooperative learning and peer-tutor-ing experiences in which teachers guide children with learning difficul-ties and their classmates in working together lead to friendly interaction, improved peer acceptance, and achievement gains (Fuchs et al., 2002a, 2002b). Teachers also can prepare their class for the arrival of a student with special needs—a process best begun early, before children have become less accepting of peers with disabilities (Okagaki et al., 1998).

GIFTED CHILDREN ● In Joey and Lizzie's school, some children were **gifted,** displaying exceptional intellectual strengths. In every grade were one or two students with IQ scores above 130, the stan-dard definition of giftedness based on intelligence test performance (Gardner, 1998a). High-IQ children, as we have seen, are particularly quick at academic work. They have keen memories and an exceptional capacity to solve challenging academic problems.

Yet earlier in this chapter, we noted that intelligence tests do not sample the entire range of human mental skills. Recognition of this fact has led to an expanded conception of giftedness in schools.

Creativity and Talent. **Creativity** is the ability to produce work that is *original* yet *appro-priate*—something that others have not thought of but that is useful in some way. A child with high potential for creativity can be designated as gifted. Because most children are not mature enough to produce useful creative works, researchers have devised tests to assess their capacity for creative thought. These tests tap **divergent thinking**—the generation of multiple and un-usual possibilities when faced with a task or problem. Divergent thinking contrasts sharply with **convergent thinking,** which involves arriving at a single correct answer and is emphasized on intelligence tests (Guilford, 1985).

Because highly creative children (like high-IQ children) are often better at some types of tasks than others, a variety of tests of divergent thinking are available (Runco, 1992; Torrance, 1988). A verbal measure might ask children to name uses for common objects (such as a news-paper). A figural measure might ask them to come up with drawings based on a circular motif (see Figure 12.7 on page 462). A "real-world problem" measure requires students to suggest solutions to everyday problems. Responses to all these tests can be scored for the number of ideas generated and their originality.

Yet critics of these measures point out that they are imperfect predictors of creative accom-plishment because they tap only one of the complex cognitive aspects of creativity. Also involved are defining new and important problems, evaluating divergent ideas and choosing the most promising, and calling on relevant knowledge to understand and solve problems (Sternberg & Lubart, 1995).

Consider these additional ingredients, and you will see why people usually demonstrate expertise and creativity in only one area or a few related areas. Even individuals designated as gifted by virtue of their high IQ often show uneven ability across academic subjects—for exam-ple, higher verbal than math scores, or vice versa (Achter, Lubinski, & Benbow, 1996). Partly for this reason, definitions of giftedness have been extended to include **talent**—outstanding per-formance in a specific field. Research consistently shows that excellence in such endeavors as cre-ative writing, mathematics, science, music, visual arts, athletics, and leadership has roots in specialized skills that first appear in childhood (Winner, 2003). Highly talented children are bio-logically prepared to master their domain of interest. And they display a passion for doing so.

At the same time, talent must be nurtured. Studies of the backgrounds of talented children and highly accomplished adults often reveal parents who are warm and sensitive, who provide a stimulating home life, who are devoted to developing their child's abilities, and who provide

The student on the left, who has a learning disabil-ity, has been fully included in a regular classroom. Because his teacher encourages peer accep-tance, individualizes instruction, minimizes comparisons with class-mates, and promotes coop-erative learning, this boy looks forward to school and is doing well.

Responses of an 8-year-old who scored high on a figural measure of divergent thinking.
This child was asked to make as many pictures as she could from the circles on the page. The titles she gave her drawings, from left to right, are as follows: "Dracula," "one-eyed monster," "pumpkin," "Hula-Hoop," "poster," "wheelchair," "earth," "moon," "planet," "movie camera," "sad face," "picture," "stoplight," "beach ball," "the letter O," "car," and "glasses." Tests of divergent thinking tap only one of the complex cognitive ingredients of creativity. (Test form copyright © 1980 by Scholastic Testing Service, Inc. Reprinted by permission of Scholastic Testing Service, Inc., from *The Torrance Tests of Creative Thinking* by E. P. Torrance. Child's drawings reprinted by permission of Laura Berk.)

models of hard work and high achievement. But rather than being driving and overambitious, these parents are reasonably demanding (Winner, 1996). They arrange for caring teachers while the child is young and for more rigorous master teachers as the child's talent develops.

Extreme giftedness often results in social isolation. Many gifted children and adolescents spend much time alone, partly because their highly driven, nonconforming, and independent styles leave them out of step with peers and partly because they enjoy solitude, which is necessary to develop their talents. Still, gifted children desire gratifying peer relationships, and some—more often girls than boys—try to hide their abilities to become better liked. Compared with their ordinary agemates, gifted youths, especially girls, report more emotional and social difficulties, including low self-esteem and depression (Gross, 1993; Winner, 2000).

Finally, whereas many talented youths become experts in their fields and solve problems in new ways, few become highly creative. The skill involved in rapidly mastering a field and thinking flexibly within it is not the same as transforming that field. Gifted individuals who are restless with the status quo and daring about changing it are rare. And before these individuals become creative masters, they typically spend a decade or more becoming proficient in their field of interest (Csikszentmihalyi, 1999). The world, however, needs both experts and creators.

Educating the Gifted. Because gifted children are especially likely to make major contributions to their societies, promoting their development is vital. These young people thrive in learning environments that permit them to take risks and reflect on ideas. When not sufficiently challenged, they sometimes lose their drive to excel. And when parents and teachers push them too hard, by adolescence they are likely to ask, "Who am I doing this for?" If the answer is not "myself," they may decide not to pursue their gift (Winner, 1997, 2000, p. 166).

Although programs for the gifted exist in many schools, debate about their effectiveness usually focuses on factors irrelevant to giftedness—whether to offer enrichment in regular classrooms, to pull children out for special instruction (the most common practice), or to advance brighter students to a higher grade. Overall, gifted children fare well academically and socially within each of these models (Moon & Feldhusen, 1994). At the same time, interventions aimed at protecting students' self-esteem are crucial in selective educational settings. In a study of more than 100,000 students in 26 countries, the more selective the high school, the lower students' academic self-esteem (Marsh & Hau, 2003). A top student in elementary school who enters a selective secondary school may suddenly find herself average or below average, with potentially detrimental effects on motivation and achievement.

Gardner's theory of multiple intelligences has inspired several model programs that provide enrichment to all students, so any child capable of high-level performance can manifest it. Meaningful activities, each tapping a specific intelligence or set of intelligences, serve as contexts for assessing strengths and weaknesses and, on that basis, teaching new knowledge and original thinking (Gardner, 1993, 2000). For example, linguistic intelligence might be fostered through storytelling or playwriting; spatial intelligence through drawing, sculpting, or taking apart and reassembling objects; and kinesthetic intelligence through dance or pantomime.

Evidence is still needed on how well these programs nurture children's talents. But so far, they have succeeded in one way—by highlighting the strengths of some students who previously had been considered unexceptional or even at risk for school failure (Suzuki & Valencia, 1997). Consequently, they may be especially useful in identifying talented low-SES, ethnic minority children, who are often underrepresented in programs for the gifted.

People usually demonstrate expertise and creativity in only one or a few related areas, so definitions of giftedness have been extended to include talent. Highly talented children are biologically prepared to master their domain of interest and experience a favorable environment for doing so. Here Laurence Tai, age 11, conducts the New York Philharmonic Orchestra as it performs "Greenwich Overture," a piece that Laurence composed.

How Well Educated Are North American Children?

Our discussion of schooling has largely focused on how teachers can support the education of children. Yet a great many factors, both within and outside schools, affect children's learning. Societal values, school resources, quality of teaching, and parental encouragement all play important roles. Nowhere are these multiple influences more apparent than when schooling is examined in cross-cultural perspective.

In international studies of reading, mathematics, and science achievement, young people in Hong Kong, Japan, Korea, and Taiwan are consistently among the top performers. Although Canadian students rank below students in Asian countries, they generally score high. American students, however, typically perform at the international average and sometimes below it (U.S. Department of Education, 2001a, 2001b).

Why do American children fall behind in academic accomplishments? According to international comparisons, instruction in the United States is not as challenging and focused as it is in other countries. In the Program for International Student Assessment, which assessed the academic achievement of 15-year-olds nearing the end of compulsory education in 27 nations, students were asked about their study habits. Compared with students in the top-achieving nations listed in Figure 12.8 on page 464, many more American students reported studying by memorizing rather than relating information to previously acquired knowledge. And in-depth research on learning environments in top-performing Asian nations, such as Japan, Korea, and Taiwan, reveals that except for the influence of language on early counting skills (see page 441), students do not start school with cognitive advantages over their North American peers (Geary, 1996). Instead, a variety of social forces combine to foster a much stronger commitment to learning in Asian families and schools:

- *Cultural valuing of academic achievement.* In Japan, Korea, and Taiwan, natural resources are limited. Progress in science and technology is essential for economic well-being, so children's mastery of academic skills is vital. Compared with Western countries, these nations invest more in education, including paying higher salaries to teachers (United Nations Development Programme, 2002).

Country	Average Math Achievement Score
High-Performing Nations	
Japan	557
Korea, Republic of	547
New Zealand	537
Finland	536
Australia	533
Canada	**533**
Switzerland	529
United Kingdom	529
Intermediate-Performing Nations	
Belgium	520
France	517
Austria	515
Denmark	514
Iceland	514
Sweden	510
Ireland	503
Norway	499
Czech Republic	498
United States	**493**
Germany	490
Hungary	488
Spain	476
Poland	470
Low-Performing Nations	
Italy	457
Portugal	454
Greece	447
Luxembourg	446
Mexico	387

International Average = 500

FIGURE 12.8

Average mathematics scores of 15-year-olds by country.

The Program for International Student Assessment assessed achievement in 27 nations. Japan, Korea, and Canada were among the top performers in mathematics, whereas the United States performed just below the international average. Similar outcomes occurred in reading and science. (Adapted from U.S. Department of Education, 2001a.)

- *Emphasis on effort.* Japanese, Korean, and Taiwanese parents and teachers believe that all children have the potential to master challenging academic tasks if they work hard enough, whereas North American parents and teachers tend to regard native ability as the key to academic success. These differences in attitude contribute to the fact that Asian parents devote many more hours to helping their children with homework (Stevenson, Lee, & Mu, 2000). Furthermore, influenced by collectivist values, Asian youths typically strive to achieve because effort is a moral obligation—part of one's responsibility to family and community. In contrast, North American young people view working hard in individualistic terms—as a matter of personal choice (Bempchat & Drago-Severson, 1999).

- *High-quality education for all.* No separate ability groups exist in Japanese, Korean, and Taiwanese elementary schools. Instead, all students receive the same nationally mandated, high-quality instruction. Academic lessons are particularly well organized and presented in ways that capture children's attention and encourage high-level thinking (Grow-Maienza, Hahn, & Joo, 2001; Stevenson, 1992). Topics in mathematics are treated in greater depth, and there is less repetition of previously taught material.

- *More time devoted to instruction.* In Japan, Hong Kong, and Taiwan, the school year is over 50 days longer than in the United States and about 30 days longer than in Canada (World Education Services, 2001). And on a day-to-day basis, Asian teachers devote much more time to academic pursuits. But Asian schools are not regimented places. An 8-hour school day permits extra recesses, with plenty of time for play, field trips, and extracurricular activities (Stevenson, 1994). Frequent breaks may increase Asian children's capacity to learn (Pellegrini & Smith, 1998).

The Asian examples underscore that families, schools, and the larger society must work together to upgrade education. In the United States, more tax dollars are being invested in elementary and secondary education, and academic standards are being strengthened. In addition, many schools are working to increase parent involvement. Parents

© CAMERAMANN/THE IMAGE WORKS

Japanese children achieve considerably better than their American counterparts for a variety of reasons. A longer school day permits frequent alternation of academic instruction with pleasurable activity, an approach that fosters learning. During a break from academic subjects, these Japanese elementary-school children enjoy a class in the art of calligraphy.

who create stimulating learning environments at home, monitor their child's academic progress, help with homework, and communicate often with teachers have children who consistently show superior achievement (Christenson & Sheridan, 2001). The returns of these efforts can be seen in recent national assessments of educational progress (U.S. Department of Education, 2003b). After two decades of decline, American students' overall academic achievement has risen, although not enough to enhance their standing internationally.

Ask YOURSELF

www

REVIEW List some teaching practices that foster children's academic achievement and some that undermine it. For each practice, provide a brief explanation.

APPLY Ray is convinced that his 5-year-old son Tripper would do better in school if only Tripper's kindergarten would provide more teacher-directed lessons and worksheets and reduce the time devoted to learning-center activities. Is Ray correct? Explain.

APPLY Sandy, a parent of a third grader, wonders whether she should support her school board's decision to teach first, second, and third graders together, in mixed-age classrooms. How would you advise Sandy, and why?

CONNECT Relate genetic–environmental correlation, discussed in Chapter 2, pages 86–89, to the development of gifted children. Which parenting and teaching practices can enhance that correlation, and which ones can undermine it?

Summary

Piaget's Theory: The Concrete Operational Stage

What are the major characteristics of concrete operational thought?

● During the **concrete operational stage**, children can reason logically about concrete, tangible information. Mastery of conservation indicates that children can **decenter** and **reverse** their thinking. They are also better at hierarchical classification and **seriation**, including **transitive inference**. School-age youngsters' spatial reasoning improves, as their ability to give directions and their understanding of **cognitive maps** reveal.

● Piaget used the term **horizontal décalage** to describe the school-age child's gradual mastery of logical concepts. Concrete operational thought is limited in that children have difficulty reasoning about abstract ideas.

Discuss recent research on concrete operational thought.

● Specific cultural practices, especially those associated with schooling, affect

children's mastery of Piagetian tasks. Some theorists believe that operational thinking can best be understood within an information-processing framework.

● Case's neo-Piagetian theory proposes that with brain development and practice, schemes demand less attention, freeing up space in working memory for combining old schemes and generating new ones. Eventually, children consolidate schemes into highly efficient, central conceptual structures and move up to a new Piagetian stage. On a wide variety of tasks, children move from a focus on only one dimension to coordinating two dimensions to integrating multiple dimensions.

Information Processing

Cite two basic changes in information processing, and describe the development of attention and memory in middle childhood.

● Brain development contributes to gains in information-processing capacity and **cognitive inhibition** during the school

years. These changes facilitate many aspects of information processing.

● During middle childhood, attention becomes more selective and adaptable. Attention (and memory) strategies develop in a four-step sequence: (1) **production deficiency** (failure to use the strategy); (2) **control deficiency** (failure to execute the strategy consistently); (3) **utilization deficiency** (consistent use of the strategy, but no improvement in performance); and (4) **effective strategy use.**

● School-age children also become better at planning. On tasks requiring systematic visual search or the coordination of many acts, they are more likely to decide ahead of time how to proceed.

● Memory strategies improve during the school years. **Rehearsal** appears first, followed by **organization** and then **elaboration.** And with age, children use several memory strategies at once.

● Development of the long-term knowledge base facilitates strategic memory processing. At the same time, children's motivation to use what they know contributes to memory development. Memory strategies are promoted by learning activities in school.

Describe the school-age child's theory of mind and capacity to engage in self-regulation.

- Metacognition expands over middle childhood as children gain a much better understanding of the process of thinking and the factors that influence it. School-age children regard the mind as an active, constructive agent, and they combine their metacognitive knowledge into an integrated theory of mind.

- Only gradually do school-age children become good at **cognitive self-regulation**—putting what they know about thinking into action. Providing children with instructions to monitor their cognitive activity improves self-regulatory skills and task performance.

Discuss current perspectives on teaching reading and mathematics to elementary school children.

- Skilled reading draws on all aspects of the information-processing system. Research shows that a combination of **whole-language** and **basic-skills approaches** is most effective for teaching beginning reading. Whole language keeps reading meaningful, whereas basic skills permit children to decode new words.

- As with reading, instruction that combines practice in basic skills with conceptual understanding is best in mathematics. Students acquire basic math facts through a combination of reasoning about number concepts and frequent practice. Experimenting with problem solving and evaluating solution techniques is essential for mastering more complex skills.

Individual Differences in Mental Development

Describe major approaches to defining intelligence.

- During the school years, IQ becomes more stable, and it correlates well with academic achievement. Most intelligence tests yield an overall score as well as scores for separate intellectual factors. The Stanford-Binet Intelligence Scale and the Wechsler Intelligence Scale for Children–IV (WISC–IV) are widely used individually administered intelligence tests.

- To search for the precise mental processes underlying mental ability

factors, researchers are combining the factor-analytic approach with the information-processing approach. Findings reveal that speed of thinking and effective strategy use are related to IQ. Sternberg's **triarchic theory of successful intelligence** extends these efforts. It views intelligence as a complex interaction of analytical intelligence (information-processing skills), creative intelligence (ability to solve novel problems), and practical intelligence (adapting, shaping, and selecting environments to meet one's desires and the demands of one's everyday world).

- According to Gardner's **theory of multiple intelligences,** at least eight mental abilities exist, each of which has a unique biological basis and a distinct course of development. Gardner's theory has been helpful in understanding and nurturing children's talents.

Describe evidence indicating that both heredity and environment contribute to intelligence.

- Heritability estimates and adoption research reveal that intelligence is a product of both heredity and environment. Studies of African-American children adopted into economically well-off white homes indicate that the black–white IQ gap is substantially determined by environment.

- IQ scores are affected by specific learning experiences, including exposure to certain communication styles and to knowledge sampled by the test. The sheer amount of time a child spends in school is a strong predictor of IQ. And **stereotype threat** can trigger anxiety that impairs children's test performance.

- Because of cultural bias in intelligence testing, IQ scores can underestimate minority children's intelligence. By introducing individualized teaching into the testing situation, **dynamic assessment** narrows the gap between a child's actual and potential performance.

Language Development

Describe changes in metalinguistic awareness, vocabulary, grammar, and pragmatics during middle childhood.

- Schooling, especially reading, contributes greatly to **metalinguistic awareness** and other complex language skills. Vocabulary continues to grow rapidly, and children have a more precise and flexible understanding of word meanings. Grasp of complex grammati-

cal constructions also improves. Furthermore, school-age children adapt to listeners' needs in challenging communicative situations, better evaluate the clarity of others' messages, and refine their conversational strategies.

What are the advantages of bilingualism in childhood?

- Children who learn two languages in early childhood separate the two language systems from the start and acquire each according to a typical timetable. When school-age children acquire a second language after mastering the first, it takes them 3 to 5 years to attain the competence of native-speaking agemates. Bilingual children are advanced in cognitive development and metalinguistic awareness.

- In Canada, language immersion programs succeed in developing children who are proficient in both English and French. Bilingual education that combines instruction in the native language and in English supports ethnic minority children's academic learning.

Children's Learning in School

Describe the impact of class size and educational philosophies on children's motivation and academic achievement.

- As class size declines, academic achievement improves. Older students in **traditional classrooms** have a slight edge in academic achievement. Those in **constructivist classrooms** tend to be critical thinkers who respect individual differences and have more positive attitudes toward school.

- Vygotsky's sociocultural theory has inspired **social-constructivist classrooms** and new approaches to elementary education, including **reciprocal teaching** and **communities of learners.** In each, learning experiences are rich in teacher–child and child–child collaboration, children acquire literacy skills in meaningful activities, and teaching adapts to each child's zone of proximal development.

Discuss the role of teacher–student interaction and grouping practices in academic achievement.

- Teaching that encourages high-level thinking and that creates a warm, stimulating, demanding academic climate fosters children's interest, involvement, and academic achievement. **Educational self-fulfilling prophecies** are most likely to occur in classrooms that emphasize competition and public evaluation, and they have a greater impact on low achievers.

● Ability grouping is linked to poorer-quality instruction and a drop in self-esteem and achievement for children in low-ability groups. In contrast, multi-grade classrooms promote academic achievement, self-esteem, and positive school attitudes. For collaboration between heterogeneous peers to lead to achievement gains, children need extensive training and guidance in **cooperative learning**.

Describe learning advantages of and concerns about computers.

● Educational software that permits children to practice basic skills and solve problems results in gains in academic performance. Word processing frees children to write longer, higher-quality text. And programming promotes a variety of complex cognitive skills. However, gender and SES differences exist in time spent with computers and confidence in using them.

Under what conditions is placement of mildly mentally retarded and learning disabled children in regular classrooms successful?

● Students with mild mental retardation and **learning disabilities** are often placed in regular classrooms, usually through **mainstreaming** but also through **full inclusion**. The success of regular classroom placement depends on tailoring learning experiences to children's academic needs and promoting positive peer relations.

Describe the characteristics of gifted children and current efforts to meet their educational needs.

● **Giftedness** includes high IQ, **creativity**, and **talent**. Tests of creativity that tap **divergent** rather than **convergent** thinking focus on only one of the complex cognitive ingredients of creativity. People usually demonstrate creativity in one or a few related areas.

● Highly talented children are biologically prepared to master their domain

of interest and have parents and teachers who nurture their extraordinary ability. Extreme giftedness often results in social isolation, and gifted youths—especially girls—report more emotional and social difficulties than their ordinary agemates. Gifted children are best served by educational programs that build on their special strengths.

How well are North American children achieving compared with children in other industrialized nations?

● In international studies, young people in Asian nations are consistently top performers. Canadian students generally score high, whereas American students typically display average or below-average performance. A strong cultural commitment to learning in families and schools underlies the high academic success of Asian students.

Important Terms and Concepts

attention-deficit hyperactivity
  disorder (ADHD) (p. 434)
basic-skills approach (p. 439)
cognitive inhibition (p. 432)
cognitive maps (p. 429)
cognitive self-regulation (p. 438)
community of learners (p. 458)
concrete operational stage (p. 428)
constructivist classroom (p. 456)
control deficiency (p. 433)
convergent thinking (p. 461)
cooperative learning (p. 459)
creativity (p. 461)
decentration (p. 428)
divergent thinking (p. 461)

dynamic assessment (p. 450)
educational self-fulfilling prophecy
  (p. 458)
effective strategy use (p. 433)
elaboration (p. 435)
Flynn effect (p. 447)
full inclusion (p. 460)
gifted (p. 461)
horizontal décalage (p. 429)
learning disabilities (p. 460)
mainstreaming (p. 460)
metalinguistic awareness (p. 457)
organization (p. 434)
production deficiency (p. 433)
reciprocal teaching (p. 456)

rehearsal (p. 434)
reversibility (p. 428)
seriation (p. 428)
social-constructivist classroom
  (p. 456)
stereotype threat (p. 449)
talent (p. 461)
theory of multiple intelligences
  (p. 444)
traditional classroom (p. 455)
transitive inference (p. 428)
triarchic theory of successful
  intelligence (p. 443)
utilization deficiency (p. 433)
whole-language approach (p. 439)

For Further Information and Help

Consult the Companion Website for *Infants, Children, and Adolescents*, Fifth Edition, *(www.ablongman.com/berk)*, where you will find the following resources for this chapter:

● **Chapter Objectives**
● **Flashcards** for studying important terms and concepts
● **Annotated Weblinks** to guide you in further research
● **Ask Yourself questions,** which you can answer and then check against a sample response

● **Suggested Readings**
● **Practice Tests** with immediate scoring and feedback

CHAPTER 13

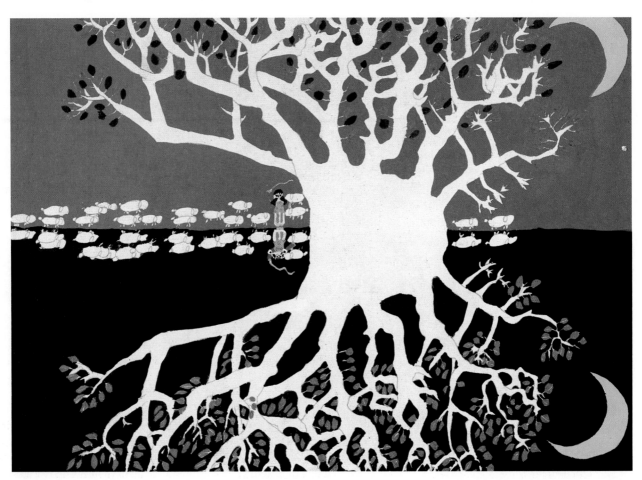

As this young painter conveys, school-age children become increasingly capable of viewing themselves and their social surroundings from diverse perspectives. Chapter 13 takes up the widening emotional and social understandings and experiences of middle childhood.

"Going Home with the Sheep"
Chun Lee
11 years, China

Reprinted with permission from the International Museum of Children's Art, Oslo, Norway.

Emotional and Social Development in Middle Childhood

*O*ne late afternoon, Rena heard her son Joey dash through the front door, run upstairs, and call up his best friend Terry. "Terry, gotta talk to you," pleaded Joey, out of breath from running home. "Everything was going great until that word I got—'porcupine,'" remarked Joey, referring to the fifth-grade spelling bee at school that day. "'P-o-r-k,' that's how I spelled it! I can't believe it. Maybe I'm not so good at social studies," Joey confided, "but I *know* I'm better at spelling than that stuck-up Belinda Brown. I knocked myself out studying those spelling lists. Then *she* got all the easy words. Did'ya see how snooty she acted after she won? If I *had* to lose, why couldn't it be to a nice person?"

Joey's conversation reflects a whole new constellation of emotional and social capacities. First, Joey shows evidence of *industriousness*. By entering the spelling bee, he energetically pursued meaningful achievement in his culture—a major change of the middle childhood years. At the same time, Joey's social understanding has expanded. He can size up strengths, weaknesses, and personality characteristics. Furthermore, friendship means something different to Joey than it did at younger ages. Terry is not just a convenient playmate; he is a best friend whom Joey counts on for understanding and emotional support.

We begin this chapter by returning to Erikson's theory for an overview of the personality changes of middle childhood. Then we look at emotional and social development. We will see how, as children reason more effectively and spend more time in school and with peers, their views of themselves, others, and social relationships become more complex.

Although school-age children spend less time with parents than they did at earlier ages, the family remains powerfully influential. Joey and Lizzie are growing up in a home profoundly affected by social change. Rena, their mother, has been employed since her children were preschoolers. In addition, Joey's and Lizzie's lives have been disrupted by divorce. Although family lifestyles are more diverse than ever before, Joey's and Lizzie's experiences will help us appreciate that family functioning is far more important than family structure in ensuring children's well-being.

Finally, when stress is overwhelming and social support is lacking, school-age children experience serious adjustment difficulties. Our chapter concludes with some common emotional problems of middle childhood.

Erikson's Theory: Industry versus Inferiority

According to Erikson (1950), the personality changes of the school years build on Freud's *latency stage* (see Chapter 1, page 16). Although Freud's theory is no longer widely accepted, children whose experiences have been positive enter middle childhood with the calm confidence Freud intended by the term *latency*. Their energies are redirected from the make-believe of early childhood into realistic accomplishment.

Erikson believed that the combination of adult expectations and children's drive toward mastery sets the stage for the psychological conflict of middle childhood: **industry versus inferiority, which is resolved positively when experiences lead children to develop a sense of competence at useful skills and tasks.** In cultures everywhere, improved physical and cognitive capacities mean that adults impose new demands. Children, in turn, are ready to meet these challenges and benefit from them. Among the Baka hunters and gatherers of Cameroon, 5- to 7-year-olds fetch and carry water, bathe and mind younger siblings, and accompany adults on food-gathering missions. In a miniature village behind the main camp, children practice hut building, spear shaping, and fire making (Avis & Harris, 1991). The Ngoni of Malawi, Central Africa, believe that once children shed their first teeth, they are ready for intensive skill training. Six and 7-year-old boys move out of family huts into dormitories, where they enter a system of male domination and instruction. And all children of this age are expected to show independence and are held accountable for irresponsible and disrespectful behavior (Rogoff, 1996).

In industrialized nations, the transition to middle childhood is marked by the beginning of formal schooling. With it comes academic training, which prepares children for the vast array of specialized careers in complex societies. In school, children become aware of their own and others' unique capacities, learn the value of division of labor, and develop a sense of moral commitment and responsibility. The danger at this stage is *inferiority*, reflected in the sad pessimism of children who have little confidence in their ability to do things well. This sense of inadequacy can develop when family life has not prepared children for school life or when experiences with teachers and peers are so negative that they destroy children's feelings of competence and mastery.

Erikson's sense of industry combines several developments of middle childhood: a positive but realistic self-concept, pride in accomplishment, moral responsibility, and cooperative participation with agemates. Let's see how these aspects of self and social relationships change over the school years.

The industriousness of middle childhood involves mastery of useful skills and tasks. As these second graders conduct an election, they become aware of one another's unique capacities and come to view themselves as responsible, capable, and helpful.

Self-Understanding

Several transformations in self-understanding take place in middle childhood. First, children can describe themselves in terms of psychological traits. Second, they start to compare their own characteristics to those of their peers. Finally, they speculate about the causes of their strengths and weaknesses. These ways of thinking about the self have a major impact on children's self-esteem.

Self-Concept

During the school years, children develop a much more refined *me-self,* or self-concept, organizing their observations of behaviors and internal states into general dispositions, with a major change taking place between ages 8 and 11. The following self-description from an 11-year-old reflects this change:

> My name is A. I'm a human being. I'm a girl. I'm a truthful person. I'm not pretty. I do so-so in my studies. I'm a very good cellist. I'm a very good pianist. I'm a little bit tall for my age. I like several boys. I like several girls. I'm old-fashioned. I play tennis. I am a very good swimmer. I try to be helpful. I'm always ready to be friends with anybody. Mostly I'm good, but I lose my temper. I'm not well liked by some girls and boys. I don't know if I'm liked by boys or not. (Montemayor & Eisen, 1977, pp. 317–318)

Notice that instead of specific behaviors, this child emphasizes competencies, as in "I'm a very good cellist" (Damon & Hart, 1988). Also, she clearly describes her personality and mentions both positive and negative traits—"truthful" but "not pretty," a "good cellist [and] pianist" but only "so-so in my studies." Older school-age children are far less likely than younger children to describe themselves in unrealistically positive, all-or-none ways (Harter, 2003).

Another change in self-concept takes place in middle childhood: Children make **social comparisons,** judging their appearance, abilities, and behavior in relation to those of others. In commenting on the spelling bee, Joey expressed some thoughts about how good he was compared with his peers—"better at spelling" but "not so good at social studies." Although 4- to 6-year-olds can compare their own performance to that of one peer, older children can compare multiple individuals, including themselves. Consequently, they conclude that they are "very good" at some things, "so-so" at others, and "not good" at still others (Butler, 1998).

Cognitive, Social, and Cultural Influences on Self-Concept

What factors are responsible for these revisions in self-concept? Cognitive development certainly affects the changing *structure* of the self. School-age children, as we saw in Chapter 12, can better coordinate several aspects of a situation when they reason about their physical world. Similarly, in the social realm, they combine typical experiences and behaviors into stable psychological dispositions, blend positive and negative characteristics, and compare their own characteristics with those of many peers (Harter, 1999, 2003). In middle childhood, children also gain a clearer understanding of traits as linked to specific desires (a "generous" person *wants* to share) and, therefore, as causes of behavior (Yuill & Pearson, 1998).

The changing *content* of self-concept is a product of both cognitive capacities and feedback from others. Sociologist George Herbert Mead (1934) described the self as a blend of what important people in our lives think of us. He proposed that a well-organized, psychological self emerges when the child's *I-self* adopts a view of the *me-self* that resembles others' attitudes toward the child. Mead's ideas indicate that *perspective-taking* skills—in particular, an improved ability to infer what other people are thinking—are crucial for developing a self-concept based on personality traits. During the school years, children become better at "reading" the messages they receive from others and incorporating these into their self-definitions. As school-age children internalize others' expectations, they form an *ideal self* that they use to evaluate their *real self*. As we will see shortly, a large discrepancy between the two can greatly undermine self-esteem, leading to sadness, hopelessness, and depression.

During middle childhood, children look to more people for information about themselves as they enter a wider range of settings in school and community. Consequently, they make frequent reference to social groups in their self-descriptions. "I'm a Boy Scout, a paper boy, and a Prairie City soccer player," Joey remarked when asked to describe himself. Gradually, as children move into adolescence, their sources of self-definition become more selective. Although parents remain influential, with age self-concept becomes increasingly vested in feedback from close friends (Oosterwegel & Openheimer, 1993).

Keep in mind, however, that the content of self-concept varies from culture to culture. In earlier chapters, we noted that Asian parents stress harmonious interdependence, whereas Western parents emphasize separateness and self-assertion. Consequently, in China and Japan, the self is defined in relation to the social group. In the United States, the self usually becomes the "property" of a self-contained individual (Markus & Kitayama, 1991). Strong collectivist values also exist in many subcultures in Western nations. In one study, researchers gathered children's self-descriptions in a Puerto Rican fishing village and an American small town. The Puerto Rican children often described themselves as "polite," "respectful," and "obedient" and justified these social traits by noting others' positive reactions to them. In contrast, the small-town children typically mentioned individualistic traits, such as interests, preferences, and skills (Damon & Hart, 1988).

Self-Esteem

Recall from Chapter 10 that most preschoolers have extremely high self-esteem. As children enter school, they get much more feedback about how well they perform compared with their peers. Grades on papers, tests, and report cards and the comments of adults and other children are integrated into self-evaluations. As a result, self-esteem differentiates, and it also adjusts to a more realistic level.

A HIERARCHICALLY STRUCTURED SELF-ESTEEM ● Researchers have asked children to indicate the extent to which a variety of statements, such as "I'm good at reading," "I'm usually the one chosen for games," and "Most kids like me," are true of themselves. By age 7 to 8, children in diverse Western cultures have formed at least four separate self-esteems: academic competence, social competence, physical/athletic competence, and physical appearance. Within them are more refined categories that become increasingly distinct with age (Marsh, 1990; Marsh & Ayotte, 2003; Van den Bergh & De Rycke, 2003). For example, academic self-worth divides into performance in language arts, math, and other subjects, social self-worth into peer and parental relationships, and physical/athletic competence into skill at various sports.

Furthermore, school-age children's newfound ability to view themselves in terms of stable dispositions permits them to combine their separate self-evaluations into a general psychological image of themselves—an overall sense of self-esteem (Harter, 1999, 2003). Consequently, by the mid-elementary school years, self-esteem takes on the hierarchical structure shown in Figure 13.1.

Separate self-esteems, however, do not contribute equally to general self-esteem. Children attach greater importance to certain self-judgments and weight them more heavily in the total picture. Although individual differences exist, during childhood and adolescence, perceived physical appearance correlates more strongly with overall self-worth than does any other self-esteem factor (Harter, 1998; Hymel et al., 1999). The emphasis that society and the media place on appearance has major implications for young people's overall satisfaction with themselves.

CHANGES IN LEVEL OF SELF-ESTEEM ● As children evaluate themselves in various areas, they lose the sunny optimism of early childhood. Self-esteem drops during the first few years of elementary school (Marsh, Craven, & Debus, 1998; Wigfield et al., 1997). This decline occurs as competence-related feedback becomes more frequent, children's performances are increasingly judged in relation to the performance of others, and children become cognitively capable of social comparison.

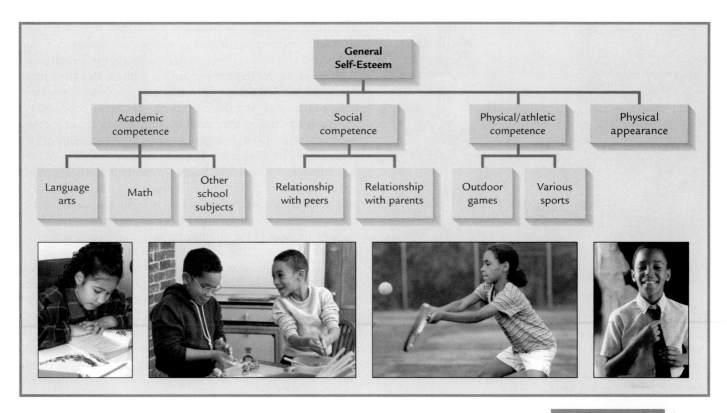

FIGURE 13.1

Hierarchical structure of self-esteem in the mid-elementary school years.
From their experiences in different settings, children form at least four separate self-esteems: academic competence, social competence, physical/athletic competence, and physical appearance. These differentiate into additional self-evaluations and combine to form a general sense of self-esteem.

(PHOTO CREDITS: *FAR LEFT:* © 2004 LAURA DWIGHT. ALL RIGHTS RESERVED; *MIDDLE LEFT:* © GEORGE DISARIO/CORBIS; *MIDDLE RIGHT:* © MITCH WOJNAROWICZ/THE IMAGE WORKS; *FAR RIGHT:* CHARLES GUPTON/STOCK BOSTON, LLC.)

To protect their self-worth, children eventually balance social comparisons with personal achievement goals (Ruble & Flett, 1988). Perhaps for this reason, the drop in self-esteem in the early school years usually is not harmful. Most (but not all) children appraise their characteristics and competencies realistically, while maintaining an attitude of self-acceptance and self-respect. Consequently, from fourth to sixth grade, self-esteem tends to rise for the majority of young people, who report feeling especially good about their peer relationships and athletic capabilities (Cole et al., 2001; Zimmerman et al., 1997). And as they evaluate their various strengths and weaknesses, individual differences in self-esteem become increasingly stable from childhood to adolescence (Trzesniewski, Donnellan & Robins, 2003).

Influences on Self-Esteem

Beginning in middle childhood, positive relationships exist between self-esteem, the values children attach to various activities, and success at those activities—relationships that strengthen with age (Marsh et al., 1998; Jacobs et al., 2002). For example, academic self-esteem predicts how important, useful, and enjoyable children judge school subjects to be, their willingness to try hard, and their achievement in those subjects. And children with high social self-esteem are consistently better liked by their classmates (Harter, 1999; Jacobs et al., 2002). Furthermore, across age, sex, SES, and ethnic groups, individuals high in self-esteem tend to be well adjusted, sociable, and conscientious. In contrast, a profile of low self-esteem in all areas is linked to anxiety, depression, and antisocial behavior (DuBois et al., 1999; Robins et al., 2001).

From age 5 on, children are aware that self-esteem has important consequences. They say that people who like themselves will do better at a challenging task and cope more easily with a peer's rebuff (Daniels, 1998). Because self-esteem is related to individual differences in children's behavior, researchers have been intensely interested in identifying factors that cause it to be high for some children and low for others.

CULTURE ● As with self-concept, cultural forces profoundly affect self-esteem. An especially strong emphasis on social comparison in school may underlie the finding that Japanese and

Children from collectivist cultures rarely call on social comparison to enhance their self-esteem. In a masquerade dance at their annual village carnival, these Caribbean children of St. Kitts display a strong sense of connection with their social group. Compared with children in individualistic societies, they are likely to be less concerned with whether another child is better at a skill than they are.

Taiwanese children score lower in self-esteem than American children, despite their higher academic achievement (Chiu, 1992–1993; Hawkins, 1994). In Asian classrooms, competition is tough and achievement pressure is high. At the same time, Asian children less often call on social comparisons to promote their own self-esteem. Because their culture values modesty and social harmony, they tend to be reserved about judging themselves positively but generous in their praise of others (Falbo et al., 1997; Heine & Lehman, 1995).

Furthermore, parents' gender-stereotyped beliefs predict sex differences in children's self-evaluations of competence in and liking for various school subjects. Girls are advantaged in language-arts self-esteem, and boys in math, science, physical/athletic, and physical-appearance self-esteem, even when children of equal skill level are compared (Fredricks & Eccles, 2002; Jacobs et al., 2002; Tenenbaum & Leaper, 2003). And although a widely held assumption is that boys' overall sense of self-esteem is higher than girls', the difference is small (Kling et al., 1999; Marsh & Ayotte, 2003). Girls may think less well of themselves because they internalize this negative cultural message.

Compared with their Caucasian agemates, African-American children tend to have slightly higher self-esteem, perhaps because of warm, extended families and a stronger sense of ethnic pride (Gray-Little & Hafdahl, 2000). And children and adolescents who attend schools or live in ethnic neighborhoods where their SES and ethnic groups are well represented feel a stronger sense of belonging and have fewer self-esteem problems (Gray-Little & Carels, 1997).

CHILD REARING ● Children whose parents use an *authoritative* child-rearing style (see Chapter 10) feel especially good about themselves (Carolson, Uppal, & Prosser, 2000; Feiring & Taska, 1996). If you think carefully about this finding, you will see that it makes perfect sense. Warm, positive parenting lets children know that they are accepted as competent and worthwhile. And firm but appropriate expectations, backed with explanations, help children make sensible choices and evaluate their own behavior against reasonable standards.

When parents too often help or make decisions for their youngsters, children suffer from low self-esteem. These controlling parents communicate a sense of inadequacy to children (Pomerantz & Eaton, 2000). And overly tolerant, indulgent parenting is linked to unrealistically high self-esteem, which also undermines development. Children who feel superior to others tend to lash out at challenges to their overblown self-images and to have adjustment problems, including meanness and aggression (Hughes, Cavell, & Grossman, 1997).

Of special concern is that American cultural values have increasingly emphasized a focus on the self, perhaps leading parents to indulge children and boost their self-esteem too much. As Figure 13.2 illustrates, the self-esteem of American young people has risen sharply over the past few decades (Twenge & Campbell, 2001). Yet compared with previous generations, American youths are achieving less well and displaying more antisocial behavior and other adjustment problems. Research confirms that children do not benefit from compliments, such as "You're terrific," that have no basis in real attainment. Instead, the best way to foster a positive, secure self-image is to encourage children to strive for worthwhile goals. Indeed, when school-age children are followed over time, a bidirectional relationship emerges between achievement and self-esteem: Good performance fosters self-esteem, and self-esteem fosters good performance (Guay, Marsh, & Boivin, 2003).

What can adults do to promote this mutually supportive relationship between motivation and self-esteem, and how can they avoid undermining it? Research on the precise content of adults' messages to children in achievement situations provides answers.

ACHIEVEMENT-RELATED ATTRIBUTIONS ● Attributions are our common, everyday explanations for the causes of behavior—our answers to the question, "Why did I (or another person) do that?" Notice how Joey, in talking about the spelling bee at the beginning of this chapter,

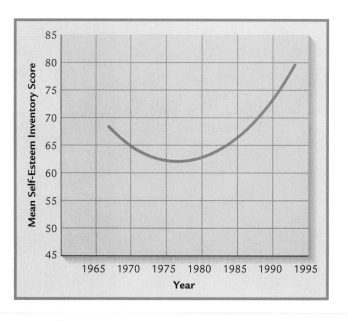

FIGURE 13.2

Generational change in American junior high school students' self-esteem from 1965 to 1995.
Self-esteem dropped slightly during the late 1960s and 1970s. From 1980 on, a period of considerable public focus on boosting children's self-esteem, average self-esteem rose sharply. Self-esteem scores for younger and older students show a similar rise. (From J. M. Twenge & W. K. Campbell, 2001, "Age and Birth Cohort Differences in Self-Esteem: A Cross-Temporal Meta-Analysis," *Personality and Social Psychology Review, 5*, p. 336. Adapted by permission.)

attributes his disappointing performance to *luck* (Belinda got all the easy words) and his usual success to *ability* (he *knows* he's a better speller than Belinda). Joey also appreciates that *effort* makes a difference; he "knocked himself out studying those spelling lists."

The combination of improved reasoning skills and frequent evaluative feedback permits 10- to 12-year-olds to recognize and separate these variables in explaining performance (Dweck, 2002). Yet children differ greatly in how they account for their successes and failures. Those who are high in academic self-esteem make **mastery-oriented attributions,** crediting their successes to ability— a characteristic they can improve through trying hard and can count on when faced with new challenges. This *incremental view of ability*—that it can increase—influences the way mastery-oriented children interpret negative events. They attribute failure to factors that can be changed and controlled, such as insufficient effort or a difficult task (Heyman & Dweck, 1998). So whether these children succeed or fail, they take an industrious, persistent approach to learning.

Unfortunately, children who develop **learned helplessness** attribute their failures, not their successes, to ability. When they succeed, they are likely to conclude that external factors, such as luck, are responsible. Furthermore, unlike their mastery-oriented counterparts, they hold a *fixed view of ability*—that it cannot be changed. They do not think that competence can be improved by trying hard (Cain & Dweck, 1995). So when a task is difficult, these children experience an anxious loss of control—in Erikson's terms, a pervasive sense of inferiority. They give up, saying "I can't do this," before they have really tried.

Children's attributions affect their goals. Mastery-oriented children focus on *learning goals*—increasing ability through effort and seeking information on how to do so. In contrast, learned-helpless children focus on *performance goals*— obtaining positive and avoiding negative evaluations of their fragile sense of ability. Over time, the ability of learned-helpless children no longer predicts how well they do. In one study, the more fourth to sixth graders held self-critical attributions, the lower they rated their competence, the less they knew about effective study strategies, the more they avoided challenge, and the poorer their academic performance. These outcomes strengthened their fixed view of ability (Pomerantz & Saxon, 2001). Because learned-helpless children fail to connect effort with success, they do not develop the metacognitive and self-regulatory skills necessary for high achievement (see Chapter 12). Lack of effective learning strategies, reduced persistence, and a sense of loss of control sustain one another in a vicious cycle (Heyman & Dweck, 1998).

INFLUENCES ON ACHIEVEMENT-RELATED ATTRIBUTIONS ● What accounts for the very different attributions of mastery-oriented and learned-helpless children? Adult communication plays a key role. Children with a learned-helpless style tend to have parents who set unusually high standards yet believe their child is not very capable and has to work much harder than others to succeed. When these children fail, the parent might say, "You can't do that, can you? It's okay if you quit" (Hokoda & Fincham, 1995). And after the child succeeds, evaluating

Repeated negative evaluations of their ability can cause children to develop learned helplessness—the belief that ability cannot be improved by trying hard. This learned-helpless boy seems to have concluded that he cannot improve. When faced with a challenging task, he is overwhelmed by negative thoughts and anxiety.

These Israeli first graders, growing up on a kibbutz, experience classroom lessons that emphasize mastery and interpersonal harmony rather than ability and competition. Here they gather outdoors on a beautiful day to learn the Alef-Bet (Hebrew letters). The teacher takes steps to instill in each child the belief that he or she can succeed.

the child's traits, as in, "You're so smart," can promote helplessness. Trait statements promote a fixed view of ability, which leads children to question their competence in the face of setbacks and retreat from challenge (Mueller & Dweck, 1998).

Teachers' messages also affect children's attributions. When teachers are caring and helpful and emphasize learning over getting good grades, they tend to have mastery-oriented students (Anderman et al., 2001). In a study of 1,600 third to eighth graders, students who viewed their teachers as providing positive, supportive learning conditions worked harder and participated more in class—factors that predicted high achievement, which sustained children's belief in the role of effort. In contrast, students with unsupportive teachers regarded their performance as externally controlled (by teachers or luck). This attitude predicted withdrawal from learning activities and declining achievement—outcomes that led children to doubt their ability (Skinner, Zimmer-Gembeck, & Connell, 1998).

Some children are especially likely to have their performance undermined by adult feedback. Despite their higher achievement, girls more often than boys blame their ability for poor performance. Girls also tend to receive messages from teachers and parents that their ability is at fault when they do not do well (Cole et al., 1999; Ruble & Martin, 1998). And in several studies, African-American and Mexican-American children received less favorable feedback from teachers (Irvine, 1986; Losey, 1995). Furthermore, when ethnic minority children observe that adults in their own family are not rewarded by society for their achievement efforts, they may try less hard themselves (Ogbu, 1997).

Finally, cultural values affect the likelihood that children will develop learned helplessness. Recall from Chapter 12 that compared with North Americans, Asian parents and teachers believe that success depends much more on effort than on ability and that trying hard is a moral responsibility—messages they transmit to children (Grant & Dweck, 2001; Tuss, Zimmer, & Ho, 1995). And Israeli children growing up on *kibbutzim* (cooperative agricultural settlements) are shielded from learned helplessness by classrooms that emphasize mastery and interpersonal harmony rather than ability and competition (Butler & Ruzany, 1993).

PROMOTING MASTERY-ORIENTED ATTRIBUTIONS ● Attribution research suggests that at times, well-intended messages from adults undermine children's competence. **Attribution retraining** is an intervention that encourages learned-helpless children to believe that they can overcome failure by exerting more effort. Most often, children are given tasks that are hard enough that they will experience some failure. Then they get repeated feedback that helps them revise their attributions, such as "You can do it if you try harder." Children are also taught to view their successes as due to ability and effort rather than to chance, by giving them additional feedback after they succeed, such as "You're really good at this." Another approach is to encourage low-effort children to focus less on grades and more on mastery for its own sake. A large-scale study showed that classrooms emphasizing the intrinsic value of acquiring new knowledge led to impressive gains in academic self-esteem and motivation of failing students (Ames, 1992). Instruction in metacognition and self-regulation is also helpful, to make up for development lost in this area and to ensure that renewed effort will pay off (Borkowski & Muthukrishna, 1995).

To work well, attribution retraining is best begun in middle childhood, before children's views of themselves become hard to change (Eccles, Wigfield, & Schiefele, 1998). An even better approach is to prevent learned helplessness, using strategies summarized in Applying What We Know on the following page.

Applying
WHAT WE **Know** / Fostering a Mastery-Oriented Approach to Learning

Provision of tasks	Select tasks that are meaningful, responsive to a diversity of pupil interests, and appropriately matched to current competence so the child is challenged but not overwhelmed.
Parent and teacher encouragement	Communicate warmth, confidence in the child's abilities, the value of achievement, and the importance of effort in success.
	Model high effort in overcoming failure.
	(For teachers) Communicate often with parents, suggesting ways to foster children's effort and progress.
	(For parents) Monitor schoolwork; provide scaffolded assistance that promotes knowledge of effective strategies and self-regulation.
Performance evaluations	Make evaluations private; avoid publicizing success or failure through wall posters, stars, privileges to "smart" children, and prizes for "best" performance.
	Stress individual progress and self-improvement.
School environment	Offer small classes, which permit teachers to provide individualized support for mastery.
	Provide for cooperative learning and peer tutoring, in which children assist each other; avoid ability grouping, which makes evaluations of children's progress public.
	Accommodate individual and cultural differences in styles of learning.
	Create an atmosphere that values academics and sends a clear message that all pupils can learn.

Sources: Ames, 1992; Eccles, Wigfield, & Schiefele, 1998.

*A*SK YOURSELF

www

REVIEW How does level of self-esteem change in middle childhood, and what accounts for these changes?

APPLY Should parents try to promote children's self-esteem by telling them they're "smart" and "wonderful"? Is it harmful if children do not feel good about everything they do? Why or why not?

CONNECT What cognitive changes support the transition to a self-concept emphasizing competencies, personality traits, and social comparisons? (See Chapter 12, pages 430–431.)

REFLECT Describe your attributions for academic successes and failures during childhood. What are those attributions like now? What experiences do you think contributed to your attributions?

*E*motional Development

Greater self-awareness and social sensitivity support emotional development in middle childhood. Gains take place in children's experience of self-conscious emotions, understanding of emotional states, and emotional self-regulation.

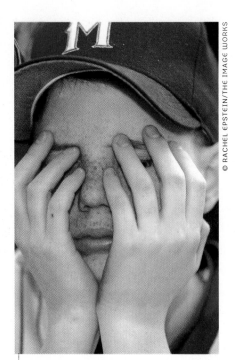

School-age children can experience shame that weakens their overall sense of self-esteem. After striking out at bat during a Little League baseball game, this boy covers his eyes in shame, perhaps in response to his parents' or coach's critical remarks. He may be saying to himself, "I'm stupid, clumsy, and no good"—thoughts and feelings that are destructive to his development.

Self-Conscious Emotions

As children integrate social expectations into their self-concepts, self-conscious emotions of pride and guilt become clearly governed by personal responsibility. Unlike preschoolers, school-age children experience these feelings without adult monitoring. A teacher or parent need not be present for a new accomplishment to spark pride or for a transgression to arouse guilt (Harter & Whitesell, 1989). Also, children do not report guilt for any mishap, as they did at younger ages, but only for intentional wrongdoing, such as ignoring responsibilities, cheating, or lying (Ferguson, Stegge, & Damhuis, 1991). These changes reflect the older child's more mature sense of morality, a topic we will take up later in this chapter.

When school-age children feel pride or guilt, they view specific aspects of the self as leading to success or failure, as in "I tried hard on that difficult task, and it paid off" (pride) or "I made a mistake, and now I have to deal with it" (guilt). They tend to feel shame when their violation of a standard was not under their control. For example, Lizzie felt ashamed when she dropped a spoonful of spaghetti and had a large spot on her shirt for the rest of the school day. But as children develop an overall sense of self-esteem, they may also experience shame after a controllable breach of standards if someone blames them for it. For example, the child who does poorly on a test and whose teacher or parent reprimands him ("Everyone else can do it! Why can't you?") may hang his head in shame while repeating to himself, "I'm stupid!" (Harter, 1999; Mascolo & Fischer, 1995).

Pride motivates children to take on further challenges. And guilt prompts them to make amends and strive for self-improvement. But profound feelings of shame (as noted in Chapter 10) are particularly destructive. They involve taking a single unworthy act to be the whole of self-worth, inducing hopelessness and passive retreat or intense anger at those who participated in the shame-evoking situation (Lindsay-Hartz, de Rivera, & Mascolo, 1995; Reimer, 1996).

Emotional Understanding

School-age children's understanding of mental activity means that they are more likely to explain emotion by referring to internal states, such as happy or sad thoughts, than to external events—the focus of preschoolers (Flavell, Flavell, & Green, 2001). Middle childhood also brings greater awareness of the diversity of emotional experiences. Around age 8, children realize that they can experience more than one emotion at a time, each of which may be positive or negative and may differ in intensity (Pons et al., 2003). For example, recalling the birthday present he received from his grandmother, Joey reflected, "I was very happy I got something but a little sad that I didn't get just what I wanted."

An appreciation of mixed emotions helps children realize that people's expressions may not reflect their true feelings (Saarni, 1999). It also fosters awareness of self-conscious emotions. For example, 8- and 9-year-olds understand that shame combines two feelings: anger at ourselves for a personal inadequacy and sadness at having disappointed another (Harter, 1999). Furthermore, school-age children display other forms of complex emotional reasoning. They can reconcile contradictory facial and situational cues in figuring out another's emotions. And they can use information about people's past experiences to predict how they will feel in a new situation. They realize, for example, that a child rejected by her best friend will probably feel sad at later meeting the friend. Younger children rely only on the current situation, saying, "She'll be happy to see her friend" (Gnepp, 1989).

As with self-understanding, gains in emotional understanding are supported by cognitive development and social experiences, especially adults' sensitivity to children's feelings and willingness to discuss emotions. Together, these factors contribute to a rise in empathy as well. As children move closer to adolescence, advances in perspective taking permit an empathic response not just to people's immediate distress but also to their general life condition (Hoffman, 2000). As at early ages, emotional understanding and empathy are linked to favorable social relationships and prosocial behavior (Schultz et al., 2001). As Joey and Lizzie imagined how people who are chronically ill or hungry feel and evoked those emotions in themselves, they gave part of their allowance to charity and joined in fund-raising projects through school, church, and scouting.

Emotional Self-Regulation

Rapid gains in emotional self-regulation occur in middle childhood. As children compare their accomplishments with their classmates' and care more about peer approval, they must learn to manage negative emotion that threatens their self-esteem.

By age 10, most children shift adaptively between two general strategies to cope with stress. In **problem-centered coping**, they appraise the situation as changeable, identify the difficulty, and decide what to do about it. If problem solving does not work, they engage in **emotion-centered coping**, which is internal, private, and aimed at controlling distress when little can be done about an outcome (Kliewer, Fearnow, & Miller, 1996; Lazarus & Lazarus, 1994). For example, when faced with an anxiety-provoking test or a friend who is angry at them, older school-age children view problem solving and seeking social support as the best strategies. When outcomes are beyond their control, as in having received a bad grade, they opt for distraction or redefining the situation in ways that help them accept current conditions: "Things could be worse. There'll be another test." Compared with preschoolers, school-age children more often use these internal strategies to regulate emotion, a change due to their improved ability to appraise situations and reflect on thoughts and feelings (Brenner & Salovey, 1997).

Cognitive development and a wider range of social experiences permit children to flexibly vary their coping strategies. And from interacting with parents, teachers, and peers, children increase their knowledge of how to express emotion in socially acceptable ways. With age, they increasingly prefer verbal strategies to overt emotional expression, such as crying, sulking, or aggression (Shipman et al., 2003). When the development of emotional self-regulation has gone along well, school-age children acquire a sense of *emotional self-efficacy*—a feeling of being in control of their emotional experience (Saarni, 1999). This fosters a favorable self-image and an optimistic outlook, which assists them further in the face of emotional challenges.

Emotionally well-regulated children are generally upbeat in mood, empathic and prosocial, and well liked by their peers. In contrast, poorly regulated children are overwhelmed by negative emotion, a response that interferes with prosocial behavior and peer acceptance (Zeman, Shipman, & Suveg, 2002). Girls with weak self-regulatory skills tend to freeze with anxiety, whereas boys more often lash out with hostility (Eisenberg, Fabes, & Losoya, 1997).

Finally, culture influences emotional self-regulation. In a striking illustration, researchers studied children in two collectivist subcultures in rural Nepal. In response to stories about emotionally charged situations (such as peer aggression or an unjust parental punishment), Hindu children more often said they would feel angry and would try to mask their feelings. Buddhist children, in contrast, interpreted the situation so they did not experience anger, saying they would feel just OK and explaining, "Why be angry? The event already happened" (see Figure 13.3). In line with this difference, Hindu mothers reported that they often teach their children how to behave emotionally. Buddhist mothers, in contrast, pointed to the value their religion places

Many children felt intensely fearful after witnessing on television the September 11, 2001, terrorist attack on the World Trade Center in New York City. At the suggestion of teachers, these children use an adaptive strategy to regulate their emotions. They offer sympathy to those directly harmed by attaching comforting messages to a flag their school made for families of victims. The flag was placed on public display.

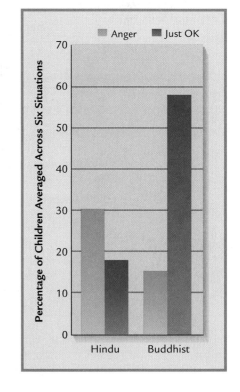

FIGURE 13.3

Hindu and Buddhist children's reports of feeling anger and just OK in response to emotionally charged situations.

Hindu children reported that they would feel more anger. Buddhist children, whose religion values a calm, peaceful disposition, more often stated that they would feel just OK. (Adapted from Cole & Tamang, 1998.)

on a calm, peaceful disposition (Cole & Tamang, 1998). In comparison to both Nepalese groups, American children preferred problem-focused over emotion-focused coping in these situations, regarding conveying anger as more appropriate. To an unjust punishment, they answered, "If I say I'm angry, he'll stop hurting me!" (Cole, Bruschi, & Tamang, 2002). Notice how this response fits with the Western individualistic emphasis on personal rights and self-expression.

Understanding Others: Perspective Taking

We have seen that middle childhood brings major advances in perspective taking—the capacity to imagine what other people are thinking and feeling—changes that support self-concept and self-esteem, understanding of others, and a wide variety of social skills. Robert Selman's five-stage sequence describes changes in perspective-taking skill, based on children's and adolescents' responses to social dilemmas in which characters have differing information and opinions about an event.

As Table 13.1 indicates, at first, children have only a limited idea of what other people might be thinking and feeling. Over time, they become more aware that people can interpret the same event quite differently. Soon they can "step in another person's shoes" and reflect on how that person might regard their own thoughts, feelings, and behavior, as when they make statements like this: "I *thought you would think* I was just kidding when I said that." (Note that this level of perspective taking is similar to second-order false belief, described on page 437 of Chapter 12.) Finally, older children and adolescents can evaluate two people's perspectives simultaneously, at first from the vantage point of a disinterested spectator and, finally, by making reference to societal values. The following explanation reflects this advanced level: "I know why Joey hid the stray kitten in the basement, even though his mom was against keeping it. He believes in not hurting animals. If you put the kitten outside or give it to the pound, it might die."

Perspective taking varies greatly among children of the same age. Individual differences are due to cognitive maturity as well as to experiences in which adults and peers explain their viewpoints, encouraging children to notice another's perspective (Dixon & Moore, 1990; FitzGerald & White, 2003). Children with poor social skills—in particular, the angry, aggressive styles we discussed in Chapter 10—have great difficulty imagining the thoughts and feelings of others. They often mis-

TABLE 13.1

Selman's Stages of Perspective Taking

STAGE	APPROXIMATE AGE RANGE	DESCRIPTION
Level 0: Undifferentiated perspective taking	3–6	Children recognize that self and other can have different thoughts and feelings, but they frequently confuse the two.
Level 1: Social-informational perspective taking	4–9	Children understand that different perspectives may result because people have access to different information.
Level 2: Self-reflective perspective taking	7–12	Children can "step in another person's shoes" and view their own thoughts, feelings, and behavior from the other person's perspective. They also recognize that others can do the same.
Level 3: Third-party perspective taking	10–15	Children can step outside a two-person situation and imagine how the self and other are viewed from the point of view of a third, impartial party.
Level 4: Societal perspective taking	14–adult	Individuals understand that third-party perspective taking can be influenced by one or more systems of larger societal values.

Sources: Selman, 1976; Selman & Byrne, 1974.

treat adults and peers without feeling the guilt and remorse prompted by awareness of another's viewpoint. Interventions that provide coaching and practice in perspective taking reduce antisocial behavior and increase empathy and prosocial responding (Chalmers & Townsend, 1990).

Moral Development

Recall from Chapter 10 that preschoolers pick up a great many morally relevant behaviors through modeling and reinforcement. By middle childhood, they have reflected on these experiences and internalized rules for good conduct, such as "It's good to help others in trouble" or "It's wrong to take something that doesn't belong to you." This change leads children to become considerably more independent and trustworthy. They can take on many more responsibilities, from running errands at the supermarket to watching younger siblings (Weisner, 1996). Of course, these advances occur only when children have had the consistent guidance and example of caring adults in their lives.

In Chapter 10 we also saw that children do not just copy their morality from those around them. As the cognitive-developmental approach emphasizes, they actively think about right and wrong. An expanding social world and gains in reasoning and perspective taking lead moral understanding to improve greatly in middle childhood.

Learning About Justice Through Sharing

In everyday life, children frequently experience situations that involve **distributive justice—beliefs about how to divide material goods fairly.** Heated discussions often take place over how much weekly allowance is to be given to siblings of different ages, who has to sit where in the family car on a long trip, and how six hungry playmates can share an eight-slice pizza. William Damon (1977, 1988) has traced children's changing concepts of distributive justice over early and middle childhood.

Even 4-year-olds recognize the importance of sharing, but their reasons are often self-serving: "I shared because if I didn't, she wouldn't play with me" or "I let her have some, but most are for me because I'm older." As children enter middle childhood, they express more mature notions of distributive justice. Their basis of reasoning follows an age-related, three-step sequence:

1. *Equality* (5 to 6 years). Children in the early school grades are intent on making sure that each person gets the same amount of a treasured resource, such as money, turns in a game, or a delicious treat.

2. *Merit* (6 to 7 years). A short time later, children say extra rewards should go to someone who has worked especially hard or otherwise performed in an exceptional way.

3. *Benevolence* (around 8 years). Finally, children recognize that special consideration should be given to those at a disadvantage—for example, that an extra amount might be given to a child who cannot produce as much or who does not get any allowance. Older children also adapt their basis of fairness to fit the situation, relying more on equality when interacting with strangers and more on benevolence when interacting with friends (McGillicuddy-De Lisi, Watkins, & Vinchur, 1994).

According to Damon (1988), the give-and-take of peer interaction makes children more sensitive to others' perspectives, and this supports their developing ideas of justice (Kruger, 1993). Advanced distributive justice reasoning, in turn, is associated with more effective social problem solving and with a greater willingness to help and share with others (Blotner & Bearison, 1984; McNamee & Peterson, 1986).

These fourth-grade boys are figuring out how to divide a handful of penny candy fairly among themselves. Already, they have a well-developed sense of distributive justice.

Understanding Moral, Social-Conventional, and Personal Matters

As their ideas about justice advance, children clarify and link moral rules and social conventions (Turiel, 1998). Over time, their understanding becomes more complex, taking into account an increasing number of variables, including the purpose of the rule; people's intentions, knowledge, and beliefs; and the context of their behavior.

School-age children, for example, distinguish social conventions with a clear *purpose* (not running in school hallways to prevent injuries) from ones with no obvious justification (crossing a "forbidden" line on the playground). They regard violations of purposeful conventions as closer to moral transgressions (Buchanan-Barrow & Barrett, 1998). They also realize that people's *intentions* and the *context* of their actions affect the moral implications of violating a social convention. In a Canadian study, 8- to 10-year-olds judged that because of a flag's symbolic value, burning it to express disapproval of a country or to start a cooking fire is worse than burning it accidentally. Older school-age children also stated that public flag-burning is worse than private flag-burning, referring to the emotional harm inflicted on others. At the same time, they recognized that burning a flag is a form of freedom of expression. Most agreed that in an unfair country, it would be acceptable (Helwig & Prencipe, 1999).

In middle childhood, children also realize that people whose *knowledge* differs may not be equally responsible for moral transgressions. Many 7-year-olds tolerate a teacher's decision to give more snack to girls than to boys because she thinks (incorrectly) that girls need more food. But when a teacher gives girls more snack because she holds an *immoral belief* ("it's all right to be nicer to girls than boys"), almost all children judge her actions negatively (Wainryb & Ford, 1998).

As children's grasp of moral rules and social conventions strengthens, so does their conviction that certain matters, such as hairstyle, friends, and leisure activities, are up to the individual. Notions of personal choice, in turn, enhance children's moral understanding. As early as age 6, children view freedom of speech and religion as individual rights, even if laws exist that deny those rights (Helwig & Turiel, 2002). And they regard laws that discriminate against individuals—for example, laws that deny certain people access to medical care or education—as wrong and worthy of violating (Helwig & Jasiobedzka, 2001). In justifying their responses, children appeal to personal privileges and, by the end of middle childhood, to democratic ideals, such as the importance of individual rights for maintaining a fair society. At the same time, older school-age children place limits on individual choice, depending on circumstances. While regarding nonacademic matters (such as where to go on field trips) as best decided democratically, they believe that the academic curriculum is the province of teachers, based on teachers' superior ability to make such choices (Helwig & Kim, 1999).

Children and adolescents in diverse Western and non-Western cultures use similar criteria to reason about moral, social-conventional, and personal concerns (Neff & Helwig, 2002; Nucci, 2002). For example, Chinese young people, whose culture places a high value on respect for and deference to adult authority, nevertheless say that adults have no right to interfere in children's personal matters, such as how they spend free time (Helwig et al., 2003). Furthermore, North American and Korean children alike claim that a child with no position of authority should be obeyed when she gives fair and caring directives, such as to share candy or return lost money to its owner. And although they recognize a parent's right to set social conventions at home and a teacher's right to do so at school, they evaluate negatively an adult's order to engage in immoral acts (Kim, 1998; Kim & Turiel, 1996). In sum, children everywhere seem to realize that higher principles—ones independent of rule and authority—must govern when people's personal rights and welfare are at stake.

As children extend their grasp of moral imperatives, they also contemplate religious and spiritual concepts. Refer to the Cultural Influences box on the following page for current evidence on how children understand the existence of God: the core idea in the vast majority of the world's religions.

As these children watch the Canada Day parade in Montreal, which celebrates the country's founding, they realize that the social convention of respecting the flag has moral implications. Any public flag-burning, they say, would harm others emotionally. At the same time, they acknowledge that destroying a flag is a form of freedom of expression that is warranted in an unfair country.

Cultural Influences

Children's Understanding of God

When asked, "What is God?" here is how several 6- to 9-year-olds responded:

- "God is a man who wears dresses [robes]."

- "You can pray anytime you feel like it, and they [Jesus and God] are sure to hear you because they got it worked out so one of them is on duty at all times."

- "God hears everything, not just prayers, so there must be an awful lot of noise in his ears, unless he has thought of a way to turn it off."

- "God is a spirit who can go anywhere." *What is a spirit?* "It's a ghost, like in the movies." (From Briggs, 2000; Gandy, 2004.)

Ideas about God differ radically from ideas about ordinary experiences because they violate real-world assumptions. Recall from Chapter 9 that between ages 4 and 8, children distinguish magical beings (such as Santa Claus and the Tooth Fairy) from reality (see page 322). At the same time, they embrace other beliefs that are part of their culturally transmitted religion. But to avoid confusion, they must isolate their concepts of God from their grasp of human agents, placing God in a separate religious realm governed by superhuman rules (Woolley, 2000). This is a challenging task for preschool and school-age children.

Previous research, strongly influenced by Piaget's theory, led to a uniform conclusion: Children assign *anthropomorphic* (human) characteristics to God, whom they view as a parentlike figure residing in the sky. Not until adolescence does this concrete image of

God as "big person" give way to an abstract, mystical view of God as formless, all-knowing (omniscient), all-powerful (omnipotent), and transcending the limits of time (Hyde, 1990).

Consider the children's responses just given, which contain a variety of concrete images—God as robed figure, as being "on duty in the sky," and as overwhelmed by the "noise in His ears." But along with these humanlike references, children included a variety of superhuman properties. New evidence reveals that even preschoolers are not limited to human, parental images of God. The typical procedures used to investigate children's religious knowledge—asking them to respond to open-ended questions—are so cognitively demanding that children often fall back on their highly detailed notions of humans to fill in for their sketchier thoughts about God.

In several studies, researchers demonstrated that when adults are given similarly demanding tasks (asked to comprehend and retell short stories about God), they, too, give many anthropomorphic responses (Barrett, 1998). And when researchers make tasks less demanding, children recognize that God has supernatural powers not available to humans, such as seeing and hearing everything. For example, nearly all 5- and 6-year-olds given a typical false-belief task (see page 337) indicated that their parents would hold a false belief, but God would not. They also said that God, but not a humanlike puppet, can see an object in a darkened box (Barrett, Richert, & Driesenga, 2001). And with

respect to God's omnipotence, even preschoolers are certain that God, but not humans, gives life to all natural things (animals, plants, and trees) (Petrovich, 1997).

Indeed, the most striking feature of children's concepts of God is their mix of tangible and intangible features. In this respect, their religious thinking is far more similar to adults' than previously thought. That children's representations of God are not restricted to a "big person" image suggests that their thinking is strongly influenced by religious education. Indeed, wide cultural variation in children's and adults' ideas exists (Barrett, 2002; Barrett & Van Orman, 1996). In studies in which school-age children drew pictures of God (which usually evokes humanlike images), Mormons, Lutherans, Mennonites, and Catholics more often represented God as humanlike than did Unitarians and Jews, in line with theological teachings of their denomination (Pitts, 1976; Tamminen, 1991). Further, children say some things about God that seem strange or funny because their culturally relevant knowledge is often incomplete.

Finally, some children are aware of the emotional comfort and guidance that visions of God can provide, as these comments indicate: "He comes down and helps you when you're sad or lonely or can't get to sleep at night." " In case you forget, he reminds you to act nice" (Berk, 2004). As we will see in Chapter 16, by adolescence (and perhaps before), religiosity is linked to psychological well-being and to prosocial attitudes and behavior.

Cognitive development, religious education, and culture combine to influence children's understanding of God. A 7-year-old and his family greet the priest after a Catholic Mass. When questioned properly, most children this boy's age indicate that God has both humanlike and supernatural powers—concepts that resemble those of adults.

© MYRLEEN FERGUSON CATE/PHOTOEDIT

Moral Education

Debate over whether and how to teach morality in the public schools is vigorous. On one side are educators who call for *character education*—teaching students to follow a common set of moral virtues, such as honesty, kindness, fairness, and responsibility (De Roche & Williams, 1998). But critics claim that transmitting a ready-made morality, such as "Be honest and work hard," ignores school-age children's developing capacity to consider multiple variables in moral decision making (Nucci, 2001). As children get older, cognitive-developmental theorists point out, they benefit from increasing opportunities for *moral discussion*—evaluating beliefs and practices on moral grounds.

Darcia Narvaez and her colleagues (2001) recommend that moral education be broadened to promote four moral components, starting at a concrete level and moving toward more abstract understandings. Each component involves a different type of knowledge essential for moral functioning:

COURTESY ALEXANDRIA NECKER

Alexandria Necker of DeWitt, Iowa, read a story about foster children being given a trash bag in which to put their belongings while being moved from home to home. On her tenth birthday, she had guests bring gifts not for her, but for area foster children. She continues to gather and distribute such gifts. Alexandria exemplifies the diverse ingredients of moral maturity—high moral sensitivity, moral judgment, moral motivation, and moral character.

● *Interpreting the situation: moral sensitivity*—using cause–effect reasoning and perspective taking to predict how one's actions are likely to affect others, resulting in awareness that a situation involves a moral issue;

● *Reasoning about right and wrong: moral judgment*—evaluating possible courses of action to determine which one is fair and just;

● *Granting moral values a high priority: moral motivation*—elevating moral values above other personal values; and

● *Having the strength of one's convictions: moral character*—controlling impulses and steadfastly behaving in accord with moral values.

At present, moral education programs for children are narrowly focused. Character education emphasizes *moral character,* whereas the cognitive-developmental approach stresses *moral judgment* (Bebeau, Rest, & Narvaez, 1999). Narvaez's four-component model offers a comprehensive basis for moral education. Children in highly successful programs should gain in each aspect of morality.

Ask YOURSELF

WWW

REVIEW How does emotional self-regulation improve in middle childhood? Do gains in emotional self-regulation have implications for children's self-esteem? Explain.

APPLY Joey's fourth-grade class participated in a bowl-a-thon to raise money for a charity serving children with cancer. Explain how activities like this one can foster emotional development, perspective taking, and moral understanding.

CONNECT Describe how older children's capacity to take more information into account affects each of the following: self-concept, emotional understanding, perspective taking, and moral understanding.

Peer Relations

In middle childhood, the society of peers becomes an increasingly important context for development. Formal schooling exposes children to agemates who differ in many ways, including achievement, ethnicity, religion, interests, and personality. Peer contact, as we have seen, contributes to perspective taking and understanding of self and others. These developments, in turn, enhance peer interaction, which becomes more prosocial over the school years. In line with this change, aggression declines, but the drop is greatest for physical attacks (Tremblay, 2000). As we will see, other types of aggression continue as school-age children form peer groups and distinguish "insiders" from "outsiders."

Peer Groups

Watch children in the schoolyard or neighborhood, and notice how groups of three to a dozen or more often gather. The organization of these collectives changes greatly with age. By the end of middle childhood, children display a strong desire for group belonging. They form **peer groups, collectives that generate unique values and standards for behavior and a social structure of leaders and followers.** Peer groups organize on the basis of proximity (being in the same classroom) and similarity in gender, ethnicity, and popularity. When these groups are tracked for 3 to 6 weeks, membership changes very little. When they are followed for a year or longer, substantial change can be observed, depending on whether children are reshuffled into different classrooms and loyalties change within the group. For children who remain together, 50 to 70 percent of groups consist mostly of the same children from year to year (Cairns, Xie, & Leung, 1998).

The practices of these informal groups lead to a "peer culture" that typically consists of a specialized vocabulary, dress code, and place to "hang out" during leisure hours. For example, Joey formed a club with three other boys. They met at recess, after school, and on Saturdays in the tree house in Joey's backyard and wore a "uniform" consisting of T-shirts, jeans, and tennis shoes. Calling themselves "the pack," the boys developed a secret handshake and chose Joey as their leader. Their activities included improving the clubhouse, trading baseball cards, playing basketball and video games, and—just as important—keeping unwanted peers and adults out!

As children develop these exclusive associations, the codes of dress and behavior that grow out of them become more broadly influential. At school, children who deviate are often rebuffed by their peers. "Kissing up" to teachers, wearing the wrong kind of shirt or shoes, tattling on classmates, or carrying a strange-looking lunchbox are grounds for critical glances and comments. These special customs bind peers together, creating a sense of group identity. In addition, by participating in peer groups, children acquire many social skills—cooperation, leadership, followership, and loyalty to collective goals. Through these experiences, children experiment with and learn about social organizations.

As with other aspects of social reasoning, children evaluate a group's decision to exclude a peer in complex ways. Most judge exclusion to be wrong, even when they view themselves as different from the excluded child. And with age, children are less likely to endorse excluding someone because of unconventional appearance or behavior. Girls, especially, regard exclusion as unjust, perhaps because they experience it more often than boys and therefore identify more strongly with excluded agemates (Killen, Crystal, & Watanabe, 2002). But when a peer threatens group functioning, by acting disruptively or by lacking skills to participate in a valued group activity (such as sports), both boys and girls say that exclusion is justified—a perspective that strengthens with age (Killen & Stangor, 2001).

Despite these sophisticated understandings, the beginning of peer group ties is a time when some of the "nicest children behave in the most awful ways" (Redl, 1966,

Peer groups first form in middle childhood. These girls have probably established a social structure of leader and followers as they gather for joint activities. Their body language suggests that they feel a strong sense of group belonging.

© MM FLASH! LIGHT/STOCK BOSTON, LLC

p. 395). From third grade on, relational aggression—gossiping, rumor spreading, and rebuffing—rises among girls, who (because of gender-role expectations) express hostility in subtle, indirect ways (Crick & Grotpeter, 1995). Boys are more straightforward in their hostility toward the "outgroup." Overt aggression in the form of verbal insults and pranks—toilet-papering a front yard or ringing a doorbell and running away—occurs among small groups of boys, who provide one another with temporary social support for these mildly antisocial behaviors.

Unfortunately, peer groups—at the instigation of their leaders—often direct their hostilities toward their own members, ejecting no-longer-"respected" children. These cast-outs are profoundly wounded, and many find new group ties hard to establish. Their previous behavior toward the outgroup reduces their chances of being included elsewhere. As one fifth grader explained, "I think they didn't like me because when I was in the popular group we'd make fun of everyone. . . . I had been too mean to them in the past" (Adler & Adler, 1998, p. 70). Aggressive rejects often join forces with likeminded peers, who actively promote one another's hostility. At the same time, some aggressive children—especially popular boys—link up with popular, nonaggressive agemates (Bagwell et al., 2000; Farmer et al., 2002). In these groups, mild-mannered children accept and even support the antisocial acts of their dominant, antisocial associates, who pick fights with other groups or bully weaker children. Consequently, teachers and counselors must target both antisocial and mixed peer groups to reduce peer aggression.

The school-age child's desire for group belonging can also be satisfied through formal group ties—scouting, 4-H, religious youth groups, and other associations. Adult involvement holds in check the negative behaviors associated with children's informal peer groups. And as children work on joint projects and help in their communities, they gain in social and moral maturity (Killen & Nucci, 1995; Vandell & Shumow, 1999).

Friendships

Whereas peer groups provide children with insight into larger social structures, close, one-to-one friendships contribute to the development of trust and sensitivity. During the school years, children's concepts of friendship become psychologically based. Consider the following 8-year-old's ideas:

> *Why is Shelly your best friend?* Because she helps me when I'm sad, and she shares. . . . *What makes Shelly so special?* I've known her longer, I sit next to her and got to know her better. . . . *How come you like Shelly better than anyone else?* She's done the most for me. She never disagrees, she never eats in front of me, she never walks away when I'm crying, and she helps me on my homework. . . . *How do you get someone to like you?* . . . If you're nice to [your friends], they'll be nice to you. (Damon, 1988, pp. 80–81)

As these responses show, friendship is no longer just a matter of engaging in the same activities. Instead, it is a mutually agreed-on relationship in which children like each other's personal qualities and respond to one another's needs and desires. And once a friendship forms, *trust* becomes its defining feature. School-age children state that a good friendship is based on acts of kindness, signifying that each person can be counted on to support the other. Consequently, older children regard violations of trust, such as not helping when others need help, breaking promises, and gossiping behind the other's back, as serious breaches of friendship (Damon, 1977; Selman, 1980).

Because of these features, school-age children's friendships are more selective. Whereas preschoolers say they have lots of friends, by age 8 or 9, children name only a handful of good friends. Girls, especially, are exclusive in their friendships because they demand greater closeness than boys (Markovits, Benenson, & Dolensky, 2001). In addition, children tend to select friends who are like themselves in age, sex, race, ethnicity, and SES. Friends also resemble one another in personality (sociability, aggression, and depression), popularity, academic achievement, and prosocial behavior (Haselager et al., 1998; Hartup, 1999). Note, however, that school and neighborhood characteristics affect friendship choices. For example, in integrated schools, as many as 50 percent of students report at least one close, other-race friend (DuBois & Hirsch, 1990).

Friendships remain fairly stable over middle childhood; most last for several years. Through friendship, children learn the importance of emotional commitment. They come to realize that close relationships can survive disagreements if both parties are secure in their liking for one another and

During middle childhood, concepts of friendship become more psychologically based. Although these boys enjoy playing baseball, they want to spend time together because they like each other's personal qualities. Mutual trust is a defining feature of their friendship. Each child counts on the other to provide support and assistance.

© RICHARD HUTCHINGS/PHOTOEDIT

resolve conflicts in ways that meet both partners' needs (Rose & Asher, 1999). As a result, friendship provides an important context in which children learn to tolerate criticism and resolve disputes.

Yet the impact that friendships have on development depends on the nature of those friends. Children who bring kindness and compassion to their friendships strengthen each other's prosocial tendencies. When aggressive children make friends, the relationship often magnifies antisocial acts. The friendships of aggressive girls are high in exchange of private feelings but full of jealousy, conflict, and betrayal. Those of aggressive boys involve frequent coercive statements and physical attacks (Crick & Nelson, 2002; Dishion, Andrews, & Crosby, 1995). These findings reveal that the social problems of aggressive children operate within their closest peer ties. As we will see next, these children often acquire negative reputations in the wider world of peers.

Peer Acceptance

Peer acceptance refers to likability—the extent to which a child is viewed by a group of agemates, such as classmates, as a worthy social partner. It differs from friendship in that it is not a mutual relationship. Rather, it is a one-sided perspective, involving the group's view of an individual. Nevertheless, certain social skills that contribute to friendship also enhance peer acceptance. Consequently, better-accepted children have more friends and more positive relationships with them (Gest, Graham-Bermann, & Hartup, 2001).

Researchers usually assess peer acceptance with self-report measures called **sociometric techniques.** For example, children may be asked to nominate several peers in their class whom they especially like or dislike, to indicate for all possible pairs of classmates which one they prefer to play with, or to rate each peer on a scale from "like very much" to "like very little" (Cillessen & Bukowski, 2000). Children's responses yield four different categories: **popular children,** who get many positive votes; **rejected children,** who are actively disliked; **controversial children,** who get a large number of positive and negative votes; and **neglected children,** who are seldom mentioned, either positively or negatively. About two-thirds of students in a typical elementary school classroom fit one of these categories (Coie, Dodge, & Coppotelli, 1982). The remaining one-third are *average* in peer acceptance; they do not receive extreme scores.

Peer acceptance is a powerful predictor of current as well as later psychological adjustment. Rejected children, especially, are unhappy, alienated, poorly achieving children with low self-esteem. Both teachers and parents rate them as having a wide range of emotional and social problems. Peer rejection in middle childhood is also strongly associated with poor school performance, absenteeism, dropping out, antisocial behavior, and delinquency in adolescence and with criminality in emerging adulthood (Bagwell, Newcomb, & Bukowski, 1998; Laird et al., 2001; Parker & Asher, 1987).

However, preceding influences—children's characteristics combined with parenting practices—may largely explain the link between peer acceptance and adjustment. School-age children with peer-relationship problems are more likely to have experienced family stress due to low income, parental changes (divorce, remarriage, death), insensitive child rearing, and coercive discipline (Woodward & Fergusson, 1999). Nevertheless, as we will see, rejected children evoke reactions from peers that contribute to their unfavorable development.

DETERMINANTS OF PEER ACCEPTANCE ● What causes one child to be liked and another to be rejected? A wealth of research reveals that social behavior plays a powerful role.

Popular Children. Although most popular children are kind and considerate, a few are admired for their socially sophisticated yet belligerent behavior. The large majority are **popular-prosocial children,** who combine academic and social competence. They perform well in school and communicate with peers in sensitive, friendly, and cooperative ways (Newcomb, Bukowski, & Pattee, 1993). In contrast, **popular-antisocial children** largely consist of "tough" boys who are athletically skilled but poor students. Although they are aggressive, their peers view them as "cool," perhaps because of their athletic ability, social dominance, and shrewd but devious social skills (Rodkin et al., 2000).

Although they are ethnically diverse, many popular-antisocial children are low-SES minority youngsters who have concluded that they cannot succeed academically. Perhaps for this reason, their peer culture encourages troublemaking behavior. Consistent with this view, in classrooms with greater numbers of aggressive children, peers are more likely to rate such children as "most liked" (Stormshak et al., 1999). So far, we do not know whether popular-antisocial children's likability protects them from future adjustment difficulties. But their antisocial activities require intervention because they often bully disliked classmates (Farmer et al., 2003).

Rejected Children. Rejected children display a wide range of negative social behaviors. The largest subgroup, rejected-aggressive children, show high rates of conflict, aggression (both overt and relational), and hyperactive, inattentive, and impulsive behavior. They are also deficient in social understanding and regulation of negative emotion. For example, they tend to be poor perspective takers, to misinterpret the innocent behaviors of peers as hostile, to blame others for their social difficulties, and to act on their angry feelings (Coie & Dodge, 1998; Crick, Casas, & Nelson, 2002). In contrast, rejected-withdrawn children are passive and socially awkward. These timid children are overwhelmed by social anxiety, hold negative expectations for how peers will treat them, and are concerned about being scorned and attacked (Hart et al., 2000; Ladd & Burgess, 1999).

As early as kindergarten, peers exclude rejected children. Rejection, in turn, further impairs these children's biased social information processing, which heightens their aggression (Dodge et al., 2003). Soon rejected children's classroom participation declines, their feelings of loneliness rise, their academic achievement falters, and they want to avoid school (Buhs & Ladd, 2001). Rejected children usually have few friends—and occasionally have none. The combination of persistent rejection and friendlessness is linked to low self-esteem, mistrust of peers, and severe adjustment difficulties (Ladd & Troop-Gordon, 2003).

Both rejected-aggressive and rejected-withdrawn children are at risk for peer harassment. But as the Biology and Environment box on the following page reveals, rejected-withdrawn children are especially likely to be targeted by bullies because of their inept, submissive style of interaction (Sandstrom & Cillessen, 2003).

Controversial and Neglected Children. Consistent with the mixed peer opinion they engender, controversial children display a blend of positive and negative social behaviors. Although they are hostile and disruptive, they also engage in high rates of positive, prosocial acts and are frequently viewed as leaders. Even though some peers dislike them, controversial children have qualities that protect them from exclusion. They have as many friends as popular children and are happy with their peer relationships (Newcomb, Bukowski, & Pattee, 1993). But like their popular-antisocial counterparts, they often bully agemates to get their way and engage in calculated, relational aggression to sustain their social dominance (DeRosier & Thomas, 2003). The social status of controversial children often changes over time, as agemates react to their mixed behavior.

Finally, perhaps the most surprising finding is that neglected children, once thought to be in need of treatment, are usually well adjusted. Although they engage in low rates of interaction, most are just as socially skilled as average children. They do not report feeling unhappy about their social life, and when they want to, they can break away from their usual pattern of playing by themselves (Harrist et al., 1997; Ladd & Burgess, 1999). Perhaps for this reason, neglected status (like controversial status) is usually temporary.

Neglected children remind us that there are other paths to emotional well-being besides an outgoing, gregarious personality style. Recall from Chapter 7 that in China, adults view restrained, cautious children as advanced in social maturity. Perhaps because shyness is consistent with a cultural emphasis on not standing out from the collective, it is associated with peer acceptance and social competence among Chinese 8- to 10-year-olds (Chen, 2002; Chen, Rubin, & Li, 1995).

HELPING REJECTED CHILDREN ● A variety of interventions exist to improve the peer relations and psychological adjustment of rejected children. Most involve coaching, modeling, and reinforcing positive social skills, such as how to initiate interaction with a peer, cooperate in play, and respond to another child with friendly emotion and approval. Several of these programs have produced gains in social competence and peer acceptance still present from several weeks to a year later (Asher & Rose, 1997). Combining social-skill training with other treatments increases their effectiveness. Rejected children are often poor students, and their low academic self-esteem magnifies their negative reactions to teachers and classmates (O'Neil et al., 1997). Intensive academic tutoring improves school achievement and social acceptance (Coie & Krehbiel, 1984).

Biology and Environment

Bullies and Their Victims

Follow the activities of aggressive children over a school day, and you will see that they reserve their hostilities for certain peers. A particularly destructive form of interaction is **peer victimization, in which certain children become frequent targets of verbal and physical attacks or other forms of abuse.** What sustains these repeated assault–retreat cycles between pairs of children?

Large-scale surveys reveal that about 20 percent of children are bullies and 15 percent victims (Nansel et al., 2001). Although most bullies and victims are boys, at times girls bombard a vulnerable classmate with relational hostility (Crick & Grotpeter, 1996). As early as kindergarten, victimization leads to a variety of adjustment difficulties, including depression, loneliness, low self-esteem, and school avoidance (Hawker & Boulton, 2000; Kochenderfer-Ladd & Wardrop, 2001).

Victims are passive when active behavior is expected. On the playground, they hang around chatting or wander on their own. When bullied, they reinforce perpetrators by giving in to their demands, crying, and assuming defensive postures (Boulton, 1999). Most lack defenders in the peer group, so bullies see them as easy prey and an opportunity to flaunt their social dominance. Biologically based traits—an inhibited temperament and a frail physical appearance—contribute to victimization. But victims also have histories of resistant attachment, overly controlling child rearing, and maternal overprotectiveness. These parenting behaviors prompt anxiety, low self-esteem, and dependency, resulting in a fearful demeanor

that radiates vulnerability (Ladd & Ladd, 1998; Pepler & Craig, 2000).

Aggression and victimization are not polar opposites. One-third to one-half of victims are also aggressive. Often these children irritate their peers, provoking attacks. And occasionally, they retaliate against powerful bullies, who respond by abusing them again—a cycle that sustains their victim status (Camodeca et al., 2002; Kochenderfer-Ladd, 2003). Among rejected children, bully/victims are the most despised, and they often experience extremely maladaptive parenting, including child abuse. Their negative home and peer experiences place them at severe risk for maladjustment (Schwartz, Proctor, & Chien, 2001; Smith & Myron-Wilson, 1998).

Interventions that change victimized children's negative opinions of themselves, that improve their social skills, and that teach them to respond to their attackers in nonreinforcing ways are vital (Gazelle & Ladd, 2002). Nevertheless, victimized children's behavior should not be taken to mean they are to blame for their abuse. Developing a school code against bullying, teaching child bystanders to intervene when it occurs, enlisting parents' assistance in changing both bullies' and victims' behavior, and moving aggressive children to another class or school can greatly reduce peer victimization, which accounts for a substantial portion of aggression in middle childhood (Olweus, 1995).

Another way to assist victimized children is to help them acquire the social skills needed to form and maintain a gratifying friendship. Anxious, withdrawn children who have a best friend are bet-

ter equipped to withstand peer attacks. They show fewer adjustment problems than victims with no close friends (Hodges et al., 1999).

Children who are victimized by bullies have characteristics that make them easy targets. They are physically weak, rejected by their peers, and afraid to defend themselves. Both temperament and child-rearing experiences contribute to their cowering behavior, which reinforces their attackers' abusive acts.

Still another approach focuses on training in perspective taking and social problem solving. Many rejected-aggressive children are unaware of their poor social skills and do not take responsibility for their social failures (Mrug, Hoza, & Gerdes, 2001). Rejected-withdrawn children, on the other hand, are likely to develop a learned-helpless approach to peer acceptance. They conclude, after repeated rebuffs, that they will never be liked (Rubin, Bukowski, & Parker, 1998). Both types of rejected children need help in attributing their peer difficulties to internal, changeable causes.

Finally, because rejected children's socially incompetent behaviors often originate in a poor fit between the child's temperament and parenting practices, interventions that focus on the child alone may not be sufficient. If the quality of parent–child interaction is not changed, children may soon return to their old behavior patterns.

Gender Typing

Children's understanding of gender roles broadens in middle childhood, and their gender identities (views of themselves as relatively masculine or feminine) change as well. We will see that development differs for boys and girls, and it can vary considerably across cultures.

Gender-Stereotyped Beliefs

During the school years, children extend gender-stereotyped beliefs acquired in early childhood. As children think more about people as personalities, they label some traits as more typical of one sex than of the other. For example, they regard "tough," "aggressive," "rational," and "dominant" as masculine and "gentle," "sympathetic," and "dependent" as feminine—stereotyping that increases steadily with age (Best et al., 1977; Serbin, Powlishta, & Gulko, 1993). Children derive these distinctions from observing gender differences as well as from adult treatment. Parents, for example, use more directive speech (telling the child what to do) with girls, less often encourage girls to make their own decisions, and are less likely to express confidence in girls when praising them, through such statements as, "You must really enjoy your work!" (Leaper, Anderson, & Sanders, 1998; Pomerantz & Ruble, 1998).

Shortly after entering elementary school, children figure out which academic subjects and skill areas are "masculine" and which are "feminine." They regard reading, art, and music as more for girls and mathematics, science, athletics, and mechanical skills as more for boys (Eccles, Jacobs, & Harold, 1990; Jacobs & Weisz, 1994). These stereotypes—and the attitudes and behaviors of parents and teachers that promote them—influence children's preferences for certain subjects and, in turn, how well they do at them. As we saw in our discussion of self-esteem, boys feel more competent than girls at math, science, and athletics, and girls feel more competent than boys at language arts.

Furthermore, girls seem to adopt a more general stereotype of males as smarter than females, which they apply to themselves. In a study of over 2,000 second to sixth graders from diverse cultures (Eastern and Western Europe, Japan, Russia, and the United States), girls consistently had higher school grades than boys. Yet despite being aware of their better performance, they did not report stronger beliefs in their own ability. Compared with boys, girls discounted their talent (Stetsenko et al., 2000). Apparently, gender stereotyping of academic talent occurs in many parts of the world.

Although school-age children are aware of many stereotypes, they have a flexible view of what males and females *can do.* As they develop the capacity to integrate conflicting social cues, children realize that a person's sex does not necessarily predict his or her personality traits, activities, and behaviors. By the end of the school years, children regard gender typing as socially rather than biologically influenced (Bigler, 1995; Taylor, 1996). Nevertheless, acknowledging that people *can* cross gender lines does not mean that children always *approve* of doing so. They judge certain violations—boys playing with dolls and wearing girls' clothing and girls acting noisily and roughly—harshly. And they are especially intolerant when boys engage in these "cross-gender" acts, regarding them as nearly as bad as moral transgressions (Blakemore, 2003; Levy, Taylor, & Gelman, 1995).

Gender Identity and Behavior

Boys' and girls' gender identities follow different paths in middle childhood. From third to sixth grade, boys tend to strengthen their identification with "masculine" personality traits, whereas girls' identification with "feminine" traits declines. Although girls still lean

During middle childhood, girls feel freer than boys to experiment with "cross-gender" activities. This 9-year-old perfects her wood-carving skills.

© DAVID YOUNG-WOLFF/PHOTOEDIT

toward the "feminine" side, they are more likely than boys to describe themselves as having "other-gender" characteristics (Serbin, Powlishta, & Gulko, 1993). This difference is also evident in children's activities. Whereas boys usually stick to "masculine" pursuits, girls experiment with a wider range of options. Besides cooking, sewing, and baby-sitting, they join organized sports teams, work on science projects, and build forts in the backyard. And more often than boys, girls consider work roles stereotyped for the other gender, such as firefighter and astronomer (Liben & Bigler, 2002).

These trends are due to a mixture of cognitive and social forces. School-age children of both sexes are aware that society attaches greater prestige to "masculine" characteristics. For example, they rate "masculine" occupations as having higher status than "feminine" occupations (Liben, Bigler, & Krogh, 2001). Messages from adults and peers are also influential. In Chapter 10, we saw that parents are especially concerned about boys' gender-role conformity. And a tomboyish girl can make her way into boys' activities without losing status with her female peers, but a boy who hangs out with girls is likely to be ridiculed and rejected.

Cultural Influences on Gender Typing

Although the sex differences just described are typical in Western nations, they do not apply to children everywhere. Girls are less likely to experiment with "masculine" activities in cultures and subcultures in which the gap between male and female roles is especially wide. And when social and economic conditions make it necessary for boys to take over "feminine" tasks, their personalities and behaviors are less stereotyped.

For example, in Nyansongo, a small agricultural settlement in Kenya, mothers work 4 to 5 hours a day in the gardens. They assign the care of young children, the tending of the cooking fire, and the washing of dishes to older siblings. Because children of both sexes perform these duties, girls are relieved of total responsibility for "feminine" tasks and have more time to interact with agemates. Their greater independence leads them to score higher than girls of other village and tribal cultures in dominance, assertiveness, and playful roughhousing. In contrast, boys' caregiving responsibilities mean that they often engage in help-giving and emotional support (Whiting & Edwards, 1988a).

Do these findings suggest that boys in Western cultures should be assigned more "cross-gender" tasks? The consequences of doing so are not straightforward. Research shows that when fathers hold traditional gender-role beliefs and their sons engage in "feminine" housework, boys experience strain in the father–child relationship, feel stressed by their responsibilities, and judge themselves as less competent (McHale et al., 1990). So parental values may need to be consistent with task assignments for children to benefit.

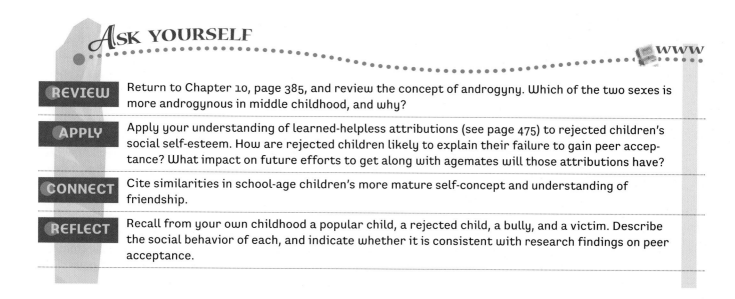

ASK YOURSELF

www

REVIEW   Return to Chapter 10, page 385, and review the concept of androgyny. Which of the two sexes is more androgynous in middle childhood, and why?

APPLY   Apply your understanding of learned-helpless attributions (see page 475) to rejected children's social self-esteem. How are rejected children likely to explain their failure to gain peer acceptance? What impact on future efforts to get along with agemates will those attributions have?

CONNECT   Cite similarities in school-age children's more mature self-concept and understanding of friendship.

REFLECT   Recall from your own childhood a popular child, a rejected child, a bully, and a victim. Describe the social behavior of each, and indicate whether it is consistent with research findings on peer acceptance.

Family Influences

As children move into school, peer, and community contexts, the parent–child relationship changes. We will see that a gradual lessening of direct control supports development, as long as it is built on continuing parental warmth and involvement.

Our discussion will also reveal that families in industrialized nations have become more diverse. Today, there are fewer births per family unit, more lesbian and gay parents who are open about their sexual orientation, and more never-married parents. In addition, transitions in family life over the past several decades—a dramatic rise in marital breakup, remarried parents, and employed mothers—have reshaped the family system.

As you consider this array of family forms, think back to Bronfenbrenner's ecological systems theory. Note how children's well-being continues to depend on the quality of family interaction, which is sustained by supportive ties to kin and community and favorable policies in the larger culture.

Parent–Child Relationships

In middle childhood, the amount of time children spend with parents declines dramatically. The child's growing independence means that parents must deal with new issues. "I've struggled with how many chores to assign, how much allowance to give, whether their friends are good influences, and what to do about problems at school," Rena remarked. "And then there's the challenge of how to keep track of them when they're out or even when they're home and I'm not there to see what's going on."

Although parents face new concerns, child rearing becomes easier for those who established an authoritative style during the early years. Reasoning works more effectively with school-age children because of their greater capacity for logical thinking and their increased respect for parents' expert knowledge (Collins, Madsen, & Susman-Stillman, 2002). Of course, older children sometimes use their cognitive powers to bargain and negotiate. "Mom," Joey pleaded for the third time, "if you let Terry and me go to the mall tonight, I'll rake all the leaves in the yard. I promise."

Fortunately, parents can appeal to the child's better-developed sense of self-esteem, humor, and morality to resolve these difficulties. "Joey, you have a test tomorrow," Rena responded. "You'll be unhappy at the results if you stay out late and don't study. Come on, no more wheeler-dealering!"

As children demonstrate that they can manage daily activities and responsibilities, effective parents gradually shift control from adult to child. This does not mean that they let go entirely. Instead, they engage in **coregulation,** a form of supervision in which they exercise general oversight while permitting children to be in charge of moment-by-moment decision making. Coregulation grows out of a warm, cooperative relationship between parent and child—one based on give-and-take and mutual respect. Parents must guide and monitor from a distance and effectively communicate expectations when they are with their children. And children must inform parents of their whereabouts, activities, and problems so parents can intervene when necessary (Maccoby, 1984). Coregulation supports and protects children while preparing them for adolescence, when they will make many important decisions themselves.

Although school-age children often press for greater independence, they also know how much they need their parents' support. In one study, fifth and sixth graders described parents as the most influential people in their lives. They often turned to their parents for affection, advice, enhancement of self-worth, and assistance with everyday problems (Furman & Buhrmester, 1992). And in a longitudinal survey of more than 13,000 nationally representative U.S. parents, those who were warm and involved, monitored their child's activities, and avoided coercive discipline were more likely to have academically and socially competent children, regardless of ethnicity, SES, and marital status. Furthermore, using these authoritative strategies in middle childhood predicted reduced engagement in antisocial behavior when children reached adolescence (Amato & Fowler, 2002).

Siblings

In addition to parents and friends, siblings are important sources of support for school-age children. Yet sibling rivalry tends to increase in middle childhood. As children participate in a wider range of activities, parents often compare siblings' traits and accomplishments. The child who gets less parental affection, more disapproval, or fewer material resources is likely to be resentful and show poorer adjustment over time (Brody, Stoneman, & McCoy, 1994; Dunn, 2002b).

When siblings are close in age, parental comparisons are more frequent, resulting in more quarreling, antagonism, and adjustment difficulties. This effect strengthens when fathers prefer one child. Perhaps because fathers usually spend less time with children, their favoritism is more noticeable and triggers greater anger (Brody, Stoneman, & McCoy, 1992; Brody et al., 1992). Furthermore, a survey of a nationally representative sample of nearly 23,000 Canadian children revealed that differential treatment of siblings increases when parents are under stress—due to financial problems, marital conflict, large family size, or single parenthood (Jenkins, Rasbash, & O'Connor, 2003). When other pressures drain their energies, parents become less careful about being fair and more responsive to personal preferences for one child over another.

Although sibling rivalry tends to increase in middle childhood, siblings also provide one another with emotional support and help with difficult tasks.

Siblings often take steps to reduce rivalry by striving to be different from one another. For example, two brothers I know deliberately selected different athletic pursuits and musical instruments. If the older one did especially well at an activity, the younger one did not want to try it. Of course, parents can reduce these effects by making an effort not to compare children. But some feedback about their competencies is inevitable, and as siblings attempt to win recognition for their own uniqueness, they shape important aspects of each other's development.

Although conflict rises, most school-age siblings rely on one another for companionship and assistance. When researchers asked siblings about shared daily activities, children mentioned that older siblings often helped younger siblings with academic and peer challenges. And both offered one another help with family issues (Tucker, McHale, & Crouter, 2001). But for siblings to reap these benefits, parental encouragement of warm sibling ties is vitally important. The warmer their relationship, the more siblings resolve disagreements constructively and turn to one another for emotional support (Howe et al., 2001; Ram & Ross, 2001). Finally, when siblings feel affection for one another, the older sibling's academic and social competence tends to "rub off on" the younger sibling (Brody & Murry, 2001).

One-Child Families

Although sibling relationships bring many benefits, they are not essential for normal development. Contrary to popular belief, only children are not spoiled. Instead, they are advantaged in some respects. North American children growing up in one-child families are higher in self-esteem and achievement motivation. Consequently, they do better in school and attain higher levels of education (Falbo, 1992). One reason may be that only children have somewhat closer relationships with parents, who exert more pressure for mastery and accomplishment. Furthermore, only children have just as many close, high-quality friends as children with siblings. However, they tend to be less well accepted in the peer group, perhaps because they have not had opportunities to learn effective conflict-resolution strategies from sibling interactions (Kitzmann, Cohen, & Lockwood, 2002).

Favorable development also characterizes only children in China, where a one-child family policy has been strictly enforced in urban areas for two decades to control overpopulation. Compared with agemates who have siblings, Chinese only children are advanced in cognitive development and academic achievement (Falbo & Poston, 1993; Jiao, Ji, & Jing, 1996). They also feel more emotionally secure, perhaps because government disapproval promotes tension in families with more than one child (Yang et al., 1995). Although many Chinese adults remain convinced that the one-child family policy breeds self-centered "little emperors," Chinese only children do not differ from children with siblings in social skills and peer acceptance (Chen, Rubin, & Li, 1995).

Gay and Lesbian Families

Several million American and thousands of Canadian gay men and lesbians are parents, most through previous heterosexual marriages, some through adoption, and a growing number through reproductive technologies (Ambert, 2003; Patterson, 2002). In the past, laws assuming that homosexuals could not be adequate parents led those who divorced a heterosexual partner to lose custody of their children. Today, a few American states and the nation of Canada hold that sexual orientation by itself is irrelevant to custody. Nevertheless, fierce prejudice against homosexual parents still prevails.

Research on homosexual parents and children is limited and based on small samples. Nevertheless, findings consistently indicate that gay and lesbian parents are as committed to and effective at child rearing as heterosexual parents (Patterson, 2001). Some evidence suggests that gay fathers are more consistent in setting limits and responding to their children's needs than heterosexual fathers, perhaps because gay men's less traditional gender identity fosters involvement with children (Bigner & Jacobsen, 1989). In lesbian families, quality of mother–child interaction is at least as positive as in heterosexual families. And children of lesbian mothers regard their mother's partner as very much a parent (Brewaeys et al., 1997). Whether born to or adopted by their parents or conceived through donor insemination, children in homosexual families are as well adjusted as other children. Also, the large majority are heterosexual (Allen & Burrell, 1996; Chan, Raboy, & Patterson, 1998; Golombok et al., 2003).

Homosexual parents are as committed to and as effective at child rearing as are heterosexual parents—and sometimes more so. Their children are well adjusted, and the large majority develop a heterosexual orientation.

Homosexual couples' joint involvement in parenting varies with the way children entered the family. When partners choose parenthood through adoption or reproductive technologies, they report more even division of child care and household tasks and happier couple relationships, which (as we saw in earlier chapters) favorably affect children's development (Chan, Rabo, & Patterson, 1998). When children resulted from a previous heterosexual relationship, the biological parent typically assumes a larger parenting role. These children face the same challenges as children in other stepfamilies—a topic we will address shortly.

Unfortunately, children of gay and lesbian parents are often teased by peers and shunned by their peers' parents (Morris, Balsam, & Rothblum, 2001). Still, they fare well emotionally and socially and may even, as a result, develop certain character strengths, such as empathy and tolerance (Ambert, 2003; Patterson, 2000). In sum, the evidence to date indicates that children of homosexuals can be distinguished from other children only by issues related to living in a nonsupportive society.

Never-Married Single-Parent Families

About 10 percent of American children and 5 percent of Canadian children live with a single parent who has never married and does not have a partner. Of these parents, about 90 percent are mothers, 10 percent fathers (U.S. Census Bureau, 2003b; Vanier Institute of the Family, 2004). More single women over age 30 in high-status occupations have become parents in recent years. However, they are still few in number, and little is known about their children's development.

In the United States, the largest group of never-married parents is African-American young women. Over 60 percent of births to black mothers in their twenties are to women without a partner, compared with 13 percent of births to white women (U.S. Census Bureau, 2003b). African-American women postpone marriage more and childbirth less than women in other American ethnic groups. Job loss, unemployment, and consequent inability of many black men to support a family have contributed to the number of African-American never-married, single-mother families.

Never-married black mothers tap the extended family, especially their own mothers and sometimes male relatives, for help in rearing their children (Gasden, 1999; Jayakody & Kalil,

2002). For about one-third, marriage occurs within 9 years after birth of the first child, not necessarily to the child's biological father (Wu, Bumpass, & Musick, 2001). These couples generally function like other first-marriage parents. Their children often are unaware that the father is a stepfather, and parents do not report the child-rearing difficulties usually associated with remarriage (Ganong & Coleman, 1994).

Still, single mothers find it harder to overcome poverty. About 47 percent of white and 59 percent of black mothers have a second child while unmarried. And they are far less likely than divorced mothers to receive paternal child support payments (Wu, Bumpass, & Musick, 2001). Consequently, many children in single-mother homes display adjustment problems associated with economic hardship (Lipman et al., 2002). Furthermore, children of never-married mothers who lack a father's warmth and involvement achieve less well in school and engage in more antisocial behavior than children in low-SES, first-marriage families (Coley, 1998). But marriage to the child's biological father benefits children only when the father is a reliable source of economic and emotional support. For example, when a mother pairs up with an antisocial father, her child is at far greater risk for conduct problems than if she had reared him alone (Jaffee et al., 2003). Overall, strengthening social support, education, and employment opportunities for low-income parents would greatly enhance the well-being of unmarried mothers and their children.

Divorce

Children's interactions with parents and siblings are affected by other aspects of family life. Joey and Lizzie's relationship, Rena told me, had been particularly negative only a few years before. Joey pushed, hit, taunted, and called Lizzie names. Although she tried to retaliate, she was no match for Joey's larger size. The arguments usually ended with Lizzie running in tears to her mother. Joey and Lizzie's fighting coincided with their parents' growing marital unhappiness. When Joey was 8 and Lizzie 5, their father, Drake, moved out.

The children were not alone in having to weather this traumatic event. Between 1960 and 1985, divorce rates in industrialized nations rose dramatically and then, in most countries, stabilized. The United States has the highest divorce rate in the world, Canada the sixth highest (see Figure 13.4). Of the 45 percent of American and 30 percent of Canadian marriages that end in divorce, half involve children. At any given time, one-fourth of American and one-fifth of Canadian children live in single-parent households. Although most reside with their mothers, the percentage in father-headed households has increased steadily, to about 12 percent in both nations (Hetherington & Stanley-Hagan, 2002; Statistics Canada, 2003b).

Children of divorce spend an average of 5 years in a single-parent home. For many, divorce leads to new family relationships. About two-thirds of divorced parents marry a second time. Half their children eventually experience a third major change—the end of their parent's second marriage (Hetherington & Kelly, 2003).

These figures reveal that divorce is not a single event in the lives of parents and children. Instead, it is a transition that leads to a variety of new living arrangements, accompanied by changes in housing, income, and family roles and responsibilities. Since the 1960s, many studies have reported that marital breakup is quite stressful for children (Amato & Booth, 2000). But research also reveals great individual differences. How well children fare depends on many factors: the custodial parent's psychological health, the child's characteristics, and social supports within the family and surrounding community.

IMMEDIATE CONSEQUENCES ● "Things were worst during the period in which Drake and I decided to separate," Rena reflected. "We fought over division of our belongings and the custody of the children, and the kids suffered. Sobbing, Lizzie told

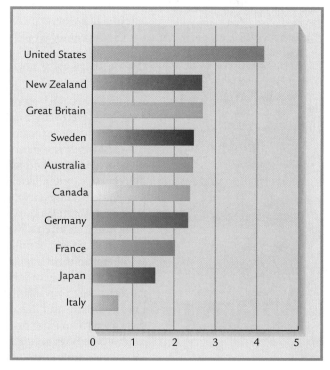

FIGURE 13.4

Divorce rates in 10 industrialized nations.

The U.S. divorce rate is the highest in the industrialized world, far exceeding divorce rates in other countries. The Canadian divorce rate is the sixth highest. (Australian Bureau of Statistics, 2003; Statistics Canada, 2003b; U.S. Census Bureau, 2003b; United Nations, 2001.)

me she was 'sorry she made Daddy go away.' Joey kicked and threw things at home and didn't do his work at school. In the midst of everything, I could hardly deal with their problems. We had to sell the house; I couldn't afford it alone. And I needed a better-paying job."

Rena's description captures conditions in many newly divorced households. Family conflict often rises as parents try to settle disputes over children and possessions. Once one parent moves out, additional events threaten supportive interactions between parents and children. Mother-headed households typically experience a sharp drop in income. In Canada and the United States, the majority of divorced mothers with young children live in poverty, getting less than the full amount of child support from the absent father or none at all (Children's Defense Fund, 2003; Statistics Canada, 2003b). They often have to move to new housing for economic reasons, reducing supportive ties to neighbors and friends.

The transition from marriage to divorce typically leads to high maternal stress, depression, and anxiety and to a disorganized family situation (Hope, Power, & Rodgers, 1999; Marks & Lambert, 1998). "Meals and bedtimes were at all hours, the house didn't get cleaned, and I stopped taking Joey and Lizzie on weekend outings," said Rena. As children react with distress and anger to their less secure home lives, discipline may become harsh and inconsistent. Contact with noncustodial fathers often decreases over time (Hetherington & Kelly, 2003; Lamb, 1999). When fathers see their children only occasionally, they are inclined to be permissive and indulgent. This often conflicts with the mother's style of parenting and makes her task of managing the child on a day-to-day basis even more difficult.

The more parents argue and fail to provide children with warmth, involvement, and consistent guidance, the poorer children's adjustment (Martinez & Forgatch, 2002; Pruett et al., 2003). At the same time, reactions vary with children's age, temperament, and sex.

Children's Age. Five-year-old Lizzie's fear that she caused her father to leave home is not unusual. The cognitive immaturity of preschool and early school-age children makes it difficult for them to grasp the reasons behind their parents' separation. Younger children often blame themselves and take the marital breakup as a sign that both parents may abandon them (Pryor & Rogers, 2001). They may whine and cling, displaying intense separation anxiety.

Older children can better understand the reasons behind their parents' divorce, which may reduce some of their pain. Still, many school-age and adolescent youngsters react strongly, particularly when parental conflict is high and supervision of children is low. Escaping into undesirable peer activities—such as running away, truancy, early sexual activity, and delinquency—and poor school achievement are common (Hetherington & Stanley-Hagan, 1999; Simons & Chao, 1996).

However, not all older children react this way. For some—especially the oldest child in the family—divorce can trigger more mature behavior. These youngsters may willingly take on extra burdens, such as household tasks, care and protection of younger siblings, and emotional support of a depressed, anxious mother. But if these demands are too great, older children may eventually become resentful and withdraw into some of the destructive behavior patterns just described (Hetherington, 1995, 1999a).

Children's Temperament and Sex. When temperamentally difficult children are exposed to stressful life events and inadequate parenting, their problems are magnified (Lengua et al., 2000). In contrast, easy children are less often targets of parental anger and also cope better with adversity.

These findings help us understand sex differences in response to divorce. Girls sometimes respond as Lizzie did, with internalizing reactions, such as crying, self-criticism, and withdrawal. More often, children of both sexes show demanding, attention-getting, acting-out behavior. But in mother-custody families, boys are at slightly greater risk for poor academic achievement and emotional adjustment (Amato, 2001). Recall from Chapter 10 that boys are more active and non-compliant—behaviors that increase with exposure to parental conflict and inconsistent discipline. Research reveals that long before the marital breakup, many sons of divorcing couples were impulsive and defiant—behaviors that may have contributed to as well as been caused by their parents' marital problems (Hetherington, 1999a; Shaw, Winslow, & Flanagan, 1999). As a result, these boys entered the period of turmoil surrounding divorce with reduced capacity to cope with family stress.

Perhaps because their behavior is more unruly, boys of divorcing parents receive less emotional support from mothers, teachers, and peers. After divorce, children who are challenging to rear generally get worse (Hanson, 1999; Morrison & Coiro, 1999). And as Joey's behavior toward Lizzie illustrates, the coercive cycles of interaction between distressed children and their divorced mothers soon spread to sibling relations (MacKinnon, 1989).

LONG-TERM CONSEQUENCES ● Rena eventually found better-paying work and gained control over the daily operation of the household. Her own feelings of anger and rejection also declined. And after several meetings with a counselor, Rena and Drake realized the harmful impact of their quarreling on Joey and Lizzie. Drake visited regularly and handled Joey's disruptiveness with firmness and consistency. Soon Joey's school performance improved, his behavior problems subsided, and both children seemed calmer and happier.

Most children show improved adjustment by 2 years after divorce. Yet overall, children and adolescents of divorced parents continue to score slightly lower than children of continuously married parents in academic achievement, self-esteem, social competence, and emotional and behavior problems (Amato, 2001). For some, persisting difficulties translate into poor adjustment in adulthood. Children with difficult temperaments are more likely to drop out of school, to be depressed, and to engage in antisocial behavior in adolescence. And divorce is linked to problems with sexuality and development of intimate ties. Young people who experienced parental divorce—especially more than once—display higher rates of early sexual activity, adolescent parenthood, and divorce in their adult lives (Wolfinger, 2000).

The overriding factor in positive adjustment following divorce is effective parenting—in particular, how well the custodial parent handles stress and shields the child from family conflict and the extent to which each parent uses authoritative child rearing (Leon, 2003; Wolchik et al., 2000). Contact with fathers is also important. For girls, a good father–child relationship protects against early sexual activity and unhappy romantic involvements. For boys, it affects overall psychological wellbeing. In fact, several studies indicate that outcomes for sons are better when the father is the custodial parent (Clarke-Stewart & Hayward, 1996; McLanahan, 1999). Fathers' greater economic security and image of authority seem to help them engage in effective parenting with sons. And boys in father-custody families may benefit from greater involvement of both parents, since noncustodial mothers participate more in their children's lives than noncustodial fathers.

After parents divorce, children in mother-custody homes who also stay involved with their fathers fare better in development. Boys often adjust more favorably when the father is the custodial parent.

Although divorce is painful for children, remaining in a high-conflict intact family is worse than making the transition to a low-conflict, single-parent household (Emery, 1999; Hetherington, 1999b). However, more parents today are divorcing because they are moderately (rather than extremely) dissatisfied with their relationship. Research suggests that children in these low-discord homes are especially puzzled and upset. Perhaps these youngsters' inability to understand the marital breakup and grief over the loss of a seemingly happy home life explain why the adjustment problems of children of divorce have intensified in recent years (Amato, 2001; Reifman et al., 2001).

Regardless of the extent of parents' friction, those who set aside their disagreements and support one another in their child-rearing roles greatly increase the chances that their children will grow up competent, stable, and happy. Caring extended-family members, teachers, siblings, and friends also reduce the likelihood that divorce will result in long-term difficulties (DeGarmo & Forgatch, 1999; Lussier et al., 2002).

DIVORCE MEDIATION, JOINT CUSTODY, AND CHILD SUPPORT ● Awareness that divorce is highly stressful for children and families has led to community-based services aimed at helping them through this difficult time. One such service is **divorce mediation,** a series of meetings between divorcing adults and a trained professional aimed at reducing family conflict, including legal battles over property division and child custody. Research reveals that mediation increases out-of-court settlements, cooperation and involvement of both parents in child rearing, and parents' and children's feelings of well-being (Emery, 2001). In one study, parents who had resolved disputes through mediation were still more involved in their children's lives 12 years later (Emery et al., 2001).

To further encourage both parents to remain involved with children, courts today more often award **joint custody**, which grants the mother and father equal say in important decisions about the child's upbringing. In most instances, children reside with one parent and see the other on a fixed schedule, much like the typical sole-custody situation. But in other cases, parents share physical custody, and children move between homes and sometimes between schools and peer groups. These transitions can introduce a new kind of instability that is especially hard on some children. Joint-custody parents report little conflict, and fortunately so, since the success of the arrangement depends on parental cooperation. And their children—regardless of living arrangements—tend to be better adjusted than their counterparts in sole maternal-custody homes (Bauserman, 2002).

Finally, many single-parent families depend on child support from the absent parent to relieve financial strain. U.S. states and Canadian provinces have procedures for withholding wages from parents who fail to make these payments. Although child support is usually not enough to lift a single-parent family out of poverty, it can ease the burden substantially. An added benefit is that fathers are more likely to maintain contact with noncustodial children if they pay child support (Garfinkel & McLanahan, 1995). Applying What We Know below summarizes ways to help children adjust to their parents' divorce.

Applying WHAT WE Know / Helping Children Adjust to Their Parents' Divorce

SUGGESTION	EXPLANATION
Shield children from conflict.	Witnessing intense parental conflict is very damaging to children. If one parent insists on expressing hostility, children fare better if the other parent does not respond in kind.
Provide children with as much continuity, familiarity, and predictability as possible.	Children adjust better during the period surrounding divorce when their lives have some stability—for example, the same school, bedroom, baby-sitter, playmates, and daily schedule.
Explain the divorce and tell children what to expect.	Children are more likely to develop fears of abandonment if they are not prepared for their parents' separation. They should be told that their mother and father will not be living together anymore, which parent will be moving out, and when they will be able to see that parent. If possible, mother and father should explain the divorce together. Parents should provide a reason for the divorce that the child can understand and assure the child that he is not to blame.
Emphasize the permanence of the divorce.	Fantasies of parents getting back together can prevent children from accepting the reality of their current life. Children should be told that the divorce is final and that they cannot change this fact.
Respond sympathetically to children's feelings.	Children need a supportive and understanding response to their feelings of sadness, fear, and anger. For children to adjust well, their painful emotions must be acknowledged, not denied or avoided.
Engage in authoritative parenting.	Provide children with affection and acceptance as well as reasonable demands for mature behavior and consistent, rational discipline. Parents who engage in authoritative parenting greatly reduce their children's risk of maladjustment following divorce.
Promote a continuing relationship with both parents.	When parents disentangle their lingering hostility toward the former spouse from the child's need for a continuing relationship with the other parent, children adjust well. Grandparents and other extended-family members can help by not taking sides.

Source: Teyber, 1992.

Blended Families

"If you get married to Wendell and Daddy gets married to Carol," Lizzie wondered aloud to Rena, "then I'll have two sisters and one more brother. And let's see, how many grandmothers and grand-fathers? Gosh, a lot!" exclaimed Lizzie. "But what will I call them all?" she asked, looking worried.

Life in a single-parent family is often temporary. Many parents remarry within a few years. Others cohabit, or share a sexual relationship and residence with a partner outside of marriage. Parent, stepparent, and children form a new family structure called a **blended, or reconstituted, family.** For some children, this expanded family network is a positive turn of events that brings greater adult attention. But most have more problems than children in stable, first-marriage families. Stepparents often introduce new child-rearing practices, and having to switch to new rules and expectations can be stressful. In addition, children often regard steprelatives as "intruders." But how well they adapt is, once again, related to the overall quality of family functioning (Hetherington & Kelly, 2002). This depends on which parent forms a new relationship, the child's age and sex, and the complexity of blended-family relationships. As we will see, older children and girls seem to have the hardest time.

MOTHER–STEPFATHER FAMILIES ● The most frequent form of blended family is a mother–stepfather arrangement, since mothers generally retain custody of the child. Boys tend to adjust quickly. They welcome a stepfather who is warm, who refrains from exerting his authority too quickly, and who offers relief from coercive mother–son cycles of interaction. Mothers' friction with sons also declines due to greater economic security, another adult to share household tasks, and an end to loneliness (Stevenson & Black, 1995). When stepfathers marry rather than cohabit, they are more involved in parenting. Perhaps men who choose to marry a mother with children are more interested in and skilled at child rearing (Hofferth & Anderson, 2003). Girls, however, often have difficulty with their custodial mother's remarriage. Stepfathers disrupt the close mother–daughter ties that often develop in single-parent families, and girls often react to the new arrangement with sulky, resistant behavior (Bray, 1999).

Note, however, that age affects these findings. Older school-age children and adolescents of both sexes display more irresponsible, acting out behavior than their peers not in stepfamilies (Hetherington & Stanley-Hagan, 2000). Parenting in stepfamilies—particularly those with stepsiblings—is highly challenging. Some parents are warmer and more involved with their biological children than with their stepchildren. Older children are more likely to notice and challenge unfair treatment. And adolescents often view the new stepparent as a threat to their freedom, especially if they experienced little parental monitoring in the single-parent family. Still, many teenagers have good relationships with both fathers—a circumstance linked to more favorable development (White & Gilbreth, 2001).

FATHER–STEPMOTHER FAMILIES ● Remarriage of noncustodial fathers often leads to reduced contact with their biological children, as they tend to withdraw from their "previous" families (Dunn, 2002). When fathers have custody, children typically react negatively to remarriage. One reason is that children living with fathers often start out with more problems. Perhaps the biological mother could no longer handle the difficult child (usually a boy), so the father and his new wife are faced with a youngster who has behavior problems. In other instances, the father is granted custody because of a very close relationship with the child, and his remarriage disrupts this bond (Buchanan, Maccoby, & Dornbusch, 1996).

Girls, especially, have a hard time getting along with their stepmothers. Sometimes (as just mentioned) this occurs because the girl's relationship with her father is threatened by the remarriage. In addition, girls occasionally become entangled in loyalty conflicts between their two mother figures. But the longer girls live in father–stepmother households, the more positive their interaction with stepmothers becomes (Hetherington & Jodl, 1994). With time and patience they do adjust, and eventually girls benefit from the support of a second mother figure.

SUPPORT FOR BLENDED FAMILIES ● Family life education and counseling can help parents and children in blended families adapt to the complexities of their new circumstances.

Effective approaches encourage stepparents to move into their new roles gradually by first building a friendly relationship with the child. Only when a warm bond has formed between stepparents and stepchildren is more active parenting possible (Visher, Visher, & Pasley, 2003). In addition, counselors can offer couples help in forming a "parenting coalition" through which they cooperate and provide consistency in child rearing. By limiting loyalty conflicts, this allows children to benefit from stepparent relationships and increased diversity in their lives.

Unfortunately, many children do not have a chance to settle into a happy blended family because the divorce rate for second marriages is even higher than that for first marriages. The more marital transitions children experience, the greater their difficulties (Dunn, 2002a). Parents with antisocial tendencies and poor child-rearing skills are particularly likely to have several divorces and remarriages. These families usually require prolonged, intensive therapy.

Maternal Employment and Dual-Earner Families

Today, North American single and married mothers are in the labor force in nearly equal proportions, and more than three-fourths of those with school-age children are employed (Statistics Canada, 2003f; U.S. Census Bureau, 2003b). In Chapter 7, we saw that the impact of maternal employment on early development depends on the quality of child care and the continuing parent–child relationship. This same conclusion applies during later years.

MATERNAL EMPLOYMENT AND CHILD DEVELOPMENT ● Mothers who enjoy their work and remain committed to parenting have children who show especially positive adjustment—higher self-esteem, more positive family and peer relations, less gender-stereotyped beliefs, and better grades in school. Girls, especially, profit from the image of female competence. Regardless of SES, daughters of employed mothers perceive women's roles as involving more freedom of choice and satisfaction and are more achievement- and career-oriented (Hoffman, 2000).

These benefits result from parenting practices. Employed mothers who value their parenting role are more likely to engage in authoritative child rearing and coregulation (see page 492). Also, children in dual-earner households devote more daily hours to doing homework under parental guidance and participate more in household chores. And maternal employment leads fathers to take on greater child-care responsibility, with a small but increasing number staying home full-time (Gottfried, Gottfried, & Bathurst, 2002; Hoffman & Youngblade, 1999). More paternal contact is related to higher intelligence and achievement, mature social behavior, and flexible gender-role attitudes (Gottfried, 1991; Radin, 1994).

However, when employment places heavy demands on the mother's schedule, children are at risk for ineffective parenting. Working long hours and spending little time with school-age children are associated with less favorable adjustment (Moorehouse, 1991). In contrast, part-time employment and flexible work schedules seem to have benefits for children of all ages, probably because these arrangements prevent work–family role conflict, thereby helping parents meet children's needs (Frederiksen-Goldsen & Sharlach, 2000).

SUPPORT FOR EMPLOYED PARENTS AND THEIR FAMILIES ● In dual-earner families, the husband's willingness to share responsibilities helps the mother engage in effective parenting. If the father helps very little or not at all, the mother carries a double load, at home and at work, leading to fatigue, distress, and little time and energy for children.

Employed mothers and dual-earner parents need assistance from work settings and communities in their child-rearing roles. Part-time employment, flexible schedules, job sharing, and paid leave when children are ill help parents juggle the demands of work and child rearing. Equal pay and employment opportunities for women are also important. Because these policies enhance financial status and morale, they improve the way mothers feel and behave when they arrive home at the end of the working day.

CHILD CARE FOR SCHOOL-AGE CHILDREN ● High-quality child care is vital for parents' peace of mind and children's well-being, even during middle childhood. An estimated 2.4

million 5- to 13-year-olds in the United States and several hundred thousand in Canada are **self-care children,** who regularly look after themselves during after-school hours. Self-care rises dramatically with age, from 3 percent of 5- to 7-year-olds to 33 percent of 11- to 13-year-olds. It also increases with SES, perhaps because of the greater safety of higher-income suburban neighborhoods. But when lower-SES parents must use self-care because they lack alternatives, their children spend more hours on their own (Casper & Smith, 2002).

Some studies report that self-care children suffer from low self-esteem, antisocial behavior, poor academic achievement, and fearfulness, whereas others show no such effects. Children's maturity and the way they spend their time seem to explain these contradictions. Among younger school-age children, those who spend more hours alone have more adjustment difficulties (Vandell & Posner, 1999). As children become old enough to look after themselves, those who have a history of authoritative child rearing, are monitored from a distance by parental telephone calls, and have regular after-school chores appear responsible and well adjusted. In contrast, children left to their own devices are more likely to bend to peer pressures and engage in antisocial behavior (Steinberg, 1986).

In this after-school program in Los Angeles, children spend time productively and enjoyably while their parents are at work. A community volunteer assists children with learning and completing homework. Children who attend such programs have better work habits and school grades and fewer behavior problems.

Before age 9 or 10, most children need supervision because they are not yet competent to deal with emergencies (Galambos & Maggs, 1991). But throughout middle childhood and early adolescence, attending after-school programs with well-trained staffs, generous adult–child ratios, positive adult–child communication, and stimulating activities is linked to better social skills and emotional adjustment (Pierce, Hamm, & Vandell, 1999). And low-SES children who participate in "after-care" enrichment activities (scouting, music, or art lessons) show special benefits, including better work habits, higher school grades, and fewer behavior problems (Posner & Vandell, 1994, 1999).

Unfortunately, good programs are in especially short supply in inner-city neighborhoods. In one survey of inner-city 10- to 14-year-olds, the vast majority did not participate in after-care activities or lessons of any kind. Instead, they watched TV and "hung out" for four or more hours each day (Shann, 2001). A special need exists for well-planned programs in these areas—ones that provide safe environments, enjoyable, skill-building activities, and warm relationships with adults.

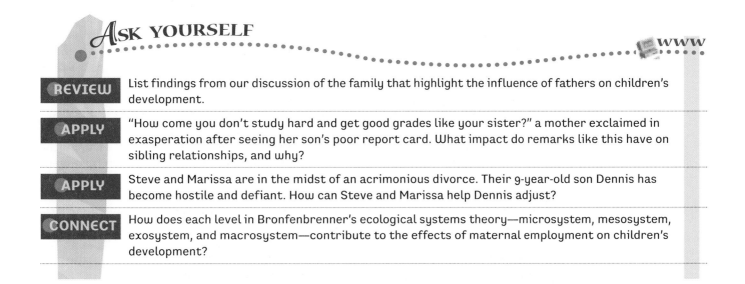

ASK YOURSELF

www

REVIEW List findings from our discussion of the family that highlight the influence of fathers on children's development.

APPLY "How come you don't study hard and get good grades like your sister?" a mother exclaimed in exasperation after seeing her son's poor report card. What impact do remarks like this have on sibling relationships, and why?

APPLY Steve and Marissa are in the midst of an acrimonious divorce. Their 9-year-old son Dennis has become hostile and defiant. How can Steve and Marissa help Dennis adjust?

CONNECT How does each level in Bronfenbrenner's ecological systems theory—microsystem, mesosystem, exosystem, and macrosystem—contribute to the effects of maternal employment on children's development?

Some Common Problems of Development

Throughout our discussion we have considered a variety of stressful experiences that place children at risk for future problems. In the following sections we touch on two more areas of concern: school-age children's fears and anxieties and the devastating consequences of child sexual abuse. Finally, we review factors that help school-age children cope effectively with stress.

Fears and Anxieties

Although fears of the dark, thunder and lightning, animals, and supernatural beings persist into middle childhood, older children's anxieties are also directed toward new concerns. As children begin to understand the realities of the wider world, the possibility of personal harm (being robbed, stabbed, or shot) and media events (war and disasters) often trouble them. Other common worries include academic failure, separation from parents, parents' health, physical injuries, the possibility of dying, and peer rejection. (Muris et al., 2000; Silverman, La Greca, & Wasserstein, 1995). Often children mull over frightening thoughts at bedtime, so nighttime fears actually increase between ages 7 and 9 (Muris et al., 2001).

Children's fears are shaped, in part, by their culture. Children in Western nations mention exposure to negative information, especially on television, as the most common source of their fears, followed by direct exposure to frightening events (Muris et al., 2001). And in China, where self-restraint and complying with social standards are highly valued, more children mention failure and adult criticism as salient fears than in Australia or the United States (Ollendick et al., 1996).

Most children handle their fears constructively, by talking about them with parents, teachers, and friends and by relying on effective coping strategies (see page 479). Consequently, fears decline at the end of middle childhood, especially for girls, who express more fears than boys at all ages (Gullone & King, 1997). But about 5 percent of school-age children develop an intense, unmanageable fear that leads to persistent avoidance of the feared situation, called a **phobia.** Children with inhibited temperaments are at high risk; they display phobias 5 to 6 times more often than other children (Ollendick, King, & Muris, 2002).

For example, in *school phobia,* children feel severe apprehension about attending school, often accompanied by physical complaints (dizziness, nausea, stomachaches, and vomiting) that disappear once the child is allowed to stay home. About one-third of children with school phobia are 5- to 7-year-olds, most of whom do not fear school so much as separation from their mother. The difficulty often can be traced to parental overprotection and encouragement of dependency. Family therapy and behavior modification procedures that reinforce the child for going to school help these children (Elliott, 1999).

Most cases of school phobia appear later, around 11 to 13, during the transition from middle childhood to adolescence. These youngsters usually find a particular aspect of school experience frightening—an overcritical teacher, a school bully, or too much parental pressure for school success. Treating this form of school phobia may require a change in school environment or parenting practices. Firm insistence that the child return to school, along with training in how to cope with difficult situations, is also helpful (Blagg & Yule, 1996).

Severe childhood anxieties may also arise from harsh living conditions. In inner-city ghettos and in war-torn areas of the world, a great many children live in the midst of constant deprivation, chaos, and violence. As the Cultural Influences box on the following page reveals, these youngsters are at risk for long-term emotional distress and behavior problems. Finally, as we saw in our discussion of child abuse in Chapter 10, too often violence and other destructive acts become part of adult–child relationships. During middle childhood, child sexual abuse increases.

Cultural Influences

The Impact of Ethnic and Political Violence on Children

Violence stemming from ethnic and political tensions is increasingly being felt around the world. Children's experiences under armed conflict and terrorism are diverse. Some may participate in the fighting, either because they are forced or because they want to please adults. Others are kidnapped, assaulted, and tortured. Those who are bystanders often come under direct fire and may be killed or physically maimed for life. And many watch in horror as family members, friends, and neighbors flee, are wounded, or die. During the past decade, wars have left 4 to 5 million children physically disabled, 12 million homeless, and more than 1 million separated from their parents (Stichick, 2001). Half of all casualties of worldwide conflict are children.

When war and social crises are temporary, most children are easily comforted and do not show long-term emotional difficulties. But chronic danger requires children to make substantial adjustments, and their psychological functioning can be seriously impaired. Many children of war lose their sense of safety, become desensitized to violence, are haunted by terrifying intrusive memories, and adopt a pessimistic view of the future. Aggressive and antisocial behavior often increases (Muldoon & Cairns, 1999). These outcomes appear to be culturally

universal, appearing among children from every war zone studied—from Iran, Bosnia, Rwanda, and Afghanistan to the West Bank and Gaza Strip (Garbarino, Andreas, & Vorrasi, 2002).

Parental affection and reassurance are the best protection against lasting problems. When parents offer security and serve as role models of calm emotional strength, most children can withstand even extreme war-related violence (Smith et al., 2001). Children who are separated from parents must rely on help from their communities. Preschool and school-age orphans in Eritrea who were placed in residential settings where they could form close emotional ties with at least one adult showed less emotional stress 5 years later than orphans placed in impersonal settings (Wolff & Fesseha, 1999). Educational programs are powerful safeguards, too, providing children with a sense of consistency in their lives along with teacher and peer supports.

The September 11, 2001, terrorist attack on the World Trade Center caused some American children to experience extreme wartime violence firsthand. Children in Public School 31 in Brooklyn, New York, for example, stared out windows as planes rushed toward the towers, were engulfed in flames, and crumbled. Many worried about the safety of family members, and some lost them. In the aftermath, most expressed intense fears—for example,

that terrorists were in their neighborhoods and that planes flying overhead might smash into nearby buildings.

Unlike many war-traumatized children in the developing world, Public School 31 students received immediate intervention—a "trauma curriculum" in which they expressed their emotions through writing, drawing, and discussion and participated in experiences aimed at restoring trust and tolerance (Lagnado, 2001). Older children learned about the feelings of their Muslim classmates, the dire condition of children in Afghanistan, and ways to help victims as a means of overcoming a sense of helplessness.

When wartime drains families and communities of resources, international organizations must step in and help children. Efforts to preserve children's physical, psychological, and educational well-being may be the best way to stop the transmission of violence to the next generation.

These traumatized victims of air raids in Kabul, Afghanistan, witnessed the destruction of their neighborhoods and the maimings and deaths of family members and friends. The children draw pictures during a therapy session at a mental health hospital. One 7-year-old depicts several of his schoolmates, who died. Without special support from caring adults, the children are likely to have lasting emotional problems.

So there really was a monster in her bedroom.

For many kids, there's a real reason to be afraid of the dark. Each year in Indiana, there are thousands of substantiated cases of sexual abuse. (Not to mention the number that goes unreported.)
The trauma can be devastating for the child and for the family. So listen closely to the children around you. If you hear something

that you don't want to believe, perhaps you should. For information on child abuse prevention, contact: Dunebrook Prevent Child Abuse LaPorte County, 7451 Johnson Road, Michigan City, IN 46360. **1-800-897-0007**. Or visit **www.dunebrook.org.**

This public service announcement reminds adults that child sexual abuse, until recently regarded as a product of children's vivid imaginations, is a devastating reality.

Child Sexual Abuse

Until recently, child sexual abuse was viewed as a rare occurrence. When children came forward with it, adults usually did not take their claims seriously. In the 1970s, efforts by professionals along with media attention caused child sexual abuse to be recognized as a serious and widespread problem. About 90,000 cases in the United States and 14,000 cases in Canada were confirmed in the most recently reported year (Trocomé & Wolfe, 2002; U.S. Department of Health and Human Services, 2003b).

CHARACTERISTICS OF ABUSERS AND VICTIMS ● Sexual abuse is committed against children of both sexes but more often against girls. Most cases are reported in middle childhood, but sexual abuse also occurs at younger and older ages. Physical disabilities, especially those that lead adults to question a child's credibility, such as blindness, deafness, and mental retardation, increase the risk. Few children experience only a single episode. For some victims, the abuse begins early in life and continues for many years (Trickett & Putnam, 1998).

Generally, the abuser is a male—a parent or someone the parent knows well. Often it is a father, stepfather, or live-in boyfriend, somewhat less often an uncle or older brother. In a few instances, mothers are the offenders, more often with sons. If the abuser is a nonrelative, it is usually someone the child has come to know and trust (Kolvin & Trowell, 1996). Abusers make the child comply in a variety of distasteful ways, including deception, bribery, verbal intimidation, and physical force.

You may be wondering how any adult—especially a parent or close relative—could possibly violate a child sexually. Many offenders deny their own responsibility. They blame the abuse on the willing participation of a seductive youngster. Yet children are not capable of making a deliberate, informed decision to enter into a sexual relationship! Even at older ages, they are not free to say yes or no. Instead, the responsibility lies with abusers, who tend to have characteristics that predispose them toward sexual exploitation of children. As Table 13.2 shows, they have great difficulty controlling their impulses and may suffer from psychological disorders, including alcohol or drug addiction. Often they pick children who are unlikely to defend themselves or to be believed—those who are physically weak, emotionally deprived, socially isolated, or affected by disabilities, such as blindness, deafness, or mental retardation (Bolen, 2001).

Reported cases of child sexual abuse are linked to poverty, marital instability, and resulting weakening of family ties. Children who live in homes with a history of constantly changing characters—repeated marriages, separations, and new partners—are especially vulnerable. But

TABLE 13.2

Factors Related to Child Sexual Abuse

FACTOR	DESCRIPTION
Abuser	Usually a male and a member of the child's family. Finds children sexually arousing, has difficulty controlling impulses, rationalizes that the victim wants sex and will enjoy it, and has learned to believe that sexual abuse of others is appropriate. May have serious psychological disturbance, including alcohol or drug addiction, and may have experienced sexual abuse as a child.
Victim	More often female than male. Abusers tend to select children who seem like easy targets—ones who are physically weak, compliant in personality, emotionally needy, and socially isolated.
Family	Often associated with poverty and repeated marital breakup. However, abuse also occurs in relatively stable, middle-SES families.

middle-SES children in stable homes are also victims, although their abuse is more likely to remain undetected (Putnam, 2003).

CONSEQUENCES OF SEXUAL ABUSE ● The adjustment problems of child sexual abuse victims are often severe. Depression, low self-esteem, mistrust of adults, and anger and hostility can persist for years after the abusive episodes. Younger children frequently react with sleep difficulties, loss of appetite, and generalized fearfulness. Adolescents may run away and show suicidal reactions, substance abuse, and delinquency. At all ages, persistent abuse accompanied by force, violence, and a close relationship to the perpetrator (incest) has a more severe impact (Feiring, Taska, & Lewis, 1999; Tricket et al., 2001). And repeated sexual abuse, like physical abuse, is associated with central nervous system damage (see Chapter 10, page 393)—an outcome that increases the risk of lasting psychological disorders.

Sexually abused children frequently display sexual knowledge and behavior beyond their years. They have learned from their abusers that sexual overtures are acceptable ways to get attention and rewards. In adolescence, abused young people often become promiscuous and are at risk for early childbearing. In adulthood, child sexual abuse is related to increased arrest rates for sex crimes (mostly against children) and prostitution (Friedrich et al., 2001; Salter et al., 2003). Furthermore, women who were sexually abused are likely to choose partners who abuse them and their children. As mothers, they often engage in irresponsible and coercive parenting, including child abuse and neglect (Pianta, Egeland, & Erickson, 1989). In these ways, the harmful impact of sexual abuse is transmitted to the next generation.

PREVENTION AND TREATMENT ● Treating child sexual abuse is difficult. The reactions of family members—anxiety about harm to the child, anger toward the abuser, and sometimes hostility toward the victim for telling—can increase children's distress. Because sexual abuse typically appears in the midst of other serious family problems, long-term therapy with children and families usually is necessary (Olafson & Boat, 2000). The best way to reduce the suffering of victims is to prevent sexual abuse from continuing. Today, courts are prosecuting abusers more vigorously and taking children's testimony more seriously (see the Social Issues: Health box on page 506).

Educational programs that teach children to recognize inappropriate sexual advances and whom to turn to for help reduce the risk of abuse (Gibson & Leitenberg, 2000). Yet because of controversies over educating children about sexual abuse, few schools offer these interventions. New Zealand is the only country with a national, school-based prevention program targeting sexual abuse. In *Keeping Ourselves Safe,* children and adolescents learn that abusers are rarely strangers. Parent involvement ensures that home and school work together in teaching children self-protection skills. Evaluations reveal that virtually all New Zealand parents and children support the program and that it has helped many children avoid or report abuse (Briggs, 2002).

COURTESY OF THE NEW ZEALAND POLICE

In Keeping Ourselves Safe, New Zealand's national, school-based child abuse prevention program, teachers and police officers collaborate in teaching children to recognize abusive adult behaviors so they can take steps to protect themselves. Parents are informed about children's classroom learning experiences and encouraged to support and extend them at home.

Fostering Resilience In Middle Childhood

Throughout middle childhood—and other phases of development as well—children are confronted with challenging and sometimes threatening situations that require them to cope with psychological stress. In this trio of chapters, we have considered such topics as chronic illness, learning disabilities, achievement expectations, divorce, harsh living conditions and wartime trauma, and sexual abuse. Each taxes children's coping resources, creating serious risks for development.

Still, many studies indicate only a modest relationship between stressful life experiences and psychological disturbance in childhood (Garmezy, 1993). In our discussion in Chapter 4 of the long-term consequences of birth complications, we noted that some children overcome the combined effects of birth trauma, poverty, and a troubled family life. The same is true when we look at findings on school difficulties, family transitions, children of war, and child maltreatment.

Children's Eyewitness Testimony

Increasingly, children are being called on to testify in court cases involving child abuse and neglect, child custody, and other matters. Having to provide information on such topics can be difficult and traumatic. Almost always, children must report on highly stressful events, and they may have to speak against a parent or other relative to whom they feel loyal. In some family disputes, they may fear punishment for telling the truth. In addition, child witnesses are faced with an unfamiliar situation—at the very least an interview in the judge's chambers, and at most an open courtroom with judge, jury, spectators, and the possibility of unsympathetic cross-examination. Not surprisingly, these conditions can compromise the accuracy of children's recall.

Age Differences

Until recently, children younger than age 5 were rarely asked to testify, and not until age 10 were they assumed fully competent to do so. Yet as a result of societal reactions to rising rates of child abuse and difficulties in prosecuting perpetrators, legal requirements for child testimony have been relaxed in the United States and Canada. Children as young as age 3 frequently serve as witnesses (Ceci & Bruck, 1998).

Compared with preschoolers, school-age children are better at giving detailed descriptions of past experiences and at making accurate inferences about others' motives and intentions. Older children are also more resistant to misleading questions of the sort asked by attorneys when they probe for more information or, in cross-examination, try to influence the content of the child's response (Roebers & Schneider, 2001).

What makes younger children more prone to memory errors? First, responding to interview questions is challenging for children whose language competence is not well developed. They often are unaware when they do not understand, and they answer the question anyway. Second, when an adult asks specific questions ("Was he holding a screwdriver?"), younger children are more likely to agree, perhaps out of a desire to please. Third, preschoolers are especially poor at *source monitoring*—identifying where they got their knowledge.

Consequently, they often confuse what they hear with what actually occurred (Poole & Lindsay, 2001). Finally, younger children are less competent at reporting their autobiographical memories in the form of clear, orderly narratives. This causes them to omit information that they remember (Gordon, Baker-Ward, & Ornstein, 2001).

Nevertheless, when properly questioned, even preschoolers can recall personally relevant events accurately, including highly stressful events. In one study, children as young as 26 months who had experienced an emergency room visit after an accidental injury accurately recalled the event 2 years later (Peterson & Rideout, 1998).

Suggestibility

Yet court testimony often involves repeated interviews. When adults lead children by suggesting incorrect facts ("He touched you there, didn't he?"), they increase the likelihood of incorrect reporting among preschoolers and school-age children alike. Events that children fabricate in response to leading questions can be quite fantastic. In one study, after a visit to a doctor's office, children answered yes to questions about events that not only never occurred but also implied abuse—"Did the doctor lick your knee?" "Did the nurse sit on top of you?" (Ornstein et al., 1997).

By the time children appear in court, it is weeks, months, or even years after the occurrence of the target events. When a long delay is combined with suggestions about what happened and with stereotyping of the accused ("He's in jail because he's been bad"), children can easily be misled into giving false information (Ceci, Fitneva, & Gilstrap, 2003). To ease the task of providing testimony, special interviewing methods have been devised for children. In many sexual abuse cases, anatomically correct dolls are used to prompt children's recall. Although this method helps older children provide more detail about experienced events, it increases the suggestibility of preschoolers, who report physical and sexual contact that never happened (Goodman et al., 1999).

Interventions

Adults must prepare child witnesses so that they understand the courtroom process and know what to expect. In

This 11-year-old testifies in court, pointing to a location on a map where he witnessed an event. Older children are better at giving detailed accounts of past experiences and resisting attempts to bias their responses. At the same time, the accuracy of their testimony depends on the way they are questioned, how long ago events occurred, whether adults have tried to pressure them, and their understanding of and comfort with the courtroom process.

some places, "court schools" take children through the setting and give them an opportunity to role-play court activities. And when questioned, children can be encouraged to admit not knowing an answer rather than guessing or going along with what an adult expects. Practice interviews about unrelated events, in which children learn to provide the most accurate, detailed information possible on four categories of information—setting, participants, actions, and conversations—are helpful (Saywitz, Goodman, & Lyon, 2002). At the same time, legal professionals must reduce the risk of suggestibility—by limiting the number of times they question children and posing questions in nonleading ways.

If a child is likely to experience emotional trauma or later punishment (in a family dispute), then courtroom procedures can be adapted to protect them. For example, they can testify over closed-circuit TV so they do not have to face an abuser. When it is not wise for a child to participate directly, expert witnesses can provide testimony that reports on the child's psychological condition and includes important elements of the child's story. But for such testimony to be worthwhile, witnesses must be impartial and trained in how to question to minimize false reporting (Bruck, Ceci, & Hembrooke, 1998).

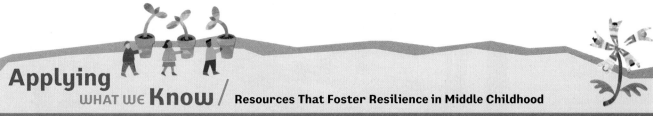

Applying WHAT WE Know / Resources That Foster Resilience in Middle Childhood

TYPE OF RESOURCE	DESCRIPTION
Personal	● Easygoing, sociable temperament ● Above-average intelligence ● Favorable self-esteem ● Persistence in the face of challenge and pleasure in mastery ● Good emotional self-regulation and flexible coping strategies
Family	● Warm, trusting relationship with at least one parent ● Authoritative child-rearing style ● Positive discipline, avoidance of coercive tactics ● Warm, supportive sibling relationships
School	● Teachers who are warm, helpful, and stimulating, who encourage students to collaborate, and who emphasize effort and self-improvement ● Lessons in tolerance and respect and codes against bullying, which promote positive peer relationships and gratifying friendships ● Extracurricular activities, including sports and social service pursuits, that strengthen physical, cognitive, and social skills ● High-quality after-school programs that protect children's safety and offer stimulating, skill-building activities
Community	● An adult—such as an extended-family member, teacher, or neighbor—who provides warmth and social support and is a positive coping model ● Stability of neighborhood residents and services—safe outdoor play areas, community centers, and religious organizations—that relieve parental stress and encourage families and neighbors to share leisure time. ● Youth groups—scouting, clubs, religious youth groups, and other organized activities—that promote positive peer relationships and prosocial behavior

Note: Just one or a few resources may be sufficient to foster resilience, since each resource strengthens others.
Sources: Conger & Conger, 2002; Masten, 2001; Pinderhughes et al., 2001; Seccombe, 2002.

Refer to Applying What We Know above for an overview of factors that promote *resilience*—the capacity to overcome adversity—during middle childhood.

Often just one or a few of these ingredients account for why one child is "stress-resilient" and another is not. Yet most of the time, personal and environmental factors are interconnected. Notice how each resource favoring resilience strengthens others. For example, safe, stable neighborhoods with family-friendly community services reduce parents' daily hassles and stress, thereby promoting good parenting (Pinderhughes et al., 2001). In contrast, unfavorable home and neighborhood experiences increase the chances that children will act in ways that expose them to further hardship. And when negative conditions pile up, such as marital discord, poverty, crowded living conditions, neighborhood violence, and abuse and neglect, the rate of maladjustment multiplies (Farrington & Loeber, 2000; Wyman et al., 1999).

Of great concern are children's violent acts. Violence committed in schools and communities by American children and adolescents with troubled lives has at times reached the level of atrocities—maimings and murders of adults and peers. Because children spend a great deal of time in school, the quality of their relationships with teachers and classmates strongly influences their social behavior (Henrich, Brown, & Aber, 1999).

Several highly effective school-based programs reduce violence and other antisocial acts by fostering social competence and supportive relationships. Among these is the *Resolving Conflict Creatively Program (RCCP),* which is used in more than 400 schools throughout the

Usually only one, or a few, factors account for why one child is resilient, whereas another fares poorly. But most of the time, one resource strengthens others. These girls, who are growing up in a low-income, inner-city neighborhood in Los Angeles, spend many free hours at a Boys and Girls Club. Enjoyable, constructive activities enhance their cognitive and social skills while reducing parental worries about their safety and well-being. As a result, parents engage in more effective child rearing, and children develop more favorably.

© AMY ETRA/PHOTOEDIT

United States, serving 175,000 students (Lantieri, 2003). RCCP provides children and adolescents with up to 51 hour-long lessons in emotional and social understanding and skills. Topics include expressing feelings, regulating anger, resolving social conflicts, cooperating, appreciating diversity, identifying and standing up against prejudice and bullying, and recognizing one's role in creating a more peaceful world. Compared with students receiving few or no lessons, second to sixth graders receiving substantial RCCP instruction less often misinterpreted others' acts as hostile, less often behaved aggressively, more often engaged in prosocial behavior, and more often gained in academic achievement. Two years of intervention, as opposed to just one, strengthened these outcomes (Aber et al., 1998). In unsafe neighborhoods, the program transforms schools into places of safety and mutual respect, where learning can occur.

RCCP, and other programs like it, underscore that academic and social development are closely connected; warm, caring ties with adults and peers promote progress in both domains. Throughout our discussion, we have seen how families, schools, communities, and society as a whole can enhance or undermine the school-age child's developing sense of competence. As the next three chapters reveal, young people whose childhood experiences helped them learn to control impulses, overcome obstacles, strive for self-direction, and respond considerately and sympathetically to others meet the challenges of the next period—adolescence—quite well.

Ask Yourself

WWW

REVIEW When children must testify in court cases, what factors increase the chances of accurate reporting?

APPLY Claire told her 6-year-old daughter to be very careful never to talk to or take candy from strangers. Why will Claire's directive not protect her daughter from sexual abuse?

CONNECT Explain how factors that promote resilience, listed on page 507, contribute to favorable adjustment following divorce.

REFLECT Describe a challenging time during your childhood. What aspects of the experience increased stress? What resources helped you cope with adversity?

Summary

Erikson's Theory: Industry versus Inferiority

What personality changes take place during Erikson's stage of industry versus inferiority?

● According to Erikson, children who successfully resolve the psychological conflict of **industry versus inferiority** develop the capacity to engage in productive work, learn the value of division of labor, and develop a sense of moral commitment and responsibility.

Self-Understanding

Describe school-age children's self-concept and self-esteem, and discuss factors that affect their achievement-related attributions.

● During middle childhood, children's self-concepts include personality traits, positive and negative characteristics, and **social comparisons.** Separate self-esteems become increasingly distinct and hierarchically organized. In addition, self-esteem declines over the early school years as children get more competence-related feedback and become capable of making social comparisons. Cultural forces also affect self-esteem, as illustrated by the influence of parents' gender-stereotyped beliefs on children's judgments of their competence at various school subjects. Authoritative child rearing is linked to favorable self-esteem.

● Research on achievement-related **attributions** has identified adult messages that affect children's academic self-esteem. Children with **mastery-oriented attributions** credit their successes to high ability and their failures to insufficient effort. They hold an incremental view of ability—that it can be improved by trying hard. In contrast, children with **learned helplessness** attribute their successes to luck and their failures to low ability. They hold a fixed view of ability—that it cannot be changed.

● Children who receive negative feedback about their ability are likely to develop learned helplessness. Supportive teachers and cultural valuing of effort increase the likelihood of a mastery-oriented approach.

● **Attribution retraining** encourages learned-helpless children to revise their failure-related attributions, thereby improving their self-evaluations and task performance. Teaching children to focus less on grades and more on mastery for its own sake also leads to gains in students' academic self-esteem and motivation.

Emotional Development

Cite changes in the expression and understanding of emotion in middle childhood.

● In middle childhood, self-conscious emotions of pride and guilt become clearly governed by personal responsibility. Experiencing intense shame can shatter children's overall sense of self-esteem.

● School-age children recognize that people can experience more than one emotion at a time. As a result, they have a better grasp of self-conscious emotions and ways to mask their feelings. They also attend to both facial and situational cues and to information about a person's past experiences in interpreting their feelings. Gains in perspective taking and emotional understanding lead empathy to increase in middle childhood.

● By the end of middle childhood, most children have an adaptive set of techniques for regulating emotion. They shift between **problem-centered coping** and **emotion-centered coping,** depending on the situation. Emotionally well-regulated children are optimistic, prosocial, and well liked by peers.

Understanding Others: Perspective Taking

How does perspective taking change in middle childhood?

● **Perspective taking** improves greatly over the school years, as Selman's five-stage sequence indicates. Cognitive maturity and experiences in which adults and peers encourage children to look at things from another's viewpoint support school-age children's perspective-taking skill. Good perspective takers show more positive social skills.

Moral Development

Describe changes in moral understanding during middle childhood, and summarize current recommendations for moral education in schools.

● By middle childhood, children follow internalized standards, so their need for adult oversight, modeling, and reinforcement declines. School-age children's concepts of **distributive justice** change from equality to merit to benevolence.

● Children also clarify and create linkages between moral rules and social conventions. In judging the seriousness of transgressions, they take into account the purpose of the rule; people's intentions, knowledge, and beliefs; and the context of their behavior. Stronger convictions about personal choice strengthen children's appreciation of individual rights, such as freedom of speech and religion.

● At present, moral education programs are narrowly focused. A comprehensive approach involves promoting four moral components: moral sensitivity, moral judgment, moral motivation, and moral character.

Peer Relations

How do peer sociability and friendship change in middle childhood?

● In middle childhood, peer interaction becomes more prosocial, and physical aggression declines. By the end of the school years, children organize themselves into **peer groups.** Although most children regard exclusion as wrong, they often direct hostility toward the "outgroup" and eject unwanted members. In groups with dominant, aggressive members, even mild-mannered children may support antisocial acts. Formal groups under the guidance of adults satisfy children's desire for group belonging while holding these negative behaviors in check.

● Friendships develop into mutual relationships based on trust. Children tend to select friends who are like themselves in age, sex, race, ethnicity, SES, personality, popularity, academic achievement, and prosocial behavior. Girls form closer, more exclusive friendships than boys.

Describe major categories of peer acceptance and ways to help rejected children.

● **Sociometric techniques** are used to distinguish four types of **peer acceptance:** (1) **popular children,** who are liked by many agemates; (2) **rejected children,** who are actively disliked; (3) **controversial children,** who are liked by some and disliked by others; and (4) **neglected children,** who arouse little reaction, either positive or negative, but are usually well adjusted.

● Two subtypes of popular children exist: **popular-prosocial children,** who are academically and socially competent, and **popular-antisocial children,** who generally are athletically skilled, highly aggressive boys who are poor students. Rejected children also fall into at least two subtypes: **rejected-aggressive children,** who show severe conduct problems, and **rejected-withdrawn children,** who are passive, socially awkward, and frequent targets of **peer victimization.** Both subgroups often experience lasting adjustment difficulties.

● Coaching in social skills, academic tutoring, and training in perspective taking and social problem solving have been used to help rejected youngsters. Teaching children to attribute peer difficulties to internal, changeable causes is also important. To produce lasting change, intervening in parent–child interaction is probably necessary.

Gender Typing

What changes in gender-stereotyped beliefs and gender identity take place during middle childhood?

● School-age children extend their awareness of gender stereotypes to personality traits and academic subjects, and girls discount their academic talent. Although children develop a more open-minded view of what males and females can do, they judge certain violations of appearance and behavior harshly and are especially intolerant when boys engage in these "cross-gender" acts.

● Boys strengthen their identification with the masculine role, whereas girls feel free to experiment with "opposite-gender" activities. Cultural distinctions between male and female roles and tasks assigned to children influence gender-typed behavior.

Family Influences

How do parent–child communication and sibling relationships change in middle childhood?

● Effective parents of school-age children engage in **coregulation,** exerting general oversight while permitting children to be in charge of moment-by-moment decision making. Coregulation depends on a cooperative relationship between parent and child.

● Sibling rivalry tends to increase as children participate in a wider range of activities and as parents compare their traits and accomplishments. Siblings often try to reduce this rivalry by striving to be different from one another. When siblings maintain warm bonds, they resolve disagreements constructively and provide one another with emotional support.

● Compared to children with siblings, only children have higher self-esteem, do better in school, and attain higher levels of education. Although only children form close, high-quality friendships, they are less well accepted in the peer group, perhaps because they have had fewer opportunities to resolve conflicts through sibling interactions.

How do children fare in gay and lesbian families and in single-parent, never-married families?

● Gay and lesbian parents are as committed to and effective at child rearing as heterosexuals. And their children are well adjusted, despite frequent unfavorable treatment from peers.

● The largest group of never-married parents is African-American young women, who postpone marriage more and childbirth less than all other American ethnic groups. Many children of never-married mothers display adjustment problems associated with economic hardship. When they lack a father's warmth and involvement, they achieve less well in school and engage in more antisocial behavior than children in first-marriage families.

What factors influence children's adjustment to divorce and blended family arrangements?

● Although all children experience painful emotional reactions during the period surrounding divorce, children with difficult temperaments and boys in mother-custody homes have more adjustment problems. Over time, children of divorce continue to score lower than children of continuously married parents on a variety of adjustment indicators. Problems with adolescent sexuality, early parenthood, and development of intimate ties surface at later ages.

● The overriding factor in positive adjustment following divorce is effective parenting. Contact with noncustodial fathers is important for children of both sexes, and outcomes for sons are better under father custody. Because **divorce mediation** helps parents resolve their disputes and cooperate in child rearing, it can help children adjust. The success of **joint custody** depends on parental cooperation, and children who experience it tend to fare better than children in sole maternal-custody homes.

● When divorced parents enter new relationships through cohabitation or remarriage, children must adapt to a **blended,** or **reconstituted, family.** How well they fare depends on which parent remarries and on the age and sex of the child. Girls, older school-age children and adolescents, and children in father–stepmother families have more adjustment problems.

How do maternal employment and life in dual-earner families affect children's development?

● When mothers enjoy their work and remain committed to parenting, maternal employment is associated with favorable consequences for children, including higher self-esteem, more positive family and peer relations, less gender-stereotyped beliefs, and better grades in school. In dual-earner families, the father's willingness to share child rearing is linked to many positive outcomes for children. Workplace supports, such as part-time employment and paid parental leave, help parents meet the demands of work and child rearing.

● **Self-care children** who are old enough to look after themselves, are monitored from a distance, and have a history of authoritative parenting appear responsible and well adjusted. In contrast, children left to their own devices are at risk for antisocial behavior. Children in high-quality after-school programs reap academic and social benefits.

Some Common Problems of Development

Cite common fears and anxieties in middle childhood.

● School-age children's fears are directed toward new concerns, including physical harm, media events, academic failure, parents' health, the possibility of dying, and peer rejection. Children with inhibited temperaments are at high risk for developing **phobias**, or intense, unmanageable fears. School phobia—severe apprehension about attending school—is an example. Severe anxiety can also result from harsh living conditions, such as constant violence.

Discuss factors related to child sexual abuse, its consequences for children's development, and its prevention and treatment.

● Child sexual abuse is generally committed by male family members, and more often against girls than against boys. Abusers have characteristics that predispose them toward sexual exploitation of children. Reported cases are linked to poverty and marital instability, but middle-SES children in stable homes are also victims. Adjustment problems of abused children often are severe. Common reactions are depression, low self-esteem, mistrust of adults, anger and hostility, suicidal reactions, and inappropriate sexual behavior.

● Because sexual abuse is related to other serious family problems, long-term therapy with children and families is usually necessary. Educational programs that teach children to recognize inappropriate sexual advances and whom to turn to for help reduce the risk of sexual abuse.

Cite factors that foster resilience in middle childhood.

● Overall, a modest relationship exists between stressful life experiences and psychological disturbance in childhood. Personal characteristics of children, a warm family life that includes authoritative parenting, and social supports at school and in the community are related to resilience in the face of stress. Often just one or a few resources favoring resilience are necessary because each strengthens others.

Important Terms and Concepts

attribution retraining (p. 476)
attributions (p. 474)
blended, or reconstituted, family (p. 499)
controversial children (p. 487)
coregulation (p. 492)
distributive justice (p. 481)
divorce mediation (p. 497)
emotion-centered coping (p. 479)
industry versus inferiority (p. 470)

joint custody (p. 498)
learned helplessness (p. 475)
mastery-oriented attributions (p. 475)
neglected children (p. 487)
peer acceptance (p. 487)
peer group (p. 485)
peer victimization (p. 489)
perspective taking (p. 480)
phobia (p. 502)

popular children (p. 487)
popular-antisocial children (p. 487)
popular-prosocial children (p. 487)
problem-centered coping (p. 479)
rejected children (p. 487)
rejected-aggressive children (p. 488)
rejected-withdrawn children (p. 488)
self-care children (p. 501)
social comparisons (p. 471)
sociometric techniques (p. 487)

For Further Information and Help

Consult the Companion Website for *Infants, Children, and Adolescents,* Fifth Edition, *(www.ablongman.com/berk),* where you will find the following resources for this chapter:

● **Chapter Objectives**
● **Flashcards** for studying important terms and concepts
● **Annotated Weblinks** to guide you in further research
● **Ask Yourself questions,** which you can answer and then check against a sample response

● **Suggested Readings**
● **Practice Tests** with immediate scoring and feedback

Milestones Development in Middle Childhood

AGE	PHYSICAL	COGNITIVE	LANGUAGE	EMOTIONAL/SOCIAL

6–8 years

PHYSICAL

- Slow gains in height and weight continue until adolescent growth spurt. (402)
- Gradual replacement of primary teeth by permanent teeth. (404)
- Writing becomes smaller and more legible. Letter reversals decline. (418)
- Drawings become more organized and detailed and include some depth cues. (418)

- Games with rules and rough-and-tumble play become common. (420–421)
- Dominance hierarchies become more stable, especially among boys. (421–422)

COGNITIVE

- Thought becomes more logical, as shown by the ability to pass Piagetian conservation, class inclusion, and seriation problems. (428)
- Understanding of spatial concepts improves, as illustrated by the ability to give clear, well-organized directions and to draw and read maps. (429)
- Attention becomes more selective, adaptable, and planful. (432–433)
- Uses memory strategies of rehearsal and organization. (433–435)
- Views the mind as an active, constructive agent, capable of transforming information. (437)
- Awareness of memory strategies and the impact of psychological factors (attention, motivation) on task performance improve. (437–438)
- By the end of this period, makes the transition from "learning to read" to "reading to learn." (439–440)
- Uses informal knowledge of number concepts and counting to master more complex mathematical skills. (440–441)

LANGUAGE

- Vocabulary increases rapidly throughout middle childhood. (451)

- Word definitions are concrete, referring to functions and appearance. (451)
- Metalinguistic awareness improves. (451)

EMOTIONAL/SOCIAL

- Self-concept begins to include personality traits and social comparisons. (471)
- Self-esteem differentiates, becomes hierarchically organized, and declines to a more realistic level. (472–473)
- Self-conscious emotions of pride and guilt are governed by personal responsibility. (478)
- Recognizes that individuals can experience more than one emotion at a time. (478)
- Attends to more cues—facial, situational, and past experiences—in interpreting another's feelings. (478)
- Understands that access to different information often causes people to have different perspectives. (480)
- Becomes more responsible and independent. (481)
- Distributive justice reasoning changes from equality to merit to benevolence. (481)
- Peer interaction becomes more prosocial, and physical aggression declines. (485)

AGE	PHYSICAL	COGNITIVE	LANGUAGE	EMOTIONAL/SOCIAL

9–11 years

PHYSICAL

- Adolescent growth spurt begins 2 years earlier for girls than for boys. (402)

- Gross motor skills of running, jumping, throwing, catching, kicking, batting, and dribbling are executed more quickly and with better coordination. (417–418)

- Reaction time improves, contributing to motor skill development. (418)
- Representation of depth in drawings expands. (418)

COGNITIVE

- Logical thought remains tied to concrete situations until the end of middle childhood. (429)
- Piagetian tasks continue to be mastered in a step-by-step fashion. (429)

- Planning improves. (433)
- Memory strategies of rehearsal and organization become more effective. (434)
- Applies several memory strategies at once. (435)
- Uses memory strategy of elaboration. (435)
- Long-term knowledge base grows larger and becomes better organized. (436)
- Cognitive self-regulation improves. (438)

LANGUAGE

- Word definitions emphasize synonyms and categorical relations. (451)
- Grasps double meanings of words, as reflected in comprehension of metaphors and humor. (452)
- Use of complex grammatical constructions improves. (452)
- Adapts messages to the needs of listeners in challenging communicative situations. (452)
- Conversational strategies become more refined. (452)

EMOTIONAL/SOCIAL

- Self-esteem tends to rise. (473)
- Distinguishes ability, effort, and luck in attributions for success and failure. (475)
- Has an adaptive set of strategies for regulating emotion. (479)
- Can "step into another's shoes" and view the self from that person's perspective. (480)
- Later, can view the relationship between self and other from the perspective of a third, impartial party. (480)
- Appreciates the linkage between moral rules and social conventions. (482)
- Commitment to personal choice strengthens and enhances understanding of individual rights. (482)
- Peer groups emerge. (485)
- Friendships become more selective and are based on mutual trust. (486)
- Becomes aware of more gender stereotypes, including personality traits and school subjects, but has a flexible appreciation of what males and females can do. (490–491)
- Sibling rivalry tends to increase. (493)

Note: Numbers in parentheses indicate the page(s) on which each milestone is discussed.

Glossary

Aboriginal Head Start
A Canadian federal program that provides First Nations, Inuit, and Métis children younger than age 6 with preschool education and nutritional and health services and that encourages parent involvement in program planning and children's learning. (p. 345)

academic preschool and kindergarten programs
Educational programs in which teachers structure young children's learning, teaching letters, numbers, colors, shapes, and other academic skills through formal lessons, often using repetition and drill. Distinguished from *child-centered preschool and kindergarten programs.* (p. 345)

accommodation
That part of adaptation in which new schemes are created and old ones adjusted to produce a better fit with the environment. Distinguished from *assimilation.* (p. 208)

acquired immune deficiency syndrome (AIDS)
A viral infection that destroys the immune system and is spread through transfer of body fluids from one person to another. It can be transmitted prenatally. (p. 115)

adaptation
In Piaget's theory, the process of building schemes through direct interaction with the environment. Made up of two complementary processes: *assimilation* and *accommodation.* (p. 208)

affordances
The action possibilities that a situation offers an organism with certain motor capabilities. Discovering affordances plays a major role in perceptual differentiation. (p. 202)

age of viability
The age at which the fetus can first survive if born early. Occurs sometime between 22 and 26 weeks. (p. 104)

allele
Each of two forms of a gene located at the same place on the autosomes. (p. 58)

amnion
The inner membrane that forms a protective covering around the prenatal organism. (p. 101)

amniotic fluid
The fluid that fills the amnion, helping to keep temperature constant and to provide a cushion against jolts caused by the mother's movement. (p. 101)

analgesic
A mild pain-relieving drug. (p. 138)

androgyny
A type of gender identity in which the person scores high on both traditionally masculine and traditionally feminine personality characteristics. (p. 385)

anesthetic
A strong painkilling drug that blocks sensation. (p. 138)

animistic thinking
The belief that inanimate objects have lifelike qualities, such as thoughts, wishes, feelings, and intentions. (p. 320)

A-not-B search error
The error made by 8- to 12-month-olds after an object is moved from hiding place A to hiding place B. Infants in Piaget's Substage 4 search for it only in the first hiding place (A). (p. 211)

anoxia
Inadequate oxygen supply. (p. 140)

Apgar Scale
A rating used to assess the newborn baby's physical condition immediately after birth. (p. 140)

assimilation
That part of adaptation in which the external world is interpreted in terms of current schemes. Distinguished from *accommodation.* (p. 208)

associative play
A form of true social participation, in which children are engaged in separate activities but interact by exchanging toys and commenting on one another's behavior. Distinguished from *nonsocial activity, parallel play,* and *cooperative play.* (p. 366)

asthma
An illness in which, in response to a variety of stimuli, highly sensitive bronchial tubes fill with mucus and contract, leading to episodes of coughing, wheezing, and serious breathing difficulties. (p. 412)

attachment
The strong, affectional tie that humans feel toward special people in their lives. (p. 264)

Attachment Q-Sort
An efficient method for assessing the quality of the attachment bond, in which a parent or an expert informant sorts a set of 90 descriptors of attachment-related behaviors on the basis of how well they describe the child. A score is then computed that assigns children to securely or insecurely attached groups. (p. 267)

attention-deficit hyperactivity disorder (ADHD)
A childhood disorder involving inattentiveness, impulsivity, and excessive motor activity. Often leads to academic failure and social problems. (p. 434)

attribution retraining
An intervention that encourages learned-helpless children to believe that they can overcome failure by exerting more effort. (p. 476)

attributions
Common, everyday explanations for the causes of behavior. (p. 474)

authoritarian child-rearing style
A child-rearing style that is low in acceptance and involvement, is high in coercive control, and restricts rather than grants autonomy. Distinguished from *authoritative, permissive,* and *uninvolved styles.* (p. 389)

authoritative child-rearing style
A child-rearing style that is high in acceptance and involvement, emphasizes firm control with explanations, and includes gradual, appropriate autonomy granting. Distinguished from *authoritarian, permissive,* and *uninvolved styles.* (p. 388)

autobiographical memory
Representations of special, one-time events that are long-lasting because they are imbued with personal meaning. (p. 224)

autonomy versus shame and doubt
In Erikson's theory, the psychological conflict of toddlerhood, which is resolved positively if parents provide young children with suitable guidance and reasonable choices. (p. 251)

autosomes
The 22 matching chromosome pairs in each human cell. (p. 57)

avoidant attachment
The quality of insecure attachment characterizing infants who usually are not distressed by parental separation and who avoid the parent

when she returns. Distinguished from *secure, resistant,* and *disorganized/disoriented attachment.* (p. 267)

babbling
Repetition of consonant–vowel combinations in long strings, beginning around 4 months of age. (p. 238)

basic emotions
Emotions that can be directly inferred from facial expressions, such as happiness, interest, surprise, fear, anger, sadness, and disgust. (p. 252)

basic-skills approach
An approach to beginning reading instruction that emphasizes training in phonics—the basic rules for translating written symbols into sounds—and simplified reading materials. Distinguished from *whole-language approach.* (p. 439)

basic trust versus mistrust
In Erikson's theory, the psychological conflict of infancy, which is resolved positively if caregiving, especially during feeding, is sympathetic and loving. (p. 251)

behavior modification
Procedures that combine conditioning and modeling to eliminate undesirable behaviors and increase desirable responses. (p. 19)

behavioral genetics
A field devoted to uncovering the contributions of nature and nurture to the diversity in human traits and abilities. (p. 83)

behaviorism
An approach that regards directly observable events—stimuli and responses—as the appropriate focus of study and views the development of behavior as taking place through classical and operant conditioning. (p. 18)

blastocyst
The zygote 4 days after fertilization, when the tiny mass of cells forms a hollow, fluid-filled ball. (p. 101)

blended, or **reconstituted, family**
A family structure resulting from cohabitation or remarriage that includes parent, child, and steprelatives. (p. 499)

bonding
Parents' feelings of affection and concern for the newborn baby. (p. 147)

brain plasticity
The ability of other parts of the brain to take over functions of damaged regions. Declines as hemispheres of the cerebral cortex lateralize. (p. 172)

breech position
A position of the baby in the uterus that would cause the buttocks or feet to be delivered first. (p. 139)

Broca's area
A language structure located in the frontal lobe of the left hemisphere of the cerebral cortex that controls language production. (p. 236)

canalization
The tendency of heredity to restrict the development of some characteristics to just one or a few outcomes. (p. 86)

cardinality
A principle stating that the last number in a counting sequence indicates the quantity of items in the set. (p. 342)

carrier
A heterozygous individual who can pass a recessive trait to his or her children. (p. 58)

central executive
In information processing, the conscious part of working memory that directs the flow of information through the mental system by deciding what to attend to, coordinating incoming information with information already in the system, and selecting, applying, and monitoring strategies. (p. 221)

centration
The tendency to focus on one aspect of a situation and neglect other important features. Distinguished from *decentration.* (p. 321)

cephalocaudal trend
An organized pattern of physical growth and motor control that proceeds from head to tail. (p. 167)

cerebellum
A brain structure that aids in balance and control of body movement. (p. 293)

cerebral cortex
The largest, most complex structure of the human brain, and the one responsible for the highly developed intelligence of the human species. Surrounds the rest of the brain, much like a half-shelled walnut. (p. 171)

cerebral palsy
A general term for a variety of problems, all of which involve muscle coordination, that result from brain damage before, during, or just after birth. (p. 140)

cesarean delivery
A surgical delivery in which the doctor makes an incision in the mother's abdomen and lifts the baby out of the uterus. (p. 139)

child-centered preschool and kindergarten programs
Educational programs in which teachers provide activities from which young children select, and most of the day is devoted to play. Distinguished from *academic preschool and kindergarten programs.* (p. 345)

child development
A field of study devoted to understanding constancy and change from conception through adolescence and emerging adulthood. (p. 4)

child-directed speech (CDS)
A form of language adults use to speak to young children that consists of short sentences with high-pitched, exaggerated expression, clear pronunciation, distinct pauses between speech segments, and repetition of new words in a variety of contexts. (p. 242)

child-rearing styles
Combinations of parenting behaviors that occur over a wide range of situations, creating an enduring child-rearing climate. (p. 388)

chorion
The outer membrane that forms a protective covering around the prenatal organism. It sends out tiny, fingerlike villi, from which the placenta begins to develop. (p. 101)

chromosomes
Rodlike structures in the cell nucleus that store and transmit genetic information. (p. 54)

chronosystem
In ecological systems theory, temporal changes in children's environments, which produce new conditions that affect development. These changes can be imposed externally or arise from within the child. (p. 29)

circular reaction
In Piaget's theory, a means of building schemes in which infants try to repeat a chance event caused by their own motor activity. (p. 210)

classical conditioning
A form of learning that involves associating a neutral stimulus with a stimulus that leads to a reflexive response. (p. 182)

clinical, or **case study, method**
A method in which the researcher attempts to understand the unique individual child by combining interview data, observations, test scores, and sometimes psychophysiological measures. (p. 36)

clinical interview
A method in which the researcher uses a flexible, conversational style to probe for the participant's point of view. (p. 35)

codominance
A pattern of inheritance in which both alleles in a heterozygous combination are expressed. (p. 59)

cognitive–developmental theory
An approach introduced by Piaget that views children as actively constructing knowledge as they manipulate and explore their world, views and cognitive development as taking place in stages. (p. 20)

cognitive inhibition
The ability to resist interference from internal and external distracting stimuli, thereby ensuring that working memory is not cluttered with irrelevant information. (p. 432)

cognitive maps
Mental representations of familiar, large-scale spaces, such as school or neighborhood. (p. 429)

cognitive self-regulation
The process of continuously monitoring progress toward a goal, checking outcomes, and redirecting unsuccessful efforts. (p. 438)

cohort effects
The effects of cultural-historical change on the accuracy of longitudinal and cross-sectional findings. Children born at the same time are influenced by particular cultural and historical conditions. Results based on one cohort may not apply to children developing at other times. (p. 43)

collectivist societies
Societies in which people define themselves as part of a group and stress group over individual goals. Distinguished from *individualistic societies*. (p. 78)

community of learners
An educational approach inspired by Vygotsky's theory in which teachers guide the overall process of learning, but otherwise, no distinction is made between adult and child contributors. All participate in joint endeavors and have the authority to define and resolve problems. (p. 458)

compliance
Voluntary obedience to adult requests and commands. (p. 280)

comprehension
In language development, the words and word combinations that children understand. Distinguished from *production*. (p. 241)

concordance rate
The percentage of instances in which both members of a twin pair show a trait when it is present in one pair member. Used to study the contribution of heredity to emotional and behavioral disorders that can be judged as either present or absent. (p. 84)

concrete operational stage
Piaget's third stage, during which thought is logical, flexible, and organized in its application to concrete information. Extends from about 7 to 11 years. (p. 428)

conditioned response (CR)
In classical conditioning, an originally reflexive response that is produced by a conditioned stimulus (CS). (p. 183)

conditioned stimulus (CS)
In classical conditioning, a neutral stimulus that, through pairing with an unconditioned stimulus (UCS), leads to a new response (CR). (p. 183)

conservation
The understanding that certain physical characteristics of objects remain the same, even when their outward appearance changes. (p. 320)

constructivist classroom
A classroom that encourages students to construct their own knowledge, through richly equipped learning centers, small groups and individuals solving problems they choose themselves, and a teacher who guides and supports in response to children's needs. Students are evaluated by considering their progress in relation to their own prior development. Often grounded in Piaget's theory. Distinguished from *traditional classroom* and *social–constructivist classroom*. (p. 456)

contexts
Unique combinations of genetic and environmental circumstances that can result in markedly different paths of development. (p. 9)

continuous development
A view that regards development as gradually augmenting the same types of skills that were there to begin with. Distinguished from *discontinuous development*. (p. 8)

contrast sensitivity
A general principle accounting for early pattern preferences, which states that if babies can detect a difference in contrast between two or more patterns, they will prefer the one with more contrast. (p. 197)

control deficiency
The inability to execute a mental strategy consistently. Distinguished from *production deficiency*, *utilization deficiency*, and *effective strategy use*. (p. 433)

controversial children
Children who get a large number of positive and negative votes on sociometric measures of peer acceptance. Distinguished from *popular*, *neglected*, and *rejected children*. (p. 487)

convergent thinking
The generation of a single correct answer to a problem. The type of cognition emphasized on intelligence tests. Distinguished from *divergent thinking*. (p. 461)

cooing
Pleasant vowel-like noises made by infants, beginning around 2 months of age. (p. 238)

cooperative learning
Collaboration on a task by a small group of students who resolve differences of opinion, share responsibility, consider one another's ideas, and work toward common goals. (p. 459)

cooperative play
A form of true social participation, in which children orient toward a common goal, such as acting out a make-believe theme or working on the same project. Distinguished from *nonsocial activity, parallel play,* and *associative play.* (p. 366)

core knowledge perspective
A perspective that states that infants are born with a set of innate knowledge systems, or core domains of thought, each of which permits a ready grasp of new, related information and therefore supports early, rapid development of certain aspects of cognition. (p. 217)

coregulation
A transitional form of supervision in which parents exercise general oversight while permitting children to be in charge of moment-by-moment decision making. (p. 492)

correlation coefficient
A number, ranging from +1.00 to −1.00, that describes the strength and direction of the relationship between two variables. (p. 40)

correlational design
A research design in which the researcher gathers information without altering participants' experiences and examines relationships between variables. Does not permit inferences about cause and effect. (p. 39)

corpus callosum
The large bundle of fibers that connects the two hemispheres of the brain. (p. 293)

creativity
The ability to produce work that is original yet appropriate—something that others have not thought of but that is useful in some way. (p. 461)

crossing over
During meiosis, the exchange of genes between chromosomes next to each other. (p. 55)

cross-sectional design
A research design in which groups of people differing in age are studied at the same point in time. Distinguished from *longitudinal design*. (p. 43)

decentration
The ability to focus on several aspects of a problem at once and relate them. Distinguished from *centration*. (p. 428)

deferred imitation
The ability to remember and copy the behavior of models who are not present. (p. 212)

deoxyribonucleic acid (DNA)
Long, double-stranded molecules that make up chromosomes. (p. 55)

dependent variable
The variable the researcher expects to be influenced by the independent variable in an experiment. (p. 40)

developmental quotient, or DQ
A score on an infant intelligence test, based primarily on perceptual and motor responses. Computed in the same manner as an IQ. (p. 230)

developmentally appropriate practice
Standards devised by the National Association for the Education of Young Children that specify program characteristics that meet the developmental and individual needs of young children of varying ages, based on both current research and the consensus of experts. (p. 232)

differentiation theory
The view that perceptual development involves the detection of increasingly fine-grained, invariant features in the environment. (p. 202)

difficult child
A child whose temperament is characterized by irregular daily routines, slow acceptance of new experiences, and negative and intense reactions. Distinguished from *easy child* and *slow-to-warm-up child.* (p. 258)

dilation and effacement of the cervix
Widening and thinning of the cervix during the first stage of labor. (p. 130)

discontinuous development
A view in which new ways of understanding and responding to the world emerge at specific times. Distinguished from *continuous development.* (p. 8)

disorganized/disoriented attachment
The quality of insecure attachment characterizing infants who respond in a confused, contradictory fashion when reunited with the parent. Distinguished from *avoidant, resistant,* and *secure attachment.* (p. 267)

distributive justice
Beliefs about how to divide material goods fairly. (p. 481)

divergent thinking
The generation of multiple and unusual possibilities when faced with a task or problem. Associated with creativity. Distinguished from *convergent thinking.* (p. 461)

divorce mediation
A series of meetings between divorcing adults and a trained professional aimed at reducing family conflict, including legal battles over property division and child custody. (p. 497)

dominance hierarchy
A stable ordering of group members that predicts who will win when conflict arises. (p. 422)

dominant cerebral hemisphere
The hemisphere of the brain responsible for skilled motor action. The left hemisphere is dominant in right-handed individuals. In left-handed individuals, the right hemisphere may be dominant, or motor and language skills may be shared between the hemispheres. (p. 292)

dominant–recessive inheritance
A pattern of inheritance in which, under heterozygous conditions, the influence of only one allele is apparent. (p. 58)

dual representation
Viewing a symbolic object as both an object in its own right and a symbol. (p. 319)

dynamic assessment
An approach to testing consistent with Vygotsky's zone of proximal development, in which an adult introduces purposeful teaching into the testing situation to find out what the child can attain with social support. (p. 450)

dynamic systems perspective
A view that regards the child's mind, body, and physical and social worlds as a dynamic, integrated system. A change in any part of the system leads the child to reorganize his or her behavior so the various components of the system work together again but in a more complex and effective way. (p. 29)

dynamic systems theory of motor development
A theory that views new motor skills as reorganizations of previously mastered skills that lead to more effective ways of exploring and controlling the environment. Each new skill is a product of central nervous system development, movement possibilities of the body, the goal the child has in mind, and environmental supports for the skill. (p. 188)

easy child
A child whose temperament is characterized by establishment of regular routines in infancy, general cheerfulness, and easy adaptation to new experiences. Distinguished from *difficult child* and *slow-to-warm-up child.* (p. 258)

ecological systems theory
Bronfenbrenner's approach, which views the child as developing within a complex system of relationships affected by multiple levels of the environment, from immediate settings of family and school to broad cultural values and programs. (p. 27)

educational self-fulfilling prophecy
The idea that children may adopt teachers' positive or negative attitudes toward them and start to live up to these views. (p. 458)

effective strategy use
Consistent use of a mental strategy that leads to improvement in performance. Distin-

guished from *production deficiency, control deficiency,* and *utilization deficiency.* (p. 433)

egocentrism
The inability to distinguish the symbolic viewpoints of others from one's own. (p. 319)

elaboration
The memory strategy of creating a relationship, or shared meaning, between two or more pieces of information that are not members of the same category. (p. 435)

embryo
The prenatal organism from 2 to 8 weeks after conception, during which time the foundations of all body structures and internal organs are laid down. (p. 102)

embryonic disk
A small cluster of cells on the inside of the blastocyst, from which the new organism will develop. (p. 101)

emergent literacy
Young children's active efforts to construct literacy knowledge through informal experiences. (p. 338)

emotion-centered coping
A approach to coping with stress that is internal, private, and aimed at controlling negative emotion when little can be done about an outcome. Distinguished from *problem-centered coping.* (p. 479)

emotional self-regulation
Strategies for adjusting our emotional state to a comfortable level of intensity so we can accomplish our goals. (p. 256)

empathy
The ability to understand another's emotional state and feel with that person, or respond emotionally in a similar way. (p. 279)

epigenesis
Development of the individual resulting from ongoing, bidirectional exchanges between heredity and all levels of the environment. (p. 88)

epiphyses
Growth centers in the bones where new cartilage cells are produced and gradually harden. (p. 168)

episodic memory
Memory for everyday experiences. (p. 334)

ethnography
A method in which the researcher attempts to understand the unique values and social processes of a culture or a distinct social group by living with its members and taking field notes for an extended period of time. (p. 37)

ethological theory of attachment
A theory, formulated by Bowlby, that views the infant's emotional tie to the caregiver as an evolved response that promotes survival. (p. 265)

ethology
An approach concerned with the adaptive, or survival, value of behavior and its evolutionary history. (p. 24)

evolutionary developmental psychology
An approach that seeks to understand the adaptive value of species-wide cognitive, emotional, and social competencies as those competencies change with age. (p. 25)

exosystem
In ecological systems theory, settings that do not contain children but that affect their experiences in immediate settings. Examples include parents' workplaces, health and welfare services in the community, and parents' social networks. (p. 28)

expansions
Adult responses that elaborate on a child's utterance, increasing its complexity. (p. 352)

experience-dependent brain growth
New growth and refinement of brain structures as a result of specific learning experiences that vary widely across individuals and cultures. Follows experience-expectant brain growth. (p. 175)

experience-expectant brain growth
The young brain's rapidly developing organization, which depends on ordinary experiences—opportunities to see and touch objects, to hear language and other sounds, and to move about and explore the environment. Provides the foundation for experience-dependent brain growth. (p. 175)

experimental design
A research design in which the investigator randomly assigns participants to two or more treatment conditions. Permits inferences about cause and effect. (p. 40)

expressive style
A style of early language learning in which toddlers use language mainly to talk about the feelings and needs of themselves and other people. Initial vocabulary emphasizes social formulas and pronouns. Distinguished from *referential style*. (p. 242)

extended-family household
A household in which parent and child live with one or more adult relatives. (p. 78)

fast mapping
Connecting a new word with an underlying concept after only a brief encounter. (p. 349)

fetal alcohol effects (FAE)
The condition of children who display some but not all of the defects of fetal alcohol syndrome. Usually their mothers drank alcohol in smaller quantities during pregnancy. (p. 113)

fetal alcohol syndrome (FAS)
A set of defects that results when women consume large amounts of alcohol during most or all of pregnancy. Includes mental retardation, slow physical growth, and facial abnormalities. (p. 113)

fetal monitors
Electronic instruments that track the baby's heart rate during labor. (p. 137)

fetus
The prenatal organism from the beginning of the third month to the end of pregnancy, during which time completion of body structures and dramatic growth in size take place. (p. 103)

Flynn Effect
The steady increase in IQ that has occurred from one generation to the next. (p. 447)

fontanels
Six soft spots that separate the bones of the skull at birth. (p. 168)

forceps
Metal clamps placed around a baby's head and used to pull the infant from the birth canal. (p. 138)

fraternal, or **dizygotic, twins**
Twins resulting from the release and fertilization of two ova. They are genetically no more alike than ordinary siblings. Distinguished from *identical*, or *monozygotic, twins*. (p. 57)

full inclusion
Placement of pupils with learning difficulties in regular classrooms for the entire school day. Distinguished from *mainstreaming*. (p. 460)

functional play
A type of play involving pleasurable motor activity with or without objects. Enables infants and toddlers to practice sensorimotor schemes. (p. 212)

gametes
Human sperm and ova, which contain half as many chromosomes as a regular body cell. (p. 55)

gender constancy
The understanding that sex remains the same even if clothing, hairstyle, and play activities change. (p. 385)

gender identity
An image of oneself as relatively masculine or feminine in characteristics. (p. 385)

gender schema theory
An information-processing approach to gender typing that combines social learning and cognitive-developmental features to explain how environmental pressures and children's cognitions together shape gender-role development. (p. 386)

gender typing
The process of developing gender roles, or gender-linked preferences and behaviors valued by the larger society. (p. 381)

gene
A segment of a DNA molecule that contains hereditary instructions. (p. 54)

general growth curve
A curve that represents overall changes in body size—rapid growth during infancy, slower gains in early and middle childhood, and rapid growth again during adolescence. (p. 290)

genetic counseling
A communication process designed to help couples assess their chances of giving birth to a baby with a hereditary disorder and choose the best course of action in view of risks and family goals. (p. 64)

genetic–environmental correlation
The idea that heredity influences the environments to which individuals are exposed. (p. 86)

genetic imprinting
A pattern of inheritance in which alleles are imprinted, or chemically marked, in such a way that one pair member is activated, regardless of its makeup. (p. 61)

genotype
The genetic makeup of an individual. (p. 53)

gifted
Displaying exceptional intellectual strengths. Includes high IQ, creativity, and talent. (p. 461)

glial cells
Cells that are responsible for myeliniation. (p. 170)

goodness-of-fit model
Thomas and Chess's model, which states that an effective match, or "good fit," between child rearing and a child's temperament leads to more adaptive functioning, whereas a "poor fit" results in adjustment problems. (p. 263)

growth hormone (GH)
A pituitary hormone that affects the development of all body tissues except the central nervous system and the genitals. (p. 294)

guided participation
A concept that calls attention to adult and child contributions to a cooperative dialogue without specifying the precise features of communication, thereby allowing for variations across situations and cultures. (p. 330)

habituation
A gradual reduction in the strength of a response due to repetitive stimulation. (p. 184)

heritability estimate
A statistic that measures the extent to which individual differences in complex traits in a specific population are due to genetic factors. (p. 83)

heterozygous
Having two different alleles at the same place on a pair of chromosomes. Distinguished from *homozygous*. (p. 58)

hierarchical classification
The organization of objects into classes and subclasses on the basis of similarities and differences. (p. 321)

Home Observation for Measurement of the Environment (HOME)
A checklist for gathering information about the quality of children's home lives through observation and parental interview. (p. 231)

homozygous
Having two identical alleles at the same place on a pair of chromosomes. Distinguished from *heterozygous.* (p. 58)

horizontal décalage
Development within a Piagetian stage. Gradual mastery of logical concepts during the concrete operational stage is an example. (p. 429)

hostile aggression
Aggression intended to harm another person. Distinguished from *instrumental aggression.* (p. 377)

identical, or monozygotic, twins
Twins that result when a zygote, during the early stages of cell duplication, divides in two. They have the same genetic makeup. Distinguished from *fraternal,* or *dizygotic, twins.* (p. 57)

imitation
Learning by copying the behavior of another person. Also called *modeling* or *observational learning.* (p. 185)

implantation
Attachment of the blastocyst to the uterine lining 7 to 9 days after fertilization. (p. 101)

independent variable
The variable the researcher expects to cause changes in another variable in an experiment. (p. 40)

individualistic societies
Societies in which people think of themselves as separate entities and are largely concerned with their own personal needs. Distinguished from *collectivist societies.* (p. 78)

induced labor
A labor started artificially by breaking the amnion and giving the mother a hormone that stimulates contractions. (p. 139)

induction
A type of discipline in which the effects of the child's misbehavior on others are communicated to the child. (p. 372)

industry versus inferiority
In Erikson's theory, the psychological conflict of middle childhood, which is resolved positively when experiences lead children to develop a sense of competence at useful skills and tasks. (p. 470)

infant mortality
The number of deaths in the first year of life per 1,000 live births. (p. 144)

information processing
An approach that views the human mind as a symbol-manipulating system through which information flows and regards cognitive development as a continuous process. (p. 23)

inhibited, or shy, child
A child whose temperament is characterized by negative reaction to and withdrawal from novel stimuli. Resembles slow-to-warm-up child. Distinguished from *uninhibited,* or *sociable, child.* (p. 260)

initiative versus guilt
In Erikson's theory, the psychological conflict of early childhood, which is resolved positively through play experiences that foster a healthy sense of initiative and through the development of a superego, or conscience, that is not overly strict and guilt ridden. (p. 358)

instrumental aggression
Aggression aimed at obtaining an object, privilege, or space with no deliberate intent to harm another person. Distinguished from *hostile aggression.* (p. 377)

intelligence quotient, or IQ
A score that reflects an individual's performance on an intelligence test compared with the performances of other individuals of the same age. (p. 230)

intentional, or goal-directed, behavior
A sequence of actions in which schemes are deliberately combined to solve a problem. (p. 211)

interactional synchrony
A sensitively tuned "emotional dance," in which the caregiver responds to infant signals in a well-timed, rhythmic, appropriate fashion and both partners match emotional states, especially the positive ones. (p. 269)

intermodal perception
Perception that combines stimulation from more than one sensory system at a time. (p. 201)

internal working model
A set of expectations derived from early caregiving experiences concerning the availability of attachment figures, their likelihood of providing support during times of stress, and the self's interaction with those figures. Becomes a model, or guide, for all future close relationships. (p. 266)

intersubjectivity
The process whereby two participants who begin a task with different understandings arrive at a shared understanding. (p. 330)

invariant features
In differentiation theory of perceptual development, features that remain stable in a constantly changing perceptual world. (p. 202)

irreversibility
The inability to mentally go through a series of steps in a problem and then reverse direction, returning to the starting point. Distinguished from *reversibility.* (p. 321)

I-self
A sense of self as agent, who is separate from the surrounding world and can control its own thoughts and actions. Distinguished from *me-self.* (p. 278)

joint attention
A state in which the child and the caregiver attend to the same object or event and the caregiver offers verbal information. Supports language development. (p. 239)

joint custody
A child custody arrangement following divorce in which the court grants both parents equal say in important decisions about the child's upbringing. (p. 498)

kinship studies
Studies comparing the characteristics of family members to determine the importance of heredity in complex human characteristics. (p. 84)

kwashiorkor
A disease that is caused by a diet low in protein and that usually appears after weaning, between 1 and 3 years of age. Symptoms include an enlarged belly, swollen feet, hair loss, skin rash, and irritable, listless behavior. (p. 180)

language acquisition device (LAD)
In Chomsky's theory, a biologically based innate system for picking up language that permits children, no matter which language they hear, to speak in a rule-oriented fashion as soon as they have learned enough words. (p. 236)

lanugo
A white, downy hair that covers the entire body of the fetus, helping the vernix stick to the skin. (p. 104)

lateralization
Specialization of functions in the two hemispheres of the cerebral cortex. (p. 171)

learned helplessness
Attributions that credit success to luck and failure to low ability. Leads to anxious loss of control in the face of challenging tasks. Distinguished from *mastery-oriented attributions.* (p. 475)

learning disabilities
Specific learning disorders that lead children to achieve poorly in school, despite an aver-

age or above-average IQ. Believed to be due to faulty brain functioning. (p. 460)

longitudinal design
A research design in which participants are studied repeatedly at different ages. Distinguished from *cross-sectional design.* (p. 45)

longitudinal-sequential design
A research design with both longitudinal and cross-sectional components in which groups of participants born in different years are followed over time. (p. 45)

long-term memory
In information processing, the part of the mental system that contains our permanent knowledge base. (p. 221)

macrosystem
In ecological systems theory, cultural values, laws, customs, and resources that influence experiences and interactions at inner levels of the environment. (p. 28)

mainstreaming
Placement of pupils with learning difficulties in regular classrooms for part of the school day. Distinguished from *full inclusion.* (p. 460)

make-believe play
A type of play in which children pretend, acting out everyday and imaginary activities. (p. 212)

malocclusion
A condition in which the upper and lower teeth do not meet properly. (p. 404)

marasmus
A disease usually appearing in the first year of life that is caused by a diet low in all essential nutrients. Leads to a wasted condition of the body. (p. 180)

mastery-oriented attributions
Attributions that credit success to high ability and failure to insufficient effort. Lead to high self-esteem and a willingness to approach challenging tasks. Distinguished from *learned helplessness.* (p. 475)

maturation
A genetically determined, naturally unfolding course of growth. (p. 13)

meiosis
The process of cell division through which gametes are formed and in which the number of chromosomes in each cell is halved. (p. 55)

memory strategies
Deliberate mental activities that improve the likelihood of remembering. (p. 334)

mental representation
Internal depictions of information that the mind can manipulate. (p. 211)

mental strategies
In information processing, procedures that operate on and transform information,

thereby increasing the efficiency and flexibility of thinking and the chances that information will be retained. (p. 220)

me-self
A sense of self as an object of knowledge and evaluation. Consists of all qualities that make the self unique, including physical characteristics, possessions, attitudes, beliefs, and personality traits. Distinguished from *I-self.* (p. 279)

mesosystem
In ecological systems theory, connections between children's immediate settings. (p. 28)

metacognition
Thinking about thought; awareness of mental activities. (p. 336)

metalinguistic awareness
The ability to think about language as a system. (p. 451)

microgenetic design
A research design in which researchers present children with a novel task and follow their mastery over a series of closely spaced sessions. (p. 28)

microsystem
In ecological systems theory, the activities and interaction patterns in the child's immediate surroundings. (p. 28)

mitosis
The process of cell duplication, in which each new cell receives an exact copy of the original chromosomes. (p. 55)

modifier genes
Genes that can enhance or dilute the effects of other genes. (p. 58)

mutation
A sudden but permanent change in a segment of DNA. (p. 61)

mutual exclusivity bias
In the early phase of vocabulary growth, children's assumption that words refer to entirely separate (nonoverlapping) categories. (p. 349)

myelination
A process in which neural fibers are coated with an insulating fatty sheath (called myelin) that improves the efficiency of message transfer. (p. 170)

myopia
Nearsightedness; inability to see distant objects clearly. (p. 405)

natural, or prepared, childbirth
An approach designed to reduce pain and medical intervention and to make childbirth a rewarding experience for parents. (p. 135)

naturalistic observation
A method in which the researcher goes into the natural environment to observe the behavior of interest. Distinguished from *structured observation.* (p. 33)

nature–nurture controversy
Debate among theorists about whether genetic or environmental factors are more important determinants of development and behavior. (p. 9)

neglected children
Children who are seldom mentioned, either positively or negatively, on sociometric measures of peer acceptance. Distinguished from *popular, rejected,* and *controversial children.* (p. 487)

Neonatal Behavioral Assessment Scale (NBAS)
A test developed to assess the behavior of the infant during the newborn period. (p. 156)

neonatal mortality
The number of deaths in the first month of life per 1,000 live births. (p. 144)

neural tube
The primitive spinal cord that develops from the ectoderm, the top of which swells to form the brain during the period of the embryo. (p. 102)

neurons
Nerve cells that store and transmit information. (p. 169)

niche-picking
A type of genetic–environmental correlation in which individuals actively choose environments that complement their heredity. (p. 87)

noble savage
Rousseau's view of the child as naturally endowed with a sense of right and wrong and an innate plan for orderly, healthy growth. (p. 13)

nocturnal enuresis
Repeated bedwetting during the night. (p. 412)

nonorganic failure to thrive
A growth disorder usually present by 18 months of age that is caused by lack of affection and stimulation. (p. 181)

non-rapid-eye-movement (NREM) sleep
A "regular" sleep state in which the body is quiet and heart rate, breathing, and brainwave activity are slow and regular. Distinguished from *rapid-eye-movement (REM) sleep.* (p. 150)

nonsocial activity
Unoccupied, onlooker behavior and solitary play. Distinguished from *parallel, associative,* and *cooperative play.* (p. 366)

normative approach
An approach in which measures of behavior are taken on large numbers of individuals, and age-related averages are computed to represent typical development. (p. 14)

obesity
A greater-than-20-percent increase over average body weight, based on the child's age, sex, and physical build. (p. 407)

object permanence
The understanding that objects continue to exist when they are out of sight. (p. 211)

operant conditioning
A form of learning in which a spontaneous behavior is followed by a stimulus that changes the probability that the behavior will occur again. (p. 183)

operations
Mental representations of actions that obey logical rules. (p. 319)

ordinality
A principle specifying order (more-than and less-than) relationships between quantities. (p. 341)

organization
In Piaget's theory, the internal rearrangement and linking together of schemes so that they form a strongly interconnected cognitive system. In information processing, the memory strategy of grouping related items. (pp. 209, 434)

overextension
An early vocabulary error in which a word is applied too broadly—that is, to a wider collection of objects and events than is appropriate. Distinguished from *underextension.* (p. 240)

overlapping-waves theory
A theory of problem solving, which states that when given challenging problems, children generate a variety of strategies and gradually select those that result in rapid, accurate solutions, yielding an overlapping-waves pattern of development. (p. 335)

overregularization
Application of regular grammatical rules to words that are exceptions. (p. 350)

overt aggression
A form of hostile aggression that harms others through physical injury or the threat of such injury—for example, hitting, kicking, or threatening to beat up a peer. Distinguished from *relational aggression.* (p. 377)

parallel play
A form of limited social participation in which the child plays near other children with similar materials but does not try to influence their behavior. Distinguished from *nonsocial, associative,* and *cooperative play.* (p. 366)

peer acceptance
Likability, or the extent to which a child is viewed by a group of agemates (such as classmates) as a worthy social partner. (p. 487)

peer group
Peers who form a social unit by generating shared values and standards of behavior and a social structure of leaders and followers. (p. 485)

peer victimization
A destructive form of peer interaction in which certain children become frequent targets of verbal and physical attacks or other forms of abuse. (p. 489)

permissive child-rearing style
A child-rearing style that is high in acceptance but overindulging or inattentive, low in control, and lenient rather than appropriate in autonomy granting. Distinguished from *authoritative, authoritarian,* and *uninvolved styles.* (p. 389)

perspective taking
The capacity to imagine what other people are thinking and feeling. (p. 480)

phenotype
The individual's physical and behavioral characteristics, which are determined by both genetic and environmental factors. (p. 53)

phobia
An intense, unmanageable fear that leads to persistent avoidance of the feared situation. (p. 502)

phonological awareness
The ability to reflect on and manipulate the sound structure of spoken language, as indicated by sensitivity to changes in sounds within words, to rhyming, and to incorrect pronunciation. A strong predictor of emergent literacy during early childhood and of later reading and spelling achievement. (p. 340)

pincer grasp
The well-coordinated grasp emerging at the end of the first year, involving thumb and forefinger opposition. (p. 191)

pituitary gland
A gland located near the base of the brain that releases hormones affecting physical growth. (p. 294)

placenta
The organ that separates the mother's bloodstream from the embryo or fetal bloodstream but permits exchange of nutrients and waste products. (p. 101)

planning
Thinking out a sequence of acts ahead of time and allocating attention accordingly to reach a goal. (p. 333)

polygenic inheritance
A pattern of inheritance in which many genes affect the characteristic in question. (p. 62)

popular children
Children who get many positive votes on sociometric measures of peer acceptance. Distinguished from *rejected, controversial,* and *neglected children.* (p. 487)

popular–antisocial children
A subgroup of popular children largely made up of "tough" boys who are athletically skilled, highly aggressive, defiant of adult authority, and poor students. Distinguished from *popular–prosocial children.* (p. 487)

popular–prosocial children
A subgroup of popular children who combine academic and social competence. Distinguished from *popular–antisocial children.* (p. 487)

postpartum depression
Feelings of sadness and withdrawal that appear shortly after childbirth and that continue for weeks or months. (p. 159)

pragmatics
The practical, social side of language that is concerned with how to engage in effective and appropriate communication with others. (p. 351)

prenatal diagnostic methods
Medical procedures that permit detection of developmental problems before birth. (p. 65)

preoperational stage
Piaget's second stage, in which rapid growth in representation takes place but thought is not yet logical. Extends from about 2 to 7 years. (p. 316)

prereaching
The poorly coordinated, primitive reaching movements of newborn babies. (p. 189)

preterm infants
Infants born several weeks or more before their due date. Although they are small in size, their weight may still be appropriate for the time they spent in the uterus. (p. 142)

private speech
Self-directed speech that children use to plan and guide their own behavior. (p. 329)

problem-centered coping
An approach to coping with stress in which the individual appraises the situation as changeable, identifies the difficulty, and decides what to do about it. Distinguished from *emotion-centered coping.* (p. 479)

production
In language development, the words and word combinations that children use. Distinguished from *comprehension.* (p. 241)

production deficiency
The failure to produce a mental strategy when it could be helpful. Distinguished from *control deficiency, utilization deficiency,* and *effective strategy use.* (p. 433)

Project Head Start
The largest federally funded program in the United States, which provides low-income children with a year or two of preschool education, along with nutritional and medical

services, and which encourages parent involvement in children's development. (p. 345)

prosocial, or altruistic, behavior
Actions that benefit another person without any expected reward for the self. (p. 364)

proximodistal trend
An organized pattern of physical growth and motor control that proceeds from the center of the body outward. (p. 167)

psychoanalytic perspective
An approach to personality development introduced by Freud that assumes that children move through a series of stages in which they confront conflicts between biological drives and social expectations. The way these conflicts are resolved determines the person's ability to learn, to get along with others, and to cope with anxiety. (p. 15)

psychophysiological methods
Methods that measure the relationship between physiological processes and behavior. Among the most common are measures of autonomic nervous system activity (such as heart rate and respiration) and brain functioning (such as the EEG and fMRI). (p. 35)

psychosexual theory
Freud's theory, which emphasizes that how parents manage children's sexual and aggressive drives in the first few years of life is crucial for healthy personality development. (p. 15)

psychosocial dwarfism
A growth disorder observed between 2 and 15 years of age. Characterized by very short stature, decreased GH secretion, immature skeletal age, and serious adjustment problems, which help distinguish psychosocial dwarfism from normal shortness. Caused by emotional deprivation. (p. 294)

psychosocial theory
Erikson's theory, which emphasizes that at each Freudian stage, individuals not only develop a unique personality but also acquire attitudes and skills that help them become active, contributing members of their society. (p. 16)

public policies
Laws and government programs designed to improve current conditions. (p. 78)

punishment
In operant conditioning, a stimulus (removal of a desirable one or presentation of an unpleasant one) that decreases the occurrence of a response. (p. 184)

random assignment
An unbiased procedure for assigning participants to treatment groups, such as drawing numbers out of a hat or flipping a coin. Increases the chances that participants' characteristics will be equally distributed across treatment conditions in an experiment. (p. 41)

range of reaction
Each person's unique, genetically determined response to a range of environmental conditions. (p. 85)

rapid-eye-movement (REM) sleep
An "irregular" sleep state in which brain-wave activity is similar to that of the waking state; eyes dart beneath the lids; heart rate, blood pressure, and breathing are uneven; and slight body movements occur. Distinguished from *non-rapid-eye-movement (NREM) sleep*. (p. 150)

recall
The type of memory that involves remembering something in the absence of perceptual support. (p. 223)

recasts
Adult responses that restructure children's incorrect speech into a more appropriate form. (p. 352)

reciprocal teaching
A teaching method based on Vygotsky's theory in which a teacher and two to four students form a cooperative group. Dialogues occur that create a zone of proximal development in which reading comprehension improves. (p. 456)

recognition
The simplest form of memory, which involves noticing whether a new experience is identical or similar to a previous one. (p. 223)

recovery
Following habituation, an increase in responsiveness to a new stimulus. (p. 184)

referential style
A style of early language learning in which toddlers use language mainly to label objects. Distinguished from *expressive style*. (p. 242)

reflex
An inborn, automatic response to a particular form of stimulation. (p. 148)

rehearsal
The memory strategy of repeating information. (p. 434)

reinforcer
In operant conditioning, a stimulus that increases the occurrence of a response. (p. 184)

rejected children
Children who are actively disliked and get many negative votes on sociometric measures of peer acceptance. Distinguished from *popular, controversial,* and *neglected children*. (p. 487)

rejected–aggressive children
A subgroup of rejected children who engage in high rates of conflict, hostility, and hyperactive, inattentive, and impulsive behavior. Distinguished from *rejected–withdrawn children*. (p. 488)

rejected–withdrawn children
A subgroup of rejected children who are passive and socially awkward. Distinguished from *rejected–aggressive children*. (p. 488)

relational aggression
A form of hostile aggression that damages another's peer relationships, as in social exclusion or rumor spreading. Distinguished from *overt aggression*. (p. 377)

resilience
The ability to adapt effectively in the face of threats to development. (p. 10)

resistant attachment
The quality of insecure attachment characterizing infants who remain close to the parent before departure, are usually distressed when she leaves, and mix clinginess with angry, resistive behavior when she returns. Distinguished from *secure, avoidant,* and *disorganized/disoriented attachment*. (p. 267)

respiratory distress syndrome
A disorder of preterm infants in which the lungs are so immature that the air sacs collapse, causing serious breathing difficulties. Also known as *hyaline membrane disease*. (p. 141)

reticular formation
A brain structure that maintains alertness and consciousness. (p. 293)

reversibility
The ability to mentally go through a series of steps in a problem and then reverse direction, returning to the starting point. Distinguished from *irreversibility*. (p. 428)

Rh factor incompatibility
A condition that arises when the RH protein, present in the fetus's blood but not in the mother's, causes the mother to build up antibodies. If these return to the fetus's system, they destroy red blood cells, reducing the oxygen supply to organs and tissues. (p. 119)

rooming in
An arrangement in which the newborn baby stays in the mother's hospital room all or most of the time. (p. 147)

rough-and-tumble play
A form of peer interaction involving friendly chasing and play-fighting that, in our evolutionary past, may have been important for the development of fighting skill. (p. 421)

rubella
Three-day German measles. Causes a wide variety of prenatal abnormalities, especially when it strikes during the embryonic period. (p. 115)

scaffolding
A changing quality of social support over the course of a teaching session, in which the adult adjusts the assistance provided to fit

the child's current level of performance. As competence increases, the adult gradually and sensitively withdraws support, turning over responsibility to the child. (p. 330)

scheme
In Piaget's theory, a specific structure, or organized way of making sense of experience, that changes with age. (p. 208)

scripts
General descriptions of what occurs and when it occurs in a particular situation. A basic means through which children organize and interpret repeated events. (p. 334)

secular trends in physical growth
Changes in body size from one generation to the next. (p. 403)

secure attachment
The quality of attachment characterizing infants who are distressed by parental separation but are easily comforted by the parent when she returns. Distinguished from *avoidant, resistant,* and *disorganized/disoriented attachment.* (p. 267)

secure base
The infant's use of the familiar caregiver as a point from which to explore the environment and to return to for emotional support. (p. 266)

self-care children
Children who look after themselves during after-school hours. (p. 501)

self-concept
The set of attributes, abilities, attitudes, and values that an individual believes defines who he or she is. (p. 359)

self-conscious emotions
Emotions that involve injury to or enhancement of the sense of self. Examples are shame, embarrassment, guilt, envy, and pride. (p. 256)

self-control
The capacity to resist an impulse to engage in socially disapproved behavior. (p. 280)

self-esteem
The aspect of self-concept that involves judgments about one's own worth and the feelings associated with those judgments. (p. 360)

semantic bootstrapping
Figuring out grammatical rules by relying on word meanings. (p. 351)

sensitive caregiving
Caregiving involving prompt, consistent, and appropriate responding to infant signals. (p. 269)

sensitive period
A time that is optimal for certain capacities to emerge and in which the individual is especially responsive to environmental influences. Development can occur later, but it is harder to induce. (p. 25)

sensorimotor stage
Piaget's first stage, during which infants and toddlers "think" with their eyes, ears, hands, and other sensorimotor equipment. Spans the first 2 years of life. (p. 208)

sensory register
In information processing, that part of the mental system in which sights and sounds are represented directly and stored briefly before they decay or are transferred to working, or short-term, memory. (p. 220)

separation anxiety
An infant's distressed reaction to the departure of the familiar caregiver. (p. 265)

seriation
The ability to order items along a quantitative dimension, such as length or weight. (p. 428)

sex chromosomes
The twenty-third pair of chromosomes, which determines the sex of the child—in females, called XX; in males, called XY. (p. 57)

shape constancy
Perception of an object's shape as the same, despite changes in the shape projected on the retina. (p. 200)

size constancy
Perception of an object's size as the same, despite changes in the size of its retinal image. (p. 200)

skeletal age
An estimate of physical maturity based on development of the bones of the body. (p. 168)

slow-to-warm-up child
A child whose temperament is characterized by inactivity; mild, low-key reactions to environmental stimuli; negative mood; and slow adjustment when faced with new experiences. Distinguished from *easy child* and *difficult child.* (p. 258)

small-for-date infants
Infants whose birth weight is below normal when length of pregnancy is taken into account. (p. 142)

social comparisons
Judgments of appearance, abilities, and behavior, in relation to those of others. (p. 471)

social learning theory
A theory that emphasizes the role of modeling, or observational learning, in the development of behavior. Its most recent revision stresses the importance of thinking in social learning and is called social-cognitive theory. (p. 19)

social problem solving
Resolving social conflicts in ways that are both acceptable to others and beneficial to the self. Involves noticing and accurately interpreting social cues, formulating goals that enhance relationships, generating and evaluating problem-solving strategies, and enacting a response. (p. 368)

social referencing
Relying on a trusted person's emotional reaction to decide how to respond in an uncertain situation. (p. 255)

social smile
The smile evoked by the stimulus of the human face. First appears between 6 and 10 weeks. (p. 254)

social–constructivist classroom
A classroom in which children participate in a wider range of challenging activities with teachers and peers, with whom they jointly construct understandings. As children appropriate (take for themselves) the knowledge and strategies generated from working together, they advance in cognitive and social development and become competent, contributing members of their cultural community. Distinguished from *traditional classroom* and *constructivist classroom.* (p. 456)

sociocultural theory
Vygotsky's theory, in which children are assumed to acquire the ways of thinking and behaving that make up a community's culture through cooperative dialogues with more knowlegeable members of society. (p. 26)

sociodramatic play
The make-believe play with others that is under way by age 2½. (p. 317)

socioeconomic status (SES)
A measure of a family's social position and economic well-being that combines three interrelated, but not completely overlapping, variables: (1) years of education and (2) the prestige of and skill required by one's job, both of which measure social status, and (3) income, which measures economic status. (p. 74)

sociometric techniques
Self-report measures that assess peer acceptance by asking peers to evaluate one another's likability. (p. 487)

stage
A qualitative change in thinking, feeling, and behaving that characterizes a specific period of development. (p. 8)

states of arousal
Different degrees of sleep and wakefulness. (p. 150)

stereotype threat
The fear of being judged on the basis of a negative stereotype, which can trigger anxiety that interferes with performance. (p. 449)

Strange Situation
A procedure that takes the baby through eight short episodes, in which brief separations from and reunions with the caregiver occur in an unfamiliar playroom. Assesses the quality of the attachment bond. (p. 266)

stranger anxiety
The infant's expression of fear in response to unfamiliar adults. Appears in many babies after 6 months of age. (p. 254)

structured interview
A method in which each participant is asked the same questions in the same way. (p. 35)

structured observation
A method in which the investigator sets up a situation that evokes the behavior of interest and observes it in a laboratory. Distinguished from *naturalistic observation*. (p. 33)

subculture
A group of people with beliefs and customs that differ from those of the larger culture. (p. 78)

sudden infant death syndrome (SIDS)
The unexpected death, usually during the night, of an infant younger than 1 year of age that remains unexplained after thorough investigation. (p. 152)

sympathy
Feelings of concern or sorrow for another's plight. (p. 365)

synapses
The gaps between neurons, across which chemical messages are sent. (p. 169)

synaptic pruning
Loss of connective fibers by seldom-stimulated neurons, thereby returning them to an uncommitted state so they can support the development of future skills. (p. 170)

syntactic bootstrapping
Figuring out word meanings by observing how words are used in the structure of sentences. (p. 349)

tabula rasa
Locke's view of the child as a "blank slate" whose character is shaped by experience. (p. 13)

talent
Outstanding performance in a particular field. (p. 461)

telegraphic speech
Toddlers' two-word utterances that, like a telegram, leave out smaller and less important words. (p. 240)

temperament
Stable individual differences in the quality and intensity of emotional reaction, activity level, attention, and emotional self-regulation. (p. 258)

teratogen
Any environmental agent that causes damage during the prenatal period. (p. 106)

thalidomide
A sedative widely available in Europe, Canada, and South America in the early 1960s. When taken by women between the fourth and sixth weeks after conception, it produced gross deformities of the embryo's arms and legs. (p. 108)

theory
An orderly, integrated set of statements that describes, explains, and predicts behavior. (p. 6)

theory of multiple intelligences
Gardner's theory, which proposes at least eight independent intelligences on the basis of distinct sets of processing operations that permit individuals to engage in a wide range of culturally valued activities. (p. 444)

thyroid-stimulating hormone (TSH)
A pituitary hormone that stimulates the thyroid gland to release thyroxine, which is necessary for normal brain development and body growth. (p. 294)

time out
A form of mild punishment in which children are removed from the immediate setting until they are ready to act appropriately. (p. 374)

toxemia
An illness of the last half of pregnancy, in which the mother's blood pressure increases sharply and her face, hands, and feet swell. If untreated, it can cause convulsions in the mother and death of the fetus. Also called *eclampsia*. (p. 120)

toxoplasmosis
A parasitic disease caused by eating raw or undercooked meat or by coming in contact with the feces of infected cats. During the first trimester, it leads to eye and brain damage. (p. 116)

traditional classroom
An elementary school classroom based on the educational philosophy that children are passive learners who acquire information presented by teachers. Children's progress is evaluated on the basis of how well they keep up with a uniform set of standards for all students in their grade. Distinguished from *constructivist classroom* and *social–constructivist classroom*. (p. 455)

transition
Climax of the first stage of labor, in which the frequency and strength of contractions are at their peak and the cervix opens completely. (p. 130)

transitive inference
The ability to seriate—or order items along a quantitative dimension—mentally. (p. 428)

triarchic theory of successful intelligence
Sternberg's theory, which identifies three broad, interacting intelligences: (1) analytical intelligence (information-processing skills), (2) creative intelligence (capacity to solve novel problems), (3) and practical intelligence (application of intellectual skills in everyday situations). Intelligent behavior involves balancing all three to achieve success in life, according to one's personal goals and the requirements of one's cultural community. (p. 443)

trimesters
Three equal time periods in prenatal development, each of which lasts 3 months. (p. 104)

trophoblast
The thin outer ring of cells of the blastocyst, which will become the structures that provide protective covering and nourishment to the new organism. (p. 101)

ulnar grasp
The clumsy grasp of the young infant, in which the fingers close against the palm. (p. 191)

umbilical cord
The long cord connecting the prenatal organism to the placenta; it delivers nutrients and removes waste products. (p. 101)

unconditioned response (UCR)
In classical conditioning, a reflexive response that is produced by an unconditioned stimulus (UCS). (p. 182)

unconditioned stimulus (UCS)
In classical conditioning, a stimulus that leads to a reflexive response. (p. 182)

underextension
An early vocabulary error in which a word is applied too narrowly, to a smaller number of objects and events than is appropriate. Distinguished from *overextension*. (p. 240)

uninhibited, or sociable, child
A child whose temperament is characterized by positive emotional reaction and approach to novel stimuli. Distinguished from *inhibited, or shy, child*. (p. 260)

uninvolved child-rearing style
A child-rearing style that combines low acceptance and involvement with little control and effort to grant autonomy. Reflects minimal commitment to parenting. Distinguished from *authoritative, authoritarian,* and *permissive style*. (p. 389)

utilization deficiency
The inability to improve performance even with consistent use of a mental strategy. Distinguished from *production deficiency, control deficiency,* and *effective strategy use*. (p. 433)

vacuum extractor
A plastic cup attached to a suction tube, used to help deliver a baby. (p. 138)

vernix
A white, cheeselike substance that covers the fetus and prevents the skin from chapping due to constant exposure to amniotic fluid. (p. 104)

violation-of-expectation method
A method in which researchers habituate infants to a physical event and then determine whether they recover responsiveness to (look longer at) a possible event (a variation of the first event that conforms to physical laws) or an impossible event (a variation that violates physical laws). Recovery to the impossible event suggests awareness of that aspect of physical reality. (p. 212)

visual acuity
Fineness of visual discrimination. (p. 156)

Wernicke's area
A language structure located in the temporal lobe of the left hemisphere of the cerebral cortex that is responsible for interpreting language. (p. 236)

whole-language approach
An approach to beginning reading instruction that parallels children's natural language learning and uses reading materials that are whole and meaningful. Distinguished from *basic-skills approach.* (p. 439)

working, or short-term, memory
In information processing, the part of the mental system where we actively "work" on a limited amount of information, applying mental strategies to ensure that it will be retained. (p. 220)

X-linked inheritance
A pattern of inheritance in which a recessive gene is carried on the X chromosome. Males are more likely to be affected. (p. 59)

zone of proximal development
In Vygotsky's theory, a range of tasks that the child cannot yet handle alone but can accomplish with the help of more skilled partners. (p. 227)

zygote
The newly fertilized cell formed by the union of sperm and ovum at conception. (p. 55)

References

Aarons, S. J., Jenkins, R. R., Raine, T. R., El-Khorazaty, M. N., Woodward, K. M., Williams, R. L., Clark, M. C., & Wingrove, B. K. (2000). Postponing sexual intercourse among urban junior high school students—a randomized controlled trial. *Journal of Adolescent Health, 27,* 236–247.

Abbott, S. (1992). Holding on and pushing away: Comparative perspectives on an eastern Kentucky child-rearing practice. *Ethos, 20,* 33–65.

Aber, J. L., Jones, S. M., Brown, J. L., Chaudry, N., & Samples, F. (1998). Resolving conflict creatively: Evaluating the developmental effects of a school-based violence prevention program in neighborhood and classroom contexts. *Development and Psychopathology, 10,* 187–213.

Abikoff, H. B., Jensen, P. S., Arnold, L. L., Hoza, B., Hechtman, L., et al. (2002). Observed classroom behavior of children with ADHD: Relationship to gender and comorbidity. *Journal of Abnormal Child Psychology, 30,* 349–359.

Abramovitch, R., Freedman, J. L., Henry, K., & Van Brunschot, M. (1995). Children's capacity to consent to participation in psychological research: Some empirical findings. *Child Development, 62,* 1100–1109.

Accutane Action Group Forum. (2003, October). General archive area. Retrieved from http://www.xsorbit1.com/users

Achenbach, T. M., Phares, V., Howell, C. T., Rauh, V. A., & Nurcombe, B. (1990). Seven-year outcome of the Vermont program for low-birthweight infants. *Child Development, 61,* 1672–1681.

Achter, J. A., Luginski, D., & Benbow, C. P. (1996). Multipotentiality among the intellectually gifted: "It was never there and already it's vanishing." *Journal of Counseling Psychology, 43,* 65–76.

Acker, M. M., & O'Leary, S. G. (1996). Inconsistency of mothers' feedback and toddlers' misbehavior and negative affect. *Journal of Abnormal Child Psychology, 24,* 703–714.

Adams, M. (2003). *Fire and ice: The United States, Canada, and the myth of converging values.* Toronto: Penguin.

Adams, R., & Laursen, B. (2001). The organization and dynamics of adolescent conflict with parents and friends. *Journal of Marriage and the Family, 63,* 97–110.

Adams, R. J., & Courage, M. L. (1998). Human newborn color vision: Measurement with chromatic stimuli varying in excitation purity. *Journal of Experimental Child Psychology, 68,* 22–34.

Adlaf, E. M., & Paglia, A. (2001). *Drug use among Ontario students, 1997–2001: Findings from the OSDUS.* CAMH Research Document Series No. 10. Toronto: Centre for Addiction and Mental Health.

Adler, P. A., & Adler, P. (1998). *Peer power.* New Brunswick, NJ: Rutgers University Press.

Adolph, K. E. (1997). Learning in the development of infant locomotion. *Monographs of the Society for Research in Child Development, 62*(3, Serial No. 251).

Adolph, K. E. (2000). Specificity of learning: Why infants fall over a veritable cliff. *Psychological Science, 11,* 290–295.

Adolph, K. E., & Eppler, M. A. (1998). Development of visually guided locomotion. *Ecological Psychology, 10,* 303–321.

Adolph, K. E., & Eppler, M. A. (1999). Obstacles to understanding: An ecological approach to infant problem solving. In E. Winograd, R. Fivush, & W. Hirst (Eds.), *Ecological approaches to cognition* (pp. 31–58). Mahwah, NJ: Erlbaum.

Adolph, K. E. A., Vereijken, B., & Denny, M. A. (1998). Learning to crawl. *Child Development, 69,* 1299–1312.

Adolph, K. E. A., Vereijken, B., & Shrout, P. E. (2003). What changes in infant walking and why. *Child Development, 74,* 475–497.

Agran, P. F., Winn, D., Anderson, C., Trent, R., & Walton-Haynes, L. (2001). Rates of pediatric and adolescent injuries by year of age. *Pediatrics, 108,* e45.

Aguiar, A., & Baillargeon, R. (1999). 2.5-month-old infants' reasoning about when objects should and should not be occluded. *Cognitive Psychology, 39,* 116–157.

Aguiar, A., & Baillargeon, R. (2002). Developments in young infants' reasoning about occluded objects. *Cognitive Psychology, 45,* 267–336.

Ahluwalia, I. B., Morrow, B., Hsia, J., & Grummer-Strawn, L. M. (2003). Who is breast-feeding? Recent trends from the pregnancy risk assessment and monitoring system. *Journal of Pediatrics, 142,* 486–491.

Ahmed, A., & Ruffman, T. (1998). Why do infants make A not B errors in a search task, yet show memory for the location of hidden objects in a nonsearch task? *Developmental Psychology, 34,* 441–453.

Ainsworth, M. D. S., Blehar, M. C., Waters, E., & Wall, S. (1978). *Patterns of attachment.* Hillsdale, NJ: Erlbaum.

Airhihenbuwa, C. A., Kumanyika, S., Agurs, T. D., & Low, A. (1995). Perceptions and beliefs about exercise, rest, and health among African Americans. *American Journal of Health Promotion, 9,* 426–429.

Akers, J. F., Jones, R. M., & Coyl, D. D. (1998). Adolescent friendship pairs: Similarities in identity status development, behaviors, attitudes, and intentions. *Journal of Adolescent Research, 13,* 178–201.

Akhtar, N., & Montague, L. (1999). Early lexical acquisition: The role of cross-situational learning. *First Language, 19,* 347–358.

Akhtar, N., & Tomasello, M. (2000). The social nature of words and word learning. In R. Golinkoff & K. Hirsh-Pasek (Eds.), *Becoming a word learner: A debate on lexical acquisition.* Oxford, U.K.: Oxford University Press.

Akimoto, S. A., & Sanbinmatsu, D. M. (1999). Differences in self-effacing behavior between European and Japanese Americans: Effect on competence evaluations. *Journal of Cross-Cultural Psychology, 30,* 159–177.

Akinbami, L. J., & Schoendorf, K. C. (2002). Trends in childhood asthma: Prevalence, health care utilization, and mortality. *Pediatrics, 110,* 315–322.

Akshoomoff, N. A., Feroleto, C. C., Doyle, R. E., & Stiles, J. (2001). The impact of early unilateral brain injury on perceptual organization and visual memory. *Neuropsychologia, 40,* 539–561.

Akshoomoff, N. A., & Stiles, J. (1995). Developmental trends in visuospatial analysis and planning: I. Copying a complex figure. *Neuropsychology, 9,* 378–389.

Alan Guttmacher Institute. (2002a). Teen pregnancy: Trends and lessons learned. Retrieved from http://www.agi-usa.org/pubs/ib_-02.html

Alan Guttmacher Institute. (2002b). Teen sex and pregnancy. Retrieved from http://www.agi-usa.org/pubs/ib_teen_sex.html

Aldridge, M. A., Stillman, R. D., & Bower, T. G. R. (2001). Newborn categorization of vowel-like sounds. *Developmental Science, 4,* 220–232.

Alessandri, S. M., Bendersky, M., & Lewis, M. (1998). Cognitive functioning in 8- to 18-month-old drug-exposed infants. *Developmental Psychology, 34,* 565–573.

Alessandri, S. M., & Wozniak, R. H. (1987). The child's awareness of parental beliefs concerning the child: A developmental study. *Child Development, 58,* 316–323.

Alexander, J. M., Fabricius, W. V., Fleming, V. M., Zwahr, M., & Brown, S. A. (2003). The development of metacognitive causal explanations. *Learning and Individual Differences, 13,* 227–238.

Alexander, K. L., Entwisle, D. R., & Kabbani, N. S. (2001). The dropout process in life course perspective: Early risk factors at home and school. *Teachers College Record, 103,* 760–822.

Alexandre-Bidon, D., & Lett, D. (1997). *Les enfants au Moyen Age, Ve–XVe siecles.* Paris: Hachette.

Alfieri, T., Ruble, D. N., & Higgins, E. T. (1996). Gender stereotypes during adolescence: Developmental changes and the transition to junior high school. *Developmental Psychology, 32,* 1129–1137.

Ali, L., & Scelfo, J. (2002, December 9). Choosing virginity. *Newsweek,* pp. 60–65.

Alibali, M. W. (1999). How children change their minds: Strategy change can be gradual or abrupt. *Developmental Psychology, 35,* 127–145.

Aligne, C. A., Moss, M. E., Auinger, P., & Weitzman, M. (2003). Association of pediatric dental caries with passive smoking. *Journal of the American Medical Association, 289,* 1258–1264.

Allen, J. P., Philliber, S., Herrling, S., & Kuperminc, G. P. (1997). Preventing teen pregnancy and academic failure: Experimental evaluation of a developmentally based approach. *Child Development, 64,* 729–742.

Allen, M., & Burrell, N. (1996). Comparing the impact of homosexual and heterosexual parents on children: Meta-analysis of existing research. *Journal of Homosexuality, 32,* 19–35.

Allen, S. E. M., & Crago, M. B. (1996). Early passive acquisition in Inukitut. *Journal of Child Language, 23,* 129–156.

Allison, D. B., & Pi-Sunyer, X. (1994, May–June). Fleshing out obesity. *The Sciences, 34*(3), 38–43.

Alpert-Gillis, L. J., & Connell, J. P. (1989). Gender and sex-role influences on children's self-esteem. *Journal of Personality, 57*, 97–114.

Alsaker, F. D. (1995). Timing of puberty and reactions to pubertal changes. In M. Rutter (Ed.), *Psychosocial disturbances in young people: Challenges for prevention* (pp. 37–82). New York: Cambridge University Press.

Amato, P. R. (2001). Children of divorce in the 1990s: An update of the Amato and Keith (1991) meta-analysis. *Journal of Family Psychology, 15*, 355–370.

Amato, P. R., & Booth, A. (1996). A prospective study of divorce and parent–child relationships. *Journal of Marriage and the Family, 58*, 356–365.

Amato, P. R., & Booth, A. (2000). *A generation at risk: Growing up in an era of family upheaval.* Cambridge, MA: Harvard University Press.

Amato, P. R., & Fowler, F. (2002). Parenting practices, child adjustment, and family diversity. *Journal of Marriage and the Family, 64*, 703–716.

Ambert, A.-M. (2003). *Same-sex couples and same-sex-parent families: Relationships, parenting, and issues of marriage.* Ottawa, Canada: Vanier Institute of the Family. Retrieved from http://www.vifamily.ca

American Academy of Pediatrics. (1997). *Breastfeeding and the use of human milk.* Retrieved from http://www.aap.org/policy/re9729.html

American Academy of Pediatrics. (1999). Contraception and adolescents. *Pediatrics, 104*, 1161–1166.

American Academy of Pediatrics. (2000). Changing concepts of sudden infant death syndrome: Implications for infant sleeping environment and sleep position. *Pediatrics, 105*, 650–656.

American Academy of Pediatrics. (2001). Implementation principles and strategies for the State Children's Health Insurance Program. *Pediatrics, 107*, 1214–1220.

American Academy of Pediatrics. (2004). *Rise in childhood obesity linked to increase in Type 2 diabetes.* Retrieved from http://www.aap.org/advocacy/archives/mardia.htm

American College of Obstetricians and Gynecologists (ACOG), Committee on Obstetric Practice. (2002). ACOG committee opinion. Air travel during pregnancy. *International Journal of Gynaecology and Obstetrics, 76*, 338–339.

American Psychiatric Association. (1994). *Diagnostic and statistical manual of mental disorders* (4th ed.). Washington, DC: Author.

American Psychological Association. (2002). Ethical principles of psychologists and code of conduct. *American Psychologist, 57*, 1060–1073.

Ames, C. (1992). Classrooms: Goals, structures, and student motivation. *Journal of Educational Psychology, 84*, 261–271.

Ames, E. (1997). *The development of Romanian orphanage children adopted to Canada* (Final Report to the National Welfare Grants Program). Burnaby, British Columbia: Simon Fraser University.

Anand, S. S., Yusuf, S., Jacobs, R., Davis, A. D., Yi, Q., & Gerstein, H. (2001). Risk factors, arteriosclerosis, and cardiovascular disease among Aboriginal people in Canada: The study of health assessment and risk evaluation in Aboriginal peoples (SHARE-AP). *Lancet, 358*, 1147–1153.

Anaya, H. D., Cantwell, S. M., & Rothman-Borus, M. J. (2003). Sexual risk behaviors among adolescents. In A. Biglan & M. C. Wang (Eds.), *Preventing youth problems* (pp. 113–143). New York: Kluwer Academic.

Ances, B. M. (2002). New concerns about thalidomide. *Obstetrics and Gynecology, 99*, 125–128.

Anderman, E. M., Eccles, J. S., Yoon, K. S., Roeser, R., Wigfield, A., & Blumenfeld, P. (2001). Learning to value mathematics and reading: Relations to mastery and performance-oriented instructional practices. *Contemporary Educational Psychology, 26*, 76–95.

Anderman, E. M., & Midgley, C. (1997). Changes in achievement goal orientations, perceived academic competence, and grades across the transition to middle-level schools. *Contemporary Educational Psychology, 22*, 269–298.

Anderson, C. A., & Bushman, B. J. (2001). Effects of violent video games on aggressive behavior, aggressive, cognition, aggressive affect, physiological arousal, and prosocial behavior: A meta-analytic review of the scientific literature. *Psychological Science, 12*, 353–359.

Anderson, D. M., Huston, A. C., Schmitt, K. L., Linebarger, D. L., & Wright, J. C. (2001). Early childhood television viewing and adolescent behavior. *Monographs of the Society for Research in Child Development, 66*(1, Serial No. 264).

Anderson, E. (1992). *Speaking with style: The sociolinguistic skills of children.* London: Routledge.

Anderson, G. C. (1999). Kangaroo care of the premature infant. In E. Goldstein (Ed.), *Nurturing the premature infant: Developmental interventions in the neonatal intensive care nursery* (pp. 131–160). New York: Oxford University Press.

Anderson, S. E., Dallal, G. E., & Must, A. (2003). Relative weight and race influence average age at menarche: Results from two nationally representative surveys of U.S. girls studied 25 years apart. *Pediatrics, 111*, 844–850.

Andersson, B.-E. (1989). Effects of public day care—A longitudinal study. *Child Development, 60*, 857–866.

Andersson, B.-E. (1992). Effects of day care on cognitive and socioemotional competence of thirteen-year-old Swedish schoolchildren. *Child Development, 63*, 20–36.

Andersson, S. W., Bengtsson, C., Hallberg, L., Lapidus, L., Niklasson, A., Wallgren, A., & Huthén, L. (2001). Cancer risk in Swedish women: The relation to size at birth. *British Journal of Cancer, 84*, 1193–1198.

Andrews, G., & Halford, G. S. (1998). Children's ability to make transitive inferences: The importance of premise integration and structural complexity. *Cognitive Development, 13*, 479–513.

Anglin, J. M. (1993). Vocabulary development: A morphological analysis. *Monographs of the Society for Research in Child Development, 58*(10, Serial No. 238).

Anhalt, K., & Morris, T. L. (1999). Developmental and adjustment issues of gay, lesbian, and bisexual adolescents: A review of the empirical literature. *Clinical Child Psychology and Psychiatry, 7*, 433–456.

Anisfeld, M., Turkewitz, G., Rose, S. A., Rosenberg, F. R., Shelber, F. J., Couturier-Fagan, D. A., Ger, J. S., & Sommer I. (2001). No compelling evidence that newborns imitate oral gestures. *Infancy, 2*, 111–122.

Annett, M. (2002). *Handedness and brain asymmetry: The right shift theory.* Hove, U.K.: Psychology Press.

Anslow, P. (1998). Birth asphyxia. *European Journal of Radiology, 26*, 148–153.

Apgar, V. (1953). A proposal for a new method of evaluation in the newborn infant. *Current Research in Anesthesia and Analgesia, 32*, 260–267.

Aquilino, W. S., & Supple, A. J. (2001). Long-term effects of parenting practices during adolescence on well-being outcomes in young adulthood. *Journal of Family Issues, 22*, 289–308.

Aram, D., & Levin, I. (2001). Mother–child joint writing in low SES: Sociocultural factors, maternal mediation, and emergent literacy. *Cognitive Development, 16*, 831–852.

Aram, D., & Levin, I. (2002). Mother–child joint writing and storybook reading: Relations with literacy among low SES kindergartners. *Merrill-Palmer Quarterly, 48*, 202–224.

Archer, S. L. (1989). The status of identity: Reflections on the need for intervention. *Journal of Adolescence, 12*, 345–359.

Archer, S. L., & Waterman, A. S. (1990). Varieties of identity diffusions and foreclosures: An exploration of subcategories of the identity statuses. *Journal of Adolescent Research, 5*, 96–111.

Ardila-Rey, A., & Killen, M. (2001). Middle-class Colombian children's evaluations of personal, moral, and social-conventional interactions in the classroom. *International Journal of Behavioral Development, 25*, 246–255.

Arnett, J. J. (1997). Young people's conceptions of the transition to adulthood. *Youth and Society, 29*, 1–23.

Arnett, J. J. (1998). Learning to stand alone: The contemporary American transition to adulthood in cultural and historical context. *Human Development, 41*, 295–315.

Arnett, J. J. (1999). Adolescent storm and stress, reconsidered. *American Psychologist, 54*, 317–326.

Arnett, J. J. (2000a). Emerging adulthood: A theory of development from the late teens through the twenties. *American Psychologist, 55*, 469–480.

Arnett, J. J. (2000b). High hopes in a grim world: Emerging adults' view of their futures and of "Generation X." *Youth and Society, 31*, 267–286.

Arnett, J. J. (2001). Conceptions of the transition to adulthood: Perspectives from adolescence to midlife. *Journal of Adult Development, 8*, 133–143.

Arnett, J. J. (2002). The psychology of globalization. *American Psychologist, 57*, 774–783.

Arnett, J. J. (2003). Conceptions of the transition to adulthood among emerging adults in American ethnic groups. In J. J. Arnett & N. L. Galambos (Eds.), *Exploring cultural conceptions of the transitions to adulthood (New directions for child and adolescent development,* No. 100, pp. 63–75). San Francisco: Jossey-Bass.

Arnett, J. J., & Jensen, L. A. (2002). A congregation of one: Individualized religious beliefs among emerging adults. *Journal of Adolescent Research, 17*, 451–467.

Arnett, J. J., Ramos, K. D., & Jensen, L. A. (2001). Ideological views in emerging adulthood: Balancing autonomy and community. *Journal of Adult Development, 8*, 69–79.

Arnold, D. H., Fisher, P. H., Doctoroff, G. L., & Dobbs, J. (2002). Accelerating math development in Head Start classrooms. *Journal of Educational Psychology, 94*, 762–770.

Arnold, K. (1994). The Illinois Valedictorian Project: Early adult careers of academically talented male and female high school students. In R. F. Subotnik & K. D. Arnold (Eds.), *Beyond Terman: Contemporary longitudinal studies of giftedness and talent* (pp. 24–51). Norwood, NJ: Ablex.

Arnold, L. E., Elliott, M., Sachs, L., Bird, H., Kraemer, H. C., & Wells, K. C. (2003). Effects of ethnicity on treatment attendance, stimulant response/dose, and 14-month outcome in ADHD. *Journal of Consulting and Clinical Psychology, 71*, 713–727.

Arnold, P. (1999). Emotional disorders in deaf children. In V. L. Schwean & D. H. Saklofske (Eds.), *Handbook of psychosocial characteristics of exceptional children* (pp. 493–522). New York: Kluwer.

Aronson, M., Hagberg, B., & Gillberg, C. (1997). Attention deficits and autistic spectrum problems in children exposed to alcohol during gestation: A follow-up study. *Developmental Medicine and Child Neurology, 39,* 583–587.

Arora, S., McJunkin, C., Wehrer, J., & Kuhn, P. (2000). Major factors influencing breastfeeding rates: Mother's perception of father's attitude and milk supply. *Pediatrics, 106,* e67.

Arsenio, W., & Fleiss, K. (1996). Typical and behaviourally disruptive children's understanding of the emotional consequences of socio-moral events. *British Journal of Developmental Psychology, 14,* 173–186.

Arterberry, M. E., Craton, L. G., & Yonas, A. (1993). Infants' sensitivity to motion-carried information for depth and object properties. In C. E. Granrud (Ed.), *Visual perception and cognition in infancy* (pp. 215–234). Hillsdale, NJ: Erlbaum.

Artman, L., & Cahan, S. (1993). Schooling and the development of transitive inference. *Developmental Psychology, 29,* 753–759.

Asakawa, K. (2001). Family socialization practices and their effects on the internationalization of educational values for Asian and white American adolescents. *Applied Developmental Science, 5,* 184–194.

Asher, S. R., & Rose, A. J. (1997). Promoting children's social-emotional adjustment with peers. In P. Salovey & D. J. Sluyter (Eds.), *Emotional development and emotional intelligence* (pp. 193–195). New York: Basic Books.

Ashley-Koch, A., Yang, Q., & Olney, R. S. (2000). Sickle hemoglobin (HbS) allele and sickle cell disease: A HuGE review. *American Journal of Epidemiology, 151,* 839–845.

Ashraf, H. (2002). U.N. pleads for better reproductive health in poor nations. *Lancet, 360,* 1843.

Aslin, R. N. (2000). Why take the cog out of infant cognition? *Infancy, 1,* 463–470.

Aslin, R. N., Jusczyk, P. W., & Pisoni, D. B. (1998). Speech and auditory processing during infancy: Constraints on and precursors to language. In D. Kuhn & R. S. Siegler (Eds.), *Handbook of child psychology: Vol. 2. Cognition, perception, and language* (5th ed., pp. 147–198). New York: Wiley.

Astington, J. W., & Jenkins, J. M. (1995). Theory of mind development and social understanding. *Cognition and Emotion, 9,* 151–165.

Astington, J. W., Pelletier, J., & Homer, B. (2002). Theory of mind and epistemological development: The relation between children's second-order false belief understanding and their ability to reason about

evidence. *New Ideas in Psychology, 20,* 131–144.

Astley, S. J., Clarren, S. K., Little, R. E., Sampson, P. D., & Daling, J. R. (1992). Analysis of facial shape in children gestationally exposed to marijuana, alcohol, and/or cocaine. *Pediatrics, 89,* 67–77.

Atanackovic, G., & Koren, G. (1999). Fetal exposure to oral isotretinoin: Failure to comply with the Pregnancy Prevention Program. *Canadian Medical Association Journal, 160,* 1719–1720.

Atkinson, J. (2000). *The developing visual brain.* Oxford: Oxford University Press.

Atkinson, R. C., & Shiffrin, R. M. (1968). Human memory: A proposed system and its control processes. In K. W. Spence & J. T. Spence (Eds.), *Advances in the psychology of learning and motivation* (Vol. 2, pp. 90–195). New York: Academic Press.

Attewell, P. (2001). The first and second digital divides. *Sociology of Education, 74,* 252–259.

Au, T. K., Sidle, A. L., & Rollins, K. B. (1993). Developing an intuitive understanding of conservation and contamination: Invisible particles as a plausible mechanism. *Developmental Psychology, 29,* 286–299.

Auinger, P., Lanphear, B. P., Kalkwarf, H. J., & Mansour, M. E. (2003). Trends in otitis media among children in the United States. *Pediatrics, 112,* 514–520.

Aunola, K., Stattin, H., & Nurmi, J.-E. (2000). Parenting styles and adolescents' achievement strategies. *Journal of Adolescence, 23,* 205–222.

Australian Bureau of Statistics. (2003). Divorce rates. Retrieved from http://www.abus.gov.au

Avis, J., & Harris, P. L. (1991). Belief–desire reasoning among Baka children: Evidence for a universal conception of mind. *Child Development, 62,* 460–467.

Axia, G., & Baroni, R. (1985). Linguistic politeness at different age levels. *Child Development, 56,* 918–927.

Axia, G., Bonichini, S., & Benini, F. (1999). Attention and reaction to distress in infancy: A longitudinal study. *Developmental Psychology, 35,* 500–504.

Axinn, W. G., & Barber, J. S. (1997). Living arrangements and family formation attitudes in early adulthood. *Journal of Marriage and the Family, 59,* 595–611.

Azar, S. T., & Wolfe, D. A. (1998). Child physical abuse and neglect. In E. J. Mash & R. A. Barkley (Eds.), *Treatment of childhood disorders* (2nd ed., pp. 501–544). New York: Guilford.

Bacharach, V. R., & Baumeister, A. A. (1998). Direct and indirect effects of maternal intelligence, maternal age, income, and home environment on intelligence of preterm, low-birth-weight children. *Journal*

of Applied Developmental Psychology, 19, 361–375.

Bachman, J. G., Wadsworth, K. N., O'Malley, P. M., Johnston, L. D., & Schulenberg, J. E. (1997). *Smoking, drinking, and drug use in young adulthood.* Mahwah, NJ: Erlbaum.

Bach-y-Rita, P. (2001). Theoretical and practical considerations in the restoration of function after stroke. *Topics in Stroke Rehabilitation, 8,* 1–15.

Baddeley, A. (1993). Working memory and conscious awareness. In A. F. Collins, S. E. Gathercole, M. A. Conway, & P. E. Morris (Eds.), *Theories of memory* (pp. 11–28). Hove, U.K.: Erlbaum.

Baddeley, A. (2000). Short-term and working memory. In E. Tulving & R. I. M. Craik (Eds.), *The Oxford handbook of memory* (pp. 77–92). New York: Oxford University Press.

Bader, A. P. (1995). Engrossment revisited: Fathers are still falling in love with their newborn babies. In J. L. Shapiro, M. J. Diamond, & M. Greenberg (Eds.), *Becoming a father* (pp 224–233). New York: Springer.

Bader, A. P., & Phillips, R. D. (2002). Fathers' recognition of their newborns by visual-facial and olfactory cues. *Psychology of Men and Masculinity, 3,* 79–84.

Baenninger, M., & Newcombe, N. (1995). Environmental input to the development of sex-related differences in spatial and mathematical ability. *Learning and Individual Differences, 7,* 363–379.

Bagwell, C. L., Coie, J. D., Terry, R. A., & Lochman, J. E. (2000). Peer clique participation and social status in preadolescence. *Merrill-Palmer Quarterly, 46,* 280–305.

Bagwell, C. L., Newcomb, A. F., & Bukowski, W. M. (1998). Preadolescent friendship and peer rejection as predictors of adult adjustment. *Child Development, 69,* 140–153.

Bagwell, C. L., Schmidt, M. E., Newcomb, A. F., & Bukowski, W. M. (2001). Friendship and peer rejection as predictors of adult adjustment. In D. W. Nangle & C. A. Erdley (Eds.), *The role of friendship in psychological adjustment* (pp. 25–49). San Francisco: Jossey-Bass.

Bahrick, L. E. (1992). Infants' perception of substance and temporal synchrony in multimodal events. *Infant Behavior and Development, 6,* 429–451.

Bahrick, L. E. (2001). Increasing specificity in perceptual development: Infants' detection of nested levels of multimodal stimulation. *Journal of Experimental Child Psychology, 79,* 253–270.

Bahrick, L. E., Netto, D., & Hernandez-Reif, M. (1998). Intermodal perception of adult and child faces and voices by infants. *Child Development, 69,* 1263–1275.

Bai, D. L., & Bertenthal, B. I. (1992). Locomotor status and the develop-

ment of spatial search skills. *Child Development, 63,* 215–226.

Bailey, J. M., Bobrow, D., Wolfe, M., & Mikach, S. (1995). Sexual orientation of adult sons of gay fathers. *Developmental Psychology, 31,* 124–129.

Bailey, J. M., Dunne, M. P., & Martin, N. G. (2000). Genetic and environmental influences on sexual orientation and its correlates in an Australian twin sample. *Journal of Personality and Social Psychology, 78,* 524–536.

Bailey, R. C. (1991). The comparative growth of Efe pygmies and African farmers from birth to age 5 years. *Annals of Human Biology, 18,* 113–120.

Baillargeon, R. (1994). Physical reasoning in infancy. In M. S. Gazzaniga (Ed.), *The cognitive neurosciences* (pp. 181–204). Cambridge, MA: MIT Press.

Baillargeon, R. (2000). Reply to Bogartz, Shinskey, and Schilling: Schilling; and Cashon and Cohen. *Infancy, 1,* 447–462.

Baillargeon, R., & DeVos, J. (1991). Object permanence in young infants: Further evidence. *Child Development, 62,* 1227–1246.

Baker, D. P., & Jones, D. P. (1993). Creating gender equality: Cross-national gender stratification and mathematics performance. *Sociology of Education, 66,* 91–103.

Bakermans-Kranenburg, M. J., van IJzendoorn, M. H., & Juffer, F. (2003). Less is more: Meta-analyses of sensitivity and attachment interventions in early childhood. *Psychological Bulletin, 129,* 195–215.

Band, G. P. H., van der Molen, M. W., Overtoom, C. C. E., & Verbaten, M. N. (2000). The ability to activate and inhibit speeded responses: Separate developmental trends. *Journal of Experimental Child Psychology, 75,* 263–290.

Bandura, A. (1977). *Social learning theory.* Englewood Cliffs, NJ: Prentice-Hall.

Bandura, A. (1992). Perceived self-efficacy in cognitive development and functioning. *Educational Psychologist, 28,* 117–118.

Bandura, A. (1999). Social cognitive theory of personality. In L. A. Pervin (Ed.), *Handbook of personality: Theory and research* (2nd ed., pp. 154–196). New York: Guilford.

Bandura, A. (2001). Social cognitive theory: An agentic perspective. *Annual Review of Psychology, 52,* 1–26.

Banish, M. T. (1998). Integration of information between the cerebral hemispheres. *Current Directions in Psychological Science, 7,* 32–37.

Banish, M. T., & Heller, W. (1998). Evolving perspectives on lateralization of function. *Current Directions in Psychological Science, 7,* 1–2.

Banks, D. (2003). Proteomics: A frontier between genomics and metabolomics. *Chance, 16*(4), 6–7.

Banks, M. S. (1980). The development of visual accommodation during early infancy. *Child Development, 51,* 157–173.

Banks, M. S., & Salapatek, P. (1983). Infant visual perception. In M. M. Haith & J. J. Campos (Eds.), *Handbook of child psychology: Vol. 2. Infancy and developmental psychobiology* (4th ed., pp. 435–571). New York: Wiley.

Banta, D. H., & Thacker, S. B. (2001). Historical controversy in health technology assessment: The case of electronic fetal monitoring. *Obstetrical and Gynecological Survey, 56,* 707–719.

Barakat, L. P., & Kazak, A. E. (1999). Family issues. In R. T. Brown (Ed.), *Cognitive aspects of chronic illness in children* (pp. 333–354). New York: Guilford.

Barber, B. K., & Harmon, E. L.. (2002). Violating the self: Parental psychological control of children and adolescents. In B. K. Barber (Ed.), *Parental psychological control of children and adolescents* (pp. 15–52). Washington, DC: American Psychological Association.

Barber, B. K., & Olsen, J. A. (1997). Socialization in context: Connection, regulation, and autonomy in the family, school, and neighborhood, and with peers. *Journal of Adolescent Research, 12,* 287–315.

Barber, J. S. (2001). Ideational influences on the transition to parenthood: Attitudes toward childbearing and competing alternatives. *Social Psychology Quarterly, 64,* 101–127.

Barker, D. (2002). Fetal programming of coronary heart disease. *Trends in Endocrinology and Metabolism, 13,* 364.

Barker, D. J., Eriksson, J. G., Forsén, T., & Osmond, C. (2002). Fetal origins of adult disease: Strength of effects and biological basis. *International Journal of Epidemiology, 31,* 1235–1239.

Barkley, R. A. (1999). Theories of attention-deficit/hyperactivity disorder. In H. C. Quay & A. E. Hogan (Eds.), *Handbook of disruptive behavior disorders* (pp. 295–313). New York: Kluwer.

Barkley, R. A. (2002a). Psychosocial treatments of attention-deficit/hyperactivity disorder in children. *Journal of Clinical Psychology, 63*(Suppl. 12), 36–43.

Barkley, R. A. (2002b). Major life activity and health outcomes associated with attention-deficit/hyperactivity disorder. *Journal of Clinical Psychiatry, 63*(Suppl. 12), 10–15.

Barkley, R. A. (2003). Attention-deficit/hyperactivity disorder. In E. J. Mash & R. A. Barkley (Eds.), *Child psychopathology* (2nd ed., pp. 75–143). New York: Guilford.

Barkley, R. A., Fischer, M., Smallish, L., & Fletcher, K. (2002). The persistence of attention-deficit/hyperactivity disorder into young adulthood as a function of reporting source and definition of disorder. *Journal of Abnormal Psychology, 111,* 279–289.

Barling, J., Rogers, K., & Kelloway, K. (1995). Some effects of teenagers' part-time employment: The quantity and quality of work make the differences. *Journal of Organizational Behavior, 16,* 143–154.

Barnes-Josiah, D., & Augustin, A. (1995). Secular trend in the age at menarche in Haiti. *American Journal of Human Biology, 7,* 357–362.

Barnett, D., Ganiban, J., & Cicchetti, D. (1999). Maltreatment, negative expressivity, and the development of Type D attachments from 12 to 24 months of age. In J. I. Vondra & D. Barnett (Eds.), Atypical attachment in infancy and early childhood among children at developmental risk. *Monographs of the Society for Research in Child Development, 64*(3, Serial No. 258), pp. 97–118.

Barnett, D., & Vondra, J. I. (1999). Atypical patterns of early attachment: Theory, research, and current directions. In J. I. Vondra & D. Barnett (Eds.), Atypical attachment in infancy and early childhood among children at developmental risk. *Monographs of the Society for Research in Child Development, 64*(3, Serial No. 258), pp. 1–24.

Baron-Cohen, S. (2001). Theory of mind and autism: A review. In L. M. Glidden (Ed.), *International review of research in mental retardation: Autism* (Vol. 23, pp. 169–184). San Diego: Academic Press.

Baron-Cohen, S., Baldwin, D. A., & Crowson, M. (1997). Do children with autism use the speaker's direction of gaze strategy to crack the code of language? *Child Development, 68,* 48–57.

Barr, C. L., Wigg, K. G., Bloom, S., Schachar, R., Tannock, R., & Roberts, W. (2000). Further evidence from haplotype analysis for linkage of the dopamine D4 receptor gene and attention-deficit hyperactivity disorder. *American Journal of Medical Genetics, 96,* 262–267.

Barr, H. M., Streissguth, A. P., Darby, B. L., & Sampson, P. D. (1990). Prenatal exposure to alcohol, caffeine, tobacco, and aspirin: Effects on fine and gross motor performance in 4-year-old children. *Developmental Psychology, 26,* 339–348.

Barr, R. G. (2001). "Colic" is something infants do, rather than a condition they "have": A developmental approach to crying phenomena patterns, pacification and (patho)genesis. In R. G. Barr, I. St James-Roberts, & M. R. Keefe (Eds.), *New evidence on unexplained infant crying* (pp. 87–104). St. Louis: Johnson & Johnson Pediatric Institute.

Barr, R. G., & Gunnar, M. (2000). Colic: The 'transient responsivity' hypothesis. In R. G. Barr, B. Hopkins, & J. A. Green (Eds.), *Crying as a sign, a symptom, and a signal* (pp. 41–66). Cambridge, U.K.: Cambridge University Press.

Barr, R., & Hayne, H. (1999). Developmental changes in imitation from television during infancy. *Child Development, 70,* 1067–1081.

Barr, R., & Hayne, H. (2003). It's not what you know, it's who you know: Older siblings facilitate imitation during infancy. *International Journal of Early Years Education, 11,* 7–21.

Barratt, M. S., Roach, M. A., & Leavitt, L. A. (1996). The impact of low-risk prematurity on maternal behaviour and toddler outcomes. *International Journal of Behavioral Development, 19,* 581–602.

Barrett, J. L. (1998). Cognitive constraints on Hindu concepts of the divine. *Journal for the Scientific Study of Religion, 37,* 608–619.

Barrett, J. L. (2002). Do children experience God as adults do? In J. Andresen (Ed.), *Religion in mind* (pp. 173–190). New York: Cambridge University Press.

Barrett, J. L., Richert, R. A., & Driesenga, A. (2001). God's beliefs versus mother's: The development of nonhuman agent concepts. *Child Development, 72,* 50–65.

Barrett, J. L., & Van Orman, B. (1996). The effects of the use of images in worship on God concepts. *Journal of Psychology and Christianity, 15,* 38–45.

Barrett, K. C. (1998). The origins of guilt in early childhood. In J. Bybee (Ed.), *Guilt and children* (pp. 75–90). San Diego: Academic Press.

Bartgis, J., Lilly, A. R., & Thomas, D. G. (2003). Event-related potential and behavioral measures of attention in 5-, 7-, and 9-year-olds. *Journal of General Psychology, 130,* 311–335.

Barton, M. E., & Strosberg, R. (1997). Conversational patterns of two-year-old twins in mother–twin–twin triads. *Journal of Child Language, 24,* 257–269.

Barton, M. E., & Tomasello, M. (1991). Joint attention and conversation in mother–infant–sibling triads. *Child Development, 62,* 517–529.

Bartrip, J., Morton, J., & de Schonen, S. (2001). Responses to mother's face in 3-week to 3-month-old infants. *British Journal of Developmental Psychology, 19,* 219–232.

Bartsch, K., & Wellman, H. (1995). *Children talk about the mind.* New York: Oxford University Press.

Basow, S. A., & Rubin, L. R. (1999). Gender influences on adolescent development. In N. G. Johnson & M. C. Roberts (Eds.), *Beyond appearance: A new look at adolescent girls* (pp. 25–52). Washington, DC: American Psychological Association.

Bates, E. (1999). Plasticity, localization, and language development. In S. H. Broman & J. M. Fletcher (Eds.), *The changing nervous system: Neurobehavioral consequences of early brain disorders* (pp. 214–247). New York: Oxford University Press.

Bates, E., & MacWhinney, B. (1987). Competition, variation, and language learning. In B. MacWhinney (Ed.), *Mechanisms of language acquisition* (pp. 157–193). Hillsdale, NJ: Erlbaum.

Bates, E., Marchman, V., Thal, D., Fenson, L., Dale, P., Reznick, J. S., Reilly, J., & Hartung, J. (1994). Developmental and stylistic variation in the composition of early vocabulary. *Journal of Child Language, 21,* 85–123.

Bates, J. E., Wachs, T. D., & Emde, R. N. (1994). Toward practical uses for biological concepts. In J. E. Bates & T. D. Wachs (Eds.), *Temperament: Individual differences at the interface of biology and behavior* (pp. 275–306). Washington, DC: American Psychological Association.

Battin, M. R., Dezoiete, A., Gunn, T. R., Gluckman, P. D., & Gunn, A. J. (2001). Neurodevelopmental outcome of infants treated with head cooling and mild hypothermia after perinatal asphyxia. *Pediatrics, 107,* 480–484.

Bauer, P. J. (1997). Development of memory in early childhood. In N. Cowan (Ed.), *The development of memory in childhood* (pp. 83–111). Hove, U.K.: Psychology Press.

Bauer, P. J. (2002). Early memory development. In U. Goswami (Ed.), *Blackwell handbook of child cognitive development* (pp. 127–150). Malden, MA: Blackwell.

Bauer, P. J. (2002). Long-term recall memory: Behavioral and neurodevelopmental changes in the first 2 years of life. *Current Directions in Psychological Science, 11,* 137–141.

Baumeister, R. F. (1998). Inducing guilt. In J. Bybee (Ed.), *Guilt and children* (pp. 185–213). San Diego: Academic Press.

Baumeister, R. F., Smart, L., & Boden, J. M. (1996). Relation of threatened egotism to violence and aggression: The dark side of high self-esteem. *Psychological Review, 103,* 5–33.

Baumrind, D. (1971). Current patterns of parental authority. *Developmental Psychology Monograph, 4* (No. 1, Pt. 2).

Baumrind, D., & Black, A. E. (1967). Socialization practices associated with dimension of competence in preschool boys and girls. *Child Development, 38,* 291–327.

Baumwell, L., Tamis-LeMonda, C. S., & Bornstein, M. H. (1997). Maternal verbal sensitivity and child language comprehension. *Infant Behavior and Development, 20,* 247–258.

Bauserman, R. (2002). Child adjustment in joint-custody versus sole-custody arrangements: A meta-analytic review. *Journal of Family Psychology, 16,* 91–102.

Bayley, N. (1969). *Bayley Scales of Infant Development.* New York: Psychological Corporation.

Bayley, N. (1993). *Bayley Scales of Infant Development* (2nd ed.). New York: Psychological Corporation.

Beal, C. R. (1990). The development of text evaluation and revision skills. *Child Development, 61*, 247–258.

Bearison, D. J. (1998). Pediatric psychology and children's medical problems. In I. G. Sigel & K. A. Renninger (Eds.), *Handbook of child psychology: Vol. 4. Child psychology in practice* (5th ed., pp. 635–711). New York: Wiley.

Beatty, W. W. (1992). Gonadal hormones and sex differences in nonreproductive behaviors. In A. A. Gerall, H. Moltz, & I. L. Ward (Eds.), *Handbook of behavioral neurobiology: Vol. 11. Sexual differentiation* (pp. 85–128). New York: Plenum.

Beautrais, A. L. (2003). Life course factors associated with suicidal behaviors in young people. *American Behavioral Scientist, 46*, 1137–1156.

Bebeau, M. J., Rest, J. R., & Narvaez, D. (1999). Beyond the promise: A perspective on research in moral education. *Educational Researcher, 28*(4), 18–26.

Behnke, M., Eyler, F. D., Garvan, C. W., & Wobie, K. (2001). The search for congenital malformations in newborns with fetal cocaine exposure. *Pediatrics, 107*, e74.

Behrman, R. E., Kliegman, R. M., & Arvin, A. M. (1996). *Nelson textbook of pediatrics* (15th ed.). Philadelphia: Saunders.

Behrman, R. E., Kliegman, R. M., & Jenson, H. B. (2000). *Nelson textbook of pediatrics* (16th ed.). Philadelphia: Saunders.

Beilin, H. (1992). Piaget's enduring contribution to developmental psychology. *Developmental Psychology, 28*, 191–204.

Beitel, A. H., & Parke, R. D. (1998). Paternal involvement in infancy: The role of maternal and paternal attitudes. *Journal of Family Psychology, 12*, 268–288.

Belizán, J. M., Althabe, F., Barros, F. C., & Alexander, S. (1999). Rates and implications of caesarean sections in Latin America: Ecological study. *British Medical Journal, 319*, 1379–1402.

Bell, A., Weinberg, M., & Hammersmith, S. (1981). *Sexual preference: Its development in men and women.* Bloomington, IN: Indiana University Press.

Bell, J. H., & Bromnick, R. D. (2003). The social reality of the imaginary audience: A grounded theory approach. *Adolescence, 38*, 205–219.

Bell, K. L., Allen, J. P., Hauser, S. T., & O'Connor, T. G. (1996). Family factors and young adult transitions: Educational attainment and occupational prestige. In J. A. Graber, J. Brooks-Gunn, & A. C. Petersen (Eds.), *Transitions through adolescence: Interpersonal domains and context* (pp. 345–366). Mahwah, NJ: Erlbaum.

Bell, M. A. (1998). Frontal lobe function during infancy: Implications for the development of cognition and attention. In J. E. Richards (Ed.), *Cognitive neuroscience of attention: A developmental perspective* (pp. 327–362). Mahwah, NJ: Erlbaum.

Bell, M. A., & Fox, N. A. (1994). Brain development over the first year of life: Relations between EEG frequency and coherence and cognitive and affective behaviors. In G. Dawson & K. W. Fischer (Eds.), *Human behavior and the developing brain* (pp. 314–345). New York: Guilford.

Bell, M. A., & Fox, N. A. (1996). Crawling experience is related to changes in cortical organization during infancy: Evidence from EEG coherence. *Developmental Psychobiology, 29*, 551–561.

Bellamy, C. (1998). *The state of the world's children 1998.* New York: Oxford University Press (in cooperation with UNICEF).

Bellamy, C. (2000). *The state of the world's children 2000.* New York: Oxford University Press (in cooperation with UNICEF).

Belsky, J. (1992). Consequences of child care for children's development: A deconstructionist view. In A. Booth (Ed.), *Child care in the 1990s: Trends and consequences* (pp. 83–85). Hillsdale, NJ: Erlbaum.

Belsky, J. (2001). Emanuel Miller Lecture: Developmental risks (still) associated with early child care. *Journal of Child Psychology and Psychiatry, 42*, 845–859.

Belsky, J., Campbell, S. B., Cohn, J. F., & Moore, G. (1996). Instability of infant–parent attachment security. *Developmental Psychology, 32*, 921–924.

Belsky, J., & Fearon, R. M. P. (2002a). Early attachment security, subsequent maternal sensitivity, and later child development: Does continuity in development depend on caregiving? *Attachment and Human Development, 4*, 361–387.

Belsky, J., & Fearon, R. M. P. (2002b). Infant–mother attachment security, contextual risk, and early development: A moderational analysis. *Development and Pathology, 14*, 293–310.

Belsky, J., & Kelly, J. (1994). *The transition to parenthood.* New York: Delacorte Press.

Bem, D. J. (1996). Exotic becomes erotic: A developmental theory of sexual orientation. *Psychological Review, 103*, 320–335.

Bempechat, J., & Drago-Severson, E. (1999). Cross-national differences in academic achievement: Beyond etic conceptions of children's understandings. *Review of Educational Research, 69*, 287–314.

Benbow, C. P., Lubinski, D., Shea, D. L., & Eftekhara-Sanjani, H. (2000). Sex differences in mathematical reasoning ability at age 13: Their status 20 years later. *Psychological Science, 11*, 474–480.

Benbow, C. P., & Stanley, J. C. (1983). Sex differences in mathematical reasoning: More facts. *Science, 222*, 1029–1031.

Benedict, R. (1934). Anthropology and the abnormal. *Journal of Genetic Psychology, 10*, 59–82.

Bennett, K. E., Haggard, M. P., Silva, P. A., & Stewart, I. A. (2001). Behaviour and developmental effects of otitis media with effusion into the teens. *Archives of Disease in Childhood, 85*, 91–95.

Berenbaum, S. A. (2001). Cognitive function in congenital adrenal hyperplasia. *Endocrinology and Metabolism Clinics of North America, 30*, 173–192.

Berenbaum, S. A., Duck, S. C., & Bryk, K. (2000). Behavioral effects of prenatal versus postnatal androgen excess in children with 21-hydroxylase-deficient congenital adrenal hyperplasia. *Journal of Clinical Endocrinology and Metabolism, 85*, 727–733.

Bergen, D., & Mauer, D. (2000). Symbolic play, phonological awareness, and literacy skills at three age levels. In K. A. Roskos & J. F. Christie (Eds.), *Play and literacy in early childhood: Research from multiple perspectives* (pp. 45–62). Mahwah, NJ: Erlbaum.

Berk, L. E. (1985). Relationship of caregiver education to child-oriented attitudes, job satisfaction, and behaviors toward children. *Child Care Quarterly, 14*, 103–129.

Berk, L. E. (1992). The extracurriculum. In P. W. Jackson (Ed.), *Handbook of research on curriculum* (pp. 1002–1043). New York: Macmillan.

Berk, L. E. (2001a). *Awakening children's minds: How parents and teachers can make a difference.* New York: Oxford University Press.

Berk, L. E. (2001b). Private speech and self-regulation in children with impulse-control difficulties: Implications for research and practice. *Journal of Cognitive Education and Psychology, 2*(1), 1–21.

Berk, L. E. (2003). Vygotsky, Lev. In L. Nadel (Ed.), *Encyclopedia of cognitive science.* London: Macmillan.

Berk, L. E. (2004). *Conversations with children.* Normal, IL: Illinois State University.

Berk, L. E., & Spuhl, S. T. (1995). Maternal interaction, private speech, and task performance in preschool children. *Early Childhood Research Quarterly, 10*, 145–169.

Berkowitz, C. M. (2004). *Talking to your kids about sex.* Somerville, NJ: Somerset Medical Center. Retrieved from www.somersetmedicalcenter .com/18417.cfm

Berkowitz, M. W., & Gibbs, J. C. (1983). Measuring the developmental features of moral discussion. *Merrill-Palmer Quarterly, 29*, 399–410.

Berkowitz, R. J., & Stunkard, A. J. (2002). Development of childhood obesity. In T. A. Wadden & A. J. Stunkard (Eds.), *Handbook of obesity treatment* (pp. 515–531). New York: Guilford.

Berlin, L. J., Brooks-Gunn, J., McCarton, C., & McCormick, M. C. (1998). The effectiveness of early intervention: Examining risk factors and pathways to enhanced development. *Preventive Medicine, 27*, 238–245.

Berman, P. W. (1980). Are women more responsive than men to the young? A review of developmental and situational variables. *Psychological Bulletin, 88*, 668–695.

Bermejo, V. (1996). Cardinality development and counting. *Developmental Psychology, 32*, 263–268.

Berndt, T. J., & Keefe, K. (1995). Friends' influence on adolescents' adjustment to school. *Child Development, 66*, 1312–1329.

Berndt, T. J., & Murphy, L. M. (2002). Influences of friends and friendships: Myths, truths, and research recommendations. In R. V. Kail (Ed.), *Advances in child development and behavior* (Vol. 30, pp. 275–310). San Diego, CA: Academic Press.

Bernier, J. C., & Siegel, D. H. (1994). Attention-deficit hyperactivity disorder: A family ecological systems perspective. *Families in Society, 75*, 142–150.

Berninger, V. W., Vermeulen K., Abbott, R. D., McCutchen, D., Cotton, S., & Cude, J. (2003). Naming speed and phonological awareness as predictors of reading development. *Journal of Educational Psychology, 95*, 452–464.

Bertenthal, B. I. (1993). Infants' perception of biomechanical motions: Intrinsic image and knowledge-based constraints. In C. Granrud (Ed.), *Visual percpeion and cognition in infancy* (pp. 175–214). Hillsdale, NJ: Erlbaum.

Bertenthal, B. I., Campos, J. J., & Barrett, K. (1984). Self-produced locomotion: An organizer of emotional, cognitive, and social development in infancy. In R. Emde & R. Harmon (Eds.), *Continuities and discontinuities in development* (pp. 174–210). New York: Plenum.

Bertenthal, B., & von Hofsten, C. (1998). Eye, head and trunk control: The foundation for manual development. *Neuroscience and Biobehavioral Reviews, 22*, 515–520.

Berzonsky, M. D., & Kuk, L. S. (2000). Identity status, identity processing style, and the transition to university. *Journal of Adolescent Research, 15*, 81–98.

Best, D. L., Williams, J. E., Cloud, J. M., Davis, S. W., Robertson, L. S., Edwards, J. R., Giles, H., & Fowles, J. (1977). Development of sex-trait stereotypes among young children in the United States, England, and

Ireland. *Child Development, 48,* 1375–1384.

Betz, C. (1994, March). Beyond time-out: Tips from a teacher. *Young Children, 49*(3), 10–14.

Beyth-Marom, R., & Fischhoff, B. (1997). Adolescents' decisions about risks: A cognitive perspective. In J. Schulenberg, J. L. Maggs, & K. Hurrelmann (Eds.), *Health risks and developmental transitions during adolescence* (pp. 110–135). New York: Cambridge University Press.

Bhandari, N., Bahl, R., Taneja, S., Strand, T., & Mølbak, K. (2002). Substantial reduction in severe diarrheal morbidity by daily zinc supplementation in young North Indian children. *Pediatrics, 109,* e86–e92.

Bhatt, R. S., Rovee-Collier, C., & Weiner, S. (1994). Developmental changes in the interface between perception and memory retrieval. *Developmental Psychology, 30,* 151–162.

Bhutta, A. T., Cleves, M. A., Casey, P. H., Cradock, M. M., & Anand, K. J. S. (2002). Cognitive and behavioral outcomes of school-aged children who were born preterm. *Journal of the American Medical Association, 288,* 728–737.

Bialystok, E. (1999). Cognitive complexity and attentional control in the bilingual mind. *Child Development, 70,* 636–644.

Bialystok, E. (2001). *Bilingualism in development: Language, literacy, and cognition.* New York: Cambridge University Press.

Bianco, A., Stone, J., Lynch, L., Lapinski, R., Berkowitz, G., & Berkowitz, R. L. (1996). Pregnancy outcome at age 40 and older. *Obstetrics and Gynecology, 87,* 917–922.

Bibace, R., & Walsh, M. E. (1980). Development of children's concepts of illness. *Pediatrics, 66,* 912–917.

Bibby, R. W. (2000). *Restless gods: The renaissance of religion in Canada.* Toronto: Stoddart.

Bickham, D. S., Vandewater, E. A., Huston, A. C., Lee, J. H., Caplovitz, A. G., & Wright, J. C. (2003). Predictors of children's electronic media use: An examination of three ethnic groups. *Media Psychology, 5,* 107–137.

Biederman, J., & Spencer, T. J. (2000). Genetics of childhood disorders: XIX, ADHD, part 3: Is ADHD a noradrenergic disorder? *Journal of the American Academy of Child and Adolescent Psychiatry, 39,* 1330–1333

Bielinski, J., & Davison, M. L. (1998). Gender differences by item difficulty interactions in multiple-choice mathematics items. *American Educational Research Journal, 35,* 455–476.

Biernat, M. (1991). Gender stereotypes and the relationship between masculinity and femininity: A developmental analysis. *Journal of Person-*

ality and Social Psychology, 61, 351–365.

Bigelow, A. (1992). Locomotion and search behavior in blind infants. *Infant Behavior and Development, 15,* 179–189.

Bigler, R. S. (1995). The role of classification skill in moderating environmental influences on children's gender stereotyping: A study of the functional use of gender in the classroom. *Child Development, 66,* 1072–1087.

Bigler, R. S., & Liben, L. S. (1992). Cognitive mechanisms in children's gender stereotyping: Theoretical and educational implications of a cognitive-based intervention. *Child Development, 63,* 1351–1363.

Bigner, J. J., & Jacobsen, R. B. (1989). Parenting behaviors of homosexual and heterosexual fathers. *Journal of Homosexuality, 18,* 173–186.

Bioethics Consultative Committee. (2003). *Comparison of ethics legislation in Europe.* Retrieved from www.synapse.net.mt/bioethics/euroleg1.htm

Birch, E. E. (1993). Stereopsis in infants and its developmental relation to visual acuity. In K. Simons (Ed.), *Early visual development: Normal and abnormal* (pp. 224–236). New York: Oxford University Press.

Birch, L. L. (1998). Psychological influences on the childhood diet. *Journal of Nutrition, 128,* 407S–410S.

Birch, L. L. (1999). Development of food preferences. *Annual Review of Nutrition, 19,* 41–62.

Birch, L. L., & Fisher, J. A. (1995). Appetite and eating behavior in children. *Pediatric Clinics of North America, 42,* 931–953.

Birch, L. L., Fisher, J. O., & Davison, K. K. (2003). Learning to overeat: Maternal use of restrictive feeding practices promotes girls' eating in the absence of hunger. *American Journal of Clinical Nutrition, 78,* 215–220.

Birch, L. L., Zimmerman, S., & Hind, H. (1980). The influence of social-affective context on preschool children's food preferences. *Child Development, 51,* 856–861.

Birch, S. H., & Ladd, G. W. (1998). Children's interpersonal behaviors and the teacher–child relationship. *Developmental Psychology, 34,* 934–946.

Biringen, Z., Emde, R. N., Campos, J. J., & Appelbaum, M. I. (1995). Affective reorganization in the infant, the mother, and the dyad: The role of upright locomotion and its timing. *Child Development, 66,* 499–514.

Bischof-Köhler, D. (1991). The development of empathy in infants. In M. E. Lamb & H. Keller (Eds.), *Infant development: Perspectives from German-speaking countries* (pp. 1–33). Hillsdale, NJ: Erlbaum.

Bjorklund, D. F., & Douglas, R. N. (1997). The development of mem-

ory strategies. In N. Cowan (Ed.), *The development of memory in childhood* (pp. 83–111). Hove, U.K.: Psychology Press.

Bjorklund, D. F., & Pellegrini, A. D. (2000). Child development and evolutionary psychology. *Child Development, 71,* 1687–1708.

Bjorklund, D. F., Schneider, W., Cassel, W. S., & Ashley, E. (1994). Training and extension of a memory strategy: Evidence for utilization deficiencies in high- and low-IQ children. *Child Development, 65,* 951–965.

Black, R. E., Williams, S. M., Jones, I. E., & Goulding, A. (2002). Children who avoid drinking cow milk have low dietary calcium intakes and poor bone health. *American Journal of Clinical Nutrition, 76,* 675–680.

Blagg, N., & Yule, W. (1996). School phobia. In T. H. Ollendick, N. J. King, & W. Yule (Eds.), *International handbook of phobic and anxiety disorders in children and adolescents* (pp. 169–186). New York: Plenum.

Blakemore, J. E. O. (2003). Children's beliefs about violating gender norms: Boys shouldn't look like girls, and girls shouldn't act like boys. *Sex Roles, 48,* 9–10.

Blanchard, R. (2001). Fraternal birth order and the maternal immune hypothesis of male homosexuality. *Hormones and Behavior, 40,* 104–114.

Blanchard, R., Zucker, K. J., Cavacas, A., Allin, S., Bradley, S. J., & Schachter, D. C. (2002). Fraternal birth order and birth weight in probably prehomosexual feminine boys. *Hormones and Behavior, 41,* 321–327.

Blasi, A. (1994). Moral identity: Its role in moral functioning. In B. Puka (Ed.), *Fundamental research in moral development: A compendium* (Vol. 2, pp. 123–167). New York: Garland.

Blass, E. M. (1999). Savoring sucrose and suckling milk: Easing pain, saving calories, and learning about mother. In M. Lewis & D. Ramsay (Eds.), *Soothing and stress* (pp. 79–107). Mahwah, NJ: Erlbaum.

Blass, E. M., Ganchrow, J. R., & Steiner, J. E. (1984). Classical conditioning in newborn humans 2–48 hours of age. *Infant Behavior and Development, 7,* 223–235.

Blatchford, P., Baines, E., Kutnick, P., & Martin, C. (2001). Classroom contexts: Connections between class size and within class grouping. *British Journal of Educational Psychology, 71,* 283–302.

Blatchford, P., Moriarty, V., Edmonds, S., & Martin, C. (2002). Relationships between class size and teaching: A multimethod analysis of English infant schools. *American Educational Research Journal, 39,* 101–132.

Blewitt, P. (1994). Understanding categorical hierarchies: The earliest levels of skills. *Child Development, 65,* 1279–1298.

Block, J., & Block, J. H. (1980). *The California Child Q-Set.* Palo Alto, CA: Consulting Psychologists Press.

Bloom, L. (1998). Language acquisition in its developmental context. In D. Kuhn & R. S. Siegler (Eds.), *Handbook of child psychology: Vol. 2. Cognition, perception, and language* (5th ed., pp. 309–370). New York: Wiley.

Bloom, L. (2000). The intentionality model of language development: How to learn a word, any word. In R. Golinkoff, K. Hirsh-Pasek, N. Akhtar, L. Bloom, G. Hollich, L. Smith, M. Tomasello, & A. Woodward (Eds.), *Becoming a word learner: A debate on lexical acquisition.* New York: Oxford University Press.

Bloom, L., Margulis, C., Tinker, E., & Fujita, N. (1996). Early conversations and word learning: Contributions from child and adult. *Child Development, 67,* 3154–3175.

Bloom, P. (1999). The role of semantics in solving the bootstrapping problem. In R. Jackendoff & P. Bloom (Eds.), *Language, logic, and concepts* (pp. 285–309). Cambridge, MA: MIT Press.

Blotner, R., & Bearison, D. J. (1984). Developmental consistencies in socio-moral knowledge: Justice reasoning and altruistic behavior. *Merrill-Palmer Quarterly, 30,* 349–367.

Bluestone, C., & Tamis-LeMonda, C. S. (1999). Correlates of parenting styles in predominantly working- and middle-class African American mothers. *Journal of Marriage and the Family, 61,* 881–893.

Blumberg, M. S., & Lucas, D. E. (1996). A developmental and component analysis of active sleep. *Developmental Psychobiology, 29,* 1–22.

Blyth, D. A., Simmons, R. G., & Zakin, D. F. (1985). Satisfaction with body image for early adolescent females: The impact of pubertal timing within different school environments. *Journal of Youth and Adolescence, 14,* 207–225.

Bobak, I. M., Jensen, M. D., & Zalar, M. K. (1989). *Maternity and gynecologic care.* St. Louis: Mosby.

Bogartz, R. S., Shinskey, J. L., & Schilling, T. H. (2000). Object permanence in five-and-a-half-month-old infants. *Infancy, 1,* 403–428.

Bogin, B. (2001). *The growth of humanity.* New York: Wiley-Liss.

Bogin, B., Smith, P., Orden, A. B., Varela, S., & Loucky, J. (2002). Rapid change in height and body proportions of Maya American children. *American Journal of Human Biology, 14,* 753–761.

Bohannon, J. N., III, & Bonvillian, J. D. (2001). Theoretical approaches to language acquisition. In J. B. Gleason (Ed.), *The development of language* (5th ed., pp. 254–314). Boston: Allyn and Bacon.

Bohannon, J. N., III, & Stanowicz, L. (1988). The issue of negative evidence: Adult responses to children's language errors. *Developmental Psychology, 24,* 684–689.

Bohman, M. (1996). Predispositions to criminality: Swedish adoption studies in retrospect. In G. R. Bock & J. A. Goode (Eds.), *Genetics of criminal and antisocial behavior.* Ciba Foundation Symposium 194 (pp. 99–114). Chichester, U.K.: Wiley.

Bohman, M., & Sigvardsson, S. (1990). Outcome in adoption: Lessons from longitudinal studies. In D. M. Brodzinsky & M. D. Schechter (Eds.), *The psychology of adoption* (pp. 93–106). New York: Oxford University Press.

Boldizar, J. P. (1991). Assessing sex typing and androgyny in children: The children's sex role inventory. *Developmental Psychology, 27,* 505–515.

Bolen, R. M. (2001). *Child sexual abuse.* New York: Kluwer Academic.

Bolger, K. E., & Patterson, C. J. (2001). Developmental pathways from child maltreatment to peer rejection. *Child Development, 72,* 549–568.

Boller, K., Grabelle, M., & Rovee-Collier, C. (1995). Effects of postevent information on infants' memory for a central target. *Journal of Experimental Child Psychology, 59,* 372–396.

Bono, M. A., & Stifter, C. A. (2003). Maternal attention-directing strategies and infant focused attention during problem solving. *Infancy, 4,* 235–250.

Bookstein, F. L., Sampson, P. D., Connor, P. D., & Streissguth, A. P. (2002). Midline corpus callosum is a neuroanatomical focus of fetal alcohol damage. *Anatomical Record, 269,* 162–174.

Boonstra, H. (2002). Teen pregnancy: Trends and lessons learned. *Guttmacher Report on Public Policy, 5*(1), 1–10.

Borke, H. (1975). Piaget's mountains revisited: Changes in the egocentric landscape. *Developmental Psychology, 11,* 240–243.

Borkowski, J. G., & Muthukrishna, N. (1995). Learning environments and skill generalization: How contexts facilitate regulatory processes and efficacy beliefs. In F. Weinert & W. Schneider (Eds.), *Memory performances and competence: Issues in growth and development* (pp. 283–300). Mahwah, NJ: Erlbaum.

Bornstein, M. H. (1989). Sensitive periods in development: Structural characteristics and causal interpretations. *Psychological Bulletin, 105,* 179–197.

Bornstein, M. H. (2002). Parenting infants. In M. H. Bornstein (Ed.), *Handbook of parenting: Vol. 1* (2nd ed., pp. 3–44). Mahwah, NJ: Erlbaum.

Bornstein, M. H., & Arterberry, M. E. (1999). Perceptual development. In M. H. Bornstein & M. E. Lamb (Eds.), *Developmental psychology:*

An advanced textbook (pp. 231–274). Mahwah, NJ: Erlbaum.

Bornstein, M. H., Haynes, O. M., Pascual, L., Painter, K. M., & Galperin, C. (1999a). Play in two societies: Pervasiveness of process, specificity of structure. *Child Development, 70,* 317–331.

Bornstein, M. H., Selmi, A. M., Haynes, O. M., Painter, K. M., & Marx, E. S. (1999b). Representational abilities and the hearing status of child/mother dyads. *Child Development, 70,* 833–852.

Bornstein, M. H., Tal, J., Rahn, C., Galperín, C. Z., Pêcheux, M., Lamour, M., Toda, S., Azuma, H., Ogino, M., & Tamis-LeMonda, C. S. (1992a). Functional analysis of the contents of maternal speech to infants of 5 and 13 months in four cultures: Argentina, France, Japan, and the United States. *Developmental Psychology, 28,* 593–603.

Bornstein, M. H., Vibbert, M., Tal, J., & O'Donnell, K. (1992b). Toddler language and play in the second year: Stability, covariation, and influences of parenting. *First Language, 12,* 323–338.

Borst, C. G. (1995). *Catching babies: The professionalization of childbirth, 1870–1920.* Cambridge, MA: Harvard University Press.

Bortolus, R., Parazzini, F., Chatenoud, L., Benzi, G., Bianchi, M. M., & Marini, A. (1999). The epidemiology of multiple births. *Human Reproduction Update, 5,* 179–187.

Bosch, L., & Sebastian-Galles, N. (2001). Evidence of early language discrimination abilities in infants from bilingual environments. *Infancy, 2,* 29–49.

Bost, K. K., Vaughn, B. E., Washington, W. N., Cielinski, K. L., & Bradbard, M. R. (1998). Social competence, social support, and attachment: Demarcation of construct domains, measurement, and paths of influence for preschool children attending Head Start. *Child Development, 69,* 192–218.

Bouchard, T. J., Jr., Lykken, D. T., McGue, M., Segal, N. L., & Tellegen, A. (1990). Sources of human psychological differences: The Minnesota Study of Twins Reared Apart. *Science, 250,* 223–228.

Boukydis, C. F. Z., & Burgess, R. L. (1982). Adult physiological response to infant cries: Effects of temperament of infant, parental status and gender. *Child Development, 53,* 1291–1298.

Boukydis, C. F. Z., & Lester, B. M. (1998). Infant crying, risk status and social support in families of preterm and term infants. *Early Development and Parenting, 7,* 31–39.

Boulton, M. J. (1996). A comparison of 8- and 11-year-old girls' and boys' participation in specific types of rough-and-tumble play and aggressive fighting: Implications for

functional hypotheses. *Aggressive Behavior, 22,* 271–287.

Boulton, M. J. (1999). Concurrent and longitudinal relations between children's playground behavior and social preference, victimization, and bullying. *Child Development, 70,* 944–954.

Boulton, M. J., & Smith, P. K. (1992). The social nature of play-fighting and play-chasing: Mechanisms and strategies underlying cooperation and compromise. In J. H. Barkow, L. Cosmides, & J. Tooby (Eds.), *The adapted mind* (pp. 429–444). New York: Oxford University Press.

Bowen, N. K., Bowen, G. L., & Ware, W. B. (2002). Neighborhood social disorganization, families, and the educational behavior of adolescents. *Journal of Adolescent Research, 17,* 468–490.

Bowlby, J. (1969). *Attachment and loss: Vol. 1. Attachment.* New York: Basic Books.

Bowlby, J. (1980). *Attachment and loss: Vol. 3. Loss.* New York: Basic Books.

Bowlby, J. W., & McMullen, K. (2002). *At a crossroads: First results for the 18- to 20-year-old cohort of the Youth in Transition Survey.* Ottawa, Canada: Human Resources Development Canada.

Boyer, K., & Diamond, A. (1992). Development of memory for temporal order in infants and young children. In A. Diamond (Ed.), *Development and neural bases of higher cognitive function* (pp. 267–317). New York: New York Academy of Sciences.

Boyes, M. C., & Chandler, M. (1992). Cognitive development, epistemic doubt, and identity formation in adolescence. *Journal of Youth and Adolescence, 21,* 277–304.

Boyle, M. H., & Lipman, E. L. (2002). Do places matter? Socioeconomic disadvantage and behavioral problems of children in Canada. *Journal of Consulting and Clinical Psychology, 70,* 378–389.

Brackbill, Y., McManus, K., & Woodward, L. (1985). *Medication in maternity: Infant exposure and maternal information.* Ann Arbor: University of Michigan Press.

Bracken, B. A. (2000). *The psychoeducational assessment of preschool children.* Boston: Allyn and Bacon.

Bradley, P. J., & Bray, K. H. (1996). The Netherlands' Maternal-Child Health Program: Implications for the United States. *Journal of Obstetric, Gynecologic, and Neonatal Nursing, 25,* 471–475.

Bradley, R. H. (1994). The HOME Inventory: Review and reflections. In H. W. Reese (Ed.), *Advances in child development and behavior* (Vol. 25, pp. 241–288). San Diego: Academic Press.

Bradley, R. H., & Caldwell, B. M. (1982). The consistency of the home environment and its relation to child development. *International*

Journal of Behavioral Development, 5, 445–465.

Bradley, R. H., Caldwell, B. M., Rock, S. L., Ramey, C. T., Barnard, D. E., Gray, C., Hammond, M. A., Mitchell, S., Gottfried, A., Siegel, L., & Johnson, D. L. (1989). Home environment and cognitive development in the first 3 years of life: A collaborative study involving six sites and three ethnic groups in North America. *Developmental Psychology, 25,* 217–235.

Bradley, R. H., & Corwyn, R. F. (2003). Age and ethnic variations in family process mediators of SES. In M. H. Bornstein & R. H. Bradley (Eds.), *Socioeconomic status, parenting, and child development* (pp. 161–188). Mahwah, NJ: Erlbaum.

Bradley, R. H., Corwyn, R. F., McAdoo, H. P., & García Coll, C. (2001). The home environments of children in the United States. Part I: Variations by age, ethnicity, and poverty status. *Child Development, 72,* 1844–1867.

Bradley, R. H., Whiteside, L., Mundfrom, D. J., Casey, P. H., Kelleher, K. J., & Pope, S. K. (1994). Contribution of early intervention and early caregiving experiences to resilience in low-birthweight, premature children living in poverty. *Journal of Clinical Child Psychology, 23,* 425–434.

Braet, C., & Crombez, G. (2003). Cognitive interference due to food cues in childhood obesity. *Journal of Clinical Child and Adolescent Psychology, 32,* 32–39.

Braine, L. G., Schauble, L., Kugelmass, S., & Winter, A. (1993). Representation of depth by children: Spatial strategies and lateral biases. *Developmental Psychology, 29,* 466–479.

Braine, M. D. S. (1994). Is nativism sufficient? *Journal of Child Language, 21,* 1–23.

Brame, B., Nagin, D. S., & Tremblay, R. E. (2001). Developmental trajectories of physical aggression from school entry to late adolescence. *Journal of Child Psychology and Psychiatry, 42,* 503–512.

Bratt, R. G. (2002). Housing: The foundation of family life. In F. Jacobs, D. Wertlieb, & R. M. Lerner (Eds.), *Handbook of applied developmental science* (Vol. 2, pp. 445–468). Thousand Oaks, CA: Sage.

Bray, J. H. (1999). From marriage to remarriage and beyond: Findings from the Developmental Issues in Stepfamilies Research Project. In E. M. Hetherington (Ed.), *Coping with divorce, single parenting, and remarriage: A risk and resiliency perspective* (pp. 295–319). Mahwah, NJ: Erlbaum.

Brazelton, T. B. (1997). *Toilet training your child.* New York: Consumer Visions.

Brazelton, T. B., Koslowski, B., & Tronick, E. (1976). Neonatal behavior among urban Zambians and Americans. *Journal of the American*

Academy of Child Psychiatry, 15, 97–107.

Brazelton, T. B., & Nugent, J. K. (1995). *Neonatal Behavioral Assessment Scale.* London: Mac Keith Press.

Brazelton, T. B., Nugent, J. K., & Lester, B. M. (1987). Neonatal Behavioral Assessment Scale. In J. D. Osofsky (Ed.), *Handbook of infant development* (2nd ed., pp. 780–817). New York: Wiley.

Bredekamp, S., & Copple, C. (Eds.). (1997). *Developmentally appropriate practice in early childhood programs* (rev. ed.). Washington, DC: National Association for the Education of Young Children.

Breedlove, S. M. (1994). Sexual differentiation of the human nervous system. *Annual Review of Psychology, 45,* 389–418.

Brehaut, J. C., Miller, A., Raina, P., & McGrail, K. M. (2003). Childhood behavior disorders and injuries among children and youth: A population-based study. *Pediatrics, 111,* 262–269.

Brehm, S. S. (2002). *Intimate relationships* (3rd ed.). New York: McGraw-Hill.

Bremner, J. G. (1998). From perception to action: The early development of knowledge. In F. Simion & G. Butterworth (Eds.), *Development of sensory, motor, and cognitive capacities in early infancy* (pp. 239–255). East Sussex, U.K.: Psychology Press.

Brendgen, M., Markiewicz, D., Doyle, A. B., & Bukowski, W. M. (2001). The relations between friendship quality, ranked-friendship preference, and adolescents' behavior with their friends. *Merrill-Palmer Quarterly, 47,* 395–415.

Brendgen, M., Vitaro, F., & Bukowski, W. M. (1998). Deviant friends and early adolescents' emotional and behavioral adjustment. *Journal of Research on Adolescence, 10,* 173–189.

Brennan, R. T., Kim, J., Wenz-Gross, M., & Siperstein, G. N. (2001). The relative equitability of high-stakes testing versus teacher-assigned grades: An analysis of the Massachusetts Comprehensive Assessment System (MCAS). *Harvard Educational Review, 71,* 173–216.

Brennan, W. M., Ames, E. W., & Moore, R. W. (1966). Age differences in infants' attention to patterns of different complexities. *Science, 151,* 354–356.

Brenner, E., & Salovey, P. (1997). Emotional regulation during childhood: Developmental, interpersonal, and individual considerations. In P. Salovey & D. Sluyter (Eds.), *Emotional literacy and emotional development* (pp. 168–192). New York: Basic Books.

Brenner, R. A. (2003). Prevention of drowning in infants, children, and adolescents. *Pediatrics, 112,* 440–445.

Brenner, R. A., Simons-Morton, B. G., Bhaskar, B., Revenis, M., Das, A., &

Clemens, J. D. (2003). Infant–parent bed sharing in an inner-city population. *Archives of Pediatrics and Adolescent Medicine, 157,* 33–39.

Brent, R. L. (1999). Utilization of developmental basic science principles in the evaluation of reproductive risks from pre- and postconception environmental radiation exposures. *Teratology, 59,* 182–204.

Bretherton, I. (1992). The origins of attachment theory: John Bowlby and Mary Ainsworth. *Developmental Psychology, 28,* 759–775.

Bretherton, I., Fritz, J., Zahn-Waxler, C., & Ridgeway, D. (1986). Learning to talk about emotions: A functionalist perspective. *Child Development, 57,* 529–548.

Breweays, A., Ponjaert, I., Van Hall, E. V., & Golombok, S. (1997). Donor insemination: Child development and family functioning in lesbian mother families. *Human Reproduction, 12,* 1349–1359.

Brezina, T. (1999). Teenage violence toward parents as an adaptation to family strain: Evidence from a national survey of male adolescents. *Youth and Society, 30,* 416–444.

Bridges, L. J., & Moore, K. A. (2002). Religious involvement and children's well-being: What research tells us (and what it doesn't). *Child Trends Research Brief.* Retrieved from http://www.childtrends.org

Briefel, R. R., Reidy, K., Karwe, V., & Devaney, B. (2004). Feeding Infants and Toddlers study: Improvements needed in meeting infant feeding recommendations. *Journal of the American Dietetic Association, 104*(Suppl. 1), s31–s37.

Brien, M. J., & Willis, R. J. (1997). Costs and consequences for the fathers. In R. A. Maynard (Ed.), *Kids having kids* (pp. 95–144). Washington, DC: Urban Institute.

Briggs, F. (2000). *Children's views of the world.* Magill, Australia: University of South Australia.

Briggs, F. (2002). *To what extent can Keeping Ourselves Safe protect children?* Wellington, NZ: New Zealand Police.

Broberg, A. G., Wessels, H., Lamb, M. E., & Hwang, C. P. (1997). Effects of day care on the development of cognitive abilities in 8-year-olds: A longitudinal study. *Developmental Psychology, 33,* 62–69.

Brody, G. H., & Flor, D. L. (1998). Maternal resources, parenting practices, and child competence in rural, single-parent African American families. *Child Development, 69,* 803–816.

Brody, G. H., Ge, X., Kim, S. Y., Murry, V. M., Simons, R. L. & Gibbons, F. X. (2003). Neighborhood disadvantage moderates associations of parenting and older sibling problem attitudes and behavior with conduct disorders in African American children. *Journal of Consulting and Clinical Psychology, 71,* 211–222.

Brody, G. H., & Murry, V. M. (2001). Sibling socialization of competence in rural, single-parent African American families. *Journal of Marriage and the Family, 63,* 996–1008.

Brody, G. H., Stoneman, Z., & Flor, D. (1996). Family wages, family processes, and youth competence in rural married African American families. In E. M. Hetherington & E. A. Blechman (Eds.), *Stress, coping, and resiliency in children and families. Family research consortium: Advances in family research* (pp. 173–188). Mahwah, NJ: Erlbaum.

Brody, G. H., Stoneman, Z., & Flor, D. (1996). Parental religiosity, family processes, and youth competence in rural, two-parent African-American families. *Developmental Psychology, 32,* 696–706.

Brody, G. H., Stoneman, Z., & Mc-Coy, J. K. (1992). Associations of maternal and paternal direct and differential behavior with sibling relationships: Contemporaneous and longitudinal analyses. *Child Development, 63,* 82–92.

Brody, G. H., Stoneman, Z., & McCoy, J. K. (1994). Forecasting sibling relationships in early adolescence from child temperament and family processes in middle childhood. *Child Development, 65,* 771–784.

Brody, G. H., Stoneman, Z., McCoy, J. K., & Forehand, R. (1992). Contemporaneous and longitudinal associations of sibling conflict with family relationship assessments and family discussions about sibling problems. *Child Development, 63,* 391–400.

Brody, L. (1999). *Gender, emotion, and the family.* Cambridge, MA: Harvard University Press.

Brody, N. (1992). *Intelligence* (2nd ed.). San Diego: Academic Press.

Brody, N. (1997). Intelligence, schooling, and society. *American Psychologist, 52,* 1046–1050.

Broidy, L. M., Nagin, D. S., Tremblay, R. E., Bates, J. E., Brame, B., Dodge, K. A., Fergusson, D., Horwood, J. L., Loeber, R., Laird, R., Lynam, D. R., Moffitt, T. E., Pettit, G. S., & Vitaro, F. (2003). Developmental trajectories of childhood disruptive behaviors and adolescent delinquency: A six-site, cross-national study. *Developmental Psychology, 39,* 222–245.

Bronfenbrenner, U. (1995). The bio-ecological model from a life course perspective: Reflections of a participant observer. In P. Moen, G. H. Elder, Jr., & K. Lüscher (Eds.), *Examining lives in context* (pp. 599–618). Washington, DC: American Psychological Association.

Bronfenbrenner, U., & Evans, G. W. (2000). Developmental science in the 21st century: Emerging theoretical models, research designs, and empirical findings. *Social Development, 9,* 115–125.

Bronfenbrenner, U., & Morris, P. A. (1998). The ecology of developmental processes. In R. M. Lerner (Ed.), *Handbook of child psychology: Vol. 1. Theoretical models of human development* (5th ed., pp. 535–584). New York: Wiley.

Bronson, G. W. (1991). Infant differences in rate of visual encoding. *Child Development, 62,* 44–54.

Bronson, M. B. (1995). *The right stuff for children birth to 8.* Washington, DC: National Association for the Education of Young Children.

Brooks, D., & Barth, R. P. (1999). Adult transracial and inracial adoptees: Effects of race, gender, adoptive family structure, and placement history on adjustment outcomes. *American Journal of Orthopsychiatry, 69,* 87–99.

Brooks-Gunn, J. (1988). Antecedents and consequences of variations in girls' maturational timing. *Journal of Adolescent Health Care, 9,* 365–373.

Brooks-Gunn, J., & Chase-Lansdale, P. L. (1995). Adolescent parenthood. In M. H. Bornstein (Ed.), *Handbook of parenting: Vol. 3. Status and social conditions of parenting* (pp. 113–149). Mahwah, NJ: Erlbaum.

Brooks-Gunn, J., & Ruble, D. N. (1980). Menarche: The interaction of physiology, cultural, and social factors. In A. J. Dan, E. A. Graham, & C. P. Beecher (Eds.), *The menstrual cycle: A synthesis of interdisciplinary research* (pp. 141–159). New York: Springer-Verlag.

Brooks-Gunn, J., & Ruble, D. N. (1983). The experience of menarche from a developmental perspective. In J. Brooks-Gunn & A. C. Peterson (Eds.), *Girls at puberty* (pp. 155–177). New York: Plenum.

Brooks-Gunn, J., McCarton, C. M., Casey, P. H., McCormick, M. C., Bauer, C. R., Bernbaum, J. C., Tyson, J., Swanson, M., Bennett, F. C., Scott, D. T., Tonascia, J., & Meinert, C. L. (1994). Early intervention in low-birth-weight premature infants. *Journal of the American Medical Association, 272,* 1257–1262.

Brooks-Gunn, J., Schley, S., & Hardy, J. (2002). Marriage and the baby carriage: Historical change and intergenerational continuity in early parenthood. In L. J. Crockett & R. K. Sibereisen (Eds.), *Negotiating adolescence in times of social change* (pp. 36–57). New York: Cambridge University Press.

Brooks-Gunn, J., Warren, M. P., Samelson, M., & Fox, R. (1986). Physical similarity of and disclosure of menarcheal status to friends: Effects of grade and pubertal status. *Journal of Early Adolescence, 6,* 3–14.

Brown, A. L. (1997). Transforming schools into communities of thinking and learning about serious matters. *American Psychologist, 52,* 399–413.

Brown, A. S., & Susser, E. S. (2002). In utero infection and adult schizophrenia. *Mental Retardation and Developmental Disabilities Research Reviews, 8,* 51–57.

Brown, B. B. (1999). "You're going out with who?": Peer group influences on adolescent romantic relationships. In W. Furman, B. B. Brown, & C. Feiring (Eds.), *The development of romantic relationships in adolescence* (pp. 291–329). New York: Cambridge University Press.

Brown, B. B., Clasen, D., & Eicher, S. (1986). Perceptions of peer pressure, peer conformity dispositions, and self-reported behavior among adolescents. *Developmental Psychology, 22,* 521–530.

Brown, B. B., Feiring, C., & Furman, W. (1999). Missing the love boat: Why researchers have shied away from adolescent romance. In W. Furman, B. B. Brown, & C. Feiring (Eds.), *The development of romantic relationships in adolescence* (pp. 1–16). New York: Cambridge University Press.

Brown, B. B., Lohr, M. J., & McClenahan, E. L. (1986). Early adolescents' perceptions of peer pressure. *Journal of Early Adolescence, 6,* 139–154.

Brown, J. R., & Dunn, J. (1996). Continuities in emotion understanding from 3 to 6 years. *Child Development, 67,* 789–802.

Brown, J. R., Donelan-McCall, N., & Dunn, J. (1996). Why talk about mental states? The significance of children's conversations with friends, siblings, and mothers. *Child Development, 67,* 836–849.

Brown, R. W. (1973). *A first language: The early stages.* Cambridge, MA: Harvard University Press.

Brown, S. L. (2000). Union transitions among cohabiters: The significance of relationship assessments and expectations. *Journal of Marriage and the Family, 62,* 833–846.

Brown, S. S., & Eisenberg, L. (Eds.). (1995). *The best intentions.* Washington, DC: National Academy Press.

Brownell, C.A., & Carriger, M. S. (1990). Changes in cooperation and self–other differentiation during the second year. *Child Development, 61,* 1164–1174.

Bruce, D., Dolan, A., & Phillips-Grant, K. (2000). On the transition from childhood amnesia to recall of personal memories. *Psychological Science, 11,* 360–364.

Bruch, H. (2001). *The golden cage: The enigma of anorexia nervosa.* Cambridge, MA: Harvard University Press.

Bruck, M., Ceci, S. J., & Hembrooke, H. (1998). Reliability and credibility of young children's reports. *American Psychologist, 53,* 136–151.

Bruck, M., Treiman, R., Caravolas, M., Genesee, F., & Cassar, M. (1998). Spelling skills of children in whole language and phonics classrooms. *Applied Psycholinguistics, 19,* 669–684.

Bruer, J. T. (1999). *The myth of the first three years.* New York: Free Press.

Bruzzese, J., & Fisher, C. B. (2003). Assessing and enhancing the research consent capacity of children and youth. *Applied Developmental Science, 7,* 13–26.

Bryant, P., & Nunes, T. (2002). Children's understanding of mathematics. In U. Goswami (Ed.), *Blackwell handbook of childhood cognitive development* (pp. 412–439). Malden, MA. Blackwell.

Buchanan, A. (1996). *Cycles of child maltreatment.* Chichester, U.K.: Wiley.

Buchanan, C. M., Eccles, J. S., & Becker, J. B. (1992). Are adolescents the victims of raging hormones? Evidence for activational effects of hormones on moods and behaviors at adolescence. *Psychological Bulletin, 111,* 62–107.

Buchanan, C. M., & Holmbeck, G. N. (1998). Measuring beliefs about adolescent personality and behavior. *Journal of Youth and Adolescence, 27,* 609–629.

Buchanan, C. M., Maccoby, E. E., & Dornbusch, S. M. (1996). *Adolescents after divorce.* Cambridge, MA: Harvard University Press.

Buchanan-Barrow, E., & Barrett, M. (1998). Children's rule discrimination within the context of the school. *British Journal of Developmental Psychology, 16,* 539–551.

Buekens, P., Kotelchuck, M., Blondel, B., Kristensen, F. B., Chen J.-H., & Masuy-Stroobant, G. (1993). A comparison of prenatal care use in the United States and Europe. *American Journal of Public Health, 83,* 31–36.

Bugental, D. B., Ellerson, P. C., Lin, E. K., Rainey, B., & Kokotovic, A. (2002). A cognitive approach to child abuse prevention. *Journal of Family Psychology, 16,* 243–258.

Buhrmester, D. (1996). Need fulfillment, interpersonal competence, and the developmental contexts of early adolescent friendship. In W. M. Bukowski & A. F. Newcomb (Eds.), *The company they keep: Friendship in childhood and adolescence* (pp. 158–185). New York: Cambridge University Press.

Buhrmester, D., & Furman, W. (1990). Perceptions of sibling relationships during middle childhood and adolescence. *Child Development, 61,* 1387–1398.

Buhs, E. S., & Ladd, G. W. (2001). Peer rejection as antecedent of young children's school adjustment: An examination of mediating processes. *Developmental Psychology, 37,* 550–560.

Bukowski, W. M. (2001). Friendship and the worlds of childhood. In D. W. Nangle & C. A. Erdley (Eds.), *The role of friendship in psychological adjustment* (pp. 93–105). San Francisco: Jossey-Bass.

Bukowski, W. M., Sippola, L. K., & Hoza, B. (1999). Same and other: Interdependency between participation in same- and other-sex friendships. *Journal of Youth and Adolescence, 28,* 439–459.

Bukowski, W. M., Sippola, L. K., & Newcomb, A. F. (2000). Variations in patterns of attraction of same- and other-sex peers during early adolescence. *Developmental Psychology, 36,* 147–154.

Burchinal, M. R., Peisner-Feinberg, E., Bryant, D. M., & Clifford, R. (2000). Children's social and cognitive development and child-care quality: Testing for differential associations related to poverty, gender, or ethnicity. *Applied Developmental Science, 4,* 149–165.

Burgess, K. B., Rubin, K. H., Chea, C. S. L., & Nelson, L. J. (2001). Behavioral inhibition, social withdrawal, and parenting. In R. Crozier & L. Alden (Eds.), *International handbook of social anxiety* (pp. 137–158). New York: Wiley.

Burhans, K. K., & Dweck, C. S. (1995). Helplessness in early childhood: The role of contingent worth. *Child Development, 66,* 1719–1738.

Burke, R. J. (2001). Organizational values, work experiences, and satisfactions among managerial and professional women. *Journal of Managerial Development, 20,* 346–354.

Burns, C. E. (2000). *Pediatric primary care: A handbook for nurse practitioners.* Philadelphia: Saunders.

Burts, D. C., Hart, C. H., Charlesworth, R., Fleege, P. O., Mosley, J., & Thomasson, R. H. (1992). Observed activities and stress behaviors of children in developmentally appropriate and inappropriate kindergarten classrooms. *Early Childhood Research Quarterly, 7,* 297–318.

Bushman, B. J., & Huesmann, L. R. (2001). Effects of televised violence of aggression. In D. G. Singer & J. L. Singer (Eds.), *Handbook of children and the media* (pp. 223–254). Thousand Oaks, CA: Sage.

Bushnell, E. W., & Boudreau, J. P. (1993). Motor development and the mind: The potential role of motor abilities as a determinant of aspects of perceptual development. *Child Development, 64,* 1005–1021.

Bussell, D. A., Neiderhiser, J. M., Pike, A., Plomin, R., Simmens, S., Howe, G. W., Hetherington, E. M., Carroll, E., & Reiss, D. (1999). Adolescents' relationships to siblings and mothers: A multivariate genetic analysis. *Developmental Psychology, 35,* 1248–1259.

Bussey, K. (1992). Lying and truthfulness: Children's definitions, standards, and evaluative reactions. *Child Development, 63,* 129–137.

Butler, R. (1998). Age trends in the use of social and temporal comparison for self-evaluation: Examination of a novel developmental hypothesis. *Child Development, 69,* 1054–1073.

Butler, R., & Ruzany, N. (1993). Age and socialization effects on the development of social comparison motives and normative ability assessment in kibbutz and urban children. *Child Development, 64,* 532–543.

Bybee, J., Merisca, R., & Velasco, R. (1998). The development of reactions to guilt-producing events. In J. Bybee (Ed.), *Guilt and children* (pp. 185–213). San Diego: Academic Press.

Byrnes, J. P. (2002). The development of decision-making. *Journal of Adolescent Health, 31,* 208–215.

Byrnes, J. P., & Takahira, S. (1993). Explaining gender differences on SAT-math items. *Developmental Psychology, 29,* 805–810.

Cabrera, N. J., Tamis-LeMonda, C. S., Bradley, R. H., Hoferth, S., & Lamb, M. E. (2000). Fatherhood in the twenty-first century. *Child Development, 71,* 127–136.

Cadoret, R. J., Cain, C. A., & Crowe, R. R. (1983). Evidence for gene–environment interaction in the development of adolescent antisocial behavior. *Behavior Genetics, 13,* 301–310.

Cain, K. M., & Dweck, C. S. (1995). The relation between motivational patterns and achievement cognitions through the elementary school years. *Merrill-Palmer Quarterly, 41,* 25–52.

Caine, N. (1986). Behavior during puberty and adolescence. In G. Mitchell & J. Erwin (Eds.), *Comparative primate biology: Vol. 2A. Behavior, conservation, and ecology* (pp. 327–361). New York: Liss.

Cairns, R. B. (1998). The making of developmental psychology. In R. M. Lerner (Ed.), *Handbook of child psychology: Vol. 1. Theoretical models of human development* (5th ed., pp. 25–105). New York: Wiley.

Cairns, R., Xie, H., & Leung, M.-C. (1998). The popularity of friendship and the neglect of social networks: Toward a new balance. In W. M. Bukowski & A. H. Cillessen (Eds.), *Sociometry then and now: Building on six decades of measuring children's experiences with the peer group* (pp. 25–53). San Francisco: Jossey-Bass.

Caldwell, B. M., & Bradley, R. H. (1994). Environmental issues in developmental follow-up research. In S. L. Friedman & H. C. Haywood (Eds.), *Developmental follow-up* (pp. 235–256). San Diego: Academic Press.

Caldwell, C. H., & Antonucci, T. C. (1997). Childbearing during adolescence: Mental health risks and opportunities. In J. Schulenberg, J. L. Maggs, & K. Hurrelmann (Eds.), *Health risks and developmental transitions during adolescence* (pp. 220–245). New York: Cambridge University Press.

Caldwell, J. (1999). Paths to lower fertility. *British Medical Journal, 319,* 985–987.

Caldwell, J. C. P., & Barkat-e-Khuda, J. F. (2002). The future of family planning programs. *Studies in Family Planning, 33,* 1–10.

Calkins, S. D. (2002). Does aversive behavior during toddlerhood matter? The effects of difficult temperament on maternal perceptions and behavior. *Infant Mental Health Journal, 23,* 381–402.

Calkins, S. D., Fox, N. A., & Marshall, T. R. (1996). Behavioral and physiological antecedents of inhibited and uninhibited behavior. *Child Development, 67,* 523–540.

Callaghan, T. C. (1999). Early understanding and production of graphic symbols. *Child Development, 70,* 1314–1324.

Callaghan, T. C., & Rankin, M. P. (2002). Emergence of graphic symbol functioning and the question of domain specificity: A longitudinal training study. *Child Development, 73,* 359–376.

Calle, E. E., Rodriguez, C., Walker-Thurmond, K., & Thun, M. J. (2003). Overweight, obesity, and mortality from cancer in a prospectively studied cohort of U.S. adults. *New England Journal of Medicine, 348,* 1625–1638.

Cameron, C. A., & Lee, K. (1997). The development of children's telephone communication. *Journal of Applied Developmental Psychology, 18,* 55–70.

Cameron, M. B., & Wilson, B. J. (1990). The effects of chronological age, gender, and delay of entry on academic achievement and retention: Implications for academic redshirting. *Psychology in the Schools, 27,* 260–263.

Cammu, H., Martens, G., Ruyssinck, G., & Amy, J. J. (2002). Outcome after elective labor induction in nulliparous women: A matched cohort study. *American Journal of Obstetrics and Gynecology, 186,* 240–244.

Camodeca, M., Goossens, F. A., Terwogt, M. M., & Schuengel, C. (2002). Bullying and victimization among school-age children: Stability and links to proactive and reactive aggression. *Social Development, 11,* 332–345.

Campbell, F. A., Pungello, E. P., Miller-Johnson, S., Burchinal, M., & Ramey, C. T. (2001). The development of cognitive and academic abilities: Growth curves from an early childhood educational experiment. *Developmental Psychology, 37,* 231–242.

Campbell, F. A., & Ramey, C. T. (1995). Cognitive and school outcomes for high-risk African-American students at middle adolescence: Positive effects of early intervention. *American Educational Research Journal, 32,* 743–772.

Campbell, F. A., Ramey, C. T., Pungello, E., Sparling, J., & Miller-Johnson, S. (2002). Early childhood education: Young adult outcomes from the Abecedarian Project. *Applied Developmental Science, 6,* 42–57.

Campbell, J. R., Hombo, C. M., & Mazzeo, J. (2000). *NAEP 1999: Trends in academic progress.* Washington, DC: U.S. Department of Education.

Campbell, R., & Sais, E. (1995). Accelerated metalinguistic (phonological) awareness in bilingual children. *British Journal of Developmental Psychology, 13,* 61–68.

Campos, J. J., Anderson, D. I., Barbu-Roth, M. A., Hubbard, E. M., Hertenstein, J. J., & Witherington, D. (2000). Travel broadens the mind. *Infancy, 1,* 149–219.

Campos, J. J., Kermoian, R., & Zumbahlen, M. R. (1992). Socioemotional transformation in the family system following infant crawling onset. In N. Eisenberg & R. A. Fabes (Eds.), *New directions for child development* (No. 55, pp. 25–40). San Francisco: Jossey-Bass.

Campos, R. G. (1989). Soothing pain-elicited distress in infants with swaddling and pacifiers. *Child Development, 60,* 781–792.

Camras, L. A. (1992). Expressive development and basic emotions. *Cognition and Emotion, 6,* 267–283.

Camras, L. A., Oster, H., Campos, J., Campos, R., Ujie, T., Miyake, K., Wang, L., & Meng, Z. (1998). Production of emotional and facial expressions in European American, Japanese, and Chinese infants. *Developmental Psychology, 34,* 616–628.

Canada Campaign 2000. (2003). *Poverty amidst prosperity—building a Canada for all children: 2002 report card.* Ottawa: House of Commons.

Canadian Broadcast Standards Council. (2003). *Voluntary code regarding violence in television programming.* Retrieved from http://www.cbsc.ca/english/codes/violence/violence.htm

Canadian Fitness and Lifestyle Research Institute. (2001). Survey of physical activity in Canadian schools. Retrieved from http://www.cflri.ca/cflri/pa/surveys/2001survey/2001survey.html

Canadian Fitness and Lifestyle Research Institute. (2002). 2000 physical activity monitor. Retrieved from http://www.cflri.ca/cflri/resources/pub.php#2001capacity

Canadian Fitness and Lifestyle Research Institute. (2003). *A case for daily physical education.* Retrieved from http://www.cflri.ca/cflri/tips/95/LT95_09.html

Canadian Institute for Health Information. (2003). Proportion of deliveries by caesarean section, excluding stillbirths. Retrieved from http://www.cihi.ca

Canadian Pediatric Society. (2003). Breastfeeding. Retrieved from http://www.caringforkids.cps.ca/babies/Breastfeeding.htm

Candy-Gibbs, S., Sharp, K., & Petrun, C. (1985). The effects of age, object, and cultural/religious background on children's concepts of death. *Omega, 15,* 329–345.

Canetto, S. S., & Sakinofsky, I. (1998). The gender paradox in suicide. *Suicide and Life-Threatening Behavior, 28,* 1–23.

Canobi, K. H., Reeve, R. A., & Pattison, P. E. (1998). The role of conceptual understanding in children's addition problem solving. *Developmental Psychology, 34,* 882–891.

Cantor, J., & Harrison, K. (1997). Ratings and advisories for television programming: University of Wisconsin, Madison, study. In Mediascope (Ed.), *National Television Violence Study: Scientific papers 1994–1995.* Studio City, CA: Author.

Capaldi, D., DeGarmo, D., Patterson, G. R., & Forgatch, M. (2002). Contextual risk across the early life span and association with antisocial behavior. In J. B. Reid, G. R. Patterson, & J. Snyder (Eds.), *Antisocial behavior in children and adolescents* (pp. 123–145). Washington, DC: American Psychological Association.

Capelli, C. A., Nakagawa, N., & Madden, C. M. (1990). How children understand sarcasm: The role of context and intonation. *Child Development, 61,* 1824–1841.

Caplan, M., Vespo, J., Pedersen, J., & Hay, D. F. (1991). Conflict and its resolution in small groups of one- and two-year-olds. *Child Development, 62,* 1513–1524.

Carey, S. (1995). On the origins of causal understanding. In D. Sperber, D. Premack, & A. J. Premack (Eds.), *Causal cognition* (pp. 268–308). Oxford, U.K.: Clarendon Press.

Carey, S. (1999). Sources of conceptual change. In E. K. Scholnick, K. Nelson, S. A. Gelman, & P. H. Miller (Eds.), *Conceptual development: Piaget's legacy* (pp. 293–326). Mahwah, NJ: Erlbaum.

Carey, S., & Markman, E. M. (1999). Cognitive development. In B. M. Bly & D. E. Rumelhart (Eds.), *Cognitive science* (pp. 201–254). San Diego: Academic Press.

Carlo, G., Koller, S. H., Eisenberg, N., Da Silva, M., & Frohlich, C. (1996). A cross-national study on the relations among prosocial moral reasoning, gender role orientations, and prosocial behaviors. *Developmental Psychology, 32,* 231–240.

Carlson, C., Uppal, S., & Prosser, E. (2000). Ethnic differences in processes contributing to the self-esteem of early adolescent girls. *Journal of Early Adolescence, 20,* 44–67.

Carlson, K. J., Eisenstat, S. A., & Ziporyn, T. (1996). *The Harvard guide to women's health.* Cambridge, MA: Harvard University Press.

Carlson, S. M., & Moses, L. J. (2001). Individual differences in inhibitory control and children's theory of mind. *Child Development, 72,* 1032–1053.

Carlton, M. P., & Winsler, A. (1999). School readiness: The need for a paradigm shift. *School Psychology Review, 28,* 338–352.

Carmichael, S. L., & Shaw, G. M. (2000). Maternal life stress and congenital anomalies. *Epidemiology, 11,* 30–35.

Carolson, C., Uppal, S., & Prosser, E. C. (2000). Ethnic differences in processes contributing to the self-esteem of early adolescent girls. *Journal of Early Adolescence, 20,* 44–67.

Carpendale, J. I. M. (2000). Kohlberg and Piaget on stages and moral reasoning. *Developmental Review, 20,* 181–205.

Carpendale, J. I., & Chandler, M. J. (1996). On the distinction between false belief understanding and subscribing to an interpretive theory of mind. *Child Development, 67,* 1686–1706.

Carpenter, C. J. (1983). Activity structure and play: Implications for socialization. In M. Liss (Eds.), *Social and cognitive skills: Sex roles and children's play* (pp. 117–145). New York: Academic Press.

Carpenter, M., Nagel, K., & Tomasello, M. (1998). Social cognition, joint attention, and communicative competence. *Monographs of the Society for Research in Child Development, 63*(4, Serial No. 255).

Carpenter, T. P., Fennema, E., Fuson, K., Hiebert, J., Human, P., & Murray, H. (1999). Learning basic number concepts and skills as problem solving. In E. Fennema & T. A. Romberg (Eds.), *Mathematics classrooms that promote understanding: Studies in mathematical thinking and learning series* (pp. 45–61). Mahwah, NJ: Erlbaum.

Carr, J. (2002). Down syndrome. In P. Howlin & O. Udwin (Eds.), *Outcomes in neurodevelopmental and genetic disorders* (pp. 169–197). New York: Cambridge University Press.

Carr, M., & Jessup, D. L. (1997). Gender differences in first-grade mathematics strategy use: Social and metacognitive influences. *Journal of Educational Psychology, 89,* 318–328.

Carskadon, M. A., Harvey, K., Duke, P., Anders, T. F., Litt, I. F., & Dement, W. C. (2002). Pubertal changes in daytime sleepiness. *Sleep, 25,* 525–605.

Carver, K., Joyner, K., & Udry, J. R. (2003). National estimates of adolescent romantic relationships. In P. Florsheim (Ed.), *Adolescent romantic relations and sexual behavior: Theory, research, and practical implications* (pp. 23–56). Mahwah, NJ: Erlbaum.

Carver, P. R., Egan, S. K., & Perry, D. G. (2004). Children who question their heterosexuality. *Developmental Psychology, 40,* 43–53.

Casby, M. W. (2001). Otitis media and language development: A meta-analysis. *American Journal of Speech-Language Pathology, 10,* 65–80.

Case, R. (1992). *The mind's staircase: Exploring the conceptual underpinnings of children's thought and knowledge.* Hillsdale, NJ: Erlbaum.

Case, R. (1996). Introduction: Reconceptualizing the nature of children's conceptual structures and their development in middle childhood. In R. Case & Y. Okamoto (Eds.), The role of central conceptual structures in the development of children's thought. *Monographs of the Society for Research in Child Development, 246*(61, Serial No. 246), pp. 1–26.

Case, R. (1998). The development of conceptual structures. In D. Kuhn & R. S. Siegler (Eds.), *Handbook of child psychology: Vol. 2. Cognition, perception, and language* (pp. 745–800). New York: Wiley.

Case, R., Griffin, S., & Kelly, W. M. (2001). Socioeconomic differences in children's early cognitive development and their readiness for schooling. In S. L. Golbeck (Ed.), *Psychological perspectives on early education* (pp. 37–63). Mahwah, NJ: Erlbaum.

Case, R., & Okamoto, Y. (Eds.). (1996). The role of central conceptual structures in the development of children's thought. *Monographs of the Society for Research in Child Development, 61*(1–2, Serial No. 246).

Case-Smith, J., Bigsby, R., & Clutter, J. (1998). Perceptual-motor coupling in the development of grasp. *American Journal of Occupational Therapy, 52,* 102–110.

Casey, B. M., Nuttall, R. L., & Pezaris, E. (2001). Spatial-mechanical reasoning skills versus mathematics self-confidence as mediators of gender differences on mathematics subtests using cross-national gender-based items. *Journal for Research in Mathematics Education, 32,* 28–57.

Casey, M. B. (1986). Individual differences in selective attention among prereaders: A key to mirror-image confusions. *Developmental Psychology, 22,* 824–831.

Casey, M. B., Nuttall, R. L., & Pezaris, E. (1997). Mediators of gender differences in mathematics college entrance test scores: A comparison of spatial skills with internalized beliefs and anxieties. *Developmental Psychology, 33,* 669–680.

Cashon, C. H., & Cohen, L. B. (2000). Eight-month-old infants' perceptions of possible and impossible events. *Infancy, 1,* 429–446.

Casper, L. M., & Smith, K. E. (2002). Dispelling the myths: Self-care, class, and race. *Journal of Family Issues, 23,* 716–727.

Caspi, A. (1998). Personality development across the life course. In N. Eisenberg (Ed.), *Handbook of child psychology: Vol. 3. Social, emotional, and personality development* (5th ed., pp. 311–388). New York: Wiley.

Caspi, A. (2000). The child is father of the man: Personality continuities

from childhood to adulthood. *Journal of Personality and Social Psychology, 78,* 158–172.

Caspi, A., Elder, G. H., Jr., & Bem, D. J. (1987). Moving against the world: Life-course patterns of explosive children. *Developmental Psychology, 23,* 308–313.

Caspi, A., Elder, G. H., Jr., & Bem, D. J. (1988). Moving away from the world: Life-course patterns of shy children. *Developmental Psychology, 24,* 824–831.

Caspi, A., Harrington, H., Milne, B., Amell, J. W., Theodore, R. F., & Moffitt, T. E. (2003). Children's behavioral styles at age 3 are linked to their adult personality traits at age 26. *Journal of Personality, 71,* 495–513.

Caspi, A., & Herbener, E. (1990). Continuity and change: Assortative marriage and the consistency of personality in adulthood. *Journal of Personality and Social Psychology, 58,* 250–258.

Caspi, A., Lynam, D., Moffitt, T. E., & Silva, P. A. (1993). Unraveling girls' delinquency: Biological, dispositional, and contextual contributions to adolescent misbehavior. *Developmental Psychology, 29,* 19–30.

Caspi, A., & Roberts, B. W. (2001). Personality development across the life course: The argument for change and continuity. *Psychological Inquiry, 12,* 49–66.

Cassidy, J. (2001). Adult romantic attachments: A developmental perspective on individual differences. *Review of General Psychology, 4,* 111-131.

Cassidy, J., & Berlin, L. J. (1994). The insecure/ambivalent pattern of attachment: Theory and research. *Child Development, 65,* 971–991.

Castellanos, F. X., Lee, P. P., Sharp, W., Jeffries, N. O., Greenstein, D. K., & Clasen, L. S. (2002). Developmental trajectories of brain volume abnormalities in children and adolescents with attention-deficit/hyperactivity disorder. *Journal of the American Medical Association, 288,* 1740–1748.

Castelli, F., Frith, C. D., Happé, F., & Frith, U. (2002). Autism, Asperger syndrome, and brain mechanisms for the attribution of mental states to animated shapes. *Brain, 125,* 1–11.

Caton, D., Corry, M. P., Frigoletto, F. D., Hopkins, D. P., Liberman, E., & Mayberry, L. (2002). The nature and management of labor pain: Executive summary. *American Journal of Obstetrics and Gynecology, 186,* S1–S15.

Catsambis, S. (1994). The path to math: Gender and racial-ethnic differences in mathematics participation from middle school to high school. *Sociology of Education, 67,* 199–215.

Catterall, J. (1998). Risk and resilience in student transitions to high school.

American Journal of Education, 106, 302–333.

Cavadini, C., Siega-Riz, A. M., & Popkin, B. M. (2000). U.S. adolescent food intake trends from 1965 to 1996. *Archives of Diseases in Childhood, 83,* 18–24.

Cavazzana-Calvo, M., Hacein-Bey, S., de Saint Basile, G., et al. (2000). Gene therapy of human severe combined immunodeficiency (SCID)-X1 disease. *Science, 288,* 669–672.

Ceci, S. J. (1991). How much does schooling influence general intelligence and its cognitive components? A reassessment of the evidence. *Developmental Psychology, 27,* 703–722.

Ceci, S. J. (1999). Schooling and intelligence. In S. J. Ceci & W. M. Williams (Eds.), *The nature–nurture debate: The essential readings* (pp. 168–175). Oxford: Blackwell.

Ceci, S. J., & Bruck, M. (1998). Children's testimony: Applied and basic issues. In I. Sigel & K. A. Renninger (Eds.), *Handbook of child psychology: Vol. 4. Child psychology in practice* (5th ed., pp. 713–774). New York: Wiley.

Ceci, S. J., Fitneva, S. A., & Gilstrap, L. L. (2003). Memory development and eyewitness testimony. In A. Slater & G. Bremner (Eds.), *An introduction to developmental psychology* (pp. 283–310). Malden MA: Blackwell.

Ceci, S. J., & Roazzi, A. (1994). The effects of context on cognition: Postcards from Brazil. In R. J. Sternberg (Ed.), *Mind in context* (pp. 74–101). New York: Cambridge University Press.

Ceci, S. J., Rosenblum, T. B., & Kumpf, M. (1998). The shrinking gap between high- and low-scoring groups: Current trends and possible causes. In U. Neisser (Ed.), *The rising curve: Long-term gains in IQ and related measures* (pp. 287–302). Washington, DC: American Psychological Association.

Center for Communication and Social Policy. (Ed.). (1998). *National Television Violence Study* (Vol. 2). Newbury Park, CA: Sage.

Centers for Disease Control and Prevention. (2003). Cases of HIV infection and AIDS in the United States, 2002. *HIV/AIDS Surveillance Report, 14.* Retrieved from http://www.cdc.gov/hiv/stats/hasr1402.htm.

Cernoch, J. M., & Porter, R. H. (1985). Recognition of maternal axillary odors by infants. *Child Development, 56,* 1593–1598.

Cervantes, C. A., & Callanan, M. A. (1998). Labels and explanations in mother–child emotion talk: Age and gender differentiation. *Developmental Psychology, 34,* 88–98.

Chall, J. S. (1983). *Stages of reading development.* New York: McGraw-Hill.

Chalmers, J. B., & Townsend, M. A. R. (1990). The effects of training in social perspective taking on socially

maladjusted girls. *Child Development, 61,* 178–190.

Chamberlain, P. (2003). Antisocial behavior and delinquency in girls. In P. Chamberlain (Ed.), *Treating chronic juvenile offenders* (pp. 109–127). Washington, DC: American Psychological Association.

Chan, R. W., Raboy, B., & Patterson, C. J. (1998). Psychosocial adjustment among children conceived via donor insemination by lesbian and heterosexual mothers. *Child Development, 69,* 443–457.

Chandler, M., Boyes, M., & Ball, L. (1990). Relativism and stations of epistemic doubt. *Journal of Experimental Child Psychology, 50,* 370–395.

Chandra, R. K. (1991). Interactions between early nutrition and the immune system. In *Ciba Foundation Symposium No. 156* (pp. 77–92). Chichester, U.K.: Wiley.

Chao, R. K. (1994). Beyond parental control and authoritarian parenting style: Understanding Chinese parenting through the cultural notion of training. *Child Development, 65,* 1111–1119.

Chao, R. K. (2001). Extending research on the consequences of parenting style for Chinese Americans and European Americans. *Child Development, 72,* 1832–1843.

Chapman, R. S. (2000). Children's language learning: An interactionist perspective. *Journal of Child Psychology and Psychiatry, 41,* 33–54.

Chase, C., Teele, D. W., Klein, J. O., & Rosner, B. A. (1995). Behavioral sequelae of otitis media for infants at one year of age and their mothers. In D. J. Lim, C. D. Bluestone, J. O. Klein, J. D. Nelson, & P. L. Ogra (Eds.), *Recent advances in otitis media.* Ontario: Decker.

Chase-Lansdale, P. L., Brooks-Gunn, J., & Zamsky, E. S. (1994). Young African-American multigenerational families in poverty: Quality of mothering and grandmothering. *Child Development, 65,* 373–393.

Chase-Lansdale, P. L., Gordon, R., Brooks-Gunn, J., & Klebanov, P. K. (1997). Neighborhood and family influences on the intellectual and behavioral competence of preschool and early school-age children. In J. Brooks-Gunn, G. Duncan, & J. L. Aber (Eds.), *Neighborhood poverty: Context and consequences for development* (pp. 79–118). New York: Russell Sage Foundation.

Chasnoff, I. J., Anson, A., Hatcher, R., Stenson, H., Iaukea, K., & Randolph, L. A. (1998). Prenatal exposure to cocaine and other drugs: Outcome at four to six years. In J. A. Harvey & B. E. Kosofsky (Eds.), *Annals of the New York Academy of Sciences* (Vol. 846, pp. 314–328). New York: New York Academy of Sciences.

Chassin, L., Ritter, J., Trim, R. S., & King, K. M. (2003). Adolescent substance use disorders. In E. J.

Mash & R. A. Barkley (Eds.), *Child psychopathology* (2nd ed., pp. 199–230). New York: Guilford.

Chavajay, P., & Rogoff, B. (1999). Cultural variation in management of attention by children and their caregivers. *Developmental Psychology, 35,* 1079–1090.

Chavajay, P., & Rogoff, B. (2002). Schooling and traditional collaborative social organization of problem solving by Mayan mothers and children. *Developmental Psychology, 38,* 55–66.

Checkley, W., Epstein, L. D., Gilman, R. H., Cabrera, L., & Black, R. E. (2003). Effects of acute diarrhea on linear growth in Peruvian children. *American Journal of Epidemiology, 157,* 166–175.

Chen, D. W., Fein, G. G., Killen, M., & Tam, H.-P. (2001). Peer conflicts of preschool children: Issues, resolution, incidence, and age-related patterns. *Early Education and Development, 12,* 523–544.

Chen, M. (2003). Wombs for rent: An examination of prohibitory and regulatory approaches to governing preconception arrangements. *Health Law in Canada, 23,* 33–50.

Chen, X. (2001). Growing up in a collectivistic culture. Socialization and socio-emotional development in Chinese children. In A. L. Comunian & U. P. Gielen (Eds.), *Human development in cross-cultural perspective.* Padua, Italy: Cedam.

Chen, X. (2002). Peer relationships and networks and socio-emotional adjustment: A Chinese perspective. In B. Cairns & T. Farmer (Eds.), *Social networks from a developmental perspective.* New York: Cambridge University Press.

Chen, X., Dong, Q., & Zhou, H. (1997). Authoritative and authoritarian parenting practices and social and school performance in Chinese children. *International Journal of Behavioral Development, 21,* 855–873.

Chen, X., Hastings, P. D., Rubin, K. H., Chen, H., Cen, G., & Stewart, S. L. (1998). Child-rearing attitudes and behavioral inhibition in Chinese and Canadian toddlers: A cross-cultural study. *Developmental Psychology, 34,* 677–686.

Chen, X., Liu, M., & Li, D. (2000). Parental warmth, control, and indulgence and their relations to adjustment in Chinese children: A longitudinal study. *Journal of Family Psychology, 14,* 401–419.

Chen, X., Rubin, K. H., & Li, Z. (1995). Social functioning and adjustment in Chinese children: A longitudinal study. *Developmental Psychology, 31,* 531–539.

Chen, Y.-C., Yu, M.-L., Rogan, W., Gladen, B., & Hsu, C.-C. (1994). A 6-year follow-up of behavior and activity disorders in the Taiwan Yu-cheng children. *American Journal of Public Health, 84,* 415–421.

Chen, Y.-J., & Hsu, C.-C. (1994). Effects of prenatal exposure to PCBs on the neurological function of children: A neuropsychological and neurophysiological study. *Developmental Medicine and Child Neurology, 36,* 312–320.

Chen, Z., & Siegler, R. S. (2000). Across the great divide: Bridging the gap between understanding of toddlers' and older children's thinking. *Monographs of the Society for Research in Child Development, 65*(2, Serial No. 261).

Chen, Z., Sanchez, R. P., & Campbell, T. (1997). From beyond to within their grasp: The rudiments of analogical problem solving in 10- to 13-month-olds. *Developmental Psychology, 33,* 790–801.

Cheng, T. L., Fields, C. B., Brenner, R. A., Wright, J. L., Lomax, T., Scheidt, P. C., & the District of Columbia Child/Adolescent Injury Research Network. (2000). Sports injuries: An important cause of morbidity in urban youth. *Pediatrics, 105,* e32.

Cherny, S. S. (1994). Home environmental influences on general cognitive ability. In J. C. DeFries, R. Plomin, & D. W. Fulker (Eds.), *Nature and nurture during middle childhood* (pp. 262–280). Cambridge, MA: Blackwell.

Chesney-Lind, M. (2001). Girls, violence, and delinquency: Popular myths and persistent problems. In S. O. White (Ed.), *Handbook of youth and justice* (pp. 135–158). New York: Kluwer Academic.

Chess, S., & Thomas, A. (1984). *Origins and evolution of behavior disorders.* New York: Brunner/Mazel.

Child Trends. (2001). *Facts at a glance.* Washington, DC: Author.

Childbirth by Choice. (1999). *Fact sheet: Unwanted pregnancy.* Toronto: Author.

Children's Defense Fund. (2003). *The state of America's children: Yearbook 2003.* Washington, DC: Author.

Childs, C. P., & Greenfield, P. M. (1982). Informal modes of learning and teaching: The case of Zinacanteco weaving. In N. Warren (Ed.), *Advances in cross-cultural psychology* (Vol. 2, pp. 269–316). London: Academic Press.

Chin, D. G., Schonfeld, D. J., O'Hare, L. L., Mayne, S. T., Salovey, P., Showalter, D. R., & Cicchetti, D. V. (1998). Elementary school-age children's developmental understanding of the causes of cancer. *Developmental and Behavioral Pediatrics, 19,* 397–403.

Chisholm, J. S. (1989). Biology, culture, and the development of temperament: A Navajo example. In J. K. Nugent, B. M. Lester, & T. B. Brazelton (Eds.), *Biology, culture, and development* (Vol. 1, pp. 341–364). Norwood, NJ: Ablex.

Chiu, L.-H. (1992-1993). Self-esteem in American and Chinese (Taiwanese) children. *Current Psychology: Research and Reviews, 11,* 309–313.

Choi, J., & Silverman, I. (2003). Processes underlying sex differences in route-learning strategies in children and adolescents. *Personality and Individual Differences, 34,* 1153–1166.

Choi, S., & Gopnik, A. (1995). Early acquisition of verbs in Korean: A cross-linguistic study. *Journal of Child Language, 22,* 497–529.

Chomsky, C. (1969). *The acquisition of syntax in children from five to ten.* Cambridge, MA: MIT Press.

Chomsky, N. (1957). *Syntactic structures.* The Hague: Mouton.

Chordirker, B., Cadrin, C., Davies, G., Summers, A., Wilson, R., Winsor, E., & Young, D. (2001). Genetic indications for prenatal diagnosis. *Journal of the Society of Obstetricians and Gynaecologists of Canada, 23,* 525–531.

Christenson, S. L., & Sheridan, S. M. (2001). *Schools and families.* New York: Guilford.

Christophersen, E. R., & Mortweet, S. L. (2003). *Parenting that works: Building skills that last a lifetime.* Washington, DC: American Psychological Association.

Chugani, H. T. (1994). Development of regional brain glucose metabolism in relation to behavior and plasticity. In G. Dawson & K. W. Fischer (Eds.), *Human behavior and the developing brain* (pp. 153–175). New York: Guilford.

Chumlea, W. C., Schubert, C. M., Roche, A. F., Kulin, H. E., Lee, P. A., Himes, J. H., & Sun, S. S. (2003). Age at menarche and racial comparisons in U.S. girls. *Pediatrics, 111,* 110–113.

Cicchetti, D. (2003). Neuroendocrine functioning in maltreated children. In D. Cicchetti & E. F. Walker (Eds.), *Neurodevelopmental mechanisms in psychopathology* (pp. 345–365). New York: Cambridge University Press.

Cicchetti, D., & Aber, J. L. (1986). Early precursors of later depression: An organizational perspective. In L. P. Lipsitt & C. Rovee-Collier (Eds.), *Advances in infancy research* (Vol. 4, pp. 87–137). Norwood, NJ: Ablex.

Cicchetti, D., & Toth, S. L. (1998). The development of depression in children and adolescents. *American Psychologist, 53,* 221–241.

Cicchetti, D., & Toth, S. L. (2000). Developmental processes in maltreated children. In D. J. Hansen (Ed.), *Nebraska Symposium on Motivation* (Vol. 46, pp. 85–160). Lincoln, NE: University of Nebraska Press.

Cillessen, A. H. N., & Bukowski, W. M. (2000). *Recent advances in the measurement of acceptance and rejection in the peer system.* San Francisco: Jossey-Bass.

Clapp, J. F., III, Kim, H., Burciu, B., Schmidt, S., Petry, K., & Lopez, B. (2002). Continuing regular exercise during pregnancy: Effect of exercise volume on fetoplacental growth. *American Journal of Obstetrics and Gynecology, 186,* 142–147.

Clark, E. V. (1990). On the pragmatics of contrast. *Journal of Child Language, 17,* 417–431.

Clark, E. V. (1995). The lexicon and syntax. In J. L. Miller & P. D. Eimas (Eds.), *Speech, language, and communication* (pp. 303–337). San Diego: Academic Press.

Clark, K. E., & Ladd, G. W. (2000). Connectedness and autonomy support in parent–child relationships: Links to children's socioemotional orientation and peer relationships. *Developmental Psychology, 36,* 485–498.

Clark, R., Hyde, J. S., Essex, M. J. & Klein, M. H. (1997). Length of maternity leave and quality of mother-infant interaction. *Child Development, 68,* 364–383.

Clarke-Stewart, A., Allhusen, V., & Goossens, F. (2001). Day care and the Strange Situation. In A. Göncue & E. L., Klein (Eds.), *Children in play, story, and school* (pp. 241–266). New York: Guilford.

Clarke-Stewart, K. A. (1998). Historical shifts and underlying themes in ideas about rearing young children in the United States: Where have we been? Where are we going? *Early Development and Parenting, 7,* 101–117.

Clarke-Stewart, K. A., & Hayward, C. (1996). Advantages of father custody and contact for the psychological well-being of school-age children. *Journal of Applied Developmental Psychology, 17,* 239–270.

Clausen, J. A. (1975). The social meaning of differential physical and sexual maturation. In S. E. Dragastin & G. H. Elder (Eds.), *Adolescence in the life cycle: Psychological change and the social context* (pp. 25–47). New York: Halsted.

Claxton, L. J., Keen, R., & McCarty, M. E. (2003). Evidence of motor planning in infant reaching behavior. *Psychological Science, 14,* 354–356.

Clements, D. H. (1990). Metacomponential development in a Logo programming environment. *Journal of Educational Psychology, 82,* 141–149.

Clements, D. H. (1995). Teaching creativity with computers. *Educational Psychology Review, 7,* 141–161.

Clements, D. H., & Nastasi, B. K. (1992). Computers and early childhood education. In M. Gettinger, S. N. Elliott, & T. R. Kratochwill (Eds.), *Advances in school psychology: Preschool and early childhood treatment directions* (pp. 187– 246). Hillsdale, NJ: Erlbaum.

Clements, D. H., & Sarama, J. (2003). Young children and technology: What does the research say? *Young Children, 58*(6), 34–40.

Clifton, R. K., Rochat, P., Robin, D. J., & Berthier, N. E. (1994). Multimodal perception in the control of infant reaching. *Journal of Experimental Psychology: Human Perception and Performance, 20,* 876–886.

Clingempeel, W. G., & Henggeler, S. W. (2003). Aggressive juvenile offenders transitioning into emerging adulthood: Factors discriminating persistors and desistors. *American Journal of Orthopsychiatry, 73,* 310–323.

Cloud, N., Genesee, F., & Hamayan, E. (2000). *Dual language instruction: A handbook for enriched education.* Boston, MA: Heinle & Heinle.

Cnattingius, S., Forman, M. R., Berendes, H. W., & Isotalo, L. (1992). Delayed childbearing and risk of adverse perinatal outcome: A population-based study. *Journal of the American Medical Association, 268,* 886–890.

Cohen, L. B. (2003). Commentary on Part I: Unresolved issues in infant categorization. In D. H. Rakison & L. M. Oakes (Eds.), *Early category and concept development: Making sense of the blooming, buzzing confusion* (pp. 193–209). New York: Oxford University Press.

Cohen, L. B., & Cashon, C. H. (2001). Infant object segregation implies information integration. *Journal of Experimental Child Psychology, 78,* 75–83.

Cohen, P., Kasen, S., Chen, H., Harmrk, C., & Gordon, K. (2003). Variations in patterns of developmental transitions in the emerging adulthood period. *Developmental Psychology, 39,* 657–669.

Cohen, S., & Herbert, T. B. (1996). Health psychology: Psychological factors and physical disease from the perspective of human psychoneuroimmunology. *Annual Review of Psychology, 47,* 113–142.

Cohen, S., & Williamson, G. M. (1991). Stress and infectious disease in humans. *Psychological Bulletin, 109,* 5–24.

Coholl, A., Kassotis, J., Parks, R., Vaughan, R., Bannister, H., & Northridge, M. (2001). Adolescents in the age of AIDS: Myths, misconceptions, and misunderstandings regarding sexually transmitted diseases. *Journal of the National Medical Association, 93,* 64–69.

Coie, J. D., & Dodge, K. A. (1998). Aggression and antisocial behavior. In N. Eisenberg (Ed.), *Handbook of child psychology: Vol. 3. Social, emotional, and personality development* (5th ed., pp. 779–862). New York: Wiley.

Coie, J. D., Dodge, K. A., & Coppotelli, H. (1982). Dimensions and types of social status: A cross-age perspective. *Developmental Psychology, 18,* 557–570.

Coie, J. D., & Krehbiel, G. (1984). Effects of academic tutoring on the social status of low-achieving, socially rejected children. *Child Development, 55,* 1465–1478.

Colapinto, J. (2001). *As nature made him: The boy who was raised as a girl.* New York: Perennial.

Colby, A., Kohlberg, L., Gibbs, J., & Lieberman, M. (1983). A longitudinal study of moral judgment. *Monographs of the Society for Research in Child Development, 48*(1–2, Serial No. 200).

Cole, D. A., Martin, J. M., Peeke, L. A., Seroczynski, A. D., & Fier, J. (1999). Children's over- and underestimation of academic competence: A longitudinal study of gender differences, depression, and anxiety. *Child Development, 70,* 459–473.

Cole, D. A., Maxwell, S. E., Martin, J. M., Peeke, L. G., Seroczynski, A. D., & Tram, J. M. (2001). The development of multiple domains of child and adolescent self-concept: A cohort sequential longitudinal design. *Child Development, 72,* 1723–1746.

Cole, M. (1990). Cognitive development and formal schooling: The evidence from cross-cultural research. In L. C. Moll (Ed.), *Vygotsky and education* (pp. 89–110). New York: Cambridge University Press.

Cole, P. M., Bruschi, C. J., & Tamang, B. L. (2002). Cultural differences in children's emotional reactions to difficult situations. *Child Development, 73,* 983–996.

Cole, P. M., & Tamang, B. L. (1998). Nepali children's ideas about emotional displays in hypothetical challenges. *Developmental Psychology, 34,* 640–648.

Cole, T. J. (2000). Secular trends in growth. *Proceedings of the Nutrition Society, 59,* 317–324.

Coley, R. L. (1998). Children's socialization experiences and functioning in single-mother households: The importance of fathers and other men. *Child Development, 69,* 219–230.

Coley, R. L., & Chase-Lansdale, P. L. (1998). Adolescent pregnancy and parenthood: Recent evidence and future directions. *American Psychologist, 53,* 152–166.

Collaer, M. L., Geffner, M. E., Kaufman, F. R., Buckingham, B., & Hines, M. (2002). Cognitive and behavioral characteristics of Turner syndrome: Exploring a role for ovarian hormones in female sexual differentiation. *Hormones and Behavior, 41,* 139–155.

Collaer, M. L., & Hines, M. (1995). Human behavioral sex differences: A role for gonadal hormones during early development? *Psychological Bulletin, 118,* 55–107.

Collie, R., & Hayne, H. (1999). Deferred imitation by 6- and 9-month-old infants: More evidence for declarative memory. *Developmental Psychobiology, 35,* 83–90.

Collins, F. S., & McKusick, V. A. (2001). Implications of the Human Genome Project for medical science. *Journal of the American Medical Association, 285,* 540–544.

Collins, W. A. (1983). Children's processing of television content: Implications for prevention of negative effects. *Prevention in Human Services, 2,* 53–66.

Collins, W. A. (2003). More than myth: The developmental significance of romantic relationships during adolescence. *Journal of Research on Adolescence, 13,* 1–24.

Collins, W. A., Laursen, B., Mortensen, N., Luebker, C., & Ferreira, M. (1997). Conflict processes and transitions in parent and peer relationships: Implications for autonomy and regulation. *Journal of Adolescent Research, 12,* 178–198.

Collins, W. A., Maccoby, E. E., Steinberg, L., Hetherington, E. M., & Bornstein, M. H. (2000). Contemporary research on parenting: The case for nature and nurture. *American Psychologist, 52,* 218–232

Collins, W. A., Madsen, S. D., & Susman-Stillman, A. (2002). Parenting during middle childhood. In M. H. Bornstein (Ed.), *Handbook of parenting: Vol. 1. Children and parenting* (2nd ed., pp. 73–101). Mahwah, NJ: Erlbaum.

Colman, L. L., & Colman, A. D. (1991). *Pregnancy: The psychological experience.* Noonday Press.

Colombo, J. (1995). On the neural mechanisms underlying developmental and individual differences in visual fixation in infancy. *Developmental Review, 15,* 97–135.

Coltrane, S. (1990). Birth timing and the division of labor in dual-earner families. *Journal of Family Issues, 11,* 157–181.

Comings, D. E., Muhleman, D., Johnson, J. P., & MacMurray, J. P. (2002). Parent–daughter transmission of the androgen receptor gene as an explanation of the effect of father absence on age of menarche. *Child Development, 73,* 1046–1051.

Comstock, G. A., & Scharrer, E. (1999). *Television: What's on, who's watching, and what it means.* San Diego: Academic Press.

Comstock, G. A., & Scharrer, E. (2001). The use of television and other film-related media. In D. G. Singer & J. L. Singer (Eds.), *Handbook of children and the media* (pp. 47–72). Thousand Oaks, CA: Sage.

Comunian, A. L., & Gielen, U. P. (2000). Sociomoral reflection and prosocial and antisocial behavior: Two Italian studies. *Psychological Reports, 87,* 161–175.

Conger, R. D., & Conger, K. J. (2002). Resilience in Midwestern families: Selected findings from the first decade of a prospective, longitudinal study. *Journal of Marriage and the Family, 64,* 361–373.

Conger, R. D., Ge, X., Elder, G. H., Jr., Lorenz, F. O., & Simons, R. L. (1994). Economic stress, coercive family process, and developmental problems of adolescents. *Child Development, 65,* 541–561.

Conger, R., Patterson, G. R., & Ge, X. (1995). It takes two to replicate: A mediational model for the impact of parents' stress on adolescent adjustment. *Child Development, 66,* 80–97.

Connolly, J. A., & Doyle, A. B. (1984). Relations of social fantasy play to social competence in preschoolers. *Developmental Psychology, 20,* 797–806.

Connolly, J., Furman, W., & Konarski, R. (2000). The role of peers in the emergence of romantic relationships in adolescence. *Child Development, 71,* 1395–1408.

Connolly, J., & Goldberg, A. (1999). Romantic relationships in adolescence: The role of friends and peers in their emergence and development. In W. Furman, B. B. Brown, & C. Feiring (Eds.), *The development of romantic relationships in adolescence* (pp. 266–290). New York: Cambridge University Press.

Connor, J. M. (2003). Physical activity and well-being. In M. H. Bornstein, L. Davidson, C. L. M. Keyes, K. A. Moore, & the Center for Child Well-Being (Eds.), *Well-being: Positive development across the life course* (pp. 65–79). Mahwah, NJ: Erlbaum.

Connor, P. D., Sampson, P. D., Bookstein, F. L., Barr, H. M., & Streissguth, A. P. (2001). Direct and indirect effects of prenatal alcohol damage on executive function. *Developmental Neuropsychology, 18,* 331–354.

Conti-Ramsden, G., & Pérez-Pereira, M. (1999). Conversational interactions between mothers and their infants who are congenitally blind, have low vision, or are sighted. *Journal of Visual Impairment and Blindness, 93,* 691–703.

Cook, T. D., Herman, M. R., Phillips, M., & Settersten, R. A., Jr. (2002). Some ways in which neighborhoods, nuclear families, friendship groups, and schools jointly affect changes in early adolescent development. *Child Development, 73,* 1283–1309.

Cooper, C. R. (1998). *The weaving of maturity: Cultural perspectives on adolescent development.* New York: Oxford University Press.

Cooper, S., & Glazer, E. S. (1999). *Choosing assisted reproduction: Social, emotional, and ethical considerations.* New York: Dimensions.

Cope-Farrar, K. M., & Kunkel, D. (2002). Sexual messages in teens' favorite prime-time television programs. In J. D. Brown, J. R. Steele, & K. Walsh-Childers (Eds.), *Sexual teens, sexual media* (pp. 59–78). Mahwah, NJ: Erlbaum.

Cornelius, J. R., Maisto, S. A., Pollock, N. K., Martin, C. S., Salloum, I. M., Lynch, K. G., & Clark, D. B. (2003). Rapid relapse generally follows treatment for substance use disorders among adolescents. *Addictive Behaviors, 28,* 381–386.

Cornelius, M. D., Day, N. L., Richardson, G. A., & Taylor, P. M. (1999). Epidemiology of substance abuse during pregnancy. In P. J. Ott & R. E. Tarter (Eds.), *Sourcebook on substance abuse: Etiology, epidemiology, assessment, and treatment* (pp. 1–13). Boston, MA: Allyn and Bacon.

Cornelius, M. D., Ryan, C. M., Day, N. L., Goldschmidt, L., & Willford, J. A. (2001). Prenatal tobacco effects on neuropsychological outcomes among preadolescents. *Developmental and Behavioral Pediatrics, 22,* 217–225.

Cosden, M., Peerson, S., & Elliott, K. (1997). Effects of prenatal drug exposure on birth outcomes and early child development. *Journal of Drug Issues, 27,* 525–539.

Costello, E. J., & Angold, A. (1995). Developmental epidemiology. In D. Cicchetti & D. Cohen (Eds.), *Developmental psychopathology: Vol. 1. Theory and method* (pp. 23–56). New York: Wiley.

Costos, D., Ackerman, R., & Paradis, L. (2002). Recollections of menarche: Communication between mothers and daughters regarding menstruation. *Sex Roles, 46,* 49–59.

Coté, S., Zoccolillo, M., Tremblay, R., Nagin, D., & Vitaro, F. (2001). Predicting girls' conduct disorder in adolescence from childhood trajectories of disruptive behaviors. *Journal of the American Academy of Child and Adolescent Psychiatry, 40,* 678–684.

Cotinot, C., Pailhoux, E., Jaubert, F., & Fellous, M. (2002). Molecular genetics of sex determination. *Seminars in Reproductive Medicine, 20,* 157–168.

Coulton, C. J., Korbin, J. E., & Su, M. (1999). Neighborhoods and child maltreatment: A multi-level study. *Child Abuse and Neglect, 23,* 1019–1040.

Courage, M. L., & Howe, M. L. (2002). From infant to child: The dynamics of cognitive change in the second year of life. *Psychological Bulletin, 128,* 250–277.

Courchesne, E., Carper, R., & Akshoomoff, N. (2003). Evidence of brain overgrowth in the first year of life in autism. *Journal of the American Medical Association, 290,* 337–344.

Cournoyer, M., Solomon, C. R., & Trudel, M. (1998). I speak then I expect: Language and self-control in the young child at home. *Canadian Journal of Behavioural Science, 30,* 69–81.

Covington, C. Y., Nordstrom-Klee, B., Ager, J., Sokol, R., & Delaney-Black, V. (2002). Birth to age 7 growth of children prenatally exposed to drugs: A prospective cohort study. *Neurotoxicology and Teratology, 24,* 489–496.

Cowan, C. P., & Cowan, P. A. (1995). Interventions to ease the transition to parenthood: Why they are needed and what they can do. *Family Relations, 44,* 412–423.

Cowan, C. P., & Cowan, P. A. (1997). Working with couples during stressful transitions. In S. Dreman (Ed.), *The family on the threshold of the 21st century* (pp. 17–47). Mahwah, NJ: Erlbaum.

Cowan, C. P., & Cowan, P. A. (2000). *When partners become parents.* Mahwah, NJ: Erlbaum.

Cowan, P. A., & Cowan, C. P. (2002). Interventions as tests of family systems theories: Marital and family relationships in children's development and psychopathology. *Development and Psychopathology, 14,* 731–759.

Cowan, P. A., Cowan, C. P., Schulz, M., & Heming, G. (1994). Prebirth to preschool family factors predicting children's adaptation to kindergarten. In R. D. Parke & S. Kellam (Eds.) *Exploring family relationships with other social contexts: Advances in family research* (Vol. 4, pp. 75–114). Hillsdale, NJ: Erlbaum.

Cowan, P. A., Powell, D., & Cowan, C. P. (1998). Parenting interventions: A family systems perspective. In I. E. Sigel & K. A. Renninger (Eds.), *Handbook of child psychology: Vol. 4. Child psychology in practice* (5th ed., pp. 3–72). New York: Wiley.

Cox, C. E., Kotch, J. B., & Everson, M. D. (2003). A longitudinal study of modifying influences in the relationship between domestic violence and child maltreatment. *Journal of Family Violence, 18,* 5–17.

Cox, K., & Schwartz, J. D. (1990). *The well-informed patient's guide to caesarean births.* New York: Dell.

Cox, M. J., Owen, M. T., Henderson, V. K., & Margand, N. A. (1992). Prediction of infant–father and infant–mother attachment. *Developmental Psychology, 28,* 474–483.

Cox, M. J., Paley, B., & Harter, K. (2001). Interparental conflict and parent–child relationships. In J. H. Grych & F. D. Fincham (Eds.), *Interparental conflict and child development: Theory, research, and applications* (pp. 249–272). New York: Cambridge University Press.

Cox, S. M., Hopkins, J., & Hans, S. L. (2000). Attachment in preterm infants and their mothers: Neonatal risk status and maternal representations. *Infant Mental Health Journal, 21,* 464–480.

Coyle, T. R., & Bjorklund, D. F. (1997). Age differences in, and consequences of, multiple- and variable-strategy use on a multitrial sort-recall task. *Developmental Psychology, 33,* 372–380.

Crago, M. B., Annahatak, B., & Ningiuruvik, L. (1993). Changing patterns of language socialization in Inuit homes. *Anthropology and Education Quarterly, 24,* 205–223.

Crair, M. C., Gillespie, D. C., & Stryker, M. P. (1998). The role of visual experience in the development of columns in the cat visual cortex. *Science, 279,* 566–570.

Cratty, B. J. (1986). *Perceptual and motor development in infants and children* (3rd ed.). Englewood Cliffs, NJ: Prentice-Hall.

Crawford, J. (1995). *Bilingual education: History, politics, theory, and practice.* Los Angeles: Bilingual Education Services.

Crawford, J. (1997). *Best evidence: Research foundations of the bilingual ecucation act.* Washington, DC: National Clearinghouse for Bilingual Education.

Creasey, G. (2002). Associations between working models of attachment and conflict management behavior in romantic couples. *Journal of Counseling Psychology, 49,* 365–375.

Creasey, G. L., Jarvis, P. A., & Berk, L. E. (1998). Play and social competence. In O. N. Saracho & B. Spodek (Eds.), *Multiple perspectives on play in early childhood education* (pp. 116–143). Albany: State University of New York Press.

Crick, N. R., Casas, J. F., & Ku, H.-C. (1999). Relational and physical forms of peer victimization in preschool. *Developmental Psychology, 35,* 376–385.

Crick, N. R., Casas, J. F., & Mosher, M. (1997). Relational and overt aggression in preschool. *Developmental Psychology, 33,* 579–588.

Crick, N. R., Casas, J. F., & Nelson, D. A. (2002). Toward a more comprehensive understanding of peer maltreatment: Studies of relational victimization. *Current Directions in Psychological Science, 11,* 98–101.

Crick, N. R., & Dodge, K. A. (1994). A review and reformulation of social information-processing mechanisms in children's social adjustment. *Psychological Bulletin, 115,* 74–101.

Crick, N. R., & Grotpeter, J. K. (1995). Relational aggression, gender, and social-psychological adjustment. *Child Development, 66,* 710–722.

Crick, N. R., & Grotpeter, J. K. (1996). Children's treatment by peers: Victims of relational and overt aggression. *Development and Psychopathology, 8,* 367–380.

Crick, N. R., & Nelson, D. A. (2002). Relational and physical victimization within friendships: Nobody told me there'd be friends like these. *Journal of Abnormal Child Psychology, 30,* 599–607.

Critser, G. (2003). *Fat land.* Boston: Houghton Mifflin.

Crockenberg, S., & Leerkes, E. (2000). Infant social and emotional development in family context. In C. H. Zeanah, Jr. (Ed.), *Handbook of infant mental health* (2nd ed., pp. 60–90). New York: Guilford.

Croninger, R. G., & Lee, V. E. (2001). Social capital and dropping out of high school: Benefits to at-risk students of teachers' support and guidance. *Teachers College Record, 103,* 548–581.

Cross, D. R., & Paris, S. G. (1988). Developmental and instructional analyses of children's metacognition and reading comprehension. *Journal of Educational Psychology, 80,* 131–142.

Crouter, A. C., & Bumpus, M. F. (2001). Linking parents' work stress to children's and adolescents' psychological adjustment. *Current Directions in Psychological Science, 10,* 156–159.

Crouter, A. C., & Head, M. R. (2002). Parental monitoring and knowledge of children. In M. H. Bornstein (Ed.), *Handbook of parenting* (Vol. 3, pp. 461–483). Mahwah, NJ: Erlbaum.

Crouter, A. C., Manke, B. A., & McHale, S. M. (1995). The family context of gender intensification in early adolescence. *Child Development, 66,* 317–329.

Crowhurst, M. (1990). Teaching and learning the writing of persuasive/argumentative discourse. *Canadian Journal of Education, 15,* 348–359.

Csikszentmihalyi, M. (1999). Implications of a systems perspective for the study of creativity. In R. J. Sternberg (Ed.), *Handbook of creativity* (pp. 313–335). Cambridge, U.K.: Cambridge University Press.

Cuddy-Casey, M., & Orvaschel, H. (1997). Children's understanding of death in relation to child suicidality and homicidality. *Clinical Psychology Review, 17,* 33–45.

Cui, X., & Vaillant, G. E. (1996). Antecedents and consequences of negative life events in adulthood: A longitudinal study. *American Journal of Psychiatry, 153,* 21–26.

Cuijpers, P. (2002). Effective ingredients of school-based drug prevention programs: A systematic review. *Addictive Behaviors, 27,* 1009–1023.

Culbertson, F. M. (1997). Depression and gender: An international review. *American Psychologist, 52,* 25–51.

Culnane, M., Fowler, M. G., Lee, S. S., McSherry, G., Brady, M., & O'Donnell, K. (1999). Lack of long-term effects of in utero exposure to zidovudine among uninfected children born to HIV-infected women. *Journal of the American Medical Association, 281,* 151–157.

Cummings, E. M., & Davies, P. T. (1994). Maternal depression and child development. *Journal of Child Psychology and Psychiatry, 35,* 73–112.

Cunningham, A. E., & Stanovich, K. E. (1998). What reading does for the mind. *American Educator,* Spring/Summer, 8–15.

Curtin, S. C., & Park, M. M. (1999). Trends in the attendant, place, and timing of births and in the use of obstetric interventions: United

States, 1989–1997. *National Vital Statistics Report, 47*(27), 1–12.

Curtiss, S. (1977). *Genie: A psycholinguistic study of a modern day "wild child."* New York: Academic Press.

Curtiss, S. (1989). The independence and task-specificity of language. In M. H. Bornstein & J. S. Bruner (Eds.), *Interaction in human development* (pp. 105–137). Hillsdale, NJ: Erlbaum.

Cutrona, C. E., Hessling, R. M., Bacon, P. L., & Russell, D. W. (1998). Predictors and correlates of continuing involvement with the baby's father among adolescent mothers. *Journal of Family Psychology, 12,* 369–387.

D'Agostino, J. A., & Clifford, P. (1998). Neurodevelopmental consequences associated with the premature neonate. *AACN Clinical Issues, 9,* 11–24.

Dahl, R. E., & Lewin, D. S. (2002). Pathways to adolescent healthy sleep regulation and behavior. *Journal of Adolescent Health, 31,* 175–184.

Dahl, R. E., Scher, M. S., Williamson, D. E., Robles, N., & Day, N. (1995). A longitudinal study of prenatal marijuana use: Effects on sleep and arousal at age 3 years. *Archives of Pediatric and Adolescent Medicine, 149,* 145–150.

Dales, L., Hammer, S. J., & Smith, N. J. (2001). Time trends in autism and MMR immunization coverage in California. *Journal of the American Medical Association, 285,* 1183–1185.

Daley, T. C., Whaley, S. E., Sigman, M. D., Espinosa, M. P., & Neumann, C. (2003). IQ on the rise: The Flynn effect in rural Kenyan children. *Psychological Science, 14,* 215–219.

Daly, K. A., Hunter, L. L., & Giebink, G. S. (1999). Chronic otitis media with effusion. *Pediatrics Review, 20,* 85–93.

Damashek, A., & Peterson, L. (2002). Unintentional injury prevention efforts for young children: Levels, methods, types, and targets. *Developmental and Behavioral Pediatrics, 23,* 443–455.

Dammerman, R. S., & Kriegstein, A. R. (2000). Transient actions of neurotransmitters during neocortical development. *Epilepsia, 41,* 1080–1081.

Damon, W. (1977). *The social world of the child.* San Francisco: Jossey-Bass.

Damon, W. (1988). *The moral child.* New York: Free Press.

Damon, W. (1990). Self-concept, adolescent. In R. M. Lerner, A. C. Petersen, & J. Brooks-Gunn (Eds.), *The encyclopedia of adolescence* (Vol. 2, pp. 87–91). New York: Garland.

Damon, W., & Hart, D. (1988). *Self-understanding in childhood and adolescence.* New York: Cambridge University Press.

Daniels, D. H. (1998). Age differences in concepts of self-esteem. *Merrill-Palmer Quarterly, 44,* 234–259.

Daniels, D. H., Kalkman, D. L., & McCombs, B. L. (2001). Young children's perspectives on learning and teacher practices in different classroom contexts: Implications for motivation. *Early Education and Development, 12,* 253–273.

Dannemiller, J. L., & Stephens, B. R. (1988). A critical test of infant pattern preference models. *Child Development, 59,* 210–216.

Dapretto, M., & Bjork, E. L. (2000). The development of word retrieval abilities in the second year and its relation to early vocabulary growth. *Child Development, 71,* 635–648.

Darling, N., & Steinberg, L. (1997). Community influences on adolescent achievement and deviance. In J. Brooks-Gunn, G. Duncan, & L. Aber (Eds.), *Neighborhood poverty: Context and consequences for children: Conceptual, ethological, and policy approaches to studying neighborhoods* (Vol. 2, pp. 120–131). New York: Russell Sage Foundation.

Darnton-Hill, I., & Coyne, E. T. (1998). Feast and famine: Socioeconomic disparities in global nutrition and health. *Public Health and Nutrition, 1,* 23–31.

Daro, D., & Donnelly, A. C. (2002). Child abuse prevention: Accomplishments and challenges. In J. B. Myers, L. Berliner, J. Briere, C. T. Hendrix, C. Jenny, & T. A. Reid (Eds.), *The APSAC handbook on child maltreatment* (2nd ed., pp. 431–438). Thousand Oaks, CA: Sage.

Daro, D., & Harding, K. (1999). Healthy Families America: Using research to enhance practice. *Future of Children, 9,* 152–176.

Darroch, J. E., Frost, J. J., & Singh, S. (2001). *Teenage sexual and reproductive behavior in developed countries: Can more progress be made?* New York: Alan Guttmacher Institute.

D'Augelli, A. R. (2002). Mental health problems among lesbian, gay, and bisexual youths ages 14 to 21. *Clinical Child Psychology and Psychiatry, 7,* 433–456.

DaVanzo, J., & Adamson, D. M. (2000). *Family planning in developing countries: An unfinished success story.* New York: Rand Corporation.

Davidson, R. J. (1994). Asymmetric brain function, affective style, and psychopathology: The role of early experience and plasticity. *Development and Psychopathology, 6,* 741–758.

Davies, T., Howell, R. T., & Gardner, A. (2001). *Human genetics.* New York: Oxford.

Davis, D. J. (2001). Neonatal subgaleal hemorrhage: Diagnosis and management. *Canadian Medical Association Journal, 164,* 1452.

Davison, K. K., & Birch, L. L. (2002). Obesigenic families: Parents' physical activity and dietary intake patterns predict girls' risk of overweight. *International Journal of Obesity and Related Metabolic Disorders, 26,* 1186–1193.

Dawson, T. L. (2002). New tools, new insights: Kohlberg's moral judgment stages revisited. *International Journal of Behavioral Development, 26,* 154–166.

Day, N. L., Leach, S. L., Richardson, G. A., Cornelius, M. D., Robles, N., & Larkby, C. (2002). Prenatal alcohol exposure predicts continued deficits in offspring size at 14 years of age. *Alcoholism: Clinical and Experimental Research, 26,* 1584–1591.

De Bruyn, E. H., Deković, M., & Meijnen, G. W. (2003). Parenting, goal orientations, classroom behavior, and school success in early adolescence. *Journal of Applied Developmental Psychology, 24,* 393–412.

De Lisi, R., & Gallagher, A. M. (1991). Understanding gender stability and constancy in Argentinean children. *Merrill-Palmer Quarterly, 37,* 483–502.

de Muinck Keizer-Schrama, S. M. P. F., & Mul, D. (2001). Trends in pubertal development in Europe. *Human Reproduction Update, 7,* 287–291.

De Roche, E. F., & Williams, M. M. (1998). *Educating hearts and minds: A comprehensive character education framework.* Thousand Oaks, CA: Corwin Press.

de Villiers, J. G., & de Villiers, P. A. (1973). A cross-sectional study of the acquisition of grammatical morphemes in child speech. *Journal of Psycholinguistic Research, 2,* 267–278.

de Villiers, J. G., & de Villiers, P. A. (2000). Linguistic determinism and the understanding of false beliefs. In P. Mitchell & K. J. Riggs (Eds.), *Children's reasoning and the mind* (pp. 87–99). Hove, U.K.: Psychology Press.

de Villiers, J.G., & de Villiers, P. A. (1999). Language development. In M. H. Bornstein & M. E. Lamb (Eds.), *Developmental psychology: An advanced textbook* (4th ed., pp. 313–373). Mahwah, NJ: Erlbaum.

de Waal, F. B. M. (1993). Sex differences in chimpanzee (and human) behavior: A matter of social values? In M. Hechter, L. Nadel, & R. E. Michod (Eds.), *The origin of values* (pp. 285–303). New York: Aldine de Gruyter.

de Waal, H. A. D. (2002). Regulation of puberty. *Best Practice and Research: Clinical Endocrinology and Metabolism. 16,* 1–12.

de Waal, H. A. D., van Coeverden, S. C., & Rotteveel, J. (2001). Hormonal determinants of pubertal growth. *Journal of Pediatric Endocrinology and Metabolism, 14,* 1521–1526.

de Winter, M., Balledux, M., & de Mare, J. (1997). A critical evaluation of Dutch preventive child health care. *Child: Care, Health and Development, 23,* 437–446.

de Wolff, M. S., & van IJzendoorn, M. H. (1997). Sensitivity and attachment: A meta-analysis on parental atnecedents of infant attachment. *Child Development, 68,* 571–591.

Deafness Research Foundation. (2003). Hear us: Incidence of deafness in newborns. Retrieved from http://www.hearinghealth.com

Deák, G. O. (2000). Hunting the fox of word learning: Why "constraints" fail to capture it. *Developmental Review, 20,* 29–80.

Deák, G. O., & Maratsos, M. (1998). On having complex representations of things: Preschoolers use multiple words for objects and people. *Developmental Psychology, 34,* 224–240.

Deák, G. O., Ray, S. D., & Brenneman, K. (2003). Children's perseverative appearance–reality errors are related to emerging language skills. *Child Development, 74,* 944–964.

Deák, G. O., Yen, L., & Pettit, J. (2001). By any other name: When will preschoolers produce several labels for a reference? *Journal of Child Language, 28,* 787–804.

Deary, I. J. (2001). *g* and cognitive elements of information progressing: An agnostic view. In R. J. Sternberg & E. L. Grigorenko (Eds.), *The general factor of intelligence: How general is it?* (pp. 447–479). Mahwah, NJ: Erlbaum.

Deater-Deckard, K., & Dodge, K. A. (1997). Externalizing behavior problems and discipline revisited: Nonlinear effects and variation by culture, context, and gender. *Psychological Inquiry, 8,* 161–175.

Deater-Deckard, K., Dodge, K. A., Bates, J. E., & Petit, G. S. (1996). Physical discipline among African American and European American mothers: Links to children's externalizing behaviors. *Developmental Psychology, 32,* 1065–1072.

Deater-Deckard, K., Pike, A., Petrill, S. A., Cutting, A. L., Hughes, C., & O'Connor, T. G. (2001). Nonshared environmental processes in social-emotional development: An observational study of identical twin differences in the preschool period. *Developmental Science, 4,* F1–F6.

Deater-Deckard, K., Scarr, S., McCartney, K., & Eisenberg, M. (1994). Paternal separation anxiety: Relationships with parenting stress, child-rearing attitudes, and maternal anxieties. *Psychological Science, 5,* 341–346.

DeBerry, K. M., Scarr, S., & Weinberg, R. (1996). Family racial socialization and ecological competence: Longitudinal assessments of African-American transracial adoptees. *Child Development, 67,* 2375–2399.

DeCasper, A. J., & Spence, M. J. (1986). Prenatal maternal speech influences newborns' perception of speech sounds. *Infant Behavior and Development, 9,* 133–150.

Deci, E. L., & Ryan, R. M. (2002). Self-determination research: Reflections and future directions. In E. L. Deci & R. M. Ryan (Eds.), *Handbook of self-determination research* (pp. 431–441). Rochester, NY: University of Rochester Press.

DeGarmo, D. S., & Forgatch, M. S. (1999). Contexts as predictors of changing maternal parenting practices in diverse family structures: A social interactional perspective of risk and resilience. In E. M. Hetherington (Ed.), *Coping with divorce, single parenting, and remarriage: A risk and resiliency perspective* (pp. 227–252). Mahwah, NJ: Erlbaum.

Degirmencioglu, S. M., Urberg, K. A., Tolson, J. M., & Richard, P. (1998). Adolescent friendship networks: Continuity and change over the school year. *Merrill-Palmer Quarterly, 44,* 313–337.

Dejin-Karlsson, E., Hanson, B. S., Estergren, P.-O., Sjoeberg, N.-O., & Marsal, K. (1998). Does passive smoking in early pregnancy increase the risk of small-for-gestational-age infants? *American Journal of Public Health, 88,* 1523–1527.

Deković, M., Noom, M. J., & Meeus, W. (1997). Expectations regarding development during adolescence: Parent and adolescent perceptions. *Journal of Youth and Adolescence, 26,* 253–271.

Delgado-Gaitan, C. (1994). Socializing young children in Mexican-American families: An intergenerational perspective. In P. Greenfield & R. Cocking (Eds.), *Cross-cultural roots of minority child development* (pp. 55–86). Hillsdale, NJ: Erlbaum.

Dell, D. L. (2001). Adolescent pregnancy. In N. L. Stotland & D. E. Stewart (Eds.), *Psychological aspects of women's health care* (pp. 95–116). Washington, DC: American Psychiatric Association.

DeLoache, J. S. (1987). Rapid change in symbolic functioning of very young children. *Science, 238,* 1556–1557.

DeLoache, J. S. (1991). Symbolic functioning in very young children: Understanding of pictures and models. *Child Development, 62,* 736–752.

DeLoache, J. S. (2002a). Early development of the understanding and use of symbolic artifacts. In U. Goswami (Ed.), *Blackwell handbook of child cognitive development* (pp. 206–226). Malden, MA: Blackwell.

DeLoache, J. S. (2002b). The symbol-mindedness of young children. In W. Hartup & R. A. Weinberg (Eds.), *Minnesota symposia on child psychology* (Vol. 32, pp. 73–101). Mahwah, NJ: Erlbaum.

DeLoache, J. S., & Todd, C. M. (1988). Young children's use of spatial categorization as a mnemonic strategy. *Journal of Experimental Child Psychology, 46,* 1–20.

Demetriou, A., Christou, C., Spanoudis, G., & Platsidou, M. (2002). The development of mental processing: Efficiency, working memory, and thinking. *Monographs of the Society for Research in Child Development, 67*(1, Serial No. 268).

Demetriou, A., Efklides, A., Papadaki, M., Papantoniou, G., & Economou, A. (1993). Structure and development of causal–experimental thought: From early adolescence to youth. *Developmental Psychology, 29,* 480–497.

Demetriou, A., & Kazi, S. (2001). *Unity and modularity in the mind and the self: Studies on the relationships between self-awareness, personality, and intellectual development from childhood to adolescence.* London: Routledge.

Demetriou, A., Pachaury, A., Metallidou, Y., & Kazi, S. (1996). Universals and specificities in the structure and development of quantitative-relational thought: A cross-cultural study in Greece and India. *International Journal of Behavioral Development, 19,* 255–290.

Dempster, F. N., & Corkill, A. J. (1999). Interference and inhibition in cognition and behavior: Unifying themes for educational psychology. *Educational Psychology Review, 11,* 1–88.

Denckla, M. B. (1996). Biological correlates of learning and attention: What is relevant to learning disability and attention-deficit hyperactivity disorder? *Developmental and Behavioral Pediatrics, 17,* 114–119.

Denham, S. (1998). *Emotional development in young children.* New York: Guilford.

Denham, S. A., Blair, K., Schmidt, M., & DeMulder, E. (2002). Compromised emotional competence: Seeds of violence sown early? *American Journal of Orthopsychiatry, 72,* 70–82.

Denham, S., & Kochanoff, A. T. (2002). Parental contributions to preschoolers' understanding of emotion. *Marriage and Family Review, 34,* 311–343.

Denner, J., Cooper, C. R., Lopez, E. M., & Dunbar, N. (1999). Beyond "giving science away": How university–community partnerships inform youth programs, research, and policy. *Social Policy Report of the Society for Research in Child Development, 13*(1).

Dennis, W. (1960). Causes of retardation among institutionalized children: Iran. *Journal of Genetic Psychology, 96,* 47–59.

Dennison, B. A., Straus, J. H., Mellits, D., & Charney, E. (1998). Childhood physical fitness tests: Predictor of adult physical activity levels? *Pediatrics, 82,* 342–330.

Derom, C., Thiery, E., Vlietinck, R., Loos, R., & Derom, R. (1996). Handedness in twins according to zygosity and chorion type: A preliminary report. *Behavior Genetics, 26,* 407–408.

DeRosier, M. E., & Thomas, J. M. (2003). Strengthening sociometric prediction: Scientific advances in the assessment of children's peer relations. *Child Development, 75,* 1379–1392.

Deutsch, F. M., Ruble, D. N., Fleming, A., Brooks-Gunn, J., & Stangor, C. (1988). Information-seeking and maternal self-definition during the transition to motherhood. *Journal of Personality and Social Psychology, 55,* 420–431.

Deutsch, W., & Pechmann, T. (1982). Social interaction and the development of definite descriptions. *Cognition, 11,* 159–184.

Dewey, K. G. (2001). Nutrition, growth, and complementary feeding of the breasted infant. *Pediatric Clinics of North America, 48,* 87–104.

Dewsbury, D. A. (1992). Comparative psychology and ethology: A reassessment. *American Psychologist, 47,* 208–215.

Diamond, A. (1991). Neuropsychological insights into the meaning of object concept development. In S. Carey & R. Gelman (Eds.), *The epigenesis of mind: Essays on biology and knowledge* (pp. 67–110). Hillsdale, NJ: Erlbaum.

Diamond, A., Cruttenden, L., & Neiderman, D. (1994). AB with multiple wells: 1. Why are multiple wells sometimes easier than two wells? 2. Memory or memory + inhibition. *Developmental Psychology, 30,* 192–205.

Diamond, L. M. (1998). Development of sexual orientation among adolescent and young adult women. *Developmental Psychology, 34,* 1085–1095.

Diamond, L. M. (2003). Love matters: Romantic relationships among sexual-minority adolescents. In P. Florsheim (Ed.), *Adolescent romantic relations and sexual behavior* (pp. 85–108). Mahwah, NJ: Erlbaum.

Diamond, M., & Hopson, J. (1999). *Magic trees of the mind.* New York: Plume.

Diamond, M., & Sigmundson, H. K. (1999). Sex reassignment at birth. In S. J. Ceci & W. M. Williams (Eds.), *The nature–nurture debate* (pp. 55–75). Malden, MA: Blackwell.

Dick, D. M., Rose, R. J., Viken, R. J., & Kaprio, J. (2000). Pubertal timing and substance use: Associations between and within families across late adolescence. *Developmental Psychology, 36,* 180–189.

Dickens, W. T., & Flynn, J. R. (2001). Heritability estimates versus large environmental effects: The IQ paradox resolved. *Psychological Review, 108,* 346–369.

Dickinson, D. K., & McCabe, A. (2001). Bringing it all together: The multiple origins, skills, and environmental supports of early literacy. *Learning Disabilities Research and Practice, 16,* 186–202.

Dickinson, D. K., & Sprague, K. E. (2001). The nature and impact of early childhood care environments on the language and early literacy development of children from low-income families. In S. B. Neuman & D. K. Dickinson (Eds.), *Handbook of early literacy research.* New York: Guilford.

Dick-Read, G. (1959). *Childbirth without fear.* New York: Harper & Brothers.

Dickson, K. L., Fogel, A., & Messinger, D. (1998). The development of emotion from a social process view. In M. F. Mascolo (Ed.), *What develops in emotional development?* (pp. 253–271). New York: Plenum.

Diener, E., Suh, E. M., Lucas, R. E., & Smith, H. L. (1999). Subjective well-being: Three decades of progress. *Psychological Bulletin, 125,* 276–302.

Dietrich, K. N. (1999). Environmental toxicants and child development. In H. Tager-Flusberg (Ed.), *Neurodevelopmental disorders* (pp. 469–490). Boston: MIT Press.

Dietrich, K. N., Berger, O. G., & Succop, P. A. (1993). Lead exposure and the motor developmental status of urban six-year-old children in the Cincinnati Prospective Study. *Pediatrics, 91,* 301–307.

Dietz, T. L. (1998). An examination of violence and gender-role portrayals in video games: Implications for gender socialization and aggressive behavior. *Sex Roles, 38,* 425–444.

DiLalla, L. F., Kagan, J., & Reznick, J. S. (1994). Genetic etiology of behavioral inhibition among 2-year-old children. *Infant Behavior and Development, 17,* 405–412.

DiMatteo, M. R., & Kahn, K. L. (1997). Psychosocial aspects of childbirth. In S. J. Gallant, G. P. Keita, & R. Royak-Schaler (Eds.), *Health care for women: Psychological, social, and behavioral influences* (pp. 175–186). Washington, DC: American Psychological Association.

DiPietro, J. A., Hodgson, D. M., Costigan, K. A., & Hilton, S. C. (1996). Fetal neurobehavioral development. *Child Development, 67,* 2553–2567.

Dirks, J. (1982). The effect of a commercial game on children's Block Design scores on the WISC–R test. *Intelligence, 6,* 109–123.

Dishion, T. J., Andrews, D. W., & Crosby, L. (1995). Antisocial boys and their friends in early adolescence: Relationship characteristics, quality, and interactional processes. *Child Development, 66,* 139–151.

Dixon, J. A., & Moore, C. F. (1990). The development of perspective taking: Understanding differences in information and weighting. *Child Development, 61,* 1502–1513.

Dixon, R. A., & Lerner, R. M. (1999). History and systems in developmental psychology. In M. H. Bornstein & M. E. Lamb (Eds.), *Developmental psychology: An advanced textbook* (4th ed., pp. 3–46). Mahwah, NJ: Erlbaum.

Dodge, K. A., Lansford, J. E., Burks, V. S., Bates, J. E., Pettit, G. S., Fontaine, R., & Price, J. M. (2003). Peer rejection and social information-processing factors in the development of aggressive behavior problems in children. *Child Development, 74,* 374–393.

Dodge, K. A., Pettit, G. S., & Bates, J. E. (1994). Socialization mediators of the relation between socioeconomic status and child conduct problems. *Child Development, 65,* 649–665.

Dodge, K. A., Pettit, G. S., McClaskey, C. L., & Brown, M. M. (1986). Social competence in children. *Monographs of the Society for Research in Child Development, 51*(2, Serial No. 213).

Doeker, B., Simic-Schleicher, A., Hauffa, B. P., & Andler, W. (1999). Psychosozialer Kleinwuchs maskiert als Wachstumshormonmangel. [Psychosocially stunted growth masked as growth hormone deficiency]. *Klinische Padiatrie, 211,* 394–398.

Doherty, G., Lero, D. S., Goelman, H., Tougas, J., & LaGrange, A. (2000). *You bet I care! Caring and learning environments: Quality in regulated family child care across Canada.* Guelph, Ontario: Centre for Families, Work and Well-Being, University of Guelph.

Donahue, M. J., & Benson, P. L. (1995). Religion and the well-being of adolescents. *Journal of Social Issues, 51,* 145–160.

Donatelle, R. J. (2003). *Health: The basics.* San Francisco: Benjamin Cummings.

Dondi, M., Simion, F., & Caltran, G. (1999). Can newborns discriminate between their own cry and the cry of another newborn infant? *Developmental Psychology, 35,* 418–426.

Donnerstein, E., Slaby, R. G., & Eron, L. D. (1994). The mass media and youth aggression. In L. D. Eron, J. H. Gentry, & P. Schlegel (Eds.), *Reason to hope: A psychosocial perspective on violence and youth* (pp. 219–250). Washington, DC: American Psychological Association.

Dornbusch, S. M., & Glasgow, K. L. (1997). The structural context of family–school relations. In A. Booth & J. F. Dunn (Eds.), *Family–school links: How do they affect educational outcomes?* (pp. 35–55). Mahwah, NJ: Erlbaum.

Dornbusch, S. M., Glasgow, K. L., & Lin, I.-C. (1996). The social structure of schooling. *Annual Review of Psychology, 47,* 401–429.

Dornbusch, S. M., Ritter, P. L., Mont-Reynaud, R., & Chen, Z. (1990). Family decision making and academic performance in a diverse high school population. *Journal of Adolescent Research, 5,* 143–160.

Dorris, M. (1989). *The broken cord.* New York: Harper & Row.

Dowd, M. D. (1999). Childhood injury prevention at home and play. *Current Opinion in Pediatrics, 11,* 578–582.

Downs, A. C., & Fuller, M. J. (1991). Recollections of spermarche: An exploratory investigation. *Current*

Psychology: Research and Reviews, 10, 93–102.

Doyle, L. W. (2001). Outcome at 5 years of age of children 23 to 27 weeks' gestation: Refining the prognosis. *Pediatrics, 108,* 134–141.

Drabman, R. S., Cordua, G. D., Hammer, D., Jarvie, G. J., & Horton, W. (1979). Developmental trends in eating rates of normal and overweight preschool children. *Child Development, 50,* 211–216.

Drew, L. M., Richard, M. H., & Smith, P. K. (1998). Grandparenting and its relationship to parenting. *Clinical Child Psychology and Psychiatry, 3,* 465–480.

Drotar, D., Pallotta, J., & Eckerle, D. (1994). A prospective study of family environments of children hospitalized for nonorganic failure-to-thrive. *Developmental and Behavioral Pediatrics, 15,* 78–85.

Dryburgh, H. (2001). Teenage pregnancy. *Health Reports, 12*(1), Statistics Canada, Cat. No. 82–003.

Dubé, E. M., Savin-Williams, R. C., & Diamond, L. M. (2001). Intimacy development, gender, and ethnicity among sexual-minority youths. In A. R. D'Augelli & C. J. Patterson (Eds.), *Lesbian, gay, and bisexual identities and youth* (pp. 129–152). New York: Oxford University Press.

Dublin, S., Lydon-Rochelle, M., Kaplan, R. C., Watts, D. H., & Crichlow, C. W. (2000). Maternal and neonatal outcomes after induction of labor without an identified indication. *American Journal of Obstetrics and Gynecology, 183,* 986–994.

DuBois, D. L., Bull, C. A., Sherman, M. D., & Roberts, M. (1998). Self-esteem and adjustment in early adolescence: A social-contextual perspective. *Journal of Youth and Adolescence, 27,* 557–583.

DuBois, D. L., Burk-Braxton, C., Swenson, L. P., Tevendale, H. D., Lockerd, E. M., & Moran, B. L. (2002a). Getting by with a little help from self and others: Self-esteem and social support as resources during early adolescence. *Developmental Psychology, 38,* 822–939.

DuBois, D. L., Burk-Braxton, C., Swenson, L. P., Tevendale, H. D., & Hardesty, J. L. (2002b). Race and gender influences on adjustment in early adolescence: Investigation of an integrative model. *Child Development, 73,* 1573–1592.

DuBois, D. L., Felner, R. D., Brand, S., & George, G. R. (1999). Profiles of self-esteem in early adolescence: Identification and investigation of adaptive correlates. *American Journal of Community Psychology, 27,* 899–932.

DuBois, D. L., & Hirsch, B. J. (1990). School and neighborhood friendship patterns of black and whites in early adolescence. *Child Development, 61,* 524–536.

Duggan, A. K., McFarlane, E. C., Windham, A. M., Rohde, C. A., Salkever, D. S., & Fuddy, L. (1999). Evaluation of Hawaii's Healthy Start Program. *Future of Children, 9,* 66–90.

Dulitzki, M., Soriano, D., Schiff, E., Chetrit, A., Mashiach, S., & Seidman, D. S. (1998). Effect of very advanced maternal age on pregnancy outcome and rate of cesarean delivery. *Obstetrics and Gynecology, 92,* 935–939.

Duncan, D. F. (1996). Growing up under the gun: Children and adolescents coping with violent neighborhoods. *Journal of Primary Prevention, 16,* 343–356.

Duncan, G. J., & Brooks-Gunn, J. (2000). Family poverty, welfare reform, and child development. *Child Development, 71,* 188–196.

Dunifon, R., Kalil, A., & Danziger, S. K. (2003). Maternal work behavior under welfare reform: How does the transition from welfare to work affect child development? *Children and Youth Services Review, 25,* 55–82.

Duniz, M., Scheer, P. J., Trojovsky, A., Kaschnitz, W., Kvas, E., & Macari, S. (1996). *European Child and Adolescent Psychiatry, 5,* 93–100.

Dunn, J. (1989). Siblings and the development of social understanding in early childhood. In P. G. Zukow (Ed.), *Sibling interaction across cultures* (pp. 106–116). New York: Springer-Verlag.

Dunn, J. (1994). Temperament, siblings, and the development of relationships. In W. B. Carey & S. C. McDevitt (Eds.), *Prevention and early intervention* (pp. 50–58). New York: Brunner/Mazel.

Dunn, J. (2002a). The adjustment of children in stepfamilies: Lessons from community studies. *Child and Adolescent Mental Health, 7,* 154–161.

Dunn, J. (2002b). Sibling relationships. In P. K. Smith & C. H. Hart (Eds.), *Blackwell handbook of childhood social development* (pp. 223–237). Malden, MA: Blackwell.

Dunn, J., Bretherton, I., & Munn, P. (1987). Conversations about feeling states between mothers and their young children. *Developmental Psychology, 23,* 132–139.

Dunn, J., Brown, J. R., & Maguire, M. (1995). The development of children's moral sensibility: Individual differences and emotion understanding. *Developmental Psychology, 31,* 649–659.

Dunn, J., & Kendrick, C. (1982). *Siblings: Love, envy and understanding.* Cambridge, MA: Harvard University Press.

Dunn, J., & Munn, P. (1986). Sibling quarrels and maternal intervention: Individual differences in understanding aggression. *Journal of the American Academy of Child Psychology and Psychiatry, 27,* 583–595.

Dunn, J., Slomkowski, C., & Beardsall, L. (1994). Sibling relationships from the preschool period through middle childhood and early adolescence. *Developmental Psychology, 30,* 315–324.

Durbin, D. L., Darling, N., Steinberg, L., & Brown, B. B. (1993). Parenting style and peer group membership among European-American adolescents. *Journal of Research on Adolescence, 3,* 87–100.

Durkin, M. S., Laraque, D., Lubman, I., & Barlow, B. (1999). Epidemiology and prevention of traffic injuries to urban children and adolescents. *Pediatrics, 103,* e74.

Durrant, J., Broberg, A., & Rose-Krasnor, L. (2000). Predicting use of physical punishment during mother–child conflicts in Sweden and Canada. In P. Hastings & C. Piotrowski (Eds.), *Conflict as a context for understanding maternal beliefs about child rearing and children's misbehavior: New directions for child development.* San Francisco: Jossey-Bass.

Durston, S., Hulshoff, P. H. E., Casey, B. J., Giedd, J. N., Buitelaar, J. K., & van Engeland, H. (2001). Anatomical MRI of the developing human brain: What have we learned? *Journal of the Academy of Child and Adolescent Psychiatry, 40,* 1012–1020.

Dweck, C. S. (2001). Messages that motivate: How praise molds students' beliefs, motivation, and performance (in surprising ways). In J. Aronson (Ed.), *Improving academic achievement: Impact of psychological factors on education* (pp. 37–60). San Diego, CA: Academic Press.

Dworkin, J. B., Larson, R., & Hansen, D. (1993). Adolescents' accounts of growth experiences in youth activities. *Journal of Youth and Adolescence, 32,* 17–26.

Dwyer, T., Ponsonby, A. L., & Couper, D. (1999). Tobacco smoke exposure at one month of age and subsequent risk of SIDS: A prospective study. *American Journal of Epidemiology, 149,* 593–602.

Dye-White, E. (1986). Environmental hazards in the work setting: Their effect on women of child-bearing age. *American Association of Occupational Health and Nursing Journal, 34,* 76–78.

Dykman, R., Casey, P. H., Ackerman, P. T., & McPherson, W. B. (2001). Behavioral and cognitive status in school-aged children with a history of failure to thrive during early childhood. *Clinical Pediatrics, 40,* 63–70.

Eacott, M. J. (1999). Memory for the events of early childhood. *Current Directions in Psychological Science, 8,* 46–48.

East, P. L., & Felice, M. E. (1996). *Adolescent pregnancy and parenting: Findings from a racially diverse sample.* Mahwah, NJ: Erlbaum.

Ebeling, K. S., & Gelman, S. A. (1994). Children's use of context in interpreting "big" and "little." *Child Development, 65,* 1178–1192.

Eberhart-Phillips, J. E., Frederick, P. D., & Baron, R. C. (1993). Measles in pregnancy: A descriptive study of 58 cases. *Obstetrics and Gynecology, 82,* 797–801.

Eccles, J. S. (1994). Understanding women's educational and occupational choices: Applying the Eccles et al. model of achievement-related choices. *Psychology of Women Quarterly, 18,* 585–609.

Eccles, J. S., & Gootman, J. (Eds.). (2002). *Community programs to promote youth development.* Washington, DC: National Academy Press.

Eccles, J. S., & Harold, R. D. (1991). Gender differences in sport involvement: Applying the Eccles expectancy-value model. *Journal of Applied Sport Psychology, 3,* 7–35.

Eccles, J. S., & Harold, R. D. (1996). Family involvement in children's and adolescents' schooling. In A. Booth & J. F. Dunn (Eds.), *Family–school links: How do they affect educational outcomes?* (pp. 3–34). Mahwah, NJ: Erlbaum.

Eccles, J. S., Jacobs, J., & Harold, R. D. (1990). Gender-role stereotypes, expectancy effects, and parents' role in the socialization of gender differences in self-perceptions and skill acquisition. *Journal of Social Issues, 46,* 183–201.

Eccles, J. S., Lord, S., & Buchanan, C. M. (1996). School transitions in early adolescence: What are we doing to our young people? In J. A. Graber, J. Brooks-Gunn, & A. C. Petersen (Eds.), *Transitions through adolescence* (pp. 251–284). Mahwah, NJ: Erlbaum.

Eccles, J. S., Templeton, J., Barber, B., & Stone, M. (2003). Adolescence and emerging adulthood: The critical passage ways to adulthood. In M. H. Bornstein, L. Davidson, C. L. M. Keyes, K. A. Moore, & the Center for Child Well-Being (Eds.), *Well-being: Positive development across the life course* (pp. 383–406). Mahwah, NJ: Erlbaum.

Eccles, J. S., Wigfield, A., Harold, R., & Blumenfeld, P. B. (1993). Age and gender differences in children's self- and task perceptions during elementary school. *Child Development, 64,* 830–847.

Eccles, J. S., Wigfield, A., & Schiefele, U. (1998). Motivation to succeed. In N. Eisenberg (Ed.), *Handbook of child psychology: Vol. 3. Social, emotional, and personality development* (5th ed., pp. 1017–1095). New York: Wiley.

Eckerman, C. O., & Peterman, K. (2001). Peers and infant social/communicative development. In G. Bremner & A. Fogel (Eds.), *Blackwell handbook of infant development* (pp. 326–350). Malden, MA: Blackwell.

Eckerman, C. O., & Whitehead, H. (1999). How toddler peers generate coordinated action: A cross-cultural exploration. *Early Education and Development, 10,* 241–266.

Eder, R. A., & Mangelsdorf, S. C. (1997). The emotional basis of early personality development: Implications for the emergent self-concept. In R. Hogan, J. Johnson, & S. Briggs (Eds.), *Handbook of personality psychology* (pp. 209–240). San Diego, CA: Academic Press.

Egan, S. K., Monson, T. C., & Perry, D. G. (1998). Social-cognitive influences on change in aggression over time. *Developmental Psychology, 34,* 996–1006.

Egeland, B., & Hiester, M. (1995). The long-term consequences of infant daycare and mother–infant attachment. *Child Development, 66,* 474–485.

Egeland, B., Jacobvitz, D., & Sroufe, L. A. (1988). Breaking the cycle of abuse. *Child Development, 59,* 1080–1088.

Ehri, L. C., Nunes, S. R., Stahl, S. A., & Willows, D. M. (2001). Systematic phonics instruction helps students learn to read: Evidence from the National Reading Panel's meta-analysis. *Review of Educational Research, 71,* 393–447.

Eiben, B., Hammans, W., Hansen, S., Trawicki, W., Osthelder, B., Stelzer, A., Jaspers, K.-D., & Goebel, R. (1997). On the complication risk of early amniocentesis versus standard amniocentesis. *Fetal Diagnosis and Therapy, 12,* 140–144.

Eibl-Eibesfeldt, I. (1989). *Human ethology.* Hawthorne, NY: Aldine.

Eichstedt, J. A., Serbin, L. A., Poulin-Dubois, D., & Sen, M. G. (2002). Of bears and men: Infants' knowledge of conventional and metaphorical gender stereotypes. *Infant Behavior and Development, 25,* 296–310.

Eiden, R. D., & Reifman, A. (1996). Effects of Brazelton demonstrations on later parenting: A meta-analysis. *Journal of Pediatric Psychology, 21,* 857–868.

Eilers, R., & Oller, D. K. (1994). Infant vocalizations and the early diagnosis of severe hearing impairment. *Journal of Pediatrics, 124,* 199–203.

Eisenberg, N. (1998). The socialization of socioemotional competence. In D. Pushkar, W. M. Bukowski, A. E. Schwartzman, E. M. Stack, & D. R. White (Eds.), *Improving competence across the lifespan* (pp. 59–78). New York: Plenum.

Eisenberg, N., Cumberland, A., & Spinrad, T. L. (1998). Parental socialization of emotion. *Psychological Inquiry, 9,* 241–273.

Eisenberg, N., & Fabes, R. A. (1998). Prosocial development. In N. Eisenberg (Ed.), *Handbook of child psychology: Vol. 3. Social, emotional, and personality development* (5th ed., pp. 701–778). New York: Wiley.

Eisenberg, N., Fabes, R. A., Bernzweig, J., Karbon, M., Poulin, R., & Hanish, L. (1993). The relations of emotionality and regulation to preschoolers' social skills and sociometric status. *Child Development, 64,* 1418–1438.

Eisenberg, N., Fabes, R. A., & Losoya, S. (1997). Emotional responding: Regulation, social correlates, and socialization. In P. Salovey & D. J. Sluyter (Eds.), *Emotional development and emotional intelligence* (pp. 129–162). New York: Basic Books.

Eisenberg, N., Fabes, R., Murphy, B., Karbon, M., Smith, M., & Maszk, P. (1996). The relations of children's dispositional empathy-related responding to their emotionality, regulation, and social functioning. *Developmental Psychology, 32,* 195–209.

Eisenberg, N., Fabes, R. A., Schaller, M., Carlo, G., et al. (1991). The relations of parental characteristics and practices to children's vicarious emotional responding. *Child Development, 27,* 1393–1408.

Eisenberg, N., Fabes, R. A., Shepard, S. A., Guthrie, I., Murphy, B. C., & Reiser, M. (1999). Parental reactions to children's negative emotions: Longitudinal relations to quality of children's social functioning. *Child Development, 70,* 513–534.

Eisenberg, N., Fabes, R. A., Shepard, S. A., Murphy, B. C., Jones, S., & Guthrie, I. K. (1998). Contemporaneous and longitudinal prediction of children's sympathy from dispositional regulation and emotionality. *Developmental Psychology, 34,* 910–924.

Eisenberg, N., Gershoff, E. T., Fabes, R. A., Shepard, S. A., Cumberland, A. J., & Losoya, S. H. (2001). Mothers' emotional expressivity and children's behavior problems and social competence: Mediation through children's regulation. *Developmental Psychology, 37,* 475–490.

Eisenberg, N., & McNally, S. (1993). Socialization and mothers' and adolescents' empathy-related characteristics. *Journal of Research on Adolescence, 3,* 171–191.

Ekman, P., & Friesen, W. (1972). Constants across culture in the face and emotion. *Journal of Personality and Social Psychology, 17,* 124–129.

Elder, G. H., Jr. (1999). *Children of the Great Depression* (25th anniversary ed.). Boulder, CO: Westview Press.

Elder, G. H., Jr., & Caspi, A. (1988). Human development and social change: An emerging perspective on the life course. In N. Bolger, A. Caspi, G. Downey, & M. Moorehouse (Eds.), *Persons in context: Developmental processes* (pp. 77–113). Cambridge, U.K.: Cambridge University Press.

Elder, G. H., Jr., & Hareven, T. K. (1993). Rising above life's disadvantage: From the Great Depression to war. In G. H. Elder, Jr., J. Modell, & R. D. Parke (Eds.), *Children in time and place* (pp. 47–72). Cambridge, U.K.: Cambridge University Press.

Elder, G. H., Jr., Liker, J. K., & Cross, C. E. (1984). Parent–child behavior in the Great Depression: Life course and intergenerational influences. In P. B. Baltes & O. G. Brim (Eds.), *Life-span development and behavior* (Vol. 6, pp. 109–158). New York: Academic Press.

Elder, G. H., Jr., Van Nguyen, T., & Caspi, A. (1985). Linking family hardship to children's lives. *Child Development, 56,* 361–375.

Elias, C. L., & Berk, L. E. (2002). Self-regulation in young children: Is there a role for sociodramatic play? *Early Childhood Research Quarterly, 17,* 1–17.

Elicker, J., Englund, M., & Sroufe, L. A. (1992). Predicting peer competence and peer relationships in childhood from early parent–child relationships. In R. D. Parke & G. W. Ladd (Eds.), *Family–peer relationships: Modes of linkage* (pp. 77–106). Hillsdale, NJ: Erlbaum.

Elkind, D. (1994). *A sympathetic understanding of the child: Birth to sixteen* (3rd ed.). Boston: Allyn and Bacon.

Elkind, D., & Bowen, R. (1979). Imaginary audience behavior in children and adolescents. *Developmental Psychology, 15,* 33–44.

Elliot, J. G. (1999). School refusal: Issues of conceptualization, assessment, and treatment. *Journal of Child Psychology and Psychiatry and Allied Disciplines, 40,* 1001–1012.

Elliott, D. S., Wilson, W. J., Huizinga, D., Sampson, R. J., Elliott, A., & Rankin, B. (1996). The effects of neighborhood disadvantage on adolescent development. *Journal of Research in Crime and Delinquency, 33,* 389–426.

Ellis, B. J., Bates, J. E., Dodge, K. A., Fergusson, D. M., Horwood, L. J., Pettit, G. S., & Woodward, L. (2003). Does father absence place daughters at special risk for early sexual activity and teenage pregnancy? *Child Development, 74,* 801–821.

Ellis, B. J., & Garber, J. (2000). Psychosocial antecedents of variation in girls' pubertal timing: Maternal depression, stepfather presence, and marital and family stress. *Child Development, 71,* 485–501.

Ellis, B. J., McFadyen-Ketchum, S., Dodge, K. A., Pettit, G. S., & Bates, J. E. (1999). Quality of early family relationships and individual differences in the timing of pubertal maturation in girls: A longitudinal test of an evolutionary model. *Journal of Personality and Social Psychology, 77,* 933–952.

Ellis, L., & Blanchard, R. (2001). Birth order, sibling sex ratio, and maternal miscarriages in homosexual and heterosexual men and women. *Personality and Individual Differences, 30,* 543–552.

Ellis, L., & Bonin, S. L. (2003). Genetics and occupation-related preferences: Evidence from adoptive and non-adoptive families. *Personality and Individual Differences, 35*, 929–937.

Ellsworth, C. P., Muir, D. W., & Hains, S. M. J. (1993). Social competence and person–object differentiation: An analysis of the still-face effect. *Developmental Psychology, 29*, 63–73.

Elsen, H. (1994). Phonological constraints and overextensions. *First Language, 14*, 305–315.

El-Sheikh, M., Cummings, E. M., & Reiter, S. (1996). Preschoolers' responses to ongoing interadult conflict: The role of prior exposure to resolved versus unresolved arguments. *Journal of Abnormal Child Psychology, 24*, 665–679.

Eltzschig, H. K., Lieberman, E. S., & Camann, W. R. (2003). Regional anesthesia and analgesia for labor and delivery. *New England Journal of Medicine, 384*, 319–332.

Ely, R. (2001). Language and literacy in the school years. In J. B. Gleason (Ed.), *The development of language* (5th ed., pp. 409–454). Boston: Allyn and Bacon.

Emde, R. N. (1992). Individual meaning and increasing complexity: Contributions of Sigmund Freud and René Spitz to developmental psychology. *Developmental Psychology, 28*, 347–359.

Emde, R. N., & Buchsbaum, H. K. (1990). "Didn't you hear my mommy?" Autonomy with connectedness in moral self-emergence. In D. Cicchetti & M. Beeghly (Eds.), *Development of the self through transition* (pp. 35–60). Chicago: University of Chicago Press.

Emery, R. E (1999). Psychological interventions for separated and divorced families. In E. M. Hetherington (Ed.), *Coping with divorce, single parenting, and remarriage: A risk and resiliency perspective* (pp. 253–271). Mahwah, NJ: Erlbaum.

Emery, R. E. (2001). Interparental conflict and social policy. In J. H. Grych & F. D. Fincham (Eds.), *Interparental conflict and child development: Theory, research, and applications* (pp. 417–439). New York: Cambridge University Press.

Emery, R. E., & Laumann-Billings, L. (1998). An overview of the nature, causes, and consequences of abusive family relationships: Toward differentiating maltreatment and violence. *American Psychologist, 53*, 121–135.

Emery, R. E., Laumann-Billings, L., Waldron, M. C., Sbarra, D. A., & Dillon, P. (2001). Child custody mediation and litigation: Custody, contact, and coparenting 12 years after initial dispute resolution. *Journal of Consulting and Clinical Psychology, 69*, 323–332.

Emory, E. K., Schlackman, L. J., & Fiano, K. (1996). Drug–hormone interactions on neurobehavioral responses in human neonates. *Infant Behavior and Development, 19*, 213–220.

Engel, N. (1989). An American experience of pregnancy and childbirth in Japan. *Birth, 16*, 81–86.

Engle, R. A., & Conant, F. R. (2002). Guiding principles for fostering productive disciplinary engagement: Explaining an emergent argument in a community of learners classroom. *Cognition and Instruction, 20*, 399–483.

Engler, A. J., Ludington-Hoe, S. M., Cusson, R. M., Adams, R., Bahnsen, M., & Brumbaugh, E. (2002). Kangaroo care: National survey of practice, knowledge, barriers, and perceptions. *American Journal of Maternal and Child Nursing, 27*, 146–153.

Enright, R. D., Lapsley, D. K., & Shukla, D. (1979). Adolescent egocentrism in early and late adolescence. *Adolescence, 14*, 687–695.

Epstein, J. L. (2001). *School, family, and community partnerships: Preparing educators and improving schools.* Boulder, CO: Westview.

Epstein, J. L., & Sanders, M. G. (2002). Family, school, and community partnerships. In M. H. Bornstein (Ed.), *Handbook of parenting: Vol. 5. Practical issues in parenting* (2nd ed., pp. 407–437). Mahwah, NJ: Erlbaum.

Epstein, L. H., Roemmich, J. N., & Raynor, H. A. (2001). Behavioral therapy in the treatment of pediatric obesity. *Pediatric Clinics of North America, 48*, 981–983.

Epstein, L. H., Saelens, B. E., Myers, M. D., & Vito, D. (1997). Effects of decreasing sedentary behaviors on activity choice in obese children. *Health Psychology, 16*, 107–113.

Epstein, L. H., Saelens, B. E., & O'Brien, J. G. (1995). Effects of reinforcing increases in active versus decreases in sedentary behavior for obese children. *International Journal of Behavioral Medicine, 2*, 41–50.

Erikson, E. H. (1950). *Childhood and society.* New York: Norton.

Erikson, E. H. (1968). *Identity, youth, and crisis.* New York: Norton.

Ernst, M., Moolchan, E. T., & Robinson, M. L. (2001). Behavioral and neural consequences of prenatal exposure to nicotine. *Journal of the American Academy of Child and Adolescent Psychiatry, 40*, 630–641.

Eshel, Y., & Kohavi, R. (2003). Perceived classroom control, self-regulated learning strategies, and academic achievement. *Educational Psychology, 23*, 249–260.

Eskilson, A., & Wiley, M. G. (1999). Solving for the X: Aspirations and expectations of college students. *Journal of Youth and Adolescence, 28*, 51–70.

Espy, K. A., Kaufmann, P. M., & Glisky, M. L. (1999). Neuropsychological function in toddlers exposed to cocaine in utero: A preliminary study. *Developmental Neurospsychology, 15*, 447–460.

Espy, K. A., Molfese, V. J., & DiLalla, L. F. (2001). Effects of environmental measures on intelligence in young children: Growth curve modeling of longitudinal data. *Merrill-Palmer Quarterly, 47*, 42–73.

Essa, E. L., & Murray, C. I. (1994, May). Young children's understanding and experience with death. *Young Children, 49*(4), 74–81.

Evans, G. W., Maxwell, L. E., & Hart, B. (1999). Parental language and verbal responsiveness to children in crowded homes. *Developmental Psychology, 35*, 1020–1023.

Evans, G. W. (2004). The environment of child poverty. *American Psychologist, 59*, 77–92.

Everman, D. B., & Cassidy, S. B. (2000). Genetics of childhood disorders: XII. Genomic imprinting: Breaking the rules. *Journal of the American Academy of Child and Adolescent Psychiatry, 38*, 386–389.

Fabes, R. A., Eisenberg, N., Hanish, L. D., & Spinrad, T. L. (2001). Preschoolers' spontaneous emotion vocabulary: Relations to likability. *Early Education and Development, 12*, 11–27.

Fabes, R. A., Eisenberg, N., McCormick, S. E., & Wilson, M. S. (1988). Preschoolers' attributions of the situational determinants of others' naturally occurring emotions. *Developmental Psychology, 24*, 376–385.

Fabes, R. A., Martin, C. L., & Hanish, L. D. (2003). Young children's play qualities in same-, other-, and mixed-sex peer groups. *Child Development, 74*, 921–932.

Facchinetti, F., Battaglia, C., Benatti, R., Borella, P., & Genazzani, A. R. (1992). Oral magnesium supplementation improves fetal circulation. *Magnesium Research, 3*, 179–181.

Fagan, J. F., III. (1973). Infants' delayed recognition memory and forgetting. *Journal of Experimental Child Psychology, 16*, 424–450.

Fagan, J. F., III, & Singer, L. T. (1979). The role of simple feature differences in infants' recognition of faces. *Infant Behavior and Development, 2*, 39–45.

Fagard, J., & Pezé, A. (1997). Age changes in interlimb coupling and the development of bimanual coordination. *Journal of Motor Behavior, 29*, 199–208.

Fagot, B. I. (1984). The child's expectations of differences in adult male and female interactions. *Sex Roles, 11*, 593–600.

Fagot, B. I., & Hagan, R. I. (1991). Observations of parent reactions to sex-stereotyped behaviors: Age and sex effects. *Child Development, 62*, 617–628.

Fagot, B. I., & Leinbach, M. D. (1989). The young child's gender schema: Environmental input, internal organization. *Child Development, 60*, 663–672.

Fagot, B. I., Leinbach, M. D., & O'Boyle, C. (1992). Gender labeling, gender stereotyping, and parenting behaviors. *Developmental Psychology, 28*, 225–230.

Fahrmeier, E. D. (1978). The development of concrete operations among the Hausa. *Journal of Cross-Cultural Psychology, 9*, 23–44.

Fairburn, C. G., Doll, H. A., Welch, S. L., Hay, P. J., Davies, B. A., & O'Conner, M. E. (1997). Risk factors for binge eating disorder: A community-based case control study. *Archives of General Psychiatry, 54*, 509–517.

Fairburn, C. G., & Harrison, P. J. (2003). Eating disorders. *Lancet, 361*, 407–416.

Falbo, T. (1992). Social norms and the one-child family: Clinical and policy implications. In F. Boer & J. Dunn (Eds.), *Children's sibling relationships* (pp. 71–82). Hillsdale, NJ: Erlbaum.

Falbo, T., & Poston, D. L., Jr. (1993). The academic, personality, and physical outcomes of only children in China. *Child Development, 64*, 18–35.

Falbo, T., Poston, D. L., Jr., Triscari, R. S., & Zhang, X. (1997). Self-enhancing illusions among Chinese schoolchildren. *Journal of Cross-Cultural Psychology, 28*, 172–191.

Fantz, R. L. (1961, May). The origin of form perception. *Scientific American, 204*(5), 66–72.

Farmer, T. W., Estell, D. B., Bishop, J. L., O'Neal, K. K., & Cairns, B. D. (2003). Rejected bullies or popular leaders? The social relations of aggressive subtypes of rural African American early adolescents. *Developmental Psychology, 39*, 992–1004.

Farmer, T. W., Leung, M., Pearl, R., Rodkin, P. C., Cadwallader, T. W., & Van Acker, R. (2002). Deviant or diverse peer groups? The peer affiliations of aggressive elementary students. *Journal of Educational Psychology, 94*, 611–620.

Farrant, K., & Reese, E. (2000). Maternal style and children's participation in reminiscing: Stepping stones in children's autobiographical memory development. *Journal of Cognition and Development, 1*, 193–225.

Farrington, D. P. (1987). Epidemiology. In H. C. Quay (Ed.), *Handbook of juvenile delinquency* (pp. 33–61). New York: Wiley.

Farrington, D. P., & Loeber, R. (2000). Epidemiology of juvenile violence. *Juvenile Violence, 9*, 733–748.

Farver, J. M. (1993). Cultural differences in scaffolding pretend play: A comparison of American and Mexican mother–child and sibling–child pairs. In K. MacDonald (Ed.), *Parent–child play* (pp. 349– 366). Albany, NY: SUNY Press.

Farver, J. M., & Branstetter, W. H. (1994). Preschoolers' prosocial responses to their peers' distress. *Developmental Psychology, 30,* 334–341.

Farver, J. M., Kim, Y. K., & Lee, Y. (1995). Cultural differences in Korean- and Anglo-American preschoolers' social interaction and play behaviors. *Child Development, 66,* 1099–1099.

Farver, J. M., & Wimbarti, S. (1995). Indonesian children's play with their mothers and older siblings. *Child Development, 66,* 1493–1503.

Fasig, L. G. (2000). Toddlers' understanding of ownership: Implications for self-concept development. *Social Development, 9,* 370–382.

Fasouliotis, S. J., & Schenker, J. G. (2000). Ethics and assisted reproduction. *European Journal of Obstetrics, Gynecology, and Reproductive Biology, 90,* 171–180.

Fattibene, P., Mazzei, F., Nuccetelli, C., & Risica, S. (1999). Prenatal exposure to ionizing radiation: Sources, effects, and regulatory aspects. *Acta Paediatrica, 88,* 693–702.

Federal Interagency Forum on Child and Family Statistics. (2003). *America's children: Key national indicators of well-being: 2003.* Washington, DC: U.S. Government Printing Office.

Federico, M. J., & Liu, A. H. (2003). Overcoming childhood asthma disparities of the inner-city poor. *Pediatric Clinics of North America, 50,* 655–675.

Feeney, J. A., Hohaus, L., Noller, P., & Alexander, R. P. (2001). *Becoming parents: Exploring the bonds between mothers, fathers, and their infants.* New York: Cambridge University Press.

Feigenson, L., Carey, S., & Spelke, E. (2002). Infants' discrimination of number vs. continuous extent. *Cognitive Psychology, 44,* 33–66.

Feingold, A. (1994). Gender differences in personality: A meta-analysis. *Psychological Bulletin, 116,* 429–456.

Feiring, C., & Taska, L. S. (1996). Family self-concept: Ideas on its meaning. In B. Bracken (Ed.), *Handbook of self-concept* (pp. 317–373). New York: Wiley.

Feiring, C., Taska, L., & Lewis, M. (1999). Age and gender differences in children's and adolescents' adaptation to sexual abuse. *Child Abuse and Neglect, 23,* 115–128.

Feldkámper, M., & Schaeffel, F. (2003). Interactions of genes and environment in myopia. *Developmental Ophthalmology, 37,* 34–49.

Feldman, R. (2002). Parents' convergence on sharing and marital satisfaction, father involvement, and parent–child relationship in the transition to parenthood. *Infant Mental Health Journal, 21,* 176–191.

Feldman, R., & Eidelman, A. I. (2003). Skin-to-skin contact (kangaroo care) accelerates autonomic and neurobehavioral maturation in preterm infants. *Developmental Medicine and Child Neurology, 45,* 274–281.

Feldman, R., Eidelman, A., Sirota, L., & Weller, A. (2002). Comparison of skin-to-skin (kangaroo) and traditional care: Parenting outcomes and preterm infant development. *Pediatrics, 110,* 16–26.

Feldman, R., Greenbaum, C. W., & Yirmiya, N. (1999). Mother–infant affect synchrony as an antecedent of the emergence of self-control. *Developmental Psychology, 35,* 223–231.

Feldman, R., Weller, A., Leckman, J. F., Kuint, J., & Eidelman, A. I. (1999). The nature of the mother's tie to her infant: Maternal bonding under conditions of proximity, separation, and potential loss. *Journal of Child Psychology and Psychiatry, 40,* 929–939.

Feldman, R., Weller, A., Sirota, L., & Eidelman, A. I. (2003). Testing a family intervention hypothesis: The contribution of mother–infant skin-to-skin contact (kangaroo care) to family interaction, proximity, and touch. *Journal of Family Psychology, 17,* 94–107.

Felner, R. D., Favazza, A., Shim, M., Brand, S., Gu, K., & Noonan, N. (2001). Whole school improvement and restructuring as prevention and promotion: Lessons from STEP and the Project on High Performance Learning Communities. *Journal of School Psychology, 39,* 177–202.

Felsman, D. E., & Blustein, D. L. (1999). The role of peer relatedness in late adolescent career development. *Journal of Vocational Behavior, 54,* 279–295.

Fennema, E., Carpenter, T. P., Jacobs, V. R., Franke, M. L., & Levi, L. W. (1998). A longitudinal study of gender differences in young children's mathematical thinking. *Educational Researcher, 27,* 6–11.

Fenson, L., Dale, P. S., Reznick, J. S., Bates, E., Thal, D. J., & Pethick, S. J. (1994). Variability in early communicative development. *Monographs of the Society for Research in Child Development, 59*(5, Serial No. 242).

Ferguson, T. J., Stegge, H., & Damhuis, I. (1991). Children's understanding of guilt and shame. *Child Development, 62,* 827–839.

Ferguson, T. J., Stegge, H., Miller, E. R., & Olsen, M. E. (1999). Guilt, shame, and symptoms in children. *Developmental Psychology, 35,* 347–357.

Fergusson, D. M., & Woodward, L. J. (1999). Breast-feeding and later psychosocial adjustment. *Paediatric and Perinatal Epidemiology, 13,* 144–157.

Fergusson, D. M., & Woodward, L. J. (2000). Teenage pregnancy and female educational underachievement. *Journal of Marriage and the Family, 62,* 147–161.

Fergusson, D. M., & Woodward, L. J. (2002). Mental health, educational, and social role outcomes of adolescents with depression. *Archives of General Psychiatry, 59,* 225–231.

Fergusson, D. M., Woodward, L. J., & Horwood, L. J. (2000). Risk factors and life processes associated with the onset of suicidal behaviour during adolescence and early adulthood. *Psychological Medicine, 30,* 23–39.

Fernald, A., & Morikawa, H. (1993). Common themes and cultural variations in Japanese and American mothers' speech to infants. *Child Development, 64,* 637–656.

Fernald, A., Swingley, D., & Pinto, J. P. (2001). When half a word is enough: Infants can recognize spoken words using partial phonetic information. *Child Development, 72,* 1003–1015.

Fernald, A., Taeschner, T., Dunn, J., Papousek, M., Boyssen-Bardies, B., & Fukui, I. (1989). A cross-language study of prosodic modifications in mothers' and fathers' speech to preverbal infants. *Journal of Child Language, 16,* 477–502.

Fernald, L. C., & Grantham-McGregor, S. M. (1998). Stress response in school-age children who have been growth-retarded since early childhood. *American Journal of Clinical Nutrition, 68,* 691–698.

Fernandes, O., Sabharwal, M., Smiley, T., Pastuszak, A., Koren, G., & Einarson, T. (1998). Moderate to heavy caffeine consumption during pregnancy and relationship to spontaneous abortion and abonormal fetal growth: A meta-analysis. *Reproductive Toxicology, 12,* 435–444.

Ficca, G., Fagioli, I., Giganti, F., & Salzarulo, P. (1999). Spontaneous awakenings from sleep in the first year of life. *Early Human Development, 55,* 219–228.

Field, T. (1994). The effects of mother's physical and emotional unavailability on emotion regulation. In N. A. Fox (Ed.), The development of emotion regulation: Biological and behavioral considerations. *Monographs of the Society for Research in Child Development, 59*(2–3, Serial No. 240).

Field, T. (2001). Massage therapy facilitates weight gain in preterm infants. *Current Directions in Psychological Science, 10,* 51–54.

Field, T., Hernandez-Reif, M., & Freedman, J. (2004) Stimulation programs for preterm infants. *Social Policy Report of the Society for Research in Child Development, 18*(1).

Field, T. M., Woodson, R., Greenberg, R., & Cohen, D. (1982). Discrimination and imitation of facial expressions by neonates. *Science, 218,* 179–181.

Fiese, B. (1990). Playful relationships: A contextual analysis of mother–toddler interaction and symbolic play. *Child Development, 61,* 1648–1656.

Fingerhut, L. A., & Christoffel, K. K. (2002). Firearm-related death and injury among children and adolescents. *Future of Children, 12,* 25–37.

Finn, J. D., Pannozzo, G. M., & Achilles, C. M. (2003). The "why's" of class size: Student behavior in small classes. *Review of Educational Research, 73,* 321–368.

Fins, A. I., & Wohlgemuth, W. K. (2001). Sleep disorders in children and adolescents. In H. Orvaschel & J. Faust (Eds.), *Handbook of conceptualization and treatment of child psychopathology* (pp. 437–448). Amsterdam: Pergamon.

Fisch, S. M., Truglio, R. T., & Cole, C. F. (1999). The impact of Sesame Street on preschool children: A review and synthesis of 30 years' research. *Media Psychology, 1,* 165–190.

Fischer, K. W., & Bidell, T. R. (1998). Dynamic development of psychological structures in action and thought. In R. M. Lerner (Ed.), *Handbook of child psychology: Vol. 1. Theoretical models of human development* (5th ed., pp. 467–562). New York: Wiley.

Fischer, K. W., & Rose, S. P. (1995, Fall). Concurrent cycles in the dynamic development of brain and behavior. *SRCD Newsletter,* pp. 3–4, 15–16.

Fischman, M. G., Moore, J. B., & Steele, K. H. (1992). Children's one-hand catching as a function of age, gender, and ball location. *Research Quarterly for Exercise and Sport, 63,* 349–355.

Fisher, C. B. (1993, Winter). Integrating science and ethics in research with high-risk children and youth. *Social Policy Report of the Society for Research in Child Development, 4*(4).

Fisher, C. B., Hoagwood, K., Boyce, C., Duster, T., Frank, D. A., & Grisso, T. (2002). Research ethics for mental health science involving ethnic minority children and youths. *American Psychologist, 57,* 1024–1040.

Fisher, J. A., & Birch, L. L. (1995). 3–5 year-old children's fat preferences and fat consumption are related to parental adiposity. *Journal of the American Dietetic Association, 95,* 759–764.

Fisher, J. O., Mitchell, D. S., Smiciklas-Wright, H., & Birch, L. L. (2001). Maternal milk consumption predicts the tradeoff between milk and soft drinks in young girls' diets. *Journal of Nutrition, 131,* 246–250.

Fisher, J. O., Rolls, B. J., & Birch, L. L. (2003). Children's bite size and intake of an entrée are greater with large portions than with age-appropriate or self-selected portions. *American Journal of Clinical Nutrition, 77,* 1164–1170.

Fisher, M., Barkley, R. A., Smallish, L., & Fletcher, K. (2002). Young adult follow-up of hyperactive children: Self-reported psychiatric disorders, comorbidity, and the role of childhood conduct problems and teen CD. *Journal of Abnormal Child Psychology, 39,* 463–475.

FitzGerald, D. P., & White, K. J. (2003). Linking children's social worlds: Perspective-taking in parent–child and peer contexts. *Social Behavior and Personality, 31,* 509–522.

Fivush, R., & Reese, E. (2002). Reminiscing and relating: The development of parent–child talk about the past. In J. D. Webster & B. K. Haight (Eds.), *Critical advances in reminiscence work: From theory to application* (pp. 109–122). New York: Springer.

Fixler, J., & Styles, L. (2002). Sickle cell disease. *Pediatric Clinics of North America, 49,* 1193–1210.

Flake, A. W. (2003). Surgery in the human fetus: The future. *Journal of Physiology, 547,* 45–51.

Flake, A. W., Crombleholme, T. M., Johnson, M. P., Howell, L. J., & Adzick, N. S. (2000). Treatment of severe congenital diaphragmatic hernia by fetal tracheal occlusion: Clinical experience with fifteen cases. *American Journal of Obstetrics and Gynecology, 183,* 1059–1066.

Flanagan, C. A., & Faison, N. (2001). Youth civic development: Implications of research for social policy and programs. *Social Policy Report of the Society for Research in Child Development, 15*(1).

Flanagan, C. A., Jonsson, B., Botcheva, L., Csapo, B., Bowes, J., Macek, P., Averina, I., & Sheblanova, E. (1999). Adolescents and the social contract: Developmental roots of citizenship in seven countries. In M. Yates & J. Youniss (Eds.), *Roots of civic identity: International perspectives on community service and activism in youth* (pp. 135–155). New York: Cambridge University Press.

Flanagan, C. A., & Tucker, C. J. (1999). Adolescents' explanations for political issues: Concordance with their views of self and society. *Developmental Psychology, 35,* 1198–1209.

Flannery, K. A., & Liederman, J. (1995). Is there really a syndrome involving the co-occurrence of neurodevelopmental disorder, talent, non-right handedness and immune disorder among children? *Cortex, 31,* 503–515.

Flavell, J. H. (1999). Cognitive development: Children's knowledge about the mind. *Annual Review of Psychology, 50,* 21–45.

Flavell, J. H. (2000). Development of children's knowledge about the mental world. *International Journal of Behavioral Development, 24,* 15–23.

Flavell, J. H., Flavell, E. R., & Green, F. L. (2001). Development of children's understanding of connections between thinking and feeling. *Psychological Science, 12,* 430–432.

Flavell, J. H., Flavell, E. R., Green, F. L., & Korfmacher, J. E. (1990). Do young children think of television

images as pictures or real objects? *Journal of Broadcasting and Electronic Media, 34,* 339–419.

Flavell, J. H., Green, F. L., & Flavell, E. R. (1987). Development of knowledge about the appearance–reality distinction. *Monographs of the Society for Research in Child Development, 51*(1, Serial No. 212).

Flavell, J. H., Green, F. L., & Flavell, E. R. (1993). Children's understanding of the stream of consciousness. *Child Development, 64,* 387–398.

Flavell, J. H., Green, F. L., & Flavell, E. R. (1995). Young children's knowledge about thinking. *Monographs of the Society for Research in Child Development, 60*(1, Serial No. 243).

Flavell, J. H., Green, F. L., Flavell, E. R., & Grossman, J. B. (1997). The development of children's knowledge about inner speech. *Child Development, 68,* 39–47.

Flavell, J. H., Miller, P. H., & Miller, S. A. (2002). *Cognitive development* (4th ed.). Upper Saddle River, NJ: Prentice Hall.

Flegal, K. M. (1999). The obesity epidemic in children and adults: Current evidence and research issues. *Medicine and Science in Sports and Exercise, 31,* S509–S514.

Fleiss, P. M. (1999). *Helping your child get a good night's sleep.* Retrieved from http://www.findarticles.com/cf_0/m0838/1999_Sept/60947818/print.jhtml

Fleming, P. J., Blair, P. S., Bacon, C., Bensley, D., Smith, I., & Taylor, E. (1996). Environment of infants during sleep and risk of the sudden infant death syndrome: Results of 1993–1995 case-control study for confidential inquiry into still-births and deaths in infancy. *British Medical Journal, 313,* 191–195.

Fletcher, A. C., Nickerson, P., & Wright, K. L. (2003). Structured leisure activities in middle childhood: Links to well-being. *Journal of Community Psychology, 31,* 641–659.

Fletcher-Flinn, C. M., & Gravatt, B. (1995). The efficacy of computer-assisted instruction (CAI): A meta-analysis. *Journal of Educational Computing Research, 12,* 219–242.

Floccia, C., Christophe, A., & Bertoncini, J. (1997). High-amplitude sucking and newborns: The quest for underlying mechanisms. *Journal of Experimental Child Psychology, 64,* 175–198.

Flom, R., & Pick, A. D. (2003). Verbal encouragement and joint attention in 18-month-old infants. *Infant Behavior and Development, 26,* 121–134.

Florian, V., & Kravetz, S. (1985). Children's concepts of death: A cross-cultural comparison among Muslims, Druze, Christians, and Jews in Israel. *Journal of Cross-Cultural Psychology, 16,* 174–179.

Flynn, J. R. (1994). IQ gains over time. In R. J. Sternberg (Ed.), *The ency-*

clopedia of human intelligence (pp. 617–623). New York: Macmillan.

Flynn, J. R. (1999). Searching for justice: The discovery of IQ gains over time. *American Psychologist, 54,* 5–20.

Fogel, A. (1993). *Developing through relationships: Origins of communication, self and culture.* New York: Harvester Wheatsheaf.

Fogel, A. (2000). Systems, attachment, and relationships. *Human Development, 43,* 314–320.

Fomon, S. J., & Nelson, S. E. (2002). Body composition of the male and female reference infants. *Annual Review of Nutrition, 22,* 1–17.

Fonagy, P., Steele, H., & Steele, M. (1991). Maternal representations of attachment during pregnancy predict the organization of infant–mother attachment at one year of age. *Child Development, 62,* 891–905.

Ford, C., & Beach, F. (1951). *Patterns of sexual behavior.* New York: Harper & Row.

Fordham, K., & Stevenson-Hinde, J. (1999). Shyness, friendship quality, and adjustment during middle childhood. *Journal of Child Psychology and Psychiatry, 40,* 757–768.

Forsén, T., Eriksson, J., Tuomilehto, J., Reunanen, A., Osmond, C., & Barker, D. (2000). The fetal and childhood growth of persons who develop type 2 diabetes. *Annals of Internal Medicine, 133,* 176–182.

Fowles, D. C., & Kochanska, G. (2000). Temperament as a moderator of pathways to conscience in children: The contribution of electrodermal activity. *Psychophysiology, 37,* 788–795.

Fox, N. A. (1991). If it's not left, it's right: Electroencephalograph asymmetry and the development of emotion. *American Psychologist, 46,* 863–872.

Fox, N. A., & Card, J. A. (1998). Psychophysiological measures in the study of attachment. In J. Cassidy & P. Shaver (Eds.), *Handbook of attachment: Theory, research, and clinical applications* (pp. 226–245). New York: Guilford.

Fox, N. A., & Davidson, R. J. (1986). Taste-elicited changes in facial signs of emotion and the asymmetry of brain electrical activity in newborn infants. *Neuropsychologia, 24,* 417–422.

Foy, J. G., & Mann, V. (2003). Home literacy environment and phonological awareness in preschool children: Differential effects for rhyme and phoneme awareness. *Applied Psycholinguistics, 24,* 59–88.

Franco, P., Chabanski, S., Szliwowski, H., Dramaix, M., & Kahn, A. (2000). Influence of maternal smoking on autonomic nervous system in healthy infants. *Pediatric Research, 47,* 215–220.

Franco, P., Danias, A. P., Akamine, E. H., Kawamoto, E. M., Fortes, Z. B., Scavone, C., & Tostes, R. C. (2002).

Enhanced oxidative stress as a potential mechanism underlying the programming of hypertension in utero. *Journal of Cardiovascular Pharmacology, 40,* 501–509.

Frank, D. A., Augustyn, M., Knight, W. G., Pell, T., & Zuckerman, B. (2001). Growth, development, and behavior in early childhood following prenatal cocaine exposure. *Journal of the American Medical Association, 285,* 1613–1625.

Franklin, C., & Corcoran, J. (2000). Preventing adolescent pregnancy: A review of programs and practices. *Social Work, 45,* 40–52.

Frederiksen-Goldsen, K. I., & Sharlach, A. E. (2000). *Families and work: New directions in the twenty-first century.* New York: Oxford University Press.

Fredricks, J. A., & Eccles, J. S. (2002). Children's competence and value beliefs from childhood through adolescence: Growth trajectories in two male-sex-typed domains. *Developmental Psychology, 38,* 519–533.

Freedman, D. S., Khan, L. K., Serdula, M. K., Dietz, W. H., Srinivasan, S. R., & Berenson, G. S. (2002). Relation of age at menarche to race, time period, and anthropometric dimensions: The Bogalusa Heart Study. *Pediatrics, 110,* e43–e49.

Freedman, D. S., Khan, L. K., Serdula, M. K., Srinivasan, S. R., & Berenson, G. S. (2000). Secular trends in height among children during 2 decades: The Bogalusa Heart Study. *Archives of Pediatric and Adolescent Medicine, 154,* 155–161.

Freeman, D. (1983). *Margaret Mead and Samoa: The making and unmaking of an anthropological myth.* Cambridge, MA: Harvard University Press.

French, S. A., Lin, B. H., & Guthrie, J. F. (2003). National trends in soft drink consumption among children and adolescents age 6 to 17 years: Prevalence, amounts, and sources, 1977/1978 to 1994/1998. *Journal of the American Dietetic Association, 103,* 1326–1331.

Freud, S. (1973). *An outline of psychoanalysis.* London: Hogarth. (Original work published 1938).

Freud, S. (1974). *The ego and the id.* London: Hogarth. (Original work published 1923)

Frick, J. E., Colombo, J., & Saxon, T. F. (1999). Individual and developmental differences in disengagement of fixation in early infancy. *Child Development, 70,* 537–548.

Fried, M. N., & Fried, M. H. (1980). *Transitions: Four rituals in eight cultures.* New York: Norton.

Fried, P. A. (1993). Prenatal exposure to tobacco and marijuana: Effects during preganancy, infancy, and early childhood. *Clinical Obstetrics and Gynecology, 36,* 319–337.

Fried, P. A. (2002a). Adolescents prenatally exposed to marijuana: Examination of facets of complex behaviors and comparisons with the influence of in utero cigarettes. *Journal of Clinical Pharmacology, 42,* 97S–102S.

Fried, P. A. (2002b). Conceptual issues in behavioral teratology and their application in determining long-term sequelae of prenatal marihuana exposure. *Journal of Child Psychology and Psychiatry, 43,* 81–102.

Fried, P. A., Watkinson, B., & Gray, R. (1998). Differential effects on cognitive functioning in 9- to 12-year-olds prenatally exposed to cigarettes and marihuana. *Neurotoxicology and Teratology, 20,* 293–306.

Friedman, J. M. (1996). *The effects of drugs on the fetus and nursing infant: A handbook for health care professionals.* Baltimore: Johns Hopkins University Press.

Friedman, S. L., & Scholnick, E. K. (1997). An evolving "blueprint" for planning: Psychological requirements, task characteristics, and social–cultural influences. In S. L. Friedman & E. K. Scholnick (Eds.), *The developmental psychology of planning: Why, how, and when do we plan?* (pp. 3–22). Mahwah, NJ: Erlbaum.

Friedrich, W. N., Grambusch, P., Damon, L., & Hewitt, S. K. (2001). Child sexual behavior inventory: Normative and clinical comparisons. *Child Maltreatment, 6,* 37–49.

Frijda, N. (2000). The psychologist's point of view. In M. Lewis & J. M. Haviland-Jones (Eds.), *Handbook of emotions* (pp. 59–74). New York: Guilford.

Frith, L. (2001). Gamete donation and anonymity: The ethical and legal debate. *Human Reproduction, 16,* 818–824.

Frith, U. (2003). *Autism: Explaining the enigma* (2nd ed.). Malden, MA: Blackwell.

Frosch, C. A., Mangelsdorf, S. C., & McHale, J. L. (2000). Marital behavior and security of preschooler–parent attachment relationships. *Journal of Family Psychology, 14,* 144–161.

Frost, J. L., Shin, D., & Jacobs, P. J. (1998). Physical environments and children's play. In O. N. Saracho & B. Spodek (Eds.), *Multiple perspectives on play in early childhood education* (pp. 255–294). Albany: State University of New York Press.

Fuchs, D., Fuchs, L.S., Mathes, P. G., & Martinez, E. A. (2002b). Preliminary evidence on the standing of students with learning disabilities in PALS and No-PALS classrooms. *Learning Disabilities Research and Practice, 17,* 205–215.

Fuchs, I., Eisenberg, N., Hertz-Lazarowitz, R., & Sharabany, R. (1986). Kibbutz, Israeli city, and American children's moral reasoning about prosocial moral conflicts. *Merrill-Palmer Quarterly, 32,* 37–50.

Fuchs, L. S., Fuchs, D., Yazdian, L., & Powell, S. R. (2002a). Enhancing first-grade children's mathematical development with peer-assisted learning strategies. *School Psychology Review, 31,* 569–583.

Fuligni, A. J. (1997). The academic achievement of adolescents from immigrant families: The roles of family background, attitudes, and behavior. *Child Development, 68,* 261–273.

Fuligni, A. J. (1998). Authority, autonomy, and parent–adolescent conflict and cohesion: A study of adolescents from Mexican, Chinese, Filipino, and European backgrounds. *Developmental Psychology, 34,* 782–792.

Fuligni, A. J. (2001). A comparative longitudinal approach to acculturation among children from immigrant families. *Harvard Educational Review, 71,* 566–578.

Fuligni, A. J., Burton, L., Marshall, S., Perez-Febles, A., Yarrington, J., Kirsh, L. B., & Merriwether-DeVries, C. (1999). Attitudes toward family obligations among American adolescents with Asian, Latin American, and European backgrounds. *Child Development, 70,* 1030–1044.

Fuligni, A. J., Eccles, J. S., Barber, B. L., & Clements, P. (2001). Early adolescent peer orientation and adjustment during high school. *Developmental Psychology, 37,* 28–36.

Fuligni, A. J., Yip, T., & Tseng, V. (2002). The impact of family obligation on the daily activities and psychological well-being of Chinese-American adolescents. *Child Development, 73,* 302–314.

Fuligni, A. J., & Yoshikawa, H. (2003). Socioeconomic resources, parenting, and child development among immigrant families. In M. H. Bornstein & R. H. Bradley (Eds.), *Socioeconomic status, parenting, and child development* (pp. 107–124). Mahwah, NJ: Erlbaum.

Furman, E. (1990, November). Plant a potato—learn about life (and death). *Young Children, 46*(1), 15–20.

Furman, W. (2002). The emerging field of adolescent romantic relationships. *Current Directions in Psychological Science, 11,* 177–180.

Furman, W., & Buhrmester, D. (1992). Age and sex differences in perceptions of networks of personal relationships. *Child Development, 63,* 103–115.

Furman, W., & Shaffer, L. (2003). The role of romantic relationships in adolescent development. In P. Florsheim (Ed.), *Adolescent romantic relations and sexual behavior* (pp. 3–22). Mahwah, NJ: Erlbaum.

Furman, W., Simon, V. A., Shaffer, L., & Bouchey, H. A. (2002). Adolescents' working models and styles for relationships with parents, friends, and romantic partners. *Child Development, 73,* 241–255.

Furstenberg, F. F., Jr., & Harris, K. M. (1993). When and why fathers matter: Impact of father involvement on children of adolescent mothers. In R. I. Lerman & T. J. Ooms (Eds.), *Young unwed fathers* (pp. 117–138). Philadelphia: Temple University Press.

Fuson, K. C. (1992). Research on learning and teaching addition and subtraction of whole numbers. In G. Leinhardt, R. T. Putnam, & R. A. Hattrup (Eds.), *The analysis of arithmetic for mathematics teaching* (pp. 53–187). Hillsdale, NJ: Erlbaum.

Fuson, K. C., & Burghard, B. H. (2003). Multidigit addition and subtraction methods invented in small groups and teacher support of problem solving and reflection. In A. J. Baroody & A. Dowker (Eds.), *The development of arithmetic concepts and skills* (pp. 267–304). Mahwah, NJ: Erlbaum.

Galambos, N. L., Almeida, D. M., & Petersen, A. C. (1990). Masculinity, femininity, and sex role attitudes in early adolescence: Exploring gender intensification. *Child Development, 61,* 1905–1914.

Galambos, S. J., & Maggs, J. L. (1991). Children in self-care: Figures, facts and fiction. In J. V. Lerner & N. L. Galambos (Eds.), *Employed mothers and their children* (pp. 131–157). New York: Garland.

Galland, B. C., Taylor, B. J., & Bolton, D. P. (2002). Prone versus supine sleep position: A review of the physiological studies in SIDS research. *Journal of Paediatric Child Health, 38,* 332–338.

Galler, J. R., Ramsey, C. F., Morley, D. S., Archer, E., & Salt, P. (1990). The long-term effects of early kwashiorkor compared with marasmus. IV. Performance on the National High School Entrance Examination. *Pediatric Research, 28,* 235–239.

Galler, J. R., Ramsey, F., & Solimano, G. (1985a). A follow-up study of the effects of early malnutrition on subsequent development: I. Physical growth and sexual maturation during adolescence. *Pediatric Research, 19,* 518–523.

Galler, J. R., Ramsey, F., & Solimano, G. (1985b). A follow-up study of the effects of early malnutrition on subsequent development: II. Fine motor skills in adolescence. *Pediatric Research, 19,* 524–527.

Galloway, J. C., & Thelen, E. (2004). Feet first. Object exploration in young infants. *Infant Behavior and Development, 27,* 107-112

Gallup Organization. (1995). *Food, physical activity, and fun: What kids think.* Chicago, IL: The International Food Information Council and The Presidents' Council on Physical Fitness and Sports.

Gandy, J. (2004). *Children explain God.* Retrieved from http://www.geocities.com/jonathangandy.geo/chilrendescribeGod.html

Ganong, L. H., & Coleman, M. (1994). *Remarried family relationships.* Thousand Oaks, CA: Sage.

Garbarino, J., Andreas, J. B., & Vorrasi, J. A. (2002). Beyond the body count: Moderating the effects of war on children's long-term adaptation. In F. Jacobs, D. Wertlieb, & R. M. Lerner (Eds.), *Handbook of developmental science* (pp. 137–158). Thousand Oaks, CA: Sage.

Garbarino, J., & Kostelny, K. (1993). Neighborhood and community influences on parenting. In T. Luster & L. Okagaki (1993), *Parenting: An ecological perspective* (pp. 203–226). Hillsdale, NJ: Erlbaum.

García Coll, C., & Magnuson, K. (1997). The psychological experience of immigration: A developmental perspective. In A. Booth, A. C. Crouter, & N. Landale (Eds.), *Immigration and the family* (pp. 91–131). Mahwah, NJ: Erlbaum.

García Coll, C., & Pachter, L. M. (2002). Ethnic and minority parenting. In M. H. Bornstein (Ed.), *Handbook of parenting: Vol. 4. Social conditions and applied parenting* (2nd ed., pp. 1–20). Mahwah, NJ: Erlbaum.

Garcia, M. M., Shaw, D. S., Winslow, E. B., & Yaggi, K. E. (2000). Destructive sibling conflict and the development of conduct problems in young boys. *Developmental Psychology, 36,* 44–53.

Gardner, H. (1980). *Artful scribbles: The significance of children's drawings.* New York: Basic Books.

Gardner, H. (1983). *Frames of mind: The theory of multiple intelligences.* New York: Basic Books.

Gardner, H. (1993). *Multiple intelligences: The theory in practice.* New York: Basic Books.

Gardner, H. (1998). Extraordinary cognitive achievements (ECA): A symbol systems approach. In R. M. Learner (Ed.), *Handbook of child psychology: Vol. 1. Theoretical models of human development* (5th ed., pp. 415–466). New York: Wiley.

Gardner, H. E. (2000). *Intelligence reframed: Multiple intelligences for the twenty-first century.* New York: Basic Books.

Garfinkel, I., & McLanahan, S. (1995). The effects of child support reform on child well-being. In P. L. Chase-Lansdale & J. Brooks-Gunn (Eds.), *Escape from poverty: What makes a difference for children?* (pp. 211–238). New York: Cambridge University Press.

Garmezy, N. (1993). Children in poverty: Resilience despite risk. *Psychiatry, 56,* 127–136.

Garmon, L. C., Basinger, K. S., Gregg, V. R., & Gibbs, J. C. (1996). Gender differences in stage and expression of moral judgment. *Merrill-Palmer Quarterly, 42,* 418–437.

Garnier, H. E., Stein, J. A., & Jacobs, J. K. (1997). The process of dropping out of high school: A 19-year perspective. *American Educational Research Journal, 34,* 395–419.

Garrett, P., Ng'andu, N., & Ferron, J. (1994). Poverty experiences of young children and the quality of their home environments. *Child Development, 65,* 331–345.

Gartstein, M. A., & Rothbart, M. K. (2003). Studying infant temperament via the revised infant behavior questionnaire. *Infant Behavior and Development, 26,* 64–86.

Gartstein, M. A., Slobodskaya, H. R., & Kinsht, I. A. (2003). Cross-cultural differences in temperament in the first year of life: United States of America (U.S.) and Russia. *International Journal of Behavioral Development, 27,* 316–328.

Gasden, V. (1999). Black families in intergenerational and cultural perspective. In M. E. Lamb (Ed.), *Parenting and child development in "nontraditional" families* (pp. 221–246). Mahwah, NJ: Erlbaum.

Gaskins, S. (1999). Children's daily lives in a Mayan village: A case study of culturally constructed roles and activities. In R. Göncü (Ed.), *Children's engagement in the world: Sociocultural perspectives* (pp. 25–61). Cambridge, U.K.: Cambridge University Press.

Gaskins, S. (2000). Children's daily activities in a Mayan village: A culturally grounded description. *Cross-Cultural Research, 34,* 375–389.

Gathercole, S. E., Adams, A.-M., & Hitch, G. (1994). Do young children rehearse? An individual-differences analysis. *Memory and Cognition, 22,* 201–207.

Gauvain, M. (1999). Everyday opportunities for the development of planning skills: Sociocultural and family influences. In A. Göncü (Ed.), *Children's engagement in the world* (pp. 173–201). New York: Cambridge University Press.

Gauvain, M., & Rogoff, B. (1989a). Collaborative problem solving and children's planning skills. *Developmental Psychology, 25,* 139–151.

Gauvain, M., & Rogoff, B. (1989b). Ways of speaking about space: The development of children's skill in communicating spatial knowledge. *Cognitive Development, 4,* 295–307.

Gazelle, H., & Ladd, G. W. (2002). *Preventing violence in relationships: Interventions across the life span* (pp. 55–78). Washington, DC: American Psychological Association.

Ge, X., Conger, R. D., & Elder, G. H., Jr. (1996). Coming of age too early: Pubertal influences on girls' vulnerability to psychological distress. *Child Development, 67,* 3386–3400.

Ge, X., Conger, R. D., & Elder, G. H., Jr. (2001). The relation between puberty and psychological distress in adolescent boys. *Journal of Research on Adolescence, 11,* 49–70.

Geary, D. C. (1994). *Children's mathematical development.* Washington,

DC: American Psychological Association.

Geary, D. C. (1995). *Children's mathematical development: Research and practical applications.* Washington, DC: American Psychological Association.

Geary, D. C. (1996). International differences in mathematics achievement: The nature, causes, and consequences. *Current Directions in Psychological Science, 5,* 133–137.

Geary, D. C. (1998). *Male, female: The evolution of human sex differences.* Washington, DC: American Psychological Association.

Geary, D. C. (1999). Evolution and developmental sex differences. *Current Directions in Psychological Science, 8,* 115–120.

Geary, D. C., & Bjorklund, D. F. (2000). Evolutionary developmental psychology. *Child Development, 71,* 57–65.

Geary, D. C., Saults, J. S., Liu, F., & Hoard, M. K. (2000). Sex differences in spatial cognition, computational fluency, and arithmetic reasoning. *Journal of Experimental Child Psychology, 77,* 337–353.

Gee, C. B., & Rhodes, J. E. (2003). Adolescent mothers' relationship with their children's biological fathers: Social support, social strain, and relationship continuity. *Journal of Family Psychology, 17,* 370–383.

Gellin, B. G., Maibach, E. W., & Marcuse, E. K. (2000). Do parents understand immunizations? A national telephone survey. *Pediatrics, 106,* 1097–1102.

Gelman, R. (1972). Logical capacity of very young children: Number invariance rules. *Child Development, 43,* 75–90.

Gelman, R., & Shatz, M. (1978). Appropriate speech adjustments: The operation of conversational constraints on talk to two-year-olds. In M. Lewis & L. A. Rosenblum (Eds.), *Interaction, conversation, and the development of language* (pp. 27–61). New York: Wiley.

Gelman, S. A., & Koenig, M. A. (2003). Theory-based categorization in early childhood. In D. H. Rakison & L. M. Oakes (Ed.), *Early category and concept development* (pp. 330–359). New York: Oxford University Press.

Gelman, S. A., & Opfer, J. E. (2002). Development of the animate–inanimate distinction. In U. Goswami (Ed.), *Blackwell handbook of childhood cognitive development* (pp. 151–166). Malden, MA: Blackwell.

Genesee, F. (2001). Portrait of the bilingual child. In V. Cook (Ed.), *Portraits of the second language user* (pp. 170–196). Clevedon, U.K.: Multilingual Matters.

Gennetian, L. A., & Morris, P. A. (2003). The effects of time limits and make-work-pay strategies on the well-being of children: Experimental evidence from two welfare

reform programs. *Children and Youth Services Review, 25,* 17–54.

Gergely, G., Bekkering, H., & Király, I. (2003). Rational imitation in preverbal infants. *Nature, 415,* 755.

Gershoff, E. T. (2002a). Corporal punishment by parents and associated child behaviors and experiences: A meta-analytic and theoretical review. *Psychological Bulletin, 128,* 539–579.

Gershoff, E. T. (2002b). Corporal punishment, physical abuse, and the burden of proof: Reply to Baumrind, Larzelere, and Cowan (2002), Holden (2002), and Parke (2002). *Psychological Bulletin, 128,* 602–611.

Gertner, S., Greenbaum, C. W., Sadeh, A., Dolfin, Z., Sirota, L. & Ben-Nun, Y. (2002). Sleep-wake patterns in preterm infants and 6 month's home environment: Implications for early cognitive development. *Early Human Development, 68,* 93–102.

Gervai, J., Turner, P. J., & Hinde, R. A. (1995). Gender-related behaviour, attitudes, and personality in parents of young children in England and Hungary. *International Journal of Behavioral Development, 18,* 105–126.

Geschwind, D. H., Boone, K. B., Miller, B. L., & Swerdloff, R. S. (2000). Neurobehavioral phenotype of Klinefelter syndrome. *Mental Retardation and Developmental Disabilities Research Reviews, 6,* 107–116.

Gesell, A. (1933). Maturation and patterning of behavior. In C. Murchison (Ed.), *A handbook of child psychology.* Worcester, MA: Clark University Press.

Gest, S. D., Graham-Bermann, S. A., & Hartup, W. W. (2001). Peer experience: Common and unique features of number of friendships, social network, centrality, and socioeconomic status. *Social Development, 10,* 23–40.

Getchell, N., & Roberton, M. A. (1989). Whole body stiffness as a function of developmental level in children's hopping. *Developmental Psychology, 25,* 920–928.

Ghim, H.R. (1990). Evidence for perceptual organization in infants: Perception of subjective contours by young infants. *Infant Behavior and Development, 13,* 221–248.

Gibbons, A. (1998). Which of our genes make us human? *Science, 281,* 1432–1434

Gibbs, J. C. (1995). The cognitive developmental perspective. In W. M. Kurtines & J. L. Gewirtz (Eds.), *Moral development: An introduction* (pp. 27–48). Boston: Allyn and Bacon.

Gibbs, J. C. (2003). *Moral development and reality: Beyond the theories of Kohlberg and Hoffman.* Thousand Oaks, CA: Sage.

Gibson, E. J. (1970). The development of perception as an adaptive process. *American Scientist, 58,* 98–107.

Gibson, E. J. (2000). Perceptual learning in development: Some basic concepts. *Ecological Psychology, 12,* 295–302.

Gibson, E. J., & Walk, R. D. (1960). The "visual cliff." *Scientific American, 202,* 64–71.

Gibson, J. J. (1979). *The ecological approach to visual perception.* Boston: Houghton Mifflin.

Gibson, L. E., & Leitenberg, H. (2000). Child sexual abuse prevention programs: Do they decrease the occurrence of child sexual abuse? *Child Abuse and Neglect, 24,* 1115–1125.

Giedd, J. N., Blumenthal, J., Jeffries, N. O., Castellanos, F. X., Liu, H., & Zijdenbos, A. (1999). Brain development during childhood and adolescence: A longitudinal MRI study. *Nature Neuroscience, 2,* 861–863.

Giedd, J. N., Blumenthal, J., Molloy, E., & Castellanos, F. X. (2001). Brain imaging of attention deficit/hyperactivity disorder: Brain mechanisms and life outcomes. *Annals of the New York Academy of Sciences* (Vol. 931, pp. 33–49). New York: New York Academy of Sciences.

Gilbert-Barness, E. (2000). Maternal caffeine and its effect on the fetus. *American Journal of Medical Genetics, 93,* 253.

Gillies, R. M. (2002). The residual effects of cooperative-learning experiences: A two-year follow-up. *Journal of Educational Research, 96,* 15–20.

Gillies, R. M. (2003). The behaviors, interactions, and perceptions of junior high school students during small-group learning. *Journal of Educational Psychology, 95,* 137–147.

Gillies, R. M., & Ashman, A. F. (1996). Teaching collaborative skills to primary school children in classroom-based workgroups. *Learning and Instruction, 6,* 187–200.

Gilligan, C. F. (1982). *In a different voice.* Cambridge, MA: Harvard University Press.

Gilliland, F. D., Berhane, K., Islam, T., McConnell, R., Gauderman, W. J., & Gilliland, S. (2003). Obesity and the risk of newly diagnosed asthma in school-age children. *American Journal of Epidemiology, 158,* 406–415.

Gillman, M. W., Rifas-Shiman, S. L., Frazier, A. L., Rockett, H. R. H., Camargo, C. A., Jr., Field, A. E., Berkey, C. S., & Colditz, G. A. (2000). Family dinner and diet quality among older children and adolescents. *Archives of Family Medicine, 9,* 235–240.

Gilvarry, E. (2000). Substance abuse in young people. *Journal of Child Psychology and Psychiatry, 41,* 55–80.

Giuliani, A., Schöll, W. M., Basver, A., & Tasmussino, K. F. (2002). Mode of delivery and outcome of 699 term singleton breech deliveries at a single center. *American Journal of Obstetrics and Gynaecology, 187,* 1694–1698.

Gjerde, P. F. (1995). Alternative pathways to chronic depressive symptoms in young adults: Gender differences in developmental trajectories. *Child Development, 66,* 1277–1300.

Gladwell, M. (1998, February 2). The Pima paradox. *The New Yorker,* pp. 44–57.

Glasgow, K. L., Dornbusch, S. M., Troyer, L., Steinberg, L., & Ritter, P. L. (1997). Parenting styles, adolescents' attributions, and educational outcomes in nine heterogeneous high schools. *Child Development, 68,* 507–523.

Gleason, T. R. (2002). Social provisions of real and imaginary relationships in early childhood. *Developmental Psychology, 38,* 979–992.

Gleason, T. R., Sebanc, A. M., & Hartup, W. W. (2000). Imaginary companions of preschool children. *Developmental Psychology, 36,* 419–428.

Gleitman, L. R. (1990). The structural sources of verb meanings. *Language Acquisition, 1,* 3–55.

Gleitman, L. R., & Newport, E. (1996). *The invention of language by children.* Cambridge, MA: MIT Press.

Glosten, B. (1998). Controversies in obstetric anesthesia. *Anesthesia and Analgesia, 428*(Suppl. 32-8), 32–38.

Glowinski, A. L., Madden, P. A. F., Bucholz, K. K., Lynskey, M. T., & Heath, A. C. (2003). Genetic epidemiology of self-reported lifetime DSM-IV major depressive disorder in a population-based twin sample of female adolescents. *Journal of Child Psychology and Psychiatry and Allied Disciplines, 44,* 988–996.

Gnepp, J. (1983). Children's social sensitivity: Inferring emotions from conflicting cues. *Developmental Psychology, 19,* 805–814.

Gnepp, J. (1989). Children's use of personal information to understand other people's feelings. In C. Saarni & P. Harris (Eds.), *Children's understanding of emotion* (pp. 151–180). Cambridge, U.K.: Cambridge University Press.

Godfrey, K. M., & Barker, D. J. (2000). Fetal nutrition and adult disease. *American Journal of Clinical Nutrition, 71,* 1344S–1352S.

Godfrey, K. M., & Barker, D. J. (2001). Fetal programming and adult health. *Public Health Nutrition, 4,* 611–624.

Goelman, H., Doherty, G., Lero, D. S., LaGrange, A., & Tougas, J. (2000). *You bet I care! Caring and learning environments: Quality in child care centers across Canada.* Guelph, Ontario: Centre for Families, Work and Well-Being, University of Guelph.

Goering, J. (Ed.). (2003). Choosing a better life? *How public housing tenants selected a HUD experiment to improve their lives and those of their children: The Moving to Opportunity Demonstration Program.* Washington, DC: Urban Institute Press.

Goin, R. P. (1998). Nocturnal enuresis in children. *Child: Care, Health and Development, 24,* 277–288.

Goldberg, M. C., Maurer, D., & Lewis, T. L. (2001). Developmental changes in attention: The effects of endogenous cueing and of distractors. *Developmental Science, 4,* 209–219.

Goldenberg, C., Gallimore, R., Reese, L., & Garnier, H. (2001). Cause or effect? Immigrant Latino parents' aspirations and expectations, and their children's school performance. *American Educational Research Journal, 38,* 547–582.

Goldfield, B. A. (1987). Contributions of child and caregiver to referential and expressive language. *Applied Psycholinguistics, 8,* 267–280.

Goldscheider, F., & Goldscheider, C. (1999). *The changing transition to adulthood: Leaving and returning home.* Thousand Oaks, CA: Sage.

Goldsmith, H. H., Lemery, K. S., Buss, K. A., & Campos, J. J. (1999). Genetic analyses of focal aspects of infant temperament. *Developmental Psychology, 35,* 972–985.

Goldsmith, L. T. (2000). Tracking trajectories of talent: Child prodigies growing up. In R. C. Friedman & B. M. Shore (Eds.), *Talents unfolding: Cognition and development* (pp. 89–122). Washington, DC: American Psychological Association.

Goldstein, E. (1979). Effect of same-sex and cross-sex role models on the subsequent academic productivity of scholars. *American Psychologist, 34,* 407–410.

Goleman, D. (1998). *Working with emotional intelligence.* New York: Bantam.

Golfier, F., Vaudoyer, F., Ecochard, R., Champion, F., Audra, P., & Raudrant, D. (2001). Planned vaginal delivery versus elective caesarean section in singleton term breech presentation: A study of 1116 cases. *European Journal of Obstetrics and Gynecology, 98,* 186–192.

Golomb, C. (2004). *The child's creation of a pictorial world* (2nd ed.). Mahwah, NJ: Erlbaum.

Golombok, S., Brewaeys, A., Giavazzi, M. T., Guerra, D., MacCallum, F., & Rust, J. (2002a). The European study of assisted reproduction families: The transition to adolescence. *Human Reproduction, 17,* 830–840.

Golombok, S., MacCallum, F., Goodman, E., & Rutter, M. (2002b). Families with children conceived by donor insemination: A follow-up at age twelve. *Child Development, 73,* 952–968.

Golombok, S., Perry, B., Burston, A., Murray, C., Mooney-Somers, J., Stevens, M., & Golding, J. (2003). Children with lesbian parents: A community study. *Developmental Psychology, 39,* 20–33.

Golub, M. S. (1996). Labor analgesia and infant brain development. *Pharmacology, Biochemistry, and Behavior, 55,* 619–628.

Gombert, J. E. (1992). *Metalinguistic development.* Chicago: University of Chicago Press.

Göncü, A. (1993). Development of intersubjectivity in the dyadic play of preschoolers. *Early Childhood Research Quarterly, 8,* 99–116.

Gonzales, N. A., Cauce, A. M., Friedman, R. J., & Mason, C. A. (1996). Family, peer, and neighborhood influences on academic achievement among African-American adolescents: One-year prospective effects. *American Journal of Community Psychology, 24,* 365–387.

Good, T. L., & Brophy, J. E. (1996). *Looking in classrooms* (7th ed.). New York: Addison-Wesley.

Goodlett, C. R., & Horn, K. H. (2001). Mechanisms of alcohol-induced damage to the developing nervous system. *Alcohol Research and Health, 25,* 175–191.

Goodlett, C. R., & Johnson, T. B. (1999). Temporal windows of vulnerability within the third trimester equivalent: Why "knowing when" matters. In J. H. Hannigan, L. P. Spear, N. P. Spear, & C. R. Goodlet (Eds.), *Alcohol and alcoholism: Effects on brain and development* (pp. 59–91). Mahwah, NJ: Erlbaum.

Goodlin-Jones, B. L., Burnham, M. M., & Anders, T. F. (2000). Sleep and sleep disturbances: Regulatory processes in infancy. In A. J. Sameroff, M. Lewis, & S. M. Miller (Eds.), *Handbook of developmental psychology* (2nd ed., pp. 309–325). New York: Kluwer.

Goodman, G. S., Quas, J. A., Bulkley, J., & Shapiro, C. (1999). Innovations for child witnesses: A national survey. *Psychology, Public Policy, and Law, 5,* 255, 281.

Goodman, K. S. (1986). *What's whole in whole language?* Portsmouth, NH: Heinemann.

Goodman, S. H., Brogan, D., Lynch, M. E., & Fielding, B. (1993). Social and emotional competence in children of depressed mothers. *Child Development, 64,* 516–531.

Goodman, S. H., Gravitt, G. W., Jr., & Kaslow, N. J. (1995). Social problem solving: A moderator of the relation between negative life stress and depression symptoms in children. *Journal of Abnormal Child Psychology, 23,* 473–485.

Gopnik, A., & Choi, S. (1990). Do linguistic differences lead to cognitive differences? A cross-linguistic study of semantic and cognitive development. *First Language, 11,* 199–215.

Gopnik, A., & Meltzoff, A. N. (1986). Relations between semantic and cognitive development in the one-word stage: The specificity hypothesis. *Child Development, 57,* 1040–1053.

Gopnik, A., & Meltzoff, A. N. (1987). The development of categorization in the second year and its relation to other cognitive and linguistic developments. *Child Development, 58,* 1523–1531.

Gopnik, A., & Meltzoff, A. N. (1992). Categorization and naming: Basic-level sorting in eighteen-month-olds and its relation to language. *Child Development, 63,* 1091–1103.

Gopnik, A., & Nazzi, T. (2003). Words, kinds, and causal powers: A theory theory perspective on early naming and categorization. In D. H. Rakison & L. M. Oakes (Eds.), *Early category and concept development* (pp. 303–329). New York: Oxford University Press.

Gopnik, A., & Wellman, H. M. (1994). The 'theory' theory. In L. A. Hirschfeld & S. A. Gelman (Eds.), *Mapping the mind: Domain specificity in cognition and culture* (pp. 257–293). Cambridge, U.K.: Cambridge University Press.

Gordon, B. N., Baker-Ward, L., & Ornstein, P. (2001). Children's testimony: A review of research on memory for past experiences. *Clinical Child and Family Psychology Review, 4,* 157–181.

Gormally, S., Barr, R. G., Wertheim, L., Alkawaf, R., Calinoiu, N., & Young, S. N. (2001). Contact and nutrient caregiving effects on newborn infant pain responses. *Developmental Medicine and Child Neurology, 43,* 28–38.

Gortmaker, S. L., Must, A., Sobol, A. M., Peterson, K., Colditz, G. A., & Dietz, W. H. (1996). Television viewing as a cause of increasing obesity among children in the United States, 1986–1990. *Archives of Pediatric and Adolescent Medicine, 150,* 356–362.

Goss, D. A., & Rainey, B. B. (1998). Relation of childhood myopia progression rates to time of year. *Journal of the American Optometric Association, 69,* 262–266.

Goswami, U. (1996). Analogical reasoning and cognitive development. In H. Reese (Ed.), *Advances in child development and behavior* (Vol. 26, pp. 91–138). New York: Academic Press.

Goswami, U. (2000). Phonological and lexical processes. In M. L. Kamil & P. B. Mosenthal (Eds.), *Handbook of reading research* (Vol. 3, pp. 251–284). Mahwah, NJ: Erlbaum.

Goswami, U., & Brown, A. (1989). Melting chocolate and melting snowmen: Analogical reasoning and causal relations. *Cognition, 35,* 69–95.

Gott, V. L. (1998). Antoine Marfan and his syndrome: One hundred years later. *Maryland Medical Journal, 47,* 247–252.

Gottesman, I. I. (1963). Genetic aspects of intelligent behavior. In N. Ellis (Ed.), *Handbook of mental deficiency* (pp. 253–296). New York: McGraw-Hill.

Gottesman, I. I. (1991). *Schizophrenia genetics: The origins of madness.* New York: Freeman.

Gottfredson. L. (1996). A theory of circumscription and compromise. In D. Brown & L. Brooks (Eds.), *Career choice and development* (3rd ed., pp. 179–232). San Francisco: Jossey-Bass.

Gottfried, A. E. (1991). Maternal employment in the family setting: Developmental and environmental issues. In J. V. Lerner & N. L. Galambos (Eds.), *Employed mothers and their children* (pp. 63–84). New York: Garland.

Gottfried, A. E., Gottfried, A. W., & Bathurst, K. (2002). Maternal and dual-earner employment status and parenting. In M. H. Bornstein (Ed.), *Handbook of parenting: Vol. 3. Being and becoming a parent* (2nd ed., pp. 207–230). Mahwah, NJ: Erlbaum.

Gottlieb, G. (1998). Normally occurring environmental and behavioral influences on gene activity: From central dogma to probabilistic epigenesis. *Psychological Review, 105,* 792–802.

Gottlieb, G. (2000). Environmental and behavioral influences on gene activity. *Current Directions in Psychological Science, 9,* 93–97.

Gottlieb, G. (2002). *Individual development and evolution: The genesis of novel behavior.* New York: Oxford University Press.

Gottman, J., Coan, J., Carrere, S., & Swanson, C. (1998). Predicting marital happiness and stability from newlywed interactions. *Journal of Marriage and the Family, 60,* 5–22.

Gould, E., Beylin, A., Tanapat, P., Reeves, A., & Shors, T. J. (1999). Learning enhances adult neurogenesis in the hippocampal formation. *Nature Neuroscience, 2,* 260–265.

Gould, J. L., & Keeton, W. T. (1996). *Biological science* (6th ed.). New York: Norton.

Gould, M., Jamieson, P., & Romer, D. (2003). Media contagion and suicide among the young. *American Behavioral Scientist, 46,* 1269–1284.

Graber, J. A., Lewinsohn, P. M., Seeley, J. R., & Brooks-Gunn, J. (1997). Is psychopathology associated with the timing of pubertal development? *Journal of the American Academy of Child and Adolescent Psychiatry, 36,* 1768–1776.

Gould, M. S., & Kramer, R. A. (2001). Youth suicide prevention. *Suicide and Life-Threatening Behavior, 31,* 6–31.

Graham, T. A. (1999). The role of gesture in children's learning to count. *Journal of Experimental Child Psychology, 74,* 333–355.

Gralinski, J. H., & Kopp, C. B. (1993). Everyday rules for behavior: Mothers' requests to young children. *Developmental Psychology, 29,* 573–584.

Granger, R. C., & Cytron, R. (1999). Teenage parent programs: A synthesis of the long-term effects of the New Chance Demonstration, Ohio's Learning, Earning, and Parenting Program, and the Teenage Parent Demonstration. *Evaluation Review, 23,* 107–145.

Granic, I., Hollenstein, T., Dishion, T. J., & Patterson, G. R. (2003). Longitudinal analysis of flexibility and reorganization in early adolescence: A dynamic systems study of family interactions. *Developmental Psychology, 39,* 606–617.

Granot, M., Spitzer, A., Aroian, K. J., Ravid, C., Tamir, B., & Noam, R. (1996). Pregnancy and delivery practices and beliefs of Ethiopian immigrant women in Israel. *Western Journal of Nursing Research, 18,* 299–313.

Grant, H., & Dweck, C. S. (2001). Cross-cultural response to failure: Considering outcome attributions with different goals. In F. Salili & C. Chiu (Eds.), *Student motivation: The culture and context of learning* (pp. 203–219). New York: Plenum.

Grant, K., O'Koon, J., Davis, T., Roache, N., Poindexter, L., & Armstrong, M. (2000). Protective factors affecting low-income urban African American youth exposed to stress. *Journal of Early Adolescence, 20,* 388–418.

Grantham-McGregor, S. M., Walker, S. P., & Chang, S. (2000). Nutritional deficiencies and later behavioral development. *Proceedings of the Nutrition Society, 59,* 47–54.

Grantham-McGregor, S., & Ani, C. (2001). A review of studies on the effect of iron deficiency on cognitive development in children. *Journal of Nutrition, 131,* 649S–668S.

Grantham-McGregor, S., Powell, C., Walker, S., Chang, S., & Fletcher, P. (1994). The long-term follow-up of severely malnourished children who participated in an intervention program. *Child Development, 65,* 428–439.

Graue, M. E., & DiPerna, J. (2000). Redshirting and early retention: Who gets the "gift of time" and what are its outcomes? *American Educational Research Journal, 37,* 509–534.

Gray, M. R., & Steinberg, L. (1999). Unpacking authoritative parenting: Reassessing a multidimensional construct. *Journal of Marriage and the Family, 61,* 574–587.

Gray-Little, B., & Carels, R. (1997). The effects of racial and socioeconomic consonance on self-esteem and achievement in elementary, junior high, and high school students. *Journal of Research on Adolescence, 7,* 109–131.

Gray-Little, B., & Hafdahl, A. R. (2000). Factors influencing racial comparisons of self-esteem: A quantitative review. *Psychological Bulletin, 126,* 26–54.

Grech, V., Vassallo-Agius, P., & Savona-Ventura, C. (2000). Declining male births with increasing geographical latitude in Europe. *Journal of Epidemiological Community Health, 54,* 244–246.

Green, G. E., Irwin, J. R., & Gustafson, G. E. (2000). Acoustic cry analysis, neonatal status and long-term developmental outcomes. In R. G. Barr, B. Hopkins, & J. A. Green (Eds.), *Crying as a sign, a symptom, and a signal* (pp. 137–156). Cambridge, U.K.: Cambridge University Press.

Greenberger, E., Chen, C., Tally, S. R., & Dong, Q. (2000). Family, peer, and individual correlates of depressive symptomatology among U.S. and Chinese adolescents. *Journal of Counseling and Clinical Psychology, 68,* 209–219.

Greenberger, E., O'Neil, R., & Nagel, S. K. (1994). Linking workplace and homeplace: Relations between the nature of adults' work and their parenting behaviors. *Developmental Psychology, 30,* 990–1002.

Greendorfer, S. L., Lewko, J. H., & Rosengren, K. S. (1996). Family and gender-based socialization of children and adolescents. In F. L. Smoll & R. E. Smith (Eds.), *Children and youth in sport: A biopsychological perspective* (pp. 89–111). Dubuque, IA: Brown & Benchmark.

Greene, K., Krcmar, M., Walters, L. H., Rubin, D. L., Hale, J., & Hale, L. (2000). Targeting adolescent risk-taking behaviors: The contributions of egocentrism and sensation-seeking. *Journal of Adolescence, 23,* 439–461.

Greenfield, P. M. (1992, June). *Notes and references for developmental psychology.* Conference on Making Basic Texts in Psychology More Culture-Inclusive and Culture-Sensitive, Western Washington University, Bellingham, WA.

Greenfield, P. M. (1994). Independence and interdependence as developmental scripts: Implications for theory, research, and practice. In P. M. Greenfield & R. R. Cocking (Eds.), *Cross-cultural roots of minority child development* (pp. 1–37). Hillsdale, NJ: Erlbaum.

Greenfield, P. M., Quiroz, B., & Raeff, C. (2000). Cross-cultural conflict and harmony in the social construction of the child. In S. Harkness, C. Raeff, & C. M. Super (Eds.), *Variability in the social construction of the child* (pp. 93–108). San Francisco: Jossey-Bass.

Greenhill, L. L., Halperin, J. M., & Abikoff, H. (1999). Stimulant Medications. *Journal of the American Academy of Child and Adolescent Psychiatry, 38,* 503–512.

Greenough, W. T., & Black, J. E. (1992). Induction of brain structure by experience: Substrates for cognitive development. In M. Gunnar & C. A. Nelson (Eds.), *Minnesota symposia on child psychology* (pp. 155–200). Hillsdale, NJ: Erlbaum.

Greenough, W. T., Wallace, C. S., Alcantara, A. A., Anderson, B. J., Hawrylak, N., Sirevaag, A. M., Weiler, I. J., & Withers, G. S. (1993). Development of the brain: Experience affects the structure of neurons, glia, and blood vessels. In N. J. Anastasiow & S. Harel (Eds.), *At-risk infants: Interventions, families, and research* (pp. 173–185). Baltimore: Paul H. Brookes.

Greer, T., & Lockman, J. J. (1998). Using writing instruments: Invariances in young children and adults. *Child Development, 69,* 888–902.

Gregg, V., Gibbs, J. C., & Fuller, D. (1994). Patterns of developmental delay in moral judgment by male and female delinquents. *Merrill-Palmer Quarterly, 40,* 538–553.

Gregory, A. M., & O'Connor, T. G. (2002). Sleep problems in childhood: A longitudinal study of developmental change and association with behavior problems. *Journal of the American Academy of Child and Adolescent Psychiatry, 41,* 964–971.

Gresham, F. M., & MacMillan, D. L. (1997). Social competence and affective characteristics of students with mild disabilities. *Review of Educational Research, 67,* 377-415.

Griffin, K. W., Botvin, G. J., Nichols, T. R., & Doyle, M. M. (2003). Effectiveness of a universal drug abuse prevention approach for youth at high risk for substance use initiation. *Preventive Medicine, 36,* 1–7.

Griffith, E. M., Pennington, B. F., Wehner, E. A., & Rogers, S. J. (1999). Executive functions in young children with autism. *Child Development, 70,* 817–832.

Grigorenko, E. L. (2000). Heritability and intelligence. In R. J. Sternberg (Ed.), *Handbook of intelligence* (pp. 53–91). Cambridge, U.K.: Cambridge University Press.

Grissmer, D., Flanagan, A., Kawata, J., & Williamson, S. (2000*). Improving student achievement: What do NAEP test scores tell us?* Santa Monica: RAND Corporation.

Grob, A., & Flammer, A. (1999). Macrosocial context and adolescents' perceived control. In F. D. Alsaker & A. Flammer (Eds.), *The adolescent experience* (pp. 99–114). Mahwah, NJ: Erlbaum.

Grody, W. W. (1999). Cystic fibrosis: Molecular diagnosis, population screening, and public policy. *Archives of Pathology and Laboratory Medicine, 123,* 1041–1046.

Grolnick, W. S., Bridges, L. J., & Connell, J. P. (1996). Emotion regulation in two-year-olds: Strategies and emotional expression in four contexts. *Child Development, 67,* 928–941.

Grolnick, W. S., Kurowski, C. O., Dunlap, K. G., & Hevey, C. (2000). Parental resources and the transition to junior high. *Journal of Research on Adolescence, 10,* 466–488.

Groome, L. J., Swiber, M. J., Atterbury, J. L., Bentz, L. S., & Holland, S. B. (1997). Similarities and differences in behavioral state organization during sleep periods in the perinatal infant before and after birth. *Child Development, 68,* 1–11.

Groome, L. J., Swiber, M. J., Holland, S. B., Bentz, L. S., Atterbury, J. L., & Trimm, R. F., III. (1999). Spontaneous motor activity in the perinatal infant before and after birth: Stability in individual differences. *Developmental Psychobiology, 35,* 15–24.

Gross, M. (1993). *Exceptionally gifted children.* London: Routledge.

Gross, S. J., Geller, J., & Tomarelli, R. M. (1981). Composition of breast milk from mothers of preterm infants. *Pediatrics, 68,* 480–493.

Grossmann, K., Grossmann, K. E., Fremmer-Bombik, E., Kindler, H., Scheuerer-Englisch, H., & Zimmermann, P. (2002). The uniqueness of the child–father attachment relationship: Fathers' sensitive and challenging play as a pivotal variable in a 16-year longitudinal study. *Social Development, 11,* 307–331.

Grossmann, K., Grossmann, K. E., Spangler, G., Suess, G., & Unzner, L. (1985). Maternal sensitivity and newborns' orientation responses as related to quality of attachment in Northern Germany. In I. Bretherton & E. Waters (Eds.), Growing points of attachment theory and research. *Monographs of the Society for Research in Child Development, 50*(1–2, Serial No. 209).

Grotevant, H. D. (1998). Adolescent development in family contexts. In N. Eisenberg (Ed.), *Handbook of child psychology: Vol. 3. Social, emotional, and personality development* (5th ed., pp. 1097–1149). New York: Wiley.

Grotevant, H. D., & Cooper, C. R. (1988). The role of family experience in career exploration during adolescence. In P. Baltes, D. Featherman, & R. Lerner (Eds.), *Life-span development and behavior* (Vol. 8, pp. 231–258). Hillsdale, NJ: Erlbaum.

Grotevant, H. D., & Cooper, C. R. (1998). Individuality and connectedness in adolescent development: Review and prospects for research on identity, relationships, and context. In E. Skoe & A. von der Lippe (Eds.), *Personality development in adolescence.* London: Routledge & Kegan Paul.

Grotevant, H. D., & Kohler, J. K. (1999). Adoptive families. In M. E. Lamb (Ed.), *Parenting and child development in nontraditional families* (pp. 161–190). Mahwah, NJ: Erlbaum.

Grow-Maienza, J., Hahn, D.-D., & Joo, C.-A. (2001). Mathematics instruction in Korean primary schools: Structures, processes, and a linguistic analysis of questioning. *Journal of Educational Psychology, 93,* 363–376.

Grusec, J. E. (1988). *Social development: History, theory, and research.* New York: Springer-Verlag.

Grusec, J. E., & Goodnow, J. J. (1994). Impact of parental discipline methods on the child's internalization of values: A reconceptualization of current points of view. *Developmental Psychology, 30,* 4–19.

Grych, J. H., & Clark, R. (1999). Maternal employment and development of the father–infant relationship in the first year. *Developmental Psychology, 35,* 893–903.

Guay, F., Marsh, H. W., & Boivin, M. (2003). Academic self-concept and academic achievement: Developmental perspectives on their causal ordering. *Journal of Educational Psychology, 95,* 124–136.

Guerra, N. G., Attar, B., & Weissberg, R. P. (1997). Prevention of aggression and violence among inner-city youths. In D. M. Stoff, J. Breiling, & J. D. Maser (Eds.), *Handbook of antisocial behavior* (pp. 375–383). New York: Wiley.

Guilford, J. P. (1985). The structure-of-intellect model. In B. B. Wolman (Ed.), *Handbook of intelligence* (pp. 225–266). New York: Wiley.

Guilleminault, C., Palombini, L., Pelayo, R., & Chervin, R. D. (2003). Sleepwalking and sleep terrors in prepubertal children: What triggers them? *Pediatrics, 111,* e17–e25.

Gullone, E., & King, N. J. (1997). Three-year follow-up of normal fear in children and adolescents aged 7 to 18 years. *British Journal of Developmental Psychology, 15,* 97–111.

Gunn, A. J. (2000). Cerebral hypothermia for prevention of brain injury following perinatal asphyxia. *Current Opinion in Pediatrics, 12,* 111–115.

Gunnar, M. R. (2001). Effects of early deprivation: Findings from orphanage-reared infants and children. In C. A. Nelson & M. Luciana (Eds.), *Handbook of developmental cognitive neuroscience* (pp. 617–629). Cambridge, MA: MIT Press.

Gunnar, M. R., & Nelson, C. A. (1994). Event-related potentials in year-old infants: Relations with emotionality and cortisol. *Child Development, 65,* 80–94.

Guo, G., & VanWey, L. K. (1999). Sibship size and intellectual development: Is the relationship causal? *American Sociological Review, 64,* 169–187.

Gustafson, G. E., Green, J. A., & Cleland, J. W. (1994). Robustness of individual identity in the cries of human infants. *Developmental Psychobiology, 27,* 1–9.

Gustafson, G. E., Wood, R. M., & Green, J. A. (2000). Can we hear the causes of infants' crying? In R. G. Barr & B. Hopkins (Eds.), *Crying as a sign, a symptom, and a signal: Clinical, emotional, and developmental aspects of infant and toddler crying* (pp. 8–22). New York: Cambridge University Press.

Guyda, H. J. (1999). Four decades of growth hormone therapy for short children: What have we achieved? *Journal of Clinical Endocrinology and Metabolism, 84,* 4307–4316.

Gwiazda, J., & Birch, E. E. (2001). Perceptual development: Vision. In E. B. Goldstein (Ed.), *Blackwell handbook of perception* (pp. 636–668). Oxford, U.K.: Blackwell.

Haan, N., Aerts, E., & Cooper, B. (1985). *On moral grounds: The search for practical morality.* New York: New York University Press.

Hack, M., Flannery, D. J., Schluchter, M., Cartar, L., Borawski, E., & Klein, N. (2002). Outcomes in young adulthood for very-low-birth-weight infants. *New England Journal of Medicine, 346,* 149–157.

Haden, C. A., Haine, R. A., & Fivush, R. (1997). Developing narrative structure in parent–child reminiscing across the preschool years. *Developmental Psychology, 33,* 295–307.

Hagekull, B., Bohlin, G., & Rydell, A. (1997). Maternal sensitivity, infant temperament, and the development of early feeding problems. *Infant Mental Health Journal, 18,* 92–106.

Haggerty, L. A. (1999). Continuous electronic fetal monitoring: Contradictions between practice and research. *Journal of Obstetric, Gynecologic, and Neonatal Nursing, 28,* 409–416.

Hahn, C.-S. (2001). Review: Psychosocial well-being of parents and their children born after assisted reproduction. *Journal of Pediatric Psychology, 26,* 525–538.

Haight, W. L., & Miller, P. J. (1993). *Pretending at home: Early development in a sociocultural context.* Albany: State University of New York Press.

Hainline, L. (1998). The development of basic visual abilities. In A. Slater (Ed.), *Perceptual development: Visual, auditory, and speech perception in infancy* (pp. 37–44). Hove, U.K.: Psychology Press.

Haith, M. M. (1999). Some thoughts about claims for innate knowledge and infant physical reasoning. *Developmental Science, 2,* 153–156.

Haith, M. M., & Benson, J. B. (1998). Infant cognition. In D. Kuhn & R. S. Siegler (Eds.), *Handbook of child psychology: Vol. 2 Cognition, perception, and language* (pp. 199–254). New York: Wiley.

Hakuta, K. (1999). The debate on bilingual education. *Developmental and Behavioral Pediatrics, 20,* 36–37.

Hakuta, K., Bialystok, E., & Wiley, E. (2003). Critical evidence: A test of the critical period hypothesis for second-language acquisition. *Psychological Science, 14,* 31–38.

Hale, C. M., & Tager-Flusberg, H. (2003). The influence of language on theory of mind: A training study. *Developmental Science, 6,* 346–359.

Halfon, N., & McLearn, K. T. (2002). Families with children under 3: What we know and implications for results and policy. In N. Halfon & K. T. McLearn (Eds.), *Child rearing in America: Challenges facing parents with young children* (pp. 367–412). New York: Cambridge University Press.

Halford, G. S. (1993). *Children's understanding: The development of mental models.* Hillsdale, NJ: Erlbaum.

Halford, G. S. (2002). Information-processing models of cognitive development. In U. Goswami (Ed.), *Blackwell handbook of childhood cognitive development* (pp. 555–574). Malden, MA: Blackwell.

Halford, G. S., Wilson, W. H., Phillips, S. (1998). Processing capacity defined by relational complexity: Implications for comparative, developmental, and cognitive psychology. *Behavioral and Brain Sciences, 21,* 803–864.

Hall, D. G., & Graham, S. A. (1999). Lexical form class information guides word-to-object mapping in preschoolers. *Child Development, 70,* 78–91.

Hall, G. S. (1904). *Adolescence.* New York: Appleton-Century-Crofts.

Hallett, M. (2000). Brain plasticity and recovery from hemiplegia. *Journal of Medical Speech-Language Pathology, 9,* 107–115.

Halliday, J. L., Watson, L. F., Lumley, J., Danks, D. M., & Sheffield, L. S. (1995). New estimates of Down syndrome risks at chorionic villus sampling, amniocentesis, and live birth in women of advanced maternal age from a uniquely defined population. *Prenatal Diagnosis, 15,* 455–465.

Hallinan, M. T., & Kubitschek, W. N. (1999). Curriculum differentiation and high school achievement. *Social Psychology of Education, 3,* 41–62.

Halpern, C. T., Udry, J. R., & Suchindran, C. (1997). Testosterone predicts initiation of coitus in adolescent females. *Psychosomatic Medicine, 59,* 161–171.

Halpern, D. F. (1997). Sex differences in intelligence. *American Psychologist, 52,* 1091–1102.

Halpern, D. F. (2000). *Sex differences in cognitive abilities* (3rd ed.). Mahwah, NJ: Erlbaum.

Halpern, L. F., MacLean, W. E., & Baumeister, A. A. (1995). Infant sleep–wake characteristics: Relation to neurological status and the prediction of developmental outcome. *Developmental Review, 15,* 255–291.

Halpern-Felsher, B. L., & Cauffman, E. (2001). Costs and benefits of a decision: Decision-making competence in adolescents and adults. *Journal of Applied Developmental Psychology, 22,* 257–273.

Hamer, D. H., Hu, S., Magnuson, V. L., Hu, N., & Pattatucci, A. M. L. (1993). A linkage between DNA markers on the X chromosome and male sexual orientation. *Science, 261,* 321–327.

Hamilton, C. E. (2000). Continuity and discontinuity of attachment from infancy through adolescence. *Child Development, 71,* 690–694.

Hamilton, S. F., & Hamilton, M. A. (2000). Research, intervention, and social change: Improving adolescents' career opportunities. In L. J. Crockett & R. K. Silbereisen (Eds.), *Negotiating adolescence in times of social change* (pp. 267–283). New York: Cambridge University Press.

Hamm, J. V. (2000). Do birds of a feather flock together? The variable bases for African American, Asian American, and European American adolescents' selection of similar friends. *Developmental Psychology, 36,* 209–219.

Hammes, B., & Laitman, C. J. (2003). Diethylstilbestrol (DES) update: Recommendations for the identification and management of DES-exposed individuals. *Journal of Midwifery and Women's Health, 48,* 19–29.

Han, J. J., Leichtman, M. D., & Wang, Q. (1998). Autobiographical memory in Korean, Chinese, and American children. *Developmental Psychology, 34,* 701–713.

Hanawalt, B. A. (1993). *Growing up in medieval London: The experience of childhood in history.* New York: Oxford University Press.

Hanawalt, B. A. (2003). The child in the Middle Ages and the Renaissance. In W. Koops & M. Zuckerman (Eds.), *Beyond the century of childhood: Cultural history and developmental psychology.* Philadelphia: University of Pennsylvania Press.

Handler, A. S., Mason, E. D., Rosenberg, D. L., & Davis, F. G. (1994). The relationship between exposure during pregnancy to cigarette smoking and cocaine use and placenta previa. *American Journal of Obstetrics and Gynecology, 170,* 884–889.

Hanel, M. L., & Wevrick, R. (2001). The role of genomic imprinting in human developmental disorders: Lessons from Prader-Willi syndrome. *Clinical Genetics, 59,* 156–164.

Hansen, M., Kurinczuk, J. J., Bower, C., & Webb, S. (2002). The risk of major birth defects after intracytoplasmic sperm injection and in vitro fertilization. *New England Journal of Medicine, 346,* 725–730.

Hanson, T. L. (1999). Does parental conflict explain why divorce is negatively associated with child welfare? *Social Forces, 77,* 1283–1316.

Harari, M. D., & Moulden, A. (2000). Nocturnal enuresis: What is happening? *Journal of Paediatrics and Child Health, 36,* 78–81.

Hardre, P. L., & Reeve, J. (2003). A motivational model of rural students' intentions to persist in, versus drop out of, high school. *Journal of Educational Psychology, 95,* 347–356.

Hardy, C. L., Bukowski, W. M., & Sippola, L. K. (2002). Stability and change in peer relationships during the transition to middle-level school. *Journal of Early Adolescence, 22,* 117–142.

Harley, B., & Jean, G. (1999). Vocabulary skills of French immersion students in their second language. *Zeitschrift für Interkulterellen Fremdsprachenunterricht, 4*(2). Retrieved from www.ualberta.ca

Harlow, H. F., & Zimmerman, R. (1959). Affectional responses in the infant monkey. *Science, 130,* 421–432.

Harnisch, D. L., Steinkamp, M. W., Tsai, S. L., & Walberg, H. J. (1986). Cross-national differences in mathematics attitude and achievement among seventeen-year-olds. *International Journal of Educational Development, 6,* 233–244.

Harris, G. (1997). Development of taste perception and appetite regulation. In G. Bremner, A. Slater, & G. Butterworth (Eds.), *Infant development: Recent advances* (pp. 9–30). East Sussex, U.K.: Erlbaum.

Harris, J. R. (1998). *The nurture assumption: Why children turn out the way they do.* New York: Free Press.

Harris, K. M. (2000). The health status and risk behavior of adolescents in immigrant families. In D. J. Hernandez (Ed.), *Children of immigrants: Health, adjustment, and public assistance.* Washington, DC: National Academy Press.

Harris, P. L., & Leevers, H. J. (2000). Reasoning from false premises. In P. Mitchell & K. J. Riggs (Eds.), *Children's reasoning and the mind* (pp. 67–99). Hove, U.K.: Psychology Press.

Harris, P. L., Brown, E., Marriott, C., Whitall, S., & Harmer, S. (1991). Monsters, ghosts and witches: Testing the limits of the fantasy–reality distinction in young children. *British Journal of Developmental Psychology, 9,* 105–123.

Harris, S., Buchinski, B., Gryzbowski, S., Janssen, P., Mitchell, G. W., & Farquharson, D. (2001). Induction of labour: A continuous quality improvement and peer review program to improve the quality of care. *Canadian Medical Association Journal, 163,* 163–171.

Harrison, A. O., Wilson, M. N., Pine, C. J., Chan, S. Q., & Buriel, R. (1994). Family ecologies of ethnic minority children. In G. Handel & G. G. Whitchurch (Eds.), *The psychosocial interior of the family* (pp. 187–210). New York: Aldine De Gruyter.

Harrison, L. J., & Ungerer, J. A. (2002). Maternal employment and infant–mother attachment security at 12 months postpartum. *Developmental Psychology, 38,* 758–773.

Harrist, A. W., Zaia, A. F., Bates, J. E., Dodge, K. A., & Pettit, G. S. (1997). Subtypes of social withdrawal in early childhood: Sociometric status and social-cognitive differences across four years. *Child Development, 68,* 278–294.

Hart, B., & Risley, T. R. (1995). *Meaningful differences in the everyday experience of young American children.* Baltimore: Paul H. Brookes.

Hart, C. H., Burts, D. C., Durland, M. A., Charlesworth, R., DeWolf, M., & Fleege, P. O. (1998). Stress behaviors and activity type participation of preschoolers in more and less developmentally appropriate classrooms: SES and sex differences. *Journal of Research in Childhood Education, 13.*

Hart, C. H., Nelson, D. A., Robinson, C. C., Olsen, S. F., McNeilly-Choque, M. K., Porter, C. L., & McKee, T. R. (2002). Russian parenting styles and family processes: Linkages with subtypes of victimization and aggression. In K. A. Kerns, J. M. Contreras, & A. M. Neal-Barnett (Eds.), *Family and peers: Linking two social worlds,* Westport, CT: Praeger.

Hart, C. H., Newell, L. D., & Olsen, S. F. (2002). Parenting skills and social/communicative competence in childhood. In J. O. Greene & B. R. Burleson (Eds.), *Handbook of communication and social interaction skill.* Hillsdale, NJ: Erlbaum.

Hart, C. H., Yang, C., Nelson, L. J., Robinson, C. C., Olsen, J. A., Nelson, D. A., et al. (2000). Peer acceptance in early childhood and subtypes of socially withdrawn behavior in China, Russia and the United States. *International Journal of Behavioral Development, 24,* 73–81.

Hart, D., & Atkins, R. (2002). Civic competence in urban youth. *Applied Developmental Science, 6,* 227–236.

Hart, D., Atkins, R., & Ford, D. (1998). Urban America as a context for the development of moral identity in adolescence. *Journal of Social Issues, 54,* 513–530.

Hart, D., & Fegley, S. (1995). Prosocial behavior and caring in adolescence: Relations to self-understanding and social judgment. *Child Development, 66,* 1346–1359.

Hart, D., Fegley, S., & Brengelman, D. (1993). Perceptions of past, present, and future selves among children and adolescents. *British Journal of Developmental Psychology, 11,* 265–282.

Hart, S., Field, T., & Roitfarb, M. (1999). Depressed mothers' assessments of their neonates' behaviors. *Infant Mental Health Journal, 20,* 200–210.

Harter, S. (1998). The development of self-representations. In N. Eisenberg (Ed.), *Handbook of child psychology: Vol. 3. Social, emotional, and personality development* (5th ed., pp. 553–618). New York: Wiley.

Harter, S. (1999). *The construction of self: A developmental perspective.* New York: Guilford.

Harter, S. (2003). The development of self-representations during childhood and adolescence. In M. R. Leary & J. P. Tangney (Eds.), *Hand-*book of self and identity (pp. 610–642). New York: Guilford.

Harter, S., & Monsour, A. (1992). Developmental analysis of conflict caused by opposing attributes in the adolescent self-portrait. *Developmental Psychology, 28,* 251–260.

Harter, S., & Whitesell, N. (1989). Developmental changes in children's understanding of simple, multiple, and blended emotion concepts. In C. Saarni & P. Harris (Eds.), *Children's understanding of emotion* (pp. 81–116). Cambridge, U.K.: Cambridge University Press.

Harter, S., & Whitesell, N. R. (2003). Beyond the debate: Why some adolescents report stable self-worth over time and situation, whereas others report changes in self-worth. *Journal of Personality, 71,* 1027–1058.

Hartshorn, K., Rovee-Collier, C., Gerhardstein, P., Bhatt, R. S., Klein, P. J., Aaron, F., Wondoloski, T. L., & Wurtzel, N. (1998a). Developmental changes in the specificity of memory over the first year of life. *Developmental Psychobiology, 33,* 61–78.

Hartshorn, K., Rovee-Collier, C., Gerhardstein, P., Bhatt, R. S., Wondoloski, T. L., Klein, P., Gilch, J., Wurtzel, N., & Campos-de-Carvalho, M. (1998b). The ontogeny of long-term memory over the first year-and-a-half of life. *Developmental Psychobiology, 32,* 69–89.

Hartup, W. W. (1999). Peer experience and its developmental significance. In M. Bennett (Ed.), *Developmental psychology: Achievements and prospects* (pp. 106–125). Philadelphia, PA: Psychology Press.

Hartup, W. W., & Stevens, N. (1999). Friendships and adaptation across the life span. *Current Directions in Psychological Science, 8,* 76–79.

Haselager, G. J. T., Hartup, W. W., van Lieshout, C. F. M., & Riksen-Walraven, J. M. A. (1998). Similarities between friends and nonfriends in middle childhood. *Child Development, 69,* 1198–1208.

Hassan, M. A., & Killick, S. R. (2003). Effect of male age on fertility: Evidence for the decline in male fertility with increasing age. *Fertility and Sterility, 79,* 1520–1527.

Hatch, M. C., Shu, X.-O., McLean, D. E., Levin, B., Begg, M., Reuss, L., & Susser, M. (1993). Maternal exercise during pregnancy, physical fitness, and fetal growth. *American Journal of Epidemiology, 137,* 1105–1114.

Hatton, D. D., Bailey, D. B., Jr., Burchinal, M. R., & Ferrell, K. A. (1997). Developmental growth curves of preschool children with vision impairments. *Child Development, 68,* 788–806.

Hauser, S. T., Powers, S. I., & Noam, G. G. (1991). *Adolescents and their families: Paths of ego development.* New York: Free Press.

Hausfather, A., Toharia, A., LaRoche, C., & Engelsmann, F. (1997). Effects of age of entry, day-care quality, and family characteristics on preschool behavior. *Journal of Child Psychology and Psychiatry, 38,* 441–448.

Hauth, J. C., Goldenberg, R. L., Parker, C. R., Cutter, G. R., & Cliver, S. P. (1995). Low-dose aspirin—lack of association with an increase in abruptio placentae or perinatal mortality. *Obstetrics and Gynecology, 85,* 1055–1058.

Hawke, S., & Knox, D. (1978). The one-child family: A new life-style. *The Family Coordinator, 27,* 215–219.

Hawker, D. S. J., & Boulton, M. J. (2000). Twenty years' research on peer victimization and psychosocial maladjustment: A meta-analytic review of cross-sectional studies. *Journal of Child Psychology and Psychiatry, 41,* 441–455.

Hawkins, D. J., & Lam, T. (1987). Teacher practices, social development, and delinquency. In J. D. Burchard & S. N. Burchard (Eds.), *Prevention of delinquent behavior* (pp. 241–274). Newbury Park, CA: Sage.

Hawkins, J. N. (1994). Issues of motivation in Asian education. In H. F. O'Neil, Jr., & M. Drillings (Eds.), *Motivation: Theory and research* (pp. 101–115). Hillsdale, NJ: Erlbaum.

Hayne, H., Boniface, J., & Barr, R. (2000). The development of declarative memory in human infants: Age-related changes in deferred imitation. *Behavioral Neuroscience, 114,* 77–83.

Hayne, H., & Rovee-Collier, C. K. (1995). The organization of reactivated memory in infancy. *Child Development, 66,* 893–906.

Hayne, H., Rovee-Collier, C., & Perris, E. E. (1987). Categorization and memory retrieval by three-month-olds. *Child Development, 58,* 750–767.

Hayslip, B., Jr. (1994). Stability of intelligence. In R. J. Sternberg (Ed.), *Encyclopedia of human intelligence* (Vol. 2, pp. 1019–1026). New York: Macmillan.

Hazan, C., & Shaver P. R. (1994). Attachment as an organizational framework for research on close relationships. *Psychological Inquiry, 5,* 1–22.

Head Start Bureau. (2003). 2003 Head Start fact sheet. Retrieved from http://www.acf.dhhs.gov/programs/opa/facts/headst/htm

Health Canada. (1999). *Injury surveillance 1999.* Retrieved from http://www.hc-sc.gc.ca

Health Canada. (2000a). *Aboriginal Head Start in urban and northern communities.* Ottawa: Minister of Health.

Health Canada. (2000b). *Canadian perinatal health report 2000.* Retrieved from http://www.hc-sc.gc.ca/pphb-dgspsp/publicat/cphr-rspc00

Health Canada. (2000c). *Paediatrics and child health: Canadian Report on Immunization, 1997.* Retrieved from http://www.hc-sc.gc.ca

Health Canada. (2001a). Percentage of teenage pregnancies ending in abortion. *Health Reports, 12,* No. 1.

Health Canada. (2001b). *Prenatal and postpartum women and tobacco.* Ottawa: Tobacco Control Programme. Retrieved from http://www.hc-sc.gc.ca/hecs-sesc/tobacco/pdf/prenatal.pdf

Health Canada. (2002a). *Breastfeeding.* Canadian Perinatal Surveillance System. Retrieved from http://www.hc-sc.gc.ca/pphb-dgspsp/rhs-ssg/factshts/brstfd_e.html

Health Canada. (2002b). The Canada Prenatal Nutrition Program. Retrieved from http://www.hc-sc.gc.ca/hppb/childhoodyouth/cbp/cpnp/index.html

Health Canada. (2002c). *Childhood injury: Deaths and hospitalizations in Canada.* Retrieved from http://www.hc-sc.ca

Health Canada. (2002d). Disease surveillance online. Retrieved from www.hc-sc.gc.ca/pphb-dgspsp/dsol-smed/index.html

Health Canada. (2002e). *Healthy Canadians: A federal report on comparable health indicators.* Retrieved from www.hc-sc.gc.ca/iacb-dgiac/arad-draa/english/accountability/indicators/html#high

Health Canada. (2002f). *Proceedings of a meeting of the Expert Advisory Group on Rubella in Canada.* Retrieved from http://www.hc-sc.gc.ca/pphb-dgspsp/publicat/ccdr-rmtc/02vol28/28s4

Health Canada. (2003a). *Acting on what we know: Preventing youth suicide in First Nations.* Ottawa: Author.

Health Canada. (2003b). Alcohol and pregnancy. Retrieved from http://www.hc-sc.gc.ca/pphb-dgspsp/rhs-ssg/factshts/alcprg_e.html

Health Canada. (2003c). Women and HIV/AIDS in Canada. Retrieved from http://www.actoronto.org/website/home.nsf/pages/womenhivaidscanada

Heath, S. B. (1982). Questioning at home and at school: A comparative study. In G. Spindler (Ed.), *Doing the ethnography of schooling: Educational anthropology in action* (pp. 102–127). New York: Holt.

Heath, S. B. (1989). Oral and literate traditions among black Americans living in poverty. *American Psychologist, 44,* 367–373.

Heath, S. B. (1990). The children of Trackton's children: Spoken and written language in social change. In J. Stigler, G. Herdt, & R. A. Shweder (Eds.), *Cultural psychology: Essays on comparative human development* (pp. 496–519). New York: Cambridge University Press.

Hedges, L. V., & Nowell, A. (1995). Sex differences in mental scores, variability, and numbers of high-scoring individuals. *Science, 269,* 41–45.

Hedges, L. V., & Nowell, A. (1998). Black–white test score convergence since 1995. In C. Jencks & M. Phillips (Eds.), *The black–white test score gap* (pp.149–181). Washington, DC: Brookings Institution.

Hediger, M. L., Overpeck, M. D., Ruan, W. J., & Troendle, J. F. (2002). Birthweight and gestational age effects on motor and social development. *Paediatric and Perinatal Epidemiology, 16,* 33–46.

Heine, S. J., & Lehman, D. R. (1995). Cultural variation in unrealistic optimism: Does the West feel more invulnerable than the East? *Journal of Personality and Social Psychology, 68,* 595–607.

Heinz, A., & Blass, J. P. (2002). *Alzheimer's disease: A status report for 2002.* New York: American Council on Science and Health.

Heinz, W. R. (1999a). Introduction: Transitions to employment in a cross-national perspective. In W. R. Heinz (Ed.), *From education to work: Cross-national perspectives* (pp. 1–21). New York: Cambridge University Press.

Heinz, W. R. (1999b). Job-entry patterns in a life-course perspective. In W. R. Heinz (Ed.), *From education to work: Cross-national perspectives* (pp. 214–231). New York: Cambridge University Press.

Helburn, S. W. (Ed.). (1995). *Cost, quality and child outcomes in child care centers.* Denver: University of Colorado.

Helwig, C. C., Arnold, M. L., Tan, D., & Boyd, D. (2003). Chinese adolescents' reasoning about democratic and authority-based decision making in peer, family, and school contexts. *Child Development, 74,* 783–800.

Helwig, C. C., & Jasiobedzka, U. (2001). The relation between law and morality: Children's reasoning about socially beneficial and unjust laws. *Child Development, 72,* 1382–1393.

Helwig, C. C., & Kim, S. (1999). Children's evaluations of decision making procedures in peer, family, and school contexts. *Child Development, 70,* 502–512.

Helwig, C. C., & Prencipe, A. (1999). Children's judgments of flags and flag-burning. *Child Development, 70,* 132–143.

Helwig, C. C., & Turiel, E. (2002). Civil liberties, autonomy, and democracy: Children's perspective. *International Journal of Law and Psychiatry, 25,* 253–270.

Henrich, C. C., Brown, J. L., & Aber, J. L. (1999). Evaluating the effectiveness of school-based violence prevention: Developmental approaches. *Social Policy Report of the Society for Research in Child Development, 8*(3).

Henrich, C. C., Kuperminc, G. P., Sack, A., Blatt, S. J., & Leadbeater, B. J. (2000). Characteristics and homogeneity of early adolescent friendship groups: A comparison of male and female clique and nonclique members. *Applied Developmental Science, 4,* 15–26.

Henshaw, S. K. (1998). Unintended pregnancy in the United States. *Family Planning Perspectives, 30,* 24–29.

Herbert, J., & Hayne, H. (2000). The ontogeny of long-term retention during the second year of life. *Developmental Science, 3,* 50–56.

Herdt, G., & Boxer, A. M. (1993). *Children of horizons: How gay and lesbian teens are leading a new way out of the closet.* Boston: Beacon Press.

Hergenrather, J. R., & Rabinowitz, M. (1991). Age-related differences in the organization of children's knowledge of illness. *Developmental Psychology, 27,* 952–959.

Herman, M. R., Dornbusch, S. M., Herron, M. C., & Herting, J. R. (1997). The influence of family regulation, connection, and psychological autonomy on six measures of adolescent functioning. *Journal of Adolescent Research, 12,* 34–67.

Hernandez, D. J. (1994, Spring). Children's changing access to resources: A historical perspective. *Social Policy Report of the Society for Research in Child Development, 8*(1).

Hernandez, F. D., & Carter, A. S. (1996). Infant response to mothers and fathers in the still-face paradigm. *Infant Behavior and Development, 19,* 502.

Herrnstein, R. J., & Murray, C. (1994). *The bell curve.* New York: Free Press.

Hespos, S. J., & Baillargeon, R. (2001). Reasoning about containment events in very young infants. *Cognition, 78,* 207–245.

Hesse, E., & Main, M. (2000). Disorganized infant, child, and adult attachment: Collapse in behavioral and attentional strategies. *Journal of the American Psychoanalytic Association, 48,* 1097–1127.

Hetherington, E. M. (1999a). Should we stay together for the sake of the children? In E. M. Hetherington (ed.), *Coping with divorce, single parenting, and remarriage: A risk and resiliency perspective* (pp. 93–116). Hillsdale, NJ: Erlbaum.

Hetherington, E. M. (1999b). Social capital and the development of youth from nondivorced, divorced, and remarried families. In A. Collins (Ed.), *Minnesota Symposia on Child Psychology* (Vol. 29, pp. 177–209). Hillsdale, NJ: Erlbaum.

Hetherington, E. M., & Jodl, K. M. (1994). Stepfamilies as settings for child development. In A. Booth & J. Dunn (Eds.) *Stepfamilies: Who benefits? Who does not?* (pp. 55–79). Hillsdale, NJ: Erlbaum.

Hetherington, E. M., & Henderson, S. H., & Reiss, D. (1999). Adolescent siblings in stepfamilies: Family functioning and adolescent adjustment.

Monographs of the Society for Research in Child Development, 64(4, Serial No. 259).

Hetherington, E. M., & Kelly, J. (2003). *For better or worse: Divorce reconsidered.* New York: Norton.

Hetherington, E. M., & Stanley-Hagan, M. (1999). The adjustment of children with divorced parents: A risk and resiliency perspective. *Journal of Child Psychology and Psychiatry, 40,* 129–140.

Hetherington, E. M., & Stanley-Hagan, M. (2000). Diversity among stepfamilies. In D. H. Demo, K. R. Allen, & M. A. Fine (Eds.), *Handbook of family diversity* (pp. 173–196). New York: Oxford University Press.

Hetherington, E. M., & Stanley-Hagan, M. (2002). Parenting in divorced and remarried families. In M. H. Bornstein (Ed.), *Handbook of parenting: Vol. 3. Being and becoming a parent* (2nd ed., pp. 287–315). Mahwah, NJ: Erlbaum.

Hetherington, P. (1995, March). *The changing American family and the well-being of children.* Master lecture presented at the biennial meeting of the Society for Research in Child Development, Indianapolis.

Hewlett, B. S. (1992). Husband–wife reciprocity and the father–infant relationship among Aka pygmies. In B. S. Hewlett (Ed.), *Father–child relations: Cultural and biosocial contexts* (pp. 153– 176). New York: Aldine De Gruyter.

Hewlett, S. (2003). *Creating a life.* New York: Miramax.

Heyman, G. D., & Dweck, C. S. (1992). Achievement goals and intrinsic motivation: Their relation and their role in adaptive motivation. *Motivation and Emotion, 16,* 231–247.

Heyman, G. D., & Dweck, C. S. (1998). Children's thinking about traits: Implications for judgments of the self and others. *Child Development, 69,* 391–403.

Heyman, G. D., & Gelman, S. A. (1999). The use of trait labels in making psychological inferences. *Child Development, 70,* 604–619.

Hibell, B. (2001). *European School Survey Project on Alcohol and Drugs.* Stockholm: Swedish Council for Information on Alcohol and Other Drugs.

Hickling, A. K., & Wellman, H. M. (2001). The emergence of children's causal explanations and theories: Evidence from everyday conversation. *Developmental Psychology, 37,* 668–683.

Hier, D. B., & Crowley, W. F. (1982). Spatial ability in androgen-deficient men. *New England Journal of Medicine, 302,* 1202–1205.

High, P. C., LaGasse, L., Becker, S., Ahlgren, I., & Gardner, A. (2000). Literacy promotion in primary care pediatrics: Can we make a difference? *Pediatrics, 105,* 927–934.

Hildreth, K., & Rovee-Collier, C. (2002). Forgetting functions of reactivated memories over the first year of life. *Developmental Psychobiology, 41,* 277–288.

Hildreth, K., Sweeney, B., & Rovee-Collier, C. (2003). Differential memory-preserving effects of reminders at 6 months. *Journal of Experimental Child Psychology, 84,* 41–62.

Hill, J. P., & Holmbeck, G. N. (1986). Attachment and autonomy during adolescence. In G. Whitehurst (Ed.), *Annals of child development* (Vol. 3, pp. 145–189). Greenwich, CT: JAI Press.

Hille, E., den Ouden, A. L., Saigal, S., Wolke, D., Lambert, M., & Whitaker, A. (2001). Behavioural problems in children who weigh 1000 g or less at birth in four countries. *Lancet, 357,* 1641–1643.

Hinde, R. A. (1989). Ethological and relationships approaches. In R. Vasta (Ed.), *Annals of child development* (Vol. 6, pp. 251–285). Greenwich, CT: JAI Press.

Hines, M., Golombok, S., Rust, J., Johnston, K. J., Golding, J., & the ALSPAC Study Team. (2002). Testosterone during pregnancy and gender role behavior of preschool children: A longitudinal, population study. *Child Development, 73,* 1678–1687.

Hines, M., & Green, R. (1991). Human hormonal and neural correlates of sex-typed behaviors. *Review of Psychiatry, 10,* 536–555.

Hirsh-Pasek, K., Kemler Nelson, D. G., Jusczyk, P. W., Cassidy, K. W., Druss, B., & Kennedy, L. (1987). Clauses are perceptual units for young infants. *Cognition, 26,* 269–286.

Hjälmäs, K. (1998). Nocturnal enuresis: Basic facts and new horizons. *European Urology, 33*(Suppl. 3), 53–57.

Ho, C. S., & Fuson, K. C. (1998). Children's knowledge of teen quantities as tens and ones: Comparisons of Chinese, British, and American kindergartners. *Journal of Educational Psychology, 90,* 536–544.

Hock, H. S., Park, C. L., & Bjorklund, D. F. (1998). Temporal organization in children's strategy formation. *Journal of Experimental Child Psychology, 70,* 187–206.

Hodapp, R. M. (1996). Down syndrome: Developmental, psychiatric, and management issues. *Child and Adolescent Psychiatric Clinics of North America, 5,* 881–894.

Hodges, E. V. E., Boivin, M., Vitaro, F., & Bukowski, W. M. (1999). The power of friendship: Protection against an escalating cycle of peer victimization. *Developmental Psychology, 35,* 94–101.

Hodges, J., & Tizard, B. (1989). Social and family relationships of ex-institutional adolescents. *Journal of Child Psychology and Psychiatry, 30,* 77–97.

Hodges, R. M., & French, L. A. (1988). The effect of class and collection labels on cardinality, class-inclusion, and number conservation tasks. *Child Development, 59,* 1387–1396.

Hoff, E., Laursen, B., & Tardiff, T. (2002). Socioeconomic status and parenting. In M. H. Bornstein (Ed.), *Handbook of parenting: Vol. 2. Biology and ecology of parenting* (pp. 231–252). Mahwah, NJ: Erlbaum.

Hoff, E., & Naigles, L. (2002). How children use input to acquire a lexicon. *Child Development, 73,* 418–433.

Hofferth, S. L., & Anderson, K. G. (2003). Are all dads equal? Biology versus marriage as a basis for paternal investment. *Journal of Marriage and the Family, 65,* 213–232.

Hoffman, L. W. (2000). Maternal employment: Effects of social context. In R. D. Taylor & M. C. Wang (Eds.), *Resilience across contexts: Family, work, culture, and community* (pp. 147–176). Mahwah, NJ: Erlbaum.

Hoffman, L. W., & Youngblade, L. M. (1999). *Mothers at work: Effects on children's well-being.* New York: Cambridge University Press.

Hoffman, M. L. (2000). *Empathy and moral development.* New York: Cambridge University Press.

Hoffman, S., & Hatch, M. C. (1996). Stress, social support and pregnancy outcome: A reassessment based on research. *Paediatric and Perinatal Epidemiology, 10,* 380–405.

Hoffman-La Roche. (2000). *FDA Dermatologic and Ophthalmic Drugs Advisory Committee Briefing Document for NDA 18-662 Accutane (isotretinoin capsules).* Retrieved from www.fda.gov/ohrms/docket/ac/00/backgrd/3639b1c

Hoffmann, W. (2001). Fallout from the Chernobyl nuclear disaster and congenital malformations in Europe. *Archives of Environmental Health, 56,* 478–483.

Hoffner, C., & Badzinski, D. M. (1989). Children's integration of facial and situational cues to emotion. *Child Development, 60,* 411–422.

Hofstadter, M., & Reznick, J. S. (1996). Response modality affects human infant delayed-response performance. *Child Development, 67,* 646–658.

Hokoda, A., & Fincham, F. D. (1995). Origins of children's helpless and mastery achievement patterns in the family. *Journal of Educational Psychology, 87,* 375–385.

Holcomb, T. F. (1990). Fourth graders' attitudes toward AIDS issues: A concern for the elementary school counselor. *Elementary School Guidance and Counseling, 25,* 83–90.

Holden, G. W., Coleman, S. M., & Schmidt, K. L. (1995). Why 3-year-old children get spanked: Determinants as reported by college-educated mothers. *Merrill-Palmer Quarterly, 41,* 431–452.

Holland, J. L. (1966). *The psychology of vocational choice.* Waltham, MA: Blaisdell.

Holland, J. L. (1985). *Making vocational choices: A theory of vocational personalities and work environments.* Englewood Cliffs, NJ; Prentice-Hall.

Hollich, G. J., Hirsh-Pasek, K., & Golinkoff, R. M. (2000). Breaking the language barrier: An emergentist coalition model for the origins of word learning. *Monographs of the Society for Research in Child Development, 65*(3, Serial No. 262).

Holmbeck, G. N. (1996). A model of family relational transformations during the transition to adolescence: Parent–adolescent conflict and adaptation. In J. A. Graber, J. Brooks-Gunn, & A. C. Petersen (Eds.), *Transitions through adolescence* (pp. 167–199). Mahwah, NJ: Erlbaum.

Holmbeck, G. N., Paikoff, R. L., & Brooks-Gunn, J. (1995). Parenting adolescents. In M. H. Bornstein (Ed.), *Handbook of parenting: Vol. 1. Children and parenting* (pp. 91–118). Mahwah, NJ: Erlbaum.

Holobow, N., Genessee, F., & Lambert, W. (1991). The effectiveness of a foreign language immersion program for children from different ethnic and social class backgrounds: Report 2. *Applied Psycholinguistics, 12,* 179–198.

Holowka, S., Brosseau-Lapré, F., & Petitto, L. A. (2002). Semantic and conceptual knowledge underlying bilingual babies' first signs and words. *Language Learning, 52,* 205–262.

Holsen, I., Kraft, P., & Vittersø, J. (2000). Stability in depressed mood in adolescence: Results from a 6-year longitudinal study. *Journal of Youth and Adolescence, 29,* 61–78.

Honein, M. A., Moore, C. A., Lyon Daniel, K., & Erickson, J. D. (2002). Problems with informing women adequately about teratogen risk: Some barriers to preventing exposures to known teratogens. *Teratology, 66,* 202–204.

Honein, M. A., Paulozzi, L. J., & Erickson, J. D. (2001). Continued occurrence of Accutane-exposed pregnancies. *Teratology, 64,* 142–147.

Hood, B. M., Atkinson, J., & Braddick, O. J. (1998). Selection-for-action and the development of orienting and visual attention. In J. E. Richards (Ed.), *Cognitive neuroscience of attention: A developmental perspective* (pp. 219–251). Mahwah, NJ: Erlbaum.

Hope, S., Power, C., & Rodgers, B. (1999). Does financial hardship account for elevated psychological distress in lone mothers? *Social Science and Medicine, 29,* 381–389.

Hopkins, B., & Butterworth, G. (1997). Dyamical systems approaches to the development of action. In G. Bremner, A. Slater, & G. Butterworth (Eds.), *Infant development: Recent advances* (pp. 75–100). East Sussex, U.K.: Psychology Press.

Hopkins, B., & Westra, T. (1988). Maternal handling and motor development: An intracultural study. *Genetic, Social and General Psychology Monographs, 14*, 377–420.

Hopkins-Golightly, T., Raz, S., & Sander, C. J. (2003). Influence of slight to moderate risk for birth hypoxia on acquisition of cognitive and language function in the preterm infant: A cross-sectional comparison with preterm-birth controls. *Neuropsychology, 17*, 3–13.

Horgan, D. (1978). The development of the full passive. *Journal of Child Language, 5*, 65–80.

Horn, J. M. (1983). The Texas Adoption Project: Adopted children and their intellectual resemblance to biological and adoptive parents. *Child Development, 54*, 268–275.

Horner, T. M. (1980). Two methods of studying stranger reactivity in infants: A review. *Journal of Child Psychology and Psychiatry, 21*, 203–219.

Horowitz, F. D. (1992). John B. Watson's legacy: Learning and environment. *Developmental Psychology, 28*, 360–367.

Hotz, V. J., McElroy, S. W., & Sanders, S. G. (1997). The costs and consequences of teenage childbearing for mothers. In R. A. Maynard (Ed.), *Kids having kids* (pp. 55–94). Washington, DC: Urban Institute.

Houts, A. C. (2003). Behavioral treatment for enuresis. In A. E. Kazdin (Ed.), *Evidence-based psychotherapies for children and adolescents* (pp. 389–406). New York: Guilford.

Howard, A. W. (2002). Automobile restraints for children: A review for clinicians. *Canadian Medical Association Journal, 167*, 769–773.

Howard, B. J., & Wong, J. (2001). Sleep disorders. *Pediatrics in Review, 22*, 327–342.

Howe, M. L. (2003). Memories from the cradle. *Current Directions in Psychological Science, 12*, 62–65.

Howe, N., Aquan-Assee, J., & Bukowski, W. M. (2001). Predicting sibling relations over time: Synchrony between maternal management styles and sibling relationship quality. *Merrill-Palmer Quarterly, 47*, 121–141.

Howe, N., Aquan-Assee, J., Bukowski, W. M., Lehoux, P. M., & Rinaldi, C. M. (2001). Siblings as confidants: Emotional understanding, relationship warmth, and sibling self-disclosure. *Social Development, 10*, 439–454.

Howes, C. (1988). Peer interaction of young children. *Monographs of the Society for Research in Child Development, 53*(1, Serial No. 217).

Howes, C. (1988). Relations between early child care and schooling. *Developmental Psychology, 24*, 53–57.

Howes, C., & Hamilton, C. E. (1993). The changing experience of child care: Changes in teachers and in teacher–child relationships and children's social competence with peers. *Early Childhood Research Quarterly, 8*, 15–32.

Howes, C., Hamilton, C. E., Phillipsen, L. C. (1998). Stability and continuity of child–caregiver and child–peer relationships. *Child Development, 69*, 418–426.

Howes, C., & Matheson, C. C. (1992). Sequences in the development of competent play with peers: Social and social pretend play. *Developmental Psychology, 28*, 961–974.

Hudson, J. A., Fivush, R., & Kuebli, J. (1992). Scripts and episodes: The development of event memory. *Applied Cognitive Psychology, 6*, 483–505.

Hudson, J. A., Sosa, B. B., & Shapiro, L. R. (1997). Scripts and plans: The development of preschool children's event knowledge and event planning. In S. L. Friedman & E. K. Scholnick (Eds.), *The developmental psychology of planning* (pp. 77–102). Mahwah, NJ: Erlbaum.

Huesmann, L. R. (1986). Psychological processes promoting the relation between exposure to media violence and aggressive behavior by the viewer. *Journal of Social Issues, 42*, 125–139.

Huesmann, L. R., Moise-Titus, J., Podolski, C., & Eron, L. D. (2003). Longitudinal relations between children's exposure to TV violence and their aggressive and violent behavior in young adulthood: 1977–1992. *Developmental Psychology, 39*, 201–221.

Huey, S. J., Jr., & Henggeler, S. W. (2001). Effective community-based interventions for antisocial and delinquent adolescents. In J. N. Hughes & A. M. La Greca (Eds.), *Handbook of psychological services for children and adolescents* (pp. 301–322). London: Oxford University Press.

Hughes, C. (1998). Finding your marbles: Does preschoolers' strategic behavior predict later understanding of mind? *Developmental Psychology, 34*, 1326–1339.

Hughes, C., & Dunn, J. (1998). Understanding mind and emotion: Longitudinal associations with mental-state talk between young friends. *Developmental Psychology, 34*, 1026–1037.

Hughes, C. A., & Filbert, M. (2000). Computer-assisted instruction in reading for students with learning disabilities: A research synthesis. *Education and Treatment of Children, 23*, 173–183.

Hughes, D. C., & Ng, S. (2003). Reducing health disparities among children. *Future of Children, 13*, 153–167.

Hughes, J. N., Cavell, T. A., & Grossman, P. B. (1997). A positive view of self: Risk or protection for aggressive children? *Development and Psychopathology, 9*, 75–94.

Human Resources Development Canada. (2000). *Dropping out of high school: Definitions and costs.* Hull, Quebec: Author.

Humphrey, T. (1978). Function of the nervous system during prenatal life. In U. Stave (Ed.), *Perinatal physiology* (pp. 651–683). New York: Plenum.

Hunsberger, B., Pratt, M., & Pancer, S. M. (2001). Adolescent identity formation: Religious exploration and commitment. *Identity, 1*, 365–386.

Hunt, E., Streissguth, A. P., Kerr, B., & Olson, H. C. (1995). Mothers' alcohol consumption during pregnancy: Effects on spatial-visual reasoning in 14-year-old children. *Psychological Science, 6*, 339–342.

Huntsinger, C. S., Jose, P. E., & Larson, S. L. (1998). Do parent practices to encourage academic competence influence the social adjustment of young European and Chinese American children? *Developmental Psychology, 34*, 747–756.

Hurewitz, F., Brown-Schmidt, S., Thorpe, K., Gleitman, L. R., & Trueswell, J. C. (2000). One frog, two frog, red frog, blue frog: Factors affecting children's syntactic choices in production and comprehension. *Journal of Psycholinguistic Research, 29*, 597–626.

Hursti, U. K. (1999). Factors influencing children's food choice. *Annals of Medicine, 31*, 26–32.

Huston, A. C., & Alvarez, M. M. (1990). The socialization context of gender role development in early adolescence. In R. Montemayor, G. R. Adams, & T. P. Gullotta (Eds.), *From childhood to adolescence: A transitional period?* (pp. 156–179). Newbury Park, CA: Sage.

Huston, A. C., Wright, J. C., Marquis, J., & Green, S. B. (1999). How young children spend their time: Television and other activities. *Developmental Psychology, 35*, 912–925.

Hutinger, P. L., Bell, C., Beard, M., Bond, J., Johanson, J., & Terry, C. (1998). *The early childhood emergent literacy technology research study: Final report.* Macomb, IL: Western Illinois University. ERIC ED 418545.

Huttenlocher, J., Haight, W., Bryk, A., Seltzer, M., & Lyons, T. (1991). Early vocabulary growth: Relation to language input and gender. *Developmental Psychology, 27*, 236–248.

Huttenlocher, P. R. (1994). Synaptogenesis in the human cerebral cortex. In G. Dawson & K. W. Fischer (Eds.), *Human behavior and the developing brain* (pp. 137–152). New York: Guilford.

Huttenlocher, P. R. (2000). Synaptogenesis in human cerebral cortex and the concept of critical periods. In N. A. Fox, L. A. Leavitt, & J. G. Warhol (Eds.), *The role of early experience in infant development* (pp. 15–28). St. Louis, MO: Johnson & Johnson Pediatric Institute.

Huttenlocher, P. R. (2002). *Neural plasticity: The effects of environment on the development of the cerebral cortex.* Cambridge, MA: Harvard University Press.

Hyde, J. S., Klein, M. H., Essex, M. J., & Clark, R. (1995). Maternity leave and women's mental health. *Psychology of Women Quarterly, 19*, 257–285.

Hyde, J. S., & Linn, M. C. (1988). Gender differences in verbal ability: A meta-analysis. *Psychological Bulletin, 104*, 53–69.

Hyde, K. E. (1990). *Religion in childhood and adolescence.* Birmingham, AL: Religious Education Press.

Hymel, S., LeMare, L., Ditner, E., & Woody, E. Z. (1999). Assessing self-concept in children: Variations across self-concept domains. *Merrill-Palmer Quarterly, 45*, 602–623.

Ianni, F. A. J., & Orr, M. T. (1996). Dropping out. In J. A. Graber, J. Brooks-Gunn, & A. C. Petersen (Eds.), *Transitions through adolescence: Interpersonal domains and context* (pp. 285–322). Mahwah, NJ: Erlbaum.

Iglowstein, I., Jenni, O. G., Molinari, L., & Largo, R. H. (2003). Sleep duration from infancy to adolescence: Reference values and generational trends. *Pediatrics, 111*, 302–307.

Inagaki, K., & Hatano, G. (1993). Children's understanding of mind–body distinction. *Child Development, 64*, 1534–1549.

Inhelder, B., & Piaget, J. (1958). *The growth of logical thinking from childhood to adolescence: An essay on the construction of formal operational structures.* New York: Basic Books. (Original work published 1955)

Innocenti Research Center. (2001). *Child deaths by injury in rich nations.* Florence, Italy: United Nations Children's Fund.

International Cesarean Awareness Network. (ICAN). (2003). International Cesarean and VBAC rates. Retrieved from www.ican-online.org/resources/statistics3.htm

Irvine, J. J. (1986). Teacher-student interactions: Effects of student race, sex, and grade level. *Journal of Educational Psychology, 78*, 14–21.

Isabella, R. (1993). Origins of attachment: Maternal interactive behavior across the first year. *Child Development, 64*, 605–621.

Isabella, R., & Belsky, J. (1991). Interactional synchrony and the origins of infant–mother attachment: A replication study. *Child Development, 62*, 373–384.

Ito, M., & Sharts-Hopko, N. C. (2002). Japanese women's experience of childbirth in the United States. *Health Care for Women International, 23*, 666–677.

Izard, C. E. (1979). *The maximally discriminative facial movement scoring system.* Unpublished manuscript, University of Delware.

Izard, C. E. (1991). *The psychology of emotions.* New York: Plenum.

Izard, C. E., & Ackerman, B. P. (2000). Motivational, organizational, and regulatory functions of discrete emotions. In M. Lewis & J. M. Haviland-Jones (Eds.), *Handbook of emotions* (2nd ed., pp. 253–264). New York: Guilford.

Jaccard, J., Dittus, P., & Gordon, V. V. (2000). Parent–adolescent congruency in reports of adolescent sexual behavior and in communications about sexual behavior. *Child Development, 69,* 247–261.

Jaccard, J., Dodge, T., & Dittus, P. (2002). Parent–adolescent communication about sex and birth control: A conceptual framework. In S. S. Feldman & D. A. Rosenthal (Eds.), *Talking sexuality: Parent–adolescent communication* (pp. 9–41). San Francisco: Jossey-Bass.

Jaccard, J., Dodge, T., & Dittus, P. (2003). Maternal discussions about pregnancy and adolescents' attitudes toward pregnancy. *Journal of Adolescent Health, 33,* 84–87.

Jacobs, J. E., & Klaczynski, P. A. (2002). The development of judgment and decision making during childhood and adolescence. *Current Directions in Psychological Science, 11,* 145–149.

Jacobs, J. E., Lanza, S., Osgood, D. W., Eccles, J. S., & Wigfield, A. (2002). Changes in children's self-competence and values: Gender and domain differences across grades one through twelve. *Child Development, 73,* 509–527.

Jacobs, J. E., & Weisz, V. (1994). Gender stereotypes: Implications for gifted education. *Roeper Review, 16,* 152–155.

Jacobson, J. L., Jacobson, S. W., Fein, G., Schwartz, P. M., & Dowler, J. (1984). Prenatal exposure to an environmental toxin: A test of the multiple effects model. *Developmental Psychology, 20,* 523–532.

Jacobson, S. W. (1998). Specificity of neurobehavioral outcomes associated with prenatal alcohol exposure. *Alcoholism: Clinical and Experimental Research, 22,* 313–320.

Jacobson, S. W., Jacobson, J. L., Sokol, R. J., Martier, S. S., & Ager, J. W. (1993). Prenatal alcohol exposure and infant information processing ability. *Child Development, 64,* 1706–1721.

Jadack, R. A., Hyde, J. S., Moore, C. F., & Keller, M. L. (1995). Moral reasoning about sexually transmitted diseases. *Child Development, 66,* 167–177.

Jaffe, J., Beebe, B., Feldstein, S., Crown, C. L., & Jasnow, M. D. (2001). Rhythms of dialogue in infancy. *Monographs of the Society for Research in Child Development, 66*(2, Serial No. 265).

Jaffee, S. R., Caspi, A., Moffitt, T. E., Belsky, J., & Silva, P. (2001). Why are children born to teen mothers at risk for adverse outcomes in young adulthood? *Development and Psychopathology, 13,* 377–397.

Jaffee, S. R., Moffitt, T. E., Caspi, A., & Taylor, A. (2003). Life with (or without) father: The benefits of living with two biological parents depend on the father's antisocial behavior. *Child Development, 74,* 109–126.

Jain, A., Concat, J., & Leventhal, J. M. (2002). How good is the evidence linking breastfeeding and intelligence? *Pediatrics, 109,* 1044–1053.

Jambunathan, S., Burts, D. C., & Pierce, S. (2000). Comparisons of parenting attitudes among five ethnic groups in the United States. *Journal of Comparative Family Studies, 31,* 395–406.

Jameson, S. (1993). Zinc status in pregnancy: The effect of zinc therapy on perinatal mortality, prematurity, and placental ablation. *Annals of the New York Academy of Sciences, 678,* 178–192.

Jamieson, J. R. (1995). Interactions between mothers and children who are deaf. *Journal of Early Intervention, 19,* 108–117.

Jang, S. J., & Johnson, B. R. (2001). Neighborhood disorder, individual religiosity, and adolescent use of illicit drugs: A test of multilevel hypotheses. *Criminology, 39,* 109–143.

Janosz, M., Le Blanc, M., Boulerice, B., & Tremblay, R. E. (2000). Predicting different types of school dropouts: A typological approach with two longitudinal samples. *Journal of Educational Psychology, 92,* 171–190.

Janssen, P. A., Lee, S. K., Ryan, E. M., Etches, D. J., Farquharson, D. F., & Peacock, D. (2002). Outcomes of planned home births versus planned hospital births after regulation of midwifery in British Columbia. *Canadian Medical Association Journal, 166,* 315–323.

Janssens, J. M. A. M., & Deković, M. (1997). Child rearing, prosocial moral reasoning, and prosocial behavior. *International Journal of Behavioral Development, 20,* 509–527.

Jayakody, R., & Kalil, A. (2002). Social fathering in low-income, African-American families with preschool children. *Journal of Marriage and the Family, 64,* 504–516.

Jenkins, J. M., & Astington, J. W. (1996). Cognitive factors and family structure associated with theory of mind development in young children. *Developmental Psychology, 32,* 70–78.

Jenkins, J. M., & Astington, J. W. (2000). Theory of mind and social behavior: Causal models tested in a longitudinal study. *Merrill-Palmer Quarterly, 46,* 203–220.

Jenkins, J. M., Rasbash, J., & O'Connor, T. G. (2003). The role of the shared family context in differential parenting. *Developmental Psychology, 39,* 99–113.

Jenkins, J. M., Turrell, S. L., Kogushi, Y., Lollis, S., & Ross, H. S. (2003). A longitudinal investigation of the dynamics of mental state talk in families. *Child Development, 74,* 905–920.

Jensen, A. R. (1969). How much can we boost IQ and scholastic achievement? *Harvard Educational Review, 39,* 1–123.

Jensen, A. R. (1985). The nature of the black–white difference on various psychometric tests: Spearman's hypothesis. *Behavioral and Brain Sciences, 8,* 193–219.

Jensen, A. R. (1998). *The g factor: The science of mental ability.* New York: Praeger.

Jensen, A. R. (2001). Spearman's hypothesis. In J. M. Collis & S. Messick (Eds.), *Intelligence and personality: Bridging the gap in theory and measurement* (pp. 3–24). Mahwah, NJ: Erlbaum.

Jensen, A. R., & Figueroa, R. A. (1975). Forward and backward digit-span interaction with race and IQ: Predictions from Jensen's theory. *Journal of Educational Psychology, 67,* 882–893.

Jensen, A. R., & Reynolds, C. R. (1982). Race, social class and ability patterns on the WISC-R. *Personality and Individual Differences, 3,* 423–438.

Jeynes, W. H., & Littell, S. W. (2000). A meta-analysis of studies examining the effect of whole language instruction on the literacy of low-SES students. *Elementary School Journal, 101,* 21–33.

Jiao, S., Ji, G., & Jing, Q. (1996). Cognitive development of Chinese urban only children and children with siblings. *Child Development, 67,* 387–395.

Jin, P., & Warren, S. T. (2000). Understanding the molecular basis of fragile X syndrome. *Human Molecular Genetics, 9,* 901–908.

Joe, S., & Marcus, S. C. (2003). Datapoints: Trends by race and gender in suicide attempts among U.S. adolescents. *Psychiatric Services, 54,* 454.

Johnson, D. E. (2000). Medical and developmental sequelae of early childhood institutionalization in Eastern European adoptees. In C. A. Nelson (Ed.), *Minnesota symposia on child psychology* (Vol. 31, pp. 113–162). Mahwah, NJ: Erlbaum.

Johnson, D. E. (2002). Adoption and the effect on children's development. *Early Human Development, 68,* 39–54.

Johnson, J. G., Cohen, P., Smailes, E. M., Kasen, S., & Brook, J. S. (2002). Television viewing and aggressive behavior during adolescence and adulthood. *Science, 295,* 2468–2471.

Johnson, M. (1991). Infant and toddler sleep: A telephone survey of parents in one community. *Developmental and Behavioral Pediatrics, 12,* 108–114.

Johnson, M. H. (1995). The inhibition of automatic saccades in early infancy. *Developmental Psychobiology, 28,* 281–291.

Johnson, M. H. (1998). The neural basis of cognitive development. In D. Kuhn & R. S. Siegler (Eds.), *Handbook of child psychology: Vol. 2. Cognition, perception, and language* (5th ed., pp. 1–49). New York: Wiley.

Johnson, M. H. (1999). Ontogenetic constraints on neural and behavioral plasticity: Evidence from imprinting and face processing. *Canadian Journal of Experimental Psychology, 55,* 77–90.

Johnson, M. H. (2001a). The development and neural basis of face recognition: Comment and speculation. *Infant and Child Development, 10,* 31–33.

Johnson, M. H. (2001b). Infants' initial "knowledge" of the world: A cognitive neuroscience perspective. In F. Lacerda, C. von Hofsten, & M. Heimann (Eds.), *Emerging cognitive abilities in early infancy* (pp. 53–72). Mahwah, NJ: Erlbaum.

Johnson, S. L., & Birch, L. L. (1994). Parents' and children's adiposity and eating style. *Pediatrics, 94,* 653–661.

Johnson, S. P. (1996). Habituation patterns and object perception in young infants. *Journal of Reproductive and Infant Psychology, 14,* 207–218.

Johnson, S. P. (1997). Young infants' perception of object unity: Implications for development of attentional and cognitive skills. *Current Directions in Psychological Science, 6,* 5–11.

Johnson, S. P., Amso, D., & Slemmer, J. A. (2003). Development of object concepts in infancy: Evidence for early learning in an eye-tracking paradigm. *Proceedings of the New York Academy of Sciences, 100,* 10568–10573.

Johnson, S. P., & Aslin, R. N. (1996). Perception of object unity in young infants: The roles of motion, depth, and orientation. *Cognitive Development, 11,* 161–180.

Johnson, S. P., Bremner, J. G., Slater, A. M., Mason, U. C., & Foster, K. (2002). Young infants' perception of unity and form in occlusion displays. *Journal of Experimental Child Psychology, 81,* 358–374.

Johnston, M. V., Nishimura, A., Harum, K., Pekar, J., & Blue, M. E. (2001). Sculpting the developing brain. *Advances in Pediatrics, 48,* 1–38.

Jones, F. (2003). Religious commitment in Canada, 1997 and 2000. *Religious Commitment Monograph No. 3.* Ottawa: Christian Commitment Research Institute.

Jones, G. P., & Dembo, M. H. (1989). Age and sex role differences in intimate friendships during childhood and adolescence. *Merrill-Palmer Quarterly, 35,* 445–462.

Jones, J., Lopez, A., & Wilson, M. (2003). Congenital toxoplasmosis.

American Family Physician, 67, 2131–2137.

Jones, M. C. (1965). Psychological correlates of somatic development. *Child Development, 36,* 899–911.

Jones, M. C., & Mussen, P. H. (1958). Self-conceptions, motivations, and interpersonal attitudes of early- and late-maturing girls. *Child Development, 29,* 491–501.

Jones, N. A., Field, T., Fox, N. A., Lundy, B., & Davalos, M. (1997). EEG activation in 1-month-old infants of depressed mothers. *Development and Psychopathology, 9,* 491–505.

Jones, S. S., & Raag, T. (1989). Smile production in older infants: The importance of a social recipient for the facial signal. *Child Development, 60,* 811–818.

Jones, W. H. (1990). Loneliness and social exclusion. *Journal of Social and Clinical Psychology, 9,* 214–220.

Jordan, B. (1993). *Birth in four cultures.* Prospect Heights, IL: Waveland.

Jordan, W. J., Lara, J., & McPartland, J. M. (1996). Exploring the causes of early dropout among race-ethnic and gender groups. *Youth and Society, 28,* 62–94.

Jorgensen, K. M. (1999). Pain assessment and management in the newborn infant. *Journal of Peri-Anesthesia Nursing, 14,* 349–356.

Joseph, R. (2000). Fetal brain behavior and cognitive development. *Developmental Review, 20,* 81–98.

Josselson, R. (1992). *The space between us.* San Francisco: Jossey-Bass.

Josselson, R. (1994). The theory of identity development and the question of intervention. In S. L. Archer (Ed.), *Interventions for adolescent identity development* (pp. 12–25). Thousand Oaks, CA: Sage.

Jovanovic, J., & King, S. S. (1998). Boys and girls in the performance-based science classroom: Who's doing the performing? *American Educational Research Journal, 35,* 477–496.

Joyner, M. H., & Kurtz-Costes, B. (1997). Metamemory development. In W. Schneider & F. E. Weinert (Eds.), *Memory performance and competencies: Issues in growth and development* (pp. 275–300). Hillsdale, NJ: Erlbaum.

Juang, L. P., & Silbereisen, R. K. (2002). The relationship between adolescent academic capability beliefs, parenting and school grades. *Journal of Adolescence, 25,* 3–18.

Jusczyk, P. W. (1995). Language acquisition: Speech sounds and phonological development. In J. L. Miller & P. D. Eimas (Eds.), *Handbook of perception and cognition: Vol. 11. Speech, language, and communication* (pp. 263–301). Orlando, FL: Academic Press.

Jusczyk, P. W. (2002). Some critical developments in acquiring native language sound organization. *Annals of Otology, Rhinology and Laryngology, 189,* 11–15.

Jusczyk, P. W., & Hohne, E. A. (1997). Infants' memory for spoken words. *Science, 277,* 1984–1986.

Jusczyk, P. W., Houston, D. M., & Newsome, M. (1999). The beginnings of word segmentation in English-learning infants. *Cognitive Psychology, 39,* 159–207.

Jusczyk, P. W., Johnson, S. P., Spelke, E. S., & Kennedy, L. J. (1999). Synchronous change and perception of object unity: Evidence from adults and infants. *Cognition, 71,* 257–288.

Justice for Children and Youth. (2003). *Corporal punishment.* Toronto: Canadian Foundation for Children, Youth, and the Law. Retrieved from http://www.jfcy.org/corporalp/corporalp.html

Justice, E. M. (1986). Developmental changes in judgments of relative strategy effectiveness. *British Journal of Developmental Psychology, 4,* 75–81.

Justice, E. M., Baker-Ward, L., Gupta, S., & Jannings, L. R. (1997). Means to the goal of remembering: Developmental changes in awareness of strategy use–performance relations. *Journal of Experimental Child Psychology, 65,* 293–314.

Kagan, J. (1998). Biology and the child. In N. Eisenberg (Ed.), *Handbook of child psychology: Vol. 3. Social, emotional, and personality development* (5th ed., pp. 177–236). New York: Wiley.

Kagan, J. (2003). Behavioral inhibition as a temperamental category. In R. J. Davidson, K. R. Scherer, & H. H. Goldsmith (Eds.), *Handbook of affective sciences* (pp. 320–331). New York: Oxford University Press.

Kagan, J., Arcus, D., Snidman, N., Feng, W. Y., Hendler, J., & Greene, S. (1994). Reactivity in infants: A cross-national comparison. *Developmental Psychology, 30,* 342–345.

Kagan, J., Kearsley, R. B., & Zelazo, P. R. (1978). *Infancy: Its place in human development.* Cambridge, MA; Harvard University Press.

Kagan, J., & Saudino, K. J. (2001). Behavioral inhibition and related temperaments. In R. N. Emde & J. K. Hewitt (Eds.), *Infancy to early childhood: Genetic and environmental influences on developmental change* (pp. 111–119). New York: Oxford University Press.

Kagan, J., & Snidman, N. (1991). Temperamental factors in human development. *American Psychologist, 46,* 856–862.

Kagan, J., Snidman, N., & Arcus, D. (1998). Childhood derivatives of high and low reactivity in infancy. *Child Development, 69,* 1483–1493.

Kagan, J., Snidman, N., Zentner, M., & Peterson, E. (1999). Infant temperament and anxious symptoms in school-age children. *Development and Psychopathology, 11,* 209–224.

Kahn, P. H., Jr. (1992). Children's obligatory and discretionary moral judgments. *Child Development, 63,* 416–430.

Kail, R. (2000). Speed of information processing: Developmental change and links to intelligence. *Journal of School Psychology, 38,* 51–61.

Kail, R. V. (2003). Information processing and memory. In M. H. Bornstein, L. Davidson, C. L. M. Keyes, K. A. Moore, and the Center for Child Well-Being (Eds.), *Well-being: Positive development across the life course* (pp. 269–280). Mahwah, NJ: Erlbaum.

Kail, R., & Park, Y. (1992). Global developmental change in processing time. *Merrill-Palmer Quarterly, 38,* 525–541.

Kail, R., & Park, Y. (1994). Processing time, articulation time, and memory span. *Journal of Experimental Child Psychology, 57,* 281–291.

Kaisa, A., Stattin, H., & Nurmi, J. (2000). Parenting styles and adolescents' achievement strategies. *Journal of Adolescence, 23,* 205–222.

Kaitz, M., Good, A., Rokem, A. M., & Eidelman, A. I. (1987). Mothers' recognition of their newborns by olfactory cues. *Developmental Psychobiology, 20,* 587–591.

Kaitz, M., Good, A., Rokem, A. M., & Eidelman, A. I. (1988). Mothers' and fathers' recognition of their newborns' photographs during the postpartum period. *Journal of Developmental and Behavioral Pediatrics, 9,* 223–226.

Kaitz, M., Meirov, H., Landman, I., & Eidelman, A. I. (1993a). Infant recognition by tactile cues. *Infant Behavior and Development, 16,* 333–341.

Kaitz, M., Shiri, S., Danziger, S., Hershko, Z., & Eidelman, A. I. (1993b). Fathers can also recognize their newborns by touch. *Infant Behavior and Development, 17,* 205–207.

Kalil, A., Schweingruber, H., & Seefeldt, K. (2001). Correlates of employment among welfare recipients: Do psychological characteristics and attitudes matter? *American Journal of Community Psychology, 29,* 701–723.

Kalinowski, T. (2002, October 25). ESL programs decline as need rises; funding formula hurts communities, school officials say. *Toronto Star,* B01.

Kamerman, S. (2000). Early childhood intervention policies: An international perspective. In J. P. Shonkoff & S. J. Meisels (Eds.), *Handbook of early childhood intervention* (2nd ed., pp. 316–329). New York: Cambridge University Press.

Kamerman, S. B. (1993). International perspectives on child care policies and programs. *Pediatrics, 91,* 248–252.

Kamerman, S. B. (2000). From maternity to parental leave policies: Women's health, employment, and child and family well-being. *Journal*

of the American Medical Women's Association, 55, 96–99.

Kandall, S. R., Gaines, J., Habel, L., Davidson, G., & Jessop, D. (1993). Relationship of maternal substance abuse to subsequent sudden infant death syndrome in offspring. *Journal of Pediatrics, 123,* 120–126.

Kao, G., & Tienda, M. (1995). Optimism and achievement: The educational performance of immigrant youth. *Social Science Quarterly, 76,* 1–19.

Kaplowitz, P. B., Slora, E. J., Wasserman, R. C., Pedlow, S. E., & Herman-Giddens, M. E. (2001). Earlier onset of puberty in girls: Relation to increased body mass index and race. *Pediatrics, 108,* 347–353.

Kaprio, J., Rimpela, A., Winter, T., Viken, R. J., Pimpela, M., & Rose, R. J. (1995). Common genetic influence on BMI and age at menarche. *Human Biology, 67,* 739–753.

Karadsheh, R. (1991). *This room is a junkyard!: Children's comprehension of metaphorical language.* Paper presented at the biennial meeting of the Society for Research in Child Development, Seattle, WA.

Karmiloff-Smith, A. (1992). *Beyond modularity: A developmental perspective on cognitive science.* Cambridge, MA: MIT Press.

Karpati, A. M., Rubin, C. H., Kieszak, S. M., Marcus, M., & Troiano, R. P. (2002). Stature and pubertal stage assessment in American boys: The 1988–1994 Third National Health and Nutrition Examination Survey. *Journal of Adolescent Health, 30,* 205–212.

Kaslow, F. W., Hansson, K., & Lundblad, A. (1994). Long-term marriages in Sweden: And some comparisons with similar couples in the United States. *Contemporary Family Therapy, 16,* 521–537.

Kasmauski, K., & Jaret, P. (2003). *Impact: On the frontlines of global health.* Washington, DC: National Geographic.

Katzmarzyk, A. (2002). The Canadian obesity epidemic, 1995–1998. *Canadian Medical Association Journal, 166,* 1039–1040.

Kaufman, J., & Charney, D. (2001). Effects of early stress on brain structure and function: Implications for understanding the relationship between child maltreatment and depression. *Development and Psychopathology, 13,* 451–471.

Kaufman, J., & Charney, D. (2003). The neurobiology of child and adolescent depression: Current knowledge and future directions. In D. Cicchetti & E. Walker (Eds.), *Neurodevelopmental mechanisms in psychopathology* (pp. 461–490). New York: Cambridge University Press.

Kavanaugh, R. D., & Engel, S. (1998). The development of pretense and narrative in early childhood. In

O. N. Saracho & B. Spodek (Eds.), *Multiple perspectives on play in early childhood education* (pp. 80–99). Albany: State University of New York Press.

Kay, M. A., Manno, C. S., Ragni, M. V., Larson, P. J., Couto, L. B., & McClelland, A. (2000). Evidence for gene transfer and expression of factor IX in haemophilia B patients treated with an AAV vector. *Nature Genetics, 24,* 257–261.

Kaye, K., & Marcus, J. (1981). Infant imitation: The sensory-motor agenda. *Developmental Psychology, 17,* 258–265.

Kearins, J. M. (1981). Visual spatial memory in Australian aboriginal children of desert regions. *Cognitive Psychology, 13,* 434–460.

Keating, D. (1979). Adolescent thinking. In J. Adelson (Ed.), *Handbook of adolescent psychology* (pp. 211–246). New York: Wiley.

Keating, D. (1990). Adolescent thinking. In S. S. Feldman & G. R. Elliott (Eds.), *At the threshold* (pp. 54–89). Cambridge, MA: Harvard University Press.

Keil, F. C., & Lockhart, K. L. (1999). Explanatory understanding in conceptual development. In E. K. Scholnick, K. Nelson, S. A. Gelman, & P. H. Miller (Eds.), *Conceptual development: Piaget's legacy* (pp. 103–130). Mahwah, NJ: Erlbaum.

Keith, T. Z., Keith, P. B., Quirk, K. J., Sperduto, J., Santillo, S., & Killings, S. (1998). Longitudinal effects of parent involvement on high school grades: Similarities and differences across gender and ethnic groups. *Journal of School Psychology, 36,* 335–363.

Keller, S. N., & Brown, J. D. (2002). Media interventions to promote responsible sexual behavior. *Journal of Sex Research, 39,* 67–72.

Kelley, S. S., Borawski, E. A., Flocke, S. A., & Keen, K. J. (2003). The role of sequential and concurrent sexual relationships in the risk of sexually transmitted diseases among adolescents. *Journal of Adolescent Health, 32,* 296–305.

Kellogg, A. (2001, January). Looking inward, freshmen care less about politics and more about money. *Chronicle of Higher Education,* pp. A47–A49.

Kelly, F. W., Terry, R., & Naglieri, R. (1999). A review of alternative birthing positions. *Journal of the American Osteopathic Association, 99,* 470–474.

Kelly, S. J., Day, N., & Streissguth, A. P. (2000). Effects of prenatal alcohol exposure on social behavior in humans and other species. *Neurotoxicology and Teratology, 22,* 143–149.

Kempe, C. H., Silverman, B. F., Steele, P. W., Droegemueller, P. W., & Silver, H. K. (1962). The battered-child syndrome. *Journal of the American Medical Association, 181,* 17–24.

Kendler, K. S., Thornton, L. M., Gilman, S. E., & Kessler, R. C. (2000). Sexual orientation in a U.S. national sample of twin and non-twin sibling pairs. *American Journal of Psychiatry, 157,* 1843–1846.

Kennedy, C. M. (1998). Childhood nutrition. *Annual Review of Nursing Research, 16,* 3–38.

Kennell, J. H., Klaus, M., McGrath, S., Robertson, S., & Hinkley, C. (1991). Continuous emotional support during labor in a U.S. hospital. *Journal of the American Medical Association, 265,* 2197–2201.

Kenyon, B. L. (2001). Current research in children's conceptions of death: A critical review. *Omega, 43,* 63–91.

Kerckhoff, A. C. (2002). The transition from school to work. In J. T. Mortimer & R. Larson (Eds.), *The changing adolescent experience* (pp. 52–87). New York: Cambridge University Press.

Kerestes, M., & Youniss, J. E. (2003). Rediscovering the importance of religion in adolescent development. In R. M. Lerner, F. Jacobs, & D. Wertlieb (Eds.), *Handbook of applied developmental science* (Vol. 1, pp. 165–184). Thousand Oaks, CA: Sage.

Kernis, M. H. (2002). Self-esteem as a multifaceted construct. In T. M. Brinthaupt & R. P. Lipka (Eds.), *Understanding early adolescent self and identity* (pp. 57–88). Albany, NY: State University of New York Press.

Kerpelman, J. L., Shoffner, M. F., & Ross-Griffin, S. (2002). African American mothers' and daughters' beliefs about possible selves and their strategies for reaching the adolescents' future academic and career goals. *Journal of Youth and Adolescence, 31,* 289–302.

Kerr, M., Lambert, W. W., & Bem, D. J. (1996). Life course sequelae of childhood shyness in Sweden: Comparison with the United States. *Developmental Psychology, 32,* 1100–1105.

Kerr, M., Lambert, W. W., Stattin, H., & Klackenberg-Larsson, I. (1994). Stability of inhibition in a Swedish longitudinal sample. *Child Development, 65,* 138–146.

Kessen, W. (1967). Sucking and looking: Two organized congenital patterns of behavior in the human newborn. In H. W. Stevenson, E. H. Hess, & H. L. Rheingold (Eds.), *Early behavior: Comparative and developmental approaches* (pp. 147–179). New York: Wiley.

Kiernan, K. (2001). European perspectives on nonmarital childbearing. In L. L. Wu & B. Wolfe (Eds.), *Out of wedlock: Causes and consequences of nonmarital fertility* (pp. 77–108). New York: Russell Sage Foundation.

Killen, M., Crystal, D., & Watanabe, H. (2002). The individual and the group: Japanese and American children's evaluations of peer exclusion, tolerance of difference, and prescriptions for conformity. *Child Development, 73,* 1788–1802.

Killen, M., & Nucci, L. P. (1995). Morality, autonomy, and social conflict. In M. Killen & D. Hart (Eds.), *Morality in everyday life: Developmental perspectives* (pp. 52–86). Cambridge, U.K.: Cambridge University Press.

Killen, M., & Smetana, J. G. (1999). Social interactions in preschool classrooms and the development of young children's conceptions of the personal. *Child Development, 70,* 486–501.

Killen, M., & Stangor, M. (2001). Children's social reasoning about inclusion and exclusion in gender and race peer group contexts. *Child Development, 72,* 174–186.

Kilpatrick, S. W., & Sanders, D. M. (1978). Body image stereotypes: A developmental comparison. *Journal of Genetic Psychology, 132,* 87–95.

Kim, J. M. (1998). Korean children's concepts of adult and peer authority and moral reasoning. *Developmental Psychology, 34,* 947–955.

Kim, J. M., & Turiel, E. (1996). Korean children's concepts of adult and peer authority. *Social Development, 5,* 310–329.

Kim, K. J., Conger, R. D., Lorenz, F. O., & Elder, G. H., Jr. (2001). Parent–adolescent reciprocity in negative affect and its relation to early adult social development. *Developmental Psychology, 37,* 775–790.

Kim, M., McGregor, K. K., & Thompson, C. K. (2000). Early lexical development in English- and Korean-speaking children: Language-general and language-specific patterns. *Journal of Child Language, 27,* 225–254.

Kim, S. Y. S., Barton, B. A., Obarzanek, E., McMahon, R. P., Kronsberg, S., & Waclawiw, M. A. (2002). Obesity development during adolescence in a biracial cohort: The NHLBI Growth and Health Study. *Pediatrics, 110,* 354–358.

Kim, W. J. (2002). Benefits and risks of intercountry adoption. *Lancet, 360,* 423–424.

King, P. M., & Kitchener, K. S. (1994). *Developing reflective judgment: Understanding and promoting intellectual growth and critical thinking in adolescents and adults.* San Francisco: Jossey-Bass.

Kinney, D. (1999). From "head-bangers" to "hippies": Delineating adolescents' active attempts to form an alternative peer culture. In J. A. McLellan & M. J. V. Pugh (Eds.), *The role of peer groups in adolescent social identity: Exploring the importance of stability and change* (pp. 21–35). San Francisco: Jossey-Bass.

Kinney, H. C., Filiano, J. J., & White, W. F. (2001). Medullary serotonergic network deficiency in the sudden infant death syndrome: Review of a 15-year study of a single dataset. *Journal of Neuropathology and Experimental Neurology, 60,* 228–247.

Kirby, D. (2002a). Antecedents of adolescent initiation of sex, contraceptive use, and pregnancy. *American Journal of Health Behavior, 26,* 473–485.

Kirby, D. (2002b). Effective approaches to reducing adolescent unprotected sex, pregnancy, and childbearing. *Journal of Sex Research, 39,* 51–57.

Kirby, D. (2002c). The impact of schools and school programs upon adolescent sexual behavior. *Journal of Sex Research, 39,* 27–33.

Kirchner, G. (2000). *Children's games from around the world.* Boston: Allyn and Bacon.

Kirk, K. M., Bailey, J. M., Dunne, M. P., & Martin, N. G. (2000). Measurement models for sexual orientation in a community twin sample. *Behavior Genetics, 30,* 345–356.

Kirk, W. G. (1993). *Adolescent suicide.* Champaign, IL: Research Press.

Kirkham, N. Z., Slemmer, J. A., & Johnson, S. P. (2002). Visual statistical learning in infancy: Evidence for a domain general learning mechanism. *Cognition, 83,* B35–B42.

Kirkman, M., Rosenthal, D. A., & Feldman, S. S. (2002). Talking to a tiger: Fathers reveal their difficulties in communicating about sexuality with adolescents. In S. S. Feldman & D. A. Rosenthal (Eds.), *Talking sexuality: Parent–adolescent communication* (pp. 57–74). San Francisco: Jossey-Bass.

Kisilevsky, B. S., Hains, S. M. J., Lee, K., Muir, D. W., Xu, F., Fu, G., Zhao, Z. Y., & Yang, R. L. (1998). The still-face effect in Chinese and Canadian 3- to 6-month-old infants. *Developmental Psychology, 34,* 629–639.

Kisilevsky, B. S., Hains, S. M. J., Lee, K., Xie, X., Huang, H., Ye, H. H., Zhang, K., & Wang, Z. (2003). Effects of experience on fetal voice recognition. *Psychological Science, 14,* 220–224.

Kisilevsky, B. S., & Low, J. A. (1998). Human fetal behavior: 100 years of study. *Developmental Review, 18,* 1–29.

Kitzmann, K. M., Cohen, R., & Lockwood, R. L. (2002). Are only children missing out? Comparison of the peer-related social competence of only children and siblings. *Journal of Social and Personal Relationships, 19,* 299–316.

Klaczynski, P. A. (1997). Bias in adolescents' everyday reasoning and its relationships with intellectual ability, personal theories, and self-serving motivation. *Developmental Psychology, 33,* 273–283.

Klaczynski, P. A. (2001). Analytic and heuristic processing influences on adolescent reasoning and decision-making. *Child Development, 72,* 844–861.

Klaczynski, P. A., & Narasimham, G. (1998a). Development of scientific reasoning biases: Cognitive versus ego-protective explanations. *Developmental Psychology, 34,* 175–187.

Klaczynski, P. A., & Narasimham, G. (1998b). Representations as mediators of adolescent deductive reasoning. *Developmental Psychology, 34,* 865–881.

Klahr, D., & MacWhinney, B. (1998). Information processing. In D. Kuhn & R. S. Siegler (Eds.), *Handbook of child psychology: Vol. 2. Cognition, perception, and language* (5th ed., pp. 631–678). New York: Wiley.

Klaus, M. H., & Kennell, J. H. (1982). *Parent–infant bonding.* St. Louis: Mosby.

Klaw, E. L., Rhodes, J. E., & Fitzgerald, L. F. (2003). Natural mentors in the lives of African-American adolescent mothers: Tracking relationships over time. *Journal of Youth and Adolescence, 32,* 223–242.

Klebanoff, M. A., Levine, R. J., Clemens, J. D., & Wilkins, D. G. (2002). Maternal serum caffeine metabolites and small-for-gestational-age birth. *American Journal of Epidemiology, 155,* 32–37.

Klebanov, P. K., Brooks-Gunn, J., McCarton, C., & McCormick, M. C. (1998). The contribution of neighborhood and family income to developmental test scores over the first three years of life. *Child Development, 69,* 1420–1436.

Klein, P. J., & Meltzoff, A. N. (1999). Long-term memory, forgetting, and deferred imitation in 12-month-old infants. *Developmental Science, 2,* 102–113.

Klenberg, L., Korkman, M., & Lahti-Nuuttila, P. (2001). Differential development of attention and executive functions in 3- to 12-year-old Finnish children. *Developmental Neuropsychology, 20,* 407–428.

Klesges, L. M., Johnson, K. C., Ward, K. D., & Barnard, M. (2001). Smoking cessation in pregnant women. *Obstetrics and Gynecology Clinics of North America, 28,* 269–282.

Kliewer, W., Fearnow, M. D., & Miller, P. A. (1996). Coping socialization in middle childhood: Tests of maternal and paternal influences. *Child Development, 67,* 2339–2357.

Klimes-Dougan, B., & Kistner, J. (1990). Physically abused preschoolers' responses to peers' distress. *Developmental Psychology, 26,* 599–602.

Kling, K. C., Hyde, J. S., Showers, C. J., & Buswell, B. N. (1999). Gender differences in self-esteem: A meta-analysis. *Psychological Bulletin, 125,* 470–500.

Klingner, J. K., Vaughn, S., Hughes, M. T., Schumm, J. S., & Elbaum, B. (1998). Outcomes for students with and without learning disabilities in inclusive classrooms. *Learning Disabilities Research and Practice, 13,* 153–161.

Klitzing, K. von, Simoni, H., Amsler, F., & Buergin, D. (1999). The role of the father in early family interactions. *Infant Mental Health Journal, 20,* 222–237.

Klump, K. L., Kaye, W. H., & Strober, M. (2001). The evolving genetic foundations of eating disorders. *Psychiatric Clinics of North America, 24,* 215–225.

Knecht, S., Draeger, B., Deppe, M., Bobe, L., Lohmann, H., Floeel, A., Ringelstein, E.-B., & Henningsen, H. (2000). Handedness and hemispheric language dominance in healthy humans. *Brain, 123,* 2512–2518.

Knobloch, H., & Pasamanick, B. (Eds.). (1974). *Gesell and Amatruda's Developmental Diagnosis.* Hagerstown, MD: Harper & Row.

Knoers, N., van den Ouweland, A., Dreesen, J. Verdijk, M., Monnens, L. S., & van Oost, B. A. (1993). Nephrongenic diabetes insipidus: Identification of the genetic defect. *Pediatric Nephrology, 7,* 685–688.

Kobak, R. R., & Hazan, C. (1991). Attachment in marriage: Effects of security and accuracy of working models. *Journal of Personality and Social Psychology, 60,* 861–869.

Kobayashi, Y. (1994). Conceptual acquisition and change through social interaction. *Human Development, 37,* 233–241.

Koch, J. J. (2002). Performance-enhancing substances and their use among adolescent athletes. *Pediatrics in Review, 23,* 310–317.

Kochanska, G. (1991). Socialization and temperament in the development of guilt and conscience. *Child Development, 62,* 1379–1392.

Kochanska, G. (1997). Multiple pathways to conscience for children with different temperaments: From toddlerhood to age 5. *Developmental Psychology, 33,* 228–240.

Kochanska, G. (1998). Mother–child relationship, child fearfulness, and emerging attachment: A short-term longitudinal study. *Developmental Psychology, 34,* 480–490.

Kochanska, G., Casey, R. J., & Fukumoto, A. (1995). Toddlers' sensitivity to standard violations. *Child Development, 66,* 643–656.

Kochanska, G., & Coy, K. C. (2002). Child emotionality and maternal responsiveness as predictors of reunion behaviors in the Strange Situation: Links mediated and unmediated by separation distress. *Child Development, 73,* 228–240.

Kochanska, G., Gross, J. N., Lin, M.-H., & Nichols, K. E. (2002). Guilt in young children: Development, determinants, and relations with broader system standards. *Child Development, 73,* 461–482.

Kochanska, G., & Murray, K. T. (2000). Mother–child mutually responsive orientation and conscience development: From toddler to early school age. *Child Development, 71,* 417–431.

Kochanska, G., Murray, K. T., & Harlan, E. T. (2000). Effortful control in early childhood: Continuity and change, antecedents, and implications for social development. *Developmental Psychology, 36,* 220–232.

Kochanska, G., & Radke-Yarrow, M. (1992). Inhibition in toddlerhood and the dynamics of the child's interaction with an unfamiliar peer at age five. *Child Development, 63,* 325–335.

Kochanska, G., Tjebkes, T. L., & Forman, D. R. (1998). Children's emerging regulation of conduct: Restraint, compliance, and internalization from infancy to the second year. *Child Development, 69,* 1378–1389.

Kochenderfer-Ladd, B. (2003). Identification of aggressive and asocial victims and the stability of their peer victimization. *Merrill-Palmer Quarterly, 49,* 401–425.

Kochenderfer-Ladd, B., & Wardrop, J. L. (2001). Chronicity and instability of children's peer victimization experiences as predictors of loneliness and social satisfaction trajectories. *Child Development, 72,* 134–151.

Koestner, R., Franz, C., & Weinberger, J. (1990). The family origins of empathic concern: A 26-year longitudinal study. *Journal of Personality and Social Psychology, 58,* 709–717.

Kohen, D. E., Brooks-Gunn, J., Leventhal, T., & Hertzman, C. (2002). Neighborhood income and physical and social disorder in Canada: Associations with young children's competencies. *Child Development, 73,* 1844–1860.

Kohen, D., Hunter, T., Pence, A., & Goelman, H. (2000). The Victoria Day Care Research Project: Overview of a longitudinal study of child care and human development in Canada. *Canadian Journal of Research in Early Childhood Education, 8,* 49–54.

Kohlberg, L. (1966). A cognitive-developmental analysis of children's sex-role concepts and attitudes. In E. E. Maccoby (Ed.), *The development of sex differences* (pp. 82–173). Stanford, CA: Stanford University Press.

Kohlberg, L. (1969). Stage and sequence: The cognitive-developmental approach to socialization. In D. A. Goslin (Ed.), *Handbook of socialization theory and research* (pp. 347–480). Chicago: Rand McNally.

Kohlberg, L., Levine, C., & Hewer, A. (1983). *Moral stages: A current formulation and a response to critics.* Basel, Switzerland: Karger.

Kohlendorfer, U., Kiechl, S., & Sperl, W. (1998). Sudden infant death syndrome: Risk factor profiles for distinct subgroups. *American Journal of Epidemiology, 147,* 960–968.

Kojima, H. (1986). Childrearing concepts as a belief–value system of the society and the individual. In H.

Stevenson, H. Azuma, & K. Hakuta (Eds.), *Child development and education in Japan* (pp. 39–54). New York: Freeman.

Kolb, B., & Gibb, R. (2001). Early brain injury, plasticity, and behavior. In C. A. Nelson & M. Luciana (Eds.), *Handbook of developmental cognitive neuroscience* (pp. 175–190). Cambridge, MA: MIT Press.

Kolominsky, Y., Igumnov, S., & Drozdovitch, V. (1999). The psychological development of children from Belarus exposed in the prenatal period to radiation from the Chernobyl atomic power plant. *Journal of Child Psychology and Psychiatry, 40,* 299–305.

Kolvin, I., & Trowell, J. (1996). Child sexual abuse. In I. Rosen (Ed.), *Sexual deviation* (3rd ed., pp. 337–360). Oxford, U.K.: Oxford University Press.

Kopp, C. B. (1994). Infant assessment. In C. B. Fisher & R. M. Lerner (Eds.), *Applied developmental psychology* (pp. 265– 293). New York: McGraw-Hill.

Korner, A. F. (1996). Reliable individual differences in preterm infants' excitation management. *Child Development, 67,* 1793–1805.

Kornhaber, M., Orfield, G., & Kurlaender, M. (2001). *Raising standards or raising barriers? Inequality and high-stakes testing in public education.* New York: Century Foundation Press.

Kotchick, B. A., Shaffer, A., Forehand, R., & Miller, K. S. (2001). Adolescent sexual risk behavior: A multi-system perspective. *Clinical Psychology Review, 21,* 493–519.

Kouvonen, A., & Kivivuori, J. (2001). Part-time jobs, delinquency, and victimization among Finnish adolescents. *Journal of Scandinavian Studies in Criminology and Crime Prevention, 2,* 191–212.

Kozulin, A. (Ed.). (2003). *Vygotsky's educational theory in cultural context.* Cambridge, U.K.: Cambridge University Press.

Kraemer, H. C., Yesavage, J. A., Taylor, J. L., & Kupfer, D. (2000). How can we learn about developmental processes from cross-sectional studies, or can we? *American Journal of Psychiatry, 157,* 163–171.

Krafft, K., & Berk, L. E. (1998). Private speech in two preschools: Significance of open-ended activities and make-believe play for verbal self-regulation. *Early Childhood Research Quarterly, 13,* 637–658.

Kramer, M. S., Guo, T., Platt, R. W., Sevkovskaya, Z., Dzikovich, I., & Collet, J. P. (2003). Infant growth and health outcomes associated with 3 compared with 6 mo of exclusive breastfeeding. *American Journal of Clinical Nutrition, 78,* 291–295.

Kramer, M. S., Guo, T., Platt, R. W., Shapiro, S., Collet, J. P., & Chalmers, B. (2002). Breastfeeding and infant growth: Biology or bias? *Pediatrics, 110,* 343–347.

Kramer, M. S., & Kakuma, R. (2002). Optimal duration of exclusive breastfeeding. *Cochrane Database of Systematic Reviews, 2002*(4). Retrieved from www.cochrane.org/cochrane/revabstr/ab003517.htm

Krascum, R. M., & Andrews, S. (1998). The effects of theories on children's acquisition of family-resemblance categories. *Child Development, 69,* 333–346.

Krebs, N. F., & Jacobson, M. S. (2003). Prevention of pediatric overweight and obesity. *Pediatrics, 112,* 424–430.

Kreppner, K., Paulsen, S., & Schuetze, Y. (1982). Infant and family development: From triads to tetrads. *Human Development, 25,* 373–391.

Krevans, J., & Gibbs, J. C. (1996). Parents' use of inductive discipline: Relations to children's empathy and prosocial behavior. *Child Development, 67,* 3263–3277.

Kroger, J. (1993). Identity and context: How the identity statuses choose their match. In R. Josselson & A. Lieblich (Eds.), *The narrative study of lives* (Vol. 1, pp. 130–162). Newbury Park, CA: Sage.

Kroger, J. (1995). The differentiation of "firm" and "developmental" foreclosure identity statuses: A longitudinal study. *Journal of Adolescent Research, 10,* 317–337.

Kroger, J. (2000). *Identity development: Adolescence through adulthood.* Thousand Oaks, CA: Sage.

Kroger, J. (2001). What transits in an identity status transition: A rejoinder to commentaries. *Identity, 3,* 291–304.

Kronenfeld, J. J., & Glik, D. C. (1995). Unintentional injury: A major health problem for young children and youth. *Journal of Family and Economic Issues, 16,* 365–393.

Kruger, A. C. (1993). Peer collaboration: Conflict, cooperation, or both? *Social Development, 2,* 165–182.

Krumhansl, C. L., & Jusczyk, P. W. (1990). Infants' perception of phrase structure in music. *Psychological Science, 1,* 70–73.

Kubik, M. Y., Lytle, L. A., Hannan, P. J., Perry, C. L., & Story, M. (2003). The association of the school food environment with dietary behaviors of young adolescents. *American Journal of Public Health, 93,* 1168–1173.

Kuczynski, L. (1984). Socialization goals and mother–child interaction: Strategies for long-term and short-term compliance. *Developmental Psychology, 20,* 1061–1073.

Kuczynski, L., & Lollis, S. (2002). Four foundations for a dynamic model of parenting. In J. R. M. Gerris (Ed.), *Dynamics of parenting.* Hillsdale, NJ: Erlbaum.

Kuebli, J., Butler, S., & Fivush, R. (1995). Mother–child talk about past emotions: Relations of maternal lan-

guage and child gender over time. *Cognition and Emotion, 9,* 265–283.

Kuhl, P. K. (2000). A new view of language acquisition. *Proceedings of the National Academy of Sciences, 97,* 11850–11857.

Kuhn, D. (1989). Children and adults as intuitive scientists. *Psychological Review, 96,* 674–689.

Kuhn, D. (1993). Connecting scientific and informal reasoning. *Merrill-Palmer Quarterly, 39,* 74–103.

Kuhn, D. (1995). Microgenetic study of change: What has it told us? *Psychological Science, 6,* 133–139.

Kuhn, D. (1999). Metacognitive development. *Current Directions in Psychological Science, 9,* 178–181.

Kuhn, D. (2000a). Theory of mind, metacognition, and reasoning: A life-span perspective. In P. Mitchell & K. J. Riggs (Eds.), *Children's reasoning and the mind* (pp. 301–326). Hove, U.K.: Psychology Press.

Kuhn, D. (2000b). Why development does (and does not) occur: Evidence from the domain of inductive reasoning. In R. Siegler & J. McClelland (Eds.), *Mechanisms of cognitive development* (pp. 221–249). Mahwah, NJ: Erlbaum.

Kuhn, D. (2002). What is scientific thinking, and how does it develop? In U. Goswami (Ed.), *Blackwell handbook of childhood cognitive development* (pp. 371–393). Malden, MA: Blackwell.

Kuhn, D., Amsel, E., & O'Loughlin, M. (1988). *The development of scientific thinking skills.* Orlando, FL: Academic Press.

Kuhn, D., Garcia-Mila, M., Zohar, A., & Andersen, C. (1995). Strategies of knowledge acquisition. *Monographs of the Society for Research in Child Development, 60*(245, Serial No. 4).

Kuhn, D., & Pearsall, S. (2000). Developmental origins of scientific thinking. *Journal of Cognition and Development, 1,* 113–129.

Kuklinski, M. R., & Weinstein, R. S. (2002). Classroom and developmental differences in a path model of teacher expectancy effects. *Child Development, 72,* 1554–1578.

Kunnen, E. S., & Bosma, H. A. (2003). Fischer's skill theory applied to identity development: A response to Kroger. *Identity, 3,* 247–270.

Kunzinger, E. L., III. (1985). A short-term longitudinal study of memorial development during early grade school. *Developmental Psychology, 21,* 642–646.

Kurdek, L. A., & Fine, M. A. (1994). Family acceptance and family control as predictors of adjustment in young adolescents: Linear, curvilinear, or interactive effects? *Child Development, 65,* 1137–1146.

Kushman, J. W., Sieber, C., & Heariold-Kinney, P. (2000). This isn't the place for me: School dropout. In D. Capuzzi & D. R. Gross (Eds.), *Youth risk: A prevention resource for counselors, teachers, and parents* (3rd

ed., pp. 471–507). Alexandria, VA: American Counseling Association.

Kutner, L. (1993, June). Getting physical. *Parents, 68*(6) pp. 96–98.

Laberge, L., Petit, D., Simard, C., Vitaro, F., & Tremblay, R. E. (2001). Development of sleep patterns in early adolescence. *Journal of Sleep Research, 10,* 59–67.

Lacourse, E., Nagin, D., Tremblay, R. E., Vitaro, F., & Claes, M. (2003). Developmental trajectories of boys' delinquent group membership and facilitation of violent behaviors during adolescence. *Development and Psychopathology, 15,* 183–197.

Ladd, G. W., Birch, S. H., & Buhs, E. S. (1999). Children's social and scholastic lives in kindergarten: Related spheres of influence? *Child Development, 70,* 1373–1400.

Ladd, G. W., Buhs, E. S., & Seid, M. (2000). Children's initial sentiments about kindergarten: Is school liking an antecedent of early classroom participation and achievement? *Merrill-Palmer Quarterly, 46,* 255–279.

Ladd, G. W., & Burgess, K. B. (1999). Charting the relationship trajectories of aggressive, withdrawn, and aggressive/withdrawn children during early grade school. *Child Development, 70,* 910–929.

Ladd, G. W., & Ladd, B. K. (1998). Parenting behaviors and parent–child relationships: Correlates of peer victimization in kindergarten? *Developmental Psychology, 34,* 1450–1458.

Ladd, G. W., LeSieur, K., & Profilet, S. M. (1993). Direct parental influences on young children's peer relations. In S. Duck (Ed.), *Learning about relationships* (Vol. 2, pp. 152–183). London: Sage.

Ladd, G. W., & Pettit, G. S. (2002). Parenting and the development of children's peer relationships. In M. Bornstein (Ed.), *Handbook of parenting: Vol. 5. Practical issues in parenting* (2nd ed., pp. 269–309). Mahwah, NJ: Erlbaum.

Ladd, G. W., & Price, J. M. (1987). Predicting children's social and school adjustment following the transition from preschool to kindergarten. *Child Development, 58,* 1168–1189.

Ladd, G. W., & Troop-Gordon, W. (2003). The role of chronic peer difficulties in the development of children's psychological adjustment problems. *Child Development, 74,* 1344–1367.

Lagattuta, K. H., Wellman, H. M., & Flavell, J. H. (1997). Preschoolers' understanding of the link between thinking and feeling: Cognitive cuing and emotional change. *Child Development, 68,* 1081–1104.

Lagercrantz, H., & Slotkin, T. A. (1986). The "stress" of being born. *Scientific American, 254,* 100–107.

Lagnado, L. (2001, November 2). Kids confront Trade Center trauma. *Wall Street Journal,* pp. B1, B6.

LaGreca, A. M., Prinstein, M. J., & Fetter, M. D. (2001). Adolescent peer crowd affiliation: Linkages with health-risk behaviors and close friendships. *Journal of Pediatric Psychology, 26,* 131–143.

Laible, D. J., & Thompson, R. A. (1998). Attachment and emotional understanding in preschool children. *Developmental Psychology, 34,* 1038–1045.

Laible, D. J., & Thompson, R. A. (2000). Mother–child discourse, attachment security, shared positive affect, and early conscience development. *Child Development, 71,* 1424–1440.

Laible, D. J., & Thompson, R. A. (2002). Mother–child conflict in the toddler years: Lessons in emotion, morality, and relationships. *Child Development, 73,* 1187–1203.

Laing, G. J., & Logan, S. (1999). Patterns of unintentional injury in childhood and their relation to socio-economic factors. *Public Health, 113,* 291–294.

Laird, R. D., Jordan, K. Y., Dodge, K. A., Pettit, G. S., & Bates, J. E. (2001). Peer rejection in childhood, involvement with antisocial peers in early adolescence, and the development of externalizing behavior problems. *Development and Psychopathology, 13,* 337–354.

Laird, R. D., Pettit, G. S., Mize, J., & Lindsey, E. (1994). Mother–child conversations about peers: Contributions to competence. *Family Relations, 43,* 425–432.

Lamaze, F. (1958). *Painless childbirth.* London: Burke.

Lamb, M. (1994). Infant care practices and the application of knowledge. In C. B. Fisher & R. M. Lerner (Eds.), *Applied developmental psychology* (pp. 23–45). New York: McGraw-Hill.

Lamb, M. E. (1997). The development of father–infant relationships. In M. E. Lamb (Ed.), *The role of the father in child development* (3rd ed., pp. 104–120). New York: Wiley.

Lamb, M. E. (1998). Nonparental child care: Context, quality, correlates, and consequences. In I. E. Sigel & K. A. Renninger (Eds.), *Handbook of child psychology: Vol. 4. Child psychology in practice* (5th ed., pp. 73–133). New York: Wiley.

Lamb, M. E. (1999). Noncustodial fathers and their impact on the children of divorce. In R. A. Thompson & P. R. Amato (Eds.), *The postdivorce family: Children, parenting, and society* (pp. 105–125). Thousand Oaks, CA: Sage.

Lamb, M. E., & Oppenheim, D. (1989). Fatherhood and father–child relationships: Five years of research. In S. H. Cath, A. Gurwitt, & L. Gunsberg (Eds.), *Fathers and their families* (pp. 11–26). Hillsdale, NJ: Erlbaum.

Lamb, M. E., Sternberg, K. J., & Prodromidis, M. (1992).

Nonmaternal care and the security of infant–mother attachment: A re-analysis of the data. *Infant Behavior and Development, 15,* 71–83.

Lamb, M. E., Thompson, R. A., Gardner, W., Charnov, E. L., & Connell, J. P. (1985). Infant–mother attachment: The origins and developmental significance of individual differences in the Strange Situation: Its study and biological interpretation. *Behavioral and Brain Sciences, 7,* 127–147.

Lammers, C., Ireland, M., Resnick, M., & Blum, R. (2000). Influences on adolescents' decisions to postpone onset of sexual intercourse: A survival analysis of virginity among youths aged 13 to 18 years. *Journal of Adolescent Health, 26,* 42–48.

Lampl, M. (1993). Evidence of saltatory growth in infancy. *American Journal of Human Biology, 5,* 641–652.

Lampl, M., Veldhuis, J. D., & Johnson, M. L. (1992). Saltation and stasis: A model of human growth. *Science, 258,* 801–803.

Landry, S. H., Miller-Loncar, C. L., Smith, K. E., & Swank, P. R. (2002). The role of early parenting in children's development of executive processes. *Developmental Neuropsychology, 21,* 15–41.

Landry, S. H., Smith, K. E., Swank, P. R., & Miller-Loncar, C. L. (2000). Early maternal and child influences on children's later independent cognitive and social functioning. *Child Development, 71,* 358–375.

Lansford, J. E., Criss, M. M., Pettit, G. S., Dodge, K. A., & Bates, J. E. (2003). Friendship quality, peer group affiliation, and peer antisocial behavior as moderators of the link between negative parenting and adolescent externalizing behavior. *Journal of Research on Adolescence, 13,* 161–184.

Lantieri, L. (2003). Waging peace in our schools: The Resolving Conflict Creatively Program. In M. J. Elias & H. Arnold (Eds.), *EQ + IQ = best leadership practices for caring and successful schools* (pp. 76–88). Thousand Oaks, CA: Corwin.

Lapsley, D. K., Jackson, S., Rice, K., & Shadid, G. (1988). Self-monitoring and the "new look" at the imaginary audience and personal fable: An ego-developmental analysis. *Journal of Adolescent Research, 3,* 17–31.

Largo, R. H., Caflisch, J. A., Hug, F., Muggli, K., Molnar, A. A., & Molinari, L. (2001). Neuromotor development from 5 to 18 years. Part 1: Timed performance. *Developmental Medicine and Child Neurology, 43,* 436–443.

Larson, R. W. (1990). The solitary side of life: An examination of the time people spend alone from childhood to old age. *Developmental Review, 10,* 155–183.

Larson, R. W. (2001). How U.S. children and adolescents spend time:

What it does (and doesn't) tell us about their development. *Current Directions in Psychological Science, 10,* 160–164.

Larson, R., & Ham, M. (1993). Stress and "storm and stress" in early adolescence: The relationship of negative events with dysphoric affect. *Developmental Psychology, 29,* 130–140.

Larson, R., & Lampman-Petraitis, C. (1989). Daily emotional states as reported by children and adolescents. *Child Development, 60,* 1250–1260.

Larson, R. W., Moneta, G., Richards, M. H., & Wilson, S. (2002). Continuity, stability, and change in daily emotional experience across adolescence. *Child Development, 73,* 1151–1165.

Larson, R. W., & Richards, M. H. (1991). Daily companionship in late childhood and early adolescence: Changing developmental contexts. *Child Development, 62,* 284–300.

Larson, R. W., & Richards, M. H. (1998). Waiting for the weekend: Friday and Saturday night as the emotional climax of the week. In A. C. Crouter & R. Larson (Eds.), *Temporal rhythms in adolescence: Clocks, calendars, and the coordination of daily life* (pp. 37–51). San Francisco: Jossey-Bass.

Larson, R. W., Richards, M. H., Moneta, G., Holmbeck, G., & Duckett, E. (1996). Changes in adolescents' daily interactions with their families from ages 10 to 18: Disengagement and transformation. *Developmental Psychology, 32,* 744–754.

Larson, R. W., Richards, M. H., Sims, B., & Dworkin, J. (2001). How urban African-American young adolescents spend their time: Time budgets for locations, activities, and companionship. *American Journal of Community Psychology, 29,* 565–597.

Larzelere, R. E., Schneider, W. N., Larson, D. B., & Pike, P. L. (1996). The effects of discipline responses in delaying toddler misbehavior recurrences. *Child and Family Behavior Therapy, 18,* 35–7.

Latz, S., Wolf, A. W., & Lozoff, B. (1999). Sleep practices and problems in young children in Japan and the United States. *Archives of Pediatric and Adolescent Medicine, 153,* 339–346.

Laucht, M., Esser, G., & Schmidt, M. H. (1997). Developmental outcome of infants born with biological and psychosocial risks. *Journal of Child Psychology and Psychiatry, 38,* 843–853.

Laumann, E. O., Gagnon, J. H., Michael, R. T., & Michaels, S. (1994). *The social organization of sexuality.* Chicago: University of Chicago Press.

Laursen, B., Coy, K., & Collins, W. A. (1998). Reconsidering changes in

parent–child conflict across adolescence: A meta-analysis. *Child Development, 69,* 817–832.

Law, K. L., Stroud, L. R., Niaura, R., LaGasse, L. L., Liu, J., & Lester, B. M. (2003). Smoking during pregnancy and newborn neurobehavior. *Pediatrics, 111,* 1318–1323.

Lazar, I., & Darlington, R. (1982). Lasting effects of early education: a report from the Consortium for Longitudinal Studies. *Monographs of the Society for Research in Child Development, 47*(2–3, Serial No. 195).

Lazarus, R. S., & Lazarus, B. N. (1994). *Passion and reason.* New York: Oxford University Press.

Leach, C. E. A., Blair, P. S., Fleming, P. J., Smith, I. J., Platt, M. W., & Berry, P. J. (1999). Epidemiology of SIDS and explained sudden infant deaths. *Pediatrics, 104,* e43.

Leaper, C. (1994). Exploring the correlates and consequences of gender segregation: Social relationships in childhood, adolescence, and adulthood. In C. Leaper (Ed.), *New directions for child development* (No. 65, pp. 67–86). San Francisco: Jossey-Bass.

Leaper, C. (2000). Gender, affiliation, assertion, and the interactive context of parent–child play. *Developmental Psychology, 36,* 381–393.

Leaper, C., Anderson, K. J., & Sanders, P. (1998). Moderators of gender effects on parents' talk to their children: A meta-analysis. *Developmental Psychology, 34,* 3–27.

Leaper, C., Tenenbaum, H. R., & Shaffer, T. G. (1999). Communication patterns of African-American girls and boys from low-income, urban backgrounds. *Child Development, 70,* 1489–1503.

LeBlanc, L. A., Goldsmith, T., & Patel, D. R. (2003). Behavioral aspects of chronic illness in children and adolescents. *Pediatric Clinics of North America, 50,* 859–878.

Lecanuet, J.-P., Granier-Deferre, C., Jacquet, A.-Y., Capponi, I., & Ledru, L. (1993). Prenatal discrimination of a male and female voice uttering the same sentence. *Early Development and Parenting, 2,* 217–228.

Lederer, J. M. (2000). Reciprocal teaching of social studies in inclusive elementary classrooms. *Journal of Learning Disabilities, 33,* 91–106.

Lee, A. M. (1980). Child-rearing practices and motor performance of black and white children. *Research Quarterly for Exercise and Sport, 51,* 494–500.

Lee, C. L., & Bates, J. E. (1985). Mother–child interaction at age two years and perceived difficult temperament. *Child Development, 56,* 1314–1325.

Lee, E. A., Torrance, N., & Olson, D. R. (2001). Young children and the say/mean distinction: Verbatim and paraphrase recognition in narrative and nursery rhyme contexts.

Journal of Child Language, 28, 531–543.

Lee, K., Cameron, C., Xu, F., Fu, G., & Board, J. (1997). Chinese and Canadian children's evaluations of lying and truth telling: Similarities and differences in the context of pro- and antisocial behaviors. *Child Development, 68,* 924–934.

Lee, K., Xu, F., Fu, G., Cameron, C. A., & Chen, S. (2001). Taiwan and Mainland Chinese and Canadian children's categorization and evaluation of lie- and truth-telling: A modesty effect. *British Journal of Developmental Psychology, 19,* 525–542.

Lee, V. E., & Burkam, D. T. (2003). Dropping out of high school: The role of school organization and structure. *American Educational Research Journal, 40,* 353–393.

Leeman, L. W., Gibbs, J. C., & Fuller, D. (1993). Evaluation of a multi-component group treatment program for juvenile delinquents. *Aggressive Behavior, 19,* 281–292.

Lefkowitz, E. S., Boone, T. L., Sigman, M., & Au, T. K. (2002). He said, she said: Gender differences in mother–adolescent conversations about sexuality. *Journal of Research on Adolescence, 12,* 217–242.

Lefkowitz, E. S., Sigman, M., & Au, T. K. (2000). Helping mothers discuss sexuality and AIDS with adolescents. *Child Development, 71,* 1383–1394.

Lehman, D. R., & Nisbett, R. E. (1990). A longitudinal study of the effects of undergraduate training on reasoning. *Developmental Psychology, 26,* 952–960.

Lehman, E. B., Steier, A., Guidash, K. M., & Wanna, S. Y. (2002). Predictors of compliance in toddlers: Child temperament, maternal personality, and emotional availability. *Early Child Development and Care, 172,* 301–310.

Lemery, K. S., Goldsmith, H. H., Klinnert, M. D., & Mrazek, D. A. (1999). Developmental models of infant and childhood temperament. *Developmental Psychology, 35,* 189–204.

Lempert, H. (1989). Animacy constraints on preschoolers' acquisition of syntax. *Child Development, 60,* 237–245.

Lengua, L. J., Wolchik, S., Sandler, I. N., & West, S. G. (2000). The additive and interactive effects of parenting and temperament in predicting problems of children of divorce. *Journal of Clinical Psychology, 29,* 232–244.

Leon, K. (2003). Risk and protective factors in young children's adjustment to parental divorce: A review of the research. *Family Relations, 52,* 258–270.

Lerner, R. M., Fisher, C. B., & Weinberg, R. A. (2000). Toward a science for and of the people: Promoting civil society through the application of developmental science. *Child Development, 71,* 11–20.

Lerner, R. M., Rothbaum, F., Boulos, S., & Castellino, D. R. (2002). Developmental systems perspective on parenting. In M. H. Bornstein (Ed.), *Handbook of parenting: Vol. 2. Biology and ecology of parenting* (2nd ed., pp. 315–344). Mahwah, NJ: Erlbaum.

Lester, B. M. (1985). Introduction: There's more to crying than meets the ear. In B. M. Lester & C. F. Z. Boukydis (Eds.), *Infant crying* (pp. 1–27). New York: Plenum.

Lester, B. M. (2000). Prenatal cocaine exposure and child outcome: A model for the study of the infant at risk. *Israel Journal of Psychiatry and Related Sciences, 37,* 223–235.

Lester, B. M., Kotelchuck, M., Spelke, E., Sellers, M. J., & Klein, R. E. (1974). Separation protest in Guatemalan infants: Cross-cultural and cognitive findings. *Developmental Psychology, 10,* 79–85.

Lester, B. M., LaGasse, L., Seifer, R., Tronick, E. Z., Bauer, C., & Shankaran, S. (2003). The maternal lifestyle study (MLS): Effects of prenatal cocaine and/or opiate exposure on auditory brain response at one month. *Journal of Pediatrics, 142,* 279–285.

Lester, D. (2003). Adolescent suicide from an international perspective. *American Behavioral Scientist, 46,* 1157–1170.

Lett, D. (1997). *L'enfant des miracles: Enfance et société au Moyen Age (XIIe–XIIIe siecle).* Paris: Aubier.

LeVay, S. (1993). *The sexual brain.* Cambridge, MA: MIT Press.

Leventhal, T., & Brooks-Gunn, J. (2003). Children and youth in neighborhood contexts. *Current Directions in Psychological Science, 12,* 27–31.

Levin, I., & Bus, A. G. (2003). How is emergent writing based on drawing? Analyses of children's products and their sorting by children and mothers. *Developmental Psychology, 39,* 891–905.

Levine, L. E. (1983). Mine: Self-definition in 2-year-old boys. *Developmental Psychology, 19,* 544–549.

Levine, L. J. (1995). Young children's understanding of the causes of anger and sadness. *Child Development, 66,* 697–709.

LeVine, R. A., Dixon, S., LeVine, S., Richman, A., Leiderman, P. H., Keefer, C. H., & Brazelton, T. B. (1994). *Child care and culture: Lessons from Africa.* New York: Cambridge University Press.

Levine, S. C., Huttenlocher, J., Taylor, A., & Langrock, A. (1999). Early sex differences in spatial skill. *Developmental Psychology, 35,* 940–949.

Levine, S. C., Huttenlocher, P., Banich, M. T., & Duda, E. (1987). Factors affecting cognitive functioning of hemiplegic children. *Developmental*

Medicine and Child Neurology, 29, 27–35.

Levinson, D. J. (1978). *The seasons of a man's life.* New York: Knopf.

Levinson, D. J. (1996). *The seasons of a woman's life.* New York: Knopf.

Levitsky, D. A., & Strupp, B. J. (1995). Malnutrition and the brain: Changing concepts, changing concerns. *Journal of Nutrition, 125,* 2245S–2254S.

Levitt, A. G., & Utmann, J. G. A. (1992). From babbling towards the sound systems of English and French: A longitudinal two-case study. *Journal of Child Language, 19,* 19–40.

Levtzion-Korach, O., Tennenbaum, A., Schnitzer, R., & Ornoy, A. (2000). Early motor development of blind children. *Journal of Paediatric and Child Health, 36,* 226–229.

Levy, G. D., Taylor, M. G., & Gelman, S. A. (1995). Traditional and evaluative aspects of flexibility in gender roles, social conventions, moral rules, and physical laws. *Child Development, 66,* 515–531.

Levy-Shiff, R. (2001). Psychological adjustment of adoptees in adulthood: Family environment and adoption-related correlates. *International Journal of Behavioral Development, 25,* 97–104.

Levy-Shiff, R., & Israelashvili, R. (1988). Antecedents of fathering: Some further exploration. *Developmental Psychology, 24,* 434–440.

Lewis, C., Freeman, N. H., Kyriadidou, C., Maridakikassotaki, K., & Berridge, D. M. (1996). Social influences on false belief access—specific sibling influences or general apprenticeship? *Child Development, 67,* 2930–2947.

Lewis, M. (1992). *Shame: The exposed self.* New York: Free Press.

Lewis, M. (1995). Embarrassment: The emotion of self-exposure and evaluation. In J. P. Tangney & K. W. Fischer (Eds.), *Self-conscious emotions* (pp. 198–218). New York: Guilford.

Lewis, M. (1997). *Altering fate: Why the past does not predict the future.* New York: Guilford.

Lewis, M. (1998). Emotional competence and development. In D. Pushkar, W. M. Bukowski, A. E. Schwartzman, E. M. Stack, & D. R. White (Eds.), *Improving competence across the lifespan* (pp. 27–36). New York: Plenum.

Lewis, M. D. (2000). The promise of dynamic systems approaches for an integrated account of human development. *Child Development, 71,* 36–43.

Lewis, M., & Brooks-Gunn, J. (1979). *Social cognition and the acquisition of self.* New York: Plenum.

Lewis, M., Ramsay, D. S., & Kawakami, K. (1993). Differences between Japanese infants and Caucasian American infants in behavioral and cortisol response to inoculation. *Child Development, 64,* 1722–1731.

Lewis, M., Sullivan, M. W., Stanger, C., & Weiss, M. (1989). Self development and self-conscious emotions. *Child Development, 60,* 146–156.

Lewis, M., Sullivan, M. W., & Vasen, A. (1987). Making faces: Age and emotion differences in the posing of emotional expressions. *Developmental Psychology, 23,* 690–697.

Lewkowicz, D. J. (1996). Infants' response to the audible and visible properties of the human face. I. Role of lexical syntactic context, temporal synchrony, gender, and manner of speech. *Developmental Psychology, 32,* 347–366.

Liaw, F., & Brooks-Gunn, J. (1993). Patterns of low-birthweight children's cognitive development. *Developmental Psychology, 29,* 1024–1035.

Liben, L. S. (1999). Developing an understanding of external spatial representations. In I. E. Sigel (Ed.), *Development of mental representation* (pp. 297–321). Mahwah, NJ: Erlbaum.

Liben, L. S., & Bigler, R. S. (2002). The developmental course of gender differentiation: Conceptualizing, measuring, and evaluating constructs and pathways. *Monographs of the Society for Research in Child Development, 62*(4, Serial No. 271).

Liben, L. S., Bigler, R. S., & Krogh, H. R. (2001). Pink and blue collar jobs: Children's judgments of job status and job aspirations in relation to sex of worker. *Journal of Experimental Child Psychology, 79,* 346–363.

Liben, L. S., & Downs, R. M. (1993). Understanding person-space-map relations: Cartographic and developmental perspectives. *Developmental Psychology, 29,* 739–752.

Liben, L. S., & Signorella, M. L. (1993). Gender-schematic processing in children: The role of initial interpretations of stimuli. *Developmental Psychology, 29,* 141–149.

Lickliter, R., & Bahrick, L. E. (2000). The development of infant intersensory perception: Advantages of a comparative convergent-operations approach. *Psychological Bulletin, 126,* 260–280.

Lidz, C. S. (2001). Multicultural issues and dynamic assessment. In L. A. Suzuki & J. G. Ponterotto (Eds.), *Handbook of multicultural assessment: Clinical, psychological, and educational applications* (2nd ed., pp. 523–539). San Francisco: Jossey-Bass.

Light, P., & Perret-Clermont, A.-N. (1989). Social context effects in learning and testing. In A. Gellatly, D. Rogers, & J. Sloboda (Eds.), *Cognition and social worlds* (pp. 99–112). Oxford, U.K.: Clarendon Press.

Lillard, A. S. (1998). Playing with a theory of mind. In O. N. Saracho & B. Spodek (Eds.), *Multiple perspec-*

tives on play in early childhood education (pp. 11–33). Albany: State University of New York Press.

Lillard, A. S. (2001). Pretending, understanding pretense, and understanding minds. In S. Reifel (Ed.), *Play and culture studies* (Vol. 3). Norwood, NJ: Ablex.

Lin, C. C., Hsiao, C. K., & Chen, W. J. (1999). Development of sustained attention assessed using the continuous performance test among children 6–15 years. *Journal of Abnormal Child Psychology, 27,* 403–412.

Lindsay-Hartz, J., de Rivera, J., & Mascolo, M. F. (1995). Differentiating guilt and shame and their effects on motivation. In J. P. Tangney & K. W. Fischer (Eds.), *Self-conscious emotions* (pp. 274–300). New York: Guilford.

Lindsey, D., & Martin, S. K. (2003). Deepening child poverty: The not so good news about welfare reform. *Children and Youth Services Review, 25,* 165–173.

Lindsey, E. W., & Mize, J. (2000). Parent–child physical and pretense play: Links to children's social competence. *Merrill-Palmer Quarterly, 46,* 565–591.

Linn, M. C., & Petersen, A. C. (1985). Emergence and characterization of sex differences in spatial ability: A meta-analysis. *Child Development, 56,* 1479–1498.

Linver, M. R., Brooks-Gunn, J., & Kohen, D. E. (2002). Family processes as pathways from income to young children's development. *Developmental Psychology, 38,* 719–734.

Lipman, E. L., Boyle, M. H., Dooley, M. D., & Offord, D. R. (2002). Child well-being in single-mother families. *Journal of the American Academy of Child and Adolescent Psychiatry, 41,* 75–82.

Lipsitt, L. P. (2003). Crib death: A biobehavioral phenomenon? *Psychological Science, 12,* 164–170.

Lissens, W., & Sermon, K. (1997). Preimplantation genetic diagnosis—current status and new developments. *Human Reproduction, 12,* 1756–1761.

Liston, R., Crane, J., Hamilton, E., Hughes, O., Kuling, S., & MacKinnon, C. (2002). Fetal health surveillance during labour. *Journal of Obstetrics and Gynecology of Canada, 24,* 250–276.

Litovsky, R. Y., & Ashmead, D. H. (1997). Development of binaural and spatial hearing in infants and children. In R. H. Gilkey & T. R. Anderson (Eds.), *Binaural and spatial hearing in real and virtual environments* (pp. 571–592). Mahwah, NJ: Erlbaum.

Livson, N., & Peskin, H. (1980). Perspectives on adolescence from longitudinal research. In J. Adelson (Ed.), *Handbook of adolescent psychology* (pp. 47–98). New York: Wiley.

Lloyd, L. (1999). Multi-age classes and high ability students. *Review of Educational Research, 69,* 187–212.

Locke, J. (1892). Some thoughts concerning education. In R. H. Quick (Ed.), *Locke on education* (pp. 1–236). Cambridge, U.K.: Cambridge University Press. (Original work published 1690)

Lockhart, R. S., & Craik, F. I. M. (1990). Levels of processing: A retrospective commentary on a framework for memory research. *Canadian Journal of Psychology, 44,* 87–112.

Loeber, R. L., Farrington, D. P., Stouthamer-Loeber, M., Moffitt, T. E., & Caspi, A. (1999). The development of male offending: Key findings from the first decade of the Pittsburgh Youth Study. *Studies on Crime and Crime Prevention, 8,* 245–263.

Loehlin, J. C. (2000). Group differences in intelligence. In R. J. Sternberg (Ed.), *Handbook of intelligence* (pp. 176–193). New York: Cambridge University Press.

Loehlin, J. C., Horn, J. M., & Willerman, L. (1997). Heredity, environment, and IQ in the Texas Adoption Project. In R. J. Sternberg & E. L. Grigorenko (Eds.), *Intelligence, heredity, and environment* (pp. 105–125). New York: Cambridge University Press.

Loganovskaja, T. K., & Loganovsky, K. N. (1999). EEG, cognitive and psychopathological abnormalities in children irradiated in utero. *International Journal of Psychophysiology, 34,* 213–224.

Longstaffe, S., Moffatt, M. E., & Whalen, J. C. (2000). Behavioral and self-concept changes after six months of enuresis treatment: A randomized, controlled trial. *Pediatrics, 105,* 935–940.

Looker, D., & Thiessen, V. (2003). *The digital divide in Canadian schools: Factors affecting student access to and use of information technology.* Ottawa: Canadian Education Statistics Council.

Lord, R. H., & Kozar, B. (1996). Overuse injuries in young athletes. In F. L. Smoll & R. E. Smith (Eds.), *Children and youth in sport: A biopsychological perspective* (pp. 281–294). Dubuque, IA: Brown & Benchmark.

Lorenz, K. Z. (1943). Die angeborenen Formen möglicher Erfahrung. *Zeitschrift für Tierpsychologie, 5,* 235–409.

Lorenz, K. Z. (1952). *King Solomon's ring.* New York: Crowell.

Losey, K. M. (1995). Mexican-American students and classroom interaction: An overview and critique. *Review of Educational Research, 65,* 283–318.

Louie, V. (2001). Parents' aspirations and investment: The role of social class in the educational experiences of 1.5- and second-generation Chinese Americans. *Harvard Educational Review, 71,* 438–474.

Louis, J., Cannard, C., Bastuji, H., & Challamel, M.-J. (1997). Sleep ontogenesis revisited: A longitudinal 24-hour home polygraphic study on 15 normal infants during the first two years of life. *Sleep, 20,* 323–333.

Lozoff, B., Klein, N. K., Nelson, E. C., McClish, D. K., Manuel, M., & Chacon, M. E. (1998). Behavior of infants with iron-deficiency anemia. *Child Development, 69,* 24–36.

Lubinski, D., & Benbow, C. P. (1994). The study of mathematically precocious youth: The first three decades of a planned 50-year study of intellectual talent. In R. F. Subotnik & K. D. Arnold (Eds.), *Beyond Terman: Contemporary longitudinal studies of giftedness and talent* (pp. 255–281). Norwood, NJ: Ablex.

Lucas, S. R., & Behrends, M. (2002). Sociodemographic diversity, correlated achievement, and de facto tracking. *Sociology of Education, 75,* 328–348.

Luciana, M., Sullivan, J., & Nelson, C. A. (2001). Associations between phenylalanine-to-tyrosine ratios and performance on tests of neuropsychological function in adolescents treated early and continuously for phenylketonuria. *Child Development, 72,* 1637–1652.

Ludemann, P. M. (1991). Generalized discrimination of positive facial expressions by seven- and ten-month-old infants. *Child Development, 62,* 55–67.

Luna, B., Thulborn, K. R., Munoz, D. P., Merriam, E. P., Garver, K. E., & Minshew, N. J. (2001). Maturation of widely distributed brain function subserves cognitive development. *Neuroimage, 13,* 786–793.

Lunenburg, F. C. (2000). America's hope: Making schools work for all children. *Journal of Instructional Psychology, 27,* 39–46.

Luria, A. R. (1976). *Cognitive development: Its cultural and social foundations.* Cambridge, MA: Harvard University Press.

Lussier, G., Deater-Deckard, K., Dunn, J., & Davies, L. (2002). Support across two generations: Children's closeness to grandparents following parental divorce and remarriage. *Journal of Family Psychology, 16,* 363–376.

Luster, T., & McAdoo, H. (1996). Family and child influences on educational attainment: A secondary analysis of the High/Scope Perry Preschool data. *Developmental Psychology, 32,* 26–39.

Luthar, S. S., Cushing, T. J., & McMahon, T. J. (1997). Interdisciplinary interface: Developmental principles brought to substance abuse research. In S. S. Luthar, J. A. Burack, D. Cicchetti & J. R. Weisz, J. R. (1997). *Developmental psychopathology* (pp. 437–456). Cambridge: Cambridge University Press.

Lutz, D. J., & Sternberg, R. J. (1999). Cognitive development. In M. H. Bornstein & M. E. Lamb (Eds.), *Developmental psychology: An advanced textbook* (4th ed., pp. 275–311). Mahwah, NJ: Erlbaum.

Lydon-Rochelle, M., Holt, V. L., Easterling, T. R., & Martin, D. P. (2001). Risk of uterine rupture during labor among women with a prior cesarean delivery. *New England Journal of Medicine, 345,* 3–8.

Lyon, G. R., Fletcher, J. M., & Barnes, M. C. (2002). Learning disabilities. In E. J. Mash & R. A. Barkley (Eds.), *Child psychopathology* (2nd ed., pp. 520–586). New York: Guilford.

Lyon, T. D., & Flavell, J. H. (1994). Young children's understanding of "remember" and "forget." *Child Development, 65,* 1357–1371.

Lyons-Ruth, K. (1996). Attachment relationships among children with aggressive behavior problems: The role of disorganized early attachment patterns. *Journal of Consulting and Clinical Psychology, 64,* 64–73.

Lyons-Ruth, K., Bronfman, E., & Parsons, E. (1999). Maternal frightened, frightening, or aytpical behavior and disorganized infant attachment patterns. *Monographs of the Society for Research in Child Development, 64*(3, Serial No. 258), 67–96.

Lyons-Ruth, K., Easterbrooks, A., & Cibelli, C. (1997). Infant attachment strategies, infant mental lag, and maternal depressive symptoms: Predictors of internalizing and externalizing problems at age 7. *Developmental Psychology, 33,* 681–692.

Lytton, H., & Gallagher, L. (2002). Parenting twins and the genetics of parenting. In M. H. Bornstein (Ed.), *Handbook of parenting: Vol. 1. Children and Parenting* (pp. 227–253). Mahwah, NJ: Erlbaum.

Lytton, H., & Romney, D. M. (1991). Parents' sex-related differential socialization of boys and girls: A meta-analysis. *Psychological Bulletin, 109,* 267–296.

Maccoby, E. E. (1984). Middle childhood in the context of the family. In W. A. Collins (Ed.), *Development during middle childhood* (pp. 184–239). Washington, DC: National Academy Press.

Maccoby, E. E. (1998). *The two sexes: Growing up apart, coming together.* Cambridge, MA: Belknap/Harvard University Press.

Maccoby, E. E. (2002). Gender and group process: A developmental perspective. *Current Directions in Psychological Science, 11,* 54–58.

Maccoby, E. E., & Jacklin, C. N. (1987). Gender segregation in childhood. In E. H. Reese (Ed.), *Advances in child development and behavior* (Vol. 20, pp. 239–287). New York: Academic Press.

Maccoby, E. E., & Martin, J. A. (1983). Socialization in the context of the family: Parent–child interaction. In E. M. Hetherington (Ed.), *Handbook of child psychology: Vol. 4. Socialization, personality, and social development* (4th ed., pp. 1–101). New York: Wiley.

MacDorman, M. F., Minino, A. M., Strobino, D. M., & Guyer, B. (2002). Annual summary of vital statistics—2001. *Pediatrics, 110,* 1037–1052.

Mackey, K., Arnold, M. K., & Pratt, M. W. (2001). Adolescents' stories of decision making in more and less authoritative families: Representing the voices of parents in narrative. *Journal of Adolescent Research, 16,* 243–268.

MacKinnon, C. E. (1989). An observational investigation of sibling interactions in married and divorced families. *Developmental Psychology, 25,* 36–44.

Macknin, M. L., Piedmonte, M., Jacobs, J., & Skibinski, C. (2000). Symptoms associated with infant teething: A prospective study. *Pediatrics, 105,* 747–752.

Madan-Swain, A., Fredrick, L. D., & Wallander, J. L. (1999). Returning to school after a serious illness or injury. In R. T. Brown (Ed.), *Cognitive aspects of chronic illness in children* (pp. 312–332). New York: Guilford.

Madole, K. L., & Oakes, L. M. (1999). Making sense of infant categorization: Stable processes and changing representations. *Developmental Review, 19,* 263–296.

Madom, S., Jussim, L., & Eccles, J. (1997). In search of the powerful self-fulfilling prophecy. *Journal of Personality and Social Psychology, 72,* 791–809.

Magnuson, K. A., & Duncan, G. J. (2002). Parents in poverty. In M. H. Bornstein (Ed.), *Handbook of parenting: Vol. 4. Social conditions and applied parenting* (pp. 95–122). Mahwah, NJ: Erlbaum.

Magolda, M. B. B. (2002). Epistemological reflection: The evolution of epistemological assumptions from age 18 to 30. In B. K. Hofer & P. R. Pintrich (Eds.), *Personal epistemology* (pp. 89–102). Mahwah, NJ: Erlbaum.

Mahon, M. M., Goldberg, E. Z., & Washington, S. K. (1999). Concept of death in a sample of Israeli kibbutz children. *Death Studies, 23,* 43–59.

Mahoney, J. L. (2000). Participation in school extracurricular activities as a moderator in the development of antisocial patterns. *Child Development, 71,* 502–516.

Mahoney, J. L., & Magnusson, D. (2001). Parent participation in community activities and the persistence of criminality. *Development and Psychopathology, 13,* 123–139.

Mahoney, J. L., Schweder, A. E., & Stattin, H. (2002). Structured after-school activities as a moderator of depressed mood for adolescents with detached relations to their parents. *Journal of Community Psychology, 30,* 69–86.

Mahoney, J. L., & Stattin, H. (2000). Leisure activities and antisocial behavior: The role of structure and social context. *Journal of Adolescence, 23,* 113–127.

Mahoney, J. L., Stattin, H., & Magnusson, D. (2001). Youth recreation centre participation and criminal offending: A 20-year longitudinal study of Swedish boys. *International Journal of Behavioral Development, 25,* 509–520.

Main, M. (2000). The organized categories of infant, child, and adult attachment: Flexible vs. inflexible attention under attachment-related stress. *Journal of the American Psychoanalytic Association, 48,* 1055–1096.

Main, M., & Solomon, J. (1990). Procedures for identifying infants as disorganized/disoriented during the Ainsworth Strange Situation. In M. Greenberg, D. Cicchetti, & M. Cummings (Eds.), *Attachment in the preschool years: Theory, research, and intervention* (pp. 121–160). Chicago: University of Chicago Press.

Major, B., Spencer, S., Schmader, T., Wolfe, C., & Crocker, J. (1998). Coping with negative stereotypes about intellectual performance: The role of psychological disengagement. *Personality and Social Psychology Bulletin, 24,* 34–50.

Makin, J. E., Fried, P. A., & Watkinson, B. (1991). A comparison of active and passive smoking during pregnancy: Long-term effects. *Neurotoxicology and Teratology, 13,* 5–12.

Malatesta, C. Z., Grigoryev, P., Lamb, C., Albin, M., & Culver, C. (1986). Emotion socialization and expressive development in preterm and full-term infants. *Child Development, 57,* 316–330.

Malina, R. M., & Beunen, G. (1996). Matching of opponents in youth sports. In O. Bar-Or (Ed.), *The child and adolescent athlete* (pp. 202–213). Oxford: Blackwell.

Malina, R. M., & Bouchard, C. (1991). *Growth, maturation, and physical activity.* Champaign, IL: Human Kinetics.

Malina, R. M., & Stanitski, C.L. (1989). Common injuries in preadolescent and adolescent athletes. *Sports Medicine, I,* 32–41.

Malloy, M. H., & Hoffman, H. J. (1995). Prematurity, sudden infant death syndrome, and age of death. *Pediatrics, 96,* 464–471.

Maloni, J. A., Cheng, C. Y., Liebl, C. P., & Maier, J. S. (1996). Transforming prenatal care: Reflections on the past and present with implications for the future. *Journal of Obstetrics, Gynecology, and Neonatal Nursing, 25,* 17–23.

Mandler, J. M. (1998). Representation. In D. Kuhn & R. S. Siegler (Eds.), *Handbook of child psychology: Vol. 1. Theoretical models of human development* (5th ed., pp. 255–308). New York: Wiley.

Mandler, J. M. (1999). Seeing is not the same as thinking: Commentary on "Making Sense of Infant Categorization." *Developmental Review, 19,* 297–306.

Mandler, J. M., & McDonough, L. (1993). Concept formation in infancy. *Cognitive Development, 8,* 291–318.

Mandler, J. M., & McDonough, L. (1996). Drinking and driving don't mix: Inductive generalization in infancy. *Cognition, 59,* 307–335.

Mandler, J. M., & McDonough, L. (1998). On developing a knowledge base in infancy. *Developmental Psychology, 34,* 1274–1288.

Mange, E. J., & Mange, A. P. (1998). *Basic human genetics* (2nd ed.). Sunderland, MA: Sinauer Associates.

Mangelsdorf, S. C., Schoppe, S. J., & Burr, H. (2000). The meaning of parental reports: A contextual approach to the study of temperament and behavior problems. In V. J. Molfese & D. L. Molfese (Eds.), *Temperament and personality across the life span* (pp. 121–140). Mahwah, NJ: Erlbaum.

Maratsos, M. (1998). The acquisition of grammar. In D. Kuhn & R. S. Siegler (Eds.), *Handbook of child psychology: Vol. 1. Theoretical models of human development* (5th ed., pp. 255–308). New York: Wiley.

March of Dimes. (2002). *Folic acid and the prevention of birth defects: A national survey of pre-pregnancy awareness and behavior among women of childbearing age, 1995–2001.* White Plains, NY: Author.

Marcia, J. E. (1966). Development and validation of ego identity status. *Journal of Personality and Social Psychology, 3,* 551–558.

Marcia, J. E. (1980). Identity in adolescence. In J. Adelson (Ed.), *Handbook of adolescent psychology* (pp. 159–187). New York: Wiley.

Marcia, J. E. (1988). Common processes underlying ego identity, cognitive/moral development, and individuation. In D. K. Lapsley & F. P. Clark (Eds.), *Self, ego, and identity* (pp. 211–225). New York: Springer-Verlag.

Marcia, J. E., Waterman, A. S., Matteson, D., Archer, S. L., & Orlofsky, J. L. (1993). *Ego identity: A handbook for psychosocial research.* New York: Springer-Verlag.

Marcon, R. A. (1999a). Differential impact of preschool models on development and early learning of inner-city children: A three-cohort study. *Developmental Psychology, 35,* 358–375.

Marcon, R. A. (1999b). Positive relationships between parent–school involvement and public school in-

ner-city preschoolers' development and academic performance. *School Psychology Review, 28,* 395–412.

Marcus, G. F. (1995). Children's overregularization of English plurals: A quantitative analysis. *Journal of Child Language, 22,* 447–459.

Marcus, G. F., Pinker, S., Ullman, M., Hollander, M., Rosen, T. J., & Xu, F. (1992). Overregularization in language acquisition. *Monographs of the Society for Research in Child Development, 57*(4, Serial No. 228).

Marcus, G. F., Vijayan, S., Rao, S. B., & Vishton, P. M. (1999). Rule learning by seven-month-old infants. *Science, 283,* 77–80.

Markman, E. M. (1992). Constraints on word learning: Speculations about their nature, origins, and domain specificity. In M. R. Gunnar & M. P. Maratsos (Eds.), *Minnesota Symposia on Child Psychology* (Vol. 25, pp. 59–101). Hillsdale, NJ: Erlbaum.

Markovits, H., Benenson, J., & Dolenszky, E. (2001). Evidence that children and adolescents have internal models of peer interactions that are gender differentiated. *Child Development, 72,* 879–886.

Markovits, H., Fleury, M. L., Quinn, S., & Venet, M. (1998). The development of conditional reasoning and the structure of semantic memory. *Child Development, 69,* 742–755.

Markovits, H., Schleifer, M., & Fortier, L. (1989). Development of elementary deductive reasoning in young children. *Developmental Psychology, 25,* 787–793.

Marks, N. F., & Lambert, J. D. (1998). Marital status continuity and change among young and midlife adults. *Journal of Family Issues, 19,* 652–686.

Markstrom, C. A., & Iborra, A. (2003). Adolescent identity formation and rites of passage: The Navajo Kinaaldá ceremony for girls. *Journal of Research on Adolescence, 13,* 399–425.

Markstrom-Adams, C., & Adams, G. R. (1995). Gender, ethnic group, and grade differences in psychosocial functioning during middle adolescence? *Journal of Youth and Adolescence, 24,* 397–414.

Markus, H. R., & Kitayama, S. (1991). Culture and the self: Implications for cognition, emotion, and motivation. *Psychological Review, 98,* 224–253.

Marlier, L., & Schaal, B. (1997). La perception de la familiarité olfactive chez le nouveau-né: Influence différentielle du mode d'alimentation? [The perception of olfactory familiarity in the neonate: Differential influence of the mode of feeding?] *Enfance, 1,* 47–61.

Marlier, L., Schaal, B., & Soussignan, R. (1998). Neonatal responsiveness to the odor of amniotic and lacteal fluids: A test of perinatal chemosensory continuity. *Child Development, 69,* 611–623.

Marsh, H. W. (1990). The structure of academic self-concept: The Marsh/Shavelson model. *Journal of Educational Psychology, 82,* 623–636.

Marsh, H. W., & Ayotte, V. (2003). Do multiple dimensions of self-concept become more differentiated with age? The differential distinctiveness hypothesis. *Journal of Educational Psychology, 95,* 687–706.

Marsh, H. W., Craven, R., & Debus, R. (1998). Structure, stability, and development of young children's self-concepts: A multicohort–multioccasion study. *Child Development, 69,* 1030–1053.

Marsh, H. W., Ellis, L. A., & Craven, R. G. (2002). How do preschool children feel about themselves? Unraveling measurement and multidimensional self-concept structure. *Developmental Psychology, 38,* 376–393.

Marsh, H. W., & Hau, K.-T. (2003). Big-fish–little-pond effect on academic self-concept: A cross-cultural (26-country) test of the negative effects of academically selective schools. *American Psychologist, 58,* 364–376.

Marsh, J. S., & Daigneault, J. P. (1999). The young athlete. *Current Opinion in Pediatrics, 11,* 84–88.

Marshall-Baker, A., Lickliter, R., & Cooper, R. P. (1998). Prolonged exposure to a visual pattern may promote behavioral organization in preterm infants. *Journal of Perinatal and Neonatal Nursing, 12,* 50–62.

Martin, C. L. (1989). Children's use of gender-related information in making social judgments. *Developmental Psychology, 25,* 80–88.

Martin, C. L., & Fabes, R. A. (2001). The stability and consequences of young children's same-sex peer interactions. *Developmental Psychology, 37,* 431–446.

Martin, C. L., Eisenbud, L., & Rose, H. (1995). Children's gender-based reasoning about toys. *Child Development, 66,* 1453–1471.

Martin, C. L., Fabes, R. A., Evans, S. M., & Wyman, H. (1999). Social cognition on the playground: Children's beliefs about playing with girls versus boys and their relations to sex segregated play. *Journal of Social and Personal Relationships, 16,* 751–771.

Martin, C. L., & Halverson, C. F. (1981). A schematic processing model of sex typing and stereotyping in children. *Child Development, 52,* 1119–1134.

Martin, C. L., & Halverson, C. F. (1987). The role of cognition in sex role acquisition. In D. B. Carter (Ed.), *Current conceptions of sex roles and sex typing: Theory and research* (pp. 123–137). New York: Praeger.

Martin, C. L., Ruble, D. N., & Szkrybalo, J. (2002). Cognitive theories of early gender development. *Psychological Bulletin, 128,* 903–933.

Martin, J. A. (1981). A longitudinal study of the consequences of early mother–infant interaction: A microanalytic approach. *Monographs of the Society for Research in Child Development, 46*(3, Serial No. 190).

Martin, J. A., Hamilton, B. E., Ventura, S. J., Menacker, F., & Park, M. M. (2002). *Births: Final data for 2001. National Vital Statistics Reports, Vol. 51, No. 2.* Hyattsville, MD: National Center for Health Statistics.

Martinez, C. R., & Forgatch, M. S. (2002). Adjusting to change: Linking family structure transitions with parenting and boys' adjustment. *Journal of Family Psychology, 16,* 107–117.

Martins, C., & Gaffan, E. A. (2000). Effects of maternal depression on patterns of infant–mother attachment: A meta-analytic investigation. *Journal of Child Psychology and Psychiatry, 41,* 737–746.

Martlew, M., & Connolly, K. J. (1996). Human figure drawings by schooled and unschooled children in Papua New Guinea. *Child Development, 67,* 2743–2762.

Martyn, C. N., Barker, D. J. P., & Osmond, C. (1996). Mothers' pelvic size, fetal growth, and death from stroke and coronary heart disease in men in the UK. *Lancet, 348,* 1264–1268.

Marzolf, D. P., & DeLoache, J. S. (1994). Transfer in young children's understanding of spatial representations. *Child Development, 65,* 1–15.

Masataka, N. (1996). Perception of motherese in a signed language by 6-month-old deaf infants. *Developmental Psychology, 32,* 874–879.

Mascolo, M. F., & Fischer, K. W. (1995). Developmental transformations in appraisals for pride, shame, and guilt. In J. P. Tangney & K. W. Fischer (Eds.), *Self-conscious emotions* (pp. 114–139). New York: Guilford.

Mason, C. A., Cauce, A. M., Gonzales, N., & Hiraga, Y. (1996). Neither too sweet nor too sour: Problem peers, maternal control, and problem behavior in African-American adolescents. *Child Development, 67,* 2115–2130.

Mason, M. G., & Gibbs, J. C. (1993). Social perspective taking and moral judgment among college students. *Journal of Adolescent Research, 8,* 109–123.

Mason, W. A., & Windle, M. (2002). Reciprocal relations between adolescent substance use and delinquency: A longitudinal latent variable analysis. *Journal of Abnormal Psychology, 111,* 63–76.

Masten, A. S. (2001). Ordinary magic: Resilience processes in development. *American Psychologist, 56,* 227–238.

Masten, A. S., & Coatsworth, J. D. (1998). The development of competence in favorable and unfavorable environments: Lessons from research on successful children. *American Psychologist, 53,* 205–220.

Masten, A. S., Hubbard, J. J., Gest, S. D., Tellegen, A., Garmezy, N., & Ramirez, M. (1999). Adaptation in the context of adversity: Pathways to resilience and maladaptation from childhood to late adolescence. *Development and Psychopathology, 11,* 143–169.

Masten, A. S., & Reed, M. J. (2002). Resilience in development. In C. R. Snyder & S. J. Lopez (Eds.), *Handbook of positive psychology* (pp. 74–88). New York: Oxford University Press.

Mastropieri, D., & Turkewitz, G. (1999). Prenatal experience and neonatal responsiveness to vocal expressions of emotion. *Developmental Psychobiology, 35,* 204–214.

Masur, E. F., McIntyre, C. W., & Flavell, J. H. (1973). Developmental changes in apportionment of study time among items in a multi-trial free recall task. *Journal of Experimental Child Psychology, 15,* 237–246.

Masur, E. F., & Rodemaker, J. E. (1999). Mothers' and infants' spontaneous vocal, verbal, and action imitation during the second year. *Merrill-Palmer Quarterly, 45,* 392–412.

Matheny, A. P., Jr. (1991). Children's unintentional injuries and gender: Differentiation and psychosocial aspects. *Children's Environment Quarterly, 8,* 51–61.

Mathews, F., Yudkin, P., & Neil, A. (1999). Influence of maternal nutrition on outcome of pregnancy: Prospective cohort study. *British Medical Journal, 319,* 339–343.

Matsuba, M. K., & Walker, L. J. (1998). Moral reasoning in the context of ego functioning. *Merrill-Palmer Quarterly, 44,* 464–483.

Matsuda, Y., Maeda, T., & Kouno, S. (2003). Comparison of neonatal outcome including cerebral palsy between placenta abruptio and placenta previa. *European Journal of Obstetrics, Gynecology, and Reproductive Biology, 106,* 125–129.

Mattson, S. N., Riley, E. P., Delis, D. C., & Jones, K. L. (1998). Neuropsychological comparison of alcohol-exposed children with or without physical features of fetal alcohol syndrome. *Neuropsychology, 12,* 146–153.

Mattys, S. L., & Jusczyk, P. W. (2001). Phonotactic cues for segmentation of fluent speech by infants. *Cognition, 78,* 91–121.

Matute-Bianchi, M. E. (1986). Ethnic identities and patterns of school success and failure among Mexican-descent and Japanese-American students in a California high school: An ethnographic analysis. *American Journal of Education, 95,* 233–255.

Maurer, D., & Lewis, T. L. (1993). Visual outcomes after infantile cataract. In K. Simons (Ed.), *Early visual development, normal and abnormal* (pp. 454–484). New York: Oxford University Press.

Maurer, D., Lewis, T. L., Brent, H. P., & Levin, A. V. (1999). Rapid improvement in the acuity of infants after visual input. *Science, 286,* 108–110.

Mayberry, R. I. (1994). The importance of childhood to language acquisition: Evidence from American Sign Language. In J. C. Goodman & H. C. Nusbaum (Eds.), *The development of speech perception: The transition from speech sounds to spoken words* (pp. 57–90). Cambridge, MA: MIT Press.

Mayeux, L., & Cillessen, A. H. N. (2003). Development of social problem solving in early childhood: Stability, change, and associations with social competence. *Journal of Genetic Psychology, 164,* 153–173.

Mayer, J. D., Salovey, P., & Caruso, D. R. (2000). Selecting a measure of emotional intelligence: The case for ability scales. In R. Bar-On & J. D. A. Parker (Eds.), *Handbook of emotional intelligence* (pp. 320–342). San Francisco: Jossey-Bass.

Mayes, L. C. (1999). Reconsidering the concept of vulnerability in children using the model of prenatal cocaine exposure. In T. B. Cohen & E. M. Hossein (Eds.), *The vulnerable child* (Vol. 3, pp. 35–54). Madison, CT: International Universities Press.

Mayes, L. C., & Zigler, E. (1992). An observational study of the affective concomitants of mastery in infants. *Journal of Child Psychology and Psychiatry, 33,* 659–667.

Maynard, L. M., Galuska, D. A., Blanck, H. M., & Serdula, M. K. (2003). Maternal perceptions of weight status of children. *Pediatrics, 111,* 1226–1231.

McCabe, A. (1997). Developmental and cross-cultural aspects of children's narration. In M. Bamberg (Ed.), *Narrative development: Six approaches* (pp. 137–174). Mahwah, NJ: Erlbaum.

McCabe, A. E., & Peterson, C. (1988). A comparison of adults' versus children's spontaneous use of *because* and *so. Journal of Genetic Psychology, 149,* 257–268.

McCall, R. B. (1993). Developmental functions for general mental performance. In D. K. Detterman (Ed.), *Current topics in human intelligence* (Vol. 3, pp. 3–29). Norwood, NJ: Ablex.

McCall, R. B., & Carriger, M. S. (1993). A meta-analysis of infant habituation and recognition memory performance as predictors of later IQ. *Child Development, 64,* 57–79.

McCartney, K., Harris, M. J., & Bernieri, F. (1990). Growing up and growing apart: A developmental meta-analysis of twin studies. *Psychological Bulletin, 107,* 226–237.

McCarton, C. (1998). Behavioral outcomes in low birth weight infants. *Pediatrics, 102,* 1293–1297.

McCarton, C. M., Brooks-Gunn, J., Wallace, I. F., Bauer, C. R., Bennett, F. C., Bernbaum, J. C., Broyles, R. S., Casey, P. H., McCormick, M. C., Scott, D. T., Tyson, J., Tonascia, J., & Meinert, C. L. (1997). Results at age 8 years of early intervention for low-birth-weight premature infants: The infant health and development program. *Journal of the American Medical Association, 277,* 126–132.

McCarty, M. E., & Ashmead, D. H. (1999). Visual control of reaching and grasping in infants. *Developmental Psychology, 35,* 620–631.

McConaghy, M. J. (1979). Gender permanence and the genital basis of gender: Stages in the development of constancy of gender identity. *Child Development, 50,* 1223–1226.

McConaghy, N., & Silove, D. (1992). Do sex-linked behaviors in children influence relationships with their parents? *Archives of Sexual Behavior, 21,* 469–479.

McCune, L. (1993). The development of play as the development of consciousness. In M. H. Bornstein & A. O'Reilly (Eds.), *New directions for child development* (No. 59, pp. 67–79). San Francisco: Jossey-Bass.

McDaniel, J., Purcell, D., & D'Augelli, A. R. (2001). The relationship between sexual orientation and risk for suicide: Research findings and future directions for research and prevention. *Suicide and Life-Threatening Behavior, 31,* 84–105.

McDonough, L. (1999). Early declarative memory for location. *British Journal of Developmental Psychology, 17,* 381–402.

McElhaney, K. B., & Allen, J. P. (2001). Autonomy and adolescent social functioning: The moderating effect of risk. *Child Development, 72,* 220–235.

McGee, G. (1997). Legislating gestation. *Human Reproduction, 12,* 407–408.

McGee, L. M., & Richgels, D. J. (2004). *Literacy's beginnings* (4th ed.). Boston: Allyn and Bacon.

McGill-Franzen, A., Lanford, C., & Adams, E. (2002). Learning to be literate: A comparison of five urban early childhood programs. *Journal of Educational Psychology, 94,* 443–464.

McGillicuddy-De Lisi, A. V., Watkins, C., & Vinchur, A. J. (1994). The effect of relationship on children's distributive justice reasoning. *Child Development, 65,* 1694–1700.

McGuffin, P., & Sargeant, M. P. (1991). Major affective disorder. In P. McGuffin & R. Murray (Eds.), *The new genetics of mental illness* (pp. 165–181). London: Butterworth-Heinemann.

McHale, J. P., Lauretti, A., Talbot, J., & Pouquette, C. (2002). Retrospect and prospect in the psychological study of coparenting and family group process. In J. P. McHale & W. S. Grolnick (Eds.), *Retrospect and prospect in the psychological study of families* (pp. 127–165). Mahwah, NJ: Erlbaum.

McHale, S. M., Bartko, W. T., Crouter, A. C., & Perry-Jenkins, M. (1990). Children's housework and psychosocial functioning: The mediating effects of parents' sex-role behaviors and attitudes. *Child Development, 61,* 1413–1426.

McHale, S. M., Updegraff, K. A., Helms-Erikson, H., & Crouter, A. C. (2001). Sibling influences on gender development in middle childhood and early adolescence: A longitudinal study. *Developmental Psychology, 37,* 115–125.

McIntosh, J. L. (2000). Epidemiology of adolescent suicide in the United States. In R. W. Maris, S. S. Canetto, J. L. McIntosh, & M. M. Silverman (Eds.), *Review of Suicidology, 2000* (pp. 3–33). New York: Guilford.

McIntyre, L., Connor, S., & Warren, J. (1998). *A glimpse of child hunger in Canada.* Quebec: Human Resources Development Canada.

McKenna, J. J. (2001). Why we never ask "Is it safe for infants to sleep alone?" *Academy of Breast Feeding Medicine News and Views, 7*(4), 32, 38.

McKenna, J. J. (2002, October 2). Personal communication.

McKeown, R. E., Garrison, C. Z., Cuffe, S. P., Waller, J. L., Jackson, K. L., & Addy, C. L. (1998). Incidence and predictors of suicidal behaviors in a longitudinal sample of young adolescents. *Journal of the American Academy of Child and Adolescent Psychiatry, 37,* 612–619.

McKown, C., & Weinstein, R. S. (2002). Modeling the role of child ethnicity and gender in children's differential response to teacher expectations. *Journal of Applied Social Psychology, 32,* 159–184.

McKown, C., & Weinstein, R. S. (2003). The development and consequences of stereotype consciousness in middle childhood. *Child Development, 74,* 498–515.

McKusick, V. A. (1998). *Mendelian inheritance in man: A catalog of human genes and genetic disorders.* Baltimore: Johns Hopkins University Press.

McLanahan, S. (1999). Father absence and the welfare of children. In E. M. Hetherington (Ed.), *Coping with divorce, single parenting, and remarriage: A risk and resiliency perspective* (pp. 117–145). Mahwah, NJ: Erlbaum.

McLanahan, S. S., & Carlson, M. J. (2002). Welfare reform, fertility, and father involvement. *Future of Children, 12,* 111–115.

McLean, D. F., Timajchy, K. H., Wingo, P. A., & Floyd, R. L. (1993). Psychosocial measurement: Implications of the study of preterm delivery in black women. *American Journal of Preventive Medicine, 9,* 39–81.

McLean, M., & Smith, R. (2001). Corticotropin-releasing hormone and human parturition. *Reproduction, 121,* 493–501.

McLean, M., Bisits, A., Davies, J., Walters, W., Hackshaw, A., De Voss, K., & Smith, R. (1999). Predicting risk of preterm delivery by second-trimester measurement of maternal plasma corticotropin-releasing hormone and alpha-fetoprotein concentrations. *American Journal of Obstetrics and Gynecology, 181,* 207–215.

McManus, I. C., Sik, G., Cole, D. R., Mellon, A. F., Wong, J., & Kloss, J. (1988). The development of handedness in children. *British Journal of Developmental Psychology, 6,* 257–273.

McNamee, S., & Peterson, J. (1986). Young children's distributive justice reasoning, behavior, and role taking: Their consistency and relationship. *Journal of Genetic Psychology, 146,* 399–404.

MCR Vitamin Study Research Group. (1991). Prevention of neural tube defects: Results of the Medical Research Council Vitamin Study. *Lancet, 338,* 131–137.

Mead, G. H. (1934). *Mind, self, and society.* Chicago: University of Chicago Press.

Mead, M. (1928). *Coming of age in Samoa.* Ann Arbor, MI: Morrow.

Mead, M., & Newton, N. (1967). Cultural patterning of perinatal behavior. In S. Richardson & A. Guttmacher (Eds.), *Childbearing: Its social and psychological aspects* (pp. 142–244). Baltimore: Williams & Wilkins.

Mebert, C. J. (1991). Dimensions of subjectivity in parents' ratings of infant temperament. *Child Development, 62,* 352–361.

Meeus, W. (1996). Studies on identity development in adolescence: An overview of research and some new data. *Journal of Youth and Adolescence, 25,* 569–598.

Meeus, W., Iedema, J., Helsen, M., & Vollebergh, W. (1999). Patterns of adolescent identity development: Review of literature and longitudinal analysis. *Developmental Review, 19,* 419–461.

Meeus, W., Oosterwegel, A., & Vollebergh, W. (2002). Parental and peer attachment and identity development in adolescence. *Journal of Adolescence, 25,* 93–106.

Mehlmadrona, L., & Madrona, M. M. (1997). Physician- and midwife-attended home births—effects of breech, twin, and post-dates outcome data on mortality rates. *Journal of Nurse-Midwifery, 42,* 91–98.

Meisels, S. J., Dichtelmiller, M., & Liaw, F. R. (1993). A multidimensional analysis of early childhood intervention programs. In C. H. Zeanah (Ed.), *Handbook of infant mental health* (pp. 361–385). New York: Guilford.

Meltzoff, A. N. (1990). Towards a developmental cognitive science. *Annals of the New York Academy of Sciences, 608,* 1–37.

Meltzoff, A. N. (1995). Understanding the intentions of others: Reenactment of intended acts by 18-month-old children. *Developmental Psychology, 31,* 838–850.

Meltzoff, A. N., & Decety, J. (2003). What imitation tells us about social cognition: A rapprochement between developmental psychology and cognitive neuroscience. *Philosophical Transactions of the Royal Society of London, Series B, Biological Sciences, 358,* 491–500.

Meltzoff, A. N., & Kuhl, P. K. (1994). Faces and speech: Intermodal processing of biologically relevant signals in infants and adults. In D. J. Lewkowicz & R. Lickliter (Eds.), *The development of intersensory perception: Comparative perspectives* (pp. 335–369). Hillsdale, NJ: Erlbaum.

Meltzoff, A. N., & Moore, M. K. (1977). Imitation of facial and manual gestures by human neonates. *Science, 198,* 75–78.

Meltzoff, A. N., & Moore, M. K. (1994). Imitation, memory, and the representation of persons. *Infant Behavior and Development, 17,* 83–99.

Meltzoff, A. N., & Moore, M. K. (1998). Object representation, identity, and the paradox of early permanence: Steps toward a new framework. *Infant Behavior and Development, 21,* 201–235.

Meltzoff, A. N., & Moore, M. K. (1999). Persons and representation: Why infant imitation is important for theories of human development. In J. Nadel & G. Butterworth (Eds.), *Imitation in infancy* (pp. 9–35). Cambridge, U.K.: Cambridge University Press.

Mennella, J. A., & Beauchamp, G. K. (1998). Early flavor experiences: Research update. *Nutrition Reviews, 56,* 205–211.

Menyuk, P., Liebergott, J. W., & Schultz, M. C. (1995). *Early language development in full-term and premature infants.* Hillsdale, NJ: Erlbaum.

Meredith, N. V. (1978). *Human body growth in the first ten years of life.* Columbia, SC: State Printing.

Mervis, C. B., Pani, J. R., & Pani, A. M. (2003). Transaction of child cognitive-linguistic abilities and adult input in the acquisition of lexical categories at the basic and subordinate levels. In D. H. Rakison & L. M. Oakes (Ed.), *Early category and concept development* (pp. 242–274). New York: Oxford University Press.

Meyer-Bahlburg, H. F. L., Ehrhardt, A. A., Rosen, L. R., Gruen, R. S., Veridiano, N. P., Vann, F. H., & Neuwalder, H. F. (1995). Prenatal estrogens and the development of homosexual orientation. *Developmental Psychology, 31,* 12–21.

Meyers, C., Adam, R., Dungan, J., & Prenger, V. (1997). Aneuploidy in twin gestations: When is maternal age advanced? *Obstetrics and Gynecology, 89,* 248–251.

Miccio, A. W., Yont, K. M., Clemons, H. L., & Vernon-Feagans, L. (2002). Otitis media and the acquisition of consonants. In F. Windsor & M. L. Kelly (Eds.), *Investigations in clinical phonetics and linguistics* (pp. 429–235). Mahwah, NJ: Erlbaum.

Miceli, P. J., Whitman, T. L., Borkowski, J. G., Braungart-Riekder, J., & Mitchell, D. W. (1998). Individual differences in infant information processing: The role of temperamental and maternal factors. *Infant Behavior and Development, 21,* 119–136.

Michael, R. T., Gagnon, J. H., Laumann, E. O., & Kolata, G. (1994). *Sex in America.* Boston: Little, Brown.

Michaels, G. Y. (1988). Motivational factors in the decision and timing of pregnancy. In G. Y. Michaels & W. A. Goldberg (Eds.), *The transition to parenthood: Current theory and research* (pp. 23–61). New York: Cambridge University Press.

Michels, K. B., Trichopoulos, D., Robins, J. M., Rosner, B. A., Manson, J. E., Hunter, D. J., Colditz, G. A., Hankinson, S. E., Speizer, F. E., & Willett, W. C. (1996). Birthweight as a risk factor for breast cancer. *Lancet, 348,* 1542–1546.

Milberger, S., Biederman, J., Faraone, S. V., Guite, J., & Tsuang, M. T. (1997). Pregnancy, delivery and infancy complications and attention-deficit hyperactivity disorder: Issues of gene–environment interaction. *Biological Psychiatry, 41,* 65–75.

Miles, H. L. (1999). Symbolic communication with and by great apes. In S. T. Parker, R. W. Mitchell, & H. L. Miles (Eds.), *The mentalities of gorillas and orangutans* (pp. 197–210). Cambridge, U.K.: Cambridge University Press.

Miller, B. C., Fan, X., Christensen, M., Grotevant, H. D., & van Dulmen, M. (2000). Comparisons of adopted and nonadopted adolescents in a large, nationally representative sample. *Child Development, 71,* 1458–1473.

Miller, C. J., Sanchez, J., & Hynd, G. W. (2003). Neurological correlates of reading disabilities. In H. L. Swanson, K. R. Harris, & S. Graham (Eds.), *Handbook of learning disabilities* (pp. 242–255). New York: Guilford.

Miller, J. G. (1997). Culture and self: uncovering the cultural grounding of psychological theory. In J. G. Snodgrass & R. L. Thompson (Eds.), *Annals of the New York Academy of Sciences* (Vol. 18, pp. 217–231). New York: New York Academy of Sciences.

Miller, J. G., & Bersoff, D. M. (1995). Development in the context of everyday family relationships: Culture, interpersonal morality, and adaptation. In M. Killen & D. Hart (Eds.), *Morality in everyday life: Developmental perspectives* (pp. 259–282). Cambridge, U.K.: Cambridge University Press.

Miller, K. S., Forehand, R., & Kotchick, B. (1999). Adolescent sexual behavior in two ethnic minority samples: The role of family variables. *Journal of Marriage and the Family, 61,* 85–98.

Miller, L. T., & Vernon, P. A. (1992). The general factor in short-term memory, intelligence, and reaction time. *Intelligence, 16,* 5–29.

Miller, L. T., & Vernon, P. A. (1997). Developmental changes in speed of information processing in young children. *Developmental Psychology, 33,* 549–554.

Miller, P. H. (2000). How to best utilize a deficiency. *Child Development, 71,* 1013–1017.

Miller, P. H., & Bigi, L. (1979). The development of children's understanding of attention. *Merrill-Palmer Quarterly, 25,* 235–250.

Miller, P. H., & Woody-Ramsey, J., & Aloise, P. A. (1991). The role of strategy effortfulness in strategy effectiveness. *Developmental Psychology, 27,* 738–745.

Miller, P. J., Fung, H., & Mintz, J. (1996). Self-construction through narrative practices: A Chinese and American comparison of early socialization. *Ethos, 24,* 1–44.

Miller, P. J., Hengst, J. A., & Wang, S. (2003). Ethnographic methods: Applications from developmental cultural psychology. In P. M. Camic & J. E. Rhodes (Eds.), *Qualitative research in psychology* (pp. 219–242). Washington, DC: American Psychological Association.

Miller, P. J., Wang, S., Sandel, T., & Cho, G. E. (2002). Self-esteem as folk theory: A comparison of European American and Taiwanese mothers' beliefs. *Parenting: Science and Practice, 2,* 209–239.

Miller, P. J., Wiley, A. R., Fung, H., & Liang, C.-H. (1997). Personal storytelling as a medium of socialization in Chinese and American families. *Child Development, 68,* 557–568.

Miller, P.A., Eisenberg, N., Fabes, R. A., & Shell, R. (1996). Relations of moral reasoning and vicarious emotion to young children's prosocial behavior toward peers and adults. *Developmental Psychology, 32,* 210–219.

Miller, R. B. (2000). Do children make a marriage unhappy? *Family Science Review, 13,* 60–73.

Miller, S. A., Hardin, C. A., & Montgomery, D. E. (2003). Young children's understanding of the conditions for knowledge acquisition. *Journal of Cognition and Development, 4,* 325–356.

Mills, R. J., & Bhandari, S. (2003). Health insurance coverage in the United States: 2002. *Current Population Reports,* P60-223. Retrieved from http://www.census.gov/prod/2003pubs/p60-223.pdf

Mills, R., Coffey-Corina, S., & Neville, H. J. (1997). Language comprehension and cerebral specialization from 13 to 20 months. *Developmental Neuropsychology, 13,* 397–445.

Mills, R., & Grusec, J. E. (1989). Cognitive, affective, and behavioral consequences of praising altruism. *Merrill-Palmer Quarterly, 35,* 299–326.

Millstein, S. G., & Irwin, C. E. (1988). Accident-related behaviors in adolescents: A biosocial view. *Alcohol, Drugs, and Driving, 4,* 21–29.

Minde, K. (2000). Prematurity and serious medical conditions in infancy: Implications for development, behavior, and intervention. In C. H. Zeanah, Jr. (Ed.), *Handbook of infant mental health* (pp. 176–194). New York: Guilford.

Mindell, J. A., Owens, J. A., & Carskadon, M. A. (1999). Developmental features of sleep. *Child and Adolescent Psychiatric Clinics of North America, 8,* 695–725.

Mischel, W., & Liebert, R. M. (1966). Effects of discrepancies between observed and imposed reward criteria on their acquisition and transmission. *Journal of Personality and Social Psychology, 3,* 45–53.

Mitchell, A., & Boss, B. J. (2002). Adverse effects of pain on the nervous systems of newborns and young children: A review of the literature. *Journal of Neuroscience Nursing, 34,* 228–235.

Mize, J., & Pettit, G. S. (1997). Mothers' social coaching, mother–child relationship style, and children's peer competence: Is the medium the message? *Child Development, 68,* 312–332.

Moerk, E. L. (1992). *A first language taught and learned.* Baltimore: Paul H. Brookes.

Moffat, S. D., Hampson, E., & Hatzipantelis, M. (1998). Navigation is a "virtual" maze: Sex differences and correlation with psychometric measures of spatial ability in humans. *Evolution and Human Behavior, 19*(2), 73–87.

Moffitt, T. E., Caspi, A., Belsky, J., & Silva, P. A. (1992). Childhood experience and onset of menarche: A test of a sociobiological model. *Child Development, 63,* 47–58.

Moffitt, T. E., Caspi, A., Dickson, N., Silva, P., & Stanton, W. (1996). Childhood-onset versus adolescent-onset antisocial conduct problems in males: Natural history from ages 3 to 18 years. *Development and Psychopathology, 8,* 399–424.

Mogford-Bevan, K. (1999). Twins and their language development. In A. C. Sandbank (Ed.), *Twin and triplet psychology.* New York: Routledge.

Mokdad, A. H., Bowman, B. A., Ford, E. S., Vinicor, F., Marks, J. S., & Koplan, J. P. (2001). The continuing epidemics of obesity and diabetes in the United States. *Journal of the American Medical Association, 286,* 1195–1200.

Moll, I. (1994). Reclaiming the natural line in Vygotsky's theory of cognitive development. *Human Development, 37,* 333–342.

Molnar, J., & Babbitt, B. (2000). *You don't have to be thin to win.* New York: Villard.

Mondloch, C. J., Lewis, T., Budreau, D. R., Maurer, D., Dannemiller, J. L., Stephens, B. R., & Kleiner-Gathercoal, K. A. (1999). Face perception during early infancy. *Psychological Science, 10,* 419–422.

Money, J. (1993). Specific neurocognitional impairments associated with Turner (45,X) and Klinefelter (47,XXY) syndromes: A review. *Social Biology, 40,* 147–151.

Monk, C., Fifer, W. P., Myers, M. M., Sloan, R. P., Trien, L., & Hurtado, A. (2000). Maternal stress responses and anxiety during pregnancy: Effects on fetal heart rate. *Developmental Psychobiology, 36,* 67–77.

Montague, D. P. F., & Walker-Andrews, A. S. (2001). Peekaboo: A new look at infants' perception of emotion expressions. *Developmental Psychology, 37,* 826–838.

Montemayor, R., & Eisen, M. (1977). The development of self-conceptions from childhood to adolescence. *Developmental Psychology, 13,* 314–319.

Moon, C., Cooper, R. P., & Fifer, W. P. (1993). Two-day-old infants prefer their native language. *Infant Behavior and Development, 16,* 495–500.

Moon, S. M., & Feldhusen, J. F. (1994). The Program for Academic and Creative Enrichment (PACE): A follow-up study ten years later. In R. F. Subotnik & K. D. Arnold (Eds.), *Beyond Terman: Contemporary longitudinal studies of giftedness and talent* (pp. 375–400). Norwood, NJ: Ablex.

Moore, D. R., & Florsheim, P. (2001). Interpersonal processes and psychopathology among expectant and nonexpectant adolescent couples. *Journal of Consulting and Clinical Psychology, 69,* 101–113.

Moore, D. S., Spence, M. J., & Katz, G. S. (1997). Six-month-olds' categorization of natural infant-directed utterances. *Developmental Psychology, 33,* 980–989.

Moore, E. G. J. (1986). Family socialization and the IQ test performance of traditionally and transracially adopted black children. *Developmental Psychology, 22,* 317–326.

Moore, G. A., Cohn, J. F., & Campbell, S. B. (2001). Infant affective responses to mother's still face at 6 months differentially predict externalizing and internalizing behaviors at 18 months. *Developmental Psychology, 37,* 706–714.

Moore, K. A., Morrison, D. R., & Green, A. D. (1997). Effects on the children born to adolescent mothers. In R. A. Maynard (Ed.), *Kids having kids* (pp. 145–180). Washington, DC: Urban Institute.

Moore, K. A., Myers, D. E., Morrison, D. R., Nord, C. W., Brown, B., & Edmonston, B. (1993). Age at first childbirth and later poverty. *Journal of Research on Adolescence, 3,* 393–422.

Moore, K. L., & Persaud, T. V. N. (2003). *Before we are born* (6th ed.). Philadelphia: Saunders.

Moore, K. L., Persaud, T. V. N., & Shiota, K. (1994). *Color atlas of clinical embryology.* Philadelphia: Saunders.

Moore, M. K., & Meltzoff, A. N. (1999). New findings on object permanence: A developmental difference between two types of occlusion. *British Journal of Developmental Psychology, 17,* 563–584.

Moore, W. S. (2002). Understanding learning in a postmodern world: Reconsidering the Perry scheme of ethical and intellectual development. In B. K. Hofer & P. R. Pintrich (Eds.), *Personal epistemology* (pp. 17–36). Mahwah, NJ: Erlbaum.

Moorehouse, M. J. (1991). Linking maternal employment patterns to mother–child activities and children's school competence. *Developmental Psychology, 27,* 295–303.

Moran, G. F., & Vinovskis, M. A. (1986). The great care of godly parents: Early childhood in Puritan New England. *Monographs of the Society for Research in Child Development, 50*(4–5, Serial No. 211).

Morelli, G. A., Rogoff, B., & Angelillo, C. (2003). Cultural variation in young children's access to work or involvement in specialized child-focused activities. *International Journal of Behavioral Development, 27,* 264–274.

Morelli, G., Rogoff, B., Oppenheim, D., & Goldsmith, D. (1992). Cultural variation in infants' sleeping arrangements: Questions of independence. *Developmental Psychology, 28,* 604–613.

Morgan, B., Maybery, M., & Durkin, K. (2003). Weak central coherence, poor joint attention, and low verbal ability: Independent deficits in early autism. *Developmental Psychology, 39,* 646–656.

Morgane, P. J., Austin-LaFrance, R., Bronzino, J., Tonkiss, J., Diaz-Cintra, S., Cintra, L., Kemper, T., & Galler, J. R. (1993). Prenatal malnutrition and development of the brain. *Neuroscience and Biobehavioral Reviews, 17,* 91–128.

Mori, L., & Peterson, L. (1995). Knowledge of safety of high and low active–impulsive boys: Implications for child injury prevention. *Journal of Clinical Child Psychology, 24,* 370–376.

Morris, J. F., Balsam, K. F., & Rothblum, E. D. (2001). Lesbian and bisexual mothers and nonmothers: Demographics and the coming-out process. *Journal of Family Psychology, 16,* 144–156.

Morrison, D. R., & Coiro, M. J. (1999). Parental conflict and marital disruption: Do children benefit when high-conflict marriages are dissolved? *Journal of Marriage and the Family, 61,* 626–637.

Morrongiello, B. A., Fenwick, K. D., & Chance, G. (1998). Crossmodal learning in newborn infants: Inferences about properties of auditory-visual events. *Infant Behavior and Development, 21,* 543–554.

Morrongiello, B. A., Midgett, C., & Shields, R. (2001). Don't run with scissors: Young children's knowledge of home safety rules. *Journal of Pediatric Psychology, 26,* 105–115.

Morrongiello, B. A., & Rennie, H. (1998). Why do boys engage in more risk taking than girls? The role of attributions, beliefs, and risk appraisals. *Journal of Pediatric Psychology, 23,* 33–43.

Mortensen, E. L., Michaelsen, K. F., Sanders, S. A., & Reinisch, J. M. (2002). The association between duration of breastfeeding and adult intelligence. *Journal of the American Medical Association, 287,* 2365–2371.

Moses, L. J., Baldwin, D. A., Rosicky, J. G., & Tidball, G. (2001). Evidence for referential understanding in the emotions domain at twelve and eighteen months. *Child Development, 72,* 718–735.

Moshman, D. (1998). Cognitive development beyond childhood. In D. Kuhn & R. S. Siegler (Eds.), *Handbook of child psychology: Vol. 2. Cognition, perception, and language* (5th ed., pp. 947–978). New York: Wiley.

Moshman, D. (1999). *Adolescent psychological development: Rationality, morality, and identity.* Mahwah, NJ: Erlbaum.

Moshman, D., & Franks, B. A. (1986). Development of the concept of inferential validity. *Child Development, 57,* 153–165.

Mosko, S., Richard, C., & McKenna, J. J. (1997a). Infant arousals during mother–infant bed sharing: Implications for infant sleep and sudden infant death syndrome research. *Pediatrics, 100,* 841–849.

Mosko, S., Richard, C., & McKenna, J. J. (1997b). Maternal sleep and arousals during bedsharing with infants. *Sleep, 20,* 142–150.

Mosteller, F. (1995). The Tennessee Study of Class Size in the Early School Grades. *Future of Children, 5*(2), 113–127.

Motl, R. W., Dishman, R. K., Saunders, R. P., Dowda, M., Felton, G., Ward, D. S., & Pate, R. R. (2002). Examining social–cognitive determinants of intention and physical activity among black and white adolescent girls using structural equation modeling. *Health Psychology, 21,* 459–467.

Mounts, N. S., & Steinberg, L. (1995). An ecological analysis of peer influence on adolescent grade point average and drug use. *Developmental Psychology, 31,* 915–922.

Mrug, S., Hoza, B., & Gerdes, A. C. (2001). Children with attention-deficit/hyperactivity disorder: Peer relationships and peer-oriented interventions. In D. W. Nangle & C. A. Erdley (Eds.), *The role of friendship in psychological adjustment* (pp. 51–77). San Francisco: Jossey-Bass.

Mueller, C. M., & Dweck, C. S. (1998). Intelligence praise can undermine motivation and performance. *Journal of Personality and Social Psychology, 75,* 33–52.

Mulder, E. J. H., Robles de Medina, P. G., Huizink, A. C., Van den Bergh, B. R. H., Buitelaar, J. K., & Visser, G. H. A. (2002). Prenatal maternal stress: Effects on pregnancy and the (unborn) child. *Early Human Development, 70,* 3–14.

Muldoon, O., & Cairns, E. (1999). Children, young people, and war: Learning to cope. In E. Frydenberg (Ed.), *Learning to cope: Developing as a person in complex societies* (pp. 322–337). New York: Oxford University Press.

Muller, F., Rebiff, M., Taillandier, A., Qury, J. F., & Mornet, E. (2000). Parental origin of the extra chromosome in prenatally diagnosed fetal trisomy. *Human Genetics, 106,* 340–344.

Müller, U., Overton, W. F., & Reene, K. (2001). Development of conditional reasoning: A longitudinal study. *Journal of Cognition and Development, 2,* 27–49.

Mundy, P. (2003). The neural basis of social impairments in autism: The role of the dorsal medial-frontal cortex and anterior cingulated system. *Journal of Child Psychology and Psychiatry and Allied Disciplines, 44,* 793–809.

Mundy, P., & Stella, J. (2000). Joint attention, social orienting, and nonverbal communication in autism. In A. M. Wetherby & B. M. Prizant (Eds.), *Autism spectrum disorders* (Vol. 9, pp. 55–77). Baltimore, MD: Paul H. Brookes.

Munro, G., & Adams, G. R. (1977). Ego identity formation in college students and working youth. *Developmental Psychology, 13,* 523–524.

Muret-Wagstaff, S., & Moore, S. G. (1989). The Hmong in America: Infant behavior and rearing practices. In J. K. Nugent, B. M. Lester, & T. B. Brazelton (Eds.), *Biology, culture, and development* (Vol. 1, pp. 319–339). Norwood, NJ: Ablex.

Muris, P., Merckelbach, H., Gadet, B., & Moulaert, V. (2000). Fears, worries, and scary dreams in 4- to 12-year-old children: their content, developmental pattern, and origins. *Journal of Clinical Child Psychology, 29,* 43–52.

Muris, P., Merckelbach, H., Ollendick, T. H., King, N. J., & Bogie, N. (2001). Children's nighttime fears: Parent–child ratings of frequency, content, origins, coping behaviors and severity. *Behaviour Research and Therapy, 39,* 13–28.

Murray, A. D. (1985). Aversiveness is in the mind of the beholder. In B. M. Lester & C. F. Z. Boukydis (Eds.), *Infant crying* (pp. 217–239). New York: Plenum.

Murray, L., & Cooper, P. J. (1997). Postpartum depression and child development. *Psychological Medicine, 27,* 253–260.

Murray, L., Sinclair, D., Cooper, P., Ducournau, P., & Turner, P. (1999). The socioemotional development of 5-year-old children of postnatally depressed mothers. *Journal of Child Psychology and Psychiatry, 40,* 1259–1271.

Mussen, P., & Eisenberg-Berg, N. (1977). *Roots of caring, sharing, and helping.* San Francisco: Freeman.

Mustillo, S., Worthman, C., Erkanli, A., Keeler, G., Angold, A., & Costello, E. J. (2003). Obesity and psychiatric disorder: Developmental trajectories. *Pediatrics, 111,* 851–859.

Mutti, D. O., Mitchell, G. L., Moeschberger, M. L., Jones, L. A., & Zadnik, K. (2002). Parental myopia, near work, school achievement, and children's refractive error. *Investigative Ophthalmology and Visual Science, 43,* 3633–3640.

Myers, M. G., Brown, S. A., Tate, S., Abrantes, A., & Tomlinson, K. (2001). *Adolescents, alcohol, and substance abuse* (pp. 275–296). New York: Guilford.

Nagin, D., & Tremblay, R. E. (1999). Trajectories of boys' physical aggression, opposition, and hyperactivity on the path to physically violent and nonviolent juvenile delinquency. *Child Development, 70,* 1181–1196.

Nagy, W. E., & Scott, J. A. (2000). Vocabulary processes. In M. L. Kamil & P. B. Mosenthal (Eds.), *Handbook of reading research* (Vol. 3, pp. 269–284). Mahwah, NJ: Erlbaum.

Namy, L. L., & Waxman, S. R. (1998). Words and gestures: Infants' interpretations of different forms of symbolic reference. *Child Development, 69,* 295–308.

Nánez, J., Sr., & Yonas, A. (1994). Effects of luminance and texture motion on infant defensive reactions to optical collision. *Infant Behavior and Development, 17,* 165–174.

Nansel, T. R., Overpeck, M., Pila, R. S., Ruan, W. J., Simons-Morton, B., & Scheidt, P. (2001). Bullying behaviors among U.S. youth: Prevalence and association with psychosocial adjustment. *Journal of the American Medical Association, 285,* 2094–2100.

Narvaez, D., Mitchell, C., Bock, T., Endicott, L., & Gardner, J. (2001). *Guidelines for developing curricula for middle school students that meet graduation standards while teaching character.* In press.

Nastasi, B. K., & Clements, D. H. (1994). Effectance motivation, perceived scholastic competence, and higher-order thinking in two cooperative computer environments. *Journal of Educational Computing Research, 10,* 249–275.

National Association for the Education of Young Children. (1998). *Accreditation criteria and procedures of the National Academy of Early Childhood Programs* (2nd ed.). Washington, DC: Author.

National Council of Teachers of Mathematics. (2000). *Principles and standards for school mathematics.* Reston, VA: Author.

National Federation of State High School Associations. (2003). *High school athletic participation survey.* Kansas City, MO: Author.

National Institutes of Health (NIH). (2003). *Genes and disease.* Retrieved from http://www.ncbi.nlm.nih.gov/books/bv.fcgi?call=bv.View..ShowSection&rid=gnd

National Sleep Foundation. (2000). *Sleep in America.* Retrieved from http://www.sleepfoundation.org

Navarrete, C., Martinez, I., & Salamanca, F. (1994). Paternal line of transmission of chorea of Huntington with very early onset. *Genetic Counseling, 5,* 175–178.

Needham, A. (2001). Object recognition and object segregation in 4.5-month-old infants. *Journal of Experimental Child Psychology, 78,* 3–24.

Neff, K. D., & Helwig, C. C. (2002). A constructivist approach to understanding the development of reasoning about rights and authority within cultural contexts. *Cognitive Development, 17,* 1429–1450.

Neitzel, C., & Stright, A. D. (2003). Mothers' scaffolding of children's problem solving: Establishing a foundation of academic self-regulatory competence. *Journal of Family Psychology, 17,* 147–159.

Nelson, C. A. (1997). The neurobiological basis of early memory development. In N. Cowan (Ed.), *The development of memory in childhood* (pp. 41–82). Hove, U.K.: Psychology Press.

Nelson, C. A. (2000). Neural plasticity and human development: The role of early experience in sculpting memory systems. *Developmental Science, 3,* 115–130.

Nelson, C. A. (2001). The development and neural bases of face recognition. *Infant and Child Development, 10,* 3–18.

Nelson, C. A. (2002). Neural development and lifelong plasticity. In R. M. Lerner, F. Jacobs, & D. Wertlieb (Eds.), *Handbook of applied developmental science* (Vol. 1, pp. 31–60). Thousand Oaks, CA: Sage.

Nelson, C. A., & Bosquet, M. (2000). Neurobiology of fetal and infant development: Implications for infant mental health. In C. H. Zeanah, Jr. (Ed.), *Handbook of infant mental* health (2nd ed., pp. 37–59). New York: Guilford.

Nelson, E. A. S., Schiefenhoevel, W., & Haimerl, F. (2000). Child care practices in nonindustrialized societies. *Pediatrics, 105,* e75.

Nelson, J. (1996). *Positive discipline.* New York: Ballantine.

Nelson, K. (1973). Structure and strategy in learning to talk. *Monographs of the Society for Research in Child Development, 38*(1–2, Serial No. 149).

Nelson, K. (1993). The psychological and social origins of autobiographical memory. *Psychological Science, 1,* 1–8.

Nelson, K. (2001). Language and the self: From the "experiencing I" to the "continuing me." In C. Moore & K. Lemmon (Eds.), *The self in time* (pp. 15–33). Mahwah NJ: Erlbaum.

Nelson, L. J. (2003). Rites of passage in emerging adulthood: Perspectives of young Mormons. In J. J. Arnett & N. L. Galambos (Eds.), *Exploring cultural conceptions of the transitions to adulthood (New directions for child and adolescent development,* No. 100, pp. 33–49). San Francisco: Jossey-Bass.

Nesdale, D., & Flesser, D. (2001). Social identity and the development of children's group attitudes. *Child Development, 72,* 506–517.

Nestle, M., & Jacobson, M. F. (2000). Halting the obesity epidemic: A public health policy approach. *Public Health Reports, 115,* 12–24.

Netley, C. T. (1986). Summary overview of behavioural development in individuals with neonatally identified X and Y aneuploidy. *Birth Defects, 22,* 293–306.

Neuman, S. B. (1999). Books make a difference: A study of access to literacy. *Reading Research Quarterly, 34,* 286–311.

Neumark-Sztainer, D., Hannan, P. J., Story, M., Croll, J., & Perry, C. (2003). Family meal patterns: Associations with sociodemographic characteristics and improved dietary intake among adolescents. *Journal of the American Dietetic Association, 103,* 317–322.

Neville, H. J., & Bavelier, D. (1998). Neural organization and plasticity of language. *Current Opinion in Neurobiology, 8,* 254–258.

Neville, H. J., & Bruer, J. T. (2001). Language processing: How experience affects brain organization. In D. B. Bailey, Jr., J. T. Bruer, F. J. Symons, & J. W. Lichtman (Eds.), *Critical thinking about critical periods* (pp. 151–172). Baltimore: Paul H. Brookes.

Newachek, P., Hung, Y.-Y., Hochstein, M., & Halfon, N. (2002). Access to health care for disadvantaged young children. *Journal of Early Intervention, 25,* 1–11.

Newborg, J., Stock, J. R., & Wnek, L. (1984). *Battelle Developmental Inventory.* Allen, TX: LINC Associates.

Newcomb, A. F., Bukowski, W. M., & Pattee, L. (1993). Children's peer relations: A meta-analytic review of popular, rejected, neglected, controversial, and average sociometric status. *Psychological Bulletin, 113,* 99–128.

Newcomb, M. D., Abbott, R. D., Catalano, R. F., Hawkins, J. D., Battin-Pearson, S., & Hill, K. (2002). Mediational and deviance theories of late high school failure: Process roles of structural strains, academic competence, and general versus specific problem behavior. *Journal of Counseling Psychology, 49,* 172–186.

Newcombe, N., & Fox, N. A. (1994). Infantile amnesia: Through a glass darkly. *Child Development 65,* 31–40.

Newcombe, N., & Huttenlocher, J. (1992). Children's early ability to solve perspective-taking problems. *Developmental Psychology, 28,* 635–643.

Newcombe, P. A., & Boyle, G. J. (1995). High school students' sports personalities: Variations across participation level, gender, type of sport, and success. *International Journal of Sports Psychology, 26,* 277–294.

Newman, C., Atkinson, J., & Braddick, O. (2001). The development of reaching and looking preferences in infants to objects of different sizes. *Developmental Psychology, 37,* 561–572.

Newman, L. S. (1990). Intentional versus unintentional memory in young children: Remembering versus playing. *Journal of Experimental Child Psychology, 50,* 243–258.

Newnham, J. P., Evans, S. F., Michael, C. A., Stanley, F. J., & Landau, L. I. (1993). Effects of freqeunt ultrasound during pregnancy: A randomized controlled trial. *Lancet, 342,* 887–890.

Newport, E. L. (1991). Contrasting conceptions of the critical period for language. In S. Carey & R. Gelman (Eds.), *The epigenesis of mind: Essays on biology and cognition* (pp. 111–130). Hillsdale, NJ: Erlbaum.

Newson, J., & Newson, E. (1975). Intersubjectivity and the transmission of culture: On the social origins of symbolic functioning. *Bulletin of the British Psychological Society, 28,* 437–446.

Nguyen, S. P., & Gelman, S. A. (2002). Four and 6-year olds' biological concept of death: The case of plants. *British Journal of Developmental Psychology, 20,* 495–513.

Ni, Y. (1998). Cognitive structure, content knowledge, and classificatory reasoning. *Journal of Genetic Psychology, 159,* 280–296.

NICHD (National Institute for Child Health and Development) Early Child Care Research Network. (1997). The effects of infant child care on infant–mother attachment security: Results of the NICHD Study of Early Child Care. *Child Development, 68,* 860–879.

NICHD (National Institute for Child Health and Human Development) Early Child Care Research Network. (1999). Child care and mother–child interaction in the first 3 years of life. *Developmental Psychology, 35,* 1399–1413.

NICHD (National Institute of Child Health and Human Development) Early Child Care Research Network. (2000a). Characteristics and quality of child care for toddlers and preschoolers. *Applied Developmental Science, 4,* 116–135.

NICHD (National Institute of Child Health and Human Development) Early Child Care Research Network. (2000b). The relation of child care to cognitive and language development. *Child Development, 71,* 960–980.

NICHD (National Institute of Child Health and Human Development) Early Child Care Research Network. (2001). Before Head Start: Income and ethnicity, family characteristics, child care experiences, and child development. *Early Education and Development, 12,* 545–575.

NICHD (National Institute of Child Health and Human Development) Early Child Care Research Network. (2002a). Child-care structure → process → outcome: Direct and indirect effects of child-care quality on young children's development. *Psychological Science, 13,* 199–206.

NICHD (National Institute of Child Health and Human Development) Early Child Care Research Network. (2002b). The interaction of child care and family risk in relation to child development at 24 and 36 months. *Applied Developmental Science, 6,* 144–156.

NICHD (National Institute of Child Health and Human Development) Early Child Care Research Network. (2002c). Parenting and family influences when children are in child care: Results from the NICHD Study of Early Child Care. In J. G. Borkowski & S. L. Ramey (Eds.), *Parenting and the child's world* (pp. 99–123). Mahwah, NJ: Erlbaum.

NICHD (National Institute of Child Health and Human Development) Early Child Care Research Network. (2003a). Does amount of time spent in child care predict socioemotional adjustment during the transition to kindergarten? *Child Development, 74,* 976–1005.

NICHD (National Institute of Child Health and Human Development) Early Child Care Research Network. (2003b). Does quality of child care affect child outcomes at age 4¹/₂? *Developmental Psychology, 39,* 451–469.

Nidorf, J. F. (1985). Mental health and refugee youths: A model for diagnostic training. In T. C. Owen (Ed.), *Southeast Asian mental health: Treatment, prevention, services, training, and research* (pp. 391–427). Washington, DC: National Institute of Mental Health.

Niehaus, M. D., Moore, S. R., Patrick, P. D., Derr, L. L., Lorntz, B., Lima, A. A., & Gurerrant, R. L. (2002). Early childhood diarrhea is associated with diminished cognitive function 4 to 7 years later in children in a northeast Brazilian shantytown. *American Journal of Tropical Medicine and Hygiene, 66,* 590–593.

Nielsen, S. J., & Popkin, B. M. (2003). Patterns and trends in food portion sizes. *Journal of the American Medical Association, 289,* 450–453.

Nilsson, L., & Hamberger, L. (1990). *A child is born.* New York: Delacorte.

Nippold, M. A. (2000). Language development during the adolescent years: Aspects of pragmatics, syntax, and semantics. *Topics in Language Disorders, 20,* 15–28.

Nippold, M. A., Allen, M. M., & Kirsch, D. I. (2001). Proverb comprehension as a function of reading proficiency in preadolescents. *Language, Speech and Hearing Services in the Schools, 32,* 90–100.

Nippold, M. A., Hegel, S. L., Uhden, L. D., & Bustamante, S. (1998). Development of proverb comprehension in adolescents: Implications for instruction. *Journal of Children's Communication Development, 19,* 49–55.

Nippold, M. A., Taylor, C. L., & Baker, J. M. (1996). Idiom understanding in Australian youth: A cross-cultural comparison. *Journal of Speech and Hearing Research, 39,* 442–447.

Nisbett, R. E. (1998). Race, genetics, and IQ. In C. Jencks & M. Phillips (Eds.), *The black–white test score gap* (pp. 86–102). Washington, DC: Brookings Institution.

Nix, R. L., Pinderhughes, E. E., Dodge, K. A., Bates, J. E., Pettit, G. S., & McFadyen-Ketchum, S. A. (1999). The relation between mothers' hostile attribution tendencies and children's externalizing behavior problems: The mediating role of mothers' harsh discipline practices. *Child Development, 70,* 896–909.

Nolen-Hoeksema, S. (2001, January). *Why women are more prone to depression than men.* Address presented at the 23rd Annual National Institute on the Teaching of Psychology, St. Petersburg Beach, FL.

Nolen-Hoeksema, S. (2002). Gender differences in depression. In I. H. Gotlib & C. L. Hammen (Eds.), *Handbook of depression* (pp. 492–509). New York: Guilford.

Norgaard, J. P., Djurhuus, J. C., Watanabe, H., Stenberg, A., & Lettgen, B. (1997). Experience and current status of research into the pathophysiology of nocturnal enuresis. *British Journal of Urology, 79,* 825–835.

Nucci, L. (2001). *Education in the moral domain.* New York: Cambridge University Press.

Nucci, L. P. (1996). Morality and the personal sphere of action. In E. Reed, E. Turiel, & T. Brown (Eds.), *Values and knowledge* (pp. 41–60). Hillsdale, NJ: Erlbaum.

Nucci, L. P. (2002). The development of moral reasoning. In U. Goswami (Ed.), *Blackwell handbook of childhood cognitive development* (pp. 303–325). Malden, MA: Blackwell.

Nuckolls, K., Cassel, J., & Kaplan, B. (1972). Psychosocial assets, life crisis, and the prognosis of pregnancy. *American Journal of Epidemiology, 95,* 431–441.

Nurmi, J., Poole, M. E., & Kalakoski, V. (1996). Age differences in adolescent identity exploration and commitment in urban and rural environments. *Journal of Adolescence, 19,* 443–452.

Nye, B., Hedges, L. V., & Konstantopoulos, S. (2001). Are effects of small classes cumulative? Evidence from a Tennessee experiment. *Journal of Educational Research, 94,* 336–345.

Oakes, L. M., Coppage, D. J., & Dingel, A. (1997). By land or by sea: The role of perceptual similarity in infants' categorization of animals. *Developmental Psychology, 33,* 396–407.

Obler, L. K. (2001). Development and loss: Changes in the adult years. In J. B. Gleason (Ed.), *The development of language* (5th ed., pp. 455–488). Boston: Allyn and Bacon.

O'Callaghan, M. J., Burn, Y. R., Mohay, H. A., Rogers, Y., & Tudehope, D. I. (1993). The prevalence and origins of left hand preference in high risk infants, and its implications for intellectual, motor, and behavioral performance at four and six years. *Cortex, 29,* 617–627.

O'Connor, A. R., Stephenson, T., Johnson, A., Tobin, M. J., Ratib, S., Ng, Y., & Fielder, A. R. (2002). Long-term ophthalmic outcome of low birth weight children with and without retinopathy of prematurity. *Pediatrics, 109,* 12–18.

O'Connor, C. (1997). Dispositions toward (collective) struggle and educational resilience in the inner city: A case analysis of six African-American high school students. *American Educational Research Journal, 34,* 593–629.

O'Connor, T. G., Deater-Deckard, K., Fulker, D., Rutter, M., & Plomin, R. (1998). Genotype–environment correlations in late childhood and early adolescence: Antisocial behavioral problems and coercive parenting. *Developmental Psychology, 34,* 970–981.

O'Dea, J. A. (2003). Why do kids eat healthful food? Perceived benefits of and barriers to healthful eating and physical activity among children and adolescents. *Journal of the American Dietetic Association, 103,* 497–501.

Ogbu, J. U. (1997). Understanding the school performance of urban blacks: Some essential background knowledge. In H. J. Walberg, O. Reyes, & R. P. Weissberg (Eds.), *Children and youth: Interdisciplinary perspectives* (pp. 190–222). Thousand Oaks, CA: Sage.

Ogbu, J. U. (2003). *Black American students in an affluent suburb: A study of academic disengagement.* Mahwah, NJ: Erlbaum.

Okagaki, L., Diamond, K. E., Kontos, S. J., & Hestenes, L. L. (1998). Correlates of young children's interactions with classmates with disabilities. *Early Childhood Research Quarterly, 13,* 67–86.

Okagaki, L., Hammond, K. A., & Seamon, L. (1999). Socialization of religious beliefs. *Journal of Applied Developmental Psychology, 20,* 273–294.

Okagaki, L., & Sternberg, R. J. (1993). Parental beliefs and children's school performance. *Child Development, 64,* 36–56.

Okami, P., Weisner, T., & Olmstead, R. (2002). Outcome correlates of parent–child bedsharing: An eighteen-year longitudinal study. *Developmental and Behavioral Pediatrics, 23,* 244–253.

Oken, E., & Lightdale, J. R. (2000). Updates in pediatric nutrition. *Current Opinion in Pediatrics, 12,* 282–290.

Olafson, E., & Boat, B. W. (2000). Long-term management of the sexually abused child: Considerations and challenges. In R. M. Reece (Ed.), *Treatment of child abuse: Common ground for mental health, medical, and legal practitioners* (pp. 14–35). Baltimore: Johns Hopkins University Press.

O'Laughlin, E. M., & Anderson, V. N. (2001). Perceptions of parenthood among young adults: Implications for career and family planning. *American Journal of Family Therapy, 29,* 95–108.

Ollendick, T. H., King, N. J., & Muris, P. (2002). Fears and phobias in children: Phenomenology, epidemiology, and aetiology. *Child and Adolescent Mental Health, 7,* 98–106.

Ollendick, T. H., Yang, B., King, N. J., Dong, Q., & Akande, A. (1996). Fears in American, Australian, Chinese, and Nigerian children and adolescents: A cross-cultural study. *Journal of Child Psychology and Psychiatry, 37,* 213–220.

Oller, D. K. (2000). *The emergence of the speech capacity.* Mahwah, NJ: Erlbaum.

Oller, D. K., Eilers, R. E., Neal, A. R., & Schwartz, H. K. (1999). Precursors to speech in infancy: The prediction of speech and language disorders. *Journal of Communication Disorders, 32,* 223–245.

Olson, H. C., Feldman, J. J., Streissguth, A. P., Sampson, P. D., & Bookstein, F. L. (1998). Neuropsychological deficits in adolescents with fetal alcohol syndrome: Clinical findings. *Alcoholism: Clinical and Experimental Research, 22,* 1998–2012.

Olweus, D. (1995). Bullying or peer abuse at school: Facts and intervention. *Current Directions in Psychological Science, 4,* 196–200.

Omar, H., McElderry, D., & Zakharia, R. (2003). Educating adolescents about puberty: What are we missing? *International Journal of Adolescent Medicine and Health, 15,* 79–83.

O'Neil, R., & Parke, R. D. (1997, March). *Objective and subjective features of children's neighborhoods: Relations to parental regulatory strategies and children's social competence.* Paper presented at the biennial meeting of the Society for Research in Child Development, Washington, DC.

O'Neill, R. M., Horton, S. S., & Crosby, F. J. (1999). Gender issues in developmental relationships. In A. J. Murrell, F. J. Crosby, & R. J. Ely (Eds.), *Mentoring dilemmas* (pp. 63–80). Mahwah, NJ: Erlbaum.

Ong, W., Allison, J., & Haladyna, T. M. (2000). Student achievement of third graders in comparable single-age and multiage classrooms. *Journal of Research in Childhood Education, 14,* 205–215.

Oosterwegel, A., & Openheimer, L. (1993). *The self-system: Developmental changes between and within self-concepts.* Hillsdale, NJ: Erlbaum.

O'Rahilly, R., & Müller, F. (2001). *Human embryology and teratology.* New York: Wiley-Liss.

O'Reilly, A. W. (1995). Using representations: Comprehension and production of actions with imagined objects. *Child Development, 66,* 999–1010.

O'Reilly, A. W., & Bornstein, M. H. (1993). Caregiver–child interaction in play. In M. H. Bornstein & A. W. O'Reilly (Eds.), *The role of play in the development of thought (New directions for child development,* No. 59, pp. 55–66). San Francisco: Jossey-Bass.

Organization for Economic Cooperation and Development. (2003). *Building partnerships for progress: Education and skills.* Paris: Author.

Ornstein, P. A., Shapiro, L. R., Clubb, P. A., & Follmer, A. (1997). The influence of prior knowledge on children's memory for salient medical experiences. In N. Stein, P. A. Ornstein, C. J. Brainerd, & B. Tversky (Eds.), *Memory for everyday and emotional events* (pp. 83–112). Hillsdale, NJ: Erlbaum.

Osborne, J. (1994). Academics, self-esteem, and race: A look at the underlying assumption of the disidentification hypothesis. *Personality and Social Psychology Bulletin, 21,* 449–455.

Osherson, D. N., & Markman, E. M. (1975). Language and the ability to evaluate contradictions and tautologies. *Cognition, 2,* 213–226.

Osmond, C., & Barker, D. J. (2000). Fetal, infant, and childhood growth are predictors of coronary heart disease, diabetes, and hypertension in adult men and women. *Environmental Health Perspectives, 108,* 545–553.

Ostrea, E. M., Jr., Ostrea, A. R., & Simpson, P. M. (1997). Mortality within the first 2 years in infants exposed to cocaine, opiate, or cannabinoid during gestation. *Pediatrics, 100,* 79–83.

Ovando, C. J., & Collier, V. P. (1998). *Bilingual and ESL classrooms: Teaching in multicultural contexts.* Boston: McGraw-Hill.

Owens, J. A., Rosen, C. L., & Mindell. J. A. (2003). Medication use in the treatment of pediatric insomnia: Results of a survey of community-based pediatricians. *Pediatrics, 111,* e628–e635.

Öztürk, C., Durmazlar, N., Ural, B., Karaagaoglu, E., Yalaz, K., & Anlar, B. (1999). Hand and eye preference in normal preschool children. *Clinical Pediatrics, 38,* 677–680.

Pagani, L., Boulerice, B., Vitaro, F., & Tremblay, E. (1999). Effects of poverty on academic failure and delinquency in boys: A change and process model approach. *Journal of Child Psychology and Psychiatry, 40,* 1209–1219.

Pagani, L., Tremblay, R. E., Vitaro, F., Boulerice, B., & McDuff, P. (2001). Effects of grade retention on academic performance and behavioral development. *Development and Psychopathology, 13,* 297–315.

Paikoff, R. L., Brooks-Gunn, J., & Warren, M. P. (1991). Effects of girls' hormonal status on depressive and aggressive symptoms over the course of one year. *Journal of Youth and Adolescence, 20,* 191–215.

Palincsar, A. S. (1998). Social constructivist perspectives on teaching and learning. *Annual Review of Psychology, 49,* 345–375.

Palincsar, A. S., & Herrenkohl, L. R. (1999). Designing collaborative contexts: Lessons from three research programs. In A. M. O'Donnell & A. King (Eds.), *Cognitive perspectives on peer learning. The Rutgers Invitational Symposium on Education Series* (pp. 151–177). Mahwah, NJ: Erlbaum.

Palmer, J. R., Hatch, E. E., Rao, R. S., Kaufman, R. H., Herbst, A. L., & Noller, K. L. (2001). Infertility among women exposed prenatally to diethylstilbestrol. *American Journal of Epidemiology, 154,* 316–321.

Palta, M., Sadek-Badawi, M., Evans, M., Weinstein, M. R., & McGuinness, G. (2000). Functional assessment of a multicenter very-low-birth-weight cohort at age 5 years. *Archives of Pediatric and Adolescent Medicine, 154,* 23–30.

Pan, B. A., & Snow, C. E. (1999). The development of conversation and discourse skills. In M. Barrett (Ed.), *The development of language* (pp. 229–249). Hove, U.K.: Psychology Press.

Pan, H. W. (1994). Children's play in Taiwan. In J. L. Roopnarine, J. E. Johnson, & F. H. Hooper (Eds.), *Children's play in diverse cultures* (pp. 31–50). Albany, NY: SUNY Press.

Parent, A., Teilmann, G., Juul, A., Skakkebaek, N. E., Toppari, J., & Bourguignon, J. (2003). The timing of normal puberty and the age limits of sexual precocity: Variations around the world, secular trends, and changes after migration. *Endocrine Reviews, 24,* 668–693.

Parer, J. T. (1998). Effects of fetal asphyxia on brain cell structure and function: Limits of tolerance. *Comparative Biochemistry and Physiology, 119A,* 711–716.

Parke, R. D., & Buriel, R. (1998). Socialization in the family: Ethnic and ecological perspectives. In N. Eisenberg (Ed.), *Handbook of child psychology: Vol. 3. Social, emotional, and personality development* (5th ed., pp. 463–552). New York: Wiley.

Parke, R. D., & Tinsley, B. R. (1981). The father's role in infancy: Determinants of involvement in caregiving and play. In M. E. Lamb (Ed.), *The role of the father in child development* (pp. 429–458). New York: Wiley.

Parker, F. L., Boak, A. Y., Griffin, K. W., Ripple, C., & Peay, L. (1999). Parent–child relationship, home learning environment, and school readiness. *School Psychology Review, 28,* 413–425.

Parker, J. G., & Asher, S. R. (1987). Peer relations and later personal adjustment: Are low-accepted children at risk? *Psychological Bulletin, 102,* 357–389.

Parks, W. (1996). Human immuno-deficiency virus. In R. D. Behrman, R. M. Kliegman, & A. M. Arvin (Eds.), *Nelson textbook of pediatrics* (15th ed., pp. 916–919). Philadelphia: Saunders.

Parten, M. (1932). Social participation among preschool children. *Journal of Abnormal and Social Psychology, 27,* 243–269.

Pascalis, O., de Haan, M., & Nelson, C. A. (1998). Long-term recognition memory for faces assessed by visual paired comparison in 3- and 6-month-old infants. *Journal of Experimental Psychology: Learning, Memory, and Cognition, 24,* 249–260.

Pascarella, E. T., & Terenzini, P. T. (1991). *How college affects students.* San Francisco: Jossey-Bass.

Pascarella, E. T., Whitt, E. J., Edison, M. I., Nora, A., Hagedorn, L. S., Yeager, P. M., & Terenzini, P. T. (1997). Women's perceptions of a "chilly climate" and their cognitive outcomes during the first year of college. *Journal of College Student Development, 38,* 109–124.

Pasquino, A. M., Albanese, A., Bozzola, M., Butler, G. E., Buzi, F., & Cherubini, V. (2001). Idiopathic short stature. *Journal of Pediatric Endocrinology and Metabolism, 14,* 967–972.

Patel, D. R., Pratt, H. D., & Greydanus, D. E. (2003). Treatment of adolescents with anorexia nervosa. *Journal of Adolescent Research, 18,* 244–260.

Patrick, E., & Abravanel, E. (2000). The self-regulatory nature of preschool children's private speech in a naturalistic setting. *Applied Psycholinguistics, 21,* 45–61.

Patterson, C. J. (2000). Family relationships of lesbians and gay men. *Journal of Marriage and the Family, 62,* 1052–1069.

Patterson, C. J. (2001). Lesbian and gay parenting. Retrieved from http://www.apa.org/pi/parent.html

Patterson, C. J. (2002). Lesbian and gay parenthood. In M. H. Bornstein (Ed.), *Handbook of parenting: Vol. 3. Being and becoming a parent* (2nd ed., pp. 317–338). Mahwah, NJ: Erlbaum.

Patterson, G. R. (1982). *Coercive family processes.* Eugene, OR: Castilia Press.

Patterson, G. R., DeBaryshe, B. D., & Ramsey, E. (1989). A developmental perspective on antisocial behavior. *American Psychologist, 44,* 329–335.

Patterson, G. R., Dishion, T. J., & Yoerger, K. (2000). Adolescent growth in new forms of problem behavior: Macro- and micro-peer dynamics. *Prevention Science, 1,* 3–13.

Patterson, G. R., & Yoerger, K. (2002). A developmental model for early- and late-onset delinquency. In J. B. Reid & G. R. Patterson (Eds.), *Antisocial behavior in children and adolescents* (pp. 147–172). Washington, DC: American Psychological Association.

Patton, G. C., Selzer, R., Coffey, C., Carlin, J. B., & Wolfe, R. (1999). Onset of adolescent eating disorders: Population based cohort study over 3 years. *British Medical Journal, 318,* 765–768.

Pauli-Pott, U., Meertesacker, B., Bade, U., Haverkock, A., & Beckman, D. (2003). Parental perceptions and infant temperament development. *Infant Behavior and Development, 26,* 27–48.

Pebody, R. G., Edmunds, W. J., Conyn-van Spaendonck, M., Olin, P., Berbers, G., & Rebiere, I. (2000). The seroepidemiology of rubella in Western Europe. *Epidemiology and Infections, 125,* 347–357.

Pederson, D. R., Gleason, K. E., Moran, G., & Bento, S. (1998). Maternal attachment representations, maternal sensitivity, and the infant–mother attachment relationship. *Developmental Psychology, 34,* 925–933.

Pederson, D. R., & Moran, G. (1995). A categorical description of infant–mother relationships in the home and its relation to Q-sort measures of infant–mother interaction. In E. Waters, B. E. Vaughn, G. Posada, & K. Kondo-Ikemura K. (Eds.), Caregiving, cultural, and cognitive perspectives on secure-base behavior and working models: New growing points of attachment theory and research. *Monographs of the Society for Research in Child Development, 60*(2–3, Serial No. 244).

Pederson, D. R., & Moran, G. (1996). Expressions of the attachment relationship outside of the Strange Situation. *Child Development, 67,* 915–927.

Pedlow, R., Sanson, A., Prior, M., & Oberklaid, F. (1993). Stability of maternally reported temperament from infancy to 8 years. *Developmental Psychology, 29,* 998–1007.

Peisner-Feinberg, E. S., Burchinal, M. R., Clifford, R. M., Culkin, M. L., Howes, C., Kagan, S. L., & Yazijian, N. (2001). The relation of preschool child-care quality to children's cognitive and social developmental trajectories through second grade. *Child Development, 72,* 1534–1553.

Pellegrini, A. D. (2002). Rough-and-tumble play from childhood through adolescence: Development and possible functions. In P. K. Smith & C. H. Hart (Eds.), *Blackwell handbook of childhood social development* (pp. 438–453). Malden, MA: Blackwell.

Pellegrini, A. D. (2003). Perceptions and functions of play and real fighting in early adolescence. *Child Development, 74,* 1522–1533.

Pellegrini, A. D., & Smith, P. K. (1998). Physical activity play: The nature and function of a neglected aspect of play. *Child Development, 69,* 577–598.

Penner, A. M. (2003). International gender × item difficulty interactions in mathematics and science achievement tests. *Journal of Educational Psychology, 95,* 650–655.

Pennington, B. F., Bender, B., Puck, M., Salbenblatt, J., & Robinson, A. (1982). Learning disabilities in children with sex chromosome abnormalities. *Child Development, 53,* 1182–1192.

Pennington, B. F., & Ozonoff, S. (1996). Executive functions and developmental psychopathology. *Journal of Child Psychology and Psychiatry and Allied Disciplines, 37,* 51–87.

Pennisi, E. (2003). A low number wins the GeneSweep Pool. *Science, 300,* 1484.

Peplau, L. A., Garnets, L. D., Spalding, L. R., Conley, T. D., & Venigas, R. C. (1998). A critique of Bem's "exotic becomes erotic" theory of sexual orientation. *Psychological Review, 105,* 387–394.

Pepler, D. J., & Craig, W. (2000). *Making a difference in bullying.* Retrieved from www.yorku.ca/lamarsh/ Making%20a%20Difference% 20in%20Bullying.pdf

Peralta de Mendoza, O. A., & Salsa, A. M. (2003). Instruction in early comprehension and use of a symbol–referent relation. *Cognitive Development, 18,* 269–284.

Perfetti, C. A. (1988). Verbal efficiency in reading ability. In M. Daneman, G. E. MacKinnon, & T. G. Waller (Eds.), *Reading research: Advances in theory and practice* (Vol. 6, pp. 109–143). San Diego, CA: Academic Press.

Perie, M., Sherman, J. D., Phillips, G., & Riggan, M. (2000). Elementary and secondary education: An international perspective. *Education Statistics Quarterly.* Retrieved from http://www.nces.ed.gov/pubs2000/ quarterly/summer/5int/q51.html

Perlman, M., & Ross, H. S. (1997). The benefits of parent intervention in children's disputes: An examination of concurrent changes in children's fighting styles. *Child Development, 64,* 690–700.

Perlmutter, M. (1984). Continuities and discontinuities in early human memory: Paradigms, processes, and performances. In R. V. Kail, Jr., & N. R. Spear (Eds.), *Comparative perspectives on the development of memory* (pp. 253–287). Hillsdale, NJ: Erlbaum.

Perry, C. L., McGuire, M. T., Neumark-Sztainer, D., & Story, M. (2002). Adolescent vegetarians: How well do their dietary patterns meet the Healthy People 2010 objectives? *Archives of Pediatric and Adolescent Medicine, 156,* 431–437.

Perry, W. G., Jr. (1970). *Forms of intellectual and ethical development in the college years.* New York: Holt, Rinehart and Winston.

Perry, W. G., Jr. (1981). Cognitive and ethical growth. In A. Chickering (Ed.), *The modern American college* (pp. 76–116). San Francisco: Jossey-Bass.

Peshkin, A. (1978). *Growing up American: Schooling and the survival of the community.* Chicago: University of Chicago Press.

Peshkin, A. (1994). *Growing up American: Schooling and the survival of community.* Prospect Heights, IL: Waveland Press.

Peshkin, A. (1997). *Places of memory: Whiteman's schools and Native American communities.* Mahwah, NJ: Erlbaum.

Peters, R. D., Petrunka, K., & Arnold, R. (2003). The Better Beginnings, Better Futures Project: A universal, comprehensive, community-based prevention approach for primary school children and their families. *Journal of Clinical Child and Adolescent Psychology, 32,* 215–227.

Peterson, C. C. (2001). Influence of siblings' perspectives on theory of mind. *Cognitive Development, 15,* 435–455.

Peterson, C., & Rideout, R. (1998). Memory for medical emergencies experienced by 1- and 2-year-olds. *Developmental Psychology, 34,* 1059–1072.

Peterson, L., & Brown, D. (1994). Integrating child injury and abuse–neglect research: Common histories, etiologies, and solutions. *Psychological Bulletin, 116,* 293–315.

Petinou, K. C., Schwartz, R. G., Gravel, J. S., & Raphael, L. J. (2001). A preliminary account of phonological and morphological perception in young children with and without otitis media. *International Journal of Language and Communication Disorders, 36,* 21–42.

Petitto, L. A., Holowka, S., Sergio, L. E., & Ostry, D. (2001). Language rhythms in babies' hand movements. *Nature, 413,* 35–36.

Petitto, L. A., & Marentette, P. F. (1991). Babbling in the manual mode: Evidence for the ontogeny of language. *Science, 251,* 1493–1496.

Petrovich, O. (1997). Understanding non-natural causality in children and adults: The case against artificialism. *Psyche en Geloof, 8,* 151–165.

Pettit, G. S., Bates, J. E., & Dodge, K. A. (1997). Supportive parenting, ecological context, and children's adjustment: A seven-year longitudinal study. *Child Development, 68,* 908–923.

Pettit, G. S., Bates, J. E., Dodge, K. A., & Meece, D. W. (1999). The impact of after-school peer contact on early adolescent externalizing problems is moderated by parental monitoring, perceived neighborhood safety, and prior adjustment. *Child Development, 70,* 768–778.

Pettit, G. S., Brown, E. G., Mize, J., & Lindsey, E. (1998). Mothers' and fathers' socializing behaviors in three contexts: Links with children's peer competence. *Merrill-Palmer Quarterly, 44,* 173–193.

Phelps, K. E., & Woolley, J. D. (1994). The form and function of young children's magical beliefs. *Developmental Psychology, 30,* 385–394.

Phillips, M. (1997). What makes schools effective? A comparison of the relationships of communitarian climate and academic climate to mathematics achievement and attendance during middle school. *American Educational Research Journal, 34,* 633–662.

Phillipsen, L. C. (1999). Associations between age, gender, and group acceptance and three components of friendship quality. *Journal of Early Adolescence, 19,* 438–464.

Phinney, J. S. (1989). Stages of ethnic identity development in minority group adolescents. *Journal of Early Adolescence, 9,* 34–49.

Phinney, J. S., & Chavira, V. (1995). Parental ethnic socialization and adolescent outcomes in ethnic minority families. *Journal of Research on Adolescence, 5,* 31–53.

Phinney, J. S., Horenczyk, G., Liebkind, K., Vedder, P. (2001a). Ethnic identity, immigration, and well-being: An interactional perspective. *Journal of Social Issues, 57,* 493–510.

Phinney, J. S., & Kohatsu, E. L. (1997). Ethnic and racial identity development and mental health. In J. Schulenberg, J. L. Maggs, & K. Hurrelmann (Eds.), *Health risks and developmental transitions during adolescence* (pp. 420–443). Cambridge, U.K.: Cambridge University Press.

Phinney, J. S., & Ong, A. (2001). Family obligations and life satisfaction among adolescents from immigrant and non-immigrant families: Direct and moderated effects. Unpublished manuscript, California State University, Los Angeles.

Phinney, J. S., Ong, A., & Madden, T. (2000). Cultural values and intergenerational value discrepancies in immigrant and non-immigrant families. *Child Development, 71,* 528–539.

Phinney, J. S., Romero, I., Nava, M., & Huang, D. (2001b). The role of language, parents, and peers in ethnic identity among adolescents in immigrant families. *Journal of Youth and Adolescence, 30,* 135–153.

Piaget, J. (1926). *The language and thought of the child.* New York: Harcourt, Brace & World. (Original work published 1923)

Piaget, J. (1930). *The child's conception of the world.* New York: Harcourt, Brace, & World. (Original work published 1926)

Piaget, J. (1951). *Play, dreams, and imitation in childhood.* New York: Norton. (Original work published 1945)

Piaget, J. (1952). *The origins of intelligence in children.* New York: International Universities Press. (Original work published 1936)

Piaget, J. (1965). *The moral judgment of the child.* New York: Free Press. (Original work published 1932)

Piaget, J. (1967). *Six psychological studies.* New York: Vintage.

Piaget, J. (1971). *Biology and knowledge.* Chicago: University of Chicago Press.

Pianta, R., Egeland, B., & Erickson, M. F. (1989). The antecedents of maltreatment: Results of the Mother–Child Interaction Research Project. In D. Cicchetti & V. Carlson (Eds.), *Child maltreatment* (pp. 203–253). New York: Cambridge University Press.

Pick, A. D., & Frankel, G. W. (1974). A developmental study of strategies of visual selectivity. *Child Development, 45,* 1162–1165.

Pickens, J., Field, T., & Nawrocki, T. (2001). Frontal EEG asymmetry in response to emotional vignettes in preschool age children. *International Journal of Behavioral Development, 25,* 105–112.

Pierce, K. M., Hamm, J. V., & Vandell, D. L. (1999). Experiences in after-school programs and children's adjustment in first-grade classrooms. *Child Development, 70,* 756–767.

Pierce, S. H., & Lange, G. (2000). Relationships among metamemory, motivation and memory performance in young school-age children. *British Journal of Developmental Psychology, 18,* 121–135.

Pierce, W. D., & Epling, W. F. (1995). *Behavior analysis and learning.* Englewood Cliffs, NJ: Prentice-Hall.

Pietro, J. A., Bornstein, M. H., Costigan, K. A., Pressman, E. K., Hahn, C.-S., Painter, K., Smith, B. A., & Yi, L. J. (2002). What does fetal movement predict about behavior during the first two years of life? *Developmental Psychobiology, 40,* 358–371.

Pinderhughes, E. E., Dodge, K. A., Bates, J. E., Pettit, G. S., & Zelli, A. (2000). Discipline responses: Influences of parents' socioeconomic status, ethnicity, beliefs about parenting, stress, and cognitive-emotional processes. *Journal of Family Psychology, 14,* 380–400.

Pinderhughes, E. E., Nix, R., Foster, E. M., Jones, D., & the Conduct Problems Prevention Research Group. (2001). Parenting in context: Impact of neighborhood poverty, residential stability, public services, social networks, and danger on parental behaviors. *Journal of Marriage and the Family, 63,* 941–953.

Pine, D. S. (2001). Functional magnetic resonance imaging in children and adolescents: Implications for research on emotion. In J. M. Morihisa (Eds.), *Advances in brain imaging* (pp. 53–82). Washington, DC: American Psychiatric Publishing.

Pine, J. M. (1995). Variation in vocabulary development as a function of birth order. *Child Development, 66,* 272–281.

Pinker, S. (1989). *Learnability and cognition.* Cambridge, MA: MIT Press.

Pinker, S., Lebeaux, D. S., & Frost, L. A. (1987). Productivity and constraints in the acquisition of the passive. *Cognition, 26,* 195–267.

Pipes, P. L. (1996). *Nutrition in infancy and childhood* (6th ed.). St. Louis: Mosby.

Pipp, S., Easterbrooks, M. A., & Brown, S. R. (1993). Attachment status and complexity of infants' self- and other-knowledge when tested with mother and father. *Social Development, 2,* 1–14.

Pipp, S., Easterbrooks, M. A., & Harmon, R. J. (1992). The relation between attachment and knowledge of self and mother in one-year-old infants to three-year-old infants. *Child Development, 63,* 738–750.

Pitts, V. P. (1976). Drawing the invisible: Children's conceptualization of God. *Character Potential, 8,* 12–24.

Pivarnik, J. M. (1998). Potential effects of maternal physical activity on birth weight: Brief review. *Medicine and Science in Sports and Exercise, 30,* 407–414.

Plomin, R. (1994). *Genetics and experience: The interplay between nature and nurture.* Thousand Oaks, CA: Sage.

Plomin, R., De Fries, J. C., McClearn, G. E., & Rutter, M. (2000). *Behavior genetics* (4th ed.). New York: Freeman.

Plumert, J. M., Pick, H. L., Jr., Marks, R. A., Kintsch, A. S., & Wegesin, D. (1994). Locating objects and communicating about locations: Organizational differences in children's searching and direction-giving. *Developmental Psychology, 30,* 443–453.

Pohl, R. (2001). *Homelessness in Canada: Part 1— An introduction.* Ottawa: Innercity Ministries.

Pohl, R. (2002). *Poverty in Canada.* Ottawa: Innercity Ministries.

Poindron, P., & Le Neindre, P. (1980). Endocrine and sensory regulation of maternal behavior in the ewe. In J. S. Rosenblatt, R. A. Hinde, C. Beer, & M. Busnel (Eds.), *Advances in the study of behavior* (pp. 76–119). New York: Academic Press.

Polansky, N. A., Gaudin, J. M., Ammons, P. W., & Davis, K. B. (1985). The psychological ecology of the neglectful mother. *Child Abuse and Neglect, 9,* 265–275.

Polka, L., & Werker, J. F. (1994). Developmental changes in perception of non-native vowel contrasts. *Journal of Experimental Psychology: Human Perception and Performance, 20,* 421–435.

Pollitt, E. (1996). A reconceptualization of the effects of undernutrition on children's biological, psychosocial, and behavioral development. *Social Policy Report of the Society for Research in Child Development, 10*(5).

Pollock, L. A. (1987). *A lasting relationship: Parents and children over three centuries.* Hanover, NH: University Press of New England.

Pomerantz, E. M., & Eaton, M. M. (2000). Developmental differences in children's conceptions of parental control: "They love me, but they make me feel incompetent." *Merrill-Palmer Quarterly, 46,* 140–167.

Pomerantz, E. M., & Ruble, D. N. (1998). The role of maternal control in the development of sex differences in child self-evaluative factors. *Child Development, 69,* 458–478.

Pomerantz, E. M., & Saxon, J. L. (2001). Conceptions of ability as stable and self-evaluative processes: A longitudinal examination. *Child Development, 72,* 152–173.

Pons, F., Lawson, J., Harris, P. L., & de Rosnay, M. (2003). Individual differences in children's emotion understanding: Effects of age and language. *Scandinavian Journal of Psychology, 44,* 347–353.

Poole, D. A., & Lindsay, D. S. (2001). Children's eyewitness reports after exposure to misinformation from parents. *Journal of Experimental Psychology: Applied, 7*, 27–50.

Popkin, B. M. (2001). The nutrition transition and obesity in the developing world. *Journal of Nutrition, 131*, 871S–873S.

Popkin, B. M., Richards, M. K., & Montiero, C. A. (1996). Stunting is associated with overweight in children of four nations that are undergoing the nutrition transition. *Journal of Nutrition, 126*, 3009–3016.

Porter, R. H., Makin, J. W., Davis, L. B., & Christensen, K. M. (1992). An assessment of the salient olfactory environment of formula-fed infants. *Physiology and Behavior, 50*, 907–911.

Porter-Stevens, C., Raz, S., & Sander, C. J. (1999). Peripartum hypoxic risk and cognitive outcome: A study of term and preterm birth children at early school age. *Neuropsychology, 13*, 598–608.

Portman, P. A. (1995). Who is having fun in physical education classes? Experiences of sixth-grade students in elementary and middle schools. *Journal of Teaching in Physical Education, 14*, 445–453.

Posada, G., Jacobs, A., Richmond, M. K., Carbonell, O. A., Alzate, G., Bustamante, M. R., & Quiceno, J. (2002). Maternal caregiving and infant security in two cultures. *Developmental Psychology, 38*, 67–78.

Posner, J. K., & Vandell, D. L. (1994). Low-income children's after-school care: Are there beneficial effects of after-school programs? *Child Development, 64*, 440–456.

Posner, J. K., & Vandell, D. L. (1999). After-school activities and the development of low-income urban children: A longitudinal study. *Developmental Psychology, 35*, 868–879.

Potter, G. B., Gibbs, J. C., & Goldstein, A. P. (2001). *EQUIP implementation guide.* Champaign, IL: Research Press.

Poulin-Dubois, D., Serbin, L. A., Eichstedt, J. A., Sen, M. G., & Beissel, C. F. (2002). Men don't put on make-up: Toddlers' knowledge of the gender stereotyping of household activities. *Social Development, 11*, 166–181.

Poulin-Dubois, D., Serbin, L. A., Kenyon, B., & Derbyshire, A. (1994). Infants' intermodal knowledge about gender. *Developmental Psychology, 30*, 436–442.

Poulton, R., Caspi, A., Milne, B. J., Thomson, W. M., Taylor, A., Sears, M. R., & Moffitt, T. E. (2002). Association between children's experience of socioeconomic disadvantage and adult health: A life-course study. *Lancet, 360*, 1640–1645.

Powell, B., & Steelman, L. C. (1993). The educational benefits of being spaced out: Sibship density and educational progress. *American Sociological Review, 58*, 367–381.

Powlishta, K. K., Serbin, L. A., & Moller, L. C. (1993). The stability of individual differences in gender typing: Implications for understanding gender segregation. *Sex Roles, 29*, 723–737.

Powls, A., Botting, N., Cooke, R. W. I., & Marlow, N. (1996). Handedness in very-low-birthweight (VLBW) children at 12 years of age: Relation to perinatal and outcome variables. *Developmental Medicine and Child Neurology, 38*, 594–602.

Pratt, M. W., Arnold, M. L., Pratt, A. T., & Diessner, R. (1999). Predicting adolescent moral reasoning from family climate: A longitudinal study. *Journal of Early Adolescence, 19*, 148–175.

Prechtl, H. F. R. (1958). Problems of behavioral studies in the newborn infant. In D. S. Lehrmann, R. A. Hinde, & E. Shaw (Eds.), *Advances in the study of behavior* (Vol. 1, pp. 75–98). New York: Academic Press.

Prechtl, H. F. R., & Beintema, D. (1965). *The neurological examination of the full-term newborn infant.* London: Heinemann Medical.

Preisler, G. M. (1991). Early patterns of interaction between blind infants and their sighted mothers. *Child: Care, Health and Development, 17*, 65–90.

Preisler, G. M. (1993). A descriptive study of blind children in nurseries with sighted children. *Child: Care, Health and Development, 19*, 295–315.

Pressley, M. (1995). More about the development of self-regulation: Complex, long-term, and thoroughly social. *Educational Psychologist, 30*, 207–212.

Pressley, M., Wharton-McDonald, R., Allington, R., Block, C. C., Morrow, L., Tracey, D., Baker, K., Brooks, G., Cronin, J., Nelson, E., & Woo, D. (2001). A study of effective first-grade literacy instruction. *Scientific Studies of Reading, 5*, 35–58.

Prevatt, F., & Kelly, F. D. (2003). Dropping out of school: A review of intervention programs. *Journal of School Psychology, 41*, 377–395.

Previc, F. H. (1991). A general theory concerning the prenatal origins of cerebral lateralization. *Psychological Review, 98*, 299–334.

Primus, W., Rawlings, L., Larin, K., & Porter, K. (1999). *Initial impacts of welfare reform on the incomes of single mother families.* Washington, DC: Center on Budget and Policy Priorities.

Prinstein, M. J., Boergers, J., & Spirito, A. (2001). Adolescents' and their friends' health-risk behavior: Factors that alter or add to peer influence. *Journal of Pediatric Psychology, 26*, 287–298.

Prinstein, M. J., & La Greca, A. M. (2002). Peer crowd affiliation and internalizing distress in childhood and adolescence: A longitudinal follow-back study. *Journal of Research on Adolescence, 12*, 325–351.

Provins, K. A. (1997). Handedness and speech: A critical reappraisal of the role of genetic and environmental factors in the cerebral lateralization of function. *Psychological Review, 104*, 554–571.

Pruett, M. K., Williams, T. Y., Insabella, G., & Little, T. D. (2003). Family and legal indicators of child adjustment to divorce among families with young children. *Journal of Family Psychology, 17*, 169–180.

Pryor, J. B., & Reeder, G. D. (1993). Collective and individual representations of HIV/AIDS stigma. In J. B. Pryor & G. D. Reeder (Eds.), *The social psychology of HIV infection* (pp. 263–286). Hillsdale, NJ: Erlbaum.

Pryor, J., & Rodgers, B. (2001). *Children in changing families: Life after parental separation.* Oxford, U.K.: Blackwell.

Prysak, M., Lorenz, R. P., & Kisly, A. (1995). Pregnancy outcome in nulliparous women 35 years and older. *Obstetrics and Gynecology, 85*, 65–70.

Pungello, E. P., & Kurtz-Costes, B. (1999). Why and how working women choose child care: A review with a focus on infancy. *Developmental Review, 19*, 31–96.

Purcell-Gates, V. (1996). Stories, coupons, and the TV guide: Relationships between home literacy experiences and emergent literacy knowledge. *Reading Research Quarterly, 31*, 406–428.

Putnam, F. W. (2003). Ten-year research update review: Child sexual abuse. *Journal of the American Academy of Child and Adolescent Psychiatry, 42*, 269–278.

Putnam, S. P., Samson, A. V., & Rothbart, M. K. (2000). Child temperament and parenting. In V. J. Molfese & D. L. Molfese (Eds.), *Temperament and personality across the life span* (pp. 255–277). Mahwah, NJ: Erlbaum.

Putnam, S. P., Spritz, B. L., & Stifter, C. A. (2002). Mother–child coregulation during delay of gratification at 30 months. *Infancy, 3*, 209–225.

Putta, L., & Spencer, J. P. (2000). Assisted vaginal delivery using the vacuum extractor. *American Family Physician, 62*, 1316–1320.

Pyeritz, R. E. (1998). Sex: What we make of it. *Journal of the American Medical Association, 279*, 269.

Quint, J. C., Bos, J. M., & Polit, D. F. (1997). *New Chance: Final report on a comprehensive program for disadvantaged young mothers and their children.* New York: Manpower Demonstration Research Corporation.

Quintero, R. A., Puder, K. S., & Cotton, D. B. (1993). Embryoscopy and fetoscopy. *Obstetrics and Gynecology Clinics of North America, 20*, 563–581.

Quist, J. F., & Kennedy, J. L. (2001). Genetics of childhood disorders: XXIII. ADHD, part 7: The serotonin system. *Journal of the American Academy of Child and Adolescent Psychiatry, 40*, 253–256.

Quyen, G. T., Bird, H. R., Davies, M., Hoven, C., Cohen, P., Jensen, P. S., & Goodman, S. (1998). Adverse life events and resilience. *Journal of the American Academy of Child and Adolescent Psychiatry, 37*, 1191–1200.

Radecki, C. M., & Jaccard, J. (1995). Perceptions of knowledge, actual knowledge, and information search behavior. *Journal of Experimental Social Psychology, 31*, 107–138.

Radelet, M. A., Lephart, S. M., Rubinstein, E. N., & Myers, J. B. (2002). Survey of the injury rate for children in community sports. *Pediatrics, 110*, e28.

Radin, N. (1994). Primary caregiving fathers in intact families. In A. E. Gottfried & A. W. Gottfried (Eds.), *Redefining families: Implications for children's development* (pp. 11–54). New York: Plenum.

Radziszewska, B., & Rogoff, B. (1988). Influence of adult and peer collaboration on the development of children's planning skills. *Developmental Psychology, 24*, 840–848.

Raffaeli, M., Bogenschneider, K., & Flood, M. F. (1998). Parent–teen communication about sexual topics. *Journal of Family Issues, 19*, 315–333.

Rahman, Q., & Wilson, G. D. (2003). Born gay? The psychobiology of human sexual orientation. *Personality and Individual Differences, 34*, 1337–1382.

Ram, A., & Ross, H. S. (2001). Problem-solving, contention, and struggle: How siblings resolve a conflict of interests. *Child Development, 72*, 1710–1722.

Ramey, C. T., Campbell, F. A., & Ramey, S. L. (1999). Early intervention: Successful pathways to improving intellectual development. *Developmental Neuropsychology, 16*, 385–392.

Ramey, S. L. (1999). Head Start and preschool education: Toward continued improvement. *American Psychologist, 54*, 344–346.

Ramey, S. L., & Ramey, C. T. (1999). Early experience and early intervention for children "at risk" for developmental delay and mental retardation. *Mental Retardation and Developmental Disabilities, 5*, 1–10.

Ramos, E., Frontera, W. R., Llopart, A., & Feliciano, D. (1998). Muscle strength and hormonal levels in adolescents: Gender related differences. *International Journal of Sports Medicine, 19*, 526–531.

Ramsay, L. J., Moreton, G., Gorman, D. R., Blake, E., Goh, D., & Elton, R. A. (2003). Unintentional home injury in preschool-aged children: Looking for the key—an exploration of the inter-relationship and relative importance of potential risk factors. *Public Health, 117*, 404–411.

Ramsøy, N. R. (1994). Non-marital cohabitation and change in norms: The case of Norway. *Acta Sociologica, 37*, 23–37.

Rank, M. R. (2000). Socialization of socioeconomic status. In W. C. Nichols & M. A. Pace-Nichols (Eds.), *Handbook of family development and intervention* (pp. 129–142). New York: Wiley.

Ranly, D. M. (1998). Early orofacial development. *Journal of Clinical Pediatric Dentistry, 22*, 267–275.

Rapport, M. D., & Chung, K.-M. (2000). Attention deficit hyperactivity disorder. In M. Hersen & R. T. Ammerman (Eds.), *Advanced abnormal child psychology* (2nd ed., pp. 413–440). Mahwah, NJ: Erlbaum.

Rasmussen, C., Ho, E., & Bisanz, J. (2003). Use of the mathematical principle of inversion in young children. *Journal of Experimental Child Psychology, 85*, 89–102.

Rast, M., & Meltzoff, A. N. (1995). Memory and representation in young children with Down syndrome: Exploring deferred imitation and object permanence. *Development and Psychopathology, 7*, 393–407.

Ratcliffe, S. G., Pan, H., & McKie, M. (1992). Growth during puberty in the XYY boy. *Annals of Human Biology, 19*, 579–587.

Ratner, N. B. (2001). Atypical language development. In J. B. Gleason (Ed.), *The development of language* (5th ed., pp. 347–408). Boston: Allyn and Bacon.

Raugust, K. (1999, October). Can you tell me how to get to Sesamestrasse? *Animation World Magazine, 4*(7). Retrieved from http://www.awn.com/mag/issue4.07/4.07pages/raugustctw.php3

Ravid, D., & Tolchinsky, L. (2002). Developing linguistic literacy: A comprehensive model. *Journal of Child Language, 29*, 417–447.

Rayner, K., & Pollatsek, A. (1989). *The psychology of reading.* Englewood Cliffs, NJ: Prentice-Hall.

Raz, S., Shah, F., & Sander, C. J. (1996). Differential effects of perinatal hypoxic risk on early developmental outcome: A twin study. *Neuropsychology, 10*, 429–436.

Redl, F. (1966). *When we deal with children.* New York: Free Press.

Reese, E., Haden, C. A., & Fivush, R. (1993). Mother–child conversations about the past: Relationships of style and memory over time. *Cognitive Development, 8*, 403–430.

Reese, E., Haden, C. A., & Fivush, R. (1996). Mothers, fathers, daughters and sons: Gender differences in autobiographical reminiscing. *Research on Language and Social Interaction, 29*(1), 27–56.

Reifman, A., Villa, L. C., Amans, J. A., Rethinam, V., & Telesca, T. Y. (2001). Children of divorce in the 1990s: A meta-analysis. *Journal of Divorce and Remarriage, 36*, 27–36.

Reifsnider, E., & Gill, S. L. (2000). Nutrition for the childbearing years. *Journal of Obstetrics, Gynecology, and Neonatal Nursing, 29*, 43–55.

Reilly, J. S., Bates, E. A., & Marchman, V. A. (1998). Narrative discourse in children with early focal brain injury. *Brain and Language, 61*, 335–375.

Reilly, T. P., Hasazi, J. E., & Bond, L. A. (1983). Children's concepts of death and personal mortality. *Journal of Paediatric Psychology, 8*, 21–31.

Reimer, M. (1996). "Sinking into the ground": The development and consequences of shame in adolescence. *Developmental Review, 16*, 321–363.

Reiser, J., Yonas, A., & Wikner, K. (1976). Radial localization of odors by human neonates. *Child Development, 47*, 856–859.

Reisman, J. E. (1987). Touch, motion, and proprioception. In P. Salapatek & L. Cohen (Eds.), *Handbook of infant perception: Vol. 1. From sensation to perception* (pp. 265–303). Orlando, FL: Academic Press.

Reiss, D. (2003). Child effects on family systems: Behavioral genetic strategies. In A. C. Crouter & A. Booth (Eds.), *Children's influence on family dynamics* (pp. 3–36). Mahwah, NJ: Erlbaum.

Renninger, K. A. (1998). Developmental psychology and instruction: Issues from and for practice. In I. Sigel & K. A. Renninger (Eds.), *Handbook of child psychology: Vol. 4. Child psychology and practice* (pp. 211–274). New York: Wiley.

Repacholi, B. M. (1998). Infants' use of attentional cues to identify the referent of another person's emotional expression. *Developmental Psychology, 34*, 1017–1025.

Repacholi, B. M., & Gopnik, A. (1997). Early reasoning about desires: Evidence from 14- and 18-month-olds. *Developmental Psychology, 33*, 12–21.

Repke, J. T. (1992). Drug supplementation in pregnancy. *Current Opinion in Obstetrics and Gynecology, 4*, 802–806.

Resnick, M. B., Gueorguieva, R. V., Carter, R. L., Ariet, M., Sun, Y., Roth, J., Bucciarelli, R. L., Curran, J. S., & Mahan, C. S. (1999). The impact of low birth weight, perinatal conditions, and sociodemographic factors on educational outcome in kindergarten. *Pediatrics, 104*, e74.

Rest, J. R. (1979). *Development in judging moral issues.* Minneapolis: University of Minnesota Press.

Reynolds, A. J., & Robertson, D. L. (2003). School-based early intervention and later child maltreatment in the Chicago Longitudinal Study. *Child Development, 74*, 3–26.

Reynolds, A. J., & Temple, J. A. (1998). Extended early childhood intervention and school achievement: Age thirteen findings from the Chicago Longitudinal Study. *Child Development, 69*, 231–246.

Reynolds, A. J., Temple, J. A., Robertson, D. L., & Mann, E. A. (2001). Long-term effects of an early childhood intervention on educational achievement and juvenile arrest. *Journal of the American Medical Association, 285*, 2339–2346.

Reynolds, C. R., & Kaiser, S. M. (1990). Test bias in psychological assessment. In T. B. Gutkin & C. R. Reynolds (Eds.), *The handbook of school psychology* (pp. 487–525). New York: Wiley.

Richard, L. S., Wakefield, J. A., & Lewak, R. (1990). Similarity of personality variables as predictors of marital satisfaction: A Minnesota Multiphasic Personality Inventory (MMPI) item analysis. *Personality and Individual Differences, 11*, 39–43.

Richards, J. E., & Holley, F. B. (1999). Infant attention and the development of smooth pursuit tracking. *Developmental Psychology, 35*, 856–867.

Richards, M. H., & Duckett, E. (1994). The relationship of maternal employment to early adolescent daily experience with and without parents. *Child Development, 65*, 225–236.

Richards-Colocino, N., McKenzie, P., & Newton, R. R. (1996). Project Success: Comprehensive intervention services for middle school high-risk youth. *Journal of Adolescent Research, 11*, 130–163.

Richardson, G. A., Hamel, S. C., Goldschmidt, L., & Day, N. L. (1996). The effects of prenatal cocaine use on neonatal neurobehavioral status. *Neurotoxicology and Teratology, 18*, 519–528.

Rich-Edwards, J. W., Colditz, G. A., Stampfer, M. J., Willett, W. C., Gillman, M. W., Hennekens, C. H., Speizer, F. E., & Manson, J. E. (1999). Birthweight and the risk for type 2 diabetes mellitus in adult women. *Annals of Internal Medicine, 130*, 278–284.

Rickel, A. U., & Becker, E. (1997). *Keeping children from harm's way.* Washington, DC: American Psychological Association.

Riegle-Crumb, C. (2000). *International gender inequality in math and science education.* Unpublished doctoral dissertation, University of Chicago.

Riggs, K. J., & Peterson, D. M. (2000). Counterfactual thinking in preschool children: Mental state and causal inferences. In P. Mitchell & K. J. Riggs (Eds.), *Children's reasoning and the mind* (pp. 87–99). Hove, U.K.: Psychology Press.

Rijsdijk, F. V., & Boomsma, D. I. (1997). Genetic mediation of the correlation between peripheral nerve conduction velocity and IQ. *Behavior Genetics, 27*, 87–98.

Rivara, F. P. (1995). Developmental and behavioral issues in childhood injury prevention. *Developmental and Behavioral Pediatrics, 16*, 362–370.

Rivara, F. P., & Aitken, M. (1998). Prevention of injuries to children and adolescents. In L. A. Barness (Ed.), *Advances in pediatrics* (Vol. 45, pp. 37–72). St. Louis: Mosby.

Rivera, S. M., Wakeley, A., & Langer, J. (1999). The drawbridge phenomenon: Representational reasoning or perceptual preference? *Developmental Psychology, 35*, 427–435.

Rivkin, M. J. (2000). Developmental neuroimagining of children using magnetic resonance techniques. *Mental Retardation and Developmental Disabilities Research, 6*, 68–80.

Roazzi, A., & Bryant, P. (1997). Explicitness and conservation: Social class differences. *International Journal of Behavioral Development, 21*, 51–70.

Robb, A. S., & Dadson, M. J. (2002). Eating disorders in males. *Child and Adolescent Psychiatric Clinics of North America, 11*, 399–418.

Roberton, M. A. (1984). Changing motor patterns during childhood. In J. R. Thomas (Ed.), *Motor development during childhood and adolescence* (pp. 48–90). Minneapolis, MN: Burgess.

Roberts, D. F., Foehr, U. G., Rideout, V. J., & Brodie, M. (1999). *Kids & media @ the new millennium.* Menlo Park, CA: Kaiser Family Foundation.

Roberts, J. E., Burchinal, M. R., & Campbell, F. (1994). Otitis media in early childhood and patterns of intellectual development and later academic performance. *Journal of Pediatric Psychology, 19*, 347–367.

Roberts, J. E., Burchinal, M. R., & Durham, M. (1999). Parents' report of vocabulary and grammatical development of American preschoolers: Child and environment associations. *Child Development, 70*, 92–106.

Roberts, J. E., Burchinal, M. R., Jackson, S. C., Hooper, S. R., Roush, J., Mundy, M., Neebe, E. C., & Zeisel, S. A. (2000). Otitis media in childhood in relation to preschool language and school readiness skills among black children. *Pediatrics, 106*, 725–735.

Roberts, J. E., Burchinal, M. R., Zeisel, S. A., Neebe, E. C., Hooper, S. R., Roush, J., Bryant, D., Mundy, M., & Henderson, F. W. (1998). Otitis media, the caregiving environment, and language and cognitive outcomes at 2 years. *Pediatrics, 102*, 346–354.

Roberts, M. C., Alexander, K., & Knapp, L. G. (1990). Motivating children to use safety belts: A program combining rewards and "flash for life." *Journal of Community Psychology, 18*, 110–119.

Roberts, R. J., Jr., & Aman, C. J. (1993). Developmental differences in giving directions: Spatial frames of reference and mental rotation. *Child Development, 64*, 1258–1270.

Robertson, J. A., Martinez, L. P., Gallegos, S., Leen-Mitchell, M. J., & Garcia, V. (2002). Accutane cases: A teratogen information service's approach. *Teratology, 66,* 1–2.

Robin, D. J., Berthier, N. E., & Clifton, R. K. (1996). Infants' predictive reaching for moving objects in the dark. *Developmental Psychology, 32,* 824–835.

Robins, R. W., Tracy, J. L., Trzesniewski, K., Potter, J., & Gosling, S. D. (2001). Personality correlates of self-esteem. *Journal of Research in Personality, 35,* 463–482.

Robinson, C. C., Anderson, G. T., Porter, C. L., Hart, C. H., & Wouden-Miller, M. (2003). Sequential transition patterns of preschoolers' social interactions during child-initiated play: Is parallel-aware play a bi-directional bridge to other play states? *Early Childhood Research Quarterly, 18,* 3–21.

Rochat, P. (1989). Object manipulation and exploration in 2- to 5-month-old infants. *Developmental Psychology, 25,* 871–884.

Rochat, P. (1998). Self-perception and action in infancy. *Experimental Brain Research, 123,* 102–109.

Rochat, P. (2001). *The infant's world.* Cambridge, MA: Harvard University Press.

Rochat, P., & Goubet, N. (1995). Development of sitting and reaching in 5- to 6-month-old infants. *Infant Behavior and Development, 18,* 53–68.

Rochat, P., Querido, J. G., & Striano, T. (1999). Emerging sensitivity to the timing and structure of protoconversation. *Developmental Psychology, 35,* 950–957.

Rochat, P., & Striano, T. (2002). Who's in the mirror? Self–other discrimination in specular images by four- and nine-month-old infants. *Child Development, 73,* 35–46.

Rochat, P., Striano, T., & Blatt, L. (2002). Differential effects of happy, neutral, and sad still-faces on 2-, 4-, and 6-month-old infants. *Infant and Child Development, 11,* 289–303.

Rodgers, J. L., Cleveland, H. H., van den Oord, E., & Rowe, D. C. (2000). Resolving the debate over birth order, family size, and intelligence. *American Psychologist, 55,* 599–612.

Rodkin, P. C., Farmer, T. W., Pearl, R., & Van Acker, R. (2000). Heterogeneity of popular boys: Antisocial and prosocial configurations. *Developmental Psychology, 36,* 14–24.

Roebers, C. M., & Schneider, W. (2001). Individual differences in children's eyewitness recall: The influence of intelligence and shyness. *Applied Developmental Science, 5,* 9–20.

Roeser, R. W., & Eccles, J. S. (1998). Adolescents' perceptions of middle school: Relation to longitudinal changes in academic and psychological adjustment. *Journal of Research on Adolescence, 8,* 123–158.

Roeser, R. W., Eccles, J. S., & Freedman-Doan, C. (1999). Academic functioning and mental health in adolescence: Patterns, progressions, and routes from childhood. *Journal of Adolescent Research, 14,* 135–174.

Rogers, C., & Shiff, M. (1996). Early versus late prenatal care in New Mexico: Barriers and motivators. *Birth, 23,* 26–30.

Rogers, L., Resnick, M. D., Mitchell, J. E., & Blum, R. W. (1997). The relationship between socioeconomic status and eating disordered behaviors in a community sample of adolescent girls. *International Journal of Eating Disorders, 22,* 15–23.

Roggman, L. A., Langlois, J. H., Hubbs-Tait, L., & Rieser-Danner, L. A. (1994). Infant day-care, attachment, and the "file drawer problem." *Child Development, 65,* 1429–1443.

Rogler, L. H. (2002). Historical generations and psychology. *American Psychologist, 57,* 1013–1023.

Rogoff, B. (1986). The development of strategic use of context in spatial memory. In M. Perlmutter (Ed.), *Perspectives on intellectual development* (pp. 107–123). Hillsdale, NJ: Erlbaum.

Rogoff, B. (1996). Developmental transitions in children's participation in sociocultural activities. In A. J. Sameroff & M. M. Haith (Eds.), *The five to seven year shift: The age of reason and responsibility,* (pp. 273–294). Chicago: University of Chicago Press.

Rogoff, B. (1998). Cognition as a collaborative process. In D. Kuhn & R. S. Siegler (Eds.), *Handbook of child psychology: Vol. 2. Cognition, perception, and language* (5th ed., pp. 679–744). New York: Wiley.

Rogoff, B. (2003). *The cultural nature of human development.* New York: Oxford University Press.

Rogoff, B., & Chavajay, P. (1995). What's become of research on the cultural basis of cognitive development? *American Psychologist, 50,* 859–877.

Rogoff, B., Malkin, C., & Gilbride, K. (1984). Interaction with babies as guidance in development. In B. Rogoff & J. V. Wertsch (Eds.), *Children's learning in the "zone of proximal development"* (New directions for child development, No. 23, pp. 31–44). San Francisco: Jossey-Bass.

Rogoff, B., Paradise, R., Arauz, R. M., Correa-Chávez, M., & Angelillo, C. (2003). Firsthand learning through intent participation. *Annual Review of Psychology, 54,* 175–203.

Rogoff, B., Turkanis, C. G., & Bartlett, L. (Eds.). (2001). *Learning together: Children and adults in a school community.* New York: Oxford University Press.

Rogol, A. D., Roemmich, J. N., & Clark, P. A. (2002). Growth at puberty. *Journal of Adolescent Health, 31,* 192–200.

Rogosch, F., Cicchetti, D., Shields, A., & Toth, S. L. (1995). Parenting dysfunction in child maltreatment. In M. H. Bornstein (Ed.), *Handbook of parenting: Vol. 4. Applied and practical parenting* (pp. 127–159). Hillsdale, NJ: Erlbaum.

Rohner, R., & Brothers, S. (1999). Perceived parental rejection, psychological maladjustment, and borderline personality disorder. *Journal of Emotional Abuse, 1,* 81–95.

Rohner, R. P., & Veneziano, R. A. (2001). The importance of father love: History and contemporary evidence. *Review of General Psychology, 5,* 382–405.

Roisman, G. I., Madsen, S. D., Hennighausen, K. H., Sroufe, L. A., & Collins, W. A. (2001). The coherence of dyadic behavior across parent–child and romantic relationships as mediated by the internalized representation of experience. *Attachment and Human Development, 3,* 156–172.

Roizen, N. J., & Patterson, D. (2003). Down's syndrome. *Lancet, 361,* 1281–1289.

Rojewski, J. W., & Hill, R. B. (1998). Influence of gender and academic risk behavior on career decision making and occupational choice in early adolescence. *Journal of Education for Students Placed at Risk, 3,* 265–287.

Rokach, A. (2001). Perceived causes of loneliness in adulthood. *Journal of Social Behavior and Personality, 15,* 67–84.

Rolls, B. J., Morris, E. L., & Roe, L. S. (2002). Portion size of food affects energy intake in normal-weight and overweight men and women. *American Journal of Clinical Nutrition, 6,* 1207–1213.

Romaine, S. (1984). *The language of children and adolescents: The acquisition of communicative competence.* Oxford, U.K.: Blackwell.

Rome-Flanders, T., & Cronk, C. (1995). A longitudinal study of infant vocalizations during mother–infant games. *Journal of Child Language, 22,* 259–274.

Rönnqvist, L., & Hopkins, B. (1998). Head position preference in the human newborn: A new look. *Child Development, 69,* 13–23.

Roopnarine, J. L., Hossain, Z., Gill, P., & Brophy, H. (1994). Play in the East Indian context. In J. L. Roopnarine, J. E. Johnson, & F. H. Hooper (Eds.), *Children's play in diverse cultures* (pp. 9–30). Albany, NY: SUNY Press.

Roopnarine, J. L., Lasker, J., Sacks, M., & Stores, M. (1998). The cultural contexts of children's play. In O. N. Saracho & B. Spodek (Eds.), *Multiple perspectives on play in early childhood education* (pp. 194–219). Albany: State University of New York Press.

Roopnarine, J. L., Talukder, E., Jain, D., Joshi, P., & Srivastav, P. (1990). Characteristics of holding, patterns of play, and social behaviors between parents and infants in New Delhi, India. *Developmental Psychology, 26,* 667–673.

Rose, A. J. (2002). Co-rumination in the friendships of girls and boys. *Child Development, 73,* 1830–1843.

Rose, A. J., & Asher, S. R. (1999). Children's goals and strategies in response to conflicts within a friendship. *Developmental Psychology, 35,* 69–79.

Rose, L. (2000). Fathers of full-term infants. In N. Tracey (Ed.), *Parents of premature infants: Their emotional world* (pp. 105–116). London: Whurr.

Rose, S. A., & Feldman, J. F. (1997). Memory and speed: Their role in the relation of infant information processing to later IQ. *Child Development, 68,* 610–620.

Rose, S. A., Feldman, J. F., & Janowski, J. J. (2001). Attention and recognition memory in the 1st year of life: A longitudinal study of preterm and full-term infants. *Developmental Psychology, 37,* 135–151.

Rose, S. A., Feldman, J. F., & Wallace, I. F. (1992). Infant information processing in relation to six-year cognitive outcomes. *Child Development, 63,* 1126–1141.

Rose, S. A., Jankowski, J. J., & Senior, G. J. (1997). Infants' recognition of contour-deleted figures. *Journal of Experimental Psychology: Human Perception and Performance, 23,* 1206–1216.

Rosen, A. B., & Rozin, P. (1993). Now you see it, now you don't: The preschool child's conception of invisible particles in the context of dissolving. *Developmental Psychology, 29,* 300–311.

Rosen, D. (2003). Eating disorders in children and young adolescents: Etiology, classification, clinical features, and treatment. *Adolescent Medicine: State of the Art Reviews, 14,* 49–59.

Rosenblatt, J. S. (2002). Hormonal bases of parenting in mammals. In M. H. Bornstein (Ed.), *Handbook of parenting: Vol. 2* (2nd ed., pp. 31–60). Mahwah, NJ: Erlbaum.

Rosengren, K. S., & Hickling, A. K. (2000). The development of children's thinking about possible events and plausible mechanisms. In K. S. Rosengren, C. N. Johnson, & P. L. Harris (Eds.), *Imagining the impossible* (pp. 75–98). Cambridge, U.K.: Cambridge University Press.

Rosenshine, B., & Meister, C. (1994). Reciprocal teaching: A review of nineteen experimental studies. *Review of Educational Research, 64,* 479–530.

Rosenstein, D., & Oster, H. (1990). Differential facial expressions in response to four basic tastes in infants. *Child Development, 59,* 1555–1568.

Ross, H. S., Conant, C., Cheyne, J. A., & Alevizos, E. (1992). Relationships and alliances in the social interactions of kibbutz toddlers. *Social Development, 1,* 1–17.

Roth, J., Brooks-Gunn, J., Murray, L., & Foster, W. (1998). Promoting healthy adolescents: Synthesis of youth development program evaluations. *Journal of Research on Adolescence, 8,* 423–459.

Rothbart, M. K. (1981). Measurement of temperament in infancy. *Child Development, 52,* 569–578.

Rothbart, M. K., Ahadi, S. A., & Evans, D. E. (2000). Temperament and personality: Origins and outcome. *Journal of Personality and Social Psychology, 78,* 122–135.

Rothbart, M. K., & Bates, J. E. (1998). Temperament. In N. Eisenberg (Ed.), *Handbook of child psychology: Vol. 3. Social, emotional, and personality development* (5th ed., pp. 105–176). New York: Wiley.

Rothbaum, F., Pott, M., Azuma, H., Miyake, K., & Weisz, J. (2000a). The development of close relationships in Japan and the United States: Paths of symbiotic harmony and generative tension. *Child Development, 71,* 1121–1142.

Rothbaum, F., Weisz, J., Pott, M., Miyake, K., & Morelli, G. (2000b). Attachment and culture: Security in the United States and Japan. *American Psychologist, 55,* 1093–1104.

Rovee-Collier, C. (1996). Shifting the focus from what to do to why. *Infant Behavior and Development, 19,* 385–400.

Rovee-Collier, C. (1999). The development of infant memory. *Current Directions in Psychological Science, 8,* 80–85.

Rovee-Collier, C., & Barr, R. (2001). Infant learning and memory. In G. Bremner & A. Fogel (Eds.), *Blackwell handbook of infant development* (pp. 139–168). Oxford, U.K.: Blackwell.

Rovee-Collier, C. K., & Bhatt, R. S. (1993). Evidence of long-term memory in infancy. *Annals of Child Development, 9,* 1–45.

Rovet, J., Netley, C., Keenan, M., Bailey, J., & Stewart, D. (1996). The psychoeducational profile of boys with Klinefelter syndrome. *Journal of Learning Disabilities, 29,* 180–196.

Rowe, D. (1994). *The limits of family influence: Genes, experience, and behavior.* New York: Guilford.

Rowe, S., & Wertsch, J. V. (2002). Vygotsky's model of cognitive development. In G. Bremner & A. Fogel (Eds.), *Blackwell handbook of infant development* (pp. 538–554). Oxford, U.K.: Blackwell.

Royal College of Obstetricians and Gynecologists. (1997, October). *Report of the panel to review fetal pain.* London: Author.

Rubin, K., Bukowski, W., & Parker, J. G. (1998). Peer interactions, relationships, and groups. In N. Eisenberg (Ed.), *Handbook of child psychology: Vol. 3. Social, emotional, and personality development* (5th ed., pp. 619–700). New York: Wiley.

Rubin, K. H., Burgess, K. B., Dwyer, K. M., & Hastings, P. D. (2003). Predicting preschoolers' externalizing behaviors from toddler temperament, conflict, and maternal negativity. *Developmental Psychology, 39,* 164–176.

Rubin, K. H., Burgess, K. B., & Hastings, P. D. (2002). Stability and social-behavioral consequences of toddlers' inhibited temperament and parenting behaviors. *Child Development, 73,* 483–495.

Rubin, K. H., & Coplan, R. J. (1998). Social and nonsocial play in childhood: An individual differences perspective. In O. N. Saracho & B. Spodek (Eds.), *Multiple perspectives on play in early childhood education* (pp. 144–170). Albany, NY: State University of New York Press.

Rubin, K. H., Fein, G. G., & Vandenberg, B. (1983). Play. In E. M. Hetherington (Ed.), *Handbook of child psychology: Vol. 4. Socialization, personality, and social development* (4th ed., pp. 693–744). New York: Wiley.

Rubin, K. H., Hastings, P. D., Stewart, S. L., Henderson, H. A., & Chen, X. (1997). The consistency and concomitants of inhibition: Some of the children, all of the time. *Child Development, 68,* 467–483.

Rubin, K. H., Stewart, S. L., & Coplan, R. J. (1995). Social withdrawal in childhood: Conceptual and empirical perspectives. In T. H. Ollendick & R. J. Prinz (Eds.), *Advances in clinical child psychology* (Vol. 17, pp. 157–196). New York: Plenum.

Rubin, K. H., Watson, K. S., & Jambor, T. W. (1978). Free-play behaviors in preschool and kindergarten children. *Child Development, 49,* 539–536.

Rubinowitz, L. S., & Rosenbaum, J. E. (2000). *Crossing the class and color lines: From public housing to white suburbia.* Chicago: University of Chicago Press.

Ruble, D. N., & Flett, G. L. (1988). Conflicting goals in self-evaluative information seeking: Developmental and ability level analyses. *Child Development, 59,* 97–106.

Ruble, D. N., & Martin, C. L. (1998). Gender development. In N. Eisenberg (Ed.), *Handbook of child psychology: Vol. 3. Social, emotional, and personality development* (pp. 933–1016). New York: Wiley.

Rudolph, D. K., & Heller, T. L. (1997). Interpersonal problem solving, externalizing behavior, and social competence in preschoolers: A knowledge-performance discrep-ancy? *Journal of Applied Developmental Psychology, 18,* 107–117.

Rudolph, D. K., Lambert, S. F., Clark, A. G., & Kurlakowsky, K. D. (2001). Negotiating the transition to middle school: The role of self-regulatory processes. *Child Development, 72,* 929–946.

Ruff, H. A., & Capozzoli, M. C. (2003). Development of attention and distractibility in the first 4 years of life. *Developmental Psychology, 39,* 877–890.

Ruff, H. A., & Lawson, K. R. (1990). Development of sustained, focused attention in young children during free play. *Developmental Psychology, 26,* 85–93.

Ruff, H. A., & Rothbart, M. K. (1996). *Attention in early development.* New York: Oxford University Press.

Ruffman, T. (1999). Children's understanding of logical inconsistency. *Child Development, 70,* 872–886.

Ruffman, T., & Langman, L. (2002). Infants' reaching in a multi-well A not B task. *Infant Behavior and Development, 25,* 237–246.

Ruffman, T., Perner, J., Naito, M., Parkin, L., & Clements, W.A. (1998). Older (but not younger) siblings facilitate false belief understanding. *Developmental Psychology, 34,* 161–174.

Ruffman, T., Perner, J., Olson, D. R., & Doherty, M. (1993). Reflecting on scientific thinking: Children's understanding of the hypothesis–evidence relation. *Child Development, 64,* 1617–1636.

Rumbaut, R. G. (1997). Ties that bind: Immigration and immigrant families in the United States. In A. Booth, A. C. Crouter, & N. Landale (Eds.), *Immigration and the family: Research and policy on U.S. immigrants* (pp. 3–46). Mahwah, NJ: Erlbaum.

Runco, M. A. (1992). Children's divergent thinking and creative ideation. *Developmental Review, 12,* 233–264.

Rushton, J. L., Forcier, M., & Schectman, R. M. (2002). Epidemiology of depressive symptoms in the National Longitudinal Study of Adolescent Health. *Journal of the American Academy of Child and Adolescent Psychiatry, 41,* 199–205.

Russell, A., Mize, J., & Bissaker, K. (2002). Parent–child relationships. In P. K. Smith & C. H. Hart (Eds.), *Handbook of childhood social development.* Oxford, U.K.: Blackwell.

Russell, A., Pettit, G. S., & Mize, J. (1998). Horizontal qualities in parent–child relationships: Parallels with and possible consequences for children's peer relationships. *Developmental Review, 18,* 313–352.

Russell, J. A. (1990). The preschooler's understanding of the causes and consequences of emotion. *Child Development, 61,* 1872–1881.

Russell, R. B., Petrini, J. R., Damus, K., Mattison, D. R., & Schwarz, R. H. (2003). The changing epidemiology of multiple births in the United States. *Obstetrics and Gynecology, 101,* 129–135.

Rust, J., Golombok, S., Hines, M., Johnston, K., Golding, J., & the ALSPAC Study Team. (2000). The role of brothers and sisters in the gender development of preschool children. *Journal of Experimental Child Psychology, 77,* 292–303.

Rutter, M. (1987). Psychosocial resilience and protective mechanisms. *American Journal of Orthopsychiatry, 57,* 316–331.

Rutter, M. (1996). Maternal deprivation. In M. H. Bornstein (Ed.), *Handbook of parenting: Vol. 4. Applied and practical parenting* (pp. 3–31). Mahwah, NJ: Erlbaum.

Rutter, M. (2002). Nature, nurture, and development: From evangelism through science toward policy and practice. *Child Development, 73,* 1–21.

Rutter, M., Pickles, A., Murray, R., & Eaves, L. (2001). Testing hypotheses on specific environmental causal effects on behavior. *Psychological Bulletin, 127,* 291–324.

Ryan, A. M. (2001). The peer group as a context for the development of young adolescent motivation and achievement. *Child Development, 72,* 1135–1150.

Ryan, A. M., & Patrick, H. (2001). The classroom social environment and changes in adolescents' motivation and engagement during middle school. *American Educational Research Journal, 38,* 437–460.

Ryding, M., Konradsson, K., Kalm, O., & Prellner, K. (2002). Auditory consequences of recurrent acute purulent otitis media. *Annals of Otology, Rhinology, and Laryngology, 111*(3, Pt. 1), 261–266.

Saarni, C. (1993). Socialization of emotion. In M. Lewis & J. M. Haviland (Eds.), *Handbook of emotions* (pp. 435–446). New York: Guilford.

Saarni, C. (1999). *The development of emotional competence.* New York: Guilford.

Saarni, C., Mumme, D. L., & Campos, J. J. (1998). Emotional development: Action, communication, and understanding. In N. Eisenberg (Ed.), *Handbook of child psychology: Vol. 3. Social, emotional, and personality development* (5th ed., pp. 237–309). New York: Wiley.

Sacks, P. (1999). *Standardized minds: The high price of America's testing culture and what we can do to change it.* Cambridge, MA: Perseus.

Sadeh, A. (1997). Sleep and melatonin in infants: A preliminary study. *Sleep, 20,* 185–191.

Sadler, T. W. (2000). *Langman's medical embryology* (8th ed.). Baltimore: Williams & Wilkins.

Safe Kids Worldwide. (2002). *Childhood injury worldwide: Meeting the challenge.* Retrieved from http://www.safekidsworldwide.org

Saffran, J. R., Aslin, R. N., & Newport, E. L. (1996). Statistical learning by 8-month-old infants. *Science, 27,* 1926–1928.

Saffran, J. R., & Thiesen, E. D. (2003). Pattern induction by infant language learners. *Developmental Psychology, 39,* 484–494.

Sahni, R., Schulze, K. F., Stefanski, M., Myers, M. M., & Fifer, W. P. (1995). Methodological issues in coding sleep states in immature infants. *Developmental Psychobiology, 28,* 85–101.

Salapatek, P. (1975). Pattern perception in early infancy. In L. B. Cohen & P. Salapatek (Eds.), *Infant perception: From sensation to cognition* (pp. 133–248). New York: Academic Press.

Salbe, A. D., Weyer, C., Harper, I., Lindsay, R. S., Ravussin, E., & Tataranni, P. A. (2002). Assessing risk factors for obesity between childhood and adolescence: II. Energy metabolism and physical activity. *Pediatrics, 110,* 307–314.

Salbe, A. D., Weyer, C., Lindsay, R. S., Ravussin, E., & Tataranni, P. A. (2002). Assessing risk factors for obesity between childhood and adolescence: I. Birth weight, childhood adiposity, parental obesity, insulin, and leptin. *Pediatrics, 110,* 299–306.

Salmela-Aro, K., Nurmi, J., Saisto, T., & Halmesmaki, E. (2000). Women's and men's personal goals during the transition to parenthood. *Journal of Family Psychology, 14,* 171–186.

Salter, D., McMillan, D., Richards, M., Talbot, T., Hodges, J., Bentovim, A., & Hastings, R. (2003). Development of sexually abusive behavior in sexually victimized males: A longitudinal study. *Lancet, 361,* 471–476.

Samuels, M., & Samuels, N. (1996). *The new well pregnancy book.* New York: Fireside.

Samuels, S. J. (1985). Toward a theory of automatic information processing in reading: Updated. In H. Singer & R. B. Ruddell (Eds.), *Theoretical models and processes of reading* (3rd ed., pp. 719–721). Newark, DE: International Reading Association.

Sandberg, D. E., & Voss, L. D. (2002). The psychosocial consequences of short stature: A review of the evidence. *Best Practice and Research in Clinical Endocrinology and Metabolism, 16,* 449–463.

Sanders, M. G., & Jordan, W. J. (2000). Student–teacher relations and academic achievement in high school. In M. G. Sanders (Ed.), *Schooling students placed at risk: Research, policy, and practice in the education of poor minority adolescents* (pp. 65–82). Mahwah, NJ: Erlbaum.

Sanderson, J. A., & Siegal, M. (1988). Conceptions of moral and social rules in rejected and nonrejected preschoolers. *Journal of Clinical Child Psychology, 17,* 66–72.

Sandman, C. A., Wadhwa, P., Hetrick, W., Porto, M., & Peeke, H. V. S. (1997). Human fetal heart rate dishabituation between thirty and thirty-two weeks gestation. *Child Development, 68,* 1031–1040.

Sandstrom, M. J., & Cillessen, A. H. N. (2003). Sociometric status and children's peer experiences: Use of the daily diary method. *Merrill-Palmer Quarterly, 49,* 427–452.

Sandstrom, M. J., & Coie, J. D. (1999). A developmental perspective on peer rejection: Mechanisms of stability and change. *Child Development, 70,* 955–966.

Sansavini, A., Bertoncini, J., & Giovanelli, G. (1997). Newborns discriminate the rhythm of multisyllabic stressed words. *Developmental Psychology, 33,* 3–11.

Sanson, A. V., Pedlow, R., Cann, W., Prior, M., & Oberklaid, F. (1996). Shyness ratings: Stability and correlates in early childhood. *International Journal of Behavioural Development, 19,* 705–724.

Santoloupo, S., & Pratt, M. (1994). Age, gender, and parenting style variations in mother–adolescent dialogues and adolescent reasoning about political issues. *Journal of Adolescent Research, 9,* 241–261.

Sapp, F., Lee, K., & Muir, D. (2000). Three-year-olds' difficulty with the appearance–reality distinction: Is it real or is it apparent? *Developmental Psychology, 36,* 547–560.

Sarrazin, G. (1999). WISC-III, *Échelle d'intelligence de Wechs pour enfants, troisième édition, adaptation canadienne-française, Manuel d'administration.* Toronto: Psychological Corporation.

Sarwaswathi, T. S., & Larson, R. (2002). Adolescence in global perspective: An agenda for social policy. In B. B. Frown, R. Larson, & T. S. Saraswathi (Eds.), *The world's youth* (pp. 344–362). New York: Cambridge University Press.

Saudino, K. J., & Cherny, S. S. (2001). Sources of continuity and change in observed temperament. In R. N. Emde & J. K. Hewitt (Eds.), *Infancy to early childhood: Genetic and environmental influences on developmental change* (pp. 89–110). New York: Oxford University Press.

Sauls, D. J. (2002). Effects of labor support on mothers, babies, and birth outcomes. *Journal of Obstetric, Gynecologic, and Neonatal Nursing, 31,* 733–741.

Savage, A. R., Petersen, M. B., Pettay, D., Taft, L., Allran, K., Freeman, S. B., Karadima, G., Avramopoulos, D., Torfs, C., Mikkelsen, M., & Hassold, T. J. (1998). Elucidating the mechanisms of paternal non-disjunction of chromosome 21 in humans. *Human Molecular Genetics, 7,* 1221–1227.

Save the Children. (2001). *Newborn health status: State of the world's newborns.* Westport, CT: Author.

Saville-Troike, M. (1988). Private speech: Evidence for second language learning strategies during the 'silent' period. *Journal of Child Language, 15,* 567–590.

Savin-Williams, R. C. (1996). Dating and romantic relationships among gay, lesbian, and bisexual youths. In R. C. Savin-Williams & K. M. Cohen (Eds.), *The lives of lesbians, gays, and bisexuals* (pp. 166–180). Fort Worth, TX: Harcourt Brace.

Savin-Williams, R. C. (2001). A critique of research on sexual-minority youths. *Journal of Adolescence, 24,* 5–13.

Savin-Williams, R. C. (2003). Lesbian, gay, and bisexual youths' relationships with their parents. In L. D. Garnets & D. C. Kimmel (Eds.), *Psychological perspectives on lesbian, gay, and bisexual experiences* (2nd ed., pp. 299–326). New York: Columbia University Press.

Savin-Williams, R. C., & Ream, G. L. (2003a). Sex variations in the disclosure to parents of same-sex attractions. *Journal of Family Psychology, 17,* 429–438.

Savin-Williams, R. C., & Ream, G. L. (2003b). Suicide attempts among sexual-minority male youth. *Journal of Clinical Child and Adolescent Psychology, 32,* 509–522.

Saw, S. M., Carkeet, A., Chia, K. S., Stone, R. A., & Tan, D. T. (2002). Component dependent risk factors for ocular parameters in Singapore Chinese children. *Ophthalmology, 109,* 2065–2071.

Saxe, G. B. (1988, August–September). Candy selling and math learning. *Educational Researcher, 17*(6), 14–21.

Sayle, A. E., Savitz, D. A., Thorp, J. M., Jr., Hertz-Picciotto, I., & Wilcox, A. J. (2001). Sexual activity during late pregnancy and risk of preterm delivery. *Obstetrics and Gynecology, 97,* 283–289.

Saylor, M. M., Sabbagh, M. A., & Baldwin, D. A. (2002). Children use whole–part juxtaposition as a pragmatic cue to word meaning. *Developmental Psychology, 38,* 993–1003.

Saywitz, K. J., Goodman, G. S., & Lyon, T. D. (2002). Interviewing children in and out of court: Current research and practice implications. In J. E. B. Myers & L. Berliner (Eds.), *The APSAC handbook on child maltreatment* (2nd ed., pp. 349–377). Thousand Oaks, CA: Sage.

Scales, P. C., & Leffert, N. (2002). *Developmental assets: A synthesis of the scientific research on adolescent development.* Minneapolis, MN: Search Institute.

Scaramella, L. V., Conger, R. D., Simons, R. L., & Whitbeck, L. B. (1998). Predicting risk for pregnancy by late adolescence: A social contextual perspective. *Developmental Psychology, 34,* 1233–1245.

Scarr, S. (1997). Behavior-genetic and socialization theories of intelligence: Truce and reconciliation. In R. J. Sternberg & E. L. Grigorenko (Eds.), *Intelligence, heredity, and environment* (pp. 3–41). New York: Cambridge University Press.

Scarr, S., & McCartney, K. (1983). How people make their own environments: A theory of genotype–environment effects. *Child Development, 54,* 424–435.

Scarr, S., Phillips, D., McCartney, K., & Abbott-Shim, M. (1993). Quality of child care as an aspect of family and child care policy in the United States. *Pediatrics, 91,* 182–188.

Scarr, S., & Weinberg, R. A. (1983). The Minnesota adoption studies: Genetic differences and malleability. *Child Development, 54,* 260–267.

Schaffer, J., & Kral, R. (1988). Adoptive families. In C. S. Chilman, E. W. Nunnally, & F. M. Cox (Eds.), *Variant family forms* (pp. 165–184). Newbury Park, PA: Sage.

Schauble, L. (1996). The development of scientific reasoning in knowledge-rich contexts. *Developmental Psychology, 32,* 102–119.

Scher, A., Tirosh, E., Jaffe, M., Rubin, L., Sadeh, A., & Lavie, P. (1995). Sleep patterns of infants and young children in Israel. *International Journal of Behavioral Development, 18,* 701–711.

Schiavi, R. C., Theilgaard, A., Owen, D., & White, D. (1984). Sex chromosome anomalies, hormones, and aggressivity. *Archives of General Psychiatry, 41,* 93–99.

Schieber, R. A., & Sacks, J. J. (2001). Measuring community bicycle helmet use among children. *Public Health Reports, 116,* 113–121.

Schieman, S., Gundy, V., & Taylor, K. (2001). Status, role, and resource explanations for age patterns in psychological distress. *Journal of Health and Social Behavior, 42,* 80–96.

Schieve, L. A., Meikle, S. F., Ferre, C., Peterson, H. B., Jeng, G., & Wilcox, L. S. (2002). Low and very low birth weight in infants conceived with use of assisted reproductive technology. *New England Journal of Medicine, 346,* 731–737.

Schlagmüller, M., & Schneider, W. (2002). The development of organizational strategies in children: Evidence from a microgenetic longitudinal study. *Journal of Experimental Child Psychology, 81,* 298–319.

Schlaud, M., Eberhard, C., Trumann, B., Kleemann, W. J., Poets, C. F., Tietze, K. W., & Schwartz, F. W. (1999). Prevalence and determinants of prone sleeping position in infants: Results for two cross-sectional studies on risk factors for SIDS in Germany. *American Journal of Epidemiology, 150,* 51–57.

Schlegel, A. (1995). A cross-cultural approach to adolescence. *Ethos, 23,* 5–32.

Schlegel, A., & Barry, H., III. (1980). The evolutionary significance of adolescent initiation ceremonies. *American Ethnologist, 7,* 696–715.

Schlegel, A., & Barry, H., III. (1991). *Adolescence: An anthropological inquiry.* New York: Free Press.

Schmid, R. G., Tirsch, W. S., & Scherb, H. (2002). Correlation between spectral EEG parameters and intelligence test variables in school-age children. *Clinical Neurophysiology, 113,* 1647–1656.

Schmidt, U. (2000). Eating disorders. In D. Kohen (Ed.), *Women and mental health* (pp. 174–197). London: Routledge.

Schmitz, M. K. H., & Jeffery, R. W. (2000). Public health interventions for the prevention and treatment of obesity. *Medical Clinics of North America, 84,* 491–512.

Schmitz, S., Fulker, D. W., Plomin, R., Zahn-Waxler, C., Emde, R. N., & DeFries, J. C. (1999). Temperament and problem behaviour during early childhood. *International Journal of Behavioral Development, 23,* 333–355.

Schneewind, K. A., & Gerhard, A. (2002). Relationship personality, conflict resolution, and marital satisfaction in the first 5 years of marriage. *Family Relations, 51,* 63–71.

Schneider, B. H., Atkinson, L., & Tardif, C. (2001). Child–parent attachment and children's peer relations: A quantitative review. *Developmental Psychology, 37,* 86–100.

Schneider, B., & Stevenson, D. (1999). *The ambitious generation: America's teenagers, motivated but directionless.* New Haven, CT: Yale University Press.

Schneider, W. (1986). The role of conceptual knowledge and metamemory in the development of organizational processes in memory. *Journal of Experimental Child Psychology, 42,* 218–236.

Schneider, W. (2002). Memory development in childhood. In U. Goswami (Ed.), *Blackwell handbook of childhood cognitive development* (pp. 236–256). Malden, MA: Blackwell.

Schneider, W., & Bjorklund, D. F. (1992). Expertise, aptitude, and strategic remembering. *Child Development, 63,* 461–473.

Schneider, W., & Bjorklund, D. F. (1998). Memory. In D. Kuhn & R. S. Siegler (Eds.), *Handbook of child psychology: Vol. 2. Cognition, perception, and language* (5th ed., pp. 467–521). New York: Wiley.

Schneider, W., & Pressley, M. (1997). *Memory development between two and twenty* (2nd ed.). Mahwah, NJ: Erlbaum.

Schneirla, T. C., Rosenblatt, J. S., & Tobach, E. (1963). Maternal behavior in the cat. In H. R. Rheingold (Ed.), *Maternal behavior in mammals* (pp. 122–168). New York: Wiley.

Schnur, E., & Belanger, S. (2000). What works in Head Start. In M. P. Kluger & G. Alexander (Eds.), *What works in child welfare* (pp. 277–284). Washington, DC: Child Welfare League of America.

Scholl, B. J., & Leslie, A. M. (2000). Minds, modules, and meta-analysis. *Child Development, 72,* 696–701.

Scholl, T. O., Hediger, M. L., & Belsky, D. (1996). Prenatal care and maternal health during adolescent pregnancy: A review and meta-analysis. *Journal of Adolescent Health, 15,* 444–456.

Schonert-Reichl, K. A. (1999). Relations of peer acceptance, friendship adjustment, and social behavior to moral reasoning during early adolescence. *Journal of Early Adolescence, 19,* 249–279.

Schonfeld, A. M., Mattson, S. N., Lang, A. R., Delis, D. C., & Riley, E. P. (2001). Verbal and nonverbal fluency in children with heavy prenatal alcohol exposure. *Journal of Studies on Alcohol, 62,* 239–246.

Schoon, I., & Parsons, S. (2002). Teenage aspirations for future careers and occupational outcomes. *Journal of Vocational Behavior, 60,* 262–288.

Schor, J. B. (2002). Time crunch among American parents. In S. A. Hewlett, N. Rankin, & C. West (Eds.), *Taking parenting public* (pp. 83–102). Boston: Rowman & Littlefield.

Schraedley, P. K., Gotlib, I. H., & Hayward, C. (1999). Gender differences in correlates of depressive symptoms in adolescents. *Journal of Adolescent Health, 25,* 98–108.

Schuengel, G., Bakermans-Kranenburg, M. J., & van IJzendoorn, M. H. (1999). Attachment and loss: Frightening maternal behavior linking unresolved loss and disorganized infant attachment. *Journal of Consulting and Clinical Psychology, 67,* 54–63.

Schull, W. J., & Otake, M. (1999). Cognitive function and prenatal exposure to ionizing radiation. *Teratology, 59,* 222–226.

Schulman, J. D., & Black, S. H. (1997). Screening for Huntington disease and certain other dominantly inherited disorders: A case for preimplantation genetic testing. *Journal of Medical Screening, 4,* 58–59.

Schulte, L. E., Shanahan, S., Anderson, T. D., & Sides, J. (2003). Student and teacher perceptions of their middle and high schools' sense of community. *School Community Journal, 13,* 7–33.

Schultz, D., Izar, C. E., Ackerman, B. P., & Youngstrom, E. A. (2001). Emotion knowledge in economically disadvantaged children: Self-regulatory antecedents and relations to social difficulties and withdrawal. *Development and Psychopathology, 13,* 53–67.

Schunk, D. H., & Zimmerman, B. J. (2003). Self-regulation and learning. In W. M. Reynolds & G. E. Miller

(Eds.), *Handbook of psychology* (Vol. 7, pp. 59–78). New York: Wiley.

Schwanenflugel, P. J., Fabricius, W. V., & Noyes, C. R. (1996). Developing organization of mental verbs: Evidence for the development of a constructivist theory of mind in middle childhood. *Cognitive Development, 11,* 265–294.

Schwanenflugel, P. J., Henderson, R. L., & Fabricius, W. V. (1998). Developing organization of mental verbs and theory of mind in middle childhood: Evidence from extensions. *Developmental Psychology, 34,* 512–524.

Schwartz, C. E., Wright, C. I., Shin, L. M., Kagan, J., & Rauch, S. L. (2003). Inhibited and uninhibited infants "grown up": Adult amygdalar response to novelty. *Science, 300,* 1952–1953.

Schwartz, D., Proctor, L. J., & Chien, D. H. (2001). The aggressive victim of bullying: Emotional and behavioral dysregulation as a pathway to victimization by peers. In J. Juonen & S. Graham (Eds.), *Peer harassment in school: The plight of the vulnerable and victimized* (pp. 147–174). New York: Guilford.

Schwebel, D. C., & Bounds, M. L. (2003). The role of parents and temperament on children's estimation of physical ability: Links to unintentional injury prevention. *Journal of Pediatric Psychology, 28,* 505–516.

Scott, K. D., Berkowitz, G., & Klaus, M. (1999). A comparison of intermittent and continuous support during labor: A meta-analysis. *American Journal of Obstetrics and Gynecology, 180,* 1054–1059.

Seccombe, K. (2002). "Beating the odds" versus "changing the odds": Poverty, resilience, and family policy. *Journal of Marriage and the Family, 64,* 384–394.

Seefeldt, V. (1996). The concept of readiness applied to the acquisition of motor skills. In F. L. Smoll & R. E. Smith (Eds.), *Children and youth in sport: A biopsychological perspective* (pp. 49–56). Dubuque, IA: Brown & Benchmark.

Seginer, R. (1992). Sibling relationships in early adolescence: A study of Israeli Arab sisters. *Journal of Early Adolescence, 12,* 96–110.

Seidman, E., Allen, L., Aber, J. L., Mitchell, C., & Feinman, J. (1994). The impact of school transitions in early adolescence on the self-system and perceived social context of poor urban youth. *Child Development, 65,* 507–522.

Seidman, E., & French, S. E. (1997). Normative school transitions among urban adolescents: When, where, and how to intervene. In H. J. Walberg, O. Reyes, & R. P. Weissberg (Eds.), *Children and youth: Interdisciplinary perspectives* (pp. 166–189). Thousand Oaks, CA: Sage.

Seidman, E., Lambert, L. E., Allen, L., & Aber, J. L. (2003). Urban adolescents' transition to junior high school and protective family transactions. *Journal of Early Adolescence, 23,* 166–193.

Seifer, R., & Schiller, M. (1995). The role of parenting sensitivity, infant temperament, and dyadic interaction in attachment theory and assessment. In E. Waters, B. E. Vaughn, G. Posada, & K. Kondo-Ikemura K. (Eds.), *Caregiving, cultural, and cognitive perspectives on secure-base behavior and working models: New growing points of attachment theory and research. Monographs of the Society for Research in Child Development, 60*(2–3, Serial No. 244).

Seifer, R., Schiller, M., Sameroff, A. J., Resnick, S., & Riordan, K. (1996). Attachment, maternal sensitivity, and infant temperament during the first year of life. *Developmental Psychology, 32,* 12–25.

Seiffge-Krenke, I. (2003). Testing theories of romantic development from adolescence to young adulthood: Evidence of a developmental sequence. *International Journal of Behavioral Development, 27,* 519–531.

Seinhausen, H. (2002). The outcome of anorexia nervosa in the 20th century. *American Journal of Psychiatry, 159,* 1284–1293.

Seitz, V., & Apfel, N. H. (1993). Adolescent mothers and repeated childbearing: Effects of a school-based intervention program. *American Journal of Orthopsychiatry, 63,* 572–581.

Seitz, V., & Apfel, N. H. (1994). Effects of a school for pregnant students on the incidence of low-birthweight deliveries. *Child Development, 65,* 666–676.

Seligman, M. E. P. (1975). *Helplessness: On depression, development, and death.* San Francisco: Freeman.

Selman, R. L. (1976). Social-cognitive understanding: A guide to educational and clinical practice. In T. Lickona (Ed.), *Moral development and behavior: Theory, research, and social issues* (pp. 299–316). New York: Holt, Rinehart, & Winston.

Selman, R. L. (1980). *The growth of interpersonal understanding.* New York: Academic Press.

Selman, R. L., & Byrne, D. F. (1974). A structural-developmental analysis of levels of role taking in middle childhood. *Child Development, 45,* 803–806.

Sen, A. (1999). *Development as freedom.* New York: Random House.

Sen, M. G., Yonas, A., & Knill, D. C. (2001). Development of infants' sensitivity to surface contour information for spatial layout. *Perception, 30,* 167–176.

Senechal, M., & LeFevre, J. (2002). Parental involvement in the development of children's reading skill:

A five-year longitudinal study. *Child Development, 73,* 445–460.

Serbin, L. A., Poulin-Dubois, D., Colburne, K. A., Sen, M. G., & Eichstedt, J. A. (2001). Gender stereotyping in infancy: Visual preferences for and knowledge of gender-stereotyped toys in the second year. *International Journal of Behavioral Development, 25,* 7–15.

Serbin, L. A., Powlishta, K. K., & Gulko, J. (1993). The development of sex typing in middle childhood. *Monographs of the Society for Research in Child Development, 58*(2, Serial No. 232).

Serpell, R., Sonnenschein, S., Baker, L., & Ganapathy, H. (2002). Intimate culture of families in the early socialization of literacy. *Journal of Family Psychology, 16,* 391–405.

Seward, R. R., Yeats, D. E., & Zottarelli, L. K. (2002). Parental leave and father involvement in child care: Sweden and the United States. *Journal of Comparative Family Studies, 33,* 387–399.

Shafer, V. L., Shucard, D. W., & Jaeger, J. J. (1999). Electrophysiological indices of cerebral specialization and the role of prosody in language acquisition in 3-month-old infants. *Developmental Neuropsychology, 15,* 73–109.

Shahar, S. (1990). *Childhood in the Middle Ages.* London: Routledge & Kegan Paul.

Shainess, N. (1961). A re-evaluation of some aspects of femininity through a study of menstruation: A preliminary report. *Comparative Psychiatry, 2,* 20–26.

Shanahan, M. J. (2000). Pathways to adulthood in changing societies: Variability and mechanisms in life course perspective. *Annual Review of Sociology, 26,* 667–692.

Shanahan, M. J., Mortimer, J. T., & Krüger, H. (2002). Adolescence and adult work in the twenty-first century. *Journal of Research on Adolescence, 12,* 99–120.

Shann, F., & Steinhoff, M. C. (1999). Vaccines for children in rich and poor countries. *Paediatrics, 354,* 7–11.

Shann, M. H. (2001). Students' use of time outside of school: A case for after school programs for urban middle school youth. *Urban Review, 33,* 339–356.

Shapiro, A. E., Gottman, J. M., & Carrere, S. (2000). The baby and the marriage: Identifying factors that buffer against decline in marital satisfaction after the first baby arrives. *Journal of Family Psychology, 14,* 59–70.

Shaver, P., Furman, W., & Buhrmester, D. (1985). Transition to college: Network changes, social skills, and loneliness. In S. Duck & D. Perlman (Eds.), *Understanding personal relationships: An interdisciplinary approach* (pp. 193–219). London: Sage.

Shaw, D. S., Winslow, E. B., & Flanagan, C. (1999). A prospective study of the effects of marital status and family relations on young children's adjustment among African-American and European-American families. *Child Development, 70,* 742–755.

Shea, B. T., & Bailey, R. C. (1996). Allometry and adaptation of body proportions and stature in African pygmies. *American Journal of Physical Anthropology, 100,* 311–340.

Shedler, J., & Block, J. (1990). Adolescent drug use and psychological health: A longitudinal inquiry. *American Psychologist, 45,* 612–630.

Sheehy, A., Gasser, T., Molinari, L., & Largo, R. H. (1999). An analysis of variance of the pubertal and midgrowth spurts for length and width. *Annals of Human Biology, 26,* 309–331.

Sheiner, E., Shoham-Vardi, I., Hallak, M., Hershkowitz, R., Katz, M., & Mazor, M. (2001). Placenta previa: Obstetric risk factors and pregnancy outcome. *Journal of Maternal-Fetal Medicine, 10,* 414–419.

Sherman, D. K., Iacono, W. G., & McGue, M. K. (1997). Attention-deficit hyperactivity disorder dimensions: A twin study of inattention and impulsivity-hyperactivity. *Journal of the American Academy of Child and Adolescent Psychiatry, 36,* 745–753.

Sherrill, C. L., & Pinderhughes, E. E. (1999). Conceptions of family and adoption among older adoptees. *Adoption Quarterly, 2,* 21–48.

Shields, A., Dickstein, S., Siefer, R., Giusti, L., Magee, K. D., & Spritz, B. (2001). Emotional competence and early school adjustment: A study of preschoolers at risk. *Early Education and Development, 12,* 73–96.

Shields, P. J., & Rovee-Collier, C. K. (1992). Long-term memory for context-specific category information at six months. *Child Development, 63,* 245–259.

Shiloh, S. (1996). Genetic counseling: A developing area of interest for psychologists. *Professional Psychology: Research and Practice, 27,* 475–486.

Shimizu, H. (2001). Japanese adolescent boys' senses of empathy (omoiyari) and Carol Gilligan's perspectives on the morality of care: A phenomenological approach. *Culture and Psychology, 7,* 453–475.

Shipman, H. L., Brickhouse, N. W., Dagher, Z., & Letts, W. J., IV. (2002). Changes in student views of religion and science in a college astronomy course. *Science Education, 86,* 526–547.

Shipman, K. L., Zeman, J., Nesin, A. E., & Fitzgerald, M. (2003). Children's strategies for displaying anger and sadness: What works with whom? *Merrill-Palmer Quarterly, 49,* 100–122.

Shoda, Y., Mischel, W., & Peake, P. K. (1990). Predicting adolescent cognitive and self-regulatory compe-

tencies from preschool delay of gratification: Identifying diagnostic conditions. *Developmental Psychology, 26,* 978–986.

Shonk, S. M., & Cicchetti, D. (2001). Maltreatment, competency deficits, and risk for academic and behavioral maladjustment. *Developmental Psychology, 37,* 3–17.

Shonkoff, J., & Phillips, D. (Eds.). (2001). *Neurons to neighborhoods: The science of early childhood development.* Washington, DC: National Academy Press.

Shulman, S., & Kipnis, O. (2001). Adolescent romantic relationships: A look from the future. *Journal of Adolescence, 24,* 337–351.

Shure, M. B. (2001). I Can Problem Solve (ICPS): An interpersonal cognitive problem solving program for children. *Residential Treatment for Children and Youth, 18,* 3–14.

Shweder, R. A. (1996). True ethnography: The lore, the law, and the lure. In R. Jessor, A. Colby, & R. A. Shweder (Eds.), *Ethnography and human development* (pp. 15–52). Chicago: University of Chicago Press.

Shweder, R. A., Goodnow, J., Hatano, G., LeVine, R. A., Markus, H., & Miller, P. (1998). The cultural psychology of development: One mind, many mentalities. In R. M. Lerner (Ed.), *Handbook of child psychology: Vol. 1. Theoretical models of human development* (5th ed., pp. 865–937). New York: Wiley.

Sidebotham, P., Heron, J., & the ALSPAC Study Team. (2003). Child maltreatment in the "children of the nineties": The role of the child. *Child Abuse and Neglect, 27,* 337–352.

Siegler, R. S. (1995). How does change occur? A microgenetic study of number conservation. *Cognitive Psychology, 28,* 225–273.

Siegler, R. S. (1996). *Emerging minds: The process of change in children's thinking.* New York: Oxford University Press.

Siegler, R. S. (1998). *Children's thinking* (3rd ed.). Upper Saddle River, NJ: Prentice-Hall.

Siegler, R. S. (2002). Microgenetic studies of self-explanation. In N. Granott & J. Parziale (Eds.), *Microdevelopment: Transition processes in development and learning* (pp. 31–58). New York: Cambridge University Press.

Siegler, R. S., & Crowley, K. (1991). The microgenetic method: A direct means for studying cognitive development. *American Psychologist, 46,* 606–620.

Siegler, R. S., & Jenkins, E. A. (1989). *How children discover new strategies.* Hillsdale, NJ: Erlbaum.

Sigman, M. (1995). Nutrition and child development: More food for thought. *Current Directions in Psychological Science, 4,* 52–55.

Sigman, M. (1999). Developmental deficits in children with Down syndrome. In H. Tager-Flusberg (Ed.), *Neurodevelopmental disorders: Developmental cognitive neuroscience* (pp. 179–195). Cambridge, MA: MIT Press.

Sigman, M., Cohen, S. E., & Beckwith, L. (1997). Why does infant attention predict adolescent intelligence? *Infant Behavior and Development, 20,* 133–140.

Signorielli, N. (2001). Television's gender-role images and contribution to stereotyping. In D. G. Singer & J. L. Singer (Eds.), *Handbook of children and the media* (pp. 341–358). Thousand Oaks, CA: Sage.

Signorielli, N., & Lears, M. (1992). Television and children's conceptions of nutrition: Unhealthy messages. *Health Communication, 4,* 245–257.

Silberg, J., Rutter, M., D'Onofrio, B., & Eaves, L. (2003). Genetic and environmental risk factors in adolescent substance use. *Journal of Child Psychology and Psychiatry and Allied Disciplines, 44,* 664–676.

Silvén, M. (2001). Attention in very young infants predicts learning of first words. *Infant Behavior and Development, 24,* 229–237.

Silverman, J. G., Raj, A., Mucci, L. A., & Hathaway, J. E. (2001). Dating violence against adolescent girls and associated substance use, unhealthy weight control, sexual risk behavior, pregnancy, and suicidality. *Journal of the American Medical Association, 286,* 572–579.

Silverman, W. K., La Greca, A. M., & Wasserstein, S. (1995). What do children worry about? Worries and their relation to anxiety. *Child Development, 66,* 671–686.

Sim, T. N. (2000). Adolescent psychosocial competence: The importance and role of regard for parents. *Journal of Research on Adolescence, 10,* 49–64.

Sim, T. N., & Koh, S. F. (2003). A domain conceptualization of adolescent susceptibility to peer pressure. *Journal of Research on Adolescence, 13,* 57–80.

Simcock, G., & Hayne, H. (2002). Breaking the barrier? Children fail to translate their preverbal memories into language. *Psychological Science, 13,* 225–231.

Simcock, G., & Hayne, H. (2003). Age-related changes in verbal and nonverbal memory during early childhood. *Developmental Psychology, 39,* 805–814.

Simion, F., Cassia, V. M., Turati, C., & Valenza, E. (2001). The origins of face perception: Specific versus non-specific mechanisms. *Infant and Child Development, 10,* 59–65.

Simmons, R. G., & Blyth, D. A. (1987). *Moving into adolescence.* New York: Aldine de Gruyter.

Simoneau, M., & Markovits, H. (2003). Reasoning with premises that are not empirically true: Evidence for the role of inhibition and retrieval. *Developmental Psychology, 39,* 964–975.

Simons, D. J., & Keil, F. C. (1995). An abstract to concrete shift in the development of biological thought: The insider story. *Cognition, 56,* 129–163.

Simons, R. L., & Chao, W. (1996). Conduct problems. In R. L. Simons & Associates (Eds.), *Understanding differences between divorced and intact families* (pp. 125–143). Thousand Oaks, CA: Sage.

Simons, R. L., Whitbeck, L. B., Conger, R. D., & Chyi-In, W. (1991). Intergenerational transmission of harsh parenting. *Developmental Psychology, 27,* 159–171.

Simons-Morton, B. G., & Haynie, D. L. (2003). Growing up drug free: A developmental challenge. In M. H. Bornstein, L. Davidson, C. L. M. Keyes, K. A. Moore, & the Center for Child Well-Being (Eds.), *Well-being: Positive development across the life course* (pp. 109–122). Mahwah, NJ: Erlbaum.

Simpson, J. A., Rholes, W. S., Campbell, L., Tran, S., & Wilson, C. L. (2003). Adult attachment, the transition to parenthood, and depressive symptoms. *Journal of Personality and Social Psychology, 84,* 1172–1187.

Simpson, J. M. (2001). Infant stress and sleep deprivation as an aetiological basis for the sudden infant death syndrome. *Early Human Development, 61,* 1–43.

Singer, L. T., Arendt, R., Minnes, S., Farkas, K., Salvator, A., Kirchner, H. L., & Kliegman, R. (2002a). Cognitive and motor outcomes of cocaine-exposed infants. *Journal of the American Medical Association, 287,* 1952–1960.

Singer, L. T., Salvator, A., Arendt, R., Minnes, S., Farkas, K., & Kliegman, R. (2002b). Effects of cocaine/polydrug exposure and maternal psychological distress on infant birth outcomes. *Neurotoxicology and Teratology, 24,* 127–135.

Singh, S., & Darroch, J. E. (2000). Adolescent pregnancy and childbearing: Levels and trends in developed countries. *Family Planning Perspectives, 32,* 14–23.

Sippola, L., Bukowski, W. M., & Noll, R. B. (1997). Age differences in children's and early adolescents' liking for same-sex and other-sex peers. *Merrill-Palmer Quarterly, 43,* 547–561.

Skinner, B. F. (1957). *Verbal behavior.* New York: Appleton-Century-Crofts.

Skinner, E. A., Zimmer-Gembeck, M. J., & Connell, J. P. (1998). Individual differences and the development of perceived control. *Monographs of the Society for Research in Child Development, 63*(2–3, Serial No. 254).

Skoe, E. S. A. (1998). The ethic of care: Issues in moral development. In E. E. A. Skoe & A. L. von der Lippe (Eds.), *Personality development in adolescence* (pp. 143–171). London: Routledge.

Slaby, R. G., & Frey, K. S. (1975). Development of gender constancy and selective attention to same-sex models. *Child Development, 46,* 849–856.

Slaby, R. G., Roedell, W. C., Arezzo, D., & Hendrix, K. (1995). *Early violence prevention.* Washington, DC: National Association for the Education of Young Children.

Slade, A., Belsky, J., Aber, J. L., & Phelps, J. L. (1999). Mothers' representations of their relationships with their toddlers: Links to adult attachment and observed mothering. *Developmental Psychology, 35,* 611–619.

Slater, A. (2001). Visual perception. In G. Bremner & A. Fogel (Eds.), *Blackwell handbook of infant development* (pp. 5–34). Malden, MA: Blackwell.

Slater, A., Bremner, G., Johnson, S. P., Sherwood, P., Hayes, R., & Brown, E. (2000). Newborn infants' preference for attractive faces: The role of internal and external facial features. *Infancy, 1,* 265–274.

Slater, A., Brown, E., Mattock, A., & Bornstein, M. H. (1996). Continuity and change in habituation in the first 4 months from birth. *Journal of Reproductive and Infant Psychology, 14,* 187–194.

Slater, A., & Johnson, S. P. (1999). Visual sensory and perceptual abilities of the newborn: Beyond the blooming, buzzing confusion. In A. Slater & S. P. Johnson (Eds.), *The development of sensory, motor and cognitive capacities in early infancy* (pp. 121–141). Hove, U.K.: Sussex Press.

Slater, A., & Quinn, P. C. (2001). Face recognition in the newborn infant. *Infant and Child Development, 10,* 21–24.

Slaughter, V., Jaakkola, R., & Carey, S. (1999). Constructing a coherent theory: Children's biological understanding of life and death. In M. Siegel & C. C. Petersen (Eds.), *Children's understanding of biology and health* (pp. 71–96). Cambridge, U.K.: Cambridge University Press.

Slaughter, V., & Lyons, M. (2003). Learning about life and death in early childhood. *Cognitive Psychology, 46,* 1–30.

Sleet, D. A., & Mercy, J. A. (2003). Promotion of safety, security, and well-being. In M. H. Bornstein, L. Davidson, C. M. M. Keyes, K. A. Moore, & the Center for Child Well-Being (Eds.), *Well-being: Positive development across the life course* (pp. 81–97). Mahwah, NJ: Erlbaum.

Slicker, E. K., & Thornberry, I. (2002). Older adolescent well-being and authoritative parenting. *Adolescent and Family Health, 3,* 9–19.

Slobin, D. I. (1985). Cross-linguistic evidence for language-making capacity. In D. I. Slobin (Ed.), *The cross-linguistic study of language acquisition: Vol. 2. Theoretical issues* (pp. 1157–1256). Hillsdale, NJ: Erlbaum.

Slobin, D. I. (1997). On the origin of grammaticalizable notions: Beyond the individual mind. In D. I. Slobin (Ed.), *The cross-linguistic study of language acquisition: Vol. 5* (pp. 265–324). Hillsdale, NJ: Erlbaum.

Small, M. (1998). *Our babies, ourselves.* New York: Anchor.

Smetana, J. G. (2002). Culture, autonomy, and personal jurisdiction in adolescent–parent relationships. In R. V. Kail & H. W. Reese (Eds.), *Advances in child development and behavior* (Vol. 29, pp. 51–87). San Diego, CA: Academic Press.

Smiley, P. A., & Dweck, C. S. (1994). Individual differences in achievement goals among young children. *Child Development, 65,* 1723–1743.

Smith, A. E., Jussim, L., Eccles, J., VanNoy, M., Madon, S., & Palumbo, P. (1998). Self-fulfilling prophecies, perceptual biases, and accuracy at the individual and group levels. *Journal of Experimental Social Psychology, 34,* 530–561.

Smith, E. P., Walker, K., Fields, L., Brookins, C. C., & Seay, R. C. (1999). Ethnic identity and its relationship to self-esteem, perceived efficacy, and prosocial attitudes in early adolescence. *Journal of Adolescence, 22,* 867–880.

Smith, G. C. S., Pell, J. P., Cameron, A. D., & Dobbie, R. (2002). Risk of perinatal death associated with labor after previous cesarean delivery in uncomplicated term pregnancies. *Journal of the American Medical Association, 287,* 2684–2690.

Smith, J. R., Brooks-Gunn, J., Kohen, D., & McCarton, C. (2001). Transitions on and off AFDC: Implications for parenting and children's cognitive development. *Child Development, 72,* 1512–1533.

Smith, J., Duncan, G. J., & Lee, K. (2003). The black–white test score gap in young children: Contributions of test and family characteristics. *Applied Developmental Science, 7,* 239–252.

Smith, K. E., Landry, S. H., Swank, P. R., Baldwin, C. D., Denson, S. E., & Wildin, S. (1996). The relation of medical risk and maternal stimulation with preterm infants' development of cognitive, language, and daily living skills. *Journal of Child Psychology and Psychiatry, 37,* 855–864.

Smith, L. B., Quittner, A. L., Osberger, M. J., & Miyamoto, R. (1998). Audition and visual attention: The developmental trajectory in deaf and hearing populations. *Developmental Psychology, 34,* 840–850.

Smith, L. B., Thelen, E., Titzer, R., & McLin, D. (1999). Knowing in the context of acting: The task dynamics of the A-not-B error. *Psychological Review, 106,* 235–260.

Smith, M. L., Klim, P., & Hanley, W. B. (2000). Executive function in school-aged children with phenylketonuria. *Journal of Developmental and Physical Disabilities, 12,* 317–332.

Smith, P. K. (2003). Play and peer relations. In A. Slater & G. Bremner (Eds.), *An introduction to developmental psychology* (pp. 311–333). Malden, MA: Blackwell.

Smith, P. K., & Myron-Wilson, R. (1998). Parenting and school bullying. *Clinical Child Psychology and Psychiatry, 3,* 405–417.

Smith, P., Perrin, S., Yule, W., & Rabe-Hesketh, S. (2001). War exposure and maternal reactions in the psychological adjustment of children from Bosnia-Hercegovina. *Journal of Child Psychology and Psychiatry and Allied Disciplines, 42,* 395–404.

Smith, R. (1999). The timing of birth. *Scientific American, 280*(3), 68–75.

Smith, R. E., & Smoll, F. L. (1997). Coaching the coaches: Youth sports as a scientific and applied behavior setting. *Current Directions in Psychological Science, 6,* 16–21.

Snarey, J. (1995). In a communitarian voice: The sociological expansion of Kohlbergian theory, research, and practice. In W. M. Kurtines & J. L. Gewirtz (Eds.), *Moral development: An introduction* (pp. 109–134). Boston: Allyn and Bacon.

Snarey, J. R., & Bell, D. (2003). Distinguishing structural and functional models of human development: A response to "what transits in an identity status transition?" *Identity, 3,* 221–230.

Snarey, J. R., Reimer, J., & Kohlberg, L. (1985). The development of social–moral reasoning among kibbutz adolescents: A longitudinal cross-cultural study. *Developmental Psychology, 21,* 3–17.

Snidman, N., Kagan, J., Riordan, L., & Shannon, D. C. (1995). Cardiac function and behavioral reactivity. *Psychophysiology, 32,* 199–207.

Snow, C. E., Pan, B. A., Imbens-Bailey, A., & Herman, J. (1996). Learning how to say what one means: A longitudinal study of children's speech act use. *Social Development, 5,* 56–84.

Society for Research in Child Development. (1993). Ethical standards for research with children. In *Directory of Members* (pp. 337–339). Ann Arbor, MI: Author.

Society of Obstetricians and Gynaecologists of Canada (SOGC). Multiple birth. Retrieved from http://www.sogc.org/multiple/facts_e.shtml

Soderstrom, M., Seidl, A., Nelson, D. G. K., & Jusczyk, P. W. (2003).

The prosodic bootstrapping of phrases: Evidence from prelinguistic infants. *Journal of Memory and Language, 49,* 249–267.

Soken, H. H., & Pick, A. D. (1992). Intermodal perception of happy and angry expressive behaviors by seven-month-old infants. *Child Development, 63,* 787–795.

Solomon, G. B., & Bredemeier, B. J. L. (1999). Children's moral conceptions of gender stratification in sport. *International Journal of Sport Psychology, 30,* 350–368.

Solomon, G. E. A., & Johnson, S. C. (2000). Conceptual change in the classroom: Teaching young children to understand biological inheritance. *British Journal of Development Psychology, 18,* 81–96.

Sondergaard, C., Henriksen, T. B., Obel, C., & Wisborg, K. (2002). Smoking during pregnancy and infantile colic. *Journal of the American Academy of Child and Adolescent Psychiatry, 41,* 147.

Sophian, C. (1995). Representation and reasoning in early numerical development: Counting, conservation, and comparisons between sets. *Child Development, 66,* 559–577.

Sorce, J., Emde, R., Campos, J., & Klinnert, M. (1985). Maternal emotional signaling: Its effect on the visual cliff behavior of 1-year-olds. *Developmental Psychology, 21,* 195–200.

Sosa, R., Kennell, J., Klaus, M., Robertson, S., & Urrutia, J. (1980). The effect of a supportive companion on perinatal problems, length of labor, and mother–infant interaction. *New England Journal of Medicine, 303,* 597–600.

Sowell, E. R., Trauner, D. A., Gamst, A., & Jernigan, T. L. (2002). Development of cortical and subcortical brain structures in childhood and adolescence: A structural MRI study. *Developmental Medicine and Child Neurology, 44,* 4–16.

Spätling, L., & Spätling, G. (1988). Magnesium supplementation in pregnancy: A double-blind study. *British Journal of Obstetrics and Gynecology, 95,* 120–125.

Spear, L. P. (2003). Neurodevelopment during adolescence. In D. Cicchetti & E. Walker (Eds.), *Neurodevelopmental mechanisms in psychopathology* (pp. 62–83). New York: Cambridge University Press.

Speece, M. W., & Brent, S. B. (1996). The development of children's understanding of death. In C. A. Corr & D. M. Corr (Eds.), *Handbook of childhood death and bereavement* (pp. 29–50). New York: Springer.

Speicher, B. (1994). Family patterns of moral judgment during adolescence and early adulthood. *Developmental Psychology, 30,* 624–632.

Spelke, E. S., Breinlinger, K., Macomber, J., & Jacobson, K. (1992). Origins of knowledge. *Psychological Review, 99,* 605–632.

Spelke, E. S., & Hermer, L. (1996). Early cognitive development: Objects and space. In R. Gelman & T. K. Au (Eds.), *Perceptual and cognitive development* (pp. 71–114). San Diego: Academic Press.

Spelke, E. S., & Newport, E. L. (1998). Nativism, empiricism, and the development of knowledge. In R. M. Lerner (Ed.), *Handbook of child psychology: Vol. 1. Theoretical models of human development* (5th ed., pp. 199–254). New York: Wiley.

Spence, M. J., & DeCasper, A. J. (1987). Prenatal experience with low-frequency maternal voice sounds influences neonatal perception of maternal voice samples. *Infant Behavior and Development, 10,* 133–142.

Spencer, J. P., Verejiken, B., Diedrich, F. J., & Thelen, E. (2000). Posture and the emergence of manual skills. *Developmental Science, 3,* 216–233.

Spencer, M. B., Fegley, S. G., & Harpalani, V. (2003). A theoretical and empirical examination of identity as coping: Linking coping resources to the self processes of African American youth. *Applied Developmental Science, 7,* 181–188.

Spencer, P. E. (2000). Looking without listening: Is audition a prerequisite for normal development of visual attention in infancy? *Journal of Deaf Studies and Education, 5,* 291–302.

Spencer, P. E., Bodner-Johnson, B. A., & Gutfreund, M. K. (1992). Interacting with infants with a hearing loss: What can we learn from mothers who are deaf? *Journal of Early Intervention, 16,* 64–78.

Spencer, P. E., & Lederberg, A. (1997). Different modes, different models: Communication and language of young deaf children and their mothers. In L. B. Adamson & M. Romski (Eds.), *Communication and language acquisition: Discoveries from atypical development* (pp. 203–230). Baltimore: Paul H. Brookes.

Spencer, P. E., & Meadow-Orlans, K. P. (1996). Play, language, and maternal responsiveness: A longitudinal study of deaf and hearing infants. *Child Development, 67,* 3176–3191.

Sperduto, R. D., Hiller, R., Podgor, M. J., Freidlin, V., Milton, R. C., Wolf, P. A., Myers, R. H., Dagostine, R. B., Roseman, M. J., Stockman, M. E., & Wilson, P. W. (1996). Familial aggregation and prevalence of myopia in the Framingham Offpring Eye Study. *Archives of Ophthalmology, 114,* 326–333.

Spindler, G. D. (1970). The education of adolescents: An anthropological perspective. In D. Ellis (Ed.), *Adolescents: Readings in behavior and development* (pp. 152–161). Hinsdale, IL: Dryden.

Spirito, A., Valeri, S., Boergers, J., & Donaldson, D. (2003). Predictors of continued suicidal behavior in adolescents following a suicide attempt. *Journal of Clinical Child and Adolescent Psychology, 32,* 284–289.

Spitz, R. A. (1945). Hospitalism: An inquiry into the genesis of psychiatric conditions in early childhood. *Psychoanalytic Study of the Child, 1,* 113–117.

Spitz, R. A. (1946). Anaclitic depression. *Psychoanalytic Study of the Child, 2,* 313–342.

Spock, B., & Parker, S. J. (1998). *Dr. Spock's baby and child care.* (7th ed.). New York: Pocket Books.

Spruijt-Metz, D., Lindquist, C. H., Birch, L. L., Fisher, J. O., & Goran, M. I. (2002). Relation between mothers' child-feeding practices and children's adiposity. *American Journal of Clinical Nutrition, 75,* 581–586.

Spurgeon, D. (2002). Childhood obesity in Canada has tripled in the past 20 years. *British Medical Journal, 324,* 1416.

Sridhar, D., & Vaughn, S. (2001). Social functioning of students with learning disabilities. In D. P. Hallahan & B. K. Keogh (Eds.), *Research and global perspectives in learning disabilities* (pp. 65–91). Mahwah, NJ: Erlbaum.

Sroufe, L. A. (1979). Socioemotional development. In J. D. Osofsky (Ed.), *Handbook of infant development* (pp. 462–516). New York: Wiley.

Sroufe, L. A. (2002). From infant attachment to promotion of adolescent autonomy: Prospective, longitudinal data on the role of parents in development. In J. G. Borkowski & S. L. Ramey (Eds.), *Parenting and the child's world* (pp. 187–202). Mahwah, NJ: Erlbaum.

Sroufe, L. A., Egeland, B., & Kreutzer, T. (1990). The fate of early experience following developmental change: Longitudinal approaches to individual adaptation. *Child Development, 61,* 1363–1373.

Sroufe, L. A., & Waters, E. (1976). The ontogenesis of smiling and laughter: A perspective on the organization of development in infancy. *Psychological Review, 83,* 173–189.

Sroufe, L. A., & Wunsch, J. P. (1972). The development of laughter in the first year of life. *Child Development, 43,* 1324–1344.

St James-Roberts, I., Goodwin, J., Peter, B., Adams, D., & Hunt, S. (2003). Individual differences in responsivity to a neurobehavioural examination predict crying patterns of 1-week-old infants at home. *Developmental Medicine and Child Neurology, 45,* 400–407.

Stams, G. J. M., Juffer, F., & van IJzendoorn, M. H. (2002). Maternal sensitivity, infant attachment, and temperament in early childhood predict adjustment in middle childhood: The case of adopted children and their biologically unrelated parents. *Developmental Psychology, 38,* 806–821.

Standley, J. M. (1998). The effect of music and multimodal stimulation on responses of premature infants in neonatal intensive care. *Pediatric Nursing, 24,* 532–538.

Stark, L. J., Allen, K. D., Hurst, M., Nash, D. A., Rigney, B., & Stokes, T. F. (1989). Distraction: Its utilization and efficacy with children undergoing dental treatment. *Journal of Applied Behavior Analysis, 22,* 297–307.

Statistics Canada. (1999). Education indicators in Canada: Equity. Retrieved from http://www.cmec.ca/stats/pceip/1999old/indicatorsite.n4/english/pages/page26e.html

Statistics Canada. (2000a). *Canadian social trends: Children's participation in sports.* Retrieved from http://www.statcan.ca/Daily/English/000912/d000912a.htm

Statistics Canada. (2000b). *Immigrant youth in Canada.* Retrieved from http://www.ccsd.ca

Statistics Canada. (2002a, October 29). Computer access at school and at home. *The Daily.* Retrieved from http://www.statcan.ca/english/edu/feature/computer/htm

Statistics Canada. (2002b). *Changing conjugal life in Canada.* Ottawa: Author.

Statistics Canada. (2002c). Crime in Canada. *Juristat, 22*(6). Retrieved from http://www.statcan.ca

Statistics Canada. (2002d). *Family studies kit.* Retrieved from http://www.statcan.ca/english/kits/Family/pdf/ch3_3e.pdf

Statistics Canada. (2002e). *Language composition of Canada, 2001 Census.* Retrieved from http://www.statcan.ca/english/IPS/Data/97F0007XCB2001000.htm

Statistics Canada. (2002f). Youth in transition survey, 2000. *The Daily.* Retrieved from http://www.statcan.ca/Daily/English/000928/d000928b.htm

Statistics Canada. (2003a). Births—shelf tables. Retrieved from http://www.statcan.ca/english/IPS/Data/84F0210XPB.htm

Statistics Canada. (2003b). Divorces. Retrieved from www.statcan.ca

Statistics Canada. (2003c). Population. Retrieved from http://www.statcan.ca

Statistics Canada. (2003d). *Television viewing data bank.* Ottawa: Author.

Statistics Canada. (2003e). Who goes to postsecondary education and when: Pathways chosen by 20-year-olds. Retrieved from http://www.statcan.ca/english/IPS/Data/81-595-MIE2003006.htm

Statistics Canada. (2003f). *Women in Canada: Work chapter updates.* Retrieved from http://www.statcan.ca/cgi-bin/downpub/freepub.cgi

Stattin, H., & Magnusson, D. (1990). *Pubertal maturation in female development.* Hillsdale, NJ: Erlbaum.

Staub, F. C., & Stern, E. (2002). The nature of teachers' pedagogical content beliefs matters for students' achievement gains: Quasi-experimental evidence from elementary mathematics. *Journal of Educational Psychology, 94,* 344–355.

Steele, C. M. (1997). A threat in the air: How stereotypes shape intellectual identity and performance. *American Psychologist, 52,* 613–629.

Steele, C. M., & Aronson, J. (1995). Stereotype threat and the intellectual test performance of African Americans. *Journal of Personality and Social Psychology, 69,* 797–811.

Steele, S., Joseph, R. M., Tager-Flusberg, H. (2003). Developmental change in theory of mind abilities in children with autism. *Journal of Austism and Developmental Disorders, 33,* 461–467.

Stehr-Green, P., Tull, P., Stellfeld, M., Mortenson, P. B., & Simpson, D. (2003). Autism and thimerosal-containing vaccines: Lack of consistent evidence for an association. *American Journal of Preventive Medicine, 25,* 101–106.

Stein, J. H., & Reiser, L. W. (1994). A study of white middle-class adolescent boys' responses to "semenarche" (the first ejaculation). *Journal of Youth and Adolescence, 23,* 373–384.

Stein, N., & Levine, L. J. (1999). The early emergence of emotional understanding and appraisal: Implications for theories of development. In T. Dalgleish & M. J. Power (Eds.), *Handbook of cognition and emotion* (pp. 383–408). Chichester, U.K.: Wiley.

Stein, Z., Susser, M., Saenger, G., & Marolla, F. (1975). *Famine and human development: The Dutch hunger winter of 1944–1945.* New York: Oxford.

Steinberg, L. (1984). The varieties and effects of work during adolescence. In M. Lamb, A. Brown, & B. Rogoff (Eds.), *Advances in developmental psychology* (pp. 1–37). Hillsdale, NJ: Erlbaum.

Steinberg, L. (1986). Latchkey children and susceptibility to peer pressure: An ecological analysis. *Developmental Psychology, 22,* 433–439.

Steinberg, L. (2001). We know some things: Parent–adolescent relationships in retrospect and prospect. *Journal of Research on Adolescence, 11,* 1–19.

Steinberg, L. D., Darling, N. E., & Fletcher, A. C. (1995). Authoritative parenting and adolescent development: An ecological journey. In P. Moen, G. H. Elder, Jr., & K. Luscher (Eds.), *Examining lives in context* (pp. 423–466). Washington, DC: American Psychological Association.

Steinberg, L. D., Fegley, S., & Dornbusch, S. (1993). Negative impact of part-time work on adolescent adjustment: Evidence from a longitudinal study. *Developmental Psychology, 29,* 171–180.

Steinberg, L., Lamborn, S. D., Darling, N., Mounts, N. S., & Dornbusch, S. M. (1994). Over-time changes in adjustment and competence among adolescents from authoritative, authoritarian, indulgent, and neglectful families. *Child Development, 65,* 754–770.

Steinberg, L., & Morris, A. S. (2001). Adolescent development. *Annual Review of Psychology, 52,* 83–110.

Steinberg, L., & Silk, J. S. (2002). Parenting adolescents. In M. H. Bornstein (Ed.), *Handbook of parenting: Vol. 1. Children and parenting* (pp. 103–134). Mahwah, NJ: Erlbaum.

Steinberg, L., & Silverberg, S. B. (1986). The vicissitudes of autonomy in early adolescence. *Child Development, 57,* 841–851.

Steinberg, S., & Bellavance, F. (1999). Characteristics and treatment of women with antenatal and postpartum depression. *International Journal of Psychiatry in Medicine, 29,* 209–233.

Steiner, J. E. (1979). Human facial expression in response to taste and smell stimulation. In H. W. Reese & L. P. Lipsitt (Eds.), *Advances in child development and behavior* (Vol. 13, pp. 257–295). New York: Academic Press.

Stenberg, C., & Campos, J. (1990). The development of anger expressions in infancy. In N. Stein, B. Leventhal, & T. Trabasso (Eds.), *Psychological and biological approaches to emotion* (pp. 247–282). Hillsdale, NJ: Erlbaum.

Stephens, K. (1999). Toilet training: Children step up to independence. *Child Care Information Exchange,* No. 125 (January/February).

Stern, M., & Karraker, K. H. (1989). Sex stereotyping of infants: A review of gender labeling studies. *Sex Roles, 20,* 501–522.

Sternberg, R. J. (1997). *Successful intelligence.* New York: Plume.

Sternberg, R. J. (2001). Beyond g: The theory of successful intelligence. In R. J. Sternberg & E. L. Grigorenko (Eds.), *The general factor of intelligence: How general is it?* (pp. 447–479). Mahwah, NJ: Erlbaum.

Sternberg, R. J. (2002a). Individual differences in cognitive development. In U. Goswami (Ed.), *Blackwell handbook of childhood cognitive development* (pp. 600–619). Malden, MA: Blackwell.

Sternberg, R. J. (2002b). Intelligence is not just inside the head: The theory of successful intelligence. In J. Aronson (Ed.), *Improving academic achievement* (pp. 227–244). San Diego, CA: Academic Press.

Sternberg, R. J., & Grigorenko, E. L. (2002). *Dynamic testing.* New York: Cambridge University Press.

Sternberg, R. J., & Jarvin, L. (2003). Alfred Binet's contributions as a paradigm for impact in psychology. In R. J. Sternberg (Ed.), *The anatomy of impact: What makes the great works of psychology great* (pp. 89–107). Washington, DC: American Psychological Association.

Sternberg, R. J., & Lubart, T. I. (1995). *Defying the crowd.* New York: Basic Books.

Sternberg, R. J., Forsythe, G. B., Hedlund, J., Horvath, J. A., Wagner, R. K., Williams, W. M., Snook, S. A., & Grigorenko, E. L. (2000). *Practical intelligence in everyday life.* Cambridge, U.K.: Cambridge University Press.

Stetsenko, A., Little, T. D., Gordeeva, T., Grasshof, M., & Oettingen, G. (2000). Gender effects in children's beliefs about school performance. *Child Development, 21,* 517–527.

Stettler, N., Kumanyika, S. K., Katz, S. H., Zemel, B. S., & Stallings, V. A. (2003). Rapid weight gain during infancy and obesity in young adulthood in a cohort of African Americans. *American Journal of Clinical Nutrition, 77,* 1374–1378.

Stevenson, H. W. (1992, December). Learning from Asian schools. *Scientific American, 267*(6), 32–38.

Stevenson, H. W. (1994). Extracurricular programs in East Asian schools. *Teachers College Record, 95,* 389–407.

Stevenson, H. W., Lee, S., & Mu, X. (2000). Successful achievement in mathematics: China and the United States. In C. F. M. van Lieshout & P. G. Heymans (Eds.), *Developing talent across the lifespan* (pp. 167–183). Philadelphia: Psychology Press.

Stevenson, M. R., & Black, K. N. (1995). *How divorce affects offspring: A research approach.* Dubuque, IA: Brown & Benchmark.

Stevenson, R., & Pollitt, C. (1987). The acquisition of temporal terms. *Journal of Child Language, 14,* 533–545.

Steward, D. K. (2001). Behavioral characteristics of infants with nonorganic failure to thrive during a play interaction. *American Journal of Maternal Child Nursing, 26,* 79–85.

Stewart, P., Reihman, J., Lonky, E., Darvill, T., & Pagano, J. (2000). Prenatal PCB exposure and neonatal behavioral assessment scale (NBAS) performance. *Neurotoxicology and Teratology, 22,* 21–29.

Stewart, R. B. (1983). Sibling attachment relationships: Child–infant interactions in the Strange Situation. *Developmental Psychology, 19,* 192–199.

Stewart, R. B., Jr. (1990). *The second child: Family transition and adjustment.* Newbury Park, CA: Sage.

Stice, E., & Barrera, M., Jr. (1995). A longitudinal examination of the reciprocal relations between perceived parenting and adolescents' substance use and externalizing behaviors. *Developmental Psychology, 31,* 322–334.

Stichick, T. (2001). The psychosocial impact of armed conflict on children. *Child and Adolescent Psychiatric Clinics of North America, 10,* 797–814.

Stifter, C. A., Coulehan, C. M., & Fish, M. (1993). Linking employment to attachment: The mediating effects of maternal separation anxiety and interactive behavior. *Child Development, 64,* 1451–1460.

Stiles, J. (2001a). Neural plasticity in cognitive development. *Developmental Neuropsychology, 18,* 237–272.

Stiles, J. (2001b). Spatial cognitive development. In C. A. Nelson & M. Luciana (Eds.), *Handbook of developmental cognitive neuroscience* (pp. 399–414). Cambridge, MA: MIT Press.

Stiles, J., Bates, E. A., Thai, D., Trauner, D., & Reilly, J. (1998). Linguistic, cognitive, and affective development in children with pre- and perinatal focal brain injury: A ten-year overview from the San Diego Longitudinal Project. In C. Rovee-Collier, L. P. Lipsitt, & H. Hayne (Eds.), *Advances in infancy research* (pp. 131–163). Stamford, CT: Ablex.

Stipek, D. (1995). The development of pride and shame in toddlers. In J. P. Tangney & K. W. Fischer (Eds.), *Self-conscious emotions* (pp. 237–252). New York: Guilford.

Stipek, D. (2002). At what age should children enter kindergarten? A question for policy makers and parents. *Social Policy Report of the Society for Research in Child Development, 16*(3).

Stipek, D. J., & Byler, P. (1997). Early childhood education teachers: Do they practice what they preach? *Early Childhood Research Quarterly, 12,* 305–326.

Stipek, D. J., & Byler, P. (2001). Academic achievement and social behaviors associated with age of entry into kindergarten. *Journal of Applied Developmental Psychology, 22,* 175–189.

Stipek, D. J., Gralinski, J. H., & Kopp, C. B. (1990). Self-concept development in the toddler years. *Developmental Psychology, 26,* 972–977.

Stoch, M. B., Smythe, P. M., Moodie, A. D., & Bradshaw, D. (1982). Psychosocial outcome and CT findings after growth undernourishment during infancy: A 20-year developmental study. *Developmental Medicine and Child Neurology, 24,* 419–436.

Stocker, C. M., & Dunn, J. (1994). Sibling relationships in childhood and adolescence. In J. C. DeFries, R. Plomin, & D. W. Fulker (Eds.), *Nature and nurture in middle childhood* (pp. 214–232). Cambridge: Blackwell.

Stodolsky, S. S. (1988). *The subject matters.* Chicago: University of Chicago Press.

Stone, M. R., & Brown, B. B. (1999). Identity claims and projections: Descriptions of self and crowds in secondary school. In J. A. McLellan & M. J. V. Pugh (Eds.), *The role of peer groups in adolescent social identity: Exploring the importance of stability and change* (pp. 7–20). San Francisco: Jossey-Bass.

Storch, S. A., & Whitehurst, G. J. (2001). The role of family and home in the literacy development of children from low-income backgrounds. In P. R. Britto & J. Brooks-Gunn (Eds.), *The role of family literacy environments in promoting young children's emerging literacy skills (New directions for child and adolescent development, No. 92, pp. 53–71).* San Francisco: Jossey-Bass.

Stormshak, E. A., Bierman, K. L., Bruschi, C., Dodge, K. A., & Coie, J. D. (1999). The relation between behavior problems and peer preference in different classroom contexts. *Child Development, 70,* 169–182.

Stormshak, E. A., Bierman, K. L., McMahon, R. J., Lengua, L. J., & the Conduct Problems Prevention Research Group. (2000). Parenting practices and child disruptive behavior problems in early elementary school. *Journal of Clinical Child Psychology, 29,* 17–29.

Strapp, C. M., & Federico, A. (2000). Imitations and repetitions: What do children say following recasts? *First Language, 20,* 273–290.

Strassberg, Z. (1995). Social information processing in compliance situations by mothers of behavior-problem boys. *Child Development, 66,* 376–389.

Straus, M. A., & Stewart, J. H. (1999). Corporal punishment by American parents: National data on prevalence, chronicity, severity, and duration, in relation to child and family characteristics. *Clinical Child and Family Psychology Review, 2,* 55–70.

Strauss, S. (1998). Cognitive development and science education: Toward a middle level model. In I. E. Sigel & K. Renninger (Eds.), *Handbook of child psychology: Vol. 4. Child psychology in practice* (5th ed., pp. 357–399). New York: Wiley.

Streissguth, A. P., Treder, R., Barr, H. M., Shepard, T., Bleyer, W. A., Sampson, P. D., & Martin, D. (1987). Aspirin and acetaminophen use by pregnant women and subsequent child IQ and attention decrements. *Teratology, 35,* 211–219.

Striano, T., & Rochat, P. (2000). Emergence of selective social referencing in infancy. *Infancy, 1,* 253–264.

Striano, T., Tomasello, M., & Rochat, P. (2001). Social and object support for early symbolic play. *Developmental Science, 4,* 442–455.

Stright, A. D., Neitzel, C., Sears, K. G., & Hoke-Sinex, L. (2002). Instruction begins in the home: Relations between parental instruction and children's self-regulation in the classroom. *Journal of Educational Psychology, 93,* 456–466.

Stromswold, K. (1995). The acquisition of subject and object questions. *Language Acquisition, 4,* 5–48.

Strouse, D. L. (1999). Adolescent crowd orientations: A social and temporal analysis. In J. A. McLellan & M. J. V. Pugh (Eds.), *The role of peer groups in adolescent social identity: Exploring the importance of stability and change* (pp. 37–54). San Francisco: Jossey-Bass.

Stryer, B. K., Tofler, I. R., & Lapchick, R. (1998). A developmental overview of child and youth sports in society. *Child and Adolescent Psychiatric Clinics of North America, 7,* 697–719.

Stunkard, A. J., Sørenson, T. I. A., Hanis, C., Teasdale, T. W., Chakraborty, R., Schull, W. J., & Schulsinger, F. (1986). An adoption study of human obesity. *New England Journal of Medicine, 314,* 193–198.

Subbotsky, E. V. (1994). Early rationality and magical thinking in preschoolers: Space and time. *British Journal of Developmental Psychology, 12,* 97–108.

Subrahmanyam, K., & Greenfield, P. M. (1996). Effect of video game practice on spatial skills in girls and boys. In P. M. Greenfield & R. R. Cocking (Eds.), *Interacting with video* (pp. 95–114). Norwood, NJ: Ablex.

Subrahmanyam, K., Greenfield, P., Kraut, R., & Gross, E. (2001). The impact of computer use on children's and adolescents' development. *Applied Developmental Psychology, 22,* 7–30.

Sullivan, M. W., & Lewis, M. (2003). Contextual determinants of anger and other negative expressions. *Developmental Psychology, 39,* 693–705.

Sullivan, S. A., & Birch, L. L. (1990). Pass the sugar, pass the salt: Experience dictates preference. *Developmental Psychology, 26,* 546–551.

Sulzby, E., & Teale, W. (1991). Emergent literacy. In R. Barr, M. L. Kamil, P. B. Mosenthal, & P. D. Pearson (Eds.), *Handbook of reading research* (Vol. 2, pp. 727–757). New York: Longman.

Sundell, H. (2001). Why does maternal smoke exposure increase the risk of sudden infant death syndrome? *Acta Paediatrica, 90,* 718–720.

Super, C. M. (1981). Behavioral development in infancy. In R. H. Monroe, R. L. Monroe, & B. B. Whiting (Eds.), *Handbook of cross-cultural human development* (pp. 181–270). New York: Garland.

Super, D. (1980). A life-span, life-space approach to career development. *Journal of Vocational Behavior, 16,* 282–298.

Super, D. (1984). Career and life development. In D. Brown & L. Brooks (Eds.), *Career choice and development* (pp. 192–234). San Francisco: Jossey-Bass.

Sureau, C. (1997). Trials and tribulations of surrogacy: From surrogacy to parenthood. *Human Reproduction, 12,* 410–411.

Sutcliffe, A. G. (2002). Health risks in babies born after assisted reproduction. *British Medical Journal, 325,* 117–118.

Sutton, M. J., Brown, J. D., Wilson, K. M., & Klein, J. D. (2002). Shaking the tree of forbidden fruit: Where adolescents learn about sexuality and contraception. In J. D. Brown, J. R. Steele, & K. Walsh-Childers (Eds.), *Sexual teens, sexual media* (pp. 25–55). Mahwah, NJ: Erlbaum.

Suzuki, L. A., & Valencia, R. R. (1997). Race–ethnicity and measured intelligence. *American Psychologist, 52,* 1103–1114.

Svensson, A. (2000). Computers in school: Socially isolating or a tool to promote collaboration. *Journal of Educational Computing Research, 22,* 437–453.

Swanson, J. L., & Fouad, N. A. (1999). Applying theories of person–environment fit: The transition from school to work. *Career Development Quarterly, 47,* 337–347.

Swendsen, J. D., & Mazure, C. M. (2000). Life stress as a risk factor for postpartum depression: Current research and methodological issues. *Clinical Psychology–Science and Practice, 7,* 17–31.

Szepkouski, G. M., Gauvain, M., & Carberry, M. (1994). The development of planning skills in children with and without mental retardation. *Journal of Applied Developmental Psychology, 15,* 187–206.

Szkrybalo, J., & Ruble, D. N. (1999). "God made me a girl": Sex-category constancy judgments and explanations revisited. *Developmental Psychology, 35,* 392–402.

Tacon, A., & Caldera, Y. (2001). Attachment and parental correlates in late adolescent Mexican American women. *Hispanic Journal of Behavioral Sciences, 23,* 71–88.

Tager-Flusberg, H. (2001). Putting words together: Morphology and syntax in the preschool years. In J. B. Gleason (Ed.), *The development of language* (5th ed., pp. 159–209). Boston: Allyn and Bacon.

Takahashi, K. (1990). Are the key assumptions of the "Strange Situation" procedure universal? A view from Japanese research. *Human Development, 33,* 23–30.

Tamis-LeMonda, C. S., & Bornstein, M. H. (1989). Habituation and maternal encouragement of attention in infancy as predictors of toddler language, play, and representational competence. *Child Development, 60,* 738–751.

Tamis-LeMonda, C. S., & Bornstein, M. H. (1994). Specificity in mother–toddler language–play relations across the second year. *Developmental Psychology, 30,* 283–292.

Tamis-LeMonda, C. S., Bornstein, M. H., & Baumwell, L. (2001). Maternal responsiveness and children's achievement of language milestones. *Child Development, 72,* 748–767.

Tammelin, T., Näyhä, S., Hills, A. P., & Järvelin, M. (2003). Adolescent participation in sports and adult physical activity. *American Journal of Preventive Medicine, 24,* 22–28.

Tamminen, K. (1991). *Religious development in childhood and youth.* Helsinki, Finland: Gummerus Kirjapaino Oy.

Tangney, J. P. (2001). Constructive and destructive aspects of shame and guilt. In A. C. Bohart & D. J. Stipek (Eds.), *Constructive and destructive behavior* (pp. 127–145). Washington, DC: American Psychological Association.

Tanner, J. M. (1990). *Foetus into man* (2nd ed.). Cambridge, MA: Harvard University Press.

Tanner, J. M., Healy, M., & Cameron, N. (2001*). Assessment of skeletal maturity and prediction of adult height* (3rd ed.). Philadelphia: Saunders.

Tardif, T., Gelman, S. A., & Xu, F. (1999). Putting the "noun bias" in context: A comparison of English and Mandarin. *Child Development, 70,* 620–635.

Taylor, J. H., & Walker, L. J. (1997). Moral climate and the development of moral reasoning: The effects of dyadic discussions between young offenders. *Journal of Moral Education, 26,* 21–43.

Taylor, J. S. (2002). Caregiver support for women during childbirth: Does the presence of a labor-support person affect maternal–child outcomes? *American Family Physician, 66,* 1205–1206.

Taylor, M. (1996). The development of children's beliefs about the social and biological aspects of gender differences. *Child Development, 67,* 1555–1571.

Taylor, M. (1999). *Imaginary companions and the children who create them.* New York: Oxford University Press.

Taylor, M., & Carlson, S. M. (1997). The relation between individual differences in fantasy and theory of mind. *Child Development, 68,* 436–455.

Taylor, M., & Carlson, S. M. (2000). The influence of religious beliefs on parental attitudes about children's fantasy behavior. In K. S. Rosengren, C. N. Johnson, & P. L. Harris (Eds.), *Imagining the impossible* (pp. 247–268). New York: Cambridge University Press.

Taylor, M., Esbensen, B. M., & Bennett, R. T. (1994). Children's understanding of knowledge acquisition: The tendency for children to report that they have always known what they have just learned. *Child Development, 65,* 1581–1604.

Taylor, M. C., & Hall, J. A. (1982). Psychological androgyny: Theories, methods, and conclusions. *Psychological Bulletin, 92,* 347–366.

Taylor, R. D., & Roberts, D. (1995). Kinship support and maternal and adolescent well-being in economically disadvantaged African-American families. *Child Development, 66,* 1585–1597.

Taylor, R. L. (2000). Diversity within African-American families. In D. H. Demo & K. R. Allen (Eds.), *Handbook of family diversity* (pp. 232–251). New York: Oxford University Press.

Telama, R., Yang, X., Laakso, L., & Viikari, J. (1997). Physical activity in childhood and adolescence as predictor of physical activity in young adulthood. *American Journal of Preventive Medicine, 13,* 317–323.

Teller, D. Y. (1997). First glances: The vision of infants. *Investigative Ophthalmology and Visual Science, 38,* 2183–2203.

Teller, D. Y. (1998). Spatial and temporal aspects of infant color vision. *Vision Research, 38,* 3275–3282.

Temple, C. M., & Carney, R. A. (1995). Patterns of spatial functioning in Turner's syndrome. *Cortex, 31,* 109–118.

Tenenbaum, H. R., & Leaper, C. (2002). Are parents' gender schemas related to their children's gender-related cognitions? A meta-analysis. *Developmental Psychology, 38,* 615–630.

Tenenbaum, H. R., & Leaper, C. (2003). Parent–child conversations about science: The socialization of gender inequities? *Developmental Psychology, 39,* 34–57.

Terenzini, P. T., Pascarella, E. T., & Blimling, G. S. (1999). Students' out-of-class experiences and their influence on learning and cognitive development: A literature review. *Journal of College Student Development, 40,* 610–623.

Tertinger, D. A., Greene, B. F., & Lutzker, J. R. (1984). Home safety: Development and validation of one component of an ecobehavioral treatment program for abused and neglected children. *Journal of Applied Behavior Analysis, 17,* 159–174.

Teti, D. M., Gelfand, D. M., Messinger, D. S., & Isabella, R. (1995). Maternal depression and the quality of early attachment: An examination of infants, preschoolers, and their mothers. *Developmental Psychology, 31,* 364–376.

Teti, D. M., & McGourty, S. (1996). Using mothers versus trained observers in assessing children's secure base behavior: Theoretical and methodological considerations. *Child Development, 67,* 597–605.

Teyber, E. (1992). *Helping children cope with divorce.* New York: Lexington Books.

Thacker, S. B., & Stroup, D. F. (2003). Revisiting the use of the electronic fetal monitor. *Lancet, 361,* 445–446.

Tharp, R. G. (1993). Institutional and social context of educational practice and reform. In E. A. Forman, N. Minick, & C. A. Stone (Eds.), *Contexts for learning* (pp. 269–282). New York: Oxford University Press.

Tharpe, A. M., & Ashmead, D. H. (2001). A longitudinal investigation of infant auditory sensitivity. *American Journal of Audiology, 10,* 104–112.

Thatcher, R. W., Lyon, G. R., Rumsey, J., & Krasnegor, J. (1996). *Developmental neuroimagining.* San Diego, CA: Academic Press.

Thatcher, R. W., Walker, R. A., & Giudice, S. (1987). Human cerebral hemispheres develop at different rates and ages. *Science, 236,* 1110–1113.

Thelen, E. (1989). The (re)discovery of motor development: Learning new things from an old field. *Developmental Psychology, 25,* 946–949.

Thelen, E. (2001). Dynamic mechanisms of change in early perceptual–motor development. In J. L. McClelland & R. S. Siegler (Eds.), *Mechanisms of cognitive development: Behavioral and neural perspectives* (pp. 161–184). Mahwah, NJ: Erlbaum.

Thelen, E., & Adolph, K. E. (1992). Arnold Gesell: The paradox of nature and nurture. *Developmental Psychology, 28,* 368–380.

Thelen, E., & Corbetta, D. (2002). Microdevelopment and dynamic systems: Applications to infant motor development. In N. Granott & J. Parziale (Eds.), *Microdevelopment: Transition processes in development and learning* (pp. 59–79). New York: Cambridge University Press.

Thelen, E., Corbetta, D., Kamm, K., Spencer, J. P., Schneider, K., & Zernicke, R. F. (1993). The transition to reaching: Mapping intention and intrinsic dynamics. *Child Development, 64,* 1058–1098.

Thelen, E., Corbetta, D., & Spencer, J. (1996). The development of reaching during the first year: The role of movement speed. *Journal of Experimental Psychology: Human Perception and Performance, 22,* 1059–107

Thelen, E., Fisher, D. M., & Ridley-Johnson, R. (1984). The relationship between physical growth and a newborn reflex. *Infant Behavior and Development, 7,* 479–493.

Thelen, E., & Smith, L. B. (1998). Dynamic systems theories. In R. M. Lerner (Ed.), *Handbook of child psychology: Vol. 1. Theoretical models of human development* (5th ed., pp. 563–634). New York: Wiley.

Thiedke, C. C. (2001). Sleep disorders and sleep problems in childhood. *American Family Physician, 63,* 277–284.

Thiedke, C. C. (2003). Nocturnal enuresis. *American Family Physician, 67,* 1499–1506.

Thoman, E., & Ingersoll, E. W. (1993). Learning in premature infants. *Developmental Psychology, 29,* 692–700.

Thomas, A., & Chess, S. (1977). *Temperament and development.* New York: Brunner/Mazel.

Thomas, A., Chess, S., & Birch, H. G. (1968). *Temperament and behavior disorders in children.* New York: New York University Press.

Thomas, J. R., & French, K. E. (1985). Gender differences across age in motor performance: A meta-analysis. *Psychological Bulletin, 98,* 260–282.

Thomas, R. M. (2000). *Comparing theories of child development* (5th ed.). Belmont, CA: Wadsworth.

Thompson, A., Hollis, C., & Richards, D. (2003). Authoritarian parenting attitudes as a risk for conduct problems: Results of a British national cohort study. *European Child and Adolescent Psychiatry, 12,* 84–91.

Thompson, J. W., Ryan, K. W., Pinidiya, S. D., & Bost, J. E. (2003). Quality of care for children in commercial and Medicaid managed care. *Journal of the American Medical Association, 290,* 1486–1493.

Thompson, L. A., Goodman, D. C., & Little, G. A. (2002). Is more neonatal intensive care always better? Insights from a cross-national comparison of reproductive care. *Pediatrics, 109,* 1036–1043.

Thompson, P. M., Giedd, J. N., Woods, R. P., MacDonald, D., Evans, A. C., & Toga, A. W. (2000). Growth patterns in the developing brain detected by using continuum mechanical tensor maps. *Nature, 404,* 190–192.

Thompson, R. A. (1990a). On emotion and self-regulation. In R. A. Thompson (Ed.), *Nebraska Symposia on Motivation* (Vol. 36, pp. 383–483). Lincoln: University of Nebraska Press.

Thompson, R. A. (1990b). Vulnerability in research: A developmental perspective on research risk. *Child Development, 61,* 1–16.

Thompson, R. A. (1994). Emotion regulation: A theme in search of definition. In N. A. Fox (Ed.), The development of emotion regulation. *Monographs of the Society for Research in Child Development, 59*(2–3, Serial No. 240).

Thompson, R. A. (1998). Early socio-personality development. In N.

Eisenberg (Ed.), *Handbook of child psychology: Vol. 3. Social, emotional, and personality development* (5th ed., pp. 25–104). New York: Wiley.

Thompson, R. A. (2000). The legacy of early attachments. *Child Development, 71,* 145–152.

Thompson, R. A. (2001). Development in the first years of life. *Future of Children, 11*(1), 21–33.

Thompson, R. A., & Limber, S. (1991). "Social anxiety" in infancy: Stranger wariness and separation distress. In H. Leitenberg (Ed.), *Handbook of social and evaluation anxiety* (pp. 85–137). New York: Plenum.

Thompson, R. A., & Nelson, C. A. (2001). Developmental science and the media. *American Psychologist, 56,* 5–15.

Thorndike, R. L., Hagen, E. P., & Sattler, J. M. (1986). *The Stanford-Binet Intelligence Scale.* Chicago: Riverside Publishing.

Thorne, B. (1993). *Gender play: Girls and boys in school.* New Brunswick, NJ: Rutgers University Press.

Thornton, S. (1999). Creating conditions for cognitive change: The interaction between task structures and specific strategies. *Child Development, 70,* 588–603.

Thorpy, M. J., & Yager, J. (2001). *Encyclopedia of sleep and sleep disorders.* New York: Facts on File.

Tienari, P., Wynne, L. C., Laksy, K., Moring, J., Nieminen, P., & Sorri, A. (2003). Genetic boundaries of the schizophrenia spectrum: Evidence from the Finnish adoptive family study of schizophrenia. *American Journal of Psychiatry, 160,* 1587–1594.

Tienari, P., Wynne, L. C., Moring, J., & Lahti, I. (1994). The Finnish adoptive family study of schizophrenia: Implications for family research. *British Journal of Psychiatry, 164,* 20–26.

Tietjen, A., & Walker, L. (1985). Moral reasoning and leadership among men in a Papua New Guinea village. *Developmental Psychology, 21,* 982–992.

Tiggemann, M., & Anesbury, T. (2000). Negative stereotyping of obesity in children: The role of controllability beliefs. *Journal of Applied Social Psychology, 30,* 1977–1993.

Tincoff, R., & Jusczyk, P. W. (1999). Some beginnings of word comprehension in 6-month-olds. *Psychological Science, 10,* 172–175.

Tinsley, B. J. (2003). *How children learn to be healthy.* Cambridge, U.K.: Cambridge University Press.

Tizard, B., & Rees, J. (1975). The effect of early institutional rearing on the behaviour problems and affectional relationships of four-year-old children. *Journal of Child Psychology and Psychiatry, 16,* 61–73.

Tofler, I. R., Knapp, P. K., & Drell, M. J. (1998). The achievement by proxy spectrum in youth sports: Historical perspective and clinical approach to pressured and high-achieving children and adolescents. *Child and Adolescent Psychiatric Clinics of North America, 7,* 803–820.

Tomasello, M. (1995). Language is not an instinct. *Cognitive Development, 10,* 131–156.

Tomasello, M. (1999a). Having intentions, understanding intentions, and understanding communicative intentions. In P. D. Zelazo, J. W. Astington, & J. Wilde (Eds.), *Developing theories of intention: Social understanding and self-control* (pp. 63–75). Mahwah, NJ: Erlbaum.

Tomasello, M. (1999b). The human adaptation for culture. *Annual Review of Anthropology, 28,* 509–529.

Tomasello, M. (2000). Do young children have adult syntactic competence? *Cognition, 74,* 209–253.

Tomasello, M. (2003). *Constructing a language: A usage-based theory of language acquisition.* Cambridge, MA: Harvard University Press.

Tomasello, M., & Akhtar, N. (1995). Two-year-olds use pragmatic cues to differentiate reference to objects and actions. *Cognitive Development, 10,* 201–224.

Tomasello, M., Akhtar, N., Dodson, K., & Rekau, L. (1997). Differential productivity in young children's use of nouns and verbs. *Journal of Child Language, 24,* 373–387.

Tomasello, M., & Brooks, P. (1999). Early syntactic development: A construction grammar approach. In M. Barrett (Ed.), *The development of language* (pp. 161–190). London: UCL Press.

Tong, S., Caddy, D., & Short, R. V. (1997). Use of dizygotic to monozygotic twinning ratio as a measure of fertility. *Lancet, 349,* 843–845.

Toomela, A. (1999). Drawing development: Stages in the representation of a cube and a cylinder. *Child Development, 70,* 1141–1150.

Toomela, A. (2002). Drawing as a verbally mediated activity: A study of relationships between verbal, motor, visuospatial skills and drawing in children. *International Journal of Behavioral Development, 26,* 234–247.

Torff, B., & Gardner, H. (1999). The vertical mind—the case for multiple intelligences. In M. Anderson (Ed.), *The development of intelligence* (pp. 139–159). Hove, U.K.: Psychology Press.

Torney-Purta, J. (2002). The school's role in developing civic engagement: A study of adolescents in twenty-eight countries. *Applied Developmental Science, 6,* 203–212.

Torrance, E. P. (1980). *Torrance Tests of Creative Thinking.* New York: Scholastic Testing Service.

Torrance, E. P. (1988). The nature of creativity as manifest in its testing.

In R. J. Sternberg (Ed.), *The nature of creativity: Contemporary psychological perspectives* (pp. 43–75). New York: Cambridge University Press.

Torrey, E. F., Bower, A. E., Taylor, E. H., & Gottesman, I. I. (1994). *Schizophrenia and manic-depressive disorder: The biological roots of mental illness as revealed by the landmark study of identical twins.* New York: Basic Books.

Touwen, B. C. L. (1984). Primitive reflexes—conceptual or semantic problem? In H. F. R. Prechtl (Ed.), *Continuity of neural functions from prenatal to postnatal life* (Clinics in Developmental Medicine No. 94, pp. 115–125). Philadelphia: Lippincott.

Toyamo, N. (2000). "What are food and air like inside our bodies?" Children's thinking about digestion and respiration. *International Journal of Behavioral Development, 24,* 222–230.

Trasti, N., Vik, T., Jacobson, G., & Bakketeig, L. S. (1999). Smoking in pregnancy and children's mental and motor development at age 1 and 5 years. *Early Human Development, 55,* 137–147.

Trehub, S. E. (2001). Musical predispositions in infancy. *Annals of the New York Academy of Sciences, 930,* 1–16.

Tremblay, G. C., & Peterson, L. (1999). Prevention of childhood injury: Clinical and public policy challenges. *Clinical Psychology Review, 19,* 415–434.

Tremblay, M. S., Katzmarzyk, P. T., & Willms, J. D. (2002). Temporal trends in overweight and obesity in Canada, 1981–1996. *International Journal of Obesity, 26,* 538–543.

Tremblay, R. E. (2000). The development of aggressive behavior during childhood: What have we learned in the past century? *International Journal of Behavioral Development, 24,* 129–141.

Tremblay, R. E. (2002). Prevention of injury by early socialization of aggressive behavior. *Injury Prevention, 8*(Suppl. IV), 17–21.

Tremblay, R. E., Japel, C., Perusse, D., Voivin, M., Zoccolillo, M., Montplaisir, J., & McDuff, P. (1999). The search for the age of "onset" of physical aggression: Rousseau and Bandura revisited. *Criminal Behavior and Mental Health, 9,* 8–23.

Trent, K., & Harlan, S. L. (1994). Teenage mothers in nuclear and extended households. *Journal of Family Issues, 15,* 309–337.

Triandis, H. C. (1995). *Individualism and collectivism.* Boulder, CO: Westview Press.

Triandis, H. C. (1998, May). *Crosscultural versus cultural psychology: A synthesis?* Colloquium presented at Illinois Wesleyan University, Bloomington, Illinois.

Trickett, P. K., Noll, J., Reiffman, A., & Putnam, F. (2001). Variants of intrafamilial sexual abuse experiences: Implications for short-and long-term development. *Development and Psychopathology, 13,* 1001–1019.

Trickett, P. K., & Putnam, F. W. (1998). Developmental consequences of child sexual abuse. In P. K. Trickett & C. J. Schellenbach (Eds.), *Violence against children in the family and community* (pp. 39–56). Washington, DC: American Psychological Association.

Trocomé, N., & Wolfe, D. (2002). *Child maltreatment in Canada: The Canadian Incidence Study of Reported Child Abuse and Neglect.* Retrieved from http://www.hc-sc.gc.ca/pphb-dgspsp/cm-vee

Tronick, E., Morelli, G., & Ivey, P. (1992). The Efe forager infant and toddler's pattern of social relationships: Multiple and simultaneous. *Developmental Psychology, 28,* 568–577.

Tronick, E. Z., Thomas, R. B., & Daltabuit, M. (1994). The Quechua manta pouch: A caretaking practice for buffering the Peruvian infant against the multiple stressors of high altitude. *Child Development, 65,* 1005–1013.

Tröster, H., & Brambring, M. (1993). Early motor development in blind infants. *Journal of Applied Developmental Psychology, 14,* 83–106.

True, M. M., Pisani, L., & Oumar, F. (2001). Infant–mother attachment among the Dogon of Mali. *Child Development, 72,* 1451–1466.

Truglio, R. (2000, April). *Research guides "Sesame Street."* Public lecture presented as part of the Consider the Children program, Illinois State University, Normal, IL.

Trusty, J. (1999). Effects of eighth-grade parental involvement on late adolescents' educational expectations. *Journal of Research and Development in Education, 32,* 224–233.

Trusty, J. (2002). Effects of high school course-taking and other variables on choice of science and mathematics college majors. *Journal of Counseling and Development, 80,* 464–474.

Trzesniewski, K. H., Donnellan, M. B., & Robins, R. W. (2003). Stability of self-esteem across the life span. *Journal of Personality and Social Psychology, 84,* 205–220.

Tuchfarber, B. S., Zins, J. E., & Jason, L. A. (1997). Prevention and control of injuries. In R. Weissberg, T. P. Gullotta, R. L. Hampton, B. A. Ryan, & G. R. Adams (Eds.), *Enhancing children's wellness* (pp. 250–277). Thousand Oaks, CA: Sage.

Tucker, C. J., McHale, S. M., & Crouter, A. C. (2001). Conditions of sibling support in adolescence. *Journal of Family Psychology, 15,* 254–271.

Tudge, J. R. H. (1992). Processes and consequences of peer collaboration:

A Vygotskian analysis. *Child Development, 63,* 1364–1397.

Tudge, J. R. H., Hogan, D. M., Snezhkova, I. A., Kulakova, N. N., & Etz, K. E. (2000). Parents' child-rearing values and beliefs in the United States and Russia: The impact of culture and social class. *Infant and Child Development, 9,* 105–121.

Tunmer, W. E., & Chapman, J. W. (2002). The relation of beginning readers' reported word identification strategies to reading achievement, reading-related skills, and academic self-perceptions. *Reading and Writing, 15,* 341–358.

Turiel, E. (1998). The development of morality. In N. Eisenberg (Ed.), *Handbook of child psychology: Vol. 3. Social, emotional, and personality development* (Vol. 3, pp. 863–932). New York: Wiley.

Turner, P. J., & Gervai, J. (1995). A multidimensional study of gender typing in preschool children and their parents: Personality, attitudes, preferences, behavior, and cultural differences. *Developmental Psychology, 31,* 759–772.

Tuss, P., Zimmer, J., & Ho, H.-Z. (1995). Causal attributions of underachieving fourth-grade students in China, Japan, and the United States. *Journal of Cross-Cultural Psychology, 26,* 408–425.

Twenge, J. M., & Campbell, W. K. (2001). Age and birth cohort differences in self-esteem: A cross-temporal meta-analysis. *Personality and Social Psychology Review, 5,* 321–344.

Twenge, J. M., & Crocker, J. (2002). Race and self-esteem: Meta-analyses comparing whites, blacks, Hispanics, Asians, and American Indians and comment on Gray-Little and Hafdahl (2000*). Psychological Bulletin, 128,* 371–408.

Tyrka, A. R., Graber, J. A., & Brooks-Gunn, J. (2000). The development of disordered eating: Correlates and predictors of eating problems in the context of adolescence. In A. J. Sameroff & M. Lewis (Eds.), *Handbook of developmental psychopathology* (2nd ed., pp. 607–624). New York: Kluwer.

Tzuriel, D. (2001). *Dynamic assessment of young children.* New York: Kluwer Academic.

Tzuriel, D., & Kaufman, R. (1999). Mediated learning and cognitive modifiability: Dynamic assessment of young Ethiopian immigrant children to Israel. *Journal of Cross-Cultural Psychology, 30,* 359–380.

Uhari, M., Mäntysaari, K., & Niemelä, M. (1996). A meta-analytic review of the risk factors for acute otitis media. *Clinical Infectious Diseases, 22,* 1079–1083.

Uhari, M., Tapiainen, T., & Kontiokari, T. (2000). Xylitol in preventing acute otitis media. *Vaccine,* *19*(Suppl. 1), S144–S147.

Ulrich, B. D., & Ulrich, D. A. (1985). The role of balancing in performance of fundamental motor skills in 3-, 4-, and 5-year-old children. In J. E. Clark & J. H. Humphrey (Eds.), *Motor development* (Vol. 1, pp. 87–98). Princeton, NJ: Princeton Books.

United Nations Children's Fund. (2000). *Child poverty in rich nations.* Florence, Italy: Innocenti Research Centre.

United Nations Development Programme. (2002). *Human development report 2002.* New York: Oxford University Press.

United Nations. (2001). *World social situation.* New York: Author.

United Nations. (2003). *World population prospects: The 2002 revision.* Retrieved from www.unpopulation.org

U.S. Census Bureau. (2003a). *International data base.* Retrieved from http://www.census.gov/ipc/www/idbnew.html

U.S. Census Bureau. (2003b). *Statistical abstract of the United States* (123rd ed.). Washington, DC: U.S. Government Printing Office.

U.S. Centers for Disease Control and Prevention. (2002). *Sexually transmitted disease (STD) surveillance.* Retrieved from www.cdc.gov/std

U.S. Department of Agriculture. (2003). *Food insecurity in households with children.* Washington, DC: Author.

U.S. Department of Education. (2001a). *Program for International Student Assessment (PISA) 2000 highlights.* Retrieved from nces.ed.gov/surveys/pisa/2000highlights.asp

U.S. Department of Education. (2001b). *Pursuing excellence: A study of U.S. twelfth-grade mathematics and science achievement in international context.* Washington, DC: U.S. Government Printing Office.

U.S. Department of Education. (2002). *Digest of education statistics 2001.* Washington, DC: U.S. Government Printing Office.

U.S. Department of Education. (2003a). *Digest of education statistics: 2002.* Washington, DC: U.S. Government Printing Office.

U.S. Department of Education. (2003b). *NAEP High School Transcript Study: The Nation's Report Card.* Retrieved from http://nces.ed.gov/nationsreportcard/

U.S. Department of Health and Human Services. (2000a). *Breastfeeding: HHS blueprint for action.* Washington, DC: U.S. Government Printing Office.

U.S. Department of Health and Human Services. (2000b). *Promoting better health for young people through physical activity and sports.* Washington, DC: U.S. Government Printing Office.

U.S. Department of Health and Human Services. (2001a). *CDC School Health Policies and Programs Study, 2001.* Retrieved from http://www.cdc.gov/nccdphp/dash/shpps/factsheets/fs00_pe.htm

U.S. Department of Health and Human Services. (2001b). *Youth violence: A report of the surgeon general.* Retrieved from www.surgeongeneral.gov/library/youthviolence

U.S. Department of Health and Human Services. (2002a). *Health United States and injury chartbook.* Washington, DC: U.S. Government Printing Office.

U.S. Department of Health and Human Services. (2002b). *National Household Survey on Drug Use and Health.* Retrieved from www.samhsa.gov

U.S. Department of Health and Human Services. (2002c). *National survey results on drug use from the Monitoring the Future Study 2002: Vol. 1. Secondary school students.* Washington, DC: U.S. Government Printing Office.

U.S. Department of Health and Human Services. (2002d). *Obesity still on the rise, new data show.* Retrieved from http://www.cdc.gov/nchs/releases/02news/obesityonrise.htm

U.S. Department of Health and Human Services. (2002e) Youth risk behavior surveillance—2001. *Morbidity and Mortality Weekly Report,* *51*(SS04), 1–64.

U.S. Department of Health and Human Services. (2003a). Births: Final data for 2002. *National Vital Statistics Reports,* *52*(2).

U.S. Department of Health and Human Services. (2003b). *Child maltreatment 2001: Summary of key findings.* Washington, DC: National Clearinghouse on Child Abuse and Neglect Information.

U.S. Department of Health and Human Services. (2003c). Fetal alcohol syndrome. Retrieved from http://www.cdc.gov/ncbddd/fas/fasask.htm

U.S. Department of Health and Human Services. (2003d). *Impaired fecundity by age and selected characteristics.* Washington, DC: U.S. Government Printing Office.

U.S. Department of Health and Human Services. (2003e). National, state, and urban area vaccination levels among children aged 19 to 35 months: United States 2002. *Morbidity and Mortality Weekly Report, 52,* 728–732.

U.S. Department of Health and Human Services. (2003f). Prenatal care. Retrieved from www.cdc.gov/nchs/fastats/prenatal.htm

U.S. Department of Health and Human Services. (2004). *National survey results on drug use from the Monitoring the Future Study 2003: Vol. 1. Secondary school students.* Washington, DC: U.S. Government Printing Office.

U.S. Department of Justice. (2003). *Crime and victims statistics.* Retrieved from http://www.ojp.usdoj.gov/bjs

U.S. Department of Labor, Bureau of Labor Statistics. (2003, February). Consumer Price Index. *Monthly Labor Review, 125*(2).

Upchurch, D. M., Aneshensel, C. S., Sucoff, C. A., & Levy-Storms, L. (1999). Neighborhood and family contexts of adolescent sexual activity. *Journal of Marriage and the Family, 61,* 920–933.

Updegraff, K. A., McHale, S. M., & Crouter, A. C. (1996). Gender roles in marriage: What do they mean for girls' and boys' school achievement? *Journal of Youth and Adolescence, 25,* 73–88.

Updegraff, K. A., & Obeidallah, D. A. (1999). Young adolescents' patterns of involvement with siblings and friends. *Social Development, 8,* 52–69.

Uribe, F. M. T., LeVine, R. A., & LeVine, S. E. (1994). Maternal behavior in a Mexican community: The changing environments of children. In P. M. Greenfield & R. R. Cocking (Eds.), *Cross-cultural roots of minority child development* (pp. 41–54). Hillsdale, NJ: Erlbaum.

Usmiani, S., & Daniluk, J. (1997). Mothers and their adolescent daughters: Relationship between self-esteem, gender role identity, and body image. *Journal of Youth and Adolescence, 26,* 45–60.

Valdés, G. (1998). The world outside and inside schools: Language and immigrant children. *Educational Researcher, 27*(6), 4–18.

Valian, V. (1999). Input and language acquisition. In W. C. Ritchie & T. K. Bhatia (Eds.), *Handbook of child language acquisition* (pp. 497–530). San Diego: Academic Press.

Vance, M. L., & Mauras, N. (1999). Growth hormone therapy in adults and children. *Drug Therapy, 341,* 1206–1215.

Vandell, D. L., & Mueller, E. C. (1995). Peer play and friendships during the first two years. In H. C. Foot, A. J. Chapman, & J. R. Smith (Eds.), *Friendship and social relations in children* (pp. 181–208). New Brunswick, NJ: Transaction.

Vandell, D. L., & Posner, J. K. (1999). Conceptualization and measurement of children's after-school environments. In S. L. Friedman & T. D. Wachs (Eds.), *Measuring environment across the life span* (pp. 167–196). Washington, DC: American Psychological Association.

Vandell, D. L., & Shumow, L. (1999). After-school child care programs. *Future of Children, 9*(2), 64–80.

Vandenberg, B. (1998). Real and not real: A vital developmental dichotomy. In O. N. Saracho & B. Spodek (Eds.), *Multiple perspectives on play in early childhood education* (pp. 295–305). Albany: State University of New York Press.

Van den Bergh, B. R. H., & De Rycke, L. (2003). Measuring the multidimensional self-concept and global self-worth of 6- to 8-year-olds. *Journal of Genetic Psychology, 164,* 201–225.

van den Boom, D. (2002). First attachments: Theory and research. In G. Bremner & A. Fogel (Eds.), *Blackwell handbook of infant development* (pp. 296–325). Oxford, U.K.: Blackwell.

van den Boom, D. C., & Hoeksma, J. B. (1994). The effect of infant irritability on mother–infant interaction: A growth-curve analysis. *Developmental Psychology, 30,* 581–590.

Van der Woerd, K. A., & Cox, D. N. (2001, June). *Assessing academic competence and the well-being of Aboriginal students in British Columbia.* Poster presented at the American Psychological Association, Atlanta.

van Hoof, A., & Raaijmakers, Q. A. W. (2003). The search for the structure of identity formation. *Identity, 3,* 271–289.

Vanier Institute of the Family. (2004). *Profiling Canada's families: II.* Ottawa, Canada: Author. Retrieved from http://www.vifamily.ca/library/profiling2/toc.html

van IJzendoorn, M. H. (1995). Adult attachment representations, parental responsiveness, and infant attachment: A meta-analysis on the predictive validity of the Adult Attachment Interview. *Psychological Bulletin, 117,* 387–403.

van IJzendoorn, M. H., & De Wolff, M. S. (1997). In search of the absent father—meta-analyses of infant–father attachment: A rejoinder to our discussants. *Child Development, 68,* 604–609.

van IJzendoorn, M. H., Goldberg, S., Kroonenberg, P. M. & Frenkel, O. J. (1992). The relative effects of maternal and child problems on the quality of attachment: A meta-analysis of attachment in clinical samples. *Child Development, 63,* 840–858.

van IJzendoorn, M. H., & Kroonenberg, P. M. (1988). Cross-cultural patterns of attachment: A meta-analysis of the Strange Situation. *Child Development, 59,* 147–156.

van IJzendoorn, M. H., & Sagi, A. (1999). Cross-cultural patterns of attachment. In J. Cassidy & P. R. Shaver (Eds.), *Handbook of attachment: Theory, research, and clinical applications* (pp. 713–734). New York: Guilford.

Varendi, H., Christensson, K., Porter, R. H., & Winberg, J. (1998). Soothing effect of amniotic fluid smell in newborn infants. *Early Human Development, 51,* 47–55.

Varendi, H., & Porter, R. H. (2001). Breast odour as the only maternal stimulus elicits crawling toward the odour source. *Acta Paediactrica, 90,* 372–375.

Vartanian, L. R. (1997). Separation–individuation, social support, and adolescent egocentrism: An exploratory study. *Journal of Early Adolescence, 17,* 245–270.

Vartanian, L. R., & Powlishta, K. K. (1996). A longitudinal examination of the social-cognitive foundations of adolescent egocentrism. *Journal of Early Adolescence, 16,* 157–178.

Vatten, L. J., Maehle, B. O., Lund, N. T., Treti, S., Hsieh, C. C., Trichopoulos, D., & Stuver, S. O. (2002). Birth weight as a predictor of breast cancer: A case-control study in Norway. *British Journal of Cancer, 86,* 89–91.

Vaughn, B. E., & Bost, K. K. (1999). Attachment and temperament: Redundant, independent, or interacting influences on interpersonal adaptation and personality development? In J. Cassidy & P. Shaver (Eds.), *Handbook of attachment: Theory, research, and clinical applications* (pp. 265–286). New York: Guilford.

Vaughn, B. E., Colvin, T. N., Azria, M. R., Caya, L., & Krzysik, L. (2001). Dyadic analyses of friendship in a sample of preschool-age children attending Head Start: Correspondence between measures and implications for social competence. *Child Development, 72,* 862–878.

Vaughn, B. E., Kopp, C. B., & Krakow, J. B. (1984). The emergence and consolidation of self-control from eighteen to thirty months of age: Normative trends and individual differences. *Child Development, 55,* 990–1004.

Vaughn, B. E., Vollenweider, M., Bost, K. K., Azria-Evans, M. R., & Snider, J. B. (2003). Negative interactions and social competence for preschool children in two samples: Reconsidering the interpretation of aggressive behavior for young children. *Merrill-Palmer Quarterly, 49,* 245–278.

Vaughn, S., & Klingner, J. K. (1998). Students' perceptions of inclusion and resource room settings. *Journal of Special Education, 32,* 79–88.

Vazsonyi, A. T., Hibbert, J. R., & Snider, J. B. (2003). Exotic enterprise no more? Adolescent reports of family and parenting processes from youth in four countries. *Journal of Research on Adolescence, 13,* 129–160.

Venet, M., & Markovits, H. (2001). Understanding uncertainty with abstract conditional premises. *Merrill-Palmer Quarterly, 47,* 74–99.

Veneziano, R. A. (2003). The importance of paternal warmth. *Cross-Cultural Research, 37,* 265–281.

Ventura, S. J., Hamilton, B. E., Mathews, T. J., & Chandra, A. (2003). Trends and variations in smoking during pregnancy and low birth weight:

Evidence from the birth certificate, 1990–2000. *Pediatrics, 111,* 1176–1180.

Ventura, S. J., Matthews, T. J., & Hamilton, B. E. (2001). Births to teenagers in the United States, 1940–2000. *National Vital Statistics Report, 49,* 1–23.

Vergnaud, G. (1996). Education, the best portion of Piaget's heritage. *Swiss Journal of Psychology, 55,* 112–118.

Vernon, P. A., Wickett, J. C., Bazana, G., & Stelmack, R. M. (2001). The neuropsychology and psychophysiology of human intelligence. In R. J. Sternberg (Ed.), *Handbook of intelligence* (pp. 245–264). Cambridge, U.K.: Cambridge University Press.

Vernon-Feagans, L., Hurley, M., & Yont, K. (2002). The effect of otitis media and daycare quality on mother/child bookreading and language use at 48 months of age. *Journal of Applied Developmental Psychology, 23,* 113–133.

Victora, C. G., Bryce, J., Fontaine, O., & Monasch, R. (2000). Reducing deaths from diarrhea through oral rehydration therapy. *Bulletin of the World Health Organization, 78,* 1246–1255.

Videon, T. M., & Manning, C. K. (2003). Influences on adolescent eating patterns: The importance of family meals. *Journal of Adolescent Health, 32,* 365–373.

Vinden, P. G. (1996). Junín Quechua children's understanding of mind. *Child Development, 67,* 1707–1716.

Vinden, P. G. (2002). Understanding minds and evidence for belief: A study of Mofu children in Cameroon. *International Journal of Behavioral Development, 26,* 445–452.

Visher, E. B., Visher, J. S., & Pasley, K. (2003). Remarriage families and stepparenting. In F. Walsh (Ed.), *Normal family processes: Growing diversity and complexity* (pp. 153–175). New York: Guilford.

Vitaro, F., Larocque, D., Janosz, M., & Tremblay, R. E. (2001). Negative social experiences and dropping out of school. *Educational Psychology, 21,* 401–415.

Vogel, D. A., Lake, M. A., Evans, S., & Karraker, H. (1991). Children's and adults' sex-stereotyped perceptions of infants. *Sex Roles, 24,* 605–616.

Vogel, L. D. (1998). When children put their fingers in their mouths: Should parents and dentists care? *New York Dental Journal, 64*(2), 48–53.

Volling, B. L. (2001). Early attachment relationships as predictors of preschool children's emotion regulation with a distressed sibling. *Early Education and Development, 12,* 185–207.

Volling, B. L., & Belsky, J. (1992). Contribution of mother–child and father–child relationships to the

quality of sibling interaction: A longitudinal study. *Child Development, 63,* 1209–1222.

Volling, B. L., McElwain, N. L., & Miller, A. L. (2002). Emotion regulation in context: The jealousy complex between young siblings and its relations with child and family characteristics. *Child Development, 73,* 581–600.

Volling, B. L., McElwain, N. L., Notaro, P. C., & Herrera, C. (2002). Parents' emotional availability and infant emotional competence: Predictors of parent–infant attachment and emerging self-regulation. *Journal of Family Psychology, 16,* 447–465.

Vondra, J. I., Hommerding, K. D., & Shaw, D. S. (1999). Stability and change in infant attachment in a low-income sample. In J. I Vondra & D. Barnett (Eds.), Atypical attachment in infancy and early childhood among children at developmental risk. *Monographs of the Society for Research in Child Development, 64*(3, Serial No. 258), pp. 119–144.

Vondra, J. I., Shaw, D. S., Searingen, L., Cohen, M., & Owens, E. B. (2001). Attachment stability and emotional and behavioral regulation from infancy to preschool age. *Development and Psychopathology, 13,* 13–33.

von Hofsten, C., & Rosander, K. (1998). The establishment of gaze control in early infancy. In S. Simion & G. Butterworth (Eds.), *The development of sensory, motor and cognitive capacities in early infancy* (pp. 49–66). Hove, U.K.: Psychology Press.

Voss, L. D., Mulligan, J., & Betts, P. R. (1998). Short stature at school entry—an index of social deprivation? (The Wessex Growth Study). *Child: Care, Health and Development, 24,* 145–156.

Vostanis, P., Grattan, E., & Cumella, S. (1997). Psychosocial functioning of homeless children. *Journal of the American Academy of Child and Adolescent Psychiatry, 36,* 881–889.

Voyer, D., Voyer, S., & Bryden, M. P. (1995). Magnitude of sex differences in spatial abilities: A meta-analysis and consideration of critical variables. *Psychological Bulletin, 117,* 250–270.

Vurpillot, E. (1968). The development of scanning strategies and their relation to visual differentiation. *Journal of Experimental Psychology, 6,* 632–650.

Vygotsky, L. S. (1978). *Mind in society: The development of higher psychological processes.* Cambridge, MA: Harvard University Press. (Original works published 1930, 1933, and 1935)

Vygotsky, L. S. (1987). Thinking and speech. In R. W. Rieber, A. S. Carton (Eds.), & N. Minick (Trans.), *The collected works of L. S. Vygotsky: Vol. 1. Problems of general psychology*

(pp. 37–285). New York: Plenum. (Original work published 1934)

Wachs, T. D. (1995). Relation of mild-to-moderate malnutrition to human development: Correlational studies. *Journal of Nutrition Supplement, 125,* 2245S–2254S.

Wachs, T. D. (1999). The what, why, and how of temperament: A piece of the action. In L. Balter & C. S. Tamis-LeMonda (Eds.), *Child psychology: A handbook of contemporary issues* (pp. 23–44). Philadelphia: Psychology Press.

Wachs, T. D. (2000). *Necessary but not sufficient: The respective roles of single and multiple influences on individual development.* Washington, DC: American Psychological Association.

Wachs, T. D., & Bates, J. E. (2001). Temperament. In G. Bremner & A. Fogel (Eds.), *Blackwell handbook of infant development* (pp. 465–501). Oxford, U.K.: Blackwell.

Wachs, T. D., Bishry, Z., Moussa, W., Yunis, F., McCabe, G., Harrison, G., Swefi, I., Kirksey, A., Galal, O., Jerome, N., & Shaheen, F. (1995). Nutritional intake and context as predictors of cognition and adaptive behavior of Egyptian school-age children. *International Journal of Behavioral Development, 18,* 425–450.

Waddington, C. H. (1957). *The strategy of the genes.* London: Allen & Unwin.

Wade, T. J., Cairney, J., & Pevalin, D. J. (2002). Emergence of gender differences in depression during adolescence: National panel results from three countries. *Journal of the American Academy of Child and Adolescent Psychiatry, 41,* 190–198.

Wadhwa, P. D., Sandman, C. A., & Garite, T. J. (2001). The neurobiology of stress in human pregnancy: Implications for prematurity and development of the fetal central nervous system. *Progress in Brain Research, 133,* 131–142.

Wagner, B. M., Silverman, M. A. C., & Martin, C. E. (2003). Family factors in youth suicidal behaviors. *American Behavioral Scientist, 46,* 1171–1191.

Wahlsten, D. (1994). The intelligence of heritability. *Canadian Psychology, 35,* 244–259.

Wainryb, C., Shaw, L. A., & Maianu, C. (1998). Tolerance and intolerance: Children's and adolescents' judgments of dissenting beliefs, speech, persons, and conduct. *Child Development, 69,* 1541–1555.

Waite, L., & Gallagher, M. (2000). *The case for marriage: Why married people are happier, healthier, and better off financially.* New York: Doubleday.

Wakat, D. K. (1978). Physiological factors of race and sex in sport. In L. K. Bunker & R. J. Rotella (Eds.), *Sport psychology: From theory to practice* (pp. 194–209). Charlotte, VA: University of Virginia. (Proceedings of the 1978 Sport Psychology Institute)

Wakeley, A., Rivera, S., & Langer, J. (2000). Can young infants add and subtract? *Child Development, 71,* 1477–1720.

Walberg, H. J. (1986). Synthesis of research on teaching. In M. C. Wittrock (Ed.), *Handbook of research on teaching* (3rd ed., pp. 214–229). New York: Macmillan.

Walden, T., Lemerise, E., & Smith, M. C. (1999). Friendship and popularity in preschool classrooms. *Early Education and Development, 10,* 351–371.

Waldenström, U. (1999). Experience of labor and birth in 1111 women. *Journal of Psychosomatic Research, 47,* 471–482.

Waldman, I. D., Weinberg, R. A., & Scarr, S. (1994). Racial-group differences in IQ in the Minnesota Transracial Adoption Study: A reply to Levin and Lynn. *Intelligence, 19,* 29–44.

Wales, R. (1990). Children's pictures. In R. Grieve & M. Hughes (Eds.), *Understanding children* (pp. 140–155). Oxford: Blackwell.

Walker, A., Rosenberg, M., & Balaban-Gil, K. (1999). Neurodevelopmental and neurobehavioral sequelae of selected substances of abuse and psychiatric medications in utero. *Neurological Disorders: Developmental and Behavioral Sequelae, 8,* 845–867.

Walker, D., Greenwood, C., Hart, B., & Carta, J. (1994). Prediction of school outcomes based on early language production and socioeconomic factors. *Child Development, 65,* 606–621.

Walker, L. (1995). Sexism in Kohlberg's moral psychology? In W. M. Kurtines & J. L. Gewirtz (Eds.), *Moral development: An introduction* (pp. 83–107). Boston: Allyn and Bacon.

Walker, L. J., Pitts, R. C., Hennig, K. H., & Matsuba, M. K. (1995). Reasoning about morality and real-life moral problems. In M. Killen & D. Hart (Eds.), *Morality in everyday life* (pp. 371–407). New York: Cambridge University Press.

Walker, L. J., & Taylor, J. H. (1991a). Family interactions and the development of moral reasoning. *Child Development, 62,* 264–283.

Walker, L. J., & Taylor, J. H. (1991b). Stage transitions in moral reasoning: A longitudinal study of developmental processes. *Developmental Psychology, 27,* 330–337.

Walkowiak, J., Wiener, J., Fastabend, A., Heinzow, B., Krämer, U., & Schmidt, E. (2001). Environmental exposure to polychlorinated biphenyls and quality of the home environment: Effects on psychodevelopment in early childhood. *Lancet, 358,* 1602–1607.

Wall, E. J. (2000) Practical primary pediatric orthopedics. *Nursing Clinics of North America, 35,* 95–113.

Wall, J., Covell, K., & MacIntyre, P. D. (1999). Implications of social supports for adolescents' education and career aspirations. *Canadian Journal of Behavioural Science, 31,* 63–71.

Wallace, J. M., Jr., Bachman, J. G., O'Malley, P. M., Schulenberg, J. E., Cooper, S. M., & Johnston, L. D. (2003). Gender and ethnic differences in smoking, drinking, and illicit drug use among American 8th, 10th, and 12th grade students, 1976–2000. *Addiction, 98,* 225–234.

Walther, F. J., den Ouden, A. L., & Verloove-Vanhorick, S. P. (2000). Looking back in time: Outcome of a national cohort of very preterm infants born in the Netherlands in 1983. *Early Human Development, 59,* 175–191.

Walton, G. E., Armstrong, E. S., & Bower, T. G. R. (1998). Newborns learn to identify a face in eight-tenths of a second? *Developmental Science, 1,* 79–84.

Wang, Q. (2003). Infantile amnesia reconsidered: A cross-cultural analysis. *Memory, 11,* 65–80.

Wapner, J. J. (1997). Chorionic villus sampling. *Obstetrics and Gynecology Clinics of North America, 24,* 83–110.

Wark, G. R., & Krebs, D. L. (1996). Gender and dilemma differences in real-life moral judgment. *Developmental Psychology, 32,* 220–230.

Warren, A. R., & Tate, C. S. (1992). Egocentrism in children's telephone conversations. In R. M. Diaz & L. E. Berk (Eds.), *Private speech: From social interaction to self-regulation* (pp. 245–264). Hillsdale, NJ: Erlbaum.

Warren, D. H. (1994). *Blindness and children: An individual difference approach.* New York: Cambridge University Press.

Wasik, B. A., & Bond, M. A. (2001). Beyond the pages of a book: Interactive book reading and language development in preschool classrooms. *Journal of Educational Psychology, 93,* 243–250.

Wasserman, G. A., Graziano, J. H., Factor-Litvak, P., Popovac, D., Morina, N., & Musabegovic, A. (1994). Consequences of lead exposure and iron supplementation on childhood development at age 4 years. *Neurotoxicology and Teratology, 16,* 233–240.

Wasserman, G. A., Liu, X., Pine, D. S., & Graziano, J. H. (2001). Contribution of maternal smoking during pregnancy and lead exposure to early childhood behavior problems. *Neurotoxicology and Teratology, 23,* 13–21.

Wasserman, G. A., & Miller, L. S. (1998). The prevention of serious and violent juvenile offending. In R. Loeber & D. P. Farrington (Eds.),

Serious and violent juvenile offenders (pp. 197–247). Thousand Oaks, CA: Sage.

Waters, E., & Cummings, E. M. (2000). A secure base from which to explore close relationships. *Child Development, 71,* 164–172.

Waters, E., Merrick, S., Treboux, D., Crowell, J., & Albersheim, L. (2000). Attachment security in infancy and early adulthood: A twenty-year longitudinal study. *Child Development, 71,* 684–689.

Waters, E., Vaughn, B. E., Posada, G., & Kondo-Ikemura, K. (Eds.). (1995). Caregiving, cultural, and cognitive perspectives on secure-base behavior and working models: New growing points of attachment theory and research. *Monographs of the Society for Research in Child Development, 60*(2–3, Serial No. 244).

Watkins, W. E., & Pollitt, E. (1998). Iron deficiency and cognition among school-age children. In S. G. McGregor (Ed.), *Recent advances in research on the effects of health and nutrition on children's development and school achievement in the Third World.* Washington, DC: Pan American Health Organization.

Watson, A. C., Nixon, C. L., Wilson, A., & Capage, L. (1999). Social interaction skills and theory of mind in young children. *Developmental Psychology, 35,* 386–391.

Watson, D. J. (1989). Defining and describing whole language. *Elementary School Journal, 90,* 129–141.

Watson, J. B., & Raynor, R. (1920). Conditioned emotional reactions. *Journal of Experimental Psychology, 3,* 1–14.

Watson, M. (1990). Aspects of self development as reflected in children's role playing. In D. Cicchetti & M. Beeghly (Eds.), *The self in transition: Infancy to childhood* (pp. 281–307). Chicago: University of Chicago Press.

Waxman, S. R. (2003). Links between object categorization and naming: Origins and emergence in human infants. In D. H. Rakison & L. M. Oakes (Eds.), *Early category and concept development: Making sense of the blooming, buzzing confusion* (pp. 193–209). New York: Oxford University Press.

Waxman, S. R., & Senghas, A. (1992). Relations among word meanings in early lexical development. *Developmental Psychology, 28,* 862–873.

Webb, N. M., Nemer, K. M., & Chizhik, A. W. (1998). Equity issues in collaborative group assessment: Group composition and performance. *American Educational Research Journal, 35,* 607–651.

Webb, S. J., Monk, C. S, & Nelson, C. A. (2001). Mechanisms of postnatal neurobiological development: Implications for human development.

Developmental Neuropsychology, 19, 147–171.

Webster-Stratton, C., Reid, J., & Hammond, M. (2001). Social skills and problem-solving training for children with early-onset conduct problems: Who benefits? *Journal of Child Psychology and Psychiatry, 42,* 943–952.

Wechsler, D. (1996). *Canadian supplement manual for the WISC-III.* Toronto: Psychological Corporation.

Wechsler, D. (2002). *WPPSI-III: Wechsler Preschool and Primary Scale of Intelligence* (3rd ed.). San Antonio, TX: Psychological Corporation.

Wechsler, D. (2003). *WISC-IV: Wechsler Intelligence Scale for Children* (4th ed.). San Antonio, TX: Psychological Corporation.

Wehren, A., DeLisi, R., & Arnold, M. (1981). The development of noun definition. *Journal of Child Language, 8,* 165–175.

Weikart, D. P. (1998). Changing early childhood development through educational intervention. *Preventive Medicine, 27,* 233–237.

Weinberg, M. K., & Tronick, E. Z. (1994). Beyond the face: An empirical study of infant affective configurations of facial, vocal, gestural, and regulatory behaviors. *Child Development, 65,* 1503–1515.

Weinberg, M. K., Tronick, E. Z., Cohn, J. F., & Olson, K. L. (1999). Gender differences in emotional expressivity and self-regulation during early infancy. *Developmental Psychology, 35,* 175–188.

Weinert, F. E., & Schneider, W. (Eds.). (1999). *Individual development from 3 to 12: Findings from the Munich Longitudinal Study.* Cambridge, U.K.: Cambridge University Press.

Weinfield, N. S., Sroufe, L. A., & Egeland, B. (2000). Attachment from infancy to early adulthood in a high-risk sample: Continuity, discontinuity, and their correlates. *Child Development, 71,* 695–702.

Weinstein, R. S. (2002). *Reaching higher: the power of expectations in schooling.* Cambridge, MA: Harvard University Press.

Weisfeld, G. (1997). Puberty rites as clues to the nature of human adolescence. *Cross-Cultural Research, 31,* 27–54.

Weisfeld, G. E. (1990). Sociobiological patterns of Arab culture. *Ethology and Sociobiology, 11,* 23–49.

Weisner, T. S. (1996). The 5 to 7 transition as an ecocultural project. In A. J. Sameroff & M. M. Haith (Eds.), *The five to seven year shift* (pp. 295–326). Chicago: University of Chicago Press.

Weisner, T. S., & Wilson-Mitchell, J. E. (1990). Nonconventional family life-styles and sex typing in six-year-olds. *Child Development, 61,* 1915–1933.

Weiss, B., Dodge, K. A. Bates, J. E. & Pettit, G. S. (1992). Some consequences of early harsh discipline: Child aggression and a maladaptive social information processing style. *Child Development, 63,* 1321–1335.

Weissman, M., Wolk, S., Goldstein, R. B., Moreau, D., Adams, P., & Greenwald, S. (1999). Depressed adolescents grown up. *Journal of the American Medical Association, 281,* 1707–1713.

Weisz, A. N., & Black, B. M. (2002). Gender and moral reasoning: African American youths respond to dating dilemmas. *Journal of Human Behavior in the Social Environment, 6,* 17–34.

Weizman, Z. O., & Snow, C. E. (2001). Lexical output as related to children's vocabulary acquisition: Effects of sophisticated exposure and support for meaning. *Developmental Psychology, 37,* 265–279.

Wekerle, C., & Wolfe, D. A. (2003). Child maltreatment. In E. J. Mash & R. A. Barkley (Eds.), *Child psychopathology* (2nd ed., pp. 632–684). New York: Guilford.

Wellman, H. M. (1990). *The child's theory of mind.* Cambridge, MA: MIT Press.

Wellman, H. M. (2002). Understanding the psychological world: Developing a theory of mind. In U. Goswami (Ed.), *Blackwell handbook of child cognitive development* (pp. 167–187). Malden, MA: Blackwell.

Wellman, H. M., Cross, D., & Watson, J. (2001). Meta-analysis of theory-of-mind development: The truth about false belief. *Child Development, 72,* 655–684.

Wellman, H. M., & Hickling, A. K. (1994). The mind's "I": Children's conception of the mind as an active agent. *Child Development, 65,* 1564–1580.

Wellman, H. M., Somerville, S. C., & Haake, R. J. (1979). Development of search procedures in real-life spatial environments. *Developmental Psychology, 15,* 530–542.

Wen, S. W., Liu, S., Kramer, M. S., Marcoux, S., Ohlsson, A., & Sauvé, R. (2001). Comparison of maternal and infant outcomes between vacuum extraction and forceps deliveries. *American Journal of Epidemiology, 153,* 103–107.

Wendland-Carro, J., Piccinini, C. A., & Millar, W. S. (1999). The role of an early intervention on enhancing the quality of mother–infant interaction. *Child Development, 70,* 713–721.

Wentworth, N., Benson, J. B., & Haith, M. M. (2000). The development of infants' reaches for stationary and moving targets. *Child Development, 71,* 576–601.

Werker, J. F., Pegg, J. E., & McLeod, P. J. (1994). A cross-language investiga-tion of infant preference for infant-directed communication. *Infant Behavior and Development, 17,* 323–333.

Werkele, C., & Avgoustis, E. (2003). Child maltreatment, adolescent dating, and adolescent dating violence. In P. Florsheim (Ed.), *Adolescent romantic relations and sexual behavior: Theory, research, and practical implications* (pp. 213–242). Mahwah, NJ: Erlbaum.

Werner, E. E. (1989, April). Children of the garden island. *Scientific American, 260(4),* 106–111.

Werner, E. E. (1993). Risk, resilience, and recovery: Perspectives from the Kauai Longitudinal Study. *Development and Psychopathology, 5,* 503–515.

Werner, E. E., & Smith, R. S. (1982). *Vulnerable but invincible: A study of resilient children.* New York: McGraw-Hill.

Werner, E. E., & Smith, R. S. (1992). *Overcoming the odds: High risk children from birth to adulthood.* Ithaca, NY: Cornell University Press.

Werner, E. E., & Smith, R. S. (2001). *Journeys from childhood to midlife: Risk, resilience, and recovery.* Ithaca, NY: Cornell University Press.

Wertsch, J. V., & Tulviste, P. (1992). L. S. Vygotsky and contemporary developmental psychology. *Developmental Psychology, 28,* 548–557.

Westen, D., & Gabbard, G. O. (1999). Psychoanalytic approaches to personality. In L. A. Pervin & O. P. John (Eds.), *Handbook of personality: Theory and research* (2nd ed.). New York: Guilford.

Wheeler, T., Barker, D. J. P., & O'Brien, P. M. S. (1999). *Fetal programming: Influences on development and disease in later life.* London: RCOG Press.

Wheeler, W. (2002). Youth leadership for development: civic activism as a component of youth development programming and a strategy for strengthening civil society. In R. M. Lerner, F. Jacobs, & D. Wertlieb (Eds.), *Handbook of applied developmental science: Vol. 2* (pp. 491–506). Thousand Oaks, CA: Sage.

Whitaker, D. J., & Miller, K. S. (2000). Parent–adolescent discussions about sex and condoms. *Journal of Adolescent Research, 15,* 251–273.

White, B., & Held, R. (1966). Plasticity of sensorimotor development in the human infant. In J. F. Rosenblith & W. Allinsmith (Eds.), *The causes of behavior* (pp. 60–70). Boston: Allyn and Bacon.

White, D. A., Nortz, M. J., Mandernach, T., Huntington, K., & Steiner, R. D. (2001). Deficits in memory strategy use related to prefrontal dysfunction during early development: Evidence from children with phenylketonuria. *Neuropsychology, 15,* 221–229.

White, L., & Gilbreth, J. G. (2001). When children have two fathers: Effects of relationships with stepfathers and noncustodial fathers on adolescent outcomes. *Journal of Marriage and the Family, 63,* 155–167.

White, M. A., Wilson, M. E., Elander, G., & Persson, B. (1999). The Swedish family: Transition to parenthood. *Scandinavian Journal of Caring Sciences, 13,* 171–176.

White, S. H. (1992). G. Stanley Hall: From philosophy to developmental psychology. *Developmental Psychology, 28,* 25–34.

Whitehead, B. D., Wilcox, B. L., Rostosky, S. S., Randall, B., & Wright, M. L. C. (2001). *Keeping the faith: The role of religion and faith communities in preventing teen pregnancy.* Washington, DC: National Campaign to Prevent Teen Pregnancy.

Whitehurst, G. J., Arnold, D. S., Epstein, J. N., Angell, A. L., Smith, M., & Fischel, J. E. (1994). A picture book reading intervention in day care and home for children from low-income families. *Developmental Psychology, 30,* 679–689.

Whitehurst, G. J., & Lonigan, C. J. (1998). Child development and emergent literacy. *Child Development, 69,* 848–872.

Whiting, B., & Edwards, C. P. (1988a). *Children in different worlds.* Cambridge, MA: Harvard University Press.

Whiting, B., & Edwards, C. P. (1988b). A cross-cultural analysis of sex differences in the behavior of children aged 3 through 11. In G. Handel (Ed.), *Childhood socialization* (pp. 281–297). New York: Aldine de Gruyter.

Whitington, V., & Ward, C. (1999). Intersubjectivity in caregiver–child communication. In L. E. Berk (Ed.), *Landscapes of development* (pp. 109–120). Belmont, CA: Wadsworth.

Wichstrøm, L. (1999). The emergence of gender difference in depressed mood: The role of intensified gender socialization. *Developmental Psychology, 35,* 232–245.

Wickham, S. (1999, Summer). Home-birth: What are the issues? *Midwifery Today, 50,* 16–18.

Wideen, M. F., O'Shea, T., Pye, I., & Ivany, G. (1997). High-stakes testing and the teaching of science. *Canadian Journal of Education, 22,* 428–444.

Wiecha, J. L., Sobol, A. M., Peterson, K. E., & Gortmaker, S. L. (2001). Household television access: Associations with screen time, reading, and homework among youth. *Ambulatory Pediatrics, 1,* 244–251.

Wigfield, A., Battle, A., Keller, L. B., & Eccles, J. S. (2002). Sex differences in motivation, self-concept, career aspiration, and career choice: Implications for cognitive development. In A. McGillicudy-De Lisi & R. De Lisi (Eds.), *Biology, society, and behavior: The development of sex differences in cognition* (pp. 93–124). Westport, CT: Ablex.

Wigfield, A., & Eccles, J. S. (1994). Children's competence beliefs, achievement values, and genderal self-esteem change across elementary and middle school. *Journal of Early Adolescence, 14,* 107–138.

Wigfield, A., Eccles, J. S., Yoon, K. S., Harold, R. D., Arbreton, A. J., Freedman-Doan, C., & Blumenfeld, P. C. (1997). Changes in children's competence beliefs and subjective task values across the elementary school years: A three-year study. *Journal of Educational Psychology, 89,* 451–469.

Wilcox, A. J., Weinberg, C. R., & Baird, D. D. (1995). Timing of sexual intercourse in relation to ovulation: Effects on the probability of conception, survival of the pregnancy, and sex of the baby. *New England Journal of Medicine, 333,* 1517–1519.

Wildes, J. E., Emery, R. E., & Simons, A. D. (2001). The roles of ethnicity and culture in the development of eating disturbance and body dissatisfaction: A meta-analytic review. *Clinical Psychology Review, 21,* 521–551.

Wilk, A. E., Klein, L., & Rovee-Collier, C. (2001). Visual-preference and operant measures of infant memory. *Developmental Psychobiology, 39,* 301–312.

Willatts, P. (1999). Development of means–end behavior in young infants: Pulling a support to retrieve a distant object. *Developmental Psychology, 35,* 651–667.

Wille, D. E. (1991). Relation of preterm birth with quality of infant–mother attachment at one year. *Infant Behavior and Development, 14,* 227–240.

Williams, K., Haywood, K. I., & Painter, M. (1996). Environmental versus biological influences on gender differences in the overarm throw for force: Dominant and nondominant arm throws. *Women in Sport and Physical Activity Journal, 5,* 29–48.

Williams, P. E., Weiss, L. G., & Rolfhus, E. (2003). *WISC-IV: Theoretical model and test blueprint.* San Antonio, TX: Psychological Corporation.

Williams, W. (1998). Are we raising smarter children today? School- and home-related influences on IQ. In U. Neisser (Ed.), *The rising curve: Long-term gains in IQ and related measures* (pp. 125–154). Washington, DC: American Psychological Association.

Willinger, M., Ko, C.-W., Hoffman, H. J., Kessler, R. C., & Corwin, M. J.

(2003). Trends in infant bed sharing in the United States. *Archives of Pediatrics and Adolescent Medicine, 157,* 43–49.

Willner, J. P. (1998). Reproductive genetics and today's patient options: Prenatal diagnosis. *Mount Sinai Journal of Medicine, 65,* 173–177.

Wilson, M. N., Greene-Bates, C., McKim, L., Simmons, T. A., Curry-El, J., & Hinton, I. D. (1995). African American family life: The dynamics of interactions, relationships, and roles. In M. N. Wilson (Ed.), *African American family life: Its structural and ecological aspects* (pp. 5–21). San Francisco: Jossey-Bass.

Winkleby, M. A., Robinson, T. N., Sundquist, J., & Kraemer, H. C. (1999). Ethnic variation in cardiovascular disease risk factors among children and young adults. *Journal of the American Medical Association, 281,* 1006–1013.

Winn, M. (2002). *The plug-in drug: Television, computers, and family life.* New York: Penguin.

Winner, E. (1986, August). Where pelicans kiss seals. *Psychology Today, 20*(8), 25–35.

Winner, E. (1988). *The point of words: Children's understanding of metaphor and irony.* Cambridge, MA: Harvard University Press.

Winner, E. (1996). *Gifted children: Myths and realities.* New York: Basic Books.

Winner, E. (1997). Exceptionally high intelligence and schooling. *American Psychologist, 52,* 1070–1081.

Winner, E. (2000). The origins and ends of giftedness. *American Psychologist, 55,* 159–169.

Winner, E. (2003). Creativity and talent. In M. H. Bornstein, L. Davidson, C. L. M. Keyes, K. A. Moore, & the Center for Child Well-Being, (Eds.), *Well-being: Positive development across the life course* (pp. 371–380). Mahwah, NJ: Erlbaum.

Winsler, A., Diaz, R. M., & Montero, I. (1997). The role of private speech in the transition from collaborative to independent task performance in young children. *Early Childhood Research Quarterly, 12,* 59–79.

Winsler, A., Diaz, R. M., McCarthy, E. M., Atencio, D. J., & Chabay, L. (1999). Mother–child interaction, private speech, and task performance in preschool children with behavior problems. *Journal of Child Psychology and Psychiatry, 40,* 891–904.

Winsler, A., & Naglieri, J. (2003). Overt and covert verbal problem-solving strategies: Developmental trends in use, awareness, and relations with task performance in children aged 5 to 17. *Child Development, 74,* 659–678.

Wiser, A., Maymon, E., Mazor, M., Shoham-Vardi, I., Silberstein, T.,

Wiznitzer, A., & Katz, M. (1997). Effect of the Yom Kippur fast on parturition. *Harefuah, 132,* 745–748.

Witherington, D. C., Campos, J. J., & Hertenstein, M. J. (2001). Principles of emotion and its development in infancy. In G. Bremner & A. Fogel (Eds.), *Blackwell handbook of infant development* (pp. 427–464). Malden, MA: Blackwell.

Wolchik, S. A., Wilcox, K. L., Tein, J.-Y., & Sandler, I. N. (2000). Maternal acceptance and consistency of discipline as buffers of divorce stressors on children's psychological adjustment problems. *Journal of Abnormal Child Psychology, 28,* 87–102.

Wolfe, D. A. (1999). *Child abuse* (2nd ed.). Thousand Oaks, CA: Sage.

Wolfelt, A. D. (1997). Death and grief in the school setting. In T. N. Fairchild (Ed.), *Crisis intervention strategies for school-based helpers* (2nd ed., pp. 199–244). Springfield, IL: Charles C. Thomas.

Wolff, P. H. (1966). The causes, controls and organization of behavior in the neonate. *Psychological Issues, 5*(1, Serial No. 17).

Wolff, P. H., & Fesseha, G. (1999). The orphans of Eritrea: A five-year follow-up study. *Journal of Child Psychology and Psychiatry and Allied Disciplines, 40,* 1231–1237.

Wolfinger, N. H. (2000). Beyond the intergenerational transmission of divorce: Do people replicate the patterns of marital instability they grew up with? *Journal of Family Issues, 21,* 1061–1086.

Wolpe, J., & Plaud, J. J. (1997). Pavlov's contributions to behavior therapy: The obvious and not so obvious. *American Psychologist, 52,* 966–972.

Wong, C. A., Eccles, J. S., & Sameroff, A. (2003). The influence of ethnic discrimination and ethnic identification on African American adolescents' school and socioemotional adjustment. *Journal of Personality, 71,* 1197–1232.

Wood, E., Desmarais, S., & Gugula, S. (2002). The impact of parenting experience on gender stereotyped toy play of children. *Sex Roles, 47,* 39–49.

Wood. S. (2001). Interview, *Frontline.* Retrieved from http://www.pbs.org/wgbh/pages/frontline/shows/fertility/interviews/wood.html

Woodhouse, B. B. (2001). Children's rights. In S. O. White (Ed.), *Handbook of youth and justice* (pp. 377–410). New York: Kluwer Academic.

Woodward, A. L., Markman, E. M., & Fitzsimmons, C. M. (1994). Rapid word learning in 13- and 18-month-olds. *Developmental Psychology, 30,* 553–566.

Woodward, L. J., & Fergusson, D. M. (1999). Childhood peer relationship problems and psychosocial adjustment in late adolescence. *Journal of Abnormal Child Psychology, 27,* e87.

Woodward, L., Fergusson, D. M., & Horwood, L. J. (2001). Risk factors and life processes associated with teenage pregnancy: Results of a prospective study from birth to 20 years. *Journal of Marriage and the Family, 63,* 1170–1184.

Woodward, L., Taylor, E., & Dowdney, L. (1998). The parenting and family functioning of children with hyperactivity. *Journal of Child Psychology and Psychiatry, 39,* 161–169.

Woolley, J. D. (1997). Thinking about fantasy: Are children fundamentally different thinkers and believers from adults? *Child Development, 68,* 991–1011.

Woolley, J. D. (2000). The development of beliefs about direct mental–physical causality in imagination, magic, and religion. In K. S. Rosengren, C. N. Johnson, & P. L. Harris (Eds.), *Imagining the impossible* (pp. 99–129). New York: Cambridge University Press.

Woolley, J. D., Phelps, K. E., Davis, D. L., & Mandell, D. J. (1999). Where theories of mind meet magic: The development of children's beliefs about wishing. *Child Development, 70,* 571–587.

Wooster, D. M. (1999). Assessment of nonorganic failure to thrive. *Infant-Toddler Intervention, 9,* 353–371.

Wooster, D. M. (2000). Intervention for nonorganic failure to thrive. *Transdisciplinary Journal, 10,* 37–45.

World Education Services. (2001). *World education database.* Retrieved from http://www.wes.org

World Health Organization. (2003a). *Oral Health Country/Area Profile Program.* Retrieved from www.whocollab.od.mah.se/index.html

World Health Organization. (2003b). *The world health report, 2003.* Geneva, Switzerland: Author.

Wright, B. C., & Dowker, A. D. (2002). The role of cues to differential absolute size in children's transitive inferences. *Journal of Experimental Child Psychology, 81,* 249–275.

Wright, J. C., Huston, A. C., Murphy, K. C., St. Peters, M., Pinon, M., Scantlin, R., & Kotler, J. (2001). The relations of early television viewing to school readiness and vocabulary of children from low-income families: The Early Window Project. *Child Development, 72,* 1347–1366.

Wright, J. C., Huston, A. C., Reitz, A. L., & Piemyat, S. (1994). Young children's perceptions of television reality: Determinants and developmental differences. *Developmental Psychology, 30,* 229–239.

Wright, J. W. (Ed.). (1999). *The universal almanac 1999.* Kansas City: Andrews and McMeel.

Wright, V. C., Schieve, L. A., Reynolds, M. A., & Jeng, G. (2003, August 29). Assisted reproductive technology surveillance—United States, 2000.

Morbidity and Mortality Weekly Report, 52(No. SS–9).

Wu, L. L., Bumpass, L. L., & Musick, K. (2001). Historical and life course trajectories of nonmarital childbearing. In L. L. Wu & B. Wolfe (Eds.), *Out of wedlock: Causes and consequences of nonmarital fertility* (pp. 3–48). New York: Russell Sage Foundation.

Wu, P., Robinson, C. C., Yang, C., Hart, C. H., Olsen, S. F., Porter, C. L., Jin, S., Wo, J., & Wu, X. (2002). Similarities and differences in mothers' parenting of preschoolers in China and the United States. *International Journal of Behavioral Development, 36,* 481–491.

Wu, T., Mendola, P., & Buck, G. M. (2002). Ethnic differences in the presence of secondary sex characteristics and menarche among U.S. girls: The Third National Health and Nutrition Examination Survey, 1988–1994. *Pediatrics, 110,* 752–757.

Wyatt, J. M., & Carlo, G. (2002). What will my parents think? Relations among adolescents' expected parental reactions, prosocial moral reasoning and prosocial and antisocial behaviors. *Journal of Adolescent Research, 17,* 646–666.

Wyman, P. A., Cowen, E. L., Work, W. C., Hoyt-Meyers, L., Magnus, K. B., & Fagen, D. B. (1999). Caregiving and developmental factors differentiating young at-risk urban children showing resilient versus stress-affected outcomes: A replication and extension. *Child Development, 70,* 645–659.

Wynn, K. (1992). Addition and subtraction by human infants. *Nature, 358,* 749–750.

Wynn, K. (2002). Do infants have numerical expectations or just perceptual preferences? Comment. *Developmental Science, 5,* 207–209.

Wynn, K., Bloom, P., & Chiang, W.-C. (2002). Enumeration of collective entities by 5-month-old infants. *Cognition, 83,* B55–B62.

Xu, F., & Spelke, E. S. (2000). Large number discrimination in 6-month-old infants. *Cognition, 74,* B1–B11.

Yale, M. E., Messinger, D. S., Cobo-Lewis, A. B., Oller, D. K., & Eilers, R. E. (1999). An event-based analysis of the coordination of early infant vocalizations and facial actions. *Developmental Psychology, 35,* 505–513.

Yan, J., & Smetana, J. G. (2003). Conceptions of moral, social-conventional, and personal events among Chinese preschoolers in Hong Kong. *Child Development, 74,* 647–658.

Yang, B., Ollendick, T. H., Dong, Q., Xia, Y., & Lin, L. (1995). Only children and children with siblings in the People's Republic of China: Levels of fear, anxiety, and depression. *Child Development, 66,* 1301–1311.

Yang, C.-K., & Hahn, H.-M. (2002). Cosleeping in young Korean children. *Developmental and Behavioral Pediatrics, 23,* 151–157.

Yanovski, J. A. (2003). Rapid weight gain during infancy as a predictor of adult obesity. *American Journal of Clinical Nutrition, 77,* 1350–1351.

Yarrow, M. R., Scott, P. M., & Waxler, C. Z. (1973). Learning concern for others. *Developmental Psychology, 8,* 240–260.

Yates, W. R., Cadoret, R. J., & Troughton, E. P. (1999). The Iowa adoption studies: Methods and results. In M. C. LaBuda & E. L. Grigorenko (Eds.), *On the way to individuality: Current methodological issues in behavioral genetics* (pp. 95–125). Commack, NY: Nova Science Publishers.

Yeates, K. O., Schultz, L. H., & Selman, R. L. (1991). The development of interpersonal negotiation strategies in thought and action: A social-cognitive link to behavioral adjustment and social status. *Merrill-Palmer Quarterly, 37,* 369–405.

Yip, R., Scanlon, K., & Trowbridge, F. (1993). Trends and patterns in height and weight status of low-income U.S. children. *Critical Reviews in Food Science and Nutrition, 33,* 409–421.

Yirmiya, N., Erel, O., Shaked, M., & Solomonica-Levi, D. (1998). Meta-analyses comparing theory of mind abilities of individuals with autism, individuals with mental retardation, and normally developing individuals. *Psychological Bulletin, 124,* 283–307.

Yirmiya, N., & Shulman, C. (1996). Seriation, conservation, and theory of mind abilities in individuals with autism, individuals with mental retardation, and normally developing children. *Child Development, 67,* 2045–2059.

Yirmiya, N., Solomonica-Levi, D., & Shulman, C. (1996). The ability to manipulate behavior and to understand manipulation of beliefs: A comparison of individuals with autism, mental retardation, and normal development. *Developmental Psychology, 32,* 62–69.

Yogman, M. W. (1981). Development of the father–infant relationship. In H. Fitzgerald, B. Lester, & M. W. Yogman (Eds.), *Theory and research in behavioral pediatrics* (Vol. 1, pp. 221–279). New York: Plenum.

Yonas, A., Elieff, C., & Aterberry, M. E. (2002). Emergence of sensitivity to pictorial depth cues: Charting development in individual infants. *Infant Behavior and Development, 25,* 295–514.

Young, J. F., & Mroczek, D. K. (2003). Predicting intraindividual self-concept trajectories during adolescence. *Journal of Adolescence, 26,* 586–600.

Youngblade, L. M., & Dunn, J. (1995). Individual differences in young children's pretend play with mother and sibling: Links to relationships and understanding of other people's feelings and beliefs. *Child Development, 66,* 1472–1492.

Youngstrom, E., Wolpaw, J. M., Kogos, J. L., Schoff, K., Ackerman, B., & Izard, C. (2000). Interpersonal problem solving in preschool and first grade: Developmental change and ecological validity. *Journal of Clinical Child Psychology, 29,* 589–602.

Youniss, J. (1980). *Parents and peers in social development: A Piagetian-Sullivan perspective.* Chicago: University of Chicago Press.

Youniss, J., McLellan, J. A., & Yates, M. (1997). What we know about engendering civic identity. *American Behavioral Scientist, 40,* 620–631.

Youniss, J., McLellan, J., & Yates, M. (1999). Religion, community service, and identity in American youth. *Journal of Adolescence, 22,* 243–253.

Yu, S., Yarnell, J. W. G., Sweetnam, P. M., & Murray, L. (2003). What level of physical activity protects against premature cardiovascular death? The Caerphilly Study. *Heart, 89,* 502–506.

Yuill, N., & Pearson, A. (1998). The developmental bases for trait attribution: Children's understanding of traits as causal mechanisms based on desire. *Developmental Psychology, 34,* 574–586.

Yuill, N., & Perner, J. (1988). Intentionality and knowledge in children's judgments of actor's responsibility and recipient's emotional reaction. *Developmental Psychology, 24,* 358–365.

Zafeiriou, D. I. (2000). Plantar grasp reflex in high-risk infants during the first year of life. *Pediatric Neurology, 22,* 75–76.

Zahn-Waxler, C., Kochanska, G., Krupnick, J., & McKnew, D. (1990). Patterns of guilt in children of depressed and well mothers. *Developmental Psychology, 26,* 51–59.

Zahn-Waxler, C., & Radke-Yarrow, M. (1990). The origins of empathic concern. *Motivation and Emotion, 14,* 107–130.

Zahn-Waxler, C., Radke-Yarrow, M., & King, R. M. (1979). Child-rearing and children's prosocial initiations toward victims of distress. *Child Development, 50,* 319–330.

Zahn-Waxler, C., Radke-Yarrow, M., Wagner, E., & Chapman, M. (1992). Development of concern for others.

Developmental Psychology, 28, 126–136.

Zahn-Waxler, C., & Robinson, J. (1995). Empathy and guilt: Early origins of feelings of responsibility. In J. P. Tangney & K. W. Fischer (Eds.), *Self-conscious emotions* (pp. 143–173). New York: Guilford.

Zahn-Waxler, C., Schiro, K., Robinson, J. L., Emde, R. N., & Schmitz, S. (2001). Empathy and prosocial patterns in young MZ and DZ twins: Development and genetic and environmental influences. In R. N. Emde & J. K. Hewitt (Eds.), *Infancy to early childhood: Genetic and environmental influences on developmental change* (pp. 141–162). New York: Oxford University Press.

Zeanah, C. H. (2000). Disturbances of attachment in young children adopted from institutions. *Developmental and Behavioral Pediatrics, 21,* 230–236.

Zelazo, N. A., Zelazo, P. R., Cohen, K. M., & Zelazo, P. D. (1993). Specificity of practice effects on elementary neuromotor patterns. *Developmental Psychology, 29,* 686–691.

Zeldin, A. L. & Pajares, F. (2000). Against the odds: Self-efficacy beliefs of women in mathematical, scientific, and technological careers. *American Educational Research Journal, 37,* 215–246.

Zeman, J., Shipman, K., & Suveg, C. (2002). Anger and sadness regulation: Predictions to internalizing and externalizing symptoms in children. *Journal of Clinical Child and Adolescent Psychology, 31,* 393–398.

Zeskind, P. S., & Barr, R. G. (1997). Acoustic characteristics of naturally occurring cries of infants with "colic." *Child Development, 68,* 394–403.

Zeskind, P. S., & Lester, B. M. (2001). Analysis of infant crying. In L. T. Singer & P. S. Zeskind (Eds.), *Biobehavioral assessment of the infant* (pp. 149–166). New York: Guilford.

Zeskind, P. S., & Ramey, C. T. (1978). Fetal malnutrition: An experimental study of its consequences on infant development in two caregiving environments. *Child Development, 49,* 1155–1162.

Zeskind, P. S., & Ramey, C. T. (1981). Preventing intellectual and interactional sequelae of fetal malnutrition: A longitudinal, transactional, and synergistic approach to development. *Child Development, 52,* 213–218.

Zhou, M., & Bankston, C. L. (1998). *Growing up American: How Vietnamese children adapt to life in the United States.* New York: Russell Sage Foundation.

Zigler, E., & Gilman, E. (1998). The legacy of Jean Piaget. In G. A. Kimble & M. Wertheimer (Eds.),

Portraits of pioneers in psychology (Vol. 3, pp. 145–160). Washington, DC: American Psychological Association.

Zigler, E., & Styfco, S. J. (2001). Can early childhood intervention prevent delinquency? A real possibility. In A. C. Bohart & D. J. Stipek (Eds.), *Constructive and destructive behavior* (pp. 231–248). Washington, DC: American Psychological Association.

Zigler, E. F., & Finn-Stevenson, M. (1999). Applied developmental psychology. In M. H. Bornstein & M. E. Lamb (Eds.), *Developmental psychology: An advanced textbook* (4th ed., pp. 555–598). Mahwah, NJ: Erlbaum.

Zigler, E. F., & Hall, N. W. (2000). Child development and social policy: Theory and applications. New York: McGraw-Hill.

Zimmer-Gembeck, M. J., Siebenbruner, J., & Collins, W. A. (2001). Diverse aspects of dating: Associations with psychosocial functioning from early to middle adolescence. *Journal of Adolescence, 24,* 313–336.

Zimmerman, B. J., & Risemberg, R. (1997). Self-regulatory dimensions of academic learning and motivation. In G. D. Phye (Ed.), *Handbook of academic learning: Construction of knowledge* (pp. 105–125). San Diego: Academic Press.

Zimmerman, P., & Becker-Stoll, F. (2002). Stability of attachment representations during adolescence: The influence of ego-identity status. *Journal of Adolescence, 25,* 107–124.

Zimmermann, P. (2000). L'attachement á l'adolescence: Mesure, développement et adaptation [Attachment in adolescence: Assessment, development, and adaptation]. In S. Larose, G. M. Tarabulsy, D. R. Pederson, & G. Moran (Eds.), *Attachment et développement* (pp. 181–204). Montreal: Quebec University Press.

Zins, J. E., Garcia, V. F., Tuchfarber, B. S., Clark, K. M., & Laurence, S. C. (1994). Preventing injury in children and adolescents. In R. J. Simeonsson (Ed.), *Risk, resilience, and prevention: Promoting the well-being of all children* (pp. 183–202). Baltimore: Paul H. Brookes.

Zucker, K. J. (2001). Biological influences on psychosexual differentiation. In R. K. Unger (Ed.), *Handbook of the psychology of women and gender* (pp. 101–115). New York: Wiley.

Zuckerman, B., Frank, D. A., & Mayes, L. (2002). Cocaine-exposed infants and developmental outcomes: "Crack kids" revisited. *Journal of the American Medical Association, 287,* 1990–1991.

Name Index

Italic n following page number indicates caption for photograph, illustration, table, or figure.

Subject Index

maternal employment. *See*
Maternal employment
middle childhood and,
492–502
never-married single-parent
families, 494–495
newborns, adjustments to,
157–161
one-child families, 96, 493
parent–child relationships,
492
reconstituted, 496, 499–500
single-parent. *See* Single-
parent families
size of. *See* Family size
socioeconomic influences
on, 74–76
stepfamilies, 496, 499–500
Family life education, for
stepfamilies, 499–500
Family planning, 95–96, 97.
See also Contraception
Family size, 95–96
child maltreatment and,
391–392
only children, 493
temperament and, 263
Family therapy. *See*
Counseling
Family violence. *See* Child
maltreatment
Fantasy play. *See* Make-believe
play
FAS (fetal alcohol syndrome),
112–113
Fast mapping, in vocabulary
development, 349
Fat, body. *See also* Obesity
baby fat, 166, 288
early childhood, 288
middle childhood, 402
prenatal development, 105,
106
Fat, dietary. *See also* Nutrition
breastfeeding and, 180
early childhood, 296
Father. *See* Families; Parent
entries; Paternal age
Father–child relationship. *See
also* Parent–child
relationship
divorce and, 496
favoritism in, 493
gay and lesbian families, 494
gender stereotyping and, 384
incest. *See* Sexual abuse of
children
maternal employment and,
500
remarriage and, 499
Father-headed households.
See Single-parent families
Father–infant relationship. *See
also* Parent–infant
relationship
attachment and, 274, 275
cultural influences on, 275
newborns, 147, 157–158, 160
Father–stepmother families,
499

Fatness. *See* Obesity
Fear
conditioning of, 183
cultural influences, 502
early childhood, caregiving
guidelines, 363–364
infancy and toddlerhood,
254–255
middle childhood, 502
peer victimization, 489
rejected-withdrawn children,
488
self-care children, 501
sexual abuse victims, 505
war, effect on children,
502–503
Fearful distress, as
temperament dimension,
259
Feeding practices. *See also*
Eating habits; Nutrition
attachment and, 265
bottle-feeding, 178–180
breastfeeding. *See*
Breastfeeding
early childhood motor
development and, 306
obesity and, 408, 410–411
Female versus male
development. *See* Gender
entries; Sex differences
Femininity. *See* Gender *entries*
Fertility drugs and multiple
births, 57
Fertilization, 99–100
in vitro. *See* In vitro
fertilization
Fetal alcohol effects (FAE),
113
Fetal alcohol syndrome (FAS),
112–113
Fetal medicine, 65, 68
Fetal monitoring, 137
Fetoscopy, 65
Fetus, period of prenatal
development, 100,
103–106
teratogens in, 107
Field experiments, 41
Fijians, moral development
among, 371
Fine motor development
defined, 187
early childhood, 306–309
enhancing, 310–311
infancy and toddlerhood,
187–191
middle childhood, 418–419
milestones, 305
sex differences in, 309–310,
419
Finland
cesarean deliveries, 139
infant mortality rate, 145
obesity incidence, 407
Firearms, childhood injuries
and death from, 300
Fires, 300
First-language learning, 237

Fitness. *See* Exercise; Health;
Nutrition
Flexibility, in middle
childhood, 417–418
Flynn effect, 447
fMRI. *See* Functional
magnetic resonance
imaging
Folic acid and prenatal health
care, 69, 118
Fontanels, 168–169
Food. *See* Eating *entries*;
Feeding practices;
Malnutrition; Nutrition;
Vitamins and minerals
Food insecurity, 181
Food supplement programs,
406
prenatal care, 118
Forceps, in childbirth,
138–139
Formal operational stage of
cognitive development,
20–21
Formula (bottle-feeding), 155,
178–180
Fragile X syndrome, 61
France
child-directed speech in, 243
infant mortality rate, 145
reproductive technology
laws, 67
welfare programs, 81
Fraternal twins, 57. *See also*
Twin studies; Twins
Freestanding birth centers,
135
Freud's psychosexual theory.
See Psychosexual theory
of development (Freud)
Friendships, 486–487. *See also*
Peer relations
attachment security and, 277
early childhood, 368
middle childhood, 486–487
sex differences in, 486
Frontal lobes, 171, 174. *See
also* Cerebral cortex
ADHD and brain activity,
434
Broca's area, 236
infantile amnesia and, 224
middle childhood, 404
Full inclusion of students with
learning disabilities, 460
Functional magnetic
resonance imaging
(fMRI), 36, 170–171
ADHD studies, 434
autism and, 339
brain growth spurts and, 174
child maltreatment victims,
393
inhibitory control and, 432
language development
studies, 237
lateralization of brain and,
291–292
Functional play, 212, 367

G
Gallbladder disease and
obesity, 407
Games. *See also* Athletics;
Play; Toys; Video games
early childhood, 304–305
language development and,
239
middle childhood, 420–423
organized games with rules,
420–423
sex differences in motor
development and,
309–310
Gametes, 55–56. *See also* Ova;
Sperm
Gardner's multiple
intelligences theory,
444–445
educational principles based
on, 461
Gastrointestinal system
breastfeeding and, 179
prenatal development of, 102
Gay and lesbian families, 494
Geese, imprinting studies, 265
Gender appropriate. *See*
Gender stereotyping
Gender constancy, 385–386
Gender differences. *See* Sex
differences
Gender gap. *See* Sex
differences
Gender identity
cognitive-developmental
theory of, 381, 385–386
defined, 385
early childhood, 385–387
emergence of, 385
gender schema theory of,
381, 386–387
middle childhood, 490–491
psychoanalytic theories of,
381
self-esteem and, 385
sex differences in
development, 490–491
social learning theory of,
381, 385
theories of, 381, 385–386
Gender-linked preferences.
See Gender typing
Gender reassignment, 383
Gender-role adoption. *See*
Gender stereotyping
Gender-role identity. *See*
Gender identity
Gender schema theory, 381,
386–387
Gender stereotyping. *See also*
Gender typing
academic subjects and, 490
cross-cultural research of
personality traits, 490
cultural influences on, 491
early childhood, 358,
381–382, 387
infancy and toddlerhood,
263, 279–280

maternal employment and,
500
middle childhood, 490–491
motor development and, 310
parental influence and, 490
reducing, 387
sports and, 419
teacher influence and, 490
television programming and,
385
temperament and, 263
toys and, 280
Gender typing. *See also*
Gender identity; Gender
stereotyping; Sex
differences
adolescence
longitudinal-sequential
study of, 45–46
aggression and, 377
child-rearing practices and,
382–384
defined, 381
early childhood, 381–387
environmental influences
on, 382–385
family influences on,
382–384
genetic influences on, 382
peer relations and, 384–385
sibling relationships and, 384
social environment's
influence on, 385
teachers influencing, 384
television influencing, 385
Gene therapy, 68–69
General growth curve, 290
Generational differences, 43,
44
Generativity, as psychosocial
stage of development, 17
Genes, 54–55. *See also* Genetic
entries
alleles, 58–59
crossing over of, 55, 56
dominant–recessive
inheritance, 58–59
heterozygous pairings, 58–59
homozygous pairings, 58–59
Human Genome Project, 68
mapping. *See* Genetic maps
modifier genes, 58
mutation, 61–62
Genetic counseling, 64–65,
69–70
Genetic diagnosis,
preimplantation, 65
Genetic disorders, 62–64
Genetic engineering, 68–69
Genetic imprinting, 61
Genetic–environmental
correlation, 87–89, 231
Genetics, 54–65. *See also*
Chromosomes; Genes;
Inheritance;
Nature–nurture
controversy
ADHD and, 434
asthma and, 412